History of
Lykens Township
Volume I

The Gratz Historical Society
2016

SUNBURY PRESS

Mechanicsburg, PA USA

Published by Sunbury Press, Inc.
105 South Market Street
Mechanicsburg, Pennsylvania 17055

SUNBURY
P R E S S
www.sunburypress.com

For information about special discounts for bulk purchases, please contact Sunbury Press Orders Dept. at (855) 338-8359 or orders@sunburypress.com.

To request one of our authors for speaking engagements or book signings, please contact Sunbury Press Publicity Dept. at publicity@sunburypress.com.

ISBN: 978-1-62006-847-2 (Hardcover)
Library of Congress Control Number: 2016954370
FIRST SUNBURY PRESS EDITION: September 2016

Product of the United States of America
0 1 1 2 3 5 8 13 21 34 55

Designed by The Gratz Historical Society
Cover by Lawrence Knorr
Edited by The Gratz Historical Society

Continue the Enlightenment!

INTRODUCTION

Although this is a narrative focusing on Lykens Township, it is impossible to record its past history without including a broad account of the things that happened in the surrounding areas of "the upper end."

As the history unfolds, it is interesting to see how each section of the upper end of Dauphin County had a part in the development of the whole area. People migrated to one section, then moved on to another part, but always leaving a trail. So that now, we can learn to follow the trail, and become aware of their whole history.

One case in point, is the settlement of the section we now know as Loyalton. Contrary to the thoughts of most of us, the first settlers to arrive in that part were not Germans! Instead, Andrew Lycans, a Swede, made the first attempt at settlement in the mid-1700s, followed shortly thereafter, by numerous people of Irish and English or Huguenot heritage. Many of them came from the Lancaster County area. Many were millwrights who came to take advantage of the wonderful source of water near the Wiconisco Creek. This was before the discovery of coal. It was not a haphazard migration, but friends told friends, and it was almost a community of people who came to settle. It soon developed into something of a family affair, as intermarriage took place among the families. In many cases, the land then was passed on to the next generations of family. Although some of the first land grants were given to investors, some members of their families stayed and today have descendants living in the area. Some of the investors were influential people from the Harrisburg area.

Because so many of the folks in the area of Oak Dale village, later Short Mountain Post Office, now Loyalton were adhering to the Wesley doctrine, a missionary soon formed a congregation of Episcopal Methodists, meeting in the vicinity of Loyalton. For years a trail of Methodist and Evangelical congregations developed first, along what is now Route 209 from Lykens to Millersburg, but later became established in other areas of Lykens Valley. Today the Loyalton area is part of Washington and Wiconisco Township, and no longer part of Lykens Township. But its' early influence must be considered part of the Lykens Township heritage.

Another early settlement in what is now Lykens Township began in the present section known as Erdman. Most of those pioneers were of German background.

There are various expressions, some passed on through several generations, that describe our desire to unearth the history of past dwellers for our present day residents.

"Any who care not about their earthly origin care little as to anything higher."

"I have but one lamp by which my feet are guided; and that is the lamp of experience. I know of no way of judging the future but by the past." – Patrick Henry

As the "Story of Lykens Township and area develops it becomes obvious that it was not a coincidence that brought several families to one area of the township. (They knew each other before they came) and had common interests where they had been.

A MOVE WESTWARD

One of the most amazing things that came to light during our research was the fact that there were specific migrations from the Lykens Township and Gratz area to the west. Some folks moved to locations, such as western Pennsylvania. Others went on to Ohio and Boone, Iowa. But we have learned more about the migration to Ogle County Illinois that took place during the 1840-1870 Period. We have not learned the specific reason why the migration took place, but a bit of early history of that territory suggests an incentive for the westward movement.

In 1818, the territory of Illinois became a state. But soon after that date, an Illinois representative succeeded in enlarging the northern boundary of the state. It included the territory that extended from Chicago, west to the lead mines near Galena. Sandwiched in between, was the vast section of forest and prairie land, which later became suitable for dairy farming. In 1831, after much conflict, the federal government moved most Illinois Indians to a western site across the Mississippi River. In 1832, the serious Black Hawk War ended the few remaining Indian attacks on the white settlers. Shortly after that, work began on the Illinois and Michigan Canal, making it possible for farm products to be shipped to the east. The influx of settlers from the east began to arrive in the new territory. It included the section below Rockford, known as Ogle County. Among the arrivals apparently were the "cousins" of many of our ancestors.

But how did people from Dauphin County actually find out about Ogle and surrounding counties in Illinois? The answer is not clear. One source of information may have been the circuit rider pastor from Halifax, Dauphin County that moved to Oregon, Illinois in the 1840's. It was a fairly common practice in those days for ambitious preachers to take on the task of bringing the gospel to settlers on the fringe of the established settlements.

Rev. Nicholas Stroh was a member of the Stroh family that settled very early near Halifax, Dauphin County. Rev. Stroh was a Lutheran minister, and in the church history of Ogle County, he is credited with organizing and establishing the Lutheran congregation called St. James at West Grove, as well as congregations at Adeline, Brookville, Mt. Morris and Oregon about 1850. All of the cemeteries at these churches have tombstones with surnames familiar to our area. Two other churches were established in the area about the same time. One was by the German Reformed, and another by the Albrights and United Brethren in Christ denomination. The Lutheran and Reformed congregations worshipped in the same building, on alternate Sundays same as here. A quote from their by-laws states that the denomination conducting the services should "have the use of the church for the entire day." Another rule was that "As long as there are three German members in either congregation, there must be some German preaching." St. James Lutheran church had two side aisles, and the men and women entered separate doors and were seated separately. It is certainly similar to the habits of the early Lykens Valley congregations of years ago. The Rev. Nicholas Stroh continued to serve the Lutheran congregation until he retired in 1880. He died New Years Day 1897, at the age of 98, and is buried in Oakwood cemetery, Mt. Morris, Ill.

The early history of the area mentions that the settlers coming in the later 1830's and early 1840's found that they had a choice of settling on the prairie or in the timber area. Most shunned the prairie, finding the timber area as the most congenial place to live. They built their houses in the timber and cleared the land for farming. Families from the Lykens Township area continued to move to Ogle County, Illinois as late as the 1870s, became established there, and today their descendants make up a goodly portion of the population. As one Illinois native said "You walk into most any cemetery in the Ogle County and surrounding area, and you think you are near Gratz!!" The names for the most part are the same: Bowerman, Kuntzelman, Schoffstall, Schreiner, Shiro to name a few. Many of the residents are aware that their roots are in Dauphin County and in particular Lykens Twp.

The reader of this history will find many references to family members that moved to Illinois. A few early letters are included, and several Civil War pension records provided personal information for this research.

TO READERS OF THIS BOOK

We know there are mistakes! Some we made, and others were inherited from well-meaning sources of information. Researchers will realize that all records are the result of human endeavors. Original records have discrepancies. Records that are transferred to hand written and typed copies trend to become even more inaccurate, for many reasons. The internet has become a place for easy access genealogy research with tremendous results as well as disheartening inaccuracy. We have done most of the work in court house, church and other original documents. We hope that our readers will enjoy the contents of this book for its history and direction in finding family ties to genealogy. We hope that the errors, particularly numerical mistakes will not prevent the reader from gleaning important, interesting as well as historical information about the area where you or your ancestors lived.

ABBREVIATIONS :

b – born   d - died   m married – dau – daughter – bapt baptized (christened)
twp – township – Co. County. Asterisks "*" in front of names reflects the line of descent from the immigrant ancestor to the present generation.

GENEALOGICAL MATERIALS

The genealogical material is placed between brackets to disassociate it from the usual text. Generations of families are separated by using different forms of printing for given names (bold or plain capital letters, underlined , small bold or plain print, or italic letters) for very recent generations. The material is compact to save space. The genealogies of the early settlers, whose families stayed here permanently, are much longer and detailed for obvious reasons. We tried to establish early family ties for all first settlers. But the backgrounds of a few early settlers unfortunately remained uncertain.

PARCEL NUMBERS

The use of parcel numbers is a rather new way of finding information in county deed records. (The new system makes it easy to locate properties, and identify the owner).

The parcel system was not available when our committee began the project of searching land records for this publication. You will notice that we included a *Parcel Map* (showing the parcel number on the owners property). The number is also used on the right side of the owners name on the book page where the property is described.

There is one problem! The deed history of Loyalton and all of this *VOLUME ONE* of the Lykens Township history. was already mostly finished when the parcel map became available. It would have been too difficult to "redo" that history to include the parcel information. Some of the Loyalton properties do include parcel numbers because they have recently changed ownership and it was easy to add the number.

ACKNOWLEDGMENTS

In addition to our "in house" committee, a special thanks to MANY folks (too numerous to mention) who shared information, and donated manuscript material and books to our library. Also those whose memories added interesting first hand information to the basic facts. Special thanks to Philip Rice who has truly been a "friend" to our library in many ways. Roger Cramer, Evelyn Hartman (now deceased), Elsie Eves, Annabelle Hoffman and shared information with us numerous times. We will never forget the impact of Dr. Glenn and Carolyn Schwalm, (now deceased), whose interest helped to establish our library. Ed Bechtel, Shirley Kiester, Sally Reiner, Mary Bateman and Kathryn Kieffer were great in providing help for the research in Loyalton. The encouragement of these fine folks and others whose help with individual genealogies helped us to reach our goal of preparing this our second large historical publication. The first publication was the "the history of Gratz." This historical search is a focus on Lykens Township, but also includes much information that pertains to the history of other areas of the "Upper End of Dauphin County."

REFERENCES & BIBLIOGRAPHY

Jay Osman was very helpful in collecting Andrew Lykens information
Court records of Lancaster County at Lancaster Co Historical Society
Lancaster County Pennsylvania Quarter Sessions Abstracts edited by Gary T. Hawbaker
The Indian Wars of Pennsylvania by C. Hale Sipe
Egle's Notes and Quieries by William Egle
The History of Dauphin County by William Egle
The Swedish Colonial Society
The Craig Report on Andrew Lycans by Dr. Peter S. Craig
The Lykens Family of Eastern Kentucky by the Magoffin County Historical Society
The Mouns Jones (Jonasson) House of Berks Co., Pa. website

THE BOOK COMMITTEE

Without these truly committed members of our research committee, we would not have the history of Lykens Township. Their focus, ambition, dedication and determination for all these years to make this project a success, is truly remarkable. We are sorry that we were unable to finish the book before the decease of some of the members. But their contribution to the cause will not be forgotten.

RESEARCH: Leah Hollenbach, Lena Kessler, now deceased, Jane Miller, Lois Schoffstall
INDEXING AND SCANNING: Ned Weaver, now deceased, Diane Schreffler, Jane Miller, Leah Hollenbach.
COMPUTER ENTRY: Leah Hollenbach, Jane Miller, Charles Schoffstall

TABLE OF CONTENTS

ILLUSTRATIONS

GENEALOGIES

Chapter 1

THE FIRST INHABITANTS
Of
LYKENS TOWNSHIP

At the present time it is believed the first humans to set foot in North America crossed the Bering Strait land bridge into Alaska some 15,000 plus years ago. These Asian immigrants would come to be known as American Indians. Unlike the generally east to west migration of our early immigrants from Europe, these nomadic people migrated from northwest to south and southeast. They arrived in the Susquehanna Valley of Pennsylvania about 10,000 BC. Based on archaeological evidence and historical records, it is probable the land of Lykens Township and vicinity was used to varying degrees by a number of tribes of American Indians in all stages of their development. In understanding the first people to inhabit the Susquehanna Valley it's helpful to know how archaeologists classify their various cultural stages, which are as follows:

COLONIAL – 1550 AD to 1800 AD
WOODLAND – 1,000 BC to 1550 AD
TRANSITIONAL – 1,800 BC to 800 BC
ARCHAIC – 8,000 BC to 1,000 BC
PALEO-INDIAN – 10,000 BC to 8,000 BC

It is unknown exactly when their language developed, but by the time the first Europeans arrived in America the Indians had an established language and names for themselves. Much of their language, and most of their names have survived to the present day.

The Susquehannock

The presence of the Susquehannock Indians on the Susquehanna River can be traced to the beginning of the Colonial stage in 1550, although many archaeologists believe the actual date to be much earlier. Until their defeat in 1675, the Susquehannocks were the dominating force in the Mid-Atlantic region. They were physically strong, intelligent, and warlike. They were already trading with the French when Captain John Smith first made contact with the Susquehannocks in 1608 while on an exploratory expedition up the Susquehanna River. It was Smith's interpreter who gave them the name "Susquehannock," probably not the name used within the tribe. Captain Smith described the Indians as "giants" with great booming voices. Exaggeration or truth, the Susquehannocks were indeed fearsome, and they ruled the length of the Susquehanna and its tributaries (from the New York State line to the Chesapeake Bay) with an iron fist. Other Indians entering the Susquehanna Valley did so at their own peril. The well-armed Susquehannocks made war at one time or another with most neighboring tribes, but especially their bitter enemy to the north the Iroquois Confederacy, also called the Five Nations. The Five Nations consisted of the Mohawk, Oneida, Onondaga, Cayuga, and Seneca tribes. They became the Six Nations after admitting the Tuscarora tribe in 1722. The territory of the Iroquois Confederacy encompassed most of what is now New York State, and they numbered as many as 12,000 at their peak in the early 1600s. The Susquehannock population at that time was about 7,000.

The Susquehannock were hunter/gatherers, but also grew squash, beans and corn. They had numerous villages along the Susquehanna and its tributaries. They lived in "longhouses" shared by a number of families, which were partitioned for privacy. The longhouses were surrounded by a stockade or fort-like structure consisting of long poles planted in the ground vertically, and then tied together. The longhouses were from 50 to 80 feet long, and from 10 to 15 feet wide, and were constructed of a pole frame covered with tree bark. The largest Susquehannock town, and probably their cultural and governmental center, was located on the Susquehanna near the mouth of the Conestoga Creek in Lancaster County. There were other villages on the main branch of the Susquehanna near Bainbridge, Middletown, Lebanon, Paxtang, Camp Hill, New Cumberland, West Fairview, Haldeman Island, Clemson Island, Liverpool, and Shamokin (now Sunbury), as well as sites on the West and North Branches.

Isaac Taylor a surveyor from Chester County made this draught of the Susquehanna River in 1701, and evidently had accompanied some Indian trader on one of his expeditions.

It shows the Indian villages near Paxtang, On Duncan's and Clemson's islands, above the Mouth of the Juniata, at now Sunbury, and on "John Penn's" Creek and the Juniata. The streams on the east side of the river are the Suatara (Swatara) and the Quatochatoon, the later being the Wiconisco or Mahantango.

(Drawing from the History of Dauphin County).

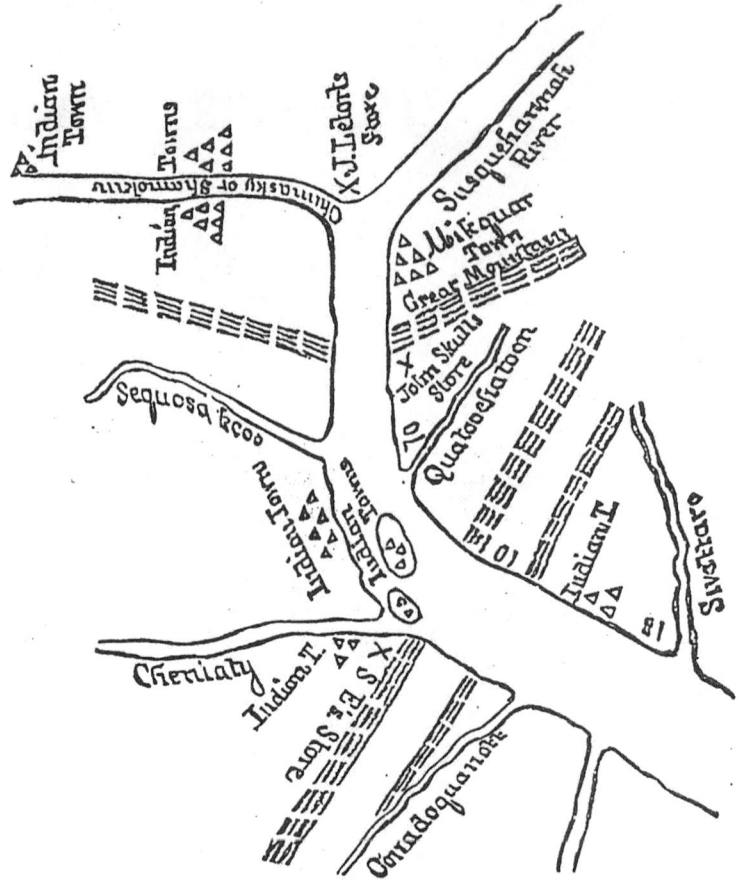

Although there are no known Susquehannock village sites in Lykens Township proper, the Susquehannock, and other Indians, undoubtedly used this land for hunting, temporary camps, travel, and possibly agriculture. Lykens Township is located between three major north/south Indian travel routes, and they would have afforded any traveler easy access to its land. The travel routes were; to the west, the Susquehanna River itself, and the Paxtang Path from Washington Boro in Lancaster County to Shamokin (Sunbury) in Northumberland County. The Paxtang Path paralleled the river to Harrisburg, crossed over Peters Mountain, and then more or less followed present day Route 147 to Sunbury. To the east was the Tulpehocken Path from Womelsdorf (near Reading) to Sunbury. It ran through Hegins, Valley View, Sacramento, and the Klingerstown gap, than merged with the Paxtang Path near Herndon.

About 1675 the Susquehannocks were defeated by the Iroquois Confederacy, and most were assimilated into its tribes in the north. Another 300 or so were expelled to the mouth of the Potomac River on the Chesapeake Bay. In 1701 the remnants of the Potomac River group were allowed to return to their original town at Conestoga. They now called themselves the Conestoga Indians, though some scholars believe that's what they called themselves all along. For the next 62 years the Conestoga lived in peace, having been converted to Christianity by Moravian missionaries. In 1763, enraged by the atrocities of other Indians, a group of settlers called "The Paxton Boys" murdered the last remaining 20 Conestoga Indians in their village, as well as at Lancaster, where the Indians had been taken for protection. That was the end of the once mighty Susquehannock Indians.

A Vacuum In The Valley

After the Six Nations defeated the Susquehannocks, the Confederacy was quick to fill the resulting void in the Susquehanna Valley. The Confederacy had three pressing concerns; the fear of another unfriendly Indian tribe taking over the Valley; the increasing encroachment of Europeans in the Valley; and the Indian refugee problem of the latter half of the 1600s caused by disease and war. Another concern was that some of the Indians simply didn't want to live near the white man.

The Six Nations came up with a solution to solve all of these problems at one time. They would allow these displaced Indians to live in the Susquehanna Valley if they would ally with the Iroquois Confederacy. This would give the Confederacy friends to the south, and slow the push of the Europeans, or so they hoped. The Confederacy gave these instructions to the refugees:

> *"Be Watchful that no body of the White People may come to settle near you. You must appear to them as frightful Men, and if notwithstanding they come too near give them a Push we will secure and defend you against them..."*

The refugees were only too happy to do so, and they came to the Susquehanna Valley from all directions. The Valley became a virtual melting pot of displaced Indians. The Tutelo, Conoy, Delaware, Nanticoke, Shawnee, Tuscarora, and various branches of these tribes filled the Susquehanna Valley. Some of them remained permanently in the Valley, and others slowly migrated north and west. These refugees left evidence of their presence all along the Susquehanna River and its tributaries in the form of place names and artifacts.

Area Artifacts

Indian artifacts can be found virtually anywhere in Upper Dauphin County, but only a few locations are said to yield large enough quantities to suggest anything other than a temporary camp (from a few months to a few years). The artifacts found are mostly in the form of tools, pottery, and projectile points, i.e., points (usually stone) made for the purpose of being affixed at the tip of a spear or arrow. Paradoxically, more projectile points are likely to be found at an older site of the pre-Colonial stages, than in the more recent Colonial and late Woodland stages. The reason is, during the late Woodland and Colonial stages, the Indians began trading with the Europeans for things they needed, eliminating their need to make them. The Indians found it was easier to trade a few animal pelts for a rifle than to make an arrowhead, and the rifle was infinitely more effective. Accordingly, artifacts from the Colonial stage are more likely to have been made from metal, wood, or glass. The more durable stone of the early stages outlasted the wood and most of the metals of the later stages, and therefore can be found in greater numbers.

Artifacts have been found in numerous areas of Lykens Township, but aside from possible closely guarded secret sites known to local artifact collectors, the finds by now are usually random. Only hints and clues of Upper Dauphin County sites can be found in historical records, with two exceptions. The Shoop site near the town of Enders, and the Clemson Island site located on Clemson Island near Halifax. The Shoop site has been dated to the Paleo-Indian stage, while the Clemson Island site appears to have been used to some extent by all stages. The Paleo-Indian and Archaic stage Indians were nomadic, and traveled with the seasons, and the migrations of the animals they depended on. Small bands of twenty to fifty would set up camps and move on when the resources were depleted, leaving behind evidence of their tool and point making. Only when the Transitional, Woodland, and Colonial Indians became engaged in agriculture did more permanent Indian villages begin to be utilized.

Clues to other Upper Dauphin County village sites are vague at best. In Egle's Notes and Queries, when talking about the disposition of Andrew Lykens' land, William Egle mentions, "there was an Indian village on the land owned by Henry Bohner." Another clue is the Indian name "Wiconisco" meaning "a wet and muddy camp," suggesting there was a camp, or camps, located along the Wiconisco Creek. Also, Andrew Lykens named four of the Indians who attacked him on March 7, 1756, suggesting they may have lived nearby. To be certain, it's possible for a persistent artifact hunter to find artifacts virtually anywhere in Lykens Township and vicinity.

Land Purchase of 1749

Although in 1681, King Charles II had granted proprietorship of Pennsylvania to William Penn, Penn adopted the policy of repurchasing the same lands from the Indians prior to it being opened for settlement. It was a policy Penn's sons continued after his death until all of Pennsylvania had been purchased in this manner. Penn's wisdom in buying land he already owned could not immediately be seen, but for certain it saved many pioneer and Indian lives, and made life easier for everyone. The tracts of land were large, and were purchased only after agreement of the terms by both parties. The negotiations went on sometimes for years.

The land that is now Lykens Township was part of the "Purchase of 1749" for which the Penn's paid the Iroquois Confederacy 500 English Pounds. This vast tract included all or parts of Dauphin, Northumberland, Columbia, Lebanon,

Schuylkill, Luzerne, Lackawanna, Carbon, Monroe, Pike, and Wayne Counties. The following document was part of the negotiations, and the terms herein were eventually adopted:

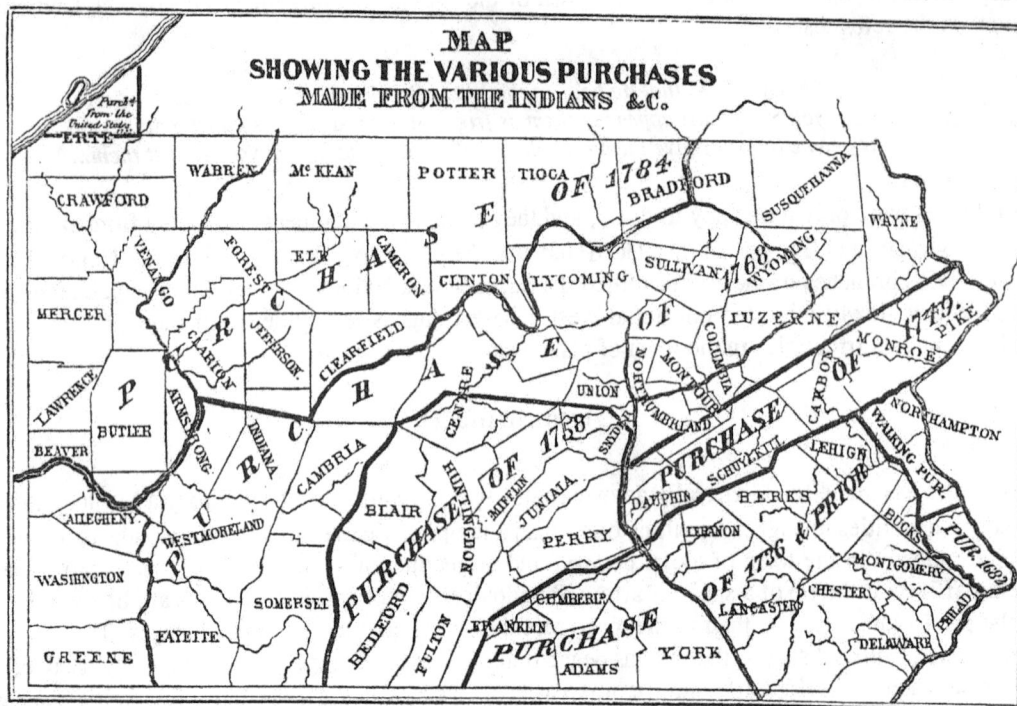

TRACTS OF LAND PURCHASED FROM THE INDIANS.

"Brethren:

We have taken into consideration your offer of the sale of some land lying on the East side of Sasquehanna and though we have no directions from the Proprietaries (who are now in England), to treat with you, yet as we judged it for their benefit and for the publick good not to reject the offer you have thought proper to make, we send you word by the Interpreter that we would not treat with you about a new purchase, but at the same time we gave you to understand that we could by no means accede to your proposal in the manner you had limited it, viz: to take land lying on the East Side of the Sasquehanna, as far as Thomas McKee's [Dalmatia], because you must be sensible that as the head of the river Schuylkill lies not far from the Sasquehanna, and not far from the head of Schuylkill there runs one of the main branches of the River Delaware, and that the Delaware Indians, in the last treaty, had granted the lands from this branch to very near the Leachawanchsein [Lackawaxen River] on Delaware. I say, considering all these things, which were explained to you on a Draught, by which it appears that all you offer is mountainous, broken and poor land, you must know that this is not worth our acceptance, but we added if you would extend your offer to go more Northerly on Sasquehanna as far as Shamokin [Sunbury], and that the tract might carry its breadth to Delaware river, so that we could in any manner justify ourselves to the Proprietors, we would close and give you a just consideration for the lands. On this you held a council and made us a second offer that you would sign a deed to the Proprietors for all that Tract of Land that lies with the following bounds, viz: Beginning at the Kittochhinny Hills [Kittatinny, or Blue Mountain], where your last purchase ends [Purchase of Oct. 11, 1736] on Sasquehanna, from thence by the courses of the River Sasquehanna to the first Mountain North of the creek called in the Onondago Language Cantawhy, and in the Delaware Language Makooniahy [Mahanoy Creek], on the said River Sasquehanna, this is the Western Boundary; then for the North Boundary by a straight line to be run from that Mountain to the main Branch of Delaware River, at the North side of the Mountain of Lechawachsein [Lackawaxen], so as to take in the waters of the Lechawachsein; the East Boundary to be the River Delaware from the North of the Viskil to the Kittochtiny; the South Boundary to be that range of the Kittochhinny Hills to the place of beginning, together with the islands of the Rivers Sasquehanna and Delaware in that Compass. Having received the second offer, though neither in this is there any considerable quantity of good land, yet in regard to your Poverty more than to the real value of the Tract we sent you word that on your Signing a deed we would pay you the sum of Five Hundred Pounds."

The gamesmanship that took place on both sides can be seen in this document. The Penns knew full well this was not "broken and poor land". The Iroquois Confederacy knew that the original offer was too small of a tract to be considered. It is also interesting to note the Penns had already purchased the extreme eastern part of this tract from the Delaware Indians as part of the infamous "Walking Purchase" of 1737. The deed for the 1749 purchase was signed on August 22 of that year. It became the first legitimate deed issued for Lykens Township land, aside from William Penn's original charter.

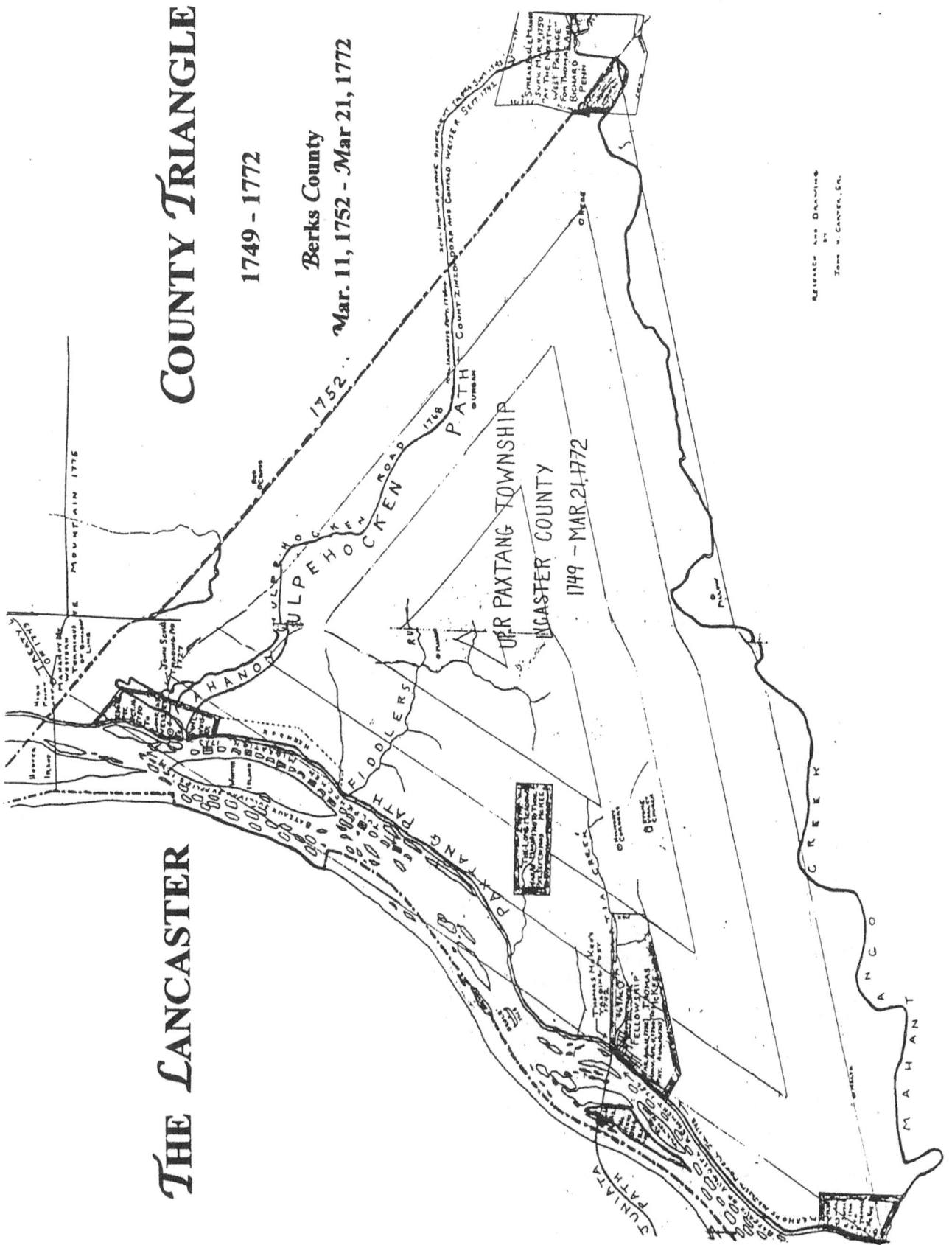

HISTORY OF LYKENS TOWNSHIP

By the 1749 treaty, Lancaster County (erected in 1729) extended to a line that passed between Bear Gap and Elysburg. The section of Lancaster County known as the township of Upper Paxtang took in all of the territory south of the line that would become Northumberland County. In 1752 Berks County was formed. It's western boundary was a straight line crossing Mahantango Creek at Klingerstown, and met the Susquehanna River at the base of Little Mountain near Herndon. Upper Paxtang Township, Lancaster County became the "Lancaster County Triangle" until 1772 when Northumberland County was formed. During all those years until 1772 when Northumberland County was formed, all of the lands surveyed or patented within this triangle were registered at the county seat of Lancaster. [A fact worth noting for land and genealogy purposes.] When Northumberland County was formed, Upper Paxtang Township was greatly reduced. In 1785 it became part of Dauphin County.

Much of the "Lancaster County Triangle" territory borders on Lykens Township. The settlers of that area have Always had strong ties with those in what would become Lykens Township.

Almost immediately after the 1749 purchase, the land was opened for settlement. Andrew Lykens was one of the first settlers to take advantage of the opportunity and was granted 250 acres on the north side of Wiconisco Creek in 1750. Land ownership in Lykens Township was thus begun.

Area Indian Names and Their Meanings

Allegheny [Delaware] – "river of the Alligewi [Indians]".
Appalachian [Choctaw] – "people on the other side".
Catasauqua [Delaware] – "thirsty earth".
Catawissa [Delaware] – "growing fat".
Chillisquaque [*] – "at the place of snow birds".
Codorus [*] – "rapid water".
Conestoga [*] – "at the place of the immersed pole"; an Indian tribe formerly called the "Susquehannock".
Conewago/Conewingo [Iroquois] – "at the rapids".
Conococheague [Iroquois] – "indeed a long way"
Conodoguinet [Iroquois] – "for a long way nothing but bends" or "long winding river".
Delaware [English] – The name given to the Lenni Lenape Indians who resided on the Delaware River. The river was named for Lord De La Warre, Governor of the English Colony at Jamestown, VA.
Juniata [Iroquois] – "a projecting rock".
Kishacoquillas [*] – "the snakes are already in their dens".
Kittanning [Delaware] – "at the place of the great river".
Kittatinny [Delaware] – "a great hill or mountain" or "loftiest mountain".
Lenni Lenape [Delaware] – "the original people" or "real people".
Mahantango [Delaware] – "where we had plenty of meat to eat".
Mahoning/Mahonoy [Delaware] – "at the lick".
Manada [Delaware] – "an island".
Mauch Chunk [*] – "the mountain of bears".
Muncy [Delaware] – "where stones are gathered together".
Nanticoke [*] – "tide water people"; name of Indian tribe originally on the Chesapeake.
Nittany [Delaware] – "a single hill or mountain".
Ohio [*] – "beautiful river".
Paxtang [Delaware] – "where the water stands" or "place of springs".
Pequea [*] – "dust" or "ashes".
Pocono [Delaware] – "a stream between mountains".
Schuylkill [Swedish] – "hidden river"; name given to a branch of the Delaware Indians.
Shamokin [*] – "the place of chiefs or rulers"; original name of Sunbury, PA.
Shikellamy [Iroquois] – "he enlightens us"; name of famous chief residing at Sunbury.
Shenandoah [*] – "it is a very great plain".
Susquehanna [*] – "the muddy river".
Tamaqua [Delaware] – "little beaver"; the name of an Indian chief.
Tuscarora [*] – "hemp gatherers"; the sixth Indian tribe admitted to the Six Nations.
Tulpehocken [Delaware] – "turtle land".
Wiconisco [*] – "a wet and muddy camp".
Wyoming [*] – "large flats" or "great meadows".
[*] – origin unknown

(Thanks to Jay Ossman for research for this chapter)

Chapter 2

THE LIFE AND TIMES
OF
ANDREW LYKENS

King Gustavus Adophus of Sweden had a dream – he wanted to start a Swedish colony in the New World, and as early as 1624 he began to plan his project. Unfortunately, before he could see his dream become reality, King Gustavus was killed in battle in 1632. After his untimely death, his young daughter Christina, now Queen of Sweden, did not let her father's dream die with him. Late in 1637 she sent two ships full of Swedish pilgrims to start New Sweden Colony, America. They arrived on the west bank of the Delaware River in March of 1638, and were so impressed with its beauty they selected that spot to make a new home. They purchased from the native Indians a stretch of land roughly between what is now Trenton, New Jersey, and Wilmington, Delaware. In the coming years many more ships with Swedish settlers would arrive in New Sweden, and the new colony grew and prospered. Andrew Lykens' great-grandfather Nils Anderssen, along with his large family, was among a later group of settlers, arriving around 1654. The Lykens family also flourished in New Sweden, on both the east and west shores of the Delaware River.

By the time Andrew Lykens was born in 1701 the family surname had gone through many variations of basically the same theme. The original came from a very complicated set of Swedish naming rules, which when simplified states the given (or Christian) name of the father becomes the child's surname. Sometimes the place of the child's birth became the surname, with the father's given name used as a middle name. This is the most likely scenario of what was to evolve into a name we recognize today as "Lykens" the name attached to a town, a valley, and a township, in Upper Dauphin County, Pennsylvania.

Not much is known about the youth of Andrew Lykens, but for certain his life centered around his church and family. He probably spent his early years working on the family farm, and attending the historic Gloria Dei (Old Swede's) Church, or Christ Church in New Sweden. About December 13, 1730, Andrew married Jennett Calhoun. (Jennett, or Jane as she was called, was a daughter of John and Jennett Calhoun.) Now married, and with the prospect of children, Andrew set out to make a home for his family and provide for their needs. This noble endeavor seemed to be the motivating factor in Andrew's life, but also the one that caused him considerable trouble, and would eventually cost him his life.

In 1732, about two years after his marriage, Andrew settled near Swatara Creek, Hanover Township, now in Dauphin County, Pa. This is the first known account of his migration. He was granted two hundred and fifty acres of land there in April 1737, and presumably he built a house, made improvements to the land, and began his family.

The land that Andrew Lycans owned near Swatara Creek was adjacent to a mill tract of land on the creek, and owned early by John Young. Another adjoining tract contained a small log house built in the 1730s and was owned by Adam Harper. It was the first frontier post and public house northwest of Philadelphia, serving weary travelers and scattered settlers. Indians continued to live in wigwams in the vicinity when the tavern post was erected. Several caves along the Swatara Creek were said to serve as a place of refuge from Indians during the early days. Another place of refuge was the so-called Fort at Harper's where early settlers could gather during troubled times. In 1756, the Indians killed five or six white persons in that immediate vicinity. Andrew Lykens escaped that episode. Today, the approximate whereabouts of Andrew Lykens' first land near Swatara Creek can be located by first finding the brick tavern that was built on the site of the old one in 1804.

During his stay in the Swatara Creek area, Andrew Lykens and his family apparently lived a relatively normal tranquil life. In the Court of the Quarter Sessions held in Lancaster on May 5, 1741, Andrew Lykens served on the jury which found a saddle thief guilty, and sentenced to a fine of ten shillings and twenty-one lashes on the bare back. But in the November 1742 Session of the same Court, Andrew was indicted for assault on one Joseph Ripeth. The details of this episode are not known other than historian William Egle's comment, "he [Andrew] took the law into his own hands." Based on that statement, one can speculate if he had taken a less drastic course, the law would have been on Andrew's side. This would not be the last time Andrew lacked the patience to wait for the slow movement of the law.

Andrew Lykens apparently possessed a spirit of adventure that stayed with him throughout his life. During the early 1740s, he sold his land on Swatara Creek, and accompanied by his brother-in-law George Calhoun, William White, and a few others, he and his family moved to settle (illegally) the lands between the Juniata River and Sherman's Creek on the west shore of the Susquehanna River. This practice of "squatting" was not uncommon in Colonial Pennsylvania, and in many cases the squatter becomes the eventual owner of the land. The authorities usually looked the other way, but this time there were extenuating circumstances and they were obligated to respond. The land had not yet been purchased from the Indians and they resented this encroachment by the white man on their property. But what the Provincial authorities saw as a far more serious matter is that the squatters were interfering with the delicate negotiations presently underway between the famed Indian agent Conrad Weiser and the Indians, for the purchase of that same land. The Indians confronted the Provincial authorities about the small Lykens settlement, and others as well, and demanded the pioneers be removed immediately. In 1748 the authorities sent the Lancaster County sheriff and other officials, including Conrad Weiser, to the Lykens settlement and they informed the settlers they must leave at once. Conrad Weiser himself accompanying the officials to the settlement attests to the seriousness of the offense. But just walking away from years of hard work must not have been an easy matter, and the settlers chose not to heed the sheriff's warning. On May 22, 1750, the under-sheriff of Cumberland County and other legal authorities were sent to the settlement, to warn the inhabitants to leave. When the men arrived with the orders, they found five log cabins owned by these people: William White, George Calhoun, William and George Galloway, one not finished but owned by David Hiddleston, and a cabin owned by Andrew Lycans. Lycans was not there, but three of the other men were taken into custody because they refused to obey orders. Two others resisted and ran away. From a safe distance they turned, and called back saying that they would not be carried to jail.

The next morning the magistrates went back to the cabin of Andrew Lycans, and found only their children home. They were told that the father and mother would be back soon. The neighbors already in custody agreed at this point that they were all trespassers. They posted a one hundred-pound bond for themselves and Lycans, and signed over custody of all the cabins to the Proprietors. The magistrates took council and decided that the cabins would have to be burned to keep anyone from coming back later to settle. The personal belongings were removed from the cabins, and as each one became empty, the sheriff burned them. That is, all but the one owned by Andrew Lycans.

The following day, May 24, 1750, the magistrates again came calling on Andrew Lycans to make him aware that his neighbors had paid bond for his appearance and immediate removal. They also cautioned him not to bring himself or them into trouble by a refusal. At this point, Mr. Lycans produced a loaded gun, and said he would shoot the first man that would dare to come closer. The magistrates were able to disarm him; he was convicted and committed to the custody of the sheriff. By coincidence a group of Indians were in the vicinity while all this was taking place. When they saw the behavior of Andrew Lycans, they insisted that his cabin should be set on fire, or they would proceed to do it. The Lycans family possessions were removed, the empty cabin burned, and Lycans was carried off to Lancaster County jail. The sheriff noted in the account of the episode, that he treated these settlers with as much kindness as possible, and offered to help them to become established else where . . . "on any part of the two million acres lately purchased of the Indians." He also said that "the cabins that were burned were of no considerable value, being such as the country people erect in a day or two and cost only the charge of an entertainment." Soon after this episode, the governing authorities considered the Indians appeased, and they quickly ordered Andrew's release.

ANDREW LYCANS RESETTLES

Most of us have heard a version of the story of the Indian raid on the Andrew Lykens farm on the Wiconisco Creek. Shortly after the episode on the west shore of Susquehanna River, Andrew Lycans made a new settlement for the third time in his life. He sought and was given permission to take up about two hundred acres of land recently opened up for settlement "near the Wiconisco Creek" in what is now Loyalton, Lykens Valley, Dauphin County.

Here the families of Lycans, Rewalt, Ludwig Shietz and possibly others "made considerable improvements." Until the spring of 1756 these pioneers on the Wiconisco were living on their land in relatively peaceful surroundings. But in 1755, General Edward Braddock and his troops were sent by England, to protect the Ohio and Allegany Valleys from takeover by the French and their Indian allies. Braddock and his forces were on their way to Fort Duquesne when surprised by the French and Indians. The British forces were annihilated and General Braddock killed. After their stunning victory the French began paying the Indians for any American scalp in an effort to terrorize the settlers and push the frontier line farther east. There was a marked increase of devastation and death caused by the Indians. All along the frontier, which at that time included the east and west shores of the Susquehanna River, the Indians massacred the settlers whenever and wherever they could. Andrew Lycans' new land on the Wiconisco Creek lay directly in their path of death and destruction.

On March 7, 1756, the day began for Andrew like many others, tending to the many chores necessary for homesteading on the frontier. This day Andrew with the help of his son John, two neighbors - John Rewalt and Ludwig Schietz, an unidentified farm hand and a young boy, went out early in the day to care for their cattle and take care of the necessary chores. Two shots rang out, and the men ran back into the house to prepare to defend them selves. While they were in the house, some Indians took cover in a nearby hog pen. By this time, the families were alerted, and three men, John Lycans (Andrews son), John Rewalt, and Ludwig Schietz already armed, crept out of the house to ward off their attackers. The Indians saw them, and each of the men received a serious gunshot wound (Ludwig in the abdomen). By this time Andrew Lycans noticed an Indian at the hog pen that he identified as Joshua James, and shot him dead. He also saw two white men running from the cover of an outbuilding. Andrew, Ludwig Schietz and a boy with him decided to try for an escape, but were quickly observed, and pursued by about sixteen Indians. The savages got close enough so that one of them, Bill Davis almost succeeded in striking the boy with a tomahawk, but Ludwig Schietz was able to kill that Indian, and Lycans killed two more and wounded several others. Exhausted and wounded the three men eventually sat down on a log to rest. The pursuing Indians observed them from a distance and then retreated to take care of their wounded. Lycans and his party managed to escape over the mountain to Hanover Township. However, Andrews' wounds were very serious, and resulted in his death sometime on the evening of March 7, 1756. Ironically, the Indians apparently were acquainted with Andrew Lykens and his neighbors. Perhaps they were neighbors from the nearby Indian encampment. A few days after the attack, an official report was written naming the attackers. They were: Bill Davis, one of the Indians killed, Tom Hickman, Tom Hayes, and Joshua James, members of the Delaware Tribe.

H. G. Stutzman in his "History of the Reformed Church of Tower City, Pennsylvania" outlines the path that the wounded settlers took when they fled this area. He writes "an old Indian trail led into the upper end of the Williams Valley from the south. This trail passed through the Swatara Gap north of Lickdale and followed the Swatara Creek to its junction with Fishing Creek at the present village of Suedberg. Thence it proceeded along Fishing Creek, through the gorge later spanned by the High Bridge, and thence along the gap in the Sharp Mountain. From there it passed northwestwardly across Stoney Mountain, emerging in Williams Valley near the Oley Bender residence."

Andrew Lycans left a wife Jane, one son, and five daughters. The whereabouts of Jane and the five daughters on the day Andrew and his party were attacked is unknown. It is also unknown when or if Jane Lykens ever returned to her land on the Wiconisco Creek (the grant was in her name). John Lycans son of Andrew recovered from his wounds. He was commissioned an officer in the Provincial Service on July 12, 1762. In June 1764, Lieutenant John Lycans was stationed at Manada Gap with fifteen men to guard against the Indians. He never lived in our area, but probably on the west side of the Susquehanna River.

Ludwig Shietz returned to Lykens Valley, raised a large family and died about 1795. His descendants stayed here, and some of them were affiliated with these churches: Hoffman, St. Johns, David's and Salem (Killinger

John Rewalt probably moved to another area of Pennsylvania. But a possible son or grandson, John Rewalt (Mar 17, 1769 – Jan 17, 1810), is buried in Hill Cemetery in Halifax. He had five children named: Elizabeth, Sally, John, William and George. This John Rewalt kept a tavern stand located on the corner of Market St. in Halifax. After he died, the tavern was purchased by Michael Shure and became known as The Travellers Inn. William White was killed by Indians on July 10, 1763 near Mexico, Juniata County. Conrad Weiser died in Berks County in 1760.

The identity or disposition of the young boy and farm hand with the Lykens party on March 7, 1756 has never been learned.

During the next years more raids from marauding Indians caused other pioneers to flee, although those assaults were not considered as serious as this one. Before too long, the white inhabitants were able to live in peace, without being molested by the Indians that continued to live in the region. The Lycans cabin survived for over one hundred years, until 1863. It is said to have been located on the land now owned by the Domer Shaffer family, about halfway between the Shaffer house and the site of the old Oak Dale Forge.

During the 1760s, this upper area was attached to Lancaster County and became part of Paxtang. In 1767, it became Upper Paxtang and during another interval of years while governed by Lancaster County, we were listed as Upper District, Wiconisco District or just plain "Upper End". Families had been slowly moving into the area, and small pockets of residents were sparsely dotting the landscape. These folks had to be independent, brave, and very hardy souls, and yet their numbers increased. The area had finally become a permanent development.

Andrew Lykens will to survive on a piece of frontier land probably brought him the honor of having his name attached to a beautiful part of Dauphin County, Pennsylvania. Many others would have quit, and with good cause, had they endured just a small part of what Andrew did. His fortitude could be compared to that of Daniel Boone, who's uncle Benjamin Boone married Susannah Lycan, Andrew's first cousin. Pioneers of this nature played a significant role in Pennsylvania's history, and in building a nation from the wilderness.

ANDREW LYKENS AND HIS FAMILY

As previously mentioned, the surname **LYKENS** went through many changes over a long period of time. It is derived from the Swedish name NILSSON [Nils Anderssen]. Other alias names include Likens, Lycans, Leyson, Lykill, Lykins, Lykings, Laicans, etc.). It comes from a small village called Laiykan, located in Gunnarskog Parish, Varmland, Sweden. It means "a clearing in the woods" or "a glen."

The original name has gone through many variations of spellings due to a very complicated set of Swedish naming rules, which when simplified states that the given (or Christian name) of the father becomes the child's surname. The variety of its spellings creates a difficult task in finding the family genealogy.

Nils Anderssen (b c1610/1620 – d c1680), and his large family are the first of the family to arrive in America. They arrived on the ship Eagle in 1654, and settled in the New Sweden Colony shortly after it was settled. They were some of the earliest immigrants to take up land along the coast of Pennsylvania, before spreading out to many other parts of the state and country. The father was a miller and he and his family first resided at Fort Christina, (present-day Wilmington). He is recorded as having made a purchase from the company store as early as June 17, 1654. His last purchase in that store was on August 8, 1655, shortly before the Dutch conquered the colony, and made it part of New Netherland.

Andrew Lycans/ Lykens
From a Description

Nils Anderssen and his unknown wife **had these children** (they all used a form of the surname Laicons): **Anders; Rachel; Esther** b c1636 in Sweden, m Robert Wallis; **Hannah** b c1638 in Sweden, m Sep 4, 1686, Daniel Howell; **Marcus/Moses** (c1640 – c1695) of Cooper's Creek, Gloucester Co., N.J.; *****Peter** b c1642 - see below; *****Michael** b c1844 - see below; **Susannah** b c1646 in Sweden; **Sarah** b c1648, m Feb 4, 1686/87 John Ironmonger.

1671, the first known record of the two brothers Peter and Michael, also locates them in Delaware. Peter was listed as working for Armegot Printz on her plantation in the New Sweden Colony. Michael Lycon secured a land patent at Shackamaxon, Philadelphia.

Both brothers eventually moved to Shackamaxon, in Philadelphia, located in the vicinity now known as Frankford. Most of the early family members were affiliated with the Lutheran denomination. From that area, the family members bravely removed to various unsettled or briefly settled areas. The story of their early ventures is most interesting.

*PETER NILSSON LYCON born about 1642 in Sweden, died about Nov.1691 in Shackamaxon, Phila Co. Another source says his will was filed 3-10-1697]. He married about 1662 in New Sweden Colony, Christina _____. Early Pennsylvania Land Records indicate that on May 26, 1684, Peter purchased 200 acres of land in Shackamaxon (Philadelphia). Peter built a mill on the land, but soon his mill was taken over by the Quakers. Despite the takeover, the mill was known as "Swedes Mill" for many years.

On September 25, 1691 a Peter Nelson received a patent for 468 acres of land "with a yearly rent of one bushel of good winter wheat for each hundred acres." (This was a yearly fee paid to the proprietors). Peter married, but the name of his wife is unknown. **Peter had these known children: Anna; Brigitta; Magdalena; Nils - see below; Hanse (1667 - Sep 19, 1751) of Pennypack Creek, Phila,** see below; **Anders Peterson (b c1670 Upland Creek, Delaware Co - d c1762, Robeson Twp., Berks Co.), m c 1694 Annika (Anna) Jonson. Anders Peterson and Annika (Jonson) Nillson had these children: Peter** (b c1704, Berks Co – d 1794 Winchester, Frederick Co, Va), m c1734 Sarah Jonson; <u>Susannah</u> (c1708 – c1784), m c1738 Benjamin Boone (b Jul 16, 1706, Devonshire, England – d Oct 14, 1762, Berks Co.), son of Squire Boone, and brother to famous Daniel Boone; Ingeborg (c1672 – after 1727), m c1690, Mouns Jonasson/Jones (b1663 – d1727, Manatawny, Pa.), a son of Jonas Nielsson and Gertrude Svensdotter. About 1700 Mouns and Ingeborg moved to what is now Douglasville, Berks Co. Their house built in 1716 in Douglasville, still stands and is on the National Registry of Historic Places. **Ingeborg and Mouns Jonasson children:** <u>Margaret</u> b c1692; <u>Peter</u> b c1694; <u>Christina</u> b c1696; <u>Jonas</u> b Sep 23, 1698; <u>Anders</u>; <u>Magdalena</u>.

<u>NILS LAICON</u>, son of Peter Nilsson Lycon above, (b 1666 - d Dec 4,1721, Northern Liberties, Philadelphia, is bur Old Swedes Church Cem, Delaware, his tombstone reads: "Here lieth ye body of Neills Laickan who died Dec ye 4th 1721 aged 55 years), who married Marie Gostenberg. Marie was a daughter of Olaf Nilsson and Cecilia Gostenberg. Nils Laicon and Marie lived in Northern Liberties, Philadelphia as early as 1756, when their daughter Bridget died.
Nils and Marie (Gostenberg) Laicon had these children: John, Peter, Christina, m Justa Justis, Jr., **Gertrude,** m Edward Hatfield; **Anna** b1695, m John Rambo; **Marie** b 1697, m Hans Keen b 1699, a son of Erick and Catherine (Classen) Keen. All of these children were born before 1699. **They also had these: Bridget** (b 1701 - d May 7, 1756 of consumption, record in Old Swedes Church), m 1st John Seeds, 2nd Thomas Milnor. They lived in New Castle Co., Delaware. Bridget's will was recorded in book D, page 206, New Castle. **Susanna** b 1703, m Thomas Rowan; **Elizabeth** m Frederick Georgen, who d before 1722. After Frederick Georgen died, Elizabeth married 2nd on Aug 15, 1722 to Maous (Louis) Keen. The record of marriage is in Old Swedes Church in Delaware and reads: " Louis Keen married Aug 15, 1722, Elizabeth, dau of Nils Laican of Lycon, oldest son of Peter Nilsson Lauken, a native of Sweden, whose name is given in the _____ Church register as Elizabeth Georgen, from whence we may infer that at time of the nuptials with Maous Keen, she was a widow."

<u>HANSE</u> LAICON son of Peter Nilsson above (b 1668 in Phila. Co. - d Sep 19, 1751, Pennypack Creek, Phila. Co, bur Old Swedes Church Cem, Delaware), married about 1689 to Gertrude Elizabeth Claussen, a dau of Jan Classen. On August 30, 1697, a Hans Lykell alias Nelson sold 175 acres of land to G. Lillington. On January 27, 1699 Andreas Lykell sold land to G. Lillington.
Hanse and Gertrude (Claussen) Lycans had these children:
_____ dau (b c1691 – d c1746, Low Darby Twp, Chester Co, Pa.), m Otto Netzelius.
Susanna (c1693 - 1744, Phila), m Lawrence Rawson.
Eva b c1695, m Olaf Mollicka in 1718.
John b 1697 in Phila, was m 1718, to Christiana Elizabeth _____. (A record indicates that John and three others broke out of Burlington County, N.J. jail on April 29, 1742. Nothing more is known about him.
Peter b Jan 2, 1698/99 near Wilmington Del - d before March 5, 1754 Winchester, Frederick Co, Va), He m Oct 22, 1719, Bridget _____, moved to Virginia. **Peter and Bridget Laicon had these children:**

Hance Lycan (Nov 24, 1727 - May 29, 1767), m Brita "Bridget" - **Jacob Gooden Lycan** son of Hance (Dec 24, 1758 - 1808/09), m Margaret Rachel Morton - Jacob Gooden Lycans son **Andrew B. Lycans** (Jan 1, 1802 - ___), m Ann Seals b Aug 14, 1809)
Eleanor (no dates)
Jacob A.
Hans Jonas -Johannes
Andrew (b 1742 - d 1781 in Virginia)
Charles (b 1746 Frederick, Virginia)
Henry (b 1750 Frederick, Virginia)

Andrew (b Dec 19, 1701 in Phila – d Mar 7, 1756 in Hanover Twp, Pa.) died from wounds received in an Indian attack at his home in Lykens Township. [See personal write-up about this incident.] He m Dec. 13,1730 in Christ Church, Phila. to Jannett (Jane) Calhoun, a dau of John and Jannett Calhoun of Paxtang, Dau Co. Lykens Township was named for Andrew Lykens, early settler of this area. Andrew was also the namesake of Lykens Valley. **Andrew and Jane (Calhoun) Lycans had these children:**
John (no dates) believed to have married Elizabeth _____, and had a son Abraham. This Abraham received a grant of 323 acres of land on February 3, 1755, in or near the mouth of the Juniata River. The land was near the area where this branch of the Lykens family apparently settled in the Juniata area. John was commissioned July 12, 1762, as an officer (Lieutenant) of the Provincial service, and was stationed at Manada Gap in 1764.

Susannah (no dates), m Sep 20, 1757 James Crampton, Paxtang, Dau Co. by Rev. John Casper Stoever.
Rebecca (no dates)
Mary (no dates), m Joseph Poultney
Margaret b c1742, m 1st on Jul 1, 1761 to William Buchanan of Carlisle, Pa. m 2nd Robert Chambers before May 23, 1780.
Elizabeth (b c1743 – d pre 1820), m Feb 5, 1771 Edmund Richardson

Hans (b c1702 - d May 20 to June 15, 1761 in Lower Dublin Twp, Phila), m Margaret Morton. **Hans and Margaret (Morton) Lycans had these known children:**
Mary
Andrew (Jan 16, 1726 - Sep 20, 1807),
Caroline

Nicholas (b c1703 – d 1766, Chester Twp., Burlington Co., N.J.), m c1728, but name of wife not known.

*MICHAEL NILSSON** (b c1644 - Sweden - d Apr 17, 1703 in Glouster, N.J.) , m c1670 to Helene Lom b 1650 in New Sweden Colony. Early Pennsylvania land records (Philadelphia) give this information: Michael Leyson (al's) Nelson received a patent for 462 1/2 acres of land March 4, 1691 from the Commissioners "under the Yearly Rent of One Bushell of wheat, which said 462 1/2 acres were the said Michaels dividend of a Tract held formerly by him in Joint Tenancy with Peter Cock by virtue of a Patent dated May 3, 1671, granted to them by Governor Lovelace for about 600 acres. He sold 327 acres of his land August 31, 1699.
Michael and Helene (Lom) Nilsson had these children (most affiliated with Swedesboro P.E. Church):
Catherine b 1671 m Laurens Hulings b before 1672, a son of Marcus Laurenszen and Brigitta Danielsson.
Anna b Aug 21, 1673 m John Rambo, Jr
Gertrude b Dec 16, 1676 m Erick Cox (Cock)
Nicholas b Feb 20, 1677 d 1733, Gloucester Co., N.J.
Mous b Mar 10, 1679 d 1727, bur Jan 17, 1728, Gloucester Co
Andrew b Mar 11, 1682 d c1733, Gloucester Co
Christina b Feb 17, 1684
Michael Likian (Lycans) b Oct 11, 1688 m Anna _____
Helene b Oct 20, 1689 m John Jones on Jul 7, 1723
Zacharius b Dec 26, 1696 d c1733, Gloucester Co

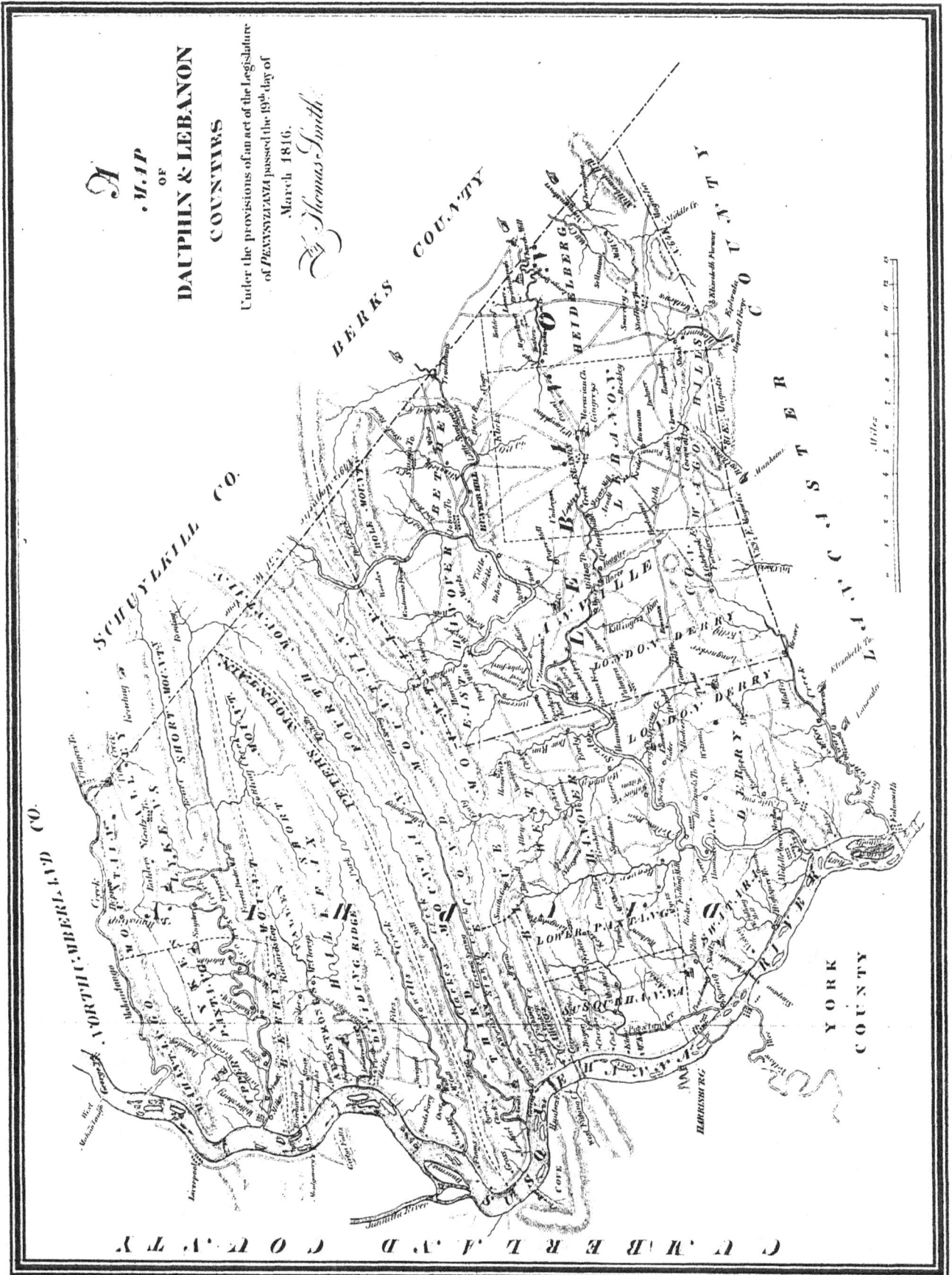

Chapter 3

𝔈ARLY 𝔏IFE 𝔍N 𝔗HE "𝔘PPER 𝔈ND"

When Andrew Lykens settled in this area he was living in Paxtang Township, one of the original townships, formed August 17, 1729. It was part of Lancaster County (which had just been split from Chester County), and covered an extensive portion of what is now Lebanon County. About 1765 Paxtang Township was separated, and Upper Paxtang was formed, covering that area we refer to as "the upper end."

Most early references to this area speak of the dense forests. Upon arrival, the first settler's task was to clear the land, and provide shelter. Little or no expenditure of money was needed. Large and beautiful timbers provided the necessary logs for the construction of their homes, and wooden pegs held them together. There was little need for nails, hammers, or glass. At first the houses were one story, one-room cabins that could be erected in a brief period of time. If there was a foundation, it consisted of a buried rock situated under each corner. Very few window openings if any, were found in these first buildings - "openings weakened the structures." The short narrow doors and floors were constructed of logs that were split lengthwise. The roof was thatched or covered with bark, later with wood shingles. The loft of the cabin served as the sleeping quarters and provided a place for storage. At first panthers, wild cats, wolves, foxes, skunks and other obnoxious things were in abundance roaming about near their homes. Squirrels, ground hogs, pheasants and partridges were also abundant. Snakes were frequently found occupying the kitchen cupboard.

The men were farmers, but had the necessary skills to build the homes, repair and build their needed equipment. A few specialized in skills such as millwrights, blacksmiths, saddlers, and shoemakers. The women engaged in providing the family needs: preparing the food for the table; clothing and linens for the home; medicinal know how. The family had to be self-reliant, there wasn't much to be purchased!

Charles F. Muench in penning the memories in 1879 of his childhood in Lykens Valley during the early 1800s, relates that after the wool from their sheep was processed into fabric, tailors and their apprentices were engaged by the farmers to come to their homes to make the necessary garments for the male members of the household for the coming winter. Women then used some of the wool to make stockings for the whole family. Shoemakers were engaged in the same manner. One pair of shoes in those days was the average supply for the lad or lass, until the next fall season. Mr. Muench also recalled that nearly every family had a patch of ground for flax raising. After a long and tedious process starting in May when the seeds were planted, and continuing for many months, the flax was ready for spinning into cloth. Spinning parties were then formed. Young girls considered it no hardship to walk three or four miles to a spinning party (the young man carrying the spinning wheel.) Half of the night was generally spent in the employment. In place of tallow candle or oil, light was furnished from pine knots properly prepared for the purpose. A hole of about 14 inches in a large chimney, with the proper flue to carry off the smoke, constituted the chandelier for the party. A large portion of the families had their own weaving looms, which afforded employment on rainy days for girls and boys. Mr. Muench wrote that his sister taught him the art and mystery of weaving before he was ten years old.

Gradually, more people arrived, and the settlements became more permanent. The pioneers had begun to relax because Indians were no longer a serious threat.

But this period of time was not without it's problems! As previously mentioned land was being cleared, and that was a difficult task. Some of the early young folks who came here had very little financial backing to purchase land. For them the task of clearing land became a method of obtaining land for themselves. At least one young man, Peter Forney saw this as an opportunity to own land. He contracted with a landowner to clear the land, earning one acre for himself, for each two acres he cleared.

Folks, who invested in large tracts of land, first of all were unable to oversee all of their land. Most of the time, when they constructed their homes, they cleared perhaps an acre or two around their homestead and fenced that area. But then they also cleared timber from other sections of their land, and soon a new crop of grass, small bushes and undergrowth replaced the forest. Sometimes contentious neighboring farmers saw this as an opportunity to graze their cattle, sheep or other animals in an area that they could easily be nourished, and were free to roam a whole season. But the neighbors were the least of the offenders. After the winter was over, large flocks of animals were driven to these more isolated regions by settlers who lived in more confining areas. It was a cheap way to fatten their cattle by letting them roam all summer in these sections. Sometimes they roamed over the fields on the farms and

14

destroyed new crops that the local farmers had planted. In the fall, young boys or older men returned to drive the cattle back home. This procedure was annoying to say the least for the native farmers. The farmers retaliated by getting the offenders attention in advertisements in appropriate newspapers. The following items applied to the early land in the Upper Dauphin area:

Advertisement appearing in the Pennsylvania Gazette for 24 April 1776:

" Upper Paxton Township, Lancaster County, April 16, 1776. Whereas we, the subscribers, and others, have these many years past suffered greatly, by reason of great numbers of cattle that have every year been brought here to pasture in Lykens Valley, which have destroyed our common pasture, to the great loss and injury of the inhabitants here; and as we conceive it to be a public nuisance, we do therefore forewarn all persons, who have been accustomed to such practices, as well as those who should incline to do so for the future, that if any cattle should be brought to Lyken's Valley aforesaid to pasture (except such as are owners of land there, and have the same seated) and such cattle should be drove away or killed, therein, as we are resolved not to suffer it any longer in the manner we have done hitherto, as we have taken due advice upon the premises. signed:

John Hoffman	Joel Ferree	Leonard Snider
Christopher Snider	Nicholas Hoffman	Melchoir Fegal
Peter Hoffman	Peter Smith	John Boshart
Jacob Harmon	Michael Deivler	
William Rider	Jacob Sherz	

Soon families were increasing; so more substantial and elaborate homes were being built. The countryside was becoming dotted with log cabins, two story houses, stables and barns, a gristmill or two and by 1780 a still. It was a peaceful and beautiful place. Glass became more readily available and affordable, so windows were cut into the walls to make the interior of the homes more cheerful. Enough land had been cleared to produce crops of food for the families and their animals. But much of the land was still covered with forests.

Prosperity is followed by taxation. The first known assessment list of Upper Paxtang (Lancaster Co.) was taken in 1778, and includes a record of the inhabitants of "Wiconisco District, taken by Peter Hoffman, Upper Paxtang, Wikiniski District." The following names appear on that list and give us an idea of how much the valley was increasing in population:

Buffington, Benj.	Hoffman, Jacob	Nigla, George	Shotz, Jacob
Bratz, Ludwick	Herman, David	Peter, Richard	Shesley, John
Conaway, Francis	Hains, Henry	Paul, John	Shesley, Jacob
Con, Daniel	Jury, Abraham	Regel, Andrew	Smith, Jacob
Cline, Widow	King, Adam	Rither, William	Snider, Leonard
Divler, Michael	Kooper, George	Ridle, George	Shotz, Ludwick
Divler, Mathias	Lerue, Francis	Seal, George	Sheadel, George
Fritz, George	Lark, Stopher	Stiver, Yost	Walker, Robert
Frelick, Anthony	Leman, Daniel	Snoak, Christian	Woodside, James
Grub's Land	Meck, Nicholas	Saladay, Michael	Weaver, Martin
Huffman, Peter	Metz, Jacob	Salady, John	Wolf, Daniel
Huffman, Hanicle	Miller, John	Stonebreaker, Nitter	Worz, Adam
Huffman, John	Matter, John	Shesley, Stophel	Weaver, Jacob
	Myers, John		Wersel, Henry
	Nighbour, Abraham		Yeager, Andrew

Freeman

Jonathan Woodside. Samuel Kessler, John Phillips, Adam Nartz, John Herman, Godlep Kline

Located Lands

Aaron Levy	Caleb Way	Nicholas Miller	Frederick Height
Bartrem Galbraith	William Poore	Patrick Work	Henry Wails
Lattis Winger	George Fry	John Shock	Samuel Sleight
Isaac Heeler	Abraham Reggy	George Muckland	George Harris
Simon Snyder	John Cline	Philip DeHause	Levy Simeons
Daniel Williams	James Beeham	Martin Cryder	Doctor Leight
Felty Overlady	Stephen Martin	Arthur Niger	John Clandining
____ Lauman	Andrew Boggs	Christian Snyder	____ Teeker

Michael Miller	Rev. Anderline	Michael Groscolp	George Ferree
Jacob Whitmore	Simon Brand	John Didde	

Above 53 years

Richard Peter, Peter Huffman, John Coulman, William Rider, Jacob Weaver, Chrisley Snoak, Jacob Shot, George Nigley, Philip Glinger, John Gilman

By an act of March 4, 1785, Dauphin County was separated from Lancaster County. Upper Paxtang at that point became part of Dauphin County. It took in all of the section north of Berry's Mountain, watered by the Wiconisco Creek and its branches. It became known as the Wiconisco or Lykens Valley, and is frequently referred to as Lykens Valley to this day. The settlers continued to have problems with farmers from other areas sending their cattle to this place to graze on private land.

Another advertisement appeared in the Readinger Zeitung, in 1794:

"Pine Creek Grazing. Notice. All and sundry are notified that any one who intends to graze cattle in our region should reconsider and that from now on this will not be tolerated . . . these rude clowns think that we must suffer this, but we are determined to find out if we are masters on our own lands or not. So much from us on Pine Creek in Berks and Dauphin Counties." [note that Schuylkill County was then part of Berks County.]
signed:

Christopher Boyer	Peter Stein
George Dieterich	Nicholas Jund
Henrich Boner	Adam Schwartz
Isreal Ritter	Daniel Schuy
Henrich Hoover	Hannes Dieterich
George Klinger	Philip Geres
Friederich Stein	Carl Kohlmann
Andreas Hoffman	Robert Osman
Alexander Klinger	

The conglomerate of settlers was for the most part of German or Swiss origin. A few were French Huguenots (among them the Salade family), and others were English (such as the Buffington's). There were also a number of Scotch/Irish. Many of the first settlers migrated here from another part of Lancaster County, Berks County, and some from what is now known as Lebanon County. Still others came from as far away as Montgomery or Chester County. Few if any came here directly after landing on American shores.

Most had come from a religious background, and desired to continue their religious practices. During the period from 1750 to 1770, the circuit ministers apparently served the few people here. One early record speaks of Reverend William Hendel who often visited Lykens Valley during the Revolutionary War. Because of the Indians, the inhabitants went to meet him, armed with weapons, and guard him to his place of destination. While he preached, the guards stood around the outside of the church buildings near the doors so that they could keep a lookout for the enemies, while they listened to the sermon. After the service, they guarded him on his way home, until he was beyond danger. Shortly after 1770, the church congregations were formed and ministers moved into the area. St. David's Church at Killinger had six baptisms performed in 1770. St. Johns "Hill" Church, St. Peter's "Hoffman" Church, and Zions "Klinger's" Church were established shortly thereafter. By 1790, a number of large families had joined one of the above named congregations. The Methodist Episcopal denomination had also established small classes or congregations in Halifax, Millersburg, and the area now known as Loyalton before 1800. [More about Lykens Township churches and their ministers in individual articles about each church.]

During the 1790s, the Federal government was in need of more money, and was already looking for new means of taxation. A decree went out to all states and territories requesting each assessor to submit an accurate description of the appurtenances (improvements) made by each resident on two acres of land surrounding his house. On October 1, 1798, Cornelius Cox, the Upper Paxton assessor filed his report on duties performed. He had made his rounds, visiting every resident in the township. He and his committee had measured each house, counted all the windows, every "light" within the windows, described each house, as well as the outhouses, placed a valuation on each property, and recorded the name of the owners. His report can still be found in federal assessment records. Mr. Cox had found a total of eighty-eight "homesteads" in the whole territory of Upper Paxton. Not one slave was found in the territory.

In January 1810, the inhabitants of Upper Paxtang petitioned the court to make another division in their township. Their request was granted September 3, 1810, and the eastern section of Upper Paxtang became Lykens Township. Lykens Township territory was reduced on March 12, 1819 by the formation of Mifflin Township, which took land from Upper Paxtang and Lykens Township. Another change took place on June 26, 1840 when the portion of land south of the north side of Thick Mountain was erected into Wiconisco Township. The last division took place on January 23, 1846 when Mifflin Township was divided, and the new portion became Washington Township. The new township bordered on the dividing line of both Mifflin and Lykens Township.

Regarding all the border changes that were made to the land originally encompassing the settlement of Andrew Lykens and that eventually became temporarily Lykens Township territory; it is difficult to focus only on the present borders of the township. While the land transactions will focus mainly on the area of present Lykens Township, a substantial amount of information is also included about the commerce in the thriving territory of Oak Dale and Loyalton. The landowners and early enterprising settlers in that area contributed much to the development of the whole Lykens Valley. It is important to remember and appreciate their contributions. Also much of the individual owners farmland on the southwestern section of Lykens Township crosses the township lines, and is included in the history.

EARLY MERCHANTS & CRAFTSMAN
Of Lykens Township 1817

Bower, Samuel	shoemaker	Hoffman, John	shreiner	Shoffstall, Ludwig	weaver
Biting, Peter	blacksmith	Hepner, Henry	grist & sawmill	Snook, Christian	cordwainer
Conrath, Christian	gristmill	Klinger, Peter	grist & sawmill	Salady, Jacob, Jr.	gristmill
Cerst (?), Georg	sawyer	Martin, Paul	distillery	Shoffstall, Samuel	shreiner
Etzweiler, Frederick	blacksmith	Kissinger, John	sawmill	Umhols, Bernard	bock?
Frantz, Jacob	meser?	Romberger, Henry	cooper	Umhols, Philip	?
Ferree, Daniel	gristmill	Reigle, John	su—mer?	Van Orman, William	hederer
Ferree, Isaac	sawyer	Reigle, Daniel	colter	Weise, John	blacksmith
Feterhof, John	miller	Shoffstall, Jonas	weller	Weise, Adam	shoemaker
Gutman, Henry	weaver	Snyder, John	blacksmith	Wels, Thomas	storekeeper
Huber, Jacob	grist & sawmill	Saladay, John, Jr.	grist & sawmill	Williard, W	weaver
Hoffman, Nicholas	sawyer	Shoffstall, Solomon	shreiner	Williard, John	weaver

EARLY MERCHANTS & CRAFTSMAN
Of Lykens Township 1831

Bower, John	tannery	Hallabach, George	blacksm & shoemaker	Shoffstall, George	carpenter
Buffington, Abram	weaver	Hennerliter, John	mason	Stough, George	shoemaker
Beck, Daniel	blacksmith	Herman, John	carpenter	Shoffstall, Ludwig	weaver
Burkart, John H.	potter	Hoffman, Jacob	carpenter	Shreffler, Conrad	blue dyer
Baney, Isaac	storekeeper	Hoffman, John, Esq	sawmill, fulling mill	Smeltz, Andrew	carpenter
Burr, Henry H	inn keeper	Hoffman, Henry	carpenter	Sassman, George	shoemaker
Buchanan, James	forge & sawmill	Keener, Philip	tavern & postmaster	Salade, John	shoemaker
Buffington, Solomon	shoemaker	McCurty, Michael	fuller	Saltzer, John D.	mason
Bird, George	weaver	Motter, George	cooper	Salade, John	shoemaker (Gratz)
Bickel, Tobias	wheel wright	Moffet, William	tannery	Steabler, George	blacksmith
Bellis, Peter	gunsmith	Muench, Chas E.	taylor	Sheffer, Jacob	brickmaker
Bressler, John	taylor	Miller, Joseph	storekeeper	Shoffstall, Moses	plasterer
Beck, John, Jr.	weaver	Motter, Baltzer	carpenter	Schreiner, Henry Esq	distillery & stone mill
Coleman, Peter	distillery	Matthias, Adonyth	turner	Troutman, Peter	weaver
Crabb, Peter	blacksmith	Miller, John	wagoner	Umholtz, Michael	carpenter
Crabb, George	blacksmith	Moyer, Jacob	shoemaker	Updegrave, Elias	carpenter
Dietrich, Emanuel	weaver	Miller, John P.	tanner	Updegrave, Solomon	shoemaker
Dornheim, Henry	doctor	Moyer, George	blacksmith	Williard, Michael	shoemaker
Dennis, James	forgman	Nolan, Rickert	mason	Welker, Peter	weaver
Enterline, Christian	hatter	Orndorf, John	doctor	Welker, John	weaver
Eckler, Jacob	tanner	O'Neil, Edmond	doctor	Witman, Jonathan	tinker
Forney, Michael	miller	Ossman, John	carpenter	Walborn, John	carpenter
Fry, John	storekeeper	Ossman, Daniel	carpenter	Welker, William	weaver

Fogel, Christofel	tanner?	Rehrer, George	carpenter	Witman, Edward	inn keeper
Forney, John	blacksmith	Riegel, Jacob	distillery	Werner, Jacob	carpenter
Frantz, Henry	weaver	Riegel, Daniel, Sr	gelder	Witman, George	hatter
Feagley, Daniel, Jr	shoemaker	Rickert, Henry	weaver	Wolf, Michael	carpenter
Ferree, Isaac	surveyor	Rickert, Martin	shoemaker	Witman, John	cigar maker ?
Ferree, Joel B.	surveyor	Romberger, Jacob	taylor	Wild, Adam	wagoner
Fry, Henry	forgeman	Romberger, Christ	cooper	Wens, John	cooper
Geyer, George	miller	Romberger, Peter	cooper	Wolf, Christian	shoemaker
Grove, George	cooper	Roads, William	blacksmith	Walborn, Michael	shoemaker
Grim, John	miller	Reedy, Leonard	gunsmith	Yerger, Henry	tanner
Ginder, John	forgeman	Rissinger, John, Sr.	carpenter, grist & saw mill		
Feagley, Jacob	sawmill	Rissinger, John, Jr.	miller	**TAVERN KEEPERS**	
Herb, Jacob	potter	Paul, John, Jr.	surveyor	Conrad Fry	
Hoffman, Georg	taylor	Shoffstall, Samuel	carpenter	Edward Witman	
Hoch, Samuel	mill wright	Shoffstall, Christian	shoemaker	John Keffer	
Hedrich, Jacob	shoemaker	Shoffstall, Samuel	carpenter	Ludwig ImShoffstall	
				Henry Burr	

EARLY ROADS OF LYKENS VALLEY

The primitive roads in the valley for the most part were actually Indian trails, or paths, which the white traders followed. The Indian village of Shamokin (now Sunbury) containing more than fifty wigwams was a central point from which numerous paths branched out in various directions. Several Indian Chiefs representing Six Nations lived there, and representatives of William Penn traveled the paths to negotiate with them for land. Various early explorers, Indian agents, traders and missionaries found these paths during the early 1700s.

Beginning long before 1800, it was not uncommon for pack horses to come into this valley loaded with merchandise, salt and iron. Barrels or kegs were hung on each side of the horse. Pack horses were generally led in droves of twelve or fifteen horses, carrying about 200 pounds weight each, going single file, and managed by two men, one going before as the leader, and the others in the rear to oversee the safety of the packs. The pack horses were generally furnished with bells which were kept from ringing during the day drive but were loose at night, when the horses were set free and permitted to feed and browse. The bells were intended as guides to help the owners locate their animals in the morning. Later, when the forge at Loyalton became operational iron ore was carried from the Conewego Hills on pack horses.

One of the principal ancient trails was identified as the Tulpehocken Path, and was known by white explorers at least by the very early 1700s. It ran from the Tulpehocken region of Berks County, north across the Blue Mountain through Pine Grove, to Keffer's Summit and West to Good Spring. It crossed the mountain north to Hegins and then west to Sacramento, Fearnot, and Klingerstown. There it entered the gap into Northumberland County eventually reaching Ft. Augusta near what is now (Sunbury). The frequent use by the Indians along the Susquehanna caused this trail to be a well beaten track which the white traders later used as a bridle path for their pack horses. Trade with the Indians became a profitable business. While this path crossed very little of the area now known as Dauphin County, it was very useful to the settlers that lived here.

By 1768, this path was surveyed in preparation for the layout of an improved trail to be used for early settlers travels. In 1805, the Pennsylvania legislature enacted a law directing the construction of a road along this Indian trail. The path was widened and graded removing steep slopes and other problems to make it accessible to wagons and carriages. This trail became known as the "Old Sunbury Road."

A portion of Tulpehocken Path at Keffer's summit turned westward over the summit and did wind through Williams Valley to the Susquehanna River in Dauphin County. This path was surveyed in about 1769 for use of the white settlers, and followed along the north slope of Stoney Mountain, passed east of Muir, then turned through Tower City to Lykens and Millersburg. It became known as the Williams Valley Road, and was in existence until 1873, then replaced by the "State Road" now known as Route 209. [This is probably the road that Peter Forney helped to build when he was a boy 14 years old. He described the road as leading from Shreiners to the Susquehanna River and being twenty miles of wilderness. He said it had only three small clearings along the route.]

Another Indian trail came into the Williams Valley from Lickdale, and following north to Talihao Gap in the Blue Mountain, came to Suedberg, and the High Bridge. From there it followed the east branch of the Fishing Creek, known as Baird's Run, to DeHaas Swamp, across Stoney Mountain, entering Williams Valley south of Orwin. (This was said to be the trail used by the Andrew Lykens party while fleeing from their attack by the Indians at Loyalton.

One other trail from Indiantown Gap across the mountain to Cold Spring, going north across Sharp and Stoney Mountains to Sand Spring in Clark's Valley led to the top of Peters Mountain at the site of the old Greenland Hotel. A member of the Ferree family established a sawmill at this sight, and a very small settlement of settlers lived there. The Greenland Road was eventually developed for stagecoach use, and a postal station was maintained at the hotel. The early trail intersected a path from the east (now site of Pottsville) that wound down the mountain to Lykens. From Lykens it continued to Loyalton, north through Pillow Gap to Sunbury. Bishop Spangenberg used this trail as early as 1742 on his mission to the Indians at Sunbury.

The earliest official records of roads established by the authorities for this region began with the road laid out about 1736 between Chester and Harrisburg on the Susquehanna River. About 1785, when Dauphin became a separate county, several roads were laid out linking Harrisburg to Middletown, Hummelstown and Jonestown.

Soon after that, a newly laid out trail made travel a bit more accessible to residents in the area of Upper Paxton Township. A petition for a Bridle Path was made "to the worshipful court of quarter sessions in the Borough of Lewisbourg, Dauphin County the third Tuesday in November 1787. [Note that Harris' Ferry was established in 1785, renamed Louisburg in 1786 in honor of Louis XVI of France, changed to Harrisburg before 1810]. The petition of the inhabitants of Upper Paxton humbly showeth that your petitioners have for a considerable time labored under much difficulty for want of a Bridle Road, being laid out from the forks of the road on the level of the North side of Peters Mountain to Reeds Ferry, the nearest and best way, it being a way that is frequently traveled by a large concourse of people from many district ports of the country and of all probability will continue to be so. Said road would be of much advantage for publick utility and afford convenience to the inhabitants of said township. We your petitioners humbly hope that your worships will take this our present distressing condition under your most wide consideration and grant us such relief as your wisdoms may think fit and as in duty bound your petitions will forever pray." The petition was signed November 11, 1787 by these Upper Paxton Twp residents: John Taylor, James Reed, Isaac Jones, George Clark, Philip Shenpacker, Martin Umbecker, John Richmond, James Buchanan, William Johnston, George Bashens. (Leonard Reedy and many other early settlers used this path to travel by horseback to Harrisburg on official business at the county seat, or for other commercial business well into the 1800s).

Roads for the use of local residents began to be built soon after 1800. The first Road Tax began in 1810, and Jacob Schneider became the Roadmaster. The next year, December 1811, plans were made for a road through Upper Paxton Twp. near Wiconisco Creek connecting Millersburg to Lykens. It intersected with the road leading from Harrisburg to Sunbury and linked with property of Daniel Ferree. [The 1816 map on page 13 identifies the existing roads at that time.]

At a Quarter Session held on May 5, 1817 permission was granted to have a road laid out from the town of Gratz to intersect the road leading from the Tulpehocken or Reading Road to Isaac Ferree's Mill at or near Christian Hoffman's land. Samuel Boyer, George Deibler, Peter Hoffman, John Hoffman, John Umholtz and George Bleystine were appointed by the court to view and lay out the road. Final confirmation was made September 4, 1817. Land for this public road was to be cleared at the width of thirty-three feet. It began at the west end of Gratz, and followed a southern direction passing by the improved land of Jacob Hoover, land of Hartman Rickert, Jacob Hoffman, Christian Hoffman and ending at the point of the Tulpehocken (the road leading to Isaac Ferree's Mill) Road to Reading, near the dwelling house of Christian Hoffman. The road has become known as Specktown Road.

In April 1822 Conrad Fry was paid for preparing 2 drafts for a State Road. Fry was paid money to survey the road from Gratz to Uniontown. On May 10, 1823, Isaac Ferree was paid for running a new road.

On January 21, 1824, permission was granted to view a road to be constructed beginning in Dauphin County and run to Reading. Several men were appointed to view the road, including these residents of Lykens Township: John Hoffman, Esq., John Shoffstall and Conrad Fry. They decided that the "best way" was to begin at the Merchant mill of Philip Messner of Mifflin Twp, intersect the public road from Millersburg to Berrysburg in Lykens Valley at the line of the land of Baltzer Romberger and John Herman. Then pass through Williams Valley at the place of Jacob Runk, and on to Reading. At the same court session, a petition was made to erect a bridge over Mahantongo Creek. Approval was made because the commissioners thought the project was too expensive for the local townships to undertake.

On August 17, 1829, a committee was appointed by the court "to view and lay out a road for public use beginning at a post in the center of Gratz. The road would cross the land of Simon Gratz, passing the schoolhouse, *pass through the unimproved land of John Philip Klinger near his barn, and end at a post on the Tulpehocken Road,* west of the school house near Klingerstown. At the north edge of Gratz, a fork or branch veered to the left, providing a road or path to the Mahantongo Mountain. By 1850, this thoroughfare became known as "the public road to Klingerstown." It's branch became the "road to Mahantongo Mountain."

The surviving account book of Adam Weise (dating from 1799 through the early 1800s) provides names of workers and interesting details about the care and construction of the early roads. Below are items found in that account book:

March 23, 1833 Subscribers paid to Jury on road

March 25, 1836 G. Stough & H. Yerges hauling stones, John Lubold for repairs on road.

March 28, 1837 M. Uhler haul planks, Peter Batteiger work timbering & laying road tax, Henry Schaefer for bridge hauling. Henry Schaefer for making bridge (this line crossed out). Walborn for hauling stone

Apr 11, 1840 to Geo Witman for pine boards, Philip Keiner and Solomon Shindel for hand boards

March 27, 1841 Geo Klinger for timber for foot bridge & Harry Wiest for spike and iron for bridge, Bowman for 1 board for bridge, Geo Witman for sign board, Thomas Elder 4 logs, Martin Rickart timber, several others for planks and timber. Also J Osman for 90 ft of boards, Jacob Ritzman timber, Saltzer timber (crossed out), Jonas Deibler 350 ft boards,

Oct 31, 1842 road tax collected in Wiconisco Twp

Apr 14, 1845 - paid to Theodore Gratz for opening road in snow

Apr 13, 1846 - paid Dan Lebo for hand boards, Jacob Wiest for mending bridge

TURNPIKES ESTABLISHED

Just prior to 1800 the age of turnpike roads had been established in Dauphin County. Large four-wheeled vehicles arched over with sailcloth coverings, and usually drawn by six powerful horses, could now convey merchandise for much further distances. These vehicles became known as Conestoga wagons. Stagecoaches were also used in this region for passenger travel.

The Dauphin Guardian newspaper dated Nov 7, 1807, describes a "New Stage Line" running from Harrisburg to Sunbury. It "starts the journey at the public house of Andrew Berryhill of Harrisburg Tuesday November at 10, and arrives at the house of Charles Hegins in Sunbury on Wednesday afternoon. It will start back on Monday and arrive at Harrisburg on Tuesday morning so the passengers can proceed and arrive in Lancaster the same day by an extra stage. The stage is new, good horses, careful drivers and cost is $3 from Harrisburg to Sunbury. Way passengers is 6 cents per mile. Fourteen pound baggage per person is allowed."

In a few years scheduled stage travel became easily available to residents of this area who wished to travel to most any other area. (Information from: Historical Sketch of Dauphin County by Geo H. Morgan, 1877

COVERED BRIDGES OF LYKENS TOWNSHIP

After the early roads were built and trailed throughout the countryside, covered bridges became a common site, and have since become one of the more nostalgic remains of our past. Although most of the lovely old wooden landmarks have disappeared, enough of them remain to make even very young folks aware of their original existence.

In our limited search for information, we have not found an exact date for the first wooden covered bridge built in Pennsylvania, or for that matter, in the United States. "The Permanent Bridge" built over the Schuylkill River in Philadelphia was constructed in 1805. This is considered the first Pennsylvania covered bridge. A bridge built in 1791, in Epsom, New Hampshire, may qualify as the earliest covered bridge built in America.

The first American patent for a covered bridge was issued to Charles W. Peale in 1797. Other designers who became prominent in the early days of bridge building included Theodore Burr. A native of Connecticut, Theodore Burr was born into a family of mill-builders in 1771. He moved to New York, and in 1800, he built his first bridge across the Chenango River. He continued in his occupation, moving to different locations, becoming noteworthy for his achievement.

By 1809, Acts of the Pennsylvania Assembly authorized the incorporation of bridge companies. Commissioners began to solicit subscriptions to stocks. By October 1809, enough shares of stock were pledged to form and incorporate the Northumberland Bridge Company, and The Harrisburg Bridge Company. Simon Gratz was among the shareholders in both of those companies. One year later, in the fall of 1811, Theodore Burr came to Northumberland and signed a contract with Northumberland Bridge Company to build a bridge across the North East Branch of the Susquehanna River. The bridge would link the town of Northumberland to Shamokin Island, and from there to Sunbury. Three other bridges would soon be constructed across the Susquehanna at other locations. This event was an important achievement for all residents of Pennsylvania. It marked the beginning of much safer and convenient travel over the large and important Susquehanna River. Up to this point, transportation across this river depended on ferrying, rafting, rowboat, canoe, or simply walking or riding a horse through the shallow areas of the waters.

This was apparently the beginning of covered bridge construction in the proximity of Lykens Township. The bridges that were built in our township were hardly designed by such an illustrious person as Theodore Burr. Often a group of farmers or businessmen would organize and agree to build a covered bridge, and maintain it. Sometimes they sold shares to finance the cost, because very little help could be expected from county or state authorities.

Most of the bridge projects were planned and built by local carpenters. They used local wood, many times oak or chestnut. They proceeded to build bridges in the same manner as any building of that period. The framework was usually laid out on the ground, and raised by men of the neighborhood. Most of the covered bridges cost less than a thousand dollars. Although perhaps not supervised by such as Theodore Burr, several local men became quality builders of bridge structures. Jacob H. Forney grew up in Killinger, Upper Paxton Township, and is remembered as one of the local builders. He was born in 1851, a son of George and Rebecca (Sultzbach) Forney.

Why were the wooden bridges that were enclosed and covered with a roof so popular during a span of over one hundred years (beginning perhaps about 1850)? Surely most of us have contemplated that question. Logically, the large timber truss construction braced and strengthened the whole structure. Enclosing the bridge floors with a cover resembling a shed or barn seemed to be an ideal way to preserve the underpinning from extreme weather. It also prevented the hot and humid summers, and freezing inclement weather of the winters, from creating adverse conditions for timbers that would otherwise be exposed.

Covered bridges served as tollhouses during earlier years. The closed-in structures also provided a safe haven for travelers during snow and rainstorms. Animals upon entering the barn-like environment were less likely to be fearful of rushing streams. The covered bridges became a great meeting place for assemblies of people, friends or for other gatherings. They were also the means of generating intriguing traditions or stories that were passed down from generation to generation. The many initials carved into the wooden walls, continue to be a reminder of the idle moments of long ago outings.

It is estimated that at one time, as many as 1,500 covered bridges were scattered across the state of Pennsylvania. They provided a means of transportation over creeks and waterways. Most of them were built in the period between 1830 and 1880. Slowly but surely, most of them have by now disappeared, with less than two hundred remaining in the whole state.

Within the confines of Lykens Township, several covered bridges were built across streams or creeks. But most of the structures provided transportation across creeks that bordered on other townships in Dauphin, Schuylkill, or Northumberland County. At this point in time, it would be difficult for us to know how many of these bridges were built. Due to population increases and new developments, new routes were established for travel. Probably some of the old original bridges were abandoned. Others perhaps were replaced by more modern structures. Sadly, Lykens Township and adjoining townships have lost most of the original covered bridges, that one time dotted this area. They disappeared one by one, victims of flood, rot, sheer neglect, vandalism, and unfortunately in the name of progress. For the sake of preserving their memory, we are documenting the several known bridges that either bordered or existed within Lykens Township. Included in this list are identified bridges from the area now known as Loyalton because it had been at one time part of Lykens Township.

Throughout the book, the covered bridges will be mentioned again when the history of their particular site will be covered. Information about some of the bridges was difficult to find. Others apparently were popular spots. We have gathered as many stories and details as possible. They can be found with the individual write-ups.

The count of covered bridges that graced our area may not be accurate. But the following bridges are known to have existed.

LOYALTON AREA OR VICINITY

Two bridges are known to have existed in this vicinity. The bridge near Oak Dale Forge earlier known as *OAK DALE STATION BRIDGE*, later *KEISTER BRIDGE*, was sixty-five feet long. It was destroyed in the 1972 flood. The bridge near Vicky's Restaurant, (specific *name unknown*), was probably replaced by a concrete bridge in 1930s. We have not found information as to the size of the bridge.

Another bridge known as *WILHOUR MILL BRIDGE* spanned the Wiconisco Creek in narby Washington Township, north west of Elizabethville for many years. This bridge measured seventy-five feet. Several years ago, it was purchased by a resident of Montgomery County, and with great care was moved from this area to Collegeville, Pa. and established in a new location where it is being preserved.

The bridge known as *RAKERS MILL BRIDGE*, also crossed the Wiconisco Creek in Washington Township. It was seventy feet long.

BRIDGES IN OR NEARBY LYKENS TOWNSHIP

Several bridges existed in this area, but only one continues to survive. The bridge near the border of Lykens and Washington Twp., called *HENNINGER BRIDGE*, crosses Wiconisco Creek. It was built about 1850, and is sixty feet long. Vandals extensively damaged the structure, but is was restored about 2003.

The shorter *SPECKTOWN BRIDGE* spanned a small stream along Specktown Road. It was destroyed because of new road construction during the 1940s. We have not found information about its size, but it had a shorter span.

A bridge over Pine Creck, along Gratz-Klingerstown Road. known as *RED BRIDGE*, was replaced by a concrete bridge in 1951.

A bridge over Pine Creek, actually in Schuylkill County, known as The *WHITE BRIDGE*, was an important means of travel between the two townships. It was eventually replaced by stone bridge.

The following bridges gave access to folks who were traveling north or northwest.

PILLOW OR PROXIMITY

Crossing the Mahantango Creek, the bridge known as PILLOW or WITMER BRIDGE was located in Mifflin Township east of Pillow. It was 105 feet long and allowed easy access between Pillow and Klingerstown. This bridge area was remembered by young folks years ago as a great place to swim. It was destroyed by the severe storm Hurricane Agnes in 1972.

On the western side of Pillow the covered bridge near the well-known mill gave access to travel toward Sunbury. That bridge was also lost in the flood of 1972.

Another bridge that crossed the Mahantango Creek near the border of Lykens and Jordan Township was known as the *TROUTMAN BRIDGE*. It was located near the road to Hebe and was 105 feet long.

The *DEIBLER GAP BRIDGE* spanned the Mahantango Creek near the boundary of Mifflin Township in Dauphin County and Lower Mahanoy Township in Northumberland County. It was near County Line. This bridge was builtt about 1852, and was 103 feet long. It was destroyed by Hurricane Agnes in 1972.

EARLY SCHOOLING IN THE "UPPER END"
(SCHOOLS OF LYKENS TOWNSHIP)

Individual write-ups for each school will be found throughout the book. But the historical background and information is given here accompanying the early general history of the valley.

In preparing for this section, the following article provided the best source of information about early education in the Lykens Valley area. D.H.E. LaRoss, Superintendent of Dauphin County Schools, did the report in 1877. He studied the history of early schools of Dauphin County, and gave the following account (printed verbatim) about our area.

Upper Paxton, the third of the original districts, extended from Gratz to Millersburg, about eighteen miles, in what is now termed Lykens Valley, and from Richards Gap to Halifax, about ten miles, in Armstrong Valley. The early settlers of Lykens Valley were principally German, and it was their custom of establishing a schoolhouse with every church, which were all German Reformed and Lutheran. These schools were supported by the patrons, at a cost of fifty cents a month. The German language was taught exclusively, up to 1815 or 1816, in both valleys, when the English was introduced, and both languages were taught in the same school.

The first school in Lykens Valley was established two or three miles from Gratz, and one hundred yards from the old Hoffman Church, in 1805. At that time, and up to 1815, a wilderness of heavy pine timber and undergrowth extended for miles along the old valley road to Millersburg.

The first teacher in this locality was Charles E. Muench, a thoroughly educated German. From 1812, and even earlier, the schools were controlled by the settlers, and assisted by the ministers and best-educated inhabitants of the valley. Orthography, Reading, Writing, and Arithmetic were the only subjects taught in all the county schools. The Bible and Psalter were the textbooks in nearly all the German schools up to 1820. The Heidelburg and Lutheran catechisms were studied by the advanced pupils, and rehearsed once or twice a week. The first parochial school was organized in Berrysburg, nearly fifty years ago. The different organized churches owned small tracts of land, from ten to twenty acres, on which a schoolhouse was erected, all one-story, and some double: one part to be occupied by the teacher and family, and the other part as a schoolroom. (In another place, the double schoolhouse is described as having two or three small rooms - one for the schoolroom, another for kitchen and bedroom). About that time, the districts now called Mifflin, Washington, Lykens, Wiconisco, and Williams, had nine schools, a territory of one hundred and fifty square miles. All the schools were taught in private houses, except three, which were built by citizens. The land, in some instances, was purchased for a few dollars, and some donated, but in either case only sufficient to hold the building. On a fixed day, they assembled at the place where the house was to be built and some went to felling trees, others to hauling the logs, and the rest erected the house. In two or three days the house was finished. The furniture was made of pine or oak boards nailed against the wall, benches made of slabs, with pins two and a quarter feet from the edge.

Other sources of information regarding early schools give a few more colorful details. In 1874 Superintendent S. D. Ingram described the first early schools as "low frame buildings." These early schools were sometimes known as "Subscription Schools." Parents had to pay tuition to the teacher, buy the books, and contribute wood for the large open fireplace in the classroom. (Parents were expected to supply wood in a proportional quantity to the number of their children enrolled in the classroom). However, it was not unheard of for some families to provide generous loads of hickory wood to warm the children, while others brought only scanty, scraggy, ill-looking heaps of green oak, white birch or hemlock. A huge amount of wood was needed for the large fireplace, as windows and doors were drafty. During the school day, bigger boys were sent out to cut enough wood to keep the fire burning. In later years stoves became popular heating facilities.

Tuition could sometimes be just as difficult to collect, as the firewood needed for the fireplace or stove. The schoolmaster had the responsibility to collect his fee, and sometimes he had to engage the help of the local Justice of the Peace. Evidence of this is found in the account books of Leonard Reedy, of Gratz.

Pennsylvania adopted several early State Constitutions. But none of them addressed the need for legislation, even of a general nature, in reference to public schools, until 1809. That year, an act was passed "for the gratuitous education of the poor." It required the assessors of each township to report the names of all children between the age of five and twelve, whose parents were unable to provide for their education. When the lists were compiled and approved by the commissioners, the parents were notified. The parents could then send their children to the nearby school at the expense of the county. The names are listed for the interest of the reader, and as research material. We

have "found" several children whom otherwise could not have been linked to their parents by other records.
(A record of "poor children" of 1822 shows a widow Hawk with two children: Philip age 9, Phebe age 7.)

By March 29, 1824, a new law provided that "every township should elect three schoolmen who should superintend the education of the poor children within their respective townships, and cause them to be instructed as other children are treated, the expense of tuition to be paid by the county." This law provided for three years of education for each child between the ages of six and fourteen.

Evidence of Lykens Township putting this law into effect is found on the 1825 tax assessment. That year the following children (residents of Lykens Township) were listed as having their tuition paid by the county:

Children of Henry Frantz & wife Magdalena: Anna Mary age 11, Elisabeth 8, Jacob 10, Lidi 7; Philip Keener and wife: Elisabeth 11, Luseda 9, Mary Magdalena 7; Peter Blease (Peas) & wife - Elisabeth 9, Marian 7.

In 1826 the new law was repealed, and the act of 1809 revived. However, in 1828, A. Maria Buffington, age 11, was listed as having her tuition paid. In 1834 the following families were listed, including name of parent, guardian or next friend and effected child.

John Vanderslice and Mary Feagley - Amelia Vanderslice age 10; John Williard and Ann Raidle - John Williard, 8; Jacob Bordner & wife Maria - William Bordner, 9; Fanny Conrad - Christiana Conrad, 6; Peter Zimmerman and wife Elisabeth - Daniel Zimmerman, 10; Sara Zimmerman, 7; Jacob Brubaker and wife Mary - Hiram Brubaker, 9; Jacob Brubaker, 7; William Rewbodem and wife Elisabeth - John Rewbodem, 10; Francis Rewbodem, 6; George Pinkerton & wife Marilet - Sires (Cyrus?) Pinkerton, 9; Hiram Pinkerton, 6; Adam Yeo (Yohe?) & wife Maria - Rebecca Yeo, 8.

About 1833, a Pennsylvania state election was held giving residents an opportunity to choose the free public schools. On December 5, 1835, the Common School system was established, and each county was divided into districts. (As noted in Dr. La Ross's report, Upper Paxton was the third district). Each district was appropriated money, but from the very beginning many districts were reluctant to accept the money. Lykens Township was one of the last holdouts. It was not yet receiving appropriations in 1844.

On the 1837 Lykens Township tax assessment, a large group of children were listed (from the township and Gratz), whose parents were unable to pay their schooling. The following parents or guardians and children were on the list:

Thomas Weinrick	- Peter Weinrick age 5
James Deiner	- James J. Daniel age 5
William Row	- Emmaline 9, Elias 5
David Rossell	- Marchad (Margaret?) 11, Peky (Becky) 9, Bobby 7
John Shaid	- John 9, Margary 7
Jacob Hoffman Jr.	- Daniel 8
George Bird	- Elizabeth 7, Salome 6
J. Jack Bird	- Angain 10
James Ferree	- Sara Elizabeth 7
George Warfel	- Carolina 11, David 8, John 6
George Pinkerton	- Maryann 11, Daisy 10, Hiram 9
Jacob Brubaker	- Adam 9, Henry 6
Henry Gerber	- Sarah 9, Darias 7, Emeline 5
George Widel	- Alabam 10, Emanuel 8
Lory Shomber	- Sarah 6
Michael Walborn	- Sally W. 7, Chatarina 5
Adam Unger	- Jacob 6
Wever & Chadarina Faust	- Mary Ann Faust 11, J. Amy Faust 8
John Miller, Mat. Deibler	- Louania Moyer, 10
Elizabeth Reedy, witow	- Henry 7, William 7 (one age)
Ludwig Schofftall	- Louis 10, Albert 8, Adam 6
Michael Katterman	- Henry Katterman, 8
Esther Fegley, witow	- Sarah Fegley, 11
Daniel Fegely	- Henry Arthur Fegley, 6
Elizabeth Rissinger, witow	- Jonas 9, Sally 8, Chatarina, 6
John Hoffman	- John Hoffman 7
Chadarina Hoover, witow	- Elizabeth Hoover 11, Paty Hoover 9, John Hoover 7
Michael McSurdy	- Margard 11, Jacob 9
Andrew Matter	- Samuel 10

EARLY LIFE IN THE "UPPER END"

In 1840, the following children were educated at the expense of the county. (Parent or guardian named, followed by name, birth and age of children.)

Michael Baney	- Adam age 10, born Nov 16, 1830; J. H. Peter 6, born Nov 22, 1834
Samuel Bowman	- Chatarina 9, born Apr 9, 1831
Daniel Fagely (Gratz)	- Henry Albert 9, born May 1, 1832; Manda 6, born Oct 28, 1834
Lewis Faust (Gratz)	- Jonas 10, b Jun 15, 1830
Jacob Hoober Jr	- Elisabeth 9, born Jan 9, 1831
Christian Hoober	- Sarah 6, born Sep 28, 1834
John Hocher	- Eli 9, born Apr 15, 1831; Sarah 7, born May 15, 1833; Samuel 6, born Jul 17, 1834
Henry Neyswender	- Rebecka 10, born Jun 25, 1830; Henry Peter 8, born Mar 12, 1832.
Michael McSurdy	- Daniel 9, born Feb 15, 1831; Sarah 7, born Jul 8, 1833.
Joseph Osman	- Chatarina 7, born Sep 7, 1833
Daniel F. Nece	- Daniel 9, born Feb 15, 1831; Mary 5, born Sep 4, 1835.
Andoney Smith	- Emmerline 6, born Dec 18, 1834
George Schindel	- Polly 6, born May 7, 1834
Solomon Schoffstall	- Sarah 7, born Jun 20, 1833, Jonas 5, born May 2, 1835.
Samuel Swartz	- Engeline 9, born Feb 9, 1831
Ludwig Schoffstall	- Philip 9, born Dec 22, 1831; Joseph 7, born Aug 15, 1833
Adam Unger	- Jacob 9, born Mar 25, 1831
John Riegel, Esq	- Obet 11, born Oct 18, 1829
Leonard Reedy	- William 11, born Mar 26, 1829; George 7, born Oct 31, 1833.
Jacob Scheel	- Jacob Coler 5, born Apr 7, 1835
John Miller (Gratztown)	- Joel 6, born Jul 25, 1834
Isaac Hern	- Wistian 5, born Oct 29, 1835
Michael Katterman	- Henry 11, born Feb 5, 1829
George Witman	- Harriet 11, born Jan 15, 1829; Henry 8, born Jan 7, 1832

In 1854, the Directors of the Common School of Lykens Township in pursuit of better education purchased ground for most of the known township schools. More details can be found under the individual write-ups of those schools. The superintendents' report of 1855 showed that the township spent $1303.11 for building purchase and repair. It was an unusually large amount of money, probably accounting for new buildings.

When the Common School finally became fully established throughout the county, numerous other problems continued. Qualified teachers were difficult to find. The county superintendent wrote at length in his annual report, about the qualities that women teachers would bring to the classroom. But until many years later, men continued to dominate the teaching field. Other problems as late as 1855, included the fact that area schools remained un-graded, and books had to be purchased by families.

In 1856, Superintendent S. D. Ingram in his annual report, elaborated on the many difficulties he encountered, or gave words of encouragement to those districts adhering to his will. In special reference to our area on another matter, he writes "Millersburg, Upper Paxton, Washington, Mifflin, Gratz, Lykens and Wiconisco are north of Berry's Mountain in the beautiful valley of Lykens. Short Mountain separates Wiconisco from Lykens. The Mahantongo Mountain is near the northern boundary. Wiconisco is a mining district. The remaining districts are agricultural. Many of them beautiful, well cultivated and thickly settled." What a contrast to the description of just forty years earlier when the same area was considered a "wilderness of heavy pine timber and undergrowth."

The 1863/64 school term was a year of serious problems. County Institute usually held in the Harrisburg school, was cancelled because of an outbreak of small pox. The Harrisburg school served as a hospital for small pox victims. Also in that year, the Harrisburg schools were jeopardized because the Civil War battles were moving closer to our area.

By 1865, Cornell's out-line map became a popular tool in the Dauphin County classrooms. Lykens Township received eight of them, one for each school.

During the early 1870s, the school directors focused their attention to providing new schools. In 1874, Superintendent S. D. Ingram mentioned in his report that " a very good brick building at a cost of $1,350 was built in Lykens Township, with the best style of furniture and property arranged." He praised the directors of the Lykens District for "commencing the good work" and, hoped that it may continue until all the low frame buildings of the district would be dispensed with. In 1875, another very good brick building built in the township, cost $1,330, and the best style of furniture cost $141.00. They constructed a third building in 1881. The remainder of the brick buildings became reality possibly before or right after 1881. One other frame building constructed in 1914 ended the era of building Lykens Township schools.

In 1894, the directors of the school boards for the first time fully complied with the new law. They furnished textbooks to the pupils in each school.

For the next sixty years, township schools routinely provided the education facilities for the young folks who lived here. Compared to modern day activities, in up-to-date buildings and classrooms, those environments may seem crude. But the schools trained many students for a lifetime of accomplishments. At the same time, they provided them with happy (and mostly innocent fun) activities with friends. As noted by many of the former pupils who registered at a featured School Booth on SIMON GRATZ DAY in the 1970s, those were "the good old days."

As a separate part of the history of the local schools, a piece from the May 12, 1910 Elizabethville Echo is printed below.

VETERAN SCHOOL TEACHERS WILL HOLD REUNION

The following gentlemen, composing the committee of teachers of forty years ago met at Hotel Snyders, Elizabethville May 6, 1910 to arrange for a reunion: Aaron Daniel, Gratz, chairman: W. B. Meetch, Isaiah T. Enders, John A. Romberger, George Washington Enders, Isaac W. Hoffman. It was decided to hold the reunion or convention in Elizabethville auditorium at 10:30 a.m. Thursday, June 7th. A program was arranged for, and that it will be a happy event goes without saying. All those who taught forty years ago and more in this favored spot Upper Dauphin, and their wives or husbands are eligible to attend. Dinner will be served at the specially favored price of fifty cents per plate.

The primary object for holding this reunion is of course, to have a social gathering - revive old friendships, and sing old favored songs, recite old recitations; and to have a profitable time reviewing the past and comparing the methods of teaching in vogue one-hundred, seventy-five, forty years ago with those of the present day. Come along old friends of education let's gather in cheerful friendship. Bring your happy SMILES.

Below will be found a list of teachers known to the committee. Will those whose names have been omitted kindly write to the chairman at once. Everyone who expects to attend on June 7th should notify Mr. Daniels at Gratz without delay or the secretary of Millersburg, so that ample preparations can be made for the dinner.

George Washington Enders, Enders
Michael Hensel, Wiconisco
Daniel Arts, Artz
D. C. Milhouse, Halifax, R.F.D.
John W. Seiders, Halifax, R.F.D
Thomas Leibruch, Halifax
Isaac W. Hoffman, Millersburg
William B. Meetch, Millersburg
H. L. Lark, Millersburg
Mrs. John Kahler, Millersburg
Josiah Weaver, R.F.D. Millersburg
B. W. Holtzman, R.F.D. Millersburg
John W. Hoffman, Gratz
Mrs. Amelia Boyer, Gratz
John D. Gise, Gratz
Aaron Daniel, Gratz
Emanuel Miller, Harrisburg
Isaac F. Enders, Harrisburg
Henry Laudenslager, Sunbury
Cyrus Snyder, Delaware
John H. Bressler, Tower City
Edwin L. Bergstresser, Selinsgrove
Daniel Lubold, Pottsville
Preston Miller, Pottsville
Henry Eisenhower, Harrisburg, Illinois
Isaac Keboch, Berrysburg
Cyrus Romberger, Lykens

Harry Snyder, Harrisburg
George Romberger, Harrisburg
Daniel Romberger, Harrisburg
J. B. Nicholas, Harrisburg
Peter S. Bergstresser, Berrysburg
Isaac Henninger, Berrysburg
Joseph F. Romberger, Berrysburg
Thomas Buffington, Berrysburg
John Miller, Berrysburg
George Washington Matter, address unknown, went west
Daniel C. Blyler, Reading
John A. Romberger, Elizabethville
Nathaniel Buffington, Elizabethville
Theodore Miller, Elizabethville
James Miller, Elizabethville
Isaiah Matter, Elizabethville
Cornelius Hoffman, Enterline
G. W. D. Enders, Fisherville
Simon O. Bowman, Millersburg
William H. Lehman, Millersburg
Charles Swab, Norristown
Mrs. Amelia Swab, Norristown
J. V. Fisher, Philadelphia
Rudolph Dornheim, Philadelphia
John O'Neal, Carolton, Pa.
William O'Neal, Carolton, Pa.
Hon. J. B. Seal, Millersburg

The above is as far as names and addresses could be ascertained; all are cordially invited to be present and it is earnestly desired that all teachers not named will send their names and addresses to the secretary, Isaac Hoffman for enrollment and say if they will be present at the meeting June 7th.

VETERAN TEACHERS REUNION

THE SECRETARIES FULL REPORT
ELIZABETHVILLE ECHO DATED JUNE 16, 1910

The first reunion of the veteran school teachers of forty or more years ago of Upper Dauphin County was held in the auditorium in Elizabethville school building June 7, 1910.

The morning session was called to order by President Aaron Daniel, Rev. O. T. Moyer selected for his scripture lesson the 13th chapter of Paul's letter to First Corinthians, it having been one of the lessons in the fourth reader that was used more than forty years ago. The Scripture lesson was followed by the prayer of Rev. Moyer.

Miss Annetta E. Romberger then entertained the audience very delightfully with an instrumental solo "Polonaise." Next in order was the election of officers. Professor P. S. Bergstresser was nominated for President, and talked about the Berrysburg Seminary. He mentioned that Jacob S. Whitman was first president (1851), L.K.Hoch was president in 1853. Isaac W. Hoffman was nominated for Secretary. He taught seven years, starting in 1854.

George W. Enders then spoke on the subject, **"THE TEACHERS OF FORTY YEARS AGO."**

"We have no idea how it was before Free Schools. The sons and daughters of the rich were given education. Poor men with no money who were unable to pay, their children had no education. In those times there were no schoolhouses, preachers were the teachers. They taught school during the week, preached on Sunday. There were three classes, first the parents who could pay for their child's education, second those unable to pay, third class having 70,000 members in Pennsylvania. These were called "witches and ghosts."

An elderly lady who attended the reunion gave an example of Subscription schools - the teachers boarded around, were paid twenty dollars per term of three or four months. They had sixty pupils, used one book, the "Psalter." Each pupil paid two cents a day and brought the teacher many things to eat. The Psalter had no pictures. After that they used the Testament. After the lady made her comments, she was asked "were the pupils as happy as now?" She replied, "yes, we had the happiest hearts - we carried our flowers in our hearts instead of on our hats."

DANIEL AUGUSTUS MUENCH
(Son of Charles Edward Muench - First Teacher)

We would be remiss not to include the following first hand account given about 1890 by Daniel A. Muench, and included in the pages of Egle's Notes And Queries - 4th Series, Volume two printed 1895, page 247 - 251)

Daniel Augustus Muench was born in Tulpehocken Township, Berks County August 1, 1804, a son of Charles Edward Muench, the German schoolmaster who taught for many years at Hoffman school. When Daniel was eight months old, the family moved to Lykens Valley, and in the winter of 1805, his father taught the first school in that part of the county. The building was located near the old Hoffman Church.

Daniel was raised on a little farm two miles west of the school, working in the fields and woods in summer, and attending the ordinary pay school for a few months in winter. It was the only preparation he had for what proved to be much of his life work - teaching school.

"Early one morning in November 1823, a little, dilapidated log school house, at a bend in the Mahantango Creek, welcomed a timid, country boy to its portals as teacher. It was my first days experience, and although it occurred sixty-seven years ago, I have a vivid recollection of its events. My first duty was to chop wood and build a fire in the large ten-plate stove, in the center of the room, a duty for which I was doubtless better prepared than for what was to follow.

The region was known as the country of the Hottentots, and I became convinced before nine o'clock that I would have more than one large unruly boy to handle. I also knew that if physical force was to rule the school, I had made a mistake in accepting it. Fortunately for me, after I had worried through that long, long first day, as I was on my way to my boarding place in the evening, I met a large, muscular farmer, who came to the rescue by stating that if at any time I needed assistance I should send for him. The next day I needed assistance and I sent for him. In a few minutes he walked into the room, armed with a dry hickory sprout. He came not to interpret the law but to execute it. The only question he asked was "who is the ringleader?" No sooner was the leader in the mischief pointed out to him than he grasped him by the arm and with a vigor that was surprising, applied the hickory to the unfortunate boy's back. Evidently, believing that 'actions speak louder than words' without uttering a word he returned to his work in the fields. I had no occasion to call in his assistance thereafter. His first impressive visit did much to assist me in completing my first term on the banks of the Mahantango without much difficulty."

Some of the normal duties that Daniel Muench performed as a teacher was to sharpen quills, which required a great deal of time. Another duty was to write copies for the pupils. These were usually short proverbs such as "Pride goes before a fall." He stated that he wrote that one hundreds of times.

He told of one experience regarding penmanship. "I was fortunate in being a good penman. On one occasion I gained the respect of an unruly boy by carefully writing, in bold letters, the headlines of his arithmetic example book. He had but little fear of the rod, but after he saw that I was a good writer he had respect for my pen."

"Classification, in my days as a teacher, was out of the question, for there were nearly as many different kinds of books as there were different pupils. The only subject in which we approached anything like classification was reading. The pupils that could read used the Testament. The length of term was from three to four months, and each pupil paid fifty cents a month for tuition. There was great uniformity in my salary. I never received less than sixteen dollars, nor more than eighteen dollars a month for my teaching. My first school was taught in 1823, and my last one in 1846. My schools, in addition to the one on Mahantango Creek, were Whitleys in Susquehanna Township; Lenkers and St. Johns in Lykens Valley; and Bowermans in Powels Valley."

Daniel Muench continued: "The old German Reformed Church near Gratz was the first that I ever attended. Reverend William Hendel, Jr. D. D. came all the way from our old home in Tulpehocken to preach for us occasionally. Among his successors, to whose preaching I often listened with great interest, were Reverend James R. Reily and Rev. Isaac Gerhart. At this old church repose the remains of both my parents."

"I have very distinct recollection of the first Sabbath School of which I was a member. It was organized at Fetterhoff Church, in Halifax Township, by John Rutter, John Zimmerman, and myself. Unfortunately we were a little in advance of the times in the neighborhood. They were not ready for such an innovation, and after a few Sabbaths we were locked out of the church and the small library that we had collected was scattered never to be brought back again."

On the subject of politics, Mr. Muench said, "I don't think I was a politician. I voted regularly, and when I was a candidate for office I was always pleased to have my friends vote for me. My first ballot was cast for Jackson for President in 1828. I had a singular experience at that election. My father had just been naturalized and he proudly walked with me to the polls and exercised his right as an American citizen for the first time with me. George Wolfe was the first governor that received my vote and my first commission as Justice of the Peace bears his signature. This commission was granted to me in 1831, and I served continuously till 1855. One life of policy I always tried to live up to while acting as Justice of the Peace was that of not sending petty, trivial cases to the court. I always felt that the courts were encumbered with many cases that should never go there."

"There is nothing particularly startling in my twenty-four years experience in this position. Perhaps the most exciting incident occurred when William F. Johnson was the Governor of the state. A murder had been committed at Christiana, Lancaster County, and there was strong suspicion that the crime was committed by fugitive slaves. Governor Johnson issued a proclamation, offering $1000.00 for the apprehension of the guilty parties. Soon after this as I was riding over Peters Mountain on horseback one afternoon, I met five burly Negroes, who asked me to direct them to a hotel. The tavern at Matamoras was the nearest place, and I directed them to go there. Soon after leaving them the thought occurred to me that they might be the murderers. I immediately took a roundabout way and rode into the village before the Negroes arrived. I told the landlord of my suspicion, and directed him to deputize a stalwart man of the village to act in that capacity. A posse of men was selected to surround the hotel, with orders not to molest them during the night unless they attempted to leave, but to be in readiness to arrest them early in the morning. The excitement in the village during the night can readily be imagined. Very few of the residents closed an eye.

With daylight came the arrest of the Negroes, and in a short time they were being carried over Peter's Mountain toward the capital. In the vicinity of Dauphin they were met by the slaveholders' agent of Harrisburg and a number of men in search of the fugitives. After considerable parleying the men released them to the agent and his men and returned to Matamoras. Soon thereafter, they were landed behind the bars in Harrisburg. After all the excitement they did not turn out to be the murderers. The agent returned them to their masters in the South, giving to my men forty dollars for their trouble, and putting the remainder of the four hundred dollars, which he received in his pocket. The price then paid for capturing fugitive slaves was eighty dollars a head."

Speaking on other subjects Daniel Muench said, "I was married on the 18th day of December 1828. Instead of the wedding party getting into cabs and driving to the depot, as is the custom nowadays, my party, which was rather a large one, had to drive several miles over the country. There was but one carriage, an old time Dearborn, in Halifax Township, and that of course was reserved for the bride and groom. All the other members of the party were obliged to ride in ordinary one-horse wagons."

"My first trip to Harrisburg from Lykens Valley was made in a crowded stage coach on the old Sunbury Road over Peter's Mountain. I made my first journey to Philadelphia in 1836. I went as far as Harrisburg by stage. There I took the horse cars for the city. I remember the journey was a very tedious and tiresome one. The horses were changed four times on the way down."

"I did considerable hunting and fishing in my younger days, and with better success than is usually the case with hunters and fishermen now a days. Then it did not require much skill to be a success in either of these sports, as game of all kinds was very plentiful. In fact, in my early boyhood days, there was more game in the Lykens Valley than most boys care for. One cold night a large bear was shot within a few yards of our house. It was in prime condition, and its large hams and shoulders supplied the community with meat for several days. It was not an unusual thing to wake up in the night and hear the cry of the wild cat in the orchard or woods near by, or the howl of the wolf on the Mahantango Mountain. Scarcely a day passed that we did not see several deer bounding through the valley. The Wiconisco Creek was well stocked with fish before the coalmines were operated. Since then, its darkened waters are undisturbed by the finny tribe. Perhaps no mountain streams in Pennsylvania afforded better haunts for the speckled trout than did Bear and Rattling Creeks, away back in 1820. Many a day, when a boy, I wandered over the mountains in the vicinity of Lykens with my associates gathering berries and hunting rabbits, and often on moonlit nights did we go in search of 'coon. Little did we think that we were treading over one of Dauphin County's greatest sources of material wealth."

To Clara

Be kind to all, be intimate with few.
And may the few be well chosen

Your Friend

(Graz Jan 10th 1886)

Chapter 4

THE LAND WHERE THE LYKENS FAMILY DWELT
(LATER BECAME FERREE LAND)

On February 7, 1765, Jane Lykens applied for a tract of land containing 201 1/2 acres and allowance, and a warrant was issued to her on February 7, 1765. The next year on June 21, 1766, Jane Lykens made application to the Proprietors for a second tract of 263 acres and 50 perches of land in the area where they lived. A survey of both tracts of land was made July 21, 1766, but a patent was never granted to her or members of her family. Instead, Joel Ferree, from Lancaster County, was granted a patent to the 263-acre tract on November 28, 1766, and on November 29, 1766, he received a patent on the 201 1/2-acre tract.

Joel Ferree took up several other tracts of land that were warranted to him in what would later become Lykens Township. On January 31, 1775, two of the tracts were patented to him. One contained 108 1/2 acres, a second one contained 395 acres. A third warrant contained 82 - 3/4 acres, but it was patented to his son Isaac April 17, 1795. Still another tract containing 47 plus acres was surveyed to Joel Ferree, but patented to Isaac Ferree on Apr 17, 1795. Two other tracts patented to Jacob Smith in 1789 and 1793, a total of 283 ½ acres became vested in Daniel Ferree on April 1, 1793. Daniel and Margaret Ferree conveyed the land to Isaac Ferree in 1815. The original Lykens family lands and the land purchased by the Ferree family were slowly purchased by new owners and later became the hub of a thriving little community.

According to early area history (refer to Biographical Encyclopedia of Dauphin Co, Pa.1896), before Joel Ferree received the patent on 108 ½ acres, he arranged to have Henry Schoffstall build a house (in 1771) on the tract, which was located near what would become Oak Dale Forge. It was said to be the second house built in the area that is now Loyalton. (Andrew Lykens house was first). The location was described as being seventy-five yards north west of the bridge that crossed Wiconisco Creek. Joel lived in the area at least briefly. In 1780 this is the only property listed in his name in all of Lancaster County (Dauphin was then part of Lancaster Co). He is listed in the "Wiconisco District." But on August 27, 1791, Joel gave two tracts of land to his son Isaac, and moved back to Leacock Township, Lancaster Co. (In the spring of 1801, Joel Ferree traveled out to Moon Township, Coraopolis to visit with the family of his first wife. While there he walked a short distance from the house to hunt. When the family discovered that he had not returned, they went in search of him and found that he had been killed. He met up with Indians, and they scalped him.)

The "window tax" taken in 1798, records Isaac Ferree as owner of this land with a 25 by 20 foot cabin and good barn, with Henry Rutter as a tenant on the property. By 1800, Isaac was living in the house, and as early as 1805, he owned a sawmill and later a powder mill. The map of 1816 (page.13) shows a place called FERREES on the northwest side of the road leading from Millersburg to Reading, beside the Wiconisco Creek. Further along the creek in a southeasterly direction, the Ferree Powder Mill is marked. It was on the opposite side of the creek from where Oak Dale Forge was later located. Isaac Ferree began to manufacture gunpowder at this mill at least by 1812. During the war of 1812 the mill produced a large quantity of its product. In 1813 the following advertisement appeared in the Harrisburg newspaper **Pennsylvania Republican.**

GUN POWDER

August 9, 1813
The subscriber has constantly for sale, the best rifle and other gunpowder (warranted equal to any made in this country), manufactured at his mill, on Wikiniski creek, Lycan's township, Dauphin county.

Isaac Ferree
N.B. Any person applying to Mr. John Howard in Harrisburg, can be supplied with the above mentioned Gunpowder in quarter casks.

J.F.

Also in 1813 the Ferree mill is mentioned in Dauphin County court records, as the starting point for a road or cart way to be built. The road was to begin near the Wiconisco Creek, at the Ferree mill. This is where the public road leading from Lycans Gap to Reading, and the road to Sunbury crossed. The new road would lead to Schuylkill County line, running between Ludwig Shitz and Jacob Snyder's farm to the road leading to Reading.

Isaac Ferree accumulated many more acres of land from many sources in Upper Dauphin County. At the time of his death on January 24,1820, he owned six tracts of land containing upwards of 1500 acres located in the area of Loyalton and Lykens, much of it inherited from his father. He also owned two tracts comprising several hundred acres of land in Mifflin Township. His son-in-law James Buchanan, the administrator of his will, made a petition to the court to have his eight tracts of Ferree land distributed. On December 2, 1823, "twelve free and honest men" made partition of the eight tracts. They could not part the land in equal amounts, but they made seven parcels from the eight original tracts. The tracts were made available to family members for choice, and they took up most of the land. **John Row**, husband of Susanna granddaughter of Isaac Ferree took a tract of over 145 acres. This land was adjacent or within the boundaries of Loyalton. **Isaac Ferree, Jr.** second son of Isaac chose another tract of over 143 acres. This land was part of the tract where the gristmill was located. **Josiah and Mary Bowman**, grandchildren of Isaac Ferree, chose a 138-acre130 perch tract in place of their mother Susanna Ferree Bowman. Some of this land was located north west of the Loyalton site. **Reuben Ferree**, third son of Isaac Ferree was given a tract of 100-plus acres. However, by an article of agreement on April 9,1827 Reuben and Nancy Ferree conveyed ownership to Nicholas Snyder. It bordered on the Wiconisco Creek, land of Jacob Dietrich, John Buffington and Christian Hoffman Jr. **Isaac Rutter**, a son of deceased Rachel Ferree Rutter accepted a tract with 138 acres 5 perches. **Two other tracts** were not sold until December 1, 1827, when John E. Forster, Merchant of Harrisburg purchased them. One tract contained 227 acres 46 3/4 perches of land. The other tract contained 191 acres 34 ½ perches. On February 4, 1828, John E. Forster sold the land with buildings to James Buchanan, coppersmith of Harrisburg, and husband of Elizabeth, daughter of Isaac Ferree.

The Ferree Family
(With help from Sharleen Ferree, Jay Ossman, & Annabelle Hoffman)

Research on the Ferree family has been time consuming, and especially difficult to gather on the early local family. The following information has been carefully gathered from numerous sources. It includes more data than is normally used, because the family was very instrumental in founding the early settlement now known as Loyalton. Also, the Ferree background is most interesting.

[The earliest known ancestor of the **FERREE** family (various spellings including Fierre, Ferry, Free, Fuehre, Fier) is DANIEL FERREE, b c1650, probably in Normandy, believed to be a son of Jean Fiere LaVerre (b in the c1624 – d before 1691), who resided in Landau, France. This was a section located less than 50 miles north of Strassburg, Germany, and was under the jurisdiction of the Holy Roman Empire. Under the reign of Louis XIV, living conditions were less than ideal for Daniel Ferree, a Huguenot, and Calvinistic in religion. He was a wealthy silk manufacturer in Landau, but after the revocation of the Edict of Nantes in 1685, he and his family gathered some trifling articles and some cash, and fled first to Strasburg, later to Lindau, Bavaria, Germany. Here Daniel died c1707, and it is reported that he was slain during the insurrection in France.

Daniel Ferree (c1650–c1707/08, in Palatinate Bavaria), m in 1675, Madam Maria de la Warrenbuer (b c1650 in Picarde, Loire, France – d 1716 in Conestoga, Lancaster County, Pa., bur in Ferree Graveyard, also known as Carpenter's Graveyard). After their marriage, Daniel and Maria Ferree lived in Picarde, later moved to Flanders, before moving to Landau in the German Palatinate. After Daniel Ferree died, his widow Maria resumed her maiden name, probably for the sake of protection. She and her family decided to come to America, and obtained a civil passport from the Court Clerk of Billingheim on March 10, 1708. The passport stated in part that it was for the "purpose to emigrate from Steinweller, via Holland and England, to the Island of Pennsylvania to reside there. That during the time that their father, the widow and the children resided in this place, they behaved themselves piously and honestly; It would have been highly gratifying to us to see them remain among us." The family sailed first to Holland, and then on to England where they arrived in London during the summer of 1708. Madam Warrenbuer's two sons, Daniel and Isaac and Isaac Le Fever are recorded as having arrived at New York with their families aboard the ship "Globe" on January 1, 1709. They had been at sea for eleven weeks, enduring a very cold and perilous trip. Madam

Warrenbuer and her remaining children apparently did not arrive in America until later. They may have made the voyage on the ship Lyon, which landed in New York in June 1710.

Madam Warrenbuer Ferree and her family of six children, three sons and three daughters joined by LeFever, Dubois and other families settled in the already established Huguenot colony at Esopus (now Kingston), New York. While in New York, Philip Ferree, the youngest son found employment with Abraham DuBois, and eventually married Abraham's daughter Leah.

Madam Ferree applied for a tract of land in Pennsylvania, and on September 10, 1712, a two thousand acre tract was granted "for whom the same was taken up or intended. But upon further consideration of the matter, it is agreed among ourselves that the said land shall be confirmed to Daniel Fiere, son, and Isaac LeFaver, son-in law of the said widow." The land was located near the head of Pequea Creek, in Strasburg Township, near present Paradise, in Lancaster County. While dividing the land, the grantors discovered that 300 hundred more acres were included with the 2,000 acres. They paid the additional twenty-one pounds on October 29, 1734, and received a new patent. In the meantime, they took up more land and received a total of five thousand acres by patent. Madam Ferree, therefore, never owned land in Lancaster County. Instead it was granted to two of her heirs for the purpose of sharing it among the other family members.

An unknown writer, familiar with the transplanted family, wrote the following account of the arrival of the Ferree family in Lancaster County, Pennsylvania in 1712.

"It was on the evening of a summer day when the Huguenots reached the verge of a hill commanding the view of the valley of the Pequea. It was a woodland scene; a forest inhabited by wild beasts, for no indication of civilized life was very near. Scattered along the Pequea, among the dark green hazel, could be discovered the Indian Wigwams, the smoke issuing there from in its spiral form. No sound was heard but the songs of the birds: in silence they contemplated the beautiful prospect which nature presented to their view. Suddenly a number of Indians darted from the woods. The females shrieked when an Indian advanced and in broken English said to Madam Ferree: 'Indian no harm white. White good to Indian. Go to our Chief. Come to Beaver.' Few were the words of the Indian. They went with him to Beaver's cabin and Beaver, with the humanity that distinguished the Indian of that period, gave up to the emigrants his wigwam. The next day he introduced them to Tawana, who lived on the great flats of Pequea and was a chief of a band of Conestoga Indians who at that time occupied this region. The friendship formed between the Red Men of the forest with Huguenots upon their arrival was maintained for many years, each race giving the other assistance in time of need."

The Ferree family settled on their newly acquired land in Lancaster County. But as this part of Pennsylvania became settled, some of the Ferree descendants migrated to the settlement developed by Andrew Lykens. Here several members of the Ferree's made major contributions to the settlements in Loyalton and Lykens. The local genealogy of the Ferree family is not complete. But the information that could be found is included.

DANIEL FERREE (c1650 – Mar 10, 1708, in Bittingheim, Bavaria, Germany) m 1669 in Steinweiler, Bavaria to Maria De Le Warrenbuer (b c1653 - d Jan 1716 in Strasburg, Lanc Co, Pa.). Her remains were buried on the original Ferree tract that eventually became walled with stone and supplied with an iron gate. It became known as the Carpenter or Ferree Graveyard, was designated for burial of members of the Ferree family. **Daniel and Maria De LeWarrenbuer Ferree had these known children:**

*DANIEL, Jr. (b 1677 Lindau, Bavaria - d Aug1762, Lancaster Co., Pa.), m c1701Anna Maria Leininger in Steinweller. Daniel Ferree made a will on Jan 25, 1744/45 in which he appointed his son Daniel as exec. but Daniel died before his father. **Before coming to America had two children:**
**Andrew b 1701, bapt. in the church at Steinweller Sep 28, 1701 – d 1739). Not much is known about Andrew, except that he had a farm in Lancaster County. Upon his death, an inventory was made of his goods. It is an interesting combination of items that gives insight into what was found on a homesteader's property at that time. Among his possessions were wheat and rye, some stacked and some in the ground: a "great" wagon, a little wagon, a plow, two mauls and three iron wedges, spade and shovel, a matock and three dung forks, two broad-axes, joyners axe and adze, carpenter tools, sythes, hinges, hand-saw, five sickles, chains, horse geer, and a mans saddle. Other household and miscellaneous items included a large bible, two feather beds, wearing clothes, pewter, box of iron, watering pot, wooden ware, two iron pot racks, four working horses, a mare and two colts, six grown cows, ten head of young cattle, eleven sheep,

swine, two chests, a spinning wheel, sled, cash received for a servant girls time. Andrew m Mary Reed.
Andrew and Mary (Reed) Ferree had these children:
***David** (1725 – May 1806), m Mary ___. **David and Mary Ferree had these children:**
+Daniel (b c1755 – d May 28, 1819,in Susquehanna Twp, according to the Oracle newspaper of
Harrisburg), m 1st Sarah Brua (___ - d between 1808 &1810). Daniel Ferree m 2ⁿᵈ Susannah Peiffer,
widow of George Peffer, on Dec 27, 1810, record Zion Lutheran Ch, Harrisburg. (George Peffer had 324
acres 135 perches of land when he died. It was sold to these people: George Deibler, Adam Rumberger,
Henry Umberger, Philip Umholtz, John Feagley). Daniel Ferree was the early settler in the vicinity of Oak
Dale Forge, Lykens Twp. whose gristmill is mentioned in the early history of what is now Loyalton. He is
listed on the tax records of 1805 and 1817. But soon after that he and his second wife Susannah moved to
Susquehanna Township, where he died.

After Daniel Ferree died, his widow Susannah gave all of her interest in the real and personal estate of
her late husband to the four children - except the things that she brought to Daniel at the time of their
marriage. An agreement was made to give $20.00 to Susannah and Sarah Peffer, two daughters of Susanna
from her former marriage to George Peffer. (**George and Susanna ___ Peffer had these children: Sarah
b Oct 31, 1803, bpat Zion Luth Ch Hbg; Samuel (b & d 1813)); Susanna ____**

On October 15, 1821, a list bearing name of items assigned to Susannah was recorded and approved
by a signature of Jacob B and Daniel L. Ferree. The following list of household furniture had been delivered
to Mrs. Susannah Ferree under agreement:

tables	1 spinning wheel	3 iron pots & 1 dutch oven
1 crout stant	2 pictures - gilt framed	1 tea kettle
1 keg of wine	1 clock and case	2 iron skillets
1/2 barrel with vinegar	1 walnut dining table	1 griddle and small skillet
13 chairs	1 breakfast table	1 waffle iron
a lot of books	1 desk and bookcase	1 small brass kettle
1 square stand	1 large looking glass	1 bread toaster & grid iron
1 single bed - bedstead	2 small pictures w/frames	1 coffee mill
3 portraits	1 maple bureau	4 flat irons
1 walnut chest	1 bed and bedstead	4 candle sticks and 1 pr snuffer
1 small looking glass	1 pr brass candlesticks	2 market baskets
1 dough trough	1 10 plate stove & pipe	1 milk cow
		1 pr hand iron shovel & tongs

Susanna signed (with an X) that she received the articles on June 8, 1819.

Daniel and Sarah (Brua) Ferree had these children:
+ + *Daniel L* (no dates) m Amelia ___ of Cumberland Co. Daniel petitioned the court June 30, 1820 to sell
the real-estate of Daniel Ferree of Susquehanna Twp.
+ + *Jacob D.* (no dates), m Sarah _____, lived in Swatara Twp., Dau Co;
+ + *Susanna* (no dates), m Henry Peiffer of Low Dau Co, possibly a son of George Peiffer whose widow
became Susanna's step mother.
+ + *Catherine* (b Apr 27, 1783, bapt Hoffman Ch in 1811 as an adult - d Aug 1, 1859), bur Hoffman Cem,
stone illegible), m in 1808 to Jacob Hoffman, Jr. (Feb 4, 1782 – d Feb 2, 1862), a son of John Nicholas
Hoffman. They lived in Lykens Twp., but Jacob also served in the Pennsylvania Legislature term of
1833/34. See [Hoffman history for more information.] **Jacob and Catharine (Ferree) Hoffman had these
children:**
Hanna b Aug 10, 1807, m John Romberger b Oct 24, 1802 ; **Amos** b Mar 25, 1809, m 1837 Amanda
Harper, dau of Thomas Harper; **Sara** (b Aug 23, 1811, bapt Sep 7, 1811 Hoffman Ch – d Sep 24, 1848,
bur Davids Cem, Killinger), m Michael Forney (1809 – 1881, bur Fetterhoffs Cem, Rife); **Elizabeth** b Nov
9, 1814; **Catherine** (b Mar 23, 1816 near Short Mt – d Dec 19, 1873 in Gratz, bur Simeon Cem), m
Abraham Hess (b Apr 7, 1817 Up Mahanoy Twp, Northld Co – d Dec 23, 1892), a son of David and
Mariah (Katerman) Hess; **Anna Maria** b Nov 1817; **David** b Aug 30, 1821; **Jacob** b Apr 20, 1825, m
Elizabeth Hoover, lived in Lykens Twp., but later moved to Williamstown.; **Daniel** b Aug 23, 1829, m
Susanna ___ b Mar 31, 1837.
+ +*Hanna* (b Aug 13, 1789 bapt Hoffman Ch in 1811 as adult - d _____) m Daniel Hoffman (Oct 9, 1785 -
Oct 26, 1830, bur Hoffman Cem), a son of John Nicholas and Anna Margaret (Harman) Hoffman. By her

husbands will Hannah was granted the family farm, with her son David to care for her. Daniel Hoffman served in the war of 1812. **Daniel and Hanna (Ferree) Hoffman had these children:** <u>Jacob</u> **David** (Jul 3, 1812- May 30, 1887, bur Millersburg), m May 19, 1836 Eva Romberger (Jun 28, 1810 – 1876), a dau of Adam and Anna Catharina (Paul) Romberger; <u>Sarah</u> b Mar 26, 1816; <u>Daniel</u> b Sep 8, 1817, m Frane Frantz; <u>Hannah</u> b Aug 17, 1819, m Isaac Uhler; <u>David</u> <u>Ferree</u> b Aug 30, 1821 m Carol Snyder; David was a J.P in Berrysburg; <u>Loretta</u> b Nov 2, 1822; <u>Joseph</u> b Oct 29, 1824 lived in Hummelstown; <u>Elmira</u> b Feb19, 1830 m John S. Musser, Dau Co Commissioner.

++<u>Sarah</u> (   ), m John Reed (- d pre 1827),of Halifax Twp
++<u>Mary</u> (   ) m Michael Shure of Halifax?

+<u>Sarah</u> (no dates) not married
+<u>Lydia</u> (no dates) m Joseph Le Fevre
+<u>Catherine</u> (no dates) m Martin Maure
+<u>Hannah</u> (no dates) m John Eliott
+<u>Andrew</u> (Nov 22, 1758 – 1831), m Mary Ferree (1763 – 1828), a dau of Peter Ferree. They were progenitors of York County Ferree family. Andrew had a son Jacob b Sep 23, 1802. ;
+<u>Elisabeth</u> m Apr 23,1795 to Arthur Travers
+<u>Susan</u> (no dates) m Jacob Trout
+<u>David</u> (1772 – 1832) m Mary Baker (1775 – 1858).

*****Joseph** (no dates) m Sarah de la Plain;
*** <u>Lydia</u> (1731 – 1778), m Samuel Le Fevre (1719 – 1789);
*****Mary** <u>Jane</u> (no dates) m Jacob Brua.

****John** (b 1703, bapt in church of Rhorbac Feb 2, 1703 – d 1773), [His will was dated Apr 8, 1773, his executors were Mary Ferree and Henry Hoke.] He m Barbara Stautenberger (b c1708 – d ____). He may have married a second time to Mary _____ . A Mary is listed as his executor in 1773. **John and Barbara (Stautenberger) Ferree had these known children:** <u>Peter</u> (1736 – 1795), m _____ (no dates), and lived in Lampeter Two, Lanc Co. Peters will is dated Nov 19, 1795, and names Jacob Shertz as his executive. **Peter Ferree and his wife _____ had these children:** <u>John</u>; <u>Peter</u>; <u>Samuel</u>; <u>Jacob</u>; <u>Hannah</u> (no dates) m Henry Hoke; <u>Mary</u> (b Dec 6, 1762 York – d Nov 15, 1828), who m Andrew or Isaac Ferree (b 1753 Lykens Valley – d Jan 24, 1820, Lanc Co, a son of Joel and Mary (Copeland) Ferree. [See write-up on Isaac Ferree elsewhere.];<u>Rachel</u>; <u>Elizabeth</u> m Joel Ferree; <u>Conrad</u>; <u>Susanna</u> (no dates), m George Cryder or Kreider; <u>Mary</u>.
****Daniel** (b1706 - d Aug1750, made will Aug 10, recorded Sep 4, 1750), m May 1, 1739 in Lancaster County, Mary Carpenter (1710 - ____), a daughter of Henry Carpenter. The wedding document has been preserved by a family descendant, and it's contents reflects the fact that French Huguenots were similar in nature to members of the Society of Friends and the Mennonite community.

"Whereas, Daniel Feire, Junior, of the county of Lancaster and province of Pennsylvania, yeoman, and Mary Carpenter, daughter of Henry Carpenter of the county and province aforesaid, spinster, having made due publication of their intention of marriage as the law directs: - These are therefore to certify all whom it may concern that on the first of May, Anno Domini, 1739, before m Emanuel Carpenter, one of his Majesty's justices of the peace for the said county, they, the said Daniel Fiere and Mary Carpenter appeared in a public and solemn assembly for that purpose appointed and meet together at the dwelling house of the aforesaid Henry Carpenter, where he the said Daniel Fiere did openly declare that he took the said Mary Carpenter to be his wife, promising to be unto her a loving and faithful husband till death should separate them, and she, the said Mary Carpenter, then and there in the assembly, did in like manner openly declare that she took the said Daniel Fiere to be her husband, promising to be unto him a loving , faithful and obedient wife till death should separate them, and for a further confirmation thereof, both the said parties to these presents have hereunto interchangeably put their hands, she after the custom of marriage, assuming the surname of her husband; and we whose names are hereunto subscribed, being witnesses present at the solemnization thereof, the year and day first above written.

Witness: *Daniel Fiere*
Emanuel Carpenter,   *Mary Fiere*

[guests present:]

Henry Hanes, Elizabeth Kemp, Paulus, Peter Apfel, Henry Carpenter, Salome Carpenter, Lawrence Hayn, Daniel Le Fevre, Henrich Zimmerman, William Buffington, Daniel Zimmerman, Hans Hauser, Gabriel Zimmerman, Jacob Carpenter, Theophilus Hartman, Christian Zimmerman, Hani Hartman, Isaac Fiere, Peter Fiere, Johann Conrad Kaempf, Isaac Le Fevre, Daniel Hartman, Johannes Volkaemmer, George Philip Dollinger, Christian Harman, Maria Herman, Abraham Fiere, Susan Zimmerman, Hester Le Fevre, Jacob Fiere, Philip Le Fevre, Samuel Le Fevre, Salome Harman, Leah Fiere, Mary Hain, Jonas Le Rou, Rachael Fiere, Isaac Fiere.

Daniel and Mary (Carpenter) Ferree had these children: <u>Salome</u> d young; <u>Mary</u> (___ d Aug 24, 1764), m John Carpenter (b ___ d 1798), a son of Dr. Henry Carpenter. **John and Mary (Ferree) Carpenter had these children:** <u>Abraham</u> (b__ d 1815, bur Ferree Cem); <u>Mary</u> (no dates) m John Smith; <u>Susan</u> (no dates) m Frederick Yeiser; <u>Daniel</u> d young.
**Joseph (no dates) married but no children.
**Philip b c1709 – nothing more known.
Elizabeth (1710 – c1765), m 1st c1728 to Abraham LeFever (Apr 9, 1706 –Nov 20, 1735), a son of Isaac and Catherine (Ferree) LeFever. **Abraham and Elizabeth (Ferree) LeFever had two known children (they are mentioned in the will of their grandfather Isaac LeFever): <u>John</u> (no dates); <u>Peter</u> (no dates: After Abraham LeFever died, Elizabeth m 2nd c1736 Christian Kemp (1714 – 1790).
Isaac (b 1715 Lanc. Co – d1782 Lanc Co), m 1st about 1738 to Elizabeth Ferree (b c1715/18 , Lanc Co – d 1752) a dau of Philip and Leah (DuBois) Ferree. **Isaac and Elizabeth (Ferree) Ferree) had these children: Mary (b 1738 – 1806); **Isaac** b c1740; **Rebecca** b c1740; **Thomas** b 1742 – d 1815 in Pittsburgh, Pa.); **Catherine** b c1744; **Susanna** b c1746; **John** (b 1748 – d 1815); **Ephraim** (b 1752 – d 1808), m Elizabeth;
Isaac is said to have m c1753, 2nd Susanna Green (b c1719 – d after 1785), **had these children: Sallie** b c1756; **Lydia** b c1758; **Joel W.** (b 1760 – d 1802, bur Lock Haven, Pa.), m Mary Bressler (b Sep 14, 1768 Stark Co, Ohio – d 1830), a dau of George and Fannie (Herr) Bressler; **Elisha** (b 1768 – d 1832);
    Before Daniel and Anna Maria (Leininger) Ferree came to America, they secured a certificate from the French Reformed Church at Pelican. It stated: "We, the pastors, elders, and deacons of the Reformed Walloon Church at Pelican, in the Lower Palatinate, having been requested by the honorable Daniel Fiere, his wife, Anne Maria Leininger, and their children, Andrew and John Fiere, to grant them a testimonial of their life and religion, do certify and attest that they have always made profession of the pure Reformed religion, frequented our sacred assemblies and have partaken of the Supper of the Lord with the other members of the faith; in addition to which they have always conducted themselves uprightly, without having given cause for scandal that has come to our knowledge. Being now on their departure to settle elsewhere, we commend them to the protection of God and to the kindness of all our brethren in the Lord Christ."
*CATHERINE (b Mar 26, 1679, Bavaria – d c1749 in Lanc Co.), m in 1703 in Bayem, Bavaria, Germany to Isaac Le Fevre (b Mar 26, 1669 France – d Oct 1, 1751 Strassburg, Lanc Co.), a son of Abraham Le Fevre. Isaac had accompanied the Ferree family in their flight from Landau, as nearly all of his family members were put to death by soldiers. **Isaac and Catherine (Ferree) Le Fevre had these children:**
Abraham (b Apr 9, 1706 – d 1735), m Elizabeth Ferree (1710 – c1765), a dau of Daniel and Anna Maria (Leininger) Ferree.
Philip b 1710 in Esopus, New York;
Daniel b 1713, said to be 1st white child to be born in Lancaster Co., Pa.;
Mary;
Esther;
Samuel (b ___ d May 1789, bur Ferree Cem), m Lydia Ferree (- d 1778), a dau of Daniel Ferree;
 George who served with distinction as a Lieutenant during the Revolutionary War. His son Daniel was a a Colonel during the War of 1812.
*JANE (no dates) m Richard Davis had no children.
*MARY (b c1683 Bavaria - c1754, Lanc Co), m Jun 30, 1715 in Emanuel Ch, New Castle, Del. to Thomas John Faulkner (b 1686 in New Castle, Del - d Mar 28,1752). **Thomas and Mary (Ferree) Faulkner had these children: Jesse; Mary C; Susanna; Eve.**
*JOHN (b 1685 - d Sep 1769), m 1st Mary Elizabeth Musgrave (b c1688 - d pre1736), a dau of John Musgrave, of Bavaria, France. After Mary died, John m in 1736 to Ruth Buffington. The record of

35

marriage is in Kennett Monthly Meeting (Quaker). He received part of the Ferree grant in 1747. **John and Mary Elizabeth (Musgrave) Ferree had these children: Mary Elizabeth b 1720; Martha b 1722; Solomon (1730 – 1782); Sarah b 1724; Daniel b c1725; Esther b 1726; Moses b 1728. John and Ruth (Buffington) Ferree had these children: Ruth b 1737 in Chester, Pa.; John (b 1739 – 1834) served as Col. in the 10th Pa Rifle Reg, and rendered distinguished service; Susanna b 1741.**

***PHILIP** (b Jul 1687 Landau, France – d May 19,1753), near Paradaise, Leacock Twp, Lanc Co, bur Old Carpenter Cem), m Jun 2, 1713 in 1st Dutch Ch, Kingston, Ulster Co, N.Y., Leah Dubois (Oct 16, 1687 – Sep 12, 1758), a dau of Abraham Dubois and wife Margaret of Esopus (Kingston), N.Y. He had worked for Abraham Dubois for about two years before he maried Leah. In 1743, Philip received a tract of land that was part of the Ferree grant in Leacock Twp, Lanc Co. He and Mary also received inherited other land in Lancaster County that had been patented to Leah's father. Philip wrote his will Mar 3, 1753, it was probated Jul 26, 1753, exec's Abraham and Jacob Ferree. **Philip and Leah (DuBois) Ferree had nine children:**

***Abraham** (b 1708, Conestoga, Chester Co, christened Aug 22, 1715, at Emanuel Church, Newcastle, Del. - d Mar 1775 in Strasbur, Lanc Co (exec's Cornelius and Joel Ferree), m in Strassburg, Lanc Co in 1736 to Sarah Elizabeth Etling (b Aug 30, 1719 – d _____), a dau of Cornelius and Rebecca (Van Meteren) Etling of Kingston, N.Y. Abraham received land in Lanc Co from his father Nov 3, 1752. After Abraham died, his widow m _____ Curgis, and moved north along the Susquehanna River. **Abraham and Elizabeth (Etling) Ferree had had these children:**

Isreal b c1751, m Margaret Dickey Abraham b c1748;

Cornelius b Sep 13, 1753, bapt 1st Ref, Lancaster, moved to Virginia;

Rebecca b c1754, m David Shriver;

Rachel (b c1755 – d 1805, Washington Co., Md), m David Muskimen (b 1732 Ireland – d 1773);

Elizabeth (b 1741 – d Dec 21, 1818 in Scioto, Ohio) m William Miller (Nov 2, 1744 – Oct 22, 1790 in Shenandoah, Va);

Mary b Jul 12, 1757, m George Grafft (Apr 6, 1739 – Apr 10, 1779), a son of John and Elizabeth (Carpenter) Grafft. Mary m 2nd on Nov 20, 1783 to Griffin W. Willett b Dec 23, 1750 in Kentucky.

***Magdalena** (b 1712 Conestoga – d May 19, 1753 in Paradise), who m Nov 24, 1749, William Buffington (b 1710 in Chester Co, d Mar 13, 1784 in Hampshire Co, Va), a son of Thomas and Ruth (Cope) Buffington. William is said to have been married previously to Alice Rupp. After Magdalena died, William married a third time to Mary _____ , a widow of Christopher Smith. **William Buffington and his wives had these children: Joel (1744 – 1821), m 1772 to Elizabeth Logan; Susannah b 1748; Thomas; Jonathan; Ruth; David (1763 – 1824); William (1765 – 1824).**

***Jacob** (b c1714 – d 1782, bur Ferree Cem), m Mary _____ (no dates), m 2nd Susan Barbara Carpenter (1735 – 1775). Jacob received land in Lanc Co from his father c1752.

***Elizabeth** (b 1715/18 – d 1752 in Paradise, Lanc Co) m c1738 to Isaac Ferree (1715 – 1782), her cousin a son of Daniel and Anna Marie (Leininger) Ferree. **Isaac and Elizabeth (Ferree) Ferree had these children: Mary (b 1738 – 1806); Isaac b c1740; Rebecca b c1740; Thomas b 1742 – d 1815 in Pittsburgh, Pa.); Catherine b c1744; Susanna b c1746; John (b 1748 – d 1815); Ephraim (b 1752 – d 1808), m Elizabeth.** After his first wife Elizabeth (Ferree) Ferree died, Isaac m about 1753 or 1754 to Susan Green (b c1719 – d after 1785). **Isaac and Susan (Green) Ferree apparently had these children:; Sallie b c1756; Lydia b c1758; Joel W. (b 1760 – d 1802, bur Lock Haven, Pa.), m Mary Bressler (b Sep 14, 1768 Stark Co, Ohio – d 1830), a dau of George and Fannie (Herr) Bressler; Elisha (b 1768 – d 1832);**

***Rachel** (b 1716 Leacock, Chester Co - d pre1753), m c1750/52 James Gardner (1712 - ____)

***Leah** (b c1724 – d _____), m after 1753 Peter Baker (b 1721 Paradise, Salisbury, Lancaster Co.

***Isaac** (b 1725 Paradise – d 1759 Rowan N.C.), son of Philip & Leah Ferree believed to have been killed by Indians in Rowan, N.C. where he lived. He was a ferry operator. He m c1750 1st to Eliz Forbes, a dau of George Forbes who wrote his will 1768. **Isaac and Elizabeth (Forbes) Ferree had these children:**
Jacob Forbes (b Aug 8, 1750 Lanc Co – d Sep 5, 1807 Allegheny Co) He m 1st on Aug 8, 1770 at St. James Episcopal Ch, Lancaster, his cousin Rachel Ferree (b 1754 – 1782), a dau of Joel and Mary (Copeland) Ferree. In 1801 Jacob Ferree, Sr with others organized a company at Elizabethtown to open

commerce down the Ohio River to New Orleans. The boat was built and launched there and loaded with grain and flour and started on its first trip May 1, 1801. The enterprise proved successful. He had also purchased an estate in Moon Township, now Corapolis in 1800. In the early spring of 1801, Joel Ferree, Sr the father of Jacob Ferree's first wife, came from Lancaster County to visit. One day he went a short distance from the house to hunt. Not returning, they went in search of him and found him dead, scalped by Indians.

When Jacob Ferree, Sr died, he left vast estates in Virginia, North Carolina and Allegheny County, Pa.

Jacob Forbes and Rachel (Ferree) Ferree had these children: <u>Joel</u> b Oct 6, 1771 Pequea Valley, Lanc Co -). He served as Colonel of the 1st Batt of Lanc associators.

<u>Olivia</u> ? (no dates) m William Moore.. He m 2nd on Jul 1, 1783, Alice Powell b 1754 of Lanc Co. ;

<u>Rebecca</u> b c1752, Lanc Co.- d 1809 in Georgetown, Ky., m John Marlatt (1748-1783, d Surry Co., N.C.

Philip Jr. (b Mar 24, 1730 in Pa. - d c1805, in Paradise, Lanc Co). He wrote his will Apr 20, 1796, it was recorded Apr 2, 1805, exec's Adam Lightner and Philip Ferree. Philip m Jun 19, 1801, Anna Copeland (b Mar 18, 1735 Lanc Co- Jul 24, 1807), bur old Ferree Cem. Philip received land in Lanc Co from his father in Nov 3, 1752 **these children were mentioned in his will.

<u>Mary</u> b 1758 m Thomas Williams

<u>William</u> b c1760 Lanc Co

<u>Elizabeth</u> (Jul 18, 1763 – 1810), m John Foster

<u>Philip</u> b 1765, m Sarah

<u>Joel</u> (b c1769 – Nov 10, 1843, Sullivan Co In.), m Aug 14, 1794 Polly Leith in Shenandoah, Va.

<u>Lydia</u> b c1771 Lanc Co

<u>Tamer</u> b 1773 , Lanc Co, m c1795, William Marsh;

<u>Rachel</u> b 1775 m Isaac Trout

<u>James</u> b 1779 m c 1804 Catherine LeFeure

<u>Abraham</u> (1778 – 1830), m Lydia LeFeure

<u>Richard</u> (Feb 21, 1770 – 1844), m Elizabeth Barr

**Joel (b Feb 19, 1731 Leacock, Lancaster, Co – d Jun 19,1801, Allegheny Co., bur Ferree Cem. Strasburg Twp., Lanc Co), a gunsmith, was married several times. Joel m 1st 1750 to Mary Copeland (b 1730 Lanc Co- d 1759 Paradise, Lanc Co). After Mary died, Joel m Nov 5, 1859 2nd Jane Johnson (c1735 – 1785, bur Ferree Cem), 3rd Susan Green (1719- after 1785, a widow of his cousin Isaac Ferree b 1715), 4th m c1788 to 1793 to Sarah Davis a widow with children, and dau of Zacharius Davis who died 1788, and was a son of James Davis whose will was written 1784.

Joel Ferree served during the Revolutionary War, using his skill as a gunsmith. He supplied firearms to the Lancaster Militia, and he is noted by the DAR as a patriot..

In the spring of 1801, Joel Ferree, Sr. took a trip from his home in Lancaster County, to Moon Twp. near Corapolis, Allegheny County to visit with the family of his deceased daughter. While there, one day he walked a short distance from the house to hunt. When he did not return to their home, the family went in search of him, and found him dead, scalped by Indians. Joel had a wife Sarah. Joel received land from his father Philip Jul 2, 1750 in Lanc Co.

[For the sake of presenting his genealogy in a more simple manner, and because of all the Ferree's Joel had the most significant effect on " Lykens Valley" his genealogy is recorded separately below.]

*JANE (b 1687 - d 1754), m Jun 30, 1715 to William Richard Davis (b c1689 Strasburg - d pre 1830), marriage recorded in Emmanuel Church, New Castle, Del. **They had no children.** He shared in the Ferree tract of land in Lanc Co.

****

*JOEL FERREE [from above] (b Feb 19, 1731 Leacock, Lancaster, Co – d Jun 19,1801, Allegheny Co., bur Carpenter Cem. Strasburg Twp., Lanc Co), son of Phillip and Mary (Copeland) Ferree above, m 1st 1750 to Mary Copeland (b 1730 Lanc Co- d 1759 Paradise, Lanc Co). All of his children were born to Mary Copeland.

After Mary died, Joel m 2nd Jane Johnson, 3rd Susan Green, 4th m netween 1788 and 1793 to Sarah Davis, a dau of Zacharius Davis who died 1788, and was a son of James Davis whose will was written 1784.

Joel wrote his will Nov 3, 1797, it was recorded Jul 13, 1801, the exec. Was Isaac Ferree, his widow was Sarah. In the will he mentions his son Isaac and his children - five sons: Joel, Isaac, Elijah, Uriah., Reuben, and seven daughters: Rachel, Susanna, Mary, Jane, Leah, Elisabeth, Rebecca. Joel also mentions his daughter Leah m to Adam Lightner, and the children of his daughter Rachel: Joel, Rebecca, Jane, and Elisabeth. He also provided for the freeing of his three negro slaves.

Joel Ferree and his wives had these children:

**ISAAC (b Oct 8, 1752 Lanc Co - d Jan 24, 1820 Lancaster Co, bur in Carpenters Cem), Mary (Copeland) Ferree was his mother. On Jun 1, 1773, Isaac m his second cousin Mary Ferree (1755 - 1806), bur in Ferree Cem with Isaac. She was a daughter of Isaac Ferree. This Isaac Ferree is the one who owned over 600 acres of land here in Lykens Valley. One tract was patented land, the other two were purchased from his father's estate. James Buchanan his son-in-law was administrator of Isaac's will. [More information below.]

RACHEL (1755 - 1782), on Aug 8, 1770, she became the wife of her first cousin Jacob Ferree (b Aug 8, 1750 Lanc - d Sep 5, 1807 in Alleghenry Co), a son of Isaac and Elizabeth Forbes Ferree, grandson of Isaac Ferree b 1725. Jacob and Rachel inherited land in Allegheny County owned by her father Joel. **Jacob and Rachel (Ferree) Ferree had these children: ELISABETH (b Jan 19, 1781 - d ___), m her cousin Isaac Ferree Jr b 1780, son of Isaac Ferree b 1753; **REBECCA** (no dates); **JANE** (no dates); **JOEL** (b ___ - d 1814), m Elizabeth Ferree, dau of Peter Ferree of Lancaster County. He became a Colonel while serving during the War of 1812 with Adam Ritschers Co of York. He died while returning from service in the Washington- Baltimore campaign. **Joel and Elizabeth (Ferree) Ferree had these children;** Susanna (Jan 11, 1804 - Oct 10, 1846, bur Oak Dake Cem), 1st wife of John Row (Feb 24, 1798 - Mar 29, 1873); Rebecca (b Oct 1809 - Jul 3, 1893, bur IOOF Cem, Lykens), m Jacob Moyer (Jul 1804 - Apr 16, 1869). Jacob was a shoemaker in 1850 in Wiconisco Twp. **Jacob and Rebecca (Ferree) Moyer had these children:** Susanna (1832 - 1916, bur IOOF Cem, Lykens), m Mar 1, 1853 Meth Ch, Halifax to John Hensel (b 1824 Adams Co - d 1912), a son of Andrew and Mary Hensel ; **Rebecca** b c1835; **Mary Jane** b c1841; **Jonas** b c1850;

**LEAH (Aug 18,1757 - May 8,1841, bur Paradise, Lanc Co), m Jan 14, 1777 to John Adam Lightner (1753 - 1798)

****

ISAAC [from above] (b Oct 8, 1752 Lanc Co - d Jan 24, 1820 Lancaster Co, bur in Carpenters Cem), was a son of Joel Ferree (1731 - 1801) and Mary (Copeland) Ferree above. On Jun 1, 1773, Isaac m his second cousin Mary Ferree (1755 - 1806), bur in Ferree Cem with Isaac. She was a daughter of Isaac Ferree. This Isaac Ferree is the one who owned over 600 acres of land here in Lykens Valley. One tract was patented land, the other two were purchased from his father's estate. James Buchanan his son-in-law was administrator of Isaac's will. **Isaac and Mary (Ferree) Ferree had these children (born in Lykens, Dau Co):

***JOEL (b 1775 Lykens – d 1819), m Elizabeth Ferree (no dates). Three of Joel's children lived in Dauphin County, and were mentioned in the will of Isaac Ferree their grandfather. **They were:** Susanna (b Jan 11, 1804 - d Oct 10, 1846, bur Oakdale Cem), m John Rowe (Feb 24, 1798 - Mar 29, 1873), lived in Washington Twp. After Susan died, John Rowe m Anna Elizabeth ____ (Jul 5, 1810 - Jul 12, 1900, bur Oakdale Cem). John Row and Anna Elizabeth ( ) had 3 children; **Mary,** living in York Co in 1823; Rebecca (b Oct 1809 – Jul 3, 1893), minor child when father died, m Jacob Mayer (b Jul 1804 – d Apr 16, 1869, bur IOOF Cem, Lykens). Lived in Wiconisco Twp in 1850. He was a shoemaker-received inheritance from Joel Ferree in right of his wife. **Jacob and Rebecca (Ferree) Mayer had these known children:** Susanna b 1833; Rebecca b c1835; Mary Jane b 1841; Jonas b c1847;

***SUSAN BARBARA (b c1776 - d Jan 23, 1804), m in 1794 to John F. Bowman (b May 10, 1771 Lanc Co - d Nov 6,1835, bur in old Meth Cem, Mbg, reburied in Oak Hill Cem c1890's). John F. Bowman was born along Pequea Creek, near Strasburg, Lancaster Co. on a mill property which was adjacent to the Ferree farm. He was a millwright, but later moved to Halifax, Dau Co, became a merchant, and later settled permanently in Millersburg. **John F. and Susan Barbara (Ferree) Bowman had these children: Eliza; Maria; George; Josiah** (1834 - Mar 6, 1896, bur IOOF Cem Lykens), m Eliza A Rutter (Jul 25, 1834 - Jan 25, 1898) . **Josiah and Eliza A (Rutter) Bowman had these children:** George J. (Jun 17, 1862 - Oct 13,

1889); **Francis C** (1864 - 1866) **Maria F.** (no dates). After Susan Barbara died, John F. Bowman married Frances Crossen. [More information in write-up on John F. Bowman.]

***RACHEL** (b c1778 Lykens Twp - d c1823) before her father according to orphan court records in Dauphin County. She m Henry Rutter (b _____ d probably 1848) . Henry and Rachel are probably the ones living as tenants in the house of Isaac Ferree in 1798. In 1800 Henry Ritter lived in Up. Paxton and had 3 young males and 1 young female in the family. A Henry Rutter of Halifax died in 1848, and Isaac and George Rutter were the executives. **Henry and Rachel (Ferree) Rutter had these children:**
Isaac lived in Dauphin Co in 1823. He is probably the Isaac, age 56, and a farmer that lived in Halifax Twp in 1850, **and had these family members:** Leah Jane; **Eliza**; **John**; **Rachel** 33, **Mary** 26, **Margaret** 23, **Joel** 20, **Henry** 17, **Rachel L.** 15; ; (the last four minors in 1823, and their father was named guardian, since their mother had previously died).
Mary m Jacob Leman and was living in Dauphin County in 1823;
George (1799 - d Dec 1884 in Mercer Co, Pa.), m Mar 25, 1823 (Davids Ch, Killinger record, Heinrich Rutter and Friedrich Lubold sponsors), to Susanna Lubold (b Jul 17, 1803 – d Jun 9, 1886), a dau of Frederick and Elizabeth (Ney) Lubold. George and Susanna lived on a farm in Halifax Twp in 1850. **George and Susanna (Lubold) Rutter had these children (some bapt Fetterhoff's Ch):** Henry b c1830, Elizabeth b c1832, **Rachel** b Mar 1, 1834; **Sarah** b c1836, **William Leitzle** b Feb 22, 1842;, **Mary Ann** b Jun 20, 1844; **Hannah M** b c1847. By 1880, George and Susanna had moved to Hempfield Twp., Mercer Co, Pa. Their son Isaac age 51, and Allen age 19, a nephew lived with them.
Leah
Jane;
Eliza (Jul 25, 1834 - Jan 25, 1897), m Josiah Bowman (1834 -
Joel W. (Jul 14, 1812 – Apr 9, 1847, bur Fetterhoff Cem);
John (Dec 2, 1808 – Nov 19, 1896, bur Fetterhoff Cem), m Margaret Ann _____ (Dec 22, 1816 – Mar 23, 1881). They lived in Halifax Twp in 1850. Margaret Rutter age 79 and Margaret Rutter age 9 lived with them. **John and Margaret Ann ( ) Rutter had these children:** George b c1837; Josiah b c1840; Isaac b c1842; William b c1847; Margaret (1849 – 1852, bur Fetterhoff Cem); Mary Jane (1856 – 1866 bur Fetterhoff Cem.)

***ISAAC Jr.** (b 1780 Dau Co – d Apr 21, 1852 Ohio?), m Elizabeth Ferree (b Jan 19, 1781 Lanc Co – d _____), a dau of Jacob and Rachel (Ferree) Ferree, lived in dau Co. Isaac Ferree, Jr. served during the War of 1812. In 1810, Isaac and his family are on the census record for Up Paxton Twp. with a young son and three young daughters. In 1820 they have 4 sons, 4 daughters. **Isaac and Elizabeth (Ferree) Ferree had these children:**
+ +**Rachel** (b Oct 9, 1805 – d Jun 23, 1874, bur unknown, recorded in Zion Luth Ch, Lykens), m 1st John Wilson, had a dau Elizabeth b c1827. Elizabeth Wilson age 9 was in the household of James Ferree in 1839, and was listed as a child whose schooling was paid by the township. Rachel m 2nd James Ferree (b c1792 - c1872). In January 1872 a Lykens newspaper records the accident of James Ferree, Esq while he was visiting with his daughter in Harrisburg. He fell on the street and broke his right arm, and sustained other injuries. The accident resulted in an attack of fever leaving him in critical condition, probably resulting in his death. James and Rachel lived in Wiconisco Twp in 1850, and he was a plasterer. At that time James W. Ferree and Elizabeth F Wilson lived in the household as well as Leah J. Sheehan age 2 months. **They had these children:** Sarah Ann b c1831 (she was listed under poor children whose tuition was paid by township; James W. b c1837,(He may be the one on the 1880 census in Wash Twp age 36, wife Catherine E 36, ch Josie E 9, Mary J 8, Dora 4, James b Aug 1879;

+ + **Jane** b c1808 m Lawrence Shomper (b c1808 -), a son probably of Lawrence Shomper b c1775. In 1820 they lived in Lykens Twp, and had 4 sons and 2 dau and a wife.. Jane and Lawrence lived in Wiconisco Twp in 1850. **Lawrence and Jane (Ferree) Shomper had these children:** Mary b c1831; Isaac b c1833 (no dates), m _____ , **had these children:** Amos b 1855; Jacob b 1857; Loran b 1859; Jane b 1883, all died young and are bur in Shomper Cem; Uriah (Apr 15, 1838 - Oct 16, 1900, bur Shomper/Sheafer Cem, Wiconisco Twp), m Sarah _____ (Dec 10, 1842 - May 19, 1914), **had these known children:** David b c1862; Daniel (b c1864, probably the one (1865 - 1937 bur Greenwood Cem, Tower

City, m Annie J ___ (1868 – 1955)) ; Mary b c1867; Cyrus b c1873; Uriah, Jr. (1878 – 1910); Isaac F b 1880; Amos b c1840; Elizabeth b c1846.

++Joel Barlow (1809 - 1880, bur Oakdale Cem), m Ann McCurtin (b Feb 22, 1814 - Jan 11, 1881), said to be a resident of Alleghany Co. when they married. Joel was a surveyor, and in 1850 they lived in Wiconisco Twp. In 1870 and 1880, Joel and Ann lived in Washington Twp., he was again listed as a surveyor. **Joel B and Ann (McCurtin) Ferree had these children:** Micah b c1834; Martha Jane b c1841; John Milton (b c1842 - ___), m 1st Sarah ___ b c1842. In 1870 John Milton and Sarah Ferree are living in a double house next to his parents in Washington Twp. and he is a butcher. **They have these children:** *Harry M* b c1862; *Emma J* (1864 - 1920, bur Salem Cem), m John K. Berksfield (1855 - 1924;. John Milton Ferree m 2nd Jul 4, 1875, Jennie Leitner, Oakdale Ch, both of Short Mountain. In 1880 Milton and Jennie lived in Williams Twp., and had *Nelson* b c1867 with them. He was a butcher; Zander (Leander S.) b c1844 - ___), m Catherine Elizabeth _____ b c1844. In 1870 Leander S. Ferree and family lived in Washington Twp and he was a butcher. In 1873, Leander S. Ferree laid out a plot plan in Loyalton. The lots were sold to numerous people and Loyalton began to grow rapidly. **Leander S. and Catherine Elizabeth ( ) had these children:** John b c1869; Josee (dau) b May 15, 1871 Oakdale; _____ b Aug 1872; Mary Jane b Apr 9, 1873 Loyalton; John G. b Jul 18,, 1874 bapt Jul 14, 1876; Dora May b Aug 11, 1875; James b Aug 1879; Joel Forbes b Dec 1, 1848, m Catherine Miller, moved to Michigan, had son Clinton Augustus bapt Mar 31, 1878 in Zion Luth Ch, Lykens; Agnes Ann b Nov 24, 1850 – d 1851); Edith Ann b Jun 26, 1855 – Aug 16, 1856); William Ward (Jan 26,1857 – Oct 13, 1885, murdered by his brother-in-law in Connellsville, Pa.). He m __ Gilman. He lived with parents in Wash Twp in 1870.

++George Washington (b Nov 21, 1810, Wash Twp - d Jan 5, 1873, bur Hoffman Cem). When he died, Frank P. Ferree and John Rush were adm. of his estate. He was m in 1834 to Leah Umholtz (Feb 7, 1815 - Jan 1888), a dau of Henry and Susanna (Hoover) Umholtz. In 1880 Leah lived alone in Lykens. George worked in the mines in Wiconisco for 25 years. **George Washington and Leah (Umholtz) Ferree had eight children:**
Cyrus (1834 – 1839);
Ann Mary (b Oct 19, 1838 – d May 25, 1895, bur Simeon Cem), m Isaac Burd (Dec 1832 – d 1865, bur Hoffman Cem). **Isaac and A. Mary (Ferree) Burd had these children:** Samuel b c1857; Elizabeth b c1858, lived with the Cyrene Bowman family in 1870, after her father died. She later m Jan 3, 1875 William Messner a son of John P. Messner of Lykens Twp; Susan b c1860; George W. (Mar 1, 1861 – Apr 6, 1889), who lived with the James Kolba family in 1870. He is buried beside his mother in Simeon Cem. His obituary describes him as an unfortunate mortal who was crippled by a mine accident early in life. The 1880 census states that he had a sore back; Henry H. b c1863, m Ida ____ lived in Mt. Carmel; Emma J b c1864 lived with her grandmother Ferree in 1880. She later married William Row of Lykens Twp.; Sarah b c1865, m Ambrose Reinhold of Williamstown; Mary Louisa m May 12, 1872 to Durrell Seesholtz in Lykens. Durrell (1846 – 1916, bur IOOF Cem, Lykens), was a son of Rebecca and _____ Seesholtz of Lykens. He was a "workman in the cars in 1870." In 1911, they lived in Harrisburg. **Mary Louisa and Durrell had these children:** *Harry F* (Jan 4, 1874 – Oct 20, 1943), Pvt in USMC, bur Simeons Cem; *Edith*; *Mary R.*
Elizabeth (Jun 4,1841 – Feb 18, 1913), not married; Henry (1844 – d Apr 14, 1903, bur Gratz Cem, according to death record), m Louisa Bellon (b Mar 1846 – d Sep 2, 1913, in Coal Twp, Northld Co, bur Simeons, according to death certif.), a dau of Mathias Bellon. Henry was a Civil War Vet. **Henry and Louisa (Bellon) Ferree had these children (some bapt Simeon Ref, Gratz):** Ida Charlotte b Jan 6, 1867; Sarah Caroline b May 27, 1868; George Franklin b Apr 9, 1870; Henry M. b c1873; ; Lizzie Louisa b Sep 6, 1875; Mary E b c1878; Hattie Leah b Sep 23, 1880, m Apr 6, 1895 Henry Lloyd Coleman – **had these children (some bapt St. Johns Luth, Lykens):** Emma Louisa b Nov 5, 1900; Harold Franklin b May 16, 1909 in Wiconisco; Anna May b Feb 2, 1911;
Eva N. b Aug 1882 – she was 2nd wife of Daniel S. Artz b 1875, a son of Preston and Mary J. Artz; Charles Adam b Dec 1885; (all baptism at Simeon Ref. Ch);
??Leah – this may be Leah J (Aug 25, 1840 – Aug 15, 1883, bur "Hill" Cem near village of Dauphin), 1st wife of George W. Hocker (Nov 23, 1846 – Nov 12, 1908). After Leah died, George Hocker m Mary J. Fleager (Nov 17, 1847 – Jun 30, 1903).
Sarah Grace (b Apr 23, 1846 (bapt Hoffman Ch) - d pre 1888), was in 1870 teaching school, later m Nathan Bressler, had a dau Sallie;

40

George W. Jr. (b c1849- d 1879), m Emma Ritzman, had a dau Hattie Louisa b Aug 12, 1876; Henry Franklin b Jul 21, 1878;

 Franklin Pierce (b May 25, 1853 – d Sep 22, 1938), m in 1878 to Catherine Ann Salada (Mar 12, 1860 – Apr 24, 1917), a dau of Henry and Elizabeth (Seiler) Salade (b Feb 1820). Franklin Pierce was a farmer, school teacher and Justice of the Peace in Lykens Twp.In 1880, Frank and his family lived in Lykens. Emma J. Burd age 17, and George F. Ferree age 11 was with them. In 1900, Elizabeth Salada b Feb 1820, mother of Catherine lived with Franklin and Catherine Ferree.

 Frank and Catherine (Salada) Ferree had these children: Sarah Edith b Nov 1877; Joseph Allen b Dec 17, 1885; Elizabeth Leah (b Apr 1, 1890, bapt Hoffman Ch - d 1897); Henry Washington (b Apr 20, 1892 -   ), moved to Fresno, Calif.; Blanche Miriam (b Sep 13, 1894 – d 1897).

Edith Ellen (Feb 16, 1855 – Jul 22, 1895, d of cancer), m Feb 22, 1879, to John Rush. John and Edith Ellen (Ferree) Rush had 6 children: Harry Edgar b Dec 27, 1879; Elizabeth Beulah b Sep 28, 1883, d young; Mary Salome b Feb 19, 1886, m Richard Schmeltz, son of Elias Schmeltz, lived in Spring Glen, Sch Co; George W. (Jul 20, 1888 – Jul 10, 1916); Sarah m Harvey Carl, lived in Gratz; Nora Ellen b May 29, 1894, these bapt Hoffman Ch., m Norman Miller, son of John Miller, lived in Berrysburg.

++Maria b c1812, m Edward Myers

++Thomas Jefferson (b c1818 d 1864, burial unknown), m Julia Ann Schuman (Mar 8, 1819 bapt Hoffman Ch - Oct 26, 1887, bur Old Stone Cem, E'ville, alone), a dau of David & Elisabeth Shuman. They lived in Washington Twp in 1850.Thomas J and Julia Ann (Schuman) Ferree had these children: William Henry (b Jan 16,1839 – d Apr 21, 1896, bur IOOF Cem, Lykens), m Sep 27, 1866 in U.Meth Ch Mbg. Anna Spicher of Liverpool, (b Mar 25, 1843 – d Dec 2, 1901, death recorded in Zion Luth, Lykens), lived in Lykens in 1880. William Henry and Anna (Spicher) Ferree had these children: Allice Barbara b Jan 13, 1868; Ida b c1870;, Newton S (b Jan 8,1872 – d Jul 26, 1894, bur IOOF Cem); Kate b c1874; Flora Jane (Oct 8, 1875 – Mar 26, 1880); William Weston b Oct 4, 1877; Joseph Jefferson b Oct 19, 1879; Charles Ray b Aug 5, 1881 – Apr 9, 1891, bur IOOF Cem); Ellen C b Jan 28, 1884; Forrest C. (b Jan 29, 1887 – 1935, bur IOOF Cem, Lykens), m Margaret E ___ (1892 - ----);

Cyrus b c1841, m Mary ____;

Elizabeth (1843 – 1920, bur Salem Union Cem, E'ville), m George K. Leiter (1841 – 1914), had a son Clayton (1882 - 1914), bur near parents.

Anna Mary b c1846, m Samuel Spicher;

Sarah Ferree (b Jul 22, 1848 – Apr 9, 1910), m John Sweezy (Oct 28, 1840 – May 5, 1902 bur Salem Union Cem, E'ville). John and Sarah (Ferree) Sweezy had these children: Clara A Sweezy (Apr 15 1880 – Jun 15, 1880 bur Motters Cem); Sarah K (d Jan 30, 1892, age 7 yr 8 mo); Minnie J. (d Jan 21, 1892 age 8 y llm 20 d); Harry E (May 2, 1881 – Apr 6, 1882); Katie J (Feb 3, 1876 – Mar 3, 1881); William C (Dec 12, 1881 – Jan 26, 1887); Sally (Jan 15, 1879 – Feb 22, 1879); Cora L (Apr 23, 1871 – Sep 1, 1872)

Jonathan (b Mar 10, 1852 – d Feb 21, 1939, bur Salem Ref. Cem, E'ville), m Apr 13, 1878 Martha Jane Enterline b Nov 19, 1859, a dau of Joseph and Catherine (Matter) Enterline), Jonathan and Martha Jane (Enterline) Ferree had these known children: Howard William b Feb 10, 1879; Mamie (c1891 - d Dec 21, 1896)

++Ann Elizabeth b c1819, m John Sheehan b c1812 in Ireland. They lived in Wiconisco Twp in 1850 and he was employed as a miner. John and Ann Elizabeth (Ferree) Sheehan had these children: Elizabeth b c1843; Joseph b c1846; Michael b c1848; Timothy b c1850.

++Uriah Dubois (Jul 1819 - Jan 9, 1894, death recorded in Zion Luth, Lykens), m Mary A. ____ (b c1826 - ___). In 1850 Uriah and Mary lived in the household of his father Isaac, and had their two children. Uriah Dubois and Mary (___) had these children: Elizabeth b c1846; Jacob b c1847.

++Isaac Newton (c1820 - 1878), m Margaret Eli

++Jacob Forbes (c1822 d Nov 4,1886, bur Cal Meth Cem, Wiconisco), m Oct 7, 1866 Hannah York. (Jan 18, 1827 - Dec 26, 1886). They were married by James Ferree, J.P. of Lykens. Before the Civil War, Jacob was a miner. He was enrolled in Co A of the 50th Regt Pa Volunteers on Aug 30, 1863, later served in Co C of the 149th Pa Vol. Until Mar 1864. He later enrolled in Co F of the 48th Pa Vol Regt. While on duty at Beaufort, S. C. in March 1862, he was unloading a wagon load of commissary stores, when the horses were frightened and pushed the wagon back. He was jammed between the wagon and a pile of boxes, hurting his left hip. He never fully recovered and also developed Rheumatism, for which he received a pension.

In 1880 Jacob and Hannah lived in Wiconisco Twp. Jacob and Hannah (York) Ferree had a son Benjamin Franklin (1868, orphaned at age 9 - 1953, bur Cal Meth Cem), m Catherine H. Mumma (1875 - 1967).

++**Leah** (b c1824 m Patrick Martin (b c1826 in Ireland - d ____). They lived in Wiconisco Twp in 1850. **Patrick and Leah (Ferree) Martin had these children:**Ann Eliza b c1842; Mary Jane b c1844;;Amanda b c1848; Rachel b 1850; John H. (b c1851 - d Jun 6, 1930, bur Calvary Meth Cem, Wiconisco), of heart disease.

***ELIJAH** (b 1781 Lykens - d c1823), m Sallie Brua lived in Dau Co. Elijah age 26 - 45 is on the 1820 census for Lykens Twp., had a wife same age, and 2 sons and 4 dau. One person in the family is involved in manufacturing.

***ELIZABETH** (c178_   Lykens, bapt May 18, 1822 as an adult - d _____, in Baltimore), m James Buchanan, a son of _____. James was involved with the Oak Dale Forge, but they later moved to Baltimore. **James and Elizabeth (Ferree) Buchanan had these children (they were all bapt the same day as their mother (May 18, 1822) in Zion Luth Ch, Hbg):**
Anna Mary Ferre b May 20, 1816; **James Evans** b Nov 17, 1817; **Uriah Ferree** b Jun 17, 1819; **Olivia Emeline** b Nov 14, 1821

***MARIA** (b 1784   ) m Jesse Cloud - lived in Baltimore

***JANE** b 1786 Lykens, m Capt. Tobin

***LEAH** b 1788 Lykens, m Joseph Wright (b _____ d before 1823), lived in Lanc Co.

***REBECCA** (b Dec 25, 1791 Strassburg, Lanc - d Jan 14, 1827, bur Old Leacock Cem, Lanc) m Mathias Slaymaker., lived in Lancaster Co.

***URIAH** (1792 - 1819, bur Ferree Cem, Lanc Co)

***REUBEN** (b 1794 Lykens - d 1827)., m Nancy Wells, and lived in Mifflin Twp as late as 1838. They later moved to Iowa. **Reuben and Nancy (Wells) Ferree had 7 children: Thomas** b c1819; **Uriah** b 1819, m Anna Gibble and lived in Nebraska; **Charles** b c1827, m Lucy Middleton; **Mary** b c1823; **James** b c1829, he may be the one that m Mary J ___ b c1839, and **had these children: Emeline** b c1869; **Sarah E** b c1864; **Mary J** b c1868; **Ida** b c1870; **Isaac H** b c 1873; **Amanda** b c1877; **Alvin H.** b c1878; **Sarah** b c1834; **Amanda** b c1837.

OAK DALE

(Later renamed Loyalton)

This area is no longer part of Lykens Township. But it was probably the very earliest settlement of what became Lykens Township, and enjoys the distinction of being the place where Andrew Lykens, namesake of our township settled. The early settlers who came here found the environment of this little area conducive and desirable for settlement. The meandering creek flowing through the rich soil was not only beautiful, but held the most promise for a valuable and likely successful investment. In those days, water was one of the principle commodities when investors looked for land to purchase. But is it possible that the early investors also had an inkling of coal being buried under the mountains? The discovery of that precious commodity became the most important element in the development of this land.

It is interesting to note that many of the very first settlers in this section were of Irish, Scotch-Irish and English descent, with a sprinkling of French Huguenots. Some followed the example of Andrew Lykens, and came here after settling in the Philadelphia area. But more came from what is now the Lancaster County part of Pennsylvania. A few of the new landowners never really lived here, but purchased tracts of land as an investment. Today, a high percentage of people of German descent own most of this land.

Oak Dale is the only area of Lykens Township known to suffer serious or fatal atrocities from the Indians. It was probably actions on both sides that brought on the bloodshed. It was also toward the end of the most dangerous period of the mid-1750s, and probably was a follow up of the events that took place in some of the surrounding counties. Traditional stories, giving other examples of problems among the settlers here in northern Dauphin County and the local Indians, have been handed down from ancestors. But few if any of them resulted in murderous consequences.

Oak Dale which is now the southern tip of Loyalton is significant in another way, because it reflects the growth that took place in this region. It was settled very early, and throughout the years became detached from Lancaster County. Then it was separated from Upper Paxton in 1810 into Lykens Township. Later, part of it became the section broken away from Lykens Township, and was located in Wiconisco Township by July 2, 1839. Another change took place on September 3, 1845, when a new township was formed, and named Washington Township, after the first President of the United States. Official records from those early years show confusion in trying to distinguish the changes in location of land, and land ownership, from one township to another.

Although the Oak Dale / Loyalton area has long been separated from Lykens Township, it is necessary to include it in the history of Lykens Township. The activities of the early Oak Dale settlement, the railroad, and in fact, the very early settlers here influenced the makeup and later development of the whole region.

MAP SHOWING PART OF WASHINGTON TOWNSHIP

Map Drawn By Fisk
Dated 1875

LAST TWO FERREE TRACTS SOLD TO JOHN E. FORSTER

The two largest tracts of land that belonged to Joel Ferree, of Lancaster County and sold to his son Isaac, remained with the family for several years, and were the last to be sold. But they became the nucleus of the early development in the vicinity. On December 1, 1827, James Buchanan, administrator of Isaac Ferree's estate sold them to John E. Forster, merchant of Harrisburg. One tract contained 227 acres 46 ¾ perches of land. The other tract contained 191 acres 34 ½ perches. On Feb. 4, 1828, John E. Forster sold the land with buildings back to James Buchanan, coppersmith of Harrisburg. Buchanan sold some land, but a large part of these two tracts became the Oak Dale Forge.

James Buchanan owned the two tracts of land for several years. But on May 17, 1841, he and his wife Elizabeth Buchanan sold a large tract of the land to Josiah Bowman. After Josiah Bowman died, his heirs George Bowman and Louisa, John R. Bowman and Anne J., Levi Bowman and Agnes, Francis S. Bowman, and C. W. Conway and his wife Susan on April 14, 1869, sold the land with two two-story frame houses and kitchen, a bank barn, wagon shop, good water and apple orchard to George Neagley. This land lay on the north side of what became the Oak Dale Forge (see1875 map), and continued north beyond the main road through what is now Loyalton.

Soon after they purchased the land, George and Caroline Neagley sold one small tract of 4 acres from their land located on the south side of Loyalton to Adam E. Wert on May 22, 1875. It was located on the south side of Oak Dale Forge. About two years later, Adam E. Wert conveyed that land to John Wommer.

On April 25, 1878, about the time that George and Caroline moved to Millersburg, they sold about 180 acres of land to Nathaniel Miller. Most of it belonged to the Oak Dale Forge and Academy complex for many years.

THE BOWMAN FAMILY
(some information from Bowman/Wainewright family history)

This **BOWMAN** family is traced to Ulie Julius Buman (1396 –1425 of Switzerland. After ten generations of living in Switzerland a family member **Wendell Bowman** (1681 – Apr 1735), son of **Hans Rudolf** b 1637 came to n America with William Penn, and settled in Lancaster County. He married Anna _____ (1685 – c1735). His brother **John** (1685 – 1738) also came to America, married Barbara _____, and had a large family. His first child **John** (1705 – 1749), m Barbara Weave b c1717, dau of John Jr. and Barbara Weave of Lancaster Co. is the ancestor of the **BOWMAN** family members listed here.

BENJAMIN BOWMAN (Jul 4, 1742 Lanc Co - Jun 29, 1822 Clarence, N.Y.), m c1768 Elizabeth Ferree (Oct 29, 1743 - Nov 4,1800), a dau of Isaac and Elizabeth Ferree. **Benjamin and Elizabeth (Ferree) Bowman had these children:**

ELIZABETH BOWMAN (no dates) m George Withers

SUSANNAH BOWMAN (Apr 17, 1769 - Jan 23, 1840), m Joseph LeFevre (1765 – 1835)

JOHN F. BOWMAN (b May 10, 1771 at Pequea Creek, near Strasburg, Lancaster Co. - d Nov 6, 1835, bur in old Methodist Cem, Millersburg. (All bodies removed from that cemetery and placed in Oak Hill Cemetery in 1895.) . He was a millwright, but later entered the mercantile pursuits. In 1809 he moved to Halifax, and became a merchant there. But in 1830, he moved on to a larger trade in Millersburg. John F. Bowman married in 1794 to Susanna Barbara Ferree (c1776 – Jan 23, 1804), a daughter of Isaac and Mary (Copeland) Ferree. **John F. and Susan Barbara (Ferree) Bowman had these children (born in Lanc Co): ELIZA** b c1794; **MARIA** (Nov 9, 1797 – May 20, 1828, bur Halifax Cem); **GEORGE** (1794 - 1860, m Louisa _____; **JOSIAH** (Mar 27, 1800 – 1863 age 62 y 9 m 15 d, bur Oak Hill Cem, Mbg),, m Elizabeth Rutter (1805 – May 17,1885 age 85). In 1850 Josiah and Elizabeth Bowman lived in Wiconisco Twp, where Josiah was listed as a farmer. Their son Isaac was a printer, John was a farmer, Josiah was a druggist. They also had Peter Zimmerman age 18 with them. **Josiah and Elizabeth (Rutter) Bowman had these children: George** (no dates) m Louisa _____; Isaac (May 18, 1825 - Sep 2, 1893, bur Oak Hill Cem, Mbg); **John R.** (Sep 19, 1828 – Mar 21, 1904, bur Mbg), m Anne J. ; **Josiah** b c1832, m Elizabeth . In 1850 they lived in Lykens and Josiah was an insurance agent; **Levi** b c1835, m Agnes; **Susanna L.** b c1837, m C. W.Conway; **Frank S.** (b Jan 24, 1844 at Loyalton - d 1901.Lebanon), m Sep 14, 1869, Mary Catherina (Wert, Mark), wid of Cyrus Mark (May 22, 1843 - Dec 6,1893), a dau of Simon Wert of Millersburg. **Frank S. and Mary (Wert, Mark) Bowman had two children:** Linn b Apr 28, 1874; Hay Wert b Jun 30, 1870 – Apr 26, 1946, bur Oak Dale Cem, Mbg), m Jun 6, 1895 Nelllie M. Bowman (Jun 25, 1874 - May 6, 1902), a

dau of Simon S. and Anne P (Jackson) Bowman. Frank S. became a lawyer, but he also established the Millersburg Sentinel. After Susanna died, John F. Bowman m in 1805, Frances Crossen b Aug 31, 1786 - d Sep 30, 1846), a dau of John Crossen. **John F. and Frances (Crossen) Bowman had these children:**
JOHN JEFFERSON (Feb 12, 1807 - Aug 13, 1894, bur Oak Dale Cem, Mbg), m Margaret Sallade (Jan 12, 1807 – Jul 13, 1894, bur Mbg) a dau of Simon and Jane (Woodside) Sallade. In 1880 they lived in Millersburg, and he was listed as a retired dry goods merchant.They had these children living in their household: Lucinda, Levi B, a tinsmith; Margaret A.. Also these brothers and sisters: Levi, Jacob, Emeline, and Hattie Troutman age 15, a servant. **John J and Margaret (Sallade) Bowman had these children:**
Mary F. b c1836. m T. Jefferson Black; Jennie E. b c1837 m Professor Charles S.Fahnestock, Chester; Delaware Co.; Lucinda (1839 – Mar 14, 1924, age 85 yrs, bur Mbg); Dr. John F.(Jan 5, 1841 – Jan 16, 1914, bur Mbg Cem) Lived in Millersburg; Simon Sallada (b Oct 13, 1842 near E'ville - d Jan 26, 1916, bur Mbg. Cem), m Jul 29, 1866, Anne P. Jackson a (1847 – Nov 4, 1923),dau of Addison and Hannah P. (Light) Jackson. Simon S. was veteran of the Civil War. **Simon S. and Anne P. (Jackson) Bowman had these children:** Sumner Sallada (Feb 9, 1867 – Jan 11, 1954), m Katherine Baker Wainwright, (Feb 2, 1882 in N.Y - Aug 22, 1944, Mbg) , ; Edmund Boohan b Nov 2, 1868;; Irene A. m J. S. Hopkinson, Supt. of the Northern Central railroad from Harrisburg to Sunbury ; Nellie M. m Hay W. Bowman, editor of Millersburg Sentinel; Hannah; James Donald; Robert Herr b Oct 27, 1889. **Levi B** (b Dec 14, 1846 in E'ville - d Mar 13, 1911, bur Mbg), m Agnes Mary ____ (1855 – 1931). Levi B. was a tinsmith, working for his uncle Levi Bowman in his store. He later succeeded his uncle in that business; **Levi B. and Agnes Mary ____ Bowman had these children:** Emma b Nov 21, 1864; Susan b Nov 4, 1866;Elizabeth .
LEVI (May 16, 1809 – Dec 6, 1894), was a tinware manufacturer in Millersburg; Margaret (Ann b May 30, 1851 – Jan 25, 1934, bur Mbg).
LOUISA b c1811 in Lancaster Co;
ISAAC (1815 – Lanc Co – 1870, Mbg)
MARY E. (b c1815 -   ), m Rev. Charles W. Jackson a Methodist Episcopal Minister who served the Halifax Circuit in 1836. Rev. Jackson had the honor of preaching the first Methodist sermon to the newly established congregation in Berrysburg. The congregation was meeting in the Yeager home because their church had not yet been built.
LUCINDA (Apr 22, 1821 – Sep 12, 1845, in Ill.) m Dr. Hiram Rutherford (Dec 27, 1815 Paxtang, Dau Co, son of Col William Rutherford – d Cole Co. Ill). After Lucinda d, Hiram m Harriet Hutchinson. In 1880 they lived in Oakland, Cole Co, Ill, & he was listed as a physician. These children lived with them: John b c1845 a clerk in a bank; Cyrus b c1851, a physician; Kate b c1858; Wilson b c1860; Anna b c1865; Luther b c1867;
JACOB (1824 – 1887, Mbg);
EMELINE (Jan 20, 1825 – Feb 26, 1883);
BENJAMIN (Apr 23, 1827 – May 24, 1910, bur Oakd Dale Cem, Mbg), m Jalania _____ (Nov 13, 1839 – Oct 15, 1903). In 1850 Benjamin was living in Up. Paxton Twp and was a boatman.
John F Bowman became a millwright while living in his native Lancaster County. But in 1809 he moved to Halifax, Dauphin County, where he was a dry goods merchant. In 1830, he moved to Millersburg and continued in that business until his death.
BENJAMIN BOWMAN b 1773
LANA BOWMAN b c1775
ISAAC BOWMAN c1779 m Elizabeth Ellemaker
MARY BOWMAN 1781 m John Guigar
JOSHUA (JOSIAH) BOWMAN b 1783]

THE NAGELY /NEAGELY FAMILY

[*JACOB NAGELY immigrant from Wurtemberg, Germany settled first in Berks County, but later moved to Lykens Valley. He had two sons. (according to Dau Co Hist)
**JOHN NAGELY (no dates) m Sara ____. In 1774 they were communicants at Salem Luth, Killinger. They apparently died before the 1790 census was taken. Nothing more has been learned about them.
 **GEORGE NAGELY (b ___ d spring 1806, probably bur David's Cem) , m Magdalena ____. In 1798 when the window tax was taken, George was noted as having a good barn and a still house, at the foot of

45

Mahantongo Mountain next to "Jo" Nagely. David's Ref. Ch death minutes record these two as the parents of Joseph. George was a communicant at Salem Luth 1773,1777, 1779, and1784. He was an elder in 1780. George Neagly wrote his will dated Jul 28, 1790, it was probated Mar 12, 1806. He mentions that he is old and weak, and specifies that his land should go to his two sons George and Joseph. His wife had apparently died, and no other person is mentioned in the will. **George and Magdalena Nagley had these two sons:**
***GEORGE** (Jul 3, 1764 bap Holy Trinity Luth, Lanc - d Nov 25, 1853, bur Oak Hill Cem, Mbg), married Hanna _____ (no dates). A record in Davids Church at Killinger states that George was confirmed in 1780 at the age of 16. His father in his will states that Geoge is the oldest son.
George and Hanna (___) Nagley had one known dau, but according to the 1810 census he had several other girls. **** Magdalena b Apr 1 0, 1789 bapt Salem Luth
***JOSEPH** (Oct 5, 1766 bap 1st Ref, Lanc. – d Jul 12, 1828, bur St. Davids Cem, Killinger), m Jul 5, 1792, Anna Maria Hoffman (b Tulpehocken, Berks Co.Jan 8, 1773 - Feb 18, 1840), a dau of Johannes and Anna Maria (Kauffman) Hoffman. Joseph was confirmed at David's Ch in 1782 at the age of 15. He and his wife Anna Maria communed at Davids Church and he was an elder in 1814. In 1798 when the window tax was taken, Joseph was noted as having an excellent barn and lived along the River Road next to George Nagely. **Joseph & Anna Maria (Hoffman) Nagley children (2 sons & 4 dau most conf at Davids Ch.) r):**
****ELIZABETH** b Jul 24, 1793, bapt Salem Luth, confirmed age 19 in 1813 at Davids Ch. She m John Holtzman as recorded in her fathers will.
****MARY MAGDALENA**, (Feb 20, 1795 – Jul 25, 1863, bur St. Johns "Hill" Cem) , m Peter Lark (Nov 20, 1795 – Aug 11, 1850) had two known dau's: **Sarah** (Sep 8, 1823 -d Dec 2, 1904 bur St. John's Hill Cem, Bbg), not m; **Catharine** (Apr 22, 1833 – May 16, 1915), m Geo W. Koppenhaver (1835 – 1884).
****DANIEL** (Nov 12, 1797 - Feb 2, 1873), m Margaret Gable (Apr 8, 1803 - Oct 17, 1875, bur St. Davids Cem), a dau of Joseph and Catharine Gable. They lived in Up Paxton Twp in 1850 and also1860, when he was listed as a gentleman. **Daniel Margaret (Gable) Nagley child: (bap Davids Ch):**
George (Aug 16, 1825 - Sep 14, 1894, bur Davids Cem, Killinger, m Caroline S. Lebo (b Jun 29, 1827, bapt David's Ch, Killinger –d Jul 23, 1921, bur Oak Hill Cem, Millersburg), a dau of Henry and Anna (Billenstald) Lebo.

In 1850 & 1860 he was listed as a carpenter and lived in Upper Paxton Twp. In 1880 George and Caroline lived in Millersburg and George was listed as a furniture manufacturer. Their daughter Emily lived with them as did Frank Sheetz age 21 a cabinetmaker.
George and Caroline S. (Lebo) Nagley had these children: Emily b c1859;(maybe)Lovina m Specht ?Arndt, Rebecca m ____Lebo, Mary m ____ Grove? **John** (Oct 10,1827 bapt David's Ch - Sep 12, 1891, bur Oak Hill Cem, Mbg), m Dec 22,1853 Elizabeth R. _____ (Jan 7, 1824 -Apr 10, 1887), dau of John and Anna Murray. John learned the trade of cabinetmaker in Liverpool, Perry Co., later moved to Freeport, Ill, then came back to Liverpool. In 1869 he established a planning mill at Millersburg; **Sarah** b c1828; **Joseph** (Oct 12,1829-1838); **Maria** Feb 25, 1833; **Catherine** b c1835; **William** b Dec 18, 1838, probably the one living in Low Mah. Twp in Northld in 1880,WifeAnnie38, ch: Milton 14 & Q. Maggie 11; **Daniel** b c1840; **Isaac** b 1842; **Margaret** (Jul 20, 1843 – Jul 24, 1911, bur David's Cem, Killinger), m D. K. Holtzman (Nov 28, 1836 – Dec 8, 1910); **Hannah** 1846.

John Nagley (1827 – 1891)

****CATHERINE** (1801 – 1889) , m Mar 23, 1823 Abraham Will (Apr 20, 1798 - Oct 1, 1828 is bur St. Davids, a son of Conrad and Catharine Will. Catharine was an unfortunate person in that she lost her husband and two children within less than two years. She never remarried. She lived with her son Isaac and family in 1880 in Up. Paxton Twp. **Abraham and Catherine (Nagley) Will had these children (bapt David's Ch): Maria** (Mar 26, 1826 – Feb 25, 1829, bur with father); **Isaac** (Aug 8, 1827 - 1891 bur David;s Cem), m Susannah Feidt (Jun 23, 1828 – Sep 8, 1902), a dau of Daniel and Lidia Feidt. Isaac and

46

Susannah (Feidt) Will had these children: Mary b c 1855; David b c1857, m Sarah Jane (1864 – 1926); Amelia b May 14, 1864; John Willaim (Dec 3, 1868 – Jun 6, 1927, bur David's Cem); **Sarah** (Dec 28, 1828 – May 14, 1830, bur David's Cem).

****<u>SARAH</u>. (no dates) A minor child when her father died, had Jacob Weaver as her guardian.

****<u>GEORGE</u> (Sep 8, 1805 - Oct 14, 1865, bur St. Davids Cem, Killinger) m Charlotta Kintzel (May 14, 1811 - Jan 2, 1852, bur St. Davids Cem, Killinger), a dau of Christian and Mary Kintzel. They lived in Up Paxton Twp in 1860. **George and Charlotta (Kintzel) Nagley had these children:**

David (Aug 25, 1833 – Aug 23, 1900, bur David's Cem), m Salome Feidt (Nov 11, 1830 – Aug 11, 1901), a dau of George and Susanna Feid, lived in Up Paxton Twp in 1860 and continued at least to 1880.
David and Salome (Feidt) Nageley had these children: (bapt David's Ch); <u>George Edwin</u> (b May 2, 1858 – May 20, 1880, bur David's Cem); <u>John Frederick</u> (May 14, 1860 – 1942, bur David's Cem), m Nora _____ (1868 – 1929); <u>Isreal Penn</u> b Mar 18, 1862 – 1940, bur David's Cem), m Ella A ___ (1868 – 1945); <u>Leah Jane</u> b c1864; <u>Amelia</u> b c1868.

Isaac (1835 – 1885, bur David's Cem), m Mary S. Seal (1842 – 1923), a dau of John H and Martha Seal.. They lived in Up. Pax Twp in 1880, and Jennie C. Miller, domestic age 20, and Martha Seal age 68, mother in law lived with them. **Isaac and Mary (Seal) had these children (bapt Davids Ch):** <u>Henry Calvin</u> b Sep 7, 1862; <u>Benton Pierce</u> ; (Aug 20, 1865 – 1942, bur David's Cem), m Minnie ___ (1868 – 1951); <u>Katie Selesta</u> b Aug 22, 1869; <u>George</u> S. b c1871; <u>Nevin Edgar</u> b Sep 8, 1880.

Henrietta b Jun 11, 1839, m Henry Sheaffer; **Catharine** (Jul 21, 1841 – 1923 bur Davids Cem), m Levi Sheetz; (**Mary Ann** b c1844, m DavidE. Feidt b Feb 17, 1844; **John A** (1846 – 1916, bur David's Cem, Killinger), m Emma S. ___ (1853 – 1931); **Daniel W.** (Nov 2, 1849 - Nov 24, 1919, bur Oak Hill Cem, Mbg, m Emma E. ___ b c1851. In 1880 lived in Millersburg and was a book keeper. **They had a dau** <u>Jelania</u> (1875 – May 15, 1919, bur Oak Hill Cem.)]

WAS HOME OF CLYDE W. CLAPSADLE
SMALL HOME AT ROADSIDE (OAK DALE FORGE ROAD)

This small portion of land belonged to the tract that Alfred and Louisiana Rowe owned. They sold a large tract to J. G. Romberger on April 2, 1924, and soon Romberger laid out in lots. On July 7, 1924, they sold this lot to H. H. and Jennie Snyder. On April 11, 1925, Patrick and Margaret Warren purchased the 19,388 square foot lot from Snyder. They may have had the present house built. It is said that "Jack" Zerbe built this one and ½ story frame house during the 1930's from old second hand lumber. Patrick and Margaret Warren lived here a few years. Patrick died in September 1937. On Dec 17, 1942, Margaret Warren conveyed to Clyde W. Clapsadle, a single man. At that time the property bordered the west side of the road, and the land of Wesley Troutman. Robert & Beatrice Bonawitz owned it next and sold to Albert G. Mauser on September 4, 1953.

[Clyde W.Clapsadle (1905 – 1980, bur IOOF Cem, Lykens), was a son of Charles and Grace Clapsadle].

UPPER DAUPHIN AREA SCHOOL DISTRICT LAND

Home of Upper Dauphin District Elementary School

Old Residential Dwelling Along Oak Dale Forge Road

This land originally belonged to the Ferree family, and after several owners, 180 acres became the property of George Neagley, as mentioned above. He sold it to Nathaniel Miller April 25, 1878. The house is old and may have belonged to James Buchanan. In 1828 he was assessed for two houses and two cabins. In 1831 he was assessed for five houses. This was probably one of the houses, and probably the one he and his family lived in. Over the next years it became part of the forge property.

Many years later in 1926, Nathaniel and Gertrude Miller conveyed the land with appurtenances to Helen Watson. Helen C. E. Watson, a widow of Elizabethville conveyed it to Irene Watson February 21, 1936.

On March 19, 1945 Mildred W. and Evan P. Hassinger, and Irene (Watson) Renn and her husband Clyde conveyed the land to Preston E. and Cora L. Klinger. Preston Klinger died February 1, 1951. At this time the land was described as being several parcels and tracts of bottom brush and mountain land with dwelling house. On May 1, 1958 Cora L. Klinger conveyed the 180 acres to Donald L. and Lois Miller. They sold the property to Upper Dauphin School District for the site of the new elementary school.

The Oak Dale Forge Complex
(Part Of Last Two Ferree Tracts Sold To John E. Forster)

Oak Dale Forge is probably the best known of the early sites in the Loyalton area. Its location was adjacent to the Indian village that according to Egle's History of Dauphin County History was located on the east, on the old Henry Bohner farm. Oak Dale Forge was the larger part of the two Ferree tracts of land James Buchanan had purchased early in 1828.

By the end of 1828, the forge had been built, and James Buchanan, forge master, and single, was listed on the tax record with four hundred sixteen acres of land containing two wooden houses and two cabins. He had another tract of one hundred twenty acres of mountain land and a sawmill. He was listed for taxes in 1831 under "dealers" of Lykens Township. Nearby coal mining was becoming an industry, causing people to settle in the area.

REMAINS OF THE OLD OAK DALE FORGE

The little settlement of Oak Dale had become reality, and now Buchanan's Oak Dale Forge was successful. The 1830 census lists him as having a hundred acres of first class land with a forge and five houses. The houses were located on the south side of the creek, and were occupied by his hired workman. At that time several men were listed in the tax record for Lykens Township as forge-man. They included James Dennis, Henry Fry, and John Ginter. In 1834, the records are more specific, listing James Buchanan as forge master with three hundred eighty one acres. It lists John Killet, George Klinger, Thomas Nutt, and Peter Zeck, as tenants of Buchanan's and working as forge-men. Other men recorded as employees at the forge, were George Conner, Samuel Boon, and Joseph Dunlap. John Spayd and Adam Wilt were employed by Buchanan as wagon-makers, and were tenants in one of his houses. Buchanan also had a sawmill, blacksmith shop, and three tracts of land. One containing two-hundred acres, one with one-hundred eighteen acres, and another twenty acres, all of them less than first class land. With the influx of people, a store and post office was needed, so James Buchanan established that facilities on his forge property about 1832 and he became the first postmaster of the Oak Dale post office. Tradition tells us that the post office facilities were housed in the farmhouse once owned by Mrs. Cora Keister. In previous days mail was brought to town by packhorse. Before that, neighbors in the forge area took turns walking weekly to Millersburg to pick up the mail. On May 4, 1837 Thomas Harper was appointed as successor to James Buchanan, but on March 31, 1838, the name of the Oak Dale post office was changed to Short Mountain and Daniel Wommer became postmaster. Uriah S. Ferree, Jr. was the next appointee and served until October 9, 1855. David K. McClure replaced him. McClure became the last postmaster of Short Mountain, and served until October 24, 1877 when it was replaced by the newly established Loyalton post office.

The Old Store At The Forge

The store that was established near the Oak Dale Forge is shown on the 1862 map as located directly across the road from the large house on the Oak Dale Forge property. Thanks to the memories of Josiah Bowman we know that his father John F. Bowman was the storekeeper at the store adjoining the forge probably up to 1835 when he died. Josiah lived with his parents at the time, and mentions that merchandise of every sort was chiefly purchased at this store. The only other store in the area was that of Henry Shaeffer's at Lykens Valley Colliery. Josiah substantiated the idea that the post office was located on the forge property, noting that Thomas Harper was the postmaster in the 1830's.

The establishment of the tavern is an interesting point. According to the details given by Josiah Bowman, there was no "public house" on the forge lands. The owners would not allow a tavern to be built on the grounds, and would not sell land for hotel purposes. We know however, that a tavern existed. In 1831, Henry H. Burr, a relative of the celebrated bridge builder, received a tavern license and opened an "excellent" public house, called "Oak Dale." It was indeed a substantial tavern, assessed at the same value as the tavern of Elizabeth Fry of Gratz. The fee was $100 dollars compared to all others in the area assessed at $50 dollars or less. Burr apparently stayed only one year, as he is not recorded as a hotelkeeper in the area after that. He may have been replaced by Adam Row whose license allowed him to be a tavern keeper in Lykens Township in 1833, when Oak Dale Forge was part of Lykens Township. According to the 1862 map, a tavern was located on the main Street in Loyalton in 1862, owned by D. H. Wommer. He may have had the hotel years before that. A few years later, Jacob B. Hoffman was a tavern keeper, probably in that same dwelling (note 1875 map). The story is told that when Jacob B. Hoffman applied for a license, the neighbors rebelled because they thought his house was not big enough to accommodate his large family and a tavern. By the mid-1830s, Oak Dale Forge was a very successful center, surrounded by many hundreds and thousands of acres of land, ready to be cleared and inhabited.

BUCHANAN FAMILY

[The ancestry of this James Buchanan has not been established, unfortunately. The following is all we have. **JAMES BUCHANAN** (b c1787 - ____), m c1815 Elizabeth Ferree (b ___ bapt May 18, 1822, as an adult - d _____), a dau of Isaac and Mary (Copeland) Ferree. **James and Elizabeth (Ferree) Buchanan had these known children** (all baptized the same day as their mother (May 18, 1822), record in Zion Lutheran Church in Harrisburg): **Anna Mary Ferree** b May 20, 1816; **James Evans** b Nov 17, 1817; **Urhia Ferree** b Jun 17, 1819; **Olivia Emeline** b Nov 14, 1821. According to the 1830 census, they had at least more children.]

On March 25, 1837, James and Elizabeth Buchanan sold 228 acres 81 1/2 perches of land in Lykens Township, with a forge and other buildings to Thomas Harper and Guilford and Simeon Harper, of Lebanon County. This land on the Wiconisco Creek was bound by land of Woodside, Nicholas Bressler, the bend of the Wiconisco Creek, James Buchanan, then crossed the creek and adjoined the land of Frederick Lubold. Richard Nolan and his wife Mary of Lykens Township, a neighbor, on the same day signed a written agreement to Harper and Guilford of Lebanon County. They gave permission "to raise and swell the water of the forge dam called Oak Dale Forge in Wiconisco Creek to the Iron Drive mark near the roots of the elm tree on the land of Richard Nolan." The tax record of 1837 lists Harper and Guilford as owners of the forge, and James Dennis, Thomas Nutt, and David Harner as tenants and forgeman. It also lists Buchanan with one hundred seventy acres and Jacob Shoop was his tenant. He had another one hundred acres of unseated land. Buchanan did not appear on tax lists or census records after that.

HARPER FAMILY

[**ADAM HARPER** (1722 - 1782) came to America and settled in East Hanover Township, Lebanon County in 1740. He married Catherine Bassler. On November 1, 1754 Adam Harper purchased a messuage, plantation and tract of land located in Swatara Township, Lancaster County from John and Margaret Young. This 242 acre tract of land was bounded by land of Andrew Lycans. A creek known as Indian Town Creek separated the tracts of land owned by Adam Harper and his contemporary Andrew Lycans. Adam Harper intended to build a mill over the creek, and also a dam. This was about two years before Andrew Lycans, who had migrated to our area, was killed in the Indian raid in what is now Loyalton (Lykens Township).

When Adam Harper purchased this Swatara Township property, it contained a small log house built in the 1730s, and thought to be even at this late date, part of the structure of the old existing tavern. This was originally the first frontier post northwest of Philadelphia. When Adam Harper purchased the property, he became a tavern keeper. At that time, it is said that Indians continued to live in wigwams in the nearby Indian village from whom the name Indiantown sprang. It is also said that Adam Harper dug a secret under-ground chamber that could be entered from a small hole in the side of the hand dug well. This was for protection from the Indians who at that time had made many raids on the white settlers. It was here that the Harper family first settled. They later moved to Dauphin County, and became residents of the section of Lykens Valley where Andrew Lykens settled.

*JOHN HARPER (b Jan 8, 1760 E. Hanover Twp, Leb Co - d Feb 19, 1827), son of Adam became the second generation of the Harper family in America. John m Barbara Backenstoss (b___ - d pre Jan 23, 1825), a dau of John and Charlotte (Schmidt?) Backenstoss. He became the owner of his father's "Harper Tavern." **John and Barbara (Backenstoss) Harper had these children:**

**CATHARINE HARPER (no dates), m Henry W. Miller in 1811 in Leb Co, moved to South Bend, Ind in the 1840s.

JOHN HARPER (b Sep 9, 1791 E. Hanover Twp, Leb Co. - d Mar 26, 1865), who married Dec 12, 1812 Elizabeth Raiguel (Jan 19, 1793 - Feb 25, 1863), a dau of Abraham and Elizabeth Raiguel of Leb Co , whose ancestors were driven from France and settled in Switzerland because of their religious associations. Later they came to America to find freedom in William Penn's colony. They settled on a very large tract of land in the area of Annville, Lebanon County. **John and Elizabeth (Raiguel) Harper had several children who remained in Jonestown, Leb. Co, or moved to Indiana.

THOMAS HARPER (b Mar 25, 1793 E. Hanover Twp, Leb Co - d Feb 25, 1866 Wiconisco Twp, Dau Co), m Sep 2, 1813, Tabor Ref Ch, Leb, Pa. to Catharine Reist (b Feb 27, 1798 Leb Co - d Jul 18, 1817, Leb Co), a dau of Peter and Catharine (Hostetter) Reist . Thomas and Catharine (Reist) Harper had these children:**

***Amanda (b Dec 8, 1815, E Hanover Twp, Leb Co - d Sep 23, 1897 Lykens Twp, Dau Co), m Amos Hoffman (b May 25, 1809 Lyk Twp - d May 29, 1897, Girardville, Sch Co), a son of Jacob and Catherine (Ferree) Hoffman.

***John C. (b Jul 6, 1817 E. Hanover Twp, Leb Co - d Jan 22, 1885 bur Chas Barber Cem, Pottsville, Sch Co), m Margaret A. Singer (___ - d Oct 29, 1895). He was a prominent Methodist Churchman. In 1850 John C. and Margaret Harper lived in Wiconisco Twp, and he was listed as a clerk. **John C. and Margaret (Singer) Harper had these children:** **Ann** b c1844; **Sarah** b c1845; **Amanda** b c1847; **Francis** b c1849.

Thomas Harper m 2nd about 1818, Barbara Reist (Oct 7, 1801 - Dec 29, 1877), a sister to his first wife. In 1850 Thomas and Barbara were living in Mifflin Twp. They had these people in their household: Thomas M age 15 carpenter, Joseph R. 13, Daniel 11, Jacob A 8, Catharine Betz 12, Joseph Gross age 42, an E. Clergyman, Simon Gross age 8. **Thomas and Barbara (Reist) Harper had these children:**

***Henrietta (1819 - Apr 5, 1852, d in Philadelphia, Pa.), m May 16, 1838 in Oakdale, (now Loyalton) Dau Co to George Rex (1815 - Apr 20, 1884, bur Schaefferstown, Leb Co), a son of Abraham and Elizabeth (Shaeffer) Rex. George was a physician.

***Rebecca b Aug 21, 1820 E. Hanover Twp, Leb Co, m Thomas Snyder , son of Thomas Snyder Sr. He was a tinsmith. They lived in Berrysburg by 1853.**Thomas and Rebecca (Harper) Snyder had these children: John Henry Harper; Emma F. Fenly; Thomas Willard** b Feb 4, 1853.

***Cornelius Augustus (b Apr 21, 1822 E. Hanover Twp, Leb Co - d Mar 27, 1895, Halifax Twp., Dau Co.), m Oct 4, 1842, by Rev. Leitzel to Sarah Uhrich (b Feb 1825 Halifax Twp, Dau Co - d Apr 7, 1894), a dau of Valentine and Jane (Sweigard) Uhrich. Cornelius was a veteran of the Civil War, with the rank of Captain in Co G 103rd Regt Pa. Volunteers. And Co K of the 173rd Drafted Militia. In 1850, Cornelius and Sarah Harper lived in Wiconisco Twp, and he was listed as a merchant. **Cornelius and Sarah (Uhrich) Harper had these children:**

Annie B; Samuel S. (Aug 26, 1843 – after 1915), Civil War Vet of Co B 9th Pa Cav, moved to Montana where he m Augusta Frances Wilkins on Dec 11, 1870 in Boulder, Jefferson Co, Mont, **had one child:** Ida L. b Sep 13, 1877, m ____ Jones of Kerman, Calif.; **Adeline** b 1845 m John P. Jenkins, moved to Bedford Co, Pa.; **Valentine U** (b Nov 18, 1849 d Mar 11, 1911 bur Fetterhoffs Cem, Halifax Twp), m Sarah E. ____ (b Sep 30, 1855 - d Apr 13, 1936); **Cornelius A. Jr.** (no dates), m Hattie J. Ellinger (b Sep 23, 1848 - d Sep 25, 1900, moved to Shamokin, Northld Co and worked in the mines; **Thomas William** (b Jan 10, 1853 - Dec 31, 1932, bur IOOF Cem, Lykens), m Jan 1, 1878 in Zion Luth Ch, Lykens to Mary Jane Rudisell (b Feb 12, 1860 - d Nov 21, 1923), a dau of David and Susanna (Row) Rudisill. **Thomas and Mary Jane (Rudisell) Harper had these children:** Anton Franklin (1878 - 1882); William Henry (1881 - 1918, bur IOOF Cem, Lykens), m 1904 to Mary J. Stuppy ; John David b 1883 , d Ft. Sam Houston, Texas; Thomas Edw (1885 - 1891, bur IOOF Cem, Lykens); Susan Isabella (1887 - 1973), m Chester Allen Rettinger (1883 - 1956), son of James F. and Kathryn (Weiss) Rettinger; Ellen Rebecca (1889 - 1972), m Malvin Snowden Finton (1895 - 1974), a son of Charles N. and Alice R. (Mumma) Finton; Cornelius Mark "Neil" (1891 - 1957) lived in Michigan; **Clara** (b 1855 - 1926), m Franklin N. Miller (1852 - 1928), lived in Fisherville, Jackson Twp., Dau Co; **Henrietta** (b Feb 25, 1857 Minersville, Sch Co - Jul 10, 1919, bur Meth Cem, Halifax), m Dec 31, 1883 to George W. Wagner (b Aug 9, 1862 Harrisburg - d 1932, Halifax), a son of William and Ellen (Lehr) Wagner. After they were married, Henrietta and George lived on her father's farm, and George farmed the land. By 1895 they moved to Halifax Twp, purchased their own farm, and became successful. **Ida** (no dates); **Nora J.** (1865 - 1872, bur IOOF, Lykens)

***<u>**Catharine**</u> b Sep 22, 1824 in E. Hanover Twp, Leb Co.
***<u>**Adaline Embig**</u> (b May 27, 1826 Leb Co - d Jan 17, 1853, Wiconisco Twp, Dau Co), m George W. Hochlander (Oct 10, 1812 - d Jan 27, 1875). He later m Mary D ____ who d Apr 25, 1901 age 76 yrs.
***<u>**Henry Clay**</u> b Jun 14, 1828 Leb Co m May 27, 1851 to Mary A. Hammer, dau of Elijah and Elizabeth Hammer. In 1850 Henry lived with the Henry Stroup family in Wiconisco Twp, and he was a merchant.
***<u>**Lafayette**</u> b c1830
***<u>**Sarah Anna**</u> b May 30, 1831, Leb Co d May 12, 1910 Wiconisco Twp, Dau Co.bur Calvery Meth, Cem). She m 1st _____ Reichert, 2nd Edward Frankenfield (Dec 28, 1828 - Jan 3, 1865), son of John and Elizabeth (Schoener) Frankenfield of Northumberland Co. Edward was a coachmaker in Berrysburg. After Edward died, Sarah lived in Wiconisco Twp. She was a public school teacher. Edward and Sarah (Harper, Reichert) Frankenfield were married Oct 4, 1853 by Rev. Sell in Berrysburg. **Edward and Sarah Anna (Harper, Reichert) Frankenfield had these children: William L** (1852 - 1925); **Harper Augustus** (Mar 2, 1855 -   Mar 27, 1939); **Annie Barbara** (1857- 1938, bur Wiconisco Cem), m James Dodds; **Lillian Eliz** (May 31, 1860 - 1943, bur Wiconisco Cem), m John Watkeys (1854 - 1894, died from wounds of a mine accident..
***<u>**Thomas H.**</u> (b Jun 16, 1834 Leb Co- d Dec 28, 1853, Berrysburg, Dau Co).
***<u>**Joseph Richard**</u> (b May 22, 1837 - d Sep 7, 1858), m Charlotte Moyer (Oct 14, 1837 - Jun 18, 1895), a dau of John George and Margaret (Tallman) Moyer of Gratz. **Joseph and Charlotte (Moyer) Harper had one child: Amanda Barbara** (b Jul 13, 1857 - d Nov 21, 1938, bur Simeon Cem, Gratz), m Nov 25, 1875 Isaac K. Hepler (Aug 5, 1838 - Jul 23, 1918), a son of George and Hannah (Kratzer) Hepler. (marriage record in Oakdale Ch record Loyalton) [Photo of Joseph Harper page 229, Comprehensive History of Gratz]
***<u>**Willard G**</u> (b 1839 - May 24, 1864), d while serving in the Civil War. He m Sep 21, 1862 Amelia P. Kottka of Lykens. She d Feb 16, 1919. **Willard and Amelia (Kottka) Harper had one child: Thomas William** b Jul 11, 1863.
***<u>**Benjamin b**</u> & d 1840
***<u>**Jacob A.**</u> (b Jul 2, 1841 - d Aug 20, 1872, bur Wiconisco Cem), m Amanda Tallman (Jan 9, 1844 Germany - Sep 30, 1902), a dau of Jacob and Christiana Tallman. In 1880 after Jacob died, Amanda lived in Wiconisco Twp. She had her children and her mother Christiana living with her, also Maggie Page age 19 listed as a servant. **Jacob and Amanda (Tallman) Harper had these children: Annie B** (1863 - 1865); **Harry T.** b c1865; **Oscar E** b c1868; **Lillie A** b c1872.
***<u>**Benjamin Franklin**</u> (May 6, 1843 – Mar 7, 1892, bur Oak Dale Cem), attended Oak Dale Church and had children baptized there. They lived in Washington Twp in 1880. On Sep 21,1862 Benjamin Franklin and Clara Rebecca Moyer (Feb 14,1846 - Mar 6, 1917) were married in Mifflinburg, Union Co by Baptist minister Rev. Isaac Myers. Benj. F. was a Civil War Vet, served in Co C 21st Cav as Pvt. **Children of Benjamin Frank and Clara Rebecca Harper: Carry** b c1862;**Harvey O.** (1863 - 1897); **Annie S** (1866 - 1954); **George D** (May 15,1869 –1945, bur Oak Dale Cem), m Annie ___ (1866 –1954), had son Benjamin F.(1896 - 1898); **Mary A** (1871 - 1880); **Charles O.** b c1876; **Amelia E.** b May 10,1878; ; **Nora Madda** (b Jun 26, 1880 – Jan 2, 1903); **Netta Malinda** b Jun 15, 1886 bapt Aug 15, 1886; **Dollie** b Jun 20, 1888.

<u>JACOB HARPER**</u> (b May 13, 1795 - d Jan 30, 1859) remained in E. Hanover Twp, Leb Co, m Mary Miller (1796 -1864). He was a Leb Co Commissioner.
<u>CHARLOTTE HARPER**</u> (c1802 - pre1840) m Johan Jacob Stein (1794-1840), lived in Jonestown, Leb Co.
<u>REBECCA HARPER**</u> (no dates), m Isreal Lang b 1798, lived in Jonestown, Leb Co.

On April 1, 1852, The Dauphin Deposit Bank of Harrisburg conveyed two tracts from the Harper interest in the Oak Dale Forge estate to Joseph McClure. The first tract contained 228 acres 81 1/2 perches of land. It was bound by the south side of Big Wiconisco Creek, the land warranted to Nathan Woodside south to the late Hugh Bitterman land, Edward Bickel, middle of creek, Josiah Bowman, late land of James Buchanan, Richard Nolan, Wiconisco Creek, and Frederick Lupold. The Second tract contained 220 acres of woodland and was bound by Thomas Harper, Simon Guilford, Frederick Lubold, and lands warranted to Mathias Freck & Simon Salade, the warrant to John Lancy (?), Samuel and William Lauzer, and the late Hugh Bitterman.

After Joseph McClure died, his widow Margaret & heirs sold the two tracts on November 5, 1862, to her son David K. and Eliza McClure. These two tracts comprised the Oak Dale Forge Estate. David K. and Eliza McClure lived here for sometime, and he became an ironmonger before moving to Berrysburg. In 1860, the McClure's lived in Wiconisco Township. Several people employed as servants lived with them: Sarah Longabaugh, age 21; Nancy Reigle age 20; Isaac Machamer age 20; Joseph Crouser age 26. Julian Bergstresser, age 36, was also with them.

Many people have recalled during the past years, that the Oak Dale Academy was located on the forge property. Not much is known about its operation, when it began or when it closed. One tradition is that it was a school for boys. Circumstantial evidence indicates that the McClure family probably had something to do with its existence. The McClure family had ties to the Beshler, Bergstresser and Lark families, of the Berrysburg Seminary. Perhaps there was an affiliation between Berrysburg Seminary and Oak Dale Academy.

A piece in the Lykens Register dated October 18, 1872 gives the following information: "REMODELING - D. K. McClure, Esq., of Oak Dale Farm, Washington Township is transforming his residence by remodeling it into the cottage style architecture. It presents a more noticeable appearance than ever, particularly to travelers on the Summit Branch Railroad."

In 1880, David and Annie McClure lived in Washington Twp, and he was listed as a gentleman. In addition to their children, Emma a schoolteacher, Joseph, John, Arthur and Gertrude, they had Ida Wert age 12 with them, listed as a servant. After his wife died, David K. moved to Upper Paxton where he lived with one of his daughters.

On January 7, 1879, David K. and Eliza McClure sold these four tracts of land to Loyetta E. Lark: 228 acres 81 1/2 perches located on the Wiconisco Creek, 220 acres comprising "Oak Dale Forge Estate," fifty acres with two story log weather boarded house, seven acre tract with one and one-half story log house and out buildings. (The last two came from the John Wommer and Henry Miller grants, were sold to Michael Sausser and Josiah Bowman, before McClure purchased on Mar 29, 1854.)

The Larks were not listed on census records, so they probably used these lands as rental properties. Shortly after, Henry I and Loyetta E. Lark moved to Peabody, Marion County, Kansas. On February 21, 1887, they sold the four tracts above plus a fifth tract containing two acres, one hundred fifty-two perches, by the middle of Wiconisco Creek to B. W. Romberger of Philadelphia. [The deed mentions that the small property of William Schoffstall had been a part of this, but not included in this sale.]

THE McCLURE FAMILY

[*JOSEPH McCLURE (b ___ - d Nov 17, 1861) , married Margaret _____, and lived in Uchalan Township, Chester County, Pennsylvania. He is descended from a family of McClures whom migrated to America from Ireland at a very early time. **Joseph and Margaret McClure had these children:**
DAVID K. (b Apr 5, 1827 in Chester Co. - Dec 12, 1911, bur Peace Ref Cem, Berrysburg), m 1855 to Ann Eliza Beshler (Apr 11, 1837 - Mar 6, 1882), a dau of Dr. H, C. and Mary (Boyer) Beshler of Berrysburg. Dr. H. C. Beshler was born in New Berlin, Snyder County. He attended University of Pennsylvania, and then practiced medicine in several places before moving to Berrysburg. Dr. Beshler died Dec 25, 1888 at the age of eighty-one. Mrs. Beshler was born in Freeburg, Snyder County. David K. McClure grew up on a farm, and worked at the Oak Dale Forge becoming an ironmonger, before owning this forge. **David K and Ann Eliza (Beshler) McClure had these children:**
 Charles B. (b Jul 5, 1856 in Wash Twp - d ____), m in Bloomsburg, Pa. Oct 4, 1887 to R. Elizabeth Hower in, Pa. a dau of Jackson Hower. Charles B. studied medicine with his grandfather Dr. Beshler, then attended University of Penn. He graduated in 1888 from Western Pennsylvania College in Pittsburgh. He practiced medicine in several places before moving to Gratz in 1894. They lived in the old house on lot thirty-four, which had been an early hotel. The McClure family lived in Gratz until December 1899, when they moved to Berrysburg. **Charles B and Elizabeth (Hower) McClure had these children: Arthur Carlton; Hiester N.** (1895 - Aug 12, 1896, bur Simeon Cem); **Dora Florence** (Nov 13, 1896 - Dec 1989, bur Clifton Cem, Fairfax, Va) . Dora never married. She was a public school teacher in Pennsylvania and Virginia, lived to the age of ninety-three.

Emma J. b c1858 - she was living at home in 1880 and was a school teacher.
H. Joseph b c1860, m Mary Elizabeth _____, moved to Philadelphia where he was a merchant.
John C. b c1866
Arthur E. b c1867
M. Gertrude (1872 - 1940, bur Peace Ref Cem), m Nathaniel Miller [see Miller genealogy]

**JAMES R (no dates), a yeoman of Chester County;
**MARY ANN (no dates) m Tyrus F. Bull, who was a merchant and lived in Philadelphia;
**MARTHA, (no dates) m William Freck of Philadelphia;
**HANNAH not married in 1862, lived in Chester County;
**RACHEL, (no dates) m ___ Butenback, but was a widow in 1862.]

THE LARK / LARCH FAMILY

[The LARK family is of Swiss origin, and settled early in Berks County.
CASPER LARK (b ___ d Sep/Oct 1766 in Heidelberg, Berks County, m Margaret _____.
Casper and Margaret Lark had these children: ANNA ELIZABETH b Jun 6, 1741;
***Christopher (STOPHEL)** (b pre 1756 - d Nov 1812), m _____, had a son **John Jost** bapt Apr 19, 1778 Bern, Berks Co;**John William** b Jan 5, 1785; **Nicholas** (b ___ d 1784, Heidelberg Twp; **Balser** (b ___ d spring 1774), Bern Twp, m Barbara, had a son **Johannes** bapt Jul 24, 1774, (mother was a wid); **Jacob; Jost; Elisabeth** m ___ Fox; **Margaret** m ___ Lower; **Catharina** b ___ Fey
Rachel

***CHRISTOPHER (STOPHEL) LARCH/LARK** (b before 1756 - d Nov 1812), m _____ before 1775. In his will Christopher mentions his patent of 260 acres
Christopher (Stophel) Lark and his wife that these children:
 GEORGE (___ - c1805), **had these children:
***Catherine
***Elizabeth
***Christopher
***Peter b Nov 20, 1795
***George (May 1, 1798 Mifflin Twp – Mar 11, 1829, bur St. Johns Hill Cem), m Elizabeth Enterline (May 15, 1799 – Jul 27, 1877), a dau of _____. George died before his father, and in his fathers will he stated " Elizabeth wid of son Geo, "shall keep the end of the house where she lives and two acres for a garden, as long as she remains a widow." Elizabeth m 2nd Capt John Snyder (1794 – 1849), widower of Anna May Wert. After her husband died, Elizabeth made her home with her son George. She was with him in 1860. **George and Elizabeth (Enterline) Lark had these children: ****Amos** d young; ******Elizabeth** b 1824 d young; ******John** (Feb 7, 1826 – c1898 , Salina , Kansas), m Leah Shoop (Feb 14, 1829 – Dec 2, 1881, bur St. Johns Hill Cem), a dau of Jacob Shoop. Early in life, John was trained as a stonemason. But later purchased a farm. John and Leah Lark lived in Mifflin Twp on a farm in 1870. Much later, after his wife died, he moved to Salina, Kansas where he is buried. **John and Leah (Shoop) Lark had these children:** George W.b Sep 20, 1851- d young; Emanuel S. b Feb 8, 1853, m in 1873 Emeline Boyer (Oct 21, 1847 – Apr 9, 1895, bur Shamokin Cem), a dau of Benjamin and Catharine(Stine) Boyer. Emanuel attended several academies in the area, than became a teacher for ten terms. He eventually moved to Shamokin. **Emanuel and Emaline (Boyer) Lark had these children:** *Charles Calvin* b Mar 12, 1874, an attorney; *Carrie Catharine* (1875 – 1893); *John Benjamin* b Dec 18, 1876; *Leah B; H. Wilson; Thomas F.*
****George b Mar 17, 1828, m Mar 2, 1854 Salome Enterline b 1831. They lived in Berrysburg and he was a merchant. In 1860 Ann Lark age 18, and Charles Dillman age 12, Solomon Enterline age 25, clerk, Elmira Thomsen age 30, servant, Washington Thomson age 35 tailor, and Jacob Mace age 24 teamster lived with the family. George's mother, widowed for the second time, also

lived with the family. In 1870 George was a morocco manufacturer. His mother Elizabeth continued to live with the family, as well as Polly Dillman age 22, listed as a domestic. In 1880 George and Salome Lark lived in Millersb urg, just two doors away from Aaron P. Lark. George was listed as a traveling boot and shoe salesman .**George and Salome (Enterline) Lark had these children:** <u>Leon</u> b Apr 5, 1855; <u>Elizabeth</u> ; <u>Frank Edward</u> b c1857, a school teacher in 1880 living with his parent in Millersburg; <u>William B</u> b c1859; <u>Mary</u> b c1865; <u>Annie L</u>. b c1868; <u>Clara Eliza</u> b Apr 4, 1871.

ELIZABETH (____ d c1795), m Philip Lenker (Jun 4, 1759 - Oct 12, 1824, bur _____). Elizabeth received money from her fathers estate. **Philip and Elizabeth (Lark) Lenker had these children:
***Anna Margaretha (Apr 6, 1784 - Oct 24, 1832), m George Weaver.
***Michael b Mar 6, 1786, m Anna Maria _____;
***Anna Maria (Aug 16, 1788 - Aug 7, 1857), m J. Geo Cooper (1788-840)
*** Elisabeth (Apr 12, 1790 - Nov 27, 1857), m John Hoke (Nov 25, 1786 - Jun 17, 1856, bur Fisherville Cem.)
***Catharine Barbara (Jan 6, 1792 - Sep 29, 1873), m Abraham Sheesley (Sep 24, 1786 - Oct 1, 1871)
***Justina (Jan 15, 1794 - Mar 13, 1841, may be bur Salem Luth Cem, Killinger) m Nov 14, 1814 (by Rev. Reily) Johannes Lebo (Jun 29, 1793 - Aug 22, 1879, bur David Cem, Killinger). [See info with Lebo family.] After his first wife Elizabeth (Lark) Lenker died, Philip m Anna Margaret Weaver (Apr 17, 1774 - Apr 10, 1838).

CATHARINE (b ____ d 1825), the 1st wife of John Bitterman (Jul 7, 1786 - Aug 25, 1853, bur St. John Hill Cem), a son of Baltzer Bitterman. **John and Catherine (Lark) Bitterman had two known children: ***David (Nov 3, 1811 - Nov 20, 1873, bur Stone Valley Cem, Dalmatia), m 1st Elizabeth Schwab (Jul 10, 1811 - Jul 30, 1842, bur St. Johns Hill Cem), a dau of Jacob and Anna Maria Schwab. He m 2nd Elizabeth Dockey (1831 - 1889, bur Stone Valley Cem), a dau of John and Mary (Shaffer) Dockey. ***Daniel (Mar 7, 1821 - Jul 5, 1884), recorded St. Johns Ch. The death record of this son Daniel mentions that he is a son of John and Catherine (Lark) Bitterman. He m Mary ____ (b c1821 - ____).Daniel Bitterman lived in Lykens Township, but later moved to Lykens and became proprietor or Railroad Hotel. In 1860 Daniel and Mary lived in Wiconisco Twp and he was listed as a tavern keeper. The had Sarah E. Shaffner age 18, listed as a servant living with them. In 1870 Daniel continued to be a hotel keeper in Wiconisco Twp., and they had Charles Hoffman age 20, Charles Miller age 20, and Jon B. Dan age 18, all carpenters living with them. In 1880 he was a stone mason. **Daniel and Mary Bitterman had these children:****** <u>George Washington</u> b c1836; ****<u>Charles</u> b c1840; ****<u>Mary Jane</u> b c1846.

PETER (Nov 20, 1795 - Aug 11, 1850 bur St. Johns Hill Cem, m Mary Magdalena Neagley (Feb 20, 1795 - Jul 25, 1863). In 1860 Mary Magdalena and her daughter Sarah lived together in Mifflin Twp. **Peter and Mary Magdalena (Neagley) Lark had these children (some bapt David's Ref Killinger):
***Elizabeth (b Jan 25, 1819 other source says Sep 14, 1820)- Sep 21,1887, bur David's Cem, Killinger), m David Weaver (Jul 5, 1813 - Mar 8, 1895).
Daniel (Jun 14, 1821 -May 16, 1896, bur St. Johns Cem, m Susanna Hoy (Oct 6, 1823 - Jan 31,1897), a dau of Peter and Susanna Hoy. Daniel and Susanna lived on a farm in Mifflin Twp. 1850 to 1880. **Daniel and Susanna (Hoy) Lark had these children:** *<u>Amanda</u> (Jun 7, 1844 - Feb 26, 1923, bur St. Johns Cem), m Oct 18, 1863 to Daniel C. Orndorf (Oct 3, 1842 - Nov 15,1870, bur Motters Cem, E'ville), a son of John and Amelia Orndorf. After Daniel died, Amanda m Henry Erdman (Sep 11, 1836 - Feb 11, 1889, killed in Wiconisco), son of George and Rosian (Hess) Erdman. They had one child:****<u>Sarah</u> 1847; ****<u>Mary</u> 1849, this is probably Mary Jane (1848 - 1931, bur St. John's Hill Cem), m Aaron Schreffler (1851 - 1920), a son of Adam and Angeline Schreffler. **Aaron and Mary (Lark) Schreffler had these children:** <u>Hannah Priscilla</u> b Feb 12, 1870; <u>Harry</u> b c1875; <u>Lillie Eveline</u> b Oct 28, 1874; <u>Iva Cordelia</u> b Oct 19, 1877;
****<u>David P</u>. (Aug 20, 1851 - Feb 24, 1911, bur Salem Luth Cem, Killinger), m Jan 22, 1882

Mary Lenker (Feb 2, 1851 – Nov 1, 1917), a dau of Philip Lenker. They lived in Curtin, Mifflin Twp;******Catherine** 1854; ******Emma** <u>Susanna</u> (Oct 15, 1856 – Aug 17, 1937, bur St. Johns Hill Cem), m Daniel D. Matter (Feb 2, 1852 – Jan 15, 1934);****<u>**Elizabeth**</u> b Apr 3,1860; ****<u>**Agnes Jane**</u> (Dec 25, 1862 – Nov 22, 1941, bur St. Johns Cem);****<u>**Anna Irene**</u> (Sep 9, 1867 – Jun 19, 1957, bur St. John's Cem), m Charles P. Metz (1867 – 1923); **** <u>**Amelia**</u> b c1870.

***<u>**Sarah**</u> (Sep 7, 1823 - Dec 2, 1904 bur St. Johns Cem), not married, lived with sister Kate and George Koppenhaver in 1880 in Berrysburg.
***<u>**Mary**</u> (Jun 3, 1824 – Apr 5, 1910, bur St. Johns Hill Cem), m 1854 Isaac Weaver (May 4, 1833 –Apr 3, 1904).[See also Weaver Genealogy]
<u>**Catharine**</u> (Apr 22, 1833 - May 18, 1915, bur St. Johns Hill Cem), m Feb 26, 1857, George W. Koppenheffer (Jul 29, 1835 – May 2, 1884), **George W. and Catharine (Lark) Koppenheffer had a son**: *<u>**Allen Lark**</u> (Jan 4, 1857 – Mar 26, 1901, bur St. Johns Hill Cem), m Mary A. ____ b c1859. **Allen L and Mary (____) Koppenhaver had a son George E.** b c1877. They lived with his parents in 1880 in Berrysburg.

CHRISTOPHER (b 1790 – Goshen, Chester Co. - c1830?), son of Stophel Lark, m Dec 25, 1814 Rachel Buffington (Apr 3, 1792 - Mar 15, 1828), a dau of George and Barbara (Hoffman) Buffington. **Christopher and Rachel (Buffington) Lark had these children:
***<u>**Simon B.**</u> (Jun 26, 1816 - Dec 20, 1851, bur Peace Ref Cem, Bbg), m Sarah Boyer (Jun 2,1818 - Feb 8, 1909).They lived in Mifflin Twp in 1850 and he was a merchant. In 1870, Sarah Lark , a widow lived in Berrysburg and her son Henry L was with her. At the time he was studying law. **Simon B. and Sarah (Boyer) Lark had one known child:**
****<u>**Henry Lewis**</u> (1852 – Mar 12, 1928, bur Oak Hill Cem, Mbg), m Sep 16, 1874 to Loyetta E. Tressler (Feb 14,1848 – Mar 12, 1928), a dau of John & Elizabeth (Loy) Tressler, founder of Tressler orphan home in Loysville. Henry was an attorney in Harrisburg. He and his wife both died at the same time in San Antonio, Texas, and their bodies were returned to Millersburg. They lived in Berrysburg in 1880, and his mother lived with them. Also Daniel Behny age 17. [The name Tressler was derived orginally from Dressler.] **H. L. and Loyetta E. (Tressler) Lark had these known children** (bapt Union Salem (Peace) Ch, Berrysburg):<u>Charles Tressler</u> (Jul 25, 1876 – Oct 3, 1946, bur Oak Hill Cem, Mbg), m Blanche ___ (b c1877 – d Jun 2 6, 1959); <u>Mabel Loyetta</u> b Mar 7, 1878, m ___ Geis, a prof. At Columbia Univ. Henry and Loyetta moved during the 1880s to Peabody, Marion Co, Kansas, later San Antonio, Texas, brought back for burial in Oak Hill Cemetery, Millersburg.

<u>**Aaron P.**</u>(Mar 7, 1819 – Jan 26, 1891, bur Oak Hill Cem, Mbg). He may have m 1st Rebecca _____ b c1825, a dau of _____. The 1850 census of Washington Twp lists Aaron Lark age 31 with Rebecca age 25, and Mary Jane age 2, Samuel Snyder 22, and Catharine Weaver 17. He m Martha _____ (Oct 19, 1826 – Feb 3, 1883), a dau of _____. They lived in Mifflin Twp in 1860, he was a storekeeper. In 1880, lived in Millersburg. He was a carpenter. **Aaron & his wife had these children:** *<u>**Mary**</u> b c1848;**** <u>**Alice**</u> b c1854, lived with parents in 1880, was a dressmaker;****<u>**Thomas S**</u>. b c1855, going to college in 1880.;

Henry L. Lark

***Mary Ann** b Aug 16, 1821

***Catharine Barbara** (Mar 29, 1824 – Apr 7, 1857, bur Grand View Cem, Pillow), m Jacob Wiest b Jan 6, 1820 – d Dec 27, 1871, at McKee's Half Falls due to an accident. Jacob Wiest was m first to Susanna Bordner (Apr 4, 1819 – Apr 21, 1846, bur Pillow), a dau of Peter Bordner. Catharine Barbara was the 2nd wife of Jacob Wiest. Jacob was a merchant in Pillow. **Jacob and Catharine Barbara (Lark) Wiest had three children**, but all died as infants. In 1850 Jacob and Catharine lived in Mifflin Twp, and had Mary Jane and James M Wiest, children from 1st marriage with them. They also had William Wiest age 17, a clerk, and Abraham Hepler 22, a laborer with them. Jacob Wiest's 3rd wife was Sarah Ann Nace.

***Hanna** (Dec 26, 1827 – 1907), m 1849 John D. Snyder (Dec 9, 1827 – 1902), a son of John Snyder b 1794 & wife Anna May (Wert) Snyder b 1799. John and Hanna lived in Mifflin Twp. in 1850 and he was listed as an ironmonger. In 1860 John was in the foundry business. Ann Snyder age 19 and Jacob Bressler age 20 a tinner lived with the family. He was a Justice of Peace for years. **John D. and Hanna (Lark) Snyder had these children:** ****Sara Jane** b c1850; ****MaryAnn** b c1854; ****Edwin G** b c1855; ****Rachael B.** b c1859; ****Joseph H.** b c1766; ****Arthur L** b c1868; ****John T.**; ****Elizabeth.**

***George** b c1828, lived with his brother Simon in 1850.]

On March 13, 1897, B. W. and Helena Romberger sold all five of the tracts located in Washington Township to Nathaniel Miller, of Elizabethville.

Nathaniel Miller grew up on the family farm in Washington Township, and remained there until the age of twenty-two. His father had a distillery, so he decided to learn the business of distilling whiskey. Soon after he became involved in the fathers' business a high tax was levied on whiskey, so they closed the distillery for four years. When his father died in 1872, Nathaniel purchased the business and continued with it the remainder of his life. He also purchased a gristmill known as Stine's Mill, and had several large farms.

THE MILLER FAMILY

[This **MILLER** family is descended from **JOHN MILLER**, (born _____ in Wurtemberg, Germany – d _____, bur Northld Co. The Dauphin County history relates that he came to America and settled near County Line in Northld Co. He m Veronica Francis Kerstetter (b Apr 9, 1752 Cleona, Lebanon Co – d _____, said to be bur Fetterhoffs Cem near Halifax). She was a dau of Sebastian and Magdleana (Deibler) Kerstetter. John and Veronica Miller were affiliated with both Zions Stone Valley Church and Salem Lutheran in Killinger. Veronica attended communion service at Salem Luth as late as 1815. After John Miller died, his widow and three sons Peter, Daniel and John moved to Armstrong Valley. Veronica died at the home of her son Daniel. **John and Veronica (Kerstetter) Miller had these children (some bapt Salem Luth, Killinger, others Stone Valley, Northld Co):**

ANNA CATHARINE MILLER (b Jun 25, 1775 – d Apr 25, 1842, bur Old Salem Cem, Killinger), m George Wirth (Apr 19, 1770 – Feb 13, 1845), a son of John Adam and Eva Elisabeth (Snoke). **George and Anna Catharine (Miller) Wirth had these children:** Elisabeth (b Oct 2, 1798 – 1845), m Jacob Ulsh (1795 – 1854), moved to Perry Co.; **Anna Catharine** (b Dec 28, - 1800 – d 1877), m Jonas Hocker (1803 – 1878), moved to Crawford Co., Ohio; **Lydia** (b Jan 26, 1805 – Apr 8, 1864, bur Salem Luth, Cem Killinger), m Daniel Feidt (1803 – 1854), a son of George and Rachel (Snyder) Feidt; **John George** (b Mar 7, 1808 – May 20, 1891, bur Salem Luth Cem), m Catherine Dreibelbis (Feb 20, 1808 – Jun 16, 1880). **John George and Catherine (Dreibelbis) Wirth had these children:** Sara Amanda (1835 – Jan 18,1839); Mariana (1836 – Jan 17, 1839); Delilah (Nov 16, 1839 – 1923), m Jacob Herbert Rowe (1841 – 1928); Mary (1844 – 1925), m Benneville W. Holtzman (Sep 12, 1845 – Sep 15, 1912), a son of John H and Elizabeth Holtzman; Malinda (b Aug 22, 1845 – d Sep 20, 1920, bur Salem Luth Cem), m John Elias Wiest (Oct 25, 1849 – 1903), a son of Elias and Catherine (Bingaman) Wiest; **John** b Oct 6, 1809;

SOPHIA MILLER (b Aug 2, 1776 – d Oct 22, 1842, bur old Salem Luth Cem), m J. Jacob Wirth (b May 21, 1764 Lebanon Co – d Jan 1,1833), a son of John Adam and Eva Elisabeth (Snoke) Wirth. **J. Jacob and Sophia (Miller) Wirth had these children:** JOHN b Dec 7, 1796 twin, m Magdalena Shoop, dau of Jacob and Catharine Shoop, moved to Ashland Co., Ohio; **DANIEL** (b Dec 7, 1796 twin – d Oct 20, 1858, bur Salem Luth Cem), m Susannah Shoop (Mar 21, 1797 – Mar 12, 1873), a dau of John Geo and Anna Maria Eliz (Deibler) Shoop; **ANNA MARIA** (b Feb 6, 1799 – d May 6, 1859, bur Zions "Hoovers" Cem, Rife), m Ludwig Paul (Jun 17, 1794 – Nov 24, 1878), a son of George and Anna Cath (Matter) Hoover; **JACOB** (b Jul 20, 1804 – d _____, bur Fetterhoff Cem, Halifax), m Sarah Eliz Faber (May 25, 1807 – Apr 5, 1902, bur St. Pauls Cem, Enterline), a dau of Adam and Sussanah (Koppenheffer) Faber; **SOLOMON** (Dec 20, 1805 – Jun 24, 1873), m Anna Mary Noll (1806 – 1890), moved to Aaronsburg, Centre Co.; **ISAAC** (b Mar 22, 1808 – d Mar 18, 1863, bur Salem Luth Cem, Killinger), m Aug 17, 1826 Elizabeth Potteiger (Nov 10, 1805 – Oct 18, 1881), a dau of John and Anna Barbara Potteiger; **HENRY** (b May 16, 1810 – Apr 13, 1880, bur St John's "Hill" Cem, Bbg), m Elizabeth Harman (Dec 5, 1813 – Oct 26, 1894), a dau of John Harman .

JOHN MILLER (Nov 5, 1777 – Jul 6, 1861, bur Miller Cem, in Jackson Twp, Dau Co), was born in Northld County, but came to Dauphin County and settled on a farm in Jackson Twp in 1817. John Miller m Anna Catherine Seiler (May 5, 1783 – Aug 24, 1865), a dau of Jost and Elisabeth (Heckert) Seiler of Stone Valley . In 1850 John and Catharine Miller lived in Jackson Twp and had Mary Schott age 14 with them. **John and Anna Catherine (Seiler) Miller had these children (some bapt Zions Stone Valley, some Salem Luth, Killinger):**

MICHAEL MILLER (b Feb 12, 1805 bapt Salem Luth Ch, Killinger, grandparents John and Veronica Miller sponsors – d Dec 27, 1864, bur Miller Cem), m 1st Mary Catharine Straw (Aug 3, 1805 – Jun 26, 1833), a dau of John Straw. **Michael and Mary Catharine (Straw) Miller had these children;** Josiah (1828 – 1898, bur Bowerman Cem, Enterline), m Catharine _____ (1829 – 1898); **Balthaser** (1830 – 1904), m Christiana _____ (1832 – 1914)); **Cyrus** (b c1830 _____), m _____ Sweigard. He was a blacksmith, died in Reading leaving a widow and four children.
Michael m 2nd Hannah Buffington Kolva (Oct 11, 1808 – Apr 24, 1890), dau of David and Eva (Schoffstall) Buffington, and widow of Jacob Kolva. Michael was a blacksmith in Jackson Twp. In 1850 Michael and Hannah lived in Jackson Twp, and had these people living in their household: Cyrus 19, a blacksmith; Jacob Kolva 19, Sarah 4 months, Benjamin Kuntzelman 3 month, Eve Kolva 21, Leah Miller 8, Hannah 5, Aaron 3, and Eve Buffington, 74, the mother of Hannah.**Michael and Hannah (Buffington, Kolva) Miller had these children (many of these family members bur St.Jacob's "Millers" Cem, Jackson Twp** Lydia (1835 – 1843); **Michael H** (1836 – 1924), m Catharine Snyder (Jan 7, 1842 – Mar 23, 1911), lived in Jackson Twp in 1870. **Michael H and Catharine (Snyder) Miller children:** Isabella b c1861; Ellen b c1864; Ira O. b 1866; Jacob b c1868; Harvey b c1869; Jennie b 1874, m Harvey H. Snyder; Edward L. b1878 **Eli** (1838 – 1843); **Samuel** (1840 – 1843); **Leah** (1842 – 1884); **Hannah** b 1844, m Jul 23, 1865 David A. Snyder (c1840 – Mar 2, 1913 **David A. and Hannah (Miller) Snyder had these children:** Wellington (no dates) lived in Tower City; Leon (no dates) lived in Gratz; _____ m J. W. Miller; **Aaron** (Jul 9, 1846 – d _____), m Florenda Bender ( ), a dau of A. Q. and Susanna (Fisher) Bender of Wash Twp. They lived in Jackson Twp on a farm. **Aaron and Florenda (Bender) Miller had these children:** Fannie, m Harry McNeal; Edwin; Ammond; Sarah; Harry; Adam.

PHILIP MILLER (Aug 25, 1807 - Nov 11, 1889, bur St. Jacob's Luth & Ref "Millers" Cem), m c1831 to Susanna Warfel (Dec 4, 1815 – Nov 19, 1842), but were divorced soon after the marriage.). Philip had a second marriage to Catharine Shott (Sep 18, 1820 – 1908), a dau of Jacob and Catharine (Messner) Schott. Philip was a wagon maker, living in Jackson Twp in 1850. At that time he had Catharine Schott 27, John Miller 16, and Hiram Schott 3 in his household, and was living next to Michael Miller. In 1860 and 1870 Philip lived with his son John and family in Jackson Twp., and he was listed as a wheelwright. Catharine (Shott) was not living with them. She married Jacob Bordner (1804 – 1879). Jacob had previously been married to Lydia Guest (c1810 – 1845. Jacob and Catherine Bordner moved to Crawford Co., and later to Wood Co Ohio.

In1880, Philip is listed as the father age 72 living with his son John B. Miller and family in Jackson Twp. **Philip Miller had one known child: John B.** (b Apr11, 1834 - d May 8, 1911, bur Millers Cem, Powell's Valley), m Catherine ____ (b Jun 26, 1832 – d Jan 9, 1902). **John B. and Catherine Miller had these children: James O** (1856 – 1921, bur Miller's Cem), m Mary ___ (1858 – 1890); **Susan J.** b c1858; **Mary E.** b c1839; **Clement W.** b c1865.

*DANIEL MILLER b Jul 10, 1811 more information below, bapt Stone Valley;

JOHN MILLER   (b Sep 21,1814 , bapt Stone Valley – d Jan 30, 1897, bur St. Jacob's Luth & Ref "Millers" Ch.) m Barbara Sweigard (Apr 25, 1818 – Feb 2, 1902), a dau of Adam and Elisabeth Sweigard.. John was a farmer in Jackson Twp in 1850. **John and Barbara (Sweigard) Miller had these children: Philip W** b c1840; **Catharine** b c1841; **Elizabeth** (1842 – 1844); **John A.** b c1844; **Benjamin** b c1846; **Henry** b c1848.
ELIZABETH MILLER (b Feb 14, 1817 bapt Stone Valley - d Apr 27, 1897), m John Lettich, all of whom lived in Jackson Twp,
CHRISTIAN B. MILLER moved to Kansas in 1886..

JOHN PETER MILLER (b May 17, 1780 bapt Stone Valley, Northld Co – d May 30, 1842, bur St. Jacob's Luth & Ref "Millers" Cem, Powells Valley), m Maria Magd Weaver (Oct 25, 1777 – Nov 13, 1854). They lived on a farm in Jackson Twp. **Peter and Maria Magd(Weaver) Miller had these children:**
Peter Miller (b Dec 14, 1805 - ____), m Susannah Snyder (b c1814 - ____), lived in Jackson Twp on a farm. In 1850 Peter and Susanna lived in Jackson Twp, his mother Magdalena age 74, Mary Ann Zimmerman age 20, Nathaniel Bressler 29, an OST preacher lived with them. In 1860 they had Caroline Seiler 15, John Snyder 11, listed as servants with them. **Peter and Susanna had these children: Sarah Anna** (1833 – 1843, bur "Miller" Cem); **Samuel B.**(Feb 4, 1838 – Oct 2, 1870, bur Fairview Cem, Jackson Twp), m Mary Fitting c1840, a dau of John and Sarah (Betz) Fitting of Jackson Twp. In 1860 they lived next to his parents.

Daniel Miller;
Mary Miller (b c1810 -   ) m Valentine Straw b c1811 - ___); **Valentine and Mary (Miller) Straw had these children: Samuel B.** b c1833;**William W.** b c1836; **Susannah** b c1839; **Mary** b c1942; **Sarah** b c1844; **Andrew E.** b c1846; **Emaline** (1849 – 1864);

Susanna Miller (Oct 14, 1818 -   m Christian Snyder ( ), lived in Jackson Twp. on a farm. **Chrstian and Susanna (Miller) Snyder had these children: Joseph; Eleanor; Isaac T; Josiah;** ____ m John L. Keiter;
Joseph Miller: Jul 21, 1821

JOHN JACOB MILLER (b Jul 10, 1782 twin – d Jan 4, 1860, bur Miller's Ch, Powels Valley), m Elisabeth ____ (Aug 6, 1793 – Mar 6, 1871)
ANNA CATHARINA MILLER b Jul 10, 1782 twin, m Michael Heckert –
ANNA MARGARETHA MILLER b Feb 12, 1784 , m George Shoop, Jr.

*DANIEL MILLER from above (b Jul 10, 1811 Low Mahanoy Twp, Northld Co – d Jul 4, 1872), m Catharine Snyder (Jun 18, 1808 – Dec 15, 1884, bur Fetterhoff Cem, near Halifax), a dau of William and Elizabeth Snyder. Daniel was a blacksmith and also had a distillery in Washington Twp until his death. They lived in Jackson Twp., Dau Co. in 1850, and in addition to their children, William Lettich age 23, a blacksmith lived with them **Daniel and Catharine (Snyder) Miller had these children:**

SUSAN (Jul 25, 1833 – 1920, bur Maple Grove Cem, E'ville) m John Frank (b 1829 – d 1873, bur Maple Grove Cem, E'ville), probably a son of David and Gertrude Frank of Jackson Twp..

Susannah in 1880 was a widow, and lived in Washington Twp with her children and her widowed mother. **John and Susannah (Miller) Frank had these children: William D.** b c1859, m Mary A ____ (1861 – 1905, bur Maple Grove Cem, E'ville); **Emma J.** b c1863; **John Albert** b c1869;

<u>JAMES</u> (b Feb 16, 1835 Jackson Twp, Dau Co – d Dec 3, 1920, bur Maple Grove Cem, E'ville), m Jul 4, 1858 to Sarah Hoffman (Dec 6, 1835 – Aug 23, 1911), a dau of Peter and Elizabeth (Hoffman) Hoffman of Halifax Twp. In 1857 he spent some time in Ogle County, Illinois, but came back within a year. In 1866 James and family moved from Jackson Twp to Elizabethville, where he did carpentry and taught school .He also clerked in the store of Fred Weaver. In 1869, he succeeded John Keiper as Secretary-Treasurer of Lykens Valley Mutual Insurance Co. In 1880, James and Sarah and their family lived in Washington Twp. **James and Sarah (Hoffman) Miller had these children: Milton A** (Jun 30, 1859 – 1937, bur Maple Grove Cem), lived in Olean, N.Y, m Susan Hoke Leopold, **had these children: Miles V.** (Oct 8, 1898 – Jul 14, 1974, bur Maple Grove Cem, E'ville), m Amy D. ___ (b Nov 1, 1905; **Eugene** (no dates); **Ruth** (no dates; **Ellen Victoria** b & d 1863; **Agnes Amanda** (Jul 24, 1865 - 1955, bur Maple Grove Cem), m Lincoln U. Bolton; **James Melvin; Susan R.** (1868 – 1954, bur Maple Grove Cem); **Elmira Salina** b Aug 19, 1869 in E'ville – d 1953, bur Maple Grove Cem, E'ville), m Harry M Cooper (1870 – 1927); **Harvey Monroe.** "Solly Hulsbuck" (Sep 27, 1871 – Jun 17,1939, bur Maple Grove Cem), m Apr 2, 1903 in Philadelphia to Rose K Sheetz (1881 – Oct 20, 1965), a dau of John Sheetz of Jefferson Twp, Dau Co. He was born in the round stone house in Elizabethville known as "Newton Hall." In addition to being a civic servant in his hometown of Elizabethville, Harvey won considerable fame as an author and poet. He wrote several books of poems and other writings, and printed them on a small hand press in his home. They were printed under the name of Hawthorne Press, Elizabethville. His small printer is now housed in the Gratz Historical Society museum. Original copies of some of his books are also in our museum. Under the name "Solly Hulsbuck" he wrote volumes of poetry and prose in English and the Pennsylvania German dialect, which contributed to his fame. He corresponded with numerous famous writers, James Whitcomb Riley, Robert Louis Stevenson, William Jennings Bryan, etc.
Harvey M and Rose (Sheetz) Miller had one one child: Sara (no dates), m J. George Ennis of Mount Penn, Pa.
Ruth (1892 – 1963), m ____ Covell Eugene K (1904 – 1972)
<u>NATHANIEL</u> (b Nov 19, 1837 in Wash Twp, Dau Co - d 1928, bur Maple Grove Cem, E'ville), was a son of Daniel and Catherine (Snyder) Miller. He m Jan 13, 1867 to Leah Holtzman (b Sep 17, 1835 - d Jan 12, 1883, bur Ref Cem, Rife) a dau of John M and Elizabeth (Novinger) Holtzman. In 1880, Nathaniel and Leah lived in Washington Township. In addition to their children, his sister-in-law, Sally Holtzman age 34, lived with them. Nathaniel died of pneumonia, and was the oldest living resident of Elizabethville. Nathaniel owned several farms in Washington Twp., including the property with gristmill known as Stine's mill.**Nathaniel and Leah (Holtzman) Miller had these children: Jane Alice** (1868 - 1869); **Stephan Allen** (Sep 22, 1870- 1915, bur Maple Grove Cem), m Anna Beadle (1871 - 1952), was a baggage master on the Summit Branch railroad; **Helen Catherine** (Dec 15, 1876 – 1937, bur Maple Grove Cem, E'ville), m ____ Watson. Nathaniel Miller m 2nd Sep 11,1883, Elmira Bailor Smith (1845 - 1905), wid of Wm Smith b Apr 28, 1849, in Juniata Twp, Perry Co., and a dau of David and Margaret (Smith) Bailor, whose family came from Berks County to Perry County years earlier. **They had one child: Ida Mary** b Sep 18, 1884, m George Harper of Phenix, Va.. Nathaniel Miller married a third time to Gertrude McClure, who was named as his wife on a deed dated 1916.
<u>ADAM S</u> (Jul 14, 1841 – Aug 18, 1921, bur Maple Grove Cem, E'ville), m Mary Kauffman, a dau of Jonas Kauffman at Pillow. **Adam S. and Mary (Kauffman) Miller had these children:** Elmer K; Mabel (no dates), m ___ Shepherd, of Cleveland, Ohio; Gertrude (no dates) m ___ Heston of Cleveland, Ohio; Inez (no dates), m ___ Ferris of Cleveland, Ohio.
<u>Mary Catharine</u> (Aug 17, 1846 –1923, bur Maple Grove Cem, E'ville), m William George Hoke, (1844 – 1915, bur Maple Grove Cem, E'ville) lived in Elizabethville. In 1880 William G and Mary C (Miller) Hoke lived in Washington Twp. next to Jonathan Hoke age 54,who was living along. **They had these children:** <u>Cora E.</u> b c1875; <u>Vergie M</u> b c1878.

Photographs Of Members of the Miller Family

James Miller & his wife Sarah (Hoffman) Miller
(James is a son of Daniel & Catharine (Snyder) Miller

Nathaniel Miller   Adam S. Miller
(sons of Daniel and Catharine (Snyder) Miller)

The Land Where The Lykens Family Dwelt

From the pages of "Penn'a-German Poems (Dialect section) by Solly Hulsbuck, printed 1906

From HARMONIES OF THE HEART By Harvey M. Miller (printed about 1902)

DOT LEEDLE BOY

I got me vonce a purty vife
  Vich luf me eferlasting much
  Budt she dond't dink dot I vas Dutch
I speak mit English, betcher life!
  Und like der vay der olt vorld runs,
    Ve haf alretty cares und joy,
    Und dhen ve got von leedle boy, --
A shtork bird bringt him vonce.

Oh, dot vas plessings all de vhile,
  Vhen somedimes yet upon mine knee
  He tells me ef'ry A –B-C
Und I bend down und kiss dot child.
  I dink ov nodings – only him,
    Und vhen ve roll upon der floor
    I like to be a boy vonce more,
Dot innocence throwed in.

Der drubbles somedimes dot I feel,
  Der vork und vorry ov der day,
  Und all der hurts und scars, I say
His leedle childhood's kiss will heal.
  I kvick forget der shtrife und fight,
    For mit his kickers in der shky
    He pokes his heel up in mine eye
Und puts him oudt ov sight.

Dhere's nodings, frients, for happy times,
  Like leedle childerns, vot's a boy
  Budt clo'es vot's holdin' new-born joy
Vhere heav'n und eart' togedder jines!
  Ehr vot's a girlie, say, but heaps
    Ov honey sweetness vhere she's plac'd
    Und all der men dhey like der taste,
Und vant alretty her for keeps.

Vot if I get me rich right quick,
  Mit landt und houses ov der best
  Is dot vot gifs a feller rest?
Dot makes von cracy loonatick!
  I vould a lawyer quick employ
    Und all ov dot mine frients present,
    Budt keep mine wife und heart's
        Content,
Und if you please, mine leedle boy.

A SONG OF CHEER

A song is worth a world o' sighs,
  An' worry doesn't pay;
When sorrow drains your tired eyes,
  Just sing it all away!
Don't mind what Fate's a-bringing,
But to your hymn-book clinging,
    Keep your grip, -
    The cheeriest trip
Is goin' to glory singing.

EN VOLENTINE

Du shae glae maidly, seez we'n rose,
Coom hare und huck dich uf mi shose,
Ich kent mit leeb dich hartzlich dricka
Und bussa bis du daidsht farshticka
O, leeva maidly, geb mer'n sign
Und sawg du bisht mi Volentine.

DER ANSER

Du gonz, du lump, du oldar gase,
Du bisht so seez das luder kase;
Du wit mich yusht far hussa flicka,
Und far di haesa shtrimplin shtricka;
Gook yusht in's glaws, so'n monkey
      shine
We sell iss blendy Volentine.

Harvey M "Solly Hulsbuck" Miller

On April 11, 1916 Nathaniel and Gertrude Miller of Elizabethville sold two different tracts of their land to George Lahr. Both tracts were in Washington Twp. One contained 126 acres 43 perches with two dwelling houses, bank barn and out buildings, and a spring of water. It was located on the side of Summit Branch Railroad, with reserved right to Cora Keister bearing date Jan 16, 1914. This land was bound by Wiconisco Creek, Charles Hoover, Nathaniel Miller (of which this was part), and the Cora Keister estate. A second tract containing 33 acres 80 perches of woodland was located on the side of Berries Mt. in Washington Twp, and was bound by the road from Loyalton to Railroad Station, Nathaniel Miller, late lands of George F. Williams (he purchased his land from Nathaniel miller in 1899 and sold it back to Nathaniel in 1916), Cora Keister, John Harman, William Schoffstall. This land was part of the property that B. N. and Helena Romberger sold to Nathaniel Miller on Mar 30, 1897. George E. and Annie Lahr of Washington Twp sold these two tracts of land to Josiah Hoover of Lykens Township.

Josiah Hoover owned these two tracts of land plus several others for many years. He sold them on December 24, 1921to Edmond Hoover. On March 31, 1925, Edmond and Lillie Hoover sold the two tracts to William Heckler. [William Heckler was born c1834 in Wurtemburg, Germany. He lived in Porter Twp., Sch Co in 1880, with his wife Caroline b c1840 in Pa., to parents who were born in Prussia. **They had five children**: William H.b 1869, settled in Lykens where he conducted the Union House Hotel beginning in 1905; Kate b c1870; Charles b c1872; Augustus b c1874; Harry b c1876.] [**HOOVER genealogy elsewhere in the book.**]

While William Heckler owned this property, the James Kissinger family lived as tenants in one of the houses on the grounds. Mildred, one of their daughters remembered that during the time that they lived there, the Oak Dale Station was a thriving place. Travel on this train was a regular practice. But not all persons alighting from the train were legitimate! In those days it was common for "bums" to hitch a ride by crawling up on a train to go to their destination with free transportation. Sometimes when the train stopped at Loyalton, the bums would alight, and walk down the road to go door to door to beg for food. Mildred recalled that their mother (Mrs. Kissinger) sometimes gave them something to eat. These beggars were smart enough to mark the fence or some other object in front of the houses where they were able to get a free meal. Sometimes they ask permission to sleep in the barn. Mr. Kissinger did not allow it because of the danger of fire. But he gave them a straw mattress and let them sleep in the small house after he collected any matches they were carrying with them.

A devastating fire of undetermined origin did destroy the huge barn early one morning in May 1932. Ray Heckler completed some chores at the barn a short time before flames were discovered in the hay mow. He called his father, but the flames spread so rapidly he was able to liberate but one horse. A mule, 3 horses and 6 head of cattle perished, ten tons of hay and all implements were destroyed. The barn was 109 feet long and 65 feet wide. The Kissinger's remembered that the Heckler barn caught fire while they lived there, and they watched as it burned to the ground.

Present Home Of Domer Shaffer Family - Earlier Home Of Josiah Hoover
This was home of Oakdale Academy. It was always an attractive property, a special feature on second floor were wall mirrors reaching from floor to ceiling. (They were sold separately when Cook sold the house).

On June 11, 1937, William Heckler transferred both tracts to Frank W. Boyer, who sold the same year to Charles W. Cook. On April 15, 1943 Charles W. and Eva Cook conveyed both to Vernon Domer and Margaret Shaffer. The Shaffer's also purchased the 2 acre 95 ¾ perches of land. After Vernon Domer Shaffer died, his widow Margaret L Shaffer turned the property over to her sons Fred E. and Thomas A. Shaffer on March 8, 1994.

[**VERNON DOMER SHAFFER** (Aug 11, 1917 - Jan 10, 1970), a son of Calvin Arthur and Laura Rebecca (Bohner) Shaffer, of Lower Mahanoy Twp, Northld Co m Margaret Johns (   ), a dau of Walter Johns. **Domer and Margaret (Johns) Shaffer had these children: Thomas; Fred** m Pat Klinger, later separated; **James** m Connie Leitzel.]

Josiah Hoover family –Seated in the yard of their home
l to r – standing: Leah (Hoover) Bender, Lottie (Hoover) Hoover, Lillian (Hoover) Shappel
Std: Edmond and Lillian (Wetzel) Hoover & Josiah and Catharine (Schmeltz) Hoover

OLD BARN ON SHAFFER PROPERTY

65

Small House Behind Mansion On Shaffer Property. Walter
Johns lived in this house, as did the James Kissinger family.

William H. Heckler

(WAS RICHARD NOLAN LAND)

This next land is located on the north east side of the forge complex and was part of the Ferree land. But in 1823, John Row inherited the land from Isaac Ferree in place of his deceased wife Susannah (Ferree). On June 2, 1836, 47 acres 115 3/10 perches of the land were sold to Richard Nolan, one of the few stone and brick masons that lived in this area between 1820 and 1860. This land adjoined the land of the Oak Dale Forge, and on March 25, 1837, Richard and Mary Nolan of Lykens Twp., conveyed the "rights to raise and swell water of the Forge dam on the Wiconisco Creek." In 1850, John Beverson age 32, lived with the Nolan family and was listed as a laborer. Many years later, Richard Nolan and his family moved to Harrisburg and on April 1, 1861, they sold this same tract to John F. Madden of Schuylkill County. The Madden family lived here for a few years, but on April 1, 1867, it was sold to Moses Nutt, "subject to payment of $700 to Richard Nolan by his death or sooner." This land at that time adjoined the land of John Row, Jacob Moyer, north to Josiah Bowman and David K. McClure, and south to Samuel Lubold. Moses and Sarah Nutt conveyed the 47 acres 115 3/10 perches of land to Charles Hoover in April 1873. The Charles Hoover family lived here in 1880.

On Apr 2, 1898 Charles Hoover conveyed the 47 acres 115 perches of land to George A. Harner. The land bordered north side of Berrys Mt., Simon Finney, to land of Peter Schoffstall north former Geo Gilbert land, s to former August Bauem land. Containing 12 acres, 140 perches. It was part of the land of Washington Matter exec of Henry Matter sold to F. D. Harner . Frederick D. Harner sold o George Harner Apr 2, 1898 deed not recorded. In March 1920, George Harner conveyed 12 acres 140 perches to Charles W. Cook, and it became part of the old forge and mansion property.

THE NOLAN FAMILY

[RICHARD NOLAN (c1801 – 1879, bur Harrisburg Cem), m apparently first Mary _____ (c1798 - ___). Richard later m widow Elizabeth Minnich (b c1823 - d c Apr 1884 in Harrisburg, bur "by U.B. rites" according to her will by her first husband." **Elizabeth had these children**: Jeremiah and Daniel Minnich, Mary m to ___ Robinson; Harriet Jane m ___ Shaffner, Catherine m _____ Everhart, John Henry Minnich. Richard and his first wife Mary lived in Wiconisco Township in 1850, and John Beverson age 32, a laborer was living with the family. Richard Nolan died in Harrisburg, and by his will he gave his wife Elizabeth "the cooking stove, small clock and bureau we generally have in our bedroom and one sink and such dishes as she and the executor agree on. Also personal things she brought here as my heirs have nothing to do with her personal property or real estate according to the agreement we entered when we married. If she marries, the executor (his son in law John Orndorf, Sr. of Wiconisco) shall sell the balance of my real estate at public sale. **Richard and Mary (_____) Nolan had these children**: Emeline (Oct 21, 1826 – Feb 29, 1904), bur Wiconisco Cem), m John Orndorf (Aug 4, 1822 – Sep 20, 1894), a son of Christian and Eva Christina (Bordner) Orndorf. **Lucinda** b c 1829, m ___ Moyer; **Lyman F.** b c1833, m Sarah _____ b c1834. Lyman was a store keeper in 1860. **They had these children;** William b c1856; Asbury b c1858; Howard H. b c1861, m Mar 29, 1881 Annie Lucas, **they had a child** Edith Cordella b Feb 5, 1882, bapt Zion Luth Ch, Lykens; Emanuel b c1864, was a shoemaker in 1880; Jacob b c1871; Lotta b c1876. **Sidney Ann** b c1835, m George Hawk; b c1830. George was a cola miner in 1880 in Lykens. **George and Sidney Ann (Nolan) Hawk had these children:** Oscar b c1857, a coal miner in 1880; Travis b c1860; Kate b c1867; George b c1877. **Dianth** b c1838.]

THE JOHN F. MADDEN FAMILY

[**JOHN F. Madden** (b c1824 – d ____), m Elizabeth ____ (maybe Wallace) b c1834. They lived in Wiconisco Twp in 1860, and he was a miner. **John and Elizabeth Madden had these children (some bapt Zion Luth, Lykens):** Alice V. b Dec 22, 1853; Martha J b Jul 14, 1856; Charles F. b Nov 17, 1858; John Elijah b Jul 20, 1864.]

THE CHARLES HOOVER FAMILY

[**CHARLES HOOVER** (Mar 10, 1850 – Feb 8, 1929, bur Maple Grove Cem, E'ville), was a son of Elias and Elizabeth Hoover. He m Leah A. Boyer (Jun 5,1839 – Apr 7, 1909). **Charles and Leah (Boyer) Hoover had these children:** Mary E. b c1873; John E. (1873 – 1957, bur Maple Grove Cem), m Katie A. ____(1877 – 1966); Isaac F.(1876 – 1961, bur Maple Grove Cem), m Carrie L. ___(1875 – 1940). [More info under Hoover family.]

HOME OF ROBERT L. & NANCY J. KEISTER
(Home of the old Oak Dale Post Office, left side of Forge in 1875, 34 acres south eastward)

This land was part of the tract that belonged to John Wommer and Henry Miller. (John Wommer owned Lykens Coal Company in 1837). John Wommer and Henry Miller conveyed 50 acres of land with 2 story log house to Michael Sausser and Josiah Bowman.

On March 29, 1854 Michael Sausser and his wife Lydia, and Josiah Bowman and his wife Elizabeth sold two tracts of land in Wiconisco Township to David K. McClure. The larger tract contained fifty acres with a two-story weather boarded log house, kitchen and log stable, and was owned by the McClure's for a long time before they sold it to Loyetta E. Lark on January 7, 1879. The smaller tract of two acres 152 perches contained a dwelling that had belonged to John Wommer. When the Lark's purchased this land, an agreement was made between a neighboring owner, William Schoffstall regarding the water rights, and a claim of Richard Budd regarding some timberland. The Lark's sold to B. W. and Helena Romberger on Feb 21, 1887. About ten years later, on Mar 13, 1897 B. W. and Helena Romberger sold to Nathaniel Miller.

Nathaniel and Gertrude Miller of Elizabethville conveyed two tracts of land on April 2, 1917 to Cora J. Keister, wife of William Keister. One tract contained an acre and thirty perches of land with a dwelling and outbuildings. The two-story log house is the home of the Oak Dale Forge post office, thus dates to as early as 1832. Oak Dale Forge post office was later renamed "Short Mountain." Many Indian artifacts have been found in the vicinity of this property.

The second tract contained 34 acres, 118 perches of land. It was boundsouth west by the land of Josiah Boyer, east to Wiconisco Creek, Nathaniel Miller, George Williams, south, Aaron Hassinger. A reserve was included in the deed record providing that "a tight chicken fence must be built around the whole tract and the private road running east and west must be open all seasons for the use of the first party."

The Keister's lived on this land for many years, and after both had died, the heirs conveyed this property containing the two tracts on January 27, 1949 to Arthur D. and Naomi O. Keister, whom with their family lived here in later years. While they lived in the house, Mary Bellon lived with them. After both Arthur and Naomi Keister died, the property was conveyed to Robert L. and Nancy J. Keister on Mar 22, 1983, and they are the present owners.

THE WOMMER FAMILY

[The WOMMER family has been traced back to **Jacob Wommer** b c1615 in Germany. The generations follow in sequence: **Michael** (1648 – 1725); **Jacob** (1680 – 1746) m to Mary Eliz Blasius (1680 – 1746); followed by **Michael** (Jan 7, 1717 – 1794), m Anna Mary Melchior b1722 in Germany. They are the first of the Wommer family to migrate to America. They settled in Bern Twp, Berks Co. Michael and Anna Mary (Melchior) Wommer had ten known children, one of them being **ADAM WOMMER** (b c1757 in Bern Twp. Berks C. – d 1809 in Catawisa Twp., Northld Co), and his wife Justina Shepler (1768 – 1817), a dau of Henry and Justina (Kraft) Schepler of Berks Co. *JOHN WOMMER son of Adam Wommer settled in Loyalton.

[*JOHN WOMMER (Mar 7, 1786 - Oct 26, 1870, bur Hoffman Cem), a son of Adam and Justina Shepler Wommer, residents of Berks Co., m Jun 12, 1807 Elizabeth Kantner (Sep 2, 1786 - Jun 12, 1853), a dau of John Jacob and Susanna (Feit or Fey) Kantner of Manheim Twp, Berks Co. In 1834 John was a tenant on a property on the Bear Gap land. He was either part owner or at least affiliated with Lykens Coal Company in 1837. In 1850 John and Elizabeth lived in Wiconisco Twp., and he was a Justice of the Peace. In 1860 John lived with his son Daniel in Wiconisco Twp. **John and Elizabeth (Kantner) Wommer had these children (some bapt Friedens Luth & Ref Ch, Norwegian Twp, Sch Co):**
**SUSANNA b Jan 25, 1813 (twin?)
**LUCY ANN b Jan 25, 1813 (twin?)
DANIEL H. (b Feb 7, 1815 Friedensburg – d Sep 1, 1875 bur Hoffman Cem), m Elizabeth _____ (Aug 19, 1817 - Apr 12, 1918), a dau of _____. In 1860 they lived in Wash. Twp and he was a tavern keeper in Loyalton. They had Amanda Derr age 14, and his father John with them. In1880 Elizabeth was living alone in Wash. Twp. **Daniel and Elizabeth Wommer had one known child: ***George W. b & d 1845;
**GABRIEL b Oct 18, 1817
**ELISABETH (Mar 19, 1819 – May 13, 1900, d in New Bloomfield, Perry Co, bur Elizabethville)
**JUSTINA (b Mar 20, 1822 in Sch Co - d Jun 19, 1891, Lykens), m Jan 30, 1841 to Levi Holwig, Sr (Dec 1819 Low Mah Twp, Northld Co - Oct 21, 1896 in Coal Dale, bur Hoffman Cem) , a son of Jacob and

Elizabeth (Charl) Holwig. After Justina died, Levi m Sallie A. Myers, and had one child ***Ida Lucille b Dec 17, 1892. **Levi and Justina (Wommer) Holwig had 7 children**: ***Levi (Mar 17, 1864 - d Feb 14, 1894, Lykens, m Ellen Heckert, dau of Frederick Heckert. Levi and Ellen (Heckert) Holwig had 11 children, 7 preceeded the father in death.;

JOHN (Oct 18, 1826 - Feb, 19, 1908, bur Hoffman Cem), m Elizabeth Jacoby (Jan 18, 1829 - May 4, 1894), a dau of Johann and Susanna Jacoby, of Sch Co. In 1860 they lived in Wiconisco Twp. In 1880, John and Elizabeth lived in Washington Twp and had two grandsons with them: Henry Rabuck age 6, Samuel Snyder age 2. **John and Elizabeth (Jacoby) Wommer had these children:
***Elizabeth b c1852; ***Malinda b c1854; ***John b c1856; ***Isabella (b Oct 10, 1858 -1924, bur IOOF Cem, Lykens), m George Snyder. **George and Isabella (Wommer) Snyder had these children:**
****Samuel Jerome b Jun 20, 1878, bapt Simeon Ref Ch, Gratz.
***Daniel (1863-1865, bur Hoffman Cem); ***Justina Margaret.(Oct 11, 1864 bapt Zion Luth Lykens - d Sep 15, 1877 bur Hoffman Cem)
**MARIA SALOME b Dec 7, 1828
**WILLIAM b 1830
**GEORGE b 1832
**CATHARINE b 1834
**MARY b 1836

THE KEISTER FAMILY
(Information from William Keister)

[The Keister family came to America in the early 1700's and settled in Berks County. The Keister family of Loyalton has not yet been traced to the immigrant, but Michael's branch moved to Hartley Twp., Union Co. **MICHAEL J. KEISTER** (b c1832 in Hartley Twp., Union Co - d Jan 13, __), m Dec 23, 1858 to Mary Emma Marr (b c1834 in Hartley Twp – d _____). **Michael and Mary Emma (Marr) Keister had these children:**
*WILLIAM ISAAC (b Oct 5, 1858 Union Co – d Nov 17, 1937), m 1st Mary Ellen Dershaman b c1864, and in 1880 they lived in Hartley Township next to his parents. William m 2nd Cora J. Platt b ___ d Aug 15, 1914) of Tower City. They came to this area early 1900.
William Isaac and Ellen (Dershaman) Keister had these children (some bapt Oak Dale Ch):
Irvin Edward b Apr 15, 1875 Snyder Co; **Mary Elizabeth b May 3, 1880 b Hartley Twp, Union Co.;Bertie (no dates) m Lloyd Franklin bapt Oct 24, 1899 County Line Ch, Northld Co
Mabel Ruthette bapt Oct 24 1899 County Line Ch, Northld Co (b ___ d Jan 31, 1966), m Irvin O. Shadle;Esther Anna bapt Oct 24, 1899 County Line Ch, Northld Co, m _____ Rickey, who died before 1948;**Grace May bapt Oct 24, 1899 County Line Ch, Northld Co (b ___ d Sep 15, 1930), leaving these children: ***Sherwood Rowe m Marguarite; ***Chester Bower; ***Harry Bellon.
** Lula Irene (Jun 18, 1901 – Jul 17, 1940), m Charles E. Saltzer. **Charles E and Lulu (Keister) Saltzer had these children:** ***Earlin R; ***Miriam.
Foster Willliam (Mar 23, 1904 – Aug 23, 1942), m Alma V Strawhecker (1914 – 1991, bur Greenwood Cem, Tower City). They lived near Oak Dale Forge. **Foster and Alma Keister had these children:
***Richard F.; ***Ronald E; *** Kenneth L; ***Doris L; *** Cloyd D.
Arthur Daniel (Apr 7, 1907 – 1977), m Naomi O. Fetterhoff (1906 – 1982 bur IOOF Cem, Lykens). **Arthur and Naomi (Fetterhoff) Keister had these children:
William Edward b Jan 21, 1928, m Jul 1, 1950 Shirley Evelyn Bush, lives in Loyalton. William and Shirley are active members of the Gratz Historical Society. **William and Shirley (Bush) Keister have these children; ****Christine Louise b May 30, 1951; ****Yvonne Marie b May 17, 1954 m Michael Eugene Marr, had these children:** Danielle J b May 27, 1971; Micelle L b Jul 18, 1979; Marie A. b Oct 20, 1980; ****Thomas Eugene b Oct 7, 1955; ****Brian Rene b Aug 10, 1957, m Sally Shade, a dau of Cyril and Lorraine (Witmer) Shade;*Dennis LeRoy b Oct 11, 1958.
***Margaret Louise b Jun 4, ____, m 1st Robert Herb, 2nd Dec 24, 1957 Galen Paul
***Grace Arlene b Feb 18, 1932, m Edwin Novinger;
***Robert Lamar b Nov 20, ___, m Nancy J. Cope, lives near Harrisburg.

***Ruth** b Jul 6, ___ , m Clarence Barge, Jr.
***Donald** (b Jun 25, ___ d Aug 25, ___)

*JONAS ELLSWORTH** (b Sep 11, 1862 Union Co – Oct 16, 1939 m Cora Adda Thomas;
*LEVI ELISHA** b Feb 27, 1865 Snyder Co, m Sarah Ann ____;
*ALBERT** b Apr 15, 1867 Clearfield Co ;
*LAURA LUSTRE** (May 8, 1870 Union Co – Feb 27, 1944), m, Irvin L. Shively
*RUFUS REUBEN** Sep 11, 1873 Union Co – Nov 3, 1958, bur Miller's Ch), m 1st Sara Parmer; 2nd
Maude Hilbert Barge, **they had these children: **Clair;**Eleanor; **Estella; **Elsie** b Nov 17, 1909 m
Andrew Harman (1897– 1970), son of ___ and Mary Alice (Mauser) Harman); **Raymond.
*MILTON** (Mar 15, 1876 – 1951), m Elizabeth Wirth
*MARY MINNIE** (Oct 3, 1878 Union Co – Apr 22, 1881)
*ELLEN ELIZABETH** b Sep 28, 1883 Union Co

THE OAK DALE COVERED BRIDGE
Crossed Wiconisco Creek Near Forge

One Of the Few Original Surviving Photo's Of The Oak Dale Forge Covered Bridge

This covered bridge gave access to the Oak Dale Station, and was one of many bridges that were built across the Wiconisco Creek. The early paths or roads were makeshift, rough and bumpy byways. Crossing the creek was a chore, until a crude style bridge made crossing easier. Early maps show that a type of bridge gave travelers assistance in crossing the Wiconisco Creek, and by 1858 a fairly good bridge was in place.

The covered bridge may have come later. The date when it was built is unknown at this time. It served the community for many years, and numerous area folks have interesting memories in relation to the bridge. Linda Bush was fond of this structure, and put her artistic talents to work by painting several pictures of it. One of her paintings was given to Eugene Fetterhoff and his wife as a Christmas present during the days when she was employed as their baby sitter. The bridge was doomed to destruction during the flood of 1972. The neighboring residents, were concerned for its safety, and doom came at two o'clock in the morning when with a thunderous crash it fell into the swollen creek. Within a short time the present cement bridge was built to replace the old landmark.

HOME OF MR. & Mrs. RONALD G. STROHECKER
(On the right side of the road after crossing the bridge – was D. McClure in 1875)

On Jun 5, 1899, Nathaniel and Elmira Miller conveyed a small tract of 105 perches with a 2 ½ story frame dwelling to George F. Williams. George and Emma Williams sold it back to Nathaniel Miller on April 1, 1916. This was part of the Oak Dale Academy property earlier owned by B. W. Romberger, and bordered at this time the other land of Nathaniel Miller and Cora Keister. On April 24, 1929 William Keister, single, sold the property to Claude E. and Maggie Keiter. On May 28, 1930 Claude E. and Maggie Keiter conveyed the land to Foster and Alma Keister, and they conveyed to Dorothy Gonder Davenport. Dorothy and her husband Howard replaced the old house with a new one, but shortly after that they moved to California. On October 9, 1951, Dorothy & Howard Davenport conveyed to Lloyd & Beulah Troutman, and on June 25, 1952 they sold to Thomas E. and Pauline Troutman. He died July 4, 1953, and his widow conveyed to Galen M. and Margaret Paul. They sold on April 28, 1958 to Ronald G. and Esther Strohecker.

[**WILLIAM P. WILLIAMS** (1839 – d May 2, 1915, bur IOOF Cem, Lykens), m Sarah Smeltzer (May 3, 1840 Mifflin Twp– Oct 12, 1917 of cancer, recorded St. Johns Luth, Lykens). They lived in Wash. Twp in 1880. **William and Sarah (Smeltzer) Williams had 9 chidren (some bapt Hoovers Ch, Rife)**: Mary Jane b Jan 8, 1863; George F. (Feb 28, 1867 – Feb 22, 1925, Lykens), m Emma Francis Warfel; John E. b 1869; Hettie E b c1876, m Wm. C. Hoover, son of Charles Hoover, of Coaldale; Samuel M b April 1880]

ROAD TO THE LEFT

After passing the home of Ronald Strohecker, a narrow unpaved lane veers off to the left. Two houses were located on the north side of the unpaved lane. They belonged to Henry Miller, and Adam Wert. Several other dwellings were located south between the unpaved road and Oak Dale Forge Road. They apparently belonged to Michael Palm in 1875. These were very old houses, dating probably back to when the forge was built. They were likely the homes of the tenants while they worked for Mr. Buchanan at the forge.

BRIAN K. AND CONNIE L. BORDNER PROPERTY
(Was Home of Ray E. Geist -H. Miller in 1875 – 6 acres)

Present Appearance Of Very Old House

**L to r: son Marlin , Ray Geist
And Wife Della In Front Of The
House Years Ago.**

**Back Of Ray Geist Home
As It Looked In The 1930s**

This land was conveyed to D. K. and Ann Eliza McClure about 1849. It was part of the Oak Dale complex, until February 2, 1875 when 6 acres 122 ½ perches of land with house was purchased by Henry O. Miller. He and his wife owned it until October 8, 1881, when it was sold to Benjamin Frank Harper. It was bound by the old forge dam, Lark land, and north to John Wommer land. After Benjamin Frank Harper died, his executor, Samuel M. Neiman, conveyed the property to George D. Harper on March 31, 1897. He owned it for many years, but sold to Della R. Geist on February 18, 1939. After her death, her only heir, Ray E. Geist became owner of the property on January 24, 1970, and he lived here for the remainder of his life. On May 23, 2000 Brian K. and Connie L.Bordner purchased this property. The very old log house has survived for many years, but has recently been enlarged and given a modern appearance.

Ray E. Geist enjoyed the outdoors, spent most of his time hunting and fishing, and had several varieties of dogs to accompany him on his adventures. The woodsy setting of his home was a suitable setting for his lifestyle. One person referred to Ray as being "one of our mountain men." Family reunion picnics were frequently held in the nearby woods.

Ray E. Geist

On left Ray and Marlin posing with collection of fox hides, dogs & guns

[HENRY MILLER (c1837 - ___), m Catherine ___ b c1850- ___), lived in Wash Twp in 1880. **Henry and Catherine (___) Miller children**: Maggie b 1871; Cyrus F b 1874; Jennie E. b 1876; John J. b 1879 .]

[JAMES GEIST (May 14, 1864 – Nov 11, 1891, Northld Co), a son of Daniel & Cicilia (Updegrave) Geist of Leck Hill, m Mary A. Rothermel (1863 – 1925). **James & Mary A. (Rothermel) Geist had these children**: EDWIN D. (Feb 26, 1885 Leck Hill, Northld Co – 1975), m Nov 16, 1907 Agnes Matter (Jan 14, 1892 – 1971). **Edwin D. and Agnes (Matter) Geist had these children**: Ray E. b Jun 9, 1908 Gratz -___), m Della Fetterhoff had a son Marlin; Russell b Oct 6, 1910), m Felma Pauline Miller b Jan

22, 1912, a dau Newton W. & Elizabeth (Art) Miller. **Russall and Felma (Miller) Geist had these children**: Robert Allen b Nov 5, 1928, m Eudorie Reitz, lives in Ephrata; Carvel Lewis b Jun 22, 1930, m Jane ___ , lives in Lock Haven; **Albert** b Oct 6, 1909; **Mary M.** b Jul 1, 192, m Ellwood Walborn; **Sarah A.** b Nov 27, 1913, m Paul Miller; **Earl M.**, m Leah Romberger; **LYNDON MAUDE M.** (Mar 31, 1889 – 1966), m HarryZacharias Buffington (Apr 29, 1891– Feb 20,1949), a son of Geo. and Mary (Laudenslager) Buffington. **Harry and Maude (Geist) Buffington had a son**: **James Harry**; FLOSSIE (Apr 11, 1890 – Mar 17, 1924), m John Paul.]

CAMP SWAMP HOLE, INC.
(Was ADAM W. WERT Land in 1875)

On June 9, 1866 David K. McClure conveyed a small tract of about four acres from his large holdings of land to John Wommer. After several years, John and Elizabeth Wommer sold the tract with appurtenances on November 22, 1873 to Adam Wert, a resident of Jackson Township. But several years later on April 16, 1877, Adam W. and Sarah Wert sold the land back to John Wommer. This land was located a short distance from the Oak Dale Station. It adjoined the land of B. W. Romberger (formerly D. K. McClure). On March 29, 1895 John and Elizabeth Wommer conveyed the same land to Frank W. Behney of Porter Township. This deed was not recorded until October 11, 1901. On December 16, 1903, Frank W. and Emma Behney conveyed the four acres and dwelling house to William M. Keiter of Jackson Township. By this time the land adjoined the land of Nathaniel Miller. William M. Keiter on February 15, 1915, conveyed the property to Bertie Ochenrider of Elizabethville. But about one year later on May 24, 1916, Bertie and James Ochenrider sold the four acres of land and dwelling to Mary Melinda Bellon, a widow. After Mary Melinda Bellon died her heirs transferred to Carrie Gonder on May 1, 1944. Carrie later married Ralph G. Snody and on September 28, 1961, they sold to Ralph F. Buffington, Jr. and his wife Marian I. Buffington. The Buffington's in turn sold to Harold E. and Ella R. Kissinger on December 19, 1986, but on February 2, 1989, Harold E. and Ella R. Kissinger conveyed to Thomas W. Miller, and he sold October 18, 1991 to members of CAMP SWAMP HOLE, INC.

RALPH & CARRIE M. SNODY HOUSE

Carrie Gonder owned part of this land and on May 31, 1949, she and her husband Ralph purchased another acre plus tract. They owned this property until their death. After Carrie died, it was conveyed to Linda and Roy E. Gonder May 3, 2001.

(MICHAEL PALM 2 ACRES OF LAND 1875 – later William Schoffstall)

This land was part of the Oak Dale Forge and had numerous owners (Sausser, Wommer, McClure, Lark). D. K. McClure conveyed to Michael Palm, and on April 25, 1878, his land was sold by sheriff sale to John Hess. The particular land consisted of about an acre with a double two-story frame dwelling, stable, smoke house and bake oven. It appears that he had maybe two other small tracts, although a record of transfer was not found. The other land might have been transferred to John Hess as well. John Wommer also had a small tract in this area that became part of the McClure property. On January 7, 1879, John Hess sold two tracts of land to H. L and Loyetta Lark. Henry and Loyetta Lark moved to Kansas sometime during the early 1880's and on August 26, 1885, they sold at least some of their land. A small tract broken from the two tracts above was sold to William Schoffstall of Washington Township. It was a two acre ninety-six perch tract of land with a two-story log weather-boarded house, a kitchen and other out buildings. This was an interesting piece of property especially because of the location, close to the Oakdale railroad station, and because of the conditions of the sale. The old railroad bed was on the land, and "it was not to be closed up for farming nor to be used in any way so as to prevent or obstruct the right of way on the railroad bed or across any of the other land owned by Loyetta E.Lark." The watercourse was also to be used by the Larks and William Schoffstall. [Note that Michael Palm and William Schoffstall were brother-in-laws, probably partly explaining the land transactions.] The house is gone for many years, and the land apparently reverted back to later owners of the forge complex.

The following piece from **The Lykens Register** dated September 13, 1900 relates an incident in the life of the William Schoffstall family.

"For sometime the rumor of danger has been hanging around Loyalton. Not bodily danger, but danger of losing one of the most estimable young ladies. The rumor was confirmed on Tuesday evening when at the house of William Schoffstall, their daughter Martha was ushered into the presence of the invited guests to the sweet strains of Mendelsohns Wedding March, played by Charles M. Coles., and joined in holy matrimony to Harry W. Weaver of Georgetown by Rev. Geiger of Pillow. The bride was dressed in India linen, beautifully trimmed, carrying a pretty bouquet, while the groom was neatly dressed in conventional black, wearing a white carnation in his lapel. The groom was attended by Lucien C. Schoffstall the brides brother and Harry C. Deppen of Sunbury while the bridesmaids were misses Sara McLaughlin of Roseberg, Perry County, and Gertrude Gise of Gratz. The groom is well known in this section and is a son of Cornelius Weaver of Kansas, who one time lived in County Line. He will soon enter Muhlenburg College in Allentown where he will prepare for the ministry. The bride is also well known and is a successful school marm. The cause of education in these parts will miss her. A bounteous wedding supper was much enjoyed by all the guests. They will soon go housekeeping in Allentown. Those present were: Noah Swanger and wife, John Robinson and wife, Charles Coles and wife, Forrest E. Schwartz and family, A. P. Schoffstall, John W. Schoffstall and wife, Mrs. Botteiger of Media, Clara Swanger of Wiconisco, Miss Bertha Schminky and Lottie Hepler and Thomas Hepler of Gratz, Jos Kramer and wife, Annie Schoffstall of Williamstown, Christ Budd and wife, Center View, Irvin Boyer and wife, Aaron Hassinger, George Harper and wife, Misses Ada Helt and Martha Swanger of Loyalton and Mrs. John Troutman of Tower City."

THE PALM /POLM FAMILY

The **PALM/POLM** family arrived in America at a very early date and settled in Berks County. Unfortunately, we have not been able to connect to those early generations. Michael is the earliest one we found.

MICHAEL F. PALM (b Dec 25, 1832 Cleveland, Ohio – d Nov 26, 1917, bur ME Cem, Williamstown), a son of _____ . (His pension record gives several dates for his birth including December 26, 1835.) Michael m Feb 27, 1865 by Rev. N. E. Bressler of Fisherville to Angeline Schoffstall (Feb 13, 1846 - Jun 19, 1909), a dau of Christian and Mary (Snyder) Schoffstall of Washington Twp. Michael and his family lived in Washington Twp., where he was employed as a blacksmith. Michael was a Civil War Vet, served in Co D, 127th Regt Pa Vol. During the battle at Chancellorsville, Michael was wounded in the foot by a large shell. He also went deaf from the roar of cannon. When he applied for a pension after the war, Henry Weiser was a witness for him, and he said Michael was a "first rate Dutchman whose word is as good as gold." His health deteriorated to the point that in July 1916 he was admitted to a government hospital for the insane. **Michael and Angeline (Schoffstall) Polm had these children (some bapt Zion Luth, Lykens): Emma** (Nov 7, 1865 – 1923), m Chas. Shutt; **Mary Ellen** b Apr 14, 1867, m John Lehman, moved to N.J.; **William** b c1868; **Albert F.** b Feb 13, 1869; **Elizabeth** b c1870; **John Henry** b Feb 15, 1871 - 1952, bur Fairview Cem, Williamstown), m Carrie A. (1874 - 1959); **Charles** b c1872; **Wilson Oscar** b Jan 3, 1875 m Mary E. ___ (May 15, 1875 - Feb 12, 1899, bur Seyberts Cem, Williamstown), Wilson m 2nd Edna E. ____; **Daniel** b c1876; Hattie b Feb 16, 1881, m Emanuel Row.

WILLIAM F. POLM (Nov 15, 1828 - Oct 19, 1874, bur Matters Cem), m 1st Elizabeth Ann ___ (Jul 4, 1836 - Jun 14, 1867), a dau of _____ . William was a Civil War Vet. **William F. and Elizabeth Ann ( ) Polm had these children: Joseph** (Jun 18, 1855 – May 14, 1881, bur Matter Cem), m Rachel ____ b c1857. Joseph and Rachel lived in Washington Twp in 1880, and had a daughter Katie Alta. b Jan 22, 1880; **Emma** b c1857; **William F** (Oct 16, 1859 - Dec 3,1871); **Alda Peora** (1866 – 1867). After his first wife died, William F. Polm m 2nd Anna Eliza _____ b c1833, wid of Solomon Rudisill (Jun 1, 1831 - Jun 16, 1897, bur Matters Cem). **William and Anna Eliza Polm had these children; Sarah Catherine** b Oct 11, 1868; **Anna** b c1872, m Rudisill; **Anna Eliza** (Mar 9, 1873 – Nov 27, 1896, bur Matters Cem), m W. S. Howard; After William died, his widow Anna Eliza lived in Washington Twp in 1880 and had the two daughters with her.

WILLIAM SCHOFFSTALL FAMILY

[WILLIAM SCHOFFSTALL, SR. (Sep 25, 1836 - 1922, bur Oak Dale Cem), a son of Christian and Mary (Snyder) Schoffstall of Loyalton, m Mary Ann. Swanger (Feb 13, 1843 - 1922), a dau of Peter and Elizabeth Swanger of Loyalton. In 1880, William and Mary A. Schoffstall lived in Washington Twp. **William and Mary Ann (Swanger) Schoffstall had these children: Annie E** b Sep 16, 1864 - d Nov 9, 1879, bur Oak Dale Cem) ;**Andrew Peter** (Jun 16, 1866 - 1937), m Sep 23, 1894 Margaret R. Welker (1877 - 1942), at the home of her parents Mr. & Mrs. Benjamin Welker of Loyalton. **Katie A** b c1868; **Sarah** b c1870; **Lucian Christian** (Jul 12, 1874 – 1951, bur Maple Grove Cem, E'ville), m Jun 15, 1901 Jennie C. Helt (1880 – 1937)(record in County Line Ch); **Martha Emma** b Dec 29, 1875, m Sep 1900 Harry W. Weaver of Georgetown see newspaper piece following this family genealogy; They lived in Allentown in 1912. **John Rudy.** (b c1878 bapt Jun 16, 1878 Oak Dale Ch) m Mary Seeshultz on June 18, 1897. (More information in Schoffstall genealogy.)

Chapter 5

LAND WEST OF FORGE & WICONISCO CREEK
(From Various Sources)

The next acreage came from various tracts and grants of land including Matter, Dietrich and Bitterman land. It is located along the western side of Wiconisco Creek beginning at a line at the north end of the Kuntzelman tracts as well as other surrounding land. Oak Dale Forge territory lies immediately to the east but is separated by Wiconisco Creek. This land was partly settled with farms and a few lots, but over many years was dispersed to various owners and is now basically woodlands.

LAND TO PHILIP WILVERT (had 68 acres in 1875)

John and Magdalena Bitterman owned this land and sold it to William and Rebecca Hawk on April 4, 1850. Josiah Boyer was the next owner and assigned it April 3, 1854 to Henry Matter. On October 25, 1856 Henry and Mary Matter conveyed two separate tracts containing 13 acres and 51 acres 79 perches, a total of 64 acres 120 perches to Philip Wilvert.

After Philip Wilvert died, his heirs conveyed his land in two separate tracts. On September 24, 1894 the 51 acres were transferred to his daughter Sarah J. Miller, wife of Daniel Miller. After Sarah J. Miller died, her son Albert Miller conveyed her land to Harvey Lupold April 1, 1927. It later became land of Glenn Snyder.

Amanda Klinger, wife of Wellington Klinger and daughter of Philip Wilvert received the 13 acre tract also on September 24, 1894. She had it for a long time, but by her will, and deed recorded Aug 1941, she transferred the same tract to Ellen R. and Roscoe Klinger.

WILBERT/WILVERT FAMILY

[We have not been able to complete the research on the Wilvert family. The following is what we were able to find.

MICHAEL WILVERT (c1755 – pre1840, **may or may not** have been the parent of all of the children below. He owned about 40 acres of land and a dwelling in Lykens Twp in 1831. (Land was part of grant Martin Nissley to Andrew Daniel, then Wilvert near Crossroads). The 1830 Lykens Twp census records Michael Wilvert as the head of house age between 70 and 80. He was apparently a widower, and had a young couple and child living with him, probably his son Michael. By 1840 Michael b c1801and his family are living in Lykens Twp.
*PETER WILVERT (   ), m Susanna _____ had these children (some bapt Fetterhoffs Ch);
Catharine (May 20, 1800 – Jul 6, 1874), m John Gipple (Aug 6, 1800 – May 31, 1874), son of George & Elis Gipple. **John and Catharine (Wilbert) Gipple had these children (some bapt Fetterhoff's Ch):
***Henrich b Dec 14, 1826; ***Emanuel b Dec 20, 1829,
** Johan Jr. b Jan 5, 1812 ; **Susanna b Jan 7, 1814; **Daniel b Mar 21, 1816;** Elisabeth b Nov 20, 1819;
*ELIZABETH WILVERT(Apr 23, 1794 – Sep 20, 1869, bur Fetterhoof Cem), m Conrad Enders (May 18, 1788 – Dec 5, 1874). He was a vet of War of 1812. **Conrad and Elizabeth (Wilvert) Enders had these children:** **Conrad b Jan 5, 1823; **Barbara b Jan 3 0, 1826; **Susannah b c1834.
*ADAM WILVERT (Dec 3 0, 1796 Fisherville – Feb 6, 1875, bur Fetterhoffs Cem), m Juliana Daniel (Feb 13, 1800 – Apr 12, 1862), a dau of Andreas and Susannah (Hoy) Daniel. Adam was a weaver. **Adam and Juliana (Daniel) Wilvert had these children (bapt Fetterhoff Ch);** **Susanna b Mar 20, 1833;
**Lydia Ann (Feb 12, 1834 – Sep 14, 1910); **Amelia b Jun 7, 1835; **Henry b Nov 25, 1837;
*MICHAEL WILVERT b c1800 m Elizabeth Daniel b Nov 10, 1802, a dau of Andreas and Susannah (Hoy) Daniel. In 1840, Michael and Elizabeth Wilvert lived next to her father, and had three children.

77

*JOHN B WILVERT (Dec 20, 1801 - Mar 5, 1863, bur Zions UB Cem Matamoras), m Catherine (Sep 18, 1803 - Dec 14, 1869). John was a mason.**John and Catherine _____ Wilvert had these children: ** Susanna** b May 12, 1824; **Maria** b Apr 5, 1828; **Catharine** b Mar 27, 1830; **John** b Dec 2, 1833;
*PETER WILVERT(May 1803 - d pre 1850), m Mary Enders (Mar 22, 1803 - Mar 22, 1875, bur Fairview Cem, Enders, a dau of John George and Catharine Bowman, a native of Lancaster Co, whom migrated toDauphin Co. In 1850 Mary Wilvert a widow lived in Jackson Twp and had these children living with her. Levi; Henry; George; Sarah. **Peter and Mary (Enders) Wilvert had these children:**
Philip (Oct 29, 1821 - Nov 2, 1893, bur Motter Cem, Wash Twp), m in 1846 Catharine Matter (Jan 26, 1823 - Mar 13, 1915), a dau of Henry and Anna Mary (Dietrich) Matter of Dietrich. In 1850 Philip and Catherine Wilvert lived next to his widowed mother in Jackson Twp. **Philip & Catharine (Matter) Wilvert children:** ***Sarah Jane** (Jan 12, 1848 –Aug 23, 1926, bur Maple Grove Cem, E'ville), m Daniel Miller (b c1846 -d 1901). In 1880 they lived in Jackson Twp. **Daniel & Sarah Jane (Wilvert) Miller children:** Emma b c1871; Albert b c1873' Katie b c1874; Clara R b c1876; Sarah b c1880; Susan m Henry Heller;
***Mary** (1852 - Dec 24, 1857), died of typhoid fever
***Lydia Ann** (Mar 14, 1854 - Oct 20, 1930, bur Motters Cem) m Feb 15, 1872 John Calvin Lentz (Feb 11, 1851 – Jun 5, 1895), a son of John F. and Sarah Ann (Hartz) Lentz. They lived in Washington Twp in 1880. **John Calvin & Lydia Ann (Wilvert) Lentz children:** John Philip (Nov 22, 1872 – Sep 30, 1941), m Gertrude Riegel; Anne Louise b Jun 20, 1874, m William Cromer; Katie E Dec 21, 1876 - Dec 5, 1915), m Harry Campbell; James Edwin (Mar 8, 1879 – May 31, 1946), m Florence Enders;Raymond Andrew (Oct 21, 1881 – 1916), m Edna Houser; Chas Warren (1884 – 1968, m Minnie Mae Riegle (1889 – 1967) dau of Clinton and Catharine (Hartman) Riegel; Daniel b 1887;; Henry H. b 1889; Allen C; Joseph ;Harry.
***John H.** (Jun 21, 1855 - Dec 25, 1857), died of typhoid Fever.
***Emeline** (1859 - 1861, bur Matters Cem)
***Amanda E**. b c1861 - d Feb 3,1942, bur Maple Grove Cem), m Wellington Klinger (Mar 18, 1858 – 1936), son of Simon & Mary Klinger. Wellington, 22 lived in Wash. Twp in 1880 with J.A. Romberger.
***CLARA R.** (Oct 7, 1863 - Apr 6, 1928, bur Maple Grove), m Feb 25, 1882 Alfred Bechtel (Feb 3, 1859 – Dec 31, 1924), a son of Simon and Susan (Messner) Bechtel of Wash. Twp. **Alfred & Clara (Wilvert) Bechtel children:** Homer (1883-1950); Clayton b 1884; Isaac b 1886;Edwin C. (Jan 24, 1891 – Feb 8, 1956, bur Maple Grove Cem, E'ville), m Hilda W. Moyer (Mar 22, 1897 – Jun 12, 1967), had a dau *Mary Ruth* (Dec 22,1922 –Dec 29,1992, bur E'ville), m Paul Franklin Keefer b Apr 23, 1918; Mary b 1893
Levi (Sep 18, 1823 – 1892), m April 1856 Julia Zimmerman( ), a dau of Adam Zimmerman of Jackson Twp. Levi was a stone mason and was engaged in canal and railroad building. They lived in Jackson Twp in 1880.**Levi and Julia (Zimmerman) Wilvert had these children:** ***Cornelius B** (Mar 18, 1857 - Apr 25, 1907, bur Enders), m Sep 2, 1881 Lydia Loudermilch b Sep 2, 1856, a dau of Michael Loudermilch He became a teacher and taught in Jackson Twp for 22 years;***Isaac** b Apr 17, 1861 - Jan 28,1889, result of mine accident Williamstown, m Savilla Boyer (no dates); ***Annie Jane** Oct 4, 1870 – Jun 22, 1930), m Albert Dietrich (1864 – 1924) of Lykens Twp.
Heinrich (Apr 16, 1826 – Oct 1, 1879,bur Enders), m 1st Catharine Matter (Apr 18, 1831 – May 26, 1857), 2nd Anna Catharine Witman (Apr 10, 1837 – Jan 27, 1872), a dau of John & Catharine (Messner) Witman; 3rd Sarah Bowman (Feb 27,1848 – Feb 5,1921), widow of Samuel Shoop anad dau of John Bowman of Enders. In 1880 Sarah (3rd wife) was a widow living in Jackson Twp. She had these children with her: Harry U. Shoop 10; Emma R Shoop 8; Carson Wilbert 3; George Wilbert 1; Henry Wilbert age 4 months.**Heinrich had these children:**
***Aaron A.** (Dec 4, 1851 – Dec 20, 1916) m Mary Jane Ender (Aug 29, 1846 – Mar 2 8, 1910, bur Enders Cem), a dau of Philip and Mary Enders.Aaron was a stonemason; ***Susan Elizabeth** (1854 – 1920), m Valentine Enders; ***Charles** b 1857 d young; ***John R** (1861 – 1881, bur Enders Cem); ***Mary C** b 1868, m Jacob Newton Ferron; ***Emma Cora** (Jul 9,1870 - Aug 9,1949), m Daniel Harrison Dietrich (Aug 16, 1866 – Apr 7, 1934), a son of Emanuel and Ellen J. (Adams) Dietrich; **Sarah J.** d young; **Carson E** (1877 – 1894, bur Enders Cem); **George G** (1878 – 1946); **Henry** b 1880 – 1953).
Maria b Apr 5, 1828;
Sarah b c1831 m Isaac Weaver.
George (Nov 22, 1830 – Oct 3, 1895, bur Longs Cem, Halifax), m Sarah Tyson (Oct 29, 1835 – Oct 3, 1915), a dau of Mary Tyson b c1815, whom lived with them in 1880 in Halifax . **George and Sarah (Tyson) Wilvert had these children:** ***Anna E**. b c1861; ***Emma R**. b c1864; ***John H.** b c1869, probably m Dollie E.Eisenhower (1872 – 1931); ***Sarah E.** b c1876.

*HEINRICH WILVERT(Oct 5, 1805 – Aug 8, 1842, bur Fetterhoff Cem), m Susanna Fetterhoff Jul 20, 1813 – Feb 7, 1878, bur Messiah Luth Cem), a dau of Philip & Eva (Boyer) Fetterhoff. After Henrich d, Susanna m ___Witman.
*GEORGE B. WILVERT (Feb 22,1812 –May 5, 1878), m Nancy Welker (Jun 24, 1813 - Feb 1, 1887). George was a carpenter, living in Matamoas in 1850. In 1880 Nancy was a widow living along. **George and Nancy (Welker) Wilvert children**; Henrietta b c1835; Josiah b c1836; Margaret b c1840; George Nathaniel (Jan 22, 1842 Halifax - Jul 23, 1912)

PETER SWANGER LAND IN 1875

This land is made up of several tracts located in Washington Twp. Between 1845 and 1850, Magdalena Bitterman sold three tracts of land (10 acres, 10 acres and 15 acres) to Frederick Guyer. It was bound by Edward Bickel and Sausser land to the north by and Wiconisco Creek to the south east. On March 20, 1853 Peter Swanger bought the three tracts. But in 1861 William Schoffstall, executor of Peter Swanger estate sold to Martha L., Clara R. and Catharine E. Swanger, Peter's daughters. Aaron A. Hassinger became the next owner April 1, 1901 of two tracts. Ten acres of mountain land, and15 acre with a two- story log dwelling bank barn, orchard and running water near the house. It bordered on the farm of Mrs. D. A. Miller & Henry Boyer, north to Benneville Boyer (this was Edward Bickel land), Michael Miller (was George Neagley land), B. W. Romberger, & Wiconisco Creek, Josiah Boyer (was George Neagley land) and late Philip Wilvert land. In March 1906 Nathaniel Miller conveyed a 1 acre 16 perch tract of land to Aaron Hassinger that bordered on the west side of the creek. This was to allow free access to an area where workman with horses and wagons were cutting down trees and marketing lumber.

Before Aaron Hassinger died, he penned his will, and Jacob E. Hassinger was the recipient of his land. Jacob and his family acquired other land and lived on this farm with frame dwelling, barn and other buildings for many years. But after his wife died, Jacob E. Hassinger conveyed two of the tracts (15 + acres and the right away along the creek to David Barge on Nov 12, 1949. The 10 acre tract was conveyed to Eugene Hassinger in Dec 1952.

Jacob Hassinger purchased 3 other tracts of land (2 acres 13 perches, 6 acres, 9 acres 101 ½ perches) that Josiah Boyer had owned and later sold to J. Clinton and Regina Boyer April 1, 1917. They sold to Jacob E.Hassinger on Jul 28, 1922. On October 8, 1949, Jacob E. Hassinger sold the same to Claude Keiser. These lots were only a part of the land that Claude Keiser accumulated. [See write-up on the "Old Claude Keiser Farm"]

EDWARD BICKEL LAND NEAR OAK DALE FORGE

An old historic site (long gone) was located near the above land. James Buchanan and Irvin & Elizabeth Moyer sold a 20 acre 26 ½ perch tract in April 1834 to Edward Bickel. Bickel received "full right and privileges to erect, build and repair, review or rebuild a dam or creek. He may swell dam up to certain mark, from lower end of the coal house, peaceably and quietly have use of and cause swelling of the dam for use of any mill or water works, without suit trouble, hindrances or molestation of said James Buchanan. Edward is not to revise to a point when it would injure or damage the mill seat of the present forge sawmill or any waterworks that could be exited at present forge." Tax records of 1834 show Edward Bickel operating a clover mill.

The Bickel family lived on this property for many years. In 1860 Edward was listed as a millwright. On April1, 1866, adm. of Edward Bickel's estate sold this land to Simon S. Bickel.In July1875, Simon S.and wife Anna Elisabeth Bickel moved to Philadelphia where Simon was a merchant. They sold this property to teacher Isaac Kemble of Tower City, He may have taught at the adjoining academy while living here. He married Matilda (Oak Dale Ch record says Kemble) on Sep 26, 1870. Isaac Kemble sold the property to Benneville Boyer March 13, 1879. By 1880, the Kemble family was back in Porter Twp, and he was teaching in the common schools of that area.

Benneville Boyer accumulated several tracts of land from several sources, deeds not recorded. On December 17, 1891. He sold the tracts containing 53 acres to his son Henry, who sold to his sister Ellen Harner, wife of Charles Harner on March 10, 1903. About six acres of it was part of the Edward Bickel clover mill property. The six acres were bound by land of Henry Boyer, Aaron Hassinger and south to Nathaniel Miller.

[The Bickel family settled first in Berks Co. They had at least 3 generations of Tobias Bickel's. The earliest Tobias had a wife Maria Elizabeth. The 2nd generation was Tobias & Salome (Galt) Bickel. The third, their son Tobias Bickel (Nov 12, 1782 Heidelberg Twp, Berks–Nov 9, 1836, bur Simeon Cem, Gratz).He owned land here in 1828, was a millwright. **EDWARD** (Mar 16, 1809- Jul 28, 1864, bur Simeon Cem), m Ann Salada (Mar 3, 1816 –Mar 19, 1903), dau of Simon & Jane (Woodside)Salada. **Edward & Ann (Salada) Bickel children**: Tobias (1839 – 1931 bur Maple Grove, Eville), millwright, m Juliana Bender (1840 – 1927), **their children**: Fanny (1864 -1941, bur Maple Grove), m Elijah E. White (1858 – 1930); Annie (1868 – 1938, bur Maple Grove), m Benj. F. Bartho (1862- 1934); **Simon** b c1842, m Annie __, **children**: Edward E. b Jun 18, 1869; Robert Elder b Mar 31, 1871; **John** (1845 -1851); Matilda b c1846, m Isaac Kemble b 1839, **had these children**: Edward b 1871; **Henry W.** (1853 – 1920, bur Maple Grove), m Aug 2, 1874 Henrietta F. Buffington (1856 – 1917), moved to Ashland, Sch Co. **children**: Susan J. b 1876; John b 1878; Earl (1888-1907, bur Maple Grove).

Jeremiah & Esther (Schmeltz) Hassinger
(1808 – 1879)   (1812 – 1881)

Dam & Ice House on Hassinger Farm

Henry T. Hassinger
(1859 – 1938)

Jacob E. Hassinger
(1836 – 1913)

Jacob & Aaron Hassinger at Farm

Jacob Hassinger Family
Jacob, Maud, Dorothy, Homer, Lester

THE SWANGER/SCHWANGER FAMILY

The **SWANGER** family is traced to the immigrant ancestor Jacob Schwanger (Oct 14,1714 Germany – 1788 Cumberland County. He married (Oct 27, 1735 Maria Susanna Leyenberger (Jun 16, 1708 – 1777) of Germany. They arrived in America Oct 20, 1747, bringing their six children with them. Of the six, we found five children, all born in Germany. **John Peter** b May 29, 1740; **Maria Magd** Jan 1, 1742; **Jacob** b May 5, 1743; **Isaac** Nov 25, 1744; **Catharine** b Oct 19, 1746. They had three more after arriving in Berks County, bapt. at Host Church:**Anna Maria** bapt Oct 22, 1749; **Eva Elisabeth** b Aug 26, 1 751; **Abraham** b Feb 16, 1757. Unfortunately we haven't been able to find the line connecting Peter Swanger a resident of Loyalton to the earlier family.

[**PETER SWANGER** (Oct 18, 1817 - Dec 4, 1873, bur Oak Dale), m Elizabeth ____ (Aug 17, 1823 - Jan 5, 1894) .Samuel Henry was adm of his will. After Peter died, Elizabeth continued to live in Wash. Twp. and in 1880 these children were with her: Catherine E age 35, Margaret A age 22, Martha L age 20, and Clara R 16. **Peter and Elizabeth (   ) Swanger had these children:**
Jared b c1837 – lived in South Chester, Deleware in 1880 and was a supt. in rolling mill. He was m to Rachel b c1846, **they had these children: John** b c1866; **Thomas** b c1869; **David** b c1878; Lottie b c1880
David b c1838 – this may be the one that lived in Harrisburg in 1880 and was a railroad employee. He m Sarah ____ b c1847, they had a son Franklin b c1880
Mary Ann. (Feb 13, 1843 - 1922) , m William Schoffstall, lived in Loyalton area...see his writeup.
Catherine E. (1844 –1929, bur Maple Grove Cem, E'ville) member of ME Church 1871
Rebecca m Peter Lebo ? or John B. Forney?
Christina (b Feb 7, 1846 – d Sep 9, 1911 in Lykens, bur Maple Grove Cem, E'ville), m John Bottiger (May 15, 1845 – Nov 15, 1872). **John and Christina (Swanger) Bottiger had these children**: A. Harvey b c1867;Mary E. (Jul 25, 1869 – Nov 27, 1935, bur Maple Grove Cem); Charles P. b c1871; KateE. b c1873. **Ellen Jane** b c1849;
Caroline (c1851 m Mar 20, 1874 James Forney (b Feb 15, 1849 - May 25, 1888, bur Oak Dale Cem) of Jackson Twp, a miner. ME record Berrysburg. In 1880, James and Caroline lived in 1880 Washington Twp next to William Schoffstall family. **James and Caroline (Swanger) Forney had these children:** Gertrude M. b c1874; Mabel H. b c1875; John K. b c1877; Annie M b1880.
Alice M (Feb 6, 1853 - Oct 9, 1889, bur Oak Dale Cem)
Peter b c1855 lived in South Chester, Delaware in 1880 and was an Engr. in a roller mill. He m Florence.
Noah b1856; **Margaret A** b1857 may have m Peter Lentz; **Samuel** b c1859
Martha L (Feb 5, 1860 – Jul 6, 1913, bur Oak Dale Cem), m Aaron E. Hassinger (1860 – 1945). She was 2nd wife. Aaron Hassinger's 1st wife Sarah Hepner (Nov 19, 1854 – Jul 12, 1897, bur St. Johns.
Clara R. (b Jun 26, 1876 – d Feb 1939) m John Phillips , had two daughters: Ruth Pinkerton (   ) m Jospeh Ritzman and had a son Dean; Pauline Olive b Mar 4, 1904, m. or was adopted by Henry Schoffstall a well-known shoemaker from Gratz.]

THE JACOB HASSINGER FAMILY
(Thanks to Nancy Schreffler for photos and help on Hassinger genealogy)

The **HASSINGER** family is traced to two known immigrants that came to America.

Herman Hassinger (b c1723 Germany - ____), settled in Berks County where he met and married Maria Engel Wagner (Dec 23, 1726 – May 15, 1785, bur Stouchsburg), a dau of John Jacob and Anna Sosphia Wagner. **Herman and Maria (Engel Wagner)Hassinger had these children (some bapt Tulpehocken or Stouchsburg, Berks Co): Margaret** b c1757; **Jacob S.** b c1759;**John Jacob** b Mar 19, 1760; **Anna Maria** Jul 19, 1763; **John** b Aug 13, 1765 m Dec 9, 1788 Catharine Sehler; **Christoph** (Jan 14, 1768 – Jul 3, 1826), m Catherine

JOHANNES HASSINGER (b c1711 Germany – d 1797 Snyder Co, bur Hassinger White Ch Cem). He is said to be a son of Anton Hassinger b pre 1691 in Germany. He married Maria Catharine Reinick, and settled in Snyder Co. **Johannes and Maria Catherine (Reinick) Hassinger had these known children:** John Jacob (Oct 14, 1731 – Jul 25, 1802, bur Hassinger Cem, Snyder Co), m 1760 Elizabeth ____ b Dec 6, 1741. **John Jacob & Elisabeth Hassinger had three knows sons:**
John Jacob, Jr. (Aug 10, 1762 – Nov 1, 1821, Old Hassinger Cem, Middleburg, Snyder Co), m Magdalena (May 27, 1771 – Dec 22, 1837, bur Beavertown, Snyder Co.)
John or Jonathan (Nov 14, 1764 – May 12, 1810, Middleburg), m Dec 1, 1794 Lanc Co toEva Catherine Bobb (Nov 11, 1770 – Oct 2, 1826).
Jeremiah (c1765 –Aug 1827, Snyder Co), m Elizabeth Bechtel, and had one known child: *Jeremiah (Dec 6, 1808 -Apr 3, 1879, bur St. Johns Hill Cem, Bbg) SEE Below.

[***JEREMIAH HASSINGER** (b Dec 6, 1808 – Apr 3, 1879, bur St. Johns Hill Cem), son of Jeremiah and Elizabeth (Bechtel) Hassinger, m Esther Smeltz (Dec 3, 1813 – Nov 5, 1881), a daughter of Andreas and Anna Maria (Waller) Smeltz. Jeremiah and Esther lived in Mifflin Twp in 1850 to 1870, where he was employed as a blacksmith. In 1880 Esther lived in Mifflin Twp, and Agnes Hoffman age 18 was with her. Her home was next to her son Jacob Hassinger. **Jeremiah and Esther Hassinger had these children:**

*MARY ANN(b Dec 6, 1834 Lykens Twp – d Aug 29, 1895, bur St. Pauls Cem, Enterline), m Nov 4, 1856, in Jackson Twp. to Cornelius Hoffman (Apr 24, 1831 – Feb 15, 1916), a son of Christian and Sarah (Tobias) Hoffman of Washington Twp. **Cornelius and Mary Ann (Hassinger) Hoffman had these children:** ****William H.** b Feb 26, 1859; ****Agnes Rebecca** b Dec 20, 1860, m Washington Sheetz of Wayne Twp.; ****Lucy Ellen** b Dec 20, 1862; ****Margaret E** b Nov 4, 1864, m William Dempsey of Wayne Twp.; ****John C.** b May 19, 1867, moved to Cass Co Ind in 1895; ****Charles D** b Sep 16, 1869, a teacher in Jefferson Twp; ****Jacob T.** b Nov 9, 1872, teacher in Wayne Twp; ****Aaron M.** b Dec 23, 1874; ****Albert H** b Aug 16, 1876 moved to Cass Co, Ind.

*JACOB H. (Jan 4, 1836 – Feb 18, 1913), m 1st Susannah Huber (Oct 25, 1838 – Feb 17, 1855). Jacob m 2nd Lydia A. Gipple (Jul 8, 1841 – Feb 3,1904), a dau of Jacob and Sarah Gipple of Washington Twp. (Both wives buried with Jacob at St. Johns Hill Cem). Jacob built the house on their homestead farm, which was located on the west side of St. John's Hill Church. In addition to farming, Jacob Hassinger became well known in the area as a skilled fence and post maker. He developed a new type fence that replaced the old "rail and rider" fence. **Jacob H and Lydia A. (Gipple) Hassinger had these children (most bapt St. Johns Hill Ch):**
**Elizabeth (no dates), m William Lentz
Susanna (Jul 26, 1857 - m Jonathan Lebo b 1852. In 1880 they lived in Mifflin Twp and Hugh Boddiger an uncle age 68 lived with them. **Jonathan and Susanna (Hassinger) Lebo had these children: Harry b c1878; Maggie b 1880.
Henry Theopholus (Dec 20, 1858 – May 25, 1938, bur St. Johns Hill Cem), m May 31, 1879, Sarah Jane Miller (Mar 26, 1856 Northld Co – Jan 3, 1912), a dau of John and Elizabeth (Hand) Miller.. In 1870, at the age of 12, Henry lived with the Samuel Clark family in Mifflin Twp, as a domestic. Henry and Sarah lived in Lykens Twp in 1880. He worked at the Loyalton Hotel taking care of the visitor's horses. He also picked up the mail in Loyalton, and took it to Elizabethville, by horse and buggy. Sarah Jane was a good seamstress and made all of the family's clothing. She was one of the many women of that day whom smoked a pipe. **Henry and Sarah Jane (Miller) Hassinger had these children: Isaac W.(1881 – 1958), m Anna E. Wingard (1887 – 1975), dau of Geo and Mary (Ender) Wingard; Homer F Oct 11, 1883 – Feb 24, 1966), went to Chicago, but later came back to Tower City; Claude R (Apr 4, 1886 – Jan 11, 1970, bur Hbg); Damon F b c1888; Carrie Elizabeth (Sep 26, 1891 – 1962, bur Maple Grove Cem, E'ville); m Isaac Reisch (1886 – 1941), a son of a son of Daniel and Elizabeth (Bowman) Reisch; Irene (1895 – 1994, bur Maple Grove Cem), m M. Stanley Quay Tschopp, (1889 – 1958), a son of Andrew and Mary (Buffington) Tschopp;
Aaron Emanuel b Dec 23, 1860 – d 1945, bur Oak Dalel Cem), m 1st Sarah Hepner (Nov 19, 1854 – Jul 12, 1897, bur St. Johns Cem),a dau of Simon and Elisabeth (Potteiger) Hepner. **Aaron Emanuel and Sarah (Hepner) Hassinger had these children: Jennie (Aug 4, 1885 – Apr 5, 1973), m John David Rowe (1875 – 1961); Cora b c1884, m Frank Weaver; Jacob Edwin (Mar 2, 1892 – Mar 2, 1955, bur St. John's Hill

Cem), m Maud Edna Miller (Apr 10, 1887 - 1919), a dau of Joel and Hannah (Schreffler) Miller. **Jacob Edwin and Maud (Miller) Hassinger** had these children: Lester Miller (Sep 15, 1903 - May 11, 1970, bur Maple Grove Cem, E'ville), m Ruby Kocher (1907 - 1997), a dau of John and Florence (Wert) Kocher. **Lester and Ruby (Kocher) Hassinger** had one child: Eugene Lester (1925 - 1973) ; **Dorothy Elva** (Mar 19, 1905 - c1939), m Charles Keiter, **had these children**: *Ruth; Helen; Charles Jr.;* Homer Edward (Jan 7, 1907 - Nov 5, 1963, bur Hoffman Cem), m Mary Jane Brown (Jul 30, 1902 - Dec 2, 1998), a dau of Charles and Polly (Rothermel) Brown of Klingerstown. **Homer and Mary Jane (Brown) Hassinger had these children**: *Jean Romaine* b Jul 22, 1931, m Leroy Kenneth Patton b Oct 3,1929; *Elva H.* b Jul 9, 1933, m William Miller of Spring Glen; *Catherine* b Oct 31, 1936, m Ralph Kieffer of Dornsife; Wilmer Aaron Abraham (Jan 28, 1912- Jun 12, 1929, bit by poisonous snake, bur St. John's Hill Cem);   Aaron m 2nd on Jan 17, 1903 at County Line, Martha L Swanger (Feb 5, 1860 – Jul 6, 1 913, bur Oak Dale Cem), a dau of Peter and Elizabeth Swanger of Washington Twp.

Emma Sybilla (Nov 30,1863 - May 29,1934, bur Simeon Cem), m 1st John E. Buffington **had these children (bapt Hoffman Ch): Milton Oliver b Nov 8, 1883; Charles Warren b Apr 29, 1886. Emma m 2nd Adam Welker, had a dau **Anna E.** (1889 - 1959), m Fremont J. Mauser (1890 - 1947); Emma m 3rd Chauncy Riegel (Aug 1,1870 - Dec 4, 1936), a son of Harrison and Hannah L (Rickert) Reigle of Lykens Twp. **Chauncy and Emma (Hassinger) Riegel had a dau** Evelyn Chrstine (1902 - 1961), m Paul Lenhart.

**Daniel b Dec 1864

**Mary b Jan7, 1866 –May 4, 1931, bur Maple Grove Cem, E'ville), m 1st Oliver T. Enders (1861 - 1907, bur Maple Grove Cem), a son of Henry and Susan (Sweigart) Enders. Mary m 2nd Isaac A..Whitman (1857   - 1919), a son of William and Susannah (Enders) Whitman. He was a carpenter.

**Amanda Agnes b Dec 31, 1867 bapt Hoffmans, m Elias Hoffman

**Sarah Elisabeth b Sep 16, 1869, m William Lentz of E'ville.

**Jacob Jeremiah (Jul 12, 1871 - Apr 1872)

**Lydia Ellen b Jan 1, 1874, bapt Hoffmans Ch

John Daniel (Mar2 or 29, 1876 - May 26, 1942), bur St. John's Hill Cem), m Jun 4, 1898, Lydia A. Shaffer (Feb 23, 1881 - Sep 5, 1949, bur St. John's Hill Cem), a dau of Michael B. and Catherine (Boyer) Shaffer of Mifflin Twp. John was a farmer and road supervisor, lived on farm near St. John's Hill Church. **John Daniel and Lydia A. (Schaffer) Hassinger had these children: Alvena (1898 - 1938), m William W. Howard (1896 - 1986); Vergia (1901 - 1986), m Harry Miller, 2nd Ray M. Musser; Clayton Daniel (1904 - 1967, bur St. Johns Hill Cem), m Irene K. Weaver (1907 - 1996), **had these children**: Marzette; Richard; Donald; Merrill; Allen Edw (Aug 5, 1906 - Aug 12,1943, bur St. Johns Hill Cem), m Laura E. Koppenhaver (1906 - 1980), a son of schoolmaster Daniel Koppenhaver and wife Carrie Ritzman **Allen E. and Laura (Koppenhaver) Hassinger had a son** Warren Elvin b Dec 12, 1926; Mellie b (1909 - 1995), m John Wesley Erdman; Myrtle C. (Feb 28,1912 - Sep 7, 1974, bur Zion Hoover Cem), m Mark W. Lenker, 2nd Leroy H. Landis (Apr 23, 1909 - 1981); John Woodrow (1916 - 1993), m Marie K. Matter; Elvin (1917 - 1998), m Hazel M. Warner; Jacob M.(1920 - 1993), m Dorothy H. Radel.

Maggie (Mar 9, 1881 - Jul 7, 1951, bur Zion Hoover Cem), m Amos Cooper (Sep10, 1872 - Nov 23, 1951). **Amos and Maggie (Hassinger) Cooper had these children: Resta; Jacob; Albert; Floyd; Orvin.

**Lillian Jane (Mar 19, 1882 - Mar 23, 1944), m Dec 7, 1907 in Berrysburg, Charles A. Enders (1884 - 1970). Charles was 1st m to Margaret Umholtz, dau of John and Ella (Hoover) Umholtz. She d in childbirth.

Charles m again Nov 14, 1945 to Carrie Hassinger Reich, sister to Lillian Jane, and widow of Isaac Reich.

*ELIZABETH b c1840

*LOUISA (Jan 8,1845 - May 20, 1896). Louisa and Cornelius Weaver had a dau Ida Almeda b Aug 6, 1868, bapt Hoffman Ch.. On Nov 13, 1871 she m Francis Koppenhaver b c1854. **Francis and Louisa (Hassinger) Koppenheffer had these children**: **Charles b c1871; **Harvey A. b c1873; **Daniel b c1878.

*AARON b c1848

*JOHN HENRY b c1852 m Sep 30, 1881, Susannah Hoke of Jordan Twp, Northld Co. **John Henry and Susannah (Hoke) Hassinger had these children** (bapt Oakdale, Loyalton): **George E b Apr 13, 1875; **Alice L b Nov 23, 1877; ** Catharine A b May 26, 1873 - d 1884;** George b c1875

*JOEL ADAM (May 3, 1853 - Aug 22, 1901), m Amelia Bohner (1854 – 1924)]

LAND TO WASHINGTON MATTER
(J. C. Harman 81 acre tract in 1875)

On April 29, 1862 Elias and Elizabeth Kuntzelman conveyed _____ acres (34?) of land in Washington Twp. to Washington Matter. This land bordered the land of David K. McClure, Henry Matter, south to Jacob Rife and Moses Nutt. Several years later, on April 4, 1866 Washington and Margaret Matter conveyed 75 acres of the land to Christian Johns of Earl Township, Lancaster Co. This land was made up of farm and woodland, and bordered the land of the estate of John Dietrich. On April 1,1873, the heirs of Christian Johns conveyed the 75 acres to John C. Harmon. His neighbors were John Boyer, Philip Wilvert, Joseph Russell, and the estate of Catherine Botts. In 1884 the land was sold to Richard Budd, a timber contractor. On Aug 19, 1903, Richard Budd sold it back to John C. Harmon. After John C. Harmon died, his heirs sold 21.646 acres of the land known as the "Richard Budd farm" on December 26, 1914 to Daniel Romberger. [See information on Kate Lebo land].

THE JOHNS FAMILY

The **JOHNS /TSCHANTZ** family has been traced back to Hans Tschantz born 1564 in Bern, Switzerland , but an accurate line of descent has not been found.

PETER TSCHANTZ (1784 - Mar 13, 1837, bur Mellinger Cem), a son of Johan and Anna Tschantz, was the immigrant ancestor for the family in this area. Peter m Maria Hess (Dec 1, 1782 - Jul 21, 1853), a dau of Christian and Ann (Litzler) Hess. They settled first in the Manheim area of Lancaster County. The name changed from Tschantz toJohns about the time they came to America.

[**JOHN HENRY JOHNS** (Apr 7, 1807 Heidelberg Twp., Adams Co - Jul 15, 1901 Wiconisco, bur Union Cem). m Catherine A. Dickey (Dec 7, 1822 Lanc Co – Jul 23, 1903). When John Henry was three years old, his parents moved from Adam County to Lancaster Co, then later moved back to Adams Co. He lived there until early adulthood and move to the west. After a few years he came back to Adams County where he married his wife. In 1840 he came to Wiconisco and remained there until his death. John Henry was over six feet tall, and although exposed to the rigors of many winters in the forests of this locality at a time when the only passage through them consisted of narrow paths, he was never known to be sick. He enjoyed outdoor life, was a great sportsman and related many of his memories of abundant deer and other game, and streams swarming with finny tribe. In 1880 John Henry and Catherine lived in Wiconisco Twp and had their granddaughter Hattie age 13 with them. **John Henry and Catherine (Dickey) Johns had these children (3 sons, 5 dau)**; **John W.** (1847 - Nov 24, 1930, of abscess on lung & heart affliction, bur IOOF Cem, Lykens, m 1st Lenora ____ (1848 - Aug 15, 1893), m 2nd 1905 Clara Miller (1855 - Jul 25, 1914), of a stroke); **Susan S.** (1851 - 1898, bur Wic Cem), m Edward Holtzman (Oct 5, 1849 - Mar 13, 1940), of Wiconisco;**Catharine** d age 16; **Rebecca** m Josiah Minnich.]

[*CHRISTIAN JOHNS (b Feb 20, 1810, Lanc Co - d Apr 26, 1871), a son of Peter Tschantz and Maria Hess, m Mary Rohrer (b Apr 12, 1809 - Aug 10, 1897), a dau of Jacob and Anna (Hartman) Rohrer of Lancaster Co. **Christian and Mary Johns had these children;**
**JACOB R. (Jul 12, 1831 - d Apr 9, 1892, bur Oak Hill Cem, Mbg), m Mary A ___ (Jul 30, 1847 - Dec 18, 1905). In 1880 they lived in Millersburg where Jacob was listed as a manufacturer in a culinary mill.Jacob R. and Mary A ( ) had these children: Anson b c1857; Christian R (b Mar 14, 1864 - d Jan 31, 1907, bur Oak Hill Cem, Mbg), m ; Sarah E b c1869; Jacob L b c1874; Emma R b c1876
**CHRISTIAN R. (c1837 - c Jun 1873?), a son of _____ m Susannah _____ b c1837. Christian and Susannah(____)Johns had these children: John B. b c1860; Jacob R b c1862, m Mary ___ ;
Christian R (Mar 14, 1864 - Oct 17, 1942, bur Mbg); Peter O. b c1866; Lydia A. b c1868. In 1870 Margaret Wise age 16, a domestic servant lived with the family.
PETER OLIVER (Jan 20, 1839 - Jul 28, 1881, bur Matters Cem), m, Jan 15, 1861 Maria Louisa Bitzer (May 20, 1839 - May 28, 1928), a dau of Christian Bitzer. They lived in Washington Twp in 1880. Peter had a sawmill, and one day he was cutting wood, when a piece flew up and hit him on the head causing his death. **Peter O and Maria Louisa (Bitzer) Johns had these children:

Wayne Bitzer (Aug 4, 1862 – Oct 3, 1930, bur Meth Cem, Halifax), m Dec 29, 1889 Emma Lizzie Eby (Mar 18, 1868 – Sep 16, 1949), **Wayne and Emma Lizzie (Eby) Johns had these children; Howard P.** (Apr 21, 1892 – May 13, 1984, bur Halifax Meth Cem), m Estella E. Harmon? (1893 – 1953)

<u>Calvin B</u> (b Jul 22, 1864 – d1949, bur Maple Grove Cem, E'ville), m Hattie M ___ ;

<u>Viola Ann</u> (Mar 12, 1866 – Jan 29, 1898), m ____ Witt;

<u>Sybilla Agnes</u> (Dec 18, 1867 – Aug 1948), m William Lewis Hoffman (May 22, 1866 – Jul 15, 1955). **William and Sybilla (Johns) Hoffman had these children: Harry H.** (Sep 6, 1889 – Dec 19, 1956), m Mabel E. Helt (1889 – 1939), 2nd Lillian M. Bair; **Mary Louisa** (Jul 28, 1895 - ___), m Dec 25, 1917 Ralph D. Snyder (1893 – 1946), had a dau <u>Arlene</u> Agnes b Feb 1, 1922 m Nov 12, 1941 Henry A. Romberger b Sep 24, 1919;

<u>Lenora</u> **Minerva** (Nov 9, 1869 – 1951), m Floyd Kemmerer (1893 – 1942), moved to Iowa.

<u>Louisa</u> **Elizabeth** (Mar 21, 1872 Loyalton – d ___), m Feb 7, 1892 Edward Franklin Miller (b Dec 17, 1869, Enterline - d May 19, 1935 Wash D.C.)

<u>John</u> **Peter** (Aug 28, 1874 – Nov 13, 1946, bur Maple Grove Cem, E'ville), m Sarah Ellen Miller (May 10, 1879 - 1964), a dau of James and Sarah Miller of Fisherville. **John Peter and Sarah Ellen (Miller) Johns had these children**: Marlin Miller (Aug 1, 1903 – 1975, bur Maple Grove Cem), m Mary Catherine Hoy (1902 – 1991), had a son <u>Marlin</u> Elmer (no dates) m Mary Waters, **had these children:** <u>Ray</u> (no dates) m Darla Radel, and had a dau *Penny R.* Ray has the garage in Gratz; <u>Stanley</u>; <u>Roger</u>.

Paul Oscar (Jan 19, 1908 – 1993, bur Maple Grove Cem, E'ville) m Ruth Susanna James (1908 – 1981)

Margaret Louisa b Jul 14, 1910, m Jul 14, 1935 Rev. Glenn E. Matter.

<u>Mary Emma</u> (1877 – 1879)

Pearl Ottilla b Nov 16, 1881, m Franz Fetterhoff, lived in Lykens. **Franz and Pearl O. (Johns) Fetterhoff had these children**: <u>Vivian</u>; <u>Harold</u>.

**MARY R (1838 – 1918, bur Maple Grove Cem, E'ville) m Fred W. Fickinger (1845 – 1939)

*DAVID JOHNS (no dates) is probably another brother to Christian and Henry]

Johns Reunion 1926

THE RICHARD BUDD FAMILY

[Richard Budd born in Queens County Ireland Apr 1,1832–d 1904, originally buried in "the old sunken" cemetery   in Williamstown, and moved to Sacred Heart Cemetery with much ceremony. He was a son of   Benjamin and Mary (Larns) Budd, and was one of five children: **Richard**; **John** went to Calif in 1854, died   there a few years later; **William** a contractor in Wmstown; **Dora** m Patrick Boerman of Phila; **Rebecca** not married lived with Richard. Benjamin   (the father) died about 1839 in Ireland, and their home was sold to an English Lord. In 1840 Mrs. Budd and the children sailed from Liverpool to New York, and then came to   Pottsville where the mother died. Richard became involved in lumbering near Pottsville. In 1861 he raised Co. K of 96th Pal Vol. and was engaged in the Civil War. He moved to Williamstown in 1864. He had married in 1852 Fanny Robison (b c1833 – Jul 30, 1880), **had these children: Christopher**, lived in Armstrong Valley; **Benjamin** d young; **John** (1852 – 1909), m Elizabeth _____ 1857 – 1934), lived in Wmstown; **George**; **William**; **Andrew** (1860 –1928,bur Sacred Heart Cem): Richard, Sr. (1861- 1925, Henry H.   bur Sacred Heart), m Mary ____ (1867 – 1941); **Allen** (1867 –1936), m May (1870 – 1948);**Joseph** d young; **Mary** d age 24; **Annie** d age 12.]

RICHARD BUDD

THE GEORGE HERMAN FAMILY

The **HERMAN/HARMAN** family came to America before the Revolutionary War, and at least three or four of them served in the militia. Jacob, Daniel and John served with Capt. Martin Weaver, and some eventually settled in Lykens Valley. David Herman served in another group. A larger account of the Herman family will be found elsewhere in this book.

George Herman was the ancestor of John C. Herman (owner of the land described above). His descendants are listed as follows:

*__GEORGE HERMAN__ (Sep 3, 1770 – Feb 17, 1848, bur St. John's Hill Cem), m Catharine M ___ (Feb 21, 1780 – Mar 17, 1845). In 1798 George was assessed for a new 30 by 25 foot dwelling house, a 45 by 20 wood barn, in Up. Pax. Twp, and lived next to Jacob Harman. They lived in Up Paxton in 1810 had 2 sons 3 dau. George made a will in which he shared his goods among the children. He designated his dwelling to his son Daniel, and he was supposed to "care for me so I don't suffer for lack of care." George and Catharine M (___) Hermann had these children (some bapt St. Johns Hill Ch);

**__John G__ b Feb 20, 1797 – Mar 8, 1866, bur St. John's Hill Cem), m Elizabeth ____ (Mar 10, 1799 – Dec 9, 1872). They lived in Washington Twp 1850, and he was a farmer. In 1860 son John & dau Susannah lived with them. Susannah was a milliner. John G. Herman's will was probated Mar 15, 1866 naming these three children: John Adam, John G., Jonathan dec'd.

 John G. and Elisabeth (___) Herman had these children
***Susannah (Nov 19, 1824 – Nov 11, 1907, bur Maple Grove Cem, E'ville). In 1860 she lived with her parents and was a milliner.
***John Adam (Feb 13, 1826 – Nov 26, 1899, bur Oak Dale Cem), m Emmaline Robinson. (Apr 4,1833 – Jan 5, 1894) lived in Wiconisco Twp in 1860 and 1880. John built the home on Daniel Romberger farm. **John Adam and Emmaline (Robinson) had these children:** Robert (Sep 10, 1858 – 1941, bur Maple Grove Cem, E'ville), m Aug 15, 1880 Sarah M. Gunderman (Feb 19, 1857 – Sep 26, 1934). **Robert and Sarah (Gunderman) Herman had these children:** Willie Otto b Aug 10, 1881; Jerry M. (1883 –1918), served during the Spanish American War, was a trumpeter in USMC 4 years; Clayton R. (Apr 18, 1885 – Aug 9, 1904); James Elmer b May 31, 1887; Jacob Oscar b Dec 21, 1892; Joseph b c1860; Henry b c1862; Eliza b c1863, m John M Harner; Mary b 1866, m Charles W. Lower; Anna or Emma E. b c1868, m

Samuel E. Schlegel; Frank b c1870, m Mary Alice, **had these children** *Emily Rebecca* b Dec 28, 1891; Susan b c1874 m John Wolf; Ellen b c1878; ***Joseph b Mar 23, 1831 – d Jan 19, 1854, bur St. John's Hill Cem). In 1850 Joseph age 20 lived with the Thomas Heller family; **William (b Jul 19, 1833 – Nov 2, 1855, bur St. John's Hill Cem);***John C. (Jul 9, 1834 - Sep 11, 1912, bur Maple Grove Cem, E'ville), m Jan 1, 1888 Emma Zimmerman (b Jul 15,1854 – d Apr 9, 1912 of diabetes), a dau of Michael Zimmerman of Washington Twp. John was a vet of the Civil War, having served in Co. K 173rd Inf, and listed as a resident of Loyalton in 1890. **John C. & Emma (Zimmerman) Harmon children**: Annie A (1888 – Sep 3,1963), of Elizabethville; John O. (1890 – d Jan 13, 1913, bur Maple Grove Cem E'ville); Margaret (1892– 1943, bur Maple Grove Cem), m Jun 15, 1907 Clayton S. Bechtel (1884 – 1926) of Elizabethville. Fannie (1896 – 1948, bur Maple Grove Cem, E'ville), m Thomas A. Amig of Illinois (1886 –1961); ***Jonathan (c1835 - ___), was married, but he died before his sister Susannah. She remembered his children in her will. He may be the one that had a daughter Kate who m Cyrus Hentsley, Lizzie m to ____ Lake.***Philip b1839 probably the one served in the Civil War; ***Martinus b 1841.]

THE DIETRICH LAND AND FAMILY

The next described land was part of several grants from Commonwealth of Pa. to Michael Dietrich in the later part of the 1700's. Several additional tracts in this vicinity were granted to other Dietrich family members, but most of their land was on the fringe of what became Lykens Township, and will not be traced in this study.

Michael Dietrich may have died before he received a patent on his land, so his two sons Jacob and John each inherited an undivided share of 229 acres 30 perches with appurtenances. Jacob and John with families, were both living on the land as early as 1805. Michael Dietrich specified that the land should be separated giving both boys individual ownership. Unfortunately documents were never prepared for the transfer in their lifetime. Jacob, one of the sons died in 1814, and several years later in 1819, a deed notes that "Michael Dietrich, grandfather died years ago." By this deed, the brother John released the half part containing 229 acres 30 perches to the heirs of Jacob and Magdalena Dietrich. Jacob had several girls and one son Jacob who inherited the land. They transferred ownership to Jacob Dietrich Jr., whom with his wife Catharine conveyed part of the land to John Matter. Another section was sold to Jacob Kuntzelman, as noted elsewhere. The area in which they settled became known as "Dietrich's".

John Dietrich the brother lived on the land he inherited in Wiconisco Twp. until his death in 1846. In his will he requested that the land be rented to a good farmer until his son John becomes 21, and then he should inherit it. (The barn was in a dilapidated condition because the railroad was built so close to the buildings. It had to be replaced (at a cost of $200), in order to sell the plantation. Twenty acres of his land was sold to pay for the new construction. The property bordered land of Henry Kuntzelman, Christian Romberger, Berry's Mountain, Jacob Dietrich, John Snyder, Henry Matter. It was eventually dispersed to several individuals.

THE MICHAEL DIETRICH FAMILY

(Some help from "Our Dietrich Lines" by William Dietrich)

The ancestry of this family goes back to **John Jacob Dietrich** (1632 - 1672), m Amelia Demuth of Pfalz, Ger & remained in their native Germany. Their son **John Jacob Dietrich** (1666-1721), m Maria Catherine, dau of Simon Moisbender, & remained in Germany, **had these children**: JOHN JACOB DIETRICH, (1695- Oct 31, 1752), m Anna Margaretta Heinrich in Pfalz, Ger. Four of their children migrated to America:GEORGE (d Earl Twp, Lanc Co, m Maria:NICHOLAS (May 15, 1727- 1813, Gettysburg), m A. Margaretta Shaffer(Nov 15, 1724-1797), dau of Johann Gerhart Shaffer. Nicholas came to America in 1749, settled in Earl Twp.;WILLIAM (1730- 1770 York Co), m Magdalena ___; MICHAEL (1736 Sims Germany - after 1800), arrived in Phila. In 1754, and settled first in Earl Twp, Lanc Co., married in 1769 to Maria Sarah Bernhard. Very little has been found mentioning Michael or his wife. They sponsored a child for Jonathan and Anna Miller at St. Johns "Hill" Church in 1788. They were buried in St. Pauls Cem, Jeff. Twp, Dau Co., which has since been destroyed. **Michael & Maria Sarah (Bernhard) Dietrich:** *JACOB DIETRICH (Feb 21, 1770 Lanc Co -1814), m A. Magdalena Hammon (Jan 22, 1776 – Mar 29, 1851, bur E'ville Cem), a dau of Philip & Mary Margaret Hammon. Jacob a Capt in War of 1812, died on way home from Frederichsburg, Md. O/C records state that Jacob died in 1814 leaving a widow Magdalena & 5 children, the oldest Jacob age 21. When he died, Jacob had a plantation with of 229 acres of land in Lykens Twp. His daughter Magd. already married to Joseph Fisher, became guardian of all the other siblings. After Jacob Dietrich died, Magdalena his widow lived in Mifflin Twp. She married John Moyer pre-1827. On November 10, 1827 John & Magdalena Moyer ("late Magd widow of Jacob Dietrich") sold the Dietrich plantation to her son Jacob, with the stipulation that her son would pay an annual dower to her in payment, as well as an eighty-dollar yearly fee. But by 1830, John Mayer left taking her money from the real estate, plus the eighty-dollar yearly sum. She testified (for the sake of receiving a divorce) that he left her destitute. She received a divorce in April 1832. Nicholas Hoffman was her petitioner for the divorce (he apparently was a relative). The orphan court settlement states that she died "leaving no husband." John Moyer continued to live in the area. In 1839 he purchased a tract of land in Mifflin Twp from Peter Moyer. In 1846 John Moyer and wife Mary sold part of the land to Joseph Lebo.

Children of Jacob and A. Magdalena Dietrich (bapt St. Johns Hill Ch, Bbg or Hoffman Ch):

**JOHN JACOB Jr. b May 1795 – d before 1848, m Catherine Fisher (d pre1848), a dau of Leonard & Susanna Fisher. They lived in Jackson Twp. Soon after the father died, the mother died also leaving several children. An orphan court record indicates that "sundry inhabitants of Washington Twp petitioned the court for a guardian for the children. John J. Dietrich was appointed.

John Jacob & Catherine (Fisher) Dietrich children (noted from orphan court record of his mother & bapt Hoffman & St. John' Ch):

*****Catherine** b Jan 4, 1816, sp Susanna Fisher, Widow; *****John Jacob** b Jul 2,1819- Nov 26,1859), m Lucinda Webner (Jul 25,1822 – Feb 19, 1902 in Lykens), dau of John & Christina (Heiser) Webner.**John Jacob & Lucinda Dietrich children:** Mary b c1845; Caroline (1847-May 31, 1996), m Apr 28, 1867 (Salem Ch, Bbg record) Frederick J. Doudon (1845 -1931), **had these children:** *Author* b c1868; *Elizabeth* b c1873; Sarah Ann (Jun 15,1849 – 1920, Saline, Il); Lucinda b c1853; Ellen Christian b Dec 5, 1856 bapt Zion Luth, Lykens; Amellia R (Oct 9, 1858- 1894), m Adam Rudisill; Rebecca. O/C paper of Dec 19, 1859 records Lucinda and names of children as heirs of John Jacob. In 1850, John J. and Lucinda Dietrich lived in Jackson Twp. In 1860 widow Lucinda and her children lived in Wic.Twp. *****Susanna** b Jul 3, 1821; *****Isaac Franklin** b 1826, m Elizabeth;*****Sarah Anna** b Aug 4,1826, m Edward Weidman Feb 25, 1866, in Bbg; *****Hanna** b Jun 29,1828;*****Samuel** (d 1893)*****Thomas** (1832 –1911), a Civil War Vet, m 1ˢᵗ Caroline Coleman (1832 - 1906), m 2ⁿᵈ Lydia Alleman (1851 – 1927); *****Joseph Russel** (1835 – 1873); *****Francis** (1839 – 1892)

**MAGDALENA b Jan 23, 1797 was under 21 when her father died. She m Joseph Fisher (Jul 24, 1796 Bethel Twp, Berks Co – May 31, 1853, d of consumption, bur E'ville), a son of Leonard & Susanna (Sausser) Fisher. They lived in Washington Twp in 1850.When her father died, Magdalena and Joseph Fisher were appointed guardian of her siblings.

Joseph and Magdalena (Dietrich) Fisher children (some bapt St. John's Hill Ch):

*****Catherine** (Jul 3, 1817 – Jan 20, 1877, bur Old Stone Ch, E'ville) m Christian Kemmerer (Aug 2, 1808 – Jan 19, 1882), **had these children:** John F. (Apr 12, 1842 – Jun 11, 1863), d during Civil War; Magdalena (1848 – 1865); Amanda (1857 – 1872); Christiana Sybilla b Aug 14, 1860 – 1861; *****John** b Apr 8, 1819; *****Susanna** (b Jan 30, 1821 – Oct 21, 1894, bur E'ville), 2ⁿᵈ wife of Adam Q Bender (Sep 1, 1808 – Jan 13, 1884). Susanna and Adam Q. bender purchased the Magdalena Dietrich homestead in E'ville; *****Amelia** (Aug 20, 1822 – Jun 20, 1868, bur St. John Hill Cem) 1ˢᵗ wf of Benjamin Romberger (Jan 17,1821 – Feb 29, 1904). They lived in Mifflin Twp in 1860 on land that they received from her father in 1836. **Benjamin & Amelia (Fisher) Romberger children:** Daniel (1844- 1870), m Mary Moyer; Joseph (1848 – 1916), m Mary Sophia Yeager (1844 – 1920), a dau of Henry Yeager; Mary b c1850; Nathan (1852- 1916), m Mary Ellen Shepley (1855 – 1923); *****Joseph A**.b Aug 24, 1824 - d ___ Illinois), m Elizabeth Mayer (Oct 17, 1825 - Jul 29, 1842), a dau of Peter and Hannah (Schoffstall) Mayer). They moved to Ogle Co.,Ill. in 1854; *****Sarah Ann** b Mar 20, 1826; *****Maria** b May 11, 1830, m William Hoffman; *****Hannah** (no dates) m John Messner;

AMELIA (Feb 14,1799–Feb 6,1885, bur Salem Luth Cem, E'ville), m Ludwig Lenker b May 30, 1798, son of Stephanus & Susanna (Deck) Lenker. **Ludwig & Amelia (Dietrich) Lenker children:

*****Catharine** (Oct 4, 1820 –1891), m Christian Matter;*****John** (Sep 9,1822 –1884), m Sarah Noll (1824 –1912), lived in Wash Twp in 1850. **John & Sarah (Noll) Lenker children:** Sarah b c1845; Geo. Wash b c1846; Mary Jane b c1847; John b c1849; *****Elisabeth** b Aug 16, 1824, m ___ Hoover;*****Jacob** b Mar 31,1827;*****Michael** b 1834;*****Joseph**; *****Stephen** *****Susanna** (1836 –1912), m Geo. W. Buffington (1832 –1871); *****Annie** b c1838 m Henry Bordner.

ANN MARIA (Polly) (Mar 15, 1803 – Nov 11, 1865), m Henry Matter (Dec 26, 1796 – Oct 1, 1868, of Lykens, bur E'ville), a son of Michael & Anna Mara (Romberger) Matter. Henry Matter was a vet of the War of 1812. In 1850 Anna Maria and Henry Matter lived in Washington Twp, and they had Rebecca 11, and Sarah Sheesley age 9 with them. **Henry & Ann Maria (Dietrich) Matter had these children: *****Elisabeth** (Feb 6, 1820 - Feb 9, 1891), m 1ˢᵗ David Sheesley, 2ⁿᵈ George Gilbert; 3ʳᵈ Philip Bowman (no dates); *****Thomas** (Apr 21, 1821 – May 1879), m

1ˢ Margaret Fetterhoff, 2ⁿᵈ Lovina Lenker; ***<u>Catharine</u> (Jan 26, 1823 – Mar13, 1915, bur Motter Cem), m Philip Wilvert (Oct 29, 1821 –Nov 2,1893). [See Wilvert family];***<u>Margaret Rebecca</u> (Mar 18, 1825 – Jun 22, 1890 in Abilene Ks), m Jacob Frederick Eisenhouer; <u>Nicholas</u> (Dec 7, 1827 – Jun 23, 1865), m Matilda Lebo; ***<u>Enoch</u> (Apr 5, 1829 – May 22, 1892), m Margaret Ann Reisch;***<u>Sarah</u> b c1830, m George R. Williard b c1826;***<u>Washington</u> (Jan 16, 1832 – Sep 26, 1878), m Margaret Kumbler (1829 – 1898); ***<u>Mary Ann</u> (May 25, 1841 – Feb 9, 1904), m Emanuel Bohner (1836 – 1904).

HANNA (Dec 24, 1812 – Oct 23, 1896, bur Peace Cem, Bbg), m Robert F. Elder (Sep 1, 1800 – Aug 13, 1854). He had about 17 acres of land in Washington Twp, bordering on land of George Lupold and heirs of Martin Paul. Robert F. and Hannah (Dietrich) Elder had a son Robert Thompson b Apr 6,1850. In 1850 Robt & Hannah Elder lived next to Michael & Elizabeth Dietrich & son Elias,14. Robert died in Derry Twp. **Robert & Hanna (Dietrich) Elder children: ***<u>Mary</u> b c1833; ***<u>David</u> (1838-1908, Masonic Home, Phila), m Catherine Stoever; ***<u>Victoria</u> b 1841; ***<u>Rosetta</u> b 1838; ***<u>Thomas</u> b 1845;, moved to Carroll Co., Ind; ***<u>Ann</u> b 1843; ***<u>Emma</u> b 1850. In 1860 Rosetta, a milliner,Victoria & Annie, teachers, & Thomas farm hand lived together in Wash. Twp.

*<u>**JOHN** DIETRICH</u> (Nov 7, 1771 Lanc Co – c May 1846), m Anna Barbara Matter (b1766 - ____). John and Anna Barbara lived in Wiconisco and Washington Township, and owned various acreages of land. Prior to his death, Johannes made a lengthy will describing his wishes for dividing his land and money. John Paul, Jr. served as executor, and is probably responsible for writing the five page will which is written in beautiful calligraphy. [John Paul, Jr. was noted for his calligraphy.] The will was penned on September 18, 1845 and probated June 1846. The will does not mention a wife. It does name six children: Emanuel, John, Jr., Peter, Catherine, Christina & Michael. Each of them inherited land and money. **John and Anna Barbara (Matter) Dietrich had these children (some bapt St. John's Hill Ch):**

<u>Emanuel</u> (Jun 24, 1797 – c May 1847), Wiconisco Twp m Anna Maria Daniel (Sep 15, 1798 – May 23, 1850), a dau of Andreas & Susanna (Hoy) Daniel. They had a 232 acre farm lying in both Wiconisco and Washington Township. Also 11 acres of mountain land with buildings in Washington Twp. **Emanual and A. Maria (Daniel) Dietrich had these children (bap St. Johns Hill & Hoffman Ch):
***<u>Jonas D.</u> (Aug 13, 1819 – Jun 17, 1891, bur Zion Meth, Jefferson Twp), m 1ˢᵗ Mary ____ (Jun 11, 1816 – Jun 18,1847), m 2ⁿᵈ Rebecca (May 19, 1818 – Mar 3, 1899). They had several children died young.
***<u>Juliana</u> b Mar 12, 1820
***<u>Maria Anna</u> b Sep 18, 1821
***<u>Isaac F</u> (Apr 27, 1823 – 1893), m Susanna McCoy (1829 –1893), lived in Wiconisco Twp in 1850, later in Jackson Twp., in 1870 Juniata Co., Tower City, Sch. later. **Isaac and Susanna Dietrich had these known children:** <u>Ann Mary</u> b c1849; <u>Emanuel</u> probably the one (1849 – 1936, bur Seyfert Cem), m Redulla __ (1855 – 1930); <u>Wilson</u> (Feb 13, 1859 Juniata Co – May 15, 1929, Reading), m Margaret McAllister (1860 – 1948), had about 11 children.
***<u>Amanda</u> (Dec 24, 1824 – Mar 5, 1896, bur Fairview Cem, Enders), m Peter J. Enders (May 28, 1824 – Oct 24, 1903), a son of John & Sarah (Ettinger) Enders of Jackson Twp. He was a shoemaker and Civil War Vet. They had about 12 children.

<u>Johannes Harper</u> (Nov 26, 1798 - cMay 1846), m Catharine Russel (1800- 1872, bur Oak Dale Cem). He died in WiconiscoTwp In his will he requests that the land be rented to a good farmer until his son John becomes 21, and then he should inherit it. (The barn was in a dilapidated condition because the railroad was built so close to the buildings. It had to be replaced (at a cost of $200), in order to sell the plantation. Twenty acres of his land was sold to pay for the new construction. The land bordered land of Henry Kuntzelman, Christian Romberger, Berry's Mtn, Jacob Dietrich, John Snyder, Henry Matter. **John H and Catharine Dietrich had these children:
***<u>John Harper, Jr.</u> (1842 – 1916, bur Calvary Meth Cem, Wic), m Mary A. Woland (1845 – 1916), a dau of John & Lydia (Heckert) Woland; ***<u>Catherine Elmira</u>. (children minors when father died)

<u>Maria Sarah</u> b May 23, 1800, bapt St. John's Hill Ch, parents John and A. Barbara Dietrich. We have no other information for her except that the Gratz Historical Society has a dower chest imprinted: **"MARIA SARA DIETRICH - Lykens Township". The only other possible candidate that we found as the owner of that chest, is the Mary Sarah Dietrich who was sponsor at the baptism of this Mary Sarah.

Peter (b Oct 16,1801, bapt Hoffman Ch -1840), m Elizabeth Buffington (Jan 31, 1811 – Apr 4, 1885, bur Straws Cem.). They lived in Wiconisco Twp. When Peter died, Jacob D. Hoffman became guardian of his four minor children. Peter received real estate posthumously from his grandfather John Dietrich. Peter's four children were named as heirs. In 1860 his 46 acres of land was sold to John A. Harman . **Peter & Elizabeth Dietrich had four children:** ***John Levi** c1829; ***Sarah Ann** (May 10, 1833– Dec 6,1863, bur Straw Cem, Enders), m Jonathan Shoop; ***Catherine Elizabeth**; ***Susanna Barbara**;

Anna Catharine (Mar 13, 1803 - Jan 15, 1866), m George Botts b 1798. [See Botts genealogy];

Christina b c1804, m George Dennis, **had these children:** Elizabeth; George, according to father's will.

Michael b Mar 10,1805 m Elizabeth Lubold b Nov 10,1812 (bapt St. Johns Ch), dau of Geo. & Elizabeth (Buffington) Lubold. In 1841, Michael released his share of his fathers land to John Dietrich Jr. Michael & Elizabeth Dietrich lived in Wash. Twp in 1850 & 1860; in Jackson Twp in 1880. Their son Elias age 25 and Lucian H. Dietrich age 5 lived with them in 1860. **Michael & Elizabeth Dietrich had one known child:**
***Elias** (1836 –Oct 23, 1902, bur Union Cem)), m Nov 22, 1860 Amanda Welker (Mar 4, 1840- 1917), lived in Wiconisco Twp in 1880 and George Welker age 27, a brother-in-law was living with them. **Elias & Amanda (Welker) Dietrich children (bapt St. Johns Luth, Lykens);**

Louisa (Apr 7, 1862- Jul 1, 1932 d from a fall from a tree), m 1st Barry Row, lived with parents in 1880, was a seamstress. Later m Elias L. Schwartz, and still later on May 28, 1887 to James William Orr.

Solomon (Apr 28, 1863 – 1931, bur Fair View Cem), m Lillian Bainbridge (1870 – 1932)

George D. (Sep 28, 1864 – Nov 5, 1943), m Mar 5, 1885 Emma D. Pell (Feb 21, 1867 – Nov 21, 1946)-

Amanda (Jul 17, 1865- Mar 8, 1947 in Ferndale, Mich, m Leopold Marks.

John C. (Sep 17, 1867- Dec 2, 1935, bur Shamokin), m Emma Elizabeth Doney (1868 – 1954).

Sarah Adaline (Jan 31,1868-1947), m Richard Williams (1868–1935).

Isaac Oliver (Apr 15, 1871 – Oct 28, 1938), m Aug 27, 1892 Sarah J. Schomper (1877 – 1950), a dau of George Schomper of Wiconisco. **Isaac and Sarah J. (Schomper) Dietrich children:** *John* (1893-1941); *George* (1895 – 1940), m Margaret Bottiger, **had these children:** *Violet* & *George* Jr.; *Harry (1897– 1962),* m Hazel Hoke (1902 –1973), **had these children;** *Helen*, m Chas Coleman; *Harry* m Barbara Hoover; *Samuel* b c1873, m Lydia Shiley; *Eva* m Clarence Miller; *Amanda* m Carl Reismiller; *Charles* m Madeline Saunders; *Sarah* m Joseph Ulsh; *Carrie* m Harold Clough;

Samuel Elias (Feb 14, 1874- 1935), m Lydia Shiley;

Alfred Monroe b Nov 14, 1875, m Annie L. __ b Jun 1875.

Catherine Rebecca Mar 25, 1878

Edward H. (Dec 23, 1880- Nov 23, 1951), m Emma Woland (1877 – 1944), lived in Michigan.

Harry Wilson (Sep 7, 1881 – 1963, bur Seibert Cem, Wic), m Sarah Ann Doud (1877 – 1946).

Mable May (Aug 21, 1883- 1961), m 1st Harry P. Fullmer, 2nd Horace Stoner Glace.

Dietrich family- stg: Harry, brother, brother, Samuel, brother. std: Sarah (Shomper)Dietrich; Amanda (Welker) Dietrich; Isaac Oliver.

THE KUNTZELMAN LAND

The land of Henry Kuntzelman was comprised of several different tracts of land, purchased on separate occasions. It was located immediately west of the Oak Dale Forge, and during the first years was in an isolated area. Later when the railroad came, his land bordered along the tracks near the Oak Dale train station. [See 1875 map.] Henry Kuntzelman purchased at least four different tracts giving him over 200 acres total. Some of the acreage came from the Commonwealth of Pennsylvania grant to Jacob Dietrich. Kuntzelman purchased 98 acres of that land from Jacob and Catherine Dietrich on May 11, 1829. Another section came from the James Way grant and was purchased in 1826. A small portion was from the Peter Henn grant, and may have been his first purchase of land. Kuntzelman purchased another tract from the heirs of Martin Paul on April 9, 1831. Henry Kuntzelman was taxed for land as early as 1820, and that year the census records him with a family, and an older female, perhaps his mother or mother-in-law. He had 135 acres of mountain land, 25 acres with a house, plus 30 acres and 31 acres in 1837, and his son Henry Kunzelman Jr was living on one of the properties that he would be inheriting from his father.

The Kuntzelman family (three generations of them) resided here, and later began to sell some of their land (several small tracts as well as larger tracts) to other settlers and investors. This was a busy and thriving area for many years while coal was being transported by rail, and passenger service was available from Oak Dale Station. However, very little evidence of its importance has survived, as much of it later became mostly woodland.

Henry Kuntzelman, Sr. was a minister in the Methodist Episcopal conference and served this area as an itinerant pastor as early as 1814. Henry (Sr.) apparently spent most of his time farming, but had a personal interest in the welfare of the Methodist Episcopal, United Brethren in Christ, and the Evangelical churches that were established near Loyalton. When he wrote his will in 1829, he considered giving his farm for the use of the Methodist Congregation "if all of his heirs died." Later he voided that part of his will, but in 1834 he did officially convey a lot containing ninety-two perches to the trustees of the Methodist and U.B. Congregations for a school and church. He gave it in "love and affection." His son Henry Jr. did inherit the remainder of his land.

On October 24, 1857, not long before his wife died, Henry (Jr.) and Elizabeth Kuntzelman conveyed this plantation of 81 acres 152 perches of land to their son Elias Kuntzelman. The land bordered the estate of John Dietrich, David Matter, north to Jacob Way and Philip Wilvert They also sold a separate two-acres with appurtenances to him.

Will of Henry Kuntzelman, Sr.

I Henry Kuntzelman Sr. of Lykens Township being of middling health of body and sound mind desire to settle my worldly affairs whilst I have strength and capacity to do so, now make and publish this my last will. He gives soul to the creator.

His real estate and personal property to his son Henry or his heirs except that his beloved wife Mary shall have the new springhouse for her only use. She shall have the clock, the brick stove, weaving loom with all that belongs to it and three beds and bedsteads, two cows and three sheep and son Henry shall find her a horse to ride at all times. She shall have her saddle and bridle and the Dearborn wagon with the harness. She shall have everything she needs out of the house and kitchen furniture and my son Henry shall find sufficient feed for her cows and sheep and shall feed them himself and take care of them. My son Henry shall find her sufficient wood – make it fine and bring it to the house and give her yearly twenty five bushels of wheat and he shall take it to the mill and bring the flour to her house again. My son Henry shall give her yearly one hundred fifty pounds swine and fifty pounds of beef, 30 pounds of sachess (sausage?) if she wants it. Also fifteen pounds heckel flax and fifteen pound of Joe ? every year and fifteen dollars in money every years.

If my beloved wife shall get sick my son Henry shall find a person to wait on her during her sickness and if a doctor she wants, he must get one and pay him. This all my son Henry must do and fulfill during her lifetime or widow hood. But if my beloved wife shall marry again she shall leave the house and premises and shall have no more than one cow, one bed and bestead, one chest and her spinning wheel. It is my wish that no appraisement and no vendue shall be and if my son Henry shall die before my wife Mary and this place shall be rented it shall not be rented without her will and consent.

(THE NEXT PART IS CROSSED OUT)

If my son Henry shall die and his heirs shall all die then it is my will that after the death of my beloved wife all my property shall be for the use of the Methodist Episcopal Church. The present property may be sold and the money put on interest but the real property shall only be rented? by and the r____ for this r---- and interest from the money if the personal shall be full amount for the _____ yearly.

(next not crossed out)
And I do hereby appoint my son Henry executive of this my last will and testament. In witness where of I Henry Kuntzelman Sr the testator have to this my will consisting of one sheet of paper set my hand and seal this fifteen day of January 1829.
N.B. my son Henry shall give my beloved wife Mary every year during her lifetime or widowhood as much salt and lard and vinegar as she needs.
N.B. And son Henry shall not sell any of my land as long as my beloved wife Mary shall live without her free will and consent.

Henry Kuntzelman Sr

The will was witnessed by Michael Dietrich, John Dietrich, Jr. (both sworn Aug 14, 1841 before John H. Hoffman Register.

THE KUNTZELMAN FAMILY
(Early information from Annette Kunselman Burgert research)

[The earliest known member of the KUNTZELMAN family is **BARTHOLOMAI KUNTZELMAN**, the immigrant ancestor whom landed in America on the ship "MOLLY" on October 16, 1741. Among the passengers was his family and brother-in-law Christian Comens, originally from Morschheim, Germany. Bartholomai was b c1696 and came from Wendelsheim, Germany. On February 16, 1737, Bartholomai, who was by then a widower, and Maria Barbara Comens, b Jul 19, 1715, a dau of John Philipps and Maria Esther Comens, were married, according to the Lutheran Church record at Wendelsheim.

After coming to America this family settled in Lebanon Township, Lancaster (now Lebanon) County as early as 1755. They later moved to Hanover Township. Bartholomai died there sometime in 1774. He penned his will on November 25,1773, it was probated at Lancaster on September 28, 1774. His wife inherited most of his estate. About a year after he died, his widow Maria Barbara married Peter Bucher. The marriage was performed by Rev. John Casper Stoever on Sep 28, 1775 in Hanover Twp.
Bartholomai and Maria Barbara (Comens) Kuntzelman had these known children:
ANNA CATHARINA b Nov 22, 1740 (nothing more known)
JOHANN PHILIPS (b Dec 23, 1737 in Wendelsheim, Germany – d Jul10,1809 in Berks Co., Pa.). He is believed to be the man named (probably by mistake) "Jacob" Kuntzelman who was married Jun 1, 1760 to Barbara Diem, at First Ref. Ch Lancaster. In all other records he is referred to as Philip. For several years Philip and Barbara lived in Hanover Township, but by 1772 had moved to Northumberland County. They later moved back to Stumpstown, the region now known as Fredericksburg, Lebanon County. Philip was an innkeeper in 1783. On May 15, 1776, he received a warrant for twenty-five acres of land in Berks County. Another tract containing 300 acres called "Indian Camp" was located on Pine Creek in Pine Grove Township, Schuylkill County. He had an inn at this location from 1796, probably until his death. It was located along the path from Tulpehocken to Sunbury. Philip Kuntzelman died in 1809, his will dated Jul 10, 1809, was probated Aug 29, 1809 in Reading, Berks Co (His residence had since become Mahantango Twp, Sch Co.) The date of death for Barbara has not been found, but it probably occurred in 1830, since final disposal of her husbands' estate took place at that time. **Philip and Barbara (Diem) Kuntzelman had these children:**
PHILIP ADAM (b Dec 23, 1761 Berks Co –d Oct 29, 1834, Broome Co., N.Y), m 1st Catharina possibly Foster or Ferster (b _____ - d Nov 22, 1822 at Nanticoke, N.Y.). About 1793, Philip Adam and his family moved to Broome County, New York. After Catharina died, Philip married Sally Moyer. **Philip Adam and Catharina Kuntzelman had these children:**
Anna Catharine (b May 12, 1781, bapt Hoffman Ch – d Oct 25, 1857 Broome Co., N.Y.), m James Clock;
John (b c1783 – d Aug 2, 1862), m 1st Wealthy Ames, 2nd Elizabeth Canfield;
John Philip (b Jan 2, 1785 bapt St. Johns Ch Fredericksburg, Leb Co – d Jan 14, 1848), m Betsey Bundy;
John Heinrich (b Nov 12, 1786 bapt Klingers Ch – d 1877), m 1st Harriet Ames, 2nd Susan Wilkinson;
John Peter b Oct 30, 1788, bapt Klinger Ch, m Feb 15, 1812 in N.Y. Jerusha Akerly, had 14 children;
Barbara (b _____ - Jun 27, 1839), m 1st ___ Bacon, 2nd _____ Roselle, 3rd ____ Akerly;
Elizabeth b c1791 Broome Co., N.Y – d 1866), m John Ames;
Jacob (b Mar 12, 1793, Nanticoke, N. Y. – d Jun 9, 1862), m Polly Gates;
Samuel (no dates), m Persis;
David b c1796, Nanticoke, N.Y.- d 1881), m Eliza Hovey

BARBARA (c1771 –d 1830 Hubley Twp, Sch Co her will probated Jul 28,), m c1790 Johan Philip Artz (b Feb 6, 1764 Tulpehocken Twp, Berks Co.- d pre Jun 23,1826 date will probated), son of Jacob & Anna Eva (Braun) Artz. **Philip and Barbara (Kuntzelman) Artz had these children (most bapt Klinger Ch:**
Maria Barbara (b Jul 12, 1791 – Feb 24, 18__), m Johann Jacob Coleman (Jul 14, 1792 – Oct 9, 1822, bur Coleman Cem, Lyk Twp);
John Michael (b Oct 20, 1792 – d Apr 25, 1842, m Catharine Ossman (Jan 5, 1795 – Jan 21, 1881, bur Artz Cem, Sacramento, Sch Co) , a dau of James and Magd Margaret Ossman.
Eve Maria (b Feb 13, 1794 – Jul 11, 1885, bur Artz Cem), m Philip Dietrich (Mar 5, 1794 – Jan 28, 1871), a son of John and Barbara Dietrich ;
Philip (Nov 6, 1795 – Jan 27, 1856), m Catharine Bressler (b ___ d 1881, bur Friedens Cem, Hegins), a dau of Michael and Barbara (Hetzel) Bressler.
Johannes (b Jul 13, 1797 – Jul 13, 1842, bur Artz Cem), m Barbara Stine (May 5, 1801 – Jan 9, 1883), a dau of Peter and Hanna Stein.
Elisabeth (b Aug 18, 1799 – d May 11, 1866, bur Artz Cem), m Peter Coleman (Jul 25, 1799 – Aug 26, 1855), a son of Carl and Barbara (Stein) Coleman.
Susanna (b Nov 11, 1801 – Jan 10, 1877, bur Simeon Cem, Gratz, Pa.), m John E. Buffington (May 29, 1799 – Feb 21, 1866)
Jacob (b Feb 8, 1803 ? - d Aug 26, 1883, bur Artz Cem), m Rachael Hartman (b Oct 15, 1801 Montg. Co, Pa. –d Sep 3, 1890), dau of Henry and Sarah (Herner) Hartman from Gratz
David (b Jun 16, 1805 – Jun 2, 1879, bur Artz Cem), m Sarah _____ (Mar 11, 1813 – Oct 18, 1876)
George b after 1806 moved to Jefferson Co, Pa.
Catharine b after 1806 m Daniel Otto (Sep 28, 1809- a son of William and Margaret (Kessler) Otto. In 1838 he purchased land in Red Bank Twp, Armstrong Co with Philip Kuntzelman
Lydia b after 1806 m George Young and move to western Pa.

JOHANNES (Oct 11, 1775 – Jan 24, 1850) bur Friedens Luth Cem, Hegins, Scho Co., m c1794 Margaretha (Mary) Reissen (?). (Jul 1775 – Dec 5, 1858). **Johannes and Margaretha (Reissen) Kuntzelman had thirteen children – eleven survived their parents (some bapt Klinger's Ch):**
Christina (no dates) d before her father, m Joseph Holdeman. Their children moved to Will Co., Ill. with their father.
John (b Dec 3,1795 Sch. Co – d Apr 14, 1871 in Red Bank Twp, Armstrong Co, Pa.), m 1st in 1817, Elizabeth Hoffa (b Jul 24, 1796 Schaefferstown, Leb Co – d Mar 3, 1841 in Erdman, Dau Co, bur Klinger's Cem), a dau of Abraham and Elisabeth (Van Der Sluess) Hoffa. He m 2nd Magdalena widow of George Ferringer, who died 1846. He may have married for a third time, to Magdalena (Otto) Kuntzelman, widow of his brother Philip. John and his family lived in Lower Mahantango Twp., Sch Co where he worked as a blacksmith from about 1817 to 1834. At this time he moved to Red Bank Twp, Armstrong Co., Pa. According to his will he had four children. Abraham b Jul 20, 1818;
Philip (c1796 – May 1846, Redbank Twp, Armstrong Co), m Magdalena Otto b Nov 6, 1795, a dau of William and Agatha (Struphauer) Otto – d Sep 24, 1865). They lived in Low Mahantango Twp as early as 1818, but in 1833 moved to Red Bank Twp, Armstrong Co., where he purchased 200 acres of land in 1834. **Philip and Magdalena (Otto) Kuntzelman had these children:** **Elias** (1822 – 1891), m Margaret Schaffner; **John P.** (1825 – 1891) m Susanna Hoffman; **Catharine** (c1826 – 1888), m Leander Weinberg and moved to Michigan; **Lavina** (1826 – 1858), m Samuel Koppenheffer; **Margaret** (1828 – 1898), m George Lenkert; **Moses** b 1829, moved to St. Joseph Co, Michigan; **William** b 1833 moved to Kalamazoo Co., Mich.; **Lydia** b 1837 moved to St. Joseph Co. Mich.
Peter (Feb 11, 1797, bap Klingers Ch – d 1873 Mercer Co), m Sara Deibler b Jun 15, 1803, a dau of Mathias and Anna Cath Eliz Etzweiler Deibler. They lived here in Upper Dau Co, but later moved to Coolspring, Jefferson Co, then Mercer Co., Pa. **They had twelve children:** **Joel** b Jun 27, 1820 bapt Hoffman Ch.
M. Catharina (Jul 22, 1800 – Nov 2, 1873), m Michael Paul (Sep 21, 1798 – May 3, 1879), a son of Elias and Elizabeth Paul. They are bur at Howerter Cem in Mahantango Valley, Sch Co.
John Heinrich bapt Sep 26, 1802 at St. Jacobs Church, Pine Grove Twp, Sch Co. - d in Armstrong Co)
George (1805 – Mar 31, 1868, d in Armstrong Co), m Martha ___ (b ---- d Oct 10, 1891), Lived in Lower Mahantango Twp, where he was employed as a miller. In 1833 they moved to Red Bank, Armstrong Co.

Jonathan (b May 15, 1806 Hegins, Sch Co – Nov 24, 1879, bur Orwin Ref Cem), m Elizabeth Henninger (Feb 2,1818 - Jul 12, 1900), a dau of George and Elisabeth (Miller) Henninger. They had eight children.
David b c1807 – d Armstrong Co. He m Catharine Ferringer, dau of George and Magdalena Ferringer, and by 1833 moved to Red Bank Twp, Armstrong Co.
Elisabeth b c1812 – d Sep 2, 1895 Armstrong Co), m Jun 16, 1833 to Henry Fetter, in Sch Co., but moved to Red Bank Twp, Armstrong Co.
Daniel (Jan 29, 1814 – Oct 13, 1894 Armstrong Co, bur New Salem Cem, Red BankTwp), m Sarah _____ (1816 – Dec 10, 1891), moved to Red Bank Twp. They had eight children.
Solomon (b c1817 Sch Co – d in Tremont, Pa.), m Lydia Bixler (Nov 14, 1822 – Jun 17, 1895, bur Salem Luth & Ref Cem, Rough & Ready, Sch Co), a dau of John and Susan (Geist) Bixler of Mahantongo Twp, Sch Co.
Michael (b 1822 Sch Co – d 1891 Ogle Co, Ill, bur North Grove Evang Cem, m Jun 6, 1847 in Pa. to Lydia Ossman (b Mar 14, 1828 Sch Co – d May 8, 1911 in Ogle Co, Ill.), a dau of Philip and Barbara (Friedline) Ossman. They moved to Armstrong Co, later to Egan, Ill.
HEINRICH (b May 17, 1783 Fredericksburg, Sch Co – d Nov 13, 1840, bur Motter Cem, E'ville, Dau Co. m Mary Ferringer (c1781 – Mar 28, 1850), a dau of George Ferringer, Sr of Low Mahantango Twp, Sch Co. Heinrich was the land owner in Loyalton as mentioned previously.
Henry and Mary (Ferringer) Kuntzelman Sr had one child:
Henry Kuntzelman, Jr. (b May 28, 1807 in Pine Valley, Sch Co – d Jan 19, 1880, bur IOOF Lykens), m Elizabeth McLean (b Jun 1, 1805 – d Dec 9, 1858) of Irish descent, born in Millersburg. Elizabeth was a dau of John and Elizabeth McClain, bapt Salem Lutheran Ch, Killinger. In 1828, Henry Kuntzelman had a farm in the area of Loyalton and some mountain land. Henry Jr. was a tenant on the farm. He continued to be a tenant until 1837 when he inherited his fathers homestead. In 1860 Henry Kuntzelman (Jr.) lived alone in a two family home. His son Moses and family lived in the other part.
Henry and Elizabeth (McLean) Kuntzelman had these children:
Elias b c1829, m Elizabeth _____ b c1829. **Elias and Elizabeth Kuntzelman had these children :**Emma J b 1849; John W. b 1850; Franklin b c1852; Catherine b c1854; Malinda (b & d 1855, bur Motter's Cem); Ann b c1856. They are probably the ones who eventually moved to Illinois;
Josiah b c1827, died in the army during Civil War;
 Amos (Mar 20, 1833 –Nov 29, 1905 of Apoplexy, bur IOOF, Lykens), m in 1851 to Sarah Hoffman (Oct 4, 1833 –d Jan 13, 1865) a dau of ___. Amos learned the trade of a tailor in Lykens, worked four years then began his own business as merchant tailor in Lykens. In 1860 Malinda Paul age 24 lived with the family and was an apprentice tailoress. When the Civil War broke out, he enlisted at Pottsville Sep. 23, 1861 in Co G 96th Regt. Pa. Vol. He became ill from exposure during the battles and was hospitalized for two months, then was discharged in June 1862. He came home and became an agent for Singer Sewing Machines, but later re-enlisted in Co B. Ninth Pa Cavalry. He was in some of the campaigns, and was appointed division tailor. After his discharge on May 29, 1865, he returned to Lykens, pursued the sewing machine business for the remainder of his life. **Amos and Sarah (Hoffman) Kuntzelman had these children:** William H. (1852 - 1934, bur IOOF Cem, Lykens), m Rebecca A _____ (1853 - 1920), he was a miner in Lykens; Isaiah b c1853, a tailor in Bainbridge, Lancaster Co; Mary b c1859, m H. E. Rumlinger, manufacturer of Phila; Clara m Charles Foster a railroader of Bradford Co, Pa. After Sarah died, Amos married Oct 23, 1865 Sarah C. Eisenhower (b Nov 7, 1832 - d May 5, 1882) of Halifax, **had one child:** Robert A.. a minor.
Moses bc1837 -), m Catherine (c1837 -). In 1860 Moses and Catheriine lived in a separate part of his father Henry Kuntzelman's house. They later moved to Nebraska. **Had these children:** Hannah b c1859; Aaron I Kuntzelman (1867- 1937 bur Fairview Cem Wmstown his wife Emma J (1874 - 1967)

ELIAS KUNTZELMAN SELLS HIS LAND

Elias Kuntzelman began to dispose of some of his land. In addition to the land he received from his father he accumulated several small tracts from other sources. He sold his land by conveying the tracts of land to several different buyers, some in the same acreage that he received. The land in this section of Oak Dale is located on the southern end of the Kuntzelman tracts. Over several years during the 1860 to 1900 period it was purchased and repurchased many times, in several cases the same persons exchanging their land. It was mostly transferred between members of the families of Botts, Russell, Nutt and Mayer who had intermarried. Some of the land of Elias Kuntzelman bordered on the old railroad tracts, and extended the small village of houses near the Oak Dale Station. It became a very attractive secluded community, each house built on a small tract of land, surrounded by enough farmland with fruit trees and gardens to keep them supplied with food. The store and the post office at the forge provided them with other essentials and kept them in touch with the outside world. The forge provided an opportunity for excellent employment of various types. Today, a visitor to this site on the north side of Berry's Mountain will find mostly grown up woods with little evidence of even foundations of those old log buildings.

LAND SOLD TO MOSES BOTTS (6 acres on 1875 Map)

On April 18, 1860, Elias and Elizabeth Kuntzelman of Wiconisco Township sold 2 acres, 115 5/10 perches to Mrs. Catharine Botts. This land adjoined the land of the old railroad, south to the land of Moses Nutt, and Catherine Botts other land, then north to Elias Kuntzelman other land. It was part of the tract of land that was patented to Michael Dietrich in September 1818, and on March 21, 1856 was conveyed to Catharine Botts (maiden name Dietrich). Apparently at least one house was on this land. Catharine and her husband George Botts conveyed it to Elias Kuntzelman in April 1860, but he sold it back to her. The two acre tract and another tract containing 130 9/10 square perches was sold on April 8, 1870 by Catharine Botts to George W. Botts of Berrysburg.

Moses Botts owned another 5 acres of land with a 2-story log house, fruit trees etc. It was bound north and west by land of John Harman, south to Joseph Russell and the railroad tracks. (This land on 1862 (map). On April 27, 1876, a sheriff sale was held transferring the land to Benjamin Wingard. After Benjamin died, his administrator, John Wingard held an auction and sold to Jacob Wingard in January 1882. Jacob Wingard conveyed to Sarah M. Barry Apr 15, 1882. After Sarah M. Barry died, the property went to Ann and John Ditterman on July 24, 1909. Eventually John and Ann Ditterman moved to Kansas, and sold to Sarah Ellen Harman, whose heirs sold to Daniel C. Romberger Dec 27, 1934. Kate M. Lebo was the next owner.

THE BOTTS /BETZ ETC. FAMILY

[The **BOTTS/BETZ** family has been elusive in doing our research. We have not been able to connect the earliest ancestors to the family that lived in this area.
*JOHN BOTTS, Sr. (-d pre 1835), m Hannah _____. They lived in Mifflin Twp., on land they purchased from George and Susanna Lebo in April 1819. Hannah sold the land to John Botts, Jr. and George Botts in 1834.
Children (some bapt St. John's Hill Ch):
**JOHN, JR (- d pre 1835).
**GEORGE b c1798 m Anna Catharina Dietrich (Mar 13, 1803 bapt St. John's Hill Church, Bbg – Jan 15, 1866), a dau of John and Anna Barbara (Matter) Dietrich. In 1850 they lived in Lykens Twp., in 1860 lived in Wiconisco Twp (the township lines changed).
George and Catherine (Deitrich) Botts had these children: (The 1st & 2nd ones, George & Hiram have not been proven)
***George W. (Dec 27, 1827 – Feb 9, 1874, bur Peace Cem, Bbg), m Susannah _____ (b Jul 25, 1823 – Mar 21,1872). In 1850 and 1860 they lived in Mifflin Twp and he was a tailor. Josiah Mertz age 12 lived with them. In 1870 George W. and family lived in Berrysburg and he was listed as an agent for sewing machines. When George W. Botts died in 1874, his tract of land in Mifflin Twp., was sold to Jonathan Roop, his house in Berrysburg was sold to Dr. Beshler and Benjamin Bordner "trustees for the Heller School Fund." Orphan Court records show that Dr. Beshler was appointed guardian of these three minor children: Ellen; William; Emma. **George W. and Susannah Botts had these known or suspected children:** Mary b c1852; Ellen b c1853; Ann b c1856; **Emma L.** b Jun 20 , 1856;; **Charles & John** H. b c1860, d young; George William (Jan 14, 1865, bapt Salem Ref, Bbg. - Apr 9, 1933, bur Maple Grove Cem, E'ville). In 1880 he lived with B. F. Koppenhaver family in Wash Twp. George m Jan 1, 1891 Mary Elizabeth Schoffstall (Aug 2, 1868 - Jan 22, 1921), a dau of Frederick and Rebecca (Hoke) Schoffstall.
George W. and Mary Elizabeth (Schoffstall) Botts had these children: G. Fred (1892 – 1969, bur Maple Grove Cem; Charles Russell (Apr 24, 1897 - Jan 8, 1967, bur Maple Grove Cem), m Sarah Anna Baker

(Dec 19,1899 – Jan 1,1981), a dau of Chas Henry and Katie Salome (Wert) Baker; <u>Morgan S.</u> (Nov 29, 1899-1957), m Miriam Snyder b1906; <u>John J.</u> (1903-1971), m Margaret C. Wise (1905-1999); <u>Mildred.</u>
*****Hiram** b c1828, m Catherine ____ b c1844. They lived in Mifflin Twp. in 1870 and he was a carpenter. **Hiram and Catherine Botts had these children:** <u>Caroline</u> b c1860; <u>Catherine</u> b c1863; <u>George W.</u> b c1866; <u>Jeremiah</u> b c1870.
*****Daniel** (Jun 3, 1833;
*****Perry** b c1840;
 *****Luisiana** b c1842;
*****Moses** (c1843 – Jul 22, 1928), m Elizabeth Wingert (1856 – Dec 30, 1928)

****WILLIAM** (Jan 15, 1801 bapt St. Johns Hill Ch Bbg – Jul 18, 1870, bur Malta Cem, Northld Co), m Barbara _____ (Aug 9, 1810 – Sep 17, 1873), lived in Low Mah Twp., Northld Co. **William and Barbara Botts had these known children (bap Stone Valley, Northld Co:)** *****John** (Dec 17, 1829 – Jan 28,1905, bur Stone Valley Cem), m Mary Anna Heckert (Feb 5,1829– bapt StoneValley – Mar 26, 1884), a dau of Solomon and Elizabeth (Shaffer) Heckert. They lived with her parents in Low Mah Twp, 1850. In 1860, lived in Up Pax Twp, and David Zerbe age 14 lived with them. They continued to lived in Up. Pax remainder of their lives. **John and Mary Anna (Heckert) Botts had these children:** <u>Catherine</u> b Sep 18, 1849 twin; <u>Anna Sarah</u> b Sep 18, 1849 twin d infant; <u>Jeremiah</u> b Apr 17, 1851, m Maggie _____, moved to Lincoln Co.Kansas; <u>Edward</u> b Sep 21, 1852, he lived with Daniel Bishoff in 1870 and was an apprentice cabinet maker. He m Henrietta Messersmith (1855 – after 1914), a dau of William A. and Catherine (Wingert) Messersmith. They lived in Lawrence, Missouri at least for awhile; <u>Benjamin</u> b Jan 17, 1855 d young; <u>Anna Maria</u> b Feb 2, 1857, m Uriah D. Ferree, lived in Harrisburg in 1905; <u>Agnes</u> b 1862, m David Zerbe, lived in County Line, Northld Co; <u>Margaret</u> (1863 – Sep 26, 1893), m Jacob M. Enterline (1864 –Jul 19, 1898), a son of Henry and Jemima (Wertz)Enterline. **Jacob & Margaret (Botts) Enterline had these children:** <u>Gertrude L.</u>b c1884, m James R. Herman; <u>Clara</u>; <u>Mary E</u>; <u>Verna M.</u>b Jul 11, 1891, m Harry Eicherly; <u>Elizabeth</u> b1865; <u>John, Jr.</u> b1870, m Irene __, moved to Kansas.
*****Magdalena Margaret** b Jun 30, 1836

****CATHARINE** (May 19, 1803 (bapt date, Cem date Mar 20, 1803) – (Jan 15, 1866, bur Motter Cem), m Isaac Hoke (Jun 9, 1803 – Dec 21, 1892), a son of Rudolph and Susanna Hoke. Isaac was a blacksmith. After Catharine died, Isaac moved to Indiana and settled on a farm, but later moved to Kansas with his daughter Emeline Shoop. Eventually he returned to Elizabethville where he died.
Isaac and Catharine (Botts) Hoke had these children: *****Catharine** b c1831, m Benjamin R. Buffington b Jan 21, 1823, son of Solomon and Elisabeth (Romberger) Buffington), moved to Calif;*****Elisabeth;** *****Emeline** m ___ Shoop, moved to Kansas; *****Mary Ann** b c1824; *****Jonathan** (b Dec 25,1825 Wash Twp – d May 2, 1903, bur Motters Cem), m 1857 Clara E. Matter. He helped to build the Summit Branch railroad. **Jonathan and Carrie E. (Matter) Hoke had these children:** <u>Catharine Malinda</u> (b 1857 d young; <u>Luciann</u> b Aug 18, 1861; <u>Aaron David</u> (Jul 25, 1868 – Nov 19, 1915 Perry Co), was a tanner and partner in Enterprise Hosiery Co. He m Sep 22, 1891 Katy E. Bowman b Mar 23, 1868, a dau of Daniel A. and Louisa (Enders) Bowman of Fisherville ; *****William** (no dates); *****Elizabeth** b c1837; *****Sarah Jane** b c1839; *****Emaline** b c1842; *****James Valentine** (Mar 10, 1850 – Feb 25, 1935, bur Maple Grove Cem, E'ville), m May7,1868 Sarah E. Grimm (Jun 2,1849 Jackson Twp – Oct 20,1927), dau of John & Susanna H (Eby) Grimm. **James Valentine and Sarah E (Grimm) Hoke had these children:** <u>Harvey</u> (1868 – after 1935, Phila); <u>Cora Ann</u> (1870 -1954, Fisherville), m Penro P. Miller (1865-1936);<u>Martha</u> (1872 – 1921, bur Maple Grove Cem); <u>Jennie S.</u> (1874 – 1915, bur Maple Grove Cem); <u>Elzsabeth</u> (1876 -1971), m Albert Bastian (1877 – 1970); <u>Sallie G</u> (1877 – 1964, bur Halifax Cem, m Parker T. Miller);<u>Susan Catharine</u> (1881-1908, bur Maple Grove Cem), m Richard J. Budd (1876 – 1949); <u>Elsie Irene</u> (1885 – 1956, bur Maple Grove Cem), m Solomon Rettinger Parmer (1881-1942), a son of Philip and Rebecca (Rettinger) Parmer.

****JACOB** (May 27, 1805 – Jul 9, 1826, bur Davids Ch Killinger) a son of John & Anna Betz-
****ISAAC** b c1808, m Susan _____ b c1809, lived in Wiconisco Twp in 1860

The next 3 (Moses, Anthony, & Joseph Botts) have not been confirmed as members of the above BOTTS family.

MOSES BOTTS (   ), m Catherine Witmer (   ). This may be the Moses Botts age 18, living with Jacob Row in Washington Twp in 1850.
Moses and Catherine (Witmer) Botts had these children (some bapt St. John's Hill Ch, Bbg):
Henry b c1853
Aby b Dec 10, 1854 sp Jacob Rau & wf St Johns
John Adam b Feb 26, 1857 sp John Weber & wife
Josiah b Nov 8, 1858 sp Anthony Betz
Mary Ellen b May 19, 1860

ANTHONY "Nathaniel" BOTTS (Aug 1822 - Mar1902 bur St. Johns Cem) m Jan 16, 1845, Catherine Rau (Sep16,1820 – Aug 7, 1883). Civil War Vet and after the war he applied for a peddlers license. . Anthony and Catherine lived in Washington Twp in 1850, listed as a carpenter; In Wiconisco Twp in1870 also listed as a carpenter. He later became employed as a saloon keeper, but in 1880 he was listed as a confectioner. **Anthony & Catherine (Rau) Botts had these children (some bapt St. Johns Hill Ch, Bbg)**
William Henry b Oct 14, 1846
Nathaniel (Oct 22, 1848 – Dec 12, 1862, bur St. Johns Cem)
Isabelle b May 14, 1851 – d Feb 27,1865. bur St. Johns Cem)
Leah J (Feb 21, 1855 – Apr 3, 1875, bur St. Johns Cem)
Mary S. (b Dec 1, 1856 – May 1, 1875)
Sarah Amanda (Mar 21, 1858 St. Johns Hill record names the mother Maria A.. Row - Aug 26, 1926), m George Adam Deibler (Jun   30, 1855 – Feb 9, 1934, bur Simeon Cem). **George A & Sarah   Amanda (Botts) Deibler had these children**: John Henry (Oct 20,   1880- Aug 22, 1936), m Thame Sevila Umholtz (1892 – 1982)
George Franklin b Sep 15, 1859
Henrietta b May 3, 1861, bapt St. John's
James Monroe b Nov 4, 1862
Daniel b May 9, 1865*
Alice Lorena b Apr 21, 1867

JOSEPH BOTTS (Batze) (_____) m Anna Mary Fisher
Children:
Rebecca b Apr 5, 1857 sp Elis Fisher

WINGERT/WINGARD FAMILY

[The earliest known immigrant ancestor of the Wingert (Wenger, Wingard, etc) family is believed to be **Hans Wingert** (1686 – Sep 8, 1750), a son of Christian and Christina (Schneiter) Wenger who left Guggesberg of near Schwarzenburg, Switzerland in 1734. He m Anna Uhlrich (1679 – after 1740 Tulpehocken Twp, Berks Co), and **had these known children**:*LAZARUS b 1715; ANNA b 1716; ____ m Johannes Carl.

*LAZARUS WINGERT (Nov 10, 1715 – Dec 16, 1796, bur St. Daniel Cem Robesonia, Pa.), came to America with his mother Anna age 56, and his sister Anna Age 19 on ship "Oliver" in August 1735. Lazarus m Nov 10,1738, Maria Catharine Lauck (Sep 7, 1711 – 1797), a dau of John Abraham Lauck (1691 – 1771, bur Tulpehocken Twp., Berks Co) and Anna Catherine (Becker) Lauck b c1689, lived in Ulster Co., N.Y. Lazarus named his wife Catherine and 17 children in his will. **Lazarus and Maria Catharine (Lauck) Wingert had these children:**
**JOHN GEORGE (c1739 – c1770, bur Tulpehocken, Berks Co)
**JOHN b Dec 26, 1740;
LAZARUS (Dec 26,1740–after 1798), m Anna Maria Sallada. By1798 when the window tax was taken, Lazarus had land with a 30 by 28 foot frame dwelling and another tract of land with a poor stable in Wiconisco Valley adjoining land of Dewald Novinger; **Lazarus & Anna Maria (Sallada) Wingert had these children: *****Maria** b Jun 31, 1763, m Henry Solomon Weiser (May 14, 1763 - ___), a son of Peter

and Catharine Weiser. **Henry Solomon & Maria (Wingart) Weiser had these children:** ****<u>Peter</u> Jan 17, 1784; ****<u>**Maria Catharine**</u> b Mar 20, 1787 m 1810 John Reigert; ****<u>**Henry Solomon**</u> b Mar 4, 1789, m Susanna Zerbe (Sep 27, 1797 – Mar 17, 1858); ****<u>**Francisca**</u> b Jun 30, 1790, m 1816 Michael Frederick.

***<u>**Lazarus**</u> b Dec 20, 1768, m Elizabeth _____, lived in Mifflin Twp in 1812.

<u>**Jacob**</u> b ___ m Maria Magd _____ (1783 – Feb 21,1832 of Gratz Cong. **Jacob and Maria Magd Wingert had 5 children** (Salem Luth & St. Johns Hill Ch): *<u>**Elisabeth**</u> b Aug 15, 1804; ****<u>John</u> (May 7, 1806 – c1851), probably the one in Wiconisco Twp in 1850 with a wife Matilda. They had Angeline Messersmith age 7 with them. In 1857 Matilda received land from John Wingert.

****<u>**Joseph**</u> (Dec 23, 1804 – May 4, 1885, bur Oak Hill Cem, Mbg), m Rosina _____ (c1818 – ___), lived in Up Paxton Twp in 1850. **Joseph and Rosina Wingart had these children:** <u>Sarah E</u> b c1837; <u>Mary M</u> b c1842; <u>Mariah</u> b c1847

****<u>**Daniel**</u> (Feb 12, 1808 – Jan 17, 1891, Bur Oak Hill Cem), m Christiana (b c1815 – Feb 14, 1878 bur Oak Hill Cem, Mbg). In 1880 Daniel was a widower living in Millersburg. He was a switch tender on the railroad. His son Francis H. age 24, a watchman on the R. R. and a dau Mary age 20 lived with him.

****<u>**Benjamin**</u> (Sep 7,1809 – Dec 28, 1880, bur Oak Dale Cem, Loyalton), m Margaret (Rebecca) A. ___ (Jan 13, 1815 – Dec 18, 1868) They lived in Wash Twp in 1850 & 1860. They owned 5 acres of land with 2 story house, out buildings, good water and fruit trees in Washington Twp bordering on land of Herman & Joseph Russell. John Wingert was adm of his fathers estate. Part of Benjamin's land was sold to son John's wife Emma in 1879. **Benjamin and Margaret Rebecca Wingart had these children;** <u>John</u> (Feb 18, 1838 – after 1880), m Emeline or Emma _____ b c1836 – lived in   Wash Twp 1870 & 1880. **John and Emma Wingart had these children:** *Florence* b c1866; *Jacob H.* b c1868; *Benjamin S.* b c1875; *Sallie E* b c1879. <u>Philip</u> b c1840; <u>William</u> b c1840 (twins? – they appear on both 1850 & 1860 census having the same age); <u>Jacob</u> b Sep 12,1843; <u>Elizabeth</u> b Sep 12,1843; <u>Aaron</u> b c 1848.

<u>ANNA CATHARINE</u> (1743 – Dec 12, 1791), m 1st John George Walborn (Mar 15, 1740 – 1770), a son of Hermanus & Margaret Fcg. She m 2nd May 26, 1772 Isaac Heller (c1750 – 1814). **Isaac and Anna Catharine (Wingert) Heller had these children:** ***<u>Susan</u> b c1772; ***<u>John Adam</u> (Oct 28, 1773 – 1860, Crawford, Ohio);***<u>Jacob</u> (Apr 15, 1777 - Mar 20, 1850, Crawford, Ohio)

<u>SUSANNAH</u> (c1745 - ___)

<u>ABRAHAM</u> (d young)

<u>JACOB</u> (b c1747 - 1791), m Anna Maria ___, **had these known children:** ***<u>Catherine</u> b Jun 11,1777 ***<u>Johannes</u> b Nov 14, 1778. Lazarus & wife Wingert were sp. for both;

<u>MARGARET ELISABETH</u> (Mar 15, 1749 – Heidelberg Twp, Berks Co –Mar 29, 1818, David's Cem, Killinger) Margaret m Feb 2, 1772 Adam Weise (Dec 23, 1751 New Goshenhoppen, Montg Co.– Oct 5, 1833, Mbg), a son of John George & Eve Weise. They moved to Lykens Valley in 1796. Margaret was his 1st wife, had 8 children. [Weise genealogy elsewhere in book.]

<u>MARY</u> b c1750

<u>MARY ELISABETH</u> (Sep 18, 1754 – Sep 17, 1835 Womelsdorf, Berks Co), m Jabetz Weiser (Jul 3, 1753 – May 16, 1829), a son of Philip & Sophia (Riem) Weiser. Jabetz served in the Berks Co. Militia. He inherited part of the old Weiser farm near Womelsdorf, where they lived. In old age he was blind, hard of hearing and spent most of his time confined to his bed. **Jabetz and Mary Elisabeth (Wingert) Weiser had 10 children:** *** John Philip (Sep 3, 1776 – 1860), m Elisabeth Shaffer;*** Mary Catharine b Nov 10, 1777; ***John b Nov 30, 1779; ***Samuel b 1781 d young; ***Solomon b 1783 d young; ***Henry Solomon b 1786; ***Eva Maria Elisabeth b 1788; ***Maria Philippina b 1790; ***Sarah b 1794; ***Rebecca b 1796.

<u>NICHOLAS</u> b c1753

<u>ANGELICA</u> b c1755

<u>VALENTINE</u> (b c1756 – 1793), m Margaret _____ **had 2 minor children:** *** _____ b c1887; ***William b   Sep 29, 1792, bapt Harrisburg. He is probably the one that became a Gratz postmaster on Dec 20, 1830 and served until 1834. Also served as tavern keeper for at least one year. In 1834 he was a chair maker. William m Elizabeth ___ & while in Gratz had at least one son. He came from Low Mah Twp and later moved back to that area.

<u>CHRISTINA</u> b c1757

<u>HENRY</u> b c1758

**MARIA SABILLA b c1759
**JOSEPH b c1761

The next two (Jacob and Isreal Wingert) have not been connected to the above Wingert family.

Jacob Wingert (Apr 14, 1796 – Oct 3, 1864, bur Fairview Cem, Fisherville), m Phebe Ann b c1808. They lived in Jackson Twp in 1850. **Jacob and Phebe Ann Wingert had these children:** Nancy b Jun 6,1825 – d 1825 age 4 mo., bur Davids Church, Killinger; Jacob b Mar 7, 1829; George F. b Dec 26, 1832 – Apr 16, 1914, bur Oak Hill Cem, Mbg), m ____ (Feb 18, 1836 – Jun 13, 1907). George was a member of First Methodist Church in 1876; John b Sep 6, 1834; Benjamin (Oct 5, 1836 – Jan 28, 1880), m Susannah ____ (Mar 28, 1834 – Jan 12, 1865, bur Fetteroff Cem).: Mary b c1838; Ann Jane b c1844; Daniel W b c1845; Catherine L b c1848

Isreal Wingart (b c1810 m Hannah b c1816. They lived in Up Paxton Twp in 1850. Hannah lived alone in 1880. **Isreal and Hannah Wingart had these children:** William C. (Jun 3, 1839 – Jul 30 , 1909, bur Oak Hill, Mbg), m Charlotte ____ (b c1839 - Mar 19, 1912). In 1880 they lived in Millersburg and he was a car inspector. **William C. and Charlotte Wingart had these children:** Mary b c1870; Anne b c1872; Edward b c1873; William b c1876; Melinda b c1879;
Angeline b c1840
Nathan b Sep 22, 1841
George b c1846, m Mary M. _____

"OLD CLAUDE KEISER FARM"
(Containing land of Botts & Russel as noted on 1875 map)

On April 18, 1860, Elias and Elizabeth Kuntzelman of Wiconisco Twp, sold two small tracts of their land. One messuage containing 6 acres 44 ¾ perches a house and other buildings, was sold to Moses and Sarah Nutt of Oak Dale. This was part of two tracts, one had belonged to Henry Kuntzelman. The other belonged to John and Catherine Bressler whom assigned to Jacob and Barbara Mayer, and they assigned to Moses Nutt on March 25, 1867. Moses Nutt, a forgeman, and his wife Sarah, on April 1, 1867, assigned 11 acres 36 perches with buildings to Joseph Ressel. On the same day they sold the 6 acres 44 ¾ perches of land to Joseph Ressel. It joined the land of (was Peter Swanger's), Wiconisco Creek and David K. McClure land. John Ressel had another 8 acres 25 perches of land that he received by the will of John H. Dietrich on January 26, 1867. It bordered on the lands of John Adam Harman, Philip Wilvert, Peter Johns.

On August 30, 1875 Joseph Ressel conveyed both tracts of land and houses to Josiah Boyer. But again on May 16, 1886, Josiah and Ann Boyer conveyed the 6 acre 44 /34 perches of land with two story frame house, smoke house and barn to Joseph Ressel.The land bordered on land of Richard Budd (late C. Johns) , south to Philip Bahney (late C. Botz), Loyalton railroad, and north to D. K. McClure. Joseph and Elizabeth Ressel sold the 6 plus acres to J. J. Nutt of Lykens on July 2, 1897. John J. Nutt died in 1915, and his heirs conveyed the property to Kate M. Lebo of Tower City on July 3, 1916. Many years later on December 31, 1938, Kate Lebo sold four tracts of land to Claude Keiser. They were as follows:

One tract was the 6 acres with frame dwelling as described above, and belonged to John J. Nutt. It bordered land of Richard Budd, Philip Barry, Lykens Valley Railroad, south to D. K. McClure.

Another tract contained 4 acres 8 perches, and was purchased from Daniel C. Romberger and his wife.

A third tract contained 27 acres of timberland near Loyalton and was sold to Kate Lebo by John M Harman.

The fourth tract contained another 27 acres that was purchased from John M and Lizzie M. Harman in 1920.

Claude Keiser received another 3 tracts from Jacob E. Hassinger on October 8, 1949. One contained 17 acres, and two others contained 7 acres. They were purchased from Daniel C. Romberger. The total acreage was 91 acres 92 perches, and bordered north line of Forge Road, land of Glenn and Jerry Snyder, Roscoe Klinger, Lykens Valley Branch of Penn Central Railroad. It included most of the land where several old house had been built in earlier times. Claude S. Keiser lived alone on this farm for many years. He died March 19, 1969, and on May 25, 1970, his heirs conveyed all of this land to Constantine and Mary K. Pellas.

THE NUTT / McNUTT FAMILY

[Members of the NUTT or McNUTT family came to America at a very early date, and settled first in New Jersey. **Jonathan Nutt** (b 1680 in New Jersey – d Oct 16, 1749 in Bucks Co, Pa.) **and his wife Susannah Lovett lived in Bucks County and had these children: John** b Oct 16, 1707; **Ann** b 1709; **Martha** (b 1712 – d 1732); **Mary** (b 1714 – d 1732).

Moses Nutt b Aug 23, 1751 in Burlington, N.J. was a son of Levi and Ann (Evins) Nutt. Moses m Feb 3, 1772 Anne Bufferin in Mansfield, N.J.

These are apparently relatives of Moses Nutt the early settler to Oak Dale Forge area. But we have not learned how he found this area. He is apparently the only one of his family to settle here.

MOSES E. **NUTT** (b Oct 17, 1819 in Speedwell, N.J. – d Mar 5, 1891 in Lykens, bur IOOF Cem), a son of John and Nance Nutt, m Sarah Elizabeth Moyer (Oct 23, 1829 – Dec 1, 1901), a dau of Jacob and Rebecca (Ferree) Moyer.

Moses came to this area early in the 1830's and settled in the region of the Oak Dale Forge. He was a skilled forgemen and was employed at the forge beginning about 1834. The family continued to live in the Oak Dale area until late in the 1870's. In 1880 Moses and wife lived in Lykens and their son John J. age 20 lived with them. **Moses and Sarah (Moyer) Nutt had these children:** Amanda b May 5, 1833 d young; **Mary** **Ann** b Jul 25, 1835 died young, both children bur Boyer Cem, Wash Twp; **Melinda** (Aug 7, 1846 – Jan 1, 1922, bur IOOF Cem., Lykens beside parents) , m Isaac E. Snyder (Oct 27, 1845 - Nov 15, 1890), a son of _____.
Martha b c1848; **Jacob John** (1852 – 1915, bur IOOF, Lykens), m Anna J. (1867 – 1947). **Jacob John and Anna J. Nutt had these children:** Myron N; Helen m James Byerly; Sarah; A William H. Smith (Jan 1, 1836 – Jan 2, 1890) is also bur with the Nutt family.
THOMAS LACY NUTT (no dates) m Anna Eliza Robison. **Thomas and Anna Eliza (Robison) Nutt had these children:** Rebecca (Mar 17, 1837 – May 7, 1915), m Mar 16, 1858 to John Pifer (b c1814 – d ___).

Moses Nutt (1819 – 1891)

The 1880 census names these children in their household: **Martha E** b c1855 in Indiana; **Sumart** (? A son) b c1860; **Lewis E** b c1863 in Ohio; **Thomas J.** b c1865 in Ohio; **Cora A.** b c1868; **Mary** b c1870; **Sinette** b c1872; **Liza** b c1874; **Emma** b c1877.
John Harper (b Aug 17, 1839 – d Apr 12, 1924, Mercer Co, Ohio, m Mar 16, 1864 Sharlotte Harner Pifer (b Nov 12, 1842 – May 7, 1916), a dau of John Pifer and his first wife Elizabeth Kimmel. (After Elizabeth died, John Pifer married Rebecca Nutt, dau of Thomas Lacy Nutt. According to records, John Harper Nutt and his sister Rebecca and their families moved to Black Creek, Mercer County Ohio before 1860, and lived In a farming region. In 1880, they lived in the same neighborhood. **John H. and Sharlotte (Pifer) Nutt had these children: Viola F.** b c1867; **Emma D.** b c1868; **Mary G.** b c1876; **James W.** b 1880.

THE RUSSELL / RESSEL FAMILY

[The earliest known ancestor of the RUSSELL family is JOHN CHRISTOPHER RESSEL (Jun 24, 1723 – Feb 21, 1793), lived in Bart Twp., Lancaster Co. He came to America on the ship St. Andrew in September 1752. He married Feb 24, 1756 Susannah Maria Haberstick, also of Lancaster County. **John Christopher and Susanna Maria (Haberstick) Ressel had these known children (b Germany): *HENRY** (b Sep 5, 1762 – Jun 10, 1818); **RACHEL** b 1764; **REBECCA** b 1766; **SUSANNA** b 1768; **MICHAEL** b 1770.

*HENRY (Sep 5, 1762 – Jun 10, 1818), m Barbara Herman (no dates). He is probably the one living in Upper Paxton Twp in 1800 having a wife, two sons and two daughters. **Henry and Barbara (Herman) Ressel had these children:**

JOHN (no dates), m Oct 10, 1809 Sarah Rau. **John and Sarah (Rau) Ressel had these children (most bapt St. John's Hill Ch);
John b Jan 18, 1814, m Christiana Dietrich (no dates) dau of John and Catharine Dietrich;
Barbara b Oct 23, 1815 sp Jacob Haag & Elis
Elisabeth b Sep 7, 1817 sp Balthaser Romberger Jr & Elis
Joseph b Jun 19, 1819
Susanna b Jul 6, 1821 sp Barbara Roessle grandmother??. She at age 19 lived with Nathaniel Row family in 1850, Wiconisco Twp.
Jeremiah b Feb 25, 1824

Joseph Ressel below has not been connected to those above, but apparently belongs to this family.

(Joseph Ressel (b Jun 20, 1836 – Nov 23, 1901, of heart disease, bur Hoffman Cem), m while on leave from military service May 10, 1864, by Rev. Bressler to Elizabeth Boddorf (b c1838 d Jan 23, 1903 of paralytic Stroke), a dau of Chriatian and Sarah Batdorf of Wic. Twp. Joseph and Elizabeth lived in Wash. Twp in 1880. He was a Civil War veteran, and a prisoner at Andersonville and other areas. **Joseph and Elizabeth (Baddorf) Russell had these children:**
Alvin S b Apr 23,c1866; **John Wesley** (Jul 21, 1867 – May 7, 1927, bur Meth Cem Wic), m Belle ___, had a dau Laura Elisabeth b Oct 24,1891, bapt Hoffman Ch; **Joseph P.** (Dec 17, 1868 – Sep 1937, bur Steelton); **Frederick L "Frank"** (Apr 22, 1870 – Feb 1940, bur in Tower City), m Jun 20, 1896 Lizzie Weaver (Oct 1878 – 1952), a dau of Peter and Mary (Eby) Weaver of Rife. **Frank & Lizzie (Weaver) Russel had these children:** Stella m Howard Klinger, lived in Loyalton; Joseph; Henry M (Aug 27, 1871 – 1952), m Minnie ___ (1871 – 1945), lived in Tower City; **Margaret L.** (Feb 16, 1873 – Jan 8, 1940, bur Wic. Cem), m Feb 5, 1895 Adam Rudisill (Mar. 28, 1857 – 1939), lived in Lykens; **Kate M.** Feb.

Joseph Russell (1836 – 1901) &
Elizabeth (Batdorf) Russell (1838 – 1903)

(Feb 20, 1875 – 1966), m William F. Lebo (1861 – 1931), lived in E'ville; **Emma E** (Feb 16,1876 – Nov 1937), m Benjamin Welker, Jr. (1876 – 1937) [see Welker genealogy]; **Sarah Annie** (Jan 12, 1880 – 1939, bur Tower City), m George Walborn (1873 – 1937), a son of Jacob & Catherine (Heinzman) Walborn lived in Tower City.]

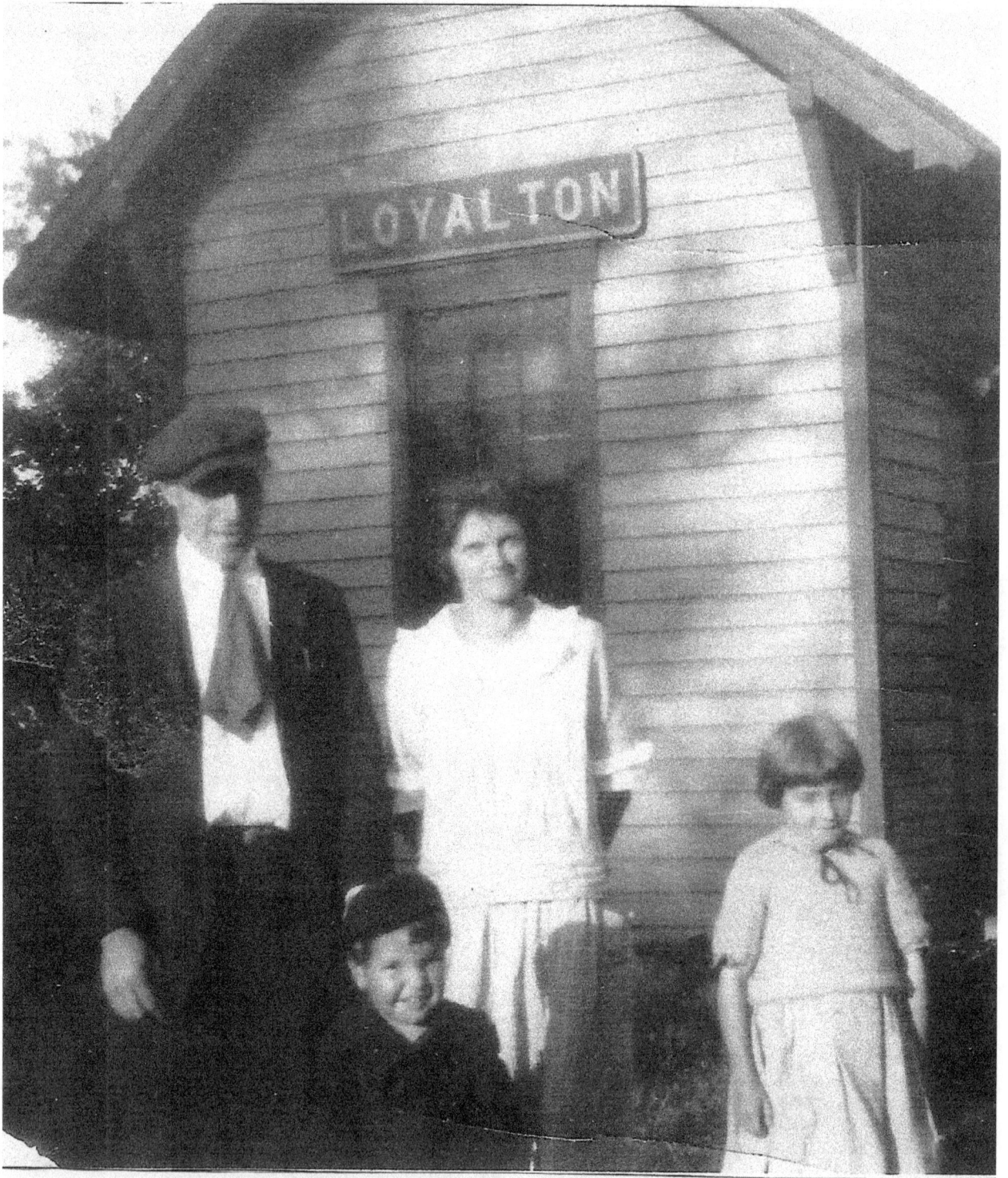

1920 – FAMILY PHOTO -- TAKEN AT OAKDALE STATION, LOYALTON, PA.

L. to R. – William Deitrich, Helen Deitrich, Son – Harold & Daughter - Kathryn

OAK DALE STATION

Large deposits of coal apparently were never found anywhere on Berry's Mountain near Oak Dale (Loyalton). Despite the fact that Oak Dale was situated very close to the end of Short Mountain, the people living in the little village were never surrounded by coal banks or other exterior reminders of the deep mines in the interior of the mountain. Although mining took place throughout much of the area in the bowels of Short Mountain, the outer surface of the mountain was only scarred near the towns of Lykens and Wiconisco, eastwardly. There the collieries were established, and the anthracite coal industry thrived for many years.

Oak Dale had earlier become established because of its proximity to the Wiconisco Creek. Water was one of the most precious commodities, and when settlers were purchasing land, it was important to locate where a good supply was available. Land adjacent to creeks was especially sought after, for all types of milling. The Oak Dale area had much to offer.

Below - 2 Views Of Tracts Near Loyalton Station - both directions
(Dated Nov 1954)

About the time that the forge was thriving at Oak Dale, coal mining was becoming a successful industry on the eastern side of the village. Transportation had become a necessity to transport coal from Lykens to Millersburg, and from that point to other localities. So the railroad became a reality. [Consult story relating to coal history, next].

Oak Dale was in a most advantageous position. The railroad would pass by the village, running along the side of Berry's Mountain. During the first years of railroading, coal was the sole or at least chief product that was transported on the Line. But gradually other uses were found for the railroad. People began to think in terms of

using the rail system for the purpose of passenger service.

Advertisements appeared in newspapers in the 1830s giving people an opportunity to ride the rail at a cost of three cents each mile. In two hours, one could travel the length of the system, from Lykens to Millersburg. However, regular service for passengers was not established until years later. The need for transportation of goods continued to increase. Each station along the way provided new services. Farmers used the service to ship or receive crops, feed, fertilizer, and to sell their produce and other products. Eventually, cattle were brought in from the west by rail.

The local mills used these facilities to their advantage in distribution of their goods.

Soon modes of transportation were needed to carry people to the train stations. Not much is known concerning the availability of special carriages. However, the local Swab Wagon Company began to build various types of vehicles that were important in serving the local residents.

CARRIAGE BUILT BY SWAB - USED TO PICK UP PASSENGERS AT THE RAILROAD STATION
(Carriage restored and owned by the Swab family. Business later Inherited By The Margerum family)

The railroad gained favor over the years, to the point that Lykens Valley residents relied on it for quick delivery of goods and transportation. The Railroad Company scheduled daily trips, and printed advance schedules of arrivals and departures. The trains stopped at each station along the way from Lykens to Millersburg, allowing about 90 minutes for a total trip. Stations were built at each little village including from Millersburg: Woodside near Rife, Crossroads (Elizabethville), Oak Dale (Loyalton), Lykens, Wiconisco, and Williamstown.

Rail transportation was now becoming important and very popular among the Upper Dauphin County citizens. According to a local newspaper of 1869 (reprinted April 17, 1896 under chronicle of history):

"On Monday a regular passenger train was started on Summit Branch Railroad, leaving Lykens at 5:50 a. m, arrives at Harrisburg 8:45. A returning trip leaves Harrisburg 4:20 p.m. and arrives in Lykens at 6:40 p.m."

Progress was being made to the point that special trains brought more varied items. Merchants in the area used the service to travel to cities to buy merchandise, and have it delivered. Residents used the service to purchase items from catalogues. A weekly mail car delivered the mail.

Beginning as early as1867, during the summer when camp meeting was held at Elizabethville, special excursion trains brought the people to the camps. The railroad tracts became a particularly popular place for young people to meet. Many photos have survived, showing groups of people of all ages congregating together.

A letter to the editor of a local paper (date and name of paper unknown) describes a ride on the train traveling along the foot of Berry's Mountain from Lykens, Oak Dale, Elizabethville, Camp Ground, Lenker's, Woodside and on to Millersburg as a wonderful experience taking in the scenic route. At one point they "rounded a curve and witnessed the 4 sides of a dwelling along the route gone for good but not forgotten." Young folks walked the tracks on Saturday or Sunday, then hiked to the top of Berry's Mountain, enjoying the cool spring water on the way. These trainmen from the local area were remembered in the letter: John H. Boechler, Robert J. Day County Herrold, Bob Gilbert, Grant Lawrence, Bob Neageley, Harrison Johnson - directing signals at tower, George Garman, C. C. Wilhelm, W. R. Trout, Fletcher fennel, J. W. Harter, W. S. Klinger, R. M. Klinger, Joe Creveling, Luke Lenker, Chas E. Manning, G. L. Seigrist, Ben Michaels, W.H. Hehn, R. E. Klinger, Wm. McKissick, Unc. Kline, Squrly Day, Chas. Keefer, G. W. Michaels, John Clemson, Charles Zigner, ___ Grimm, and Charles (Windy) Freeburn.

As previously mentioned, the village of Oak Dale enjoyed all of the commercial successes of the mining era without becoming commercialized. Many of the residents were employed at the mines. Local people became established in businesses in the town. They supplied many of the needs for residents of the area, but the small complex remained a very attractive village. The Oak Dale Station gave the residents access to travel never before offered to people of the Lykens Valley. It was a very attractive place to live. Oak Dale was probably the smallest or one of the smallest stations built along the route. It could probably be described as a "whistle stop." One elderly historian from the area said that it became known as "Old Loyalton Huckleberry Train Station."

Chapter 6

A Brief History Of The Area Coal Industry

It was on a Sunday afternoon in 1825, that two residents made an amazing discovery. The discovery would eventually change the environment for the whole surrounding area. On that afternoon, Jacob Burd Sr., and Peter Kimes, went for a walk. They were living near the lower end of Short Mountain, and their walk took them to an area of that mountainside. As they neared the higher surface, the two men stopped to rest, and to gaze at the very beautiful valley below them.

While the two men enjoyed the magnificent scene, one of them idly scratched in the ground with his walking stick. Looking down on the ground, he noticed that the black dirt near their feet resembled coal. The two men were immediately impressed! Only thirty-four years had passed since the discovery of anthracite coal in Eastern Pennsylvania. The two Sunday hikers were aware of the earlier find.

It didn't take long for the news of Burd and Kimes discovery to spread. A few days later, a group of men dug an excellent quality of coal in that area. Soon after that, these energetic men cut out a road that led to the coal find. Before long, horse drawn wagons laden with coal could be seen rolling down the mountain. Early records reveal the names of James Todarff, John Brown, and William Hall as the first miners. William Hall may be the ancestor of Thomas Hall who opened "Tommy Hall's Tunnel" in later years, and lived in Gratz.

The discovery of coal was the beginning of a new and different commercial market for this otherwise large, beautiful farm country, interspersed with developing villages, and sandwiched between ranges of mountains. The land that had been a worthless mountain tract had now become valuable. It contained a good crop of what became known in anthracite trade, as Lykens Valley red ash coal. Odorless, smokeless and more easily kindled, this coal burned more freely than white ash coal. It wasn't long until numerous investors sought after the land. It was the beginning of the coal industry in this area. It also probably accounts for another fact that is unique to this area. Many of the early houses built in Lykens Valley during that period did not contain fireplaces.

It is interesting to note that both Burd and Kimes were tenants (not owners) on land in this area. The tax record lists Burd as a laborer, Kimes as a farmer in 1820. Peter Kimes was affiliated with Hoffman's Church. He and his wife Nancy had a family of seven children. One of the children, Peter Nathaniel, born December 6, 1824, was baptized at Hoffman's Church. A girl by the name of Anna (Nancy) Kimes, confirmed at Hoffman's in 1826, is noted as married. She may actually be the wife of Peter, using a second given name.

Whether either man ever personally profited greatly from their discovery is not known. The tax record in 1831 lists Kimes with 700 acres of mountain land in Lykens Township. Kimes owned it in partnership with three other persons, Hoch, Loy, and Dunkel. Apparently coal had not yet been discovered on their land, or at least it was not being mined. Even in those early years, the tax record did mention the presence of coal in lands when they were assessed. This land was not specified as coal land. However, by 1834 Kimes and his friends had become affiliated with Haldeman and Elder, whose land holdings were extensive.

The tax records from 1828 to 1832 show a surge of interest in mountain land on Short Mountain. While many individuals and groups of people purchased large tracts, not all investors were fortunate in receiving land containing a good source of coal. Conrad Fry, tavern keeper of Gratz, was one person who did purchase twenty-five acres of actual coal land. But until about 1830, coal was mined in small and scattered quantities.

One of the big winners in the coal discovery was of course Simon Gratz. Whether he was aware of the possible coal veins, or if it was purely coincidental, Simon Gratz was in an advantageous position, by the discovery of coal. He had earlier inherited a grant of about 400 acres of land from Aaron Levy, patented to Simon Gratz on May 1, 1830. Although located on Short Mountain, his land was not the land on which the initial coal was found. In addition to this tract of land, Simon Gratz owned several more hundred acres. He also obtained other hundreds of acres of land in partnership with Sheaffer, Elder, Haldeman, and Schreiner. Simon Gratz is considered one of the founders of our anthracite coal industry.

About 1830, Simon Gratz with some of his close associates formed the Wiconisco Coal Company. President Simon Gratz, and the following men, comprised the company; Samuel Richards, George H. Thompson and Charles R. Thompson all acquaintances from Philadelphia; Henry Schreiner a native Philadelphian who had settled in Gratz in 1819; Henry Sheafer who had originally settled in Halifax.

When the Wiconisco Coal Company developed, these same men were instrumental in organizing the Lykens Valley Railroad Company, and Lykens Valley Coal Company. A bill passed in the state legislature on April 7, 1830 gave the men permission to construct the railroad. Mr. Ashwin, an English Civil Engineer, laid out the railroad bed for this company, on the north foot of Berrys Mountain. It trailed along the north side of Berry Mountain from Lykens, passing through Oak Dale, Elizabethville and eventually arriving at Millersburg and the Susquehanna River. Construction took place under the direction of civil engineer John Paul, Jr. The many talented Mr. Paul built and owned the two rather unusual stone houses on the main street in Elizabethville. Henry Sheaffer was Superintendent of the project, and Simon Sallada another impressive man, who settled in Elizabethville, was the director. John Paul, Jr. using his expertise took into consideration that the railroad would pass through Elizabethville, which was 700 feet above sea level. He graded the railroad bed into an inclined plane to make use of gravity as the coal was transported from there to Millersburg.

A Brief History Of The Area Coal Industry

This was the fourth railroad in the United States, and the first in Dauphin County, built for the purpose of transporting anthracite coal. The project completed in October 1833 consisted of a sixteen-mile long, single railroad track. It was constructed of white oak rails and flat iron bars that could handle ten small cars. Horse and mule power pulled the cars along the tracks from Lykens to Elizabethville. From below Elizabethville, gravity took over for the rest of the journey.

When the rail was completed, the men realized that they needed another source of transportation to carry goods from Millersburg to other locations. The Susquehanna River was usually too shallow to ship coal in this manner. The solution was an alternative route to get the coal cars to the other side of the river. On April 19, 1834, the first attempt was made to send a flatboat load of coal cars across the Susquehanna River to the Pennsylvania Canal at Mount Patrick. There, forty-three tons of coal were sent down chutes onto a canal boat, and floated down the river to Columbia, Lancaster County. The process of this trial run was considered successful. The same procedure became common practice. After each delivery of coal (mostly in large lump form), the empty cars were pulled back to the mines by horse or mule power, and loaded for another shipment.

Michael Sheafer (Dec 1, 1803 – Nov 30, 1849), son of George Sheafer of Halifax Twp, and his son Henry J. were very involved in the development of the local coal industry. Before 1831, when the Lykens Valley Coal Company was organized and commenced operations at "Bear Gap" the company built a large log frame house, and Michael Sheafer moved into it for the purpose of boarding the workmen and entertaining the members of the company. At that time most of the Upper End (Lykens, Wiconisco and Williamstown) was a vast wilderness, with a few log huts scattered around. Michael Scheafer was one of the contractors who helped to build the Lykens Valley Railroad, and make improvements at the mouth of the Wiconisco Canal feeder. He also had an early contract for delivery of the coal that was floated across the river to Mount Patrick on the Pennsylvania Canal.

By 1837, the Lykens Coal Company had built houses on their property, within what was then Lykens Township. The actual location of the houses has not been learned, but the tax record for that year shows the names of tenants living in those company houses, and their occupations with the coal company: Jacob Brubaker, blacksmith; Jonathan Bordner, collier; William E. Clark, laborer; Dennis Ely, laborer, James Ferree, collier; John Hawk, laborer; George Pinkerton, carpenter; Michael Shaeffer, innkeeper; Henry Shaeffer, agent; George Warfel, collier; and John Wommer, collier. Other private held land bordered along the railroad tracts. One known person, John Dietrich, had a farm adjoining the railroad, and had a negative experience. The railroad bed was built close to his barn and out buildings causing them to become dilapidated and rendering them useless. To prepare the property for sale, the heirs had to sell a small acreage separately to pay the cost to rebuild the barn.

Although the new industry was pleasing to all persons involved, it soon became evident that in the long run it was not a true success. A single poorly constructed track, with coal cars driven by mule power, frequently were derailed, making coal delivery to Millersburg sometimes a two-day trip. The coal shipments continued until 1845, when the railroad had worn out. For about three years, shipment by this means was suspended.

In the meantime, a bill introduced by Simon Salada in the state legislature, eventually passed and made it possible to extend the original canal from Millersburg to Clarks Ferry.

While the canal was being constructed, Lykens Valley Railroad was being re-graded & rebuilt using heavy iron rails and wooden cross ties to support the newer heavier cars that could carry larger loads of coal. A new sixteen-ton locomotive with steam engine named "**Lykens Valley**" was the first of several locomotives that were used to power these newer cars. A second engine was named **Simon Gratz**, in honor of the illustrious founder. About that same time, the first Lykens Valley Coal Breaker became a reality. In 1848 the coal industry had a totally new start in Lykens Valley.

Pennsylvania Rail Road Coal & Iron Company (no date)

Over the next years, the railroad had many successes, and other years that were not so healthy. In 1865, Lykens Valley Railroad Coal Company filed for bankruptcy, and Josiah Caldwell from Massachusetts became an important figure in the management and improvement of the company.

On February 1, 1865, an agreement was signed between officials of Lykens Valley Railroad and Coal Company, and Summit Branch Railroad Company that changed the administration of the railroad. It allowed Summit Branch Railroad Company to rent the facilities on a long-term basis. As per the agreement, Summit Branch Railroad Company would pay an annual rent of $62,500, payable monthly in equal portions to Lykens Valley Railroad and Coal Company. It was for the use of the railroad now completed to Millersburg, using all lateral railroad lands, including the lands known as Beuhler lands and Williams Valley in Dauphin County, and all things needed that connected to the railroad owned by the first party. The contract was made to begin on March 1, 1866, to be valid for a period of 999 years. Other items in the contract made Summit Branch Railroad Company responsible to "keep everything connected to railroading in good order and repair" Maintenance of the machine shops, water tanks, buildings, locomotives and rolling stock, was included in the agreement. Care of the motor power for transportation of coal and other property, the road, and also of transportation of passengers, if any, was included. They were to convey property and merchandize of any parties, retain all tolls, and pay all taxes.

LYKENS VALLEY COAL "PIONEER"

First Motorized Coal Car In America (1887)

On July 25, 1867, another agreement was made between J. J. Wallace of Lykens and Frederick Weaver of Washington Township. With this agreement, a transportation line was established to deliver goods and merchandise between Lykens Valley and a point on 12th and Market Street in Philadelphia. (In later years, this point was the site of the Wanamaker Department Store.) The contract marked the beginning of a freight business that enhanced railroad trade. In 1868, this firm built the first railroad stations at Lykens and Williamstown. When the partnership began, J. J. Wallace produced two (numbered two and five) railroad cars, and was in charge of collecting the freight and managing the Lykens, Williamstown and Wiconisco stations. Frederick Weaver had three rail cars (numbered one, three and four), and was in charge of all the other stations, apparently from Elizabethville to Millersburg. In 1875, Mr. Weaver built the railroad station building in Elizabethville, and it has continued to exist until this day. Rail service continued for many years, under many different circumstances, and finally closed in 1981.

THE FREDERICK WEAVER FAMILY

[**FREDERICK A. WEAVER, Jr.** (b Feb 18, 1830 – d Nov 16, 1898, E'ville), was a son of Frederick b c1810 & Elmira (b c1812) Weaver. Frederick, Sr., came from Prussia, and settled first in Westmoreland Co. where he was a blacksmith. He later moved to Pottsville, Schuylkill County. While in Pottsville he married Caroline Conrad who died before 1860, probably buried in Pottsville. He moved to Berrysburg and purchased a lot from J. W. Beshler on April 11, 1855. But he sold it the next year on April 10, 1856 to Mary Delb and her husband John. When he sold the lot he was listed as a coach maker. In 1860 Frederick Weaver purchased a lot from Daniel J. Boyer. That year he was listed on the census in Berrysburg as a blacksmith. Elmira his wife, Sophia 24, daughter, Charles 5, Clara 1, was also listed. In 1865 he sold the property in Berrysburg and moved to Washington Township.

Frederick Weaver Jr, manufactured carriages and had a general mercantile business. In 1860 he and his wife Catharine lived in Berrysburg, and had Mary Bordner 18 and Lovina McCurtain 15 hired as servants and living in the household. He also had these coach maker apprentices: John Null 20, Isaac Rutter 19, William Hunter 18, Nicholas Moyer 20, and William Weidman 27 a journeyman. By 1865 he lived in Elizabethville and established the merchandise business of Fred Weaver & Son. By 1875 he was a partner in the distilling business. First with Miller, later with Gilbert, and eventually it became a successful family enterprise of Weaver & Son. Harry (the son) went on to become a very outstanding, enterprising citizen of Elizabethville. His involvement in various business operations and community projects benefited the town in many ways. Subsequently, generations of the Weaver family followed in his footsteps.

Frederick and Caroline (Conrad) Weaver had these children:
Henrietta (no dates), m Daniel Martin;
Christina b c1850 m William A.. Kottka b c1849a son of William (b c1810 - 1886) & Amelia Kottka of Wash. Twp. William Sr. was a widower living alone in Wash Twp. in 1880 next to his son William A. Kottka. In 1880, William A. Kottka was listed as a miller. Samuel Collier age 22 lived with them and was an apprentice miller. **Wm A. and Christina (Weaver) Kottka had these children:** <u>Ray Wm</u> b Nov 21,1871; <u>Katie Elva</u> b Apr 25, 1873; <u>Julia A</u> b c1877;
Sophia b c1851 listed as a sibling in Dau County birth records in 1853.
A son ___ b Apr 3, 1853, d young;
Caroline L. b Jan 14, 1856, m Edward G. Collier who d Jan 9, 1898, E'ville. **Edward G. and Caroline L. (Weaver) Collier had these children:** <u>Catherine A.</u> b c1875., m ___ Schaeffer of Berks Co; <u>William R.</u> b c1878; <u>Ray C.</u> b c1879; <u>Sylvia</u> b c 1885; <u>F. Reed</u> b c1887; <u>Christine</u> b c1894;

After Caroline his wife died, Frederick married Catharine Anna Helfrich (b Apr 30, 1834 Lehigh Co– d Apr 16, 1915 E'ville), a dau of Levi and Elizabeth (Wanner) Helfrich, granddaughter of Daniel and Maria Magdalena (Hoch) Helfrich of Lehigh and Berks Co. Frederick and Catherine lived in Mifflin Twp in 1860 as mentioned above. However, none of his children from the first wife lived with them. **Frederick & Catharine (Helfrich) Weaver had one son: Harry H.** (Sep 13, 1861 - Aug 24, 1924, bur Maple Grove Cem), m Jul 11, 1880 Josephine Schramm (c1867 - 1935), a dau of Hiram and Catharine Schramm. **They had these children:** <u>Frederick Blair</u> bapt. Jan 11, 1881, m Beula Miller; <u>Donald E</u> b Sep 20, 1881; <u>Lottie Beatrice</u> b Jul 20,1884, m Clarence Snyder; <u>Ida Pauline</u> b Dec 9, 1885, m Zena Miller; <u>Herbert H.</u>, <u>Howard H.</u>, m Miriam Bauder; <u>Richard L.</u> (Oct 23, 1895 - Feb 1, 1959), m Grace McLanachan (Feb 6, 1896– Jan 29,1963), a dau of Samuel Boyce McLanachan (Oct 27, 1863–Feb 28, 1905, bur Bbg) and wife *Virginia Hackman (Mar 25, 1868 - Apr 13, 1940), a dau of Rev. Henry and Mary Catherine (Hoke, Romberger) Hackman. **Richard L. & Grace (McLanachan) Weaver had these children:** <u>Dorothy</u> b Feb 8, 1919, m Henry Kiehl; <u>Richard S.</u> (Feb 1, 1921 - Nov 19, 1980), m Lena Forney; <u>Ned McLanachan</u> b Sep 19, 1924, m Leah Elizabeth Radel b May 16, 1921 and **had two sons:** *Anthony Michael* b Feb 5, 1946; *James Richard* b Mar 13, 1953; <u>Ruth H.</u> b Dec 18, 1929, m Donald Cook; <u>Scott A.</u>; Stella C m Galen Ulsh; Lottie d Jul 1, 1911 within months of her marriage to Clyde Eyster; Pauline m Clarence Snyder; Anna J. m Abner Rossman; Vivian C; Maude m Samuel H. Knisely; Daisy m John Franklin Cook; Mabelle m Col Philip Regar.

THE HACKMAN FAMILY

[Rev. Henry E. Hackman (Sep 15, 1824 - Dec 27, 1896, bur Matter Cem), a pastor in U.B. church, and son of Ephraim and Maria Magdalena (Orwig) Hackman of Sch Co, m 1st to Sarah ___ (1827 - 1862). m 2nd Mary Catherine (Hoke) Romberger (1837 - 1918). **Henry Hackman children to Sarah:** Anne b c1848; m Michael Hicker; **Mary** (Nov 30,1849 - 1929), m 1st Cornelius Hoy (1841 - 1880), bur Bbg. On Nov 7, 1891, Mary m 2nd William B. Lenker, widower of Amanda Deibler; **Alice** b c1851; **Edwin** (Jul 30, 1855 - Jun 21, 1936, Oberlin, Pa.), m Henrietta Stull; **Clara** b c1858; **Horace** b c1860, m Mollie Schoffstall; **Wilson Howard** (Feb 9, 1861 - Nov 15, 1928, bur Ebenezer Cem, Lebanon). **Henry Hackman children to 2nd wife Mary Catherine:** Ida; Elizabeth (1865 - 1886, bur with father); *Virginia (Mar 25, 1868 - Apr 13, 1940), m Samuel Boyce McLanachan (Oct 27, 1863 - Feb 28, 1905); **Laura** b 1870, m Harry Stine]

LAND OWNERS ELDER AND HALDEMAN

After the first wave of landowners purchased land from the Commonwealth of Pennsylvania, and villages began to be established, other individuals desired to purchase land in the area. Two residents of Harrisburg became perhaps the largest owners of land in the vicinity of what is now Loyalton. It is doubtful however, that either man ever lived here.

THOMAS ELDER (b Jan 30, 1767 -d Apr 29, 1853 in Harrisburg), son of Robert Elder (Jun 11, 1742 - Sep 29, 1818) and Mary J. (Thompson) Elder (1750 - 1813), is descended from a family that came to America very early. His grandfather Reverend John Elder born Jan 26,1706 in Edinburg, Scotland, died Jul 17,1792 in Paxtang Twp, Dau Co), Rev John Elder came from Lough Neagh, county Antrim, Ireland to Pennsylvania in 1730. John Elder graduated from University of Edinburgh, studied divinity, and in 1732 was licensed to preach the gospel. He ministered to several different Presbyterian congregations in the area of Harrisburg.

During the French and Indian War men from Reverend Elder's congregation were prompt to offer their services to protect the inhabitants. Rev. Elder became their enthusiastic captain and trained them as scouts. They were a very disciplined group, and these mounted rangers became well known as the "Paxtang Boys." Day and night during those traitorous times, Rev. Elder gathered the women and children together and prayed for his congregational charges. During at least two summers every man attending Paxtang Church carried his loaded rifle with him and Rev. Elder had two in the pulpit. On July 11,1763, he became a colonel, commanding the blockhouses and stockades from Easton to the Susquehanna. During the later part of 1763, many murders were committed in Paxtang, culminating in the destruction of the Indians on Conestoga Manor and at Lancaster. The rangers in Colonel (Rev.) Elders Company participated in the destruction, but it has never been proven that the Rev. Elder had previous knowledge of the plot. The men became known as the "riotous and murderous Irish Presbyterians." When the British army overran New Jersey, Rev Elder went to church that Sunday as usual. Instead of a sermon, he began a short and hasty prayer, and then called upon the patriotism of his congregation to come to the defense of their country. Three of his sons joined the march, one of the sons, John was only sixteen years old. During those years, Rev (Col) John Elder wrote letters to John Penn, Esq. and others, notifying them of the hostile activities and sufferings of the people in the settlements.

Rev. John Elder, a handsome, portly man, over six foot tall, continued in the ministry of his original congregations for fifty-six years. He died in 1792, and was buried in Old Paxtang Church yard. He married in 1740, Mary Baker (b1715 in Antrim, Ireland, d 1749 in Paxtang). His second wife was Mary Simpson (1732 - 1786).

Reverend John Elder destined his son Robert Elder (father of Thomas) for the ministry. But The French and Indian War changed his plans. As mentioned above he became a ranger with his father on the frontiers and continued throughout the war years to help in the field or in organizing the Associators. After the war, he went back to farming avoiding public office, preferring the quiet of domestic life.

Thomas Elder studied law in Philadelphia, and was admitted to the Dauphin County bar in 1791. He served as a private in Captain Dentzels Company during the Whiskey Insurrection. In 1812 he organized a company to erect the Harrisburg Bridge, first built over the Susquehanna, and for many years the longest in the Union. He served in many other capacities of public and private service. He married March 23, 1799, Catharine Cox who died June 12, 1810, a daughter of Colonel Cornelius Cox of Estherton, Pa. He married again on May 30, 1813 Elizabeth Shippen Jones (Dec 13, 1787 – Oct 31, 1871), a dau of Robert Strettell Jone and Ann Shippen of New Jersey.

Thomas Elder is mentioned here, because of his interests in the coalfields, and his many investments in land in Lykens Township and surrounding area. Also, because at least one member of his family (probably a cousin) lived in this area for some time.

ROBERT T. son of Thomas Elder (b Sep 1,1800 in Derry Twp - d Aug 13, 1854, bur Hanover Presbyterian Cem), m Hannah Dietrich (b c 1812 - d after 1894), a dau of Jacob and Magdalena Dietrich. Robert learned the hatter trade in Philadelphia, and then moved to Paxtang, Dauphin County and manufactured and sold hats. He moved to Washington Twp. before his marriage and purchased 220 acres of woodland, which he cleared and improved. Robert Elder and his family appeared on the census record for 1850 in Washington Twp., with no occupation. Robert & Hannah had nine children - some of them are: Mary b c1833; Jane b c1835; Rosetta b c1837; David D. b Mar 16, 1838, m Kate Stoever b Jan 30, 1866, a dau of Rev. C.F. and Louisa G. Stoever of Mechanicsburg. David grew up in this area until the age of twelve and then lived with an uncle in Derry Twp, attending school there for one year. His father died when he was sixteen, leaving him on his own. He became employed in several book and stationery shops, and then became a partner with J. W. Miller. In 1877 he purchased the business and with his brother traded under the name of David D. Elder and Co. In 1884 he sold the business to

David Bently, and manufactured wallpaper until 1892. He moved to his farm in Washington Twp, and took up agricultural pursuits. He was a veteran of the Civil War. David D. and his wife Kate had five children, three daughters and two sons. **Victoria** b c1840; **Ann** b c1845; **Thomas** b c1846; **Emma** b c1849; _____ b

JACOB M. HALDEMAN (b _____ d Dec 15, 1856), was the second son of John Haldeman (1753 - 1832) and Mary (Breneman) Haldeman. He was a descendant of Caspar Haldeman of Thun, Switzerland. The first of the family to come to America was **Jacob Haldeman** (b 1722 in Canton of Neufchatel - d Dec 31, 1784 in Lancaster Co, Pa. **John Haldeman** son of Jacob Haldeman (1753 - 1832), and father of Jacob M. Haldeman settled in Locust Grove, Lancaster County. He had numerous tracts of land and engaged in business pursuits with several different partners in Philadelphia, the China trade, and was a member of the first General Assembly of Pennsylvania.

Jacob M. Haldeman was well educated and inherited the business traits of his family. At the age of nineteen he was sent on horseback by his father to Pittsburgh, making his journey through many Indian settlements, to purchase flour to send down the river in flat-boats to New Orleans.

About 1806, assisted by his father, he purchased the waterpower and forge at the mouth of Yellow Breeches Creek in what is now New Cumberland and became established in the iron business.

The village was first known as Haldemans, before becoming New Cumberland. He added a rolling and slitting mill, and by his energy and industry soon became one of the foremost iron manufacturers in the state. During the War of 1812 he supplied the government with iron that was made into guns. With the success of these enterprises, he expanded his interests, and soon invested in land here in Lykens Township.

An island known as Haldeman's Island was located near the western shore of the Susquehanna River. A Swedish family of Hulings settled on nearby Duncans Island as early as 1735. Mr. Hulings established a ferry at the foot of Haldeman's Island that crossed the mouth of the Juniata River. He also built a causeway at one end for pack-horses to pass. This was the beginning of the white mans settlement on land where Indian villages were abundant. The first white settlements were by permission from the Indians, but later resulted in the vast conflicts that resulted in massacres.

As previously mentioned, on August 12, 1812 the Harrisburg Bridge Committee was formed to build a bridge across the Susquehanna joining the western shore near the Haldeman Island. Thomas Elder and Jacob M. Haldeman had been affiliated in business opportunities in places near Harrisburg and Cumberland County. Now Thomas Elder served as President, Jacob M. Haldeman was one of the Directors of the bridge committee. With their guidance the first foundation stone was laid on December 2, 1812. In October 1816 the first toll was received. They continued to be part of this organization and thirty-three years later, they were the only two of the original members still living. This account gives insight into the personal relationship of these two men.

In 1828, soon after coal was discovered here in Lykens Township, Thomas Elder and Jacob M. Haldeman began to purchase many acres of land. That year they were assessed as partners for 435 acres, mostly mountain land. Thomas Elder owned 300 acres of mountain land. By 1831 they had accumulated 1800 acres of unseated land, and another 300 acres of coal land. Some of this land was occupied by tenants and was located in or near what is now Loyalton. In 1834, Thomas Elder had 480 acres of regular land, 1137 acres of coal land. Jacob M. Haldeman had a total of 1879 acres of land. In 1837 Thomas Elder had 122 acres of regular land. Together, Elder and Haldeman owned 480 acres of regular land, and 2300 acres of coal land. In 1840 most of the land became Wiconisco Township. After these many years, most of these acres continue to be mountain land.

LOCATION OF AND WHAT BECAME OF THEIR LAND

Elder and Haldeman received land from many sources. Some of their land came in large tracts. Others were small tracts, purchased from owners who perhaps had a change of circumstances, changed their mind about settling here, or perhaps discovered land that better fit their needs. Much of the land was on the north east side of Loyalton on or near Short Mountain. Therefore most of the mountain or coal land remained unsettled. The following tracts or parts of tracts became part of the more domesticated section of the area.

LAND FROM JAMES WAY PATENT

In Feb 1826, Commonwealth of Pennsylvania conveyed a tract of land to George Pierce, executor of the estate of James Way. The land was made up of two tracts containing a total of 378 acres 120 perches. It had been surveyed in two pieces on May 25, 1773, one tract to Jacob Way, one to Benjamin Way. By separate deeds (one in August 1811 to Jacob Way, and one in January1812 Benjamin Way), both men conveyed their respective rights in the land to Caleb Way. In March 1812, Caleb Way died, and his son James became executor of his estate. James died in March 1825, after appointing George Pierce his executor. This land had previously been in Lykens Township, but then through redistricting became part of Wiconisco Township. It was also part of the tracts of land that Thomas Elder and Jacob M. Haldeman owned though divers conveyances.

On May 3, 1826, George Pierce, executor of James Way disbursed with many acres of land by conveying several tracts to various buyers. One tract containing 95 acres, 147 perches sold to Henry Kuntzelman. On September 13, 1830, Henry Kuntzelman and his wife conveyed their tract of land to Thomas and Jacob M. Haldeman. This tract was located along the road from Millersburg to Williams Valley, and was bounded by Christian Hoffman's land, the Wiconisco Creek, and had been part of the land conveyed to Rachel and Jane Ferree. On May 3, 1826, George Pierce, executor of James Way conveyed another tract of 131 acres 40 perches of land to Samuel ImSchoffstall, but a few years later, on January 13, 1831, Samuel and Catherine ImSchoffstall sold this land to Thomas Elder and Jacob M. Haldeman. A third tract belonging to James Way containing 44 acres 146 perches of land was conveyed May 3, 1826, to Christian Hoffman Jr. But Christian Hoffman and his wife on January 14, 1831 conveyed the same to Thomas Elder and Jacob M Haldeman. A fourth tract of James Way land containing 52 acres 68 perches with appurtenances was conveyed on May 31, 1826, to Daniel G. Hoffman, whom with his wife Susannah transferred it to Thomas Elder and Jacob M. Haldeman on January 22, 1831.

In 1831, the tax record reflects two tracts of (James) "Ways" land containing 250 acres, now owned by Elder and Haldeman. In 1834 and 1837, the tax record shows 244 unseated acres that were previously owned by Kuntzelman, ImSchoffstall, G. Hoffman, Christian Hoffman, Jr. and James Way.

Thomas Elder died in 1853, and on March 26, 1855, his attorney conveyed his half of the land to John Jacob Dietrich and Daniel Reise. A portion of this land known as Elm was conveyed August 1, 1857, to William Kottka, who had just recently moved into the area. The ground in Elm was laid out in lots by Daniel Hoffman in 1855, and William Kottka received one of those 40 x 140 foot lots.

THE HENRY BOHNER FARM
(Historically Remembered As The Old Indian Campground)

This tract of land may well prove to be the earliest settlement in the area near Loyalton. It is said to have a unique historic background that takes it back to an early period when it was the site of an Indian village. Egles in his History of Dauphin County mentions that when Andrew Lykens was here, the Indian village was adjacent to his land. The spring near the house in which the Henry Bohner's lived, was the head of the run that emptied into the head of the Forge dam. It was called "Indian Town Run." Egles also mentions that Joel Ferree occupied this very early house, probably the first in the area built between 1795 - 1800. (He died in Baltimore in 1812).

Jacob and Benjamin Way were the early owners of this land and by a succession of transactions Joel Ferree, Christain Hoffman, Thomas Elder and Jacob M. Haldeman, Adam and Catherine Romberger, followed by their son Daniel Romberger possessed the land. On August 4, 1860 Daniel and Hannah Romberger sold 100 acres, 75 perches of the land to Jacob Lubold, a resident of Wiconisco Township. In April 1871, Rebecca Lubold sold the land of Jacob Lubold to John M. Row.

A Brief History Of The Area Coal Industry

By sundry transactions John M. Row for years had been both accumulating and dispersing much land, without officially recording deeds. Thus from here on it is difficult to trace some of his land to the earlier owners.

Deed Volume T – 45 – 409

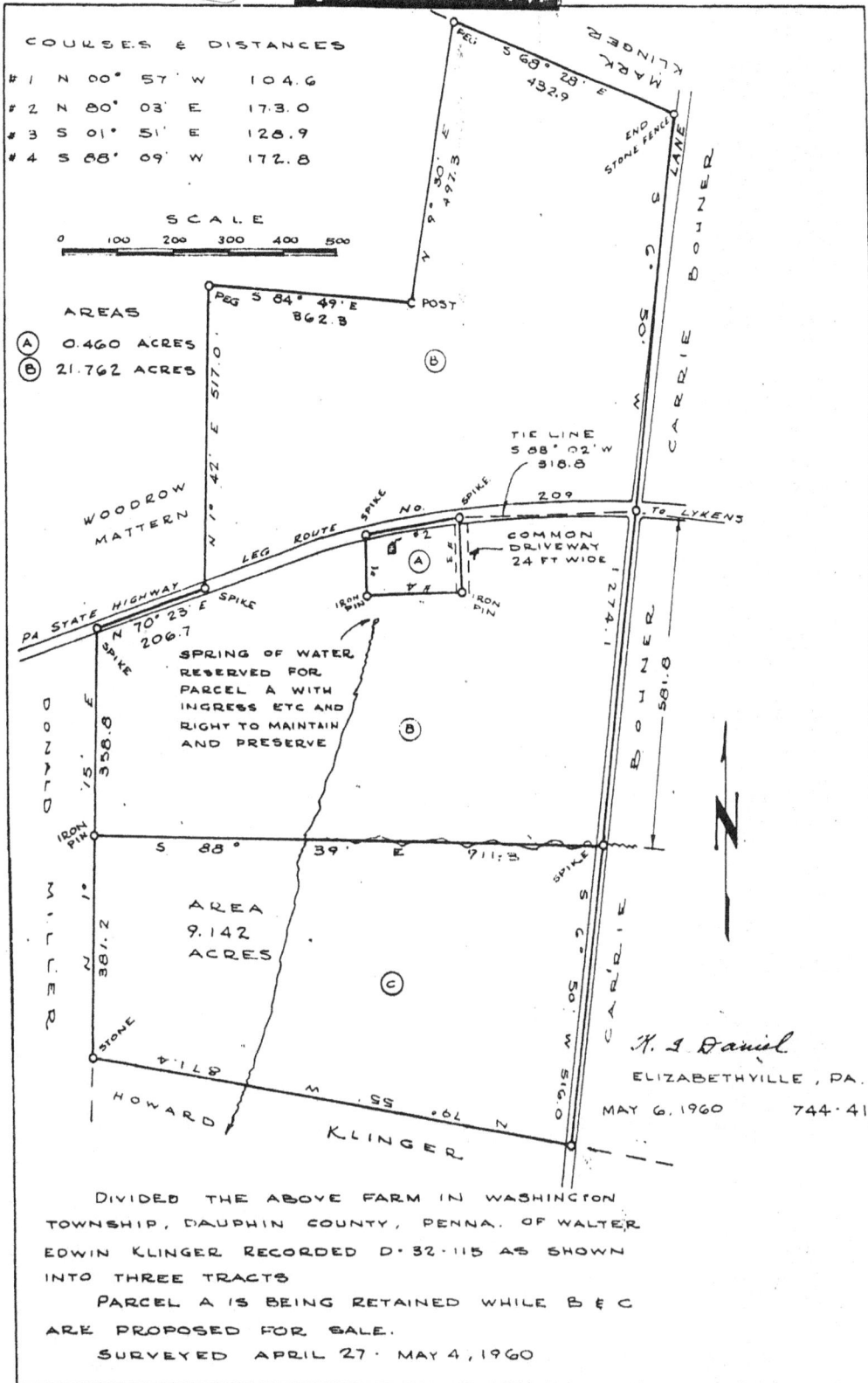

COURSES & DISTANCES

# 1	N 00° 57' W	104.6
# 2	N 80° 03' E	173.0
# 3	S 01° 51' E	128.9
# 4	S 88° 09' W	172.8

SCALE

0   100   200   300   400   500

AREAS

(A) 0.460 ACRES
(B) 21.762 ACRES

AREA 9.142 ACRES

SPRING OF WATER RESERVED FOR PARCEL A WITH INGRESS ETC AND RIGHT TO MAINTAIN AND PRESERVE

COMMON DRIVEWAY 24 FT WIDE

TIE LINE S 88° 02' W 318.8

R. I. Daniel
ELIZABETHVILLE, PA.
MAY 6, 1960   744·41

DIVIDED THE ABOVE FARM IN WASHINGTON TOWNSHIP, DAUPHIN COUNTY, PENNA. OF WALTER EDWIN KLINGER RECORDED D·32·115 AS SHOWN INTO THREE TRACTS

PARCEL A IS BEING RETAINED WHILE B & C ARE PROPOSED FOR SALE.

SURVEYED APRIL 27 · MAY 4, 1960

A survey taken May 6, 1960, showing a modern plan of the land in the vicinity of the early Indian village site.

Two other patents were backdated January 31, 1775 to Joel Ferree from John Penn. Isaac Ferree son of Joel Ferree inherited his land. When Isaac died the land was divided and his granddaughter (3rd daughter of his son Isaac), Rebecca Ferree, wife of Jacob Mayer inherited part of it. On June 7, 1836 Jacob and Rebecca Mayer conveyed a portion of their land containing 47 acres 115 perches with houses to John M. Row. Thomas B. Mayer received the remaining land and after he died it was sold to Anna R. Lubold in 1922. Ralph W. Klinger purchased the four acres in 1942, and his widow sold to Ella J. Graeff on July 5, 1977. Later that year on November 1, 1977 Ella J. Graeff conveyed the same property to Eugene P. and Kay A. Matter.

On November 8, 1873, the heirs of John M. Rowe sold part of his plantation and land containing 41 acres 7 and 8/10 perches to Henry Bohner. The deed mentions that some of this land had belonged to Jacob and Rebecca Mayer, and some had previously by sheriff sale been owned by Lewis Heilner and Josiah Bowman. The land bordered on John M. Row's other land, the east side of a lane, Isaac Lubold, south to Thomas B. Moyer, north to Peter O. Johns, Charles Hoover, and the Daniel Klinger estate. Henry died in September 1908, but previously wrote a will bequeathing the plantation to his wife Kate. Several months later in February 1909 Kate sold some of the property to her son Ray H. Bohner. She reserved for herself a small tract containing 11,250 square feet, and on that land she had a two-story frame house built. Ray owned the farm by 1919.

On January 30, 1930, Ray H. and Carrie Bohner conveyed the house and land of his mother to Joseph A. and Annie M. Riegel of Washington Township. The land borders on the highway from Loyalton to Lykens. On Oct 2, 1991, Anna M. Riegel, widow of Joseph "Jasper" Riegel sold the premises to Gerald Riegel, the present owner.

Another tract of 30 acres 27 perches of land with appurtenances, was sold by Rebecca, widow of Jacob Moyer to Daniel and Emaline Klinger in 1870. Rebecca had inherited the land from her Ferree family. Edwin and Kate Klinger were the next owners, followed by their son Walter E. Klinger. In May 1960, Walter conveyed the land in two tracts: Nine plus acres (tract C) to Short Mountain Sportsman Club, the other 21 plus acres (tract B) to William H. and Joy Snyder. A small tract (A) with house was reserved for himself. "Access to a spring of water located 81 feet from the southern line of tract A were reserved for parcel A . [Notice survey printed below.] The spring near the house in which the Henry Bohner's lived, was the head of the run that emptied into the head of the Forge dam. It was called "Indian Town Run." Egles also mentions that Joel Ferree occupied this very early house. The small tract (A) is possibly the house referred to by Egles. [A public sale held probably in the 1980s was located at a house in this vicinity. A person attending that sale noted that it was a very old dilapidated house. The floors were treacherous and part of one section of the floor fell in during the sale. Perhaps it was the old house referred to above.]

William H. Snyder conveyed 84 acres of land to Nicholas and Linda Lire in 1976, part of it being the above described acreage. The 84 acres were resold in 1984, to Kenneth and Fae Horning, apparently present owners. This described area is most likely the site of the Indian Village.

[**BOHNER** genealogy information elsewhere in book.]

MICHAEL E. RIEGEL (1870 – Sep 1, 1940, bur Hoffman Cem), m Mary M ____(1876 – 1948).
Michael E. and Mary M (__) Riegel had these children: **JOSEPH ANDREW**, also known as Jasper A. (Jun 2, 1894 bapt Hoffman Ch – d Nov 6, 1961,bur Hoffman Cem), m Jun 30, 1925 Anna May Lebo?.
Joseph and Anna May Riegel had a son Gerald. **FORREST** (1898 – 1933, bur Hoffman Cem) WWI soldier]

ONE ACRE 40 PERCHES OF LAND TO PETER BOHNER
(Now Raymond C. and Olive M. Bechtel land)

On April 9, 1838, John and Susan Row conveyed 1 acre 40 perches of land to Jacob Row. Jacob Row and his wife owned this small lot until January 16, 1860 when they sold it to Henry Bohner, Jr. On February 21, 1874, Henry and Kate Bohner sold to Peter Bohner. On December 11, 1905, after Peter Bohner died, his executor Peter A. Matter conveyed the small tract with house and other buildings to John H. Troutman. The land was bound by road to Lykens, north to Thomas B. Moyer and Daniel Wommer land. John H. Troutman died August 12, 1930, his wife died May 30, 1968. The heirs Elmer A. and Mary Troutman, Eva Alvesta and Mark F. Klinger, Clayton G. and Ruthe E. _____ conveyed October 18, 1968 to Forrest L. Troutman. On May 6, 1972, Forrest L. Troutman died and on June 29, 1972 his administrator conveyed the one acre 40 perch tract to Raymond C. and Olive M. Bechtel of Lykens. The old buildings are now gone, apparently a vacant piece of land.

A Brief History Of The Area Coal Industry

LAND TO PETER O. JOHNS
(ten acres 1875)

John and Ann Ellizabeth Row conveyed ten acres of land to Peter O. Johns March 25, 1873. After Peter died, Maria his wife sold his land. These ten acres with appurtenances were conveyed to John B. Straub on June 16, 1882. They were on the south side of the road from Millersburg to Lykens, and were bound by land of Isaac Lubold, south to Moses Nutt (now Charles Hoover) John Row (now Henry Bohner) south to the public road. John E. and Salome Straub assigned the land back to Maria L. Johns in March 1884, and after some years, on March 31, 1900, she conveyed the 10 acres to Michael E. Riegel. After Michael and his wife Mary died, the administrators of his estate, Joseph also known as Jasper A. Riegel and Helen M. Warfel sold the 10 acres with appurtenances to Kenneth Bain on March 13, 1950. Kenneth Bain died October 11, 1975, and the property was conveyed May 11, 1977 to Robert J. Barder, Jr and Rosanna Ritzman of Tower City.

ISAAC LUPOLD FARM
(115 acres in 1875)

This land was part of the James Way grant. Egle tells in the History of Dauphin County, that this site was the location of the second house built in the area between 1795 and 1800. George Setzler is said to be the builder. [A John and Elisabeth Setzler had a daughter Susanna b Jul 2,1814, bapt. at St. John's Hill Church.]
Samuel Lupold became the owner of 113 acres of the land, and after his death it was conveyed to Isaac S. Lupold on January 1, 1872. The land was bound by Short Mt. Coal Company, south to Moses Nutt and John Row. On June 15, 1888, Isaac and Catharine Lupold sold 39 acres 140 perches of the land to A. F. Engelbert.

THE WALLACE FARM

Farm As It Looks Today

Another early settlement that is now just over the border in Wiconisco Township, was the farm that belonged to John J. Wallace. According to Egle's history, from 1795 to 1800 only three houses were built between Oak Dale Forge and the site of the town of Lykens. One was located on the Henry Bohner property, and occupied by Joel Ferree Jr. who died in the War of 1812 in Baltimore. The second house was built by George Setzler on what became Isaac (Seebolt, Lubolt ???). The third was a cabin built on what would become the John Wallace property [See 1875 Wiconisco Twp. map near border of Washington Twp]. Peter Schoffstall built the house and he lived there for a time before Peter Minnich owned it. In later years Solomon Schoffstall lived in this cabin, but he eventually erected the old log house that survived for many years.

It was originally part of the James Way tract, and later sold (about 1826) to Daniel Hoffman. On April 22, 1869, a public sale was held and 130 acres of land was conveyed to J. J. Wallace and William Hoke. It bordered land of Gideon Shadel, Elias Snyder, other land of William Hawk, and the road leading from Millersburg to Pottsville.

114

When that transaction was made, 80 acres of land were in fine cultivation. It had a two-story stone house, a two story weather-boarded house, a fine log bank barn and a ½ story springhouse. There was a spring of never failing water and an apple orchard. During the next few years, the stone house apparently disappeared.

John J. Wallace later moved to Lykens, and sold this land with "two-story structure", 2 story weather-boarded house with basement, a fine bank barn, a spring and apple orchard to Anthony F. Engelbert on March 27, 1883. Anthony F. Engelbert died in 1894, and his estate was conveyed to Ramon Shadle on February 24, 1903. Ramon Shadle died in 1943, and his widow and son conveyed three tracts of land to Robert C. Matter November 20, 1943. The tracts contained 9 acres 143 perches, 4 ½ acres, and 100 acres 75.3 perches. Two days later, Robert Matter sold to Etta Shadle. On May 1, 1954, Etta Shadle conveyed three tracts from the land to Lloyd and Beulah Troutman. But on June 12, 1954, the Troutman's sold the same three tracts to Charles E. Wolfe of Elizabethville. Years later, on March 9, 1970, Charles E. Wolfe conveyed to Margaret M. and Arthur Markovitz, and on March 30, 1982, they conveyed to Amos D. and Anna S. Lapp.

THE WALLACE FAMILY

[ROBERT WALLACE (1796 - 1871) m Isabella ___(Apr 29, 1794 –Nov 30, 1860), came from Ayrshire, Scotland to America and brought their family with them. They had one known child:
CRAWFORD WALLACE (Dec 15, 1825 - Feb 8, 1893, bur IOOF Cem, Lykens), son of Robert Wallace (1796 - 1871) and his wife Isabella (1794 - 1860), came with his parents from Scotland was a coal miner in 1880. He m Jeannet ____ (1828 - May 7, 1905), born in Scotland. In 1880 they lived in Wiconisco Twp., and had Ellen Hutchinson age 24, a music teacher b in Scotland with them. Crawford and Jeannet Wallace had these children: Jeannet b c1852 was a seamstress at home in 1880; John C. b c1855 Scotland was a coal miner in 1880 next to Crawford Wallace, m Sarah E b c1859, had these children: Mary E b c1877; Jennie G b c1879. Alfred b c 1857 coal miner; Sidney b 1860 coal miner; William b c1862;Maggie H. (1864 - 1887); Lewis B (1865 - 1910), clerk in store in 1880; Daisy b c1869; Maud b c1871;
WILLIAM WALLACE (no dates, d in Harrisburg), m Elisabeth Christomer, a native of Leb Co., d near Dauphin . William was of Scotch-Irish descent, whose occupation was charcoal burning, later farmer. They had these known children: THOMAS; LEGRAND (Jan 23, 1823 - bapt as adult Dec 11, 1852, St.Johns Bbg - ____), did not marry, lived with his brother John. (record gives parents as Wm and Elis Wallace.)
JOHN JAMES (b Oct 20 1824, Leb Co, bapt as adult Dec 11, 1852 St. Johns Bbg (record names parents William and Elisabeth Wallace), d Mar 11, 1906). He was m in 1849 to Elizabeth Snavely (Apr 8, 1831 in Cornwall Twp., Leb Co - Sep 26, 1914), a dau of Thomas and Mary A. (Lemon) Snavely. John J. was employed by the railroad, taught school, and in 1860 was constable in Wiconisco Twp. He also owned a boat that he used on the canal. In 1867 he and Frederick Weaver became partners and operated the line until 1877. John James and Elizabeth (Snavely) Wallace children (some bapt St. John's Hill, Bbg, some Zion Luth Lykens: Mary Elisabeth (Jun 25,1852, bapt St. Johns Hill Ch– 1856); William L. (Nov 22, 1856 - June 14, 1923, bur IOOF Cem), m Apr 1883 in Hughesville, Lycoming Co. Emma Snyder (May 12, 1856 Port Carbon, Sch Co. - 1937). By the age of 11 he worked in his fathers railroad office at Lykens, but in 1872 transferred to Williamstown and was station agent. Later for 9 months he tried the tea business in Williamsport. In 1888 he became chief clerk in the NC Railroad Co at Lykens. William & Emma (Snyder) Wallace children: Verdilla; Clara; Cloyd; Mary; Herbert; John G b c1858, moved to Phila; Alfred b c1860, moved to Phila; Samuel T. (1862 - 1935, bur IOOF, Lykens), m Emma Klinger (Jul 1864 - 1915). Samuel was a brakeman on the railroad between Renovo & Harrisburg. Then became proprietor of the Glenn House in Lykens for two years. He opened a boot & shoe trade in Lykens in 1895. Had son C Lee (1884 - 1960); Amy Estella b Jul 10, 1867, m Henry Harter; Jennie Elisabeth (Jul 26, 1872– Dec 1876); ELIZABETH; HARRIET (no dates) m James Shaw; MARY; WILLIAM H. (1835 - ___), m Pricilla ___ (Dec 25, 1842 - Dec 29, 1912, bur Lykens). They lived in Lykens Twp in 1880, he was a miner.They had these known children (some bapt Zions Luth Ch, Lykens):Charles Bell b Dec 30, 1864; Carolina b 1865; Harriet L b Nov 11,1867; Arthur W. b 1870; Thomas Lester (Jul 7, 1872 - Jan 24, 1890, pneumonia, bur IOOF Cem); William Henry (May 21, 1874 - 1934, bur Calvary Meth Cem); Howard Sylvester b Sep 3, 1876; Mamie Dell b May 28, 1878; Roy Lagram b Sep 18, 1881; John Edgar b May 29, 1884.]

[ANTHONY F. ENGELBERT(b c1832 - d Jan 6, 1894, bur Calvary Meth Cem, Wiconisco), m Sarah E. ____ (b c1836 - d Dec 4, 1908). Her parents were from Wales. Anthony is listed with a general business in

1880. Amanda Matter age 18 lived with the family. **Anthony F. and Sarah E. Engelbert children: Annie Mary** (Sep 13, 1861 – Dec 23, 1952, bur Calvary Meth Cem), m _____ Sanner; **John Robert** (Jul 25, 1865 – Oct 30, 1894, bur Calvary Meth Cem), m Florence Alvord b Mar 24, 1867, a dau of Jacob & Lucy Ann Alvord, postmaster of Lykens. John met an untimely death. He, his wife and sister traveled to Millersburg that morning, and started for home in the evening. As they neared the Red Tavern the two ladies continued their journey, while John turned his horse to the tavern. There he met his good friend Philip Hawk, who noticed that John was intoxicated, and invited him to stay over night. Unwilling to spend the night, John headed for home. But as he approached Uriah Koppenhaver's home, he decided to seek entry to their home in hopes of getting warm. He tied his horse to a post and abruptly gained entry to the house in a way that aroused suspicion. The frightened mother and 19 year old son were home alone, and thinking he was a burglar, the son using an old musket, shot and killed him; **Amy E.** b Jul 15, 1870; **Catharine Irene** (Jun 18, 1873 – Jul 19, 1943,bur Calvary Meth Cem); **Harry A.** (Jul 31, 1877 – Jan 5, 1903, bur Calvary Meth Cem).]

[**PETER MINNICH** (b Up Pax Sep 17, 1785 – d Sep 25, 1855 Wash T. bur Rife Cem), a son of George & Anna Barbara Minnich, m Feb 21, 1808 Anna Maria Matter (b Mifflin Twp Jan 21, 1790 – Jan 29, 1871). He a veteran of War of 1812. **Peter and Anna Maria (Matter) Minnich children (some bapt St. Johns Hill Ch); Peter** b Feb 19,1808; **Johannes** (May 24,1809–Jun 22, 1894); **Michael** (Sep 24,1811– Mar 10, 1891), m Lucy Ann ___ b c1813, they had these children: **Jeremiah** b c1834; **Josiah** b c1837; **Cyrus** b c1839; **Uriah** b c1842; **Elias** b c1844; **Sarah Malinda** bJun 5, 1847; **Catherine** b c1849 Rife. In 1850, they lived in Wash Twp. and Mary Riegel age 58 lived with them; **Daniel** b Sep 24, 1811; **Elizabeth** (Dec 29, 1813 - 1882), m John Travitz (1810 – 1880); **Catharine** Nov 24, 1815 bapt St.Johns Hill; **Sarah** (Dec 17,1817 – May 10, 1880) -mother named Ava Maria – May 10, 1890, bur St.Jacob Cem, Waynesville), m Jacob Gipple (Jan 16, 1815– Sep 23, 1882), a son of Christian & Johanna (Stroh) Gipple, **had son Joseph** b Jul 28, 1857.]

LAND FROM THE JAMES WAY ESTATE

Another patent from Commonwealth of Pennsylvania dated February 2, 1826 was issued to George Pierce, executor of the estate of James Way, and contained 180 acres of land in Lykens Township. May 3, 1826 became the transfer date for this tract, when it was conveyed to Rachel Wilson and Jane Ferree who was married to Lawrence Shomper. On March 9, 1832, Rachel Wilson, Lawrence Shomper and Jane his wife appointed Joel B. Ferree as their attorney to sell the land that was bound by land of Thomas Elder on the west and north, Peter Romberger on the east, Joseph S. Barnett and Jacob Haldeman on the south. It was conveyed March 27, 1832 to Michael of Lykens Twp. This area became the town of Lykens, thus ending its affiliation with Lykens Township.

THE JAMES WAY FAMILY

[This family of Quaker background is traced back to **ROBERT WAY** (b Feb 21, 1667 England – d1722 Kennett, Chester Co), a son of Edward Way of Great Marlow, England. Robert Way had lived in Wiltshire, England before coming to America. He settled in Chester County and continued in the Quaker religion. They had ties to the Buffington family, probably in several ways. **Robert and Hannah Hickman (b 1673 – d aft 1727), had these children: John** (1694 - 1777), m Anna Hannum (1705 - 1800), and among their children was **Caleb** (1732 - 1812). **The children of Caleb Way were:** Eldest child *James Way (1763 - 1825) mentioned below; William Way received a patent in June 1809 on land called "Mill Place" located in Up Paxton, later Lykens Twp. He died unmarried. His land was sole to Solomon ImSchoffstall; Phoebe Way; Ann Way m ___ Pierce; Jacob Way; Rebecca Way m Woodward; and youngest child Mary Way b Apr 1, 1785, whom m George Pierce (b 1780 – d Oct 15, 1835, West Caln, Chester Co). George Pierce served as executor of his brother-in-law James Way's estate, and conveyed the land that James Way owned here in Lykens and Wiconisco Twp to several separate buyers; **Robert** (1696 - 1736) moved to Suffolk, Mass.; **Joseph** (1697 - after 1755), m Sarah Pyle; **Jacob** (1698 - 1777), m Sarah Hannum; **Elizabeth** (1700 - Oct 6, 1764), m Sep 2, 1738 to John Buffington a son of Richard and Phoebe (Grubb) Buffington; **Francis** (1702 - 1785); **Caleb** (1704 – c1782); **James** (1708 - 1759), m1738 Mary Kerlin; **Benjamin** (1710 - 1758), m Mary Painter, a dau of Samuel and Eliz (Buxcey) Painter.

*JAMES WAY(b Aug 26, 1763 Chester, Pa – d Mar 11, 1825 in Phila.), a son of Caleb Way (Nov 30, 1732 – Nov 16, 1812) and Rebecca Mendenhall b 1736, of Chester Co. James m 1st in 1787 Sarah Trego b 1763. He m 2nd Jan 19, 1815 Ann Johnson Howell (b 1791 in Md. – d Jul 29, 1864). His 3rd wife was Sarah Buffington Tinker b c1763. **James Way and his wife Ann Johnson Howell had these children**: **Amanda** (Oct 3, 1815 – pre1878), m John H. Frick; **William Penn** (Feb 7, 1818 in Md – d pre 1895), m c1844 Amanda Stenmetz b 1823; **John Tunis** b Dec 14, 1819 in Md.; **Charles W.** b 1821 in Md.; **George Pierce** (Jun 21, 1823 – Oct 2, 1897), lived in Yonkers, N.Y;]

THE SHORT MOUNTAIN MURDER IN 1857
(All For A Watch!)

Throughout the history of the Upper End of Dauphin County, serious crimes were uncommon. Our years of research have uncovered only a handful of murders or suspicious deaths. Three of them occurred during the 1850s. One took place in Gratz when George Hoffman was murdered at a Militia gathering in 1856. Another took place in Elizabethville July 1859 when Nancy Bender Hawk was found hanging from a tree. The one described here took place in May 1857. It was such a phenomenon that the "Daily & Weekly Telegraph" of Harrisburg published a complete history of the trial in a book. Thanks to Tom Buffington of Loyalton, we have a photocopy of the original book in our library.

On the evening of May 25, 1857, as three women (Sarah Schoffstall Lebo wife of Daniel, Mrs Sarah Hoover wife of Samuel, & Mrs. Angeline Shoop, wife of Frederick were crossing Short Mountain, a peculiar smell attracted their attention. Making a search, they found the decayed body of a person laying a few rods from the path that crossed the mountain. They raised an alarm and soon a crowd had congregated together. Among them was William Williams, who appeared calm and totally unconcerned about the matter. He remarked that perhaps he had been the last person to see Hendricks alive, as he had been at his house three weeks before. Hendricks had not been seen since. Esquire Ferree held an inquest, appointed a jury, and deputized constable Richard Nolen as foreman of the inquest.

The jury of inquest identified the body as that of Daniel Hendricks. John S. Updegrove, one of the jurors, stated that Hendricks had been boarding with him at the time of the murder, and that he had a watch in his pocket the morning he left home. They searched the pockets of the deceased, but found only a piece of the watch-guard attached to his vest buttonhole. By-standers knew that Williams had a watch similar to the one described by Updegrove. The jury started for Williams' house, about three-fourth mile distant, and reached it by midnight, arousing the sleeping family. Williams opened the door, the jury and others entered the house, and told him that they came to make inquiry about the watch. He was sworn, but denied having the watch. He stated that Hendricks had been to his house "last Sunday three weeks ago." Williams gave him liquor, both started over the mountain to Gratztown. Williams accompanied him as far as to the mines. He said Hendricks did not have a watch that day, but he knew he owned one.

The jury then separated, agreeing to meet at squire Ferree's office at five o'clock next morning. The body was left unguarded during the remaining part of the night. After the meeting they traveled toward Williams house to arrest him, but met him a short distance from the house, on his way to work. After several denials Williams admitted that he had Hendricks watch "for a debt." Williams was taken before Esquire Ferree, and confined in a properly guarded room, at Miller's Hotel in Lykenstown. The jury accompanied by Dr. Withers then proceeded to where the body of Hendricks lay, to complete their examination. Grizzly details describe the examination! A coffin was then prepared. The body was buried at the site at the expense of the county. The Inquest then went to Williams house where they found a gun, the bore of which was sufficiently large to admit the pebble found in the body of Hendricks. Williams was indicted for the murder on August 27,1857. After a hearing before the Justice, he was immediately conveyed to Harrisburg, and committed for imprisonment in Dauphin County prison. A trial was held in November and on the 18th he was convicted of first-degree murder. A motion for a new trial was overruled. The prisoner was sentenced to be hanged. After the hanging the body was placed in a coffin, removed to the Poor House burying ground and interred.

William Williams born in 1828 was a son of John and Catherine Williams and grew up in Clarks Valley. His mother died soon after he was born. He and several siblings were under the care of their father, known as the "blind basket maker" who became blind after a severe case of small pox. William became an apprentice carpenter to Jacob Fite of Clarks Valley, later worked at Victoria Furnace where he met Emeline Row b Aug 16,1830, a dau of John & Susannah (Ferree) Row. They married before 1850 against her parents' wishes. William and Emeline appear on the 1850 census in Wiconisco Twp., without children. They had a child that died young, and Adam born Sep 14,1852, bapt Nov 14, 1852, with sponsors William & Barbara Rau. Emeline died shortly after that. A year later, William married Justina Haines, had a daughter Mary born after his conviction in January 1858. Mary lived with the Gideon

Shadel family in1860. William lived in the Lykens area ten years, worked at Short Mountain Coal Company. He was remembered as being "wild, reckless and immoral."

Daniel Hendricks grew up elsewhere and came to this area apparently to work in the mines. He was married and had two children, but separated from his wife about two years before he was murdered. His wife "ran off" with a Mr. Fisher, but after Hendricks was murdered she came back to their house to get some hymns and her wedding cap out of a bureau. Hendricks was noted as a heavy drinker with a temper, and immoral.

Tom Buffington and Ed Bechtel were familiar with the fact that the grave of Daniel Hendricks was on the site of the murder. When the account of the murder and trial was found, they ventured up along the path on Short Mountain and found the grave with tombstone in place.

William Williams (1828 – 1857)

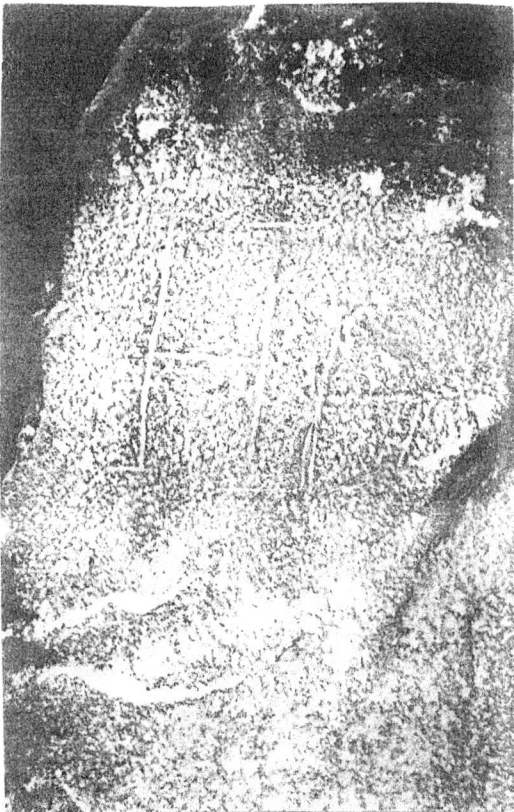

Thomas "Buff" Buffington holding gravestone of Daniel Hendricks on Short Mountain where Hendricks was murdered and later buried. Ed Bechtel took the photo Aug 24, 2006 when they hiked to the location.

Gravestone of Hendricks murder victim

Chapter 7

THE VILLAGE OF LOYALTON
(Earlier Known as Short Mountain)

Oak Dale established about 1830, for many years enjoyed commercial success, and was the central focus for everything that went on in the surrounding community. But as time passed, more commercial enterprises sprung up along the main road leading from what became Lykens to Millersburg. More houses were built, and by 1875, Short Mountain Post Office and village was noted on the map. The name Loyalton (village) came at a later time.

During the early years, Commonwealth of Pennsylvania granted land located in what became Short Mountain (now Loyalton) to a number of individuals. While the forge area flourished, other nearby sites became successful ventures as well.

TWO AERIAL VIEWS OF LOYALTON (BOTH UNDATED)

Looking Westward Over Loyalton Photo Taken 1950s

The two aerial views of Loyalton (one above, the other on the following page) were taken in recent years, but the exact date is not known. These photos were taken from opposite ends of the town and give a special view of this beautiful little village surrounded by fields and woods.

Looking Eastward Toward Loyalton Photo Taken c1970

OLD LANDMARKS IN THE VILLAGE

The Oak Dale Forge was the center of attention in the early days. But several sites near or in what would later become Loyalton are significant for their historic or traditional influence. They are worthy of being mentioned. Several of these sites have been obliterated over these many years; some can no longer be recognized. The following sites have been established as having historic value.

THE GRISTMILL PROPERTY

Two Views Of The Early Gristmill (Much Later Referred To As Fisher's Mill)
(The Ferree mill was here pre-1800, the brick mill was assessed in 1828)

120

Home Of Mr. & Mrs. George Luther
(Built c1830 Part of Gristmill Property)

The land for the gristmill originated from parts of two early patents. Some of the land came from a tract that Jacob and Margaret Neff owned and conveyed to John Field on October 31, 1779. John and Deborah Field sold the tract on February 19, 1787 to Samuel McCrory of Armagh Township, Mifflin County. Samuel McCrory, by his will recorded in Lewistown, conveyed the same tract with houses to Eleanor Stahlman on February 6, 1806. Eleanor Stahlman of Lower Mahantango Township, Schuylkill County, widow of John Stahlman, conveyed the same to Henry Shubert, surveyor, on April 1, 1830.

Two other tracts were patented to Timothy Horsfield, Esquire of Bethlehem executor of the estate of William Parsons of Easton, Northampton County. One tract containing 283 1/2 acres of land was situated on the Wiconisco Creek, bounded by vacant land, and crossing Wiconisco Creek. Another tract containing 405 acres had some type of appurtenances. As executor of William Parson, Timothy Horsfield on November 4, 1768 sold the two tracts of land to Benjamin Spyker, who lived in Lancaster County before 1749.

THE SPYKER FAMILY

[The Spyker family originally lived in Lancaster County, but later moved to Tulpehocken Township, Berks County. **PETER SPYKER, esq.** (Oct 7, 1711 - Jul 18, 1789, bur Tulpehocken Trinity Ref Cem) , is the earliest known ancestor. He m Maria Margaret Seidel (Mar 21, 1721 - Oct 16, 1781). Peter was licensed in 1774, as an Indian trader, served as an officer in the Provincial Army during the French and Indian War. In the beginning of the Revolution, he assisted in   organizing Berks County Militia, and went to the Constitutional Convention Jul 15, 1776. **Peter and Maria Margaret (Seidel) Spyker had these known children:**

PETER b c1743, m _____ (no dates). Peter had a dau Elizabeth (b c1769 – d Apr 2, 1826), m c1792 to Michael Dechard (b 1771 – d Apr 20, 1837 in Winchester, Tenn.), a son of Johann Peter Dechard (b Aug

LOYALTON ROLLER MILLS – LOYALTON, PA.

Located – South of town.

23, 1736 Hesse, Germany – d Dec 6, 1783 in Sinking Springs, Berks Co and his wife Elizabeth (____)
Dechard.

BENJAMIN (b Mar 16, 1747 – Berks Co – d before 1790), m c1769 to Maria Catherine Lower (b Aug 9,
1748 - ___), a dau of Christian and Anna Cath Elizabeth (Seybert) Lower. **Benjamin and Maria Catherine
(Lower) Spyker had these known children (records in Trinity Church in Reading):** Jonathan b Mar 13,
1780, Stouchburg; Eleonora Charlotta b Nov 23, 1783; Elizabeth (no dates) m Jan 6, 1793, Michael
Dechert, son of Peter Dechert of Reading; Lucretia (no dates) m Apr 6, 1794 Jacob Dechert, son of Peter
Dechert. **Jacob and Lucretia (Spyker) Decherd had one known child:** Peter Spyker Dechard b Sep 8,
1796 – d Feb 12, 1823 in Chambersburg; ; **David** b May 19,1786 in Reading area; **Benjamin** b Jul 18,
1789.]

ELISABETH b c1748
ANNA CATHARINA b Dec 20, 1750, bapt Trinity Luth, Lancaster
MARGARET BARBARA b Dec 30, 1751, m Jacob Gartman on Feb 15, 1773.
JOHN HENRY b Aug 29, 1753 – d Jul 1, 1817, Lewisburg, Union Co), m 1776 to Maria Weiser (1754 –
1829)
GEORGE PETER b Nov 25,1756, m 1798 to Susanna Kurtz
JOHN (b c1760) m Elisabeth ____ (no dates), and had **these known children bapt at Trinity Church in
Reading: Peter** b Aug 19, 1788, m Elisabeth ___ (no dates). Peter was appointed as postmaster of Gratz on
Jun 9, 1823, and served for one year. He is assessed for a property in Gratz from 1822 to 1825, and then
crossed out. Peter and Elizabeth sold a property in Mifflin Twp on September 20, 1823 to Jacob Dietrich;
Johann b Aug 4, 1791; **George** b Apr 6, 1795; **Elisabeth** b Sep 3, 1797; **Sara** b Feb 15, 1800; **Carolyus** b
Jan 11, 1803.]

On June 17, 1774 Benjamin Spyker, the elder, of Tulpehocken Township, Berks County, a saddler, and
Margaret Barbara his wife sold the 283 1/2 acres of land to Christian Lower, a miller, also of Tulpehocken
Township, and Wendel Seibert of Bethlehem Township, blacksmith. This tract of land adjoined Wiconisco Creek and
another tract of vacant land.

On August 8, 1777, Christian Lower, miller, of Tulpehocken Township, Berks County and Anna Elizabeth
his wife, Wendel Seibert, yeoman of Bethel Township, Berks County and his wife Catharine sold the 283 1/2 acre
tract of land to Jacob Smith, a mason of Coventry Township, Chester County. (At the time of this sale, the land was
located in Lancaster County, since Dauphin County was not yet formed.)

Jacob and Margaret Smith sold this plantation of 283 1/2 acres and another small tract containing 21 acres,
to Daniel Ferree of Strasburg, Lancaster County, on April 1, 1793. The land, bound by Wiconisco Creek, was now
in Upper Paxton Township, Dauphin County, because the new county of Dauphin was formed in 1785.

Daniel and Susannah Ferree conveyed 120 acres of their land to Isaac Ferree on March 16, 1815, but the
land was by that time located in Lykens Township, which had been separated from Upper Paxton Township in 1811.
This acreage was part of the land Jacob Smith conveyed to Daniel Ferree in April 1793, and part of the patent that
Daniel Ferree received in 1804.

On November 23, 1818, the real estate and personal property of Isaac F. Ferree was conveyed to Elijah
Ferree, Joel Leightner and Mathias Slaymaker in trust to dispose. The three trustees conveyed 120 acres of land with
appurtenances, located in Lykens Township, to Michael Deppen on March 27, 1823. It was bound by land of Adam
Row, south to Isaac Ferree, south to corner of Daniel Hoffman, west to Peter Schoffstall, north to Andrew Riegel.

Michael and Sarah Deppen of Lykens Twp held this property only briefly, and sold to Henry Shubert of
Lower Mahanoy Township, Northumberland County in March 1825.

After purchasing land from both grants, Henry Shubert was assessed in 1828 for 125 acres, one brick
gristmill, one wooden house and one cabin. In 1831 his land was assessed in three parts. He had two 50-acre tracts of
un-cleared land, 25 acres of seated land containing the brick mill and wooden house. He also had 30 acres with a
house, and Christian Battorf was a tenant in that house in 1831 and 1832.

On March 30, 1831, Henry and Susanna Shubert purchased another small tract containing four acres, eleven
and one-half perches with wooden house from Jonas Hoffman. (Christian Hoffman conveyed this small tract of land
to Jonas Hoffman on May 16, 1826 with appurtenances, and it was part of the early Hoffman settlement at the end of
Short Mountain). In 1831 and 1832 John Wens occupied the house.

In 1834 Henry Shubert was assessed for the flourmill, and Gotlieb John Smith was listed as his miller. Other
tenants on the property were: Thomas Morrisville a cooper, and Charles Green, tanner and Henry Boddeiger. In

addition to farming and milling, Henry Shubert took up surveying. On the tax record for 1837 Henry Shubert was assessed for individual parcels of land. One tract of 124 acres contained the old log building and a newly built brick building. George Geiger was a tenant on that property. A small four- acre tract with log house was the residence of John Maxwell, listed as the miller. Michael Riegel lived in a wooden house on the remaining 70 acres. John Lubolt, a furrier and Thomas Maxwell, cooper were tenants on the property. The mill property became a thriving enterprise.

The Shubert family eventually moved to Pottsville, Schuylkill County, and on March 29, 1842, they sold both tracts and appurtenances to Peter Boyer of Lower Mahanoy Township, Northumberland County. The first tract of one hundred twenty acres bordered the land of Adam Row, Isaac Ferree, John Schoffstall and Andrew Riegel. The four acres, eleven perches bound by the bank of the Wiconisco Creek, bordered the land of Thomas Elder, Jacob M. Haldeman, Adam Row estate, and other land of Henry Shubert. [Only church record found was Henry Shubert bereft of his parents by sudden death Aug 6, 1829 age 2 yrs bur Hoffman Cem]

THE TANNERY
(Building destroyed c1919)

Most of the tannery land belonged to the same land grants and had the same previous ownership as the gristmill described above. About the time (1842) Peter Boyer purchased that land, the new boundaries were formed for Lykens, Wiconisco and Washington Township. Part of the land of Peter Boyer, yeoman and his wife Catherine was assessed in Wiconisco Township and part in Washington Twp.

On January 11, 1850, Peter and Catherine Boyer sold eighteen acres, one hundred thirty eight perches of their land with the mill to Daniel Good, tanner of Gratz. This part of their land was located on the eastside of Wiconisco Creek, and was bound by other land of Peter Boyer, Jacob Emerich, Mary Delb, Josiah Bowman, and Daniel Hoffman estate.

Daniel Good came to this area from Selinsgrove, Northumberland County, after he learned the tanning trade working as an apprentice with a Mr. Ulrich, probably a relative. He settled first in 1834, as a tenant on the William Moffet tannery property here at Loyalton.

The William Moffet tannery was located on two acres of land that was part of the grant patented July 23, 1762 to the estate of William Parsons of Easton, Northampton County mentioned above. It had the same succession of owners until the Ferree family purchased it. On January 1, 1808, Daniel and Sarah Ferree conveyed two tracts, 150 acres and 21 ½ acres to Michael Shuer, a house carpenter living in Halifax Twp. A reserve on the land gave Daniel Ferree the "privilege of conducting and leading the water of the spring through the land to his mills." On March 15, 1811, Michael and Mary Shuer (of Halifax Twp), conveyed the 150 acre tract of land to Adam Rowe and his wife Christiana, residents of Lancaster County. This land bordered the Wiconisco Creek, land of Andrew Riegel, Daniel Ferree, Isaac Ferree, and Christian Hoffman. It continued to have water reservations to the spring at the corner of the mill house. On April 22, 1815, Adam Rowe, yeoman, and Christiana his wife sold two acres from their land to William Moffet, a tanner. These tracts were in Lykens Township, opposite to each other along the highway between Williams Valley and Millersburg. William Moffet had these two acres of land for a long time, along with another tract of 14 acres 156 perches with buildings that he purchased from Levi and Susanna Buffington on May 1, 1818. The land was from the Peter Henn (Hain) grant patented March 6, 1792. By1828, William Moffet had died, and his heirs had tenants living on both tracts. Adam Row was a tenant on the two acres and was the tanner. From 1831 to 1832, Christ Fogel lived in the log house on the small tract where the tan yard was. Peter Dietrich lived in a house on the 13 acres until 1834. Daniel Good in 1834 was the resident and tanner on the tan yard property. By 1840 he was the owner.

THE SHUER/SHEARER FAMILY

[**MICHAEL SCHAUER** (b in Bavaria, Germany, set sail with his family from Massenbach, Creichgau, Germany, for America in 1710. His family arrived, but it is believed that he died at sea on the voyage to New York. He married Anna Magdalena _____ b c1679 in Germany. **Michael and Anna Magdalena ( ) Schauer had these children (all b Massenbach, Wurtemburg, Germany):**
JOHANN HANS MICHAEL (May 30, 1699–Aug 16, 1772 in Berks Co., bur Daniels Corner Church, Robesonia, Berks Co.). He married in 1717 in New York to Elisabetha Catharina Lauck (bapt Oct 7, 1696 –

d ____), a dau of Johann Valentine and Anna Catharina (Ruhl) Lauck. **Johann Hans and Elisabetha Catharina (Lauck) Schauer had these children:**
JOHANN ADAM (b c1718 in America – d c 1762), m Anna Elisabetha Koch on Jun 16, 1748;
ELISABETHA b Feb 1, 1720;
MAGDALENA b c1722 Berks Co, m Johann Heinrich Fiedler Jun 13, 1744 in Berks Co;
ANNA CATHARINA b c1724 m Henrich Frey Aug 30, 1743;
MICHAEL (b Aug 17, 1726 Berks Co – d pre 1771, Berks Co)
ANNA CHRISTINIA b c1728 Berks Co
ANNA MARIA b Nov 19, 1730 Berks Co.
MARIA CATHARINA b c1732
EVA ROSINA b 1733 Berks Co, m Johann Mathias Wenrich !! in 1754 in Berks Co
MARIA SIBILLA b c1736, m Johann Adam Pfattheicher
SUSANNA b c1738

Johann Adam (b 1701 - ____), m Maria Elisabetha Fritz on Apr 3, 1720 in Claverack, Germany
Anna Magdalena b Apr 2,1704, Massenbach, Wuerttemberg, Germany
Maria Catharina (b Sep 4,1706 - ____), m Henrich Busch in Germany

[**MICHAEL SHUER OR SHEARER** (b c1788 - did not find connection to above family), m Catharine _____ (b Mar 17, 1791 - d Sep 27, 1851, bur Hoffman Cem), a dau of _____. Michael and Catharine Shuer were in this area as early as 1815 when a child was baptized at Hoffman Church. He purchased land from Adam and Ann Mary Heller in March 1819, and sold it to his son Joseph in 1860. The land was in Berrysburg. They lived in Mifflin Twp in 1850. Their daughter Sarah lived with them, and they also had two children:William Myers age 1, and Catharine Jew? Age 2 with hem. In 1860 Michael was listed as a shoemaker. Sarah, probably his daughter lived with him. Their son Joseph and wife Christiana Shearer lived next door, and Joseph was employed as a stage driver. **Michael and Catharine ( ) Shearer had these children: JOSEPH** (Mar 17, 1814 – Apr 7, 1872, bur ME Cem, Berrysburg), m 1st Elizabeth ____ (Feb 29, 1816 – Mar 3, 1851). Joseph m 2nd Christiana ____ b c1830 - ___). Joseph was a stage driver in 1860 in Mifflin Twp. After Joseph died, Christiana m Jul 29, 1875, John Miller of Halifax, recorded in Meth Ch records, Berrysburg. **SALOME** b Oct 22, 1815, bapt Hoffman Ch; **LOUISIANA** b Aug 20, 1819, bapt St. Johns Hill Ch **CATHARINE** b c1820 **MICHAEL** (Jul 12, 1821 – Jan 19, 1876, bur Hoffman Cem) ; **AMANDA** b Oct 12, 1831; (Joel Shearer 51, Up Pax in 1880 had Mary 36, Chas 10, Miranda 6 Sylvania 3]

THE MOFFET FAMILY

[**WILLIAM MOFFET** (Feb 2, 1787 – Oct 23, 1834, bur Hoffman Cem), m Maria ____(Feb 5, 1794 – Apr 26, 1822). In 1820 the Moffet family lived in Lykens Twp, had 1 young son and 4 young daughters and one person was in manufacturing. When William Moffet died, Henry Kuntzelman became the guardian of his young children, but in 1838, Samuel Schoffstall became the guardian in place of Henry Kuntzelman. **William and Maria (__) Moffet had these children:** Annie (no dates), m ___ Dale (b __ d pre-1842), moved to Columbia Co., Pa.; **Jane** (no dates), m William F. Sellers of Montg. Co, Pa.; **Eleanor** (no dates) m William Bingham of Huntington Co., Pa.; **Nathaniel** (1822- d young, bur Hoffman Cem).
    After his first wife died, William Moffet married Elizabeth Row, a dau of John Row.]

According to the GOOD HISTORY, by Christiana Boyer Latsha, Daniel Good made "weekly trips from Loyalton to Gratz to supervise the work at the latter place." By 1837, the Good family had moved to Gratz where they owned another tannery. In 1837 Isaac Burd lived on the two acres and apparently was working for Daniel Good.

The "Manufacturer's Tax Schedules Of Pennsylvania" records Daniel Good with three employees in 1850, to whom he paid out a total of thirty-six dollars per month in wages. The only necessary raw materials were hides and bark. (The bark coming chiefly from oak trees produced tannic acid. Hides contain gelatin, and when combined with the tannic acid, it converts the hides to leather.) The tannery at Gratz operated by horsepower, but the one in Loyalton was operated by waterpower. Tanneries were important because they supplied sole and upper leather for shoes, and harness leather made from calf, horse, kid and sheepskins. Other skins from animals such as deer and dog were tanned. Hides of this type were in great demand to supply the several resident boot and shoemakers and saddlers who lived in each town, Plasterers used plenty of animal hair (available at the tannery) in finishing the inside wall of the early homes.

After Daniel Good died, his heirs sold this same acreage and the mill to Daniel A. Good, son of Daniel Good, Esquire. On January 29, 1877 Daniel A. and his wife assigned their property to John Hess to sell. On March 23, 1878, the property located on the west side of the creek was assigned to Jeremiah C. Good. The neighboring properties at this time were owned by Jacob Emerich on the north, Josiah Bowman, south, Daniel Hoffman, deceased, Peter Boyer and Mary Delb. A news article dated April 11, 1884 mentions that J. C. Good moved to Loyalton to take over the Good mill, and he would supply the region with flour and feed. On October 26, 1887, the gristmill and tract of land was conveyed to Lykens Valley Coal Company (now of Washington Township). Many years later on November 8, 1906, Lykens Valley Coal Company sold the same acreage and mill to Peter A. Matter. Several other transfers of ownership were made after that and in 1918 Edwin C. Bechtel became owner of over 5 acres of the land with frame dwelling, barn and tannery buildings. (This was probably the individual tract that was part of the whole complex) He conveyed it to David R. Matter in 1919, but the deed to that transaction mentions the dwelling and barn, but states that it was the "late tannery." The tannery building may have been destroyed.

THE GUTH / GOOD FAMILY
(Information from Christiana Boyer Latsha and Susan Killingbeck through Muench family. More info in Comprehensive History of Gratz)

[The **GUTH** or **GOOD** family has been traced back to Zurich, Switzerland where the first known person of this surname, **Rudolph** Guth was born in 1370. The lineage from that point includes a long list of generations, beginning with **Walti** b 1402, **Klaus** b 1435, **Hans** b 1468, **Hans** b 1500, **Walti** b 1538, **Melchoir** b 1563, **Thomas** b 1606, **Rudolph** b 1645, **Rudolph** (1674 – 1706). All of the generations to this point lived in Zurich, Switzerland. Rudolph m Susanna Jaggi (1675 – 1706), and moved to Zweibrucken, Germany where they both died of disease. They had a son **Lorentz** b 1703 in Zweibrucken, m Maria Salome Goertsch in 1733. They came to America about 1738, purchased several tracts of land and settled in Lehigh County. He died in 1782. They had a son **Adam** (b Oct 2,1754 Bucks Co – d May 5, 1826 in Selinsgrove, Northld Co), m Dorothea Strickler (1758 –1829) in 1778 and had a large family.

The children of Adam and Dorothea (Strickler) Good included **ADAM GOOD** (Dec 10, 1779 – 1842, Penn Twp, Snyder Co), settled a few miles west of Selinsgrove, on land he purchased in 1813. He was a farmer and blacksmith. On Dec 1, 1799, Adam married Magdalena Mary Ulrich (Oct 16, 1778 - Oct 15, 1848, bur in Union Luth & Ref Cem. in Selinsgrove). She was a dau of John George Ulrich, Jr. (1753 – 1825), a son of John George Ulrich, Sr. (1726 – 1781), and Catherine Laudenslager (1757 – 1827), a dau of George and Catherine Laudenslager. **Adam and Magdalena (Ulrich) Good had these children:** *George b Nov 9, 1800; *Magdalena b Dec 28, 1802; *Charles b Sep 9, 1805; John b Apr 19, 1807; *Daniel (Oct 26, 1809 - Nov 21, 1870);*Elizabeth (b Oct 28, 1811 Penn Twp, Snyder Co – d Oct 2, 1879, bur Luth & Ref Cem, Kratzerville, Snyder Co), m c1829 John Michael Bieber (1811 – 1886) of Penn Twp; *Catherine b Dec 13, 1813; *Susanna b Mar 20,1816; *Adam (Oct 12, 1818 – Jun 30, 1901), m Jul 30, 1840, Mary Slear; *Amelia b Jan 1, 1822.

*DANIEL GOOD** (Oct 26, 1809 – Nov 21, 1870), m Margaret Reedy (Apr 12, 1812 – Sep 3, 1885), dau of Leonard Reedy the gunsmith, and his wife Elizabeth (Braun) Reedy. **Daniel and Margaret (Reedy) Good had these children:**
SARAH (b Oct 11, 1834 in Loyalton - d May 1, 1876, in Gratz, bur Simeon Cem), m Samuel Schoffstall (Jun 6, 1830 - Mar 10, 1895, bur St. Peters Luth. & Ref Cem, Orwin, Sch Co), son of Henry Schoffstall. Samuel Schoffstall learned the tanning rrade with his father-in-law. **Samuel and Sarah (Good) Schoffstall had these children: ***Henry (Aug 26, 1854 - ____), m Carolina Ritzman:***Daniel (Mar 4, 1857 - 1930), m Louisa Miller (1857 - 1903), bur in Greenwood Cem, Tower City), probably dau of Jacob and Mary Ann Miller of Lykens Twp; ***John (Nov 11, 1858 -May 22, 1873), m Sarah Brown Fenstermacher; ***Milton (Jun 3, 1862 - ____), m ____ Minnich; ***Mary b Dec 12, 1864, m Henry Schlegel; ***Catharine Amelia b Nov 23, 1870, m George Hunter.

After Sarah Good Schoffstall died, Samuel m Sarah Julian Geiss, they had a son: Charles Elmer b c1878.

JEREMIAH (b Apr 2, 1836 in Lykens Twp - d Feb 26, 1905, in Boone, Iowa), m Oct 30, 1855 Lovina Kissinger b c1836, dau of John and Margaret Kissinger of Lyk Twp. **Jeremiah and Lovina (Kissinger) Good had 15 children: ***Julianna** b Jan 9, 1856, m Jul 22, 1909, Hiram Gladstone of Des Moines, Iowa; ***George W.** b in Gratz, Mar 25, 1857, m Mar 4, 1877 to Lillie I. Robinson of Berrysburg, worked in the tannery at Gratz until 1889, when he went to Ogden, Iowa; ***Margaret Elizabeth** (Feb 4, 1859- d young); ***Mary Jane**. b in Gratz Oct 26, 1860, m Oct 20, 1877 William F. Bohner, a stage driver in Gratz They moved to Iowa in 1890; ***Milton H**. b in Gratz Dec 21, 1861, m Aug 20, 1887, Irene Lorenson of Hastings, Neb. in 1912, he became a partner in GOOD AND CARYELL, Grain dealers of Cummings, Kan;. ***John Daniel** b in Gratz Nov 19, 1865, m Feb 28, 1893, Effie Bell Hannum of Boone, Iowa; ***Edwin** (b in Gratz Nov 20, 1864 - d Dec 13, 1893 in Boone, Iowa), m Viola Johns of Loyalton, was a miner while living in Gratz, later moved to Iowa, where he was a farmer until his death; ***Sarah Louisa** (Dec 26, 1866 - Dec 15, 1889, bur Simeon Cem), m George Sitlinger; ***Susan Adeline** b in Gratz, Sep 3, 1868, m Dec 25, 1887, Theophilus M. Koppenhaver, lived near Loyalton on a farm; ***Jacob Franklin** b in Gratz, Dec 30, 1870, moved to Iowa, and m Carrie M. Bowman, on Feb 13, 1895; ***William Lloyd** b in Gratz, Dec 4, 1872, went West; ***Katherine Louella** b in Gratz, May 21, 1874, moved to Iowa, m 1st 1893, Fred Lilyard, 2nd in 1907, John Wm. Nesselroad; ***Carrie** b Mar 10, 1876, d young; ***Charles** b Jan 16, 1878, d young; ***Henry** b Sep 19, 1880, d young.

CATHARINE (b in Gratz Nov 5, 1837 - d c1921), m Feb 16,1857 Josiah P. Stine (Sep 9, 1837 - Nov 29, 1907), of Lykens Twp. **Josiah P and Catharine (Good) Stine had these children: ***Franklin Peter**; ***Daniel M; ***Mary L.**

DANIEL A. (b in Gratz Feb 16, 1840 - d Apr 2, 1922, bur Simeon Cem), m Sep 2, 1860, Sarah D. Hess (1839 - Feb 3, 1909), a dau of Solomon and Eva (Saltzer) Hess. He was a miller & carpenter. **Daniel and Sarah had these children: ***Mary L.** (b Wash Twp Dec 7, 1861 - d 1939), m Oscar T. Tobias, lived in Gratz; ***Ellen Margaret** (Aug 7, 1863 - 1875); *** **Solomon S** b Feb 9, 1865 in Wash Twp, m Feb 28, 1892 to Agnes E. Klinger, had two sons: Roy D.; Warren L. Solomon Good served as apprentice to Jonas Swab, then followed the trade of flour and feed miller. He left this area and lived in many places along the East Coast. ***Ariel Daniel** b in Wash Twp Oct 28, 1866, m Jun 8, 1898 Gertie A. Schoffstall of Williams-town. **Ariel and Gertie (Schoffstall) Good had these children:** Effie; Leonard; Earl F; Sarah D., who lived in Loyalton; John W. lived in the Harrisburg area. John W. suggested the idea of marking the site where the Daniel Good Tannery was located in Gratz. He also made the idea possible by providing the funds for the stone and plaque; Ariel Daniel Good was a mill-wright and merchant at Loyalton. ***Jennie C** b Wash Twp. Nov 20, 1871, m Jan 21, 1889, Grant Williard, a miner. They lived in Lykens and **had these children:** Maud (no dates) m Fred Daniel; Tillie; Mayme; John; Norman; Henry; Allen; Darwin. Daniel A. Good lived in Washington Twp, worked as a fuller, later traveled extensively for the mill furnishing companies.

MARY A. b at Gratz Nov 6, 1842, not married. Mary worked as a clerk in her sister Emma's store in Gratz, was assistant postmistress for several years, and was an able seamstress. She later moved to Phila, where she was proprietress of a boarding house.

JOHN L. (b Gratz Apr 9, 1845 – Jun 8, 1928 Ogden, Iowa), served during the Civil War, m Jan 17, 1867, Cassiah Schreffler. In 1869, moved to Pilot Mound, Iowa. He engaged in farming and stock-raising, also served four years in Iowa State Legislature. **John L and Cassiah (Schreffler) Good had these children: ***Anna Margaret** (1868 – 1962), m Henry Dockey Dec 25, 1886 in Pilot Mound, Iowa ***Hattie A**. d young; ***Daniel Abner** (1871 – 1943) m Minnie Reutter in Pilot Mound, Iowa; ***Charles Grant** (1872 – 1957), Iowa; ***Minnie Estella** (1878- 1970, Webster Iowa), m Henry W. Wolf 1909 in Pilot Mound, Iowa; ***Katie Della** (1883 – 1908); ***Lucille May** (1891 – 1918, childbirth).

***EMMA JANE** (b in Gratz Oct 5, 1847 - d Apr 24, 1906, of appendicitis, bur in Phila), m Oct 24, 1867, Jonathan A. Umholtz. **Jonathan A. and Emma Jane (Good) Umholtz had these children;** Chas W.; Henry Lloyd; Mary Jane; Nora Jane; Hattie M; Arthur E.

AMELIA b Nov 19, 1849 in Gratz, m Feb 2, 1873, John Franklin Boyer, son of William S. and Christiana Boyer. **John Franklin & Amelia (Good) Boyer had these children: ***Carrie M; ***Josey D; ***Katie G; ***Cynthia; ***Louise Ann.**

HENRY W. b at Gratz Apr 5, 1852, m Apr 6, 1871, Eliza Enterline of Gratz; He was a carpenter for the Reading Company, later a house carpenter in Tremont. **Henry and Eliza had these children: ***Harry** b

in Gratz Sep 8, 1871, moved to Tremont; ***John** b in Gratz Jun 20, 1873, m May 22, 1892 Jennie
Williams of Spring Glen, moved to Lykens where he worked as a saddler, barber, and miner.]

On March 28, 1907, Peter A. and Carrie A. Matter conveyed the gristmill property of 18 acres 138 perches
to James C. Fisher. It was described as adjoining the land of Washington Kessler (late Jacob Emerick), Nathaniel
Miller (late Josiah Bowman), south to west side of Wiconisco Creek, William L. Hoffman (Daniel Hoffman), north
to J. W. Boyer (late Peter Boyer), north to other land of J. W. Boyer (late Andrew Riegel), north to Harry
Zimmerman (late Peter Boyer), south to east side of Wiconisco Creek, Amos Radel, and other late land of Jacob
Emerick, and back to Washington Kessler land.

Fisher Home Immediately After The Devastating Agnes Hurricane

James Fisher died in 1915, and his wife Elizabeth continued to live here until her death on March 5, 1939.
The heirs continued to own this property for many years. Unfortunately, in 1972 the destructive hurricane Agnes
Swept through Lykens Valley and did much damage to area property. A few residents in Loyalton were particularly
hard hit by rushing water from Wiconisco Creek. Some folks left their homes during the storm, but Raymond Fisher
who lived alone decided to stay. Eventually, as the water rose higher and higher from Wiconisco Creek, he decided
he had no alternative but to move to higher ground. He gathered a few necessities, a chamber pot, crackers, a six-
pack of soda, a pack of cookies and a calendar and retreated to the second floor of his house. He was trapped there
for more than two days. A National Guard helicopter circled the home three times but could not see Raymond.
Raymond was slowed by age and the helicopter circled the house faster than Raymond could move to a window to be
seen. Neighbors and friends made several rescue attempts, but the water was too swift. When the water velocity
finally diminished he was removed by boat.

About one year after the flood, on July 14, 1973 Raymond Fisher sold the old mill property to George and
Elizabeth Luther of Edgewater, Maryland. On May 14, 1976, George E. and Elizabeth H. Luther of Washington
Township transferred the property to Shagbark, Inc. In recent years, George E. Luther has used the land to produce
blueberries. During the season, acres of blueberries are open to the public to pick. It is a delightful experience to fill
a container with the large blue berries, while viewing the scenery around you and hearing the chirping birds above.
Mr. Luther also built a small produce stand near the road for the convenience of passing motorists.

[**JAMES CLARK FISHER** (Aug 24, 1850 – Apr 5, 1915, bur Simeon Cem, Gratz), son of _____
m Elizabeth _____ (1856 - Mar 5, 1939), a dau of _____ . In 1880, James and Elizabeth lived in Eldred
Twp., Sch Co. George Sitlinger age 17, a cousin, lived with them **James and Elizabeth (___) Fisher had
these children: Flora A** b Aug 1876, m Fred Hudach, **had 2 children:** Flora and Carl ; **Amelia Minerva**

(Nov 16, 1878 – Jan 27, 1912, bur Simeon Cem). She was not married, lived with her sister in Johnstown, died of a heart attack; **Raymond W.** (1892 – 1977, bur Simeon Cem) lived in Elizabethville; **Gertrude M.** (   ), m C. R. Helt, lived in Johnstown. The family lived in New Jersey in 1912.

THE BENJAMIN E. CRABB FARM
(G. A. Boyer 84 acres in 1875)

Although this farm is not in the town of Loyalton, it is close enough to recognize it here as part of the early settlement of the village. The land belonged to Henry Shubert; he sold March 29, 1842 to Peter Boyer who died in 1852. On May 25, 1855, the heirs conveyed 84 acres 151 ¼ perches of land, with frame dwelling, barn and other buildings to his son Gabriel Boyer. This land bordered land of Michael Sausser heirs, Andrew Riegel heirs, Daniel Good, and Catherine Boyer. Gabriel and his wife Matilda lived here in 1860, and had George Shumber age 17 living with them. In 1870 William Messner age 13 lived with them. In 1880, Matilda's father John Ginter lived with them. (John Ginter was an early settler, but his land was further west, and will not be discussed in this history). At the age of 82, he was a widower, was retired from his farm and was working at the forge. Gabriel Boyer was a miller while they lived here, but they eventually moved to a farm near Millersburg.

THE GINTER FAMILY

[*JOHN GINTER (b Oct 11, 1797 bap Oley Ref Ch - d Mar 1, 1882), was a son of Jacob Ginter of Oley Twp, Berks Co. He m Christiana Moyer (Apr 19, 1800 - Jul 17, 1876), both bur Peace Ref Cem, Berrysburg . John was confirmed at Hoffman church May 1, 1836, and the record states that he was married. They lived in Loyalton where John was employed as a forgeman at the Oak Dale Forge as early as 1831. He also was a farmer in 1850. By 1860, John and Christianne were settled in Washington Twp, where he was listed as a farmer. In 1870 John and Christiana Ginter had Polly Troutman age 22, living with them. **John and Christiana (Moyer) Ginter had these children :**
ROBERT (b _____ d before 1882), lived in Clinton, Henry Co., Missouri. **Robert & his wife had (5) child: ***Udora Sephania b Nov 11, 1855 m H. H. Adlesperyer; *****John C.** b Oct 8, 1857; *****Francis Rosela** b Aug 8, 1860, m F. M. Bates;*****Commodore S.** b Feb 8, 1863; *****William F.** b Oct 7, 1866.
ELIZABETH (Dec 8, 1823 - Jul 5, 1882), m 1st Cyrus Buffington (Dec 30, 1821 - Jul 16, 1856), a son of George and Catherine (Yeager) Buffington of Washington Twp. both bur Peace Ref Cem, Berrysburg. Elizabeth was confirmed at Hoffman Ch Apr 23, 1842. **Cyrus and Elizabeth (Ginter) Buffington had these children: ***Thomas (Dec 8,1841 - Jun 17, 1916), bur Peace Ref Cem, Bbg) *****Jeremiah** (Jul 20, 1847 - Feb 20, 1848; *****Alfred C** (b & d 1849); *****Robert; **Leah Jane;** After Cyrus died, Elizabeth

m 2nd **Samuel Umholtz, had these children:** ***Adaline m George Welker; ***Harvey m Katie Welker; ***William m Katie Thomas.

**JACOB (no dates), confirmed at Hoffman Ch Apr 26, 1840. moved to Chatfield, Fillmon Co., Minn. A Jacob and Elisabeth Ginter had Rachel Rebecca b Dec 24, 1847, John William b Nov 27, 1846, Daniel Amos b Sep 9, 1849, bapt Salem Luth

MATILDA (Oct 12, 1827 - May 23, 1893), m Gabriel Boyer (Feb 25, 1825 - Nov 14, 1887, bur Bbg). **Gabriel and Matilda (Ginter) Boyer had these children (some bapt Peace Ref Ch, Berrysburg): ***John I (b & d 1852) ***Joseph (b Dec 25, 1854 - 1855); ***Frances D. (b & d 1856); ***John Wesley A. b Nov 14, 1857;

**LOUISA ANN b c1831 m Benneville Kissinger, (Jan 3, 1830 - May 18, 1880, bur Simeon Cem), a son of John and Margaret (Hawk) Kissinger. Benneville was a stone mason.

HARRIET (b c1835- _____) m John T. Hoffman (Jul 12, 1837 - Feb 22, 1897), bur Peace Ref Cem, Berrysburg, a son of Christian and Sarah (Tobias) Hoffman. In 1860 she was single, living with her parents, and was a milliner. In 1870 & 1880, John G. and Harriet lived in Washington Twp on a farm. **John G. and Harriet (Ginter) Hoffman had these children: ***Sarah R b c1862; ***Jacob H. (1867 - 1877), bur Peace Cem;

**FRANCES b ___ m Dr. ?Jacob Shope d before 1883;

ANNA JANE (Dec 19, 1837 - Feb 4, 1917), m Josiah Boyer (Dec 21. 1831 - Jan 31, 1917), bur Maple Grove Cem, Elizabethville c1842. In 1870 they lived in Washington Twp, and he was a farmer. **Josiah and Anna Jane (Ginter) Boyer had these children: ***David A b c1861; ***Malinda b c1863.

**SARAH b c1844 m Emanuel Klinger of Atwood, Indiana

JOHN W. b c1849 m Nov 28, 1876 Emma Jane Bowman Oak Dale record. **John W. and Emma J. (Bowman) Ginter had these children: ***Corah Eva b Nov 23, 1886 bapt Oak Dale Ch.]

On April 1, 1929, John Wesley Boyer executor of Gabriel Boyer estate conveyed four separate tracts to Fred E. and Carrie Kocher. In addition to the 84 acres 151, ¾ perch homestead, he received 37 acres 69 perches that Peter Bohner conveyed to Peter A. Matter. It was bound by land of Michael Sausser estate, north to middle of Wiconisco Creek, and Gabriel Boyer's other land. A third tract of 3 acres 3 ¾ perches was located along the road from Loyalton to Elizabethville, next to William Matter (former Josiah Boyer land), and the school lot that had been a part of this land. (On October 4, 1876 Benneville Boyer sold 30 perches of land to the School District for Washington Twp. This land originally belonged to Peter Boyer, and was sold to Hannah Uhler April 9, 1852, who sold to Catharine Boyer March 30, 1860; her heirs assigned to Benneville and Catherine Boyer May 1872, and on January 5, 1882, it was sold to Gabriel Boyer.)

The fourth tract was a lot located along the road from Loyalton to Berrysburg and adjoined the first and third tract. This land was the site of the old Methodist Episcopal church, and was conveyed by trustees of the church to John Wesley Boyer on October 27, 1895, about the time that it was replaced by the Oak Dale Church. Fred and Carrie Kocher sold all four tracts to Edward and Goldie Crabb on March 29, 1944. They continued to own the two large tracts of land for many years, but after Edward H. Crabb died, the heirs conveyed the 84- acre farm, and the 37 acre tract to Benjamin E. and Marion Crabb in May 1963. They are the present owners.

On August 4, 1945, Edward and Goldie Crabb sold the two smaller tracts to Clyde J and Effie Miller. That land was bound by Wiconisco Creek, west along Edward Crabb other land and land of Peter and Carrie Matter. Clyde J. Miller died Feb 17, 1947 and the land became owned by Effie Miller. On Feb 25, 1959 Effie Miller widow of Washington Twp conveyed to Claude S. Miller. On July 3, 1976 this land (310 by 791 foot) was conveyed by Kay E. Rice executor of Claude Miller to George E. and Elizabeth H. Luther of Edgewater, Md.

BOYER FAMILY

[The Ancestor of this family was **JOHN BOYER** (b 1727 in Germany - d 1777 in Amity Twp, Berks Co. He m Elizabeth Specht. They had a **son PHILIP BOYER** (Dec 14, 1754 – Jul 31, 1832) who m Christina Weaver (1754, of Amity Twp, Berks Co - 1832), **had these children::** Michael; Jacob; John; *PETER; Mary m George Koch; Daniel (1792 – 1825).

*Peter Boyer (Jan 15, 1787 - d Mar 6, 1852, bur Hoffman Cem), m Catharine Herb (Jun 27, 1791 - Dec 15, 1875), of Berks Co. Peter was a skilled mason, and worked in that trade most of his lifetime. He moved from Berks County to Northumberland County in 1834, and in 1842 moved to Washington Twp, Dau Co. where he operated the mill. He was also a stonemason and farmer. He was a strong man, noted for his courageous disposition and was known locally as "Wammas" Boyer. After his death, his wife Catherine lived with their son Josiah. **Peter and Catharine (Herb) Boyer had these children:**

Benjamin (b Aug 8, 1813 Amity Twp, Berks Co - d Dec 10, 1887, bur Stone Valley Cem), m Catherine Stine (b Aug 22, 1814 Hubley Twp Sch Co - Sep 27, 1887). **Benjamin and Catherine (Stine) Boyer had these children: ***Elias; ***John E. (b 1841 Northld Co - d 1895, Gratz, bur Hoffman Cem), m Mary Moyer (1844 - 1927), a dau of Philip Moyer; ***Benjamin A. (Mar 17, 1853 - Aug 31, 1916, bur Stone Valley Cem), m Elizabeth Coleman (Jul 19, 1849 - Jan 18, 1941), a dau of John (Jr) and Catherine (Artz) Coleman. **They had two known sons:** *Charles I* (1876 - 1966) and *John B* (1882 - 1948), both bur Stone Valley Cem with parents. [See lengthy newspaper article about Elizabeth in Comprehensive History of Gratz]; ***Hannah m William Seiler; ***Emaline m Emanuel Lark; ***Caroline (Jul 13, 1850 – Mar 10, 1924), m Jeremiah Lenker Mar 7, 1850 –May 6, 1930, bur Wolfs X Roads Cem);***Daniel of Jordan Twp.

**Elias (Oct 25, 1815 - Jan 16, 1891, bur Stone Valley), m Mary _____ (Jun 11, 1817 - Aug 30, 1885)

**Isaac (Mar 23, 1818–Jul 3, 1901, bur Pillow), m Catherine Deppen b c1821 lived in Pillow, was a miller.

**Mary Ann (no dates) m Jonas Witmer

**Rachel (1823 - Dec 30, 1906), m Elias Buffington (Mar 25, 1824 - Dec 12, 1895), a son of John E and Susanna (Artz) Buffington) - see Buffington information.

**Hettie (no dates), m Daniel Hoffman

Gabriel (Feb 25, 1825 – Nov 14, 1887, bur Berrysburg), m Matilda Ginter (Oct 12, 1827 – May 23, 1893), a dau of John Ginter. **Gabriel and Matilda Boyer had one child: ***John Wesley. A. (Nov 14, 1856 - Oct 14, 1887, bur Maple Grove Cem, E'ville), m May 5, 1878 to Lydia Ann Row (b Oct 18, 1858 – Jul 1925), a dau of John M. and Elizabeth (Wolf) Row. In 1880, they lived with his parents in Washington Twp. and had a child Frances Ellen. b Oct 15, 1880.

Abraham (b Apr 11, 1827 Berks Co - d Sep 28, 1894, bur Stone Valley Cem) m Catharine Anderson (Mar 17, 1832 - Jun 1, 1908), a dau of John and Mary (Harold) Anderson. **Abraham and Catharine (Anderson) Boyer had these children: ***S. Pierce b Jan 12, 1853, m Mar 1883 to Susan Michael, a dau of Jacob and Catharine (Bobb) Michael, and lived in Northld Co; ***Amelia m Henry Kieffer of Dau Co; ***John; ***Elias D lived in Up Augusta Twp, Northld Co; ***Hannah m John Lahr, lived in Pillow; ***Peter b Apr 15, 1867, m Catharine Troutman, lived in Pillow.

**Catherine (Apr 14, 1829 - Jan 19, 1883, bur Hoffman Cem), m Jonas Willier (Oct 8, 1820 – Dec 19, 1867), a son of Adam and Sarah (Reisch) Williard. [See Williard write-up for more info.]

Josiah (b Dec 21, 1831 Berks Co (twin) - d Jan 31, 1917, bur Maple Grove Cem, E'ville), m Aug 7, 1856 to Anna Jane Ginter (Dec 19, 1837 – Feb 4, 1917), a dau of John Ginter. They lived in Wiconisco Twp. in 1860, later in Washington Twp. **Josiah and Anna Boyer had these children: ***David; ***Adam; ***Alfred, moved to Tower City and was a merchant; ***Cornelius b c1858; ***Samuel b 1850; ***Albert D b c 1861; ***Malinda E (1862 – 1950, bur Maple Grove Cem, E'ville), m Robert Lenker (Aug 31, 1859 - Apr 9, 1935); ***John C (Sep 1, 1872 – Mar 12, 1943, bur Maple Grove Cem), m Regina E. Feb 24, 1876 – Nov 21,1969). He studied medicine in Phila, became a doctor.

Benneville b Dec 21, 1831 (twin) – Mar 27, 1902, bur Maple Grove Cem, E'ville) , m Catharine _____ (b Oct 1, 1832 – d Feb 21, 1917). They lived in Wiconisco Twp in 1860 next to his brother Josiah. In 1880, they were assessed in Washington Twp. living on adjoining properties, and their son Henry lived with them.. Benneville and Catharine Boyer had these children:** ***Irvin D. (1851 – 1931, bur Maple Grove Cem), m Susan ___ (1856 – 1932), and lived near his parents in Washington Twp. **Irvin and Susan Boyer had these children:** *Kate M.* b c175; *William Henry* (1877 – 1957, bur Maple Grove Cem, E'ville), m Annie B. ___ (1878 – 1948); ***Henry (1855 – 1934, bur Maple Grove Cem, E'ville), m Mary ___ (1863 – 1923); ***Francis b c1858.

John (Apr 8, 1833 - Nov 14, 1916, bur Hoffman Cem), m Elizabeth Swab (Feb 1, 1839 - Sep 14, 1893), he had Elias Buffington for a guardian when father died. John and Elizabeth Boyer lived in Washington Twp in 1880. **John and Elizabeth (Swab) Boyer had these children: ***Isaac F b c1868; ***George b c1872; ***Katie E b c1876; ***William Monroe b c1879.

**Sarah Ann (Sep 8, 1840 - Oct 11, 1912, bur Hoffman Cem), m Jonas W. Hoffman (Jun 15, 1838 - Feb 14, 1887, bur Hoffman Cem), Civil War Vet, a son of John and Elizabeth Hoffman

Leah Ann b c1842, m Charles Hoover b c1850. They lived in Washington Twp in 1880. **Charles and Leah Ann (Boyer) Hoover children; ***Mary E b c1873; ***John E b c1874; ***Isaac F b c1876.]

THE STONE HILL SCHOOL

The exact date that this school was built has not been learned. But a deed transaction dated March 1865 mentions that school lot number two borders the land being sold. This building continued to be the center of education in Loyalton until the big merger during the 1950's when Upper Dauphin School District became the center for all township schools in the area. On January 3, 1959, the School District of Washington Township conveyed Stone Hill School building to J. Boyd and Mary L. Crouse. They sold to Gilbert and Margaret Burrell on January 4, 1966. It has been a residence since that date. The names of several early teachers have been learned. S. S. Good taught in 1886, C. I. Lubold in 1894 and 1895, B. U. Longabach in 1896, and Edwin Bechtel in 1912. The earliest school photo found was of the term 1886/87. It appeared in the Harrisburg paper in 1952, was identified by members of the Good and Ginter family. Agnes Klinger, standing to the right of teacher S. S. Good, became his wife in 1892.

Stone Hill School 1886. l to r, **Front Row:**; Charles Hoke; John Forney; Frank Eby; John Schoffstall; Ed Troxell; Claude Troutman. **2nd Row:** Martha Schoffstall; Charles Troxell Gertie Gunderman; Annie Moyer; Mazie Lubold; Estella Shadle; Katie Troxell; Millie Harper; Mable Forney; Adaline Gunderman; Lydia Snyder; Jane Troutman; Katie Rowe; Alfred Rowe; Charles Rowe; Edward Moyer. **3rd Row:** Mollie Rowe; Annie Lubold; Mattie Harper; Wm J. Ginter; Ray Bohner; Ira Rowe; Harry Yohe; Daisy Eby; Jacob Snyder. **Top Row:** Amelia Lubold; Mary Hoover; Katie Miller; Louisa Johns; Agnes Klinger; S. S. Good, teacher; Jennie Good; John Hoover; Charles Lehman; Lewis Rowe; Isaac Hoover; Lucian Schoffstall; Joseph Rowe.

Stone Hill School- March 18, 1915 – Teacher Meta Radel. Top Row: Mary Grubb; Anna Rowe; Bessie Snyder; Maude Snyder; Prudence Harner; Pauline Grubb; Mary Mumma; Lula Kiester; Florence Rowe. 2nd Row: Emily Keiter; Sarah Keiter; Bessie Troutman; Pauline Bower; Marlyn Johns; Helen Troutman; Mildred Lower; Sarah Good; Laura Buffington; Laura Grubb; Leona Snyder; Lloyd Harner; Amy Snyder; Elmer Klinger; Stella ____ ; Leonard Good; 3rd Row: Foster Kiester; Wm Keiter; Marlyn Snyder; Arthur Kiester; John Buffington; Paul Johns; Wm. Troutman; Earl Good; Warren Hoke; Lloyd Rowe. Pupils absent, not on picture: Herman Lower; Walter Rowe; Claude Troutman; Andrew Keiter; Forrest Grubb; Anna Kissinger; Leon Kissinger; Russel Crabb; Alma Grubb; John Lubold.

Stone Hill School c1930 – l to r: Front Row: Jr. Kemble, ___, John Troutman, Paul Troutman, Bill Kline, Roy Gonder, Lawrence Engle. 2nd Row: Marlin Engle, _____, Jean Romberger, _____, _____, Bobby Weaver, Rich Harner, Edward Bechtel, _____. 3rd Row John Lebo, Paul "Silas" Troutman, Bob Bonawitz, Lilly Weaver, Bob Smeltz, Arlene Troutman, Sherwood Rowe, Ray Hechler. 4th Row: Bob Hechler, Fred Harner, Eleanor Hechler, Beatrice Harper, _____, Kathryn Troutman, Mary Bruner. Teacher: Margaret Kerstetter.

132

Stone Hill School 1947/48
Back row l to r: Palmer Riegel, Dale Williard, Carl Brunner, John Warfel, teacher Mrs. Cora Erdman Welker. 3rd row: Anna Troutman, Janet Henninger, Carolyn Riegel, Nancy Long, Hilda Miller, 2nd row: Larry Shaffer, Chester Wise, Clair Bush, Benny Crab, Harry & Harold Dietrich. 1st row: Faye Shaffer, Catherine Hassinger, Barbara Hoover, Ruth Keister, Kay Yerges, Kitty Swab, Betty Klinger.

Photo from Margaret Johns Matter – year unknown- not identified

THE WORLD WAR II HONOR ROLL
(No Longer Existing)

The citizens of Loyalton as a patriotic gesture constructed this very attractive memorial in honor of those who served their country during World War II. At a service of dedication this statement was made:

"We give this to you as a memento of the service that was held to honor the service men who entered the Armed Forces from this community."

The following names are listed on the roll:

Henry Heim	Warren D. Romberger	Park L. Ferree
Merlin C. Hoover	Arthur S. Rowe	Carl N. Miller
Eldred L. Kocher	Lee Artz	Eugene L. Hassinger
Earl F. Good	Burnett L. Kocher	Harold E. Matter
Harry A. Travitz	Paul W. Buffington	Mark C. Maurer
Raymond E. Snyder	Mark M. Lubold	William H. Byerly
Carl H. Burrell	Kenneth Lettich	Harold C. Hoover
Charles D. Bellis	Charles W. Lahr	Gilbert E. Burrell
Lewis W. Lahr	Robert D. Bonawitz	Marlin E. Shoop
Robert M. Smeltz	Paul A. Troutman	John W. Troutman
Lloyd M. Bellis	Raymond D. Weaver	Austin H. Swab
Harold D. Dietrich	Edwin L. Novinger	Roy E. Gonder
John M. Foley	Gilbert W. Hoover	
Lloyd H. Helt	Jonas J. Hoffman	
Ralph C. Snody	Nevin H. Lahr	
Paul S. Romberger	Edward E. Bechtel	
Roy N. Miller	Richard E. Harner	
Nevin F. Shadle	Marlin H. Lahr	
Daniel Minnich	Clarence J. Mauser	
William R. Williard	Cyril H. Devers	

THE VILLAGE OF LOYALTON

RESIDENTS OF LOYALTON INCLUDED
IN THE 1890 CENSUS OF CIVIL WAR VETERANS & WIVES
(CENSUS TAKEN BETWEEN JUNE 1, 1890 & JULY 1, 1890)

Samuel Gunderman	Co. F 46th Inf	– (Right foot shot off)
Daniel Klinger	Co K 26th Vol Inf	
Peter B. Lyeter		
Joseph Russell		
Benjamin F. Harper	Pvt Co 21st Cav	
John Wingert	Co K 26th Inf	
Benjamin Weeber	Co F 200th Inf	
Jacob Klinger	Co K 26th Vol Inf	
Jonathan Klinger	Co K 26th Vol Inf	- Corp.
James M. Koppenhaver	Co A 210th	- Elizabethville
John C. Harman	Co K 173rd Inf Draft	- Loyalton
Urich Koppenhaver	Co H 192nd Inf	
Henry C. Evitts	Co I 177th Inf	
Michael Matter	Co B 9th Cav	- Elizabethville
Jacob Forney	Co H 192nd Vol	
John Sweesy	Co D 188th	
Hirman Schram	Co E 28th	
Samuel Wert	Co H 192nd	
Philip Hawk	Co G 16th Cav	
John M Robson	Co I 15th Vol	
John Snyder	Co A 210th	
Peter Motter	Co D 127th Pa Vol	
Samuel Eberly	Co A 167th	
Jacob Swab	Co H 210th	
Sarah widow f Jacob Swab		
Adam W. Wert	Co H 130th Vol	
Samuel E. Blyler	Co C 36th Malitia	
Jacob L. Weaver	Co B 9th Cav	
Jacob Zerby	Co B 9th Cav	
Jonas Row	Co F 16th Cav	
William F. Polm wife Ann	Co E 18th Cav	
Amos Schoffstall	Co I 177th	- Berrysburg
Samuel Bechtel	U.R. S	- Elizabethville

LOYALTON BASEBALL TEAM BIG WINNER

On December 23, 1925, John G. and Amelia Romberger conveyed 6 acres 79 perches of land to The Loyalton Community and Pastime Association for $1200. The land had previously been owned by Alfred H. and Lousianna Row and they conveyed it to the Romberger's on April 2, 1924. The association had just become incorporated on September 2, 1925. The group desired to "provide a public park and play ground to promote and conduct such kinds of innocent sports and amusements as may from time to time be needed by the residents of the township." The following directors were chosen for the first year: C. S. Grubb, J. S. Zerbe, A. D. Good, Clayton A. Bechtel, R. E. Bohner, Chas W. Buffington, Marlin Johns.

Soon after the land was purchased an enthusiastic group of men and boys with the help of horses worked hard to construct part of it into a baseball diamond. When the field was ready the men formed the Loyalton baseball team and joined the Twin Valley League. They won the championship the very first year! It was a great start for a team that for many succeeding years ended the season by winning the championship. Because Loyalton had the distinction of having especially good players, young men from the surrounding towns were pleased to play on their team.

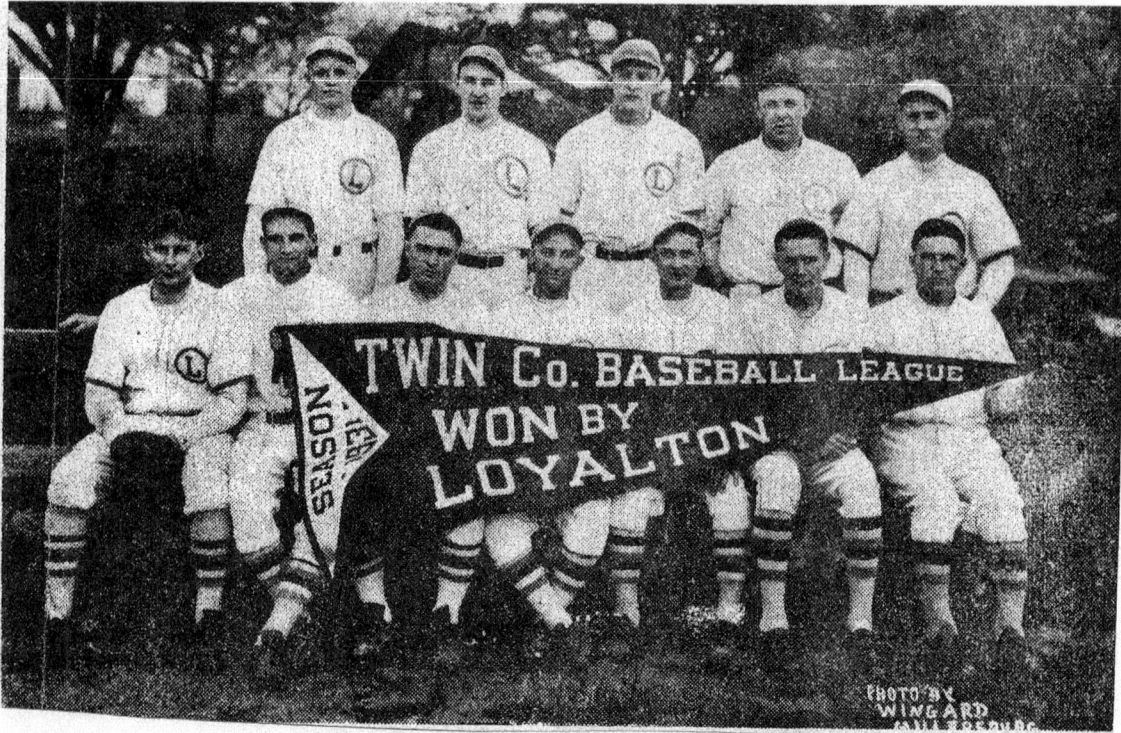

Loyalton Baseball Team League Champions 1931
- Seated l to r: Earl Good, Paul Johns, Elwood Hoover, Marlin Johns, Lester Miller, Patsy Noble, Lent Hoover. Stding: James Byerly, John Byerly, Bill Byerly, Sol Row and Arthur Grubb (well known player tried out in 1928 with Danville, Il 3-I League.)

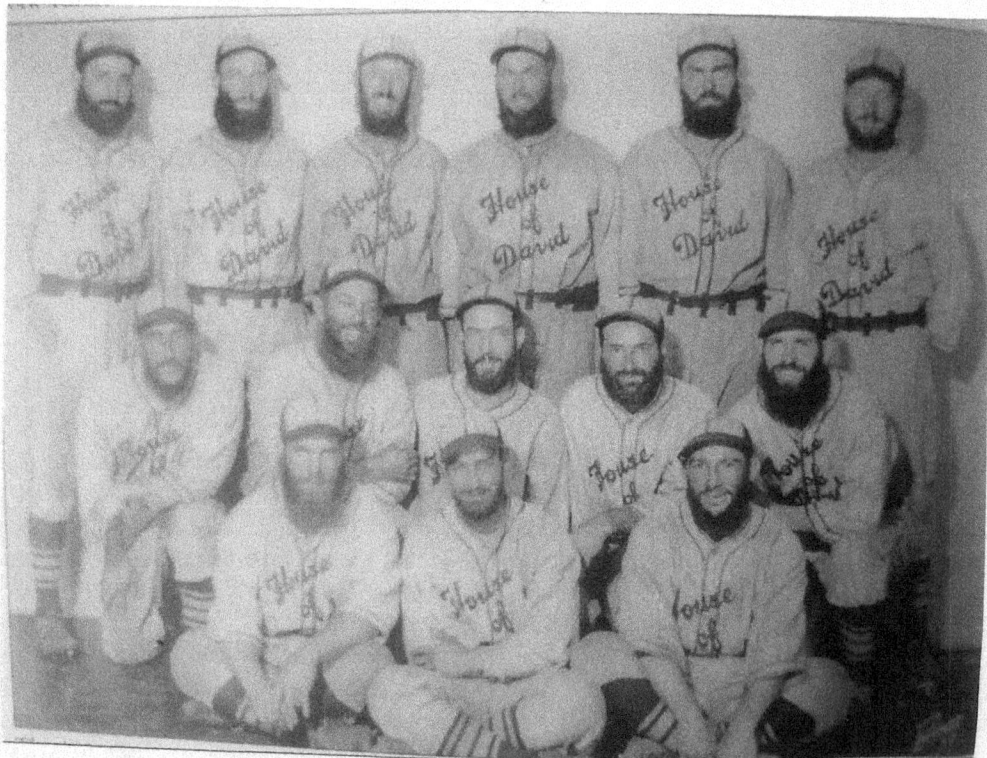

House Of David Professional Team

Several persons remember in the years that the town team won the championship they had at least one visit from the "Israelite House of David" team. They were unlike any other team. They were established in 1903 as a religious group in Benton Harbor, Michigan. Then in 1915 they organized a baseball team, and traveled all over the country playing wherever they could schedule a game. They had long hair and beards resembling Biblical characters, and the ability to win most of their games.

Loyalton Team Twin County Champions 1951
Back row l to r: Marlin Johns, Jr., Harry (Buzz) Hepler, Myles Kahler, Jack Hepler, Donald Hoffman, Dale Williard, John Harris, Palmer Riegel. Front row: Bob Harris, Robert Bonawitz, Cylon Williams, Glenn Hepler, Bruce Hoover. Batboy Lynn Harris.

Throughout the many years of baseball the Loyalton teams collected their share of champion winnings and had the pennants to prove it. A few years ago, Bob Bonawitz an active member of the Gratz Historical Society donated the pennants for display in the large baseball exhibit area of the society museum. Bob also donated pictures of the teams. Bob was proud to have these items displayed and preserved so that future generations could have the pleasure of seeing the Loyalton awards.

HISTORY OF IMMANUEL CHURCH OF LOYALTON
(And It's Predecessors)

Immanuel Evangelical Church of Loyalton is the outgrowth of two religious organizations, which were established in this immediate area many years ago.

The first known religious organization to be established in the vicinity of Loyalton was the Methodist Episcopal congregation. It was through some early Irish Methodists who had settled in Halifax about 1782, Daniel Miller, founder of Millersburg, and a missionary by the name of William Ross, that Methodism was introduced to this area. In addition to the Halifax class and the Millersburg class (first held in 1801), another class was formed in Lykens Valley "near Gratz." The last one was probably the group who met near Loyalton. All three of these groups belonged to the Dauphin Circuit, and along with probably four or more other congregations shared the same ministers.

IMMANUEL EVANGELICAL CHURCH OF LOYALTON

The Methodist Episcopal Congregation near Loyalton apparently continued to meet in private homes for several years. A list of the early itinerant ministers was preserved in the Quarterly Conference records. There were many preachers because usually two preachers served as a team, and served only one or two years in each circuit. Starting in 1802 these ministers served: Jacob Gruber, Anning Owens, Henry Boehm, Joseph Osborne, Joseph Stephens, William Hunter, Daniel Ireland, Thomas Birch, William Hoyer, Jacob Miller, James Mitchell, Thomas Bowing, William J. Bethel, John Fernon, William Fox, etc -------.

Henry Kuntzelman, Sr. listed as a preacher in 1814 and 1815 settled in the vicinity of Loyalton, purchased a farm in 1831, and continued to live here. Several years later on October 20, 1834 Henry Kuntzelman and his wife Mary, of Lykens Township, conveyed a small tract of ninety-two square perches of land in Mifflin Township to the trustees of the Methodist and U.B. in Christ Congregation in Union. The trustees were John Matter, Isaac Matter and Henry Kuntzelman, Jr. The land was conveyed for "the love and affection" for the use of a school and meeting house of the Methodist and U.B. Congregation. It is not clear whether this was two separate buildings or one to be used for both school and church activities in the style of the old colonial meeting house.

During those early years, another group of Evangelically minded people began to meet as a Prayer Meeting class. They too held worship and Bible Study services in private homes. When their numbers increased, members of the Methodist Episcopal Church invited the Evangelical Congregation to worship in their meetinghouse. They continued to worship in the Methodist Meeting house, and eventually the Methodists decided to build another church.

On December 9, 1852, Hannah Uhler sold one-half acre (80 square perches) of land to "Trustees and successors in office in trust for the use of members of Methodist Episcopal Church." The trustees were Aaron P. Lark, Thomas Snyder, John Robinson, Elias Kuntzelman and Daniel Dieter. Under the leadership of Rev. Ruben Deisher and Rev. Joseph Specht, the people gave their liberal support. The guidance of Lay leaders Daniel Romberger, Benjamin Wingart, Charles Klinger, Alex Klinger, and P. Harmon enabled the church body to reach their goal. The new church was built, and Zion Church at Oak Dale was dedicated, Christmas Day in 1859, "for the service of the Trinity of God to Worship the Lord therein in Spirit and Truth, and for to Preach His Holy word." Rev. S. Neitz preached the dedication sermon. By 1876, the Oak Dale church was free of all debt. Steady progress was made and the congregation grew. During the next few years, the congregation became associated with the "Old Lykens Valley Circuit." In future years, other name changes were made in the circuit, but usually four or more churches belonged to the same one. In the1870s, Berrysburg, Gratztown, Oak Dale and Weaver's congregation constituted the Berrysburg Circuit.

The Village Of Loyalton

Camp meetings were popular dating back to a much earlier time. It is recorded that in 1867 a train was run on the Summit Branch Railroad to accommodate those of the citizens who desired to attend the campmeeting at Millersburg. The church minutes beginning in 1876, record the yearly camp meeting events of these churches. In 1876, camp meeting was held in the grove of Alexander Klinger at the crossroads. The churches of this circuit sponsored the grove meetings that attracted many people. People from a distance (and even local people) brought tents and stayed at least several days. That year sixty-eight tents were pitched. In 1878, a camp meeting was held at Oak Dale, and seventy-six tents were pitched. In succeeding years, camp meetings were held in Jonathan Klinger's woods, a place "below Elizabethville," and in 1886 in Captain Budd's woods at Oak Dale Station. Overall, the Oak Dale congregation remained in a very prosperous condition, and grew in numbers.

At a meeting of the Annual Conference and quarterly Conference held in 1893 an important decision was made. The following statement was recorded:
"The trustees of Berrysburg and Oak Dale Church of the Methodist Episcopal Church, in the United States of America, shall sell the property." On October 27, 1893, Daniel Bordner, Valentine Lenker, Samuel Snyder, N. K. Miller, R. I. Robinson, and John R. Hoover, all of Berrysburg sold the property to John M. Boyer for thirty dollars. These men were the Trustees of Methodist Episcopal Church of Berrysburg and Oak Dale. An exception was made however, "reserving the building there-on which was formerly a church, with the right of removal of the same to the use and benefit of Josiah Boyer. Also excepting and reserving the space of said lands occupied by graves of deceased persons until such time (if such time shall ever be) when the dead will be removed there from."

By 1895 the Oak Dale membership had increased and it was said that the location was inconvenient for most of the people. Besides, the building had deteriorated. The members decided on a new building to be located in the village of Loyalton. After consulting with the Quarterly Conference, permission was granted "providing $1,200 in good subscription" could be secured before starting. The trustees, Edward Romberger, John M. Row and Henry F. Raker, representing the congregation, purchased a lot of ground from Sarah M Weiss and her husband William in 1897 for $100. By several different conveyances, this land had been owned by Henry C. Beshler, Benjamin J. Snyder, Amanda Hoke, and Sarah M. Weiss.

Mr. Charles Lebo of Berrysburg began construction, and the church was dedicated November 28, 1897, as Immanuel Evangelical Church of Loyalton. The bell from the old Zion Oak Dale church building has been mounted in a brick cubicle near the front of the present church.

The original building has seen numerous changes. The choir loft and chairs were added in 1922. In 1932, the building was enlarged, with the addition of a Sunday school room, a social room and a kitchen. The lighting system was upgraded, and in 1937 renovations were made in the chancel, and new furniture was added.

During the early 1940s, the congregation decided to purchase stained glass windows for the sanctuary of the church. They were receiving donations from members of the church for the windows, but one special contribution came from another source. This was about the time of World War II, and one of the residents of Loyalton, Robert "Rube" Aboff had a son who was in the service. The Aboff family was of Jewish ancestry, but Rube volunteered to pay for a window "if the congregation would say a prayer for his son." The stained glass window purchased by the Aboff family continues to survive, and is the only one displaying a Jewish Star of David.

Over many years social gatherings of members of the congregation were common practice. The following account dated 1922 describes one of the events:

The Loyalton & Oak Dale Sunday School held their annual picnic in Zerbe's Grove, Saturday, August 26, 1922 promptly at 9:30. The village was thrilled by the sweet strains of music of the Williamstown Band as they marched through the streets of the beautiful village. This band is one of the strongest musical organizations in the county, consisting of forty pieces and proved themselves as efficient in ability as the number could merit.

The picnic is growing each year and is fast becoming the great picnic of the Upper End. The weather was ideal and from morning until late in the evening automobiles kept rolling in. The grove is located at the foot of Berries Mountain only a stone's throw from the P.P.R. Station. It abounds in beautiful shade trees and is supplied with good mountain water.

Rev. A. E. Miller had charge of the program in the afternoon. Devotional services were conducted by Rev. Kuhn of Elizabethville. Able addresses were delviered by Lieut-Governor E. E. Beidleman, Rev. P. M. Holdeman, Rev. Campbell and Charles Passe. Following the addresses were amusements of various sorts consisting of different races and games, followed by a festival in the evening at which time the band again proved faithful.

Zion Church At Oak Dale

(Nov 5 to 9,1973 torn down by Cemetery Association: Carson Underkoffler, Dean Hartman, Mark Wise.)

The following pastors served Immanuel Church beginning 1897:

Rev. C. C. Moyer 1897	Rev. C. E. Horner 1924 – 1928	Rev. Arthur Lucas	1957 - 1959
Rev. C. E. Eagle ?	Rev. Albert Buck 1928 - 1930	Rev Lloyd Helt	1959 - 1964
Rev. D. A. Brown ?	Rev. Walter Sinclair 1930 - 1935	Rev. Keith Wise	1964 - 1967
Rev. C. N. Wolfe 1900 - 1904	Rev. Paul Gottschalk 1935 - 1939	Rev. Donald Van Kirk	1967 - 1976
Rev. O. T. Moyer 1908 - 1910	Rev. Lloyd Helt 1939 - 1942	Rev. Donald Raffensperger	1976 - 1987
Rev.J. S. Farnsworth 1910 -1912	Rev. Charles Kindt 1942 - 1946	Dr. P. Dale Neufer	1987 - 1990
Rev. Bean ?	Rev. Chester Strohl 1946 – 1949	Rev. Henry Gable	1990 - 1992
Rev. L. H. Yergey 1917-1921	Rev. Harold M. Young 1949-1953	Rev. Philip Sabas	1992 -2000
Rev. A. E. Miller 1921-1924	Rev. Elwood Heisler1953-1957	Rev. Edw. Diagostino	2000-2005
		Rev. Fred Rudy	2005

Peter John & Sarah Miller, (dau **James & Sarah Miller),** **Fisherville,** married April 7, 1901, after Sunday service, over 200 people attending. They had a noon lunch with minister & others, left on honeymoon to Niagara Falls. It was 1st wedding in Immanuel Church.

"The Bell Placed Here In Memory Of Oak Dale U.M. Church"

140

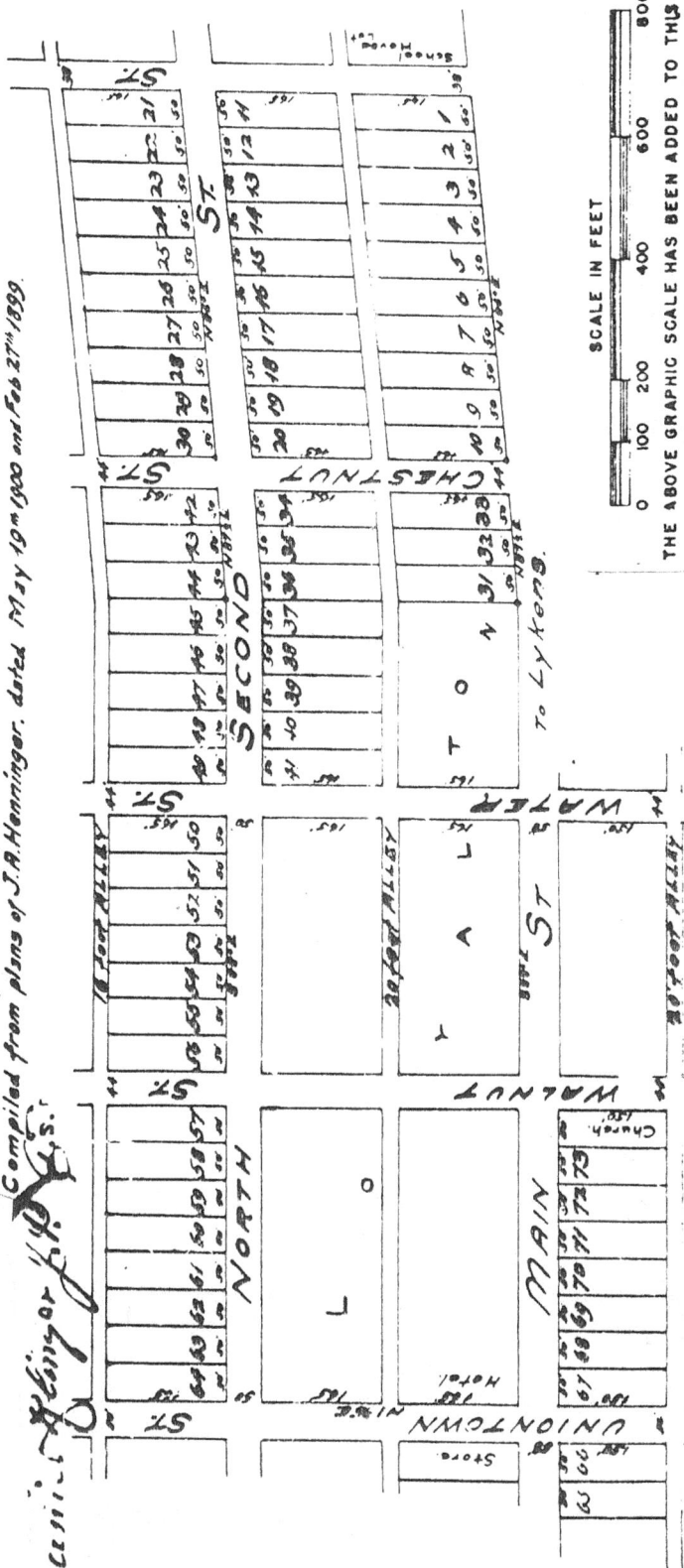

PLAN OF
SARAH M. WEISS'
ADDITION TO THE TOWN
LOYALTON

Compiled from plans of J.A. Henninger, dated May 19th 1900 and Feb 27th 1899.

SCALE IN FEET

0 100 200 400 600 800

THE ABOVE GRAPHIC SCALE HAS BEEN ADDED TO THIS
PHOTOGRAPHIC REPRODUCTION OF THE ORIGINAL PLAN.

Howard A. LeVan, Jr.
Registered Professional Engineer.
Pennsylvania 4621

PARCEL MAP OF LOYALTON

The parcel numbers represent the present owners of the lots.
(Some parcel lots may be missing for various reasons)

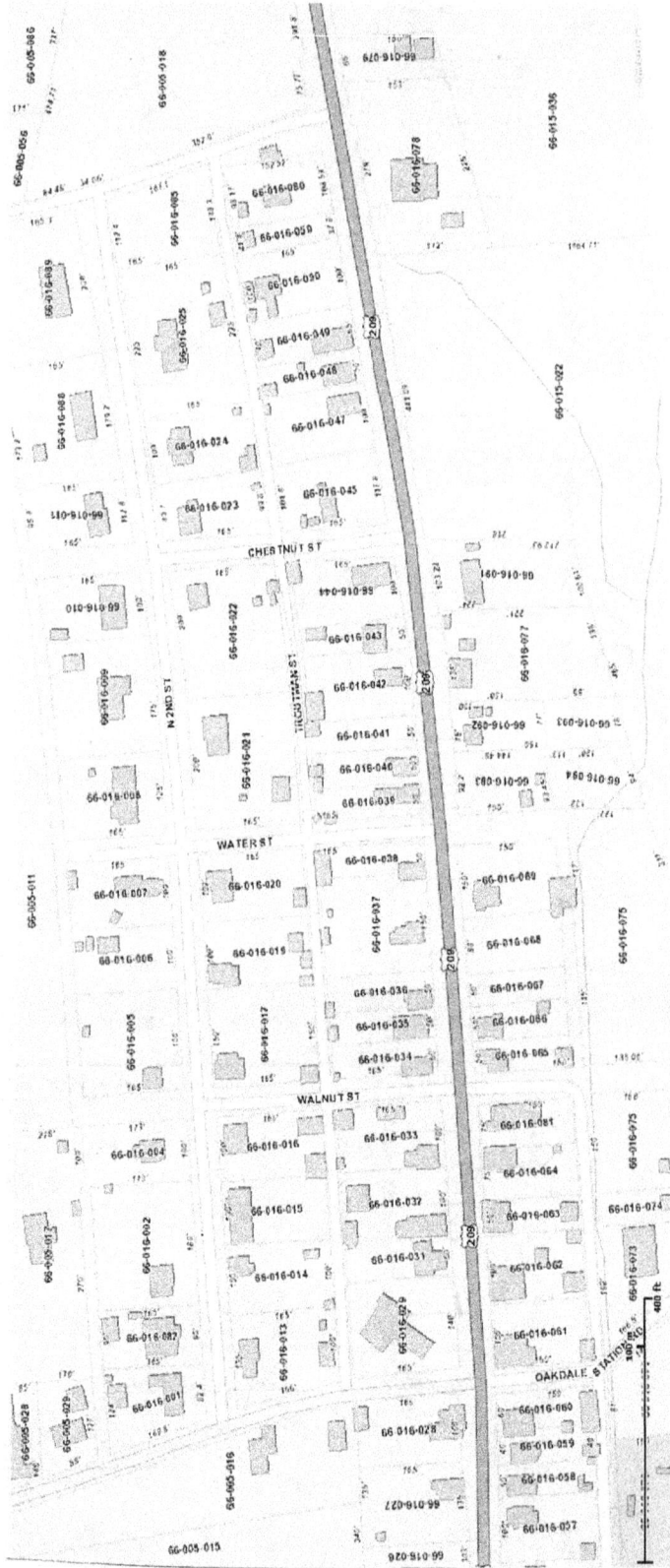

Chapter 8

THE NEW LOYALTON BEGINS IN 1875

In 1875, Dr. Henry C. Beshler laid out 107 plus acres of land in lots and had it surveyed by Daniel Hoffman. It became known as what was called the L. S. Ferree Plan. The result was the expansion of the area north of Oakdale Forge, now known as Loyalton. Various people purchased the land for various purposes, some commercial enterprises, but mostly residential homes.

Ownership of this land is traced back to the William Parson grant, and after several other conveyances, Michael Shuer conveyed 150 acres to Adam Rowe. Other lands were purchased and Adam Rowe, Sr. became the owner of a large amount of land in this vicinity. After Adam Rowe, Sr. died in 1830, John Paul, Jr. surveyed the land and the estate was prepared for distribution. John Rowe his son had already been a tenant living in a large 50 x 50 foot wooden house on 50 acres of his father's farmland. John was given this land in August 1839, as his share of his father's estate.

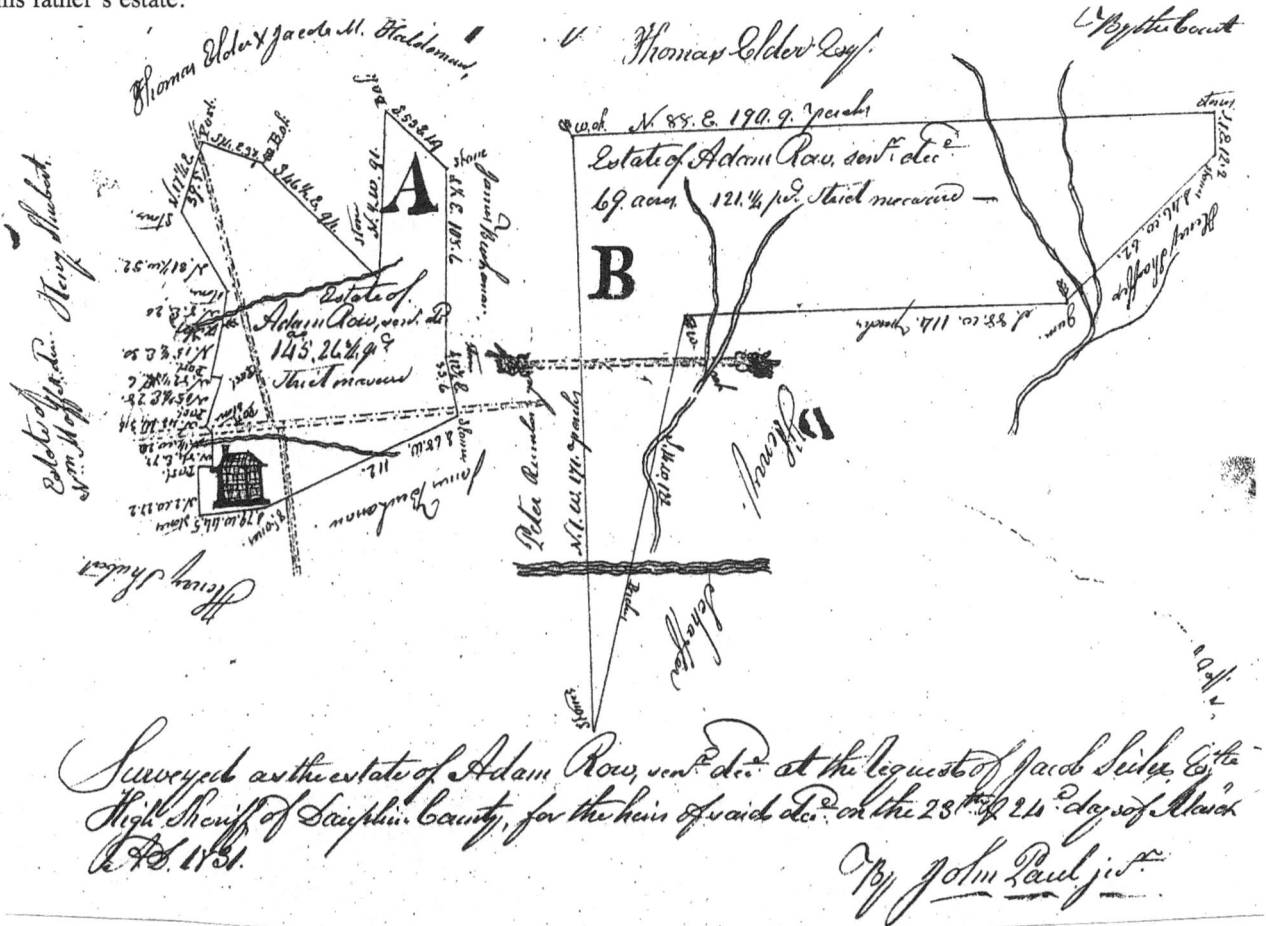

Henry Shubert was named trustee of the estate of Adam Rowe Sr. He conveyed the remainder of the land to Adam Rowe Jr. on April 1, 1835. Adam Rowe Jr. and his wife by deed of trust for the creditors, assigned all the property and personal goods of Adam Rowe Sr. to Daniel Riegel on December 27, 1842. On February 3, 1843, the plantation was scheduled for public vendue to either rent or lease to the highest bidder for one year from April 1, 1843, to April 1, 1844. It was struck down to Josiah Bowman. He leased the farm by verbal contract to Adam Rowe to manage the farm, agreeable to certain stipulations and contracts. Josiah Bowman was not happy with the understanding. In July 1843, Adam Rowe Jr. assigned all the crops, fall wheat, winter grain already harvested and in the barn, hay, second crop oats in ground, corn, potatoes, corn fodder, cows, hogs, sheep, and young cattle. In short, all property was to go to Daniel Riegel. This action was recorded on July 27, 1843.

On November 14, 1844, Daniel Riegel, assignee of Adam Rowe conveyed 86 acres of land to Jacob Emerich with dower to widow Mary, (whom by this time had married John Delp a wagon maker), and a right of way to the mill of Daniel Good. Another tract of 30 acres 87 perches of land was sold to Cornelius A. Harper on April 12, 1845. Cornelius A. and Sarah Harper sold their tract of land (by that time in Wiconisco Twp) on March 29, 1847, to Jacob Emerich a resident of Wiconisco Twp. Neighboring lands were: other land of Adam Rowe, John Rowe, Josiah Bowman, Peter Boyer and Mary Delp.

THE ADAM RAU/ ROW/ ROWE FAMILY
(Some information from Evelyn Row & Evelyn Hartman)

[ADAM ROW (Sep 21, 1770 - Sep 5, 1830, bur St. John's Luth, Berrysburg), m Mar 28, 1797 to Christiana Diller (b Sep 16, 1772 – Churchtown, Lanc Co - d Feb 21, 1823), a dau of John and Magdalena (Sherk) Diller. They were married in her parents home, by Rev. Traugott Frederick Illing, of the Episcopal Church in Churchtown. The tombstone of Adam Rowe had this inscription: "Don't mourn for me now, I am dead and moldering in my grave, but look to Christ the living head who all mankind can save." John Rowe oldest son of Adam and Christiana (Diller) Rowe inherited this land. (The other children will be found listed in the extensive history of the Rowe family in this book.)

*JOHN (b Feb 24, 1798, Lanc Co. - d Mar 29, 1873, Wash Twp, bur Oakdale Cem with both wives), son of Adam and Christiana (Diller) Rowe, m Susannah Ferree (Jan 11,1804 - Oct 10, 1846 bur Oak Dale Cem), a dau of Joel and Elizabeth (Ferree) Ferree. After Susannah died, John m Anna Elizabeth __ (1810 – 1900), had 3 children. **John and Susannah (Ferree) Row had 13 children (some bap St. Johns Hill Ch):**
**Mary Lovina (May 25, 1822 - Dec 25, 1826, death recorded in St. Davids Ch, Killinger);
Nathaniel b May 11, 1824, m Alabama Weidel b c1828, a dau of George and Nancy (Radel?) Weidel, lived in Wiconisco in 1850, and Susanna Russel age 19, C.F. Johns age 20, a tinner, and Nathaniels brother age 24, lived with them. **Nathaniel and Alabama (Weidel) Rowe children: ***Oliver b c1848; ***Mary Ann b c1849; ***John Wesley (1854 – 1857) ***Francis M b Sep 24, 1855.
Joel (Oct 30, 1825 - Sep 22, 1895, of cancer, bur Calvary Meth, Wic.), m Elizabeth ____ (Feb 22, 1825 - Mar 19, 1896). In 1860, they lived in Lykens Twp, Elizabeth Fagely age 72, a widow lived with them. In 1880 they lived in Wic. Twp. **Joel and Elizabeth Rowe children:*Emma b c1850; ***John b c1852; ***Charles b c1855; ***Mary b c1857; ***Rebecca b c1859;*** Sarah (1865 – Mar 30, 1904);***Susan b 1866.**
**Christina Elizabeth b Feb 16, 1827, m William Meyers b 1812. They lived in Lykens in 1880 and had Joseph Laudenberger age 21 with them
Lemuel (Nov 30, 1828 - Dec 18, 1900, bur IOOF Cem, Lykens), m 1858 Elmira Hawk (Aug 15, 1831 - Aug 17, 1892), a dau of Mathias and Magdalena Rowe. Lemuel hauled logs for the mines, by 1860 was a miner. He later was in an ice cream business with his son George. **Lemuel & Elimira (Hawk) Rowe child:
Mary Ellen (Jan 5, 1854 – Jul 11, 1908, bur Lykens), m William Mummy, **had these children:** Chas Henry b Jun 10, 1873; William Franklin b Aug 21, 1874; John Wellington b Oct 9, 1880; ***George Oliver (1858 – Apr 17, 1936, bur Simeon Cem, Gratz), m Elmira Unger (185 – Dec 30, 1925), a dau of _____ ; *** Sarah b 1859;William H. (Feb 10, 1864 – Jul 8, 1925, bur Simeon Cem), m Emma Jane Burd (May 4, 1863 – Feb 26, 1927), a dau of Isaac and A. Mary (Ferree) Burd. Emma lived with her grandmother Ferree in 1880 in Lykens Twp. **William & Emma (Burd) Rowe children (some bap Hoffman Ch):** Jennie M. (1882 – 1887, bur Simeon Cem, Gratz) ****Mary Elmira b Mar 24, 1884, m __ Hoyer; ****Beulah May b Dec 11, 1889, m Norman Kessler; ****Elizabeth Louise b Oct 7, 1892, m E. E. Shoop; Nora O. b May 1895; Florence b 1900.
*** Sarah b 1859; 3 others died before parents.
**Elmira b Aug 16, 1830;
Susan (Jan 11, 1831 – Jul 14, 1903, bur IOOF Cem, Lykens) m David Rudisill (Jan 1, 1831 – Nov 18, 1908). They lived in Lykens in 1880. **David & Susan (Rowe) Rudisill children: ***Adam b c1857; ***Clara b c1864; ***Alfred b c1868.
John M (Feb 4, 1835 – Dec 12, 1906, bur Maple Grove Cem, E'ville), m Jan 11, 1858 Elizabeth Wolf Klinger (May 20, 1836 – Oct 19, 1911), widow of Daniel Klinger, and dau of Michael & Catharine (Romberger) Wolf. Daniel Klinger d 1856, the same year they married, leaving a son _____ (1856 – 1876). **John M and Elizabeth (Wolf Klinger) Rowe children: ***Nathaniel; ***Ellen (Mar 23, 1860–1933) m Wm Neiman (1854 – 1923, bur Schweitzer Cem, Bbg);*Elizabeth (no dates) m William Meyers of**

Lykens (he died before 1900); *****Lydian** (Oct 13, 1858 - Jul 25, 1925, bur Maple Grove Cem), m May 5, 1878 John Wesley Boyer (Nov 14,1857 - Mar 1, 1948), a son of Gabriel and Matilda (Ginter) Boyer): *****SydneyAnn** (1863 - 1945), m Feb 10, 1884 Fred Mucher (1855 - 1937), son of John & Lana Mucher. *****Amos F**. (1865 - 1937, bur Calvary Cem, Wic.), m Sarah Kate Hawk (1865 - 1942), a dau of George & Sydney Hawk; *****Joseph E.** (Feb 14, 1872 - Apr 9, 1948, bur Maple Grove Cem, E'ville), m Susan A. ____ (May 15, 1877 —Mar 25, 1976); *****Beulah M.** (Jul 9, 1882 - Oct 21, 1936, of Diabetes, bur Simeon Cem, Gratz), m Jan 14, 1903 James Kessler (Sep 3,1873 - Mar 30, 1937).

****Cornelius** (b c1839 - Feb 12, 1890, bur Calvary Meth Cem, Wiconisco), m Eve Bleistein (c1839 - Apr 4, 1925), a dau of Joseph and Eva (Matter) Bleistein, lived in Wiconisco Twp in 1860 and 1880 and was a farmer and teamster. **Cornelius and Eva (Bleistein) Rowe had these children:** *****Sarah** b c1863; *****Albert** (1864 - 1922), m Ida C. ____ (1865 - 1907); **Theodore** or Absalom (Feb 2,1864–Apr 21,1921, bur Cal Meth Cem, Wic.), m Eertha "Ida" Williard (Dec 6, 1865–Jun 14, 1907), a dau of George D. & Amanda Barbara (Miller) Williard. He was a teamster at age15; *****John** b c1869.

****Leah Jane** (b Jan 11, 1840- d Nov 3, 1907), m John W. Eby (Jun 7, 1838-Aug 18, 1885, bur Wiconisco.

****Sarah Jane** b c1842

****Amanda** (c1844 - 1916, bur Old Union Cem, Lykens), m Daniel Shomper (Sep 20, 1844 - Dec 9, 1875), a son of Daniel and Elizabetrh (Rickert) Shomper.

****Walter F.** (1846 - 1915, bur Fairview Cem, Wmstown), m Christiana Rowe (1848 - 1921), a dau of Martin and Susanna (Fagley) Rowe. In 1880 they lived in Williamstown and had Samuel Rubendahl age 11 a step-son with them. **Walter F. and Christiana (Rowe) Rowe children:** *****David** b c1871; *****Ellen L** b c1872;*****Emanuel** b1874; *****Mary A** b c1876; *****Susan** b c1878; *****Franklin Ellsworth** b Jun 15,1880; *****Kate M** (1882– 1956, bur Fairview Cem, Wmstown); **After Susannah died, John Rowe m Anna Elizabeth** ____ (Jul 5, 1810 - Jul 12, 1900, bur Oakdale Cem), a dau of _____, In 1850, John and Ann Elizabeth Rowe lived in Wiconisco Twp, two doors away from William Rowe.

In 1860 John lived in Wiconisco Twp and had wife Ann Elizabeth with him. Also children Walter, Adam, Eleanor, Alfred and Gottlieb Bower age 48 a shoemaker. **John & Anna Elizabeth Rowe had a son:** ****Adam DAVID** (Jul 17, 1849 - Aug 30, 1935 bur Maple Grove Cem, E'ville) m Hannah Amelia Wirt (Apr 4, 1855 - 1924). Adam and Hannah lived in Washington Twp in 1880. His mother Anna Elizabeth (2nd wife of his father John) age 69 lived with them. **Adam D. & Hannah (Wirt) Rowe children:** *****Catherine E** (1873 - 1946, bur Maple Grove Cem, E'ville), m William Mumma (1874 -1961);*****John David** (1875 - 1961, bur Maple Grove Cem, E'ville), m Jennie E Hassinger (Aug 4,1880 - Apr 5, 1923), a dau of Aaron Hassinger. When Jennie became sick and confined to her bed, she was told by Dr. Barto that her problem was that she was "just worn out." Bob Smeltz passed on some advice given to him by Jacob Smeltz. He suggested that she drink eggnog with whiskey every day. She did, and in two weeks time (by Christmas that year), she was able to come downstairs! She lived in a nursing home for ten more years. **John David and Jennie E (Hassinger) Rowe children:** Walter Emanuel (1901-1951, bur Maple Grove Cem, E'ville), m Della Mae Snyder (1898 - 1975), had dau Ethel Elizabeth (1923 - 1970), m Eldred L. Kocher; Annie (1903 - 1981), m Harry J. Harper (1899- 1943), had a dau Beatrice A.; Violet (1916-2003), m Ralph Deibert; *****Ira F.** 1877-1954, bur Maple Grove Cem, E'ville), m Annie C (1879-1947);*****AlfredH.** (1879 -1957, bur Simeon Cem, Gratz), m Louisiana Catherine Kessler (1877 - 1975), **had these children:** Lillian R.(1905 - Oct 11, 1967, bur Maple Grove Cem), m Claude S. Miller (1898 - 1976); Pauline M; Florence.*****Clinton** (no dates), m Aug 25, 1900 Katie N. Michael;*****Elmer Newton** b Dec 11, 1886; *****Hannah**; *****Adam**.

****Erlena Catharine** (Nov 10, 1852-1920, bur E'ville), m David Bonawitz (Jan 3,1851-Jul 12, 1939). David was an apprentice to a cabinet maker in his youth, became a carpenter in Rife. They lived in Up Pax Twp in 1880. **David and Catharine (Rowe) Bonawitz children:*******Rosie E** (1874 - 1963), m Nathan E. Snyder;*****Ira Charles**.(1876-1947), m Mary J. Troutman (Jun 10, 1883-1970), a dau of Daniel and Sarah Troutman.*****Ira C. and Mary J. (Troutman) Bonawitz children:** Eva E b 1902, m George W. Snyder (1897-1946); Howard D.b1905, m Mary L. Jury; Charles E. (1907 - 1969, bur Wmstown), m Florence M. Seager; Robert O. b Oct 12,1918, m 1st Beatrice A. Harper b1921, 2nd Phyllis Hoover Daniel.*****Annie E** 1878-1946), m Hiram Killinger;*****George Alfred** (1880–Dec 8, 1928, bur Eville), m Carrie Grubb (1883-Apr11,1951), a dau of Henry and Isabella Grubb;*****Lydia E.** (1882-1947), m John H.Weaver (1879-1952) *****Frances** b1887 m Roy P.Walters (1884-1963);*****Esther** (1895 -1968), m Wm. Bowers (1891 - 1953).

****Eleanor** b c1853

Alfred C. (1854 – 1912, bur Oak Dale Cem), killed in mines, m Jane Peters (1858 – 1922), a dau of
_____ and Mary A. Peters. In 1880 Mary A. Peters age 60 "mother in law" lived with Alfred and Jane.
Alfred C and Jane (Peters) Rowe had these children (bapt Oak Dale Ch):***Lewis F.** (1874 – 1952, bur
Maple Grove Cem), m Maggie E _____ (1874 – 1947); ***Charles A** b c1878;***Mary Annie Elizabeth**
b Mar 14, 1879; ***James Alfred Daniel** b Mar 6, 1884;*** **Walter Edmund** b Oct 4, 1886; *** **Laura**
_____***Jennie** b Jun 18, 1891; ***Carrie Louisa**. m Adam Row, they had no children.

Jennie E. Hassinger Rowe (Mrs. John) on porch
At her old log house near Short Mountain, Loyalton

FAMILY OF DAVID & ERLENA (ROW) BONAWITZ
Standing l to r: Frances, George, Ann, Ira, Rosie, Seated: Lydia, father David, Esther, mother Erlena

THE ADAM ROWE FAMILY
L to r: front row – Adam D, Newton, wife Hannah; Standing: Ira, John, Alfred, Clinton, Catherine

On April 1, 1854, Jacob and Catherine Emerick conveyed the plantation (both tracts) with 114 acres of land to Christian ImSchoffstall. On March 18, 1865, Christian and Mary ImSchoffstall of Wiconisco Twp. transferred the 114 acres of land and property to David K. McClure, also of Wiconisco Twp. Adjacent to this property were the lands of John Rowe, south to Josiah Bowman, the school (lot #2), Daniel Warner, north to Daniel Good, Molly Crawford, the public road, John Bowman, then south to the land of Thomas Elder (deceased), and Jacob M. Haldeman. Several small lots or tracts were sold from the 114 acres during the next several years.

On April 4, 1874, David K. McClure and his Elizabeth sold 107 acres 30 4/10 perches of the above land to H. C. and Mary Beshler of Berrysburg, subject to the privilege of conducting water from a spring and meadow to the mill of Daniel Good. This acreage bordered the land of Daniel Warner, George Neagly, Daniel Good, Mrs. Amanda Rowe, and Daniel Romberger. Dr. Beshler and L. S. Ferree developed a plot plan (known as the L. S. Ferree plot plan), surveying this area into lots for purchase (This plan was not found recorded in Dauphin County court records). For financial reasons H. C. Beshler assigned the tract to Jacob L. Snyder on July 12, 1886. It was then assigned to John D. Snyder. Benjamin J. Snyder received it September 26, 1887 when he was the highest bidder at a public vendue held at the public house of David Hoffman in Loyalton..

On January 9, 1892, Benjamin J. Snyder conveyed the 107 acres of land belonging to Henry C. and Mary Beshler of Berrysburg to Amanda Hoke, wife of Josiah Hoke. This land bordered the Wiconisco Creek, land of Nathaniel Miller, the public road, across the road to land of J. W. Boyer, William Walter, Joel Miller and the public road to Williamstown. Also land of Amelia Gunderman south, Benjamin Welker, the school house, and the public road to Lykens and Mrs. Williams land.

Amanda Hoke sold land to Reuben Kessler, and then sold the remainder of her land to Sarah Weiss October 1, 1895. The new plot plan became known as the SARAH M. WEISS ADDITION TO THE TOWN OF LOYALTON. Several more plans were developed in later years.

[JOHN DIETRICH SCHNEIDER (Sep 23, 1783-Dec 12, 1837, bur Stone Val Cem), m Salome Witmer (Mar 3, 1789-Sep 20 , 1871), a dau of Mathias & Barbara (Shaffer) Witmer. They lived in Low Mah Twp., Northld Co. John Dietrich & Salome (Witmer) Schneider had these children:

*JOHN A. (Nov 15,1811 – Jul 1, 1881, bur St. Lukes Cem, Malta), m Lydia Ann Lower (May 23, 1808 – May 6, 1864) a dau of Daniel and Sophia Lower. They lived in Low Mahanoy Twp, Northld Co in 1860 and at that time son Jacob age 20, and three Lower children – Benneville 7, Charles H 9, and Rebecca 17 lived with them. **John A. and Lydia (Lower) Snyder had these children**:
**Luisiana (Mar 27, 1833 – Jul 17, 1840)
Jacob L. (b Feb 8, 1840 Low Mahanoy Twp Northld Co – d Jan 27, 1895, bur Vera Cruze, Northld Co), m Mar 24, 1861 Elizabeth Messner (Dec 11, 1841 – Aug 13, 1921), a dau of Philip and Anna Maria (Dockey) Messner of Stone Valley, Northld Co . Jacob and Elizabeth Snyder lived in Washington Twp in 1880 and Jacob was a wheelwright. His father John A. Snyder age 68, a carpenter lived with them. He was a partner of Reuben Kessler in the distillery at Loyalton. **Jacob L and Elizabeth (Messner) Snyder had these children (some bapt Stone Valley): Mary Alice b May 16, 1862; Henry M b c1866, lived in Shamokin in 1895; John Albert b Sep 10, 1871, lived in   Shamokin in 1895; Maggie M b Feb 26,1876; Lidia Ann b Sep 16, 1877;]
*Lydia b c1812
*William b Dec 2, 1815

[ABRAHAM SNYDER (Jan 7,1814 – Jun 21, 1888, bur Meth Cem, Bbg), m Hannah Bordner (Jan 29, 1821 – Apr 8, 1900), lived in Berrysburg where he was a shoemaker in 1850 & 1860. George Feit age 18 lived with them in 1850. **Abraham and Hannah Snyder had these known   children:** Anna Elizabeth b c1840;   Silvester b c1844; Benjamin J. (b c1847-____), m Susan ___ b c1852. In 1880 they lived in Uniontown and he was a moulder. **Benjamin J. and Susan ( ) Snyder had these children (some bapt County Line Ch, Low Mahanoy Twp, Northld Co):** Sarah J. b c1872; Katie J b c1874; Charles B. b c1876; Mary L b Dec 8, 1878; Dora May b Sep 7, 1877; Wellington E. b Feb 28, 1880; Harry Edward b Jun 5, 1882; Joseph Franklin b Sep 7, 1883; Daniel b c1848; Franklin b c1850; Fanny b c1864.
 M. Ellen (Mar 21, 1851 – Dec 31,1891);

Henry Nelson Hoke Family c1923
l to r: 1st row seated: Anna Hoke Travitz; Henry Nelson; Paul A.; Sarah Ida Radel; Edna Hoke Shadel. 2nd row standing:Hazel Dietrich; Harry H. Jr.; Ray Nelson; William Hoke; Mabel m Newton Row; Florence; Minnie missing

THE HOKE FAMILY

This information is not complete. We are sharing what we were able to find.

RUDOLPH HOKE (b c1755. – d Jan 7, 1827 Mifflin Twp), m Susanna____. He was the first of the family to arrive in Lykens Valley. He was here by 1800 when he had four sons and three daughters in the family. His Sons Jonas & Isaac Hoke were adm. of his estate. Orphan Court records of 1831 name the children. **Rudolph & Susanna Hoke had 10 children:**

*JOHN B. (Feb 24, 1802 – Jan 12, 1861, bur Peace Cem, Bbg), m Jan 1, 1824 Elisabeth Snyder Hoffman (May 11,1803 – Jul 11,1889, in Berrysburg), a dau of Leonard Snyder and widow of Daniel Hoffman. They lived in Wash. Twp in 1850. In addition to their children, Ann Mary (Shott) Snyder age 72 widow of Leonard Snyder, Jr, was with them. In 1860 John and Elisabeth Hoke lived in Washington Twp. Beside several children (William, Rebecca, and Jacob), Henry M Snyder, widower age 82 was with them. In 1870, Elisabeth was a widow, lived in Berrysburg. Her son Jacob was with her, and her daughter Rebecca married to Frederick Schoffstall. In 1880 Elizabeth lived with her son Jacob and his family. **John and Elisabeth (Snyder Hoffman) Hoke children (some bapt Hoffman Ch):**

Josiah b Mar 21, 1825 – Feb 12, 1894, bur Peace Ref Cem, Berrysburg, heart problem), m Amanda ____(Sep 4, 1823 – Mar 12, 1909). They lived in Mifflin Twp in 1850, and Peter Baney age 15 lived with them. In 1860 they were in Wiconisco Twp, living next to Michael Sausser. Their son Joseph, also Clara Sausser 17, servant and Jonathan Harman 28 was with them. In 1870 they were in Wash. Twp., and Josiah was listed as a broker. **Josiah and Amanda (___) Hoke had one known child: **Joseph A.** (b Oct 4,1854 – Jul 5, 1923, bur St. John's Hill Cem), m Mar 26,1878 Sarah Elizabeth Snyder (Jan 30, 1862 in Malta, Northld. Co – Sep 13, 1922), a dau of Samuel Solomon and Catherine (Swab) Snyder. In 1880 Joseph and Sarah Elizabeth Hoke lived with his parents Josiah and Amanda Hoke. **Joseph and Sarah Eliz (Snyder) Hoke had a dau** **Carrie Amanda** (b Sep 21, 1878 – Nov 6, 1950, bur Maple Grove Cem), m Nov 16, 1899 Peter Adam Matter (Jun 28, 1862 – Dec 24, 1943), son of Jeremiah Adam and Rebecca (Bohner) Matter. [More genealogy information with Matter family.]

Elizabeth b Jan 14, 1828; **Mary Ann b May 17, 1830, m ___ Fuller; **Catharina b Jan 29, 1833; **John B. (Jun 20, 1835 – 1900), m Oct 17, 1838 Sarah Hoffman b 1841, **had 16 children – these known: Sarah Eliz (Apr 30,1860– 1941), m Rudolph Schneider; Jane; Charles Franklin b 1861; Geo McClellan b1863; John Henry b1864; Catherine Rebecca b1872; Josiah b1873; Margaret Ellen; Samuel Tilden b 1876; John B.; Robt Lee b 1883;

**William (Nov 22, 1837 – 1910, bur Maple Grove Cem, E'ville), m Anna Jane (1842 – 1922), lived in Wash Twp in 1880. William was a reaper agent. Susan Lubold age 11 lived with them.

**Leonard (b Nov 17, 1839 – Jun 9, 1842)

Rebecca (Jun 26, 1842 – 1874), m Frederick Schoffstall (1837 – 1920, bur Peace Cem, Berrysburg), a son of Peter Schoffstall. At the age of 9, Rebecca lived with the Christian B. Miller family. **Frederick & Rebecca (Hoke) Schoffstall had these children; **Mary Eliz** (Aug 2, 1868 – Jan 22, 1921), m 1891 to George William Botts, **had these children:** **Frederick; Russell; **Morgan;**John; **Mildred; **Charles W. (1870 – 1951, bur Peace Cem), m Mollie Snyder (1853 – 1930). After Rebecca died, Frederick m Mary Ellen Botts (Jun 13, 1852 – Apr 28, 1918), a dau of George W. Botts.

Jacob H. (May 8, 1846 – Mar 9,1897, of consumption, bur Peace Cem, Berrysburg), m Sarah ___ (1845 – 1934). They lived in Berrysburg in 1880 and his mother Elizabeth lived with them. **Jacob and Sarah Hoke had these children: **Elizabeth b c1871; **Jennie (1872 – 1926); **Flora b c1875; **Alice b c1878.

*ISAAC (Jun 9, 1803 – Dec 21, 1892, bur Motters Cem), m Catharine Botz (Mar 20, 1803 – Jan 15, 1866), a dau of John and Hannah Botts. They lived in Wash Twp. in 1870 next to Henry I Miller. **Isaac and Catharine (Botz) Hoke children:** **Mary Ann b c1824; **Jonathan "Jonas" (Dec 25, 1825 –May 2, 1903, bur Motter Cem), m Clara Matter ( ), lived in Elizabethville. Jonathan was a shoemaker. He helped to build the Summit Branch Railroad. In 1880 Jonathan lived alone. He moved to Jackson Twp. **Jonathan and Clara (Matter) Hoke had a son** Aaron D. b Jul 25, 1868, m Katy E. Bowman of Wmstown. He became a currier, later moved to Phila, later to Middletown and worked for a leather co. In 1895 came back to Elizabethville, was a partner with Buffington, Enders & Hoke in the Enterprise Hosiery Co. **They had 2 children:** Wilmer b 1893; Elsie Irene b 1895.;

William b c1829; **Catharine Sep 26,1831–Dec7,1921 Los Angeles,Ca); Elisabeth b c1837; Sarah Jane b 1840;Emeline b 1842, m ___ Shoop, moved to Kansas;**Valentine (1845–Nov 24, 1893, death record states he died of drink & exposure), m May 7, 1868 Sarah E. Grimm b _____ . He lived in Halifax at the time of his death.

*SARAH (no dates), m Daniel Minnich; *JACOB (no dates); *POLLY (no dates) m William Simon; *ADAM (no dates)- This may be the Adam Hoke b c1800, living with Isaac Hoke b c1830, Catharine b c1825, & their children Alfred 2 and Valentine 3 months in W.T. in 1850 W.T.; *ELIZABETH (no dates); *SAMUEL (no dates)
*HENRY (c1810 Lanc Co –Apr 5,1855 of consumption in Wash Twp, bur St.Johns Hill Cem), m Mary _____ b c1801? Lived in Mifflin Twp in 1850. **Had these children: **Susanna b c1831;**Sarah b c1839;**Rebecca b c1841; **John b c1842.
*JONAS (no dates). This may be the one on the 1850 census b c1805, m to Julia b c1806 living in Wash T. In 1880 Jonas age 72 was recorded as the father-in-law living with John and Caroine Chubb age 25.

THE JACOB HOKE FAMILY, Etc.

JACOB HOKE b c1793 m Anna Margaret Radel (b 1796 - d ___), a dau of Michael and Margaret Radel of Stone Valley. Jacob and Anna Margaret lived in Up Paxton Twp in 1850. In 1860 Jacob Hoke age 60 lived in Mifflin Twp and his son Josiah age 30, his wife Sarah age 19 and infant dau Adaline Margaret with him. **Jacob and Margaret (Radel) Hoke had these children (some bapt St. John's Hill Ch); **HANNAH b Aug 4, 1817; **MICHAEL (Mar 1, 1819 – 1849), m _____. When Michael died, the grandmother Margaret Hoke petitioned the orphan court for a guardian for the two minor children. George Neagley was chosen. **Michael had two known children: ***Jonathan;***Elizabeth; **JONAS b Oct 6, 1820; **ELIAS b Aug 22, 1825, m Sarah Goodman b c1826. In 1860 they lived in Mifflin Twp & he was a blacksmith. **Elias and Sarah (Goodman) Hoke had these children: ***William Henry (1848 – 1909, bur Klinger Cem), m Anna Eliza ___ (Oct 7, 1847 – Mar 17, 1883) lived in Wash Twp., in 1880. **Wm H. & Anna Eliza Hoke had these children:****John H. b c1870; ****Emma Jane b c1871;****James M b c1874; ***Zacariah (1850 – 1864, bur Pillow Cem); ***Ann Margaret b Jan 8, 1853; ***Catherine (Jun 18, 1856 – Nov 18, 1924, bur Pillow, Dau Co), m John H. Witmer (May 8, 1851 – Feb 7, 1915). **John H. & Catherine (Hoke) Witmer had these children: ****Joseph (1876 – 1955_); ****Elizabeth (1877 – 1949), m John Adam Snyder b 1875. **John Adam and Elizabeth (Witmer) Snyder children: Della Mae (1898 – 1975); John Alvin (1900 – 1904); Katie Eliz (1903 – 1949); Blanche Alvena (1907 – 1959); Maude LuEllen (1909 -1943);****Mary Edna (1880 – 1923);****John Emory (1883 – 1956);****Sarah b c1858.

JOSIAH (Sep 15, 1830 – May 17, 1886, bur St. John's Hill Cem), m Nov 13, 1859 to Sarah A. Fagely (Jan 25, 1841 - Nov 27, 1902), a dau of Henry and Adaline Fagley. They lived in Mifflin Twp in 1870. **Josiah and Sarah (Fagely) Hoke had these children: ***Adaline Margaret (Apr 9, 1860 – Jul 3, 1942, bur Zion (Hoover) Cem, Rife), m Jacob Novinger (Jun 11, 1855 – Apr 8, 1939), a son of Jacob N. and Anna Mary (Harman)Novinger;*Henry Nelson (Feb 19, 1862 - Jul 21, 1934, bur Maple Grove Cem), m Sarah Ida Radel (1865 – 1953), a dau of Solomon &Catherine (Shaffer) Radel.**They had these children:****Annie Alverta (Aug 1,1885 – May 22, 1935, Loyalton, bur Maple Grove Cem), m Mar 21, 1908 Jacob Irvin Travitz (Oct 5, 1882 – Jan 2, 1922) a son of Simon and Eliza E. (Grim) Travitz.;****Edna Lena (Jul 3, 1887 – 1979), m Clayton Perry Esquella Shadle (Aug 27, 1880 – Oct 10, 1966), a son of Benjamin and Sallie (Sitlinger) Shadle. Perry owned a hotel in Big Run;****Hazel(no dates), m Harry O. Dietrich; ****Mabel Estella (Dec 13, 1889 – 1974), m Elmer Newton Rowe (Dec 11, 1886 – 1953), a son of Adam Diller and Hannah Amelia (Wert) Rowe;

Josiah Hoke (1830 – 1886)

****William Clarence (Mar 11, 1892 – 1973, bur Simeon Cem Gratz), m Katie L Koppenhaver (1889 – 1964), a dau of Theophilus M and Susan Adeline (Good) Koppenhaver;****Harry Hoyt Josiah (Aug 22, 1894 –Nov 19,1944), m 1st Mable Hoffman d Oct 27, 1918, had 2 children: Leon (Apr 6, 1916 – killed Aug 14, 1956), m Ethel Koppenhaver; Chas E (Oct 21, 1918 – killed Nov 11, 1956), m Dora Emma Morgan. Harry m 2nd Maude B. Shade widow of Herbert Dunleavy (1898– 1977), a dau of Henry M and Martha Jane (Wolfe) Shade, had 4 children: Clayton E. b May 28, 1921, m Lorraine H. Hand; Marlin W. b Oct 1923, m Beverly; Violet S b Feb 1926, m Clifford W. Herb; Harry E b Jan 1929, m Patty Jean Reiber.****Minnie Irene (Jun 22, 1898 – 1990, b Wiconisco), m Charles M.Heim (1889 – 1958);**** Roy Nelson (Sep 1900 -1924, bur Maple Grove Cem);****Hazel Gertrude (Aug 19, 1902 – Dec

149

bur Wiconisco), m Harry Oliver Dietrich (Oct 14, 1897- 1962, bur Cal Meth Cem, Wiconisco),a son of Isaac Oliver and Sarah Jane (Shomper) Dietrich; ****Florence Catherine (Oct 10, 1904 - 1995, bur Maple Grove Cem), m 1st Fred C. Heim, 2nd Francis E. Crosson; ****Paul Allen (May 27, 1909 - 1922, bur Maple Grove Cem). ***Jonathan (1864 - Jan 24, 1952, bur St. Johns Hill Cem), m Ellen Stoneroad (1860 - 1933);*** Mary Alice (Apr 10, 1866 - 1920, bur St. Johns Hill Cem), m Jacob W. Welker (Jul 26, 1869 - Feb 16, 1949), a son of Wm Henry & Elizabeth (Shoop) Welker;***Charles D.(Sep 2,1869–May 22, 1900 consumption, bur St. Johns Hill Cem), m Jane Rothermel (Aug 18, 1877 - 1936). They lived in Berrysburg; ***George (1871 - 1906), lived in Lykens.
**CHARLOTTE b c1837, lived with her parents in 1860 in Mifflin Twp.

Following are other early Hoke settlers in upper Dauphin County. The relationship has not been confirmed.

VALENTINE HOKE (___ Dec 9, 1837, bur E'ville). Nothing more found.

JOHN HOKE (Nov 25, 1786 - Jun 19, 1856, bur Fetterhoff Cem), m Elizabeth Lenker (Apr 12, 1790 - Nov 27, 1857, dau of Philip & Elizabeth (Larch) Lenker, lived in Halifax Twp. **John & Eliz. Hoke had 6 children:**
Hugh; **Jonathan (b ____ -d c1882?), m Rebecca;Elizabeth b Sep 18, 1817, m Samuel Gray;**Sarah m John Chubb;**Lydia;**Josiah b Mar 21, 1825. All children lived in Halifax area when John Hoke died.
CHRISTIAN HOKE (1796 –1873, bur Dau Cem, Dau Co), m _____ **had these children:** Christiana (1816 - 1884, Bur Dau); David b Jul 19, 1821; Catharine b c1830

JACOB HOKE (   ), m Elizabeth ____, **Children:** Jacob b Apr 3, 1817 Shoop Ch, Lower Pax. Twp; Christian b Nov 18, 1819; Phillippus b Dec 17, 1822 bapt Fetterhoff Ch, Halifax Twp

MICHAEL HOKE (Mar 6, 1810 - Nov 7, 1900 bur E'ville), m Lydia Gonder (Nov 25, 1811 - Jul 8, 1900), lived in Wash Twp in 1850 & 1860, he was a tailor. **Michael and Lydia (Gonder) Hoke children:** John (Feb 4, 1831 – Mar 22, 1859, bur Hoover's Cem, Rife), a shoemaker; Hannah b c1836; Catharine b c1838; Jacob b c1842, may have m Catherine ___ b c1845, had dau Mary M b c1869. He was a shoemaker in 1870 in Wash Twp; Hiram b c1844; Wm b c1844; Ellen Jane b c1846; Mary b c1848; James W. (1851 - 1938), m Mary E. ___ (1854 - 1920). They lived in Mifflin Twp in 1880; he was a plasterer.

LEANDER S. FERREE FAMILY

[LEANDER S. FERREE (b c1844 - d Apr 21, 1882), a son of Joel Barlow and Ann (McCurtin)Ferree, m Catherine Elizabeth _____ b c1844. **Leander and Catherine Eliz. Ferree had these children some bapt Meth Episcopal, Bbg): John b c1869; Josie E (female) b May 15, 1871; Mary Jane b Apr 9, 1873; John G b Jul 18, 1874; Dora May b Aug 11, 1875; James B. b Aug 1879; Rosy A.** [See also Ferree genealogy.]

THE BESHLER FAMILY

[HENRY C. BESHLER (Jan 5, 1807 - Dec 8, 1888, bur Peace Cem, Bbg), m Mary Boyer (Oct 23, 1814 - b in Freeburg, Snyder Co - Oct 25, 1894). Dr. Beshler and his wife came to Berrysburg from New Berlin, Snyder County before 1850, and he was first listed as a merchant in 1850. By 1860 he became a doctor. In addition to his immediate family, these people lived in the household: J. F. Miller, son-in-law and agent for reaper, and John Hawk age 20, listed as a servant. Dr. Beshler practiced medicine in Berrysburg for the remainder of his life. **Henry C. and Mary (Boyer) Beshler had these children:**
EMMA JANE (b Mar 6, 1835, Freeburg - 1919), m Jul 4, 1855 J. Frank Miller (Jun 13, 1830 in Annville, Leb Co, - d Nov 10, 1904, bur Peace Cem), a son of Isaac and Mollie (Fernsler) Miller. J. Frank early in life moved to Iowa, then to Ohio, where he worked at a grist mill, until he became ill. He came back home and taught school at Annville.In 1854, he moved to Princeton, Illinois and engaged in the grain business.He also worked with the "under ground railroad while there, and received a commission as first Lieutenant in the Illinois State militia. He served in co B 9th Regt. Pennsylvania cavalry during the Civil War, with Col.Williams and Capt E. G. Savage. He was eventually promoted to Major, and served during numerous battles throughout the war. After the war he resided in Berrysburg, where he served as

postmaster, and was a merchant . **J. Frank and Emma Jane (Beshler) Miller had these children: Henry I.** b Feb 24, 1857, m Addie Moyer of Pillow. He was a teacher; **ANNA LAURA** b Aug 24, 1859, m George D. Romberger, insurance agent of Berrysburg.

<u>ANN ELIZA</u> (Apr 11, 1837 – Mar 6, 1882, bur Peace Cem, Bbg), m David K. McClure, a son of Joseph and Margaret McClure of Oakdale (now Loyalton). **David K and Ann Eliza (Beshler) McClure had these children: Charles B.** (b 1856 in Wash Twp – d ____), m Oct 4, 1887 to R. Elizabeth Hower in Bloomsburg, Pa. a dau of Jackson Hower. Charles B graduated in 1888 from Western Pennsylvania College in Pittsburgh. He practiced medicine in several places before moving to Gratz in 1894. They lived in the old house on lot thirty-four that had been an early hotel. The McClure family lived in Gratz until December 1899, when they moved to Berrysburg. **Charles B and Elizabeth (Hower) McClure had these children: Arthur Carlton: Hiester N.** (1895 – Aug 12, 1896m, bur Simeon Cem): Dora Florence (Nov 13, 1896 - Dec 1989), bur Clifton Cem, Fairfax, Va.). Dora never married. She was a public school teacher in Pa. and Virginia, lived to the age of ninety-three.

 <u>JOHN G.</u> (1840 – Apr 1869, bur Peace Cem, Bbg), m Jennie ___ (Feb 6, 1839 – Feb 2, 1867). John became a doctor, but he died very young at the home of Dr. McClure in Oakdale.

 <u>ANNA M.</u> (Jul 22, 1866 – May 7, 1909, bur St. John's Hill Cem), m Mar 5, 1890 Dr. W. Edwin Bonawitz (Jan 30, 1866 – Oct 2, 1911), a son of Jonathan and Margaret (Rutter) Bonawitz ; _____ m Isaac Hoke; _?_____ (maybe Henrietta b c1840 on 1870 census Berrysburg as wife of John W. Deibler ? OR Cate with John W. Deibler 1880 both b c1845 (from deed we have in library.)

THE OLD ALFRED H. ROW FARM
(D. BESHLER IN 1875)

This land was part of the large acreage owned by Adam Row, Sr. (Some inherited from the Ferree family). Christian Schoffstall became the owner of this part in 1854, followed by David K. McClure, H. C. and Mary Beshler, Amanda Hoke, the Sarah Weiss lot plan, and Reuben Kessler. On April 2, 1910, George W. Kessler conveyed several tracts of land to Alfred H. Rowe, including this 14 acre 82 perch parcel with the old log dwelling and bank barn. The land bordered along the south side of Main Street between lot 68 and 72, the south side of an alley to Reuben Kessler, and bordering on land of Nathaniel Miller.

The 14 acres 82 perches with dwelling house and bank barn was located directly behind the Snyder store, and the old log farm house (believed to be the oldest or one of the oldest existing houses in Loyalton) was on the right (west of the road). The exact date of the house is not known but it appears on the 1858 map as the dwelling of Christian Schoffstall, and was probably there much earlier than that. Soon after Alfred Rowe purchased the farm, he replaced the barn with a new, more modern structure with stanchions for his dairy cattle. In later years the barn was turned into a residential and commercial enterprise.

On August 16, 1922 the Washington Camp 454 POS of A purchased the barn and 7500 square feet of land from Alfred H. Row. The upper levels were converted into apartments, and the bottom level consisted of a bar, restaurant, dance hall and barber shop.

Alfred Row Barn In Background, Girl Unidentified

Below - Unidentified Boys Playing Crochet Near Barns (c1907 – 1915)

151

Square dances were held weekly. In 1925 Paul and Abby Gotshall) Schreffler, residents of Elizabethville operated the restaurant and bar. Mary Brown (later Mrs Homer Hassinger) was a waitress. Whenever business was slow, Mary fried onions. The aroma soon brought in new business. Silas Troutman was the errand boy for the barber. He & Mary agreed that their least favorite job was keeping the spittoons bright and shiny.

On January 20, 1943, the Washington Camp POS of A sold the property to Peter A. and Carrie Matter. Loyalton Fish and Game Association used the restaurant in the 1950s to hold their fish fries. After Peter and Carrie Matter died, the property was sold to Ralph P. and Caroline Matter, and on June 16, 1959 they sold to Robert C. and Helen Matter. Robert Matter owned this complex for many years and changed it into a compound of apartments. Robert C. Matter d Nov 25, 1983, and Helen E. Matter became the owner. On April 12, 1984, Helen Matter, widow conveyed the same to Steven T. Herrold of Herndon.

THE FARM HOUSE

The log dwelling is very old. As previously mentioned it is earlier than 1858, but it may have been owned by the Row family as early as 1828. Alfred Row sold to J. G. Romberger, he sold the 22,741 square feet and log house to Wesley I and Catherine L. Troutman Apr 2, 1924. After Wesley died, Catharine L Troutman sold to Claude S. and Lillian Miller July 17, 1936. While the Miller's owned it, John and Evelyn (Troutman) Sleighter family lived here, and in the '40s, Mr. and Mrs. Weaver were residents. The Weaver's operated a loom for weaving rugs. Lillian Miller died Oct 11, 1967 giving title to Claude. After Claude Miller died, his executor Kay Rice conveyed this and three lots (21-22-23) to Dennis E. and Joanne E. Row on September 7, 1976. They are the present owners.

On the west side of the farm, a large shed became a shirt factory about 1901, and provided employment for area residents. Ross Blyler was the overseer. The factory workers produced only one item – shirt sleeves. They were made for the Gratz Shirt Factory.

The Old Barn At Present Appearance – An Apartment Complex

THE REUBEN KESSLER DISTILLERY
(6400 sq ft from Dr. H. C. Beshler/ L. S. Ferree Plan)

This land is located on the south side of Main Street, and was adjacent to the Alfred H. Rowe farm. In more recent times the land fronting on Main Street was purchased and became a residential property, owned by Bruce and Helen Hoover. It will be discussed separately.

On April 28, 1874, several days after they purchased their land, Henry C and Mary Beshler of Berrysburg sold a lot containing 6400 square feet in Loyalton, to Jacob L. Snyder of Washington Twp. It was situated along the road from Loyalton to Millersburg, and bounded by Henry C. Beshler's other land, land of George Williard, and Jacob Hoffman. Jacob L. and Elizabeth Snyder received at least two other tracts of land from Dr. Henry C. Beshler, in separate transactions. Those two tracts were apparently assigned to Jacob L. Snyder, as no recorded deed has been found. After purchasing the land, Jacob carried on a wagon business. He and Reuben Kessler became partners and together also built a distillery on the land. Jacob sold his share of the business to Reuben Kessler shortly before his death.

[Jacob L. Snyder (Feb 7, 1840 – Jan 27, 1895, d in Loyalton, bur St. Luke's Cem, Malta, Northld Co), m Elisabeth ____ (Dec 11, 1841 – Aug 13, 1921). **Jacob L. and Elisabeth Snyder had these known children**:Lydia Ann b Sep 16, 1877; James; Henry, both moved to Shamokin; Jacob Hilbert b Jul 10, 1881. More genealogy elsewhere.]

On January 10, 1894, Jacob L. and Elizabeth Snyder of Loyalton sold all of the above land and distillery to Reuben Kessler of Lykens Township. Reuben and his sons became owners of the distillery. Included with the land was an engine, a sawmill and fixtures, boring machine, line shaft and all other machinery tools. It was located on the south side of the public road, and bounded by land of Edward Klinger, Mrs. Amanda Hoke and Joel A. Miller. Reuben Kessler received another 18,630 square feet of land from Amanda Hoke on August 11, 1894. They received two more lots from Sarah M. Weiss on March 27, 1901. (The last two tracts belonged to separate lot plans laid out by Amanda Hoke and Sarah M. Weiss and are discussed elsewhere.)

Reuben Kessler was a skilled brew master, his two sons also engaged in the business. The eldest son George "Wash" attended the local schools and was an excellent student. He followed his father and became the brew master.

James the second son was known as Jim. He hated school, because the only language they spoke at home was the Pennsylvania Dutch.

From the beginning, Reuben traveled to the coal region to sell his whiskey. He always concealed one jug among all the jugs on the wagon to hold the money. As soon as Jim became old enough to drive a team of horses, he followed in his fathers footsteps and began to deliver brew to the taverns. Each morning he would prepare the wagon for the days deliveries. The first thing he did was put some straw in the wagon box. He would then place the barrels and gallon jugs of whiskey in such a way that they would not spill or be broken. He always had two extra jugs - one full jug that provided free samples for the customers; one empty jug used for a cash box. These jugs were placed under the wagon seat. He was now ready to start on his routine journey.

In the warmer seasons, as he drove along the countryside, Jim would be observing the fields looking for the farmers. If he saw one plowing or doing some other chore, Jim would stop and give the farmer a free drink. Most likely the farmer would respond by paying a dollar for a full jug, and immediately hide it in the fencerow. Some of the Kessler jugs have survived and Bob Smeltz, a descendant has some of these ceramic type unmarked jugs in his basement. He remembers that his grandmother Row had huge jugs of whiskey in her basement when he was a child. If Bob had a sore throat, she would give him a spoonful of whiskey from those jugs.

Advertisement Print Calendar From Kessler Brewery

At the end of the day, after all his other deliveries were made, Jim would visit one of his father's farms in Lykens Township (either the one at Specktown or the one along Cross Roads). The one at Specktown had a large tavern house located on the farm, and it did a thriving business. A small log house near by was where the tenant farmer lived. It was here in the surrounding fields of this farm (as well as the other farm) that supplies such as corn, barley, and rye was grown for the distillery. During harvest time the grain was taken to Fishers gristmill to be ground.

The Kessler business at first included a wagon factory, and then a blacksmith shop to make the iron parts for the wagons. Later the distillery was located on the top floor of the building and the bottom floor continued to hold all the plans for building wagons. This two-story building was located on the lot where the home of Harold Hoover was constructed in the later 1940s and where Bruce and Helen Hoover lived until his death. The barn at the end of the Hoover property was the steer barn. The steers were fed the mash from the distillery.

Reuben and Elizabeth Kessler owned this distillery property for many years, and Reuben dispersed his product to a wide area surrounding Loyalton. On January 11, 1911, Reuben and Elizabeth Kessler sold the distillery known as number forty-four of the Ninth District of Pennsylvania, to his son, James A. Kessler. An additional covenant went with it, agreeing that "it was to be used for the purpose of distilling spirits, and subject to provision of law and a lien on the property for taxes should have priority over title to distillery premises. In case of forfeiture of distillery premises, or any part for violation of revenue laws of the United States, Reuben and Elizabeth Kessler shall be discharged and not responsible." The old original building containing the wagon shop, blacksmith shop and then the distillery provided a unique setting in Loyalton of by-gone days. Jake Novinger was for sometime the blacksmith. A coach shop was located on the lot next to the distillery. The Kessler Distillery was very productive, until prohibition days when the whole production came to an end. George Snyder bought the business at public sale in October 1920 and tore the buildings down. James Kessler bought the blacksmith shop, wagon shop and bonded warehouse with several lots.

Elizabeth (Sweigart)
Kessler
And
Reuben Kessler

Wedding Photo
Feb 26,
1871

THE KESSLER FAMILY

[*ABRAHAM KESSLER (b Nov 30, 1818, Sch Co – d Jun 12, 1881), a son of Michael Kessler, Jr. (Feb 21, 1794 – Apr 4, 1879 Hegins Twp., Sch Co., bur Weishample Cem) and Magdalena Arnold. Abraham m Catherine Riegel (Oct 13, 1816 –Nov 15, 1892, d at the home of her son), a dau of Andreas (Jr) and Elizabeth (Stein) Riegel. **Abraham and Catherine (Riegel) Kessler had one child:**
 REUBEN (Jun 18, 1846 Sch Co. - d Sep 16, 1915, bur Simeon Cem), m Feb 26, 1871, Elizabeth Sweigart (May 10, 1848 - Oct 22, 1931), a dau of Philip and Susan (Fauber) Sweigart of Jackson Twp. Elizabeth suffered four years with asthma before her death. **Reuben & Elizabeth (Sweigart) Kessler children (most bapt Simeon Ref Ch):**
 George W. (Jun 7, 1872–Jan 4, 1912, bur Simeon Cem, Gratz), m Katie F. Harman (Sep 26, 1876 - Jul 30, 1945), a dau of John G. Harman. George and Katie had no children;
James Andrew (Sep 3,1873–Mar 30, 1937, bur Simeon Cem), m Beulah M. Rowe (Jul 9,1882–Jan1937), a dau of John D. Rowe. James died at the home of Chas Hoffman of Elizabethville; **Louisiana Catharine** (Dec 27,1877 –1975, bur Simeon Cem, Gratz), m Alfred H. Rowe (1879–Feb 11, 1957), a son of Adam D. & Hannah (Wirt) Rowe, **had 3 children;** Lillian R.(1905 - 1967), m Claude S. Miller; **Pauline M** ( ), m Darwin Rebuck, had a dau Kay E., m Wm Rice; **Florence** (d Jan 1, 1924), m ___ Smeltz, had son Robert. Abraham Philip (Jul 11, 1893 - 1895, bur Simeon Cem).
[See other **Kessler genealogy** on page 293.]

The Old Covered Bridge In Loyalton

(Near what was Vicki's Valley Inn)

Early Photo of Loyalton Covered Bridge

The date of this old covered bridge, a remnant of the horse and buggy days, is not known. However, it stood firm for many years against all types of conditions, giving access to travelers as they passed over the Wiconisco Creek. But late in 1931, the structure was weakened by a blaze, believed caused from a cigarette cast aside by a motorist. It was repaired, but deemed too weak to support heavy traffic. A detour was established in December 1931. Motorists first used a township dirt road past Good's Mill, more than a mile in length. However, this road passed over an iron bridge that was too light, so it was closed. It forced motorists to use a detour 8.44 miles in length from the west side of Loyalton to Berrysburg, over the concrete highway to the Hoffman Church and crossroad to Loyalton.

A protest induced officials to reinforce the lighter bridge to shorten the detour. Steel beams were used to strengthen the Loyalton bridge. The roof and wooden sides were removed, and guardrails were placed. Harry A. Long of Port Royal and a crew of twenty-five men did the construction at a cost of about $3,000.

Many folks from the past had memories of the old wooden bridge. One memory concerned young Raymond Fisher who came to town and lived at the nearby Fisher's Mill. He loafed at the Snyder store (as many other folks), and when the store closed, walked home through the covered bridge. Raymond had relatives in Germany, and during the First World War, he was sympathetic to the German cause. Loyalton residents were not pleased with his attitude. So some young men made a straw stuffed dummy to resemble a German soldier, and dropped it on Raymond when he was walking home in the dark, through the covered bridge. Very scared he ran home and never mentioned the war again.

A Walk Down Main Street

(Focusing On Turn of The Century, But Including Later Buildings)

This is a good place to pause and remember a very special member of the Gratz Historical Society. Robert Bonawitz, a resident of Loyalton for most of his life became a member of our Society when he married Phylis Hoover Daniels and moved to Gratz. Bob was an energetic person whose interest in history and civic goodwill motivated him to join the crew of men whose efforts kept our building and surroundings in good condition. His carpentry skills were especially useful. But above all we wish to posthumously acknowledge his contribution to the library of our society and now this book. With the help of other residents of Loyalton, Bob on his own initiative collected information and brought it to the library either to be copied or as donations. His activities occurred long before we thought of publishing this book. Most of the photos in this section of the book are the results of his thoughtfulness. Too bad he is no longer with us to share his vast knowledge of oral history of his community.

We also need to acknowledge the help received from member Catherine Hassinger Kieffer. Catherine grew up in Loyalton and was able to relate information about the land owners and the individuals of her acquaintance that she knew during her "growing up years" and to the present time. Her help is very appreciated. Edward Bechtel is another person whose contribution of information, pictures, and microfilm research of newspapers has been very worthwhile. His cousin Tom Buffington has more recently joined the team and has also contributed very good information. One more dedicated genealogist should be mentioned here – Evelyn Hartman. She has developed a wide range of family information from the Loyalton (and other) areas, and has contributed much genealogy.

The following information may not completely cover the details of ownership of all the houses and lands that make up the nucleus of Loyalton. The main objective is to point out some of the earlier history, and chronicle life in the village as it emerged to the present time.

West Main St, Looking Eastward
On Left Travitz house, Helt Store, On Right Geo W. Snyder small house, Elwood Hoover House, Snyder Store

This early photo was taken from somewhere on the east side of the bridge over Wiconisco Creek. It is a view of Loyalton showing opens fields, lean telegraph poles and typical deep rutted dirt road leading into the village. Today, the "open fields" on the south side of the road are developed and most of the land has become commercialized. Beginning on the south side of the street the restaurant known as Vicki's Valley Inn is the first building to come into view.

TIMOTHY KOPPENHAVER 66-016-051
(Was VICKI'S VALLEY INN)

This property was part of the land owned by Alfred H. Rowe. On April 2, 1924 Alfred H. Rowe sold the land to John G. Romberger. He had it surveyed by G. W. Huntzinger in May 1924, and laid out in lots. Later that year on November 10, 1924 Jonathan Zerbe purchased 9 lots (#15 to 23). On October 23, 1926 he conveyed a substantial part of lots 19 and 20 to Jacob Bloom and Robert Aboff of Harrisburg. (Aboff also owned extended adjoining acreage). On Dec 24, 1929, Minnie wife of Jacob Bloom conveyed their undivided share of the property to her brother-in-law Robert Aboff (better known as "Rube").

By 1930 a building was constructed on this site. Older folks from the community remembered that the heavy timbers used in the construction came from the old Clark's Ferry bridge. Dynamite boxes were used for the rough lumber in the building. When the building was finished, Robert and Ida (Bloom) Aboff conducted a business here known as the "Aboff Bar and Pool Hall." During the 1930's and '40's it was a special bar and restaurant where people gathered for live music and dancing. Square dancing was especially popular. String instruments accompanied by a local caller provided background music for the people who gathered for the frequent entertainment. "Cock

Fights" became a weekly entertainment. By the 1940's part of the building served as a garage. Gas pumps were installed in front of the building, and auto supplies were available for purchase inside. A steel beam under what is now the dining room floor, supported the weight of cars that were driven in for repairs. A coal yard was located behind the building. Rube hired young boys to unload coal, paying them twenty-five cents to unload five ton of coal.

Robert Aboff's son served during World War II. At that time, the local church was being remodeled and Mr. Aboff volunteered to pay for one of the new stained glass windows being installed in the church. In return he wished that the members of the church would pray for the safe return of his son. The window that he sponsored is on the east side of the sanctuary, and the only one displaying the Star of David.

Robert Aboff and his wife eventually moved to Lykens where they owned the "Joe End Store." They remained in Lykens until his death. Robert was born in 1900 and died summer of 1969, leaving his wife Ida and two sisters, Mrs. Faye Berk of Harrisburg and Mrs.Jerri Felix of Miami, Florida. He was buried in Chisuk Emuna Cemetery in Harrisburg

While Rube owned this building, Woodrow "Pete" Kennedy worked for him, and later he and his wife Carol purchased the business. While he owned the building, it continued to be an entertainment center, with "floor shows" and traveling bands providing weekend attractions. In 1969 "Pete Kennedy's Valley Inn" was sold to Leona Reisch. In 1972, during the Agnes hurricane this building was seriously damaged. In fact, patrons barely escaped the rising flood waters. The building was in disrepair until 1976 when Marlin Shade, Jr bought it. It became known as the "Valley Inn" and in addition to fine food, live entertainment by his own band "The Vagabonds" became a weekly feature. The group also accepted outside engagements. Several years ago a new owner became the proprietor and the restaurant has become known as "Vickie's Valley Inn.

"Vicki's Valley Inn" was a popular place to eat, and was in business for many years. Several years ago a heavy rain storm created heavy flooding to the area. The building became seriously damaged, and the restaurant was closed. On September 5, 2001, the property was purchased by Timothy Koppenhaver, and he is the present owner.

JESSICA A. McQUIRE 66-016-053
5480 Route 209

The next four lots (15 – 18) are from the J. G. Romberger plan surveyed and laid out by G. W. Huntzinger, known as the South Side Addition to Loyalton. In November 1924 Jonathan Zerbe purchased these lots. When "Rube" Aboff purchased the adjoining lot and buildings, he also purchased two tracts made up of these four lots with a one story frame dwelling. On November 6, 1967, Ida and Robert Aboff conveyed one tract to Jerry P. and Constance Solence. They conveyed the second tract to Jerry and Constance Solence on May 19, 1969. After many years, on November 19, 1996, Jerry and Constance Solence conveyed both tracts to John M. and Caroline L. Pugh.
On September 16, 2008 Jessica A. McGuire became the owner.

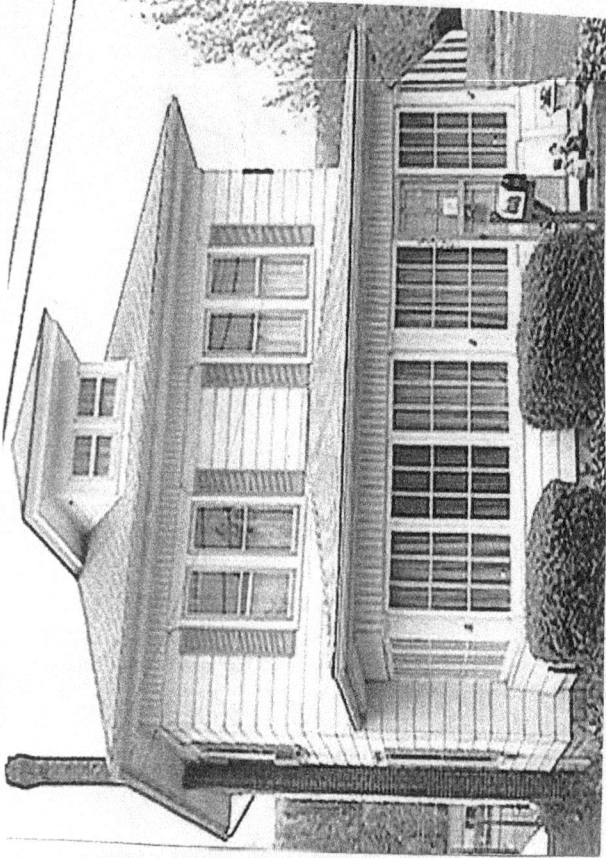

Hilario j and Rose A. Gonzales 66-016-057

Dagen Garage   66-016-055

Jessica A. McGuire 66-016-53

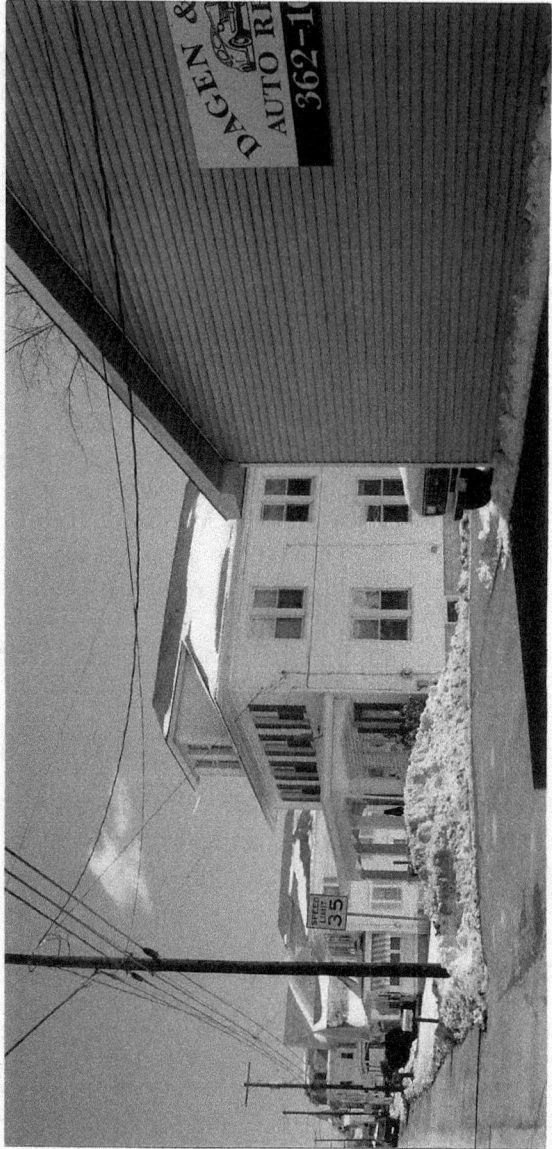

The Bruner Family 66-016-056

THE NEW LOYALTON BEGINS IN 1875

DAGAN'S GARAGE 66-016-055
(Was Marlin Johns Garage & Home)
(lots 9, 10, 11, 12, 13, 14 of J. G. Romberger Plan)

These six lots joining each other are located on the south side of Main Street, and are part of the J. G. Romberger plan. They were conveyed to John P. and Sarah E. Johns on April 2, 1924. John P. Johns built the garage and a double brick house on their land. They owned this property for a long time. John P. and his son Marlin M. Johns and their families shared the brick house. In March 1945 they conveyed both lots to Marlin M. and Mary K. Johns. On July 27, 1974, their son Marlin E, Jr. and his wife Mary J.(Waters) Johns became the next owners. The Johns family had an auto repair shop and garage here for a number of years. But on July 16, 1988, James W. and Marie A. Casner became owners, and after that on June 27, 2008 the property became Dagan's Garage owned. by Steven L. Dagen.

THE BRUNER FAMILY 66-016 -056
5500 Main Street

These lots # 7 and # 8 were part of the southwest addition of J. G. Romberger plan, and were conveyed to John P. and Sarah E. Johns on April 2, 1924. On March 22, 1945 John P. and Sarah E. Johns conveyed these two lots to Marlin M and Mary K. Johns. The two Johns families shared the brick house. After Mary and Marlin Johns died, Bryan R., Richard A. and Bradly A. Bruner became the owners of the property as of June 28, 2007..

HARRISON MILLER FAMILY

[*SAMUEL COLEMAN MILLER* (Feb 9, 1839- Jul 12, 1879) of Sch Co., m Catherine Kimmel Updegrave b 1842, Sch Co. d after 1880). Soon after Samuel died, Catherine, now a widow and her children moved to Perry Twp., Snyder Co. and appear on the 1880 census. She was left with a large family, the smallest child only seven months old – apparently born after Samuel's death. The census lists these members of her household: Riley 19, James 17, Jonathan 15, Albert 12, Harrison 11, Oscar 7, Henry 5, Ella 2, Ida 7 month Elizabeth Tressler, other 16. *Samuel Coleman & Catherine (Kimmel Updegrave) Miller had these children (from another source)*: John U. b c1865; *Harrison U.* b 1870 (see below); Henry U. b c1872; Oscar U.b c1873; Jannie Barbara b c1875; Ludella Harriet b c1878; Ida Catherine b c1879.
Harrison Updegrave (Nov 10, 1870 – Jun 25, 1942, bur Maple Grove Cem, E'ville), m Emma Jane Huntzinger (1869–1943). *Harrison and Emma Jane (Huntzinger) Miller had these children*:
William Harrison (1896 – Dec 7, 1963, bur St. Johns Hill Cem), m Florence Sarah Matter (Mar 28, 1903 – Oct 31, 1980), a dau of Balthaser L. and Sarah Priscilla (Lubold) Matter. *William Harrison and Florence (Matter) Miller had these children*: Shirley Romaine b Oct 20, 1925, m Harry F. Peck; Robert William b Jul 30, 1922; Barbara M b May 15, 1932.
Claude S. (1898 – Jan 14, 1976, bur Maple Grove Cem, E'ville), m Apr 9, 1927 Lillian R. Rowe (1905 – Oct 11, 1967), a dau of Alfred and Louisiana Kessler Row . *Claude and Lillian (Rowe) Miller had these children: Kay E.* b _____ m William Rice.
Clyde Jacob (aks "Cloyd" (May 12, 1904 – Feb 17, 1947, bur Maple Grove Cem) killed in Shiro Mines accident), m Nov 2, 1929 Effie Emeline Klinger (Jun 6, 1907- Jun 27, 2006), a dau of Edwin M. and Katie L. (Hoffman) Klinger of Loyalton. Effie later m Daniel Row. *Clyde Jacob and Effie (Klinger) Miller had these children*: Betty R. (Apr 14, 1931 - Jul 31, 2002, bur Maple Grove Cem), m Ralph E. Lebo Jr. (Sep 19, 1927 – Jul 18, 2002), a son of Ralph Edwin and Lottie Irene (Leitzel) Lebo. *Ralph E. and Betty (Miller) Lebo had these children*: Barbara Ann b 1956 m John F. Diakow, a son of John F. and Martha P (Klinger) Diakow; Hilda G. b Sep 29, 1933, m Jonathan D. Klinger b Sep 18, 1927.
Laura K. (Sep 16, 1905 – Feb 8, 1989, bur Simeon Cem, Gratz), m Albert Leroy Sitlinger (Feb 2, 1903 – Sep 1973), a dau of Samuel J. and Bertha D. (Riegel) Sitlinger. [See Sitlinger family for more details.]
Raymond D. b Aug 17, 1907 – d 1988), m Margaret Sarah Kerstetter (1908 – pre 1988)).
[More information in genealogy of Joseph "Jost" Miller]

Robert E. (Jr.) and Dawn M Liddick 66-016-059

John C. & Marlene Forney 66-016-058

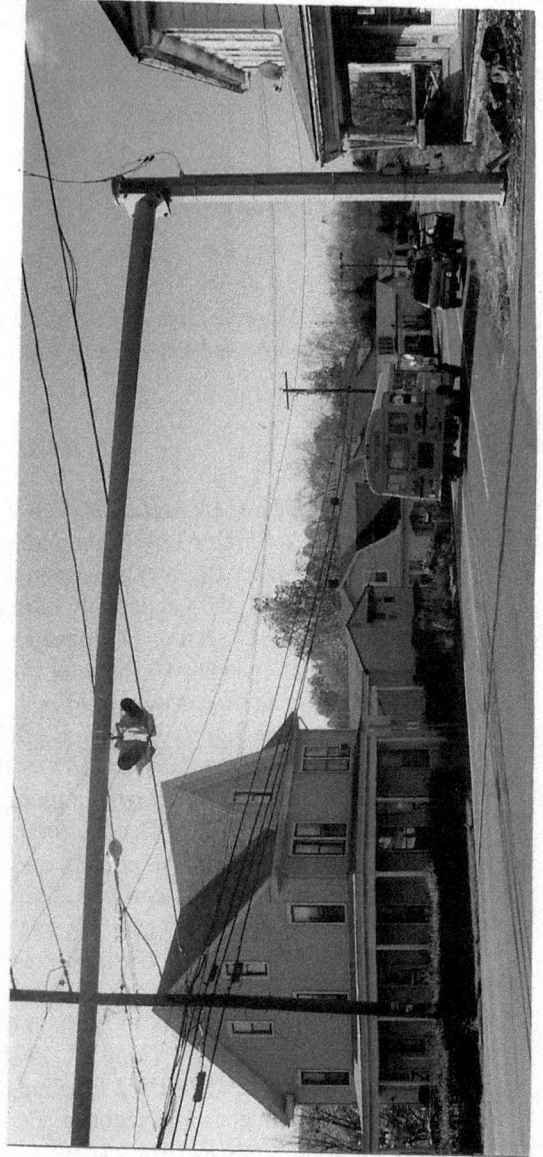

Hilario J. and Rose A. Gonzales 66-016-060

HILARIO J. AND R OSE A. GONZALES 66-016-057
5508 Route 209

John G. and Amelia Romberger, conveyed these lots to Lillian Rowe on August 31, 1925. Lillian married Claude S. Miller and they conveyed these lots to Ellen and Isaiah Daniel. They sold them back to Lillian and Claude Miller. After Claude Miller's death in 1976, his executive Kay Rice conveyed the lots to John F. and Barbara (Lebo) Diakow in 1976 (Barbara a daughter of Betty (Miller) Lebo) . On December 22, 1978 John F. and Barbara A. Diakow conveyed to Gary E. Lenker and Daniel M. Lenker, partners. But on April 20,1979 the Lenkers transferred the four lots to Chester L. & Donna Hubler. On April 8, 1988, Betty J. Schreffler became the owner of these four lots located on the south side of the State Highway. On October 19, 2006, all four lots were sold to Justin D. and Jane A. Morgan. Several years later on May 28, 2009, the Morgan's sold to Hilario J. and Rose A. Gonzales.

DAREN DANIEL HOFFMAN 66-016-058
Route 209 - Main Street

These two lots were part of the land that Alfred H. and Louisiana K. Row conveyed to J. G. Romberger on Apr 2, 1924. He sold the same day to George W. and Eva Snyder, they sold March 30, 1925 to Edmond Hoover. The land bordered on south side of state highway beginning at northeast corner of the 2 lots conveyed here by other land of grantor, south 150 feet to stake on north side along alley, north to lot of John G. Romberger north to stake south side of highway, along highway 50 feet each lot fronting 25 feet by 150 feet deep. Catharine Hoover Spotts, and her daughter Ruby and husband Rudy Bressler were tenants on the property in 1932. John and Evelyn (Troutman) Sleighter lived here in the 1940s. Benjamin F. Wise purchased this house from the heirs of Edmond Hoover after he retired from his dairy farm in Washington Twp. Ben kept busy by being the school bus driver during the 1950's. After Benjamin Wise died, this property was conveyed to John C. and Marlene Forney. Daren Daniel Hoffman became the next owner on June 17, 1994.

The Wise Family

[*B. Frank Wise* (b Dec 9, 1866 - d May 20, 1947, bur Maple Grove Cem) m May 7, 1893 Maggie R. Klinger (1872 – 1948), a dau of Jacob and Mariah (Harner) Klinger. B. Frank Wise lived with his uncle and aunt Jonathan and Hettie Klinger in 1880 in Wash Twp. *B. Frank and Maggie R. (Klinger) Wise had these children*: *Hattie Naomi* b Aug 27, 1898, m Lester A. Enders; *Daniel Klinger* b Aug 17, 1899; *Charles Marlin* (Nov 10, 1903 – 1971, bur Maple Grove Cem), m Katie J. Lenker (Jul 15, 1902– 1969), *had these children*: Neal Franklin b Apr 22, 1928;; *Mark Franklin* b Oct 25, 1905 m E. Fay   Dockey (Nov 12, 1909 –1995*), had these children*: Mark Chester b Jul 13, 1935;, m Doris Strohecker ; *Truman William* (Nov 18, 1908 – Jan 7, 1992, bur Maple Grove Cem), m Melva (Mildred) I. Gotshall   (1911 - ___). He became a minister. *Truman and Melva (Klinger) Wise had these children*: Kenneth Wellington b Feb 27, 1928; Truman Gerald b Sep 18, 1929 of Catawissa; Dolores Elaine b Sep 1, 1935, m ___ Rebuck;*;* Jean m ___ Strohecker; *Daniel K* m Mame ____ *, had these children*: June Eleanore b Jun   11, 1925; Fay Pauline b Mar 16,1927; Daniel Richard b Mar 7, 1929;]

ROBERT E. JR. AND WIFE DAWN M. LIDDICK 66-016-059
5518 W. Route 209

These two lots #65 and 66 are part of the land that was surveyed from the premises of Amanda Hoke October 1, 1895 to Sarah M Weiss, and laid out February 4, 1898. Andrew Weiss, son of Sarah M. and William H. Weiss was the next owner and sold in 1902 to William L. Hoffman. He sold to D. A. Good Feb 9, 1907, but the deed was not recorded. The lots were transferred from D. A. Good to Charles S. Grubb on May 8, 1909. The lots are located on the south west corner of Main and Union Street, running 100 feet along the front on Main Street and 150 feet along east side of Union Street to an alley and contain a 2 ½ story frame dwelling. Shortly after Charles S. Grubb bought these two lots, he separated them by selling lot #65 on October 15, 1910 to Sarah A. Miller (Mrs. James Miller). During the 1920s a large shed at the end of this lot was turned into a factory operated by Ross Blyler. This factory produced only shirt sleeves for the shirts manufactured in the factory in Gratz.

Charles S. Grubb continued to own lot *#66* until his death. By his will made Dec 1, 1923, and probated Jan 2, 2, 1929 he gave this property to Annie M. Grubb. Annie M. Grubb sold Jun 10, 1948 to C. Elwood and Myrl (Grubb) Hoover. Elwood is remembered as being the school bus driver and Washington Township road supervisor. He also had a milk route for the Bonawitz and Romberger dairies. On April 7, 1970 C. Elwood and Myrl Hoover conveyed to Marguerite and Arthur S. Rowe. It has remained in the Rowe family, to Marguerite after Arthur died, then to Dennis E Rowe and Bradley A. Rowe, and in 2006 to Casey L. Rowe. On November 23, 2009 Robert E. and Dawn M. Liddick became the present owners.

HILARIO J. & ROSE A. GONZALES 66-016-060
5522 Route 209

As noted above, shortly after Charles S. Grubb purchased lots # 66 & #65, he separated them by selling this lot *#65* containing 6000 square feet on October 15, 1910 to Sarah A. Miller (Mrs. James Miller). This lot bordered the western side of lot 66, measured150 by 40 Feet and contained a frame dwelling house. An agreement was made to allow this property access to the cesspool on the other part of the lot. After Sarah A. Miller died, the property was sold to Charles A. Rowe on Dec 6, 1920, and he sold to George W. Snyder on March 17, 1923. On March 8, 1969, Eva Snyder widow of George W. Snyder, (and others) conveyed this lot to Arthur Sherwood and Maguerite (Snyder) Rowe. While they owned it, Marguerite was a beautician, and had a beauty parlor in this house. In 1995 Marguerite Rowe, by then a widow, conveyed this property to Hilario J. and Rose A. Gonzales of Millersburg. Hilario Gonzales has completely rebuilt and restructured the house.

[CHARLES S. GRUBB (Apr 9, 1882 – Dec 22, 1928, of heart attack bur Maple Grove Cem, E'ville), a son of Henry A. and Isabella L (Hess) Grubb, m Jul 18, 1903 Annie M. Miller (Jul 17,1883–Jun 11, 1971)   a dau of James and Sarah A. Miller of Loyalton. *Charles S. and Annie M. (Miller) Grubb children*: *Myrl Emily* (1905-1977, bur Maple Grove), m 1925 Charles Elwood Hoover, a son of Edmond and Lillian (Wetzel) Hoover. *Charles Elwood and Myrl (Grubb) Hoover children*: Harold C. (c1926 – Jul 28, 2001), m Annie B. Schell, *had two children*: Harold C. "Butch" and Todd E; *Arthur James Henry* (Nov 16, 1907 – Mar 8, 1988, bur Fairview Cem, Wmstown), m Ruth L. Bond (b 1907 Wmstown – d 1988), a dau of Thomas and Ellen (Price) Bond of Williamstown. He was at one time mayor of Williamstown; *Ruth N.* (Feb 27, 1912 - Jan 10, 2007, bur Greenwood Cem, Tower City) m   Francis A. Reichenbach, a district judge in Up Dau Co; *Catharine L.* b & d 1913.[More information in Hess family genealogy.]

[DAVID O. SNYDER (Feb 24, 1867 – Aug 12, 1921, bur Maple Grove Cem, E'ville), a son of David and Hetty Snyder of Northld Co, m Dec 29, 1888 Jane S. Bender (Jun 22, 1866 – Mar 17, 1927), a dau of Jonathan and Christine (Bechtel) Bender. *David O. & Jane S. (Bender) Snyder children (some bapt Salem Ref, E'ville)*:David E (1895 – 1947), bur Maple Grove), m Maude Shell of Carsonville; *William F.* b Feb 9, 1889; *Ralph David* b Oct 20, 1893; *David E* (1895 –1947), m Maude Shell (1895 –1975); *George Washington* b Feb 22, 1897- Jun 9, 1946, bur Maple Grove   Cem), m Oct 8, 1921 Eva E. Bonawitz (Dec 7, 1902 – Jun 9, 1946); *Amy Annie* b Jun 30, 1906.]

Next properties located on north side of Main road (Route 209) between Wiconisco Creek & Crossroads

GEORGE E. LUTHER, JR. & BETTY A. LUTHER 66-005-014

House Being Destroyed By Storm 1972

This lot has the same history as lots one to four. It was from the L. S. Ferree plan and was assigned to John D. Snyder on January 9, 1890. He sold it to David F. Hoffman on March 11, 1890, and it was eventually sold to John S. and Susanna Boyer. On March 6, 1908 they sold this one acre tract of land to Harvey Grubb. The land was located on the north side of Main Street bounded by land of Clark Fisher, north to Washington Kessler estate, south to land of Jacob I. Travitz. On April 29, 1913 Harvey Grubb conveyed the property to Samuel E. Spotts. Samuel E. Spotts died in 1918, and much later on April 1, 1937 his widow Catherine Spotts transferred the same to John B. and Sallie L. Hull. They sold to Margaret A. and Henry V. Shadle on February 5, 1943. Margaret continued to live here after her husband died until 1972 when the house was completely destroyed as hurricane Agnes swept through the area. On June 15, 1979 Margaret A. Shadle, widow sold her one acre lot to George E. and Elizabeth H. Luther (owner of former gristmill property.) On September 27, 1991, this and adjoining lots one to four were sold to George E. Jr. and Betty A. Luther his wife. On November 9,   2010 Nicholas A. Schaffer and Janine Smith became the present owners.

THE TRAVITZ FAMILY

[*JOHN TRAVITZ* (Jul 12, 1810 - Mar 1, 1880, bur Millers Cem, Powells Valley), m Elizabeth Minnich (Dec 2, 1813 - Jun 23, 1882), a dau of Peter and Anna Maria (Matter) Minnich. John and Elizabeth Travitz lived in Jackson Twp in 1850. Elizabeth was a widow in 1880 living in Jackson Twp and had her grand-daughter Alice Hoffman 14 with her. *John and Elizabeth (Minnich) Travitz children:* WILLAM (Jan 5, 1835 - Jan 29, 1853); *SUSANNAH* b c1837; *SARAH* b c1839; *REBECCA* b c1840; *PHILIP* b c1842; *SIMON* (b May 10, 1844 Jackson Twp - d Jun 29, 1917, bur Fairview Cem, Enders) , m 1st Mary ____ (Oct 19, 1849 - Jun 5, 1872, bur Fetterhoff Cem), m 2nd Feb 15, 1874 in Williamstown to Eliza E. Grim (May 6, 1853 - May 22, 1924), a dau of Solomon and Sarah (Frank) Grim, lived in Jackson Twp in 1880. He was a vet of Civil War.
Simon and Mary Travitz had this child: Anna J. b c1872. *Simon and Eliza E (Grim) Travitz children (many bapt Jan 25, 1909, recorded in Oak Dale Ch Record);*
Charles C. b c1876 m Lizzie L ____, *had these children*: Katie Irene b May 30 , 1899 bapt Salem Luth E'ville; Sallie Gertrude b Feb15,1901; Carrie Cecelia b Jan 31,1902; John F.b c1878; Susan R. b c1879;*William Henry* b Oct 13,1880-1968, bur Maple Grove Cem), m Beulah A. Evitts (1890-1967); *JacobIrwin* (b Oct 5,1882 Armstrong Valley – d Jan 2,1922 of pneumonia, bur Maple Grove Cem, E'ville), m Mar 21, 1908 Annie Alverta Hoke (Aug 1,1885 – May 22, 1935), at the home of her parents Henry Nelson and Sarah Ida (Radel) Hoke. *Jacob Irwin and Annie Alverta (Hoke) Travitz children*: Lucy May b Jun 14,1909, m 1926 1st Harry M. Bruner (Nov 23, 1906 – May 31, 1932, by auto accident bur Maple Grove Cem). *Their children*: Betty Alverta b 1927; Harry; Lucy m 2nd in 1941 Charles A. Wingert (Aug 18, 1915 – Oct 8,1976, bur Maple Grove Cem.); *Harry Alvin* (Feb 8,1912-Dec 4,1974, bur Cal Meth Cem, Wic.), m 1st Anna M. Kute b 1922, m 2nd Annie C. Johns b 1914. *Kathryn Alverta*. (Feb 10,1915 - Dec 26,1926, bur beside parents); *Katie Laura* b Dec 6,1885, m ____ Weaver; *James Harrison* b Mar 16,1890; *Mary Ellen* b Jun 11,1891; *Peter Elias* (1893 –1909, bur Fairview Cem Armstrong Valley); *Robert Alvin* b Jan 5, 1895-1910); *PETER* b c 1846; *MARY* b c1848; *JOHN* (Mar 17,1852 –Apr 2, 1853, bur Millers Cem)

THE SPOTTS FAMILY

[*HENRY MORRIS SPOTTS* b c1861, a son of Samuel and Mary A. (Phillips) Spotts of Stone Valley,   Northld Co, m Emma Louisa Snyder b c1864. In 1880, Henry lived in Wash Twp with the Emanuel Boyer family, was employed by them. *Henry Morris and Emma Louisa (Snyder) Spotts children*: Katie b c1882; *Etta Elizabeth* (Mar 25, 1885 - Apr 11, 1975, bur Maple Grove Cem, E'ville), m Roman Veneda Shadle (b Sep 5, 1882 Loyalton – d Sep 1, 1943); *Samuel Edwin* (1886 – 1918, bur Hoffman   Cem), m Aug 14, 1908, Amelia Catherine Hoover (Dec 15,1889-1979), a dau of Edmund & Lillian (Wetzel) Hoover. *Samuel E. and Amelia Catherine (Hoover) Spotts children: Harold Hoover* (Mar 29, 1909-May 7, 1992, bur Simeon Cem), m Ruth Bowman (Aug 20, 1912 - Mar 3, 1991), a dau of Nerwin and Dora (Eby) Bowman. *Ruby* (Jan 19, 1913 - Jan 31, 1884), m Rudy Bressler]

THE BENJAMIN SHADLE FAMILY

[*BENJAMIN SHADLE* (b Jul 3, 1848 Hegins Twp., Sch Co – d Jan 11, 1919, bur Maple Grove Cem, E'ville), m Jan 10, 1875 Sarah Sitlinger (Sep 1, 1853 – Dec 3, 1923), a dau of Isaac and Mary (Shade) Shadle. *Benjamin and Sallie (Sitlinger) Shadle had these children*:

CARRIE LILLIE (Aug 12, 1875 – Jul 22, 1940, bur Maple Grove Cem), m Isaac Franklin Hoover (1876 – Feb 1961), son of Charles and Leah Ann (Boyer) Hoover.

ESTELLA b Aug 12, 1875

HATTIE PERSTELLA (Oct 1877 – June 17, 1913, Loyalton, bur Maple Grove Cem), m Apr 4, 1897 Frederick Charles Harner (Aug 16, 1876 – Sep 16, 1932, son of Charles F. and Ellen (Boyer) Harner.

CLAYTON PERRY ESQUELLA (Aug 27, 1880 – Oct 10, 1966, bur Maple Grove Cem), m Edna Lena Hoke (Jul 3, 1887 – Jun 9, 1979) a dau of Henry Nelson and Sarah Ida (Radel) Hoke

ROMAN VENEDA (b Sep 5, 1882 Loyalton – d Sep 1, 1943, bur Maple Grove Cem), m Jan 3, 1903 Etta Elizabeth Spotts (Mar 25, 1885 – Apr 11, 1975), a dau of Henry Morris and Emma Louisa (Snyder) Spotts *Roman and Etta (Spotts) Shadle had these children:*

Sally Louisa (Jul 14, 1903 – Sep 1, 1977), m John Benjamin Hull (1895 Loyalton – Mar 8, 1973)), a son of William R and Clara S. (Lebo) Hull.

Nevin (Apr 15, 1909 – Jul 14, 1994))

Henry Veneda b Feb 11, 1906 in Big Run – d Jan 17, 1964, bur Maple Grove Cem, E'ville) m Margaret Arlene Kissinger b May 28, 1911, a dau of Thomas and Eva (Umholtz) Kissinger. *Henry Veneda and Margaret Arlene (Kissinger) Shadle had one child*: *Evelyn Marie* b Jan 6, 1929, m Dean Schelgel Hartman b Feb 24, 1927, a son of Homer Isaac and Bertie Elizabeth (Schlegel) Hartman. [More info with Kissinger genealogy.]

THE ETZWEILER AND HELT GENERAL STORE 66-016-028

H. C. Beshler and his wife conveyed lot number 9 and 10 to Catherine E. Ferree on March 29, 1875. Several years later on June 1, 1888, Catherine Ferree sold lot nine to Fannie K. Laird of Fisherville. William Lewis Hoffman became a tenant and by 1902, he and Wayne B. Johns established a store on the premises. By 1905, Hoffman and W. B. Johns were mentioned as storekeepers "dividing their stock of general merchandise" and were preparing to be in business separately. William Lewis and Sybilla Hoffman sold out to Edward Etzweiler. By October 1906, Etzweiler and Helt were partners, and had made a trip to Philadelphia to purchase their new stock of fall and winter goods.

On November 2, 1907, Fannie Laird and her husband sold this lot to A. D. and S. S. Good. On August 13, 1909, S. S. and Agnes E. Good conveyed their interest in the property to A. D. Good. The Good family had a mercantile business while they owned it, and later tenant Umholtz had a business in the building.

Charles W. Hepner was the next owner, having purchased the two lots, dwelling house and store property on October 3, 1921. He was the merchant until his death on November 16, 1927, and by his will his wife Sylvia S. Hepner inherited the house and lots. When Sylvia S. Hepner died her daughter Blanche M. Deppen inherited it.

L to r: Albert Enders, Al Rowe, unidentified patron photo taken 1934.

TROY AND CRYSTAL BOYER 66-015-028
(was ETZWEILER – HELT STORE)

Blanche and her husband Harvey lived in Pillow and on December 3, 1936 they sold the two lots to Jonathan S. Zerbe of Loyalton. But a few months later in June 1937, he conveyed both of these lots plus the two he owned to the east to Walter S. Zerbe and Lottie Zerbe. During the 1930's the building became what was then called a "beer garden." In 1934 Albert Enders was the bartender and the existing picture below shows Albert with two patrons, Al Rowe to the left and an unidentified friend.

Many years later, on June 3, 1964, Lottie M. Zerbe conveyed these lots to Catherine B. Zerbe. On December 29, 1972 Catherine B. Zerbe conveyed the two lots to James H. and Audry Schreffler. Several years later on April 12, 1978, Arland and Gertrude Scheib became the owners, but sold on June 13, 1989 to Michael L. Garnick. On August 4, 2009 Eric J. Garnick became the next owner. Several years later on June 28, 2012 Eric J. Garnick conveyed the property to Troy and Crystal Boyer, the present owners.

This apparently was an unusual event that took place during the 1930s at the junction of what is now Route 209 and Crossroads. Photo from Bob Fromme

THE ETZWEILER FAMILY
(Some information from Cornelius E. Koppenheffer and Irene Baker)

[The earliest found ancestor of this family was ***Johan George Etzweiler***, immigrant from Stein on the Rhine in Switzerland to America with his family while a young man (about 1740). He married Elisabeth Miller, and apparently settled first in Lancaster County, where at least one of their children was baptized. He later in 1775 settled in Buffalo Valley. During the conflict after the Revolutionary War, George joined the group of Frontier Rangers whose duty it was to protect the settlers from roving Indians. On May 26, 1780 George and three other soldiers were killed one mile south of Mifflinburg, Union County. They had just returned to French Jacobs Mill from patrolling the neighborhood, and were washing themselves when the Indians attacked them. A monument has been placed on the site of the encounter. After George Etzweiler was killed, Maria m Michael Schadle.

[*Johan George and Elisabeth (Miller) Etzweiler had two known children*: a dau *Anna Barbara* born Apr 3, 1748, and a son *GEORGE ETZWEILER Jr.* bapt Jan 13, 1745 at the Reformed Church in Lanc. – d 1780). George Etzweiler, Jr. m Jul 1, 1767 Maria Elisabeth Schora "Jury" (b Jun 7, 1744 in Switzerland, a daughter of Abraham Schora Sr. and Catharine (Guerne) whom later came to Upper Paxton Twp. *George and Maria Elisabeth (Schora) Etzweiler had these children: *CATHARINA ELISABETHA** (Feb 15, 1768 – May 28, 1838), m Matthias Deibler Sr (Dec 14, 1763 –   Mar 10, 1837), a son of Michael & Anna Maria Deibler, and lived in Lykens Township.[More information in Deibler genealogy.]
GEORGE Jr (Apr 27, 1773 - Apr 27, 1828), m Jan 13, 1795 Elisabetha Welker (Dec 27, 1777 - pre 1813, Strausberg, Lanc Co.), a dau of Valentine & Henrietta Welker. After his first wife died, George m about 1813 Mary Berkert, bur at Millersburg. He had a total of 17 children, half of whom died young. *George and Elisabeth (Welker) Etzweiler had 10 ch 6 sons 4 dau (4 sons d before him – those found):* **George* b Feb 19, 1796 David's Killinger Ch, m Maria ____, *had these children (Bapt David's Ref Ch, Killinger):* ***Friedrich*** b May 7, 1819; ***David*** b Feb 15, 1824;

166

John b c1804, m Dec 19, 1826 Anna Groh b Nov 26, 1808, a dau of Jacob and Elisabeth Groh of Mbg, **had these children: ***Susanna b Dec 20, 1828 bapt David's: *****John D.** (Nov 18, 1830 – Nov 14, 1897, bur Oak Hill Cem, Mbg), m Sarah Henninger (Jul 15, 1835 – Apr 18, 1883) in Juniata County. He was a wagon maker. **John D. and Sarah (Henninger) Etzweiler had these children:** Jerome; Charles; Josiah; William; *****Mary Jane** b c1835; *****Susannah** b c1838; *****Lydia** b c1842; *****Theodore** b c1845; a***** dau** b c1848

George b c1807 m Mary A. _____ b c1809. They lived in Up Paxton Twp in 1850, and he was listed as a potter. They had Emanuel Moyer 23 a boatman with them. **George and Mary A Etzweiler children (bapt Davids, Killinger):*Adaline** b c1833; *****Aaron** b c1834;*****Margaret** (Dec 24, 1835 – Jan 31, 1921), m William Augusta Jodon; ***** Leah Elizabeth** b Apr 27,1838; *****Catharine** b c1844; *****Christina** b c1846; *****Mary** b c1850.

George Etzweiler (1773 – 1828), m 2ⁿᵈ to Maria Berkert (b c1781 – d after 1850), had 7 ch 4 sons 3 dau (3 sons 1 dau died before father). In 1850 Mary (Berkert) Etzweiler age 69 lived next to George Etzweiler age 43 and his wife Mary A. age 41. Mary Etzweiler had Jane Moody 50 and Mary Jane 26 with her. **George and Maria (Berkert) Etzweiler had these known children:**

Joseph b Mar or Jul 2, 1817 Union Co d Jul 2, 1825 cause Hitzigen Fieber;**Frederick** b May 7, 1819 bapt Davids Killinger;****Mary Jane** b c1824 – lived with her widowed mother in 1850; ****David** b Feb 15, 1824;****Anna** b Oct 28, 1835 – date given; ****Margaretha** b Dec 24, 1835 date given.

*FRIEDERICH (c1775 – Sep 15, 1843), m 1ˢᵗ Catharina Elisabetha Gruber (c1777 – 1809), a dau of George and Ellizabeth (Emerick) Gruber. He m 2ⁿᵈ Christina Dorothea Wolfe (Jan 28, 1787 – Jun 29, 1879, bur in Millersburg, Ohio). Friederich & Christina Etzweiler were communicants at Klinger Church in1814. About 1820 Friedrich and his second wife Christina along with most of his children from both wives, left Millersburg, Penna. and settled in Wayne Co., Ohio. The two oldest children, Daniel and Elisabeth, were already married and remained here in the area of Elizabethville. In Ohio Friederich became a blacksmith and stayed in that area the remainder of his life. **Friederich and Catherine Elis (Gruber) Etzweiler known children (some bapt. Klingers, St. John's Hill, and David's at Killinger Church):**

Daniel (Apr 9, 1800 – Sep 15, 1878, bur St. James Cem, Carsonville), m Christina Smith (Oct 10, 1802 – Sep 27, 1889), of Northumberland County. They lived on a farm in Washington Township. In 1880 Christiana a widow lived with her son Henry in Jefferson Twp. **Daniel and Christiana (Smith) Etzweiler had these children 8 sons, 3 daughters:

***Lydia b Mar ? 24, 1822 sp Friedrich and Christina Etzweiler

***Jonathan (Apr 13, 1825 - _____), m Mary Hoover b c1827. They lived in Wayne Twp in 1880. **Jonathan and Mary (Hoover) Etzweiler had these known children:**

Samuel (Apr 12, 1846 in Jefferson Twp – 1916, bur Bowerman Cem, Enterline), m Jun 1867 Catherine Mader (_____ - 1921), of Middle Paxton Twp. Samuel was a CW vet. They lived in Wayne Twp in 1880 and had Reuben Buffington age 18 with them. **Samuel and Catherine (Mader) Etzweiler had these children (some bur Bowerman Cem, not dates):** *Susan; Daniel; Elias; George W;David H* (1858 – 1931, bur Bowerman Cem, Enterline), *Emma J ___* (1864 – 1925); *Ellen* b c1865; *John W.* (1874 – 1888); *Jane* b c1876;*Mary A.* b c1878. David b c1859; John b c1863.

***Daniel (1828 – Jun 11, 1896), m Dec 26, 1848 Mary Eberly of Armstrong Valley (bc1828 – d Oct 31, 1903. **Daniel and Mary (Eberly) Etzweiler had these children:** Lydia Ann b c1879; Elizabeth b c1880.

***Elias (Sep 15, 1829 – Apr 9, 1909, bur Maple Grove Cem, E'ville), m Eliza Riegel (May 12, 1827 – Feb 3 1903), a dau of Daniel and Catherine Hoffman Riegel . They lived in Jefferson Twp, had Lizzie Laudenslager age 18 with them in 1880. He was a Civil War Vet;

***Michael (b Nov 15, 1831 in E'ville – d Dec 14, 1893) , m Sep 27, 1855 Catharine Bordner (b Mar 12, 1838 – Oct 5, 1899), a dau of Jacob and Mary (Snyder) Bordner of Lykens Twp. He was a Civil War Vet. In 1880, the family lived in Jefferson Twp. and he was a blacksmith. **Michael and Catharine (Bordner) Etzweiler had these children:** Amanda b 1856; Rebecca b 1858; Christiana b1860 d young; Anna Sophia b 1864 d young; William H b Aug 28, 1866, m Amelia Enterline (May 10, 1870 – Dec 16, 1954). After William H. died, Amelia m Nathan Zimmerman of Armstrong Valley. William and his brother Jacob worked together as blacksmiths. **William H and Amelia (Enterline) Etzweiler had these children:** *Thomas G* b 1891, m 1913 Sarah A. Herb; *Emma* b 1892; *Michael J* b 1894; *Gertrude E* b Sep 1895. All of the siblings but William H. moved to Mercer County. Nathaniel E b 1869; Jacob F (b Jul 7,1871 – Oct 6,

1952), m Dec 25, 1894 Jennie G. Lehr (1875 – 1948), dau of Emanuel and Isabella Lehr of Enterline; Simon b 1875 d young; Carrie E. b 1878.

***Adam b Aug 15, 1833

***Catherine b c1835, m Levi B. Ditty;

***Elisabeth (no dates) m Samuel D. Klinger

***Mary E m Frederick Fauber

***Peter (b Sep 26, 1843 – Jun 2, 1923, bur Maple Grove Cem, E'ville), m Catharine _____ b c1859. Peter and Catharine listed as wife lived in Halifax Twp in 1880, and addition in to children Charles 11, Samuel 8, Edward 5, Adam 1, they had J.Buffington age 19, and J. Woland age age 4 living with them, listed as servants. Peter apparently m 1st to Jane Amanda ___ (Apr 3, 1853 – Sep 23, 1929, bur beside him in Maple Gove Cem). Peter Etzweiler had these children:

 Charles (1868 – 1934), m Alice L. _____ (1872 – 1950, bur Maple Grove Cem); Samuel b c1872; Edward (May 17, 1875 – May 28, 1938, bur Maple Grove Cem, E'ville), m Anna Susan Helt (Feb 8, 1879 – Sep 24, 1943), a dau of Daniel D. & Catherine (Snyder) Helt. Had the store in Loyalton.

 Adam (Jul 22, 1878 – Apr 30, 1940, bur Maple Grove Cem), m Jan 1, 1899 Mary Alice Gottschall (Jul 29, 1877 – Aug 4,1954), a dau of Solomon and Ceclia Gottschall of Carsonville.

***Henry (Sep 20, 1846 – Feb 23, 1896, bur Bowerman Cem), m Catharine Snyder of Jefferson Twp had two known children: Michael Irwin b May 8, 1885, bapt St. Johns Lykens – Feb 4, 1914, killed in mines); Emma Christiana b Jun 18, 1886

**Elizabeth (Nov 23, 1802 – Nov 6, 1878), m Michael Runk (b Jan 20, 1799 - d Apr 5, 1860, bur old cem E'ville), a son of John Jacob and __ (Hayman) Runk. Michael and Elizabeth (Etzweiler) Runk had one dau ***Catharine (Jan 20, 1822 – Mar 27, 1845, bur Old Stone Cem, E'ville), m John Keiper (Jul 4, 1810 – Aug 16, 1854)

**Catharine b Sep 8, 1805, m Mathias Deibler, Jr, had a child Sara b Mar 9, 1819, bapt Hoffman Ch.

**Peter (no dates) m Sarah Harner and moved to Ohio

**Johannes b Feb 19, 1809 bapt St. John's Hill

Children of Frederick and Christina Dorothea (Wolfe) Etzweiler:

Johan Jacob b Dec 24, 1810, bapt Klinger's Ch; **George (no dates);Abraham b Apr 27, 1814;

**Anna Maria b Dec 5, 1817 bapt David's Killinger; **Jonas b Oct 20, 1819 bapt David's Killinger

*MARGARETHA b c1774

* Daniel b c1775

*ELISABETH (Dec 7, 1780 – May 9, 1844)

THE HELT FAMILY

[*CHRISTIAN HELT (no dates), m _____ . He was a farmer in Clark's Valley. Christian Helt and wife had these children:

**DAVID (Mar 2, 1817 – May 30, 1883, Jackson Twp), m Elizabeth Miller (1824 – Jan 22, 1901), a dau of _____ . They lived in Clark's Valley. David and Elizabeth (Miller) Helt had 8 children:

***John F. (Jan 14, 1841 – Mar 15, 1910, bur Enders), m Oct 1861 Margaret Enders (b Jan 9, 1840 - d Nov 21, 1894), a dau of Philip Enders and granddaughter of John Conrad Enders of Jackson Twp. (John Conrad Enders opened the first "Public Road" leading from Halifax, via Fisherville and Elizabethville. It linked the stage route from Harrisburg, via Gratz to Pottsville). In 1867 formed a mercantile partnership with George W. Enders, later purchased Enders half. John was a Civil War Vet. John F. and Margaret (Enders) Helt had two children: Anna J. m Dr. C. C. Miller of Halifax; Ira M b Aug 17, 1865 m Aug 17, 1890 Maggie Philips, dau of William Philips.

***Henry (Jun 1843 – Jan 24, 1886, of consumption, bur IOOF Cem, Lykens), m Sarah A ____ b c1846, had these children: Leonard Absalom b Mar 15, 1870 bapt Hoffman Ch – d May 10, 1889, bur IOOF Cem, Lykens); Sady E. b c1876; Raymond b c1879; Edith Ann b Sep 16,1885;.

***Catharine (1849 –1905, bur Maple Grove Cem, E'ville), not m.

***Emeline m David Smink

***William

***Daniel David** b Oct 14, 1857 – Mar 20, 1937 bur Maple Grove Cem, E'ville), m Catherine Snyder (Apr 24, 1853 – Jan 26, 1909), a dau of James and Lydia (McCully) Snyder of Jackson Twp. They lived in Jackson Twp in 1880. *Daniel David and Catherine (Snyder) Helt had these children:*
Charles Franklin (Jun 12, 1875 – Mar 16, 1948), m Amy Gertrude Fisher b Oct 19, 1881
Sarah Elizabeth (May 12, 1877 – Feb 26, 1952, bur Maple Grove Cem, E'ville), m Apr 9, 1895 Charles Edgar Uhler (1874 – 1944); Anna S b c1879.
Adam (1878 – 1940, bur Maple Grove Cem), m M. Alice ____ (1877 – 1954)
Anna Susan (Feb 8, 1879 – Sep 24, 1943) m Edward Etzweiler (May 17, 1875 – May 28, 1938)
Jennie (Oct 9, 1880 – Nov 28, 1937, m Lucien Christian Schoffstall (Jul 12, 1873 – Jul 11, 1951);
Lydia Alice (Mar 18, 1883–May 2, 1942), m Apr 10, 1909 Norman L. Riegle (Oct 4, 1886–Nov 11, 1942)
James David (b Sep 11, 1884 Jackson Twp – d Oct 7, 1953, bur Maple Grove Cem, E'ville), m Loie O Hensel (Feb 17, 1894 – 1978). They moved to Lykens in 1909, where he became involved with J. S. Reiff in the furniture and undertaking business.
James David & Loie O. (Henzel) Helt child: James D. Jr. (1919   1976, bur Cal Meth Cem, Wiconisco), m Elsie Williams b Jun 10, 1921.;
Ada Irene (Nov 9, 1886 – Sep 13, 1960), m Fred Ricker (Feb 1, 1889 – Nov 9, 1953)
Mabel Edna.(May 20, 1889–Dec 5, 1939), m Aug 20, 1910 Harry H. Hoffman (Sep 6,1889–Dec 19,1956)
Harvey Daniel (Jul 12, 1891 – Feb 4, 1943, bur Maple Grove Cem, E'ville), m Jan 1, 1910 Edna Klinger (Feb 24, 1892 – 1985), a dau of Preston A. and Anna (Hoffman) Klinger
Raymond Clair (Jul 9, 1893 – May 29, 1958), m Beatrice E. Kratzer b Aug 9, 1893
Arthur Leonidas b Nov 7, 1895 m Helen Kniley b Apr 11, 1893.

Very old view of Main Street. From the left is the Zerbe hotel, Solomon Good home, and the Landon Hoover home.

THE FOLLOWING PROPERTIES ARE LOCATED BETWEEN CROSSROADS AND WALNUT STREET ON THE NORTH SIDE OF THE STREET

THE ZERBE (INDIAN HEAD) HOTEL 66-016029
(Replaced by service station after hotel destroyed by fire)

South East Room - Inside of Loyalton Hotel (people unidentified)

This is one of the lots that Dr. H. C, Beshler sold to Jacob L. Snyder. He and his wife Elizabeth conveyed it to Peter O. Johns on November 1, 1874. The lot bordered east by David Klock, northwest by William Schoffstall, south by the public road to Lykens. A large two-story frame tavern stood on the lot.

Mariah widow of Peter O. Johns sold this lot in 1882 to Edward A. Hess. He and his wife Mary conveyed the same to David F. Hoffman in March 1889. David F. Hoffman and Jacob Messner of Tower City had a joint association to the hotel, but on April 1, 1892, Jacob Messner purchased the property from David F. and Caroline Hoffman. He sold to Jonathan Zerbe during the later1890s. Jonathan S. Zerbe purchased two adjoining lots (lots 12 & 13 from the Ferree plan) September 29, 1903 from Jacob and Emma Messner. The sign on the following photo of the tavern is proof that the tavern was here while David F. Hoffman owned the premises, and helps to date the picture to about 1890.

Soon after Jonathan Zerbe (known as "Jack") owned the property, Annie Klinger became the mainstay in the Zerbe household. Her husband Preston A. Klinger died in 1895 at the age of 29, leaving her with small children. She became the hotel cook and raised her own and the Zerbe children. (Annie was a daughter of David F. and Carolyn (Whitman) Hoffman. Henry Hassinger took charge of the livery stable.

170

Jonathan & Julia (Messner) Zerbe with children
Walter & Lottie or Bertha

Jonathan Zerbe grew up on a farm in Low Mahanoy Twp, Northld Co, but when he was sixteen years old, his mother died, and two years later his father also died, both of small pox. He began to work for A. D. Lentz and continued with him for five years, as a farm hand. In March 1878, he went to Kansas, and again worked as a farm hand for almost one year. When he came back to Pennsylvania he married and moved to Tower City, where he worked in the mines for 12 years. In 1892, he became a partner with his brother-in-law Jacob Messner in the hotel business on this lot, and eventually became sole owner.

A.. D. Lentz, the farmer for whom Jonathan worked, in later years wrote a complimentary piece about Jonathan Zerbe. He praised him as the best farm hand he ever had in his employ, a willing worker, and perfectly honest in handling large sums of money. One day Lentz lost his purse with over eight hundred dollars. Jonathan found it, and returned the whole amount to him. Lentz mentioned that he raised him and had him under his care during a time when young men are "apt to become bad and vicious." But Jonathan always respected his advice, as if it were from his own father. Lentz was very thankful for what Jonathan had done for him.

A piece in the local paper of September 20, 1906, told of a robbery that took place near Zerbe Hotel. "A bold highway robbery took place on top of the hill on the Uniontown road about one-fourth mile from Loyalton about nine o'clock on Saturday evening. Frank Wiest the butcher living near Uniontown Gap was returning from the Lykens market, where he had made his regular collections. When he reached this point a daring thief rushed up to the team and while it was in motion, struck Mr. Wiest a terrible blow on the head with a billy. At the same moment an accomplice rushed to the other side of the wagon and both boarded it at once. An encounter ensued during which the victim was horribly beaten with the weapon the thugs carried, and was robbed of about $70. Mr. Wiest was left unconscious but shortly revived and turned his team back toward Loyalton when he was met by Peter Matter and Edward Grubb. The latter took charge of the team and brought the unfortunate man to Loyalton, where he was taken to Zerby's hotel. Dr. Lebo of Gratz was hurriedly summoned and dressed the wounds and on Sunday afternoon he was considered able to be removed to his home where he is expected to recover. One of the thieves lost his hat in the scuffle and it is likely that both will soon be apprehended and brought to justice." Another similar event took place on a Saturday evening in April 1914. Some thieves stole meat from Jonathan Zerbe. On Sunday the three men were caught near Lenker's station roasting the meat for their supper. They were taken to Lykens the same evening by the constable and a few other men.

Jonathan S. Zerbe purchased the lot on the east side of his hotel lot known as lot #13 from Preston Klinger on September 16, 1927. On February 21, 1928, he sold half of it to his neighbor Solomon Good.

On June 28, 1937, Jonathan S. Zerbe sold both properties (with four lots) to his son Walter S Zerbe. While Walter and his wife owned this hotel, it was one of the places for Loyalton residents to gather, the other being the

Interior Of Hotel While The Snyder Family Owned It.

Snyder store across the street. Warren Hoke was sometimes the bartender. But often times Lottie Zerby was in charge. She was a friendly person, just several inches taller than five foot, and weighed 300 pounds. In later years, Clyde and Betty Snyder owned this business, as can be seen by the sign on the picture on the previous page. (Clyde was a son of Howard & Rosie Snyder of Greenbriar, Northld. Co. Betty a dau of Charles & Edna (Knohr) Ramberger of Rough & Ready.) Eventually Mabel P and Michael Korpa owned this land and conveyed it August 18, 1959 to Gary L. and Gail E. Burrell. Mabel and Michael Korpa owned lot 12 and ½ of 13 briefly and sold June 25, 1973 to John C. and Marlene Forney. They sold June 29, 1994 to Daren Daniel Hoffman. All the physical memories of this beautiful old building were eventually destroyed by fire.

After the fire destroyed the hotel, this vacant lot became the site of the present gas station.

ZERBE/ ZERBY ETC. FAMILY

[The *Zerbe* family came from France, some settled in Schoharie Valley of New York, later moved to Tulpehocken Twp, Berks Co. *DANIEL ZERBE* (b May 10, 1787 Berks Co – d Jan 9, 1858 Low Mahanoy Twp, Northld Co, bur Stone Valley Cem), m Maria Elizabeth Wirth (b Sep 24, 1788 – Apr 5,1857), a dau of J. Henrich and Elizabeth (Enderline) Wirth of Low Mah Twp. Daniel migrated to Lower Mahanoy Twp by wagon, and was one of the early settlers in the region.

Daniel and Maria Elizabeth (Wirth) Zerbe had eight children; THOMAS (Jan 5, 1809 - Jun 27, 1894), a dau of Martin and Elisabeth (Michael) Garman, lived in Lower Mahanoy Twp.

Thomas and Elizabeth (Garman) Zerbe had these children: Josiah b Sep 14, 1838, killed by a bull while he was working at his barn in Kansas;

Thomas b May 3, 1840, m Jul 29, 1860, St. John's Ch, Bbg, Catharine Messner b Apr 28, 1843 - , a dau of Philip and Anna Maria (Dockey) Messner of Low Mah Twp, Northld Co. Thomas was a watchman on the railroad.

Thomas and Catharine (Messner) Zerbe had these children: Charles Adam b Mar 14, 1862; *Jonathan W.* b 1864; *James W.* b 1866, lived in Reading; *Joseph H.* b Mar 19, 1870, m Catherine Wright; *Daniel W.* b 1873, soldier in Phillipines;

Sarah b Oct 9, 1842, m Henry Miller and lived in Shamokin; *Rebecca* (no dates) m George Heitzman, moved to Kansas; *Benjamin* (no dates) moved to Snyder Co.; *Catherine Mary Janee* b Feb 4, 1855, m Elias Paul, moved to Shamokin; *Elias Solomon* b Sep 16, 1857, moved to Altoona;

JOSEPH ( ), m Catharine Meck (, bur Dalmatia), lived in Lower Mahanoy Twp. *Joseph and Catharine (Meck) Zerbe had these children; Elizabeth* b Jun 1, 1842; *Henry* Civil War Vet; *Joseph* b 1847; *Daniel* b Feb 11, 1853; *George*; _____ dau not married; *Samuel* b Jul 16, 1860; *Jonas*

JOHN b _____ died of small pox, m late in life, no children.

DANIEL (Aug 1811 – Feb 8, 1861, bur St. Valley Cem), not married

GEORGE (b ----- d 1875, of small pox, bur Stone Valley Cem, Northld Co), m Phoebe Spangler (b ___ - 1873 of small pox), a dau of _____. They lived on a farm in Lower Mahanoy Twp. George Zerbe was a Civil War Veteran. *George and Phoebe (Spangler) Zerbe had these children: William D.; Ellen m William Alleman;*

Jonathan (b Nov 16, 1857 Low Mahanoy Twp, Northld Co – d1941, bur Maple Grove Cem, E'ville), m Oct 28, 1879, Julia Messner (1857 – 1897), a dau of Philip and Anna Mary (Dockey) Messner. *Jonathan and Julia (Messner) Zerbe had these children:*

Harry Franklin (Jul 11, 1883 – 1884, bur Maple Grove Cem); *Mary Bertha* (1887 – 1944), m Elmer Romberger (b ___ d Nov 5, 1942); *Lottie May* (Oct 19, 1891 – 1970), not married;

Walter Scott (Feb 28, 1895 , bapt St. Johns Ch, Lykens – Oct 25, 1956, bur Maple Grove), m Catherine Bailer.He was a WW1 Veteran. He was a WWI veteran, owned Lykens Mercantile Co. *Walter & Catherine (Bailer) had these children*: *John Bailer* moved to Indiana; _____ m John William Runyon, Jr., lived in Delmar, N.Y. *SUSANNA* (no dates) , m John Meck, lived in Williamstown, Pa.; *REBECCA* (no dates) m Adam Bowman, moved to Illinois; *CATHARINE* (no dates) m David Schwartz, moved to Michigan; *ELIZABETH* (no dates) m Adam Alleman, lived in Lower Mahanoy Twp]

JACOB MESSNER FAMILY

[*JACOB MESSNER* (Mar 22, 1861 - Nov 25, 1943, bur Oak Hill Cem, Mbg), a son of Philip and Anna Maria (Dockey) Messner , m Emma L. Searer (Jul1862 – Dec 26, 1932), a dau of George Searer of Low Paxton Twp. Jacob was born in Low Mahanoy Twp, Northld Co, but his parents moved the family to Tower City about 1871 where the father became established in his carpenter business. He erected twenty-seven houses and many roads and bridges, before going back to his native county. After his marriage, Jacob Messner engaged in contracting and building houses, then in 1891 became employed by the Pennsylvania Railroad Compnay in bridge and carpenter work between Harrisburg and Renovo repairing bridges damaged in the great flood of 1891. In 1892, he became a partner in hotel keeping with Jonathan Zerbe in Loyalton but the partnership was dissolved in 1901, when he moved to Millersburg. *Jacob and Emma L. (Searer) Messner had these children*: *George* (Jun 1880 – 1976), m May 3, 1900 Annie C. Hoke (1880 Dalmatia, Northld Co – 1961); *Philip A.*; *Mary E.* b May 1886; *Estella* b Dec 1889; *Harry A* b Jul 1892; *Lloyd H* b Dec 1895; *Eva* b Oct 1899.

SERVICE STATION 66-016-029 & 030

This building has the same history as the above account of the hotel. Several years after Daren Daniel Hoffman received it, this land was sold to the Garnick family.

On June 19, 1995 Tower Sales purchased the lot. Soon after they purchased the land they established the service station which continues to be in business.

THE HOME OF CHESTER H. & JAYME L. GROSSER 66-016-031
(WAS THE SOLOMON GOOD HOME)

This lot #14 was part of the L. S. Ferree / Henry C. Beshler plan. On Jan 18, 1875 John Wommer Sr. purchased the lot (the 1875 map shows Wommer as the owner). Two years later, May 18, 1877, John and Elizabeth Wommer sold the same lot to Anne Ferree. After Anne Ferree died, her executor Uriah Ferree conveyed the one-fourth acre property with frame dwelling (50 feet by 165 feet) to John H. Dietrich on Apr 1, 1882. John H. and Mary Elisabeth Dietrich sold it to Thomas C. Baddorf on March 6, 1884. On April 20, 1892 Baddorf conveyed it to Solomon S. Good. On Feb 21, 1928, Solomon and Agnes Good purchased half of lot # 13 on the west side of their property from Jonathan S. Zerbe.[Lot #13 deed states "third lot from east side of Intersection of the road to Gratz and road to Millersburg." It was part of the L. S. Ferree tract, was sold to Peter Johns, his heirs sold it to Edward and Mary Ann Hess in March 1882. David F. Hoffman purchased it March 19, 1884 and he and Caroline sold February 15, 1893 to Preston Klinger. It was sold to Jonathan Zerbe in 1927.] Many years later, in June 1952 Solomon S. and Agnes Good sold the whole property (one and ½ lot) to their son Roy D. Good. On Jun 12, 1953 Myles H. and Carly Kahler became the owners. On May 1, 1959 Myles H. and Carly Kahler conveyed the property to Marvin J. Hornberger. [Good genealogy elsewhere in book.]

Much later, David R. Herb, single and Linda D. Herb, single conveyed these premises to David L. Snyder and Dorreen (Willier) Snyder on Mar 12, 1982. On May 22, 1990 David L. and Dorreen Snyder sold the property to John B. and Joan C. Stehman, but on May 25, 1993 they sold to Chester H. and Jayme L. Grosser.

[**THOMAS C. BADDORF** (Jul 2,1851-Aug 24,1913, bur Oak Dale), a son of Peter and Elisabeth (Welker) Baddorf of Lykens Twp, m Mary L. Peters (Mar 31,1858 – Aug 3, 1924). In 1870, Thomas lived with the Henry Wise family and was an apprentice blacksmith.By 1880 Thomas and Mary Batdorf were married and living in Washington Twp. **Thomas C. and Mary L. (Peters) Baddorf had these children (at least 5 of them bapt Oak Dale Ch on Mar 12, 1894): James Edward** b Feb 15, 1886, m Feb 8, 1908 Beulah Irene Wert; **Oscar Nuton** b Aug 15, 1887; **Francis** b Mar 12, 1887, bapt Mar 12, 1894; **Joseph Warren** b May 29,1889 bapt Mar 1889-1928); **Harvey Clarence** b Jan 21,1890; **Cora Annetta** b Apr 18,1892; **Estella Louisa** b Jun 5,1893;**Alvin Thomas** b Jun 26,1897. [More info- **BADDORF** genealogy elsewhere in book].

HOME OF LYNN & Peggy P. Kahler
(WAS THE LANDON HOOVER HOME)
(Lot #15 & 16 Dr. Beshler/L.S. Ferree Plan)

Lots 15 & 16 belonged to the Beshler/ Ferree plan, and was first conveyed to Jacob L. Snyder. This house was first built as a double house, both parties sharing the attic because there was no partition dividing it. Later Fred C. Harner & Mary A. his wife owned it, and they sold to Edmond Hoover & Lillie Oct 18, 1928. Wellington M Hoover of Sunbury and Lottie E Hoover of E'ville heirs of Edmond Hoover sold to Landon J. Hoover & Fay M. on May 26, 1948 with frame dwelling. Landon and Fay Hoover lived on the west side of the house, and his father lived on the east side. Other tenants were Mellie and Minnie Riegel with children Carolyn & Palmer, and Silas Troutman and his mother. The house was eventually converted to a single dwelling. Landon J. and Fay M. Hoover conveyed to Myles H. and Carly V. (Hoover) Kahler on May 25, 1959. On January 30, 1996, Miles H. and Carly V. Kahler conveyed this property to Lynn B. and Peggy P. Kahler. [Hoover genealogy elsewhere in book.]

THE HARNER FAMILY

[***FREDERICK HARNER SR.** (b Oct 5, 1782 Germany – d Apr 24, 1870, bur Simeon Cem. Gratz), m Mary Schurr (Nov 8, 1779–Nov 20, 1849). **Frederick & Mary (Schurr) Harner had these known child:**: ****FREDERICK D.** (b Jun 19, 1816 Pine Grove – d Nov 10, 1894 of pneumonia, bur Matter's Cem), m Aug 13, 1840 Rebecca Hoffman (Nov 21, 1820 – Dec 18, 1891 of heart failure), a dau of George and Rebecca (Kuntzelman) Hoffman. **Frederick and Rebecca (Kunzelman) Harner had these children:** *****Jeremiah H** (Sep 11, 1841 – Apr 8, 1922), m Lucy Collier (b ____ - d 1897). Jeremiah worked as an engineer on the Lykens Valley Branch railroad. **Jeremiah and Lucy (Collier) Harner had these children:** Kathyn R.b c1872, m ____ Sharp; Mary 1875; Pearl E b c1879; *****Sarah** (Mar 26, 1842 - Jan 26, 1891), m Henry Martz. (one dau m Gordon Smith). *****Mariah** (Sep 1, 1844 - Dec 22, 1922, bur Maple Grove Cem, E'ville), m Jacob Klinger (Apr 19, 1838 – Aug 23,1903), 1880 lived in Wash Twp. With them were: Theodore Matter17, James M Romberger 15 and Hannah Harner 65, aunt. **Jacob and Mariah (Harner) Klinger had these children:**

Maggie R.(1872–1948, bur Maple Grove Cem) m May 7, 1893 B. Frank Wise (Dec 9, 1866 – May 20, 1947); **Frederick E** (1874 – 1942, bur Maple Grove Cem), m Susan A ___ (1875 – 1950); **Wm A** (1876 – 1959, bur Maple Grove Cem); **Sally b** c1879; **Catharine Edith** b Jun 30, 1886.

***William F. (b Jul 29, 1846 - d Oct 1, 1895 bur E'ville Cem) m Sarah Lebo (b ___ d Feb 12, 1924). He was a fireman at the mines. In 1880 they had Emma Lebo age 23 a Tailoress with them. **William F and Sarah (Lebo) Harner had these children**: **Jennie E** b c1876; **Amy R**; **Florence M.**

***George A. (Oct 30, 1848 – Jan 18, 1924, bur E'ville), m Minerva Gilbert (1850 – 1914), **had these children**: Carrie E b c1874; lived in Wash T in 1880

***Henry (Mar 3, 1851 – Mar 2, 1864)

***Charles F. (Aug 12, 1853 – Mar 19, 1926, bur Oak Dale Cem), m 1st Mar 15,1876 Ellen Boyer. 2nd Mary Hoke; **Charles F. and Elle (Boyer) Harner had these children**); **Frederick Charles** (Aug 16, 1876 – Sep 16,1932, bur Maple Grove Cem, E'ville), m 1st Apr.1891 Hattie P. Shadle (Oct 26, 1877 – Jun 17, 1913), 2nd Mary A Hoke (Nov 23, 1882 – Jul 29, 1955); **Fred and Hattie P. (Shadle) Harner children:** **Floyd Benjamin** (Jul 18, 1904 – Oct 27, 1961, bur Maple Grove Cem, E'ville), m Leona Miriam Snyder (Jul 22,1907 – Aug 23, 1988), a dau of Harvey H. and Jennie Dorcia (Miller) Snyder, had a son Richard and dau Ethel m 1st to ___ Buffington of E'ville, had two sons Thomas and David. She m 2nd to Pershing Henninger; **Prudence** m Ralph Burrell. Floyd was employed by Reiff & Nestor in Lykens.
Annie Catharine (Mar 27, 1882 – Jun 26, 1891, bur Oak Dale Cem); **Minnie E.** (Sep 26, 1884 – Dec 17, 1912, bur Oak Dale Cem), m H.A. Romberger; **Edwin Lot** (Mar 21, 1893 – Nov 4, 1909, bur Oak Dale Cem) ;

***Isaac (May 7, 1855 – Jul 21, 1928, bur E'ville), m Mary Evitts (1861 - 1953), had a son Lester Isaac b Mar 12, 1897. Isaac worked on the railroad

***Catharine (Oct 28, 1857 – Mar 3, 1955), m Jan 17, 1880 Franklin Shadle (1848 – 1891);

***Jonathan (Sep 9, 1860 – Mar 27, 1865)

***Emma L. (Oct 2, 1863 – Sep 29, 1952), m Feb 21, 1893 George H. Swab (1867 – 1949);

***Edmon (Dec 5, 1867 – Nov 14, 1906), m Clara Romberger (1864 – 1950)

ELIZABETH (Jun1,1820–Sep 6,1855, bur Simeon Cem), m Samuel Umholtz (Dec14,1814–Mar 18, 1883), son of Philip and Ann Mary (Willier) Umholtz. **Elizabeth and Samuel (Harner) Umholtz children:
***Emanuel (Jul 30, 1843 – Sep16, 1904), The custom of tolling the Simeon church bell for a funeral began with his funeral. He m Oct 23, 1866 Mary Hartman (Sep 7 or 26, 1840 – Dec 13,1908), a dau of Henry Hartman. Emanuel was a Civil War veteran. **Emanuel and Mary (Hartman) Umholtz had these children:** Isaac (Apr or May 15, 1867 – Oct 25, 1901, bur Simeon Cem), d in mining accident of fractured skull m Nov 2, 1884 Emma Cecilia Williard (bur Simeon Cem, no dates), a dau o f John L. and Eliza (Thomas) Williard, and had a son Elmer (1885 – 1972). They lived at S. Pine St. Gratz at time of his death; **Ida Elizabeth** (Jul 29, 1868 – Apr 19, 1937), m George Daniel, a son of George and Elizabeth (Hoffman) Daniel ;
Isaac (1845 – Apr 2, 1865), killed in battle during Civil War, bur Poplar Grove Mat'l Cem, Petersburg, Va.; ***Sarah b c1847, m Henry Ritzman; ***Henry M (1848 – 1851);Mary Ellen (Oct 21, 1849 – Jan 2, 1915), m Elias Klinger; ***Louisa b c1851, m Jacob Zimmerman of Williamstown; ***Edward (Jul 15, 1854 – Jul 4, 1936 in Newton, Kansas), m Catharine Buffington (1860 – 1929), a dau of Samuel and Sarah (Umholtz) Buffington of Gratz; ***Leah b c1856.

After Elizabeth died, Samuel Umholtz m Apr 5, 1857, 2nd Abbie Maurer, but they divorced March 1858. He m 3rd Elizabeth Ginter (Dec 8, 1823 – Jul 5, 1882), a dau of John and Christiana (Moyer) Ginter, widow of Cyrus Buffington (1821 – 1856). [Ginter gen. Elsewhere.] **Samuel and Elizabeth (Ginter) Umholtz had these children:** Adaline (Sep 8,1860–Jan 19,1916, bur Simeon Cem), m George A. Welker (1862 –1933); **Harvey** (1862 – 1888, killed in Shiro Mines, bur Simeon Cem), m Katie Welker; **William P.** (Apr 4, 1865 – Jan 7, 1923), m Catharine N. Thomas (Jan 29,1872 –Dec12,1916), a dau of Edward and Elizabeth (Hoffman) Thomas. **William P and Catharine (Thomas) Umholtz children:** **Edmund Harrison** (1889 –1891); **Chas H** (1890 -1898); **Carrie Elizabeth** (1893 –1955), m Guy R. Klinger; **James Albert** (1894–1895); **Walter Franklin** (1900 - ___), m Fae Klinger; **Clayton Jacob** (1903 – 1990), m Hannah C. Buffington; **Florence** (1905 – 1975, bur Simeon Cem), m Harrison Jacob Sitlinger; **Grace** (1907–1979), m Elwood Romberger.]

[**LANDON JOSIAH HOOVER** (Jul 2, 1909 – 1958, bur Hoffman Cem), a son of Edmund and Lillian (Wetzel) Hoover, m Faye M. Hoffman (b 1911 - 2003), a dau of _____ **Landon J. and Faye M. (Hoffman) Hoover** had these children: **Carley** b 1930 m Myles Kahler; **Bruce Harold** (Jun 25, 1931 – Jul 10, 2006), m Helen Maletich; **Barbara** b 1935 m Harry Dietrich; **Lou** Gehrig (b – d Feb 19, 1995), named for baseball player. (For more information see Hoffman genealogy).]

HOME OF TERRY A. SULTZBAUGH
(WAS THE PAUL JOHNS HOME & Dairy Lots 17 & 18 of the Ferree Plan)

Very Early View Of John P. Johns House

These two lots were from the Ferree plan. They were sold to Daniel A. Good, but after he died, his heirs Mary and O.T Tobias and Sarah D. Good conveyed to Harvey E. Smeltz Jun 3, 1922. Harvey E. Smeltz and Alma (Star) Smeltz conveyed to John P. Johns and Sarah Jan 9, 1925. On March 22, 1945 John P. and Sarah E. Johns conveyed these two lots to Paul and Ruth Johns. After Ruth and Paul Johns died, their daughter Betty Budrow conveyed this property to Florence E. Dockey of Wiconisco on June 30, 1993. Florence Dockey died in 1998, and her property was sold to Terry A. Sultzbaugh.

JOHNS DAIRY

In 1910, John Peter Johns established a dairy on his farm on Stone Hill at the east end of Loyalton. It became a thriving enterprise, and continued for many years. About the time that the Johns family purchased this lot, the dairy business was moved from the farm to this property. Paul Johns the son took over the business.

A supply of milk was purchased from various farmers in the area. Twice each day, members and employees of the Johns family made the rounds to the farms and collected the milk, bringing it to the farm and later to the small building on this lot for processing. While gathering milk they also purchased produce, eggs and chickens for resale to their customers. Each day, they sold about 200 quarts of milk. They had twenty-four cases of quart bottles (twelve in a case), and nine cases of pints. Another case of half-pints contained chocolate milk. Every Saturday was a special treat. Johns made ice cream that sold out as soon as it was made.

Silas Troutman worked full time for the dairy from 1930 to 1941. This was during the depression years. He worked seven days a week, and his starting salary was five dollars per week, plus one quart of milk. When Silas and Lucy married in 1941 he was earning thirteen dollars per week. Margaret Johns Matter was also helping in the dairy. Her job was to bottle all the milk after Silas washed the bottles and cans. When he had the bottles and cans ready, Silas contacted Margaret by speaking through a funnel that carried his voice to her.

During the depression, the federal government gave people vouchers to buy milk, but the milk had to be pasteurized. Johns milk was raw, so Margaret wrote to the milk marketing board asking for permission to sell raw milk. They were given authorization because they always passed inspection. Eventually, J. P. Johns purchased the Troxell Dairy located in Big Run. They continued to operate the dairy for many years. The little house that housed equipment to operate the dairy has survived and is on this lot.

On March 22, 1945, John P. Johns and Sarah E conveyed this property to Paul and Ruth Johns. The lots were described as being bound on the north by an Alley, east by Walnut St., South by Main St. west by lot 16, measuring 100 feet front by 165. A note of interest to folks who collect local dairy milk bottles: Years later When Paul Johns dug out beside the house to build a porch, he thought of a way to dispose of the unneeded milk bottles he was storing. He broke them up and buried them in the cement under the porch! [See **Johns genealogy for family information.**]

[**JOHN E. SMELTZ** (b Feb 8, 1877 - d Feb 1922, murdered), a son of Daniel and Amanda Smeltz, m on Jan 7, 1896 to Sarah E. Rowe (1881–1941, bur Oak Dale). **John E. and Sarah (Rowe) Smeltz had these children: Harvey E. "Harp"** (1897 – 1929, in a mining accident, bur Calvary Meth Cem Wmstown), m 1st Florence Rowe, a dau of Alfred and Kate (Kessler) Rowe. He m 2nd H. Irene ___ (1903 –1923). He later married Bertha Esterline (1886 – 1973, bur Calvary Meth Cem, Wic.), widow of Frederick Esterline (1886 – 1918). **Lloyd A.** (1899 –1966, bur Fairview Cem, Wmstown), m Elsie Warfield (Jul 21, 1891 - Sep 1952), a dau of George Warfield; **Lloyd A. and Elsie (Warfield) Smeltz children:** ____ m Ben Kelly; ___ m Ray McCready; Lloyd Jr.; John; Marlin; **Robert b** ____, m Mary Hoffman, a dau of Charles Hoffman, has a son Larry**; Edwin** b c1904;**Marlin Daniel** b Sep 9, 1908; **Clarence F** (1912– 1913); **Melvin** (1916 – 1963), bur Maple Grove Cem, E'ville, m Gladys E. Markel (1918 – 1965)]

THE NEXT LOTS ARE LOCATED BETWEEN WALNUT STREET AND WATER STREET
(North Side of Main Street)

This photo shows the latest "look" of the old Johns home. Also the little building that housed the dairy equipment. To the right is the home of Rev. & Mrs. Jeffrey Wagner.

REV. & MRS. JEFFREY WAGNER
(Lot #19)

This 50 by 165 foot lot #19 located on Main Street was from the L. S. Ferree plan. H. C. Beshler conveyed it to Cornelius Gunderman on Mar 15, 1884. Cornelius Gunderman conveyed to Henry A. Grubb on March 31, 1900. Henry Grubb died May 23, 1910, and by his will conveyed the property to his wife Isabelle. After her death the "mansion dwelling" was to be sold and the money divided among the heirs. Isabelle died July 24, 1944 and on October 14, 1944 Frederick H. Lahr and Carrie M. Bonawitz, administrators of the estate of Henry A. Grubb conveyed the property to Frederick H. Lahr. The lot was located on the northeast corner of Main and Walnut Street. On Jun 21, 1957 Frederick H. and Ruby Lahr conveyed the 2 ½ story single frame dwelling and barn to Barbara L.

Hoover. After Barbara married Harry A. Dietrich he shared ownership with her. On July 23, 1971, Barbara L and Harry A. Deitrich conveyed this 2 ½ story frame dwelling and lot to William J. and Linda K. Scheib. On May 1, 1984, they conveyed to Deborah A. and Scott A. Snyder. Rev. Jeffrey A. & Nancy L. Wagner became the owners on July 28, 1994. He is the minister at Hoffman's Church.

JONATHAN AND HILDA KLINGER 1957
(Was The Home Of Citizen Cornet Band 1895 – Now Vacant Lot))
Lot #20

Loyalton Cornet Band
Date of photo not known. L to r – 1st row: Thomas Schaffner, Ray Helt, Walter Zerbe.
2nd Row: William Mumma, John Hoover, Ray Bohner, Nathan Snyder, Clinton Rowe, Harvey Helt, ____, ____, Harry Gunderman. 3rd row: John Rowe, Walter Rowe, ____, ____, John P. Johns, Samuel Spotts, Daniel Kissinger, Jim Helt, Fred Harner, Edwin Linger or Charles Rowe.

Loyalton Band Members: l to r – Harvey Matter, Loy Miller, Charles Koch – Year unknown

Rev. and Mrs. Jeffrey A. and Nancy L. Wagner 66-016-034

Jonathan and Hilda Klinger 66-16-035

Jessica L. Savage 66-016-032

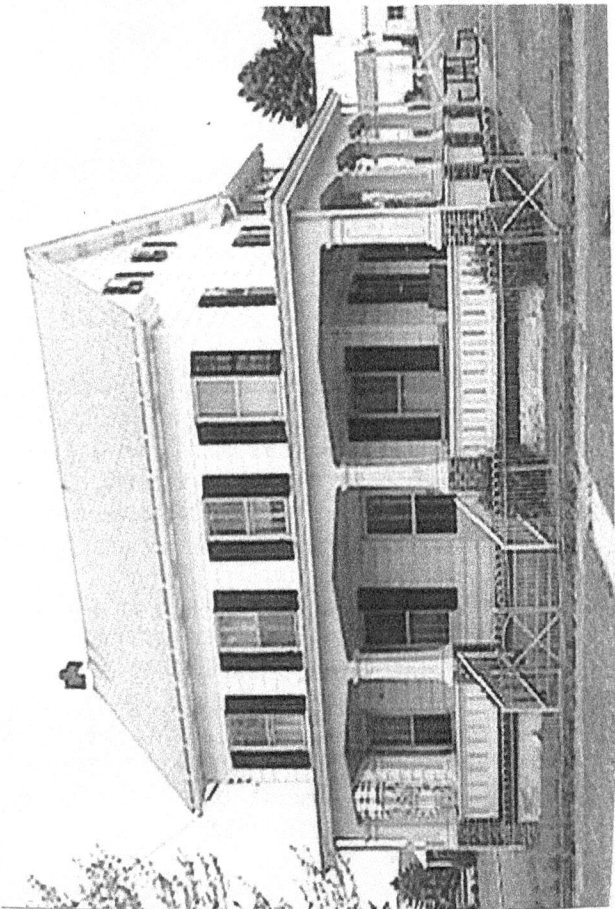

Robert G. and Carolyn J. Sites 66-016-033

This lot was taken from the L. S. Ferree plan and was sold to by Dr. Beshler to Jonathan Hawk on August 1, 1876. In October 1895 Jonathan and Malina Hawk conveyed the lot to Wayne B. Johns, S. S. Good, and C. I Lubold, Trustees of The Citizen Band of Loyalton. The lot bordered along lot 19, ran 60 feet eastward along Main Street to lot 21 owned by Samuel Gunderman. The band group on May 14, 1910 became incorporated into The Citizen Cornet Band of Loyalton. On September 21, 1912, Wayne B. Johns transferred the property to the group under the new name. Many Civic and social activities took place here. The band had regular practice sessions, and put on many fund raising affairs including the annual week long Band Fair, cakewalks, and games of chance.   The band was very popular throughout the many years of its existence. Samuel Spotts was remembered as a person that could "make his slide trombone talk," Nate Snyder was a talented cornet player. Fred Daniels an accomplished musician could play a number of instruments. These talented musicians were called upon to entertain at Loyalton events, and also in surrounding areas. They were well received.

On October 5, 1946 The Citizen Cornet Band conveyed this property to Earl F. Good. Earl F. Good died on August 4, 1951 and his heirs conveyed the property to Emory B. and Dora (Koppenhaver) Miller on March 20, 1952. Emory and Dora Miller conveyed to Susan C. Good on July 15, 1952. Susan C. Good married John Deibler and on August 24, 1957 they sold this property to Jonathan and Hilda Klinger. The original building was torn down during the 1940s.

This photo shows to the left the home of late Effie Miller, now John & Hilda Klinger.
Vacant lot between, was Loyalton Band lot. House to right was Emory Miller, now. Parke Hoover

PARKE AND KELLY HOOVER 66-016-037

This lot #21 was part of the L. S.Ferree tract and was first purchased by Jacob E. and Carrie S. Boyer. They sold October 28, 1911 to Emory B. Miller. Emory Miller while he lived here ran the delivery truck for the Lykens Mercantile. Many years later Emory and his wife Dora conveyed this property to their daughter Susan C. Miller on January 29, 1940. (She m Earl Frank Good 1906 – 1951). Susan later married John C. Deibler, and on August 24, 1959, they sold this property to Jonathan and Hilda Klinger. [See Christopher Miller genealogy below.] Kenneth and Jean Zerby became the owners, but sold to Parke and Kelly Hoover on November 29, 2010..

[EARL W. ZERBY (Mar 18, 1887 -   *), a son of William and Elizabeth Zerby, m in 1906 Clara Bitterman (Dec 11, 1886 - - Sep 10, 1925, of cancer, bur POS of A Cem, Lykens), a dau of Henry & Bertha Bitterman. Earl and Clara (Bitterman) Zerby children: William H b 1907, m Mildred Thompson, a dau of John H. and Elizabeth (Morgan) Thompson; Ray b 1910; Verna Bertha b Apr 23, 1912, m Clarence D. Polm, a son of John and Carrie (Hand) Polm;; Elizabeth Elizabeth (Dec 14, 1914 - Dec 15, 2007):Kenneth Mark (Mar 12, 1917 - Aug 20, 2010): Harold Edward (Jul 13, 1919 - Aug 19, 1987 Calif); Edith Elizabeth b Dec14, 1914; Kenneth Mark (Mar 12, 1917 - Aug 20, 2010), m Georgina Duncan b 1921, a dau of Georgge W. and Amelia (Hand) Duncan); Harold Edward b Jul 13, 1919; Betty Jean bapt Dec 31, 1922]*

181

THE CHRISTOPHER MILLER FAMILY

[CHRISTOPHER MILLER b in Germany, m Margaretha Barbara Schuppinger b pre 1734. Christopher and Margaretha Barbara (Schuppinger) Miller had a son:
JOHANNES (b c1751 Wurttemburg, Ger – d 1812, County Line, Northld Co, Pa.), m Fronica Kerstetter (b Apr 9, 1752 Leb Co, Pa. – d 1818 bur Fetterhoffs Cem, Fisherville), a dau of Sebastian and Magdalena (Deibler) Kerstetter. Johannes and Fronica (Kerstetter) Miller had a son Johannes (Nov 5, 1777 – Jul 6, 1871, bur St. Jacobs (Millers) Cem, Jackson Twp, Dau Co.), m Anna Catherine Seiler (May 5, 1783 – Aug 21, 1865), a dau of Jost and Elizabeth (Heckert) Seiler. Johannes and Anna Catherine (Seiler) Miller had a son John T. S."Hontz" (Sep 21, 1814 Low Mah. Twp, Northld. Co. – Jan 30, 1897, bur St. Jacobs (Millers) Cem Jackson Twp. Dau Co), m Barbara Sweigard (Apr 25, 1818 – Feb 2, 1902), a dau of John Adam and Mary Elizabeth (Warfel) Sweigard. John "Hontz" and Barbara (Sweigard) Miller had a son Henry A. (Sep 3, 1848 – Jun 15, 1907, bur Millers Cem), m Catharine Naomi Paul (Feb 15, 1849 – Jun 28, 1902), a dau of Jacob and Sarah (Schreffler) Paul. Henry A. & Catharine (Paul) Miller were parents of:
Emory Benton Miller (Feb 26, 1869 bapt Salem Ch, Bbg. – Mar 17,1956, bur Maple Grove Cem), m Dora Alice Koppenhaver (Mar 20, 1881 – Nov 6,1953), a dau of Wm. S. and Susanna (Rogers) Koppenhaver.
Emory and Dora (Koppenhaver) Miller had one daughter: Susan (b Aug 11, 1910- ___ , bur E'ville), m Earl Franklin Good (1906 – Aug 4, 1951), a son of Ariel Daniel and Gertie A. (Schoffstall) Good. Susan and Earl Good had two children: Linda Susan b 1947 m James A. Nessport; Elaine Marie b 1949, m Milan J. Smolko. Susan Miller Good later m John C. Deibler (Aug 12, 1892 – Jan 29, 1980), a son of Daniel Jacob and Sarah Louisa (Stine) Deibler.]

[JOHN MILLER (b Nov 5, 1777 Northld Co - d Jul 6, 1861, bur Miller's Cem, Enterline), m Anna Catharine Seiler (May 5, 1783 – Aug 24, 1865). John Miller came to Jackson Twp, Dau Co and purchased a farm in 1817. John and Anna Catharine (Seiler) Miller had these children:
MICHAEL (b Feb 12, 1805 Northld Co – d Dec 27, 1864, bur Miller Cem, Enterline), m 1st Mary Catharine Straw (Aug 3, 1805 – Jun 26, 1833), a dau of John and Barbara (Sweigard) Straw of Jackson Twp. Michael was a farmer and blacksmith.Michael and Catharine (Straw) Miller had these children:
Josiah (Dec 25, 1828 – Jul 3, 1898, bur Bowermans Cem, Enterline), m Catherine ___ (1829 – 1899);
Balthasar (Feb 28,1830 – Jun 19, 1904, bur Miller Cem, Jackson Twp), m Christina Miller (Dec 4,1832 – Jun 24, 1914 of injuries from a fall), a dau of John Jacob and Elizabeth (Heckert) Miller;
Cyrus (b Jackson Twp Feb 21, 1831 – d ___ in Reading, Berks Co), m Elizabeth Sweigard b c1831, a dau of Peter and Eva Maria (Metz) Sweigard. Cyrus was a blacksmith in 1850, by 1880 was employed at Short Mt. Colliery as a stable boss.Cyrus and Elizabeth (Sweigard) Miller had these children: Cyrus R. (1850 – 1922), m Catherine Minnich/Mench (1850 – 1928), a dau of Michael and Ruth Ann (Kern) Mench. Cyrus R. and Catherine (Mench) Miller had these children (some bapt Luth Ch. Lykens): Franklin Elias b Aug 28, 1870; Mary Ellen b Dec 7, 1872 Clara Rebecca b Mar 6, 1874; Sadie J b c1876; Cyrus E b c1878; Jennie Margaret b Sep 12, 1880; Lottie Ann b Nov 4, 1882; Lydia Lucian b Apr 28, 1887; Martha Hildegard b Apr 1,1889.
George W. (Jun 3, 1854 –1855); Melinda (1856 – 1923), m David Hoffman (Jan 8, 1852 – 1923), a son of George and Susan (Miller) Hoffman. (The marriage record states that Melinda was a dau of Cyrus and Elizabeth Sweigard Miller;

After Mary Catharine died, Michael m Hannah Buffington (Oct 11, 1808 – Apr 24, 1890 bur Miller Cem), a dau of David D. and Eva Sarah (Schoffstall) Buffington, and widow of Jacob Kolva. Michael and Hannah (Buffington) Miller had these children: Lydia (1835 – 1843); Michael H. (Jun 15, 1836 – Jan 14, 1924 of gangrene, bur Miller Cem), m Catharine Snyder (Jan 7, 1842 – Mar 23, 1911), a dau of Daniel and Elizabeth (Hetrick) Snyder; Eli (1838 – 1843); Samuel (1840 – 1843); Leah (1842 – 1884); Hannah b (Apr 18, 1844 – Apr 16, 1923, bur Maple Grove Cem), m Jul, 23 1865 David A. Snyder (b Jan 27,1840 – d Mar 2, 1913), a son of Daniel and Elizabeth (Hetrick) Snyder, had 3 children: Wellington Nevin (Nov 16, 1870 – Mar 3, 1923), m Mary Etta Botteiger (1866 – 1940), a dau of John Henry and Mary Rachel (Fry) Botteiger; Fannie S. b Nov 15, 1873, m Thomas Bateman; Leon Grover (1885 – 1977, bur Maple Grove Cem, E'ville), m Sarah Strayer (b Mar 20, 1883, d Feb 7, 1967), a dau of Aaron B. and Harriet E (Grim) Strayer; John Aaron (Jul 9, 1846 – Dec 25, 1923, bur Maple Grove Cem), m Florenda Bender (Oct 17, 1840 – Feb 18, 1902), a dau of Adam Q and Susanna (Fisher) Bender.]

STEVEN E. & WANDA S. DAGEN 66-016-038
(was Hilda M. & John Klinger)
(S. L. Ferree plan)

This 50 x 165 foot lot, containing 18,250 square feet and located on the northwest corner at the intersection of Main and Third Streets (Water St.) was part of the Ferree Beshler plan and was sold to Jacob L. Snyder on March 24, 1876. On May 11, 1898 Elizabeth Snyder conveyed this lot to Edwin M Klinger, a butcher and carpenter. While Edwin M and his wife lived here, their daughter Effie was born in this house.

On March 26, 1910, when Effie was one year old, her parents exchanged homes with the grandfather Klinger (who lived in a home on the site of Horning's store). The heirs of Emeline Klinger sold the lot with dwelling and out buildings to Walter Klinger on May 4, 1929, and he transferred to Effie E and Clyde J. Miller on Feb 5, 1938.

When Clyde was 42 years old he decided to work the abandoned Shiro mine on Short Mt. (Big Run side, directly across from where Hornings store is today). Preston and his son Johnny Klinger were in the deal. One Monday morning Jakie had already left for the mine. Effie heated leftover Sunday dinner (chicken corn soup) for Preston & Johnny. When they entered the mine, their carbide lights went out. They made it out before the timbers broke. But Clyde "Jakie" was caught in the cave-in and suffocated. Effie always feared the mines but Jakie told her "there's always another way out." This time there wasn't.

Effie later married Daniel Row. Effie continued to enjoy good health for years and died in 2006, at the age of 99. After Clyde died, Effie married Daniel Row and included the new husband on the deed on December 16, 1975.

On Feb 19, 2003, Effie Row sold lot #25 with dwelling to (her daughter) Hilda and John Klinger. It was conveyed to Steven E. and Wanda S. Dagen on Nov 14, 2006.
[See HARRISON MILLER genealogy page 160].

From Left: Home of Effie Miller, Rebecca E.Knapp, was Cheri P. Rinkevich, Marcella (Matter) Walborn

Was WILLIAM MUMMA
Lot #24

Lot #24 – Edwin and Kate Klinger owned this lot and conveyed to his mother Emeline Klinger March 26, 1910. After she died her heirs conveyed the lot and dwelling to Clyde J. and Effie Miller in May 4, 1929.

EFFIE E. ROW, HILDA M. AND JOHN KLINGER
(Lot 25 of the S. L. Ferree plan)

This 50 x 165 foot lot, containing 18,250 square feet and located on the northwest corner at the intersection of Main and Third Streets was part of the Ferree/ Beshler plan and was sold to Jacob L. Snyder on March 24, 1876. On May 11, 1898 Elizabeth Snyder conveyed this lot to Edwin M Klinger, a butcher and carpenter. On March 26, 1910 Edwin M. and Kate L. Klinger transferred to Emeline Klinger. The heirs of Emeline Klinger sold lot #25 with dwelling and out buildings to Walter Klinger on May 4, 1929, and he transferred to Effie E and Clyde J. Miller on Feb 5, 1938. After Clyde died, Effie married Daniel Row and included the new husband on the deed on December 16, 1975. On Feb 19, 2003, Effie Row conveyed lot #25 with dwelling to (her daughter) Hilda and John Klinger.

House On Left Michael D. & Debra J. Curtis, On Right: STEVE & ANGELA ROMANOFSKY

CHERI P. RINKEVICH HOME
(Lot #26)

This lot containing 8,250 square feet was part of the Beshler/ Ferree plan. On March 24, 1876 H. C. Beshler conveyed it to C. W. Lower. The deed described it as adjoining an alley to the north, east to lot 27, south to Main Street, and west to 3rd (Water) Street. Charles W. and Sarah Lower conveyed the property to David Klock before October 1884. Daniel E. Snyder became the owner and he sold to Jacob L. Snyder on October 3, 1884. On February 11, 1888 Jacob L. Snyder sold to Joel A. Miller with a two-story frame dwelling.

Later, Isaac Henninger became the owner, and he and his wife Sara conveyed lot 26 to Henry Boyer on March 14, 1908. Henry Boyer died April 22, 1934, leaving two children Charles E. and Carrie M. Batdorf. The lot was conveyed to Carrie and her husband Adam S. Batdorf, who died April 18, 1952. On October 1, 1959 widow Carrie Batdorf sold to J. Boyd Crouse and on August 28, 1961, he sold to Elwood E. Kissinger.

On May 4, 1973, Elwood E. Kissinger and Jean E. his wife conveyed to Russell E. and Marcella A. Walborn. They sold on May 27, 1987, to Glen E. Keister and Jenny. A. Solence as joint tenants. (Lot #26). Glen E. Keister, single conveyed the lot to Jenny A. Solence on June 4, 1987. Jenny A. Solence on Sep 26, 1991, sold back to Glen E. Keister, later who married Chritine L. Keister. On April 4, 1996, Glen E. and Christine L. Keister conveyed these premises to Cheri P. Rinkevich.

THE CHARLES W. LOWER FAMILY

[**Charles West Lower** b May 1855 – Feb 20, 1916, bur Oak Dale Cem),a son of Reuben and Elizabeth Esther (Shaffer) Lower of Stone Valley. He m 1st Sarah E. _____ (Dec 2, 1855 – Jun 20, 1884, bur Malta Cem, Northld Co). They are on the 1880 census in Low Mah Twp, Northld Co. He is listed as a wagoner. He m 2nd Marianda Snyder (Feb 22,1851 – d Sep 19, 1886) a dau of Adam and Cath (Bingaman) Snyder, a widow of Emanuel Shaffer (1851–1884). Charles W. Lower m Aug 28,1888 3rd Mary L. Herman (Jun 1,1866 – Feb 17,1931, bur beside him in Oak Dale Cm). **Charles W. & Mary (Herman) Lower children (some bapt Stone Valley, some at Oak Dale Ch):** Lawrence Herbert b Aug 20, 1889, he and Fannie M. Bamberger had a son Charles Lawrence b Sep 22, 1907; Estella Edna May b July 17, 1893; Mary Ellen b (Aug 10,1897, bapt Oak Dale Ch. – Jun 9, 1986, bur Oak Dale Cem), m Boyd Crouse (Jul 1, 1887–Jul 20, 1876); Mildred Alberta b Dec 17,1904. **Pauline Emily** (Apr 6,1907- 1975, bur Maple Grove Cem, E'ville) m Kenneth Bain (1903–1982). Had a son Kenneth C.(1930 – 1987, served in US Marine Corp in Korea.]

THE ABRAHAM MILLER FAMILY

ABRAHAM MILLER (Dec 4,1799–Feb1,1867, bur St. John's Hill Cem), m 1st Anna Maria Matter (b ___ - d before her father who d1847, had 6 children), 2nd Anna Bitterman (c1820 - Oct 31, 1889). Abraham Miller and family lived in Mifflin Twp. In 1860 they had Rebecca age 9 with them. **Abraham Miller had these children:** SARAH (Sep14,1823– Jan 13, 1878), m David Dubendorf (Nov 27,1821–Apr 29,1854, d of Small Pox, bur Simeon Cem, Gratz), a son of Samuel Tobias and Elizabeth Dubdendorf. **David & Sarah (Miller) Dupendorf children:** Elizabeth b c1846; Mary Ann b c1848. Sarah later m Benjamin Koppenhaver (1801 – 1871, bur St. Lukes Cem, Malta, Northld Co). Benjamin Koppenhaver was 1st m to Johanna Radel (1797 – 1860, bur St. Johns Hill Cem).
SIMON (Jul 28, 1825 - Mar 1863, killed in explosion in Treverton), m Katharine Kobel;
DANIEL (Aug 30,1826–Aug17,1892, bur St. John's Cem), m Elizabeth Herb (Dec 12,1829-Jul ,1899). They lived on a farm in Mifflin Twp. in 1860. **Daniel and Elizabeth (Herb) Miller children:** Amanda b c1852; Sarah b c1854; John b c1857; Fiana b c1859.
CATHARINE (no dates), 2nd wife of George Ossman b c1826
ANNA (May 19, 1830 - ____), m Elias Werner b 1823 - ____), lived in Berrysburg in 1860. **Elias and Anna (Miller) Werner children:** Isaac b c1851; Abraham b c1853; Josiah b c1855; Daniel b c1857; George b c1860; John b c1866; Rebecca b c1868.
JOSIAH A. (Nov 28, 1834 – Jun 23, 1889, bur St. Johns Hill Cem), m Mary "Polly" Cooper (Aug 19, 1838 – Apr 16, 1917), a dau of John Cooper. They lived in Mifflin Twp in 1870, had Charles Miller age 11 with them. In Washington Twp in 1880. **Josiah A. and Mary (Cooper) Miller had these children (bapt St. Johns Hill Ch):** Agnes b c1859; Joel Abraham (Aug 11, 1863– Jan 15,1939, bur St. John's Hill Cem),

m Hannah Priscilla Schreffler (Feb 12, 1870 – Oct 21, 1900), a dau of Aaron and Mary Jane Schreffler.
Joel Abraham & Hannah Priscilla (Schreffler) Miller children: <u>Maude Edna</u> (Apr 10, 1887 - 1919), m
Jacob Edwin Hassinger (1892 – 1955); **Mattie Irene** b Sep 15, 1888; **Lula Olera** (Nov 4, 1889 – Dec 13,
1954); **Mary** b 1892;**Loy Aaron** b Dec 6, 1894; **Ralph** 1901;**Ada**; **George "Butch"**;
Amanda Ann (Feb 21, 1865 – 1867); **Henry Wilson** (May 24, 1866 – Nov 12, 1952, bur St. Johns Hill
Cem), m Alice L.__ (Jan13,1867– Apr 12, 1947); **M. Isaac** b Apr 1,1873; **Ida Polly May** b Jan 19, 1875.
JOHN N, moved to Valley View
REBECCA (no dates), m Augustus Lantz of Dalmatia.

HOME OF _____
LOT #27

   Lot #27 was part of the McClure land that was sold to Dr. Beshler. Dr. Beshler conveyed the lot and house
to Isaac Hoke Mar 13, 1885. The lot was bound on the north by and alley, east by lot 28, south to Main Street, west
to lot 26, measured 50 by 165 and contained 8,250 square feet. It was part of the L. S. Ferree plan.

Verna Bruner

Temporary page

[**ISAAC HOKE** (b c1823 - d Sep 1, 1898, Loyalton), a son of _____Hoke, m 1ˢᵗ to Catherine _____
(Nov 25, 1824 – Sep 2, 1874, bur Millers Cem, Powells Valley). In 1850 Isaac and Catherine Hoke lived in
Wash Twp and had Adam Hoke age 50 with them. Isaac was a blacksmith. **Isaac and Catherine (_____)
Hoke had these children: Alfred J** (Nov 1, 1847 – Jan 1, 1934, bur Miller's Cem Powells Valley), m 1ˢᵗ
Sarah A _____ (Feb 12, 1853 – Nov 19, 1889, bur Millers Cem with Alfred). m 2ⁿᵈ Mary _____ (Mar 1,
1852 - May 18, 1907, bur E'ville); **Valentine** (1850 – 1935, bur E'ville), m May 7, 1868 at Salem Ch,
Berrysburg Sarah E. Grimm (1851 – 1927), lived in Jackson Twp in 1880, **had these children:** Harvey b
c1868; Cora A b c1870; Martha M b c1872; Jennie S b c1875; Sallie G b c1878; Lizzie A b c1879; **Charles**
(b & d 1857); **Caroline** of T.C.; **Malinda Agnes** b c1865, m Henry F. Rebuck.
   After Catherine died, Isaac m 2ⁿᵈ on Jan 25, 1877 to Rebecca Moyer Lubold (b Mar 23, 1836 - d Feb
13, 1913, bur E'ville) a dau of Jacob and Rebecca (Ferree) Moyer and widow of Jacob Lubold (b Sep 18,
1837 - d c1873), a son of Samuel and Catharine (Williard) Lubold. In 1880, Isaac and Rebecca lived in
Wash Twp. [**Jacob and Rebecca (Moyer) Lubold had these children: Susan Lubold** m M. A. Miller;
Annie Lubold b c1863, m Harper T. Bressler of Tower City; **Samuel Franklin Lubold** b c1870, moved to
Phila; **William P, & Fred Lubold** both moved to Shamokin; **Jacob A lbert Lubold** b May 10, 1860 of
Millersburg.] Her brothers & Sisters were Susan Moyer (1832 – 1916),   m John Hensel (b Bloomfield,
Perry Co Dec 11, 1824 – d 1912 Lykens, bur IOOF Cem). Susan & John drove to Halifax Mar 1, 1853 to
Meth Episcopal parsonage and were married. **John and Susan (Moyer) Hensel had these children –most
bur IOOF, Lykens): Thomas A** (1853 – 1921); **John Frank** 1854 – 1921); **Rebecca (1855 – 1905), m**
Edw Harris (1854 – 1929); **Jennie** m Richard James; **Chas & Jacob** d young.; **Annie** m _____ Hoke;

Brothers of Rebecca?**James B** Moyer; **Thomas Beaver** Moyer (b Jul 29, 1847 – d Dec 8, 1921), died as a
result of an auto accident. He was walking to the Immanuel Church in Loyalton for prayer meeting on
Wednesday night when he was hit by a car in front of Fred C. Harner's home. The car was coming from
Gratz.   Thomas Moyer m 1ˢᵗ Mary Klinger (Dec 3, 1846 – Jul 4, 1908), **and had these children:** John E.;
Maggie m Isaac M. Henninger, Annie, m Charles Lubold. In 1910, after Mary died, Thomas and Sallie
Grimm were married.
THIS SHOULD GO WITH J LUBOLD P 260, JACOB MOYER OR FERRE FAMILY.
THIS PAGE NOT DONE

JOHN A. LEITZEL
Lot #28

This lot # 28 was part of the McClure land that was sold to Dr. Beshler Apr 14, 1874. On August 28, 1876 Dr. H. C. Beshler conveyed the lot to Charles F. Kauderman and George Wise his son-in-law with buildings. In April 1883 George Wise, (a blacksmith) by then a widower of Gratz conveyed his one-half of the lot to Henry F. Rabuck of Loyalton. The lot was described as being bound on the north by an alley, East by lot 29, south to Main St. and west by the other half of this lot. Charles F. Kauderman conveyed his half of the lot to Isaac Hoke, the deed was recorded in August 1886. After Isaac Hoke died, his widow Rebecca conveyed this lot to Mary L. Lower on April 1, 1901. Mary L. and her husband Charles W. Lower sold this property to Jane P. Row (wife of Alfred C. Row). Newspaper Feb 28, 1901 says A. C. Row purchased Hoke homestead of C. W. Lower.

(deed 4337 p 043 – dated March 2002) says Alfred Row owned this
E-44-205 1959 Alfred H. Row to John A. Leitzel double frame dwelling on lot 28. Reuben Kessler trust to Alfred H. Row 1921.

Maybe photo of Bob Bonawitz & wife etc.

needs help

MICHAEL D. & DEBRA J. CURTIS.
(Lots #29, #30, & #31)

On January 9, 1890, Sheriff William Sheesley sold a number of (Beshler) lots in Loyalton to John D. Snyder. They were owned by Henry C. Beshler, and were part of the plan of lots laid out by L. S. Ferree in 1873, and later sold to Henry C. Beshler. On March 11, 1890, John D. Snyder and Hannah his wife sold two of the lots to David F. Hoffman. They were lots 29 and 30, located along Main Street. David F. and Caroline Hoffman assigned both lots to John K. McGann of Wheatland farm in Jackson Twp, on February 18, 1893, for the sake of their creditors. Several months later on November 14,1893 David F. Hoffman's **lot number 29** was sold to Cornelius Gunderman, but Gunderman moved to Millersburg and on March 16, 1904 he sold to Jonathan Zerbe. Charles A. Hoover was the next owner, and he sold October 2, 1909 to Frederick C. Harner of Loyalton.

Lot number 30 was conveyed to Henry M. Spotts on November 14, 1893. He later moved to Wiconisco Township and on April 26, 1897 Henry M. and Emma L. Spotts sold to Frederick C. Harner.

Frederick C. Harner and his wife Mary A, on April 2, 1923, conveyed the two lots numbered **29 and 30,** along with lot ***number 31** to Harry J. and Annie E. Harper. After Harry J. Harper died in 1943, Annie E. Harper his widow and his daughter Beatrice became owners of lots 29 and 30 (and #31below). Later Annie E Harper became the wife of Fred Markel, and on March 30, 1948 Beatrice (by then married to Robert Bonawitz) granted her one-half interest in the properties to her mother Annie E. Harper Markel. James L and Sharon E. (Bonawitz) Rissinger became the owner of these two lots in 1982, but on July 29, 1993, they conveyed to Michael D. and Debra J. Curtis.

*Lot number 31** was also part of the L. S. Ferree plan, but Sarah M. and William H. Weiss had purchased the land from Amanda Hoke on October 1, 1895. Sarah M and William H. Weiss sold the lot to Frederick C. Harner on June 4, 1900. On April 2, 1923, conveyed the two lots numbered 29 and 30, along with lot **number 31** to Harry J. and Annie E. Harper. After Harry J. Harper died, Annie E. Harper deeded this lot and lots 29 and 30 to herself and her daughter Beatrice on January 31, 1944. Later Annie E Harper became the wife of Fred Markel. On March 30, 1948 Robert and Beatrice Bonawitz granted their one-half interest in the properties to Annie E. Harper Markel. On September 5, 1953 Annie Harper Markel conveyed this lot to her daughter Beatrice and husband Robert Bonawitz. Robert and Beatrice Bonawitz had a new home constructed on this property. On Nov 13, 1986 Robert and Beatrice Bonawitz conveyed the property to Steven R. and Judy (Heim) Meredith. They in turn conveyed to Bradly Schmick on Sep 28, 1998.

[**HARRY J. HARPER** (1899 – 1943, bur Maple Grove Cem, E'ville), a son of George D. Harper m Feb 12, 1921 Annie E. Rowe (1903 – 1981), a dau of John D. and Jennie (Hassinger) Rowe. **Harry J and Annie E (Rowe) Harper** had these children: **Beatrice Arlene** (May 19, 1921 – 1981), m Robert Bonawitz (1918 – 1996), had dau **Sharon** m James Rissinger;After Harry died, his widow Annie m Fred B. Markel (1906 – 1984)]

HENRY F. REBUCK FAMILY

[**HENRY F. REBUCK**(Apr 1860 – 1939, bur St. Peter Cem, Red Cross, Norhtld Co), son of Peter S. and Lydia (Ferster) Rebuck, m Malinda Agnes Hoke (1865 - ____), a dau of Isaac and Catharine Hoke. **Henry F. and Malinda Rebuck** had these children: **Carrie M.** b Feb 1882 m John Walborn; **Dora W.** (Oct 31, 1883 - 1959), m Peter Schwartz; **Katie Agnes** (Nov 1885 – 1946, bur Herndon), m Chas F. Rothermel; **Bertha E** b Nov 1887 m Jacob Stettler; **Elizabeth Ellen** (Mar 21, 1890 – d age 94) m 1st William H. Hoch (1890–1918, bur Himmel Cem), m 2nd John Troutman 1885–1953, bur Himmel Cem); **Harry E** (Jun 1892 - 1976), m Mabel Kahler (1898 – 1980); **Charles P**. b 1895 , m Mary Hoover; **Fred P** (Jul 1897 – 1922), m Edna Kahler; **George Victor** b Sep 1899 –d Dec 1990), m 1925 Edna Kahler Rebuck; **James Wilson** (no dates) m Annie Schreffler; **Beulah** b 1902 m Wilbert Foulds; **Lloyd** (1907 - 1960), m Stella Smeltz.]

STEVE & ANGELA ROMANOFSKY
(Lot # 32 & 33)

These two lots #32 & 33 were from the Sarah M. Weiss addition and are located on the corner of Main and Chestnut Streets containing a 2 ½ story single dwelling. Sarah M and William Weiss conveyed to John Wesley Boyer June 4, 1900. John Wesley Boyer died Mar 9, 1948 and his heirs conveyed to Paul W. Romberger, his grandson, only child of Frances E. Boyer his daughter. She died Apr 8, 1911. Paul W. Romberger and Iva sold this to Jacob and Mary Smeltz on July 13, 1948. While they owned the property, widow Catharine Troutman lived in the small summerhouse on the lot for a brief time. Jacob Smeltz died November 17, 1963, and Mary his widow conveyed the residence to John J. and Carolyn Wiest September 2, 1965.

John J. Wiest conveyed these two lots to Donald E. and Constance J. Matter on September 2, 1966. While they lived here Constance operated a beauty shop in the house. On December 19, 1988, they conveyed the same to Jeffrey L. Seiler and Amy B. Ciccocioppo. On March 27, 1997 Jeffrey L and Amy B. (Ciccocioppo) Seiler conveyed these two lots to Steve J. and Angela M. Romanofsky with 2 ½ story frame house and garage.

The next lots were from the plan laid out by J. G. Romberger, located on the north side of Main Street. Alvin Hoffman purchased the lots, and in 1930, with the help of his brother built three bungalow type new houses. Alvin Hoffman died, and his widow Amanda E. Hoffman sold them.

These Three Similar Houses belong to from left: David & Kathy Reisch, Karen Hoffman, Donald & Arlene (Roadcap) Hoffman.

HOME OF DAVID & KATHY S. REISCH
(North side of Main St. & East corner of Chestnut Street First House lots #10, 9)

Located on the north side of Main Street, is located on the east corner of Chestnut. On March 9, 1946, after Alvin died, Amanda E. Hoffman, widow conveyed the two lots and house to Arthur and Mable (Hoffman) Byerly. Mark Byerly and Anna Byerly (sister & brother) were the next owners. On January 14, 1992, Mark A. Byerly and his sister Anne Troutman, widow conveyed to Mark A. Byerly and his wife Grace R. Byerly. On February 12, 2005, Mark A. and Grace R. Byerly conveyed the two lots to their daughter Kathy S. Reisch and husband David.

HOME OF KAREN HOFFMAN
(Second House lots 8,7,6,5)

Lots from the J. G. Romberger plan, and numbered 8, 7, 6 and 5. Amanda E. Hoffman, widow, conveyed these lots and house to Charles D. and Darlene (Roadcap) Hoffman on March 9, 1946. They lived in this house until his death.. Charles D. Hoffman and Darlene A. his wife on March 23, 1992 conveyed these lots to Donald C. and Arlene F. Hoffman. On February 5, 1996, Donald C. and Arlene F. Hoffman conveyed to Daren Daniel Hoffman their son. These lots are bound by north side of Main Street (Route 209), eastwardly 100 feet to western line of lot # 9, then northward along lot 9 for 165 feet to the eastern line of lot #4, then along #4 southward to Route 209.

HOME OF DONALD C. & ARLENE F. HOFFMAN
(Third House)

This house built by Alvin Hoffman to become a rental property. The first known tenants to live here were Ira & Mary (Troutman) Bonawitz & H. Edward & Ruth Collier. Later, Gilbert & Peg Burrell & Clyde & Mary Forney lived here. When Charles D. and Darlene A. Hoffman owned the house they remodeled it and Donald & Arlene (Roadcap) Hoffman became the owners.

[**Alvin G. Hoffman** (Oct 6, 1875 – Nov 24, 1934), m Amanda or Amelia E. Troutman (b c1890 - d age almost 100), **had these children: Charles D.** b c1903, m Darlene _____ **had these children: Donald C.** m Arlene Roadcap, **had a son** <u>Daren Daniel</u> ,who d 2006, m Karen;; **Foster**, **Mary** m Robert Smeltz.; **Mabel Pauline** b Sep 22, 1908, m Michael Korpa; they lived in 2 of the houses. The 3 a double house was built for income.

**The next properties are located on the south side of Main Street
between Oak Dale Forge Street and Walnut Street.**

THE HARVEY SNYDER STORE
(Lots 67 & 68 Sarah M. Weiss Plan)

The John's Family When They Owned The Store

Amanda Hoke sold these two lots numbers 67 and 68 in 1895 to Sarah Weiss. Her representative Andrew Weiss sold to Wayne B. Johns on March 6, 1902. Wayne Johns was first in business on the northwest corner of Main Street with William Lewis Hoffman. But the two men had a disagreement, and Wayne decided to move to this location. The beautiful building was built here about 1904, and became the W. B. JOHNS GENERAL STORE. About ten years later, Wayne and Emma Johns conveyed these two lots and business to Daniel Helt, and moved to a farm in Matamoras. Their son Howard, a young man helped them on the farm, for several years, and later became a minister. Daniel D. and Adeline Helt conveyed the business to Harvey H. Snyder on April 1, 1920.

The Snyder family continued in the store business for many years. Harvey was also postmaster with post office facilities housed in the store. He employed his son-in-law Clayton A. Bechtel, to run a huckster route four days each week. He first used a horse and wagon to get around the area. Monday and Friday the trip was to Big Run and Coaldale with a few stops in Lykens. Tuesday the route was to the Specktown and Lykens Township area. Thursday the truck went to Armstrong and Small Valley. Eventually a 1937 Chevy panel truck replaced the horse and wagon.

After Harvey died in 1948, his widow sold the two lots with three-story frame dwelling and store July 3, 1948 to daughter Amy and her husband Clayton. They continued in the business.

On June 26, 1951, Clayton became ill while working on the "Specktown Route", came home to the store building, laid on the couch, and died of a heart attack. His son Edward E. Bechtel then quit working in the shoe factory in Millersburg and took over the huckster truck. In the mid-1950s the Chevy was replaced with an International Metro Truck. With the larger truck there was an aisle for people to walk in through the truck and select their own groceries and household items. Area farmers and other folks sold products such as produce, eggs, and other commodities for the store inventory, and some of those items were available on the truck. Meats were stored in a chest cooler, and there was always candy for the kids. At this time the store and post office opened from 7 AM to 8 PM. Amy Bechtel and Melva Sitlinger tended the store. Melva was postmistress from 1940 to 1963, and also employed at the store.

Very Old Photo Giving Westward View Into Loyalton
House On Left Gone, was home of Chas & Mary Lower, later Kenneth & Pauline (Lower) Bain.
Home in distance Was William Boyer, Then Jacob Smeltz.

1924 Sunday School Picnic At "Picnic Woods" in Loyalton
l to r identifiable: Marlin Snyder, Clayton Bechtel & Amy, Jennie Snyder, Harvey
Snyder. Ed. E. Bechtel child in high chair

Many people bought groceries on credit "put it on the book" and then settled up on payday. Most people settled on payday. But during the depression years dozens and dozens of unpaid bills accumulated by customers.

On Friday morning, February 8, 1963 Ed Bechtel did not feel well while on the "Big Run/Coaldale route." He drove home, laid on the couch and passed away the same way his dad Clayton did. He died of a heart attack at the age of 39. The truck was sold and that was the end of the huckster route. The store remained open until September 6, 1969 when it closed due to Amy's advancing age. The post office was moved two houses to the east but Loyalton Post Office closed permanently in September 1971. The town was served by rural delivery. This building became an apartment complex in 1975. For several years the third floor was used for Lodge meetings, plays, and other community activities.

Snyder Store – left - Melva Sitlinger, postmistress, Harvey and Jennie D. (Miller) Snyder - 1947

Clayton A. Bechtel with horses, Harvey A. Snyder at rear of wagon

Mr. & Mrs. Harvey Snyder

THE GEORGE SNYDER FAMILY
(Some information from Robert G. Fisher's publication & Evelyn Hartman)

[**GEORGE SNYDER** (b c1734 in Ger. -d c1832, supposedly aged about 100 years). He m Anna Elizabeth Riegel (Apr1,1738 –d supposedly post-1823 in Ohio). Her parents George Wilhelm and Anna Maria (Plattner) Riegel settled first in Tulpehocken area of Berks Co. and were married there Jan 12,1736 in Tulpehocken Church. George and Anna Elizabeth Snyder came to the Armstrong Valley in Dauphin County. In 1798 he was listed as a resident owning a one-story wooden house with three windows, and 24 lights (panes). The house measured 24 by 24 fee on two acres of cleared land. He also had an 11 by 11 foot shop. His tract totaling 193 acres of land adjoined Berry's Mountain. A nearby neighbor was Stophel Sheesley. **George and Anna (Riegel) Snyder had a son**: GEORGE (b c1755 – d 1845 in Jackson Twp), m Sep 29, 1778 in Cocalico Ref Ch, Ephrata Twp., Lanc Co to Catherine Ammon (no dates), a dau of Philip and Maria Magdalena Ammon. **George and Catherine (Ammon) Snyder had these children:**
WILLIAM (Jun 9, 1779 Berks Co – Sep 23, 1852 Centerview, Jackson Twp), m Anna Elizabeth Deibler (Oct 26, 1784 – Jan 7, 1852, Jackson Twp), a dau of George and Anna Elizabeth (Clingman) Deibler; **JACOB** (1781–1861), m Margaret Bender (1781–1865); **GEORGE** (c1782–1815); **JOHN, SR.** (Aug 10, 1798– Dec 8,1873, bur Salem Old Stone Cem, E'ville), m Sarah Zimmerman (Jul 4,1805–May 10,1871), a dau of Christian B. and Anna Margaretha (Miller) Zimmerman. They lived in Jackson Twp. **John & Sarah (Zimmeroan) Snyder children: Catharine** b Jun 3,1822; **Nicholas** (1824 –May 15, 1891, bur Old Stone Cem)), m Susanna McCully (1832 -1861); **Margaret** b Jul 4,1827; ***James** (1830–1903) see below: **William** b1837, m Catharine _____ ; **Sarah Ann** (Aug 22,1840 –Mar 20,1881, bur Old Stone Cem), m Joseph Boyer.

[***JAMES SNYDER** (Feb 20, 1830 – Jun 14, 1903, bur Maple Grove Cem, E'ville), a son of John and Sarah Snyder above, m Apr 25, 1852 Lydia McCully (Aug 21,1834–Feb 14,1908), a dau of Robert & Anna Catharine (Lubold) McCully. They lived in Jackson Twp in 1880, and he was a farmer. James was a Civil War vet; later hotel keeper when he owned the "Mountain House." **James and Lydia (McCully) Snyder known children;**
CATHARINE A. (Apr 25, 1853 – Jan 26, 1909, bur Maple Grove Cem), m **Daniel David Helt** b Oct 14, 1857–Mar 20, 1937), a son of Harry and Sarah Helt.
CHARLES (Jul 1855 –1918), m Sarah E. Hoffner;
ISABELLE (Oct 10,1858 –1919), m Simon Dietrich
SUSAN (Dec 2, 1861–1901), m John Hoffner ;
HARVEY H. (May 30, 1868 – Jan 6, 1948, bur Maple Grove Cem., E'ville), m Dec 24, 1892 Jennie Dorcia Miller (Mar 2,1874–1953), a dau of Michael N. and Catherine (Snyder) Miller of Jackson Twp. .
Harvey and Jennie (Miller) Snyder had these children:
Amy Estella (Jun 30, 1893 – Jan 23, 1975, bur Maple Grove Cem), m Clayton A. Bechtel (Apr 11, 1893 – Jun 26, 1951). **Clayton A. and Amy E (Snyder) Bechtel had these children:**
Kathryn Elmira b Aug 11, 1915, m William Robert Williard b 1910, a son of William Burton and Mary Elverida (Frantz) Williard.
Edward E. (Jul 30, 1923 – Feb 8, 1963, bur Maple Grove Cem), a WWII Veteran;
Orpha Alva (b Dec 10, 1896 Jackson Twp – d Jul 16, 1957, bur Fairview Cem, Enders). m Joel Elsi Enders (b Nov 25, 1883 Fisherville – d 1963). Joel was a railroad freight handler.
Iva J. (1898 – 1979, bur Maple Grove), m Paul W. Romberger (1900 - 1972), a son of Elmer Wesley and Frances E. (Boyer) Romberger. Had son Robert Elmer b Sep 19, 1924, m Gloria Nelson
Nellie Catharine b & d Apr 1903
J. Marlin (1905 – 1959, bur Maple Grove Cem) m Mary Snyder (1907 – 1978)
Leona Miriam (Jul 22, 1907 – Aug 23,1988, bur Maple Grove Cem), m Floyd Benj. Harner (Jul 18, 1904 Oct 27, 1961), a son of Frederick Charles and Hattie Persillia (Shadle) Harner;]

THE BECHTEL (BAGDEL) etc FAMILY

[The earliest known ancestor of the Bechtel family is **JOHN BURKHART BECHTEL** (no dates) of East Nantmeal Township Chester County, Pa. **John Burkhart Bechtel married Gertrude Reifschneider (no dates) had these children:**

*CATHERINE BECHTEL (Feb 28, 1755 - 1826, no tombstone found), m 1773 John Martin Lubolt (Nov 5, 1727 - Feb 7, 1810, bur St. John's "Hill" Cem), eldest son of Johannes Lupold. [More information with Lupold/Lubold genealogy.]

*JOHN GEORGE BECHTEL (c1762 - spring of 1811 Up Pax Twp, bur St. Johns "Hill" Cem), m c1786 Anna Maria _____ (Oct 19, 1754 Chester Co - d Feb 25, 1832), lived in Wiconisco Twp. **John George and Anna Maria (___) Bechtel had eight children (some bapt St. Johns Ch, Berrysburg and Hoffman Ch):**

**Maria Catharine Bechtel (b Jun 17, 1787 bapt Zion "Klinger's Ch– d Aug 6, 1869, bur Salem Luth, E'ville), was probably never married. In 1850 Catharine Bechtel age 62, said to be blind, lived with Mary Doughtery age 40 and her family. The 1860 census shows Catharine Bechtel, 73, spinster living in the home of Solomon Rudisil 28, Annie E.24, Oscar A 1.

Johan Burchard Bechtel –eldest son (Mar 14, 1792 - May 24, 1853 of palsy & dropsy, bur Salem Cem, E'ville), m Anne Catherine Albright (b May 16,1798 Up Pax Twp –d Mar 14, 1855), a dau of Johann Henry and Catherine Elizabeth (Schoh) Albright/Albrecht. **John Burghart & Catherine (Albright) Bechtel had these children, bapt St. Johns:

***Catharine b c1815 Wash Twp, m Jonathan Lebo

***John (May 30, 1816 - Jan 11, 1873 bur Salem Luth Cem, E'ville), m Elizabeth _____ (Dec 25, 1810 - Sep 3, 1889), lived in Jackson Twp in 1850, by 1870 in Wash. Twp. **John and Elizabeth ( ) Bechtel had these children:** Samuel b c1838, m 1ˢᵗ Aug 1, 1861 Hannah Snyder (Nov 1, 1843-Nov 28, 1879, bur Salem Luth Cem E'ville);**Elmira** b c1841;**William** b c1845; **Sarah Ann** b c1850, m ___ Lehman; **Isabella** b 1858.

Probably *****Elias** (Jul 12, 1817 - 1872, bur Old Stone Cem, E'ville, m Rebecca _____

***George (Mar 26, 1819 - Apr 11, 1861,bur Salem Luth, E'ville), m Christiana Smith (Sep 13, 1823 - Oct 29, 1874, bur Old Stone Cem, E'ville), a dau of Johannes and Anna Maria (Koppenhaver) Smith. George and Christiana lived in Wic.Twp in 1850 and beside their children, Jonathan Harman age 17 lived with them. They lived in Wash. Twp in 1860, and he was a farmer. **George and Christiana (Smith) Bechtel had these children:**

Thomas b c1841, m Kate Bistline and lived at Newport;

Mary b c1842;

Simon b c1843, m Rebecca ___ b c1850, lived in Wash. Twp in 1880. Simon's occupation was listed as "gathering bones.**" Simon and Rebecca Bechtel children:** *Harry A* b c1870, listed in 1880 as "picking bones"; *Christina* b c1874;

Henry (b Nov1, 1845 – d Jun 29,1908, bur Seyberts Cem, Williamstown), m Amanda Rowe (Feb 27, 1847 – Apr 21,1923), a dau of Jacob and Susannah Rowe. They lived near Fisherville, he was a plasterer. In 1880 they lived in Williamstown and he worked in the mines. They had Catharine Hain 56, listed as servant with them. **Henry and Amanda Bechtel had these children:** *Bella* b c1873, m John Russell; *Chas E* (c1876 – d Oct 28, 1932), m Elizabeth Kauffman; *George J.*b Sep1879 moved to Gary Indiana;

Elias (Jul 12, 1847 – Sep 14, 1872), m Rebecca b c1848 (both bur Salem Luth, E'ville). After Elias died Rebecca m John Helt.

Ann Elisa b Mar 24, 1849, bur Salem Luth, E'ville;

John Adam (b Nov 13, 1854 – d Sep 26, 1912, bur Maple Grove Cem), m 1872 Amanda Dubendorf (Apr 23, 1850 – Sep 14, 1935), a dau of Samuel and Lydia Margaret Radel Dubendorf of Mifflin Twp. John Adam was employed by Swab Wagon Company in the blacksmith shop. When he died the Swab employees collected $ 18.00 to be dispersed as follows: $10.75 floral offering and expressage, $6.00 for digging grave, balance to go to the family. **John Adam and Amanda (Dubendorf) Bechtel had these children:** Ella (1885 – 1956, bur Maple Grove Cem, E'ville) m Charles Hummel (1883 - 1958); Estella May b Mar 14, 1888;

Joseph Franklin b Nov 12, 1858, lived in Harrisburg in 1912;

Christina (1861 – 1863, bur E'ville);

Manerery (female) b c1868; **Katie** b c1875;

***Jacob (Dec 2, 1820 - Aug 17, 1888), m Catherine Michael (Jun 8, 1821 - Dec 24, 1864), a dau of William and Barbara Michael. **Jacob and Catherine (Michael) Bechtel had these children:** *Sarah* (b Apr 25, 1841 – d Jun 19, 1925), m 1ˢᵗ Philip Warfel, after his death m Nathan Enders (1848 – 1913, bur Enders); *John* (1843 – 1859); *Aaron* b1847 moved to Kansas; *William* (b c1848 – Jan 8, 1917), m Emma Warfield b 1858, lived in Washington Twp. William was a stone mason; *Harvey* b c1850; *Edward* b c1852; *Rebecca* b 1853; *James* (1854 – Jul 9, 1920 of a mining accident), m Elmira Travitz (1857 – 1918, bur Greenwood Cem, Tower City). **James and Elmira (Travitz) Bechtel had these children:** *Frank W.* (1875 – 1934), m Maggie Klein (1876 – 1934); *John* 1878 – 1948, m 1ˢᵗ Stella ___, 2ⁿᵈ Jennie Wren; *Edward* (1881

– 1908, killed in mines), m Edna Hornish; *Ralph* (1885 – 1904, killed in mines); *Carrie* b c1891, m Noah Adams; *Clayton A.* (1893 – 1951, bur Maple Grove Cem, E'ville), m Amy E. Snyder b 1893;Ray b Nov 2, 1895 m Rebecca Thompson of Sheridan; *Isaac & Isabella* b c1856; *Peter* b c1857; *Catherine* (1859 – 1943), m Andrew Fox; *Amos* b c1861; *Philip* b c1862. Jacob Bechtel m 2nd Elizabeth Eby.

*****Elizabeth** (b Dec 20, 1822 Wash Twp. – d Jun 7, 1878, bur Old Stone Cem, E'ville), m Jonathan Lebo (Nov 10, 1817 – Oct 20, 1868), a son of Johannes and Justina (Lenker) Lebo of Wash Twp. **Jonathan and Elizabeth (Bechtel) Lebo children;** **Eliza** b c1841; **Catherine** (Feb 24, 1843 – Aug 2, 1919), m William C. Blaine (Aug 11, 1840 – Dec 1896); **Emeline** (Oct 14, 1844 – Jan 6, 1929, bur Oakdale Cem, Wash Twp), m Daniel A. Klinger (Jan 12, 1834 – Jan 13, 1908), a son of Alexander and Magdalena (Smeltz) Klinger of Washington Twp.; **Isaac** b Jul 16, 1846; **Priscilla** b Apr 9, 1848; **Jonathan** b 1849; **Sarah Ellen** b Aug 25, 1851; **Simon Peter** (May 1,1854 –Jun 12, 1918, bur Maple Grove Cem, E'ville), m Sarah Jane Cooper (Oct 16, 1854 – Nov 28, 1927), a dau of Amos and Mary Cooper. **Mary Frances** b Jul 29, 1858;

*****Simon** (Feb 19, 1825 – Nov 4, 1884, bur Old Stone Cem, E'ville), m Sep 28, 1845 to Anna Susannah Lusethe Messner (Sep13, 1828 – Mar 30, 1883), a dau of Philip Jacob and Mary Magdalena (__) Messner. **Simon and Anna Susanna (Messner) Bechtel children:** **Isaac** (Jan 2,1846 –Sep17, 1860, bur Old Stone Cem, E'ville); **Daniel** (Mar 30,1850–Mar 27,1864, bur Old Stone Cem); **Sarah** (Aug 25,1852–Feb 4, 1865, bur Old Stone Cem); **Mary A.** (May 26, 1856 – Nov 13, 1865, bur Old Stone Cem); **Alfred** (Feb 3, 1859 – Dec 31, 1924, bur Maple Grove Cem, E'ville), m Feb 25, 1882 Clara R. Wilbert (Oct 7, 1863 – Apr 6, 1928), a dau of Philip and Catharina (Matter) Wilbert of Wash Twp. **Alfred and Clara (Wilbert) Bechtel children:** *Homer C.* (1883 – 1950), m Annie Williard; *Clayton S.* (1884 – 1926, bur Maple Grove Cem, E'ville), m Margaret Harman (1892 – 1943). Clayton S. and Margaret (Harman) Bechtel had these children: Raymond Clayton; Harold Homer; Velva m ___ Fisher; Mary m ___Kieffer; Elva (1912 – 1939); Elma m ___Troutman; *Isaac D* (1886 – 1949); *Edwin C* (1891 – 1956, bur E;ville), m Hilda Moyer (1897 – 1969). He was a vet of WWI and a teacher; *Mary C* b 1893; *Ellen L* b1894, m Harold L. Romberger, a son of Daniel W. Romberger; *Eva S* b 1897, m Walter Schwalm (1897–1942); *Ira A* b Jan 9, 1900, m Mary W. Strawser; **Malinda** (May 6,1862 –Feb 21, 1937, bur Maple Grove Cem), m Aaron Shoop (May 3, 1855 – Jan 2,1931), a son of Daniel and Catherine (Enders) Shoop); **Nathaniel** (Jul 16,1865 – Nov 22, 1920, Reinerton, Sch Co), m 1st Sarah Elisabeth Kolva a dau of Jacob and Fannie (Schoffstall) Kolva). 2nd ____ Evitts; **Abraham** (Aug 8,1867 – Dec 26, 1924), m Katharine Shoop (1868 – 1952); **Kate** (Nov 12, 1869 – Jun 1, 1927, bur Maple Grove Cem, E'ville), m 1st 1887 John Shadle (Nov 27, 1867 – Jun 26, 1894, killed by electricity). She m 2nd Jun 26,1897, to Robert Bowerman (1862–1952), bur beside him.

*****Isaac** (Dec 11, 1827 – Apr 12, 1891, bur St. Jacob Cm), m Magdalena H _____ (Jun 11, 1829 – Dec 19,1887). They lived in Halifax Twp in 1880 and had Sarah E. Sheetz age 21, and Albert Faber 16 listed as servants living with them. **They had these children**: John O. b c1859;

****Elizabeth** b c1794 – (a son of Elizabeth Bechtel – David McElcar (May 27, 1822 – Nov 3, 1841, bur St. Johns Luth Bbg may be her son).

****Mary 1** b c1796 - was over 14 years of age when father died

****Magdalena** (b Nov 16 or 19, 1797, bapt Hoffman Ch – d Feb 16, 1871, bur Hoffman Cem), m c1816 William Lettich/ Ledich (Dec 17, 1792 – Oct 17, 1871). In 1860, William and Magdalena lived in Wash, Twp. Their widowed daughter Magdalena John and her young son Henry lived with them. **William and Magdalena (Bechtel) Lettich had these children (some bapt Hoffman, some St. Johns (Hill) Ch:** probably *****Jacob** b c 1815, m Catherine ____ b c1828, lived in Washington Twp. I n 1850, had a son Peter b c1849, and Eliza Bechtel age 14 lived with them;

*****Peter** (Jun 15, 1817 – 1877, Henry Co, Ohio, bur Union Cem, Napoleon Twp), m Catharine Harmon (b c1813, Dau Co – d Apr 1875), a dau of Simon and Susannah (Harmon) Matter of Ashland Co., Ohio. In 1860 Peter and Catharine lived in Freedom Twp, Napoleon Co., Ohio. Their son Simon 16, Sarah A. Shindel 20 lived as a domestic, and George Lettich age 30 lived with them. Simon m Della McDaniels

*** **Elizabeth** (Nov 9,1818 – Dec 12, 1886, bur Motters Cem, Wash Twp), m Dec 6, 1836, Jacob Matter (Jul 2, 1813 – Feb 12, 1875), a son of John Michael and Anna Maria (Romberger) Matter. They lived in Washington Twp in 1860, and he was a farmer. Elizabeth Shoop age 18 lived with them. **Elizabeth and Jacob Matter children: Ann Mary** b Aug 1,1837; **Emanuel T.**(Oct 18, 1839 – Oct 30, 1895, bur Wmstown Cem, Dau Co.), m Josephine _____. He was a Civil War Vet; **Elizabeth** (Sep 25, 1841 – Oct 17, 1926, bur Maple Grove Cem), m c1859 Joel Shoop (Jan 13, 1835 – Oct 20, 1903); **Catharina** (Feb 3, 1843 – Apr 8, 1904, bur St. Johns (Hill) Cem, Bbg), m Jun 26, 1859 Joseph Enterline (Sep 15, 1838 – Apr 9,

1894), a son of John K. and Lovina (Groff/Grove) Enterline; <u>Cornelius</u> (Sep 15, 1844 – Dec 21, 1871), Civil War Vet; <u>William</u> b May 28, 1846; <u>Adaline</u> (Sep 4, 1847 – Mar 12, 1864, bur Motter Cem, Wash Twp), m Emanuel M. Wetzel; <u>Henry Jacob</u> (Feb 26, 1849 – Feb 23, 1865, bur Motters Cem; <u>Isaiah Elmer</u> (Dec 22, 1851 – Feb 21, 1926 d Eldred Twp, Sch Co, bur Maple Grove Cem, E'ville), m Apr 2, 1871 Emma Catherine Forney (May 14, 1851 – Aug 1, 1906), a dau of John F. and Susanna (Lenker) Forney. Isaiah m 2nd after 1906, Annie M.Peters Comfort, who d May 20,1938. <u>Mary</u> <u>Magdalena</u> (Apr 21, 1853 – Mar 18, 1887, bur Motter Cem, Wash Twp), m Oct 16, 1873 U.B. Parsonage, Lykens to Phillip Heller (Dec 12, 1852 – Mar 19, 1945, bur Maple Grove Cem. at the age of c93 years), a son of Thomas and Elisabeth (Matter) Heller; <u>Sarah Jane</u> (b & d 1855, bur Motters Cem); <u>James Peter</u> (1856 – 1 857, bur Motter Cem); <u>Thomas Milton</u> b May 2, 1858, m Fietta _____.

***<u>Johannes</u> (Apr 22,1820 –Mar 30,1893, Cass Twp, Webster City, Hamilton Co, Iowa), m Apr 4, 1844 Elizabeth Miller (Feb 14, 1817–Apr 27,1897, bur St. Jacob's (Miller's) Cem, Jackson Twp, Dau Co), a dau of Johannes and Anna Catharine (Seiler) Miller. John and Elizabeth Ledich lived in Washington Twp in 1850, and **had these children**: <u>Mary</u> (Aug 15, 1844 – Sep 19, 1875, bur Long's Cem, Halifax), m Benjamin F. Eisenhower (Feb 15, 1843 – Aug 3, 1874), a son of Benjamin and Mary Magdalena (Chubb) Eisenhower; <u>Katharine</u> b c1846, m ___ Sweigard; <u>John</u> <u>Edward</u> b c1850, m C. E. Fetterhoff (1851 – 1872, bur Longs Cem, Halifax). Johannes Lettich moved to Dubuque Co, Iowa about 1855, purchased land, had a blacksmith shop. He m 2nd Aug 26, 1855 in Dubuque, Iowa, J. Ellen Kephart (1823 Bellefonte, Pa,- Oct 23, 1869 in Iowa). **Johannes and J. Ellen (Kephart) Lettich children**: <u>Henry</u>; <u>Nettie</u>; <u>Daniel W.</u> Johannes Lettich m 3rd Apr1,1877 Elizabeth McIntosh b in England, had no children. John Lettich was a Civil War Vet.
***<u>Salome Sarah</u> (Oct 25, 1822 – Jul 8, 1877, bur Motter Cem), m Dec 6, 1836, Joseph Keen (Jul 4, 1814/1815 – d Mar 28, 1900), a son of Henry and Nancy Keen. **Salome and Joseph Keen children**: Daniel b c1842, was a carpenter, and lived with his parents in 1860; <u>Frank</u>; <u>Henry</u>; <u>Joseph</u> b c1844, was an apprentice carpenter and lived with his parents in 1860; <u>William</u> b c1848; <u>Sarah</u> <u>Ann</u> (Oct 17,1849 –Dec 7, 1907, bur Motter Cem), m Oct 3, 1865, Michael Matter (Apr 28, 1842 – Dec 4, 1912 , Hillsboro, Highland Co, Ohio, bur Motter Cem (stone has no dates), son of Christopher and Catharine (Lenker) Matter. He was a Civil War Vet; <u>Edward F.</u> b c1850. In 1880 Joseph Keen, widower, lived with his dau Sarah.
***<u>Magdalena</u> (Aug 9, 1823 – May 3, 1891, bur Hoffman Cem), m Feb18, 1858 in Dau Co to Henry John (b Rheinbaiern, Europe – d between 1858 and 1860). She lived with her parents in 1860,recorded as a widow. **Magdalena and Henry John had a son bapt St. John's (Hill) Ch**: <u>Heinrich Louis</u> b Dec 10, 1858. Henry John apparently died, and Magdalena m Feb 11, 1864 Balthaser Matter (Mar 8,1798 – Aug 30, 1868, bur St. John's (Hill) Cem), a son of Johannes Jacob and Catharine (Bitterman) Matter. **Magdalena & Balthaser Matter had a son <u>Balthaser Lettich Matter</u>** (Apr 22,1864, bapt St. Johns Ch - Aug 4, 1949, bur St. John's (Hill) Cem), m c1887 Sarah Priscilla Lubold (Feb 10,1869 –Jan 14,1955), a dau of Aaron Adam & Sarah (Rogers) Lubold. Magdalena (Lettich Johannes) Matter m 3rd (after 1868), Peter Daniel Batdorf (Jan 20, 1814 – Dec 5, 1880, bur Hoffman's Ch Cem), a son of Peter and Maria Catherine (Steiner) Batdorf.
***<u>Jacob</u> (Oct 18, 1825 – May 27, 1910, bur Colemans Ch Cem Lyk Twp), m Catharine Burger (Jul 31, 1828 – May 17, 1910). **Jacob and Catharine (Burger) Bechtel children**: <u>Amanda</u> (no dates), m ___ Reed, lived in Delaware; <u>Daniel</u> (no dates) lived in Lykens; <u>Ellen</u> (no dates) m Frank Klinger of Spring Glen; <u>John Henry</u> (Jun 11, 1859 – Aug 8, 1931, bur Fearnot Cem), m Jun 9, 1878 Sevilla Carl (Jun 15,1858 - Jul 11, 1935), a dau of Jacob and Polly Carl. **John Henry and Sevilla (Carl) Lettich children**: <u>Jane</u> (no dates) m William Harner of Tremont; _____ m Lloyd Poffenberger of Tower City; Charles N (Jan 1888 – Nov 13, 1940 killed in mines); <u>William Harrison</u> (Sep 19, 1894 - Apr 21, 1932), killed in mines, m _____, **had these children**: *Elsie*; *Marvin*; *Leonard*; <u>Catharine</u> (b Mar 17, 1853 Low Mahantango Twp Sch Co - d _____) m Samuel Gunderman (1842 - 1916), lived in Millersburg [more information with Gunderman family];<u>Lena</u>; <u>Mary</u>; <u>Sally</u>; <u>Hiram T.</u>
***<u>William</u> (Sep 1827 - ____), m Mary A. Wagner (Sep 14, 1829 – Oct 12, 1902, bur Mt. Zion, Pa.
***<u>Catharine</u> (May 1, 1829 – Mar 19, 1896, bur Coleman Cem, Lyk Twp) m Jacob Koppenhaver (Sep 2, 1825–Jun 21,1887), a son of John Jacob and Anna Maria (Rebuck) Koppenhaver. [see Koppenhaver gen.]
***<u>George</u> (b c 1830 – d Jun 28, 1864, Freedom Twp, Henry Co, Ohio)
***<u>Anna Maria</u> (b Jul 8, 1832 – d Feb 24, 1905, bur Zion (Klinger's) Cem, Lyk Twp), m Jacob W. Tobias (Feb 4, 1833 – Jan 2, 1889), a son of Joseph and Anna Mary "Polly" Wiest. **Jacob W. and Anna Maria (Lettich) Tobias children**: <u>Polly</u>; <u>Alice</u>; <u>Maggie</u>; <u>William</u>; <u>Joseph</u>. Anna Maria m 2nd Charles Wetzel.
***<u>Benjamin</u> b c1838

***Amanda** (Dec 18, 1840 – Aug 19, 1890, bur David's Cem, Hebe, Jordan Twp, Northld Co), m Henry W. Deppen (Sep 16, 1833 – Oct   20, 1902), a son of Abraham and Barbara (Wiest) Deppen.
****Johan George Bechtel** b Feb 18, 1804 bapt Hoffman Ch – was a minor child when father died.
***JOHN BECHTEL** (   ), m Barbara _____ . **John and Barbara (   ) Bechtel children;**
****JOHN GEORGE** b Jun 1, 1787, bapt Zion (Klingers Ch)
***PHILIP BECHTEL** (   ) m Magdalena - **had these child bapt St. Johns Ch**: Johan Jacob b May 31, 1785. **Philip and Maria Catharine Bechtel** had Johannes b ___5, 1791 bapt St. Johns]

Old Photo - Looking Westward On Main St., 1st House On The Left Was Home Of Paul Bruner, 2nd House Melvin Riegel, & the church. On The Right, 1st Building Is The "Band Hall."

GENE B, WOLFGANG & DENNIS M. GATLING
(Lot # 69 & 70)

This 7500 square foot lot was owned by George W. and Kate Kessler. On April 2, 1910 they sold it to Alfred H. Rowe. On March 2, 1922, Alfred H. Rowe conveyed the lot to Michael M. Piltz, and he maintained a two-story concrete block and frame garage and dwelling. After Piltz had the garage it became known as the Inch Garage. On May 11, 1928 Michael M and Sadie Irene Piltz conveyed the lot to Lottie M. Zerbe. Two other brief owners were John Romberger and Norm Eshelman. By 1932 William L. Gaugler owned the lot and Harry and Loretta Gaugler Collier conducted a "tea room" and restaurant in the building. A jukebox provided music for dancing. On April 24, 1964, Dora D. Gaugler conveyed these premises to Arthur L. and Shirley L. Klouser. Arthur hung his barber pole in front of the building and for many years it became his barbershop. Shirley Klouser died March 12, 1977 and on September 25, 1992, Arthur L. Klouser conveyed to Gene B. Wolfgang and Dennis M. Gatling. The building is now an apartment complex.

THE GAUGLER FAMILY

[The GAUGLER, etc family settled very early near Trappe, Montg Co., then Berks Co, but some descendants later migrated to Snyder Co. **JACKSON W. GAUGLER** b c1825, m Lydia ____ b c1827, lived in Selingrove, Snyder Co. in 1880. **They are the parents of: Adda** b c1857, a music teacher in 1880, **Libbie L** b c1860; **Kertz E** b c1862; **Newton C.** (Feb 28, 1863 – Mar 12, 1901, bur Maple Grove Cem).

Byran R. & Heather R. Huff 66-016-063

Marcella A. Walborn 66-016-066

Larry E. & and Karan K. Conley 66 016 062

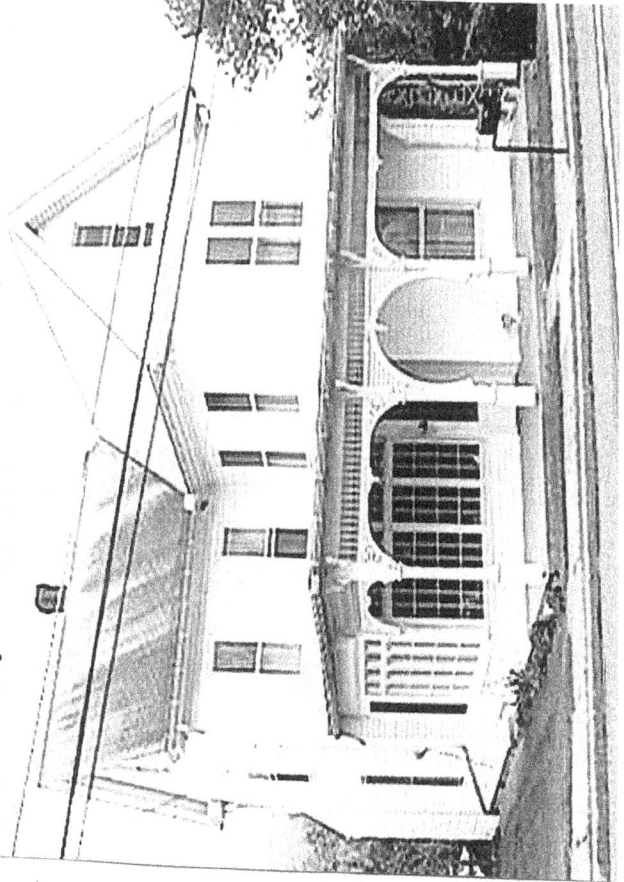

Galen & Margaret Kiester Paul 66-016-064

Franklin b c1867; **Dessie A.** b c1869; **Charles** b c1873.
Jackson W. Gaugler may also be the parent of **Henry S.** (May 19, 1849 - Jan 29, 1914, bur Maple Grove Cem, E'ville), m Emich ___ Jul 22, 1848- May 30, 1908). **Henry & Emich Gaugler were the parents of William L.** (1879 -1964, bur Maple Grove Cem), m Dora D. _____(1879 -1966), **William L. and Dora D. Gaugler had these children (some bapt Salem Ref., E'ville):** Lauretta Luella (Nov 26, 1905 -1983, bur Maple Grove Cem), m Harry W. Collier (1896 -1964); Elva Mattis b Apr 3, 1908, m Charles L. Williams, **had these children (bapt Zion Luth. Lykens):** Lauretta Margaret Lower b Jan 16, 1931; George Lamar Lower b Dec 1,1932; Kenneth Donald b Jul 30, 1939.

THE PILTZ FAMILY

[**MICHAEL M. PILTZ** (no dates) m Sadie Irene _____
Lula m Henry Seidel had a son Otto Henry b Mar 11, 1888
Edward Piltz m Oct 15, 1887 Anna A. Yentsch, a dau of August Yentsch, **had these children**: Chas Edward b Apr 29, 1888; **Martha Emma** b Jan 18, 1890; **Wm August** b Oct 25, 1891; **Leana Christian** b Jan 20, 1893, m Sam Kolva; **Edward Harman** b Aug 20, 1894; **Margaret Emma** b Jan 8, 1896, m Nov 4, 1916 Chas R. Etzweiler; **Abby Katie** b Mar 2, 1899, m Apr 12, 1918 Samuel E. Long; **Howard Henry** b Apr 29, 1901; Helen Irene b Mar 28, 1903; **Frederick Joseph** b Mar 7, 1906;

HOME OF BRYAN R. BRUNER & HEATHER R. HUFF
(WAS HOME OF PAUL "SILAS" TROUTMAN Lot #71)

This 7500 square foot lot belonged to George W. and Katie Kessler. On Apr 2, 1910 George W. Kessler sold to Alfred H. Rowe, and he conveyed to Washington Camp 454 P O S Of A on Aug 16, 1920. On Apr 27, 1922 Jonathan Zerbe purchased it and he conveyed to Melva Sitlinger Aug 29, 1940. Melva Sitlinger was Loyalton's post mistress for many years (located in Snyder's, and later Bechtel's Store), and lived in an apartment in the store building. But when she purchased this lot, "Shmuck" Forney of Berrysburg built her a house. Melva and her daughter Lucy with husband Paul "Silas" Troutman lived here. The post office was eventually moved to this location, and a craft shop opened in the house. After Melva retired, Lucy became the postmistress for a short time until it closed in the 1960s. Loyalton has become an R. D. Lykens address. Melva Sitlinger died April 10, 1985, and on August 30, 1985 Lucy H. and Paul W. Troutman became the owners. On March 18, 1987, Scott A. Klouser purchased the home, but on March 11, 1994 sold to Todd E. and Eileen M. Taylor. On April 27, 1994, they conveyed these premises to Bryan R. Bruner and Heather R. Huff, the present owners.

L to R: Immanuel Church, Homes of Margaret Kiester Paul and Bruner/Huff

HOME OF MARGARET KIESTER PAUL
(Lot #72 & 73)

These two lots were part of the plan of Sarah Weiss. She sold September 18, 1900 to Elmer W. Romberger. Elmer was an active member of the church and community. His first wife was a daughter of Wesley Boyer. When she died young, Elmer married Bertha Zerbe. She had been the Superintendent for Red Lion School District. Bertha's brother Walter owned the Lykens Mercantile, and Elmer became associated with him. Elmer also owned the farm north of Loyalton now owned by the Bush family. He died on this farm while hunting pheasants. Two ring necks were found on the ground nearby him.

On Jun 4, 1943, after Elmer W. Romberger died, his son Paul W. Romberger sold lots 72 & 73 to the trustees (William E. Matter, Paul Johns, John Sleighter, Marlin Shoop, and Mark E. Klinger) of Immanuel Evangelical Church for a parsonage. The house was later purchased by Galen and Margaret Kiester Paul, and they are the present owners.

IMMANUEL CHURCH

Information for this lot and the church is detailed in another section of the Loyalton history.

This next portion includes the properties located between Walnut and Water Street on the south side of the street.

KENNETH LEE HOFFMAN)
(Lot "E")

This lot known as lot "E" contains 7500 square feet and was part of the Amanda Hoke tract. She sold to Sarah Weiss. On February 4, 1898 the land was laid out as the Sarah A. Weiss addition and on March 11, 1898 Sarah Weiss conveyed the property to Wayne B. and Emma L. Johns, They sold to Francis Gunderman. On June 20,1933 Francis Gunderman died and his widow Mary E. Gunderman sold to Melvin K. and Minnie Riegel on April 14, 1941. It was described as being located on the Southeast corner of Main and Walnut Street. On Dec 31, 1968, Minnie Riegel widow of Melvin, conveyed this property to Ronald H. and Barbara Ann Barge. On December 30, 1981, they conveyed to Kurt H. and Susan A. Rutzmoser, who in turn conveyed to Kenneth Lee and Debra Lee Hoffman On June 27, 1984. Kenneth Lee Hoffman became sole owner on July 30, 1988.

[*MELVIN K. RIEGEL* (1915 – 1960, bur Maple Grove Cem, E'ville), m Minnie M. Smeltz (1914 – 1993), a dau of Jacob and Mary Smeltz of Lykens Twp. *Melvin K. and Minnie (Smeltz) Riegel had these children*: *Carolyn* b Sep 18, 1934; *Palmer* b 1935. *More information in Riegel genealogy*.]

HOME OF MARCELLA A. WALBORN   66-016-066 & 067

These two lots "D" & "C" have a similar background and eventually were owned by the same persons. Both lots were part of the Sarah Weiss survey of February 1898. Sarah and William Weiss sold lot "C" to John D. Rowe on March 11, 1898. He had a house built on the land in 1902, but he and his wife Jennie sold to Adam D. Rowe on September 27, 1909. Sarah Weiss conveyed lot "D" to Adam D. Rowe on September 27, 1909, giving him a total of 15,000 square feet. He was a shoe repairman while he lived here. On April 20, 1927, Adam D. Rowe conveyed lot "C" with 50 feet frontage along Main Street to Paul A. Bruner. He conveyed lot "D" to John D. Rowe on September 21, 1935. John D. Rowe sold lot "D" to William F. and Catharine Mumma, and they sold to their daughter Estella A. and her husband Paul A. Bruner on August 16,1946, making the Bruner's owners of both lots. After Paul Bruner died, Estella sold both lots on January 30, 1969 to Donald C. and Margaret Matter. After Margaret died, Donald C. Matter conveyed to his daughter Marcella A. Walborn on January 13, 1993. [More information in Mumma genealogy.]

HOME OF STEVEN E. AND WANDA HOOVER 66-016-068 & 069
(2 LOTS, , WAS KESSLER DISTILLERY Lot "B")

This lot was from the Sarah Weiss plan, and on March 27, 1901, Sarah and her husband conveyed it to Reuben Kessler. On March 16,1921, it was conveyed to James A. Kessler, and he sold in 1944 to Ida Aboff and her husband, but the deed was not recorded. Ida Aboff conveyed to C. Elwood Hoover on Aug 5, 1944, of the same year, and he had a house built on the 13,200 square foot lot in the 1950s. Shortly after the house was built, C. Elwood and Myrl Hoover conveyed the property to Bruce and Helen Hoover on September 8, 1955. In the picture, part of the outbuildings from the Kessler distillery era can be seen in the background. Bruce died July 19, 2006, Helen died Oct 14, 2006. On October 19, 2009 Jeffrey Hoover, executor of Helen Hoover conveyed the property to Steven E. and Wanda S. Dagen, present owners.

[*C. Elwood Hoover* (Oct 3,1903 – Jan1975), a son of Edmund and Lillian (Wetzel) Hoover, m Myrl E. Grubb (1905 – 1977), a dau of Charles S. and Annie M. (Miller) Grubb. *C. Elwood and Myrl E. (Grubb)Hoover had child*: *Harold C.* (Jan 3, 1926 Jul 28, 2001), a Master Sgt at the time of his death, m Anna B. Schell (1925 – 200_), a dau of Charles & Laura (Bourmer) Schell. *They had a son*: Todd E. ( ), m Susan Loudon, *had these children*: *Jaren Todd* (Oct 13, 1988 - Apr 17, 2008); *Owen*; *Namen*; *Hanlen*.
Bruce H. Hoover (Jun 25, 1931 - Jul 19, 2006), son of Landon & Faye (Hoffman) Hoover, m Helen M Maletich (1925 - 2006), a dau of John L. and Sophia Maletich, *had a son* Jeffrey Hoover.]
See more HOOVER Genealogy elsewhere in the book.

199

HOME OF THOMAS L. AND JUDITH BUFFINGTON 66-016-083 & 092
(Lots from Rev. Crouse lot plan)

This lot has the same general history as the adjoining lot toward the east. The lot was owned by the Kessler family, then Catherine L. Row, and later J. Boyd and Mary Crouse. Rev. and Mrs. Crouse moved to Loyalton during the 1950s and when they purchased the lot, they built this ranch style house. Rev. Crouse was the choir director for Immanuel Church. After Reverend Crouse died, Mary his widow developed a subdivision on her land dividing it into several separate lots. She sold parcel B on July 27, 1977, to Dana and Judith Michael. An adjoining "lot 7" was purchased by Joseph M and Miriam Hill in 1965, and sold to Dana and Judith Michael on July 16, 1976. On November 14, 1986, Dana A. and Judith E. Michael conveyed the two tracts to Thomas L. and Judith A. Buffington. A third lot from the Crouse plan "parcel A" was sold to Lou G. Hoover on July 27, 1977, and when he died in 1995 it was conveyed to Tad P. Kahler. In October 2004, he sold to Thomas and Judith Buffington the present owners

HOME OF RONALD GEARHART 66-016-077
(Old House, site of early tavern)

This lot is intriguing because it is an historic site, but mystifying because it's history is difficult to find. The earliest known owner of the land was Henry Shubert who owned it in 1834. John and Daniel Wommer later owned it, followed by Nathaniel Miller.

The interest begins with the 1875 map which marks this spot as the site of a hotel. It also shows Jacob B. Hoffman owning three acres of land. We know that Jacob was a tavern keeper here briefly during the 1870s, before moving on to Williams Township, where he was again working as a hotel keeper. When he applied for a liquor license in Washington Twp., the neighbors rebelled, stating that his dwelling was not big enough to house his large family and to provide space for a hotel. George and Lavina Williard purchased this land in 1877, and their heirs conveyed to Jacob and Amanda Kissinger. On April 2, 1892, Jacob and Amanda Kissinger transferred to David F. Hoffman, and he and his wife Caroline Hoffman on March 17, 1894 conveyed to Edwin Klinger. The lot contained 4 acres 7/10 perches.

On March 31, 1897, Edwin L. and Kate L. Klinger sold to Reuben Kessler, and after Reuben died, his widow Elizabeth Kessler sold the four acres April 30, 1921 to Catherine L. Row, wife of Alfred Row. The land bordered on the south side of the public road through Loyalton, by James A. Kessler, (Late Reuben Kessler), south to Nathaniel Miller. On August 19, 1961 Catherine L. Row conveyed the acreage to J. Boyd and Mary Crouse. After her husband died, Mary L. Crouse divided her land into a subdivision, and this was parcel "C".

Mary L. Crouse widow, conveyed to Eugene T. and Eva M. Clancy Jul 27, 1977. Eva died and Eugene Clancy conveyed to Lawrence H. Lower Jan 5, 1983. Lawrence died shortly thereafter, and by his will he gave to his sister Mary Lower Crouse May 1, 1984. Mary L. Crouse, widow, conveyed to Ronald E & Peggy Ann (Bruner) Gearhart June 22, 1984.

EDITH A. KISSINGER 66-016-091

This land borders route 209 and the land of Upper Dauphin School Distrct. It has about the same early background as the previous property, and through the years was transferred to many different owners. Eventually Nathaniel Miller owned it and on September 2, 1883 conveyed to George and Lavina Williard. John K. McGann purchased the acreage in August 1894, but sold it to Edwin M. Klinger. Three years later Edwin M and Kate L. Klinger sold to Reuben Kessler. On April 30, 1921 Catherine L. Row purchased the property, and after many years, she sold on August 19, 1961 to J. Boyd and Mary L. Crouse. Williard M. and Emma C Kissinger were the next owners, and after Williard M. Kissinger died, his widow Emma C. Kissinger shared ownership with her daughter Edith A. Kissinger. On January 25, 1999 Edith A. Kissinger became the sole owner.

THE NEXT SECTION IS SOUTH SIDE OF NORTH SECOND STREET
between South Crossroads Street and Stone Hill Road.

L to r: Photo of North Second Street Looking East (taken about 1908)
Houses identified as now belonging to: Brian Coleman, Willard Wiest, Gary Sweigard

HOME OF GARY SWEIGARD 66-016-013
1100 N. Second St. 1900 house

These three lots were part of the "Addition to Loyalton" of 1899. Andrew Weiss heirs conveyed them to George W. Kessler in 1905. After George died, Kate Kessler in June 1914 conveyed them to Charles F. Harner. The two lots front on the south side of North Second Street and lot number five. The "Triangular lot "A" fronts on North Second Street and to the east side of Crossroads Road. Charles worked in the mines, and was responsible for drilling holes with a hammer before dynamite was used. Working in coal dirt breathing the dust resulted in lung disease, and he died of miner's asthma. Just before his death, he told Kate Row "I don't mind dying, but it's for such a long time."

Charles F. and Ellen Harner sold this property to Fred C. and Mary Harner on February 15, 1926. After Fred C. Harner died, his widow Mary conveyed August 31, 1936 to Floyd B. and Leona M Harner. They were residents of this property the remainder of their lives. Leona died Aug 23, 1988. On December 2, 1988, the heirs of Leona Harmer sold to Gary H. Sweigard.

WILLARD E. AND DIANE E. WIEST 66-016-014
1150 N. 2nd Street 1900 house

These lots were from the plan laid out by Henninger for Sarah Weiss in 1899. On October 4, 1899, Sarah Weiss conveyed these two lots 5 & 7 to Maria L. Johns. Several years later on October 31, 1903 Maria L. Johns conveyed both lots to Alice Lettich. On March 4, 1910 Alice and her husband Daniel Lettich conveyed the lots to George R. Lesher, and he in turn conveyed to Amanda Smeltz. John E. and Amanda Smeltz sold the two lots to James A. Kessler in April 1920. Arthur and Sarah (Good) Miller became the owners and built a new house about 1940. Sarah was the "Avon lady" for years and Arthur owned a business out of the home, installing storm windows. Nathan E. and Rosie E. Snyder owned it later. Nathan died in 1946, and Rosie died in 1963. The executors of Rosie E. Snyder conveyed to her sole heir Galen D. Snyder on December 2, 1963. Margaret E. Snyder his widow conveyed to Charles J. Henninger on April 6, 1971, and on May 10, 1988, Charles J. Henninger, widower sold to Lewis H. and Carolyn E. Leeper. They sold to Willard E. and Diane E. Wiest on January 27, 1999.

[DANIEL M. LETTICH (Jan 2,1870 – Mar 30, 1957, bur Maple Grove Cem, E'ville),, a son of Jacob & Catherine (Hartman) Lettich, m Oct 10, 1894 Alice L. Yohe (1874 – 1944), a dau of Angeline Yohe..
They had these children: Ray L. (1899 – 1949, bur Maple Grove Cem), m Dora E. ___ (1899 – 1971) ; Lottie A b 1905, m Loy A Miller , a son of Joel and Hannah (Shaffer) Miller.]

L to r: Home of: Willard & Diane Wiest, Karl Dietrich, and Brian Coleman

Gary Sweigard 66-016-013

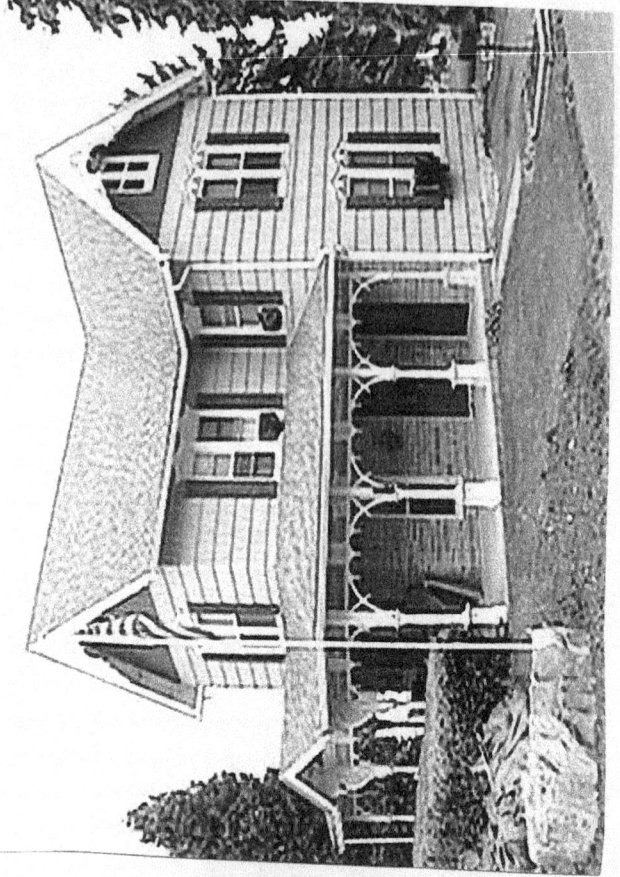

Brian K. Coleman 66-016-016

Edith A. Kiissinger 66-016-091

Karl B.Dietrich 66-016015

HOME OF KARL B. DEITRICH 66-016-015
(Lots #9 & #11 North Second Street – Under Side)

Same early history as adjoining lots. S. S. Good owned and sold to Myles Kahler on September 27, 1957. The Kahler's sold to Harry A. Dietrich, and he sold these two lots to Rudolph and Ruby Bressler. The house was built in the 1970s. Rudolph died January 31, 1984, and his estate was sold to Karl B. Dietrich on July 16, 1985.

HOME OF BRIAN K. COLEMAN 66-016-016
(LOT 13 & 15 (south side of North Second Street and Walnut St. _South Side_)

Sarah and William Weiss sold this lot to Solomon S. and Agnes Good on March 8, 1899. They owned it until February 25, 1949, then conveyed it to Aerial D. Good. He conveyed March 19, 1953 to Leonard D. and Hilda Good, and they to William L. and Dora Gaugler on May 28, 1955. After William Gaugler died, Dora his widow conveyed the property to Harry M. Joyce L. Bruner, they sold June 17, 1966 to Daniel H and Vivian R. Crabb. Vivian conveyed her share to Daniel H. Crabb on September 26, 1973, and Daniel H. and Sandra A. Crabb sold to Brian K. Coleman and Donetta M. Reedy of Millersburg on December 14, 1996.

MARY ELLEN BYRNE & KATHLEEN H. BOYER 66-016-017
(From J.A. Henninger - Sarah Weiss survey of 1899 lots 17, 19, 21, North 2nd & Walnut Sts. _South Side_)

Sarah Weiss sold lot #19 to Clinton I. and Katie W. Rowe and they sold to Irvin D. and Susan Boyer on August 4, 1902. William H. and Annie B Boyer owned lot 17 and conveyed it to Irvin D. Boyer on Apr 20, 1909. After Irvin Boyer died, his widow Susan, widow Kate Feidt, and William H. and Annie B. Boyer conveyed the two lots to William H. Boyer on June 2, 1932. Robert and Mary (Hoffman) Smeltz became tenants. Lot # 17 with two-story frame dwelling was on the southeast corner of Walnut and North Second Street, adjoining vacant lot #19. Eugene L. and Theresa M. Hassinger became the next owners.

Lot #21 was owned by Alice L. and Daniel M. Ledich, and on April 8, 1918 they conveyed to Annie R. Lubold. Annie R. Lubold died Dec 19, 1941 and the lot was conveyed to Rudolph P. Bressler by her heirs. Rudolph P. Bressler sold to Eugene L and Theresa M. Hassinger on August 29, 1958. Eugene died on August 22, 1973, and his widow Theresa M. Hassinger conveyed all three lots to her daughters Mary Ellen Byrne and Kathleen H. Boyer of West Chester on April 9, 1996. [See Hassinger genealogy elsewhere in book.]

[IRVIN D. BOYER (Jun 16, 1851 – Dec 12, 1931, bur Maple Grove Cem, E'ville), a son of Benneville and Catherine (Musser) Boyer, m Susan Bohner (Sep 7, 1856 – d Oct 2, 1932), a dau of Nicholas and Lydia ((Spatz) Bohner. *Irvin D. and Susan (Bohner) Boyer had these children*: *Kate M.* b 1875 m Wm A. Feidt; *William H.* (1877 - 1957), m Annie B. Grubb (1878 – 1948)]

HOME OF CHRISTINE TODD AND YVONNE MARR 66-016-019
(LOT # 23 of Sarah Weiss plan – next to vacant lot - _South Side_)

This lot was owned by Benjamin Wingard before 1910. He sold it to John M. Harman on December 5, 1913. John M and Lizzie M. Harman conveyed the property to Henry Boyer on May 14, 1918. On March 29, 1923 Henry and Mary Boyer sold to William Lewis Hoffman, the first postmaster in Loyalton. William L. Hoffman also sold McNess products, and was part owner of the store on the northwest corner of the square. When William

Hoffman purchased this property, the lot was bound on the east by lot of William F. Mumma (earlier owned by John Row estate), on the west by the late John Fawber's lot. On September 1, 1949, William Lewis Hoffman, by then a widower, sold to Jacob E. Hassinger. He owned the property until it was sold in1955.to William and Shirley (Bush) Kiester. [See Kiester genealogy elsewhere in book.]

THE FAWBER, FABER, ETC. FAMILY

[The **FAWBER** family descends from immigrant Frederick Adam Faber, born May 29, 1717 in Baden, Ger -d Bethel Twp., Lebanon Co. Aug 25, 1767, bur Bethel Moravian Cem). He m 1st Anna Maria Hautsch of Lanc Co. She d c1758. He m 2nd in 1759, Elizabeth (Meily Spitler), 1723 – 1773), a dau of Jacob Meily & widow of John Spittler, Jr. Their **JOHANNES** (Feb 7, 1750 – c1808), m Margaret Rudy (Dec 13, 1753 – Oct 4, 1825, bur Jonestown Cem,). The Fawber family moved to Dauphin County during the early 1800s.

*JOHN FAWBER, Jr. (Mar 30, or Apr 12,1777, Leb Co – Jul 15, 1828, bur Hill Ceem,Halifax), a son of John and Margaret (Rudy) Fawber, m 1805 Maria Magdalena Rudy (Nov 6, 1784 or May 14, 1784 – Jan 16, 1845, bur Bowerman Cem.), a dau of Jonas and Barbara Rudy. **John and Maria Magd (Rudy) Fawber had 10 children (6 sons, 4 dau) – these are known children):**
MICHAEL (Aug 8, 1808 – Jul 7, 1855, bur Bowerman Cem), m Elizabeth ___ (Apr 21, 1806 – Jun 10, 1872). They lived in Jefferson Twp., in 1850. **Michael and Elizabeth Fawber had these known children:** Samuel (Mar 22, 1831 – Dec 26, 1905, bur Bowerman Cem), m Amanda ___ (Mar 13,1838 – Sep 28, 1913). They lived in Jefferson Twp. in 1880. **They had these known children:** John H. (1860-1926); Peter N. b c1868; Edward L. b c1870; Elizabeth b1873; Mary E. b c1874; Frederick b c1833, m Elizabeth ___ (May 31, 1841 – Feb 18, 1917, bur Maple Grove Cem, E'ville);Joseph (Jan 1836 - Jefferson Twp - Aug 13, 1897, bur Bowerman Cem), m Margaret Rebecca (1842 –1926); **Jospeh and Margaret Rebecca Fawber children:** Lydia J. b ___ m Oct 1922, Ralph E. Smeltz; Albert lived in Lancaster Co in 1897; Ambrose b c1866; John A. b c1868; Milton b c1874; Charles b c1876; Alvin b ___, m _____, had these children (bapt Zions Luth, Lykens): Harvey Thomas b May 4, 1908; Emma Jane b 1910 John; Harvey, lived n Phila in 1897;
Sarah b c1837; Isaac b1839; Nathaniel b c1844; Susannah b c1847;
CATHARINE (Jan 14,1810- Oct 15, 1892), m John Baker (1804– 1876, bur Bowerman Cem, Enterline).
JOHN (Aug 31,1811 –May 1, 1885, bur Fetterhoff Cem), m Elizabeth Fetteroff (Nov 19, 1815 – Jun 7, 1860, a dau of Philip and Eve (Boyer) Fetteroff. In 1850 John and Elizabeth lived in Jackson Twp. **John and Elizabeth (Fetteroff) children (bapt Fetteroff Ch):** Philip Frederick b Oct 1, 1835; Susanna Maria b Feb 16, 1838;Sarah Delila b Mar 22, 1846; John A. (1847 – 1916), m Sarah J. Meckley (1854 – 1915, bur Messiah Luth Cem, Fisherville), a dau of Samuel and Sarah Meckley. They lived in Jackson Twp in 1880. He was a Civil War Vet. **John A. & Sarah J. Fawber children:** Anna A (1872 – 1909), m S. J. Zearing; Rosa Elizabeth (Jun 20,1877 – Dec 5, 1959, bur Fisherville), m John C. Bixler (Jun 9,1872 – Mar 5, 1942, a son of Cornelius & Catherine A. (Miller) Bixler; Mary C. (1885 –1960); Ellen b 1879.
GEORGE (Aug 3, 1813 – Oct 1, 1895, bur Old Cem, E'ville), m 1838, 1st Esther Filbert, 2nd Elizabeth Lehr (May 17, 1834 – Sep 17, 1898) . George lived alone in Wash Twp in 1870. In 1880 he had Elizabeth age 35 with him.
ADAM (Feb 4, 1815 – Oct 1, 1895, bur Berrysburg), m Susannah Koppenhaver (Apr 3, 1819 – Nov 3, 1889), a dau of Frederick & Maria Elizabeth (Gross) Koppenhaver. They lived in Washington Twp in 1850,1860, 1870. In 1870 they have Emanuel Harman 8, grandson, Solomon Wert 3, and Susan Hoke 1 yr. with them. In 1880, Susanna age 64 is listed as Adams wife. **Adam and Anna Fawber had these children:** John Frederick b c1842; Mary b c1844, m 1st Frederick Harman, 2nd John Isaac Paul; Margaret m George Brenneman; Matilda m William McGinnis Sarah Elizabeth b c1849, m Adam Wert; Eliza b c1850; Beulah or Leah b c1851, m John Keiter; Catharine b c1853; Thomas b Jun 11, 1854; Rebecca b Feb 25, 1856, m George Brenneman; Peter b c1858; Emma J. b1860, m Adam Lyme
JACOB (Jul 25, 1819 – Feb 26, 1891, bur Fisherville), m Catharine ___ (Mar 1, 1831 – Sep 3, 1908). They lived in Jefferson Twp in 1850, and had John Sheesly age 73 and Sarah Sheesly age 83 with them. **Jacob and Catherine ( ) Fawber had these children;** Amos b 1850, m Catharine b c1852. They lived in Harrisburg in 1880. **Had these children;** Mary b c1872; David b c1875 ;
MAGDALENA b Aug 23, 1822, bapt David's Ch, Killinger; **SUSANNA** b Nov 26, 1825, bapt David's Ch, Killinger – May 12, 1869), m 1st ___ Lehr, 2nd Philip Sweigart (1820 – 1894).

Photo l to r: Gary H. Sweigard, William & Shirley Kiester, Betty R. Miller

JACOB B. HOFFMAN FAMILY

[*JACOB B. HOFFMAN* b Apr 20, 1825 – d _____ , bur   ), a son of Jacob and Catharine (Ferree) Hoffman, m Elizabeth Hoover (b c1830 - d   ), a dau of _____. In 1870 Jacob and Elizabeth Hoffman lived in Washington Twp. In 1880 they lived in Williams Twp. and he was a tavern keeper. *Jacob B. and Elizabeth (Hoover) Hoffman had these children (some bapt Hoffman Ch):* *LUZETTA* b Feb 21, 1849; *FRANCES ELEANOR* b Jan 20, 1850; *MARYELLA* b c1860; *ALAINE* b c1862; *WILLIAM LEWIS* (May 22, 1866 – Jul 15, 1955), m Sybilla Agnes Johns (Dec 18, 1867 – Aug 1948), a dau of Peter O. and Maria L (Bitzer) Johns. *William & Sybilla (Johns) Hoffman children*: *Harry H* (Sep 6, 1889 – Dec 19, 1956), m Mabel E. Helt (1889–1939), 2ⁿᵈ Lillian M. Bair, moved to Ephrata before 1931; *Mary Louisa* (Jul 28, 1895 - ___), m Dec 25,1917 Ralph D. Snyder (1893 –1946), had a dau *Arlene Agnes* b Feb 1, 1922 m Nov 12, 1941 Henry A. Romberger b Sep 24, 1919.; *JACOB G.* b c1871; *EDWARD G* b c1872. [More genealogy under Hoffman and Johns families].

THE WILLIAM KIESTER FAMILY
LOT #25 NORTH SECOND STREET – SOUTH SIDE – VACANT

On October 1, 1895, Amanda Hoke conveyed a tract of land to Sarah and William Weiss. They conveyed to Franklin W. and Emma Bahney on March 27, 1901. After Franklin W. Bahney died Emma married John A. Fawber, and they sold the land to Sybilla A. and William L. Hoffman on March 27, 1920. After Sybilla died, William L. Hoffman sold to Jacob Hassinger September 1, 1949, whose heirs conveyed to William and Shirley Kiester on September 9, 1955, The property continued to remain in the family.

[*FRANK W. BAHNEY* (Nov 18, 1865 – Oct 3, 1902, bur St. John's Hill Cem), m Emma Shaffer (Apr 1, 1863 – Aug 15, 1934), a dau of Solomon & Susanna (Hepner) Shaffer of Stone Valley, Northld Co. *Frank W. and Emma Bahney children: Susan Elizabeth* b Nov 2, 1890; *Harry D.* (Dec 31, 1892 – Apr 19, 1969, bur Maple Grove Cem, E'ville), m Sadie H. Schreffler (1889 – 1975); *Charles C.* b Jan 1896]

HOME OF NATHAN E. DAGEN 66-016-020
(Lot # 27 & 29 North Second Street – <u>South Side</u>) 1900 house

These two lots number 29 & 27, containing a 2 ½ story frame dwelling and located on North Second Street were from the Henninger survey. The adjoined Water Street on the east, and on the west by lot 25. Edwin M and Katie Klinger conveyed the two lots to Henry H. and Daisy Hoffman on March 29, 1902. Henry H. and Daisy Hoffman conveyed them to John M. Rowe on March 29, 1905. John M. Rowe died in 1911 and his heirs conveyed on March 3, 1920 to William F. and Catharine Mumma. William F. and Catherine Mumma conveyed them to their daughter Mary A. (Mumma) Troutman and her husband John W. Troutman on August 16, 1946, with a request that she not sell them for ten years. On October 19, 1960 Mary A. Mumma Troutman was designated trustee of the land. After Mary died (Aug 30, 1964), John W. Troutman and Paul A. Troutman executor of Harry N. Troutman

Gary H. Sweigard 66-016-020

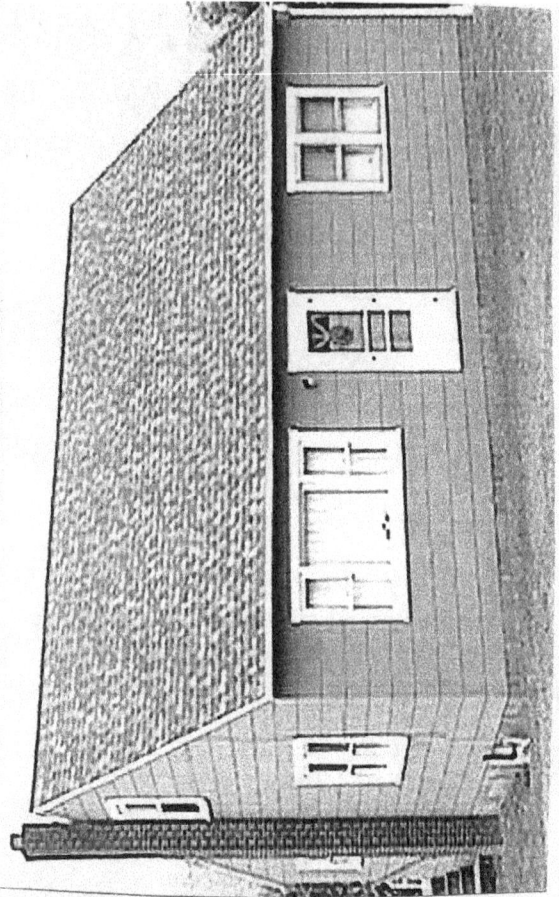

Benjamin M and Ashley M. Blazer 66-016-022

William and Shirley Kiester 66-016-019

Virginia Bruner 66-016-021

conveyed the two lots to Charles E. Wolfe, widower on Feb 16, 1967. Gary H Sweigart and Fredricka Rose Williams were the next owners On November 25, 1975.. On Jul 23, 1980 Gary H. Sweigard became the sole owner of this lot with two and one-half story frame dwelling. Gary H. Sweigard died on November 14, 2014. The property was sold on Jun 29, 2015 to Nathan E. Dagen, the present owner.

[*HENRY H. HOFFMAN* (1879 – 1958 bur Fairview Cem. Enders), m Daisy M. Heller (1881 – 1963). *Henry H. and Daisy Hoffman children (some bapt Oak Dale Ch)*: *Lester William* b Apr 8, 1904; *Walter Henry* (May 20, 1906 – 1973, bur Fairview Cem); *Mary Elizabeth* b Sep 11, 1908.]

THE MUMMA FAMILY

[*SAMUEL MUMMA* (Oct 1822 – Sep 12, 1870), m Annie Davis (c1822 - Oct 16, 1898). They lived in Wiconisco Twp in 1860 and 1870 and Samuel was listed as a powder maker. In 1880 Annie was a widow in Lykens and had her four youngest children with her. *Samuel & Annie (Davis) Mumma children*:
MARY b c1842;
REBECCA b 1843 m Edward Zerby b c1838. They lived in Lykens, he was a miner. *Edward & Rebecca (Mumma) Zerby children*: *Charles* b c1860; *Lilly Ann* b c1863; *William G* b c1865; *Franklin* b c1867; *Frederick* b c1870;
MARTIN (1844–1915, bur IOOF Cem. Lykens), m Susan ____ (Jan 4,1844 – Apr 24,1887). They moved to Millersburg.*Martin and Susan (___) Mumma children (some bapt Zion Luth, Lykens)*: Amelia Anna Elizabeth (Oct 10, 1867 – Nov 14, 1870); *Samuel William Franklin* b Aug 21, 1872; *George Oscar Clayton* (Dec 5, 1874 – Aug 1, 1886); Charles Henry b Jun 10,1873; *Charles Edwin Ray* b Sep 16, 1877 – Dec1879); *Harry Martin Welton* b Apr 26,1885. After Susan died Martin m Mary M. Carl Oct 4, 1891.
Possibly Samuel b c1845 – tanner with Frances Barlier family in 1880 in Lykens.
WILLIAM W. (1848 – Jan 4, 1917, pneumonia, bur IOOF Cem, Lykens), m Jun 8, 1873 Mary Ellen Rowe (Jan 5, 1853 – Jul 11, 1908). *William and Mary Ellen (Rowe) Mumma had these children:*
Charles Henry (Jun 10, 1873 – 1950, bur Maple Grove), m Apr 22, 1899 Anna J. Leiter b Mar 29, 1878 – d 1950), a dau of George K. and Mary E. or Eliz Ferree(?) Leiter of E'ville.
William Franklin b Aug 21, 1874 – d 1961, bur Maple Grove Cem), m Catharine E. Rowe (1873 – 1946) a dau of Adam D. Rowe. *William F. and Catharine (Rowe) Mumma had these children*: Mary A. (1898 – 1964), m Harry N.Troutman (1893 – 1967); Estella Alberta (Jul 20, 1905 – 1969, bur Maple Grove Cem, E'ville), m Paul A. Bruner (1905- 1965). *Paul A. & Estella Alberta (Mumma) Bruner children*: Margaret (1926 – 1980), m Donald Matter, a son of Peter Matter, had two children: *Don; Marcella,* m Russell E. Walborn; William b 1928 m Verna and 2 dau's *Virginia* b 1956, m ___Teeter, *Peggy* m Ronald Gearhart.
John Wellington b Oct 9, 1880 – Feb 28, 1913, bur beside parents) m Jun 24, 1905 Margaret E. Tschopp, *had a dau Mary Ellen* b Jul 21, 1906, m Harry Kniley. After John Wellington died, Margaret m Thomas H. Chaundry on Apr 12, 1918.
After his wife Mary Ellen died, William W. Mumma m Nov 18, 1905 Mary L. Wagner (1854 – 1938) of Sunbury. *William W. and Mary E. (Wagner) Mumma had these children*: *William Rutherford* b Jul 10, 1909; *Robert Wallingford* b Apr 18, 1915; *Harold* b Aug 14, 1917; *Mary Elizabeth* b Jun 10, 1920; *Pearl Arlene* b Mar 4, 1923;
AMANDA b c1851 m ____ Ferree, moved to West Va.;
JOHN (b Jun 29, 1852 – d Nov 1, 1909, bur Old Lykens Union Cem), m Mary Jane (b Apr 2, 1854 – Feb   25, 1907). They lived in   Lykens in 1880 and he was a brakeman. *John &Mary Jane Mumma had these children*: William Walter b Mar 20, 1884 – d Feb 23, 1925, bur IOOF Cem, Lykens), m Nov 18, 1905 Mary L. Wagner ;
SARAH b Mar 31, 1854 m ____ Frank of Millersburg;
HENRY (b Apr 13, 1856 – d Oct 18, 1897, bur Old Lykens Cem), m Alice ___ b c1856, *had these children*; Henrietta b c1875; Annie b c1878. Henry m 2nd on Jul 19, 1886 Sarah Ellen Welker b c1866, a dau of Benjamin and Elizabeth (Gunderman) Welker.
FRANKLIN (Feb 11, 1859 – Sep 22, 1906, bur Old Lykens Cem), m Aug 16, 1888 Katie Wert (Oct 8, 1868 – Oct 19, 1908), a dau of John Wert, lived in Coaldale *Frank and Catherine (Wert) Mumma had these children (some bapt St. Johns Luth, Lykens)*: Lester Lorance b Dec 29, 1889; James Norman b Jul   13, 1891, d young;; Annie Venetta b Jun 26, 1893; Harry Clayton b Mar 22, 1895; ELLA Victoira b c1861 m B. Frank Stoner of Lykens, ;
EDWARD b c1874 moved to Millersburg;

HOME OF VIRGINIA BRUNER 66-016-021
(North Second Street Adjoining Water Street)

These four lots from the J. G. Romberger tract were sold to Alfred H. Row, later to Reuben Kessler. On March 8, 1923, the Reuben Kessler estate conveyed to William F. Mumma. He later sold to William A. and Verna Mumma June 4, 1956. On February 20, 1993, they sold to their daughter Virginia L. Bruner, the present owner.

HOME OF BENJAMIN M. & ASHLEY M. (HARTLIEB) BLAZER 66-016-022
(North Second Street – South Side)

These lots were from the J. G. Romberger plan, and were sold to Clara R. & Harvey Lupold on July 16, 1924. They sold to Clyde J. Miller & Effie April 18, 1945. After Clyde died, Effie E Miller sold to Robert H. and Mary Smeltz on August 20, 1947. Robert built this house in the early 1950s, and this became their permanent residence. On June 25, 2009 Mary M & Robert H. Smeltz sold to Larry E. & Ann L. Smeltz. On March 12, 2013 Larry E. and Ann L. Smeltz sold to Benjamin M and Ashley M. (Hartlieb). Blazer.

HOME OF ROBERT K. & HOLLY B. SAVILLE 66-06-023
(North Second Street Adjoining Chestnut Street – South Side)

During the 1920's, Homer Hassinger won these two lots in a lottery. In 1960 he sold to his daughter Elva and her husband William Miller. Shortly after that they built this new house. William and Elva (Hassinger) Miller had these children: Marilyn b Jun 19, 1957; William J. b Jan 2, 1959; Lee J. b Aug 11, 1965. William Miller passed away Jan 9, 1999, and since then Elva sold to Robert K. and Holly B. Saville on March 23, 2015.

HOME OF RONALD L. AND KATHLEEN HIRSCH 66-016-024
(1420 North Second Street)

J. G. and Amelia Romberger conveyed four lots (#32-33- 34- and 35) to Wallace and Francis Troutman on June 14, 1924. The Troutman's sold the same lots to Quay M and Kate N. Cooper on June 6, 1925. In May 1960 Quay Cooper sold the four lots to Leo J. Hirsch and Linda Neubold Hirsch. On February 28, 1964 Leon J. and Linda Hirsch sold the four lots to Ronald L. and Kathy Hirsch. They had the house built on their land.

HOME OF KERRY AND BRANDY MARIE WIEST 66-016-025
(North Second Street between Hirsch lot and Stone Hill Road – South Side)

This land was part of the plan laid out by J. G. Romberger. On January 8, 1992, Donald C. and Arlene Hoffman conveyed a group of lots to Daren D and Karen A. Hoffman. They built a house on part of the land. Daren D. Hoffman died, and his widow remarried to Joseph P. Kierstead. On November 13, 2009, Karen A. and Joseph P. Kierstead conveyed their home to Kerry and Brandy Marie Wiest.

THE NEXT SECTION IS NORTH SIDE OF NORTH SECOND STREET
between South Crossroads Street and Stone Hill Road.

HOME OF JAMES W. AND BEVERLY J. TRAVITZ 66-016-001
1105 North Second Street - 1962 house

This land was part of the Sarah Weiss plan that was later conveyed to Andrew Weiss. On April 16, 1904 Andrew Weiss conveyed to D. A. Good. On October 18, 1939 the heirs of Daniel A. Good (O. T. and Beulah Tobias, Solomon Good, etc) conveyed part of the tract of land to Earl F. Good. On May 24, 1947, Earl F. and Susan C. Good sold part of the tract to Floyd Harner, and in 1952 Floyd divided the land into lots known as the "Harner's Addition." Floyd and Leona N. Harner conveyed lot # 9, located on the north side of North Second Street, east side of the public road from Loyalton to Pillow to Paul W. Troutman & Lucy H. in 1961. On Nov 16, 1994 Paul W. and Lucy Troutman sold to James W. & Beverly J. Travitz of Lykens.

[*FREDERICK HARNER, SR* (Oct 5, 1782 Ger- Apr 24, 1870 bur Simeon Cem, Gratz), m Mary Shurr (Nov 8, 1779 – Nov 20, 1849. Frederick & Mary Shurr. *They had a son Frederick D* (Jun 19, 1816 Sch Co. Nov 10, 1894), m Aug 13, 1840 Rebecca Hoffman (Nov 21, 1820 – Dec 18, 1891), a dau of George and Rebecca (Kunzman) Hoffman. Their son *Charles* (Aug 12, 1853 – Mar 19, 1926, bur Oak Dale Cem, Loyalton), m 1st Ellen Boyer (no dates, bur Oak Dale), 2nd Mary Hoke Sep 1914

[*FLOYD BENJAMIN HARNER* (Jul 18, 1904 – 1961, bur Maple Grove Cem., E'ville), a son of Frederick C. & Hattie Harner, m Leona M. Snyder (1907 – 1988). *Floyd & Leona N. (Snyder) Harner had these children*: *Richard Eugene* (1924 - 1064), m Georgiana F. Klinger (1922 - 1965); *Ethel L.* b1926, m William Leroy Buffington (1907 – 1966, bur Maple Grove Cem, E'ville), a son of Herbert E. and Cora A. (Batdorf) Buffington.. *William L. & Ethel (Harner) Buffington had two children*: *Thomas* b Feb 2, 1946, m Judith A. Shaffer b Nov 14, 1947, a dau of Newton E. and Adella (Dreibelbis) Shaffer; *David*. Ethel later m Pershing Henninger.]

HOME OF STEVEN & WANDA DAGEN 66-016-082
1125 North Second Street – North Side) 1970 house

This is part of the Harner Addition. Floyd & Leona M.Harner became the owner. On June 2, 1961 they sold to Ethel L. Buffington. On April 25, 1968, C. Elwood & Myrl E. Harner became the owners. Harold died January 8, 1975, and Myrl died April 14, 1977. Steven E. and Wanda S. Dagen became the present owners on March 6, 1988.

HOME OF JENNIFER L. AND VINCENT A. LIDDICK 66-016-002
1145 N. Second Street 1951 house

These two lots were from the Harner Addition. Lot # 6 was sold in December 1952 by the Harner's to William H. and Gladys Bonawitz. Howard D. and Mary L. (Jury) Bonawitz purchased #7 from Floyd and Leona Harner on Jun 20, 1953. On September 29, 1960 William H. and Gladys sold lot #6 to Howard D. and Mary L. Bonawitz. Mary died first, and after Howard died Dec 3, 1993, his executor conveyed the property on July 15, 1994 to Jennifer L Kissinger. She and her husband Vincent A. Liddick became owners on September 25, 1998.

HOME OF TYRONE P. AND VIRGINIA R. TROUTMAN
(North Second Street- North Side)

This land has the same history of the previous tract, being part of Harner Addition. Paul W. and Lucy H. Troutman purchased it from Floyd B. and Leona M. Harner, and on March 18, 1967 conveyed lot #1 to their son Tyrone P and wife Virginia. On October 17, 1985 the Troutman's conveyed the other part to their son Tyrone P. Troutman and his wife Virginia R. Tyrone and Virginia Troutman conveyed both lots to Terry L. Bowser and Lisa C. Schwalm on May 15, 1995.

[*WESLEY IRVIN TROUTMAN* (Feb 3, 1880 – Jul 1, 1930, bur Maple Grove Cem), a son of Benneville Troutman & Hannah Wiest. He m Catharine Louisa Rebuck (Feb 6, 1880 – Oct 12, 1964), a dau of William and Lovina (Kehres) Rebuck. *Wesley and Catharine (Rebuck) Troutman children*: *Claude A.* (1902 – 1979), m Florence E.

Bonawitz ((1903 - 2000), a dau of George A. and Carrie (Grubb) Bonawitz; **William O**. (1903–1969), m Blanche Kratzer (1908–1982); **Bessie** b 1906, m Lawrence Weller; **Mabel** (1908 - 2001), m Leon J. Kissinger (1905 - 1965); **Vera Alverda** b 1911; **Evelyn** (1913– 1977), m John L. Sleighter; **Paul Wesley "Silas"**(Apr 13,1916 – Dec 20, 2007) m Lucy Hannah Maria Sitlinger b Jul 4, 1923, dau of Melva Naomi Sitlinger. **Paul Wesley and Lucy (Sitlinger) Troutman children**: <u>Judy</u>, m Joe Kleinbauer; <u>Tyrone Paul</u> b 1943, m Virginia Helt; **Joseph Martin** b 1918.]

HOME OF JEREMY D. AND DAWN L. HOFFMAN BUSS 66-016-004
1195 N. Second Street   house 1938

Earl F. Good purchased a tract of land in the Harner Addition, and after his death part of the tract was conveyed to Sarah D. and Arthur R. Miller on December 7, 1973. In 1991, Arthur Miller died, and on August 24, 1994, his widow Sarah D. Miller conveyed the property to her daughter Helen Unger of Texas. On January 16, 1995. Helen A. and Harleth Unger conveyed to Jeremy D. and Dawn L. Hoffman Buss on July 25, 2000.

L to r: Homes of: James W. & Beverly Travitz, Steven & Wanda Dagen, Vincent & Jennifer Liddick

HOME OF STEVEN AND WANDA DAGEN 66-016-005
(Lot #8 Harner Addition on North Second Street– <u>North Side</u>)

This lot has the same history as the previous one. Floyd B. and Leona M. Harner conveyed to Harold C. Hoover Sr.and wife Anna B. (Schell) Hoover. On January 2, 1978 they conveyed to Harold C. Hoover, Jr. and wife Barbara Hoover and Todd E. Hoover. The Hoover family conveyed to Steven and Wanda S. Dagen on March 16, 1988. They are the present owners.

BONAWITZ FAMILY
(Some help from genealogy by Oby Bonawitz)

[The earliest known immigrant of the BONAWITZ family is ***ADAM** Bonawitz. He settled in Berks County as early as 1754, and married Juliana. Adam Bonawitz had a son: *George* (b ___ d 1793), served in the Berks Co. Militia in 1780-81, was also a weaver. He moved to Tulpehocken Twp by 1788, was listed in 1792 as a laborer, "sickly and poor." He m Elizabeth Wenrich (Jan 30, 1756 - 1840), a dau of Matthias Wenrich II. *George and Elizabeth (Wenrich) Bonawitz children (some came to Upper Dau Co. will be discussed here)*:
*****George Michael** (Mar 22,1774 – Sep 18, 1854, bur Peace Cem, Bbg), m 1st Maria Catherine Koppenheffer b Nov 17, 1767, 2nd Elizabeth Matter. George moved to Berrysburg, Dau Co about 1801.

George *Michael & Maria Cath had these children*: ****Jacob and ****Michael moved to Ohio; ****John (1801 – 1885, bur Bbg cem), m Salome Schoffstall (Jun 11, 1813 – Sep 19, 1841), no surviving children. m 2nd Catherine (Harman, Messner), wid of John Messer (1805 – 1870), lived in Mifflin Twp. Dau Co; *John and Catherine (Harman, Messner) Bonawitz children*: *****Jonathan (1833 – 1913, bur Bbg), m Margaret Rutter (1840 – 1911), a dau of Henry Rutter of Halifax; *****Sarah (1835 – 1869, bur Stone Valley), m Jacob Lenker (1833 – 1869; *****Daniel D.* (1805 - 1886, bur Rife Cem), m Mariah Jane Maurer (1812 – 1881), lived in Millersburg. *Daniel D & Mariah Jane (Maurer) Bonawitz children*: *****Elizabeth b 1837, m Charles Longabach; *****Kathryn b 1839 m Aaron Snyder (1839 – 1877, bur Rife Cem); *****William Henry (1841 – 1906, bur Killinger Cem), m Mary Holtzman; *****Jonas (1843 – 1923, bur Rife Cem), m Magdalena Hepner; *****Lydia (1846 – 1936), m David R. Bordner, moved to Michigan; *****David M. (1851 – 1939), m Erlena Catherine Rowe lived in Up. Paxton Twp. David served as an apprentice to a cabinet maker, and became a lifetime master carpenter at Rife *David M.and Erlena Catherine (Rowe) Bonawitz children*: ******Rosie (Feb 21,1874 – Mar 5, 1963), a dau of David M. & Erlena Catherine (Rowe) Bonawitz, m Jul 10, 1897 at Berrysburg to Nathan E. Snyder (b ___ d May 10, 1946). He was a blacksmith, *Children*: ********Annie C.*b Jan 19, 1898, m William Sweigard; *******Estella I b Oct 19, 1899, m T. Snyder; *******Harvey E b Nov 13, 1902, m Catharine Shaffer; ********Galen D.* Jun 17,1905, m Margaret Snyder; ********Henry J.* (1907 – 1921);*******Allen b Feb 1, 1911, m Emma Warfel.
***Ira Charles (1876 -1947) , m Mary J. Troutman b1883, a dau of Daniel & Sarah Troutman. *Ira Charles & Mary (Troutman) Bonawitz children;* ****Eva E b Dec 7, 1902, m George W. Snyder; ****Howard D b May 15, 1905, m Mary L. Jury b 1912, he was a carpenter; ****Charles E (1907- 1962), m Florence Seager; *****Robert O.* b 1918, m Beatrice A. Harper b 1921, he was a carpenter; ***Anna Elizabeth (1878 – 1946), m Hiram Killinger (1871 – 1958), he was a carpenter. ***George Alfred (1880 – 1928), m Carrie Grubb (1883 – 1951), a dau of Henry & Isabella Grubb, he was a miner and carpenter; ***Lydia Erlene (1882 – 1947), m John H. Weaver (1879 – 1952); ***Frances b 1887, m Roy P. Walters (1884 – 1963); ***Esther (1895 – 1968), m William Bowers (1891 – 1933).

*****Isaac (1854 – 1939), m Catherine Sultzbaugh, a dau of Joseph & Mary (Landis) Sultzbaugh, lived in Up. Paxton Twp.*Isaac & Catherine (Sultzbaugh) Bonawitz children*: ******William H (1879 – 1964), m Lydia A. Romberger (1880 – 1959); ******Joseph Daniel b1882, m Florence Sweezy, a dau of John & Sarah (Ferree) Sweezy; ******Lillian b 1899, m Henry Oscar Williard; .

****Elizabeth (1809 – 1898, bur St. Davids Cem, Killinger), m Henry Botteiger (1809 – 1865); *Maria Catherine* (1811 – 1892, bur Lykens Cem), m 1st Michael Radel (1807-1864), 2nd Jacob Witmer (1807 – 1885) [See Matter history for children with Elizabeth Matter.]

***Catherine (1776 – 1826), m Jacob Yeagley.
***Christina b 1778 m John bischoff in 1801, lived near Berrysburg.
***Elizabeth b 1779 , George Price, lived in Lebanon Co.
***John b 1780 m Susanna Burckhart, lived in Middle Paxton Twp, Dau Co.
***Peter b 1784 m Susanna Schaefer, lived in Low Paxton Twp.
*** *Eva Rosina* b 1787, m John Blatt, lived in Lebanon Co.
***Mary b 1788 m George Hager;
***Adam 1792 – Oct 5, 1876, m Elizabeth Runkel lived in Lykens Twp, but moved to Venango Co.

HOME OF NATHAN E. AND STEVEN E. DAGEN
(From J. G. Romberger Plan "Eastside Addition")

This is a tract of 6 lots (#50– #55) that were part of the J. G. Romberger plan, known as the "Eastside Addition." They were purchased by Walter Zerbe and Catharine, and Lottie a single woman. On January 10, 1950 they sold the land to Ralph E. and Betty R. Lebo. This land, located east of Walnut Street on North 2nd Street, began on the southwest corner of lot 50 and ran to lot 56.

After they both had died, (Ralph died Jul 18, 2002, Betty Jul 31, 2002), their executor conveyed the property to Barbara A. (Novinger) Scheib on October 31, 2002. On May 13, 2003, Ricky L. Lesher and Barbara (Scheib) Lesher sold to Nathan E. and Steven E. Dagen.

HOME OF ROY D. AND REBECCA S. KLINGER 66-016-006 & 007
1295 N. 2nd Street & 2013 House (two tracts)

This property is made up of two tracts of ground that belonged to the J. G. Romberger plan. The first tract contained lots #56 to #59 on the North side of 2nd Street. Galen D. and Margaret E. Snyder purchased this tract and later sold to their daughter Evelyn and her husband Thomas Lehman on April 27, 1961. The Lehman's moved to Loyalton from Sunbury, and he was a foreman in the Lykens shirt factory.

The second tract contained lots #60 to #63, adjoining the first tract. It was also part of the J. G. Romberger plan and was sold to Floyd Harner on July 17, 1924. He sold to Gladys K. and Paul E. Lupold on January 16, 1937. On October 4, 1946 they sold to Evelyn A. and Thomas K. Lehman with a frame bungalow. Evelyn died on February 7, 1986. Thomas Lehman sold both properties to Rebecca S. and Roy D. Klinger on February 21, 1986. They are the present owners.

[*Thomas K. Lehman (1914 - 1988, bur Halifax Cem), m Evelyn A. _____ had these children*: Linda (   );
Rebecca (   ), m Roy D.Klinger, a son of Jonathan and Hilda (Miller) Klinger.

HOME OF KAREN E. BURRELL 66-016-008
(Was home of REVEREND GLEN AND MARGARET MATTER)
J. G. Romberger Plan
1305 North second Street – North Side)

This land was from the J. G. Romberger Plan. On September 18, 1945, Ira F. and Annie C. Row conveyed the lot to Quay and Kate A. Cooper. Darvin and Pauline Rabuck and Ruth Markel, single became the next owners. On April 25, 1978 they sold to Glenn and Margaret (Johns) Matter.

The lot remained vacant until Reverend Glenn and Margaret (Johns) Matter retired and moved back to Loyalton. After purchasing the lot, they had this ranch style home built about 1978. They both resided here until his death on April 24, 2005, and now Margaret continues to make her home until her death on August 8, 2009.

Glenn E. Matter was born in Millersburg May 28, 1914, a son of William E. and Hattie (Burrell) Matter.As a young adult he attended Albright College and became a pastor in the United Methodist Church, serving in several different places. Glenn E. Matter and Margaret L. Johns born Jul 14, 1910, a daughter of John Peter and Sarah Ellen (Miller) Johns were married July 14,1935. *They have two children*: *Jon W.* m to Ruth; *Paul E.* m to Lois.

HOME OF MARLIN AND DORIS C. BILLHIME 66-016-009
1351 North 2nd Street - North Side) house built 2005(

These lots are from the J.G. Romberger Plan. John Peter & Sarah E. Johns later purchased them. After John Peter Johns died, his widow Sarah sold them April 2, 1949 to Quay N, and Kate Cooper. On May 7, 1974 Quay M. Cooper's executor sold to Pauline Rebuck and Ruth Markel. Pauline Rebuck died (Nov 5, 1985), and her undivided interest in the property was conveyed to Darwin F. Rebuck. Darvin F. Rebuck and Ruth M. Markel became joint owners of these lots on July 17, 1987. Darvin F. Rebuck died in 1990, and Ruth M. Markel died June 24, 1996. Kay E. Rice a cousin became her executor. Kay and William Rice purchased the property on June 12, 1997. On October 18, 2002, William and Kay E. Rice conveyed the same to Marlin and Doris C. Billhime of Treverton.

[*BENJAMIN IRVIN MARKEL (1874 – 1937, bur Maple Grove Cem), a son of John and Anna (Lenker) Markel, m Emma Jane Wert (Jun 8, 1875 -Jun 13, 1939). *Benjamin Irvin and Emma Jane (Wert) Markel children*:
**J. Edwin (Jul 1901 – Jun 11, 1947, bur Maple Grove), m Mary E. ___ b 1905;
Fred Benjamin (Aug 23, 1906 – Mar 2 0, 1984, bur Maple Grove Cem), m 1st Pauline M. Row (1909 – Nov 5, 1985, bur Maple Grove Cem), a dau of Alfred H. and L. Catherine (Kessler) Row.. *Fred & Pauline Markel had a dau:* * Ruth M (Aug 30, 1927 – Jun 24, 1996, bur Maple Grove Cem). Fred m 2nd Aug 20, 1953, Annie E. (Rowe) Harper (1903 – 1981), widow of Harry Jacob Harper (1899 – 1943);
**PAULINE M. (1908 - Nov 5, 1985, bur Maple Grove Cem), m Darvin F. Rebuck (1923 – 1990), a son
**Jay Leon b 1909 m May 15, 1926 Velma Jane Stine (1908- 1955), a dau of Harry & Katie (Warful) Stine;
**Beatrice Marsella b Jan 6, 1914, m Eugene Meckley;
** Carrie Anna b Dec 11, 1918;

L to r: Homes of Marlin & Doris Billhime, Ray & Mamie Kratzer, Jefrey & Coleen Markel

HOME OF ROY R. & MAMIE KRATZER 66-016-010
(1395 North Second Street - North Side) 1961 house
From the J. G. Romberger plan, these lots were sold to Alfred H. Row. After his death, they were sold August 10, 1957 to Pauline M. and her husband Darwin F. Rebuck. On October 22, 1962 Darwin F. and Pauline M Rebuck transferred ownership of the lots to Pauline M Rebuck and Ruth M. Markel, joint tenants. Pauline M Rebuck died November 5, 1985, Darwin Rebuck died March 4, 1990): Ruth M. Markel became owner. Ruth M. Markel died June 24, 1996, and the property was sold on October 14, 1996 to Ray R. and Mamie L. Kratzer the present owners.

HOME OF JEFFREY L. AND COLEEN M. MARKEL 66-016-011
1435 North Second Street bordering east side of Chestnut St
These four lots (#80 -#83) were part of the J. G. Romberger plan. They were purchased by Beulah Lubold, who sold to Jennie D. Snyder. On March 27, 1950, Jennie D. Snyder sold the four lots to Gilbert E. Burrell, whom with his wife Margaret E. sold to Robert H. & Mary (Hoffman) Smeltz Oct 19, 1959. After Mary died, Robert and his son Larry conveyed on Dec 22, 2004, the lots to Jeffrey L and Colleen M. Markel.

[JEFFREY LEE MARKEL b Sep 17, 1962 , a son of Donald Eugene and Norma P. Pinkerton Markel, m Coleen Marie Troutman b Mar 18, 1963, a dau of Dallas and Eileen (Underkoffler) Troutman. *They have these children*: Brent; Collin Edward.]

HOME OF WILLIAM AND KAY E. RICE 66-016-088
1445 North Second Street 1969 house

This lot was also part of the J. G. Romberger plan. It was conveyed to William A. and Kay E. Rice, and they were the owners for many years.

HOME OF ROBIN C. SCHORR 66-016-089
(Corner of North Second Street and Stone Hill Road, house 1969)

L to r: House of Kay Rice & Bob Matter corner of 2nd & Stonehill

This lot was part of the land owned by Alfred H. Row. He sold November 30, 1957 to Claude S. Miller. On July 9, 1968, Claude S. Miller, conveyed to Glenn D. Wolfgang. Robert C. and Helen (Drum) Matter became the next owners on December 5, 1978. On June 12, 2000, Helen (Drum) Matter, widow sold the property to Ronald P. Weaver On August 11, 2014, he sold to Robin C. Schorr the present owner.

Claude & Lillian Miller

l to r: Louisianna (Kessler) Row, Pauline & Ruth Row, and Mrs. Reuben Kessler

The next several pages are devoted to photos of the houses located on the north side of second Street. They are identified by their parcel numbers, making it easy to find the original write-ups of the each individual property.

{The parcel numbers were not available when the research of this book was begun, making it necessary to "make room". for the photos at this later date.]

HOME OF ROBERT K. & Holly B. Saville 66-016-023

HOME OF RONALD L. AND KATHLEEN HIRSCH 66-016-024

Steven and Wanda Dagen 66-016-082

Nathan E. and Steven E.Dagen 66-016-005

James W. and Beverly J. Travitz 66-016-001

Vincent A. and Jennifer L. Liddick 66-016-002

Karen E. Burrell 66-016-008

Jeffrey L. and Coleen M. Markel 66-016-011

Roy D. and Rebecca S. Klinger 66-016-007

Ray R. and Mamie Kratzer 66-016-010

Chapter 9

NORTH FROM LOYALTON ALONG SOUTH CROSSROADS ROAD
(EAST & WEST SIDE OF ROAD)

Most of the land in this last section of Loyalton belonged to the Ferree family, and was inherited by the next generation of family members.

A tract that was inherited by the Bowman family was sold on April 12, 1869 to George Neagley. On April 1, 1878 George and Caroline Neagley conveyed 9 acres 95 perches of land with improvements to Charles Yohe. This land bordered the public road that at that time lead from Wiconisco to Millersburg, north to John M. Row land, south to land of Rebecca Gunderman. After Charles Yohe died, his widow Angeline and the children on March 11, 1899 sold the property to Daniel Wiest. On March 30, 1901 Daniel Wiest sold to George D. Kissinger. It bordered the land of Michael Gunderman, Charles Lebo and the road to Lykens. Many years later on July 19, 1943 George D. Kissinger sold to Woodrow E. Mattern. [See survey on page 112, land of Mattern, joined].

THE YOHE FAMILY
(Some help from Carol (Yohe) Golla)

MICHAEL YOHE (Mar 31, 1747 Baden, Bavaria– Dec 14, 1833 Wash Co., Pa.), m Anna Maria Shouse (1752 – 1832), **known children: JACOB** (1765 Easton, Northampton Co– 1828 Pottsville,Sch Co), **known children: Adam** (1785 – 1872), m Christiana Ann Sloppey (Jan 25, 1789 – Nov 11, 1837), **had these children** (b Jefferson, Pa.) : **Henry** b 1826; **Benjamin** (Dec 15, 1827 – Dec 15, 1894), m Barbara Smith (1827 – 1905) ; **William** (1789 Pottsville – 1827); **Benjamin** b 1790 Pottsville;

[**WILLIAM H. YOHE** (b c1824 - d Jun 28, 1882 in Valley View, bur Friedens Cem., Hegins, Sch Co with wife Annie), was probably a son of William Yohe of New Castle Twp, Sch Co. In 1810, he had a tavern that was on the border of Norwegian and New Castle Twp. His wife was a dau of John Boyer. William H. Yohe m first Maria Ossman (Dec 31, 1833 - Dec 29, 1855, bur St. Pauls (Artz) Cem in Sacramento, Sch Co). Marie Ossman was a dau of Phillip and Barbara Ossman. In 1880, William H. and Annie Yohe lived in Hegins, Sch Co. and had their son Ellsworth age 17, Isaac Yohe age 21, a nephew (probably Charles Yohe's son), and Hannah Artz age 56 with them. **William and Annie (Ossman) Yohe had a child Francis Edward** b Jun 1, 1851, died young and is buried with his mother.

William H. Yohe later m Annie _____ (Feb 23, 1833 - Jul 29, 1902, bur Friedens Cem, Hegins Sch Co.) **William H and Annie (___) Yohe had these children: Mary** b c1849; **Maclada** b c1853; **Cinderella** (1856 - 1861, bur Simeon Cem, Gratz).. A large tombstone surrounded by a sturdy iron fence marked her grave until the severe blizzard of 1993. During the storm a large tree fell over and destroyed that small section of the grave yard; **William H.** (b & d 1862, bur Simeon Cem); **Charles M** (1863 - 1864); **Ellsworth** b c1863; **Levi E.** (d Mar 21, 1913, age 52), m Amelia (Jan 29, 1863 - Jan 15, 1900, bur Friedens Cem. Hegins). Levi was the only member of the family to stay in this area. After William H. Yohe died, his widow Annie married William Scheib, but nothing more is known about him.

CHARLES YOHE (Apr 16, 1823 - Mar 9, 1898, of lung disease, bur Hoffman Cem) ,is believed to be a son of William and _____ (Boyer) Yohe above or Benjamin and Sarah Yohe. He m Angeline Henninger (Oct 17, 1830 – Sep 1, 1910), a dau of Sebastian Henninger of Lykens Twp. In 1870, the Yohe family lived in Washington Twp, and he was farming. Sebastian Henninger age 80, father of Angeline lived with them. Also Jane L Smith age 10, and Andrew Shitz age 18. Charles and Angeline lived in Washington Twp in 1880. Charles was a Civil War Vet. **Charles and Angeline (Henninger) Yohe had these known children (some bap Salem Ref, Eville & St. John's Luth, Lykens): William Henry** (bapt at Hoffman Ch Nov 12, 1848 – d Jul 19, 1911), m Isabella Bechtel (Nov 1859 – Jan 19, 1901), and lived in Washington Twp in 1880. **William and Isabella (Bechtel) Yohe had these children: Jennie May** (Nov 12, 1872 – Dec 8, 1957), m John Harvey Klinger; ; **Harry Edwin** (Oct 2,1876 – Jun 23, 1926); **Angeline** (Jan 6,1878 Dayton, Sch Co – Apr 30, 1892, Shamokin), m Jacob C. Shaffer; ; **Estella** b Jul 2, 1879; **Jonathan Albert** b Jan 11, 1881; **James Monroe** (1882 – 1938);**Amy Malinda** b Jan 1886; **Arthur Allen** (1887 – 1966); **Clara** (1890 – 1915);Edward (1892 – 1968, Tacoma, Wa); **Walter** (1894 – 1960); **Claude** (1896 – 1956); **Frederick** (b 1898 Gowen City – d 1960 Danville), m Violet Keen; **Isaac** (1857 – 1923, bur Greenwood Cem, T.C.), m Ida

____ (1865 – 1924), moved to Tower City; **Sarah Malinda** (1859 - 1863, bur Salem Union Cem, E'ville) **Ida May** b Aug 19, 1869, bapt Salem Ref, E'ville – 1867 – 1851, bur Maple Grove Cem), m John F. Smeltzer (1867 – 1966); **Katie Adeline** (Aug 24, 1872 – 1932, bur Maple Grove Cem), m Charles F. Eby (1870 – 1938); **Alice L** (1874 – 1944, bur Maple Grove Cem), m Daniel M Lettich (1870 – 1957).

THE ROW FAMILY FARM & OTHER ACREAGE
(Some Became John David Row Farm)

An area on the eastern border of Washington Township containing 20 acres (part of land from Ferree family to Row family), was inherited by John M. and Elizabeth Row, and sold to Nathaniel Row January 18, 1851. Nathaniel and Alabama Row sold to Daniel Wommer April 1856. He and his wife Elizabeth sold to Adam D. Row with appurtenances Apr 1, 1874. On February 16, 1901, Alfred C. Row conveyed 6 acres of that tract to Charles A. Row, and he conveyed to Frank and Cora Weaver April 16, 1920. Several years later on March 23, 1928, Frank and Cora Weaver sold their land to Annie and Gideon Bruner. The Bruner's sold to Alfred H. Row.

Adam D. Row, a blacksmith conveyed three other tracts of cleared and mountain land, (a total of about 14 acres) from the twenty acres mentioned above, to John David Row, a carpenter on September 27, 1909. A very old log house was on the land. A dirt lane leading from Water Street to Short Mountain gave access to this property. The land was located adjacent to the home of the late Gideon Bruner. This was the old family homestead.

When John D. Row built his house on Main Street, he and his father traded houses. John David's daughter Annie (married to Harry J. Harper) received the farm land and sold it on June 26, 1967, to her daughter Beatrice married to Robert O. Bonawitz. After Beatrice died, Robert and their daughter Sharon (Mrs. James Rissinger) sold small tracts to Robert L. and Linda L. Stoneroad and Tyrone P. Troutman, Jr., forming a small settlement of new homes. Eventually the old log house was accidentally burned to the ground. Later Sharon and Jim Rissinger built a new house on the site of the old log structure.

l to r: Annie Row Harper Markel, Beatrice Harper Bonawitz, Jennie Hassinger Row On the Porch Of The Old Log House

New Home Built By Sharon & Jim Rissinger On Site Of Old Row Farm House

HISTORY OF LYKENS TOWNSHIP

Cornelius and Eva Row sold about fifteen acres (in 3 separate tracts), to Rebecca wife of Michael Gunderman. It became a very early homestead as early as 1846, on the eastern edge of Wash Township. [See 1875 map.]

A large portion of the land inherited by John M. Row from Isaac Ferree was sold to Sarah Weiss, and became the "New Loyalton." The heirs of Sarah Weiss sold a tract of 38 acres 100 ¾ perches to George W. Kessler, and he sold to Alfred H. Row on April 2, 1910. That land bordered along North Second Street, west across Crossroad Road to the Good Tannery, north to about the area that later became the Homer Hassinger farm.

ROBERT L. & ELIZABETH JOHNSTONE?
HOME BEFORE LESTER HASSINGER (North Crossroad Road)

This land was part of the land owned by Sarah M. Weiss, and sold to George W. Kessler.

Mickie Row was a member of the Citizen Band. He had in his possession a unique stone about eight inches round and full of holes. He found it in the swamp near his house, had it analyzed and learned that it was a meteorite. He displayed it beside his well. While Micky lived here, a solid fence of rose bushes, all colors extended from his place to the house of Emma Row (later home of Lester Hassinger.)
1940-50s a tall man card shark owned it. He won Irish Sweepstakes – and put up brown stone house. Maybe Bob Bowman.

HOME OF WILLIAM E. STEELE
(North Crossroads Road – was Lester Hassinger's)

This land was part of the land that Sarah M Weiss owned and sold to Andrew Weiss. In April 1904, Andrew Weiss conveyed to George W. Kessler and on August 298, 1906, they conveyed to Emma J. Radel, wife of Amos A. Radel. On May 26, 1911, Emma J. Radel sold the land to Mary Williard, and she sold to Emma J. Rowe on July 3, 1919. The heirs of Emma J. Rowe, Beulah and Norman Lubold, Elizabeth and E. E. Shoop, M. E. and J. A. Rittner, and Florence and George Bateman conveyed the property to Lester and Ruby Hassinger on June 27, 1928. It contained two separate tracts, one had the two-story frame dwelling and ½ acres of land, the adjoining small tract contained 51 square perches. It was bound by land of Juliann Row, Albert Row, west by J. C. Fisher and south by Mrs. George W. Kessler.

During the 1950 to 1970s Lester had a coal washery across the street on the site of the new housing development. After both Lester and Ruby Hassinger died, the executrix, Mary Ellen Bryne sold February 26, 2003 to Brent R. and Estreya L. Woodcock. They sold to William E. Steele October 2004.

[EMMA J. BURD (Jan 21, 1864 – Jul 17, 1912, bur Simeon Cem), m Amos A. Radel (Apr 20, 1859 – May 4, 1936), a son of Solomon & Catherine (Shaffer) Radel. **Amos A. and Emma J. (Burd) Radel had these children (some bapt Simeon Ch, Gratz): Jacob Clarence** b Sep 15, 1897; **Florence Emily** b Jan 14, 1902;

[EMMA JANE BURD (May 4, 1863 – Feb 26, 1927), a dau of Isaac and A. Mary (Ferree) Burd. , m Oct 6, 1883, William H. Row (Feb 10, 1864 – Jul 8, 1925, bur Simeon Cem, Gratz), a son of Lemuel and Elmira (Hawk) Row. **William H. and Emma Jane Row had these children (some bapt Simeon Luth, Gratz): Jennie** d young; **Mary Elmira** b Mar 24, 1884 m ___ Hoyer (   ), **had a dau** Leah; **Beulah Mary** b Dec 11, 1889, m Norman E. Lubold, lived in Lykens Twp in 1920. **Norman & Beulah May (Row) Lubold children:** Emma b c1913 **James** b c1916; Glen b 1919;
Elisabeth Louisa b   Oct 7, 1892 m E. E. Shoop;
Nora O. b May 1895, m J. A. Rettner;
 Florence b 1900, m ___ Bateman..]

PROPERTY GONE WITH NO TRACE
(Was HOME OF MAGDALENA CRAWFORD 1858 (Samuel Gunderman in 1875)

Peter Boyer received this land in 1842, and conveyed ½ acre of his land to Magdalena Crawford about 1850. She is listed as owner on the township map of 1858. Magdalena Crawford continued to live on the property until her death. She had been married to John Crawford, and they lived in Lykens Twp as early as 1820. But things were not going well with the family. [Details & information on the Jacob Sierer property.] Magdalena and John Crawford were divorced about 1842. By 1850 John lived with the Amos Hoffman family. Magdalena lived here in Wiconisco Twp., and had her two daughters Matilda and Susanna with her. According to orphan court records these two children were "insane" and after Magdalena died, they were taken to the home for insane in Swatara Twp., Harrisburg. In 1880 they were listed as servants, and John Lyme steward, and his family had charge of the home.

After Magdalena died, her son Elias Crawford arranged for a public sale to be held on July 27, 1867 at her home. However, no one bid on the property. Elias arranged for another sale to be held on November 8, 1867, and at that time Samuel and Catharine Wolf presented the highest bid of $101.50. The property was described as having a two story log house and frame stable on the land. It was located near the brickyard beside the Wiconisco creek.

Samuel and Catherine Wolf of Lykens Township owned the property briefly, then conveyed the ½ acre to Samuel Gunderman on May 20, 1868. At that time a stable and fruit trees were on the land.

THE CRAWFORD/ CROFFERT FAMILY

[The **CRAWFORD** family settled in the Stouchsburg area of Berks Co. We have found the following two family members believed to be brothers.
*JOHN CRAWFORD (no dates), m Catherine _____ , and lived in Stouchsburg, Berks Co. **John & Catherine Crawford had one known child: <u>SUSANNA CATHARINA</u>** b Oct 7, 1774, bapt Stouchsburg.

*FREDRICH CRAWFORD (   ), m Catharine _____ , lived in Stouchsburg, Berks Co. before coming to Up. Dauphin. **Fredrich & Catharine Crawford known children (some bapt Stouchsburg, St. Jacob's Luth, Pine Grove Twp, Klinger Ch, Lykens Twp): <u>POLLY</u>** b Jun 27, 1796; **<u>JOHANNES</u>** b Mar 7, 1798; **<u>CATHARINA</u>** b Oct 1, 1802; **<u>SUSANNA</u>** b Nov 20, 1807.

[**JOHN CRAWFORD** (b c1795 – d after 1850), m in Lykens Twp Dec 5, 1819 Magdalena Romberger (1801 – Feb 3, 1867) death record in Hoffman Ch book). a dau of Adam & Anna Catharine (Paul) Romberger. On Nov 23, 1842, John filed for a divorce claiming that Magdalena deserted him in August 1839. The divorce file mentions that she was Magdalena Romberger. Orphan court records, and Romberger sponsors for the children support that fact. Also a deed for a nearby property states "Mary Romberger (alias Crawford). **John and Magdalena Crawford had these known children (some bapt Hoffman Ch): Catharine** b 1820 m Adam Johnson; **Elisabeth** (Oct 20, 1821 –May 29,1902) m Daniel D. Bohner b 1821, a son of Jacob & Catherine (Deibler) Bohner; **Elias** b May 6,1824, m Catherine _____ b c1833, lived in Susquehanna Twp, Juniata Co in 1860. **Elias and Catherine Crawford children:** Benneville b c1847; John R. b c1850; Mary b c1853; **Angeline** b Dec 11, 1826, m Charles Frederick b c1817, moved to Laney Town & Big Mountain area of Northld Co. In 1880 **Charles and Angeline (Crawford) Frederick children in their household:** Nelson b c1858; Caroline b c1862; Sarah C. b c1870. **Matilda** b Feb 19, 1829; **Louisiana** b Mar 9, 1831; **Jeremiah** b Jul 7, 1833 - __), m Anna Mary Tschupp b Jul 7, 1833, a dau of Johannes and Sarah (Wertz) Shoop. Jeremiah and Anna Mary "Polly" Crawford lived in Susquehanna Twp, Juniata Co in 1860. **They had these children: <u>Sarah</u>** b Dec 18, 1851, bapt Stone Valley Ch; <u>Hiram</u> b c1853; <u>James</u> b c1856; <u>Amos</u> b Mar 21, 1858; <u>John</u> b c1861; <u>Jeremiah</u> b c1867.
MICHAEL CRAWFORD (   ), m Elisabeth _____ **Michael and Elisabeth Crawford had one known child: Isreal** b Feb 12, 1832, bapt Klingers Ch, m Phebe b c1836, lived in Ringgold, Jefferson Co. in 1880. **Isreal and Phebe Crawford children: <u>Samuel</u>** b c1859; <u>Frederick</u> b c1863; <u>William</u> b c1865; Frank b c1870; <u>Cora</u> b c1872; <u>John</u> b c1875; <u>Lydia D.</u> b c1879.

[**Samuel Gunderman** (1842 – Nov 17, 1916, bur Oak Hill Cem, Mbg), was a Civil War veteran, and while serving at Canasaw Mountain in June 1862, he received a gunshot wound that severed his right foot. He later received an artificial foot from the government. He married Josephine Anna Long of Halifax. Samuel applied for a Civil War pension, and the record shows his brother Michael making the following statement as a witness: "Samuel and Anna were married at a very young age before the war and lived in a house in the little saloon below Loyalton. They lived together for twenty years, and then were separated and Josephine went off to Cleveland and we never saw her again." Josephine Anna Died in Cleveland about 1914, and is buried in Monroe Street Cemetery. More information in GUNDERMAN genealogy.]

On January 27, 1884, Samuel and Catharine Leidig were married by Justice of the Peace George Hoffman. On April 26, 1882, Samuel Gunderman conveyed the ½ acre of land to Jennie A. Walter. It was described as being along the road from Loyalton to Uniontown, adjoining the land of Benjamin Welker, H. C. Beshler, and west to Daniel A. Good's land. Jennie A. Walter transferred the land to Jacob F. Long on May 8, 1894. At that time it was described as adjoining the land of Henry Zimmerman estate, Jacob Hoke estate, Short Mountain Coal Company. Several months later, Jacob F. Long conveyed the land to Felix H. Rissinger on August 24, 1894. Felix Rissinger sold the land and house to Benjamin Welker on Jan 16, 1909. It has since apparently become part of an adjoining property.

Another small tract may have joined this one. Two one acre tracts were owned by Adam and Christiana Row, and were surveyed with privileges to William Moffet. In April 1842, the Moffet heirs sold to Adam Row, and after he died the property belonged to his wife Mary. She later married John Delp, and in 1858 Mary and John Delp sold to Anna Ferree. She sold to Charles F. Harner on April 1, 1884. [John Delp died about June 1861.]

HOME OF JOHN M. TSCHOPP66-005-004
(Was Homer Hassinger Farm)

This small farm is made up of three tracts of land, each having a different background of ownership. The 1858 map shows three families living in this immediate area on small parcels of land. They were Mrs.Crawford, J. Delp, and Wolf. By 1875 Three new families lived on this land: S.Gunderman, B. Welker, and L.Litener. A deed of purchase has not been found for Litener. The foundation of an old house was known to exist on the north side of the Homer Hassingerfarm, perhaps another early homestead.

One tract of this land containing 7 acres 29 perches belonged to Peter Boyer, and after his death, his heirs conveyed the acreage with a dwelling and out buildings to Daniel Wolf in April 1855. Daniel and Catherine Wolf assigned the same land to "Mary Romberger (alias Crawford)" March 14, 1859, recorded July 1861. Mary assigned the same land to Sarah Crabb September 28, 1865, and Sarah and William P. Crabb assigned to George Williard on April 1, 1868. George and Lavina Williard sold the property to Benjamin Welker April 1, 1874, and Benjamin conveyed to his wife Elizabeth Welker on November 12, 1877. [On 1875 map]. Joel A. Hassinger became the next owner in April 1884, and sold March 29, 1890 (along with the 4 acre tract) to Harry T. Zimmerman..

Another smaller tract containing 3 acres 1 perch was owned by Jacob and Catherine Emerick. On March 8, 1852 they sold to John and Lydia Brosius, they in turn sold November 22, 1856 to John and Mary Delp. [On 1875 map]. John Delp died about 1861, and his children, (Solomon, George and wife Catherine, Lydia and husband John Brosius), conveyed the land to Daniel and Hannah Romberger on April 5, 1876. They sold to Cornelius and Polly Gunderman on April 22, 1878. The Gunderman's transferred the same land to Adam Weaver on February 23, 1887. Adam and Sarah Weaver sold to Mary Klinger March 31, 1894. Mary Klinger of Uniontown sold to George O. and Daisy Boyer April 2, 1900, and they sold to Harry Zimmerman February 16, 1905.

A third tract containing 4 acres 136 perches of land was owned by Alfred H. Row (and has the same background).. He sold to Joel A. and Amelia Hassinger. On March 29, 1890, Joel and Amelia Hassinger conveyed to Harry T. Zimmerman. Prior to the time when Homer Hassinger owned the farm, the Wesley Troutman family lived here, and later Clinton Rowe and his family. The farm then was abandoned for sometime.

On April 14, 1934 the heirs of Harry Zimmerman conveyed the combined three tracts to Homer and Mary Hassinger in the form of a mini farm. The nucleus of the complex was the 7 acres with dwelling.

When the Hassinger family bought the farm, it had no running water, so the whole supply of water had to be carried from the spring at the bottom of the hill behind their barn. That meant water for drinking, washing, cooking, and laundry. Also for the cows,pigs, chickens, geese and horse. In 1936, a well was dug on the farm. They sold milk to a nearby dairy, and Mary worked as a cook at the Barn Bar & Restaurant.

On March 17, 1948, Homer E. and Mary J. Hassinger purchased another 17 acres of land from Harvey I. Crabb. It was located across the road from their original property, and was part of the land that Alfred H. and Louisa K. Rowe conveyed to J. G. Romberger in April 1924. J. G. Romberger conveyed to William W. Crabb in that same year. Frank Wagner rented a small plot of ground from the Hassinger's in the late 30's and built and ran a coal shaker for about ten years. The Hassinger's conveyed several plots of ground to separate individuals, and several new houses were built on this land. Homer and Mary lived here for the remainder of their lives. Homer died Nov 5, 1963, and Mary died in 1998. The farm was conveyed October 8, 1999 to John M. Tschopp.

[*HOMER EDWARD HASSINGER* (Jan 7, 1907 – Nov 5,1963 bur Maple Grove Cem, E'ville), a son of Jacob and Maud (Miller) Hassinger, m Mary "Polly" Jane Brown (Jul 3, 1902 – Dec 2, 1998), a dau of Charles and Polly (Rothermel) Brown from Lykens Twp. *Homer Edward & Mary (Brown) Hassinger children: Jean Romaine* m Leroy Patton of Halifax; *Elva* b Jul 9, 1933, m William Miller of Spring Glen, *they had these children: Marilyn Marlene* b 1957; *William Jacob* b 1959; *Lee Jay* b 1965; *Catherine* b Oct 31, 1936 m Ralph Kieffer of Dornsife, near Rebuck – *had these children: Glenn Edward* b 1957; *David Burlington* b 1960; *Miles Eugene* b 1961; *Carol Louise* [*more Hassinger info elsewhere.*]

THOMAS L. JR. AND WIFE KAREN E. ROBERTS 66-005-0041
215 South Crossroads Rd.

This land has the same history as the adjoining properties. After Homer Hassinger died, his widow Mary Jane Hassinger conveyed this 2 acre lot to Carl W. and Linda N. Back on April 21, 1976. Several years later on March 16, 1990 Carl W. and Linda N Back conveyed to Thomas L. and Karen E. Roberts, the present owners.

HOME OF MICHAEL D. & GLORIA J. USUKA

On October 31, 1972 Mary Jane Hassinger, widow conveyed an acre of ground to Michael D. and Gloria J. Usuka. They had a brick ranch style house built on the lot. They continue to reside here.

HOME OF EDWARD J. & LINDA M. BECHTEL

On June 27, 1973 Mary Jane Hassinger, widow conveyed a tract of land known as lot # 4 to Edward J. and Linda M. Bechtel. That same year Silas Troutman constructed this ranch style brick home on their lot. The Bechtel's continue to reside here.

SMALL TRACTS SOLD FROM HASSINGER FARM

Mary J. Hassinger, widow conveyed two tracts of land totaling 3.39 acres (1970 & 1988) to Clair E. and Jeannie R. Williard. The land was bound by corner of land of Mary J. Hassinger and former Herman T. Phillips. It was part of the premises that M. D. Zimmerman sold to Homer E. and Mary J. Hassinger on April 14, 1934, and also part of premises that Harvey I. Crabb sold to the Hassinger's on March 17, 1948.

Another tract of land beginning at Crossroads Road, on the corner of lands of Karen E. and Thomas L. Roberts Jr. borders on the Wiconisco Creek. In April 1 976 Mary J. Hassinger sold a 2.660 acre tract to Carl W. Back, Jr and Linda M. his wife. On March 16, 1990, Carl W. and Linda M. Back granted the premises to Thomas L. and Karen E. Roberts. The land bordered on land of Ruby Hassinger, and George Luther.

LOUIS M. & STEPHAN A. MELSKY
(WAS THE WILLIAM CRABB FARM)

This farm, located on the eastside of the Crossroads Road, has the same background as the Bush farm. After several early owners, it became part of the Romberger land. After Daniel Romberger died, his widow Elizabeth and other heirs, in 1883 conveyed their fifty-acre homestead made up of farm and timberland, to Cyrus Romberger and John A. Romberger. The next year, on April 1, 1884, Cyrus and Elizabeth Romberger and John A. and Emma Romberger conveyed the fifty-acre farm to Elizabeth Welker, wife of Benjamin Welker. It was sold subject to an agreement that concerned the use of the timber on the land. This land bordered Short Mountain Coal Company, H. Beshler, Gunderman, Josel Hassinger, and Edward Romberger.

Benj. F. Welker Family –top row l to r: Wm. F.(1868–1921); Marg (1876 -1942); Benj. Jr. b 1874; Jenny A. (1879 –1913); Front: Eliz Gunderman Welker; Chas 1883 –1973); Benj Sr. 1849 – 1926)

The Welker's lived here until April 6,1918, when the Welker heirs sold this fifty-acre farm to William H. Crabb. The Crabb family owned the property until March 17, 1948 when they sold the fifty acre farm with timberland to Herman T.& Evelyn I. Phillips. On July 3, 1995, the Phillips' sold to Louise M and Stephan A. Melsky. Several years later on May 12, 2003 Robert C. and Melisse E, Wise became the owners, and they sold November 12, 2012 to Brian C. and Hope R. Egli. On November 12, 2014, Christian B. and Lillian R. Stoltzfus became the present owners.

Jonas Sarah (Kocher) Welker family - Children not in order: Hannah b 1843, Jacob 1846, Sarah 1848; Benj. 1850, Isaac 1852, Geo W. 1854, John A.1856

William Henry Welker (1835 –1922) & wife Elizabeth (Shoop) Welker (He was a Civil War Vet)

THE BENJAMIN WELKER FAMILY

[*ELIZABETH GUNDERMAN WELKER* (May 13, 1844 - Sep 26, 1908, bur Hoffman Cem, alone) , dau of Mic hael and Rebecca (Riegel) Gunderman, m Wash Twp. Sep 15, 1867 by Rev. M. Fernsler. Benjamin Welker (Nov 10, 1849 - Apr 1, 1926, d of blood poisoning, bur Fairview Cem, Williamstown, alone. Benjamin was a son of Jonas and Sarah (Kocher) Welker of Washington Twp. Benjamin was a Civil War Veteran, applied for peddlers license Feb 15, 1900 under the Vet Law. A copy of a Fraktur from his pension record is housed in the Gratz Hist Soc library with the pension records. Before Elizabeth died, she composed a will dispersing her goods in such a way that it displeased her husband. *Benjamin & Elizabeth (Gunderman) Welker children (some bap Zion Luth, Lykens:* *SARAH ELLEN* b _____ m Jul 19, 1886, Henry Mumma of Lykens. Benjamin Welker was listed as the parent; *WILLIAM FRANCIS* (May 26, 1868 – Apr 18, 1921 in mining accident, bur Greenwood Cem., Tower City), m Harriet Amelia Jury (Jul 26, 1868 – Oct 12, 1939), a dau of John Henry and Susannah (Knoll) Jury; *JOHN E.* (1870 - 1871); *EMMA REAN* b Jul 29, 1872 - d Oct 25, 1873, bur Hoffman Cem); *BENJAMIN FRANKLIN* (Aug 12, 1874 – Mar 1937, bur Lykens), m Emma Russell (Nov 1876 – Nov 1937), had a son bapt Hoffman Ch: *Joseph Benjamin* (Nov 3, 1896 – 1956), m Irene Starnowsky; *MARGARET REBECCA ELIZABETH* (Dec 2 0, 1876 - d Jun 10, 1942, bur Fairview Cem, Williamstown), m Sep 22, 1894 at the home of her parents to Andrew Peter Schoffstall (Jun 1866 Mexico, Juniata Co - Feb 1937), a son of William and Mary (Swanger) Schoffstall. Andrew P moved to Loyalton, later to Lykens and was in restaurant business in Lykens Hotel. He was killed in an auto accident while traveling to Pottsville to see his wife who was in the hospital.

JENNIE AGNES (Nov 16, 1879 – Dec 7, 1913), m May 28, 1898 in Donaldson to Samuel Shell (Jan 1,1832 – Dec 18, 1905, bur Greenwood Cem, Tower City). *Samuel and Jennie Agnes Welker Shell had two children: Charles R.* b Mar 21, 1901, lived in Lykens; *Carrie E* b Aug 23, 1903. Jennie Agnes was the 2nd wife of Samuel Shell. His first wife Hannah ____ (1838 - 1895), is buried with Samuel. He was a Civil War Vet, in Co. C, 36th Regt, Penna Militia; *CHARLES R.* (Sep 17, 1883 – May 1973, bur Fairview Cem), m Virginia A. Zimmerman (Dec 1, 1881 – Mar 8, 1955), a dau of Reuben & Priscilla (Kinsinger) Zimmerman;

[*HERMAN T. PHILLIPS* Mar 29, (1916 - Oct 29, 1994), bur Simeon Cem, a son of Oscar Howard & Margaret E (Strayer) Phillips. He m Evelyn I. Snyder(b 1918- ____), from Mahantongo area. More info under Philips family genealogy.]

THE CRABB / KRAPP FAMILY

Some members of the Crabb family settled early in Berks County. A George Krapp and wife had a son George baptized c 1781 in Stouchburg Church.

GEORGE CRABB – two early members of the family lived in this vicinity. George lived in Mahanoy Twp., Northld Co. *A George and Sarah Crabb had three children (some bapt Hoffman Ch): GEORGE* b May 1812; *JOHANNES* b Sep 6, 1815 ; *John and Maria Crabb of Hebe had these children (some bapt Klinger Zion Ch): Johannes* b Jun 8, 1847; *Magdalena* b May 13, 1819;

*PETER CRABB b c1787 may be a son or brother of George Crabb. He m Mary Magdalena b c1804. She may have been his second wife. They both either died before 1870 or moved to another area. *Peter and Mary Magdalena Crabb had these children:*

**HENRY (Apr 13, 1817 – Feb 18, 1856), m Lydia Ann Schoffstall (May 26, 1826 – Sep 10, 1873), a dau of Henry Schoffstall. Henry and Lydia Crabb are bur in Simeon Cem, but not next to each other. They lived in Gratz in 1850. *Henry and Lydia Ann (Schoffstall) Crabb had these children:*

William P. (Apr 28, 1843 - May 1, 1917, bur Maple Grove Cem, E'ville), m Nov 9, 1870, Sarah Welker (Dec 19,1847 - Aug 24, 1922), a dau of _____. In 1860 William lived with Samuel and Sarah Schoffstall. In 1880 he and Sarah lived in Lykens Twp and he was employed as a miller. *William and Sarah (Welker) Crabb children: ****Jonathan or John E* (Dec 31, 1871 – Mar 22, 1926, bur Maple Grove Cem, E'ville), WW1 Vet.;** Katie Ann* b Mar 6, 1875, bapt Hoffman Ch – d 1951, bur Maple Grove Cem, E'ville), m Henry Ulsh (1869 – 1929); *****William Wilson* (Mar 29, 1876 – Jan 3, 1948); *****Sadah* b c1878 m ___ Farnsler, moved to Harrisburg; *****Harvey I* (1879 – 1971, bur Hoffman Cem), m Carrie A.____ (1886 – 1980) *Harvey I and Carrie A _____ Crabb children:* Freeman Harvey b May 7, 1903 Russell Appleton b Nov 2, 1904, m Jan 7, 1922, Alverda Schlegel; Alma Catherine b Mar 20, 1907, m ; Nevin Mathew b Mar 28,1909, m Anna Daniel; Lillie b c1912; Kenneth b c 1914 Lamar E.b Sep 10, 1925; ****Issac* b c1845; ****Amanda* b c1847 m James Kolva; *James and Amanda (Crabb) Kolva children (some bapt Ref. Simeon Ch: ****William* Theodore b Nov 9, 1868; *****Henry Joseph* b Nov 17, 1870; *****Lydian* b May 24, 1872; *****Ida* Elisabeth b Feb 11, 1874, bapt Hoffman Ch.
****Lloyd F. (1884 – 1958, bur Maple Grove Cem); *****Edward H* (1888 – 1960, bur Maple Grove Cem), m Sallie M. (1881 – 1940);
**BENJAMIN b c1824, m Mary Ann Enty b c1832, of Sch Co. After the Civil War, Benjamin lived in Sacramento where he was employed as a blacksmith, working for Edward Wiest at the hotel. In 1870, Benjamin, his wife and four children lived in Gratz. He continued work as a blacksmith along with his brother Jeremiah and another relative George Crabb. They all lived in the same house. Benjamin also lived in Berrysburg at one time, and later moved to Fountain, Sch Co. He eventually moved to Porter Twp, where he and his brother Jeremiah were partners in a blacksmith shop located beside the old Williams Valley mine between Reinerton and Muir. *Benjamin and Mary Ann (Enty) Crabb children: ***Ellen* b 1853 m Jan 18, 1874 to Jeremiah Moor of Williamstown. She m 2nd Calvin Phoenix (1853 – 1936), and Martin. She is bur in Shamokin, Northld Co; ****Jeremiah* b c1855; ****William* b c1864; ****Laura* b c1866;
***Benjamin W. b 1869.

**JEREMIAH b c1826, m before 1880 Lugitta b c1855. Tombstones have not been found. In 1850 and 1860 they lived with his parents in Gratz, and he was employed as a blacksmith. In 1870 he continues to be a blacksmith, and Mary age 46 and Amanda age 24 (probably his sisters) lived with him. Jeremiah and Lugitta had a son William b c1876.

EDWARD (Nov 12, 1832 - Oct 26, 1886, bur Simeon Cem), m Catherine Jones b c1847. In 1850 Edward lived with the Samuel Umholtz family. IN 1870 Edward was a shoemaker in Gratz. **Edward and Catherine (Jones) Crabb had these children: *****William** b c1864; *****Ida** b c1868; *****Margaret** b 1870; *****Mary** b c1874; *****George E** (1877 - 1879, bur Simeon Cem); *****Sadie Minerva** (1880 - 1881, bur Simeon Cem). Edward was a veteran of the Civil War.

**ELIZABETH (Aug 21, 1836 - Sep 3, 1855, bur Simeon Cem)

**MARY ANN (Sep 14, 1838 - Sep 14, 1857)

**SARAH b c1841 probably m William Brown and had twin dau's Mary Ann and Sarah Ann b c1858. In 1860, William and Sarah Brown lived in a section of her parents home.

JOHN PETER b c1843 m in 1866 in Gratz to Anne E. Engleman. They were married by the Justice of the Peace Keiser. An infant born to them is bur in Simeon cem. **They had two other children: *****Wellington** b Oct 7, 1869; *****Engleman** b Oct 19, 1873. John Peter Crabb was a blacksmith. He lived in Gratz until 1866, then moved to Wiconisco where he was shoeing horses for the coal company. He later moved to Pittsburgh in 1873, to Tower City in 1875, and eventually moved to Harrisburg permanently. His occupation was consistently work as a blacksmith. He was a veteran of the Civil War.

**AMANDA b c1846.

LEVI LITENER (3 acres)

(This acreage has not been identified. The property apparently disappeared and the land became part of an adjoining tract.

THE LITENER/LYTER/LEITER FAMILY

[The Lyter (Leiter, Litener, many spellings) family is descended from Jacob Lyter (b c1706 – d Feb 1764), a Swiss immigrant. He came to Lancaster County during the early part of the 1700's but later migrated to Washington County, Maryland. Most of the family was of the Mennonite faith. **Jacob Lyter had these children:** **John** b c1734; **Christian** b 1736; **Abraham** b1740; **Elisabeth** b 1741; **Jacob** b1749; **Peter** b c1751 – d 1792 Lanc Co; **Barbara**; **Anna** (no dates) m Peter Good; **Veronica.**

*CHRISTIAN LYTER (b Ger   - d age 104 yrs old, died one morning while eating breakfast according to Dau Co Hist.). **Christian Lyter m _____ and had these children:**

PETER b Mar 25, 1789 in Low Pax Twp – d Feb 12, 1870 bur Meth Cem, Halifax), m Jane Page (Dec 19, 1788 - Dec 16, 1865). **Peter and Jane (Page) Lyter had these children;

***JOSEPH P (Nov 19, 1810 - Nov 6, 1881, bur Fairview Cem, Fisherville), m Elizabeth Bowman (Aug 30, 1814 - Jul 26, 1906) Lived in Jackson Twp in 1880. Joseph and Elizabeth Lyter had a son **John Harrison** b Nov 8, 1841 bapt Fetterhoff Ch. He m Sarah A ___ b c1842, had a son Joseph A. b c1865. They lived in Jackson Twp in 1880 and he was blacksmith;

Peter B. (Sep 16, 1842 – Jan 3, 1892), bur Fairview Cem, Fisherville), m at Matamoras Mar 4, 1869 to Mary Malinda Sweigard b 1852. Peter served in Co E of the 9th Pa Cav during the Civil War. In March 1865 while serving he was taken prisoner at Monroe Cross Roads, N.C. and taken to libby Prison. He was a huckster and carpenter in civilian life, and they lived in Halifas, Enders and Elizabethville. In 1880 they lived in Washington Twp where he was a hotel keeper. They had Victoria Bechtel age age and Samuel Zerfing with them in 1880. **Peter and Mary Malinda (Sweigard). Lyter had these children:** Robert E. b c1870; Harry W. b c1872; John Harrison (Nov 18, 1877 - Jan 14, 1935, bur Maple Grove Cem E'ville). After Peter died, Mary M Sweigard Lyter m Sep 6, 1910 to Philip Hawk. [See write-up in Hawk family history.]

***CHRISTIAN b May 23, 1812, Low Pax Twp – d Jul 9, 1874, bur Meth Cem, Halifax), m Catharine Bowman b Sep 16, 1818 – d Jan 10, 1896) . He moved to Halifax with his father in 1831, learned the trade of blacksmith. He also traveled over many parts of this region as an auctioneer. **Christian and Catharine (Bowman) Lyter had these children:** Ellen **Victoria** b Jan 20, 1840 bapt Fetterhoff's Ch.

***HENRY** (Jan 15, 1816 – Jun 10, 1896, bur Longs Cem, Halifax), m Susannah Miller (May 3, 1822 - Nov 28, 1903). Henry and Susanna lived in Halifax Twp in 1880. **Henry and Susanna (Miller) Leitner had these children: Sarah Jane** (Jan 27, 1841 – Nov 6, 1918) bur Fetterhoff Cem), m Samuel B. Chubb (Nov 22, 1835), son of Henry and Nancy (Miller) Chubb; Emma L b c1864 lived with them in 1880, as did I. S. Dunkel age 15. Samuel Chubb was a Civil War Vet.

***ABRAHAM** (1819 – 1898), m Magdalena ___ (1826 – 1902). They lived in Halifax in 1880 and their two sons Amon age 33 a stone cutter and Albert 25 also lived with them.

***DANIEL** (Oct 6, 1821 – May 6, 1883), m Mary Amelia Hoffman (Jun 19, 1823 – Sep 11, 1866, bur Meth Cem, Halifax), a dau of Daniel George and Susanna (Harman) Hoffman. Daniel was a Civil War Vet.

***JOHN** (no dates)

***MOSES** (b 1827 - _____), m Mary M _____ (Aug 27, 1831 – May 25, 1856). After she died he apparently m Sarah A _____ b c1838. **Moses Lyter had these children: Thomas L** b c1855; **Franklin W** b c1860; **Harry F** b c1868; **Rodey W** b c1873. Moses and Sarah lived in Harrisburg in 1880, and he was supervisor of an ice business. His son Thomas drove an ice wagon, son Franklin worked at the ice house.

***LOUISA** (no dats) m _____ Utz

***BETSY** (no dates) She is probably the Elizabeth b c1814, m Henry Bowman (no dates). In 1880 Elizabeth Bowman lived in Dauphin (town) and her son Henry age 22 a bridge carpenter lived with her. Henry's wife Lillie b c1861 also with her.

[LEVI LEITNER (b c1818 – d ____), parents unknown, but probably Peter & Jane (Page) Leitner, m Hannah Boyer (b c1824 – d), a dau of _____. In 1850 and 1860 Levy and Hannah Leitner lived in Washington Twp. where he was farming They apparently moved to Walker Twp., Juniata County after that. In 1880, Levi Lightner 64, Hannah 52 and dau Emma 16 were on the census for that area. . **Levi and Hannah Litner had these children: SARAH ANN** b c1839; **CATHARINE** (1841 – 1912), 2nd wife of Christian Schoffstall *1812 – 1879); **FIETTA JANE** b c1843 m Aug 12, 1860, Daniel Keen, record in St. Johns Hill Ch; **LAVINA** b c1845, m Apr 26, 1868 Emanuel Romberger, record in Salem Union Ch, Berrysburg; **HANNAH EMELIA** b Dec 10, 1848, Bapt Rife Ch; **NATHANIEL** b Mar 12, 1852, bapt St. Johns Hill Ch; **ELIAS FRANKLIN** b Feb 22, 1855, bapt Zion Hoover Ch, Rife, he lived with the John M Robinson family in Williamstown in 1880.;

Perhaps the next one is also a son of Levi Leitner above:
Emanuel W. Lyter b c1849 m Sep 21, 1871 St. Johns Hill Ch to Lydia Ann Schreffler b c1853, both from Mifflin Twp. [In Seyburt Cem, Williamstown – Emanuel Lyter (1859 – 1899), Lizzie A (1867 – 1933)] Emanuel and Lydia Lyter lived in Uniontown in 1880, and he was a miller. George Weaver age 20 lived with them and was an apprentice miller. Phoebe Weaver single also lived with them and was listed as a servant. **They had these children**: William Harvey b Sep 25, 1872, bapt Salem Ref, E'ville; Minnie Ursula b Jun 9, 1874; Sarah Louisa b Mar1, 1876 bapt E'ville; Charles b c1878.

LAND FROM PETER SCHOFFSTALL GRANT TO SAUSSER
(Near Wiconisco Creek In What Is Now Washington Twp.)

The next section of land is located west along Crossroads Road leading north out of Loyalton. It was part of early Lykens Township, but now some was situated in Washington Township. Much of this land is from a grant of 157 ½ acres that Commonwealth of Pennsylvania surveyed to Peter (Im)Schoffstall on December 3, 1787, patented on July 2, 1804. The grant was known as "Sheepwith." The original patent was divided into two separate tracts.

Another section containing 202 acres of land was conveyed by the executors of Rudolph Kelker, Jr. to Peter Schoffstall on August 13, 1791, After Peter Schoffstall died, the land was divided and distributed. In most cases each of the children mutually assigned the tracts to the different heirs.

Samuel and Daniel Schoffstall and their sister Eva, widow of David Buffington were the recipients of some of this land, but they conveyed to their brother Christian Schoffstall He in turn conveyed several separate tracts to numerous buyers during the 1830's one of them being John Paul, Jr. and to Jacob Wolf, whom apparently had an affiliation in business or otherwise with the family. [Schoffstall genealogy elsewhere in book.]

LAND OF MICHAEL SAUSSER
126 acres

On March 1, 1837 by a bill of sale, Samuel Schoffstall and Sarah conveyed 126 acres 44 perches of land with buildings and improvements to David Schoffstall and Jacob Wolf. On Nov 14, 1837 David and Hannah Schoffstall of Mifflin Twp & Jacob and Juliann Wolf of Lykens Twp sold to Michael Sausser, a saddler of Lykens Twp. This land was partly in Mifflin and partly in Lykens Township and bordered the land of David Schoffstall, Henry Matter, Emanuel Dietrich, John Dietrich, Sr, Daniel Hoffman, Henry Shubert, Jacob Wolf, Frederick Lubold, Henry Shubart, Andrew and Jacob Riegle, John Hoke.

Another tract of about forty acres of land from the Peter Schoffstall grant was sold to Christian Schoffstall and later to Michael Sausser, giving him about 180 acres. Many years later, after Michael died, his daughter Sarah and her husband Dr. Nathan W. Stroup received the land. Sarah sold it to her son Michael E. Stroup on May 22, 1888. He kept most of it until his death in 1931.

THE SAUSSER FAMILY

Work has not been completed on this family. However apparently these belong to the SAUSSER family that settled first in Berks County.

MICHAEL SAUSSER b c1731 in Berks County, m Anna Cunigunda Wagner b c1737, a dau of John Mathais and Anna Elisabeth (Stumpp) Wagner. **Michael and Anna Cunigunda (Wagner) Sausser had these known children:**

*SUSANNA (Jun 8, 1755 -) – conf. Stouchsburg 1772 age 16

*JACOB b Aug 20, 1757, bapt Host Ch, probably the one confirm at Stouchsburg 1774 age 16;

*CATHARINA ELISABETH b Oct 4, 1759

*MICHAEL (Nov 15, 1765 - Aug 27, 1821), m at Stouchburg Ch Oct 16, 1787 Catharine Klar b 1767 to Philip Klar. **Michael and Catharine (Klara) Sausser had these children (some bapt Tulpchocken)** **Johannes** b Mar 22, 1788; **Johan Jacob** (bapt Aug 17,1789 – d Nov 27, 1858), m Catharine Gechter. **Johan Jacob and Catharine (Gechter) Sausser had these children:**

***Jonathan (b Apr 2, 1813 bapt Salem Hetzel Ch, Pine Grove Twp Sch Co – d Apr 8, 1900, bur Peace Ref Cem, Bbg), m Rebecca Miller (May 11, 1810 - Aug 3, 1871 of Apoplexy). Jonathan and Rebecca lived in Mifflin Twp in 1850 and he was a coachman. They had several people living with them: Jacob Shroffler age 19, a potter, Emanuel Salada age 17, a blacksmith, Daniel Yeager age 16 a potter, Benjamin Koppenheffer age 20, a blacksmith.In 1870 they lived in Berrysburg. **Jonathan and Rebecca Sausser children:** Floriana b c1834; William T. (b c1834 – d Apr 10, 1912 in Cleveland, Ohio. He was brought back for burial in Oak Hill Cem, Mbg), m Sarah ____ b c 1836, In 1860, William lived in Mifflin Twp and was listed as a stone cutter. He may have been the family member who began the tombstone monument business. **William and Sarah ___ Sausser children:** Angelina M b Jul 17, 1856, bapt Bbg; Clinton b c1857; Franklin Monroe (Aug 13, 1861 – d Feb 23,1864 of diphtheria); Henry Monroe b Aug 3,1863; Caroline b c1837; Christian b c1838; Persival b c1841, m Lydia Sirtell(?) Nov 8, 1867. He was a veteran of the Civil War; Anthony b 1844; Emma R. b c1848, m Dec 26, 1865, John Henry Messner b __ a son of John Messner; Abby Ellen b Jun 12,1851 – Apr 23, 1923, bur Oak Hill Cem, Mbg), m Meth Episcopal Ch, Mbg Apr 7, 1867 to John W. Sneeder (1844 – Apr 15, 1889); Clinton Willoughby (May 21, 1854 – Nov 19, 1911, bur Friedens Cem, Hegins), m Mary Ellen Lentz (Sep 10,1857 – Mar 1, 1940), a dau of William and Mary (Enterline) Lentz. In 1880 they lived in Tyrone, Blair County and he was listed as a marble cutter. **Clinton & Elizabeth Sausser children:** Mary B. b1880; Irvin Earl (Feb 10, 1888 – Dec 28, 1060, bur Hegins). After Rebecca died, Jonathan m Julia Ann ____ b c1833, and lived in Berrysburg. **They had two known children:** Alberta Catharine b Nov 25, 1872, bapt Peace Ch Bbg; Annie M. b c1875.

***Salome b Jul 22, 1814; ***Lydia (Nov 20, 1817- Aug 24, 1887, bur Ch of God Cem, Hegins Twp), m Daniel Laudenslager (Oct 23, 1819 -1883), a son of Jacob & Elizabeth (Coleman) Laudenslager. **They had these children:** Mary b c1844; Ann b c1846; Charles I (Mar 1, 1849 – Nov 12, 1936), m Katherine Romberger a dau of William & Sarah (Kocher) Romberger of Lykens Twp. In 1850, Lydia's mother Catharine Sausser lived with them; ***Maria Anna b Mar 23, 1819

William (Sep 4, 1799 – Mar 89, 1864, bur Oak Hill Cem, Mbg), m Catherine _____ b c1803. William was a saddler in 1850 in Up Paxton Twp. **William and Catherine (___) children:** Elizabeth b c1834; Carla b c1843; Emma b c1846. A Michael Sausser (married) was conf at Hoffman May 1834.

Michael (Feb 24,1810 – Feb 26, 1884 or 5, bur Maple Grove Cem, E'ville) m Lydia Moyer b Apr 5, 1807 – Jun 30, 1870). They lived in Wiconisco Twp in 1860 and he was listed as retired. In 1880 he lived with his daughter Sarah and family. **Michael and Lydia (Moyer) Sausser had these children:** Sarah (May 21, 1834 – Aug 5, 1888, bur Maple Grove Cem, E'ville), m Apr 30, 1868 to Nathan W. Stroup b Jan 13,1843 near Millerstown, Juniata Co, a son of Samuel B. and Sarah (Weller) Stroup, whom in 1876 moved to South Bend, Ind. (They eventually came back and are bur in Maple Grove Cem). Nathan attended the McAllister Academy, then came to Wash.Washington Twp to teach school. He began to read medicine with his uncle J. B. Stroup before graduating from Univ. of Pa. in 1855, then began practicing medicine in Elizabethville in 1856. In 1880 N.W. and Sarah Stroup lived in Wash. Twp, and had these people living with them: Maggie Kitzmiller age 20, a servant, Aaron Sweigard 14, a hostler, Michael Sausser father of Sarah.

Nathan W. Stroup

[Dr. John Calvin Stroup (Jan 8, 1860 – Feb 11, 1917, bur Maple Grove Cem), a son of Dr. John B. Stroup of Elisabethville, m Mary E. _____(Jul 23, 1866 – May 4, 1941), **had these children:**Paul Eugene b Mar 25, 1894; Clayton Dewey b Jun 25, 1898; Emma May b Oct 10, 1901; Mary Gladys b Dec 18, 1908.]

N. W. and Sarah (Sausser) Stroup had one child: Michael E (Aug 16, 1873 – Oct 29, 1931, bur beside his mother in Maple Grove Cem). He m Blanche R. ___ (Mar 27, 1876 – Aug 1, 1967, bur Maple Grove Cem). Michael and Blanche Stroup had a son Nathan W. Michael graduated from Franklin & Marshall and became a lawyer. After his wife Sarah died, Nathan Straub m Aug 29, 1889 to Susan Alexandra, widow of Dr. Allerton Aldrich of Meadville, Pa.

Jeremiah (Apr 27, 1819 – Oct 29, 1908, bur Oak Hill Cem, Mbg), m Sarah ____ (Oct 5, 1828 – Nov 5, 1901). Jeremiah was a saddler and Horseman, and they lived in Millersburg in 1880. Frank A. Harner age 29 lived with them. **Jeremiah and Sarah Sausser had these children;** Frank (Sep 1850 – 1921, bur Oak Hill Cem, Mbg), m Louisa Kriencamp (Jun 29, 1863, Ger – d 1938 in Lanc Co). **Frank and Louisa (Kriencamp) Sausser had these known children:** William Clayton (b Oct 4, 1888, bapt Ref Ch Mbg – d Jul 20, 1863, but Oak Hill Cem), m Nov 22, 1911 to Mary Amelia Matter (1893 – Apr 23, 1975), a dau of Peter A. and Rebecca (Batdorf) Matter.

THE HOFFMAN LAND AT SHORT MOUNTAIN

This land is part of the original tract of 607 ½ acres of land that Commonwealth of Pennsylvania warranted to Leonard Miller on August 21, 1751. Leonard Miller conveyed some land to Jacob Witmer and Peter Hoffman on December 1, 1753. Shortly after that, Jacob Witmer died, and his right was conveyed to Peter Hoffman. By his will written August 2, 1785, Peter Hoffman devised 214 ¼ acres of land called "Campton" to his son Christian. The land was not surveyed until June 1791. The patent was granted April 25, 1797, and Christian Hoffman was the owner of the land with appurtenances. On that same day, April 25, 1797, Nicholas Hoffman received a patent for 98 acres, 80 perches. This too was part of the tract that Leonard Miller originally took up, and adjoined the land of Christian Hoffman. Christian Hoffman had previously received a tract of land containing 81 1/2 acres from Commonwealth of Pennsylvania on February 17,1785, and a third tract of 100 acres mountain land was surveyed to him November 18, 1794. The three tracts of land gave Christian Hoffman a total of 395 acres and 18 perches. The so called "window tax" of 1798, records Christian Hoffman with two tracts of land, each containing 200 acres. One tract contains a cabin measuring 20 x 18 feet, and a poor barn. The other tract is unseated. Both tracts join the land of Nicholas Hoffman in "Wiconisco Valley." In 1815 Christian Hoffman is listed as having a blacksmith shop. In 1828, Christian Hoffman, Senior had a tenant on his land.

THE JOHN PTER HOFFMAN FAMILY

The **JOHN PETER HOFFMAN FAMILY** has had an early and continued effect on the area of Lykens Township, and the whole Lykens Valley. Much has been written about the family. Some has proved to be accurate, other information is traditional, possibly true, but unfounded. The following information is a compilation of all of the material discovered.

JOHN PETER HOFFMAN was born in 1709 in Germany, near the Swiss border. In company with other family members and friends, he sailed from Rotterdam, Holland in the ship ROBERT AND ALICE, commanded by Walter Goodman, the master, arriving in Philadelphia on September 3, 1739. Among the passengers qualifying for entrance to the port, were these Hoffman brothers: Peter, Daniel, Hannis (John), and Martin. John Peter Hoffman first settled in Berks County, where he worked as a carpenter. During those early years, Indians and early settlers continued to clash, causing problems for all folks involved. The Provincial Army became a necessary force to exact order. John Peter Hoffman and neighbors served as soldiers in that Army.

Peter Hoffman, a carpenter by trade, married Maria Sara whose maiden name may have been Seiler or Snyder. The date and place of the marriage is unknown, but a Peter Hoffman applied to the Colonial Authorities in Pennsylvania to marry on April 9, 1743. The name of the intended bride was not given. The Hoffman family settled in Berks County, and attended St. John's (Host) Church near Bernville, Tulpehocken Township from 1749 to 1770. He took the Oath of Allegiance on Oct 11, 1751.

According to tradition, about 1753, John Peter Hoffman decided to venture further into the wilderness. He and others of his family came to the area by horseback and cleared land at the end of Short Mountain in Lykens Valley. There they built cabins. John Peter built a small log house just across the road from the Paul Bush residence, "near a fine stream." He and his family lived here in their new settlement for several years. It is believed that two children Margaret and Christian were probably born here, since no baptismal records have been found in Berks County. The house that they lived in was sturdy, and survived for over one hundred years. Its last purpose was to serve as a blacksmith shop about 1850.

John Peter Hoffman was a contemporary of Andrew Lycans, Ludwig Shott, John Rewalt and others. They were the focus of the marauding Indians, who drove off the early settlers in 1756. Traditionally, we are told that Peter Hoffman and the Indians were on friendly terms and that when the Indians descended, they saved the cabin belonging to Hoffman, but burned all the others. Since the first Hoffman cabin supposedly survived until past 1850 when it continued to be used as a blacksmith shop, this is apparently a true account of the Indian raid.

John Peter Hoffman returned to Berks County, but several years later, about the spring of 1770, he came back, and brought his family with him to this valley. They determined to stay, so resisted later Indian escapades, and managed to make a permanent settlement. They erected more cabins, cleared the land and followed farming. This time they made provision for a house of worship, and St. Peter's (Hoffman) Church was established on their land about 1771.

John Peter Hoffman lived out his days in his home at the end of Short Mountain. Here he and his wife continued to raise their family, and see their children grow in numbers into a substantial crowd of descendents. Maria Sarah Hoffman died before her husband, but he lived to the age of eighty-nine, and died in 1797. He was buried by request, on Hoffman land at the end of Short Mountain. Here lie twenty-six contemporaries of John Peter Hoffman. However, the names of some of those whose bodies lie there are not now known. According to tradition, the early graves had wooden markers.

Lillian Keiper Blanning, one of the avid researchers of Hoffman genealogy in later years, remembered how the graveyard looked when she was a child. Lillian was born about 1874, and as a child she visited the area. She observed that the field was not completely cleared, and that a path led to the area where the original stones lay. She went there with her Uncle Joseph Buffington, and enjoyed picking dandelions in that field. Lillian also remembered the old blacksmith shop across the street.

The open fields of the Bush and other local farms, and the banks of the area streams have been a fascinating place to find Indian artifacts. Many folks in past years have accumulated credible collections of articles attributed to Indian life in this region. Other areas of Lykens Township also have yielded Indian objects that prove that Indians lived here many years before the white settlers arrived.

We are fortunate that members of the Hoffman family took an early interest in researching their family genealogy. In 1913 plans were made to hold the first Hoffman Reunion. It was held on the third Saturday in August at Buffalo Park in Halifax, Pa.

Reunions were held at regular intervals since then, and much history was accumulated. It was through the efforts of the Reunion Committee that the Hoffman Marker has been placed in the field where the original cemetery was established.

THE SHORT MOUNTAIN CEMETERY

The plantation on which this graveyard was established has become well known to anyone interested in the history of the area. It is truly an historical setting and has been visited by many folks throughout the years who wish to tread on the soil where their ancestors lived. A large tombstone standing alone in the field honors the twenty-six pioneers whose remains have been there since the 1700s. The Hoffman Association erected the tombstone in 1924. An inscription on the stone reads:

**JOHN PETER HOFFMAN
PIONEER**
Arrived from Holland
in 1739
Settled here 1750
Born 1709 - Died 1798
His remains with those
of 26 contemporaries
lie buried here.
Erected by
Hoffman Association
1924

A Very Early Photo Of The Barn That Was Located On What Is Now The Bush Farm

THE JOHN PETER HOFFMAN FAMILY

(In addition to our own detailed research, information from Annabelle Hoffman, Nancy Houston, Myra Marks and others have contributed. This has been a time consuming and difficult search, even with the help from a number of devoted researchers. We hope there are not too many discrepancies!)

[JOHN PETER HOFFMAN (b 1709) AND WIFE MARIA SARA HAD THE FOLLOWING CHILDREN:
+JOHN HOFFMAN (b Mar 11, 1747 bapt Host Ch – conf Host Ch 1765 - d Nov 1, 1818, will probated Mar 1819, bur Hoffman Cem with unmarked graves), m Anna Maria Kauffman (b____ d Aug 19, 1822), a dau of John Kauffman. She was confirmed in 1767 at Host Church. John was called "Alt Hannas." It is said that he resided for a time near Hoffman church on the farm later owned by George Williard. He was a farmer and served as Justice of the Peace from 1771 to his death. John served during the Revolutionary War in numerous patrols on the frontiers. He participated in the Battle of Long Island on Aug 27, 1776. He was serving as Captain Albright Deibler's Lieutenant in the Company of Associators from Lancaster (now Dauphin) County. While covering General George Washington's retreat from their encounter with the Hessians' first engagement for the British, Captain Deibler was mortally wounded and the entire company taken prisoner. John Hoffman assumed command as captain, and continued in that rank after their release. He also comanded the Upper Paxtang Company in the expedition up the West Branch of the Susquehanna in 1778. John Hoffman penned his will on September 16, 1813. It was probated March 17, 1819. John and Anna Maria (Kauffman) Hoffman had these children:
++ANNA MARIA (b Jan 8, 1773 bapt Host Ch – d Feb 8, 1840, bur David's Cem Killinger), m Jul 5, 1792 Joseph Negley (Sep 15, 1766 – Jul 12, 1828), a son of George and Magdalena Negley. Joseph and Anna Maria (Hoffman) Negley had these children (some bapt Salem Luth:
+++Elizabeth (b Jul 24, 1793 – d Mar 1831, bur St. John's Hill Cem), m John Holtzman. +++Magdalena (no dates), m Isaac Will, probably a son of Conrad Will, buried in St. David's Cem, Killinger. +++Daniel (Nov 12, 1797–Feb 2, 1873, bur David's Cem, Killinger), m Margaret Gable (Apr 3, 1803–Oct 17, 1875). +++George (Sep 8, 1805 – Oct 14, 1865, bur David's Cem, Killinger0, m Charlotte Kintzel b c1837. +++Catherine (no dates) m _____ Swab; +++Sarah (no dates), m

++JOHN JR. (b Jun 11, 1776 bapt David's Ch - d Mar 2, 1851 Up Swatara). Details of the life of John Hoffman Jr. have been difficult to substantiate. According to the Dauphin Co. History and other early sources, he was called "Young Honnas" and lived near his father John in Lykens Twp during the first part of his life. He was "the first local preacher in the valley, and built the first fulling and carding mill in the Upper End" (later owned by Samuel Wolf). He married 1st Christina Deibler (Jun 11, 1773 - Feb 12, 1815, bur Hoffman Cem), a dau of Albright and Anna

Catharine (Shoop) Deibler. She bore him at least his first three children. The fourth child, John b Aug 13, 1804, bapt at Hoffman Ch, names Anna Maria as the mother, and he is named as an heir in his father's estate. (Christina did not die until 1815). John Hoffman later moved to the Camp Curtin area of Harrisburg where he owned a dairy farm that later became the Geyer dairy farm. He was a Justice of the Peace and steward of the almshouse 1824 – 1839. He was first elected register of wills term 1839–1844. [Before that it was an appointed position]. The HARRISBURG CHRONICLES gave this report September 4, 1826: "Mrs. John Hoffman died of apoplexy on Tuesday last. Mrs. Hoffman consort of John Hoffman, Esq. steward of the Dauphin County Poorhouse." John married next, Elizabeth Knupp (Apr 18, 1796–Aug 21, 1868), probably the mother of the last children. After John died, orphan court records name these heirs: widow Elizabeth, grandson Daniel Sheesley son of deceased son Daniel; Susan deceased; Christiana, deceased; grandchildren George & Elizabeth children of son John, deceased; George; Henry; Adam; David. **John Hoffman and wives had these children (most bapt Hoffman Ch):**

+ + +Susanna (b Apr 19, 1795 - ____), m George Fleisher

+ + +Elizabeth (b c1799 recorded in Hoffman baptisms, but no date given, probably died young.

+ + +Daniel D. (b Feb 19, 1800 – d Jan 18, 1823, bur Hoffman Cem), m Elizabeth Snyder (May 11, 1803 – Jul 11, 1889) , a dau of Leonard Snyder, Jr. and his wife Anna Maria nee Schott. **Daniel and Elizabeth (Snyder) Hoffman children (some bapt Hoffman Ch):** Isaac b Feb 9, 1821; Daniel Jr b Jan 21,1823. Daniel was a distinguished civil engineer and resided in Phila.This may be the one that lived in Wiconisco Twp in 1850 and was a surveyor. He was m to Hester __ b c1826 and had a son John b c1844. After Daniel died, his widow was m Jan 1, 1824 by Rev. Isaac Gerhart to John Hoke (Feb 24, 1802 – Jan 21, 1861). John Hoke and Elizabeth are both buried Peace Cem, Berrysburg. In 1850 John & Elizabeth lived in Wash Twp, had Ann Mary Snyder age 72 with them. In 1860 John & Elizabeth lived in Wash Twp. and had Henry M. Snyder age 82, widower with them. By 1870 John Hoke had died, and Elizabeth was living in the same house as the Frederick Schoffstall family.She had her son Jacob with her. **John and Elizabeth (Snyder Hoffman) Hoke children (bapt Hoffman Ch):** Josiah b Mar 21, 1825; Elizabeth b Jan 14, 1828; Maria Anna b May 17, 1830; Catharine b Jan 29, 1833; John b Jun 20, 1835; William b Nov 22, 1837; Leonard (Nov 17, 1839 – 1842); Rebecca b Jun 26, 1842, m Frederick Schoffstall b c1838, had a dau *Mary E* (Aug 2, 1868 – Jan 22, 1921), m Jan 1, 1891 Geo Wm Botts, **had these children:** *Frederick*, *Russell*, *Morgan*, *John*, *Mildred*; Jonathan b May 8, 1846.

+ + +Christina (b Apr 27, 1802 d pre 1851), m Christian Schaffner (Nov 1, 1798 - Jan 12, 1835, bur Hoffman Cem), a son of Martin and Fanny (Haldeman) Schaffner. They settled on a farm owned by Christina's father. **Christian and Christina (Hoffman) Schaffner had these children (most bapt Hoffman Ch):**

Amanda (no dates), m Peter Sellers;

Obed b Mar 12, 1826, drowned at the age of eight years;

Daniel b August 6, 1827, may have m Elisabeth ___ . When Daniel was eight years old his father died. At the age of 12, he became a farm hand, and a short time later moved to Gratztown where he became employed at a store and tavern "boy of all work." After that he went to Schuylkill County and later to Haernerstoen to live with his brother Martin. There he learned the carpenter trade. He came back to Lykens Twp for schooling and lived with his mother. He worked as a carpenter in summer and taught school in winter in the Lykens Valley for ten years. He served during the Civil War, then back to Haernerstown where he met and married Salome Haerner, dau of Jacob and Salome (Beinkoman) Haerner. **They had these children (all b in Berrysburg):** *Lorence* bapt Nov 6, 1853 Hoffman Ch; *Franklin Jacob* b Jan 9, 1854, became an attorney in Hummelstown. *Daneil Webster* b Feb 17, 1857, went to Myerstown and became a doctor.

David b Mar 4, 1829;

Eli b Jan 13, 1831, moved to Savannah, Illinois;

Fronica b Dec 27, 1832, m William Swab b c1829, in1880 they lived in Millersburg and he was a commercial salesman. They had one known son Howard b c1856. In 1880 he lived with his parents, was a clerk in the bank.

Salome Christina b Dec 5, 1834, m William Shartzer.

Martin P (1837 – 1918, bur Hoffman Cem), m Anna Maria Miller (1840 – 1915), a dau of _____ . **Martin P. and Anna Maria (__) Schaffner had these children (bapt Hoffman Ch):** *Karl Henry* b Feb 4, 1861; *Maria Susannah* b Dec 1, 1862; *William Isaac Lincoln* b Jan 24, 1866; *Sarah Jane* b Nov 9, 1871; Vesty Ann b Jan 25, 1875; *Jacob Edwin* b Apr 19, 1877; *George Martin* b Mar 5, 1879; *Joseph Clay* b Apr 15,1881; *Thomas Foster* b Nov 18, 1884;

+ + +John III (b Aug 13, 1804 - d 1851), **had two children:** George; Elizabeth, mentioned in grandfather John Hoffman (b 1776) estate as heirs, children of John b 1804.

+ + +George (no dates) mentioned in Adm of father's estate;

+ + +Henry (no dates) lived in Harrisburg;

+++Adam (b Oct 9, 1833 – d Mar 4, 1873), m Levina Atticks. (She was a widow in Middleton, Dau Co in 1880. Adam and Levina (Atticks) Hoffman had these children: *John W.b 1857*; *Mary*; *David b 1861*; *Harry*; *Irene* b 1870; *Adam A* b 1873.

+++David R (Aug 9, 1838 – Dec 24, 1863), m Dec 24, 1863 Mary Ellen Hoyer b Oct 28, 1843 Wash Co, Md, a dau of Benjamin Franklin and Margaret Ann (Kershner) Hoyer. **David and Mary Ellen (Hoyer) Hoffman had these children:** *Edward*; b & d Nov 1865; *Ellie* b Sep 22, 1867, m Jun 12, 1888 Robert F. Ligan.

+++Mary Ellen d Mar 20, 1848 age 1

++SUSANNA (b Nov 15, 1779 – d before husband probably 1813) [another record states Jan 8, 1829 bur Hoffman Cem], m Jacob Frantz (b ____ d summer of 1830). (other source states she d age 86) [See Frantz genealogy]

++ELIZABETH (b Jul 12, 1781 – d ____), m 1st Jun 16, 1800 John Hoffman (Feb 10, 1776 – Jun 8, 1814, bur Hoffman Cem), a son of Daniel and Eva Marie (Emmert) Hoffman of Rehrersburg, Berks Co, grandson of Frederick Ludwig Hoffman, schoolmaster at Altalaha Lutheran Church. It is said that they resided on the farm near Hoffman church later owned by George Row. In his will, John gave his 125 acre farm to his wife. **John & Elizabeth (Hoffman) Hoffman children (mentioned in his will):**

+++John b Apr 15, 1801; +++Daniel b Oct 15, 1803; +++Jacob b Jul 29, 1807; +++Jonas b Oct 18, 1812. After John died, Elizabeth was married Apr 7, 1822 to Samuel Loscher, widower, by Rev. Isaac Gearhart at David's Ch, Killinger.

++CATHERINE (Jan 16, 1784 – Apr 18, 1835, bur in Hoffman plot at foot of Short Mt.), m John Buffington (Jan 3, 1778 – Jun 30, 1839), a son of Benjamin and Mary Catharine (Deibler) Buffington. Catharine was the widow of Captain Albright Deibler. Benjamin, Catharine, and Benjamin's first wife Mary (Mercy) Frisell Buffington are also buried at Short Mt. John Buffington was County Commissioner from 1822 – 1824. They lived on the farm adjoining land of Robert Elder, later Jacob Hartman. **John and Catharine (Hoffman) Buffington children (most bap either Hoffman's or St. John's "Hill" church) :** +++Maria b Jul 6, 1803; +++Catharine b Feb 17, 1810; +++Elizabeth b Mar 16, 1812; +++Salome b Dec 2, 1814; +++Johannes b May 22, 1817, m Mary Messner (b ___ - d in Pillow); +++Lydia b Jun 5, 1821, m John P. Messner, bur Salem (Peace UCC Cem) Berrysburg; +++Hanna b Aug 24, 1825 m Daniel Yeager; +++George b Oct 27, 1828, not married; +++Susan (no dates).

++JACOB b Jan 28, 1789, m Catherine Koppenhaver (no dates) a dau of Martin and Susanna (Artz) Koppenhaver of Lykens Twp., and moved to Pottsville, Schuylkill Co. He was referred to as "Alt Jake" **Jacob and Catherine (Koppenhaver) Hoffman had these children (bapt Hoffman Ch):** +++Elizabeth (Nov 9, 1814; +++Peter b Jun 8, 1816; +++Anna Maria b Nov 24, 1817; +++Sarah b Mar 16, 1819; +++David b Aug 30,1821; +++Catharine b Sep 1, 1824; +++Daniel b Aug 2 3, 1829, m Susanna Griffith (Mar 31, 1837 in Scotland – d Jan 3, 1884), a dau of ___ and Agnes Griffith. Daniel and family lived in Porter Twp, Sch Co in 1880. **Daniel and Susanna (__) Hoffman had these children:** Catharine b Sep 28, 1855; James G. b Jul 6, 1857; Agnes b Jul 13, 1859; Daniel b Aug15, 1861; Joseph b Feb 8, 1863; Catharine b Mar 9, 1865; David b May 3, 1867; William F. b Apr 2, 1869; George W. b Feb 28, 1872; Alexander b May 15, 1874; Charles F. b Sep 28, 1878.

++MARY MAGDALENA (Jul 10, 1791 –Sep 23, 1857, bur Luth & Ref Cem, Berrysburg), m 1814 Thomas Koppenhaver (b Sep 18, 1791 Bethel Twp – d Apr 20, 1826, bur Hoffman Cem), a son of John and Maria Margaretta (Zerbe) Koppenhaver. **Thomas and Mary Magdalena (Hoffman) Koppenhaver had these children (most bapt Hoffman's Ch):** +++Jonathan b May 28, 1815, bapt St. Johns "Hill" Ch, moved to Campbelltown; +++Johannes b May 2, 1817; +++Sarah b May 3, 1820, m Frederick W. Evitts; +++Anna Maria b Jan 11, 1823;+++Elizabeth b Jul 5, 1825 m Frederick W. Evitts.

++BARBARA (Dec 23,1800 – Sep 29, 1879, bur Matters Cem. near Loyalton), m John N. Specht (Aug 26, 1801 – Sep 2, 1866) and lived in Washington Twp. **John and Barbara (Hoffman) Specht had these children;** +++Jeremiah (Dec 16, 1822 – May 26, 1888), m Catharine ____ b c1831. In 1880 they lived in Washington Twp, and their son John W. age 21 lived with them; +++Catherine (Aug 25, 1829 – Mar 24, 1916), m Isaiah Matter; +++Eliza (Dec 7, 1835 – Nov 22, 1906), m Henry Snyder; +++Sarah (Feb 6, 1840 – Oct 30, 1904, bur Wiconisco), m 1859 by Rev. Moyer in U. B. Church, E'ville to Tyrus Snyder (Jan 12, 1839 – May 17, 1919 In 1880 they lived in Wiconisco Twp. Tyrus was a tanner and railroader. He was a Civil War vet. and was buried with a military funeral in Wiconisco Cem. **Tyrus and Sarah (Specht) Snyder had these children:** George F b Nov 20, 1859; Margaret Ann b Jul 4, 1861; John Calvin b Jul 11, 1863; Ira Alvin b c Aug 10, 1864; Andrew Harvey b Oct 10, 1865; Ellen Jane b Oct 2, 1868, m ___ Klinger; Maria Elizabeth b Oct 4, 1870; Carrie Catherine b Apr 6, 1872; Mary Louisa b May 20, 1874;Samuel Edward b Sep 2, 1876; Harry Monroe b Jan 2, 1878; Etta May b Aug 21, 1880; Katie Irene b Mar 20, 1884; William (no dates)..

North From Loyalton Along South Crossroad Road

+JOHN NICOLAUS HOFFMAN (b ____ bapt Host Church Tulpehocken May 4, 1749 - conf Host Ch 1767 - d Apr 28, 1814, bur in unmarked grave in Hoffman Cem, recorded by Rev James Ross Reily), m Apr 22, 1772 Anna Maria Margaretha Herman (b Nov 7, 1753 Heidelberg Twp, Berks Co - d Jan 9, 1826 Lykens Twp), a dau of Johannes and Catharine Herman. John Nicholas and Margaretha Hoffman lived on the farm later owned by Benjamin Rickert near Short Mountain. He owned a large tract of land cut up into many farms. He deeded land to the Hoffman Church congregation for a church and school. Nicholas was a soldier of the American Revolution, served part of the time with Captain Albright Deibler and Captain Martin Weaver. He was in the battles of Brandywine and Germantown and Long Island where he was first a Lieutenant, later Captain. He is listed on the Revolutionary monument at the site of the old Hoffman Church. **John Nicholas and Margaretha (Herman) Hoffman had these children (some bapt Salem & David's Ch, Killinger, Hoffman Ch:**

++ CATHARINE (b Feb 7, 1773, bapt Wirth Salem Ch, Killinger - d ____ an elderly lady), m Peter Schoffstall, Jr. (b c1770 - ____). [See write-up of Peter Schoffstall, Jr. for more information.]

++ANNA MARIA (Feb 12, 1775, bapt by Rev. Hendel in David's Ref Ch Killinger. No other information.

++ MARIA SUSANNA CATHARINE (May 5, 1776, bapt David's Ref - d Oct 31, 1826, bur in Hoffman plot, Short Mt.), m Jun 22, 1794 Levi Buffington (1761 - c1842), a son of Benjamin and Mary (Frisell) Buffington. . [See write-up on Levi Buffington for more information.]

++JOHN PETER (Sep 22, 1778 bapt Wirth Salem Ch - d c1864, possibly bur Hoffman Cem), m Susanna Magdalena Lubold (1776 - ____), a dau of John Martin and Catherine (Bechtel) Lubold, who came to this area about 1785. This Peter Hoffman was referred to as "Gross Peter." He was a farmer, owned the farm that later belonged to William Hawk. He was a soldier of the War of 1812. **John Peter and Magdalena (Lubold) Hoffman had these children:**

+++Ellizabeth (Sep 22, 1800 - Mar 7, 1876, bur Simeon Cem, Gratz), m Philip Keiser (Oct 18, 1800 - Jun 6, 1839), a son of Philip (Sr.) and Eva (Zimmerman) Keiser. Philip Keiser was a tailor in Gratz. After he died, about 1843, Elizabeth m George Erdman, a widower of Northld Co. who died 1858. George was a son of George Erdman, Sr. and his wife Dorothy (Miller) Erdman. After George died, Elizabeth lived alone in Gratz. **Philip and Elizabeth (Hoffman) Keiser had these children:**

Daniel (b Nov 17, 1820 Low Mahantongo Twp, - d Feb 4, 1877 record in Evang Luth Ch, Lykens). Early in life Daniel moved to Gratz where he learned the tanning trade. He m Apr 14, 1840 Elizabeth Matter, a dau of Baltzer and Catharine (Ritzman) Matter. She d Sep 26, 1852, age 31, is bur in Union Cem, Lykens. Daniel and his family later moved to Elizabethville. After a few years they moved to Center County, Pennsylvania near Pine Grove Mills. He continued to work in the tannery business. In the spring of 1850, he again moved his family in a "Prairie Schooner" (covered wagon) back to Lykens. It was a three day trip. Daniel went into the hotel business in what became known as "Union House" in Lykens. It was about this time that his wife died. In 1852 he built a powder mill, dry house and storage house along Rattling Creek near the Glen. The mill was run by water power from a dam at the base of "Love Rock." He furnished powder to the mines, and also to the construction crew when they were building the Northern Central Railroad from Harrisburg to Millersburg. It took two days to haul a load of twenty-five open kegs of powder to Harrisburg with a horse and wagon. The journey took them across Berry and Peter's Mountains to get there. **Daniel and Elizabeth (Matter) Keiser had these children:** Henry (Oct 26, 1840 - Mar 15, 1933), m Mar 1864 Sarah Workman. He was a Civil War veteran and kept a diary throughout his army career; Mariah (Dec 31, 1841 - Nov 9, 1908, bur IOOF Cem in Lykens), m 1st Richard Owens of Phila. After her divorce, Mariah m Joseph Dunlap (Feb 2, 1838 - Jan 26,1914), a Civil War veteran. After the war he became a butcher, later worked at the colliery. **Joseph and Mariah (Keiser) Dunlap had five children:** J. Harper; Rosa Bell; Joseph Henry; William Keiser; Agnes J. After her father died, Mariah cared for her youngest brother Samuel for a few years before he went to live with the Jacob Hartman family in Lykens Twp. In later years, when Samuel's young wife died in childbirth, Mariah took the infant daughter Cora into her home and raise her to adulthood. Cora was m to Jay William Rothermel of Pillow, and they lived n a farm adjoing the fair ground in Gratz; John d young ; William (Aug 15, 1844 - 1921), m Nov 1865 in Gratz to Ellen Hoover who d Aug 11, 1880 in Delaware from burns received from coal oil. After Ellen died, William m 2nd Dec 21, 1886 in Smyrna, Delaware, to Minerva Jane Walt b Jun 3, 1846, a dau of Henry and Catharine Walt. He was a boat builder in Liverpool, Perry Co, Pa.; George (1846 - 1863), served in the Civil War, came home and died several months later of typhoid fever; Elizabeth (Jan 20, 1848 - 1896), m Levi Workman; Catherine (1849 - 1854); Susannah b Jan 15, 1851 m Edwin Wilson.

Daniel Keiser's second wife was Amanda Zerby, b Aug 15, 1832, a dau of Henry and Christina (Romberger) Zerby. Daniel and Amanda m Oct 9, 1853. **Daniel and Amanda (Zerby) Keiser had twelve children (some died young);** Ellen (May 31, 1856 - 1910), m Lewis Jackson; Daniel (1857 - 1905); Morris (1859 - 1917), m Ellen M. ___ (Mar 13, 1868 - Oct 20, 1898, bur Wiconisco Cem); Albert (1861 - 1908), m Catharine Hawk, a dau

235

of Philip Hawk; *Edward Mead* (Jun 6, 1863 – Mar 13, 1935, bur IOOF Cem., Lykens), m Ida C. Herb (1884 – 1932); *Emma* (Jul 10, 1868 – Feb 6, 1885, age 16, bur Wiconisco Cem). She m Daniel Wert and had a son Edward b 1883, died age seven months; *Flora Allie* b Jan 31, 1870 (twin) – d Oct 5, 1898), had a child Goldy; *Laura Agnes* b Jan 31, 1870 (twin) d in infancy; *Joseph* b Jun 16, 1871, lived with brother William in Delaware after his father died, m Gertrude Powers of West Virginia; *Samuel* b Aug 19, 1872, lived with sister Mariah after his father died. He later came to Lykens Twp and lived with the Jacob Hartman family during his youth. He eventually moved back to Lykens, worked in the mines and m Cora Host. Cora died one month after her first child *Cora Valeria* was born in 1894. Cora Valeria m May 30, 1912 Jay William Rothermel, had two children Miriam b Oct 20, 1912; Clifford b May 26, 1914. Samuel Keiser later m Elizabeth Diane Dockey, a dau of Benjamin Dockey of near Pillow. Daniel Keiser and Amanda divorced Oct 6, 1874. She m Feb 10, 1877, John Bird b Sep 19, 1837 of Williamstown, also a Civil War Veteran. John Bird had previously been married to Amanda Hand, who remarried to Elias Haas. She died in 1897. Amanda Zerby Keiser d Dec 25, 1906, age seventy-four, is bur Wiconisco beside her husband John Bird. Daniel Keiser was elected to serve in the State Legislature for the terms 1863/64. He also was a veteran of the Civil War.

Elizabeth (Apr 18, 1823 – Mar 10, 1882), m John Umholtz (Mar 30, 1818 – Oct 17, 1888), and lived in Gratz. **John and Elizabeth (Keiser) Umholtz had these children:**

Sarah (Feb 13, 1842 – Dec 3, 1925), m Samuel Buffington (May 26, 1837 – May 18, 1910, bur Simeon Cem, Gratz), lived on a farm in Lykens Twp., later moved to Gratz

Edmond L. (Apr 7, 1843 – Jan 10, 1882, d of small pox, bur Simeon Cem, Gratz), m 1st Catherine Buffington b 1860 –d Jan 23, 1929, Newton, Kansas), a dau of Samuel and Sarah (Umholtz) Buffington. [See write-up on Samuel Buffington for details.]

Eliza (Jul 1847 - Nov 11, 1917), m Harry Hess (Oct 22, 1845 – May 31, 1928), a son of Solomon and Eva (Saltzer) Hess. [See write-up on Harry Hess for more details.]

Jacob (no dates), m Catharine Sheets. Jacob and Catharine (Sheets) Keiser had one known child: Ellen (no dates) m Edmond Umholtz. Jacob and Catharine divorced. Prior to the Civil War, Jacob enlisted in the Kansas Volunteer Cavalry Regt, stationed at Ft. Levenworth. He belonged to a group of soldiers wo were guarding the territory against the Indians. He came back to this area and re-enlisted in the Army where he served for the duration of the war. He eventually settled in Kansas or California where he married again and had several children.

John (b Feb 3, 1826 - d young)

Philip (Nov 24,1830 – Sep 7, 1857, bur Simeon's Cem). He m Elizabeth Kissinger and lived in Gratz. **Philip and Elizabeth (Kissinger) Keiser had three children, 2 died young :** *Amanda* (no dates) the only survivor m Percival Reichenbach and moved to Cumberland Co, Pa.

Jonas b Mar 4,1834, m Lucinda Julia Strayer b 1838, a dau of Valentine and Catherine Strayer. Jonas was a Civil War veteran. Before the war he was a "contracting carpenter" – people supplied their own material, he made an estimate and did the work. He also taught school during the winter months between 1855 and 1863, and was a Justice of the Peace. In 1860, he kept a tavern in Gratz. Jonas and the family eventually moved to Shamokin, but later moved to the state of Delaware. **Jonas and Lucinda Julia (Strayer) Keiser had these children:** *Martha* b 1856; *Kate*; *Pruella* d young; *Winfield*; *Anna*; *Lillian* (no dates), m ____ McCoy.

Sarah (Mar 3, 1836 – Sep 19, 1905, bur Lykens Cem), m in 1854 to Daniel Herb (Feb 2, 1831 – Nov 14, 1885), a son of Adam and Magdalena (Spatz) Herb of Up. Mahantongo Twp, Sch Co. Daniel and Sarah Herb lived in Lykens. **Daniel and Sarah (Keiser) Herb had eight children,** but only *Ida* reached adulthood. She m Edward M Keiser and lived in Lykens.

+ + +**Daniel** (Aug 27, 1803 – c1876, age 73 in Crawford Co., Pa.), m Elizabeth Rissinger (b Oct 30, 1801 – d after 1880), a dau of Michael and Eva Rissinger. Daniel was a carpenter. They moved to Crawford County, Pa. **Daniel and Elizabeth (Rissinger) Hoffman had these known children:** Josiah b c1828, m Fannie ____ b c1836. They moved to Wayne, Crawford Co with his parents before 1880. **Josiah and Fannie Hoffman had these children:** *Adeline* b c1859; *Charles C.* b c1861, in 1880 he was "sick with kidney"; *George M* b c1863; *Ulysus E* b c1865; *Sarah* b c1869; *Benjamin* b c1872. In 1880 they lived in Wayne, Crawford County, and Elizabeth Hoffman age 78, mother of Josiah lived with them; Catherine (no dates); Jonas (no dates) lived in Lykens and was a carpenter.

+ + +**John Jacob** (Aug 6 1805 – ____), m Elizabeth Erdman (b Dec 9, 1814 Mahantongo Twp., Sch Co. - d Sep 3, 1889, record of death in St. John's Luth Ch in Lykens, bur IOOF Cem). Elizabeth was a dau of J. Erdman and

wife. Jacob and his family lived in Lykens. In 1860 Benjamin Umberger age 26, a brakeman, lived with them. He was a tailor, but later a saloon keeper in Wiconisco. **Jacob Peter & Elizabeth (Erdman) Hoffman children (11):**
Miranda (1834 – 1914, bur IOOF Cem, Lykens), m Emanuel Hoffman (1828 – 1916), lived in Lykens. In 1860 Lucy Hoffman age 14 was with them. **Emanuel and Miranda (Hoffman) Hoffman had these children:** *Anna* b c1855, m Francis Hoffman; *William H* (1859 – 1939, bur near parents), lived with his parents in 1880 and was a machinist; *Calvin* b c1863, m Kate Gardner; *Maggie* b Sep 3, 1868;
Anna Maria (Apr 2, 1837 – Jun 9, 1908), m Philip Hawk (Aug 2, 1836 – Jul 21, 1914), a Civil War Vet;
Henry b c1840, m Emma Smith b 1846, he was a brakeman in 1860, moved to Phila after 1880;
Jonathan (Sep 22, 1841 – Jan 30, 1872), m ___ Kute;
Emaline (May 6, 1843 – Mar 13, 1878), m John H. Mark b c1839. In 1880, John , a widower, lived in Wiconisco and was a shoemaker. **John H. and Emaline (Hoffman) Mark had these children:** *Flora* b c1865; *Harry* b c1868; *Rosa* b c1874; *Cora* b c1876.
Louisianna (Apr 15, 1848 – Dec 24, 1925, Bur IOOF Cem, Lykens), m Jacob Alvord (Mar 21,1837 – Mar 21, 1907) of Lykens, a Civil War Vet;
Charles b c1849, m Lucinda Wommer b c1852, he was an engineer on the railroad in 1880, **they had one known child:** *Jacob* b c1872;
James (Oct 13, 1850 – Jan 18, 1928 bur IOOF Cem), m Elizabeth Woland (Sep 5, 1866 – 1927). **James and Elizabeth (Woland) Hoffman had these known children:** *William* b c1870, he was picking slate in 1880; *Charles Edward* b Aug 14, 1872; *Kate* b c1875;
Mary Ellen (1853 – 1914), m George H. Seal (1849 – 1915). George was a telephone operator in 1880, and in 1880, Ellen's mother Ellizabeth lived with them.
George b c1855

+ + +Catherine (Sep 10, 1807 – Sep 2, 1864), m Daniel Riegel (Jun 1, 1804 – Jun 2, 1855), a son of _____. Daniel was a County Commissioner in 1852-54. They resided in Gratz. **Daniel and Catherine (Hoffman) Riegel had these children:**
Elizabeth (May 12, 1827 – Feb 3, 1855), m Elias Etzweiler, lived in Jackson Twp
Josiah R. (Nov 30, 1829 – Jan 6, 1886), m Amanda Kissinger (May 8, 1831 – Jul 3, 1897), a dau of Jacob and Susannah Kissinger. Josiah was a Civil War Vet.
Jonas (Jun 11, 1835 – Nov 1, 1889, Sch Co) m Dec 28, 1856 by J. P. Jonas Laudenslager to Rebecca Holtzman of Tower City. Jonas was a veteran of the Civil War. After the war he worked in Williamstown as a clerk in a store, later at the braker of the mines.
Harrison (Jan 15, 1841 – Jul 31, 1899), m Hannah Rickert (May 22, 1847 – Jul 11, 1919) , a dau of Martin and Elizabeth (Yerges) Rickert. Harrison was a Civil War Veteran, worked at the Lykens Valley Coal Company, then moved to his farm in Lykens Twp.

+ + +**John Peter** (b Oct 27, 1809 bapt St. John's Hill Ch– d Feb 8, 1887), m Elizabeth Umholtz (Apr 23, 1806 – Mar 4, 1886), a dau of J. Philip and Ann Maria (Williard) Umholtz. John and Elizabeth Hoffman's gravestone is bolted together with iron bars under a maple tree in front of Hoffman's churchyard. He and his family lived on a farm near Short Mountain. In 1880 John P and Elizabeth Hoffman lived in Lykens Twp and had Joseph Hoffman age 20, a hired boy with them. **John Peter and Elizabeth (Umholtz) Hoffman had these children:**
Henry B (b Sep 22, 1828 – d Aug 2, 1893), m Aug 12, 1849 in Berrysburg to Catherine Kissinger (Jun 2, 1829 – Jun 10, 1900). In 1850 Henry B. was a fuller in Wiconisco Twp. He was not able to serve during the Civil War because of a diseased eye. So he served on the staff of Governor Pollock with the rank of Colonel and represented Dauphin County in the Legislature sessions of 1866-1869. He lived in Harrisburg. **Henry B. and Catherine (Kissinger) Hoffman had these children:** 4 ch d young; *Lillian Amanda* (1852 – 1936), m 1st Emmanuel Kicher 2 ch then divorced. She m 2nd David Wetzler had dau Maria Cath b 1891; *George* (1864 – 1929), m Mary Lenker..
John Peter III (Jun 20, 1830 – Apr 5, 1900, bur IOOF Cem, Lykens), m Mary ____ (b 1830 – d Sep 1, 1898). He lived in Powells Valley. He was a Civil War Vet.
Elizabeth b c1836, m Hiram Kimmel of Donaldson.
Jonathan (Jonas) (Jul 13, 1838 – Feb 14, 1887, bur Hoffman Cem), m Jan 2, 1859 by Rev D. Sell in Berrysburg to Sarah A. Rickert (Sep 8, 1840 – Oct 11, 1912), a dau of Martin and Elizabeth Rickert. In 1880 he was a miner. **Jonas and Sarah A. (Rickert) Hoffman had these children:** *William H* (Apr 6, 1860 - Mar 19, 1927), m Lydia ____ (May 13, 1865 – Apr 24, 1914). Lived in Gratz in 1912. **William and Lydia (____) Hoffman had theses children:** *Eugene*; *Clinton* (1863 – 1940, bur Simeon Cem), m Harriet Umholtz (1859 – 1922), lived in Gratz; *Henry*

Monroe b Aug 14, 1865; *Charles Penrow* b May 14, 1872; *George Washington* b Nov 14, 1873, m Jennie _____. They lived in Gratz in 1912. **George Washington and Jennie (   ) Hoffman had these children:** *Earl*; *Russel*; *Emily*; *Alvin Guerney* (Oct 6,1875 – Nov 24, 1934, bur Hoffman Cem), m Amanda Elizabeth Troutman (Feb 6, 1879 – Jan 12, 1975), a dau of Daniel and Sarah (Williard) Troutman. **Alvin Guerney and Amanda (Troutman) Hoffman had these children:** *Chas D* b Sep 28, 1902, m Darlene Miller, **had these children:** *Donald C* m Arlene Roadcap; *Mary* (adopted) b Sep 22, 1908 m Arthur Byerly; *Edward* (Jul 3, 1877 – Jan 1, 1933, bur Lykens Cem), m Maida ___ (Nov 11, 1881 – Oct 11, 1957); *Sarah* b Oct 3, 1879; *Mary Ellen* b May 1, 1881, m Isaiah Keiter; *Arthur* (1883 – 1957, bur Simeon Cem), m Maude ____ (1893 – 1965);; *Catherine* (no dates) m ___ Sergeant, lived in Lykens in 1912; *Kinda* (no dates) m _____Rickert and lived in Coaldale in 1912; *Jacob A.*; Catherine b c1841, m John Kicher ? who died in the Soldier's home in Ohio.

+ + +**Jacob P.** (b Jan 14, 1812 – bapt St. Johns Hill Ch – d Feb 3, 1874, bur IOOF Cem, Lykens), m Eliza ____ (Dec 9, 1814 – Sep 3, 1889)

+ + +**Jonas** (Oct 23, 1813 – Sep 28, 1889, Lykens), m Elizabeth Lebo (Dec 19, 1813 – Aug 23, 1876), a dau of George and Susannah Elizabeth (Enterline) Lebo. In 1850 Jonas and Elizabeth lived in Lykens Twp and had David Lebo age 23 with them. According to a local newspaper piece written in September 1869, Jonas was keeping a public house on the road between Donaldson and several other towns in Schuylkill County .One day his dog apparently hydrophobic bit him in the breast. His two sons Cornelius and Francis were near by and attempted to manage the dog, but it bit them as well. The dog was shot but they all survived. Jonas a widower lived in Lykens Twp in 1880. He had his daughter Rosiana age 28 and two grandsons, Grant Hoover age 12 "driving in the mines" and Henry Hoffman age 21 with him. **Jonas and Elizabeth (Lebo) Hoffman had these children (some bapt Hoffman Ch):**

Sarah (Oct 1, 1833 – Jan 13, 1865, bur IOOF Cem, Lykens), m Amos Kuntzelman (b Mar 20, 1833 - d Nov 29, 1905). **Amos and Sarah (Hoffman) Kuntzelman had these children:** *William H.* (1852 – 1934, bur IOOF Cem), m Rebecca A. ___(1853 – 1920). William lived with his parents in 1880 and was a coal miner. *Molly* b c1859, lived with parents in 1880 and was a tailoress; *Clara* b Nov 28, 1860; *Juliann* (Apr 2, 1863 – d 1864); *Robert* b c1873.

Catharine (Dec 19, 1834 – Jul 13, 1874, bur Calvary Meth Cem), m Jonas Faust (Jun 15, 1830 – Feb 13, 1884), probably a son of Lewis and Catherine (Kissinger) Faust

Susannah (b 1838 - d ___), m John Schreffler of Lykens.

Henry b 1839 m _____ Cooper, moved to Crawford County.

Lydia A (Aug 11, 1842 – Feb 11, 1909, bur Greenwood Cem, Tower City), m Emanuel J. Schoffstall (Apr 19, 1839 – Sep 1, 1886, bur Lykens), a son of Henry and Rebecca (Wells) Schoffstall. Emanuel had a restaurant in Lykens in 1874. After he died, Lydia m Henry K. Updegrove (d May 1891), proprietor of Tower City House.

Elizabeth b Oct 28, 1844, m 1st Jacob Clouser (1843 – 1919, bur Fairview Cem, Williamstown) a Civil war vet , 2nd Charles Shoemaker.

Adeline (Sep 12, 1846 – May 1940), m John Birkleback, lived in Shaft, Sch Co., Pa.

Amanda bapt Feb 4, 1849, m John Klinger

Rose Ann b Sep 18, 1849, m George Radle or Riegle

Cornelius (   ), m Elizabeth Zerbe

Francis (Nov 26, 1852 - ____), m _____ Hoffman

+ + +**Hannah** (Dec 20, 1815 – Jan 23, 1881, bur Simeon Cem), m Samuel Thomas (Aug 18, 1811 – Aug 27, 1874), a son of _____. **Samuel and Hannah (Hoffman) Thomas had these children (some bapt Hoffman Ch):**

Sarah A. (May 22, 1837 – Sep 22, 1886, bur Simeon Cem), m Daniel Strayer (Sep 27, 1822 – Oct 16, 1898), a son of Valentine and Catharine (Bealy) Strayer.

Elizabeth (Feb 13, 1851), m Henry Willier

Edward (Apr 1, 1840 – Apr 1, 1872, bur Simeon Cem), was killed in the mines by a fall of rocks. Edward m August 30, 1868, by Rev. Weidner of Oakdale Ch to Elizabeth Hoffman (May 9, 1848 – Oct 22, 1922, bur Evang Cem, Williamstown), a dau of Squire George and Hannah (Welker) Hoffman. Edward Thomas was a Civil War veteran, said to be wounded at Gettysburg, assigned to care for the Colonel's horses as he recuperated. **Edward and Elizabeth (Hoffman) Thomas had two children:** *Mary* b c1871, worked in Phila, m A. Rimage; *Catherine* (Jan 29, 1872 – 1916), m William T. Umholtz (1865 – 1923), a son of Samuel Umholtz. After Edward was killed, Elizabeth m Edward McNutt in 1885, for whom she worked as a housekeeper, during his first wife's fatal illness. They had no children.

Catherine (Dec 21, 1846 – Jan 27, 1886), m Martin Koppenhaver.

+ + +<u>George</u> (Apr 25, 1818 – Apr 6, 1837), m Susanna Enterline.

+ +<u>**ELIZABETH**</u> (Jul 12, 1780 – c1871), m Jacob Hawk, moved to Sugar Valley, Pa. **Jacob and Elizabeth (Hoffman) Hawk had these children (bapt Hoffman Ch):**

+ + +<u>**Elizabeth**</u> b Oct 20, 1810; + + +<u>**David**</u> b Feb 3, 1817; + + +<u>**Benjamin**</u> b Feb 11, 1819;

+ +<u>**JACOB**</u> (Feb 4, 1782 – Feb 2, 1862, bur Hoffman Cem, stone broken), m 1808 to Catharine Ferree (Apr 7, 1783 – Aug 1, 1859), a dau of Daniel and Sara (Brua) Ferree. In 1850 they lived in Wiconisco Twp. They had Mary Romberger age 11, and John Forney age 12 with them. **Jacob and Catharine (Ferree) Hoffman had these children (bapt Hoffman Ch):**

+ + +<u>Hannah</u> (Aug 16, 1807 – Aug 14, 1858, bur Hoffman Cem), m Jan 2, 1827, John Romberger (Oct 24, 1802 – May 29, 1891), a son of Adam and Anna Maria (Werner or Paul **CHECK THIS**) Romberger. **John and Hannah (Hoffman) Romberger had these children:** <u>William</u> b Dec 30, 1827; <u>Elisabeth</u> b May 15, 1829; <u>Sarah</u> b Sep 15, 1830; <u>Henry</u> (Jan 3, 1833 – Dec 16, 1912), m Elisabeth Hoover (1832 – 1907); <u>Amos</u> (Sep 12, 1834 – Jun 21, 1892), m Justina ___ ; <u>Mary Ann</u> b 1836; <u>Jacob</u> b 1839;

+ + +<u>Amos</u> (Mar 25, 1809 – May 19, 1897 in Girardville bur Old Meth Cem, Berrysburg), m 1837 to Amanda Harper (Dec 18, 1815 – Sep 23, 1897), a dau of General Thomas Harper. [Amos was previously m to Elizabeth Miller (Nov 8, 1811 – Oct 30, 1836), a dau of Henry and Catharine Miller. Her tombstone states that she is the wife of Amos Hoffman, and is located beside the graves of the parents of Amos Hoffman (Jacob & Cath) in Hoffman Cem]. Amos served for several years as steward of the almshouse and later lived on his farm in Lykens Twp. During the Civil War period, five of their sons were in the Union Army. They lived in Berrysburg in 1880. **Amos and Amanda (Harper) Hoffman had these children:**

<u>Henry H.</u> b c1838, served in the 8th Illinois Cavalry Co, became blind toward the end of the Civil War from exposure.

<u>Thomas William</u> (Sep 1839 – Apr 18, 1905, bur Sunbury, d in Scranton), m by Rev. Jeremiah Schindel, Jun 27, 1865 to Sarah I. Schindel, a dau of Solomon and Elizabeth (Fry) Shindel. **Thomas W. and Sarah (Schindel) Hoffman had these children:** *Sue S.* b Jul 24, 1866, m ___ Zerfing, lived in Port Treverton; *Mary H.* b Oct 1, 1868, m ___ Boyer of Port Treverton; *Elizabeth* b Jul 19, 1876, lived in Port Treverton, had a store in partnership with his brother Jacob. After his first wife Sarah died, Thomas W. Hoffman m Helen Fisk on Apr 5, 1892 in Dansville, N.Y.. Helen (1848 – 1941), was a dau of George C. and Elizabeth (Karcher) Fisk of Dansville, and Helen was a doctor. She died at the age of 92. Thomas W. Hoffman was a member of the 72nd Phila Fire Zouaves for three years, and other volunteer groups, during the Civil War. He was promoted to the rank of Lt. Colonel, and was one of only three hundred men to receive the Congressional Medal of Honor during the war of the Rebellion. He received the medal July 19, 1895 for preventing a retreat of his regiment during the battle while Captain of Co A, 208th Pa. Inf at Petersburg, Va Apr 2, 1865.

<u>Jacob Franklin</u> (Dec 25, 1841 – ___ bur Herndon), m 1st Martha Witmer (___-Oct 16, 1902), a dau of Abraham Witmer of Juniata Co. **Jacob and Martha (Witmer) Hoffman had two sons:** *Charles H*; *Edwin S*. Jacob Franklin m 2nd Jan 2, 1905 Mary Agnes Blasser, dau of Abraham D. Blasser. Jacob was a soldier during the Civil War, with the rank of Captain, and served under General Hartranft as did his brother Thomas. He recieved a wound of the right thigh in the assault of Ft. Steadman, where there was a loss of 4,500 men. After the war, Jacob and his brother Thomas embarked in the general merchandise business at Port Treverton, Snyder County. They continued in the business for thirty years.

<u>Edwin A.</u> (1845 - ___), m Sarah E. Gingrich. He was a Civil War veteran, with the rank of Sergeant.

<u>John Harper</u> (Nov 7, 1846 – Feb 15, 1938, at Milheim, bur Williamstown), m Aug 1870 to Mary Swab (no dates). During the Civil War, John Harper was a drummer. At the age of sixteen he went to Uniontown (Pillow) to learn the tanning trade. After the was he began his own tanning business and had a general store in Berrysburg. He eventually purchased a textile mill in Williamstown. **John Harper and Mary (Swab) Hoffman had these children:** *William* b c1872; *Elsie*; *Edward Harper*, moved to Phila; *Charles Edgar* b c1879; *Henrietta* (no dates) m John Smich; *Sally* d young; *John Robert*; *Carrie May*; *Joseph*.

<u>Henrietta</u> (1849 - ___) m William Williard, lived in Girardville. She lived with her parents in 1880, has Raymond Hoffman age 3, listed as grandson of her parents.

<u>George M.</u> b c1850, m Mary Shindel b c1843. He was employed by Reading Railroad Company in Shamokin. But in **1880 lived in Hubley Twp, Sch Co. with children:** *Charles* age 7 and *Lizzie* 7 months.

<u>Charles H.</u> (no dates), m moved to the south

<u>Joseph W.</u> (___ m Susan Seebold, lived in Millersburg, where he was Supt of the Standard Oil Plant.

Adeline (no dates) m Charles Koser and lived in Millersburg.
Oscar (b Apr 17, 1857, d young)

+ + +Sarah (Aug 23, 1811 – Sep 24, 1848, bur David's Cem, Killinger), m Michael Forney (May 31, 1809 bapt Salem Luth, Kilinger- Feb 24, 1881, bur Fetterhoff Cem. In 1880, Michael Forney a widower lived in Halifax Twp with the J. Andre family. He was age 71 and working at the mill. [Michael apparently had a family connection to the Andre's. J. Andre was a miller age 50, Angeline 44, Hannah M 15, Susan A 11, Ida M 7, Carrie A. 5, Daniel A 2.] **Michael and Sarah (Hoffman) Forney had these children**: Sarah b c1836; Samuel (Oct 24, 1840 – Jul 8, 1865, bur David's Cem, Killinger), m Amanda _____ (Jan 16, 1845 – May 31, 1928). He was killed during the Civil War; Jacob b c1845. [More information with Forney genealogy.]
+ + +Catharina (b Mar 23, 1816 – m Abraham Hess [See write-up on Abraham Hess for more information.]
+ + +Elizabeth b Dec 13, 1821
+ + +Jacob B. b Apr 20, 1825 m Elizabeth Hoover (b 1830 - ___), a dau of _____. In 1870 Jacob and Elizabeth Hoffman lived in Washington Twp Jacob was a hotelkeeper in 1880. **Jacob B. and Elizabeth (Hoover) Hoffman had these children (some bapt Hoffman Ch)**: Luzetta b Feb 21, 1849; Frances Eleanor b Jan 20, 1850; Maryella b c1860; Alaine b c1862; William Lewis. (May 22, 1866 – Jul 15, 1955), m Sybilla Agnes Johns (Dec 18, 1867 – Aug 1948), a dau of Peter Oliver and Maria Louisa (Bitzer) Johns of Loyalton; Jacob G. b c1871; Edward G b c1872.
+ + +Daniel (Aug 23, 1829 – m Susanna Griffith (Mar 31, 1837 in Scotland – Jan 3, 1884), a dau of Agnes Griffith (1804–Apr 7, 1882), who lived with Daniel & Susanna in Porter Twp, Sch Co in 1880. **Daniel and Susanna (Griffith) Hoffman had these children(some bapt St. John's Evang Luth Tremont)**: Daniel Lincoln b Aug 15, 1860; Joseph Henry b Feb 8, 1863; Cath Amanda b Mar 9, 1865; David Ellsworth b Mar 3, 1867; William Francis b Apr 2, 1869; George Washington b Feb 28, 1872; Alexander Wallis b May 15, 1874. .
+ +DANIEL (Oct 9, 1785 – Oct 26,1830), m Hannah Ferree (Aug 13, 1789 – after 1850), a dau of Daniel and Sarah (Brua) Ferree. Daniel served during the War of 1812. Daniel made a death bed will in which he requested that his farm should go to his wife as long as she lives, and that David should stay on the farm and take care of his mother. The court granted the farm to Hannah in the care of her son David. Hannah was a widow in Wiconisco Twp in 1850 and had Catherine Bitterman age 15 with her. **Daniel and Hannah (Ferree) Hoffman had these children (some bapt Hoffman's Ch, St. John' Hill Ch)**:
+ + +David Ferree (Jul 24, 1809 – Oct 24, 1867, bur Old Meth Cem, Bbg)), m 1st Hannah Snyder (Apr 26, 1809 – May 4, 1845), a dau of Nicholas Snyder. **David F and Hannah Hoffman had these children**: Daniel Cyrus b c1833 – c1878), moved to Jefferson Co, Ky, and was employed as a yard master at a railway depot. He m c1869 to Rebecca Wass; Nicholas A. b c1835, lived in W. Va. Civil War Vet; Marietta b c1837, m Wm Lodge; Ann Elizabeth (1839 – 1840). After Hannah died, David F. m c1847 Lydia Matilda Gray (1823 –Jul 23, 1886 in Harrisburg), probably from the family of one of the ministers in Berrysburg. In 1850 David F and Lydia lived in Mifflin Twp and he was listed as a carpenter. He was said to be a master chair maker. In addition to their children, they had with them Salome Etzweiler age 7, David Hoffman 14, Elizabeth 13, and Emelias Esterholtz 7. **David F. and Lydia M (Gray) Hoffman had these children**: Erastus B. (Nov 21, 1847 – Dec 5, 1921, Phila., bur Hbg), a gunsmith & locksmith, m 1st Mary Alice Swoyer, divorced, m 2nd Susan Atticks, lived in Hbg, **had these children**: *Maria Jennie* (Jul 16,1875 – 1925, m John M. Zimmerman (1873 – 1950); *Frank H.* (1878 – c1920); *Clarence S.*(1880 – 1903); John H. b Mar 1849 Bbg, m Anna M. ___ was a postal clerk; William J. b 1850 d young; Clara; Nelson (Oct 13,1854 – Dec 1926, Hbg); Millard F. b1857, was a druggist; Rebecca b c1858; Frank C (1860 – c1920), was a printer & telegraph, m Annie E _____; Charles C. b c1867, m Lillian Frenece.
+ + +Jacob D. (b Jul 3, 1812 – d May 30, 1887, bur Mbg), m May 19, 1836 Eva Romberger (Jun 28, 1810 –Sep 1876), a dau of Adam and Anna Catharine (Paul) Romberger. They lived on a farm in Wiconisco Twp in 1850. **Jacob David and Eva (Romberger) Hoffman had these children**: Isaac White (Mar 5, 1837 – 1924, bur Millersburg), m 1st on Nov 6, 1856 to Sarah Francis Martin (Aug 4, 1844 – Dec 17, 1874), a dau of Dr. H. G. and Elizabeth Martin of Covington, Pa. Isaac m 2nd Nov 6, 1879 to Marian Meck (1853 – 1920). Isaac White Hoffman was the ticket and freight agent for the North Central and Pa Railroad at Millersburg. Also served as Director of the First National Bank of Millersburg; Adam (1838 – 1902 Harrisburg), m Margaret C. Bush; Hannah (1840 – 1870), m James Schreiner; Sarah (1842 – 1926) m James Schreiner, her sister's widower, lived in Brooklyn, N.Y; Adaline (1845 – 1915), m Mathias Wilson McAlarney in Mifflinburg; Elmira (1847 – 1930), m John McAlarney, and moved to Harrisburg where John was employed as an Agriculture agent; In 1880, Elmira's father lived with them, and Rosanna Wilson age 66, an aunt also lived with them. Rebecca b c1849; George b c1850.
+ + +Sarah b Mar 26, 1816, m Benjamin Muench, **had these children**: Benjamin & Elizabeth.

240

+++**Daniel C.** b Sep 8, 1817 - bapt Hoffman Ch, (but mother's name is given as Catherine), m Franie Frantz b c1821. They lived in Wiconisco Twp in 1860 and he was a miner. In 1880, Daniel C. Hoffman lived in Wiconisco Twp. His wife was apparently deceased. Three children lived with him; Sarah age 33, Frank age 27, Mary E. age 25, and two grandchildren: Hannah E. age 5 and Wilson L. age 3. **Daniel C. and Franie (Frantz) Hoffman had these children:** Sarah b c1846; Hannah b c1849; Frank b c1853; Mary b c1856; Charles b c1859.

+++**Hannah** b Aug 17, 1819 m Isaac Uhler (no dates), a miller. Isaac died before 1880, and Hannah lived in Jackson Twp. alone. **Isaac and Hannah (Hoffman) Uhler had these children:** Ann E. Apr 3, 1839 - May 17, 1842, bur Hoffman Cem); John 1840 - 1842); Jacob;

+++**Lucetta** (Nov 2, 1822 - Sep 4, 1823, bur Hoffman Cem)

+++**Joseph** b Oct 29, 1824, m Sarah C. ___ b c1834, lived in Hummelstown where he kept a hotel. In 1880 Amos S. Miller age 32, horse dealer, Charles L. Fox age 32, and George Wilson age 21, hostler lived with the family. **Joseph and Sarah (____) Hoffman had these children:** Kate C. b c1856; Joseph F b c1858, worked in a saddle shop; Lizzie b c1860; Edward A b c1866; Sadie C b c1868; B.C. b c1871.

+++**Elmira** b Feb 19, 1830 m John S. Musser, Dau Co Commissioner, lived in Millersburg.

++**JOHN NICHOLAS (Jr.)** (Nov 5, 1790 - Feb 21, 1874, said to be bur in Hoffman Cem), m 1810 to Maria Margretha "Polly" Novinger (b Jun 13, 1789 - Sep 7, 1861 Halifax Twp), a dau of Dewalt and Mary (Woodside) Novinger. John Nicholas and Polly lived in Lykens Twp, but later moved to Halifax Twp. where he died. John Nicholas was referred to as "Yung Nickel." **John Nicholas and Polly (Novinger) Hoffman had these children (some bapt Hoffman & St. John's Hill Ch):**

+++**John Nicholas III** (Apr 29, 1811 - ____), m Elizabeth Buffington (Mar 16, 1812 - Mar 4, 1870, bur Salem Union Cem, Bbg), a dau of John and Catherine Buffington. He lived in Washington Twp and was proprietor of the Red Tavern at "crossroads" (Elizabethville). He was also director of the poor. **John Nicholas and Elizabeth (Buffington Hoffman had one known child:** Mary L. Elizabeth b Jun 1, 1844, m Elias Jury b c1848. In 1880 Mary Elizabeth and Elias Jury lived with her parents and he was a revenue officer. Anna Snyder 18, and Samuel Reichart age 61 also lived with them, listed as a servant:

+++**Jonathan** (Jan 1, 1813 - Jun 29, 1884, bur Fetterhoff's Cem), m Aug 9, 1843 Joannah Hoffman (Jun 28, 1824 - Dec 30, 1893), a dau of Daniel G. and Susannah (Harman) Hoffman. They lived on a farm in Fisherville. **Jonathan and Joannah (Hoffman) Hoffman had these children (bapt Fetterhoff's Ch):** Nicholas (b & d 1844) Mary Elizabeth (Aug 7, 1845 - Dec 21, 1922, bur Oak Hill Cem, Mbg), m William Bender (1842 - 1923); James b 1847; Chas Frank (1848 - 1940), moved to Minn; Isaac B. (1850 - 1901), m Mary Ellen Bressler; Geo D. (1852 - 1922); Samuel (1853 - 1885, bur Fetterhoff's Cem); Jacob (1856 - 1929, bur Wiconisco), m Catharine Smith (1854 - 1937); Sarah Jane b 1858, m __ Vanderhoft; Susannah b 1860 d young; John W. d young; Jonathan Wellington (1864 - 1943 in Indiana).

+++**George** (Oct 26, 1814- Feb 8, 1896, bur Longs Cem, Halifax), m Susanna Miller (Aug 18, 1820 - Jun 8, 1896), a dau of John and Eva Miller. In 1880 George Hoffman 65 and Susanna age 60 lived in Reed Twp. and Laura Miller age 13 listed as servant lived with them. **George and Susanna (Miller) Hoffman had these children (some bapt at Fetterhoff's Ch):** John b Aug 16, 1837; Jacobus b Oct 18, 1838 ; Margaret Ann (b Nov 26, 1840 - 1957) Sarah Jane (1842 - 1902, bur Fetterhoff Cem), m Uriah Bowman (1837 - 1912), a cabinet maker in Fisherville, a son of Abraham and Anna Eliz (Frost) Bowman; Daniel b 1846; Elizabeth b 1848 m Charles Smith; David (Jan 8, 1852 - 1945, bur Dauphin Hbg), m Melinda Miller (1856 - 1923), a dau of Cyrus and Elizabeth (Sweigert) Miller. He was a stone cutter and mason, built many homes and churches in Harrisburg; Susanna (1854 - 1937, bur Long's Cem Halifax), m Wm Tyson; Charles b & d 1857; William W (1859 - 1906), m Martha ___, bur longs Cem; Samuel (Oct 14, 1860 - Nov 12, 1945, bur Long's Cem), m c1880 Emma S. Derr (Oct 8, 1870 - Oct 29, 1937), a dau of Richard and Lucetta (Zimmerman) Derr. **Samuel and Emma (Derr) Hoffman children;** *George* b 1882; *Lottie* b 1884; *Edward* b 1888; *Lucetta* b 1892; *Stella* b 1895; *Sarah* b 1890; *Robert* (1897 - 1954), m Ella Eva Hawk (1898 - 1982), a dau of George and Mary Magd (Hawk) Hawk. **Robert and Ella Eva (Hawk) Hawk children:** *Thelma* m James Hammaker; *Robert* b 1921 m Annabelle Crabb b Aug 22, 1924, a dau of Russell and Katie (Schlegel) Crabb; *Gladys* b 1923 m Derald Matter; *William* b 1928 Shizako Kawano; *Larry* b 1933 m Joyce Fuller; Jacob b c1863 moved to Chicago, was a detective at Palmer House.

+++**Margaret** b Dec 13, 1816

+++**Elizabeth** b Jan 1, 1819 not married

+++**James Benton**(Mar 11, 1821 - Jan 19, 1896, bur Fetterhoff's Cem), m Margaret Amelia Reisch (Mar 23, 1829 - Dec 14, 1893), a dau of George and Julian (Zimmerman) Reisch. They lived on the old homestead near McClellan, Pa. **James B. and Margaret (Reisch) Hoffman children:** William Henry (Apr 18, 1850 - Mar

17,1894, killed in a mine accident), m Henrietta Franci Deibler (Sep 1853 - Mar 1914), a dau of David and Susan (Workman) Deibler. **William and Henrietta (Deibler) Hoffman children**: *Emma Jane* (1874 - 1953, bur Hbg Cem), m John Harper Hartman worked for the railroad in Harrisburg. He was a volunteer and served during the Spanish American War; Margaret; *George*; *Frank J.* b 1879; *Daisy Louise* b 1878; Hiram B (1852 - 1862); Margaret Ellen b Apr 15, 1853; Isaac Sylvestor (1855 - 1938), m Margaret Amelia Shott (1854 - 1939).

+++**Isaac** (Apr 3, 1823 - Jun 3, 1895, bur Low. Fisherville Cem), m Elizabeth Witman (Jun 9, 1827 - Nov 7, 1887), a dau of Samuel and Susanna Witman. Isaac was a Civil War veteran, and a Dauphin County Commissioner. In 1880, Emma Bowman 21, listed as servant and grandson Edward Enterline age 6 lived with them. **Isaac and Elizabeth (Witman) Hoffman children (bapt Fetterhoff's Ch):** Mary Catherine b Apr 12, 1846 - 1914, bur Fairview Cem, Enders), m Charles Greiner; David Franklin (b Apr 12, 1846 - d Apr 16, 1893 bur Fisherville), m Carolyn Witmer; Samuel Luther (1850 - 1938, bur M.E. Cem Halifax), m Catharine Bowman (1850 - 1913), dau of Philip and Mary Ann (Fetterhoff) Bowman; John Henry (1856 - 1940, bur Fisherville), m Mary Louise Tobias (1861 - 1927), a dau of Daniel and Mary (Klinger) Tobias; Sarah Eliz b1857 , m Rev. Isaac Jacob Reitz of Evan Cong Ch; Isaac Aaron b1860 - __ bur Fisherville Cem), m Mary E. Shepley (1859 - 1893), a dau of Samuel and Agnes Shepley; Cornelius b c1862;

+++**Anna Maria** b Mar 17, 1825, bapt St. David's Killinger

+++**Sarah** b c1827 m John Sheaffer, a son of Daniel and Mary Shaffer. They had a dau Mary (no dates) m William B. Meetch. He was elected register of the County.

+++**Jacob** b c1830

++**SARAH** (Feb 4, 1793 - ____), m Jonathan Snyder, moved to Canton, Ohio where she died over 90 years old. **Jonathan and Sarah (Hoffman) Snyder had one known son: Daniel J.**

++**JOHN** (b Dec 9, 1794 - d Aug 10, 1854, bur Peace Cem), m Elizabeth Bordner (Aug 28, 1800 - 1873). They lived in Berrysburg, and he was a tailor. He served in the war of 1812. He was referred to as "Schneider Hannes." **John and Elizabeth (Bordner) Hoffman had these children:** Mary b c1817, m George Hawk b c1817, lived in Mifflin Twp in 1850 & was a plasterer. **They had these children:** Amanda b c1841; Jonathan b c1843; Samuel b c 1844; Emanuel b c1846; Benj. F. b c 1848; Phebe A. b 1850. They later moved to Mercer Co. Rebecca b Dec 30, 1819; Salome b Sep 24, 1821, m Aaron Matter; Elisabeth b Dec 2, 1823, m George Daniel b Aug 15, 1822, a son of Andreas (Jr) and his wife Susanna (Williard) Daniel; Hannah b Sep 4, 1825 , m George Messner, moved to Ogle Co, Ill., later to Kane Co., Ill; Juliana b Feb 7, 1830, m John Laudenslager, a son of Jacob and Sophia (Reddinger) Laudenslager; Phoebe Ann b Jul 22, 1832 - May 1 , 1886, bur Simeon Cem), m Henry Kauderman (1828 - 1897); Edward b Aug 5, 1834; John b Mar 20, 1836 - d Sep 27, 1907, bur Peace Cem), m Elizabeth Smith (Jul 4, 1846 - d Sep 16, 1908 of cancer of the stomach), a dau of Jacob and Sarah (Breigel) Smith. John was a Civil War Vet; William H. b 1838; Benjamin F. 1840 moved to Ogle Co., Ill; Susan m ____ Forney, moved to Ogle Co., Ill. Amanda b Sep 14, 1844, m Aaron Zerby; Isaac b Apr 6, 1846;; Catharine m Joel Matter . (All of these are named as heirs of Elizabeth Hoffman in March 1874 (Misc Bk K – I-725).

++**MARGARET** (1796 - 1894)m Alexander Klinger (b Jun 4, 1793 - d ___), a son of Philip and Magdalena Klinger. Moved to Crawford Co. Pa. [See Klinger genealogy]

++**JOHN GEORGE (Squire)** (Mar 13, 1798 - Aug 12, 1887, burial place unmarked, but most likely on south side of Simeon Church). George grew up near the end of Short Mountain. He came to Gratz while he was a very young man, about 1820, and resided on lot number twenty. By trade, George was a tailor, but as early as 1834 he received an appointment to the office of Justice of the Peace. He served in that position for many years (not consecutively) up to 1881.There are numerous court records that attest to his activities in performing those duties. In 1859 he was elected Burgess of Gratz. Squire Hoffman lived to the age of ninety, apparently had a keen memory even in old age. It is thought that he was the source for many things that were recorded about Gratz during the latter part of the 1800's.

George Hoffman m 1st Catharine Troutman (Jan 29, 1797 - Mar 18, 1846, bur Simeon Cem), a dau of Jacob and Anna Mary (Williamson) Troutman. The Troutman home was located near Hebe. **George and Catharine (Troutman) Hoffman had these children (some bapt Hoffman Ch):**

+++**William** (Jan 8, 1820 - ____), m Amanda or Amelia _____ b c1817. They lived in Gratz, and he was a tailor. By 1880, William had died, and his wife moved to Phila. Several of the children lived with her. Two grandchildren, Bayard Kissinger age 17, a bartender, and Annie Schaver age 7, lived with her. **William and Amanda Hoffman had at least six children:** Catharine b c1844; Maria E (1846 - 1851 bur Simeon Cem); Charles A b c1851 lived with his mother in 1880 and was a tailor; Isabella b c1852; Priscilla b c1853; William R. b c1857, lived with his mother and was a baker; Barnard b c1863 (maybe this is the one listed above as a grandson); Ambrose Perry b Aug 31, 1865, was a bartender in 1880.

+ + +Marie (Jan 15, 1822 – Oct 1900, d at the home of her dau Ella), m Dec 22, 1846 Thomas Radel (Jun 30, 1823 – 1861), a son of Philip and Elisabeth Radel. [More information in Radel genealogy.]

+ + +John Henry (1826 –1831, bur Simeon Cem)

+ + +George Jr (b 1826 – murdered Sep 24, 1856, near Laudenslagers Hotel in Gratz during militia encampment, probably bur Simeon Cem. George m Aug 9, 1851 Caroline Burrell, but deserted about one year later, and divorced Dec 7, 1853. They were apparently on friendly terms, as it is said that Caroline visited with George as he lay mortally wounded. He was a tailor in Gratz.

+ + +Jonathan (Jul 14,1827 – 1887), lived with Solomon Laudenslager in 1850, and was listed as a carpenter. Later in 1850 he m Rebecca Umholtz (Aug 28, 1830 – Mar 6, 1907), a dau of Michael and Rebecca (Herman) Umholtz of Gratz. Jonathan and Rebecca moved to Harrisburg where he worked as a carpenter. In 1854 they moved to Lafayette County, Wisconsin. In 1880 they lived in Lafayette Co and Jonathan was a carpenter. Five of their children were with them. They are buried in Leadmine, Wisconsin. **Jonathan and Rebecca (Umholtz) Hoffman had these children**: Francis Carson b Jul 3, 1851 in Hbg, m Aug 6, 1873 Monelvia Shafer; Henry b 1853 in Hbg lived with his parents in 1880 and was a carpenter; George b c1858, was born in Wisconsin, and in 1880 was a carpenter; Mary J b c1863; Martha b c1866; Emma b c1869(last four b in Wisconsin).

+ + +Jane b 1829 m ___ Crimby

+ + +Isaac b 1833 (an Isaac Hoffman m Jun 28, 1863 by Rev. Christian L. Hartman in Gratz to Catharine Andre b Feb 9, 1835 Montg Co dau of Geo Andre. **They had these children:** Mary b c1870; Annie b c1878. + + +Harriet b 1837

After his first wife died, Squire John George Hoffman m Hannah Welker (1817 – Mar 1885), bur Simeon Cem (Evang section). She was a dau of John and Elizabeth (Messerschmitt) Welker. The death record for Hannah was found in the Gratz news of the Valley Echo newspaper, Mar 14,1885, bur tombstone had not been found.
Squire George and Hannah (Welker) Hoffman had these children:

+ + +Elizabeth (May 9, 1848 – Oct 22, 1922, bur Evang Cem, Williamstown), m 1st Aug 30, 1868, Edward Thomas b Apr 1, 1840, son of Samuel and Hannah Thomas. They were m by Rev. Wm. Weidner of Oakdale Church. Edward Thomas served during the Civil War, said to be wounded at Gettysburg, assigned to caring for the Colonel's horses as he recuperated. Edward later worked in the mines, as early as 1870, and on April 1, 1872, he was killed at the Short Mountain Colliery by a fall of rock. His young children went to live with their Hoffman grandparents by 1880. **Edward and Elizabeth (Hoffman) Thomas had these children:** Mary b c1871, worked in Phila, m A. Rimage; Catherine (Jan 29, 1872 – 1916), m William T. Umholtz (1865 – 1923), a son of Samuel Umholtz. [More details in Umholtz genealogy.]. Elizabeth m 2nd in Williamstown in 1885 to Edward McNutt for whom she worked as a housekeeper, during his first wife's fatal illness. There were no children to this marriage.

+ + +Caroline b 1849 m ___ Wenzel. She is probably the mother of George L. Hoffman d Jul 15, 1871 age 1 month, bur Simeon Cem. She and her husband lived in Shamokin by 1887.

+ + +Luther b & d 1851

+ + +Margaretha b 1853 m 1st Daniel I. McNoldy (1849 – 1877), a son of William and Mary McNoldy. He was working in the "tunnel" in 1870, died in 1877. They had one child: Annie Eliz b Nov 30, 1874, in 1880 was living with her Hoffman grandparents. Margaretha m 2nd Edward Yoder, and lived in Shamokin by 1887.
Priscilla b 1857 m William Lewis, lived in Shamokin by 1887.

+MARIA CATHERINE HOFFMAN (1751 bapt Jul 1, 1751 – conf Host Ch 1767 –Oct 4, 1819), m Andreas Riegel, Sr. (b c1750 – d May 14, 1815), both probably bur in cemetery near end of Short Mountain. [More information under Andreas Riegel write-up.]

+ANNA MARGARETHA HOFFMAN(b c1753, confirmed at Host Ch Christmas Day 1769, m 1st Adam Steinbrecher (b 1728 – d after 1774), a son of Johan Dietrich Steinbrecher. **Adam and Anna Margaretha (Hoffman) Steinbrecher had one dau:** + +CATHERINE (Apr 2, or May 3, 1774 – Sep 21, 1845), m Peter Klinger (1773 – 1858, bur Klinger Cem). [More information on write-up of Klinger family]. Shortly after her birth, Adam Steinbrecher died. Anna Margaretha Hoffman m 2nd Martin Newbecker, widower of Margaret Spahr.
Anna Margaretha m Martin Newbaker who died before 1805 (when his wife was noted as a widow). He had been married to Margaret Spare. He served during the Revolutionary War. **Martin and Anna Margaretha (Hoffman Steinbrecher) Newbaker had these children:**

+ +JOHN b 1777

++**MARY MAGDALENA** (Sep1, 1779–Jul 15, 1826, bur Hoffman Cem no stone), m Dec 23,1804 Jonas Schoffstall (May15,1782– Feb 23, 1856, bur Ogle Co, Ill), a son of Peter Schoffstall. [More info in Schoffstall gen.]

++ **MARIA SARA** b Jun 24, 1782 m John Wells, resident of Mifflin Twp, Dau Co.

++**ELISABETH** (no dates) m Joseph Keller

++**JOHN MARTIN** b Mar 11, 1791

+**CHRISTIAN HOFFMAN** (1752 – 1842, bur Fetterhoffs Cem – marked with new Rev. stone lying flat on ground given by War Dept.), m Susanna Deibler (no dates, no stone), a dau of Capt. Albright Deibler. Albright lost his life at the battle of Long Island during the Revolutionary War. Christian was referred to as "der alt Christel". He and the family lived on the old homestead at Short Mountain.**Christian and Susanna (Deibler) Hoffman children (bapt Hoffman & St. John "Hill" Ch) :**

++**ANNA MARY** (1784 -Feb 6, 1869, death recorded in Zion Luth Ch Hbg), m John Pehs/Pease, lived at Sands Spring, Clark's Valley. **John and Anna Mary (Hoffman) Pehs children (bapt Hoffman & St. John's "Hill" Ch, Fetterhoff Ch):**Christian b Aug 1, 1805; **Margaretha** b Jul 15, 1807, m 1st ____ Riegel, 2nd ____ Dubendorf; **Christian** (no dates) m Rosina; **Angelina** (no dates), m John Ebersole; **Juliana** ; **Elizabeth** b Jul 29, 1825, m ____Zimmerman; **Jacob**; **John**; ++**CHRISTINA** b Dec 25, 1789 ;++**ELIZABETH** b Nov 8, 1791

++**JOHN BENJAMIN** (Sep 17, 1793 – Apr 30, 1875, bur Bowerman Cem, Enterline), m Apr 26, 1814 by Rev. Reily to Barbara Margaret Bowman (May 19, 1795 – Oct 12,1861), a dau of John and Margaret Barbara Bowman. John Benjamin served in the War of 1812. They lived in Jefferson Twp in 1850, and he was a blacksmith and vet of War of 1812. **John Benjamin and Barbara Margaret (Bowman) Hoffman children:** George b Jan 14, 1816 m Martha Zeiders, probably moved to Indiana, had these children: Cornelius b Jan 30, 1837, bapt Fetterhoff's Ch; Elmira b c1840; Phebe b c1842; Emanuel b c1844; Isaiah b c1847; John (b Apr 4, 1818 – d Mar 31, 1890, bur Bowermans Cem, Enterline), m Anna Mary Enterline b Apr 14, 1820, a dau of Peter and Susannah (Messner) Enterline.They lived in Jefferson Twp in 1850. **John and Anna Mary (Enterline) Hoffman had these children:** Susannah (Mar 12, 1842 – Aug 27, 1897), m Nathaniel Zimmerman (1840 – 1888), a son of John and Lydia (Bowman) Zimmerman; Elias (Mar 16,1845 – Feb 24, 1872, bur Bowerman Cem), not married; Aaron (Aug 8, 1847 – Dec 26, 1865, bur Bowerman Cem), not married; Jonathan (Nov 25, 1849 – Aug 31, 1876, bur Bowerman Cem), m Catharine Emma Sheetz, whom after Jonathan's death m Leonard Hawk; Mary Ellen (Oct 2, 1853 – Aug 9, 1883, bur Bowerman Cem), m Washington Sheetz (1846 – 1919);Harvey b c1855 m Jane Travitz; Sarah Catharine (Feb 21, 1857 – Jun 22, 1931), m Sep 1, 1878 Joseph Andrew Lebo (1853 – 1936), son of Joseph and Sarah (Shepley) Lebo. Susanna b 1820 d young; Christian (Nov 11, 1821 – Jul 23, 1899), m Susannah Enterline (Feb 18, 1823 – Jul 25, 1900), a dau of Peter and Susannah (Messner) Enterline, lived in Jefferson Twp; Margareta b Sep 12, 1824, m Jonathan Spayd; Sara Ann (Feb 14, 1827 – Jul 19, 1905), m Thomas Leinbaugh Lebo (1826 – 1897), lived in Perry Co; Josiah Peter (Mar 10, 1829 – Jul 23, 1891, bur Bowerman Cem), m Emelin Bordner (1835 – 1912); James (1831–1899, bur Bowerman Cem), m Julia A. Sheetz (1839 –1913); Peter Albright (1833 – 1891), m Sarah Adaline Hochlander; Lydia Anna (1839 – 1857), not married.

++**DANIEL GEORGE** b Jul 1, 1796 – d ___ probably bur old Meth Cem, Halifax), m Susanna Harman (Nov 6, 1799 - ___), a dau of John and Elizabeth Harman. Daniel served in the War of 1812. They lived on a farm near Fisherville. **Daniel George and Susanna (Harman) Hoffman children:** Amelia (1823 - 1866) m Daniel Lyter (1821 – 1883), a son of Peter and Jane (Page) Lyter. After Susanna d, Daniel George Hoffman m her younger sister Elizabeth (Harman) Hoffman b Sep 6, 1802, widow of John Hoffman. **Daniel George and Elizabeth (Harman, Hoffman) Hoffman children:** Joannah (1824 – 1893), m Jonathan Hoffman (1813 – 1884), a son of Nicholas Hoffman, Jr.; Elizabeth (1827 – 1910), m 1st John Hoffman (1820 – 1860, died of typhoid fever), son of Peter and Elizabeth Hoffman; Charles (no dates) not married. .

++**PETER** (Mar 19, 1798 – Apr 1, 1868, bur Messiah Cem, Fisherville)), m Elizabeth Hoffman (Dec 7, 1802 - bapt Hoffman Ch - Dec 11, 1871), a dau of John George and Rebecca (Gunderman) Hoffman of Berrysburg. Peter served in the War of 1812. **Peter and Elizabeth (Hoffman) Hoffman children (some bapt Hoffman Cem):** Elizabeth m Abraham Boyer (Jun 11, 1815 – Oct 21, 1866, bur Messiah Cem, Fisherville); John (Aug 6, 1820 – Aug 27, 1860 of typhoid fever, bur Fisherville), m Elizabeth Hoffman (1st cousin), a dau of Daniel and Susanna (Harman) Hoffman; George (Dec 18, 1822 – Jan 3, 1857); Catharine Susanna b May 1, 1825, m William Taft; Jacob B (Jul 11,1830 – Sep 17, 1897), m Barbara A. Keiter (1839 – 1915), Fisherville; Henry W. (Oct 30, 1831 – 1917), m Susan Keiter, a dau of Samuel and Susanna (Shott) Keiter; Sarah (Dec 9, 1835 d Aug 23, 1911)), m James Miller (b Feb 16, 1835 – d Dec 3,1920, bur Maple Grove Cem, E'ville). **James and Sarah (Hoffman) Miller had these children:** Milton (b ___ d Apr 2, 1937), m Susan Hoke Lupold; Ellen Victoria d young; Agnes A. m Lincoln U Bolton;Lena E m Harry M Cooper; Harvey M. (Sep 27, 1871 – Jun 17, 1939), m Apr 2, 1903 Rose K.

Sheetz, dau of John and Sarah (Park) Sheetz; **Rebecca** (Nov 4, 1838 – Mar 30, 1926, after fracturing a hip bone by a fall down stairs), m Lewis Matter (Feb 6, 1837 – 1902), a son of John Michael and Margaret Rebecca (Kinerson) Matter; **Lydia Elmira** (1841 – 1912), bur Fetterhoff's Cem), m George W. Frank; **Isaac Petrus** b 1843 d young;; **Mary Ann** (1846 – 1920, b Meth Cem, Williamstown), m George W. Bowerman (1841 – May 1,1925), a son of John A. & Anna Mary (Woland) Bowerman), grandson of John and Anna Margaretha (Ditty) Woland. Civil War Vet

++CHRISTIAN Jr. (Jul 30, 1799 – Jun 1, 1870, bur Salem Luth Cem, Bbg), m Sarah Tobias (Oct 5, 1802 – Dec 5, 1870), a dau of ____ Tobias. **Christian J. and Sarah (Tobias) Hoffman Children**: <u>Susan</u> m John Null; <u>Catharine</u> m George Dunkel; **William** (Aug 5, 1823 –1894 in Victoria, Cass Co, Neb), m Mary Fisher; <u>Sarah</u> b Dec 5, 1825, m Benjamin Swab, moved to Mercer Co, until 1848 then moved to Kansas; **Mary Magdalena** b Apr 12,1828, m May 4, 1848 John B. Umholtz of Halifax Twp; <u>Cornelius</u> b Apr 24, 1831– Feb 15,1916, bur Bowerman Cem, Enterline), m Nov 4, 1856 Mary Ann Hassinger (Dec 6, 1834 – Aug 29, 1895, a dau of Jeremiah and Esther (Smeltz) Hassinger of Lykens Twp. Cornelius taught school 12 years in Wash Twp. **Cornelius and Mary Ann (Hassinger) Hoffman children**: <u>William H.</u> b Feb 26,1859; <u>Agnes Rebecca</u> b Dec 20, 1860, m Washinton Sheetz; <u>Lucy Ellen</u> b Dec 20, 1862, m ____Lenker; <u>Margaret E</u> b Nov 4, 1864, m William Dempsey; <u>John C.</u>b May 19, 1867, moved to Cass Co., Ind.; <u>Charles Darwin</u> b Sep 16, 1869, a teacher in Jackson Twp; <u>Jacob Tobias</u> b Nov 9, 1872, a teacher; <u>Aaron M.</u> b Dec 23, 1874; <u>Albert Nathaniel</u> b Aug 16, 1876; **Peter** (Feb 22, 1833 – Feb 15, 1895), m Catharine Lenker, had a son <u>George W.</u> b Mar 13, 1858, bapt Salem Union Ch Bbg; **Rebecca** b Nov 13, 1834, m Emanuel Forney. After Emanuel died, Rebecca lived with a son near Fisherville; **John Tobias** (b Jul 13, 1837, m Harriet Ginter, lived in Up. Paxton Twp., by 1880 they lived in Washington Twp. **Henry H** (Dec 16, 1839 – Feb 9, 1920)., m Aug 6, 1863 Sarah Alice Novinger (Mar 20, 1845 – Sep 23, 1906), a dau of Jonathan C. and Catharine (Hoffman) Novinger. They moved to Kansas where they died; **Susan** (b Dec 27, 1842 – Fall of 1895), m John Knoll. They moved to Mercer Co, later to Cincinnati, Ohio; **Emma J.** b Apr 22, 1846, m Joseph Tyson. After her husband died, Emma and her twin dau's Anne and Jane joined the Henry and Alice (Novinger) Hoffman's migrating to Logansport, Indiana. In June1872 they moved on to Kansas. Emma m Richard Rowe later in 1872 and in spring of 1880 the Rowe family migrated to Arkansas, and later to Oklahoma; **Susannah** b c1843, m John Noll; **Sarah Catharine** b Nov 4, 1847 m George Dunkle, moved to Mercer County, and later to Butler Co., Pa.

++SUSANNAH (Jul 19, 1801 – 1895, bur Fetterhoff Cem), m Philip Shott (Jun 25, 1791 – Jan 1, 1854).**Philip and Susannah (Hoffman) Shott children**: <u>Christian</u> m Elizabeth Becker; <u>Jonas</u>; <u>George W.</u>; <u>Sarah</u>; <u>Susannah</u>, m Isaac Novinger; <u>Leconia</u>.

++ELIZABETH b Nov 25, 1802

++JONAS DAVID (Mar 10, 1805 – Jun 7, 1849, bur Halifax ME Cem), m Rebecca Collier (Dec 4, 1803 – Feb 2, 1858). In 1850 Rebecca, a widow lived in Matamoras with her children; **Jonas David & Rebecca (Collier) Hoffman children**: <u>Joseph</u> b c1827; <u>Jonas</u> b c1830; <u>Elmira</u> (1840– Mar 17, 1861); <u>Lydia</u> (May 3, 1839 – Aug 26, 1857);

++SARA b Feb 25, 1806

++SIMON b Sep 23,1808 d young

++PHILIP (May 21,1811 – Mar 2, 1881, bur St. James Cem), m 1st Catharine Zeigler b Aug 9, 1814 – d before 1880, bur Bowerman Cem), m 2nd m Susanna Heiges (Aug 24, 1826 – Jun 20, 1884, bur Low Messiah Luth Cem, Fisherville), a dau of John Heiges, originally from York, Pa. Philip grew up on the family farm in Lykens Valley, but about 1836, he and his brother –in-law Jonathan C. Novinger, Jr moved to Powells Valley, took up land, cleared it and began farming. Their first early log cabin was destroyed by fire, and nothing was saved but Novinger's gun. The old cabin was replaced with new buildings and the family lived there for many years. Philip was also Justice of the Peace from 1848 to 1853. During those early years the family had few visitors from Lykens Valley, their nearest neighbors. When visitors arrived, they blew a tin horn a yard long to call others in the valley to greet the visitors and exchange news. Jonathan received a letter from the west which was carried by horseback to the Crossroads (then Elizabethville) the nearest post office. The letter took three months to arrive at it's destination. Jonathan and Catharine Novinger eventually moved to Logansport, Indiana. Philip Hoffman was the mail carrier between Carsonville and Elizabethville until Carsonville became a post office. He also donated land for St. James Lutheran Church, and his time to help build the church. In 1880, in addition to their children Philip and Susanna had Catherine E. Kissinger age 4, listed as a niece living with them on their farm in Jefferson Twp. **Philip and Catharine (Zeigler) Hoffman had these children**: <u>Catherine</u> b 1834 d young; **Lydia** (May 4,1835 – Aug 19, 1884, bur St. James Cem, Carsonville), m John Woland (Oct 22, 1830 – Dec 16, 1910), a son of John and Lydia Woland; **Joseph R.** (Oct 18, 1838 – 1877, bur Bowerman Cem), m Mary Bordner (Mar 4, 1842 – 1922), bur Long's Cem, Halifax with 2nd husband Henry Landis. Mary was a dau of Jacob and Maria (Snyder) Bordner; **John Philip** (Aug 8, 1842 – Mar 3, 1909, bur Fairview Cem), m Catherine Anspach. He was a Civil War Veteran; **Susannah** (Apr 1845 – 1913), m Peter Albright Hoffman (Aug

245

8, 1833– Oct 13,1891, a son of John B. and Barbara (Bowman) Hoffman; <u>William H Grant</u> b Feb 4, 1866 –1946), m Esther Weidner; <u>Savilla</u> b Jun 16,1868;<u>Edward L.</u> .b Aug 31,1870.

++CATHERINE (Sep 14, 1814 – Sep 15, 1883), m Jonathan C. Novinger, Jr, (Feb 18, 1808 – Sep 18, 1875), a son of Jonathan C and Christina (Werfel) Novinger. The family moved to Adair County, Missouri in 1848.

+ANNA ELISABETH HOFFMAN (Sep 4, 1757 – Apr 15, 1832), m Ludwig Sheetz (b ____ d Apr 24, 1823).
Ludwig and Anna Elisabeth (Hoffman) Sheetz had these children:

++CATHARINE b Mar7, 1784 m Joseph Harmon, moved to Ohio by 1818; ++SUSANNA b Dec 24, 1787 m Jul 27, 1806 Johannes Riegel;++JOHANNES b Mar 13, 1791 m Elizabeth____;++ELIZABETH b Jul 22, 1793; ++ANNA MARIA b Aug 17, 1795 m Christian Yerges

+CHRISTINA HOFFMAN b Jul 23, 1760, m Christian Seyler; +BARBARA HOFFMAN (May 31, 1763 – Jun 20, 1827), m Sep 2, 1782 George Buffington (Feb 8, 1759 – Mar 26, 1830). They are probably bur in Hoffman family plot. [More information on write-up of Buffington family.]

PHOTOS OF HOFFMAN FAMILY

Family Of Cornelius Hoffman – Sons standing.
Dau's Stded: Margaret, Ellen,Agnes , Cornelius (1831-1916)

Identified as John Peter Hoffman (1778–1864)
Son of Nicholas Hoffman

Catherine (Hoffman) Novinger

JONAS HOFFMAN TRACT

On May 16, 1826, Christian Hoffman and Susanna his wife sold 4 acres, 11 perches of the first tract to Jonas Hoffman. It was part of the early Hoffman settlement at the end of Short Mountain. Jonas and his wife owned this small tract with appurtenances for several years, but on March 30 , 1831, they sold it to Henry and Susanna Shubert.. In 1831 Henry Shubert was taxed for this four-acre property with wooden house, and John Wens was an occupant in the house. Since traditional stories point to the early existence of cabins that were built along the creek on the Hoffman property, it is easy to suspect that this was the very early Hoffman home. It soon became part of the adjacent tannery complex, and the actual site of the tan yard that (although long ago destroyed) is now remembered as the Daniel Good tannery.

THE PRESENT DAY BUSH FARM

AERIAL VIEW OF THE CLAIR BUSH FARM TAKEN MID 1940'S

It is a fact that Christian Hoffman and other Hoffman family members were some of the first early settlers to come to the area of what is now upper section of Dauphin County. They were permanent and well established residents before the land was officially patented to them. In 1800, Christian, Nicholas, John Hoffman and their families all lived in the same vicinity. In 1810, the families of Jacob, Nicholas and Christian Hoffman lived in this area. By 1820, Christian Hoffman, Sr., Christian Hoffman, Jr., and Peter Hoffman were neighbors. The remaining evidence, the tombstone, and recorded memories of earlier family members indicate that the Hoffman family did indeed settle there, and stay for many years.

About two years after Christian Hoffman sold the four acres of land to Jonas Hoffman, on April 5, 1828, he sold the remainder of all the land containing 391 acres and 18 perches, to Thomas Elder and Jacob M. Haldeman, tenants in common. The 1831 tax record confirms the fact that Elder and Haldeman owned three tracts containing 390 acres, and a wooden house is on the land. A Michael Uhler is occupying the land.

In 1853, Thomas Elder died, and on March 1, 1855, his widow and children conveyed his undivided share of the land with appurtenances to Adam Romberger. On March 24, 1857, Adam and Catherine Romberger assigned an undivided half of their plantation to Daniel Romberger. Two years later, On April 1, 1859, After Jacob M.

Haldeman died his heirs sold the other half of the undivided 391 acres of land to Daniel Romberger. That transfer made Daniel Romberger sole owner of the 391 acre, 18 perch plantation.

In 1857 when this land was sold, it was located partly in Lykens Township, partly in Wiconisco Township. It bordered the middle of Wiconisco Creek, land of Daniel Riegel, south to Little Wiconisco Creek, Jacob Hoffman, east to the estate of Hartman Rickert, Jacob Moyer and James Buchanan, then north to Adam Row, and Big Wiconisco Creek. In 1859 Daniel and Hannah Romberger sold 5 acres 64 ¼ perch of woodland to Isaac Romberger. The land was located on Short Mountain at "the coal road."

The present farmhouse was built by Robert F. Harman according to information received from Evelyn Hartman. Daniel and Hannah Romberger and family lived here for many years. After Daniel died, his heirs conveyed 223 acres, 111 perches of the land to Edward Romberger on May 10, 1883. Edward Romberger died in Washington Township, on March 22, 1907, and was survived by his widow Marcy C. and these **two children**: Elmer W., and Alice C. who married P. W. G. Raker. The two children shared the undivided farm, but on March 31, 1915, Alice conveyed her interest in the farm to her brother Elmer.

During his lifetime, Elmer was a mercantile agent, working for his brother-in-law from Lykens. He distributed goods to many of the local stores, including those in Gratz. Bertha was noted for her cleanliness, and enjoyed having her house in order. It was not unusual in those days to place paper under the carpets. So at house cleaning time, the ladies took up the carpets, and put clean paper underneath them.

An incident is remembered that took place in the depression years. One year, for Christmas Elmer gave Bertha a fifty dollar bill (which was considered a very valuable gift during those years.). A friend came to visit, and Bertha, eager to show her gift, went upstairs to get the money. Then instead of taking it up again, Bertha laid the money under the stair carpet, planning to take it upstairs later. She completely forgot about the money. Next spring when she housecleaned, she changed the paper under the carpet as usual, and the money was burned with the paper!

[**DANIEL ROMBERGER** (Feb 27, 1816 – Jul 28, 1882, bur EUB Cem, Bbg), a son of Adam and Catharine Paul) Romberger, m Hannah Bergstresser (Sep 26, 1818- Feb 13, 1889). In 1850 they lived in Lykens Twp. and had Emaline Zerby age 18, dau of Henry Zerby with them.In 1870, Daniel and Hannah lived in Washington Twp, and Sarah Hoffman age 14 lived with them.
Daniel and Hannah (Bergstresser) Romberger had these children:
ADAM b c1839; **EDWARD** (Jul 31, 1841 - Mar 22, 1907, bur Maple Grove Cem, E'ville), m Jan 10, 1867 Sarah Klinger (Mar 29, 1842 - Jan 26, 1894), a dau of Alexander Klinger. Edward was a teacher in Williamstown, but later took up farming. **Edward and Sarah (Klinger) Romberger had these children:**
Alice Celeste (Mar 23, 1870 - Dec 29, 1946), m P. W. G. Raker (1861 - 1933); **Elmer W.** (Sep 6, 1872 - Oct 31, 1942, bur Maple Grove Cem). He was hunting and had just shot a rabbit, when he suffered a heart attack. He m 1st Frances E ____ (Nov 30, 1878 - Apr 8, 1911). Elmer m 2nd on July 13, 1912, Bertha M. Zerbe (1887 - 1944, bur with parents in Maple Grove Cem) , a dau of J. S. and Julia A. Zerbe. **Elmer W. and Frances E. Romberger had one child:** **Paul W**. 1900 - 1972, bur Maple Grove Cem) , m Iva J. (1898 - 1979). After his first wife Sarah died, Edward m 2nd Feb 9, 1899 to Widow Mary Hackman.
CYRUS b c1843; **SAMUEL B**. b c1845; **JOSIAH** b c1854; **JOHN E.** b c1850; **HENRY H**. b c1852 [More info under writeup of Romberger genealogy.]

Elmer W. Romberger died on October 31, 1942, leaving a widow Bertha M. Romberger and a son Paul W. Romberger. On March 29, 1943, Paul W. and Iva J. Romberger inherited the land of his father with a two and one half story frame dwelling and bank barn. "Escepting and reserving there from a certain plot of ground in the center thereof being a size ten foot by fifteen foot piece upon which John Peter Hoffman is buried." Paul Bush later became the owner and today the farm continues to be owned by the Bush family, with Clair Bush as owner since 1981.

The Bush family has been in the dairy business for many years, and they have a large herd of dairy cows. Linda, deceased wife of Clair Bush, was a very active member of the Gratz Historical Society. She had a talent to do herb gardening, display flowers, and do various exhibits for Simon Gratz Days. When she died suddenly at the age of fifty, she was sorely missed in the Gratz Historical Society.

THE BUSH / BUSCH FAMILY
(Some help from Steve Troutman, Helen Patrick Bowman & Paul Bush family)

[***CHRISTIAN BUSH** (Mar 4, 1766 Rockland Twp, Berks Co- Aug 4,1823, Northld Co), son of Jacob & Maria Bush, m Catharina ____(c1768 - Mar 14, 1848), lived in this area in 1813 when they were communicants at

Klingers Church. Among the children of Christian Bush are: **JOHANNES** (Nov 30, 1796 – Jul 10, 1857, bur Hebe Cem), m Catharine Thomas (Apr 28, 1800 – Oct 2,1854h, a dau of Gotfried & Anna Maria Thomas. **Christian & Catharine Bush known children are: ***Moses** (Sep 29,1830 – Mar 22, 1870), Fremont, Snyder Co), m Jun 6, 1854 Elizabeth Bowman (Jun 8, 1835 – Aug 5, 1887, bur Pillow), dau of George & Esther Bowman, **had these children:****Franklin** b Jul 23,1854 –Aug 3, 1936, Barry Twp., Sch Co., m Frances Troutman;****John B.** (1855 –1867, Fremont, Pa.);**** **Mary** b 1857;****Daniel** (Nov 14, 1859 – 1939, Bbg); ****George** (1860 – 1925, Bellvue, Ohio); ****Maria Alien** b Jun 11, 1861; ****James Morris** (Oct 26, 1862 - Sep 20, 1934 in Kansas); ****William** (1864 – 1867, Fremont).

JACOB (Mar 14, 1799 –Mar 3, 1879, bur Hebe), m Catharine Barbara Paul (Jul 2, 1801 – Apr 6, 1872). **Jacob and Catharine Barbara Bush children (some bapt Klinger Ch):**
Elizabeth** (Jul 6, 1822, bapt Zion Luth Ch – Dec 24, 1915 (bur Hebe), m Daniel Troutman (Oct 23, 1817 – Nov 14, 1880, murdered by robbers in his home);Catharine** b Dec 14,1823, m George Delb; ***Jacob** (Aug 16, 1825 bapt Zion Luth Ch– Feb 27, 1896, bur Hebe), m Mary Matilda b c1836, in Jordan Twp. Lived in 1880 beside his brother Elias Bush. **Jacob & Mary children:****Sarah** b c1865; ****Catharine** b c1873; ****Elizabeth** b c1874; ****Millie** b c1875.
***Elias** (Jul 26, 1827 – Apr 22, 1902, bur Hebe), m Sarah Kissinger (Jan 6,1823 –Apr 5, 1887, bur Hebe), a dau of Geeorge & Catharine (Hoover) Kissinger, widow of Elias Klinger. In 1880 Elias and Sarah Bush lived in Jordan Twp., Northld Co. beside his brother Jacob. Their son Elias age 16 and Franklin Bush a nephew age 20 with them. Henry Stroup age 80 also lived with them. **Elias and Sarah (Kissinger, Klinger) Bush children: ****Elias K.** (Jul 6, 1864 – Aug 12, 1938, bur Greenwood Cem, Tower City), m 1884 Catharine Masser (Mar 10, 1866 – Jun 20, 1919), a dau of Moses Masser. **Elias K and Catharine (Masser) Bush children:** *Moses M.* (Dec 6, 1885 – Jul 4, 1965, bur Greenwood Cem, Tower City), m Cecelia E. Kessler (Jul 23, 1889 – Feb 27, 1974). **Moses and Cecilia E. (Kessler) Bush children:** *Paul H.* (Dec 24, 1908 – May 25, 2002), m Florence E. Romberger (Jun 16, 1911 – Sep 9, 1988), dau of Harvey & Dorothy (Platt) Romberger. **Paul H. and Florence E (Romberger), Bush children:** *Shirley E.* b Jan 31, 1931, m Jul 1, 1950 William Keister b Jan 21, 1928. **Shirley E and William Keister children:** *Christine* b May 30, 1951, m William Todd; *Yvonne* b May 17, 1954 m Michael Marr; *Thomas* b Sep 7, 1955; *Brian* b Aug 10, 1957, m Sally Shade b 1960, a dau of Cyril and Lorraine (Witmer) Shade of Gratz; *Dennis* b Oct 11, 1958, m Jutta Bingert. *Clair H.* b Mar 1, 1936 m Linda Eilene Matter (Aug 22, 1939 - Feb 12, 1995), a dau of Chester and Carrie (Miller) Bush. **Clair H. and Linda E (Matter) Bush children:** *Kenneth* b Sep 15, 1958; *Brad* b Aug 10, 1961, m Darla Shuey, **had son** *Joshua* b Nov 7, 1983; *Joseph* b May 17, 1963, m Monda Ditty, **had these children:** *Carrie* b 1992; *John Joseph* b 1995; *Kay M.* b Feb 6, 1940 m Richard Mauser, **had these children:** *Cindy,* m Larry Doyle; *Sandy* m Lester Eppley; *Ruth* m Steve Snyder; *Rachel* m Scott Deitrich; *Richard* m Michele; *Nancy* m Shawn Scheib; *Alice* b 1942, m Ken Parmer, **had these children:** *Kim* m Gary McDormott; *Jeffrey* m Caroline Waldron; *Suzanne* m Joseph Leighton; *Lisa* m David Ditty; *David P* b 1949, m Linda Kolva.
William N. (Sep 4, 1911 – Feb 1, 1937), m Grace Romberger (1914 – 1981). **William N and Grace (Romberger) Bush children:** *Lois* b 1935 m Thomas Lappenger; *Lee* b 1937 m Kim Okizumo; *Albert* m Dora Lauver; *Alvin* b May 6, 1915 m Grace Unger (1916–1992), **had these children:** *Ronald* (1937- 2001), m Judy Carl; *Carol* b 1940, m Thomas Bixler; *Terry* m Penny Shuttlesworth; *Earl* (1919 – 1982); Irene m Stanley Lebo.

Emma Jane (b Sep 7, 1887, m George Shadle, **George and Emma Jane (Bush) Shadle children:** *Harold; Helen; Alma; Alice; Anna; Irvin; George; Gene; Katie Elmira* b Dec 26, 1890, m 1906 Howard Masterson; *Ira C.* b Jun 1896, m Jenny Adams, **had these children:** *Roy; Dorothy; Carlos Wilson* (b Nov 16, 1900 – d 1937), m Ellen Updegrove b 1900; *Clayton John* (Oct 20, 1903 – 1947), m Mary Deiter, **had these children:** *Marlin; Raymond; Grace. Mary* b 1907, m Gurney Slingwine

***Benjamin** (Jul 13,1832 – Aug 9, 1911, bur St. Pauls Cem, Sacramento), m Catharine ___ Aug 7, 1839 – Jun 1, 1857). He apparently m 2nd Sarah Troutman b c1833, a dau of George T. & Christina (Klark) Troutman. They had one known child: James Monroe bJul 12, 1867. In 1880 they lived in Hubley Twp., Sch Co. They had Ida Bush age 10, Sylvester Bohner age 6 and Jere Bohner age 4 with them. Also Rebecca Wiest age 7.
ELIZABETH (Jun 10, 1803 _ Apr 10, 1876), m Martin Paul, Jr. b c1800; **GIDEON** b c1804, m Esther, moved to Jefferson Co;**SAMUEL** (Nov 5,1807– Oct 14,1877, bur Hebe), m Mary Hollenbach (Aug 10,1839 – Aug 19, 1893). **Children:**Catherine b1Aug 10, 839; Lydia b Jan 4,1843; Henry (May 7, 1845 - Mar 26, 1928, bur Simeon Cem, Gratz), m Sarah (1840 – 1903); Mary; Daniel; **WILLIAM** b c1808; **CATHERINE** b c1810, m Abraham Brosius **HESTER** b c1816, m John Greisinger.]

RANCH HOUSE ON THE FARM OWNED BY CLAIR BUSH

MR. & MRS. RODNEY SHADE LAND
(WAS PETER BOHNER LAND 1875 – Old House Now Gone)

This Was The Old Original Farm House

This land is part of the 607 ½ acre tract that Commonwealth of Pennsylvania warranted to Leonard Miller on August 21, 1751. By sundry conveyances, part of the land was conveyed to Andrew Riegel Sr. After the death of Andrew Riegel, Sr., the land was divided into three tracts, and his son Jacob Riegel received one of them.

In 1828 Jacob Riegel had 70 acres of land with a wooden house and distillery, and was listed on tax records as a farmer. He continued to have a distillery as late as 1837 when this became part of Washington Twp.

At a public vendue held March 27, 1847 the land, a house and barn was sold to John George Daniel. This plantation adjoined the land of Michael Sausser, John Hawk, Frederick Lubold, and Catherine Rodebach. On April 4, 1855, John George Daniel and his wife sold toThomas and Barbara Harper.They conveyed on March 29, 1858 to William Hawk. But on March 28, 1867, William and Rebecca Hawk sold the farm to Peter Bohner of Washington Township. [Hawk history elsewhere in book.]

Peter Bohner owned the property in Washington Twp. for many years. By 1880, he was a retired farmer. Jeremiah and Rebecca Matter, his son-in-law and daughter lived with him. Jeremiah was a plasterer.

After Peter Bohner died the property was sold on January 24, 1891 to Daniel Klinger, and he conveyed to Peter A. Matter, whom with his family lived here for a long time. Peter was hit and killed by a car on Christmas Day 1943, while walking in front of the Loyalton Hotel. His widow kept the farm until her death, and then it was divided between their sons Nevin and Ralph Matter. Eventually Nevin obtained the whole farm, and after he died in 1970, his widow Gertrude owned it. After her death in 2003, it was sold to Jane and Rodney Shade.

THE BOHNER/BAHNER FAMILY
(Some information from the Bohner genealogy written by Herbert M Bohner and Joseph and Sarah Meiser).

[Members of the **BOHNER** family are descended from **Helmar Bahn** the earliest known ancestor. He lived in the area of Reichenbach, Germany, and died about 1700. He had a son **Johann George** (b ___ d Jan 13, 1752), who married August 6, 1719 Anna Gela Ludolph (b ___ d Jun 22, 1736), both lived in Reichenbach at the time of their marriage. Johann George and Anna Gella Ludolph had a son **Johann Heinrich** (bapt Jun 6, 1728 - ___), m Catharina Elisabeth Faupelin of Reichenbach, and had a son *Johann Nicolaus b 1754.

*JOHAN NICHOLAUS BOHNER (son of Johann Heinrich b c1728 above) entered the army of Friedrich II, Langraf of Hessen-Cassel about 1775. In December 1775, a contract with the British Col. William Faucitt, was the beginning of a new life for Johann Nicolaus Bohner. Thousands of soldiers were on their way to North America by February 1776, to help the British cause against the American Colonists. After numerous battles, Nicolaus and many other soldiers were captured on December 26, 1776, and taken to a prison in Lancaster. Eventually he became a member of a Hessian Regiment, deserted, and settled in Heidleberg Twp, then Lykens Valley. He was granted a tract of 2041/2 acres of land called "Poland."

J. Nicholas (b 1754 Reichenbach, Ger - d Feb 5, 1824 bur Zion Stone Valley Ch, Northld Co), m Margaret Steger (Feb 26,1754–Aug 13,1831), dau of Adam Steger of Lanc. Co. **J. Nicholas and Margaret (Steger) Bohner children:****Maria Elisabeth bap May 22,1779, m George Stump moved to Ohio;**J. Jacob (Nov 8,1783-Dec 20,1863), m Catharine Deibler (May 16,1789-Sep 27,1855);**J.Henry (Dec 31,1786- Sep 27,1871), m 1st. Maria Elisabeth Brosius (Nov 7, 1790 - Jun 3, 1830). He m 2nd Esther Troutman (Oct 16,1807- Mar 8,1870);**J. Frederick (Jun 20,1790 - Mar 12, 1831), m Eva Brosius (Jul 2,1792 - May 27,1872); **Johannes (Sep 4,1792- Jun 7,1880), m Maria Delp (Nov 5,1789- Dec 1, 1868)

[*PETER BOHNER (Oct 1, 1817, bap Zion Stone Valley Ch - Nov 7, 1890 bur Hoffman Cem), a son of Henry and Maria Elisa (Brosius) Bohner (above), m Elisabeth Yearty (May 7, 1816 - Aug 9, 1874), a dau of Peter and Anna Maria (Umholtz) Yertz. In 1860 Peter and Elizabeth Bohner lived in a separate part of the house of Peter and Anna M. (Umholtz) Yertz in Wash Twp. Their children Rebecca age 17 and Anna E age 7 lived with them **Peter and Elisabeth (Yearty) Bohner children:**
HENRY (Dec 13, 1841- Sep 10, 1 908), m Kate ___(Dec 3, 1841 – Nov 13, 1919). They lived on a farm near Loyalton. **Henry & Kate (___) Bohner children:*Ray E. (1879 -1936), m Carrie M. Cresswell (1879- 1955). **Ray E. and Carrie (Cresswell) Bohner children:** Ray Jr. (May 15,1897- Nov 2, 1932); Albert; Shirley; Harold (no dates) m Ruth Ritzman. **REBECCA (Apr 15,1843- Mar 31,1884, bur Hoffman Cem) m Dec12, 1861 Jeremiah A. Matter (Apr 18,1836-Mar 29,1912, bur Wic Cem), son of Solomon Matter. [Info with Matter family below].
**ANNIE E. Mar 25, 1853 - Mar 4, 1871, bur Hoffman Cem)

To the right Rebecca Matter believed to be Rebecca Bohner Matter (m to Jeremiah Matter).

ALEXANDER KLINGER FAMILY
(Some information from Winifred (Matter) Gould)

[ALEXANDER KLINGER (May 28, 1805 - May 2, 1876, bur Oak Dale Cem), a son of Peter and Catherine (Steinbruck) Klinger, m Magdalena Schmeltz (Jan 18, 1805 – Jun 11, 1878), a dau of Andreas and Anna Maria (Waller) Schmeltz. Alexander Klinger a farmer, and his family lived in Washington Twp as early as 1850 and remained there until their death. He was instrumental in establishing Oakdale Evangelical Church. In 1870 Alexander and Magdalena lived alone in Washington Twp. between the residents of their sons Jonathan And Elias.. **Alexander and Magdalena (Schmeltz) Klinger children:**
*SIMON (Dec 27,1827 - Mar 20,1901, bur Maple Grove Cem), m Mary ____ (Jul 2,1838 – Jun 29, 1908). They lived in Washington Twp in 1860. **Simon and Mary Klinger children:**
Alfred (Dec1851 – 1923, bur Maple Grove Cem, E'ville), m Nov 19,1876 Maria Elizabeth Troutman (Jan1858 –1928), **had these children:** Agnes b Oct 1878; Annie B. b Nov 1879; Homer Ramer b Mar 6, 1883; Moody b Feb 1885; Minnie Bulah b Sep 11, 1887; William b Feb 1890; Bernice Pauline b Dec 31, 1895; Olive Maria b Sep 26, 1901;
John Henry (Mar 22, 1853 –Jun 6, 1901, bur Oakdale Cem), m Catherine ___ (Sep 4,1861 - Nov 25,1937); James b c1856, m May 14, 1880 (Oakdale Ch record) Mary E. Kerstetter
Wellington (Mar 18, 1858 – Feb 4, 1936, bur Maple Grove Cem, E'ville), m Jul 8, 1880 Amanda E Wilvert (Feb 1862 – Feb 3, 1942). **Wellington and Amanda (Wilvert) Klinger children (bapt Oakdale Ch):** Roscoe Milton b Apr 25, 1885; Ralph Wilbert (Jul 11, 1898 – 1970, bur Maple Grove Cem, E'ville) m Kathryn S. b 1911.
Jeremiah (Dec 29, 1861 – Nov 20, 1939, bur Rife Cem), m Agnes S. ___ (1876 – 1946)
Frances (no dates) m _____ Holtzman?; Annie (no dates) m Willis O'Neill
*BENNEVILLE (Dec 19, 1829 – Jun 14, 1849, bur Oakdale Cem, Wash Twp).
*CATHARINE b Aug 24, 1831, m Jacob Bowman (b c1830 – d ____, a son of Abraham and Anna Elizabeth (Frost) Bowman.
*DANIEL (Jan 12, 1834 – Jan 13, 1908, bur Oakdale Cem, Wash. Twp), m Mar 16, 1860 Emeline Lebo (Oct 14, 1844 – Jan 6, 1929), a dau of Jonathan and Elizabeth (Bechtel) Lebo of Washington Twp. Daniel was a watchmaker and farmer. He was a veteran of the Civil War. **Daniel and Emeline (Lebo) Klinger had these children:** Almeda M. (1863 – 1947, bur Maple Grove Cem, E'ville), m Rev. George Burrell (1858 – 1923), a son of _____. **George and Almeda M. (Klinger) Burrell had these children (bapt Oakdale Ch):** Daniel Walter b Oct 30, 1886; William Ray b Jan 21, 1890; John David b May 16, 1891; Hattie Eva (Jan 30, 1893 – 1956, bur Maple Grove Cem, E'ville), m Howard W. Gonder (1890 – 1932); Lillie May b Nov 11, 1895, she may have m J. Stewart Black of Harrisburg; Kirby Jonathan (Feb 16,1865 – Jan 24, 1926, bur Oakdale Cem), m Maggie McClata Shadle (Sep 26, 1863 – Apr 3, 1942), a dau of William and Maria Catherine (Strohecker) Shadle. **Kirby Jonathan and Maggie (Shadle) Klinger children (bapt Oakdale Ch);** Homer b Feb 21, 1886, m Gertrude ___; Dosie Darlene b Jan 31, 1888, m Franklin H. Henninger; Hermie Phoebe (Feb 16, 1890 – Aug 4, 1958), m Charles Neiman (Sep 24, 1881 - ____), a son of Isreal (Jul 10, 1820 – Nov 19, 1886, bur Oakdale Cem) and Sue Neiman. **Charles and Hermie (Klinger) Neiman children (bapt Oakdale Ch);** Delton Wilbur b Nov 7 1907; Melvin Arlington b Sep 15, 1911; Ronie Druella b Dec 3, 1892, m Harvey J. Matter; Katie Emeline b May 14, 1895, m Joseph E. Koppenhaver; Mary Almeda b June 24, 1904; Ferle Machala b Nov 8, 1905; Preston A. (1867 – 1895, bur St. John's Hill Cem, Bbg), m Anna ____(1871 – 1927). **Preston A. and Anna Klinger children:** Laura Agnes b Apr 2, 1890; Edna Irene b Feb 24, 1892, m Harvey D. Helt of Lykens; Preston Elias b Jan 28, 1895, m Cora ____, lived in Illinois; Edwin M. (Aug 1869 – 1948), m May 25, 1890 Katie L. Hoffman (1873 – 1963), **Edwin and Katie (Hoffman) Klinger children:** Walter Edwin b Oct 12, 1897; Effie Emeline b Jun 6, 1907, m Clyde Miller;Agnes (Jan 1873 – 1952), m Dec 28, 1892 Solomon Good (Feb 9, 1865 – 1954), a son of Daniel and Sarah T. (Hess) Good, and **had 2 children:** Roy b Jan 14, 1895; Warren L. b Oct 1896. JACOB (Apr 9, 1838 - Aug 23, 1903, bur Maple Grove Cem E'ville), m 1872 Maria Herner (Sep 1,1844 – Dec 12, 1922). Jacob and Maria Klinger lived in Washington Twp in 1880, and with them were Thodore Matter age 17, ___ Romberger age 17, both listed as servants. **Jacob and Maria (Herner) Klinger children: Maggie** b c1872; **Frederick E** (1874 – 1942, bur Maple Grove Cem, E'ville), m Oct 2, 1897 Susan A. Hetrick (1875 – 1950); **William A.** (1876 – 1959, bur Maple Grove Cem); **Sarah** b Nov 1878; **Catherine Edith** b Jun 30, 1886; JONATHAN (b Mar 26, 1840 – 1922, bur Maple Grove Cem, E'ville), m Apr 20, 1869 Hettie Uhler (1847 – 1932), a dau of Michael and Hetty (Wetzel) Uhler. He was a

*Civil War Vet. Mary Kerstetter age 5 lived with them in 1870; **SARAH** (b c1842   ), m Jan 10, 1866 Edward Romberger (Aug 31, 1842 – Mar 22, 1907, a son of Daniel and Hannah (Bergstresser) Romberger; **ELIAS** (b Nov 26, 1843 – Jan 11, 1908, bur Simeon Cem), m Aug 2, 1868 in Oakdale Church to Mary Ellen Umholtz (Aug 20, 1848 – Jan 2, 1915). They lived in Washington Twp in 1870, but the wife was named Mary. **Elias and (Ellen Umholtz) Klinger children:** Lotta b c1868. **MARIETTA** (b Jan 3, 1847 – Jul 5, 1908, bur Oakdale), m Thomas Moyer (Jul 31, 1847 – Dec 8, 1921). Thomas Moyer may have m Sallie Grmm on Jan 26, 1910 (Oakdale record).]

L. to r: Charles Row; Ralph Matter; Harper Hocklander; William Matter; Clayton Sausser.
Back row: Robert Matter; Donald Matter; Albert Foster; Nathan Matter

THE JEREMIAH A. MATTER FAMILY
(Information from Winifred Matter Gould)

[*JEREMIAH A. MATTER (Apr. 8, 1836 – March 29, 1912, bur Wiconisco Cem), a son of Solomon Matter, m Dec 12, 1861 Rebecca Bohner (Apr 15, 1843 – Mar 31, 1884), a dau of Peter and Elizabeth (Lentz, Yertz) Bohner. **Jeremiah A. and Rebecca (Bohner) Matter had two known children:** **PETER ADAM MATTER** (Jun 28, 1862 – Dec 24, 1943, killed by a car Christmas Day in Loyalton, bur Maple Grove Cem, E'ville), a son of Jeremiah A. and Rebecca (Bohner) Matter, m Feb 22, 1885, Rebecca Batdorf (Jul 16, 1863 – Sep 4, 1898, bur Hoffman Cem), a dau of Jonas and Lucetta (Rickert) Batdorf. **Peter Adam and Rebecca (Batdorf) Matter had these children (all born in Loyalton):** Ralph Peter (Feb 25, 1886 – Jul 23, 1968 in Tioga Co), m Edna Caroline McLean (Nov 7, 1911 – 1993); Minnie Eva (Dec 11, 1887 – Dec10, 1966, bur Fogelsville, Lehigh Co), m James A. Haas (1867 – 1942); Anna Virginia (Jan 17, 1889 – Jan 1985,bur Calvary Meth Cem, Wiconisco), m Harper Hochlander (1883 – 1962); William Edward (Mar 1, 1890 – Oct 11, 1958, bur Maple Grove Cem, E'ville), m Hattie Burrell (1893 – 1986), **had two children:** Glenn b May 18, 1914, m Margaret Johns b Jul 14, 1910, a dau of John P. and Sara E. Johns. Harold b 1924 Clayton Isaiah (Jan 20, 1891 – 1974, bur Maple Grove Cem); MaryAmelia (Sep 19, 1892 – 1975, bur Oakhill Cem,Millersburg), m Clayton Sausser; Harvey Jeremiah (Apr 8, 1894 – 1970, bur Oak Hill Cem, Mbg), m Ronie Druella Klinger (Dec 3, 1892 – 1979), a dau of Kirby Jonathan and Maggie McClata (Shadle) Klinger; Jennie Pauline (1895 – 1971), m Charles S. Row (1896 - 1967. Lulu Agnes (Jan 12, 1897 – 1974, bur Calvary Meth Cem, Wiconisco), m Albert K. Foster (1894 – 1969); John (Mar 17, 1898 – 1900). After Rebecca died Peter Adam Matter m Nov 16, 1899 Carrie Amanda Hoke (Sep 21, 1878 – Nov 6, 1950, bur Maple Grove Cem, E'ville), a dau of Joseph and Lizzie Hoke. **Peter Adam and Carrie Amanda (Hoke) Matter had these children:** Paul (Aug 7, 1900 – 1935, bur Meth Cem, Wmstown), m Emma Frye; Joseph (1902 – c1918), d in Texas during WWI. (He left home and joined the army under another name); Kathleen (1904 – 1946, bur Maple Grove Cem) m Mark Stine b 1896; Nevin (Dec 6, 1906 – 1970, bur Maple Grove Cem), m Gertrude I. Harner, a dau of Charles E. and Laura C. (Keefer) Harner; Nathan A. (Dec 25, 1909 – 1951, bur Maple Grove Cem), m Avis A. Stine; Robert (Mar 30, 1912 – 1980, bur Muir Fairview Cem), m Helen Drumm (1907 – 1999); Donald

(May 18, 1918 – 1993, bur St. John's Hill Cem), m Margaret A. Bruner (1926 – 1980); <u>Peter</u> *A.* (Jul 8, 1920 – 2002, bur Reigles Bible Fellowship Cem, Mbg), m Mary Eva Stroup. **LULA MAY MATTER** (Oct 11, 1881 – 1942, bur Calvary Meth Cem, Wiconisco), m Andrew Dodd (1877 – 1958), they had one son <u>Lester</u> b 1908. [More info under larger Matter genealogy.]

Matter Reunion 1940 –1st row std: Warren Schlegel, ___, Marian Row, Nevin Matter Jr., Winifred Matter, ___, Evelyn Matter, Helen Matter, Loretta Stine, Lyle Matter, Mary Matter dau of Nevin, Yvonnne Matter, Gertrude Matter, Leroy, Matter, Nathan son, Gerald Matter, Pauls son; Mary Matter, Harvey dau. Std 2nd row: Agnes Foster, Mary S. Matter & son Robt; Lula Matter Dodd, Mary Anna Matter & Adam Matter Jr., Peter Matter, Carrie Matter, Anna Hocklander, & Harper, Kathleen Stine. Stding: Jon Matter, Glenn's son, Harold Matter, Wms son. 3rd row: Albert Foster, Clayton Matter, Donald Matter, Peter Matter, Alice Hoke, Warren Hoke, Elwood Row, Chas Row, Harvey Matter, Jennie Row, Nevin Matter, Mrs. Stine (Avis' Mother), Avis, Nathan Matter, Mark Stine, ___ Arlene Matter, Mark Matter, Mildred Matter, Richard Matter, LeRoy Matter, Ronie Matter, Ralph Matter, Ruth Matter, Robt Matter, Wm Matter, Hattie Matter. 4th row: Harold Row, Ethel Row, Carolyn Matter (Ralph's wife), Hattie Dodd, ____ Marlin Matter.

Peter Matter Children With His 1st Wife, Rebecca Batdorf: l to r -back Harvey; Ralph; William; Clayton; Front- Amelia Matter Sausser; Jennie Matter Row; Eva Matter Haas; Agnes Matter Foster; Anna Matter Hocklander.

CHAPTER 10

SOUTHWEST LYKENS TOWNSHIP

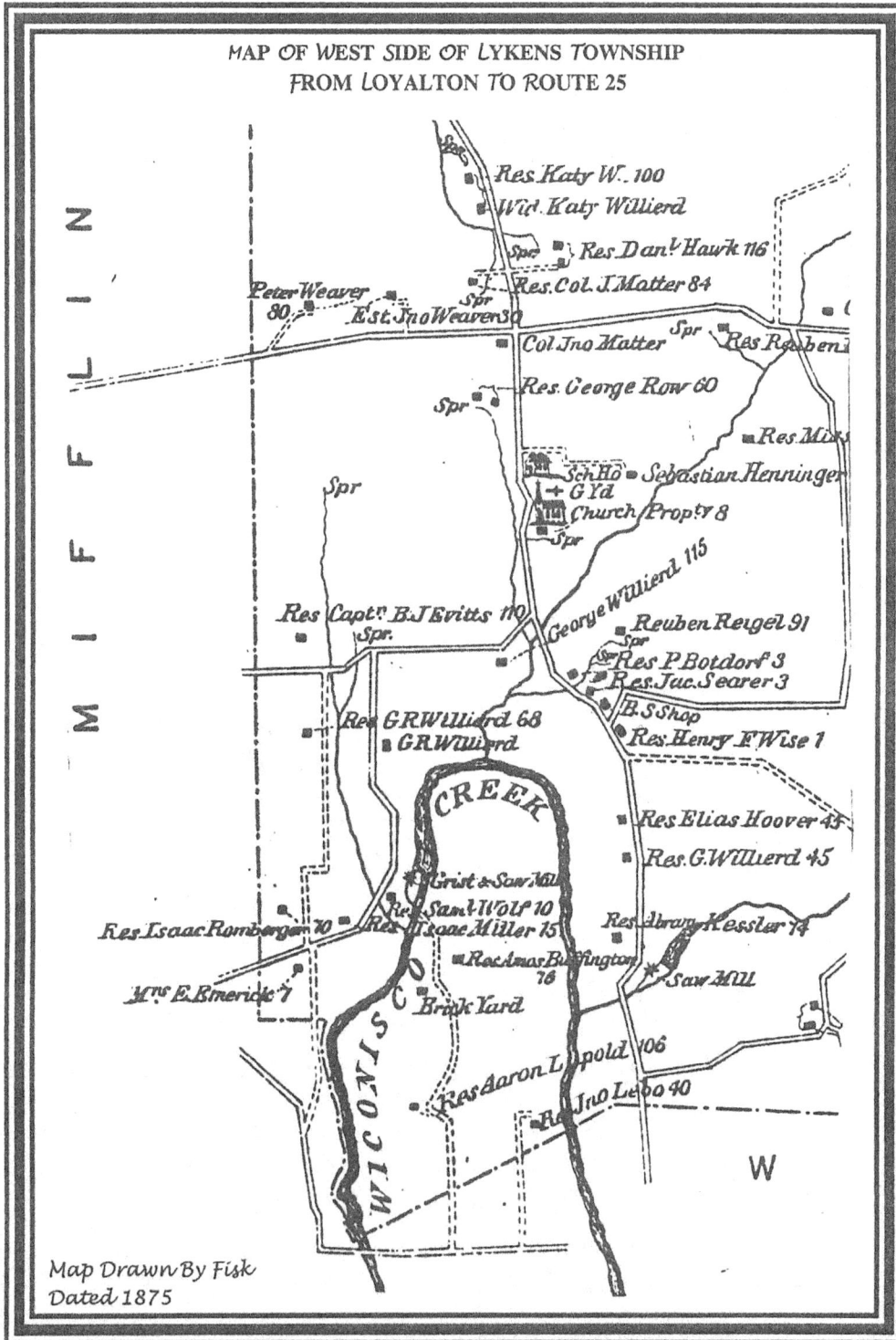

Note: This 1875 map is included to help the readers find properties of interest. By following sequence of ownership, the land can be located to 1875, then up to present time.

The history that was covered in the book to this point was in fact within the boundaries of the original Lykens Township. But over the years that land was divided between Washington, Wiconisco, and Mifflin Township. In this segment (as the map shows), we are concentrating on the land that extends into the very westerly section of present day Lykens Township. It also slightly covers the land that crosses the lines of each township reaching from Loyalton northward to the Crossroads, because some of the farms continue to be located in two townships. Notice that in most cases, the name of the 1875 owner is given along with the name of the present owner. It should be easier in that manner to precisely locate the land in the township, and it can be traced from there up to the present time.

It may seem unimportant to include the names of adjoining landowners in describing some of the properties. However, in some situations knowing the names of bordering landowners is very important in accomplishing the research. It should also be helpful to readers in locating land on the map.

In this next area, as in all other areas of the township, grants were transferred to various individuals from the Commonwealth of Pa. The Snyder family accumulated large holdings of land, (well over 400 acres) on all sides of Wiconisco Creek through grants or early transfers to them from other individuals. The Snyder's had settled in the Wiconisco Creek area just after 1750. They had one of the very early mills – located west of the present border of Lykens Twp. It was the prominent occupation of the family for many years. It was eventually sold to other settlers. The Lubold, Umholtz, Leonard Snyder, Leonard Miller, Frantz, and Specht families also owned portions of the fertile land bordering or near the Wiconisco Creek. Some of these lands are being discussed next.

The HENNINGER COVERED BRIDGE

This is the only surviving covered bridge to remain in the area. Many old original covered bridges had been constructed over creeks, and through the years escaped damage from natural causes or human negligence. But in 1972, Hurricane Agnes created serious flooding and destroyed a total of nine of the remaining structures. This one escaped. Known as Henninger Bridge #111 it spans the Wiconisco Creek at a location near the joint of Lykens and Washington Townships. Of Buur-arch construction it is eighty five feet long, and about sixteen feet wide. In recent years malicious vandalism, imposed serious damage to this structure. However, because of it's historic significance, it has been restored to a good state of preservation. A new bridge has been constructed to give access across the creek. The old covered bride stands stately nearby, surrounded by a small picnic area reminiscent of "the old days" when traveling folks lingered for a respite from their journey. Through the years many folks have gathered unique memories of events that took place in and around this bridge. But we have not been able to have access to them!

THE DELMAR WEAVER FARM
1875 - JOHN LEBO LAND 40 ACRES 1875 – AARON LUBOLD (106ACRES)

Aerial View Of Present Delmar Weaver Farm – Taken Probably 1940s

Pictures of the buildings on the old Lubold property (to right & below) were taken shortly before the buildings were removed. We understand the house was taken to Carlisle to be reassembled and restored. The barn was destroyed. Although the buildings no longer exist, the pictures survive to remind us of an early settlement within our Lykens Township.

257

Jonas & Kate Lubold With Family Probably Taken pre1900

This is a very old Lykens Township homestead. On July 2, 1822, a tract of 29 acres, 45 perches, was surveyed to John & Sarah Rodebach, and they had a house and barn by 1825. The Rodebach's sold it March 28, 1855 to Thomas & Barbara Harper. Between 1855 and 1862 this property exchanged ownership frequently. It was owned by The Harper's, Jonas Hoffman Sr. & wife Elizabeth, and Samuel Lubold. Elizabeth Hoffman repurchased the farm in March 1862, and she and her husband Jonas sold March 30, 1872 to John Lebo who now had a total of 39 acres. After several more sales the land was sold to Benneville and Phoebe A. Bohner in April 1878. In 1883 Benneville Bohner built a new bank barn and house and was taxed for it in 1884. In April 1888, the Bohner's sold their farm to Daniel Jury of Wiconisco Twp. When Daniel Jury died his estate was conveyed to Peter O. Gearhart on March 4, 1905.

About that same time in 1905, Peter O. Gerhart purchased another tract of land containing 106 acres. This was a unique piece of property because it was part of several grants that were accumulated by Martin Lubold, then his son Frederick, and had remained in the family four generations. The family was here before 1790, when the "window tax" recorded Martin Lubold with an 18 x 16 cabin, a middling barn, and living next to Leonard Snyder. By 1834 the Lubold's had two log houses. Frederick Lubold inherited the property and passed it on to his son Samuel. In the spring of 1873, it was one of two tracts that the heirs of Samuel Lubold conveyed to his son Aaron Lubold. By 1902 Aaron Lubold and his wife Katie had both died, and in March 1905 the 106 acres were sold to Peter A. and Cora Gerhart. On Nov 1, 1905 they conveyed both the 39 acres and 106 acres to Kate Lubold, wife of Jonas Lubold. On November 14, 1947 Kate C. and Jonas Lubold conveyed the 39 acres with buildings to Jonas A. Lubold. On February 16, 1960 by the will of Jonas A. Lubold this land with dwelling bank barn and other buildings was inherited by his widow Florence.

Florence Lubold died on January 23, 1970, and her daughter Nancy J. Buffington of Valley View became the owner of this and other Lubold family lands. The land was divided into separate tracts. On May 26, 1970, Nancy J. and Robert J. Buffington sold two tracts (99 acres & 29 acres) of her inherited land to Calvin B. and Elizabeth M Mauser.

On February 26, 1973, Calvin B. and Elizabeth M. Mauser sold the two tracts of land to Robert J. and Jean L. Rodichok. The 99 acre 98 perch tract is primarily in Lykens Township. The tract of 29 acres and 7 perches began at the line of the first tract and ran north to Paul H. Bush land, the Wiconisco Creek, towards the former Matter Estate.

On March 21, 1991, Robert J. and Jean L. Rodichok conveyed this farm consisting of both tracts (plus 5 acres that was sold by Claude S. Miller to Robert and Jean Rodichok Oct 19, 1976), to Delmer L. and Susan E. Weaver of New Holland, Pa. A tree lined private lane leads to this beautiful farm.

[Delmar L. Weaver m Susan Martin. The Weaver family came to Lykens Township from Lancaster County.
Delmar L and Susan (Martin) Weaver have these children: April b Apr 30, 1979, m Jul 2001 Jason Martin;
Cherry b Mar 9, 1981; **Anthony** b Oct 21, 1983; **Crystal** b Aug 8, 1986; **Carmen** b Jun 26, 1990; **Austin** b Jun 22, 1995.]

THE LUBOLD (LUPOLD, ETC) FAMILY

We are thankful to the person (identity not now known) who gave this genealogy to our library years ago.

[The family name is derived from two primitive German words, meaning valiant people. The name appears in history as early as 900 A. D. when a Count Luitpold, as it was then written, was Margrave of the East Mark, the beginning of Austria. The Leopold dynasty ruled Austria for several centuries. The family coming to America may have descended from the royal family, or perhaps an early member was in the employ of the royal family.

The immigrant ancestors of this family came on the ship Peggy, and landed in Philadelphia October 16, 1754. The father **Johannes and son Johan Martin** took an oath of allegiance to the king of Great Britain when they arrived. Several other members of the family, mother and siblings were also among the immigrants. Johannes, his wife and children settled in Pottstown, where he was employed as early as November 1754 by John Potts, the English Quaker, later founder of Pottstown. Johannes and his wife remained in the area until his death about 1769. Nothing more is known about his wife. **Johannes Luppolt and his wife had these children (all born in Germany):** *Martin b 1727; **Maria Agnes** m Nov 28, 1757 to Frederick Beeler, lived in Pottstown; **Karl**; **Ludwig** (Oct 9, 1741 - Jul 28, 1796), m Rebecca; **John** b 1743, m Dec 28, 1764, Elizabeth Reifschneider; **Anna Maria** (Sep 28, 1745 - Dec 31, 1809), m Apr 8, 1778, Michael Moser. Martin was the only one of the children to come to Lykens Valley. In recording the following Lubold genealogy, only the family members that came to Lykens Valley are included.

* **JOHN MARTIN LUBOLD** (Nov 5, 1727 - Feb 7, 1810, bur St. Johns Hill Cem, Berrysburg), m 1773, Catherine Bechtel (Feb 28, 1775 - 1826), a dau of Burkhart and Gertrude (Reifschneider) Bechtel, of Nantmeal Twp, Chester County. Martin married later in life, because he made his home with his parents, and took care of them until their death. When Martin and Catherine married, they moved first to Douglas Twp, and lived there during the Revolution. In 1785, when Dauphin County was formed, Martin sold his property, and moved to Lykens Valley. He came at the same time that his father-in-law moved his family to this area. Martin purchased a tract of 120 acres of land on the west side of the peninsula formed by Wiconisco Creek, directly across the creek from Burkhart Bechtel's tract, about a mile from the west end of Short Mountain. A small clearing had been made on the land, but the higher parts was a forest of pine and mixed trees. The bottom land along the creek was covered with large white oak trees. The family cleared the land and lived on it until the death of Martin in 1810. **John Martin and Catherine (Bechtel) Lubold had these children:**
FREDERICK (b May 4, 1774 in Douglasville - d Apr 18, 1849, bur St. Johns Hill Cem, Berrysurg), m Dec 12, 1797, Elizabeth Ney (Mar 14, 1779 - Sep 5, 1854), a dau of Michael and Justina (Bardt) Ney. Frederick bought several farms in this area, and was a successful farmer. In 1850, Elizabeth Lubold age 71 lived in Mifflin Twp, and the tax record states she was a farmer. She had Martin Lubold age 31, laborer, & Emma McCurty age 9 with her. **Frederick and Elizabeth (Ney) Lubold had these children:**
***Elizabeth (Jan 9, 1800 - Mar 8, 1814)
***Samuel (Sep 15, 1801 - Mar 1, 1871, bur Hoffman Cem), m Sep 5, 1824, Catherine Williard (Apr 21, 1802 - Jan 29, 1855), a dau of Peter and Catharina (Hoffman) Williard. They lived in Wiconisco Twp in 1850, and family tradition tells us that it was in a stone house that he built two miles west of Lykens. **Samuel & Catherine (Williard) Lubold children (some bapt Hoffman Ch):**
 Elizabeth (Sep 25, 1826 - Jan 3, 1907), m Daniel Updegrove (Apr 9, 1824 - Jul 21, 1891, bur Tower City). They lived in Wiconisco Twp in 1850, and he was a tailor, but later moved to Tower City. **Daniel and Elizabeth (Lubold) Updegrove had these children:** Aaron (May 24, 1844 - Mar 6,1893); Charles b c1849; Edward (May 24, 1863 - Nov 7, 1877); Ida (Feb 28, 1861 - Sep 5, 1910), m Ellis J. English; Henry.
Sarah (Sep 20, 1828 - Apr 18, 1893), m Mar 25, 1847 Gideon Shadel (Feb 15, 1825 - Oct 9, 1896), lived in Big Run. **Gideon and Sarah (Lubold) Shadel had these children:** Samuel Penro (1848 - 1891), m Mary Byerly (1853 - 1915); Frank (1853 - 1925)
Ann Mary (May 2, 1830 -), was the 2nd wife of Joseph Gardner.

<u>Magdalena</u> (Apr 18, 1832 – May 10, 1876), m Aug 1, 1857 in Freeport, Pa. To Jonas Garman. He was a druggist and died in Lykens in 1898.

<u>Frederick</u> (Jun 15, 1833 – Feb 20, 1865), m Elizabeth Uhler (Mar 14, 1835 – May 2 6,1906), a dau of Michael and Hester Uhler of Washington Twp. In 1860, they lived in Lykens Twp, and Elias Matter age 5, was with them. Also Martin Lubold age 39, listed as a servant, was in the household.

<u>Aaron</u> b Sep 8, 1834 – May 31, 1887), m Sarah Rogers (Feb 10, 1839 – Oct 9, 1902), a dau of Henry and Elizabeth (Latshaw) Rogers. He eventually purchased the old Lubold homestead and he and his family continued to live there. In 1870, Martin Lubold age 50, lived with the family. **Aaron and Sarah (Rogers) Lubold had these children:** <u>Elizabeth Agnes</u> b Jun 28, 1860, m Frederick Steltz of Phila.; <u>Clara J.</u>(Apr 26, 1862 – Feb 24, 1937, bur Maple Grove Cem, E'ville), m Frank Buffington (Jun 3, 1858 – Mar 13, 1938) of Elizabethville: <u>Monroe</u> (Sep 13, 1863 – Dec 19, 1935), m Christine Battorf (Mar 25, 1858 – Jan 22, 1931); <u>Amelia Isador "Ida"</u> b Nov 3, 1865, m 1891 Samuel Byerly b Sep 18, 1869, son of Jacob Byerly; <u>Minerva Candace</u> (Sep 26, 1867 – 1915), m Harry Dinger, of Herndon; <u>Sarah Priscilla</u> b Feb 10, 1869, m Baltzer Matter b Apr 22, 1864, of Loyalton, had a son ;<u>Aaron Jerome</u> b Dec 18, 1888.

<u>Harvey Ellsworth</u> b Jun 15, 1871; <u>Wilson E</u> b c1873; <u>Cora Elrette</u> b Apr 16, 1875; <u>Jennie A</u> b Jul 10, 1877; <u>Jonas Aaron</u> b Jan 27, 1880, m Katie C. ____ . **Jonas A. and Katie C (____) Lubold had these children:** *Florence* (1903 – Jan 23, 1970), m George Long **had a dau** *Nancy* b Jul 24, 1933, m Robert Buffington; *Carrie A* b 1906

<u>Rebecca</u> (Jun 10, 1835 – Dec 4, 1854), m Josiah Boyer

<u>Jacob</u> (Sep 18, 1837 – Feb 4, 1870, bur Hoffman Cem), m Rebecca Moyer (1836 – 1913), a dau of Jacob and Rebecca (Ferree) Moyer, **had a son** <u>Jacob Albert</u> b May 10, 1860

<u>Amanda</u> b Jan 4,1840 m Joseph Gardner, 1st wife

<u>Sarah</u> b Nov 8, 1840, bapt Hoffman Ch

<u>Catherine Anna</u> b Dec 3, 1841 m Henry Bohner of Loyalton

<u>Adam</u> b Apr 1, 1842

<u>Samuel</u> b Jan 30, 1843 – 1876), m Louisa (Jul 19, 1846 – Jan 19, 1918). **Samuel and Louisa F. ( ) Lubold had these children:** <u>Catharine Jane</u> b Oct 9, 1864, m David Schwalm; _____ b 1866 m William Dickey, 2nd Jacob Rice;

<u>Isaac</u> (Jan 10, 1845 –Apr 29, 1898, bur Hoffman Cem), m Catherine Snyder (Jun 6,1846 – Mar 3, 1917, a dau of Elias Snyder. Isaac and Catherine lived on a farm in Washington Twp in 1880. **Isaac and Catherine (Snyder) Lubold had these children:** <u>Charles Irvin.</u> b Jun 11,1867; <u>Martha Amelia</u> b Dec 11, 1872, m ____ Hartman of Curtin; <u>Mary M</u> b c1876, m _____ Riegle of Loyalton: <u>Anna Carrie</u> b Jan 25, 1879; <u>Samuel J.</u> b Mar 28, 1885, lived in Loyalton; <u>Charles I.</u> Lived in Loyalton.

***Susanna** (Jul 17,1803 – Jun 9,1886), m George Rutter, lived on a farm near Halifax until 1856, moved to Mercer County where he died in Dec 1884. Most of their children went with them, but their <u>son Jacob</u> m Sarah Henninger, dau of Sebastian and Barbara (Carl) Henninger of Lykens Twp.

***Catherine** (Aug 2, 1805 – Oct 18, 1844, bur Simeon Cem, Gratz), was 2nd wife of Michael McCardy (b ___ - d c1860)), he originally came from Womelsdorf. In 1840 he lived with the Frederick Lubold family and was a fuller. **Michael and Catherine (Lubold) McSurdy had these children (they were listed on the record of parents for whom the county paid for the children's schooling):** <u>Margaret</u> b c1826; <u>Jacob</u> (b c1828) m Catharine Hornberger of Ashland, Sch Co., Pa; <u>Daniel</u> b Feb 25, 1831, m Catharine Wolf b c1836, lived in Lykens Twp in 1860, with the Henry Schriner family, and he was working as a sawyer. They later move to the Minersville area. **Daniel and Catharine (Wolf) McSurdy had these children:** *Catharine* b c1852; *Elizabeth* b c1854; *Emma* b c1856; *Catharine* b c1859. Michael (1835 – 1921, bur St. John's Kimmels Ch Barry Twp Sch Co), m Mary Gehres (1841– 1917), lived in Minersville and Barry Twp.; <u>Sarah</u> b Jul 8, 1833, m George Sharp, moved to Pottsville; Susan (Feb 24, 1836 – Feb 27, 1904), m William Strut of Pottsville; <u>Emma</u> (1840 – Mar 23, 1926), m John Robinson, lived in Williamstown; <u>Mary Ann</u> (Nov 9, 1842 – Jan 4, 1901), m Samuel Rickert, lived in Williamstown. Michael, Mary Ann and Emeline were all young children when their mother died. John Rodebach became the guardian of Michael. After Catharine died, Michael McCurdy, Sr. m Elizabeth (Klinger) Fagely, widow of Daniel Fagely. Michael and Elizabeth were married on May 26, 1849, by Daniel Good, J. P.of Gratz. In 1850,

Elizabeth McCurty age 40 lived in Lykens Twp, and had Maria Fagley age 11, Daniel Fagely age 5, and Amanda McCurty age 5/12 month with her. She lived next to Daniel Lubold. Elizabeth (May 21, 1809 – Mar 7, 1892), Simeon Ch. Record.
***Hannah b Jun 2, 1808 d ____
***Salome (Apr 8, 1810 – Dec 22, 1875, bur Fetterhoff Cem), m Peter Forney (Apr 7, 1804 - Dec 14, 1866), lived on a farm near Fisherville. [More info on genealogy of Forney family.]
***Jacob b May 21, 1812, m Eliza Witman;
***Martin (Jan 20, 1815 – Apr 10, 1876, bur St. John's "Hill" Cem), not m.
***Daniel (Feb 25, 1819 – Jan 25, 1905, bur Fetterhoff Cem), m Susan Henninger (Dec 13, 1822 – Feb 4, 1879), a dau of Sebastian and Barbara (Carl) Henninger. They lived in Wiconisco Twp in 1850, later on a farm near Fisherville. **Daniel and Susan (Henninger) Lubold had these children:** Augustus (Oct 23, 1842 – Aug 4, 1855); David (Dec 1, 1844 – Jan 11, 1850); Cornelius (Dec 11, 1846 – Jan 8, 1850); Elias b Nov 18, 1848, m Saran Ann Miller; Elizabeth (Feb 10, 1850 – Oct 23, 1933); John Frederick b Oct 4, 1853 ≤ 1946, bur Maple Grove Cem, E'ville), m Jul 4, 1880 in Berrysburg to Mary Ellen Romberger (1859 – 1944). **John Frederick and Mary Ellen (Romberger) Lubold had these children (some bapt Berrysburg):** Mabel Edna b May 25, 1881; Lloyd b Oct 24, 1883; Estella May b Aug 7, 1887; Samuel (Nov 22, 1855 – Feb 13, 1863); Amanda b Oct 16, 1857, m John M. Rutter; Sarah (1860 – Dec 24, 1862); Daniel G. b Oct 27, 1862 m Irene Workman; Thomas b Oct 17, 1865 m Margaret Eisenhower; John Ellsworth b Jan 24, 1868 m 1st Margaret Sheetz b Sep 9, 1866 Wayne Twp – d Dec 14, 1918, bur Selinsgrove Cem), a dau of Josiah Sheetz. John and Margaret (Sheetz) Lubold had six children. After she died John m 2nd Mrs. Minnie Hare.

MAGDALENA (1776 - ____) m John Peter Hoffman (b Sep 27, 1778 – d 1864), a son of John Nicholas Hoffman. [See family information in Hoffman genealogy]
CATHERINE (b 1785 - d Aug 29, 1860, bur Hoffman Cem), m Hartman Rickert Jr (Dec 31, 1780 – Jun 8, 1828), a son of Johann Henrich and Maria Magdalena (Koob) Rickert [See family information in Rickert genealogy]
GEORGE (, bur Klinger Cem), m Elizabeth Buffington (b Dec 23, 1782 – d ____), a dau of George and Barbara (Hoffman) Buffington. They lived on a farm on Little Wiconisco Creek. **George and Elizabeth (Buffington) Lubold had these children:**
***Joseph (Oct 9, 1805 – Jun 14, 1861, bur Klingers Cem). Joseph was not married. He wrote his will a few days before his death stating that he wished tobe buried at Klinger's Church. He gave all his personal property and estate to his brother Martin "without interference of my relatives."
*** Anna Catherine (May 11, 1807 – May 25, 1885, bur, bur Maple Grove Cem, E'ville), m Robert McCulley (Jul 14, 1810 – Jun 5, 1881), lived in Armstrong Valley. In 1832 they lived in Elizabethville, where Robert built the old red tavern on "Professional Hill," the present location of the Kepler Convalescent Home. This was a two story frame building, and workmen constructing the Lykens Valley Railroad stayed here while they were employed by the railroad company. A water trough, with constant running water was in front of the building. **Robert and Anna Catherine (Lubold) McCulley had these children:** Susanna (Dec 13, 1832 – Apr 25, 1861), m Nicholas Snyder; Lydia (Aug 21, 1834 – Feb 14, 1908), m James Snyder (Feb 2, 1830 – Jun 14, 1903), brother of Nicholas. He was a Civil War Vet. **James and Lydia (McCulley) Snyder had these children:** Charles E. (Jul 15, 1855 – Jun 2 9, 1918), m Ellen Hoffner. CattharineA (Apr 25, 1858 – 1909, bur Maple Grove Cem, E'ville), m Daniel D. Helt (1857 – 1937); Isabella (Oct 10, 1859 – Jun 19, 1919), m Simon A. Dietrich (1855 – 1938); Susan (Dec 2, 1861 – May 9, 1901, bur Maple Grove Cem), m John Hoffner (Oct 4, 1856 – Apr 19, 1937); Harvey (May 30, 1868 - ____), m Jennie D. Miller; Elizabeth (Aug 3, 1836 – Oct 6, 1917), m Nov 5, 1854 1st George Snyder (no relative of above); m 2nd Jacob Swab (Apr 7, 1832 – Mar 13, 1908); Sarah (no dates) m Elwood Shoop, moved to Iowa; Josiah (Nov 3, 1840 – Oct 30, 1925), m 1st Sarah Grim, 2nd Mary Hoke. He d May 10, 1935 in Monroe, Iowa; Lovina (no dates) m Nathan Grim; Catherine (no dates) m William Bixler; Amos (no dates) m Kate Gipple; Caroline (no dates) m Cyrus Minnich..
*** Susanna (Jan 13, 1809 – 1888, bur Harrisburg). Susan m 2nd Daniel Brosius. In 1850, Daniel and Susanna lived in Mifflin Twp, where he was a laborer. **Daniel and Susanna (Lubold) Brosius had these children:** Joel b c1840; Benjamin b c 1841; Sarah b c1842; Samuel b c1843; Catherine b c1844; Elizabeth b c1849.

*** **John** (Oct 30, 1811 – Jan 10, 1879, bur Klinger Cem), m Catherine Sassaman (no dates), no burial location, possibly died young. John Lubold lived on a farm north of Gratz. **John Lubold had these children:** George (Sep 27, 1837 – Oct 3,1918, bur Klinger Cem), m Christine Miller (Jul 10, 1837 – Jul 13, 1914), lived in Erdman, and by 1880 lived in Shamokin, Northld Co. Their son Charles age 13 lived with them; Philip (no dates) m Mary Masser of Erdman; Charles (no dates) m Kate Miller, of Klingerstown; Jacob (no dates) m Etta Bowman, of Klingerstown; Elizabeth (no dates) m Peter Roshon, of Lavelle; Lovina (no dates) m John W. Merket of Phila.; Henrietta (no dates) m Henry Lebo of Loyalton.

*** **Elizabeth** b Nov 10, 1812 m Michael Dietrich

*** **Jacob** (Jan 28, 1816 – Dec 12, 1896, bur Salem Meth Cem, Barry Twp), m Mary Mattern (Oct 8, 1814 – Nov 20, 1898), a dau of Daniel Mattern. He was a farmer in Powells Valley, but later moved to Weishample. **Jacob and Mary (Mattern) Lubold children;** Samuel b 1842; lived in Mt. Carmel, Northld Co; Nathan (1844 – 1884); Elias bApr 25, 1847, m Louisa Paul (   ), a dau of Josiah Paul of Mt. Carmel; Susan b Aug 5, 1849), m 1ˢᵗ Jacob Engle, 2ⁿᵈ Philip Shoop, lived in Carsonville, Dau Co; John b 1851, m Sarah Swinehart, lived in Ft. Springs, Sch Co; Mary b 1854, m John Welker, lived in Carsonville; Joel (1856 – 1939, bur Salem Meth Cem, Barry Twp), m Dina J. Morris (1863 – 1950), lived in Mabel, Barry Twp, Sch Co.; Daniel (Jul 3, 1858 – Feb 18, 1934, bur Salem Meth Cem, Barry Twp), m Flora Behny (May 4, 1866 – Nov 17, 1933), lived in Mabel, Barry Twp.

***Martin** (Aug 10, 1818 or 1820 – Mar 2, 1895), m Sarah Miller (Sep 23, 1833 – ____), lived in Hegins, Sch Co. Martin was a woodman and sawyer. **Martin and Sarah Lubold children:** Amanda b c1859; Martin b c1862; Reily b c1868; Anna M. b c1873; Simon b c1876.

*** **Sarah** b Jul 28, 1820 m John Rissinger

*** **Lydia** (no dates) Jacob Kelly (1ˢᵗ wife)

*** **Mary** (no dates), m Jacob Kelly (2ⁿᵈ wife)

JOHN (Jun 6, 1790 bapt St. John's Hill Ch – May 24, 1883), m Barbara Daniel (Aug 3, 1793 – Sep 23, 1868), a dau of Andreas and Susanna (Hoy) Daniel of Lykens Twp. They lived near Hoffman Church, then moved to Fisherville, and later Millersburg. In 1852, they moved to Cochranton, Pa. John was said to be tall, and that "in stature and character he was a good type of the older generations of the family." **John and Barbara (Daniel) Lubold children (some bapt Hoffman Ch):**

***Daniel** (Feb 18, 1816 – 1892), m Hannah Harner (Oct 23, 1811 – Jun 29, 1882, bur Oak Dale Cemetery, Loyalton). After Hannah died, Daniel Lubold moved to Cochranton, apparently with his parents. He was listed on the 1860 census for Crawford Co, with his second wife. He was a wheelwright. He m 2ⁿᵈ Mrs. Elizabeth (Reese) Foote.

***John S.** (b c1818 – d c1892), m Sarah M. Wiley b c1824. They lived in Wiconisco Twp in 1850, but later moved westward, as did many other members of this family. **John S. and Sarah (Wiley) Lubold had these children:** John Henry (1842 – 1900), m Elizabeth Soliday of Leetonia, Ohio; Aaron b 1854, m Mena Stokes of Cherry Run. He was a farmer and lumberman.

***Samuel** b c1819 ,m Catherine Bonawitz [This may be the couple that had children bapt St. Johns. **These are their children:** Sarah b Nov 8, 1840, m John Hollenbach of Michigan; Adam b Apr 1, 1842, m Sarah Rousch; John b Mar 18, 1846; Elizabeth; Samuel m Susan Dietrich; Lincoln.

***Martin** (1826 – 1898), m Mary Weaver, lived in Crawford Co, was a Civil War Veteran.

***Juliana** b Jul 22, 1820

***Catharina** b Mar 17, 1822

***Elizabeth** (Jan 1, 1824 – Dec 15, 1901) m Peter Keiter

***Jacob** (Dec 11, 1827 – Jun 22, 1903), m Sophia Rousch

***Susan** b Oct 9, 1829, m Augustus Stoyer

***Barbara** b Nov 24, 1831 m Thomas Haas

***Catherine** b Jun 3, 1834 m Elias Noll

THE LEBO/ LeBEAU / LEPPO FAMILY

Some of this is from the work of Richard Alan Lebo – **The Lebo Line**
Some is from the booklet "**The Lebo Family**," written by Joseph B. Lebo for the 1956 reunion, and some from work of **E. H. Wiser**. Other information from our own research.

[The immigrants of the LEBO family were French Huguenots. During the seventeenth century, they lived in the upper Rhine Country of Germany. But when the "Treaty of Nantes" was revoked, many people were persecuted for their religious beliefs. Many thousands of refugees fled to England, where they tented in the crowded streets of London. Queen Anne eventually, in 1710, prepared ships to bring about 3000 of them to our shores, which were then her colonies.

After the long trip, they arrived in New York, and scattered to different places. Some of them, including the Lebo immigrants and other families who eventually settled in Upper Paxton area, went up the Hudson to the place now known as Newburg. Disliking the hardships and disappointments of that area, sixty families from the Schohorie and Mohawk settlement came down the Susquehanna River to the Tulpehocken area of Berks Co. in 1723. From there some of them migrated to Lykens Valley.

The first known Lebo ancestor (from our research) was **John** born about **1683** in the Palatine, Europe, and died in **May 1759** in Reading, Berks Co. He brought his family to America in the early 1700s. He became a member of Skippack Reformed Church in Montgomery Co. on May 10, 1730. He owned land in several areas of Berks Co. John Lebo married twice. His first wife was Judith, but nothing is known of her except that she probably died c1711. The second wife Anne Mary survived him. John mentions eleven children in his will. He died **leaving a wife and these children: Peter, b 1706, Abraham b 1708, Margaret b 1710; Paul; Maria Magdalena; Jacob; Mary; Leonard; Anna Elizabeth; Isaac; Henry.** Two children of John Lebo (1683 –1759), had ties to Dauphin County. **Peter (1706–1783) & Abraham Lebo (1707 -1775).**

+**PETER LEBO** (b c1706 in Germany – d Feb 15, 1783 in Newmanstown, Heidelberg, Berks Co.) He became naturalized in 1765 in Phila. He may have married twice, first to Susanna ____. Margaret (1717 – c1751) was named as his wife in his will. They had a large family.   Some of the descendants of their son Peter moved to the area of Upper Dauphin County, and are included in this genealogy below.

***PETER LEBO** (b Jan 1, 1735 Tulpehocken – d Oct 1807) married Anna Catherine Jordan b Jan 15, 1744 in Ger, a dau of Philip Adam Jordan & Eva Barbara Wagoner. They remained in Tulpehocken area of Berks Co. In his will he named his son Philip as administrator, but Philip renounced, so son Christopher replaced him. **Peter and Anna Catherine (Jordan) Lebo children (most bap Host Ref Ch, Tulpehocken):**

JOHANN PHILIP Mar 5, 1769 – Nov 9, 1839), came to Upper Paxton Twp, Dauphin County about 1798. Philip Lebo appears to have married twice, the first wife Anna Maria Wohlford was bap Apr 22, 1760 at Millback Ref Ch – d c, a dau of Conrad and Maria Margaret Wohlford of Millcreek Twp, and died before 1834. The second wife was Anna Margaret ____ (b Aug 22, 1791 – Dec 22, 1865, bur Old (Werth)Cem, Killinger). When Philip died in 1839, he left a family that was not too happy with his will. His wife Margaret stated that he was of "unsound mind at present." Margaret was to get one bedstead and bedding, a spinning wheel and reel, household furniture and kitchen utensils necessary for her own use, one stove and pipe, one cow, eight bushels of wheat, four bushels of rice, and one fat hog, 100 to 150 pounds, yearly. She should also receive hay and fodder, and the privilege of the bake oven, springhouse and cellar. All that, as long as she is a widow. The children were unhappy with the distribution of money. **Johann Philip and Anna Maria (Wohlforht) Lebo children:

***JOHANNES (b Jun 22, 1793, bapt Altalaha Evang Luth Ch, Berks Co – d Aug 22, 1879, bur Davids Cem, Killinger). He m Nov 15, 1814 (by Rev. Reily), Justina Lenker (Jan 15, 1794 – Mar 13, 1841, bur David's Cem, Killinger), a dau of Philip and Elizabeth (Lark) Lenker. He probably married Anna Maria Schott after his first wife died. In 1850 he lived in Upper Pax.ton Township, and his three daughters, Elizabeth, Catharine, and Mary lived with him. Also Nathanial Lehr age 21, a laborer. His wife had already died. **Johannes and Justina (Lenker) Lebo had these children:**

Philip (Sep 6, 1815 – Apr 30, 1896, bur Old Stone Church Cem, E'ville), m Barbara Moyer (Sep 3, 1822 – Aug 24, 1875). They lived in Washington Twp in 1850, 1860 and 1870 and he was   a farmer. **Philip & Barbara (Moyer) Lebo children (b Pa.):**

 Philip b Mar 8, 1845, m Kate Nace b Aug 1842, moved to Illinois, **had these children:** Emery b c1873; Eugene b c1878; Moved to Ogle Co, Il.about1880; Eliza **Ann** (Sep 18, 1847 – Jan 19, 1920, bur St. Johns Cem, Berrysburg), m Oct 8, 1867 Cornelius S. Hartman (Mar 8, 1844 – Dec 11, 1905); **John J.** (Sep 18, 1847 – 1935), m Sarah Lark (Nov 1846 – Apr 12, 1927), **John J. & Sarah (Lark) Lebo children:** Cora L. b c1871; Harry E. b c1873, moved to Ogle Co., Ill; **Sarah M** (May 19, 1852 –Feb 11, 1924), m Wm. H. Harner (Jul 29, 1846– Oct 1, 1895); **Aaron S** Jan 5, 1854 – 1905), m Emma Jane Meyers (1865 – 1945), moved to Ogle Co., Il; **Wm H.** (Oct 25, 1855 – Jan 13, 1890, bur Old Stone Cem, E'ville); Emma **Annie** (b & d 1857); **Edwin F**. b May 8, 1858; **Rebecca Jane** (Nov 18, 1859 – 1863); **Mary Diane** (Jul 28, 1862 – Aug 2, 1913, bur St Johns Cem, Berrysburg), m Dec 28, 1879 to John D. Hartman (Sep 18, 1854 – Mar 9, 1924); **Emanuel Nathaniel** b c1863, m Dec 4, 1881 Mary Agnes Metz (1864 – 1947) in Salem Ref Ch E'ville; .

Elizabeth (Oct 25, 1816 – May 7, 1880, bur Davids Cem, Killinger, with parents)
Jonathan (Nov 10, 1817 – Oct 20, 1868), m Elizabeth Bechtel (Dec 20, 1822 – Jun 7, 1878), moved to Juniata Co. **Jonathan & Elizabeth (Bechtel) Lebo children:** Eliza (Sep 15, 1840 – Jun 1906), m Jacob R. Miller; **Catherine** (Feb 24, 1843 - Aug 22, 1919), m Wm C. Blaine Perry Co; **Emaline** Oct 14, 1844 – Jan 6, 1929), m Daniel L. Klinger (1834 – 1908); **Isaac** (Jul 16, 1846; **Jonathan** b c1849; **Sarah Ellen** (Aug 25, 1851 – Apr 28, 1938), m George Wash. Matter (Aug 14, 1843 – 1907); **Simon Peter** (May 1, 1854 – 1918), m Sarah Jane Cooper (1854 -1878).

Leah b Nov 10, 1819
Catharine (Aug 21, 1820 – Sep 10, 1876, bur Davids Cem, Killinger, with parents)
Daniel (Mar 6, 1822 – Apr 5, 1904, bur Davids Cem, Killinger), m Jemina Cooper (Mar 13, 1829 – Jun 28, 1907), a dau of Johannes and Maria Cooper. Daniel and Jemina lived in Upper Paxton. In 1880 Sarah Matter age 11 and Jacob Matter age 45, a stone mason lived with them. **Daniel and Jemina (Cooper) Lebo children: Jacob; John;** Amanda (1848 – 1896); ___ m George M Deibler, or John W. Heckert, lived in Matterstown;

Susanna b May 1, 1823; **Sarah J.** b Jan 17,1827 d young.; **Maria** b Feb 2, 1837

*****CATHARINE** (Jun 14,1795 – Dec 13, 1833), m John H. Seal (Mar 14, 1797 – Jan 12,1875, bur Davids Cem, Killinger), a son of Heinrich and Catharina (Lietner) Seal. John H. Seal m Martha ___ (1813 – 1882), after Catharine died. **John H. and Catharine (Lebo) Seal children (bapt David's Ch, Killinger):**
Susanna (Jan 1, 1817 – Feb 17, 1881) m Daniel Heckert (Aug 25, 1810 – Feb 21,1892, bur Davids Cem, Killinger);
 Josiah (May 5, 1820 – 1892, bur Davids Cem, Killinger); **George** b Mar 27, 1829; **Salome** b Apr 3, 1832.

*****GEORGE** (Oct 22,1796 –Dec 1,1882), bur Oakhill Cem, Mbg), m Susanna Deibler (c1801-1869), a dau of George Deibler. George and Susanna (Deibler) Lebo children (some bapt Davids, Killinger, St. Johns Hill):

George b Jun 12, 1816; **David** (Apr 16, 1821 – Nov 10, 1865), , m Mary Heineke (Feb 14, 1826 – Sep 24, 1909). **David & Mary (Heineke) Lebo known children;** Jeremiah (May 1, 1851 – Jun 2, 1933), m Sarah Elizabeth Wirt (Mar 30, 1853 – Mar 31, 1915); **Susannah** (May5, 1853 – May 12, 1935), m David W. Deibler (Dec 7, 1850 – Nov 15, 1925); **John David** (Jan 26, 1862 – Apr 30, 1926), m Savilla C. Dollinger (Feb 12,1865 – Jan 1938) a dau of William S. and Amelia (Harman) Dollinger, who lived in Mifflin Twp in 1860. Amelia was a dau of Daniel and Mary Harman; **Mary Amelia** m Sovorrah Dressler; **Leah** d young; Barbara b Apr 4, 1823, sp Barbara Deibler, m ___ Walborn; Maria b Jun 14, 1825 m Henry Shaffner b Oct 9, 1817 bap David's Ch Killinger, son of Henry & Susanna Shaffner; **Matilda** (May 31, 1827 – Aug 27,1917), m __ Kuntzelman; **Anna Catharina** (Nov 11,1829 –Dec 23,1914, bur Maple Grove Cem, E'ville)

264

m Jeremiah Speck (Dec 16, 1822– May 26, 1888, bur Maple Grove Cem, E'ville); **Susannah** b c1831 m
___ Weaver; **Michael** b Apr 14,1832; **Sarah** b c1834, m ___ Smeltzer; **William** b c1835; **Amanda** b c1838.
***PHILIP** (no dates) mentioned in fathers will.
***HENRY** (Sep 6, 1800 – Nov 9, 1856, bur Davids Cem, Killinger), m May 11, 1823, Anna Mary
Billenfeld (Nov 3, 1802 – May 30, 1882), records in Davids Ch, Killinger. In 1850 Henry and Anna lived in
Up Paxton Twp.**Henry and Anna Mary (Billenstald) Lebo children (some bapt Davids, Killinger): Anna
Delila** (Feb 11, 1825 – Aug 1826); **Carolina** (Jun 29, 1827 – Jul 23, 1921 bur Oak Hill Cem, Mbg) , m
George Neagley (Aug 16,1825 – Sep 14,1894), a furniture maker; **Nathaniel** (Feb 26, 1829 – Apr 23, 1885,
bur Davids Cem), m Mar 1864 Mary Selene James (Oct 14, 1841 – Apr 5, 1907), a dau of Isaac and Agnes
(Albright) James, of Armstrong Valley; **Maria Anna** b Jan 8,1831, m John Grove, moved to Harrisburg;
Louisa (Oct 16, 1833 – Jan 31, 1909), m Sep 26, 1861 St. John's Hill Ch to Jared Specht (Jan 19, 1840 –
Apr 23, 1892, bur Oak Hill Cem, Mbg), **had a dau Mary Salome** b Apr 8,1864, bapt Zion Ch., Rife; **John
B.** (Sep 30, 1838 -Jan 15, 1862, bur Davids Cem, Killinger), m Rebecca ___ (1845-1917);**Wilhelm** (Jan 2,
1836 –Feb 24,1897, bur Longs Cem Halifax), m Phoebe ___ (c1842 – d Aug 6, 1882); **Rebecca** (Jul 1845-
Jan 15, 1917), not married, lived in Millersburg; **Henry** (1848 – Oct 9, 1893, bur David's Cem), m Hannah
___ (1842 – Aug 25, 1893).

***JACOB** (Jan 16, 1805 – Feb 24, 1876, bur St. Jacob's Cem Waynesville), m Catharina Kramer (Feb 16,
1807 – May 17, 1875, bur Jacob's Luth & Ref Cem(Millers), Jackson Twp., Dau Co) ch: **Jeremiah** (Jul 10,
1829- Jan 28,1854, bur Powell's Valley Meth Cem); **Uriah** (Feb 1831– Apr 10, 1903), m Susanna Sweigard
(Dec 22, 1842 – Dec 4, 1922, bur St. Jacob's Cem Waynesville); **Lydia** (Jul 5, 1840 – Mar 29, 1856);

***DANIEL** (Sep 2, 1807 – Oct 8, 1870), m Sarah _____ (1812 – 1832), lived in Halifax area. He m 2nd
Margaret or Rebecca ___ b c1807 -). **One child: Angeline** (1829–1830)
PHILIP (1809 – 1878), lived in Halifax.
***JONAS** "Jonathon" (Dec 20, 1811 – Feb 15, 1852, bur Bowerman Cem, Enterline), m Catharine Shott
(Apr 16,1809 –Dec 8, 1859), a dau of Peter and Elizabeth Schott. They lived in Jefferson Twp in 1850, and
he was farming. **Jonas & Catharine (Shott) Lebo children: Fanny** b c1832; **Samuel** (Dec 3, 1834 – Feb 8,
1858, bur Bowerman Cem); **Daniel** (Jan 12, 1837 – Jul 17, 1928), m Susanna Hoy (Feb 16, 1838 – Mar 8,
1913), a dau of Peter Hoy; **John** b c1839; **Peter** (Jan 1, 1842 – Nov 1, 1915), moved to Warren Co., Iowa
where he m Mary Ann Owen (1840–1897), both buried there; **Mary Ann** (Mar 10,1844 –Sep 25, 1910, bur
Wallace Cem, Warren Co, Iowa, m Ist 1865 in Pa. Mathew Alben Taylor (1841–1926); **Isaac** (Aug 24,1847
– Aug 28,1917, bur Straws Cem, Jackson Twp), m Catherine Travitz (Nov 22,1852- Oct 3, 1912). **Isaac
and Catherine (Travitz) Lebo children**: S. Jane (1873 – 1954, bur Maple Grove, E'ville) m George E.
Romberger (1868 – 1941) of E'ville; _____ m Elijah Dietrich of Lykens; **Sarah** b c1850.

***JOSEPH** (Sep 25, 1814 – Sep 25,1893), m Sarah Shepley (Oct 27, 1816 - Mar 29, 1860, bur Bowerman
Cem, Enterline), a dau of John and Susannah Shepley. They lived first in Upper Paxton Twp, later in
Jefferson Twp where he was a farmer and shoemaker. In 1880 Joseph lived in Halifax Twp and Mary age 53
was listed as his wife. **Joseph and Sarah (Shepley) Lebo children: Elsie Ann** b c1837, moved to Nebraska;
Elmira (Mar 20, 1839 –Mar 18,1858, bur Bowerman Cem); **William Harrison** (Sep19, 1841– Feb 6, 1916,
bur Halifax), m Nov 1869 to Angeline Tobias (Sep 8, 1851 – Apr 1, 1924), a dau of Daniel W. and Mary
Tobias.Joseph was a carpenter, and lived in Wayne Twp, Dau Co. He was a veteran of the Civil War; **John**
b c1843, moved to Illinois; **Samuel Alfred** (Feb 14, 1844 – Dec 30, 1893, bur Pillow Union Cem), m
Elisabeth Schoffstall (Mar 7,1848 - Apr 14, 1902), a dau of Christian and Mary (Snyder) Schoffstall. Samuel
& Elisabeth Lebo lived in Lykens Twp in 1880, and he was farming. **Samuel and Elisabeth (Schoffstall)
Lebo children**: Charles L b c 1865 m Catharine Jane Weaver (Jan 1869 – May 10, 1943), lived in Bbg;
John Henry (Dec 4,1866 –c1935), m Apr 22, 1888 in Berrysburg to Henrietta Lubold (May 18, 1870 – Feb
12, 1925), they divorced; **William F** b c1869; **Ira M.**(Mar 9,1871 –Jul 25, 1945), m Kathryn Polm (Jan 22,
1880 – Mar 8, 1962, bur Maple Grove Cem); **Mary E** b c1873, m ___ Welker; **Joseph A** b Feb 17, 1875 –
Apr 27, 1893, bur Pillow Cem), m Sarah C. ___ (Feb 21, 1857 – 1931), a dau of John and Mary (Enterline)
Hoffman;**Jenny A** b c1877; **Sally** b Mar 1880; **Meda Gertrude Alice** (Jan 2, 1884 – Feb 4, 1960, bur
Simeon Cem, Gratz), m 1st Lloyd Matter; m 2nd in 1905 · Victor E. Scheib (Oct 10, 1859 – Mar 11, 1917,
bur Klingers Cem). **Stella** b Feb 20, 1881 m Joseph Thomas; **Ursula V** (Nov 8, 1887 – Sep 12, 1912, bur
Old Union Cem, Lykens), m Aug 26, 1905 to William Franklin Matter (Dec 6, 1874 – Dec 6, 1898). **Mary**

b c1847 moved to Harrisburg; **Sarah** b c1848, moved to Kansas; **Charles P.** b 1852 moved to Illinois; **Susan A.** moved to Nebraska; **Joseph Andrew** (Apr 23,1853 –Jun 6, 1936), m Sep 1,1878, Sarah Catherine Hoffman (Feb 21, 1857 – Jun 22, 1931), a dau of John and Mary (Enterline) Hoffman of Berrysburg.

*****JAMES "Jacobus"** (Jun 19, 1816 – Dec 11, 1886, bur Davids Cem, Killinger), m Annie Jane Novinger (1819 – Dec 28, 1903). They lived in Upper Paxton Twp. **James and Annie Jane (Novinger) Lebo had these children: Sarah** b Sep 17,1839, m Nathaniel Martz (May 1835 – c1860), lived in Northld Co; **Samuel** b Feb 10, 1841, merchant in Pillow; **Jonathan** (May 1, 1843 – Dec 3, 1895), m Mary J ___ (Jun 30, 1849 – May 14, 1922, bur David's Cem), lived in Upper Paxton Twp; **James M** (Oct 26,1844 – 1926, bur Jacobs Cem, Halifax Twp), m Sep 30, 1869 to Mary Catherine Taylor (Sep 5, 1848 – 1925), a dau of William and Eliza (Brought) Taylor of Halifax. They were married about four o'clock in the morning, to enable them to take an early train for Harrisburg, where they enjoyed the State fair then in progress. From there they traveled to Warren County, Iowa to visit the brides relatives. When they came home, they "went housekeeping" with one chair, and a stove and table borrowed from the brides parents. The Taylor family were of Scotch-Irish descent, and settled in Halifax. They also owned 600 acres of land in Iowa. **Christiana** b c1846 m David Kehler; **George Washington** (May 20, 1848 – 1922, bur David's Cem, Killinger), m Clara Jury (Oct 3, 1854 –1937), lived in Upper Paxton Twp.; **Mary Jane** (1850 – 1929, bur David's Cem, Killinger), m Edward Schreffler (1855 – 1934), lived in Upper Paxton Twp; **Catharine E** (1853 – 1915, bur David's Cem), m John A. Shott (Apr 13, 1852 – Nov 29, 1911) of Millersburg; Jacob H. (May 25, 1855 – Nov 29, 1923), m Josephine F. Cooper (Dec 9, 1854 – May 17, 1914), a dau of Elizabeth Matter; **Alice** (1859 – 1949) m Henry J. Zearing (May 1, 1859 – Oct 17, 1922), lived in Harrisburg.

*****LEVI** (Sep 30,1834 – Jan 24, 1916, bur Salem Luth Cem, Killinger), m Mary Jane Buck. (1841 – Jan 13, 1906). He was mentioned in the fathers will as son of second wife.

*****MARIA "POLLY "**(Feb 2, 1837 -   ), m Philip Shaffer

****ELISABETH LEBO** (Feb 8, 1774 - Apr 8, 1844, bur St. John's Hill Cem, Bbg). The tombstone records info – married 48 years, had 9 children – 5 son 4 dau's), m Jun 13, 1791 in Stouchsburg to John George Holtzman (b Mar 1, 1765, Tulpehocken Twp, Berks Co – d Nov 11, 1838 Mifflin Twp, Dau Co.), a son of Henrich and Anna Maria Holtzman. They had 9 children. [For more information see Holtzman genealogy];

****ANNA CATHARINE LEBO** (Jun 7, 1772 – May 30, 1813), m 1st Jacob Snyder b c1768, m 2nd Gottfried Holzman (b Jun 8, 1768, a son of Henrich Holtzman lived in Berks Co.;

****CHRISTOPHER** (Aug 24, 1773 – Oct 14, 1815), m Mary Catherine Bordner (1781 – 1844). His will did not mention children.

** **JOHN PETER LEBO**b Jan 26, 1777, lived in Berks Co.

** **MARIA LEBO** (1779 – 1819), lived in Berks Co., not married. She named her brother-in-law Executor of her estate.

****ANNA MARGARETHA LEBO** b Feb 23, 1782, m 1804 Thomas Kurr b c1780;

** **SUSANNA LEBO** (Mar 3,1787 – Dec 18, 1843, bur St. David's Cem, Killinger), m Nov 16, 1806 Peter Hoy (Jul 26, 1779 – Apr 26, 1858), a son of Bernard and Anna Margaretah Hoy, moved to Upper Paxton Twp., and lived in Millersburg. **Peter & Susanna (Lebo) Hoy had known children: Jacob** (Mar 26, 1808 – Jan 29, 1887), m Elisabeth Romberger (Mar 24, 1812 – Aug 16, 1854), lived in Dau Co; **Christian** (Jul 18, 1818 – Dec 31, 1888, bur Davids Cem, Kilinger), m Leah Novinger (Jun 27, 1818 – Jun 29, 1881)

****EVA MARGRETHA LEBO** (Oct 23, 1790 – Jul 26, 1872, bur Himmel Cem, Rebuck, Northld Co), m 1808 , Stouchsburg to Gotfried Schreffler (Nov 26, 1787 – Feb 12, 1870), a son of Gotfried and Hannah Schreffler, and moved to Washington Twp, Northld Co. They are bur in Himmel Cem, Rebuck. **Gotfried & Eva Margaretha (Lebo) Schreffler children: Jonas** b Jan 17, 1817; **Elizabeth** b Apr 4,18190, m Nicholas Adam; **Joseph John** ()ct 20, 1820 – Oct 15, 1895), m Salome Rebuck (Nov 5, 1821 – Mar 17, 1895, bur Himmel Cem)', a dau of Gotfried & Catharine Rebuck; **Gottfried** (Oct 23,1822 – Jun 26, 1885, bur Leck Hill), m 1st Christiana Hepner (Sep 25, 1820 –Nov 24, 1860), 2nd Catherine Howerter (1830 – 1903), dau of Solomon & Maria (Kahler) Howerter; **Daniel** (1827 – 1908), m 1st Sallie Schankweiler (1825 – 1882), 2nd Dina Bohner (1833 – 1907); Eva b Feb 1, 1829 in Hebe; **Lidia** Ann b Feb 1, 1831.]

+**ABRAHAM LEBO** (b c1708 – 1775), m Mar 22, 1742 in Swatara Twp to Anna Margaretha Schueler (1721-pre1761), in Frederick County, Md. Abraham lived in the Tulpehocken area of Berks Co, and several of his children were bapt. in Stouchsburg and Trinity Ref Ch in that region.

Abraham Lebo was father of these children (some bapt Trinity Ref, Tulpehocken & Stouchburg)– some had descendants in Dau Co:

*ANN MARIA b Nov 15, 1744, m Christian Keen b c1740;

*ABRAHAM (Dec 29, 1747 – Feb 1787), m Margaret ___ (b c1752 , Frederick, Md.;

*JOHANNA MAGDALENA (b Sep 6, 1751 – d 1833), m 1766 to Johann George Philip Gebhart (1743 – 1815 Berks Co), she later moved to Ohio. **They had a dau** **Catherine Gebhart** (Jul 9, 1767 – pre 1815), m 1784 *John Adam Lebo (Aug 12, 1753 – 1803), moved to Up Pax.Twp in 1796 – below).

*JOHN ADAM (Aug 12, 1753 – May 8, 1803 in Up Pax Twp), m Catherine Gebhart (1767 – pre 1815), a daughter of Johann George Philip Gebhard, (see above). John Adam Lebo and family moved to Dauphin Co about 1796.

John Adam and Catherine (Gebhart) Lebo children (some bapt Host & Tulpehocken Ch):

**Margaret Elizabeth (Jul 31,1785 – Apr 18, 1858, bur St. John Hill Cem, Bbg), m John Adam Weiss (Jan 24, 1780 in Hagerstown, Md – Jan 28, 1854). John Adam Weiss had previously been married to Eve Bordner whose death occurred within the year of their marriage. John Adam and Margaret Elisabeth Lebo lived in Mifflin Twp in 1850, and had Susanna b c1808 with them. John Adam and Margaret Elizabeth (Lebo) Weise children (some bapt Salem, some David's Ch Killinger); [Info under Weiss genealogy.]

Johannes (b Mar 31, 1787 Heidelburg Twp, Berks Co bap Altalaha Luth Ch – d Jan 1, 1854 in Washington Twp, Dau Co. of Angina Pectoris, bur St. Johns Cem, Berrysburg but no marker), m Catharine Riegel (c1790 – c1813).had these known children:*****William** b Jul 15, 1810; ***Elizabeth b c1811, m Adam Cooper b Aug 27, 1809. They lived on a farm in Jackson Twp as early as 1850. **Adam and Elizabeth (Lebo) Cooper children**: ****Caroline b c1833; ****James b c1834;****Margaret b c1838; ****Priscilla b c1840; ****Nancy b c1843; ****Catharine b c1845; ****Elizabeth b c1849; ***Katerina b May 9, 1813.

Johannes Lebo (b 1787) m 2nd Mary _____. She was named in Dauphin Twp death records as his wife at the time of his death. It also states that he is buried in St. Johns Cem. John & Mary Lebo children:

*** Sarah b c1819, m Henry Yeager b c1819, lived in Washington Twp in 1850, in 1860 in Mifflin Twp. listed as a stone cutter. By 1870 the family resided in Berrysburg where he had established a factory known as The Marble And Granite Works and was listed as a tombstone maker. His son John was an apprentice stone cutter. **Henry & Sarah (Lebo) Yeager children:** ****Adaline b c1841; ****Nathaniel b c1842, he was a marble stone cutter. He m Annie ___ b c1846, they had a dau *Mary A* b c1869; Sophia b c1844; Sarah b c1846;Pricsilla b c1847, in 1870 worked as a cook in a hotel in Berrysburg for Benjamin Bordner; John b c1852, in 1870 a stone cutter; Margaret b c1855; Charles b c1857; Savella b c1859; Alice b c 1860; Alice b c1861; Lillie b c1867.

Thomas b c1824, m Sarah A. ___ b c1826. In 1850 Thomas and Sarah lived next to his parents in Washington Twp. In 1880 they lived in Spring Twp., Perry County. **Thomas and Sarah A. Lebo children**: ****James b 1849; ****Kate b c1857; ****Christian b c1862; ****Anne b c1864;*Sallie b c1867; ****Sophia b c1869;**** Matilda J. b c1876.

*** Pricilla b c1827, m David Snyder b c1827, lived in Washington Twp in 1850;

**George (Apr 2, 1790 near Rehrersburg, Berks Co. – Feb 11,1844, bur Old Harrisburg Cem, reburied in Harrisburg Cem to make way for Pennsylvania Railroad Station). He was a veteran of the War of 1812. George Lebo m Susanna Elizabeth Enterline (Aug 20,1789 -1834), a dau of Michael and Elisabeth (Snoke) Enterline of Mifflin Twp.

George & Susanna (Enterline)Lebo children:

***DANIEL (b Feb 10, 1812 – d Feb 20, 1871, of pneumonia, bur St. Johns Hill Cem, Berrysburg with 2nd wife), m Sarah Row (Oct 12,, 1821 – Feb 6, 1843, bur St. Johns Hill Cem with Row family), a dau of Wendel Row. Daniel m 2nd Sarah Schoffstall (May 5, 1824 – May 30, 1883, bur St. Johns Hill Cem), a dau of Emanuel and Catharine Schoffstall.Daniel owned a small farm in Mifflin Twp midway between St. John's and Hoffman's Church. He also was a carpenter, and in April 1864, he and the family moved to Lykens to continue as a carpenter. He and his two brothers, William and David, assisted in building the first Lykens coal breaker. **Daniel & Sarah (Row) Lebo had these children:**

****<u>Joseph</u> (Jul 30, 1839 –Aug 23, 1920), m Susannah Matilda Moyer b c1841. He was an apprentice carpenter in 1860, lived in Oregon in 1906. **Joseph & Susannah Matilda (Moyer) Lebo had these children**: <u>George McClellan</u> b Jan 1, 1862; <u>Daniel Monroe</u> b Apr 16,1864; <u>Sarah Rebecca</u> b Mar 19, 1866; <u>Emma Jane</u> b Dec 16, 1868, m Wm.Drenkel; <u>John Harvey</u> b Mar 1,1870; <u>Mary Catharine</u> b Aug 20, 1872 m Solomon Matter, 2nd John Harman; ****<u>Sarah Ann</u> (Jun 13, 1841– Sep 12,1926), m Dr. Henry R. Lehr (1838 – Jan 13,1909). Sarah Ann, age 8 was living with the Solomon Martz family in 1850);

Henry and Sarah Ann (Row) Lehr had these children: <u>Monroe D.</u>, a doctor; <u>J. Frank</u>; <u>Abraham</u>; <u>Elizabeth</u> m __ Uhler; <u>William</u> <u>Henry</u>; <u>Sarah L</u>; <u>John H.</u>; **Caroline** b Nov 17, 1842, m John Harman, had a dau *Adeline*.

Daniel and Sarah (Schoffstall) Lebo had these eleven children:
****<u>John</u> b Feb 14,1844 - Dec 26, 1922), m Sep 7, 1866, Sarah Ann Row (May 3, 1849 – Feb 8, 1927), a dau of Henry and Susannah (Matter) Row. He was a Civil War Vet in Co H, 210 th Regt Pa. Volunteers.
John and Sarah Ann (Row) Lebo had these children (some bapt St. Johns Hill Ch: Maggie Cerilla (Dec 26, 1867 - Mar 9,1887, bur St. Johns Hill Cem, Berrysburg);Charles Clinton Nov 12, 1869 - Dec 17, 1958, bur Orwin Cem, Sch Co) William Grant (Aug 30, 1871 - Feb 8, 1872, bur St. Johns Cem); Isaac Oliver (Sep 9, 1874 - ___-; Jonathan Edward b Dec 27, 1876; Anna Rebecca b Dec 27, 1878 , m ___ Keilman; Kate Ellen (b Jul 26,1880 m John Peter Schwalm; Cordella (b Dec 27, 1882 - ____), m Harvey Snyder; Joseph Oscar b Oct 1, 1884; Lottie May b Mar 21, 1887;
**** <u>Isabella</u> (Apr 29, 1845 – Jan 9, 1906), m William Bailey of Pillow;
****<u>Wilhelm E</u> (Oct 1, 1847 – Nov 10, 1920), m Jun 17, 1873 Sarah Catharina Boyer (May 17, 1856, a dau of William S. and Christiana Boyer of Gratz. They were married in the home of her parents in Gratz, by Rev. Thomas Steck children. **William E & Sara Catharine (Boyer) Lebo had these children:** <u>William Ellerslie</u> (May 30, 1874 – Apr 14, 1941), m Pruella Huntzinger (Oct 3,1874 – Jul 8, 1946), a dau of Josiah and Lydia (Schwalm) Huntzinger of Hegins. Both William and Pruella are bur in Simeon Cem. **William E. & Pruella (Huntzinger) Lebo children:** *Gertrude Estella* (Dec 7,1897 –1962, bur Simeon Cem), m Allen Walton; *Guy Luther* (Aug 27, 1899 – discrepancy with birth date – tombstone states 1897 – d 1962); twins *Ernest Laplace* & *Esther Pruella* (b & d 1902); *Ellerslie* (Apr 3, 1903 –1954 bur Simeon Cem), m Marguerite Simon (1912 – 1947), dau of Mr. and Mrs. Burton C. Simon of Philadelphia. Ellerslie first attended Muhlenberg College, later Lutheran Theological Seminary in the city of Philadelphia. He became an ordained Lutheran minister in 1929. He became widely known for his ability as an authority on church architecture. His services as a consultant and designer were sought, for over forty churches in New Jersey and Pennsylvania. **Ellerslie and Marguerite (Simon) Lebo had two children: (twins):** *Ann* m Samuel H. Dyke, *Burton C* lived in Millersville; *Elsie Eva* (twin) b Apr 3, 1903 m May 9, 1925, John William McKinley Kratzer bAug 3, 1903. *Bertha* b 1906, m Hiester Blyler (1900 - ___), a son of Charles M. Blyler (Feb 7,1864 – Dec 29, 1913), and his wife Elizabeth (Hess) Blyler (Mar 3, 1865 – Apr 15, 1935); *Arland Arthur* (Aug 19, 1909 – 1991), a doctor in Lititz, (donated numerous family medical items to Gratz Hist. Soc.). <u>Minnie *A*</u> b b 1876 m James Zerfing (Sep 7, 1876 – Aug 26,1942); <u>Christiana</u> (no dates) m Mar 27, 1900 in Valley View, Rev H. W. Snyder of Drehersville; <u>Lizzie Gertrude</u> m William A. Saltzer, **had these children:** *Joseph Albert* b Feb 7, 1907; *Lebo*; *Mark*; *Mary* m __ Hoberg.
<u>Bertha</u> m __ Butterweck; <u>D. Austin</u>, a doctor; <u>Clara Mabel</u> b Apr 3, 1886 bapt Friedan's Ref Hegins Pa. m ____Herb; <u>John Boyer</u> b Jun 15, 1887, bapt Friedan's Ref; <u>Joseph B</u> m Elizabeth Klinger, **had these children:** Howard m Ruth Coleman; Ivan; Mary. Ivan B. (no dates) m ___ Miller.
****<u>Edward</u> (b Jan 8, 1849 – d Feb 19, 1917);
****<u>Emanuel</u> (b Mar 26, 1851 – Dec 31, 1911)
****<u>Catharine Elizabeth</u> (1853 – 1890), m Daniel Schrawder b1850 of Berrysburg.
****<u>Amos</u> (1854 – 1926), m Elizabeth Shaffer b 1854;
****<u>Ann</u> b c1855; ****<u>Daniel</u> b1857;
****<u>Leah</u> b 1859;
****<u>Mary Alice</u> (1860 – 1915), m Ira Walcott;
****<u>Henry G.</u> (1866 – 1955)

***<u>ELIZABETH</u> (Dec 19, 1813 –Aug 23, 1876, bur Ioof Cem, Lykens) m Jonas Hoffman (Oct 23, 1813 – Sep 28, 1889), a son of John Peter and Susanna Magd (Lubold) Hoffman. Jonas was a farmer, but he later took up hotel keeping at Union Hotel in Lykens. **Jonas and Elizabeth (Lebo) Hoffman children:** <u>Sarah</u> (Oct 4, 1833 – Jan 13, 1865), m Amos Kuntzelman, who died in Lykens Nov 29, 1905. They lived in Lykens in

1880. **Amos and Sarah (Hoffman) Kuntzelman children**: <u>William</u> b c1852; <u>Molly</u> b c1859; <u>Robert</u> b c 1873; <u>Susanna</u> (b c1834 -) m John Schreffler (b c1830   ), he was a carpenter and they lived in Gratz in 1860. Later they moved to Ohio, where two of their sons supposedly changed their names. **John and Susanna (Hoffman) Schreffler had these children**; <u>Newton</u> b c1855; <u>George</u> b c1857; <u>Ellen</u> b c1858; <u>Sarah</u> b c1860 <u>Catherine</u> (Dec 20, 1834 – Jul 13, 1874, she died of small pox, bur Wiconisco Calvary Cem), m 1853 to Jonas Faust (Jun 15, 1830 – Feb 13, 1884. Jonas later m Sarah Delcamp in 1875 (Hoffman) . **Jonas and Catherine (Hoffman) Faust had these children:** <u>Clara</u> (c1854 – 1861); <u>Agnes</u> (b c1856; <u>Delilah</u> (b & d 18857); <u>Elizabeth</u> (bc1859; <u>Henry C</u> b c1863; <u>William</u> (Nov 1, 1864 – Jul 24, 1874, bur beside parents); <u>Mary</u> b c1866; <u>Sallie</u> b Sep 20, 1868; <u>Harry</u> b Sep 27, 1870; <u>Charles B</u> Dec 18, 1872.; **Henry** b c1839, m ____ Cooper, moved to Crawford County. **Cornelius** b c1841, m Elizabeth Zerby; **Lydia** (Aug 11, 1842 – Feb 11,1909, bur Greenwood Cem, Tower City), m Emanuel Schoffstall (Apr 19, 1839 - Sep 1, 1886, bur St. Pauls Cem, Tower City) Emanuel and Lydia lived in Lykens in 1880. **Emanuel and Lydia (Hoffman) Schoffstall had these children**:George; Charles b c 1862 , moved to Pittsburgh; ____ m John Goehrig, moved to Williamsport. Henry b c1867; Maggie b c1874.After Emanuel Schoffstall died, his widow married Henry K Updegrove, proprietor of the Tower City House. They had no children, he died May 1891.; **Elizabeth** b c1845n m Jacob Klouser, 2nd Charles Shoemaker; **Adeline** b c1846, m __ Birkleback; **Amanda** b 1849, m John Klinger; **Rose Ann** b 1859, m Jun 22, 1884, George Radel ; **Francis** b Nov 26, 1852, m _____ Hoffman. [More info in Hoffman genealogy].

GEORGE JR b Jan 12, 1816, moved to a western state. This one may have m Susanna Enterline – **had ch bapt St. Johns**: Michael b Apr 14, 1832;

WILLIAM (Feb 11, 1821 – Jan 8, 1882, bur Lykens Cem), m Angeline Keen (Mar 19, 1822 – Jan 20, 1907). **William and Angeline (Keen) Lebo had these children (bapt St. Johns Ch):** <u>Mary Jane</u> b Aug 15, 1845; <u>Anna Eliza</u> b Sep 11, 1852; <u>Sarah Ellen</u> (b Feb 26, 1855 – d Jul 27, 1914, of a stroke, bur Lykens), m Jan 21, 1873 to Jonathan Stein (b Lykens Twp Feb 9, 1851 – d 1874), a son of _____.Jonathan was a painter and grainer, excellent musician playing cornet and sometimes leader of the Lykens band. He traveled with the Sells Brothers Circus as one of the band members and player of steam calliope. He was the senior member of the firm of Stein Bro's, owner of "The Big Store" in Lykens. On the day of his death, Jonathan took his horse to the race track to give it exercise. He fell from the cart, catching lightly at the wheel in the fall. The horse stopped instantly. Jonathan was taken home, where he died of a stroke. In 1880, Sarah his widow and their young dau <u>Jennie Arlene</u> b Oct 13, 1873, lived with her parents; **Samuel** b c1857;

JOHANNES (Nov 20, 1823 – Apr 29, 1906, bur Red Cross Cem, Northld Co), m Anna Maria Kobel (1830 - Nov 12, 1915), moved to Northld Co;

MARIA b Jun 14, 1825; **DAVID** (Aug 8, 1826 – Sep 6, 1903, bur Zion Cem, Dauphin), m in Zion Evang Ch Middle Paxton Twp. Sarah Hoover (Sep 1833 – 1909) In 1850, he lived with his sister & brother-in-law.)

MICHAEL (Apr 14, 1832-Aug 17, 1894, bur IOOF Cem, Lykens)

ANNA CATHARINE (Oct 11, 1835 – Aug 17, 1894), m Isreal Lucas, lived in Wiconisco.

After his first wife Susanna died, George Lebo m Lydia, **had two known children:**

AMANDA b 1839 m John Ferree; **HENRY** b 1841, killed while serving in the Civil War.

Peter (Sep 29, 1793, bapt Host Ch, Tulpehocken Twp, also came to Upper Dauphin Area. He married Mary Sheif b c1796. **Peter & Mary (Sheif) Lebo children:

John J. Washington (Jul 16, 1814–Jun 12, 1889, bur St. Johns Cem, Berrysburg), m Jun 12, 1836, Barbara Botteiger (May 11,1813 –Feb 13, 1891), dau of John and Barbara Botteiger. John W and Barbara Lebo lived in Mifflin Twp in 1850 and 1860, and he was listed as a laborer. In 1850 Hugh Botteiger age 30, a carpenter was with them. In 1860 beside the children Mary Lebo age 64 apparently his widowed mother was with them **John Wash. & Barbara (Botteiger) Lebo had these children**: <u>Mary Ann</u> ; <u>Sarah Jane</u> b c1839; <u>Daniel M.</u> b c1842; <u>Jeremiah</u> (Dec 19, 1843- 1912), m Emaline Bressler (1847 – 1928); <u>Emanuel</u> (1846 – 1926), m Sarah E. Martz; <u>Cornelius</u> b c1849, m Elizabeth Snodgrass; <u>Jonathan</u> (Mar 26, 1851 – Jul 1, 1911, bur St. Johns Hill Cem), m 1877 Susanna Hassinger (Jul 26, 1857 - Sep 12, 1928), a dau of Jacob and Lydia Hassinger of Washington Twp. **Jonathan and Susanna (Hassinger) Lebo children:** ____ m H. B. Evitts of Llewelyn; ____ m Walter Weiss; ____ m J. J. Sulzbaugh of E'ville Homer lived in Gratz; C. C. of E'ville.

*Maria Margaret (Dec 12, 1796 – Dec 20, 1843, bur Hoffman Cem), m John Hoover (Sep 17, 1796 – Mar 17, 1877), a son of Jacob and Eva Catharine Elizabeth (Sierer) Hoover of Lykens Twp.

[Hoover genealogy elsewhere in book.]

THE SNYDER/SCHNEIDER/ ETC FAMILIES

JOHANNS/HANS SCHNEIDER (b Dec 1687, probably in Geneva, Switzerland – d Jul 1743 in Oley, Berks Co, m Catharina _____ (b 1688 Geneva, Switzerland – d Mar 27, 1774 in Oley, Berks Co). Johannes and Catharina Schneider had at least five children. Theae are known: **Jacob** b c1718 of Oley; ***Heinrich** b 1721; **Peter** b 1723; **Susanna** (no dates); **Barbara** b c1727, married to Nicholas Keim of Reading.
***HENRICH SCHNEIDER** (b 1721 Alsace Twp, Berks Co – d 1762/63, bur Oley Farms Cemetery), m Katherina Keim (b ___ d May 8, 1793), a dau of Johannes & Kathrina (Moyer) Keim, Sr. of Palatinate, Germany. Henry penned a will that was probated June 1763 in Berks Co. Henrich and Kathrina (Moyer) Keim had these children: <u>JOHN</u> ; <u>HENRICH</u> ; <u>ABRAHAM</u>; *<u>LEONARD (SR)</u>; <u>JACOB</u>; <u>DIETRICH</u>; <u>CATHERINA</u>. Leonard Snyder, Sr. (1739 - 1801), one of the sons of Henrich migrated to the Lykens Valley. In 1798 He was assessed for a 33 x 30 foot wooden one story house with six windows, on two acres. What is known of his children and early generations is recorded below. Information of the succeeding descendants of his children may be found in other sections of this publication.

THE LEONARD SCHNEIDER SNYDER FAMILY
(With help from Albert Wm. Snyder of Albuquerque, N. Mex, and others)
(The family of George Schneider/ Snyder will appear in another area. A connection probably exits between these two families, but we haven't found it.)

***LEONARD SNYDER** (b 1739 Ger – d Mar 16,1801, age sixty), record at St.Johns Church, Berrysburg, m Dec 20, 1768, New Hanover Luth Ch, Catharine Miller (1739 – Jul 30, 1799). Soon after Leonard Snyder died, his oldest son petitioned the court for an inquest to value his 450 acres of land. Since several of his children were under age, a guardian had to be chosen for them. Stophel (Christopher), Samuel and Jacob Snyder chose Jacob Smith of West Hanover as their guardian As was the practice in those days these twelve "honest" men were chosen to value the real estate: John Hoffman John McCleery, Thomas Burrell, Christian Hoffman, John Miller, Daniel Miller, Nichols Hoffman, James Clark, Baltzer Peterman (Bitterman), John Powell, Jacob Swab and Adam Weise. They decided that the land could not be fairly divided. Sometime later, in June 1802, Jacob Smith guardian of the minor children petitioned the court to say that the former petition of Leonard Snyder, Jr. contained false information. Leonard Snyder before his death had composed a will, and it was probated November 17, 1801, in which he made provision for dividing his real estate. In July 1802, the valuation of the real estate was quashed.

The will of Leonard Snyder was written on February 21, 1800, but apparently not found until after the early court proceedings were completed. Leonard had given a detailed plan for disposal of his land. Leonard Jr. was to receive the two hundred acres where he was presently living. Nicholas should receive the gristmill, sawmill and 100 acres where the mills are located, from the bridge downward, and the water rights. Catharine should receive 400 pounds, 100 when she marries, and 25 pounds yearly. Jacob should be given the plantation called "Yeagers Hill" and 200 pounds from his brother Leonard. Christopher should be furnished with a property later. Leonard and Nicholas were obligated to collect the money owed to the estate, and then buy Chirstopher a place. Samuel to receive the old plantation, but pay 150 pounds and share the orchard for ten years. The two younger sons of Leonard Snyder were "to be sent to school and taught English and German and to cypher." (In those early days, public schooling had not been initiated. Parents paid schoolmasters for the children's education.)

Leonard and Catharine (Miller) Snyder had these children:
***LEONARD JR.** (May 1, 1772 – Jan 17, 1815, bur St. John's Hill Cem, Bbg), m Anna Maria Shott (Nov 7, 1776 – Nov 15, 1852) a dau of Jacob and Elizabeth Shott. He came to Lykens Twp where he married his wife. Leonard owned land lying partly in Lykens Twp and partly in Mifflin Twp. In1850 after her husband died, Anna Maria lived with her daughter Elizabeth and family in Washington Twp. **Leonard and Anna Maria (Shott) Snyder had these children (some bapt Hoffman ch):**
****JOHN** (Aug 1, 1795 – May 4, 1850, bur Hoffman Cem), Anna Maria Wert (Jan 6, 1798 – Jan 2, 1836). A dau of Jacob & Sophia (Miller) Wert. John received a farm lying on the west side of Wiconisco Creek, some of the land in Lykens and some in Mifflin Township. John was an outspoken advocate of the public school system to replace the subscription schools. After Anna Maria died, John m Elizabeth Enterline (c1810 -1869), the widow of George Lark, had no children.

John and Anna Maria (Wert) Snyder had these children (some bapt Hoffman Ch):

***JACOB (Sep 23, 1816 – Feb 19, 1901, bur Peace Ref Cem, Bbg), m Sarah ____ (Mar 3, 1819 – Jan 3, 1890). In 1860 they lived in Mifflin Twp, in 1880 in Berrysburg.

 ***CATHARINE b May 25, 1820, not mentioned in fathers estate;

***ELIZABETH b Mar 4, 1822;

***LEONARD b Feb 15,1825, m Lydia possibly Hepner lived in Lykens Twp in 1854.
Leonard and Lydia Snyder had these children (some bapt Hoffman Ch): Sarah Jane b Feb 9, 1847.

***JOHN D. (Dec 9, 1827 in Lykens Twp- 1902, bur Meth Cem, Berrysburg), m 1849 to Hannah Lark (Dec 26, 1827 - 1907), a dau of Christopher and Rachel (Buffington) Lark. John grew up in Lykens Twp. and at the age of sixteen moved to Berrysburg. He was employed at the foundry owned by Shaffer & Wenrich, and eventually purchased the company. For fifty years he manufactured stoves, plows and other iron products. He also owned a farm in Mifflin Twp., and built the first brick house in Berrysburg. He was a Justice of the Peace for thirty- five years, and became an associate justice in 1872. The family belonged to the Methodist Episcopal Church in Berrysburg. In 1860, John and Hannah Snyder had Ann Snyder age 19, noted as a servant, and Jacob Bassler age 20 noted as a tinner living with them in Mifflin Township. **John D. and Hannah (Lark) Snyder children:** Sarah Jane b c1850, m Peter S. Bergstresser; Jennie; Mary Ann b c1853; Edwin C. (Aug 20, 1855 – Apr 7, 1882, bur Meth Cem); Rachel b c1859; Catherine E (1862 d 1864); Joseph H.(1865 - 1943 bur Meth Cem); Arthur L. b c1868; Elizabeth d young.

JOHN D. SNYDER (1827 - 1902)

***EMANUEL (c1831 – after 1850), lived in Halifax

***MARIA ANNA (Oct 31, 1832, bapt Hoffman Cen - m May 30, 1854 John Schoffstall (Nov 18,1833 – Apr 4, 1918, bur Simeon Cem), a son of Samuel and Elizabeth (Smeltz) Schoffstall. John Snyder (maybe her brother) helped her apply for a divorce in 1859, because of threats of abuse. She" moved out" in 1860,   and appears on the 1860 census for Lykens Twp living with her parents and noted as a "grass widow." But   she apparently came back to John In 1870 John and Mary are living in Gratz with their two children Daniel and John H. **John and Maria Anna (Snyder) Schoffstall had these children:** Daniel (Sep 20, 1854 – Nov 28, 1890, bur Simeon Cem, Gratz). He died of dropsy. His baptismal record has not been found, but Rev. Pflueger's record of death states that Daniel was bapt by Rev. F. Waltz, his grandparents John Snyder and wife were sponsors. John H. (1863 – 1955, bur Simeon Cem), m Catharine L. Witmer (1865 – 1925, bur Fairview Cem, Wmstown), a dau of Henry and Amanda (Fagely) Witmer of Gratz. By May 1899, John and Catharine Schoffstall lived in Wiconisco. **John H. and Catharine (Witmer) Schoffstall had these children:** Mary Lillie b Jun 8, 1885, m ___ Hoffman, d spring 1988 said to be age 101; Lizzie Amanda b Apr 25, 1887; Harry Calvin b Nov 22, 1891; John Henry b Sep 7, 1897; Albert b Apr 24, 1899.

***SAMUEL SNYDER (He may be a son b1836 – d 1885, bur St. Johns Hill Cem, Bbg), m Catherine Schwab (1837 – 1926), a dau of _____. They lived in Wash. Twp in 1880. **Samuel and Catherine (Schwab) Snyder children:**
Daniel E. (1859 – 1924, bur St. Johns Hill Cem), m Lydia Romberger (   ), a dau of _____
He was a blacksmith. **Daniel E. and Lydia (Romberger) Snyder children:** John Nathan b Apr 19, 1882; Emma Louisa. b May 30, 1864, bapt Hoovers Ch
Nathan E. (b c1870 – d 1946), m Rosie E. _____ (1874 – 1963, bur St. Johns Cem). **Nathan E. and Rosie E. (Bonawitz) Snyder children:** Estella I (1899 – 1966); Henry J. (1907 - 1921); Harvey; Annie; Galen; Allen.

**SAMUEL (Nov 10, 1799 – Jul 4, 1826), record of death in Davids Ch Killinger, noting that he was a son of Leonard, m Anna Maria _____ (no dates). Samuel died without issue, so his share of 200 acres from his father's estate evetnually went to his brother John.

ELISABETH (May 2, 1803 – Jul 11, 1889, bur Peace Cem, Bbg), m 1st Daniel Hoffman (Feb 19, 1800 – Jan 16, 1823, bur Hoffman Cem), a son of John and Christina (Deibler) Hoffman. Elisabeth received 100 acres lying on the south side of Wiconisco Creek, from her fathers estate. She sold it to her brother John in 1836. **Daniel & Elisabeth (Snyder) Hoffman children: *****ISAAC** (Feb 9, 1821 - ____); *****DANIEL JR**. b Jan 21, 1823, was a distinguished civil engineer, lived in Phila. His son **John R.** was a civil engineer employed by Summit Branch Railroad and Coal Co. in Pottsville. After Daniel Hoffman died Elisabeth m Jan 1, 1824 by Rev. Isaac Gerhart to John Hoke (Feb 24,1802 – Jan 21,1861). In 1850 Anna Mary (Shott) Snyder lived with her daughter & son-in-law John Hoke in Mif Twp. **John & Elisabeth (Snyder Hoffman) Hoke children:***JOSIAH** (Mar 21, 1825 – Feb 12, 1894, bur Peace Cem, Bbg), m Amanda ____ (Sep 4, 1823 – Mar 12,1909);*****ELISABETH** b Jan 14, 1828;***** MARY ANN** b May 17,1830;*****CATHARINA** b Jan 29,1833; *****JOHN** b Jun 20,1835; ***** WM** b Nov 22,1837;*****LEONARD** (Nov17,1839–1842);*****REBECCA** b Jun 26,1842;*****JONATHAN** b May 1846.

*CARL NICHOLAS (Apr 14, 1776 bapt David's Ch Killinger – Apr 23, 1835), m Rebecca Wells (b c1785- d Mar 1862), a dau of Samuel and Mary (Glenn) Wells of Germantown. Her parents were married in Sept 1776 in Old Suede's Church at Phila. Rebecca Lived in Mifflin Twp in 1850 and had her daughter Leah Jane age 20 with her. Rebecca lived alone in Mifflin Twp. in 1860. **Carl Nicholas & Rebecca (Wells) Snyder had 11 children:**
*William (b ____ - , was oldest, inherited land in Halifax. When his mother died was living in Ohio.
**____ b 1796;
Mary (1803 – May 12, 1879, Meth Episcopal record), m John Moyer b c1804, lived in Mifflin Twp in 1850 & 1860. John & Mary (Snyder) Moyer children:Maryann** b 1827;**Leonard** b 1827, carpenter;**Rebecca** b 1829; **Abie** b1830;**Jacob** b 1834, brick grazer; **Nicholas** b1839**; James,** blacksmith; **John; Alfred; Emasah; Henrietta**
**Elizabeth m Thomas Griffith
**Hannah (Apr 26, 1809 – May 4, 1845), m David Ferree Hoffman (Jul 24, 1809 – Oct 24, 1867, bur Old Meth Cem, Bbg), a son of Daniel and Hannah (Ferree) Hoffman. [More info in Hoffman genealogy.]
James b c1813 m Sarah ____ was a carpenter in Mifflin Twp in 1850, **had these children: John b 1837; Nicholas 1840; James 1843; Sarah Jane 1847;
Nicholas b c1820, m Mary ____, **had these children: Sarah Jane; William Henry (1842– 1921, bur Fetterhoff Cem, Halifax) m 1st Margaret McClellan, 2nd Katie Elizabeth Keefer; Samuel;Elizabeth; Uriah; James; Rebecca; John; Alfred; Emassh; Henrietta.
Thomas - This may be the one m Rebecca Harper. He was a tinsmith. **Had these children: John; Henry; Harper; Emma; Thomas Williard b Feb 4, 1853 Bbg;
**Catherine, m Jonathan Yeager;
**Rebecca
Samuel, (Jun 5, 1827 – Nov 1904) m 1850 to Ann Maria Miller b c1834, a dau of John and Leah (Bowne) Miller of Lebanon Co and Orwigsburg. They lived in Mifflin Twp in 1860. Samuel joined the Meth Church in Berrysburg in 1848, sang in the choir, taught vocal music to the children in the church. **Samuel and Ann Maria (Miller) Snyder had these children: Clara b c1850, She is on the 1870 census as having been adopted by John Miller, living about two doors away from her parents; **Sarah** b c1850 **Charles B.** b c1852, lived in Harrisburg; **Ida E.** b c1854; **Franklin M** b c1856, lived in Harrisburg; **Minnie** b c1864; **Katherine** m ____ Willus, lived in Everett; **Ella R.** b c1868, lived in Reading; **Nellie** b c1870; **Lena M** b c1873, m ____Hoover; **Harry E.** b 1875.
**Leah Jane b c1830, m ____ Boyer of Freeburg.

*SAMUEL (Aug 4, 1787 bapt St. Johns – d May 2, 1841, bur St. John's Hill Cem), m Elisabeth ____ (Nov 17, 1790 – d Mar 20, 1864). No children mentioned in estate papers. Elizabeth apparently lived alone in Wash. Twp in 1860. When Elizabeth died her heirs were her nephew Aaron Lark, niece Hannah wife of John D. Snyder.
*CATHARINE b Aug 4, 1787 (is she a twin?) m Peter Rouch
*JACOB probably m Catharine ____ **had these children (bapt St. John's Hill Ch):** Catharine b Nov 23, 1801 sp Margaret Lubold or m Margaretha ___ ch Elisabeth b Mar 1, 1802 sp John Enterline and Charlotte
*CHRISTOPHER (not much information has been found on Christopher. In the records of his father Leonard's estate (after 1801) it is mentioned that his brothers Leonard and Nicholas were "obligated to collect the money owed to the estate, and then buy Chirstopher a place." Also Christopher died in Lykens Valley about 1819, and his brother Nicholas was administrator of his estate.

FARM OF HENRY W. & LORRAINE A. HENNINGER 66-004-006
JONATHAN E. KOPPENHEFFER (133 ACRES IN 1875)

This land is located partly in Mifflin Township and partly in Lykens Township, lying west of Wiconisco Creek. It was derived from two separate tracts that originally were part of a grant to Leonard Snyder. The land was distributed to several members of the Snyder family. John Snyder eventually became the owner of this parcel bound by land of John Umholtz, Daniel Lebo, south by land of John Hoke, east by Frederick Lubold heirs, Samuel Snyder and Aaron Lebo. On April 8, 1852, John D. Snyder, administrator of the estate of John Snyder conveyed 149 acres 110 ¼ perches of land with buildings to Jeremiah Harner. The 1855 tax record mentions that Jeremiah Harner had 150 acres with a two-story log house and bank barn, and Peter Schoffstall was a tenant on the property.

On March 3, 1866 Jeremiah and Rebecca Harner conveyed the plantation to Jonathon E. and Juliana Koppenheffer. After Jonathan died in March 1882 his numerous acreages were conveyed to his children. His son John H. received this land in two separate tracts on March 11, 1882. One tract contained 84 acres 97 perches with the old log house which he had been living in since 1868. The other tract contained 60 acres 46 perches. William M and Sophia Henninger eventually became the owners, and they conveyed 84 acres 97 perches and 21 acres 63 perches to Melvin A. and Anna C. Henninger in February 1956. Melvin A. Henninger died December 16, 2000, and the farm became owned by his wife Anna C. Henninger. After Anna C. Henninger died on February 7, 2003, the executor of her estate conveyed the 84 acres 97 perches with the house and barn and the 21 acres to her son Henry W. Henninger and his wife Lorraine on April 15, 2003. The land bordered on the old mill dam and Melvin Henninger land.
[*SEE info in HENNINGER GEN elsewhere I book.]*

THE KOPPENHEFFER/ KOPPENHAVER ETC FAMILY

The earliest found ancestor of the **KOPPENHEFFER** family is Thomas Koppenheffer, born c1708 in Wurttemberg, Germany, and came to Philadelphia on September 11, 1728 with his wife Anna Maria Zinn. They settled first in Berks County.
MICHAEL KOPPENHEFFER (1733 – Nov 5, 1823), a son of Thomas and Anna Maria Koppenheffer was born in Lancaster Co. He belonged to the militia during the Revolutionary War, and was a farmer in Bethel

Twp, Berks County until 1801 when he purchased a farm in Mifflin Twp., Dau Co. Michael m Maria Eva
_____, and they had seven children born in Berks Co, all of whom settled in Lykens Valley.
*MARTINUS (Mar 7, 1760 – Jan 18, 1825, bur Coleman' s Church), m May 2, 1786 Susanna Artz.
Martinus and Susanna (Artz) Koppenheffer children:
**Elizabeth (Sep 6, 1787 – Jun 2, 1826, bur Hoffman Cem), m Sep 20, 1812 Jacob Moyer [see Moyer
genealogy]
**Michael (1788–1839), m Susanna Coleman b Sep1793. **Michael & Susanna (Coleman) Koppenheffer
children:**Catharine m James Porter;***Henry;***Daniel;***Samuel;***Angeline m Martin
Schrecongost ***George; ***Susanna m Isreal Himes.
**Catharine (no dates) m Jacob Hoffman Jr. [see HOFFMAN genealogy]
**Jacob (May 14, 1795 – Oct 25, 1865), m Anna Maria Rehbock (Oct 20, 1794 – Mar 23, 1866). **Jacob
and Anna Maria (Rehbock) Koppenheffer children:** ***Jacob; ***Phillip; ***Lydia; ***Daniel.
**John H. b Jul 19, 1797, m Elisabeth Wolf b 1799. **John H. and Elisabeth (Wolf) Koppenheffer
children:** ***Simon b c1819; ***Catharine; ***Mary; ***Martin; ***Sarah; ***John; ***Christina.
**Susanna b Aug 17, 1799
**Frederick (Dec 27, 1803 – Jun 26, 1875), m Susanna Harner (Oct 5, 1805 – Oct 8, 1881), moved to
Schuylkill Co. **Frederick and Susanna (Harner) Koppenheffer children:**Catharine m 1st George
Maurer, 2nd George W. bard;***George moved to Cedar Co, Iowa;***Martin, lived in Sch Co;***Mary m
Solomon R. Enterline; ***Thomas J:***Elizabeth m Jacob H. Zimmerman;***Sarah m John M Coleman;
*** Henry ***Susanna; ***David.

*MARIA ELISABETH b May 1, 1763, m Dec 21, 1782 William Bordner (1757 – Jan 8, 1827), a son of
Jacob and Sarah (Balt) Bordner. [see Bordner genealogy]
*JOHANNES b Aug 2 8, 1765 Berks Co – Apr 6, 1854, bur St. John's Hill Cem), m Jun 2, 1789 Anna
Maria Margaretta Zerbe (Jun 7, 1766 – May 19, 1851). They lived in Mifflin Twp in 1850 . Son John age
50 and Harriet Harner age 17, lived with them. **Johannes and Anna Maria (Zerbe) Koppenheffer
children:** **Thomas b Sep 18, 1791, Bethel Twp, - Apr 20, 1826 bur Hoffman Cem), m 1814 Mary
Magdalena Hoffman (Jul 23, 1791 – Sep 23, 1857, bur Luth & Ref Cem, Bbg); **Thomas and Mary Magd
(Hoffman) Koppenheffer children:** ***Jonathan lived in Campbelltown; ***John; ***Sarah (1820-1841),
m Frederick W. Evitts (1819-1899);***Anna Maria; ***Elizabeth (1825-1905),m Frederick W. Evitts, after
her sister died.**Maria Elizabeth b Nov 4, 1793 m John Enterline (Apr 28, 1788 – Oct 5, 1849), a son of
John Michael & Maria Elizabeth (Snoke) Enterline [See Enterline genealogy]; **Michael (Jan 3 0, 1797) -
Dec 18, 1889 bur St. Johns Hill Cem), m Anna Maria Bordner (Sep 6, 1793 – Jul 9, 1868, bur Bowerman
Cem, Enterline), a dau of Peter and Catharine (Datterman) Bordner. He was a farmer and weaver [See
Bordner genealogy];**Maria Catharine b Apr 10, 1798, m Daniel Schwab, a son of John Jacob and Mary
(Hetzel) Schwab, and moved to Tuscarawas Co., Ohio;**Johannes (Feb 20, 1800 – Nov 13, 1850, bur St.
John's Hill Cem); **Heinrich F (Aug 20, 1805 – Apr 19, 1870), bur Loysville, Perry Co), m Dec 25, 1825
Esther Daniel (Sep 2, 1806 – Feb 22, 1864). **Heinrich and Esther (Daniel) Koppenheffer children:**
Andrew D;Emanuel D (1830 – 1851);***Catharine;***William D;***Edmund D; ***Henry D;
Solomon D; ***Sarah A; ***Anna Jane;Persidia; ***Elizabeth; ***Percival D.; **Jonathan E.(Jan
18, 1808- Nov 2, 1878, bur St. John's Hill Cem), m 1827 to Julianna Swineford (Jun 26, 1806 – Apr 3,
1884). **Jonathon E. and Julianna (Swineford) Koppenheffer children (most family members bur St.
John's Hill Cem):** Harriet b Oct 13, 1828, m Daniel W. Leffler (Nov 18, 1827 – Feb 7, 1908, bur Hoover
Cem), son of Benjamin & Catherine Leffler, had a son: Erastey Hitchcock b May 17, 1851;Edward E. (Jan
22, 1830 – Oct 15, 1907), m on May 1,1859 Hannah Romberger (1834– Aug 7, 1911); Elisabeth b Mar 10,
1832; Persidia (Jan 25, 1834 –Aug 1, 1857) ; Sophia b c1835, m John H. Feather, moved to Mich. ; John
Henry (Jun 21, 1838- Sep 14, 1900), m 1st Nov 22, 1860 Lydia Moyer (Jun 21, 1868– Jan 28,1868), dau of
Daniel & Lucetta Moyer. Married 2nd before 1870,Catharine Zerfing. In 1870 John lived in Wash Twp, had
Mary age 10, Ida and Kate Zerfing with him; William S. (Mar 25, 1841 – Apr 23, 1926), m 2nd Susannah
Rogers (1844 – 1931), children: Persida Condidus b Oct 30, 1870; Oscar Elwood b Nov 3, 1872; Julia Eliz
b May 25, 1876;Wilson b Jan 11, 1879; Benjamin F. (May 12,1844 – Jun 2,1894, died of heart failure), m
Nov 13, 1869 Melissa J. Gilger; Rebecca b Aug 25, 1844; Daniel B.b Jul 30, 1846, m Sarah Jane Sheaffer;
Mary Jane b Mar 29, 1 847, m; Emaline b Nov 16, 1849; Frederick Lafayette(Dec 7,1850– Jun 10, 1930,
bur St.John's Hill Cem), m Sarah Kathryn Swab (Dec 14,1851- Dec 24, 1927), a dau of Daniel & Sarah

(Heller) Swab. **Frederick L and Sarah K (Swab) Koppenheffer children**: ***Jonathan Daniel (Mar 24, 1876 - Feb 6, 1955), m Mary R. Witmer (Mar 26, 1879 - Aug 8, 1915), **their children**: Verna m Ben Hossler; Marion m John Miller; Sarah; ***Sallie Emelia (1878-1950), m Elmer E. Dockey of Pillow; Annie Sophia (1881-1963), m John O. Diebler; Rena (1885 - 1960), m Jesse Sheetz); Estella; ***George W. (1887 -1963), m Maggie M. Erdman. **George & Maggie (Erdman) Koppenheffer children**: *Myron* m Grace Miller; *Rhea* m Mark Philips; *Nevin* m Grace Teats; *Carol* m Woodrow Kennedy; *Roger* (1923-2000),*Lucille* m Lester Witmer. ***Edward Elwood (1889 - 1965), m Esther Mae Romberger b May 20, 1891, a dau of John E. and Sarah (Lehman) Romberger of Mifflin Twp. **Edward & Esther (Romberger) Koppenheffer children**: *Frieda* b Aug 21, 1912; *Talma* b Oct 19, 1914, m John E. Novinger; *Winifred* b Apr 15, 1916, m Merle Romberger b Feb 2, 1916.

***MARIA CATHARINE** b Nov 17, 1767 , m George Bonawitz (Mar 22, 1774 - Sep 18, 1854, bur Peace CEm, Bbg. He was a tailor and farmer near Berrysburg. [More information in Bonawitz genealogy page 209]

***MICHAEL** (Sep 5, 1772 - Mar 7, 1844, bur St. John's Hill Cem), m Catharine Garrett b c1774, a dau of George Garret, lived in Mifflin Twp. In 1850, Catherine lived with her son Benjamin & family. **Michael and Catharine (Garrett) Koppenheffer children**: **Michael b c1798, m Maria Elisabeth Schaffner, moved to Stark Co. Ohio. Michael m 2nd Elisabeth Sauer.

****Benjamin** (Feb 22, 1801 twin- Apr 10, 1871, bur St. Luke's Cem Malta, Northld Co), m Johanna Radel (Sep 27, 1797 - Sep 19, 1860, bur St. Johns Hill Cem), a dau of John and Susan (Schroyer) Radel. Benjamin m 2nd Sarah Miller (Sep 14,1823 - Jan 12, 1878). **Benjamin & Johanna (Radel) Koppenheffer children**: *** Catharine b Feb 22, 1822; ***Mary Ann (Jan 1,1824 - 1847); ***Denah (Sep 11, 1825 - Nov 21,1899), m John Lehman; ***Joel b Mar 30, 1827, m Jujn 12, 1859, Mary Ann Herman; ***Benneville m Susanna Witmer; ***David b c1833, m on Feb 14, 1858, Catharine Ann Kemmerer; ***Sarah b c1834, m John N. Miller;***John Henry b c1836, m Mar 29, 1856 Sarah Kebach; ***Jonathan (Nov 12, 1837 - Sep 12, 1860)

****Jonathan Mark** (Oct 13, 1802 - Jul 3, 1891), m Catharine Hepner (Feb24, 1809 - Apr 18, 1885), a dau of George and Eva (Weiser) Hepner. **Jonathan Mark & Catharine (Hepner) Koppenheffer children**: Emanuel b c1827, a plasterer; Moses (Jul 25, 1831 - Jan 25, 1904, bur Rife Cem), m Elizabeth Ritzman (1839 - 1921); Sarah b c1833; George b c1835; John b c1837; Elizabeth b c1840; Catherine b c1842; Rebecca b c1844; Mary Jane b c1846; Emaline b 1850.

****Johannes** (b Dec 21, 1803, m Sarah Elisabeth _____, d at least by 1849 in New York State.

****Thomas** (Aug 1, 1806 - 1849, d in Jackson Twp, Northld Co., bur Bbg), m Barbara Bitterman (Jun 14, 1816 - Jun 1, 1877). Barbara later m William Snodgrass.

****Catharine** b Nov 25, 1810, m Michael Bordner,son of William & Maria Elisabeth (Koppenheffer) Bordner

****Daniel** (Jul 18, 1814 - Sep 19, 1873, bur Rife Cem), m Veronica Bordner (Sep 10, 1817 - Jul 3, 1895), a dau of Peter and Margaret (Novinger) Bordner. [See Bordner genealogy.]

****Henry C.** (1815 - 1855), m Elizabeth ___ (1825 - 1856, bur St. John's Hill Cem). Henry was a weaver. **Henry C. and Elizabeth Koppenheffer children**: ***Emma Jane b c1847, m Jacob Keagy; ***Sarah A ; ***Preston W b 1850; ***Charles W; ***Mary Elizabeth.

****Sarah** b Mar 17, 1817, m Asa, Potteiger, a son of Peter and Margaretta (Hopple) Potteiger. They lived in Williamstown. **Adam and Sarah (Koppenheffer) Potteiger children**: ***Elizabeth; ***Peter m Mary (Klinger) Shade; ***Louise m ___ Wagner; ***John m Mary E ___ ; ***Leah Jane; ***Zacherius; ***Elias; ***Sarah; ***Francis, m Elizabeth Catherine Shoop.;

****Elizabeth** b Jun 20, 1818, m Elijah F. Brua, lived in Mifflin Twp., **had a dau** ***Leah b c1843.

****George** (Dec 21,1821–Apr17, 1852 bur Hbg Cem), m sisters, 1st Elizabeth Enterline (May 16,1819–May 5, 1845 bur St. John's Hill Cem). m 2nd Sarah Enterline (Feb 3, 1823 - Jan 29, 1865, bur Speeceville Cem), dau's of W. & Mary Enterline. George Koppenheffer was Register of Dauphin Co Wills at time of his death. [See Enterline Gen]

***FREDERICK** (Jun 24, 1776 - Nov 7, 1858, bur St. John's Hill Cem), m Maria Elizabeth Gross (Dec 28, 1783 - Jan 10, 1854). The lived in Wash. Twp on a farm he purchased in 1806. **Frederick and Maria Elizabeth (Gross) Koppenheffer children**: **Anna Maria (Dec 22, 1802 - Jan 17, 1854, bur St. John's Bbg), m 1st Johannes Schmidt (Sep 16, 1797 - Feb 22, 1833), m 2nd John Lebo, **had these children**: ***Christianna m George Bechtel; ***Simon m Anna Mary Michael; ***Enoch m Susanna;. **Elizabeth (Feb 21, 1805 - Apr 2, 1874, bur Bbg), m Jonathan Holtzman (Oct 1, 1808 - Jul 21, 1881). Had a farm in

Mifflin & Lykens Twp. **Jonathan and Elizabeth (Koppenheffer) Holtzman children:** ***Mary m Isaac App; ***Jonathan B; ***Edward; ***David K., m 1st Mary Mattis, m 2nd Margaret Neagley; ***Elizabeth, m Wm Straub; ***Jonathan m Elizabeth Weaver. **Simon b Dec 24, 1810 - Dec 16, 1856, bur St. John's Hill Cem), m Leah Enterline (Apr 4, 1817 - Feb 25, 1849), a dau of John Paul and Anna Mary Enterline. They had a farm in Mifflin Twp. **Simon and Leah (Engerline) Koppenheffer children:** ***Mary; ***Daniel S (May 20, 1837 - Sep 2, 1867), m Jul 22, 1858 Sarah Lenker (May 19, 1839 - Dec 27, 1867); ***Elizabeth; Emmanuel; ***Leah. **Eva (Apr 11, 1813 - Dec 30, 1893, bir Bbg), m Gotleib Esterhelt, of Berrysburg. **Gotleib and Eva (Koppenheffer) Esterhelt children:**** Emanuel b 1844; ***Amelia b 1846; ***Isaac b 1848.**Susannah (Apr 3, 1819 - Nov 3, 1889, bur Bbg), m Adam Fawver (Feb 4, 1815 - Oct 1, 1895), son of Johannes & Magdalena (Ruby) Fawver. They had a farm in Wash. Twp. **Adam and Susannah (Koppenheffer) Fawver children:** ***Leah m John Keiter;***John F.; ***Sarah Elizabeth, m Adam Wert; ***Margaret m Geo Brenneman; ***Tillie m Wm McGinnis; ***Mary m 1st Frederick Harman, m 2nd John Isaac Paul;***Rebecca m 1st __ Fichinger, m 2nd ___ Hoy; ***Emma m Adam Lyme. *EVE CHRISTINA (Oct 21, 1778 - Mar 27, 1812, bur Hoffman Cem), m Jacob Moyer (Feb 22, 1774 - Feb 6, 1859). They lived on a farm in Lykens Twp. [See Moyer genealogy].

PETER SCHOFFSTALL (42 acres – 1875 MAP)

This land was from the John Umholtz, Jr. tract, which was partly in Mifflin and Lykens Twp. On March 3, 1852, John Umholtz Jr and his wife Mary sold 15 acres 95 perches to Daniel Lebo. On March 23, 1861 Lebo sold 25 acres 146 perches of land to Jacob Hoffman of Northld Co. Jacob and Eva Elizabeth Hoffman sold the same to Daniel and Sarah Lebo. On Apr 19, 1866 Daniel Lebo and Sarah of Wiconisco Twp conveyed both tracts (total of 41 ac 81 p) to Peter Schoffstall of Wash Twp. He assigned the land to his sons William and Amos Schoffstall The adjoining land was owned by John Umholtz estate, Isaac Romberger, Jonathan E. Koppenheffer, and Elias and George Williard. The Schoffstall's owned the land until April 2, 1900 when they sold toA. Frank Miller. James Enders became the next owner. The old house exists, but is not in good condition.

[PETER SCHOFFSTALL (1807 – 1879), m Mary Ann ____(1808 – 1875). **Peter & Mary had these children:**
AMOS b Dec 1835. In 1880 he lived in Washington Twp and his brother William age 35 and Catherine Schoffstall age 38 (her relation unknown) was living in the household.
EMALINE ELISABETH b c1834, m Aug 22, 1858 Emanuel Williard
FREDERICK b Jun 1838 – d 1920, bur Peace Cem), m Rebecca Hoke (1842 - 1874), m 2nd Mary Ellen Botts (Jun 13, 1852 – Apr 28, 1918), a dau of George W. Botts. Ellen was with Frederick in 1880 and they were living near Berrysburg. **Frederick and Rebecca (Hoke) Schoffstall had two known children:**Mary Elizabeth (b Aug 2, 1868 Wash Twp – d Jan 22, 1921, bur Maple Grove Cem, E'ville), m Jan 1, 1891 by Rev. Derr to George Wm Botts (1865 – 1933).They lived south west of Berrysburg. **George Wm and Mary Elizabeth (Schoffstall) Botts children:** Fred; Russell; Morgan; John; Mildred; Charles W. (1870–1951, bur Peace Cem, Bbg), m Jul 6, 1902 Mary Snyder (1853 – 1930). MARY ANN b c1839; WILLIAM b c1840 m Sarah (Mar 12,1841 – Jul 4, 1876, bur Peace Cem); LYDIA ANN b c1842; ISAAC (Jul 30, 1848 – Sep 16, 1865, bur St. Johns Hill Cem)] (More Schoffstall Genealogy elsewhere in the book).

[ABRAHAM MILLER (Dec 4, 1799 - Feb 1, 1867, bur St. Johns Hill Cem), m 1st Maria Matter, 2nd Anna Bitterman (b __ d Oct 321, 1889). **Abraham Miller had these children:**
DANIEL (Aug 30,1826 –Aug 1 7, 1892, bur St. Johns Hill Cem), m Elizabeth Herb (Dec 12, 1829 – Jul 5, 1899). They lived in on a farm Mifflin Twp in 1860 and 1870. **Daniel and Elizabeth (Herb) Miller children:** Amanda b c1852; Sarah Catharine b Mar 27, 1855 ; John b c1857; Caroline b 1860; Samuel b c1862; A. Frank (1863 - 1926), bur St. Johns Hill Ch),Sarah ____ (1863 - 1950); Perry b c 1866' Willington b c1869. (See also Abraham Miller genealogy p185].

B. WEAVER   2 1/2 ACRE TRACT & 11 ACRE TRACT
J. SCHOFFSTALL 11 ACRE TRACT (both on 1875 map)

John Umholtz owned a large tract of land. After he died, his heirs sold this part to John B. Umholtz on September 10, 1859. John Tobias was the next owner but sold in 1865 to Daniel Schomper. Two years later he sold the house and land to Elias and Elizabeth Hepler of Eldred Twp., Schuylkill Co on May 22, 1867. The property in Washington Twp was sold again in 1869 to Benjamin Weaver of Dauphin County.

On April 4, 1910, after Elizabeth, widow of Benjamin Weaver died the heirs sold the house and 2 1/2 acres to Frederick Schoffstall. Bound by James Enders estate (late Jacob Holtzman), south, to land earlier owned by Daniel Lebo, south to other land of Frederick Schoffstall (was owned by Peter Herman), north to Isaac Bonawitz land (late Elias Williard land). Frederick Schoffstall moved to Elizabethville, and on December 13, 1919, he sold this property along with another 11 acres to J. S. Lahr of Pillow. Frederick Schoffstall had purchased the 11 acre tract from a Sheriff sale on April 4, 1878. The 11 acres were bound on the north by land of John A. Weaver (late Jacob Snyder), east by William Henninger (late Jonathan Koppenheffer), south by A. Klinger, north by Nathan Snyder, west by J. A. Harman (now Frederick Kocher). J. S. Lahr conveyed the land on April 2, 1928 to Clarence J. and Amelia Wolfe. Amelia died May 27, 1959 and Clarence died Nov 1, 1966. The land was given to Jay and Joyce Wolfe October 19, 1964 with the two story frame house, the present owners.

[BENJAMIN WEAVER (Apr 19,1830 – Apr 21, 1897, bur Hoffman Cem), a son of Jacob and Catharine (Romberger) Weaver, of Mifflin Twp, m Elisabeth Bordner (Apr 8, 1836 - Feb 18, 1910, bur St. John;s Cem, Berrysburg). In 1860, Benjamin and Elizabeth Weaver lived in Mifflin Twp., with no children. In 1870 and 1880, they lived in Washington Twp, and he was a laborer. **Benjamin and Elizabeth (Bordner) Weaver had these children (some bapt Union Salem, Berrysburg); Sarah Ellen** b Mar 3, 1861; **Adam** (Jun 7,1864 – 1925, bur Hoffman Cem), m Sarah ____ (1853 – 1896). He m 2nd Jan 23, 1897 by Rev. Stouffer to Lydia A. Groff of Washington Twp.; **Mary Catherine** b May 10,1867, m Frank Bellon, lived in Lykens Township; **Jonas** (Aug 16, 1869 – 1869);**John Henry** b May 22, 1879, m Lydia _____.]

HOME OF LEE I AND JEAN HENNINGER
(Was ISAAC ROMBERGER LAND -70 acres 1875)

This land was part of two original tracts of land that were granted by Commonwealth of Pa. to William Row in 1814 and 1815. William Row conveyed part of the land to George Matter, a cooper and blacksmith. Another earlier original tract of 214 acres was warranted to Henry Stump in 1791, and patented in 1794 to William Frantz. In 1804 by his will, William Frantz gave 164 acres to his sons Henry, a weaver, and Jacob, a farmer. The land was transferred several times to family members Jacob & Catherine Werner, Jacob Frantz and John Hoffman, then in 1824 to George Matter, a cooper and blacksmith. In 1838, George Matter and the heirs of Jacob Frantz sold 72 acres 93 ¾ perches of land to John and Elizabeth Snyder, and on April 1, 1846 they sold to Isaac Henninger. Isaac and Catherine Henninger sold the land (two tracts 44 acres 87 ¾ perches and 28 acres 6 perches) to Leonard and Lydia Snyder in 1851.

In 1854, the two tracts parted company when Leonard and Lydia Sndyer sold the wester section of the land (the 44 acres) with a two-story log house and log bank barn to Isaac Romberger. The neighbors were George Lebo, north, John Umholtz, John Hoffman, heirs of Thomas Koppenheffer and Isaac Miller.

The remaining 28 acres were traded several times again by various conveyances. They were owned by Thomas Koppenheffer, his son Jonathan E. Koppenheffer, and then sold April 1853 to Isaac Miller. Isaac and his wife Elizabeth sold to Isaac Romberger in 1859, bringing both tracts back to the same owner. Isaac Romberger and his family lived here for many years, but eventually moved to Mifflin Twp., and on March 30, 1903 sold to their son Philip Romberger. Many years later Philip Romberger by then a widower, moved to Berrysburg and on October 1942 sold the property to Charles E. and Clara Henninger.

On June 12, 1970, after Charles E. Henninger died, his widow Clara E. Henninger conveyed the most of the 72 acres to her son Lee I. Henninger. A smaller lot on the farm had been sold to her daughter and husband Margaret and Charles Leer in 1951 for a home.

ISAAC ROMBERGER FAMILY

[*ISAAC ROMBERGER* (b Jun 26, 1821 – d Sep 26, 1912, bur Hoffman Cem), a son of Adam and Catharina (Paul) Romberger, m Lydia Michael (b Dec 14, 1827 – d Jun 17, 1870), a dau of _____. Isaac and Lydia lived in Mifflin Twp in 1850, and had George R. Shitz age 19, labr with them.
Isaac and Lydia (Michael) Romberger children:
REBECCA b Jun 17, 1846 – d Oct 23, 1941, bur Pomfret Man. Cem., Sunbury), m John J. Batman;
SARAH (Apr 24, 1850 – Sep 7, 1866, bur Hoffman Cem); **MARY JANE** (1852 – 1928), m Nov 13, 1875, Henry W. Henninger (1846 -   ). *Henry and Mary Jane (Romberger) Henninger children (some bapt E.C church Berrysburg)*: Mary E. b c1880; John Isaac b May 29, 1896;
PHILIP (b1854 – d May 29, 1947, Berrysburg, bur Hoffman Cem), m Leah J. Matter (Aug 19, 1856 – Nov 12, 1923). Philip lived in Lykens Twp in 1880, and had H. Schoffstall age 17, a servant, and M. A. Hassinger age 14, servant with them. In 1920 Philip and Leah had these people in their household: Homer P. age 23, Annie I age 20 maid on home farm, Carrie age 3. *Philip and Leah J (Matter) Romberger children*: Sada Ellen b Mar 27,1876, m William H. Howard ; Elisabeth Alverta (Jul 3, 1878 – May 12, 1961, bur Hoffman Cem), m John H. Lower (1877 – 1941); Lydia A (Aug 29, 1880 – Jun 27, 1959, bur Hoffman Cem), m William H. Bonawitz (1879 – 1964); Charles Isaac (Dec 9,1881 - ___, bur Hoffman Cem), m Minerva Latsha (Sep 12, 1879 – Aug 12,1921), a dau of Samuel and Anna (Haines) Latsha; Harry Richard (Feb 7, 1885 – 1951, bur Maple Grove Cem, E'ville; Daniel Clarence (Nov 4, 1890 - ___), bur Maple Grove Cem)), m Della May Enders b Dec 19, 1888; Homer Philip bapt Jun 7, 1896 – d Jul 8, 1916), m Jul 8, 1916 Anna I. Lyter;
EMALINE (1856 – 1857, bur Hoffman Cem); **ADALINE ELISABETH** b Aug 19, 1858, m Frank Beisel, 2nd Harvey A. Lehman. In 1880, Frank and Adaline lived in L. T. and had dau Katie M age 1 (Katie m Sep 8, 1900 James Troutman), and Harry Hepner 16, servant with them. They lived next to Joseph Lebo.
LYDIA ANN (Feb 1861 – 1946, bur Pillow), m Daniel E. Snyder (Dec 3, 1859 – Sep 15, 1924, bur St. John's Hill Cem), a son of Samuel & Catherine (Schwab) Snyder. *Daniel and Lydia Ann (Romberger) Snyder had six children*: John Nathan (Apr 19, 1882- Apr 25, 1968, Wmstown); Mabel Edna b Jan 5, 1884; Sarah Catherine b Jan 2, 1886, m Robert H. Wessner; Samuel Isaac (Jan 30, 1888 – 1971); Harry Paul b Jan 25, 1891; Charles E. Dec 1892, m Verna Hornberger. Daniel eventually left Lydia and her children. She moved to Pillow where she opened a millinery shop, her only support to raise her children.
HENRIETTA (Sep 26, 1863 – Jan 14, 1919, d of the flu), m Oct 25, 1885, Isaac Henninger (May 16, 1862 – Jun 28, 1943), a son of Sebastian and Christianna (Deibler) Henninger.

JOHN ELMER (Aug 2, 1867 – Apr 8, 1926, Hoffman Ch record), m Sarah E. Lehman (Oct 19, 1859 – Nov 6, 1931), a dau of John and Dena (Koppenheffer) Lehman. **John Elmer and Sarah E. (Lehman) Romberger children:*****Esther May** b May 20, 1891, m Edward Koppenheffer; ***William Allen (1892 – 1965), m Mabel Deibler;*** **Mary Ellen** b Oct 14, 1897, m George Finkbone (1893 – 1954); *** **Roy John** b 1904 m _____ Schell.

 After his first wife died Isaac Romberger m _____ (b ____ d c1901).

Isaac Romberger

Lydia Ann (Romberger) Snyder and her 6 children
She operated a millinery shop in Pillow to support her
children as they were growing up, after her husband
left her.

Lydia Michael Romberger

Isaac and Lydia (Michael) Romberger Family (Photo pre 1894) l to r: row 1 – Isaac & Henrietta (Romberger) Henninger; James & Rebecca (Romberger) Bateman. row 2 – Frank and Adaline (Romberger) Beisel; Isaac Romberger (father); Lydia (Michael) Romberger (mother); Lydia Romberger) Snyder; row 3 - Henry & Mary Jane (Romberger) Henninger; Philip & Leah (Matter) Romberger; John Elmer and Sarah (Lehman) Romberger.

THE FRANTZ FAMILY

Not much has been learned about the **FRANTZ** family. They probably settled first in Berks County, but moved to the Lykens Valley before 1800. They may have stayed only a brief time.

WILLIAN FRANTZ (c1750 – 1804/5 – will dated Jul 28, 1804 probated Feb 11, 1805), m Margaret
_____. He Came to Upper Paxton Twp. and was recorded on the 1798 window tax as being next to Jacob Herman, having a 45 x 20 foot wood barn, on 108 acres of land. **William and Margaret Frantz children:**

CATHARINE b ___ bapt Feb 27, 1774, Bern Ch –), m Jacob Werner. **Jacob & Catharine (Frantz) Werner children (some bapt Hoffman & St. John's Hill Ch); Magdalena** b Feb 5, 1801; **Jacob** b Apr 23, 1804; George b Mar 30, 1806; **Kasper** b Oct 5, 1808; **Anna Maria** b Oct 6, 1809; **Catharine** b Sep 24, 1811; **Susanna** b May 4, 1814; **Daniel** b Jun 3, 1817; **Elizabeth** b Aug 24, 1815.

ADAM (c1785 – after 1824) m Oct 6, 1811 Susanna Giesman (Nov 10, 1788 Tulpehocken Twp., Berks Co – Feb 15, 1827 Mifflin Twp), a dau of John Wilhelm Giesman. **Adam and Susanna (Giesman) Frantz had these children (bapt Hoffman, St. Johns "Hill" and Davids Ref ch):** William b Oct 23, 1812; Jacob b Feb 23, 1814; Christina b Jan 26, 1818; Susannah b Mar 23, 1819 – d Jul 31, 1861 of a hernia, bur St. John's Hill Cem), m Daniel Row (Jul 10, 1813 – Jul 31, 1871 of Brights disease), a son of William & Barbara (Rudy) Row;. **Daniel and Susannah (Frantz) Row children (bapt St. Johns Hill Ch):** Emilie b Jun 9, 1854; Leah Jane b May 16, 1857; Adeline b Jan 2, 1860; Sara b Jun 21, 1824
JACOB (d Jul 1830 will), m Susanna Hoffman (b ___ d 1813), a dau of John Hoffman Sr. Jacob was assessed for land in Lykens Twp as early as 1817 and continued to his death in 1830. Jacob named his brother-in-law John N. Specht as his executor. "Nothing to be sold until mother dies, then divide among

brothers & sisters. **Jacob and Susanna (Hoffman) Frantz had these children (some bap Bern Ch. Berks Co:**_____ - b ____ bapt Oct 16, 1774; William b__ bapt Aug 31, 1777 ; Conrad b ___ bapt Apr 15, 1781.
MARIA (   ) m Christopher ·Beystel
HENRY (   ), m Magdalena _____ (   ). They lived in Lykens twp in 1820. In 1825, Henry and Magdalena Frantz were listed in Lykens Twp., as having these "poor" children whose school tuition was paid by the county: Anna Mary age 11, Elizabeth age 8, Jacob 10, Lydia 7. In 1828 he was a weaver, and a tenant Jacob Frantz property. **Henry and Magdalena (   )Frantz had these children (bapt Hoffman and St. John's "Hill" Ch)**: Hannah b Nov 9, 1808; Daniel b Oct 9, 1810; Anna Maria b Sep 1812; Jacob b Mar 17, 1814; Elizabeth b Sep 7, 1815; Sara b Apr 5, 1820; Margaretha b Apr 24, 1822.
WILLIAM; ELIZABETH (   ), m William Young, she was a widow when her father died; SARA not mentioned in her fathers will; **JOHN; ISAAC; DANIEL** (   ), m Catharine _____ (   ). In 1834, Daniel was living as a tenant on the property of Widow Hoffman.**Daniel and Catharine Frantz had these children**: Benjamin b Sep 12, 1833; Uriah Nov 2, 1834, m Sarah Witmer (May 9, 1837 –Jul 25, 1880), a dau of Jacob & Sarah (Hepner) Witmer of Northld Co, eventually moved to Snyder Co.]

KEITH AND HELEN MASSER FARM
AMOS BUFFINGTON 76 Acres (1875 map)
(Buildings Recently Destroyed c2005)

This land was a westerly part of the original grant of 607 ½ acres of land that Commonwealth of Pennsylvania warranted to Leonard Miller August 21, 1751.. By sundry conveyances, Andrew Riegel, Sr., a Revolutionary War soldier, received 3ll acres of this tract in 1791, and he and his wife Catherine resided on this plantation until his death. They had a sawmill tract that bordered Big Wiconisco Creek. Their neighbors were Peter Schoffstall, Frederick Lubold, the Hoffman's, Isaac Ferree and John and Magdalena Bressler. After Andrew Riegel died, an inquest was held at his home on May 23, 1815, and the land was divided into three separate tracts.

Photo Taken In 1998 – Buildings Destroyed about 2005

In December 1819, Magdalena Riegel, daughter of Andrew Riegel, received this 42 acre part of the above land, containing a cabin and access to waterways. At the time Magdalena was married to John Bressler, but he died in 1822, and for several years Michael McCurty was a tenant on the property. Magdalena remarried about 1827 to Mathias Hawk, but continued to be assessed for this property as Magdalena Bressler until 1834, and had Abraham Bressler as a tenant. After Mathias Hawk died in 1831, Magdalena married John Bitterman. In 1843, Magdalena had her son-in-law Daniel Keen, a blacksmith living on the property. By 1849, John Bitterman had died and Daniel Stine was a tenant living on the 40 acres with two-story log house and bank barn and kitchen.

About 1858, Magdalena Bitterman sold about 35 acres of this farm to Joel and Caroline Daniel and moved to Lykens. She died there in 1868. By her will gave to these children: Nicholas Bressler $75, Amanda Bitterman now single $60, Catharine Mayer $20, ("to make even"), and then divide balance into seven equal shares. John Bressler to get $20, and Susanna Guyer's share to be divided between her and her three children. Her son George Hawk was to pay $200 for the lot next to the one he owned, and the money divided among her children. Magdalena appointed her son William Hawk to settle her estate "without extra ordinary expense and abstaining from giving to laws (lawyers ?)"

In April 1875, Joel and Caroline Daniel sold this farm to Amos Buffington, who had purchased a 34 acre tract from John Daniel in April 1863. On March 24, 1888, Samuel Wolfe became the owner, and years later in 1901, Samuel Wolfe conveyed to Elmer and Mary Wolfe. In May 1924 Henry E. and Mabel Lahr became owners and they sold to Paul H. and Florence E. Bush in April 1950. The heirs of Paul Bush sold to Helen and Keith E. Masser in 2003.

THE MAGDALENA RIEGEL FAMILY

[MAGDALENA RIEGEL (Jun 24, 1793 – Mar 24, 1868, bur IOOF Cem, Lykens), a dau of Andreas & Anna Catherine (Hoffman) Riegel, m 1st John Bressler (Aug 30, 1788 –1822/1823, bur Hoffman Cem), a son of Nicholas & Magdalena (Stoner) Bressler. **John & Magdalena (Riegel) Bressler children (some bapt Hoffman Ch):**
*Mary Ann Bressler b c1808
*Susanna Bressler b Aug 3, 1813, m Hugh Betterman (b ___- Jun 1841), possibly bur St. John's Hill Cem), a son of John & Catherine (Lark) Bitterman. **Hugh & Susanna (Bressler) Bitterman children:**
Amanda b c1836 lived with her mother & step-father in 1850 in Wiconisco Twp; Cyrus (Apr 21, 1837 – Jun 5, 1926), m Louisa McCoy (1840 –1892). [more info in Bitterman genealogy.]
Catherine Ann (no dates) m ___ Moyer, moved to Kansas. After Hugh died, Susanna m John Frederick Guyer (May 25, 1820 Ger –d 1884), Albany, Kansas). He was a stone mason. **John Frederick & Susanna (Bressler, Bitterman) Guyer children: William Warren** (1846 – 1864); **Louisa** b c1849 m ___ Dreibelbis, moved to Kansas; **Joseph Henry** (no dates).
*Magdalena Bressler (Feb 2,1818- Jul 15, 1894, bur Calvary Meth Cem, Wic), m Capt Daniel Keen (Feb 26, 1816- Dec 185_), a son of Henry & Anna Keen. **Daniel & Magdalena (Bressler) Keen children:** John H. (1840 –1919, bur Calvary Cem), m Anna Mary Mace (1838 Bbg –1921), a dau of John Mace a weaver. **John H. & Anna Mary (Mace) Keen children: Clay** b 1860, a teacher in 1880 living at home; **Ambrose** b c1864; **Edward** b c1867; **Annie** b c1871; **George** b c1874; **Benjamin** b c1877; **Samuel** (Sep 18, 1844 – 1917, bur Calvary Meth Cem), m Miriam __(1848 –1932); **Edward; Mary Amanda** b Jun 6, 1849, bapt Hoffman Ch; **George W.**(Jul 14, 1850 – Sep 16, 1907, bur near parents); **Charles; Daniel N.** (Apr 20, 1853 – Sep 13, 1861, bur beside parents);
*Nicholas Bressler (Apr 7, 1820 – Jan 26, 1880, bur Hoffman Cem), teamster with Reuben Riegel family in1850. did not marry.
*John Bressler b Feb 21, 1823 m Catherine ___ b c1828. They lived in Wiconisco in 1850 & 1860 , Sarah Hoover age 12, Mary Ann Yeager 14, lived with them in 1850. **John & Cahterine Bressler children:** Amanda b c1844; Elizabeth b c1846; William (1849 – 1867); Catharine b c1850; George b c1853; Sarah b c1857.

After John Bressler Sr (b 1788) died, Magdalena married Matthias Haag//Hawk (May 7, 1771 – Apr 4, 1831, bur Hoffman Cem alone), a son of John George Hawk. Matthias Hawk had been married to Susanna Deibler (Jun 30, 1778 – Jul 2, 1824, bur Hoffman Cem).**Matthias & Magdalena (Riegel, Bitterman) Hawk children:**
*Susan Hawk (no dates) m ___ Bressler, **had these children:** Simon; Catherine; Hannah; G. H.; Matthias; Lavina; Sarah; several living in Michigan and some in Ohio.
*Catherine Hawk (no dates) m Andrew Smeltz of Lykens Twp.
*Hannah Hawk (no dates) m ___ Novinger
*Mary Hawk (no dates) m ____ Ritzman

*Elizabeth Hawk (no dates) m John Folk or Adam Folk

*George Hawk (Mar 18, 1830 – Jan 22, 1909, bur old Luth & Ref Cem, Lykens), m Sydney Nolan b Nov 16, 1834 a dau of Richard Nolan. In 1880 they lived in Lykens & he was a coal miner. George & Sydney (Nolan) Hawk children: Oscar L. (1857 – 1924, bur in old Luth & Ref Cem); Travis L (Mar 25, 1861 – Sep 26, 1931, bur Old L & Ref Cem), m Ida M. ___ (Aug 20, 1873 - Sep 17, 1916); Kate b c1867; George b c1877, from mothers will received "half-lot where he lives" [see also Richard Nolan gen].
*Wilhelm (Mar 9, 1828-Jan 21, 1905, bur Calvary Meth Cem), m Rebecca Laudenslager (1831 – Nov 29, 1912). They lived in Wiconisco Twp in 1880, he was a tailor. Wilhelm & Rebecca (Laudenslager) Hawk children: Orsula b c1858, a teacher with parents in 1880; William B b c1865; Anna b c1869.
*Elmira (Aug 15, 1831 - Aug 17, 1892), m Lemuel Row (Nov 30, 1828 - Dec 18, 1900, bur IOOF Cem), a son of Joel & Elizabeth Row, lived in Lykens in 1880. Lemuel & Elmira (Hawk) Row children: George C b c1859; W. H. b c1862; Charles b c1873.
After Mathias Hawk died, Magdalena m 3rd John Bitterman (Jul 7, 1786 – Aug 25, 1853), a son of Baltzer Bitterman. John Bitterman married 1st May 8, 1825 to Anna Deibler (Dec 20, 1795 Lanc – Mar 6, 1826, bur St John;s Hill Cem), a dau of Daniel & Anna Maria Deibler. (Her death and marriage records in Davids Ch, Killinger). (Anna Maria Deibler had been married first on Apr 9, 1820 to Jacob Schuman (Aug 31, 1794 – Nov 10, 1831), but for only 9 weeks. John & Anna (Deibler) Bitterman child: Daniel (Mar 7, 1821 – Jul 5, 1884, death recorded in St. Johns Lykens, bur IOOF Cem), m Mary _____. Magdalena & John Bitterman children: Amanda b c1834, lived with her sister Susanna's family in 1850. Mentioned in mother Magdalena's will in 1868 as "now single"; Catherine m ___ Moyer.]

THE AMOS BUFFINGTON FAMILY

[AMOS BUFFINGTON (1829 – 1882), a son of John E. and Susanna (Artz) Buffington m Louisa Scheib (b c1834 - d1880), a dau of Michael Scheib of Lykens Twp. Before she died in 1880, Louisa wrote a will in which she states that the note, which George Williard holds against her shall be paid out of her share coming to her from her father Michael Scheib. Her husband Amos shall use the remainder of the money to educate the children. In 1880 they lived in Lykens Township, and Ferdinand Enders, a grandson, age 1, lived with them. Amos and Louisa (Scheib) Buffington children: Charles William b May 21, 1855; Adam b May 7, 1858; Daniel Franklin b Aug 9, 1859; John E. b c1859; Elmira b Jan 14, 1861, m Levi Miller; Emma J. b c1863; Maryetta b Jul 29, 1864; George Lincoln b Jul 29, 1866; Sarah A. b 1870; Christian b Mar 20, 1870; Elias b Apr 21, 1872; Susan Malinda b Jun 21, 1874. [More Buffington info elsewhere in book.]

HOME OF RAY E. AND CAROLYN BARRY
ISAAC MILLER 15 acres (1875 map)

Isaac Miller had come to Lykens Township from the Lower Tulpehocken area of Berks County at least by 1840. He purchased two tracts of land on April 6, 1840 from John and Barbara Speck (12 acres149 perches & 17 acres). At that time he had three young boys and four young girls in the household. Isaac Miller sold the 12 acres on April 3, 1847 to Solomon Martz. He kept the 17 acres containing a two-story log house and log barn.

By 1858 Isaac Miller had accumulated 44 acres with a middling log house and log barn. By 1864 he sold all but 15 acres. By 1880 Isaac became a widower, and his daughters Rebecca and Caroline and grandson William H. Howard lived with him. Isaac Miller died before 1891. His daughter Caroline owned the property until her death in 1921.

During the early 1900's the highly contagious animal sickness "foot and mouth" disease broke out in this area. A number of cattle were stricken, and their carcasses were buried somewhere on this farm.

In 1920, Caroline Miller, age 73, had a boarder named Benjamin "Franky" Latsha age 73 living with her. Their dwelling was divided into a two-family house. William and Susan Koppenhaver had two rooms on the first floor and two on the second on the west side of the house. Each year Caroline planted a garden and her neighbor James Troutman usually plowed and harrowed for her. Florence and Irene Troutman (teenagers) planted their potatoes, and later they helped to harvest them. After Caroline died, her house became the property of her son William H. Howard. He had married Sadie Romberger daughter of Philip and Leah Romberger in 1895. During their early marriage, William and Sadie lived on the farm owned by St. John's Hill Church. He farmed and was the sexton of the church for twenty-seven years. He was also Superintendent of the Sunday school and served as tax collector and school board director in Mifflin Twp. After they received this property, William and Sadie tore down the old house and built a new one about 1932.

The Willliam Henry Howard Family Sitting On The Porch Of Their Old House
l to r: Charles; William (son); William (father); Faye; Isaac; Sadie (mother) Edward
A "New" House Replaced This Old Original Log House in 1932

William H. Howard died in 1950. Ownership of two separate tracts (17 and 5 acres) was transferred to his widow Sadie. It bordered the public road to the bridge, land of Charles Henninger, and the middle of Wiconisco Creek. The five acre tract had earlier belonged to the Samuel Wolfe mill property, and when it was sold was described as "beginning at the low water mark on the Wiconisco Creek, along line of Caroline Miller north to the land of late Catherine A. Wolfe, along north side of tract by William Howard, by creek to bridge" to give the privilege of digging a run on the straight line." An interesting notation on the deed of transfer of the 17 acres from William Howard to his widow Sadie states "number one (17 acres) has been held openly, notoriously and against the whole world for a period of more than 22 years by William H. Howard." Perhaps there was a problem with the border!

On June 15, 1956, the heirs of Sadie Howard conveyed the two tracts of land and buildings to Harlan O. and M. Virginia Martz. After several years, on February 28, 1970 Harlan Martz and wife conveyed to Ray E. & Carolyn Barry, the present owner.

THE ISAAC MILLER FAMILY

[ISAAC MILLER (b c1801 Low Tulpehocken Twp, Berks Co - Feb 28, 1883, burial unknown), m Eva Elizabeth ___ (b c1800 – d before 1880). **Isaac and Eva Elizabeth Miller children:** _____ dau b c1825; _____ son b c18__; ____ dau b c1830; *PERCIVAL (b Jul 5,1831 Berks Co – d Sep 9, 1855, bur St. Johns Hill Cem), probably the one age 17, a carpenter living with the Daniel Lebo family in 1850; *REBECCA (1833 – 1911, bur St. Johns Hill Cem). **Rebecca and Charles Howard had a son **William Henry Howard** (Jan 8, 1865 – Apr 16, 1950, bur St. John's Hill Cem), m 1895 Sadie Ellen Romberger (Mar 27, 1867 – Apr 22, 1956, bur St. Johns Hill Cem), dau of Philip and Leah (Matter) Romberger. Sadie's death was caused by getting too close to a brush fire. Her clothing caught fire, she died several days later. William

Henry & Sadie Ellen (Romberger) Howard children: ***William W. b Oct 1896, m Alvena Hassinger (1896 – Sep 19, 1938), a dau of Jacob and Lydia (Gipple) Hassinger, **and had these children:** Phyllis m Morris Lebo; Francis m Lewis Lahr; Leona m George Moore; Kathryn m Paul Teats; John m Lois Cornelius; ***Isaac L. (Mar 22, 1898 - ___, bur St. John's Hill Cem), m Hattie I Klinger (Sep 13, 1900 - Apr 6, 1969). **Isaac L and Hattie I (Klinger) Howard children:** Loretta b Aug 31, 1919, m George Boyer Jr., a son of George & Sadie (Miller) Boyer of Mbg; Norwood Oct 21, 1920 –Feb 19,1939), killed in an independent mine accident; Mary Ellen b Nov 29, 1921, m John Hoover b Jun 14,1919, a son of Paul & Lizzie (Klinger) Hoover; Alberta b Nov 3, 1923, m Homer Deibler, 2nd Paul Brown; Robert Feb 4, 1925 – 1969), m Marie Hartman; Mark b Oct 10, 1926,m Wilma Shambrook; Eugene b Nov 7, 1927, m Dorothy Peifer; Pearl b Sep 9, 1930 twin, m Marlin Buffington; Fearl b Sep 9, 1930 twin, m Gerald Lenker; Harold b Apr 12, 1931 twin, m Rose Dickerson of England; Donald b Apr 12, 1931 twin, m Kathryn Mowery; Richard Jan 31, 1934, m Dorothy Shaffer; Kenneth b Jun 19, 1935;***Edward b Nov 1900 m Cleota Munch; ***Charles E. b Jan 9, 1902 – Jan 15, 1979, bur St. John's Hill Cem), m Hazel Smeltz.Charles a self employed painter and decorator, living in Berrysburg. **Charles E. and Hazel (Smeltz) Howard had a dau** ____ m Robert Barry;*** Faye b Sep,1903 Clarence W. Bingaman; Mary A. (May 25, 1836 – Jul 18, 1857, bur St. Johns Hill Cem), m Daniel Wert; Caroline (1844 – Dec 19, 1921, bur St.Johns Hill Cem).]

THE MARTZ – WOLFE MILL PROPERTY
(Samuel Wolfe in 1875)

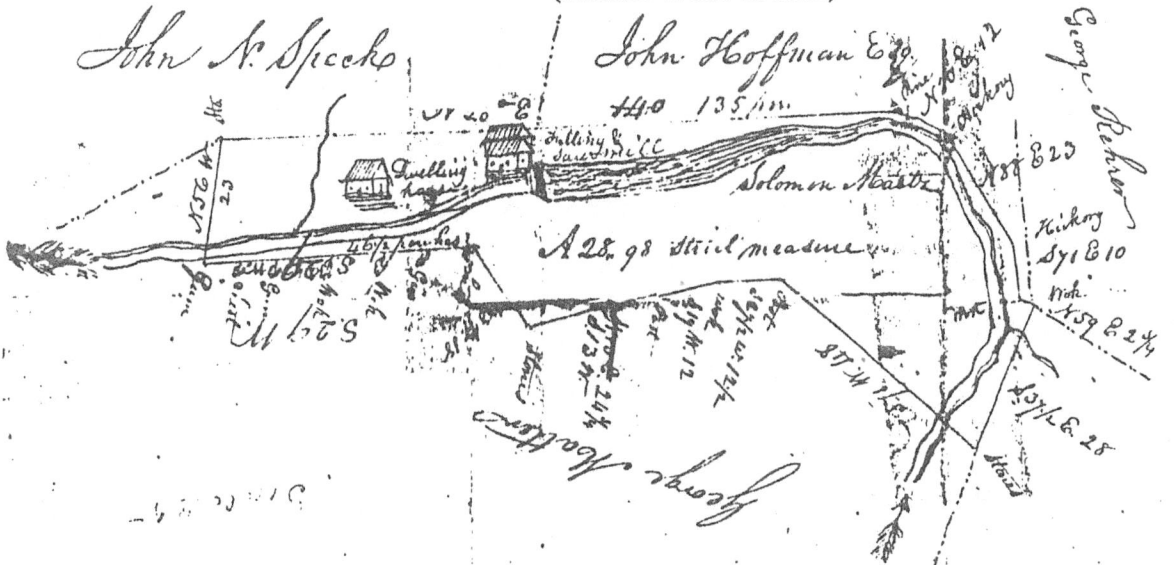

An interesting survey produced on February 26, 1840, showing the gristmill tract

This is part of the land that was granted to Leonard Miller on August 21, 1751. Andrew Riegel became owner of 311 acres of the land when it was surveyed in 1791, and later his heirs distributed the land by dividing it into several tracts. On Jun 17, 1819, John Riegel, eldest son of Andrew Riegel received 125 acres 30 perches. On May 17, 1822. John and Susanna conveyed 26 acres 75 perches as collateral for a debt to John Hoffman, Esquire, and he was assessed for the 26 acres with fulling mill and saw mill from 1826 to 1831 when a carding mill was added. The Hoffman's moved to Upper Swatara Township, but continued to own the land in Lykens Township. In their absence tenants occupied the land and took care of the mill. In 1828 Nicholas McSurdy lived on the property. Sam Hollensworth was the fuller in 1834. By 1837 Solomon Martz was listed on the tax record as fuller and tenant on the property, and it contained a saw mill, fulling and carding mill. The 1843 record shows two log mills (saw, carding and fuller), a two-story house and log barn.

On February 26, 1840, Joel B. Ferree resurveyed the mill tract containing 28 acres 98 perches in preparation for sale. On March 21, 1840, John Hoffman and his wife conveyed this tract with log house and various other buildings to Isaac Martz, making this acreage part of the Martz family complex. Isaac Martz and his wife conveyed the 28 acres, a house, log barn, fulling and sawmill to Gideon Shadle on March 29, 1856, whom in 1858 was recorded as a fuller. The property was resold on April 23, 1859 to Samuel Wolf. But two years later on April 1, 1861 Samuel conveyed to Enoch and Margaret Ann Matter and moved to Millersburg where their son Charles Elmer was born November 20, 1863. Enoch Matter moved to Sacramento, California and appointed Elias Matter to sell his property back to Samuel Wolf (April 4, 1864). On July 11, 1867, Samuel Wolf purchased a very small tract of land from the estate of John Hoffman of Swatara Twp. It contained one acre 113 3/10 perches with buildings. This deed was not recorded until June 1908.

On April 4, 1842, George and Hannah Holtzman of Lykens Township conveyed another tract containing one acre 110 perches of land to Solomon Martz. This small tract was adjacent to the larger tract above, and was also bound by land of John Snyder, Isaac Miller to the north, Solomon Martz's other land, by Wiconisco creek and then south along Big Wiconisco creek. It was part of a warrant from Commonwealth of Pennsylvania to William Row on August 16, 1814. On April 3, 1815, William Row sold it to George Matter, a cooper, and he assigned it December 26, 1840 to George Holtzman, also a cooper. That year Holtzman was assessed for the acre with a house. The tax record for 1840 names Solomon Martz as a fuller, and in 1843 he is listed as having a house, barn and two log mills, one of them a sawmill, the other a carding mill. In 1850 they lived in Lykens Twp. and had Sarah Ann Lebo age 8 with them, Obed Reigle 20, Margaret Maurer 16, Emaline 4, Henry W. 2, Francis 10/12 mo. They lived beside Samuel Thomas

In his will, written Oct 28, 1850, Solomon gave all the property (almost 40 acres with a log house and frame barn) to his wife Elizabeth. Soon after Solomon Martz had died, Elizabeth married George Emerick and moved to Uniontown (Pillow). In 1855 tenant Josiah Schoffstall a shoemaker, lived in the log house and bank barn property. 1858 John Scheibley, a tenant farmer lived on the premises. By 1864 Samuel Wolf had purchased the land including the saw and grist mill.

Samuel Wolfe became a well-known millwright. He constructed several mills in the area, including Shiffers and Raker's mills. It is not certain whether the mill on his property was the original one built much earlier. But it was known as an unusual mill for this area because it did not have a race.

Samuel Wolfe had grandchildren living in the immediate area of his mill. They loved to come and spend time at the mill. They had their own projects, and took advantage of the numerous supplies that Samuel Wolfe had on hand. Samuel enjoyed their company, but one day, he became annoyed because his supply of nails had dwindled, so he told his son, "keep the kids at home, they are stealing all my nails."

After Samuel Wolfe's wife died, he continued to live here on this property. But on May 26, 1903, he sold the two tracts of land to his son Joseph F. Wolfe, who was living in Wiconisco. One tract was the mill property containing twenty-eight acres, ninety-eight perches, and which had served him so well. The other tract was the small one-acre, one-hundred-thirteen perches that he purchased from John Hoffman. In return for receiving the two properties, Joseph F. Wolfe had to promise to "Comfort and support and maintain his father Samuel Wolfe, give him board, lodging, wash his garments and if sick or feeble to aid him." Joseph was to administer to his wants during his natural life, and defray the expense of a decent internment. This document was recorded June 2, 1903.

In 1908, Samuel Wolfe was doing some work around the mill, and saw a beehive inside the building near the tip of the roof. The bees were pesky, so Samuel put kerosene on a piece of cloth attached to the end of a long stick, and lit it. When he pushed the stick up to the nest to smoke out the bees, the nest caught fire.

The building was soon enclosed in a blaze, and the whole mill burned to the ground. Samuel died shortly after the fire. Later, the old house burned down, and today only the stone foundation is left.

After Samuel died, Joseph F. and Catherine Wolfe moved to Wiconisco. They sold the two tracts (by now considered one tract), on July 27, 1911, to William H. and C. Elmer Wolfe, executors of Samuel Wolfe's estate. After many years, this land was sold again. Catherine A. Wolfe died on September 5, 1931. Her undivided share of the property was transferred to her husband William H. Wolfe and children: Charles K. and Salome Wolfe, John H. Wolfe, and Sallie D. (Mrs Charles Kissinger).

When William H. Wolfe died on January 9, 1943, they divided the estate as established by his will. Marlin E. H. Wolfe became owner of three-quarter interest, Lillian W. Schwartz received one-fourth interest. After Lillian died, Marlin received full ownership of the property. When Marlin E. H. Wolfe died, the property was conveyed to his children.

THE MERTZ /MARTZ FAMILY

[The immigrant ancestor of the MARTZ, Johannes Henry Martz (b c1708 –c1786), a son of John Martz of Germany, arrived in Philadelphia in 1737 on the ship "Edinburgh." He settled in Longswamp Twp., Berks County near the Mertz Church. Henry married Anna Maria Rossman. After Henry Martz died, three of his sons came to Northumberland County - about1787. Philip (1738 –1803); Henry David b Jul 20, 1749, m Barbara Miller;*John Jacob (Aug 18, 1740–Feb 22, 1803, bur Sunbury) m Margaret Miller who d Nov 23, 1811. John Jacob & Margaret (Miller) Martz had eleven children: Their son Jacob Martz b 1777, eventually moved from Northumberland County to Dauphin County.

JOHN JACOB MARTZ (Aug 18, 1741 Berks Co –Feb 22, 1803, bur Sunbury), Henry settled in Rockland Twp, Berks Co., after his arrival from Germany in 1737, and took up milling. He m Margaret Miller (___ - Nov 23, 1811), and had eleven children.
*JACOB MARTZ (Dec 25, 1777 - Aug 28, 1857, bur Davids Killinger Cem), m 1st Catherine ___, 2nd Sarah Jury (Oct 31, 1787 - Oct 11, 1856, bur Davids Killinger. Jacob age 71 was a tailor in Up Paxton, in 1850 had a wife Sarah 61, and these people in their household: Samuel Forman 35 miller, Sarah 28, Sarah 10, Emanuel 7. **Jacob and 1st wife Catharine Martz had these children (some bapt. Davids & Salem Killinger Ch): Maria Margaret** b Sep 1, 1801, m ___ Messerschmidt; **Elizabeth** b Nov 4, 1803; **Juliana** b Feb 26, 1808; **Sarah was the mother of the remainder: Daniel** b Aug 6, 1809 bapt Salem Luth Killinger - ___), m Hannah_ b c1810 - ___), lived in Wash Twp. in 1860, had Henry A. Martz with them; **Sarah** b Jan 18, 1811, bapt Stone Valley Ch; **Jacob** (Dec 16, 1812 – Mar 12, 1882, bur Killinger), m 1st Rachel Welker (May 10, 1809 –Apr 12, 1860), a dau of John Welker. They lived in Up.Paxton where he was a farmer &butcher. **Jacob & Rachel (Welker) Martz children:** Uriah (Dec 15,1832 - Jan 17,1904), m Hannah Miller (Feb 16, 1835- Jan 25, 1906); John W. (Aug 13, 1834 – 1920), m 1854 to Mary Ann Witmer (Jul 18, 1833 – Feb 21, 1809), dau of Peter & Elizabeth (Philips) Witmer, and moved to Northld Co. He was a tailor & postmaster. Hannah m Adam Naubringer, 2nd Elias Witmer; Sarah b c1837 m Henry Kissinger; Elizabeth & Amanda both died of typhoid fever; Ann Mary b c1846, m Jerry Hoy; Jeremiah b c1848 m ___ Hoffman. Jacob m 2nd Sarah (Weaver) Schreffler, widow of Peter (Oct 8, 1825 – Mar 5, 1911). **Jonas** b 1815, m Caroline ___ (Dec 27, 1825 - Jun 23, 1859, bur Motters Cem), lived in Up Paxton Twp.,in 1850, and had Catharine Martz 11, and Henry Martz 14 with them. Jonas was a tailor. **Jonas and Abaline Martz had these children:** Susannah Cevilla (Sep 23, 1845 - Dec 30, 1870, bur St. Johns Hill Cem), m Jonas Row (May 11, 1839 - ___), a son of Jacob and Susan Matter Row. **Jonas and Susannah Cevilla Martz children:** Ida Ellis b May 15,1864, bap St. Johns Hill Ch; Benjamin b c1847, Isaiah b c1849. Jonas probably m 2nd Maria ___ b c1839, **had these children:** Clinton b c1869; Milton (1872 –1925, bur Maple Grove Cem); Sarah b 1874; Ida b c1877; __ dau b 1879. **Charles** (1813 – Sep 11, 1900, bur Oak Hill Cem, Mbg, m Catharine ___. Lived in Up Paxton in 1850 & 1860, was a tailor. **Children:** Nathaniel b 1835 lived in Up Pax. Twp 1860, was a tailor; Cornelius b c1846, m Mary Buffington, was Civil War Vet. **Susanna** (Sep 1826- Aug 31, 1898 of heart disease) m Simon Romberger (Jan 14, 1824 – Sep 28, 1904); He was a tailor, lived in Millersburg in 1880; Amos.]
*Solomon Martz (Oct 31, 1808 - Oct 28, 1850, bur Hoffman Cem), m Elizabeth Moyer (Nov 4, 1817 – Feb 12, 1896), a dau of John Jacob & Eva Christina (Koppenhaver) Moyer. We have not been able to identify the parents of Solomon Martz. He doesn't appear to fit into the Jacob Martz family. Elizabeth was 1st married to George Emmerick - see Emerick family.

THE EMERICH / EMERICK FAMILY

[The immigrant ancestor of the Emerich / Emerick family was **Johann Michael Emerick** (Mar 2, 1659 Hesse, Germany – d Jun 1, 1744 in Tulpehocken Twp, Berks Co.). He came first to Ulster, New York State. He later settled in Tulpehocken, Berks Co, married Dec 18, 1709 Elizabeth ____ (Nov 1, 1687 Ger.– Oct1752), They had a son Leonard Emerick b c1722 in N.Y., later lived in Berks Co., m May 21, 1751 Catharina Forry, a dau of John Forry. They were the parents of John Michael Emerick (1757 – 1835) below.

[**JOHN MICHAEL EMERICK** (Sep 6, 1757 – Nov 14, 1805, bur on private farm, Mahanoy Twp, Northld Co), m Dec 18, 1781 Anna Catharine Pontius (Apr 14, 1757 – Mar 11, 1838), a dau of John Pontius. **John Michael & Anna Catharine (Pontius) Emerick children (some bap Stone Valley or Himmel's Ch, Northld Co):**
*JOHN (Dec 10 , 1781 – Feb 18, 1859, Butler Ohio), m Margaret ____ ,moved to Ohio;
*ELIZABETH b Aug 11,1785–Jun 26, 1861), m Henry Latsha, son of Henry and Catharine (Shott) Latsha;
*SAMUEL b Dec 9, 1786
*GEORGE (Mar 9, 1788 – May 29, 1871, bur Stone Valley Cem), traveled to Northld Co in a wagon in 1813. He m Eva Magdalena Zartman (Oct 8,1795 –Feb 28,1876), dau of Martin & Susan (Fitler) Zartman. **George & Eva Magdalena (Zartman) Emerick children:** **George b Apr 13, 1813 – Jan 18, 1886, bur Stone Valley Cem, m Sarah Brosius (May 20,1817– Feb 24,1853), a dau of John and Catharine (Spotts) Brosius. George married 2nd Oct 1853, Elizabeth Moyer Martz (Nov 4, 1817 – Feb 12, 1896), widow of Solomon Martz, dau of John Jacob & Eva Christina (Koppenhaver) Moyer . **George and Sarah (Brosius) Emerick children:** Mary Ann b c1844; Isabella b c1845; John b c1846 Caroline b c1848; Edwin M (Jul 31, 1855, m Alice Wiest; Elizabeth b Dce 27, 1 857, m Henry Bickel **Jacob (Dec 21,1814 – Sep 15, 1800, bur Pomfret Manor Cem, Northld Co), m Catharine Lenker (Aug 28, 1819–May 15, 1860, bur Peace Ref Cem, Bbg), a dau of _____. Jacob and Catharine Emerick lived in Wiconisco Twp in 1850, and he was listed as a farmer. Isaac Weaver age 17, & Mary Forney age 20, lived with them. In 1860, the family lived in Wash. Twp, but Catherine is not listed on the census, she may have died before the census was taken. **Jacob and Catherine (Lenker) Emerick children:** Emanuel b c1839; Hannah (b Oct 16, 1842 – Dec 29, 1905), m Jan 8, 1865, David K. Lenker (Dec 31, 1841 – Mar 3, 1922), son of Philip and Salome (Holtzman) Lenker, in Washington Twp (record in Union Salem Church, Berrysburg ; Amanda b Aug 20, 1845, bapt Hoffman Ch–d 1935, bur beside mother); Cornelius b 1848; Mary J. b c1850; George b c1852. **Rebecca Margaret (Sep 12, 1816 – Sep 27, 1878, bur Stone Val Cem), m Charles Brosius (Sep 5, 1814 – Feb 4, 1889), a son of John and Catharine (Spotts) Brosius; **Benjamin (Feb 1, 1818 – May 5, 1842, bur StoneVal Cem), m Susanna Forney;**Sarah (Nov 7, 1819–Aug 10, 1845, bur Pillow Cem), m Jonas Snyder (no dates);**John (Dec 2, 1821 –Feb 18, 1896, bur Brookville Cem, Ogle Co, Il), m Matilda Smith (Sep 5, 1826 – Apr 12, 1908). ; **Elias (Sep 16, 1824 – Mar 2, 1898, bur Stone Val Cem), m Anna M. Stine (Nov 12,1828–Apr 2,1880), of Pine Grove, Sch Co;**Catherine b Nov16,1826, m John Stein;**Mary b Sep 2, 1828 m Isaac Martz;**Susannah (1831–1842);**Michael (Nov 27,1832 –Dec 26,1899), m Hannah Tressler (Jan 20,1832 –May 5,1918);**Joseph b Nov 27,1834 m Catherine Row b 1827, lived in Wic. Twp in1880. **Joseph & Catherine Rowe (Emerick) children:** Wm H. b 1859 Rebecca b 1860; Mary b 1866.
*SARAH MARIA (Apr 28, 1789 – Dec 14, 1872, bur Stone Valley Cem, Northld Co), m Jacob Spotts (Jun 8, 1788 – Jun 14, 1852), a son of John & Anna M. (Keiser) Spotts;
*CATHARINE b Mar 11, 1791 – Sep 18, 1860), m J. Michael Lenker (Feb 6, 1792 – Sep 20, 1867, bur Stone Valley Cem, Low Mah Twp), a son of J. Adam & Anna Maria Lenker; *ANNA MARY (1792 – c1854), m Martin Kerstetter;
*MICHAEL (Oct 9,1794 –Jun 29, 1875), bur Stone Valley Cem), m Hannah Rothermel (Jul 23, 1806 – Oct 15, 1882), a dau of Abraham & Catharine (Yeager) Rothermel.]

THE SAMUEL WOLFE FAMILY

Members of the WOLF/WOLFE family originally settled in Berks County, but migrated to the Lykens Valley well before 1800. Henry appears to be the first one, and is listed for taxes in the Wiconisco

Valley 1780. By 1790 when the "window tax" was taken, Henry and Adam wolf were both listed as having adjoining land with "poor cabins" and lived next to Henry Schoffstall. Jacob, Christian, John and David Wolf were also early settlers, but apparently moved on to other places.

[HENRY WOLFE (no dates may be John Henry (Jan 1, 1730 – Jul 7, 1803, rec in Trinity Luth, Reading), m Susanna _____ (no dates). While in Berks County he was a tile maker. **Henry and Susanna Wolfe had several children (bapt Trinity Luth Reading, Berks Co).**
John Henry b Jul 21, 1767; **Maria Christina** b Dec 23, 1769 – Apr 8, 1790, bur Reading, Berks Co)
Margaretha b Aug 1, 1772 – Aug 5, 1776, bur in Reading, Berks Co); **Susanna** b Jun 18, 1779 – Dec 1783, bur Reading, Berks Co); **Catharine** b May 8, 1783; **Elisabeth** b Sep 29, 1785

ADAM WOLFE (no dates) m Christina ____ They had at least 4 or 5 children in Lykens Twp. by 1800)
Peter b Jun 21, 1795; **Elizabeth** b Jan 5, 1798; **Johannes** b May 26, 1799 (St. Johns

HENRY WOLFE ( ), m Eva Calhoun - she was a widow in 1820, died before 1825 – **children (bap Hoffman & St. John Hill , Klingers Ch):**
*Andreas b Feb 10, 1784
*Christina Dorothea b Jan 28, 1787–1872),
*Eva Dorothea b Oct 7, 1789 -bap records Dorothea as mother – d Apr 20, 1872, bur Pillow Cem), m John D. Saltzer (Feb 18, 1791 – Sep 9, 1855). [Refer to Saltzer genealogy.]
*Magdalena b Oct 7, 1790
*Maria Catharine b Jul 11, 1793
*Susanna b Sep 19, 1796, had a dau Eva b Mar 16, 1807, no father given.
*Michael b Mar 6, 1799 bap source (Jul 18, 1798 – Jan 19, 1874, cem source bur St. Johns Hill Cem) m Christiana Romberger (Dec 14, 1809 – May 11, 1885). In 1870 Christiana was living in Lykens Twp, had Elias 22 & his wife Catherine 22, & 2 children, Mary J 3, Charles M 1 with her. Also Elizabeth McCarty 15, a domestic, Maria Wolf 33, and Christiana 2. Michael was a mason in 1825 in Lykens Twp. Christiana lived with the Elias Wolf family in 1880.**Michael and Christiana (Romberger) Wolfe children:**
Simon (Dec 16, 1826 – Mar 23, 1879, bur Coleman Cem), m Sarah Walborn (1835 – Feb 7, 1913), a dau of Christian (Mar 17, 1802 – Dec 29, 1871) and Judith (Hartman) Nov 10, 1804 – Mar 30, 1853) Walborn. **Simon and Sarah (Walborn) Wolf children: ***Sarah b c1851; ***Charles** b c1858.
Michael (Dec 6, 1828 – Jun 7, 1891, of dropsy, bur Simeon Cem), m Sep 30, 1849 Susanna Salada Jun 27, 1828 – Oct 17, 1891), a dau of Jacob and Anna Maria (Coleman) Salada. In 1870 they lived in Lykens Twp and he was a drover. In 1880 they were in Gratz, had carrie Saltzer 2, gr.dau with them. **Michael & Susanna (Saldad) Wolfe had 8 children: ***Mary Ann b c1851; ***Elizabeth** b c1853; ***Susan** b c1855; ***George** b c1857; ***Barbara E** b c1860; ***Catherine A** b c1862; ***Adaline** b c1868;

Samuel (Apr 25, 1829 - Mar 14, 1908, bur Hoffman Cem), m Catherine Ann Buffington (Nov 6, 1834 - Jul 15, 1898), a dau of George and Catharine (Yeager) Buffington. Samuel came to Lykens Township about 1856 and remained here until his death. In 1860 & 1870 he was a sawyer & miller. **Samuel & Catherine Ann (Buffington) Wolfe children (7):
***Mary b c 1855;
*** Joseph Franklin (1856 - 1934, bur Calvary Cem, Wiconisco), m Catharine Miller (Jun 10, 1856 - Dec 4, 1933), a dau of Jacob and Abby (Snyder) Miller. Joseph and Catherine moved to Virginia with her parents, but moved back to Pennsylvania before 1900.
***Martha Jane (Sep 30, 1861, m Henry M. Shade Sep 26, 1851), a son of _____.**Henry M and Martha Jane (Wolfe) Shade children: Jennie May** b Mar 12, 1880, bapt Hoffman Ch;
***Willliam Henry (Dec 5,1862 - 1945, bur Hoffman Cem), m Apr 1883 to Catherine A. Daniel (Jun 1857 –Sep 25, 1931), a dau of _____. **William and Catherine (Daniel) Wolfchildren: Edward** (Sep 26, 1884 - Sep 17, 1906, bur Hoffman Cem), was employed by the mines, and was on a freight train running between Harrisburg and Lykens. He was killed by an accident while he was breaking on the train; **Charles E** (Jul 24,1889 - Nov 1946, bur E. Harrisburg Mausoleum), m Ellen Salome, moved to Harrisburg where in 1913, he opened the first public storage garage in the city. It was located at Walnut and Strawberry Streets. This enterprise was made possible by his father, who was overcome by the grief of losing his other son in a mining accident. He mortgaged his farm, to finance an auto business for his son Charles, so that he would

not take up mining. Charles became a very successful buisnessman. **Charles K and Ellen Salome Wolfe children: Earl W; Paul; Charles K. Jr.;**

Sallie D b Aug 1893, m Charles E. Kissinger, a son of Daniel and Mary (Klinger) Kissinger. **Charles and Sallie (Wolfe) Kissinger children: Edna Katharine** b May 4,1915, m Charles Stutzman;**Earl** (1918 - 1993, bur Hoffman Cem), m Margaret Lowery b 1922; **Pauline** m James Wetzel; **Charles Jr.** m Eilene Hain. **John H.** b c Dec 1894, m Emma Willier, lived in Harrisburg. **John H. and Emma (Willier) Wolfe had a dau: Lois**, m John Haffley, lives in West Chester, Pa. In 1900 William H and Catherine lived in Lykens Twp, he was a farmer, and had these additional people with them: Edward Daniel brother-in-law b 1861, noted as a landlord, Charles Snyder adopted, b;Aug 1886; Erma B. Snyder adopted b c1888.

Charles Elmer (Nov 20, 1863 - Nov 3, 1923, of Brights disease, bur Hoffman Cem), m Dec 25, 1895 Mary E.Hawk (May 11, 1866 - Apr 30, 1932), a dau of Jonathan & Malinda (Matter) Hawk. They were married by Rev. J. Stauffer. Charles Elmer was a deacon at Hoffman Church for fourteen years, "was always in his pew" and was Supt. of the cemetery. **Charles Elmer and Mary (Hawk)Wolfe children:**
Lillian b c1902

Marlin Elmer Hawk (b Lykens Twp Oct 20, 1910 - d Mar 24, 1998,a resident of Millheim, Pa.), m Aug 13, 1938 Prudence E. Shultzabarger who died Mar 18, 1991. Both buried Fairvew Cemetery, Millheim. Marlin was a graduate of Penn State University class of 1938 with a degree in Forestry and Civil Engineering. He was employed in the lumber industry in the Pacific Northwest, the south and New England. He worked as a layout engineer on the campus of Penn State during construction of three major dormitory complexes. He also owned the M.E. Wolfe Lumber Co from 1950 to 1962. He later was self-employed as a licensed surveyor until retirement in the early 1980s.

Marlin had an avid interest in every phase of history and belonged to many history-oriented organizations, including Gratz Historical Society. He shared his knowledge of Lykens Township, his family, and local schools with our Society. We always looked forward to seeing him on special occasions, such as Simon Gratz Day. But any unexpected visit to our library was also very welcome.
Marlin had two sons and a daughter.

***Emma Agnes b c 1865, m _____ Gordon and lived in Pottsville;

*** John Harvey (1869 – 1941, bur Oakd Dale Cem), married Susan Harman (Sep 14, 1872 – 1951) lived in Loyalton. He purchased the Harman family homestead in Mifflin Township in 1912. The first house on this property was a log house but it was destroyed by fire. About 1862 the family began to build a new brick house. The bricks were made in a kiln that was located on the property in the vicinity where the housing development is now located. But while the house was being built, one of the sons _____ was called to the service. He was killed in the war, and someone else was hired to help to finish the house. The house contains two fire places, one in the kitchen and one in the basement.. **John H and Susan (Harman) Wolfe had a son: Ivan H.** b Jun 1900 , m Laura Michaels. **Ivan H. and Laura (Michaels) Wolfe had 2 sons** *Ivan* b 1933, *John M.* Ivan m 2nd Marion Mace, a dau of Chester & Maude (Kroh) Mace, **had three step children:** Nancy I., Wayne I.

***Solomon S. b c1870, moved to Merchantville, N. J.;
***Nathan Edwin (Aug 11, 1875 - 1897, bur Oak Dale Cem) died of typhoid fever.]
**Catherine b c1834;
**Elizabeth b c1836;
**Maria b c1839, with mother in 1870, and may have had a child Christiana age 2; **Amanda b c1840;
Lydia b c1845; **David b c1847; **Elias (Sep 1848 – Aug 18, 1920, bur Coleman Cem), m Feb 10, 1866 Catherine Salada (May 1848 – Sep 27, 1927), a dau ofJacob and Anna Maria (Coleman) Salada. **Elias & Catherine (Salada) Wolfe children: Mary Jane b c1867; Charles b c1869; Ida C b c1871; Annie A b c1874; Hattie b c1878; Jacob Milton b Jun 3, 1880; **Daniel (Sep 18, 1852 – Nov 4, 1925, bur Coleman Cem), m Sarah ____ (Dec 19, 1845 – Jul 4, 1918), had a son Harvey F. b c1870;

THE SPECK/SPACHT/SPECHT/ ETC FAMILY

JOHN SPECHT (Mar 14, 1786 – Dec 12, 1856, bur Hoffman Cem), is the first settler of that name to come to Lykens Valley. He appeared on the tax record of 1825 in Lykens Township. In 1828, John N. Specht was a fuller, had 36 acres of land and a log house. He also became a deacon in Hoffman Church that same year.

In1840 and 1850 the family lived in Mifflin Twp . **John and Elizabeth (   ) Specht had these children (some bapt Hoffman Ch)**
Anna Catharine b Jun 11, 1813; **Daniel** b Mar 22, 1815; **Jacob** b Aug 15, 1821, m Angeline b c1829, lived in Mifflin Twp and was a carpenter in 1850 next to his parents; **Susana** b Jan 23, 1824, may have m George Deibler (Apr 9, 1825 – Jul 4, 1890, bur Hoffman Cem. **Had these children: Henrietta** b Mar 19, 1847; **Susanna** b Dec 25, 1849; **Lydia** (May 18, 1826 – Mar 16, 1855, bur Hoffman Cem); **Johannes** b Sep 26, 1828; **Anna Maria** (Jan 1, 1831 – 1832);

[**DANIEL SPECHT** (May 10, 1793 – Jul 24, 1870, bur Pillow Cem) m Mary (Jul 16, 1796 – Feb 2, 1863). They lived in Mifflin Twp in 1850 & 1860. Dr. Benjamin Leinbauch lived with them in 1860. **Daniel and Mary Specht children:**
Levi b c18 27
Josiah (Dec 17, 1829 – Sep 6, 1853, bur Pillow Cem)
Asa (Jul 19, 1837 – Nov 3, 1865), m Catharine Snyder (Apr 26, 1837 – Nov 24, 1906, bur EUG CEm, Bbg). They lived in Uniontown. After Asa died, Catherine m Jonathan Miller. **Asa and Catherine (Snyder) Specht children (all minors when their father died.) Daniel; Henry; Levi; L. Ellington** (Mar 26, 1864 – Jan 19, 1892, bur Bbg).

JOHN N. SPECK Jr (Aug 26, 1801 – Feb 9, 1866, bur Matters Cem, E'ville), son of _____ m c1824 Barbara Hoffman (Dec 23,1800 – Sep 29, 1879), a dau of John and Anna Mary (Kauffman) Hoffman. John Speck and family lived in Washington Twp in 1850 and 1860. By 1860, their dau Sarah was married to Tyrus Snyder, and they and their young baby Sarah lived with her parents. Tyrus was a journey man. **John and Barbara (Hoffman) Speck had these children:**
JEREMIAH (Dec 16, 1822 – May 26, 1888, bur Maple Grove Cem), m Aug 23, 1868 Mary Koppenheffer, a dau of Jonathan Koppenheffer, had son William Edward b Mar 3, 1871, bapt St. Johns Hill Ch Jeremiah Speck lived in E'ville in 1860. Jeremiah left Mary later in the year that they were married. He m 2nd Catharine Kuntzelman (Nov 11, 1829 – Dec 23, 1914). In 1880 they lived in Washington Twp and had son John W. age 21 with them. He was a farmer. **Jeremiah & Catherine (Kuntzelman) Speck children: Isaiah** (1856 – 1935, bur Maple Grove Cem), m Malinda ___ (1849 – 1935); **John Wesley** (Jan 8, 1859- Mar 10, 1888 bur Maple Grove, m Dec 22, 1883 Emma J. Frank.. He was a deacon & S. S. Supt. In Salem Ref. Church.
CATHERINE (Aug 29, 1829 – Mar 24, 1916, bur Fairview Cem, Jackson Twp, Dau Co), m Isaiah Matter (Sep 4, 1827 – Sep 22, 1900);
ELIZABETH (Jan 26, 1835 – Nov 22, 1906, bur Meth Cem, Valley View), m Henry Snyder (Jul 19, 1832 – Apr 10, 1889). Henry was an apprentice tanner in 1850 living with David Matter. When they married, Henry and Elizabeth lived next to his parents. They moved to Valley View by 1870, where he established his own tannery located north of Main Street on Church Road. In 1880 they lived in Hegins Twp, Sch Co and William Kehler a nephew age 4 lived with them. **Henry and Elizabeth (Speck) Snyder children: James** b c1857; **Calvin** b c1860; **Kate** b c1861; **Charles** b c1865; **Sarah** b c1867; **Clara** b c1873; **Mary A** b c1875.
SARAH (Jan 6, 1840 – Sep 30, 1904 bur Wiconisco Cem), m Tyrus Snyder (Jan 12, 1839 – May 17, 1919). They lived in Wiconisco Twp in 1880. **Tyrus and Sarah (Speck) Snyder children: George F** b Nov 20, 1859; **Margaret Ann** b Jul 4, 1861, m ___Dietirch; **John Calvin** b Jul 11, 1863; **Ira Alvin** b Aug 10,1864; **Andrew Harvey** b Oct 10, 1865; **Ellen Jane** b Oct 2, 1868, m ___ Klinger; **Maria Elizabeth** b Oct 4,1870, m ___Bateman; **Carrie Catherine** b Apr 6, 1872, m ___Ritzman; **Mary Louisa** b May 20, 1874; **Samuel Edward** b Sep 2,1876; **Harry Monroe** b Jan 2, 1878; **Etta May** b Aug 21,1880, m ___Yentch; **Katie Irene** b Mar 20, 1884, m ___ Davidson;
BENJAMIN SPECHT (1810 -   ), m Elizabeth ____ (Dec 10, 1821 – Nov 25, 1882,bur stone valley). They lived in in Up Pax Twp in 1860 &1880. They had fifty-five acres of land that they conveyed to Jared Specht in 1869. **Benjamin and Elizabeth Specht children: Jared** (b Jan 19,1840 – Apr 23, 1892, bur Oak Hill Cem, Mbg), m Sep 26, 1861 Louisa Lebo (Dec 17, 1835 – Jan 31, 1904). **Jared & Louisa (Lebo) Specht children: Alvaretta** (b & d 1862, bapt Stone Valley, bur Davids Ref Killinger; **Mary Salome** b Aug 4, 1864, bapt Rife; **Elizabeth A** b c1866; **Franklin** b c1868; **Frederick** b c1870; **Rebecca** b c1871; **Kate A.** b c1874, m ___Davidson; **Henry B** b c1877. In 1860 Jared lived in Up Paxton with the Andrew Miller family, and was a farm hand, in 1880 he and his family also lived in Up Paxton. **Maria** b Oct 6, 1844 bapt Stone Valley; **Jeremiah** (Mar 31, 1849 – Aug 9, 1881, bur Stone Valley)

291

GERALD F. WIEST FARM
ABRAHAM KESSLER FARM (74 acres 1875)

The Farm House As It Looked Long Ago, Possibly Just after it was Built In 1915

A NEW BARN ON THE OLD FOUNDATION
(The Very old barn was torn down while the Billow's owned the farm, because the roof caved in from a heavy snow)

       This land was originally part of the 607 1/2 acre warrant to Leonard Miller on August 21,1751. Surveys of the land were made in 1791 and Andrew Riegel, Sr. purchased 311 acres. He and his wife Catherine resided on this plantation which was bound by neighbors Peter Schoffstall, Frederick Lubold, Jacob Hoffman, Jr, Christian Hoffman, Isaac Ferree, and John Bressler. Their land was also bound by a "sawmill tract," and joined the Big Wiconisco Creek at the east crossing. The 1798 "window Tax" describes the property as having a poor cabin, good smithshop, and poor stable, joining neighbor Nicholas Hoffman.

       After Andrew Riegel, Sr. died, an inquest was held on May 23, 1815, at the home of his widow Catherine Riegel. The land was divided into three tracts. Daniel Riegel Sr. third son of Andrew Riegel chose to have this forty-one acre, thirty perch farm. He received it on December 18, 1819.

       On the tax record of 1828, Daniel Riegel Sr. a farmer was taxed for the land and a log house. By 1831, he had taken up the occupation of gelder. Daniel Riegel Sr. bequeathed this property to his son Daniel Riegel, Jr. He too was listed as a gelder for several years, just as his father had been in previous years.

[DANIEL RIEGEL SR (b Sep 21, 1774 Berks Co - d Feb 8, 1839, bur Hoffman Cem, alone), a son of Andreas Riegel, Sr and his wife Catherine Hoffman. He m Nov 29, 1803, Catharine Harmon b c1780, a dau of John and Anna Maria (Heller) Harman **Daniel (Sr.) and Catharine (Harmon) Riegel children (some bapt St. Johns, Bbg): Daniel (Jr)** (b Jun 1, 1804 - Jun 2, 1855, bur Simeon Cem, Gratz), m Dec 24, 1826, Catharine Hoffman (Sep10, 1807 - Sep 2, 1864), a dau of Peter and Magdalena (Lubold) Hoffman; **John** b Oct 1806 - d pre-1838), m Susanna Louisa Muench, a dau of Rev. Carl Muench, early teacher.[more Riegel genealogy elsewhere in book.]

On April 1, 1850, Daniel and Catherine (Hoffman) Riegle sold his forty acre 142 perch farm to Abraham Kessler, who had come to this area from near Hegins, Schuylkill County. The 1855 tax record mentions a log house one and one-half story barn. The 1864 tax record mentions that Abraham Kessler "is in the army." (We did not look for a record of army service for Abraham.) He purchased another twenty-five acres from Daniel and Hannah Romberger on April 2, 1860. Another eight acres were purchased in 1865 from Joel and Caroline Daniel. The land was located along the Big Wiconisco Creek, and on the west side of the public road to Oak Dale. It gave Abraham Kessler a total of about 74 acres. When they first moved to the farm, the Kessler family lived in an old original log house which was probably located behind what is now the summer house. Abraham Kessler revitalized or rebuilt the old Riegel vertical sawmill and dam near Little Creek, and the dam to run the mill. It was built about the same time that a new bridge was constructed over the creek (about 1866), on the road from Loyalton to the Crossroads. The saw mill was located several hundred yards east of the bridge. Abraham operated the saw mill from about 1866 to his death in 1881, producing much lumber. His only child Reuben grew up in Lykens Township, attended the schools there, and helped his father on the farm and at the saw mill. After Abraham died, his son Reuben took over and ran the mill until about 1894, when the saw mill either deteriorated or was destroyed by flooding.

Eventually Reuben built the existing large house (about 1915), and his son James became the occupant. In 1920, James and Beulah lived here and had Henry Koppenhaver age 11 living with them. Reuben hoped to build a stone house, so he had his workers gather a reserve of cut stones for its construction. Unfortunately, Reuben died in 1915 before construction began.

In 1894, Reuben began a new venture, when he became involved in a distillery built about 100 feet east of the entrance to the present Upper Dauphin Area Milddle School in Loyalton. He engaged in the manufacture of whiskey for many years. His son George became the brew master, and continued in that role until his death in 1912 at the age of forty. Reuben then hired a brewmaster to take his place, and the distillery continued to prosper. [See page 154 for info on the brewery.].

Reuben Kessler owned this farm and the next adjoining farm for the remainder of his life. During his lifetime he appointed Alfred H. Row, trustee to manage his estate in the interest of his son James. When Reuben died in 1915, at the age of sixty-nine, James began to manage the farms and distillery. He hired tenant farmers, but spent much of his time on this farm and at what had been the tavern/farm property. The trust continued to be in effect until April 1, 1921, when James became the owner of the properties. Finally on April 2, 1930, James A. and Beulah Kessler, by then residents of Loyalton, sold two tracts of land, the adjoining forty-nine acres fifteen perches, and this seventy-four acres ninety-seven perches (a total of 123 acres, 112 perches) to Samuel F.and Lucy A. Billow of Herndon.

[Personal information about the Kessler family given by Marlin Dietrich, now deceased. More Kessler genealogy on page 155.]

THE KESSLER FAMILY

[**HANS ABRAHAM KESSLER** (c1720 Ger –Jul 1768, Berks Co.), came to America in 1741, settling in Heidelberg Twp., Berks Co., m Maria Magdalena Mary ___. **They had these children: *CATHARINE** b c1753, m Daniel Becht; ***ELIZABETH** b c1753, m Conrad Gabel; ***HENRY** b c1754, m Susanna ____; ***JOHN PHILIP** b c1756;
***MICHAEL, Sr.** (c1758 Heidelberg, Berks Co – c1820, Mahantongo Twp., Sch Co), m Apr 18, 1783 Magdalelna "Polly" Grim (b ___ d pre 1838). He served in the Berks Co. Militia. About 1800 Michael moved to Hegins Twp., Sch Co and built a gristmill. He gave land for 1st school and church in the township. **Michael & Polly (Grim) Kessler children:**
****MARGARET "GRETA"**b Mar 5, 1784, m William Otto;

GEORGE (Feb 19, 1786 – Mar 29, 1866), m Eva Dietrich (Sep 21, 1787 – Aug 19, 1860), bur Barry Twp., Sch Co.), a dau of John and Maria Barbara (Geiss) Dietrich; **They had these children:** ELIAS (Sep 2, 1831 – Nov 26, 1903), m Catherine Diehl (Dec 30, 1828 – Feb 2, 1914);

EVA b 1788, m Jacob Heberling

BARBARA b 1790, m Leonard Dietrich (1799 – 1865), lived in Schuylkill Co., later Crawford Co.

ABRAHAM b c1792

MICHAEL , Jr. (Feb 21, 1794 – Apr 4, 1879 Hegina Twp, Sch Co., bur Weisample Cem), m Magdalena Arnold. **Children:** ***ABRAHAM** (Nov 30, 1818 – Jun 12, 1881), [More information on him page 155]; ***MICHAEL** (Nov 11, 1820 – Jan 6, 1896, of pneumonia, bur Ch of God Cem), lived in Hegins Twp, not married; ***JOHN M** (Nov 13, 1822 – Hegins Twp – Mar 16, 1909 of pneumonia), moved to Hegins Twp with father, m 1845 Elizabeth Wolfgang (Apr 12, 1825 – Dec 26, 1896). He was a miller; ***CHRISTINA** (Nov 13, 1824 – Sep 27, 1910, bur Ch of God Cem), m John Lucas (May 28, 1820 – Aug 24, 1897), of Barry Twp., Sch Co; ***PHILIP** (Mar 17, 1827 – May 16, 1896, bur Ch of God Cem), m Esther ___ . He was a farmer & mason; ***CATHARINE** (1829 – 1897, bur Ch of God Cem), not m; ***HARRIET** b1831, m Joseph Straub, purchased the Kessler family mill. They had a dau **Sarah Elizabeth** (1857 – May 5, 1888), m Samuel E. Schwalm; ***MAGDALENA** b c1834, m Gabriel Barth of Hubley Twp. **Michael & 2nd wife Catherine (Boyer) Kessler children:** ***WILLIAM** (Sep 27, 1838 – Apr 10, 1917, bur Ch of God Cem), m Abbie ___ (1846 – 1913); ***LEVI** b 1840, m Rebecca Hoch; ***CAROLINE** b 1843, m Daniel Deibert; ***JOEL** (Mar 4, 1846 – Dec 14, 1908, bur Ch of God Cem), m Sarah Jane Hoch (Oct 10, 1847 – Jun 16, 1932); ***ELIAS** (Aug 25, 1849 – Jul 11, 1885, bur Weishample Cem), m Elizabeth Stutzman (Oct 15, 1847 – Mar 24, 1932), a dau of Peter & Polly (Artz) Stutzman.

DANIEL b 1796, lived in Low. Mahantongo Twp.

JOHN b c1798, lived in Low. Mahantongo Twp.

*MAGDALENA b c1760 m John Koch (no dates), a son of Christian Koch.

*PETER b c1762, m Nov 11, 1788 Magdalena Weiss, had these children: **John b Aug 22, 1789;

**Magdalena b Mar 22, 1791;

*ANNA MARY b c1764, m Conrad Gobel]

The Billows lived on this large farm complex, and while they resided here, a memorable event occurred in June 1936. Samuel Billow had hitched two horses to a cultivator on which he was sitting directly behind the horses, and was working in his corn field. Thunderstorm clouds were overhead, but rain had not yet fallen, when a bolt of lightening struck the horses killing one instantly, the other died a moment later. Miraculously, although seated on the partly steel cultivator, Samuel was not injured. During the same storm, high winds blew down the steeple of Hoffman's Reformed Church; Heavy timbers of the steeple crashed through the slate roof and ceiling into the auditorium of the church. A window was broken and several pews were damaged. The wind blew a barn on the nearby Albert Shade farm four inches from its foundation. A section of the roof was ripped from Simeon Church in Gratz. Trees were uprooted in the valley between Berrysburg and Gratz.

In 1943, Samuel and Lucy Billow's property was described as having a frame dwelling, bank barn, usual out buildings, and an extra barn erected on the smaller 49 acre tract. About 1949, Samuel F. and Lucy A. Billow had their land resurveyed. (They sold 57 acres to Paul Romberger - see writeup on the bordering farm owned by Geo Williard in 1875).

Several years later on May 1, 1953 Samuel F and Lucy A. Billow sold a tract of land containing six acres ninety two perches to Ernest Lenker. The last mentioned tract originally was part of the seventy-four acres described above. It bordered on the creek on the east side of Crossroads. Ernest E. and Edna I. Lenker had a 1 ½ story dwelling built on the land. Ernest has since died. Edna his widow continues to own the land.

Samuel F. Billow died, July 9, 1961, and Lucy gave her daughter Hazel V. Billow part ownership of her remaining land containing sixty-six acres, one hundred nine perches. On November 1, 1963, Lucy A. and Hazel V. Billow sold 2.846 acres of their land to Ernest E. and Edna I. Lenker. Years later on March 31, 1994 Woodrow W. Wiest sold 66 acres 109 perches (minus the small tracts) to Gerald F. Wiest the present owner.

[The **Billow** family came to Lykens Valley from Perry County. William Billow and his wife Ellen (Kumbler) Billow lived in Perry Co. Their son **Samuel F.** (1897 Perry Co – Jul 9, 1961, Lykens Twp), m

Lucy A. Reiger (1907 – Feb 16, 2001), a dau of Charles L. and Myrtle Y.(Kniss) Reiger of Herndon. *Samuel F. and Lucy A. (Reiger) Billow children*: *Hazel V* (no dates) m ___ Palmer of Elizabethville; _____ m Christian Ammann of Bethlehem; *Lloyd J.* (Sep 6, 1899 – 1978) bur Bbg), m Mary E. Klinger, and had these children: *Donald* b 1927; *Albert Lloyd* b May 17, 1928; *Jea*n (b___ d 1978), m M _____ Schumaker. *Robert* (no dates) , lived in Mechanicsburg.]

FARM OF GERALD F. AND LINDA K. WIEST
(George Williard 45 acre farm in 1875, later Reuben Kessler)

This land is a combination of three smaller tracts of land. It came originally from the Peter Hoffman Jr, tract that was sold to Nicholas Hoffman, then Jacob Hoffman who sold to Amos Hoffman on April 5, 1833. Amos Hoffman sold 15 acres on March 8, 1849 to Christian Moyer. He sold to David and Elizabeth Bitterman on April 4, 1855, and they sold March 22, 1860 to George Williard. Another tract of 17 acres from Capt. Benjamin Evitts in 1859, and a third tract that Amos Buffington sold in 1870 to George Williard combined to contain a total of 49 acres 15 perches. On March 27, 1884, after George Williard died, William Schweitzer the administrator of his estate sold this 49 acres of land to Reuben Kessler.

The Kessler family owned this and the adjoining farm for many years. The history of ownership is the same from this point until 1949, when Samuel F and Lucy Billow resurveyed their land. On March 12, 1949, Samuel F. and Lucy A. Billow conveyed a large portion of their resurveyed land containing 57 acres to Paul A. and Salome M. Romberger. The Romberger's owned this farm for many years until Paul died in April 1986. Salome M. Romberger sold 55 acres 93 perches to Ronald E. Romberger on July 7, 1997. Ronald E. and Lynne Eileen Romberger sold the same acreage with dwelling house, barn and garage to Gerald F. and Linda K. Wiest on July 13, 2006.

[*PHILIP ROMBERGER* (Aug 1854 - 1947, bur Hoffman Cem) m Leah J. Matter (1856 - 1923). *Philip and Leah J. (Matter) Romberger had a son:*
**HARRY R.* (Feb 1885 - ___), m Jun 13, 1906 Mary I Hoover b 1890 - 1969), a dau of D. Frank and Susan Hoover. *Harry R. and Mary I (Hoover) Romberger children:*
HARVEY A. b 1907 m Jan 13, 1923 Susan M. Long b 1907, a dau of George W. and Annie (Moyer) Long. *Harvey A. & Susan M. (Long) Romberger children*:*Betty b 1926, m Harold Cooper b 1921, *Son* of John & Myrtle (Fennel) Cooper.
***LILLIE A b1909 m Feb 24, 1926, Blaine A. Hoffman b1906, son of Albert and Mary L.(Schoffstall) Hoffman.
***PAUL ALVIN (Oct 15, 1915 – Apr 1986), m Salome M. _____, *had a son* ****Ronald E. b Oct 11, 1941, m Lynne Eilene _____. *They had a son* *****Ronald E. b Feb 2, 1958,
***LEAH A. (Apr 22, 1918 - May 4, 2012), m Earl M Geist, a son of Gary Geist]

FARM OF MARVIN C. KIEFFER
(ELIAS HOOVER 45 ACRE FARM IN 1875 - BRICK HOUSE built c 1883)

This land belonged to the Hoffman grant, and was conveyed to Jacob Hoffman. On May 6, 1818, Jacob Hoffman sold 16 acres (allowing fifteen feet for a road), to George Stouch. The neighbors were Jacob Hoffman, Jr., John Riegel and John Lubold. The George Stouch family lived here from1828 to 1831, and was assessed for a wooden house. He was a shoemaker. In 1833, George Stouch purchased an adjoining tract of 31 acres from John and Magdalena Rehrer. This land was also part of John Hoffman's warrant mentioned above. Peter and John Stouch, young adults lived here with their parents until about 1847 when the family moved to Halifax. On April 1, 1847 George sold three tracts of land in Lykens Township to Elias Hoover. Two of the tracts (the 31 acre and 16 acre tract) are mentioned above.

Elias Hoover lived here for many years. In 1855 he was assessed for 45 acres with a one and one half story house, log barn and carriage. In 1870, John Bressler age 22 lived with Elias and Elizabeth Hoover and was working in a brickyard. [Note on the 1875 map there is a brickyard located on the land surrounded by Wiconisco Creek.] In 1880, son Daniel Franklin Hoover and his wife Susan Amanda lived with Elias and Elizabeth. In 1883, Elias Hoover was taxed for a brick house and log stable on his 45 acre farm.

On March 18, 1901 two of the tracts from the estate of Elias Hoover were conveyed to his son Daniel F. Hoover. The 16 acre tract was farmland adjacent to Daniel Troutman land. The adjacent 31 acres was the homestead with farm buildings and a dwelling house. Daniel Frank and Susan Amanda Hoover owned this homestead for many years until Daniel Frank died May 29, 1931. Susan Amanda became the owner and continued to own the two tracts (now considered one tract containing a total of 45 acres) until her death on July 20, 1946. Several months later on Sep 30, 1946 her daughter Mary Ida and husband Harry Romberger became the new owners of the homestead.

Harry Romberger died in 1951, and Mary Ida Romberger died in 1971. Several years later on June 18, 1988, the farm was conveyed to Marvin C. Kieffer. He is the present owner.

THE STOUCH/ STOUGH FAMILY
The STOUCH FAMILY did not stay in this area very long.
Listed below are the ones that settled here at least briefly.

[GEORGE STOUCH (Mar 16, 1792 – May 21, 1857, bur Fetterhoff's Cem), m Susanna ____ (Mar 28, 1819 – Jan 7, 1899). According to the 1820 census for Lykens Twp, he had 2 sons under 10, and a wife b c1795. That wife may have died before 1840, because the census for that year has George here in Lykens Twp, with a son 20 to 30 years old. George was a shoemaker. He and his family moved to Halifax before 1850, and in that year he was not married. His dau Rebecca and Amanda Sherer age 18 lived with him. **George and Susanna (   ) Stouch children: Peter** b c1816, m Susannah b c1821, lived in Halifax Twp in 1850, and had Aaron Bressler age 15, and Philip Beisel age 13 with them. **Peter and Susannah Stouch had these children:** <u>Sarah</u> b c1843; <u>Mary</u> b c1848. **John** b c1818, m Mary ___ b c1822, lived in Halifax Twp in 1850, **had a dau** <u>Mary Ann</u> b c1848; **Rebecca** b c1821;

JACOB STOUCH (   ), m Catharine _____. Jacob and Catharine (   ) Stough had these children (some bapt Klinger Ch, Lykens Twp, and some Himmels Ch, Northld Co):
<u>JOHN</u> <u>HENRICH</u> b Apr 20, 1779, bapt Stouchburg Ch;
<u>JOHN</u> b Jan 21, 1784 (bapt Himmels Ch, Northld Co);
<u>ANNA MARIA</u> b Sep 26, 1785; <u>SUSANNA SOPHIA</u> b Mar 14, 1787 (bapt Himmels Ch);
<u>JONATHON</u> b Nov 29, 1788 , bapt Klingers; <u>MARIA SARA</u> b Jan 23, 1791, bapt Klingers
JOHN JACOB STOUCH (b Dec 15, 1780 in Tulpehocken Twp, Berks Co – d Jul 5, 1815, bur Hoffmans Cem). His tombstone written in German states in part: "Here rests the souless body of John Jacob Stauch, through the way of death earlier goes to eternity." He m Sarah Bleystein about 1806. Jacob Stouch had 50 acres of land in Lykens Twp. at the time of his death. It was sold to Jacob Eyerly of Up. Paxton Twp on October 28, 1815. **Jacob and Sarah (Bleystein) Stouch had two sons and a dau:**
JOSEPH (Oct 23, 1807 – Feb 8, 1845, bur St. Johns Hill Cem), m in 1835 to _____, had 5 children;
SARAH b c1811
JACOB b Feb 18, 1816, bapt Hoffman Ch – born after father died?

ELIAS HOOVER FAMILY

[ELIAS HOOVER (Aug 3, 1823 - Mar 20, 1900, bur Hoffman Cem), a son of John and Margaret (Lebo) Hoover, m Elizabeth Daniel (Sep 4, 1826 - May 13, 1856, died same day as her four month old son, bur Hoffman Cem), a dau of Andrew Daniel Jr and his wife Susanna. **Elias and Elizabeth (Daniel Hoover had these children:** <u>MARY</u> b c1843; <u>SARAH</u> b Oct 20, 1845; <u>EDWARD</u> (Apr 24, 1848 - Oct 5, 1893), m Mary Ann Geise (Sep 12, 1854 – Nov 13, 1919); <u>CHARLES</u> (Mar 1, 1850 - Feb 8, 1929, bur Maple Grove Cem, E'ville), m Leah _____ (Jun 5, 1839 - Apr 7, 1909), a dau of _____; <u>AMANDA</u> b c1852; <u>FREDERICK</u> (d May 13, 1856 age 4 months). After Elisabeth (Daniel) Hoover died, Elias married Nov 11, 1856 Elizabeth (Riegel) Witman (b Aug 20,1820 - d Apr 19, 1906 of dropsy), a dau of Andreas and Elisabeth Riegel. The death record called Elisabeth a "farmer lady." **Elias and Elizabeth (Riegel) Hoover had this known child: <u>DANIEL</u>**

FRANKLIN (Feb 17, 1860 - May 29, 1931, bur Hoffman Cem), m Susan Amanda Kolva (1863 –Jul 20, 1946). **Daniel Franklin and Susan Amanda (Kolva) Hoover children: Annie Clara** b Jul 26, 1879; **Mary Ida** (1890 - 1971), m Harry Richard Romberger (Feb 7, 1885 –1951, bur E'ville), a son of Philip and Lea Jane (Matter) Romberger. **Harry R. and Mary Ida (Hoover) Romberger children: Harry A.** (1906 – 1989, bur Hoffman Cem), m Millie R._____ (1912 – 1979); **Lillie E.** b c1909; **Paul Alvin** b Oct 15,1915; **Lea M.** b c1918.] (More information with HOOVER genealogy.]

John C. and Mellisa M. Rudy, Jr.,
(HENRY F. WISE PROPERTY 1 acre in 1875)

This property has the same early ownership as the Elias Hoover farm. (Land from the Hoffman family to George Stouch later to Elias Hoover).On September 28, 1863, Elias and Elizabeth Hoover conveyed part of their tract containing 1 acre 37 perches of land to Joseph Buffington with house, outhouses, barns etc. When Joseph Buffington owned this property, it was described on the tax record as having a log house, smith shop and blacksmith shop. Joseph was a blacksmith and carpenter.

JOSEPH BUFFINGTON (b Aug 24, 1824, bapt St. Johns Hill Ch, Berrysburg - d 1906, bur ___), a son of Isaac and Hannah (Fisher) Buffington, m Sarah Riegel (c1836 - _____), a dau of _____. Joseph and Sarah Buffington lived in Lykens Township in 1880 and he was a blacksmith. They had Catherine Foust age 30 lived with them.
Joseph and Sarah (Riegel) Buffington had these children: Sarah b c1852; **Aaron** b c1858 -), m Marietta _____ (b c1860 - ----). He was a coal miner in 1880 and they lived in Williamstown. **Aaron and Marietta Buffington had these children: Charles E.** (1876 – 1879, bur IOOF Cem, Lykens); **Hannah Susannah** b Jul 30, 1857, bapt Hoffman Ch; **Catherine** b c1858; **John Isaac** b Jul 1, 1859.]

On April 1, 1870, Joseph and Sarah Buffington sold 1 acre, 37 perches of land, a dwelling house and blacksmith shop to Henry F. Wise. He was a resident of Mifflin Township, and was not married at the time. Shortly after he purchased this property, Henry F. Wise was married to Sarah. In 1870, Henry and his wife had Thomas Baddorf age 18 with them, and he was an apprentice blacksmith. They lived on this property until Henry died. Charles W. Wise, administrator of his estate sold the log house and blacksmith shop to Jacob Novinger at a public vendue on March 8, 1884. Sarah Buffington the widow may have moved to Wiconisco, since that is where she is buried.

On March 14, 1900, Jacob Novinger and Adaline Margaret his wife sold the property to Alvin G. Hoffman. He and his family lived here for many years. After Alvin died, Amanda his wife continued to own this home and land, but later she moved to Berrysburg, and on June 12, 1961, she conveyed the property to Michael and Mabel P. Korpa. On February 15, 1974 Michael and Mabel Korpa sold this same parcel, dwelling and another small parcel containing 21 perches of land to Donald L. and Carolyn A. Warfel. Years later, on July 3, 1991, Donald L. and Carolyn A. Warfel sold to John C. and Mellisa M. Rudy, Jr., present owners.

THE WISE/Weiss FAMILY

[This Weise (Weiss, Wise, etc) family came to Upper Dauphin area at a very early period. The first settler here was ADAM WEISE (b Dec 23, 1751 in New Goshenhoppen, Philadelphia County, Pa.-d Oct 5, 1833 bur Davids Cem, Killinger), a son of John George and Eve Weise. The family moved to Heidelberg Twp, Berks County. When Adam was a young man he married Feb 2, 1772, Margaret Elizabeth Wingard (Mar 15, 1749 – Mar 29, 1818, bur David's Cem), a dau of Lazarus and Catharine Elizabeth Wingard.]

Adam Weise served as a sergeant in the Maryland Cavalry during the Revolutionary War, having enlisted at Hagerstown. After the war ended, he settled in Dauphin County. He was one of the few men from this area to apply for a pension. The rules were strict. It was necessary to appear in court, to testify and give an account of the activities that would make the soldier eligible for the pension. Adam Weise appeared in court and gave a description of his experiences during the war. The Gratz Historical Society has a copy of his pension record. It is included in the "Commemorative History Of The Town Of Gratz."

Adam Weise served a total of seven months in the service of the United States. After the war, he and his first wife Margaret Wingert, with their family lived in Hagerstown, Maryland. But by 1782, they were living in Upper Paxton Township, Dauphin County. The Biographical Encyclopedia of Dauphin County gives a description of where he settled.

"He settled at this time on the north side of Wiconisco Creek, on the road (as now known) leading from Cross-Roads to Berrysburg, formerly Hellerstown. He settled on what is generally known as the Elder farm, and very likely he owned the land on both sides of the creek, for he owned three-hundred-acres or more. When I (his youngest son) was ten or twelve years old, in passing along on that road in company with old men of the valley, I was shown the place where they said my father's blacksmith shop had stood, which was a little back in the field from the road, southwest from the old residence which is still standing (1896), but has been remodeled and repaired at different times. I was also shown where he had his coal-pit or hearth, which was about a hundred yards slightly northwest from where the shop stood, in the woods. Blacksmiths used nothing but charcoal in those days, and most of them burnt or charred their own coal. It should be remembered, also, that nearly all of what is now Washington and Mifflin townships to the Susquehanna River was included in Upper Paxtang Township. The Indians were very troublesome, and from this and other causes the family removed to Bethel Township, Berks County, in 1788. Mr. Weise moved back to Lykens Valley to the old place in the year 1796, and in 1802 took up his residence in Millersburg." According to tradition, their house was on the southwest corner of Union and Race Streets, and the third to be built in that village. He also built a blacksmith shop, and continued in that business until his death.

[The land where Adam Weise first lived along the Wiconisco Creek as described above, apparently was in what is now Mifflin Township. But in 1811 (before townships were separated) he had land that was assessed in Lykens Township. Adam Weise received 182 acres of land in Upper Paxton Twp. from Bartram Galbreath in 1798. The land had been surveyed in 1767 to Galbreath. Adam also received 64 acres in Upper Paxton Twp. from John A. Harman on January 18, 1802. The 64 acres were part of land surveyed to Simon Snyder August 1772, and sold to John A. Harman in 1785. Adam Weise received his own grant of 115 acres May 5, 1808. Adam Weise, Esquire and his son Adam Weise, Jr. sold 51 acres of that grant to Leonard Fisher in 1828. Most of his lands appear to be situated between Elizabethville and Berrysburg, just as it was stated by the son of Adam Weise in his memories above.]

On February 1, 1799, he was commissioned by Governor Mifflin to serve as a justice of the peace. He continued to serve in that capacity until his death in 1833. His account book has survived and is being preserved by the Gratz Historical Society. It has many entries concerning citizens of Gratz.

The Weise/Wise Descendants

ADAM AND MARGARET ELIZABETH (WINGARD) WEISE had these children;
*CATHERINE ELIZABETH b Nov 21, 1772 in Heidelberg Twp, m Apr 7, 1795 (by Rev. William Hendel) George Gunderman, **had these known children bapt at Tulpehocken Ch: ** Salome** b Aug 30, 1795; **Elizabeth** b Jan 14, 1799.
*ANN ELIZABETH (b Apr 28, 1774 in Hagerstown, Md. – d 1839, bur Old Luth Cem, Killinger, Up Pax. Twp), m Apr 5, 1797 Philip Shaffer. He d Mar 23, 1814 in Up Pax Twp. She probably later m Uriah German.
*JOHN (b Aug 13, 1776, Hagerstown, Md. – d Jan 30, 1826, bur Killinger), m Jun 7, 1801 Elizabeth Bordner, a dau of Michael Bordner of Up Pax Twp. **They had 15 children 8 sons, 7 dau, these have been accounted for (most bapt St. Johns Hill Ch): **John George** b Feb 2, 1805; **Henrich** b May 16, 1809; **Catharine** b Apr 18, 1811; **Adam** b Mar 21, 1814; **Susanna** b Jul 1, 1817; **Jacob** b Mar 10, 1819; **Jonas** b May 11, 1821; **Christina** b Mar 10, 1823;**Elias** b Nov 21, 1824.
*ANNA MARY b Jun 28, 1778 Hagerstown, Md, m Nov 7, 1797 in Up Pax Twp, Michael Shadel.
*JOHN ADAM (b Jan 24, 1780 in Hagerstown, Md.- d Jan 28, 1854 or 1856 of consumption, bur St. Johns Hill Cem), m 1st Eve Bordner (b Nov 27, 1774 – d within a year after marriage). He m 2nd Elizabeth Lebo (b Jul 31, 1785 – d Apr 18, 1858), both wives were from Up Pax Twp, bur with husband. **John Adam and Elizabeth (Lebo) Weise children: **Catharine** (Jan 13,1805 – May 12,1828, bur St. Johns Cem), m Michael Herman; **Susanna** b Sep 1806 bapt Hoffman Ch; **Elizabeth** (Oct 17, 1808 – Apr 17, 1850 bur St. Johns Hill Cem), m Michael Schmeltzer (Nov 1806 – Feb 7, 1890). In 1880 Michael Schmeltzer was living in Mifflin Twp.His dau Liddie E. age 38, and two grandchildren Elmer E 12, and Charles E. 4 lived with him;**Maria** b Nov 5, 1809; **Maria Margaret** b Dec 15, 1813;**Eva** b Mar 4, 1817; **Peter** (Apr 4, 1822 – Sep 9, 1884) died at 10 p.m. in Mifflin Twp., bur Hoffman Cem. He m Lucetta W. Forney (Jun 14, 1826 - Jan 22, 1902), a dau of John and Maria M. Forney. In 1880, Lizzie Whitmer age 26 lived with the family. **Peter and Lucetta W (Forney) Wise had these children (some bapt Hoffman Ch): ***Sarah** (Dec 3, 1844 - Mar 28, 1875, bur Hoffman Cem; ***Henry F.** (owner of this land), (b c1847 – d pre Mar 1884, bur unknown), m Sarah Jane _____ (1852 – 1916, bur Calvary Meth Cem, Wiconisco), a dau of _____. In 1880, Henry and Sarah and five of their children lived with his parents in Mifflin Twp.**Henry F. and Sarah ( ) Wise children bapt Peace Ch, Berrysburg):** *Charles Edward* b Jan 30, 1869, *William Penrose* (Feb 14, 1871 - 1928, bur Calvary Meth, Wiconisco), not married; *David Grant* b Nov 14, 1873, lived in Lykens; *Mary* (May 12, 1875 - Sep 15, 1901, bur Calvary Meth Cem, Wic.), m George W. Kelly, **had one known son: *George L;* *Emma Plett* b Apr 25, 1876;*Henry L.*b 1877, lived in Wiconisco, not married; *John Bonhard* b Nov 24, 1879; *Francis E.* lived in Wiconisco, not married; *Carrie Amanda* (1882 - 1963), m John Wesley Holtzman (Nov 30, 1878 - Nov 20, 1966), a son of Edward and Susan (Johns) Holtzman of Lykens. ***Isabella** (Jul 18, 1853 - Dec 25, 1853, bur Hoffman Cem);***Adam** b Jun 30 1858;***CharlesW** ( ), m Mary Jane Rickert, lived in Williamstown; ***John A.** b c1859; ***W. Fred** b1861 moved to Polo, Ill; ***Charles R**. Peter & Lucetta Wise had at least four infants buried at Hoffman Cem.

*JOHN GEORGE b Jan 7, 1786 in Up Pax Twp, m Charlotte Moore in 1808.
*ANNA MARGARET b Feb 14, 1789 in Bethel Twp, Berks Co, m Nov 6, 1808 Michael Shoop in Up Pax Twp.
*ANNA MARIA b Jul 21, 1791 in Bethel Twp, Berks Co, m 1811 Abraham Jury in Up Pax Twp.

    After forty-six years, Margaret died, and Adam married a second time on August 23, 1818 to Mary Bitterman Keely, widow of George Keely of Middleburg, Snyder Co. Mary b Mar 20, 1765 in Montgomery County, was a dau of Jacob and Mary Bitterman. About two years later, Mary died and was buried beside Adam's first wife, at Davids Cem, Killinger. Adam Weise married the third time on Dec 10, 1820 to Catharine Neiman Patton, widow of James Patton of Middleburg, Snyder County. Catharine (Nov 10, 1785 – Apr 30, 1863, bur Luth & Ref Cem, Berrysburg), was a dau of Conrad and Catharine Neiman.
Adam and Catharine (Neiman, Patton) Weise children:
*ABEL b Oct 3, 1821 in Millersburg, m _____ lived in Lykens.
*HANNAH b Feb 3, 1823 in Millersburg
*FREDERICK NEIMAN b Aug 25, 1825 in Millersburg, probably the F.N. Weise recorded in Zion Luth Ch, Lykens, d Jul 6, 1901, bur IOOF Cem.

THE JACOB NOVINGER FAMILY

[JACOB NOVINGER (Jun 11, 1855 – Apr 8, 1939, bur Zion Luth Cem, Rife), a son of Joseph N. (1810 – 1881, bur Rife Cem) and MaryAnn (Harman) Novinger (1823 – 1898), and grandson of James (1779 – 1837) and Elizabeth (Messner) Novinger (1786 – 1858) early settlers in Up. Paxton Twp. Jacob m Adaline Margaret Hoke (Apr 9, 1860 – Jul 3, 1942, bur Hoovers Cem, Rife), a dau of Josiah and Sarah A (Fagely) Hoke. Jacob was a blacksmith, and raised produce. **Jacob and Adaline Margaret (Hoke) Novinger had ten children: Raymond** b Mar 1, 1879, m Mary Shoop; **Joseph A.** b Jun 2, 1880; **Harry Walter** (Feb 16, 1883 – Apr 27, 1907, bur Rife Cem); **Dora** b Apr 1884, m ___ Bretz; **Charles E.** (Aug 19, 1886 – Mar 16, 1975, bur Hbg); **Lizzie Verna** (Apr 5, 1888 – Jun 14, 1966, bur Rife Cem), m 1904 to John W. Wagner of Gratz ; **Ansella C.**(1890 – 1901 bur Rife Cem); **Edna R.** b 1891; **Carl C** (1893 – 1968); **Kathryn S.** b 1894.]

THE ALLEN GUERNEY HOFFMAN FAMILY
More information with Hoffman genealogy

[Allen Guerney Hoffman (Oct 6, 1875 - Nov 24, 1934, bur Hoffman Cem), a son of Jonas and Sarah (Rickert) Hoffman, m about 1899 to Amanda Elizabeth Troutman (Feb 6, 1879 – Jan 12, 1975), a dau of Daniel B. and Sarah (Williard) Troutman. Alvin was a carpenter. **Alvin G. and Amanda E. (Troutman) Hoffman children: Charles Daniel** b Sep 28, 1902 m Jun 22, 1929 Darlene A. Miller. **Charles and Darlene (Miller) Hoffman had these children:** Donald Carl b Apr 12, 1932, m Aug 5, 1955 Arlene Roadcap b Apr 25, 1934 in Falksrun, Va. **Donald and Arlene (Roadcap) Hoffman children:** Karen Yvonne b Apr 11, 1958 m Kirk Hartlaub b 1957; Sharon Lynne b Jun 24, 1962, m John-Mark Ambler b 1961, they are missionaries; Daren Daniel b May 1, 1969, m Karen Adams; **Mary** (no dates), m Robert H. Smeltz.

Mabel Pauline (Sep 22, 1908 – Sep 20, 1992), m 1st Oct 16, 1926, Arthur Ira Byerly (Oct 31, 1902 - Apr 12, 1985), m 2nd about 1947, Michael Korpa. **Arthur & Mabel (Hoffman) Byerly children:** Pauline (1927–1 929); Mark Arthur b 1930, m Grace Rebecca Hoffman b 1927 in Halifax; Anna Marie b Jan 1932, m Jan 11, 1925 in Panama, Bruce James Troutman (1929 – 1989)]

HOME OF MR. AND MRS. RALPH D. GONDER
(THE JACOB SIERER PROPERTY - 3 acres 1875)

This land is also part of the original tract of 140 acres known as "Hempfield" that Commonwealth of Pennsylvania granted to John Hoffman. He sold to Jacob and Catherine Hoffman in 1813. On December 13,

1823, Jacob Hoffman and wife Catherine sold 43 acres 33 perches to George Rehrer. Jacob Seiler, Dauphin County Sheriff on August 19, 1833; sold the "chief" part of George Rehrer's tract to John Rehrer. John and Magdalena Rehrer sold part of their larger tract of land to George Rehrer, April 6, 1834. Several years later, George Rehrer, on January 22, 1838, sold a small tract of three acres, with buildings to John Crawford. Soon after purchasing this property, the Crawford's ran into marital problems.

[The Crawford family had lived in Lykens Township for several years. In 1820, John is listed as a manufacturer. They apparently were in dire straits at least part of the time while living in Lykens Township. They were tenants living on the property of Jacob Riegel in 1834, and resided on the property of John Tobias in 1837. During the 1830s for several years, their children were listed under "poor children" whose schooling was paid by the county. In 1832, Catherine 11, and Elizabeth 10, and Eli 7, were listed. In 1835 Elias 10 and Abby 8 were on the list. None are listed again until 1839 when Matilda age 9, and Jeremiah age 5 are listed. By that time they had purchased this property. But according to a record in Dauphin County Court, in August 1839, Magdalena "deserted" John, and on October 7, 1842, he filed for divorce. By 1850, John Crawford age 53 was living with the Amos Hoffman family and was listed as a laborer. Magdalena age 47, (called Polly on the census) lived in Wiconisco Township near Loyalton, and two of their daughters Louisiana and Matilda lived with her. A Charles Crawford age 17 lived with the Michael Spotz family in Mifflin Twp. [See also page 219 for Crawford Info.]

John and Magdalena Crawford sold their home and 3 acres on April 2, 1840 to Jonas Hoffman. From 1840 to 1849, Jonas Hoffman was assessed for three acres, a two-story house and stable, and was listed as a carpenter. About fifteen years later, on March 21, 1855, Jonas Hoffman and his wife sold the three acres to Henry Kauderman. Edward O. and Sarah Reedy owned it briefly in 1860, then sold to Jacob Sierer, whose will directed that the property be conveyed to John Evitts and his wife. On May 25, 1863, the heirs of Jacob Sierer signed a release. His request was honored on May 17, 1884.

THE SIERER/ SEARER FAMILY

[The **SIERER** family descended from immigrant **Jacob Sierer** (Jan 23, 1713 Alsace, Ger- Jan 21, 1785), who came to America in 1743. He settled in Berks County. Jacob Sierer married four times. The name of his first wife is unknown. The second wife was Anna Catharine Schmidt b c1723, to whom he was married Dec 1, 1743 in Evang. Luth Ch, New Holland. In 1756, he married Maria Catharine Bender b 1737, married 1770 the fourth wife Mary Margaret_____ who d Mar 1794. **The children of Jacob Sierer:**
*_____ b Jan 19, 1748 Stouchburg;
*ANNA EVA (no dates), m 1754 Johann Friedrich Wieland;
*MARIA VERONICA (1743 – Mar 28, 1828), m in 1764, Friedrich Deck, had these children (bapt Rehrersburg, Berks Co): **ANNA MARIA b Dec 14, 1767; **JOHAN JACOB b Mar 18, 1779.
*JOHANNES (Mar 7, 1745 – Feb 1, 1813), m Susanna Dups, a dau of John Dups of East Hanover Twp. They had this known child (bapt Rehrersburg, Berks Co:** MARIA ELISABETH b Mar 11, 1783.
*ANNA MAGDALENA b Jan 21, 1749.
*MARIA b Jun 8,1751, died young.
*JOHN JACOB (Nov 5, 1753 - pre 1785)
*GEORGE (1755 - 1804), m in 1788 to Catherine Elizabeth Rith (1759 - 1849);
*JOHN CONRAD b Feb 1756, m Jul 1777 to Anne Marie Stauch (no dates). **John Conrad and Anne Marie (Stauch) Sierer children: **ELISABETH (Nov 15, 1782 - Feb 2, 1858, bur St. Johns "Hill" Cem), m Balthaser Romberger (Dec 28, 1778 - Jun 16,1839), a son of Balthaser and Anna Maria (Trout) Romberger, lived in Wiconisco Township. **Balthaser and Elisabeth (Sierer) Romberger children: Polly** m Daniel Matter; Catharine m Philip Matter; **George**; Elizabeth m Jacob Hoy; **Susan** m Jonas Bordner; Rebecca m Jeremiah Harner; **Hannah** m Jacob Woodside; **Benjamin** ; Balthaser; CONRAD b Mar 7, 1788, Stouchburg; **ANNA MARIA b Feb 18, 1790, Stouchburg;
*EVA CATHERINE (Mar 22, 1757 - Feb 6, 1849), m Jacob Hoover, lived in Lykens Twp, Dau Co. [see write-up of Jacob Hoover for more information]
*JOHN NICHOLAS (Oct 10, 1760 - 1822), m Mary Barbara Schnug (no dates). **John Nicholas and Mary Barbara (Schnug) Sierer had these children: **MARIA BARBARA b Jul 12, 1784; **SUSANNA b May 14, 1791; **JOHNJACOB b Jul 26, 1793; **CATHERINE ELISABETH (Apr 12, 1798 - Aug 22, 1877, bur

Hoffman Cem), m Samuel Williard (May 6, 1779 - Jun 9, 1853), a son of John Peter and Magdalena (Jury) Williard. Catherine Elizabeth was the 2nd wife of Samuel Williard. [More information in the Williard genealogy]; *CHRISTOPHER (1762 - 1827), m Aug 28, 1781 Catherine Deck, dau of Joh N Deck (Stouchburg). This Christopher is probably the one living in Lower Paxton Township in 1815, when he writes his will. He names Barbara his wife, and Magdalena and Christopher Minch as his heirs.
*ELIZABETH (no dates)
*CATHERINE (no dates), m John Frederick Deck, **had this known child: **CHRISTOPHER** b May 20, 1788. Most of the above baptism's are from Tulpehocken Church records.

[JOHN SIERER (Oct 26, 1781 - Oct 16, 1861, bur Hoffman Cem), (not sure of his parents maybe Jacob and Margaret), m Susanna Stump (Apr 22, 1789 - May 18, 1852). They lived in Mifflin Twp.in 1850. **John and Susan (Stump) Sierer children** (some bap St. Johns Hill Ch): JACOB (Apr 22, 1805 - Apr 29, 1884, bur Hoffman Cem), m Elizabeth Derk (Aug 2, 1811 - Jul 16, 1880), a dau of John and Susanna (Stump) Derk; ELIZABETH b Jul 1, 1809; GEORGE (Mar 22, 1811 - Oct 29, 1881, bur Hoffman Cem), m 1st Lydia, had a dau Sarah b Oct 25, 1829, m 2nd Angaline _____ (Dec 28, 1822 - Jun 15, 1863). Angaline is bur beside George in Hoffman Cem. George was a carpenter; Catharine b Feb 6, 1815..

HENRY SIERER(Aug 13, 1832 - Nov 26, 1905 bur Wiconisco Cem), (parents unknown), m Rachel Tschopp (b Apr 18, 1830 Low Mah Twp, Northld -d Sep 8, 1881, bur Hoffman Cem). Henry and Rachel Sierer lived in Lykens Twp in 1860 beside George W. Williard, Jr.
[From the Adam Weise account book we have this information from 1864: "A stray cow came to the premises of Henry Sierer in Lykens Twp, Dau Co. After considerable time the cow was advertised in at least six different places for ten days for the owner to come, but as no owner did appear, the cow was advertised for sale, and after the cow was advertised ten days more, said cow was disposed of by a public sale held for that purpose on Saturday 16th day of January 1864. And was sold by George Hoffman Constable of Borough of Gratz to Henry Sierer for the sum of $12.00. The expenses were as follows to wit: Henry Sierer for keeping the cow three months $7.75, George Hoffman for selling said cow $1.00, H. A. Feagley for crying said sale $1.00, John Ossman for clerking the sale $2.25, total $12.00."]
By 1880, they lived in Wiconisco Twp. **Henry and Rachel (Tschopp) Sierer had these children:** Mary E. (1848 -1921, bur Calvery Cem, Wic.), m John A. Evitts (1850 - 1912), **had dau Anna Alverta** b Feb 6, 1874 bap Hoffman Ch; Samuel b c1859, probably had son Jacob F. (1861 - Feb 1921, bur Wiconisco Cem), m Matilda (1858 – 1946); Charles H. (Aug 30 , 1862 –Apr 17, 1917, bur Cal Meth Cem, Wic)), m Emma L. Kocher (1862 – 1946, a dau of Josiah and Amelia Kocher **had several children bapt St. Johns Ch, Lykens, most died young; John** b 1868

On April 6, 1893, John Evitts and wife conveyed the inherited property to Henry W. and Maria Ida Willier. This property was destined to change ownership again. Henry W. and Maria Ida Willier sold the same three acres to Lizzie E. Riegel March 31,1896. Another transaction took place on March 17, 1900, when Lizzie E. Riegel sold the same property to Josiah Hoover. They sold on April 1, 1903, to Ira F. and Annie C. Row Jr.

On September 15, 1932 Ira F.and Anne C.Row Jr conveyed the property with frame dwelling and out buildings to their son Daniel A. Row. The following day Daniel A. Row sold to Ira F. and Annie C. Row.

The Row family lived here for many years. Annie died on February 18, 1947 and on May 10, 1947, Ira F. Row conveyed the three acres with frame dwelling and out buildings to Ray E. and Josephine D. Gonder.

After Roy died, Josephine D. Gonder sold the property to their son Ralph D. Gonder and his wife Rhonda Dee Gonder on July 21, 1993. [For more information see Rowe genealogy elsewhere.]

HOME OF CYNTHIA A. AND WALTER A. SCHAEFFER
(PETER BODDORF LAND 3 ACRES 1875)

This land is a small part of the original grant known as "Hempfield" and patented to John Hoffman 1801. He sold to John and Ann Mary Hoffman 1813; they to their son Jacob Hoffman. On August 19, 1833 Dauphin Co Sheriff Seiler sold the 105 acres (more or less) of land and buildings of Jacob Hoffman Jr to John Rehrer. He and his wife Magdalena sold 108 acres 102 perches of land and buildings to George Rehrer in 1834. George and Ann Mary Rehrer sold a small tract of their land containing three acres, sixty-five perches on June 25, 1845 to Peter Baddorf.

Peter and John Baddorf had come to this area from Berks County with their father as early as 1812. Other members of the family followed. Peter Baddorf was living as a tenant on the land of Jacob Umholtz at the time that he purchased this property containing a two-story log house and small bank barn. He was a carpenter and continued in that occupation until his death in 1880. The tax record of 1883 shows this property as the Peter Baddorf estate. (Peter Baddorf (1814 -1880) below, son of George Peter Baddorf (1768 -1854) was the owner of this lot.)

After Peter Baddorf died this property was owned by his widow Magdalena. In her will dated July 14, 1888 she requested that Balthaser L. Matter be given the residence. Many years later, on June 24, 1940, Balthaser L. and Sarah P. Matter sold three acres sixty-five perches of land and the home to Mildred M. Matter of Reading, Pennsylvania, who was not married at the time. But the next year, on October 2, 1941, Mildred M. Matter sold it back to Balthaser and Sarah Matter.

On December 5, 1955 Homer C. Matter and Warren B. Matter executors of Sarah P. Matter conveyed this same property to Phyllis and John M. Peifer. Both John and Phyllis Peifer died, and the home was sold February 27, 1996 to Cynthia A. and Walter A. Schaeffer.

THE BADDORF /BATDORF / FAMILY
(Some info gathered by Kathleen Amick Temple)

[The earliest of the **BADDORF** (Batdorf, Bottorf, etc), family is traced to Westphalia, Germany where the first ancestors lived. The earliest known ancestor was (1) **JOHANNES JACOB BATDORF (1534 - 1584)**, a minister in Westphalia. His son (2) **JOHANNES BATDORF SR.** (b 1564 in Westphalia - d in Basel, Switzerland), was a teacher of the Hebrew language. (3) **JOHANNES BATDORF JR. (no dates)**, born and died in Basel, Switzerland, was also a professor of religion in 1647. (4) **JOHANNES JACOB PETER BATDORF** (b Basel, Switzerland b ___- d 1709 in London. England, m c1696 Anna Maria Catharine _____ (b Switzerland -d 1747 in Pa.)

John Jacob Peter and Anna Maria Catharine left Switzerland because of terrible persecutions, and lived in Palatine, Germany. Their five children were born there. More persecution, extremely cold weather that killed their crops, high taxes, and plundering of French and German robber Barons caused the family to leave Germany, for Rotterdam, Holland. They traveled to London, to accept Queen Anne's offer of transportation to New York. The father died before they left London, and three of the children died aboard ship during the voyage to America.

The widow, a son and daughter survived, but were met with suffering from cold and lack of subsistence when they got to New York June 10, 1710. After she arrived in New York, Anna Maria Catharine Batdorf married Johannes Zeller. **Johannes Jacob Peter and Anna Maria Catharine Batdorf had these surviving children:**
*CATHARINA ELIZABETH BATDORF (b c1697 Germany - d 1764 Heidelberg Twp, Berks Co, bur Little Tulpehocken Cem), m Rev. Christian Wilhelm Walborn (Apr 1692 - Dec 11, 1769, Heidelberg Twp, Berks Co, bur Little Tulpehocken Cem)
*JOHANNES MARTIN BATDORF (b Sep 1699, Badorf Village, Stuttgart, Ger - d after 1782, Berks Co, Pa.), m c1717 in New York to Maria Elisabeth Walborn (b Oct 25, 1696 Germany - d Leb Co, Pa.), dau of Johann and Anna Elisabeth Feg Walborn. Martin Batdorf was twelve years old when he arrived in New York with his mother and sister. In 1723 Martin and his wife Maria Elisabeth came to Pennsylvania from Schoharie, N.Y. in company of 150 men, women, and children. They cut a road from Schoharie to the headwaters of the Susquehanna River, and floated down the river in their flatboats and canoes. They drove the cattle along the banks of the stream, than turned up Swatara Creek to the western part of Berks and Lebanon Counties. They built a home on a small branch of the Tulpehocken Creek, over a mile northeast of the present town of Myerstown, Lebanon Co. **Johannes Martin and Maria Elisabeth (Walborn) Batdorf children:**
**Catherine Elisabeth or Margaretha Elisabeth bap Jun 1716, m Christian Walborn Jr. (1739 - Mar 13, 1814);
Hermanus (b c1718 Schoharie, N.Y - d c1763, Tulpehocken, Pa.), m 1st c 1743 Maria Barbara Anspach (b Jan 28, 1719, N.Y - d c1751), a dau of Johan Balthaser and Anna Maria Anspach. **Hermanus and Maria Barbara (Anspach) Batdorf children:
***Anna Maria Catharine b Mar 11, 1744, m Christian Korsnitz (1732 -1814) in Berks Co.;
Maria Elisabeth b Feb 29, 1746, m Michael Katterman, **had these children:** ****John b Nov 19, 1768; ****Catharine b Nov 22, 1771;*George b Feb 9, 1773;**** Elisabeth b Jul 9, 1774; ****Ann Margaret b Feb 20, 1776; Michael b Apr 14, 1778.
George Peter (b Dec 23, 1748 – Mar 30, 1826), m Dec 10, 1771 Anna Maria Karr, dau of Thomas Karr, bur Christ Luth, Berks Co; **George Peter and Anna Maria (Karr) Batdorf known child:** * John b Feb 3, 1773.
*** Martin b Jan 2, 1751;
*** Christina (no dates)

After Maria Barbara (Anspach) Batdorf died, Hermanus m Elisabeth Catherine Rieth b Oct 10, 1734, a dau of John Casper and Anna Margaretha Rieth of Berks Co. **Hermanus & Elisabeth Catherine (Rieth) Batdorf children:** *** Michael b Jan 25, 1754, m Catharine ____, **had these children:** Johannes b Dec 19, 1785; Johan Willhelm b Sep 9, 1788; George Peter b Jan 5, 1791; Salome b Mar 9, 1795; ***David b Mar 12,1755, moved to Maryland;***Philip b Jan 23, 1757, moved to Maryland; ***Christian b 1758; ***Casper_b Dec 14, 1758 - d 1836,Ohio.
John Adam (b1720, Schoharie, N.Y.- d Oct 10,1757, Berks Co.), m 1745 Anna Elisabeth Zeller b1725. **John Adam & Anna Elisa (Zeller) Baddorf children:*Martin b Oct 30,1748;***Peter b Dec 3,1749; ***Andreas b Jun 6,1751;***Eva Elisabeth b Mar 8,1753;***Henrich b May 17,1754;***Simon b Sep 26, 1756.
**Anna Eva b c1721, m Jacob Weiser
Maria Elisabeth (1722 - 1749, York, Pa.), m Capt. Simon Koppenheffer, Berks Co., **had a son Simon b Feb 13, 1758, bapt Stouchberg
Christian (1724 - May 16, 1781, Tulpehocken Twp), m 1748, Eva Regina Karsnitz b c1725, dau of John Karsnitz of Berks Co. **Christian and Eva Regina (Karsnitz) Baddorf had these known children: ***Christian b Jun 1, 1748; ***Maria Elisabeth b May 15, 1749; ***Christophel (Sep 2, 1751 – Aug 8, 1818, Stouchburg); ***Catharine b Mar 31, 1753; ***Johannes b Apr 23, 1755; ***Anna Regina b Feb 5, 1757; ***Eva b Jun 24, 1759; ***Johannes b Jan 18, 1761 – May 5, 1835);***Maria Barbara b Mar 1, 1763; ***Christina Elisabeth b Aug 9,1764; ***Benjamin b May 24, 1767;
**Anna Eva Maria b 1725 m Michael Koppenhaver (1733 - 1823), son of Thomas and Anna Maria Koppenhaver. [More info under Koppenhaver genealogy.]
George Peter (1725 - 1792, bur Christ Luth Ch, Stouchburg, Pa.), 1st m Sep 1, 1748, Eva Elisabetha Reith,(c1725 - Dec 1772 (or Jan 31, 1773), bur Christ Luth Ch, Berks Co),dau of Peter and Anna Catharine Reith, **George Peter and Eva Elisabetha (Reith) Baddorf children: ***Maria Barbara b Nov 21, 1749, not mentioned in fathers estate; ***Hermanus b Feb 17, 1751; ***Maria Elisabeth b Sep 30, 1753; ***Leonard b Mar 4, 1755; ***Anna Maria b Feb 9, 1757; ***Catharine b Apr 4, 1761; Eva b Feb 24, 1763, m Philip Heivner;; George Peter Baddorf married 2nd c1773, Anna Elisabetha Goldman. **George Peter and Anna**

Elisabetha (Goldman) Baddorf had these children: ***John Jacob (Sep 19, 1774 – Mar 31, 1844); ***Margaret Elisabeth b Oct 20,.1776; Jonas b Dec 3, 1780;

Henrich (1732 – Aug 15, 1808, Northld Co), m c1756 Anna Maria Saltzgaber, Berks Co. Henrich & Anna Maria (Saltzgaber) Baddorf known children (bapt Stouchburg, Berks Co):*Eva b May 20, 1756; ***John Michael b Jul 10, 1758; *** Maria Elisabeth b Aug 13, 1760; ***John Adam b Dec 7, 1761; ***Martinus b Sep 26, 1763; ***Maria Barbara b Mar 25, 1766; ***George Peter (b Feb 11, 1768 Berks Co - d c1854, in Ashland Co, Ohio), m Catherine Steiner (c1772 – 1830 in Ohio). He was a farmer and carpenter. Peter was assessed as a resident in Lykens Twp as early as 1815. In 1820 both father and son had land here. George Peter and Catherine (Steiner) Baddorf had these children: (bapt St. Johns & Hoffman Ch);

****JOHN (Aug 12, 1794 – Mar 1, 1872, Wayne Co, Ohio), m Catherine Daniel (Dec 10, 1795 – Jan 21, 1876), a dau of Andreas and Susanna (Hoy) Daniel. After selling their lot (#22) in Gratz, they probably lived in Lykens Township, or at least owned land there until about 1837. They were gone after that. John and Catherine (Daniel) Baddorf children (all recorded in St. John's Ch record, Berrysburg: *****JACOB (Feb 25, 1817 - Jun 8, 1824, bur Hoffman Cem);*****JOHN b Oct 26,1818;*****WILHELM b Jul 27, 1820; ***** ELISABETH b Dec 27, 1822; *****JONATHAN b Dec12, 1824;*****JULIANA b Dec 13, 1826; *****CATHARINE b Mar 24, 1828; *****LEVINA b Nov 2, 1831.
****CATHERINE (Oct 31, 1796 – Nov 7, 1884, Perry Co), m Peter Romberger (Nov 12, 1795 – Dec 19, 1873), a son of Henrich and Elizabeth (Hoffman) Romberger. He was a vet of War of 1812.
****CHRISTINA b Feb 10, 1799
****EVA b Jul 24, 1802
****CHRISTIAN BADDORF (Dec 6, 1803 - d Feb 17, 1885, bur Seyberts Cem, Wmstown), m Sarah Romberger (b Feb 14, 1804 – d Apr 11, 1884), a dau of Heinrich and Elizabeth (Hoffman) Romberger. In 1837 Christian Baddorf and family lived in Lykens Township. Two of their children, Peter age 11, and Jonathan age 7, were listed under "poor children" whose schooling was paid by the county. In 1839, Christian age 9, and Amos age 6 were listed as poor. By 1850, Christian Baddorf was a farmer living with his family in Wiconisco Twp. Christian and Sarah (Romberger) Baddorf had these children: *****PETER (b Jul 14,1825 – Oct 16, 1858, bur Calvary Meth, Wiconisco);*****JONATHAN b c1829; *****CHRISTIAN JR. (Dec 10, 1828 – Apr 5, 1876, bur St. Pauls Luth, Tower City). Before Christian Baddorf died, he named his brother Amos executor of his estate. However, Amos refused to serve. The father Christian Baddorf was a witness to the statement of Amos. Christian Baddorf Jr m Sarah _____ (Nov 22, 1827 - Dec 9, 1863). Christian and Sarah Baddorf, Jr had these children (bapt Zions Ch, Lykens); Mary J. b Jul 27, 1853; Sarah E. b Apr 19, 1855; S.A.E b Aug 29, 1856;*****AMOS (Mar 5, 1831 –Jul 3, 1916, bur Calvary Meth Cem, Wic), m Susan _____ (Nov 16, 1826 – May 28, 1892), lived in Wiconisco Twp in 1880 and was a coal miner. Amos and Susan Baddorf had these children: Andrew b & d 1856;Matilda b c1859; Anna b c1862; Rose b c1867; George A. b c1871; *****HENRY b c1835, m Lucinda _____, had three children that d young; *****ELIZABETH b c1837;*****AMANDA b c1841; *****DANIEL (Feb 15, 1841 – Mar 24, 1905, bur Wiconisco Cem), m Elizabeth _____ (1842 – 1923). Daniel served in Co K of 173 Pa Regt drafted militia during the Civil War. He was discharged Apr 7, 1863 due to physical disability (Rheumatism in the knee). They lived in Williams Township in 1880, where he was a huckster. Daniel and Elizabeth Baddorf children: Mary J. b c1862; Malinda b c1865; Chas W. b c1867; Carrie L. b c1877;
*****PHILLIP b c1844; *****MARY J. b Jul 27, 1853; *****SARAH E. b Apr 19, 1855.
****JOHN JACOB (May 8, 1805 – Jul 10, 1870, Delta, Fulton Co. Ohio)
****PETER (Jan 20, 1814 - Dec 5, 1880, bur Hoffman Cem), his death date recorded in Hoffman Ch book, gives name of both parents, Peter and Maria Catherine(Steiner) Baddorf. He m 1st Elizabeth Welker (Nov 23, 1812 - Jul 7, 1868. bur Hoffman Cem), death recorded in Hoffman Ch book. Peter Daniel Baddorf m 2nd about 1869, Mary Magdalena Ledig "Lettick" (Aug 9, 1823 - May 3, 1891, bur Hoffman Cem), a dau of William Ledich (Dec 17, 1792 - Oct 17, 1871) & Magdalena (Bechtel) Lettick (Nov 16, 1797 - Feb 16, 1871) . She was the widow of Balthaser Matter who died in 1868. Peter and Elizabeth Baddorf and family lived in Lykens Twp in 1850 and 1860, and he was a carpenter. By 1870 Peter and Mary Magdalena are married, and Peters daughter Amanda age 14 is with them. Mary Magdalena's two sons from her first marriage, Henry Matter age 11, and Balthaser Matter age 6, also lived with them. In 1880, Peter and Magdalena had Baltzer Matter 16, and Zelonia

Deiter age 14, hired servants with them. **Peter and Elizabeth (Welker) Baddorf children (some bapt Hoffman, some St. John's Hill Ch):**

*****JONAS (May 20, 1837 - Aug 26, 1874, died of smallpox, bur Hoffman Cem), m Sarah Miller (Feb 22, 1837 – Jan 29, 1901, bur Calvary Cem, Wiconisco); Jonas and Sarah (Miller) Baddorf had three minor children when he died: *Sarah; Hannah; Rebecca.*

*****ELIZABETH (1839 – no dates, bur Hoffman) , m Jun 1864 Joseph Russell (Jun 20, 1836 – Nov 23, 1901, bur Hoffman Cem), lived in Washington Twp. was Civil War Vet. [more info under Russell genealogy.];
*****SUSANNAH Feb 26,1842, m ___ Miller;
*****JOHN W. (Oct 19,1843 – Oct 3, 1921), m 1ˢᵗ Annie M. Thompson (Sep 6, 1848,- Aug 1876, bur Hoffman Cem), had son *John E.*(1866 – Feb 17, 1911, died in explosion at Short Mt. Slope), m Lizzie Row, a dau of John Row. John W. Batdorf m 2ⁿᵈ Mary A. Haine (1829 – 1925, bur Calvary Meth Cem, Wic. Twp);
***** SARAH (Sep 25, 1845 – Nov 11, 1922, bur E'ville), m Oct 18, 1863 James H. Smith (1842 – Feb 16, 1904), lived in Wiconisco Twp in 1880. **James & Sarah (Baddorf) Smith children bapt St. Johns, Lykens):** *George F.* (1864 –1947), m Mary ___(1865 –1939); *Daniel* b 1869; *Mary* (1874 –1942), m Thomas Hess; *Samuel* (1876- 1963), m Angeline Hoffman (1883 – 1952); *Kate* (1878 – 1969), m Henry Heggins; *Sarah Bertha* b Feb 9, 1889;
***** PETER (Feb 21, 1848 - Nov 25, 1932, bur Calvary Meth Cem, Wic), m Mary Sierer (Jul 16, 1852 - Aug 5, 1908), dau of Henry & Rachael (Tschopp) Searer, lived in Wiconisco Twp in 1880, where he was a carpenter. **Peter and Mary (Searer) Baddorf children (some bapt St. Johns, Lykens):** *Emma* (1875 – Mar 1950, bur Lykens), m James Messner; *Elwood H.* b c1877; *Edmund Fred.*(1878 - Jun 3, 1939, m Aug 24, 1899 Jennie G. Rusbatch (1879 – 1962); *Artz Clayton* b Oct 12, 1884; *Peter Clay* b Oct 29, 1886; *Rayman Claud* b Oct 9, 1887; *Elizabeth Ann* b Jul 27, 1890, m Wm. Kolvach; *Lucy May* b May 22, 1895, m Gordon Matter;
*****THOMAS (Jul 2, 1851 -1913), m Mary Peters (Mar 31, 1858 – Aug 3, 1924, bur Oak Dale Cem), dau of Samuel and Mary Ann (Swartz) Peters of Snyder Co, lived in Wash Twp in 1880. In 1870 Thomas was with the Henry Wise family in Lykens Twp. **Thomas & Mary (Peters) Baddorf children:** *George F.* b c1876; *Edwin C.* b c1878;
***** LOUISA (Nov 3, 1853 – Jan 29, 1926, bur Meth Cem, Wmstown), m William A. Frantz d 1900, had these children: *William* b 1872; *Emma* (1876 – 1949), m Oswald H. Leuschner (1869 – 1927, bur Tower City); *Annie* b 1876; *John E.* (1879 – 1943);
*****AMANDA (Mar 2,1856 – Aug 13, 1908, bur Wiconisco), m Aug 19,1888 James W. Shoop (Sep 20, 1858 – Jan 7, 1940), **had these children:** *Alberta* m Charles Kuntzelman; *Jennie* m Thomas Schreffler; *Maud* m Lester Martz.
****SARAH b May 14, 1815, bapt St. Johns Hill Ch
****JOHANNES b Jan 9, 1817, bapt St. Johns;
****CATHERINE b Mar 5, 1819 bapt St. Johns;
****THOMAS (Sep 3, 1820 bapt St. Johns Hill – May 21, 1899, Freeport, Stephenson Co., Il., a son of Peter and Catherine Baddorf Jr , m Magdalena McNeal (Feb 18, 1821 Pa. - Jul 26, 1881). **Thomas and Magdalena (McNeal) Baddorf had these children (some bapt Dau Co):*******Matilda b c1842; *****Amanda b c1844, m Frederick Merrill in 1859 in Il;*****Mary Jane b Jun 2, 1846, m John Burckhart in 1865, in Il; *****Sarah b c1848 Dau Co;*****Jonathan A b c1851; *****Ramsey M. May 1853 Pa. - Sep 21, 1916, Freeport, Il. m Louisa Marie Zimmer in 1880, Il.; *****Joanna b c1858 Ogle, Il; *****William H.(Jul 21, 1858 – Jan 1861 in Il.);*****Edward W. b c1862, m Jennie Cummersford in 1882 in Il.. After Magdalena d, Thomas Baddorf m Caroline Pralle in 1883.
The following three children of Peter Baddorf were listed under "poor children" whose school tuition was paid by the county in 1832.
****JONATHAN b Dec 11, 1822, m May 3,1857 Lucetta Rickert (Jan 30, 1840 - Apr 22, 1867), Jonathan and **Lucetta (Rickert) Baddorf children (bapt Hoffman Ch):** *****John Henry (Jul 14, 1858 – 1931, bur Wiconisco Cem), m Amelia Siemons (1858 – 1940) , had these children: Harry; Bessie; Elsie;*****Edward Franklin b Nov 30, 1859 *****Hannah Rebecca b Jul 16, 1863
****DANIEL b Aug 19, 1824 bap Hoffman Ch, - d May 13, 1903, bur Calvary Meth Cem, Wic Twp.) m Christiana Zimmerman (1825 - 1902)
****JACOB b Apr 3, 1826;
****ELIZABETH b Apr 5, 1828;

***<u>Catherine Elisabeth</u> b Sep 10, 1775, dau of Henrich and Annie Marie Baddorf

<u>Catharina Maria Anna</u> b c1734, m Christian Noecker (Mar 3, 1744 - Jun 1809). Christian and Catharine Maria Anna (Baddorf) Noecker **had these known children: <u>Elisabeth</u> b Jun 9, 1767; <u>Johannes</u> b Dec 22, 1768; <u>Christian</u> b Nov 21, 1770; <u>Catharine</u> b Jan 21, 1772; <u>Jacob</u> b Dec 1773; <u>Christopher</u> bap Dec 28, 1775; <u>Henrich</u> b Feb 4, 1778; <u>Benjamin</u> b Jan 12, 1780;

[This next one was not identified with the Baddorf family above.
****<u>John</u> (c1786 -   ), m Mary Grow (1787 -1877) moved from Berks to Jackson Twp, Northld Co by horse and wagon, and owned a small farm. They are buried at United Evang Cem Mahanoy. **John and Mary (Grow) Baddorf had these children (some bapt Stone Valley):**
Catherine (Nov 22, 1807 - Jun 11, 1883), m Samuel Heim; Marie (   ), m Samuel Eisenhart of Shamokin; Joseph, (b Jan 10, or 28, 1812 in Reading - Dec 12, 1894, bur Stone Valley Cem, Northld Co) came with father to Northld Co, learned blacksmith trade, worked in Low Mahanoy Twp. m 1st Sarah Bohner (Dec 25, 1812 - Mar 31,1870), m 2nd Lydia Hepner (Dec 28, 1828 - Oct 2, 1906), dau of Peter and Magdalena Hepner, had seven children - one was Levi B. b Sep 12, 1843, m Harriet Zartman, dau of Adam and Susan (Forney) Zartman; **John** b May 18, 1820; **Sarah; Rebecca; Eliza; Harriet; Tillie; Lucy Ann** m Peter Kniss. David (Dec 12, 1816 - Sep 28, 1901, bur Stone Valley Cem), m Charlotte Kemp (Jan 29, 1819 - Dec 31, 1897).]

BALTHASER L. MATTER FAMILY

[**BALTHASAR L. MATTER** (b Apr 22, 1864 - d Aug 4, 1949, bur St. John' Cem)), a son of Balthasar and Magdalena (Ledig) Matter, m Sarah P. Lubold (Feb 10, 1869 - d Jan 14, 1955), a dau of Aaron and Sarah (Rogers) Lubold. **Balthaser & Sarah P. Lubold Matter children (some bapt Hoffman Ch): Aaron Jerome** b Dec 18, 1888; **Warren B.** (1889 - 1968, bur St. Johns Cem); **Beulah Lucretia** b May 16, 1891; **Charles Homer** b May 1, 1892; **Verna Cordelia** b Feb 4, 1894; **Mildred M.** (1901 - Sep 12, 1975 bur St. Johns Cem), 2nd wife of Theoron Fulkroad; **Florence** b 1903; **Laura** b 1905; **Myrtle** b c1908 m Mar 14, 1925, Eston L. Dockey.]

HOME OF MARK AND RUTH ANN SIMS
(Part of George Williard tract in 1875)

This lot was part of the Hoffman land sold to Rehrer, then in 1849 to George Williard. On January 1, 1885, the heirs of George Williard conveyed a large tract of 108 acres 102 perches of land to Daniel B. Troutman. After Daniel B. Troutman died, his widow Sarah owned the land, and after her death, the heirs sold three acres 141 perches of land and house to Lloyd I. and Beulah M. Troutman on March 16, 1946. Several months later, on August 28, 1946, the Troutman's conveyed the same property to Arthur and Alverta Wentzel. Arthur Wentzel died February 8, 1947, and Alverta owned the premises. Shortly thereafter, Alverta married James R. Enders and lived in Dalmatia. On September 10, 1949, they leased the property to Homer J. and Grace Hains with the option to buy. On October 28, 1959, James R. and Alverta Enders, and Homer J. and Grace B. Hain joined in the conveyance to Ruth Ann and Mark Richard Sims. The 3 acre 141 perch property containing a 2 ½ story frame dwelling and other buildings adjoined the public highway between Loyalton and Uniontown, the land of Charles Riegel, the estate of John Riegel, and south to Matters. Mark and Ruth Ann Sims are the present owners. About 2003, a disastrous fire completely destroyed the old house and it was replaced by a new one.

[**MARK RICHARD SIMS** is a son of Henry Sims (1902 – 1957, bur Calvary Meth, Cem) and Helen (Dewalt) Sims (1904 – 1986) of Williamstown. He m Ruth Ann Klinger, a dau of Stanley and Katie Klinger. **Mark and Ruth Ann (Klinger) Sims children:**
Allen , has 2 children: Dillon: Megan m _____ Abrahms; **Brian**, m Deana Pickel, 2 sons: Kyle; Kurt
Carolyn m Rodney Fenstermacher; **Doreen** m Duane Dockey – 2 sons

JEFFREY J. AND WENDY L. HENNINGER FARM
(GEORGE R. WILLIARD -68 acres 1875– refer to map for location)

This land was part of a large original tract that Commonwealth of Pennsylvania patented to Leonard Miller on August 21, 1751, Andrew Riegel purchased 311 acres in 1791. His heirs sold a tract of land to John and Ann Mary Hoffman; They sold to John Hoffman, Esquire and his wife Elizabeth on September 15, 1813. Their heirs sold a large tract of land to Adam Williard in April 1852. He assigned 55 acres 134 perches of that land to George R. Williard in December 1853. Adam Williard conveyed another tract of 100 acres with log house and log bank barn to his daughter Sarah and Joseph Laudenslager. George and Carolyn Wiest received it next, and on April 1, 1859 sold to Benjamin J. Evitts. That same day, Benjamin J. Evitts conveyed part of the land containing 12 acres 22 perches to George R. Williard, giving Williard a total of 68 acres. Many years later, on March 1, 1879 George and his wife sold the two tracts to John Henninger of Mifflin Township. They bordered on neighboring tracts of Isaac Miller, Isaac Romberger, Israel Neiman, and George Williard.

On December 12, 1900, the heirs of John Henninger conveyed the two tracts (68 acres) in Lykens Twp. and other accumulated land, (some acreage in Mifflin Twp) to Henry Henninger. On September 4, 1925, the heirs of Henry Henninger sold the two tracts to John I. and Mabel Henninger. Mary E. Henninger received the land on May 3, 1929, and on Dec 9, 1943, she conveyed the same to Paul E. Henninger. During the 1960's Paul E. Henninger sold several building lots from the larger acreage to Clarence and Marie Enders, Dale S. Hoffman and possibly others. The remainder of the farm was conveyed to their son James F. and Marie Y. Henninger on November 3, 1972. They in turn conveyed to Jeffrey J. and Wendy L. Henninger on Dec 30, 1982; they are the present owners. The old house has been replaced by a new brick house.

DANIEL A. AND BARBARA L. LOUGHANS FARM

(Was Capt. Benjamin J. Evitts 110 acres in 1875, & later Troutman Dairy)
(We are grateful to Florence Troutman Young for sharing many of her memories growing up on this farm . Also Paul Troutman Jr for Troutman Dairy history)

This farm is part of a grant of 165 acres that Commonwealth of Pennsylvania warranted to Nicholas Sins in Apr 1779. The land was eventually patented to John Hoffman in 1801, and the Hoffman family lived here a long time. On April 28, 1852 Adam Willier purchased 145 acres 134 perches of the land from the heirs of John Hoffman, Esquire. He divided the land and assigned 55 acres 134 perches of it to George Willier on December 26, 1853. On that same date Willier assigned his plantation of 100 acres 112 perches of land to Sarah and Joseph

Laudenslager. The Laudenslager's sold the 100 acres to George and Caroline Weist on March 31, 1855. Several years later on April 1, 1859, the Wiest's sold the old homestead with 61 acres 40 perches and what was described as a two-story log rough cast house, springhouse, log barn and necessary out buildings to Benjamin J. Evitts. About 1872, George Willier conveyed his 55 acre tract to Benjamin J. Evitts, giving him substantial acreage, which was partly in Lykens and Mifflin Township.

The Loughans Farm From A Recent Photo

While B. J. Evitts lived on this farm, he became a member of the local militia and at first served as a cook. When the Civil War became reality, the 177th Regiment of Pa. drafted Militia was activated. On Nov. 2, 1862, Co. I of the 177th Regiment was formed and on November 25th, Evitts became captain, and served in that capacity until Aug. 5, 1863. His brother Henry C. Evitts was a private in the company. Many of the men from this area were assigned to Evitts' Company, at least for part of the time during the war. After the war ended, Capt. Evitts was called upon on numerous occasions to testify, or substantiate the claims given by the men in his company, as they applied for pensions. When the war ended, Capt. Evitts returned to this farm. He and his first wife Sarah lived here until her death in 1876.

After Sarah died, Benjamin J. Evitts decided to disperse of some of his lands. One reason was because he had accumulated some debts (possibly during the war) that he hoped to satisfy. Another reason was probably because in January 1877, B. J. married Sarah Geise Garber, widow of Civil War Veteran George Garber. Capt. and Sarah Evitts decided to move to Gratz, where he continued his occupation as tailor, and served as postmaster of Gratz for several years. His new wife had a small shop on the western end of Gratz that she opened after her first husband died. She sold needles, thread and various and sundry items that would be needed by the housewife. She also sold children's shoes. When she married Evitts she continued in this business.

Capt. Evitts assigned his land to H. L. Lark in January 1878, with directions to sell. A public vendue was held in April 1879, and the two tracts (55 acres and 61 acres) were sold to Franklin Beisel of Mifflin Twp. By this time the old log house had become weather-boarded. The old log barn continued to have its early style straw roof.

THE EVITTS FAMILY

[GEORGE EVITTS (b Mar 1797 in Lanc Co - d Mar 22, 1864, bur Peace Cem, Berrysburg), believed to be the son of Joseph and Margaret or Rebecca (Rutter) Evitts (1743- after 1790). Another death date given for George

Evitts is Apr 7, 1865. George m Salome _____ (Mar 13, 1800 - Aug 31, 1871) also of immigrant parents. Very little is known about George Evitts. Members of the Evitts family believe that the ancestor settled first in Cumberland County, Maryland. A record appears in the account book of Leonard Reedy in March 1830. Dr. John Orndorff was demanding payment from George Evitts for medical attention and medicine received. Payment and costs ($4.08) paid in October 1830. George Evitts has not been found on the census record for 1850. However, a tombstone record indicates he lived until 1865. His wife Salome (Sarah) was with her son Benjamin J. in 1850, 1860, and 1870. **Children of George and Salome Evitts:**

FREDERICK (1819 -1899, bur Peace Cem, Berrysburg), m 1st Sarah Koppenhaver (May 3,1820 - 1841), m 2nd Elizabeth Koppenhaver (Jul 5, 1825 - Oct 6, 1905), both wives bur near him in Peace Cem. They were sisters, and their parents were Thomas and Mary Magdalena (Hoffman) Koppenhaver. In 1850 and 1860 Frederick lived in Washington Twp, and was a tailor. **Frederick had five children: Anna Maria**, a dau with wife Sarah, she probably died young; the next children were born to 2nd wife Elizabeth: **Sarah** (1851 - 1875, bur Peace Cem); **John P.** (1852 - 1932, bur Peace Cem), m Mary A. (1850 - 1931); **George F.** (Aug 1854 – 1926, bur Wiconisco Cem), m c1875 Sarah A. Neiffer (Aug 13, 1857 – Feb 1939), a dau of W. G. Neiffer, lived in Lykens in 1900.;

HENRY C. (Oct 4, 1820 - Apr 23, 1904, bur Maple Grove Cem, E'ville), m by Rev Hemping in Washington Twp in 1840 Ellen "Nellie" Messner (1822 - 1903), a dau of Phillip Messner. They lived n Jackson Twp in 1850, and he was farming. John Seiler age 12 lived with the Evitts family in 1850. By 1870, they lived in Lykens Twp. **Henry and Ellen (Messner) Evitts had these children: Benjamin** (1844 - 1852);**Aaron** (b Jan 25, 1847 Up Paxton Twp- d May 10, 1916, in Minersville, bur E'ville),m 1st Mary Jane Romberger, dau of Isaac Romberger, divorced May 1871. Aaron m 2nd in Pillow by Rev. Engle Aug 4, 1883, to Clara H. Barr. He served in Civil War 177th Co. I. **Aaron and Clara (Barr) Evitts children:** Grace b Feb 24, 1884; Asa Burton b Jul 22, 1885;

Charles b 1849, probably d young; **John A.** b May 18, 1850, m Mary Sierer (no dates). John lived with his parents on a farm in Lykens Twp in 1870. **John and Mary (Sierer) Evitts children:** Annie Alverta b Feb 6, 1874; Margaret b Aug 1, 1855; Mary b Sep 13, 1861 - 1953), m Isaac Harner (c1855 - 1928, bur Salem Union Cem, E'ville); others d young. Henry Evitts served with his brother Capt B.J. Evitts in Co I, 177th Inf during the Civil War. He was a Pvt and served as a wagoner. After he came home from the service, Henry lived first in Upper Paxton, then in 1864 moved to Washington Twp. He later lived in Lykens Twp for eleven years before moving back to Elizabethville. He received an invalid pension because he suffered from chronic diarrhea brought on by exposure to bad weather and unfit water during his service time.

CATHARINE b c1830, who lived with her brother Benjamin in 1850.

BENJAMIN J. (Sep 20, 1822 - Mar 30, 1909, bur Peace Cem Berrysburg with first wife), m 1st Sarah Ann Yeager (Dec 1, 1836 - Jan 12, 1876), a dau of Peter and Elizabeth (Matter) Yeager of Mifflin Twp. After they married, Benjamin and Sarah (Yeager) Evitts lived in Mifflin Twp. In 1850, Benjamin was a tailor. Nicholas Hoffman and Henry Bressler lived with the family, perhaps as apprentice tailors. Also living with Benjamin and Sarah were Benjamin's mother Salome Evitts age 56, and his sister Catharine age 20. B. J. Evitts' mother continued to live with the family until her death, about 1871. Letters of Adm. were filed for her in January 1872, with sureties J. Tobias and B.F. Evitts. B. J. Evitts died at the home of his son William near Loyalton.

Benjamin and Sarah (Yeager) Evitts children:

Margaret Ellen (Nov 12, 1848 – Sep 16, 1907), died at the home of her daughter, m Charles A. Hoover (Jun 22, 1850 - Mar 28, 1916), son of John and Elizabeth Hoover, **had these children:** Sarah m Harry Strayer; Mary Jane b Oct 11, 1872, m Clayton Haag of Phoenix, Arizona; Christiana Alverta b Dec 25, 1873, m T. T. Wierman of Sunbury; William Henry (Feb 3, 1876 -Oct 1937, m Mar 16 1907 Rebecca Kissinger, **had these children:** _____ m George Kimmel of Valley View; _____ m Carlos Hoffman; _____ m Ralph Kessler, Spring Glen, _____ m Louis Zimmerman of Valley View; Florence, m William Moyer of Annville;; Blanche; Charles; Walter Elwood b Apr 2, 1878, lived in Gratz; William lived in Tremont in 1907; Margaret Ellen (Sep 14, 1880 - Sep 19, 1927, bur Hoffman Cem), m Simon L. Daniel (Oct 1, 1882 - Oct 25, 1926); Henrietta Lovera Feb 7, 1884 , m Leo Troutman , lived in Fear Not; Allen Luther b Feb 23, 1886, m Hannah,, lived Lower Northld Co; Paul (c1895 - 1951, bur Hoffman Cem), m Lizzie Klinger (1898 - 1968); Clarence lived in Dornsife;

John Philip b Jun 2, 1852, an apprentice house carpenter in 1870. He m Mary _____ b c1852, had these children: Elizabeth b c1872; Annie A b c1874; Ira W. b c1877. The family lived in Lykens Twp in 1880. (This may or not be the John (1850 - 1912) and Mary E. (1848 - 1921) Evitts bur in Calvary Meth Cem in Wiconisco.

Capt Benjamin J. Evitts
Civil War Veteran

Sarah (Yeager) Evitts
Wife of Capt B. J. Evitts

Flossie & Beulah Evitts
Daughters of William Evitts

Edward Evitts grandson of William Evitts
& unidentified friend
Holding Capt. B. J. Evitts sword & gun

William Evitts Sons: Walter, Ed, Ben, Henry, Fred

William Evitts grandchildren: Albert & Roy Evitts, Verna Travitz, Ruth Evitts, Lloyd Evitts

William Evitts girls – Laura, Beulah, Flossie, Verna
Their children: Verna Travitz, Ruth Evitts

William Evitts Family – Fred, Laura ,Henry, Flossie, Ben, Verna, Orpha, Ed. Gr. Child: Verna, Albert, Ruth, Lloyd, Roy, Beulah, Walter & wife Mabel, parents Sarah & William Evitts

<u>William Albert</u> (Sep 5, 1854 - 1928), m Sarah Adaline Daniel (Apr 1859 - 1925) both bur Hoffman Cem
William and Sarah Adaline (Daniel) Evitts children: <u>Perla May</u> b May 19, 1879; <u>Frederick Weidel</u> b Sep 4, 1900; <u>George Washington</u> (1881 – 1882); <u>Beulah Agnes</u> b Jan 21, 1890;
<u>Henrietta Catharine</u> (Sep 13, 1860 - Oct 30, 1936), m Charles Weiss (1858 - 1936), both bur Simeon Cem [see Information under Weiss family.]
<u>Salome E.</u> b Feb 17, 1865
<u>Joseph</u> (no dates) lived in Ashland
_____ m David White of Williamstown

After his first wife died, in a ceremony performed by Rev. J. S. Newhart on January 20, 1877, Sarah Ann Geise Garber became the new bride of Benjamin J. Evitts. They were married in Sarah's home in Gratz. Sarah Ann (May 1, 1845 - May 17, 1934, bur Simeon Cem), was a dau of Benjamin and Margaret (Umholtz) Geise, grew up in Lykens Twp, and attended Geise School. She m 1st George W. Garber (b Dec 15, 1843 Deer Park, Sch Co -d Sep 10,1873, age 29, bur IOOF Cem, Pottsville). He served during the Civil War in Co D, 25th Regt Penna Vol. Sarah and George Garber married about 1865, while she was living near Gratz. It was a rough stormy day. The ceremony took place in Berrysburg at the home of Rev. Yost, the Evangelical minister. Sarah's bridesmaid was her twin sister Mary, who later married Jacob Shiro. In the evening after the wedding, the newly weds were serenaded by a group of friends. Edward A. Hoffman was among the friends, and he recalled the event many years later. During their marriage, Sarah and George lived in both Pottsville and Gratz. George and Sarah (Geise) Garber had these children: Ida Celeste (Garber) b in Gratz Aug 15, 1866, m May 13, 1884 to Dr. G.M. Schminky, son of Dr. Isaiah S. Schminky; George Garber (1870 - 1941, bur Simeon Cem), lived in Holidaysburg, Pa., name of his wife unknown; Harvey Garber b c1873, m Mary ___, lived in Progress, Pa.
Benjamin and Sarah Ann(Geise, Garber) Evitts children:
<u>Joseph Benjamin</u> was b Aug 17, 1878. He was a coal miner in 1900, and living with his parents. He also taught in the schools of Gratz, later moved to Lebanon. He married, but name of wife is not known.
<u>Charles A.</u> (May 22, 1881 - 1959, bur Simeon Cem), m Mary E. Strayer (1886 - Apr 3, 1936). Charles worked at a sawmill in 1900, lived with his parents. **Charles and Mary (Strayer) Evitts children**: <u>Allen</u> Blair (May 22, 1906 - 1958, bur Simeon Cem), m Ruth Tregallas; <u>Robert</u> Henry b Jun 29, 1913.]

About a year after they moved to this farm, Frank Beisel was patching the roof and his two year old daughter Katie was playing in the barn yard. She noticed a mother pig and her baby pigs nearby, and Katie wanted to play with them. The mother pig grabbed Katie's face in her mouth. When her father saw it, he jumped from the barn roof and rescued Katie. But serious damage was done to her face. Katie had stitches on both sides of her face, in front of her ears. She had scars the rest of her life.

In 1883, the Beisel family built a new barn. They continued to use the original wagon shed and summer house. About ten years later, in 1893, they tore down the old house, and used the logs from it to construct the new one. While the house was under construction, the family made meals and ate in the summerhouse. The parents and three of the children slept in the summerhouse. The other children slept in the wagon shed.

To the left:
Franklin & Adeline (Romberger) Beisel – Picture Taken about 1877

"New House" Built 1893 by Beisel.
Beisel Family Photo taken
Between 1894 & 1900.
L to r: Kate, John, Carrie, Harry, Adeline (Romberger) Beisel Lehman, Cora, Sam Kocher (hired man), Charles Beisel.

About a year after the new house was built Franklin Beisel died, on November 4, 1894. His widow remained on the farm for about seven years, and hired Reuben Anders to work as the farmhand. Her newly wedded daughter Katie and husband James M. Troutman came to live with Mrs. Beisel about 1900, and helped to maintain the farm.

Shortly after Jim and Katie moved to the farm, about 1902, Jim established the Troutman dairy. In April 1905 Mrs. Beisel sold her sixty-one acre farm to Katie and James. She was married to Harvey Lehman and she and her new husband moved to Elizabethville. In 1910, in addition to their children James and Kate Troutman had Henry ____ age 21, a servant, and Beulah Matter 17, a servant living in their home.

A Family Gathering: Photo Taken about 1907.
Front Row – l to r: Cora Troutman dau of James; **Paul Henninger** son of Mary Henninger; **Walter Henninger** son of Will & Sophia Latsha Henninger; **Row 2: Henry Henninger; Isaac Romberger; Wm Koppenhaver. Row 3: Jane Romberger Henninger** wife of Henry; **Mary Henninger** dau of Jane & Henry; **Sophia Latsha Henninger** holding her dau Anna; **Mrs William (Susanna) Koppenhaver; Row 4: Katie (Beisel) Troutman** (Mrs James), dau of Frank & Adaline Romberger Beisel Lehman; **John Henninger,** son of Henry & Jane; **Harry Beisel** son of Frank & Adaline; **Row 5: James M Troutman** son of Daniel; **John Beisel** son of Frank & Adaline; **Will Henninger** oldest son of Henry & Jane.

313

While Jim owned the farm, a rail fence was built around all six fields and the fruit orchard. A lane on the east, and west of the buildings led to the back- fields. The cows were taken to the fields, and the girls were given the task to "mind" them. When the children turned eight, they helped to milk the cows each morning before they went to school. At an early age, they also helped to do other farm work. They harrowed the fields. During hay time, using forks, the children made piles of hay in rows so that later a wagon could be driven between the piles to be loaded and delivered to the barn. The children also helped to harvest the grains.

The children of James M. Troutman remembered many incidents that occurred while growing up. Florence was especially interested in sharing her memories, so she wrote the book "Farm Life In The Early 1900's Lykens Valley." It was printed in 2004.

During the years after 1900, it was common for roaming gypsy families to travel through this area, especially at Gratz fair time. Florence remembered that in the summer of 1912, three gypsy families camped on the Troutman farm across from the milk house along the water gutter. They had spring wagons and tents to live in, and used strings to tie chickens to the wagon wheels. A lot of willow trees grew along the water gutter, so they peeled the bark from the thin branches and wove baskets with them. The gypsy children played with the Troutman girls while they were in the area, and one night all the girls slept together. The end result was a case of head lice for the Troutman's!

The James M. Troutman family lived here for many years. During those years they conveyed several lots to family members for use as building lots. On March 22, 1947 they conveyed almost two acres of land to Paul E. and Margaret Troutman. On January 24, 1950, they sold almost a half- acre of land to John E. and Sarah Troutman. Several other small lots were sold. This area of the township more or less became a "Troutman" area.

On Jan 1,1962 James M. and Katie M. Troutman conveyed this 61 acre, 40 ½ perch farm in Lykens Township and four other tracts of land lying in Mifflin and Lykens Township to the Troutman Family Trust. On Feb 5, 1990, Daniel A. and Barbara J. Laughans purchased about fifty acres of the land in Lykens Township. They continue to be the owners and residents.

THE HISTORY OF TROUTMAN'S DAIRY
(Thanks to Paul Troutman, Jr. & Florence (Troutman) Young for this information)

Troutman Dairy started in 1902 when James M. Troutman bought Stine's Dairy from Homer and Mark Stine, located northeast of his farm. As part of the purchase he received a milk wagon.

The Troutman's gathered a herd of milking cows and soon began to deliver milk to Lykens with the horse and wagon. They filled large cans with milk, and at each house, a person would bring their container to the wagon. Using a dipper, Jim would fill their container from the can. In later years, milk was sold to customers from cans that had a faucet. He dispensed milk into a large measuring cup and then into the buyer's container.He eventually expanded his route and supplied milk to Elizabethville, Gratz, Berrysburg, Pillow and Herndon. In 1916 James purchased a new red Studebaker truck, and in the 1920's began selling milk again at the insistence of his customers. By about 1927, milk was sold raw in bottles. He bought a new cream-colored 1928 Studebaker truck and his daughter Florence began to deliver the milk. Initially, the milk was processed in the summer house that had a spring fed water trough used to keep the milk cool. In 1930 a milk house was built along the township road, and in 1950 they purchase equipment to pasteurize and homogenize milk.

In 1929, James purchased Oscar Zimmerman's Dairy, located north of Elizabethville. In 1939 they began to deliver milk to Allie Daniels store, Shimmels store, Smith's Restaurant and probably Hannah Daniel's restaurant or Rothermels Cafe (now Reed's Inn) in Gratz. They also delivered to customers in Berrysburg.

James Troutman would occasionally race another milkman, Elmer Romberger, using their milk wagons. Once after a snowstorm when he was using a team of horses and a sled, James was fined in Lykens for driving the wrong way on a one-way street. John Troutman also liked to hurry along, and drove the 1928 Studebaker from Gratz to Berrysburg floored in five minutes!

In 1945, James bought the Lloyd billow Dairy, north of the Cross Roads, and had Lloyd continue to deliver milk until his son Paul Troutman came home from the army in late1945. The Troutman's added a route to Pillow and Herndon. Paul Troutman believed in service to the customer. He was better than the mailman. He delivered milk every day but Sunday, and twice on Saturday to make up for the lack of delivery on Sunday. During severe snow storms, paths were shoveled and fields were used to get the milk through to the customers before the township roads were plowed. One Saturday night, Paul, and Paul Jr., his son spent the night at Troutman's Gap, near Pillow, because they couldn't get home in a snowstorm.

James M. Troutman retired in 1962, and turned ownership and management of the dairy over to his two sons, John and Paul. By 1983, Steve Troutman took over the business. With the advent of mergers Steve eventually gave up his home delivery service, but continued to deliver to wholesale customers in an expanded area of our region for sometime.

THE BEISEL FAMILY (and various early spellings)
(Information shared by James D. Beissel, III and Ruth Young)

This family has been traced to Xaver Bus who was born about 1370 in Eberbach, Germany. From this early progenitor came Peter Baus b c1395, Peter Buessel b c1425, ____ Buessel b c1465, Hans Beussel b c1500, Peter Beisel b c1535, Peter Beisel b c1565, Peter Beisel b c1580, Johann Wilhelm Beisel (Jan 21, 1616 – Nov 20, 1679), Johann Jakob Beisel (Oct 26,1660 –Aug 25, 1691), Johann Peter Beisel b Jul 5, 1688, **Hans Peter Beissel, Sr.**(Feb 25, 1726 - Aug 12, 1783), the immigrant to America who arrived in Philadelphia Aug 17, 1733, settled In Lehigh County. He later moved to the village of Leck Kill, Northld Co. **Hans Peter Beisel Sr. children:**
HANS PETER BEISEL, JR. (1754, Northampton Co – 1829, Up. Mahanoy Twp., Northld Co), served in the Northumberland County Militia.
*JOHANNES JACOB (Jan 8, 1758 Northampton Co – Sep 12,1829, bur Howerter Ceml, Northld Co), born in Lehigh Co. He joined the Pa. Militia at the age of 17, and in 1783 he was listed as a Lieutenant in the Militia of Northampton Co. He moved to Northld Co before1800. Jacob Beissel m Gertrude Wagner (Nov 10, 1760 - May 23,1859, bur St. John's Cem, Leck Hill, Northld Co), a dau of Jacob and Louisa (Ries) Wagner). **Johannes Jacob and Gertrude (Wagner) Beisel known children (some bapt Howerter' Ch, Northld Co):**
DANIEL H. BEISEL, SR. (Apr 10, 1782 in Lehigh Co – Mar 1, 1860, bur St. John's Cem, Leck Hill), m 1st Elizabeth Hetterich (May 8, 1791 – Nov 14, 1846), a dau of J. Nicholas and Anna Catherine (Brosius) Hettrich, m 2nd Anna Catharina Maurer (Jun 13,1793 – Jan 4, 1874), wid. of George Hornberger, Sr. of Leck Kill, had 7 more children. **Daniel H. and Elizabeth (Hetterich) Beisel children (some bapt Howerter Ch, Northld Co):
***MARIA b Mar 26, 1808; ***SALOME b Sep 6, 1809; ***LYDIA (Apr 14, 1811 – Nov 30, 1890, bur Dunkelberger Cem, Rockefellow Cem), m John Dunkelberger (Sep 16, 1806 – Mar 23, 1892); ***ANNA b Apr 3, 1812; *** ELIZABETH (May 9, 1816 – Jan 6, 1894), m 1st Michael ___, 2nd Peter Reitz (Jun 11, 1810 – Mar 3, 1886); ***MAGDALENA B c1818, m Michael Hoak; ***ABRAHAM b Jul 13, 1821; ***HARRIET (Apr 23, 1823 - Jan 7, 1894, bur Himmel's Cem), m 1st John Clark; 2nd Charles Rothermel (Aug 18, 1808 – Mar 18, 1897), widower of Elizabeth Bower; ***LUCETTA (Dec 13, 1824 – Aug 23, 1904, bur Klinger Cem), m John Klinger Wiest (Jan 14, 1821 – Apr 20, 1877), a son of Samuel and Eve (Klinger) Wiest. John K. Wiest went to California during the gold rush of 1849, and most of his children settled in either Oregon or Washington State.
***RACHEL (no dates); ***HANNAH bAug 28, 1827;
***DANIEL1 H. (Jr.), (b Up Mahanoy Twp, Northld Co Jun 28, 1829 – d Nov 25, 1904, bur St. John's Cem, Leck Hill), m Appolonia (Abbie) Hornberger (Jan 1, 1828 – Feb 4, 1907), a dau of George and Catherine Hornberger. **Daniel H. and Appolonia (Hornberger) Beisel children (some bapt Howerter's Ch): George Washington b Sep 2, 1847; Sarah Ann b Mar 8, 1849; Jeremiah b Jul 29, 1850; John b Apr 1, 1852;**
***BENNEVILLE b Jan 9, 1831, m Catharine ___, **had these children: Andreas b Jan 13, 1851; Edwin b Jul 31, 1852;**
***WILLIAM (b Nov 16, 1833 Up Mahanoy Twp – d Jul 3, 1869, bur Himmels Cem, Northld Co), m Maria Brosius (Mar 18, 1836 – Feb 11, 1874), a dau of Peter and Catharina Brosius. **William and Maria (Brosius) Beissel children:**
****Franklin (b Sep 2,1856 Leck Hill, Northld Co - d Nov 4, 1894 of brain disease,bur Hoffman Cem, later removed to Maple Grove Cem, E'ville), m by Rev. Engle May 5, 1877, Adaline Elisabeth Romberger (Aug 19,1858- 1953), a dau of Isaac and Lydis (Michael) Romberger. In 1880, Frank and Adaline Beisel lived in Lykens Township, had Harry Hepner age 16, and Katie L. Daniel age 14 living with them, listed as servants. **Franklin and Adaline (Romberger) Beisel had 3 sons 4 dau, these known children: Katie Marie (Aug 31,1878 – Dec 18, 1962), m Sep 8, 1900, James Monroe Troutman (b Oct 6, 1881 – d Jul 30, 1977, but Hoffman Cem), a son of Daniel B. and Sarah (Williard) Troutman, who lived on the neighboring farm. James worked briefly in the mines on Short Mountain after their marriage; Emma Elizabeth (Sep 19, 1881 – 1883); Carrie b May 10, 1883; Charles b 1885; Cora b 1887; John b Dec 3, 1891; Harry b Jan 29, 1893.** After Franklin Beisel died, his wife married Harvey A. Lehman

**ELIZABETH BEISEL b Aug 12, 1783, m Ludwig Byerly
**CATHARINE BEISEL (b Feb 24, 1786, Lehigh Co – d Jan 23, 1867, bur Jacob's Cem, Hebe), m Jacob Brosius (May 4, 1785 – Apr 20, 1847)
**SALOME BEISEL (Oct 27, 1789 – Feb 14, 1849, bur Zion Cem, Pitman), m George Hepler (Jun 22, 1790 – Feb 24, 1867, lived in Mahantongo Twp., Eldred Twp, Sch Co.
JOHN BEISEL (Jun 18, 1791–Oct 3, 1851, bur Jacob's Cem, Leck Kill)), m Maria Schaffer (1796– 1874, bur Shamokin Cem). **John and Maria (Schaffer) Beisel children: JACOB b Jul 1, 1824; SAMUEL b Jun 27, 1826;
**JACOB, JR. (no dates), m Maria "Polly" Bally
**RACHEL BEISEL (Jul 11, 1797 – Dec 29, 1862), m Daniel Schwartz (Dec 2, 1794 – Sep 30, 1857)
**SAMUEL H. BEISEL b Sep 6, 1803
PETER BEISEL (Oct 29,1801–Feb 16,1873 bur St. John's Cem, Leck Hill) m Magdalena Heim (Aug 25,1808 –Apr 2,1879), dau of John Heim of Up Mahanoy Twp, Northld Co. Peter & Magdalena (Heim) Beisel children:**
MOSES (1829 – 1854, bur St. Johns Cem, Leck Hill, Northld Co), m Magdalena Schankweiler (Sep 24, 1830 – Dec 15, 1909, bur Leighton, Pa.), a dau of Solomon Schankweiler (1796 – 1870, bur Himmel Cem, Northld Co.) & his wife Elizabeth Schmidt Schankweiler (1798–1830), of Up Mah Twp, Northld Co. [After Moses Beisel died, his widow Magdalena married John K. Wetzel, **they had these children (some bapt Howerter's Ch, Northld Co):** Daniel b Sep 7,1857; William Henry b Dec 30,1864; Andrew Johnson b Nov 7,1866; John b Feb 21, 1869) **Moses and Magdalena (Schankweiler) Beisel had one known child:**
Adam S. (Oct 15, 1853 – Jun 23, 1917, bur Lehighton, Pa.) was born near Gratz, according to family tradition. Adam's father died when he was one year old. His mother married a second time and had several children. When Adam was about thirteen, his mother took him aside and told him the sad news. There was no longer enough room or money to allow him to remain at home. She told him to go to the adjoining farms and ask for employment. Adam did just that, and was able to find employment and a new home.

Adam was a strong and healthy young man. He was also, not too surprisingly, kind of rough and tough during his young years. Perhaps it was the motivation he needed to become successful. He saved his money to attend Kutztown for two years, and start his career as a teacher. He apparently came to Gratz soon after Graduating from college, about 1877, and became the Principal of the Gratz School and Academy. While here, he became acquainted with Mary Sebold, a clerk in Isaac Hepler's store. On November 15, 1879, Adam and Mary married at Myerstown, in a ceremony performed by Rev. B. D. Albright. Adam was 26 and Mary was 16! Mary (Mar 4, 1863 – Dec 22, 1932), was a daughter of George Washington and Charlotte (Moyer) Sebold of Gratz. **Six children were born to Adam and Mary Beisel:** Minnie May b in Gratz Jul 19, 1880; James Monroe b in Gratz Mar 6, 1882; William Walter b in Gratz, (Jul 22, 1883 – d Jul 21, 1889); Bessie Blanche b in Lansford, Carbon Co Jan 3, 1892 – d Feb 21, 1892, bur Gratz Cem; Florence Louise (Mar 3, 1894 – d Jul 19, 1894 bur Gratz); Marie b Lehighton, Aug 2, 1895.

Mr. Beisel related to his descendants the fact that he had three "bad times" during his lifetime. They were, the time that he had to leave home, the loss of his son to typhoid fever, and a financial bank crisis later in life. In March 1890, the Beisel family moved to Lehighton, where he continued in education. He also became involved and was very successful in promoting many community activities. He died of a heart attack while unloading rocks from a wagon on land that he was planning to develop for housing.. [Photos & more information on the Adam Beisel family in "Comprehensive History Of Gratz.]
ELIZABETH b Sep 14, 1831; MARIA b Mar 20, 1833;

THE LEHMAN (LAYMAN) FAMILY

[SAMUEL LEHMAN(Apr15,1797 – Oct 12, 1859, bur St. John's Hill Cem), m Ann Mary Romberger (b c1801 –d pre 1867), a dau of Adam Romberger. Samuel was a carpenter and they lived in Mifflin Twp in 1850. **Samuel and Ann Mary (____) children (some bapt St. Johns Hill Ch);**
ADAM b c1817, m Elizabeth ____ b c 1815, **Adam and Elizabeth Lehman children:** William b c1842; Emanuel b c1743; Solome b c1848. They lived in Up. Paxton Twp. in 1850 &1880. He was a blacksmith.
JOHN (Jun 10,1821 – Jan 27, 1893, bur St. John's Hill Cem), m Dinah Koppenhaver (Sep 11, 1825 – Nov 21, 1899), a dau of Benjamin & Hannah Koppenhaver.. They lived in Mifflin Twp on St. John's Hill Church farm for twenty-eight years, during and after the Civil War years. In addition to farming, John was a shoemaker.

John and Dinah (Koppenhaver) Lehman children: Anna Elizabeth b Oct 7, 1845, m Dec 26, 1867 Allen Swab, lived in Elizabethville; **Henry** b pre-1850, m Sarah Bechtel, later moved to Iowa; **Mary** b Dec 20, 1850, m Samuel Daniel Jury, lived in Wiconisco; **John** b Feb 25, 1853, m Lizzie Wentzel, lived in Hickory Corners, Northld Co; **Hannah** b Mar 4, 1854, m Isaac Fetterhoff, lived in Elizabethville; **Amanda** (Feb 22, 1849 - Oct 3,1857; **William E.** (Feb 7, 1857 - 1931, bur St. John's Hill Cem), m Phoebe L. Matter (1868 - 1950); **Sarah Ellen** b Oct 1 9, 1859, m John Romberger; **Charles Daniel** b Sep 19, 1864, m Katie Klinger;
JACOB b c1823 m Amanda _____ b c1836. In 1860 they lived in Mifflin Twp and he was a plasterer. Jacob and Amanda ( ) Lehman children; Nathaniel b c1846; Peter b c1848; Clara b c1851.
MOSES b Feb 9, 1824
SAMUEL (c1830 - ___), m Catherine _____ b c1833 -), a dau of _____. In 1850, Samuel was living with the Philip Matter family & he was a shoemaker. They lived in Up. Pax. Twp in 1880. **Samuel & Catherine Lehman children; Wm** b c1851; **Emma** b c1853; **Mary** b c1855; **Samuel** b c1858; **Catherine** b c1858. ANN MARY b c1832; CHRISTIANA b c1834; ELIZABETH b Dec 22, 1819; BASTIAN b c1839; LYDIA b c1842

THE DANIEL DAVID BUSH TROUTMAN FAMILY

[DANIEL DAVID BUSH TROUTMAN (Jun 20, 1849 - Feb 3, 1917, bur Hoffman Cem), son of Daniel and Elizabeth (Bush) Troutman, m c1875 Sarah Caroline Williard (Aug 9, 1856 - Oct 31, 1945), a dau of _____
Daniel and Sarah (Williard) Troutman children (total of 9);
*ISAAC (Oct 17, 1875 - Feb 1960), m Mary Margaret Hoffman (Oct 11, 1874 - Aug 8, 1953), a dau of _____. **Isaac and Mary Margaret (Hoffman) Troutman children (some bapt Hoffman Ch):**
Clara Elva (May 1, 1897 - Sep 12, 1990), m Mar 1917, Charles Edward Henninger (Oct 7, 1888 - Aug 1964). **Charles Edward and Clara Elva (Troutman) Henninger children:** Margaret Etta b Apr 13, 1917 - 199_), m Jun 2, 1935, Charles Frederick Leer (Sep 16, 1906 - Nov 24, 1974 in Lyk Twp); Pershing Allen b Sep 16, 1918, Lykens Twp , m 1st Jul 26, 1950, Barbara Anita Sultzbaugh (Aug 6, 1931 - Oct 28, 1961). m 2nd Dec 31, 1964 Ethel Louise Harner b Jun 24, 1926. Lee Isaac (Aug 14, 1920 - 2003), m Jan 31, 1953, Jean Katherine Straub b Jul 12, 1928 in Klingerstown, had a dau Yvonee Elva b Feb 17, 1955. Russell Edward b Oct 9, 1928 in Lyk Twp, m in Lyk Twp, Jun 30, 1967, Nell Ann Wolf b Aug 14, 1943 in Birmingham, Al. **Russell and Nell (Wolf) Henninger children:** Erica Dawn b Mar 18, 1972 m Stephen Savage; Emily Ann b Sep 16, 1979; Elizabeth Claire and Elaine Julia (twins) b Jul 24, 1981.
Harry A. (Aug 15, 1901 - Oct 17, 1988), m Edna Wise b Jul 15, 1905. **Harry A. and Edna (Wise) Trouotman children:** Louise Elaine b 1930, m Robert Hoenstine; Mary Ellen b 1931, m Wm Carroll; William Isaac b 1933, m Andrea Smith; Shirley Ann b 1935; Karen Sue b 1945, m Richard Spielman; Timothy Ned b 1946, m Marnie Ruth Williams; Hettyh Lynne b 1950, m Norman Metzger
Mary Sara Amanda (1906 - 1907)
Ella P. (Aug 29, 1918 - c2002), m Jun 23, 1946, Philip Claire Crotty b Nov 27, 1922 in McVeytown, Pa. **Philip & Ella P (Troutman) Crotty children:** Dennis b 1947; Larry b 1953; Craig b 1952.

*JOHN HENRY (Jun 3, 1877 - 1929), m Cora May Rothermel (Aug 23, 1876 - May 30, 1968). **John Henry and Cora May (Rothermel) Troutman children:**
Forrest Lincoln (Apr 30, 1900–May 1972); **Erhlen Orion** (1902 -1943); **Vesta** (1905 –1995), m Mark F. Klinger (1902 - 1981); **Elmer Albert** bApr 3, 1907, m 1st 1933, Mary Docky (1914 - 1994), m 2nd Anna Lebo in 1994; **Clayton George** b Aug 10, 1910, m Ruth Elizabeth Clark b1924.
*AMANDA ELIZA (Feb 6, 1879- Jan 12, 1975, bur Hoffman Cem), m Alvin Guerney Hoffman (Oct 8, 1875 – Nov 24, 1934). **Alvin & Amanda (Troutman) Hoffman children:** Charles D. b 1 902; Mabel Pauline b 1908.
*JAMES MONROE (b Oct 6, 1881 - Jul 30, 1977, bur Hoffman Cem), m Sep 8, 1900 Katie Maria Beisel (Jul 31, 1878 - Dec 18, 1962), a dau of Franklin and Adeline (Romberger) Beisel. **James M and Katie Maria (Beisel) Troutman children;**
Cora Mae (Feb 7,1901 - Jun 11, 1993), m Jun 2, 1917 Earl Barry (b Jun 2, 1897 Halifax - Dec 13, 1962). **Earl and Cora Mae (Troutman) Barry children:**
Floyd John James (Sep 19, 1917 - May 22, 1941), m Jun 2, 1939, Mildred Lebo b Jan 25, 1917; Ralph Earl (Apr 16, 1919 - Aug 15 1942), m Oct 5, 1940, Pauline Gallnett b Oct 22, 1919 in Donlys Mills, Pa.; Mildred

Norma b Feb 26,1921, m Apr 8, 1944, Joseph Herbert Hartman (Jun 2,1924– Jan 23,1993); **Ella Mae** b Feb 7, 1923 in Lykens, m Jun 2,1946 in Halifax; Charles D. Bellis (Jan 25,1918 Gratz – Oct 16, 1990 in Orlando, Fla. Albert **Troutman** (Dec 22, 1924 – Aug 11, 1995), m Apr 8, 1945 Joyce Marie Stoneroad b Oct 8, 1927; **Robert Paul** (Sep 3, 1926 – Aug 30,1995), m Jun 30,1951 Rosena L. Howard b Nov 20,1928; **Dorothy Irene** b Jun 16, 1929, m Aug 16,1947, Kenneth Deibler b Mar 30,1923;**William Lawrence** b Apr 21,1931 m Aug 1,1954, Janice Louise Smeal b Mar 12, 1934; **Mary Sara Marie Adeline** b Dec 17, 1932, m 1952 Guy Hoffman (1930 –1977). Roy **Edwin** b Apr 12, 1940, Lykens Twp m 1958 Carolun Louise Starr b Feb 13, 1942 in Lykens Twp. **Lester Eugene** b Jul 26, 1942 m Sep 4, 1960 Edythe E. Zerby b Dec 9, 1943, E'ville.

Irene Carrie b Apr 10, 1903, m Jan 27, 1927 George Luther Koppenhaver (Nov 30, 1900 – May 20, 1976).
George Luther and Irene Carrie (Troutman) Koppenhaver children:
Bruce Daniel b Sep 29, 1927 m Elsie May Schwalm b Sep 11, 1939 in Halifax; Sara Marie b Nov 20, 1929 m Stanley Whittier Doe of South Portland, Maine; **Larry James** b Nov 21, 1936, m Virginia Kay Miller of Elizabethville; Richard Eugene b Sep 8, 1938, m Loretta May Walborn of Millersburg; **Paul Edward** bJan 15, 1945 m Arline Emma Crocker of Great Falls, Montana

Albert Franklin Daniel b Feb 3, 1906
Florence Lauretta b Jun 18, 1908 m Clarence Shober Young (1906 – 1991) of Denver, Pa. Clarence and Florence (Troutman) Young children: _____ son; Ruth b 1945, m Ronald E. Deppen; m 2ⁿᵈ Lawrence Zerby

Laura Evelyn (Nov 30, 1909 – 2002), m May 15, 1926 Albert Ray Reed (Nov 4, 1903 – Jan 14, 1981)
Albert Ray and Laura Evelyn (Troutman) Reed children: Betty Marie b Nov 6, 1926, m Jun 7, 1947, Ray Lester Leitzel bAug 5, 1925, of Hebe; Lucille Evelyn b Jun 9, 1929 m 1948 Dale Leroy Leer (Jan 5, 1929 – 1978, bur Dillsburg); Barbara Lorraine b Jul 19, 1932 m 1953 Peter Joseph Burke, Jr of Binghamton, N.Y.; James William b Mar 3, 1937 m Ruby Lenker b Mar 2, 1935 in Pillow; Kenneth Albert b May 7, 1939 m Linda Lorraine Whitcomb b May 15, 1942 in Tower City; Mary Ann b Aug 13, 1942 m Lee F. Fetterhoff of Wmstown. **Charles (no dates)**
John Edward b Sep 3, 1913 m Sarah Elizabeth Reisch (1911 – 1984, bur Maple Grove Cem, E'ville)
Paul Eston, Sr (Aug 5, 1915 – May 18, 1988, bur God's Missionary Cem, Lyk Twp), m Margaret Alice Dressler b Feb 21, 1915 in Halifax

*MARY JANE (Jun 10, 1883 – 1970), m Charles Bonawitz (1876 – 1947); *CHARLES FREMOUR (Dec 1886 – 1976); *SALLIE VERNA (Jun 27, 1894 – Jan 10, 1898, bur Hoffman Cem);ELSIE (Jul 18, 1898- Dec 19, 1952), m Jay A. Troutman (1893 – 1952)

MR AND MRS. PERSHING HENNINGER FARM
(was George Williard land in 1875)

Barn On Isaac Troutman Farm

This farm is made up of two tracts from various sources. A 12 acre 149 perch tract was from a warrant that Commonwealth of Pennsylvania issued to Henry Stump on June 8, 1791, patented in 1804 to William France (Frantz). William Frantz by his will gave his plantation of 164 acres to his sons Henry, a weaver by trade and Jacob a farmer. They sold some of their land to Jacob and Catherine Werner, and they sold in 1808 back to Jacob Frantz and John Hoffman. On March 9, 1821, some of land including the 12 acres, was conveyed to Barbara Hoffman, a daughter of John and Anna Mary Hoffman. Barbara later married John N. Speck, listed as a fuller. On April 6, 1840 Barbara and John N. Speck sold to Isaac and Elizabeth Miller, former residents of Low. Tulpehocken Twp., Berks Co. After that Solomon Martz, John H. Koppenheffer and Samuel Wolf owned it before it was purchased by Isaac Troutman on July 27, 1904.

Isaac Troutman Homestead

The second tract of 14 acres 155 perches also came from the Hoffman land through Jacob Hoffman who sold to George Rehrer in 1823. George Rehrer and his wife sold to George Williard in April 1849. The Williard heirs sold the 14 acres to Isaac Troutman March 30, 1901. Isaac Troutman sold both tracts (12 and 14 acres) to son Isaac and wife Mary Troutman Aug 2, 1952. After Mary died, Isaac conveyed both to Charles and Clara Henninger. They sold in June 1970 to Pershing and Ethel Henninger the present owners.

During his earlier years, Isaac Troutman and his wife lived with his parents and he walked to the mines for a long days work. He eventually purchased a tract of land on Short Mountain near Specktown. This land provided the wood he needed to build a barn. In his spare time after work or on Saturday, he went to the mountain and cut down trees, and sawed them into boards. After he purchased land from his father (about 1903), he used this wood to build a new barn on the land. They painted the barn white. A few years later, they built their house. Isaac Troutman had a dairy and many cows. They delivered milk to Gratz, Herndon and Lykens.
(Thanks to Ella Troutman Crotty for the insight into the personal life of Isaac Troutman).

Isaac & Mary (Hoffman) Troutman On Wedding Day

Isaac Troutman was a very busy man. He was a trustee of Hoffman Church, and for years dug all the graves. He was also assessor for Lykens Township. Each year of assessment he walked the township all the way to Spring Glen. He was also a carpenter, and among his projects, he helped to build the barn at Edward Dietrichs farm. Isaac was often called upon to deliver calves at area farms, and was gone all hours of the day and night. He charged one dollar for his service. Isaac was also a butcher, and each fall and winter he was busy helping many of the farmers when they scheduled a butchering day. His pay was usually a pan of scrapple, one ring of sausage, and a piece of pork.

Mrs. Troutman had a beautiful garden and yard. She and Isaac were both very neat and particular about their environment. Isaac liked to have everything new and up to date, so he loved to buy the latest items available. One day he was visiting with Mr. and Mrs. Morris Shade. He noticed that they had a new Silvertone victrola, and thought it was wonderful. So he went to Sears Roebuck in Harrisburg and bought one for his family. Isaac also purchased one of the first Pullman cars made.

Clara Troutman, a daughter was a musician. She played the organ at Hoffman Church for years and years. The family owned a piano at home for her to play. When Isaac learned of the new "player piano's" he made a trip to Harrisburg and ordered and paid for one, but he never told his wife. One day the delivery truck from the Troup Music Store rolled up to the Troutman house to deliver their new piano. Mrs. Troutman came to the door and when they told her their mission she told them there was some mistake. So they had to show her the paid invoice. The men unloaded the new piano, and took the old one with them. The Troutman's began to collect piano rolls and accumulated a great collection of rolls that were stored in a nearby cupboard. They had songs like Barney Google, Three O'clock In The Morning, and religious songs.

Isaac and Mary Troutman conveyed the 12 acre 149 perch and 14 acre 154 perch tracts to Charles E. and Clara Henninger Jun 17, 1957. After her husband died, widow Clara E. Henninger conveyed both tracts to Pershing and Ethel Henninger on June 12, 1970. On Mar 16. 1993, Pershing Henninger conveyed a residential building lot on the corner of Dairy Road to David E. and Marilyn Troutman. Pershing Henninger is the present owner of the farm and original dwelling and barn. [More info in Henninger genealogy.]

JAMES E. AND SHARON L. TROUTMAN FARM
(GEORGE WILLIARD -115 acres In 1875 – corner of Dairy & Crossroads Road - refer to map for location)

This land is part of the original tracts that Commonwealth of Pennsylvania patented to John Hoffman March 2, 1801. He received additional land and on September 14,1813, John Hoffman and his wife sold 218 acres 17 perches to Jacob Hoffman, Jr.

On December 13, 1823, Jacob Hoffman, Jr and Catherine sold the small part of the tract, containing forty-threeacres thirty-three perches to George Rehrer. George Rehrer accumulated other land, but Jacob Seiler, Dauphin County Sheriff on August 19, 1833, sold the "chief" part of George Rehrer's land containing 108 acres 102 perches to John Rehrer.

In 1834, John Rehrer and wife Magdalena sold it back to George Rehrer and Ann Mary. On April 2, 1849, the Rehrer's sold 108 acres 102 perches with two-story log house and bank barn to George Williard, but the deed was not recorded until March 20, 1854. This land bordered land of Peter Boddorf, Elias Hoover, edge of Wiconisco Creek, toward Solomon Martz, John Hoffman, George Row, the church land, John Forney, and Henry Hartman. The Williard family owned this farm for many years. But on June 1, 1886, George Williard heirs, (Lovina his widow and the children) sold the plantation to Daniel B. Troutman, husband of Sarah Williard one of the children.

320

George Williard

Lovina (Deibler) Williard

Aerial View Of Farm
At Corner Of Derry
Road & Crossroads .
Old Barn Burned
1947, Rebuilt 1948

James Troutman family –
On dairy farm.
Standing l to r:
Laura, Albert (d 1920)
Cora, Irene, Florence.
Seated: James & wife
Kate, Paul, John

Daniel B. Troutman was born in the area of Dauphin County known as "Spain" located near Pillow. His father Daniel Troutman was the victim of a murder by intruders to his farm. Daniel B. Troutman and his family came to Lykens Township, were listed next to Elias Hoover on the 1880 census, and lived here for many years. Before his death Daniel B. Troutman wrote a will in which he designated this farm to be inherited by his wife Sarah. Before her death, Sarah by her will designated the farm by then containing 91 acres 84 perches to James M. Troutman. He received it August 8, 1919. James M. and Katie M. Troutman conveyed this and four other tracts of land to the Troutman Family Trust On January 1, 1962. On January 21, 1987 James E. and Sharon L. Troutman became the owners of all five tracts.

The Daniel Troutman Family Reunion
Photo taken in June 1914 in a wooded area, now cleared, north of the farmhouse owned by James M. Troutman. Seated in center: Elizabeth Bush Troutman, wife of Daniel Troutman. l to r standing: Harriet Troutman Zimmerman; Samuel Zimmerman, Sarah Troutman Troutman (Mrs. Jacob Troutman), Catharine Troutman Carl (Mrs. Samuel K. Carl), Maria Elizabeth Troutman Klinger (Mrs. Alphus Klinger), Hiram Troutman & wife Amelia A., Lovina Troutman Walters (Mrs. Frank Walters), Daniel Bush Troutman, Sarah Williard Troutman (Daniel's wife), James B. Troutman, Mary & husband George Washington Troutman, Amanda & husband Abraham L. Troutman). Photo from Troutman Family History by Steve E. Troutman.

FRANK R. AND LESLIE E. HERB FARM
(REUBEN RIEGEL FARM -91 acres 1875)

This property is made up of parts of two larger tracts that belonged to the Hoffman family. Commonwealth of Pennsylvania granted one tract of 202 acres known as "Hickory Bottom" to Nicholas Hoffman, warranted January 7, 1785, surveyed March 1785, patented February 26, 1796. The other large tract of 270 acres, known as "Walnut Bottom" was warranted April 23, 1785, surveyed June 2, 1785, patented February 26, 1796 to Peter Hoffman, Jr. On August 10, 1799, Peter Hoffman sold this second tract to Nicholas Hoffman. From here, the land was sold off in numerous parts to several people. Nicholas and Margaret Hoffman sold parts of these tracts to Daniel Hoffman on June 30, 1809, containing about135 acres. The land changed ownership again when

Daniel and Hannah Hoffman on March 1, 1811 sold to Christopher Snyder. One year later, Christopher Snyder sold April 13, 1812 to Hermonius Zerby, who owned the land for many years. When Hermonius Zerby died, his son William sold 87 acres, 99 perches of land with buildings to Peter Forney on April 4, 1830. While Peter Forney owned the land Jacob Harman was a tenant on the property. About the time that Peter Forney bought this property, John Forney purchased a nearby farm, making this a "family territory".

Peter Forney and wife Margaret sold part of two tracts April 2, 1839 to Henry Hartman containing 87 acres 92 perches. Henry Hartman also received a small tract of land from Adam and Catherine Romberger in 1839. Combined the tracts contained 91 acres 111 perches.

When Peter Forny sold his farm he kept some of the land for himself. He and his wife Margaret lived on 20 acres of land in 1850 in Lykens Township. Their daughter Hannah, Matilda Jacobs age 19, Jacob Deibler 15, and Reuben Disher age 25, a clergyman lived with them. By 1860, Peter and Margaret moved to Mifflin Twp., and they had Matilda Shroner 29 a widow, and her son Isaac age 5 with them .By 1870, Margaret died, and Peter a retired widower was living in Berrysburg with their daughter Hannah now married to John Q. Adams.

Very Old Home As It Presently Looks

When they first purchased this land, Henry Hartman had George Lebo as a tenant on the farm. Then for many years, John Hartman Jr., son of Henry and Magdalena Hartman lived here. It may be that Henry and Magdalena purchased this farm for John. The Hartman's lived on a very large farm in Washington Township, where they did extensive farming, and raised cattle. They also owned and operated a gristmill in Washington Township.

On April 1, 1859, Henry and Magdalena Hartman sold eighty-seven plus acres, plus a four acre tract to John Hartman Jr., stipulating a dower for Henry and Magdalena. Adam Ramberger and his wife Catherine sold the small tract to Henry Hartman on April 2, 1839. The farm now contained ninety-one acres, one hundred-eleven perches. In 1849, this property is described on the tax record as having a two-story frame house, and a log bank barn. It may have been the same house that had been built on the land as early as 1820. On December 7, 1870, Dauphin County Sheriff Christian Weikel offered this farm at public auction, and the ninety-one plus acres were sold to Reuben Riegel.

THE ZERBY FAMILY

[HERMANUS ZERBY and his family arrived in Lykens Township as early as 1812, when he purchased this eighty-seven acre farm. He was probably a son of Benjamin Zerby who lived n the Tulpehocken area of Berks County. Benjamin Zerby had a son Binjamin b May 17, 1763, and another son Hermanus b March 20, 1765, bapt "Little Tulpehocken" Church. Mary the wife of Hermanus Zerby preceded him in death. She died after 1813,

when she was listed on a deed for land that she and Hermanus Zerby sold. She does not appear on the 1820 census for Lykens Township. Hermanus Zerby died about November 1832, and **left the following six children:** **WILLIAM** (Dec 13, 1801 - May 24, 1877, bur Union Luth Ref Cem, Lykens, Wiconisco Twp), m Susanna Kissinger (Nov 23, 1808, bapt Klinger Ch - d Jul 2, 1888, bur Lykens Cem.), a dau of George and Catharine (Hoover) Kissinger. William purchased a farm located within the borders of Gratz, and lived there until about 1845, when they moved to Wiconisco Twp. In 1880 Susanna Zerby by then a widow, lived in Lykens and had her son Charles and granddaughter Kate Miller age 7 with her. **William and Susanna (Kissinger) Zerby children:** son b before 1830; **Elizabeth** (Nov 1, 1822 - Jul 22,1852, bur Simeon Cem), m Jacob S. Ossman, her tombstone mentions that she is a dau of William Zerbe; probably **Emaline** b c1832, living with the Daniel Romberger family in 1850; **Louisa** (Dec 8, 1833 Gratz –Jul 16, 1911, Lykens), m 1st John R. Fisher (no dates), **had these children:** Charles W. (1859 – 1929, bur with parents); Ida b c1864; Henry Gordon (Jul 5, 1866- Mar 22, 1888); Maggie b c1869; Emma Amelia b May 25, 1871; Edward Lloyd (Jun 9, 1873 – 1930, bur IOOF Cem), m Agnes Reiff (1872 – 1912); Jacob Ralph b Aug 19, 1875; probably **Mary** (836 – 1862), who was living with the Theodore Gratz family in 1850. **Edward W** (Jul 5, 1838 – Feb 6, 1894, bur Lykens), m Rebecca maybe Mumma (1843 – 1909), lived in Wiconisco in 1870, in Lykens 1880, in both places he was employed as a miner. **Edward and Rebecca (Mumma) Zerby children:** Charles (1860 – 1879, bur beside parents); Lydia b c1863, m Lewis Sarge; William G (1865 – 1949, bur POS of A Cem, Lykens), m Elizabeth ___ (1868 – 1930); Samuel Franklin (1867 - 1870); Frederick b c1870; Catharine Ellen b Feb 6, 1871; Maggie Edith b Jan 19, 1879; **Catherine** (1844 -1866, bur beside parents); **Frederick P.** (Jan 10, 1845 – May 27, 1863); **Charles M**. b c1846, in Gratz, lived with his parents in 1870. He died Mar 22, 1895 by accidental drowning in the Wiconisco Creek, bur Wiconisco Cem, according to obituary. **Anna M**. b c1848; **Amelia** (no dates).
SAMUEL (____), m Anna Barbara Klinger b Jun 14, 1805, a dau of George and Charlotte (Deibler, Snyder) Klinger. Samuel and Barbara lived in Lykens Township through their first years of marriage. During the 1830s Samuel was assessed a tax on money he had "out on interest," probably an inheritance from his father's estate. By 1837, they were no longer living in Lykens Township. **Samuel and Barbara (Klinger) Zerby children:** Samuel b Aug 13, 1834, bapt Klingers Ch; Elizabeth b Jun 21, 1836, bapt Klingers Ch.
JACOB moved to Virginia;
HENRY b c1804, first lived in Lykens Twp. In 1837, he was a tenant on a Simon Gratz property. He later moved to Williamstown. Henry m 1st Christina Romberger (Jun 6,1809 - Feb 9, 1849,bur Calvary Meth Cem, Wiconisco), a dau of Adam and Catherine (Paul) Romberger. **Henry & Christina (Romberger) Zerby children:** Cyrus; Emanuel W. (no dates), m Catherine ___. **Emanuel & Catherine Zerby children:** *Edward Ellsworth* b May 22, 1863; *Cyrus Emanue*l b Jun 30, 1867; *Maggie Louisa* b Jan 23, 1869; *Catherine Elizabeth* b Feb 21, 1872; Amanda (Aug 15, 1832 - Dec 25, 1906), m 1st Oct 9, 1853, Daniel Keiser, 2nd m Feb 10, 1877 to John Bird (Sep 19, 1836 - Oct 21, 1910), both Amanda and John Bird are bur Calvary Meth Cem, Wiconisco. **Amanda had a total of twelve children.** Sarah b c1831, m David Zimmerman b c1826, lived in Wiconisco Twp in 1850;Emeline b c1834, m Joseph Romberger;Adam (Apr 11,1838- Sep 27,1856, bur Calvery Meth Cem) After Christina died, Henry apparently married a second time to Catherine ___ b 1829, and had these children: Mary A b & d 1853); Henry b Oct 1851; Margaret (b & d 1855); Samuel b1860; Ida S b c1870.
ELIZABETH (no dates), m Isaac Hottenstein, moved to Union County, Pa.
JOHN (no dates), in 1837 was a tenant on Samuel Schoffstall's property. He later moved to Pottsville.

These also lived in this area.
Lazarus Zerby (1827 – 1905, bur Meth Cem, Wmstown). He was a carpenter in 1880, had a wife Louisa b c1835, a son John A. b c1868 & Oscar b c1875.
Henry Zerby (1829 – 1922), Civ War Vet, wife Sarah d Nov 9, 1906, bur Calvary Meth Cem. Lived in Wmstown in 1880.
Peter Zerby b c1822 lived in Lykens Twp in 1880, had a wife Susan b 1827.

THE FORNEY FAMILY AND GENEALOGY

[The **FORNEY** family came to "Williams Valley' from Heidelberger Township, Berks County about 1790.and lived in several locations in the area. Peter Forney was from the first generation that came. He brought his family, and perhaps brothers with him. Peter is listed on the "window tax assessment of 1798 with a 20 x 16 foot cabin and poor stable. In 1800 he was living in Upper Paxton and had sixteen people living in his household. He died in Mifflin Twp in 1812, but the site of his grave is unknown. Nothing is known of his wife. The following obituary applies to his Peter. It is included here since it is an example of life among the early settlers.

"Peter Forney of Berrysburg, died January 23, 1873 age eighty-nine years, three months, twenty-five days. His funeral was Sunday in Union Salem Church. He was born September 23, 1783, in Heidelberg Township, Berks County. Mr. Forney came with his parents to Williams Valley when he was seven years old. At the age of fourteen he helped to make the road from Shreiners to the Susquehanna River, a distance of about twenty miles. At that time it was all wilderness, with only three small clearings along the route. At the age of twenty-five, he came to Lykens Valley and located at Berrysburg. The town was not yet laid out. He lived here sixty-five years until his death. His wife preceded him in death by seven years. The first land he obtained by grubbing, which he did on equal shares. In this manner, he was able to get ten acres for himself.

In 1812, he married Margaret Romberger, a daughter of Adam Romberger of this same area. When Mr. Forney asked Mr. Romberger for his daughter, he was asked how he intended to support her. The emphatic answer was "by the grubbing how." After their marriage, they were soon ready to move into their new home. The entire household goods consisted of - well - it was all put in a wheel barrow and taken to their place of abode. The house or hut they moved into had no floor. A large stump which was enclosed served for a table. The first crops they raised were taken home in a spread. Thus they commenced life in the wilderness, and lived together fifty-three years. They had eight children, twenty-five grandchildren, and thirty great-grandchildren.

In 1814, Mr. Forney was commissioned by Governor Simon Snyder's Company, First Lieutenant, tenth Regiment, First Brigade, 6th Division, Pa. Militia, composed of Dauphin, Lebanon, Berks, and Schuylkill counties.

Mr. Forney was a blacksmith, made his own farm utensils (wagon and thresher included), and worked a great deal at masonry. He did the mason work on Union Salem Church in Berrysburg, free of charge. In early life, he killed two panthers and four bears in Lykens Valley."

PETER FORNEY (____ - c1812), m Anna Catharine ____, Peter and Anna Catherine children:
*CATHERINE (b   - d c1863 – mentions a brother Peter in her will
*ANN (no dates) m Samuel Baer, died before her father – mentioned in orphan court records of Peter Forney as late wife of Samuel Baer and legatee of Peter Forney
*JOHN GEORGE b Mar 20, 1776 bapt Tulpehocken - tombstone May 12, 1777– Oct 12, 1828 bur St. Johns' Hill Cem.) m Catharine ___(Mar 6, 1778 - Apr 41, 1850, bur Fetterhoff Cem). **John George and Catherine Forney had 6 children 2 minors when he died:**
**John b Feb 2, 1802 – Sep 26, 1828, bur St. Johns Hill cem)
Peter (Apr 17, 1804 Leb Co to George Forney - Dec 11, 1866, bur Fetterhoffs Cem), m Salome Lubold (Apr 8, 1810 - Dec 25, 1875), a dau of Frederick and Elizabeth (Ney) Lubold of Douglas Twp, Berks Co, lived northwest of Fisherville, Dau Co. **Peter and Salome (Lubold) Forney had these children (some bapt Fetterhoffs Ch: Jacob b Apr 28, 1833, m Eliza Witman, had these children (bapt Fetterhoffs Ch): Sarah Elmira b Sep 7, 1855; **Emma Jane** b Feb 16, 1857; **Mary Ellen** b Jan 14, 1864. **Elizabeth** (Jun 19, 1834 - Mar 25, 1913), m Daniel Bowman (Nov 20, 1831 - May 1, 1880);**Emanuel** (Apr 24, 1837 - Sep 20, 1890, bur Fetterhoff Cem), m Rebecca Hoffman (Nov 13, 1834 – 1917), a dau of Christian & Sarah (Tobias) Hoffman; **John R.** (Dec 15, 1838 - Jul 2, 1886, bur Sweitzer Cem, Berrysburg;), m Catherine (Jun 20, 1839 - Jan 26, 1876); **Sarah Jane** (Sep 6, 1839 - Apr 16, 1915), m John Young; **John Aaron** b Jun 21, 1840, m Hannah Sweigard (1839 – 1927, bur Longs Cem., Halifax); **Frederick** (Sep 3, 1843 - Apr 25, 1911), m Susan Hoff (Sep 14, 1849 - Feb 11, 1911); **George Franklin** (Mar 14, 1846 -Jul 25, 1890, bur Fetterhoffs Cem), m Sarah Hess; Catherine (no dates) m Benjamin Bowman (Mar 1, 1840 – Jan 16, 1894).

**Catherine (Mar 16, 1807 - Feb 15, 1863, bur Hoffman Cem)
**Michael (May 31, 1809, bapt Salem Luth, Killinger - Feb 24, 1881, bur Fetterhoffs Cem.), m Sarah Hoffman (Aug 23, 1811 - Sep 24, 1848 bur Davids, Killinger), dau of Jacob & Cath (Ferree) Hoffman. Michael was a tenant on the farm of Widow Elizabeth Fry in 1834. He m 2nd about 1849, Susanna Shott Lenker (May 19, 1817 - May 15, 1877). She was the widow of J. Christian Lenker (1801 – 1846, bur E'ville.) In 1850 they lived in Up

Paxton and had Sarah, Samuel & Jacob, children of Michael and his first wife. Also Susanna Lenker's children from first marriage: Christian 8, Hiram 5. They lived in E'ville in 1860. By 1880 Michael was a widower for the second time, and lived with the J. Andre family in Halifax. J. Andre was a miller making flour, and Michael Forney was working for him. **Michael & Sarah (Hoffman) Forney children:** Sarah b c1836; Samuel (Nov 23, 1840 – Aug 7, 1865), killed during Civil War, m Amanda ___ (Jan 16, 1845 – May 31, 1928) ; Jacob b c1845; Hiram b c1846; William F (Nov 15, 1859 – Sep 2, 1929, bur Fetterhoff Cem), m Mary J ___(Jul 7, 1855 – May 19, 1895), **had these children:** Jacob E (1882–1904);Anna F (1898–1968, bur Fetterhoff Cem), m Paul R.Yeager (1893 – 1954)

**Daniel (Oct 27, 1812 – Sep   9, 1830, bur St. John's Hill Cem), m Elizabeth ___ (___ Sep 30, 1830)
**George – over 14 when father died
**Henry – minor when father died
**Simon (Jun 22, 1817 - Apr 11, 1869), m Hannah (Jun 25, 1814 - Apr 1, 1893, bur Fetterhoffs)
*PETER (b Sep 29, 1783 - d Jan 23, 1873, near Berrysburg, bur Sweitzer Cem), m Eva Margaret Romberger (Aug 10, 1795 - Aug 11, 1865, bur St. Johns' Hill Cem), a dau of Adam and Anna Maria (Werner) Romberger. A record from the Civil War pension office shows Peter Forney as serving in the war of 1812. During May 1813, he was with a detachment of men who marched from Lancaster on the afternoon of Friday May 13th to Strasburg, where they were quartered for the night, then went on to New London cross roads. They reached Elkton, Md. at two o'clock in the morning of the 15th. They returned to Lancaster on the 29th, and were discharged on the 30th by commanding officer, Capt James Humes. **Peter and Eva Margaret (Romberger) Forney had eight children:**

CATHERINE (Dec 17, 1812 – Nov 25, 1902), m William Metz (May 28, 1812 – May 10, 1866, bur Peace Cem, Bbg; In 1870 Catherine and her daughter Hannah lived together. Iin 1880 Catherine was alone in Mifflin Twp. **William and Catherine (Forney) Metz children: Michael (1839 – 1885, bur St. John's Hill Cem), m Mar 24, 1861 Mary Lenker (Jul 8, 1840 – 1917), a dau of Nicholas and Catherine (Yeager) Lenker; John (1842 – 1918), m Jan 18, 1859 Mary Gilbert (Sep 26, 1838- Jan 10, 1894, bur Peace Cem, Bbg) Susanna b 1842;_ Elizabeth (Mar 13, 1843- Jan 10, 1858). Hannah b c1851, m Elias Zartman; Mary b c1855

SUSANNA (Feb 17, 1816 – Apr 19, 1893), 2nd wife (m Jul 8, 1843) of Adam Zartman (Aug 1, 1810 - Dec 28, 1889, bur St. Johns Luth Cem, Jackson Twp), a son of William & Sarah (Herb) Zartman. Adam was killed in an accident caused by a fast moving train on the Pennsylvania Railroad as he was trying to cross the tracks at Herndon. Adam Zartman had previously been m to Susanna Reitz who d Nov 23, 1842, and had five children (Henry b 1834; Hannah b 1835; Lydia b 1837; Abigail b 1838, Eliza b 1841). They lived on a farm in Jackson Twp., Northld Co. **Adam and Susanna (Forney) Zartman children: Sarah b Apr 15, 1845; Harriet b Oct 7, 1846; Polly b Jun 20, 1849; Phoebe b Nov 24, 1850; Elias b Sep 14, 1852, m Jan 1873 to Hannah Metz, dau of William and Catherine (Forney) Metz of Bbg (above); Michael b Apr 13, 1854;Malinda b Jul 25, 1856; Lucy Ann b Oct 22, 1858;

MARY ANN (Oct 29, 1819 - Apr 26, 1902, bur Stone Valley Cem), m George Spatz (Jul 28, 1818 - Nov 8, 1875), son of Jacob and Sarah M (Emerich) Spatz of Stone Valley Area. **George and Mary Ann (Forney) Spatz children: Philip (Jan 5, 1844 - Dec 25, 1864, bur Stone Valley Cem).

HANNAH b c1833, m Jan 13, 1853, U.B. Ch , Mifflin Twp, John Q. Adams, b c1828, son of William T. and Mary Adams of Clinton Co. John was a minister of the gospel. In 1870 Hannah and John Q Adams lived in Berrysburg and her father Peter Forney age 87 lived with them. **John Q and Hannah (Forney) Adams children: William O. b c1855; Elsworth b c1861; Ulyses b c 1866; Lillian b c1868.

*ANNA MARIA b Mar 1, 1789
*JOHN (Aug 7, 1791 - May 2, 1866), m Anna Maria Moyer (b Sep 9, 1797, bapt Rehrersburg, Berks Co - d Aug 28, 1873, bur Hoffman Cem), dau of Jacob and Eva Christina (Koppenhaver) Moyer. In 1850, John Forney and Mary were head of house. George and Susanna and one year old Mary Jane lived with them. Also Sarah Brown age 10 and Susanna Daniel age 82 lived with them. In 1870, George Forney's mother Mary age 72 lived with the family. **John and Anna Maria (Moyer) Forney children:**
**JOHN F. (b Mar 30, 1822 Mifflin Twp,- Feb 4, 1901, bur Forney Cem), m in Mifflin Twp Dec 30, 1844 Susan Lenker (Jan 2, 1826 - Apr 8, 1900), a dau of Jacob and Rebecca (Hoy) Lenker. John lived with his "stepfather" Benjamin Reigle after their marriage for a few years (Not sure how he was a stepfather, but in 1850

John & Susan lived two doors away from Benjamin Riegel in Mifflin Twp.). Later John bought a 20 acre farm near Berrysburg and engaged in gardening for three years, sold that place and went back to one of Benjamin Riegel's houses for three years. He then bought 109 acre farm in Up Paxton and continued to live there. He also bought a mill in 1886. Before that, at the age of 16 he drove a huckster team to Pottsville for Benjamin Riigel.

John and Susan (Lenker) Forney children:

George W. (c1847 - Jan 26, 1917), m Susan Lenker (Aug 20, 1854 - Nov 8, 1925); Wiliam H. (Sep 25, 1849 - May 15, 1897), m 1st Lizzie Whitcomb of Centre Co., 2nd Lizzie Lenker; Kate m Joseph Matter - lived in Washington Twp; Sarah (Sep 4, 1856 –Dec 16, 1919), m Harry Keiffer (Oct 19, 1838 – Dec 27, 1901), lived in Elizabethville; **Daniel Peter b c1855, m Mary E. ____ b c1859, lived in Up Paxton; John L m Annie Bohner - lived in Up Paxton; Jacob Elmer b c1864, m Bertha Enders - lived in Up Paxton; ELizabeth Alice b c1866 m Carson Kramer of Millersburg; Hannah; Susanna; Carrie Agnes (1868 – 1911) m Michael.D. Bonawitz (1862 – 1935, bur Rife Cem), head miller for John Forney at Rife. Alfred (Oct 1, 1855 - Mar 26, 1864)

**GEORGE (Apr 5, 1823 - Nov 30, 1901, Ogle Co., Ill), m Susanna Hoffman (Nov 8, 1827 - Oct 27, 1896), a dau of John and Elizabeth (Bordner) Hoffman. . George and Susanna (Hoffman) Forney had twelve children (some bapt Hoffman Ch): Mary Jane b Oct 7, 1848, m 1868 John Riegel (1844 – 1915), a son of Reuben and Amy (Stine) Riegel. [See Riegel genealogy]; Sarah Anne b Jan 1, 1852, m Samuel Zoller; John Franklin (Oct 29, 1856- May 8, 1942, Lincoln Twp., Ogle Co, Illinois); Catherine b May 7, 1860, m Michael J. Wertz b 1850 DuPage Co., Il; Harriet b c1860; Emma Elizabeth (Feb 8, 1862- Dec 27, 1881) Ida S. (Aug 23, 1873 – Mar 31, 1894, Forreston Twp., Ogle Co, Il), m Samuel G. Byers;

**LUCETTA (Jun 14,1826-Jan 22,1902), m Peter Wise (Apr 4,1822–Sep 9,1884) –[Wise genealogy page 300]

*JOHN JACOB (May 22, 1795 - Dec 2, 1880, bur Davids Cem, Killinger), m 1st Catharina Messner (Jun 8, 1802 – Dec 21, 1840, bur David's Cem), a dau of Michael and Margaretha Messner. After Catharina died, John Jacob m 2nd Susannah ____ (b Oct 23, 1801 - Oct 23, 1878). (dates from old cem rec housed in David's Ref Ch Killinger). John Jacob is probably the one bapt at David's Ch in 1841 age 44. In 1880 Jacob was a widower living in Up Pax Twp with his son-in-law John G. Seal. He was a blacksmith. **Jacob & Catharine (Messner) Forney children (some bapt Davids Ch, Killinger– there are discrepancies between bapt & cem records.))):**
SARAH (Oct 16, 1821 – Oct 30, 1911, bur Davids Cem), m John G. Seal (Mar 27, 1810 – Jun 7, 1886). They lived on a farm in Up Pax Twp & in 1880, their dau Lydia A 15, Amanda 28, & granddaughter Sarah A 15, lived with them. **John G. and Sarah (Forney) Seal children: Catherine b 1843; Amanda b 1845; William H (Aug 4, 1846- Nov 25, 1897, bur David's Cem), m Amelia _ 1845 – 1919); Mary b 1848; Lydia A. b 1865. **JONAS (JONATHAN) (Apr 22, 1823 – Jun 21, 1881, bur Oak Hill Cem, Mbg), m Angaline ____ (c1830 – 1919). They lived in Up. Pax Twp in 1860, but later moved to a farm in Liverpool, Perry Co. **Jonas & Angaline Forney children:** John (1848- 1929); George b c1852; Amelia b c 1853; Jane b c1855; Mary M. b c1856; Elisabeth b c1858; William C. b Feb 1860; Cornelius b c1863; N. Pierce b c1867; Franklin b c1869; Jacob b c1872..
**CHRISTIAN (Jun 9, 1826- May 13, 1909, bur Oak Hill Cem, Mbg), m Amanda __(Apr 4, 1826 – May 24, 1903). He was a blacksmith.
GEORGE (Feb 26, 1828- Feb 1, 1868, bur David's Cem, Killinger), m Rebecca Sultzbach (Apr 14, 1827 – Mar 21,1883) lived in Up Paxton Twp in 1860. He was a master shoemaker . **Geo. & Rebecca Forney children:
Jacob H. (Oct 3, 1851 near Killinger - 1923, bur Davids Cem, Killinger), , m 1st Mar 20, 1876 Salome Weaver (1847 - Jun 17, 1885), dau of William J. & Elizabeth Weaver. **Jacob H. and Salome (Weaver) Forney children:** Anna Nora b Oct 18, 1876; Minnie Dora b Jul 2, 1878; Sallie M (Jun 5, 1885 - 1899, bur Davids Cem) and Marie, identical twins b Jun 5, 1885, the mother died Jun 17, 1885.
Jacob H m 2nd Mar 20, 1886 Sarah D. Woland (1840 - 1924), bur Davids Cem), dau of Andrew and Lydia (Schreffler) Woland. . Jacob H began to learn the trade of stone masonry at the age of 19, with William Seal of Up Paxton Twp., staying with him for ten years. Then he engaged in business for himself. He was very proficient, and helped to build many area bridges including these: Rockville at Harrisburg, the one across Pine Creek near Gratz; Dieblers in Upper Paxton; Bechtels in Washington Twp. He also did the masonry in the foundations of large area barns. They include those of John Deibler, Henry Williard, William Lehman, Mrs. Catherine Wert. Also did masonry for Catholic church in Williamstown, church in Lykens, and school in Uniontown. Jacob eventually retired from stone masonry and went to farming.

Mary J b Mar 7, 1856, m Alfred Seiler; **Amanda Alice** (Nov 18, 1865 – Nov 17, 1890), m 1ˢᵗ Charles Stroup, 2ⁿᵈ Charles Deibler.

SUSANNA , m George Heckert; ****MARY m Levi Miller:****MARGARET REBECCA** (Nov 25, 1833 – Dec 24, 1903), m Joseph Wert (Sep 8, 1828 – Dec 3, 1 881, bur Davids Cem, Killinger), a son of Isaac and Elizabeth Wert. Joseph was a carpenter.

CATHERINE b Aug 6, 1834, m B. J. Steever. She was a seamstress in 1860; ****AMANDA b Mar 19, 1838, m Hiram Miller.

THE HARTMAN FAMILY

[**HENRY HARTMAN, Jr.** (Jan 19, 1794 - Sep 11, 1879, bur Simeon Cem), son of Henry and Sarah (Herner) Hartman. Henry the father came from Germany to Montgomery County, later came to Williams Valley. Henry Jr. m Magdalena Schoffstall (Oct 27, 1797 - Apr 16, 1879), a dau of Peter and Catharine (Hoffman) Schoffstall. Henry was a mason and farmer. They were the parents of **JOHN** (Apr 15, 1819 - Aug 1, 1894, bur Simeon Cem), m Mary Ritzman(Jul 25, 1823 - Jan 29, 1903), dau of Jacob Ritzman and his first wife Elizabeth (Matter) Ritzman. **John and Mary (Ritzman) Hartman children: Henry J.** (Jun 13, 1841 - Dec 17, 1861, bur Simeon); **Aaron** (b Mar 12,1843 - Jul 11, 1905), m Mary Romberger (May 7, 1848 - Nov 20, 1943); **Jacob** b c1846; **Jonathan** b c1848; **Elizabeth** b c1853; **Charles** b c1856; **Solomon** (Jul 14, 1858 - Sep 16, 1872); **Milton** (Feb 15, 1863 - Aug 12, 1865). [More information on a larger HARTMAN genealogy elsewhere in the book.]

During the years that Reuben Riegel owned this farm, he continued the practices of his father of having tenant farmers living here. From 1867 to 1871, Henry and Lydia (Shaffer) Miller and their young family lived here. Henry was originally from Liverpool, Lydia from Stone Valley. They had just come back from Kansas, having decided after one year that they preferred to live in their native Pennsylvania. After they left this farm, the Miller family moved to Hegins Township where they stayed several years. Later, they purchased a farm in Barry Township, Schuylkill County, and made their permanent settlement.

Reuben Riegel by his will written December 18, 1878, published December 6, 1880, conveyed this land to his son John Riegel, and he and his family moved here from the family homestead that he and brother Andrew had shared. Amos Radel age 21, listed as a servant lived with John and his family.

On November 10, 1911 John Riegel sold two acres, ninety-five perches of land to his son-in-law, Cloyd E. Weaver. Soon after purchasing this land, Cloyd and Cora Weaver had a house constructed on the land. But due to a dispute in the family, they had the house moved or reconstructed in Big Run, about a mile east of Loyalton. After John Riegel died, his heirs on April 28, 1917 sold the remainder of the ninety-one acres, 111 perches of land to Harry E. Klinger.

Harry E. Klinger and family lived here for many years. He was a teacher in several of the public schools in Lykens, Mifflin and Washington Twp. He also taught in the Gratz School. During the summer he devoted his time to farming. He raised dairy cows. It kept him busy milking early in the morning before school, and again in the evening after the school day was over. He was remembered as being short, and frequently smoking a cigar.

Many years later after his wife Mary Jane died, Harry E. Klinger moved to Middletown, Pa.. He sold the farm on September 9, 1968 to Rudolph and Margaret Stary and George Mazur, Jr. and wife Jean. One year later they sold to Spread Eagle Farm, Inc. On August 26, 1974, it was sold to Franklin R.Herb.

When Frank R. and Leslie E. Herb purchased this property, they enlarged the house almost double in size. The original part of the house has very large old log construction in the basement. The name Riegel is carved on the rafters in the attic. Other buildings were on the property including the still existing large old barn. A spring located near the creek at the bottom of the hill southwest of the house for many years supplied the residents of the house with plenty of water. A small frame structure protects the spring. A windmill that pumped water to the buildings also has survived and is located near the house. After many years, Frank R. and Leslie E. Herb sold the farm to Gerald F. and Linda K. Weist in 1995.

A small lot was separated from the farm in recent years. A new home was constructed and has become the residence of Leslie E. Herb.

ST. PETERS (HOFFMAN'S) CHURCH

THE NEW ST. PETER'S (HOFFMAN) CHURCH
A sea of parked cars that transported many folks to the dedication service held in 1959 for the new church

On November 29, 1805, a deed in Dauphin County deed transferred ten and one-half acres of land from John Hoffman, Esquire and Ann Mary his wife, to Jacob Laudenslager, Peter Willier Senior, William Bordner and Andrew Daniel, joint trustees elected by the German Reformed religious society now composing a congregation at the church called at present Hoffman's Church, and for the use of the said congregation for a burial ground and school, and other religious exercises. "All that messuage and tract of land situate and lying and being in said Township of Upper Paxton." Charles E. Muench and Michael Enterline witnessed the deed, and Adam Weise recorded it. This was part of a tract of 354 acres of land and allowances that Commonwealth of Pennsylvania by patent on March 2, 1801 did grant unto John Hoffman. This land is part of three warrants. One tract of 165 acres 80 perches known as "Hempfield" was warranted on April 22, 1774, surveyed April 4, 1785 to Nicholas Sins. Another tract of 140 acres also known as "Hempfield" was warranted October 19, 1774, and surveyed April 5, 1785. Another tract warranted March 26, 1773. All three were patented March 2, 1801 to John Hoffman, with appurtenances.

By the time this deed was recorded, a log church had been constructed on the land, and a small, but apparently thriving congregation was established. The only date given for the foundation of Hoffman's congregation was recorded on a paper taken from the cornerstone of the 1885-1887 church. On that paper was written "founded 1771." The paper was discovered after the church burned in 1958.

Although an official date has not been declared, the first church register is proof of the early baptisms. They begin on July 24, 1791, when Reverend Anthony Hautz served as pastor. The first known confirmation class held July 18, 1791, admitted the following people to membership in the church: Jacob Troutman, Abraham Troutman, Peter Hohn, George Hohn, Johannes Hoffman, Abraham Wilgert, Jacoby Astman, Peter Schoffstall, Jacob Weber. In addition to his personal entries, Reverend Hautz collected records of baptisms performed by other persons who served this congregation between 1781 and 1786.

It is well to mention here, that the precious old leather-bound church record book dating from 1771 was missing for many, many years. After the fire in 1958 that destroyed the second church, it was learned that the original church record escaped destruction because it was housed in the home of the secretary of Hoffman's Church.

The early congregation met in homes, likely an adjacent Hoffman residence. Itinerant ministers often served the congregation. They traveled many dangerous and treacherous miles, to serve the people in these more primitive areas.

The early notes recording the effort put forth to build the church denotes enthusiasm. The first settlers had come to this wilderness area and wished to create a permanent place to worship - one of the most important segments of their lives. The log of expenses to build the church begins May 20, 1792 when an entry states that Frederick Stein collected three pounds, eighteen shillings, nine pence to pay for the ten and one-half acres of land. Seven shillings, six pence were paid to the "land measurers" for the surveying of the ten and one-half acres of land.

In preparation for the construction of the church, Heinrich Hahn and Johannes Hoffman were hired as the master builders. Levi Buffington was also mentioned as "church carpenter" and was given a budget of fifty pounds to have the work done. Out of that money he had to pay Johannes Hoffman, Heinrich Hahn, Christian Hoffman, John Nicholas Hoffman, Johannes and Wilhelm Bordner, Andreas Riegel, Johannes Kaufman, Peter Bellis, Jr., George Buffington.

During the course of construction, Johannes Hoffman and Heinrich Hahn traveled to Harrisburg several times to purchase nails, glue and paint, and window glass. Sometimes living expenses were charged for the trip. It is difficult to comprehend much travel over those early roads. The arduous task of bringing back supplies, possibly by packhorse, is even more amazing. Jonathan Crill, Christian Hoffman, Michael Sierer, Adam Heller, John Nicholas Hoffman, Peter Schoffstall and Johannes Bordner received money for shingling the church. Church windows and cement purchased in June 1793, cost five shillings, eight pence. Window glass was again purchased in September 1793, at a cost of four pounds and four shillings. In October 1793, Nicholas Hoffman was paid four pounds, ten shillings, three pence for 2000 feet of lumber. Philip Klinger was paid two shillings, three pence "for alcohol, which he brought with him." Johannes Bashort was paid six shillings, ten pence for paint "he brought with him." Peter Allman and Christian Hoffman were paid for "bord."

On June 2 9, 1794, after the new log church was occupied, the first recorded officials of Hoffman Church were documented. Frederick Stein and Peter Willier became Elders. Johannes Bordner was elected Deacon.

The new log building was a sturdy edifice, made from the rugged virgin timber cut in the surrounding forest. It was built along simple lines of architecture. Along the northern end of the interior of the church, a wine-glass pulpit and chancel enclosed the communion table. A balcony surrounded three sides of the auditorium, the choir and organ occupied the rear balcony. The entrance to the church was located on the south wall, giving an impressive view of the elevated pulpit, and presenting a reverent atmosphere for the preacher as he relayed the Word of God to his congregation. This log building served for over a century when it was deemed fitting to have a more improved edifice.

In 1885, When Rev. W. G. Engle (1872 - 1889) was pastor of this church, the old log church was razed. Many of the old logs were used in the construction of the new frame church. The second church was built about 1886, approximately on the site of the old church in the cemetery. It was dedicated in November 1886. The structure was typical of the architecture of that day, with its Gothic windows and recessed alcove for the pulpit. An organ was placed in the sanctuary. A ninety-foot steeple graced the exterior of the building. To build the steeple, the carpenters required six white pine logs, each log forty-five feet long.

In June 1936, a fierce thunderstorm passed through the area, doing much damage along its path. The twenty foot steeple was hit by a bolt of lightning at it's base, tumbled into the church sanctuary, and buried several rows of pews.

When the second church was built, the large boulder bearing the bronze tablet, a mute tribute by the D.A.R to the Revolutionary soldiers, stood near the entrance of the church. Today that same boulder can be seen in the churchyard.

To right: The Second Hoffman's Church Building

An article in the MILLERSBURG HERALD, dated Friday October 29, 1886 announces the coming dedication services for Hoffman's church:

"The new Hoffmans church in Lykens Valley will be dedicated with appropriate ceremonies on Sunday November 7th. It is positively stated that this is the oldest congregation in Lykens Valley. The original church torn down a year ago or more was over a hundred years old. It was the place of the people who inhabited the valley in the early history for many miles around. The dedication of the new modern structure will be an event of great interest that can hardly fail to bring together a vast concourse of people. The denomination is German Reformed. Rev. W.G. Engle of Uniontown is pastor in charge."

The Interior Of The New Edifice Taken c1908

In 1907 improvements were made when a heating system was installed and the interior of the church was painted. Electric lights were installed in the church in 1938.

The second church survived for many years, but on Saturday evening, November 8, 1958, a passing motorist noticed flames in the vestibule of the church. Seven area fire companies responded to the call, but high winds fanned the flames, and the seventy-three year old church was totally destroyed. In the midst of the fire, the bell fell, half melted, into the ruins. The Boyer family had donated this silver-toned bell. The thousand pound bell could be heard for a long distance. The sound of its ringing or tolling brought back many memories to many people. Later the bell was salvaged, and on May 30, 1971, was mounted on a cement pedestal on the cemetery as a memorial to the second church.

After the fire in 1958, plans were immediately made for a new brick veneer church to be built across the road from the former building. Because of money from an insurance policy, and generous donations of members and friends in both money and labor, the church was completed debt free in 1959. The cornerstone was laid August 9, 1959, and the building dedicated November 29, 1959.

New additions have since been made to the church and surroundings. In 1977, a wooden pavilion was finished, which is used for Praise services, hymn singing, fellowship, and family gatherings.

First person memories have a way of presenting a picture in the most effective manner. We include the following memories of Lee E. Boyer in regard to Hoffman Church. These are excerpts from the address he gave for the Bell Memorial service at St. Peter's (Hoffman) Church on May 30, 1971.

"THE CHURCH" was, is, and always will be comprised of PEOPLE. In view of this, it is interesting to note the crop of people who heard and responded to the peals of the church bell around and just after the turn of the century. I shall name the people as I remember they were called in conversation before and after church services.

Just next to the church, was the "Ike" Stine family, then the "Nate" Rombergers, "Corneil "Kochers, John Kochers, John Lowers, "Jim" Troutmans, "Hen" Henningers, "Ike" Troutmans, Mrs. "Dan" Troutman, Frank Hoovers and Harry

HISTORY OF LYKENS TOWNSHIP

Rombergers, Charles Hoovers, "Sim" Daniels, "Al" Hoffmans, Josiah and Edmund Riegels, Charles and "Guernie" Riegels, George Lahrs, "Young" John Riegels, Andrew Riegels, Cloyd Weavers, George Straubs, "Old" John Harris's , Charles Kochers, "Dan"Shades, "Bill" Wolfes, the Boyers, Henry Williers, Betsy Hoag, "Ike Henningers, "Charles" Browns, John Harmans, "Rial" Weavers, "Dafe" Troutmans, Will Henningers, and the Louden Family.

The church and Sunday school was by far the main social center for the people. Here they gathered regularly, a bit early so they could talk before the scheduled services and lingered after service to get the news of the week past and the week coming.

The John E. Boyer family placed the bell in the old church steeple in 1887, in memory of their ancestor Peter Boyer. Each Sunday, it was rung three times. Early in the morning it was a notice bell. Secondly, it marked the beginning of Sunday school, and the third time, it was the beginning of the church service.

During these years, Reverend Calvin P. Wehr served as pastor. He grew up in the strict Dutch environment of the Lehigh Valley, and he preached in German occasionally. In those early days, we had afternoon church services every other time. Since we had church services only every two weeks, it meant that once a month we had morning church, and once a month afternoon church service. We did not care much for afternoon services, but I never heard any objection to having church services only every two weeks.

One of the interesting factors of Reverend Wehr's pastorate was the type of horses he drove. They were genuine racehorses that had made records on the track. I remember one ride I was privileged to be given. I was thoroughly delighted with the horse's gait; he did it so rhythmically, and with apparent ease and eagerness. When the automobile era came along, Reverend Wehr purchased a Dodge touring car. There was a heart-felt question as to what should be done with the sorrel trotter named Rubin Golddust. He was much too precious to be sold on the open market., too spirited to be put to sleep. So, he was literally pensioned to the John A. Harmon stables on the Annie Boyer farm, near Berrysburg.

Reverend Wehr believed in the significance of education and, wove related thought into his preaching. When he wished to emphasize culture, he would speak of the works of Michaelangelo and Leonardo da Vinci. These names baffled the farmer boys like myself. We wondered what kind of chaps these fellows were. Their names didn't sound at all like Hoover, Troutman, or Weaver - or even like Boyer or Henninger! Then when Pastor Wehr wanted to convey the idea of comprehensiveness, he would say "from alpha to omega." That would hold us; we knew absolutely nothing about the Greek alphabet.

In catechizing, I well remember how he explained to us the meaning of "eternity." Now that concept was another pretty big "pill" for us farmer boys to swallow. But preacher Wehr made it meaningful by saying, "Suppose a robin came from heaven every hundred years, and took one bill full of earth back to heaven. Eternity would be a longer period of time than it would take the robin to carry the whole earth back to heaven." I must admit that the language was beautifully simple, and the illustration truthful.

The church bell used to toll. Often times when we were in the field and would hear the bell on a weekday, we would immediately stop the team and listen to learn whether or not the bell was tolling. If it was we would stop working and count the number of times it tolled. Then we would wonder who died and would try to correlate the number of tolls with the estimated age of some supposedly sick church member. But this wasn't the end of the tolling. On the day of the funeral, we would all gather at the church awaiting the arrival of the horse-drawn hearse. When someone saw the hearse approaching, the bell would be tolled again until the coffin was taken into the church. It was at such times, when one was standing on the church grounds, that one would really hear the volume and tone of that thousand pound bell.

c hal   Earlier, I mentioned the coming of the use of automobiles. I also mentioned that the church was a social entity. Believe me that, as the several families purchased autos to come to church, automobile interest reached the fever point. As I look back, I am surprised at the variety of cars that came to church and Sunday school. Ike Troutman's had a Pullman, Jim Troutman's a Studebaker, Charlie Kocher's a big long yellow Jackson with thirty-six inch tires, Bill Wolfe's a Maxwell, John Lowers and Hen Henninger's Fords, Frank Hoovers a Dodge, Charl Henninger a Baby Grand Chevrolet and Harry Henninger a 490 Chevrolet. Al Hoffman's had an Overland, and when Charl Wolfe's came up from Harrisburg for communion or some special service, they came in a Peerless Eight. Some of the cars had carbide lights, others Presto lights, and still others electric lights. Some had gas tanks under the front seat, others in the cowl, and still others at the rear ends. Some cars needed to be cranked; others had self-starters - either compressed air or electric. Discussion of the characteristics provided untold interest and conversation, which probably increased the church attendance!

Every family was looking forward to owning a car sometime; the sooner the better as far as the young fellows, and girls, I guess, were concerned. The church parking lot served as an automobile demonstration center. If you like the gas tank to be out of sight under the front seat with no unsightly gas cap on the cowl, and no pressure pump to bother with, you chose that type of car. Sometimes the under-the-seat-tank-cars got a little low in gasoline, so when they started up the hill from the church, they sometimes sputtered and even sometimes stopped dead before reaching the top. "The gas isn't running front to the engine," we'd say. So what would they do? Simply back down the hill, turn around, go up the hill backwards, turn around again on top of the hill and then, off on their way! The church (the old one that was then across the road), was sitting back far enough so that cars could be backed against the church at right angles and still not have the front ends interfere with traffic on the road. This presented a lenging situation: Could the car be taken out of it's parked position, headed up the hill, shifted into second gear, and make the hill? Some could, others could not. Those that couldn't had to shift back into low gear, and grind and groan to the top at a snail's pace. Don't forget that the driver figured in this business too, and believe me, he got his just due - praise or mockery.

Such are the memories of the experiences to which the peals of the Boyer bell beckoned us. It called the membership together for programs central to their lives. The fundamental outcomes or benefits cannot be measured. Our intellectual teaching was profound, but the emotions were not neglected.

332

When we think of growing up in the church, how all of us cherish the words "Holy, Holy, Holy, Lord God Almighty," "Breathe On Me Breath of God, fill me with life anew," or "Jesus keep me near the cross, there's a precious fountain . . . . .

CONFIRMATION PICTURES OF ST. PETER'S (HOFFMAN'S) CHURCH

St. Peter's (Hoffman) and Salem (Berrysburg) Church Confirmation March 18, 1951, with Pastor Marks
l to r – top row: Allen Schroyer; Ronald Miller; Owen Holtzman; William Straub; Dale Miller; Theodore Romberger; Edward Charrot. middle row: Shirley Hartman; Mae Wolfe; Lorraine Witmer; Janette Engle; Barbara Straub; Miriam Potter; Elaine Schroyer. 1st row: Eileen Hain; Shirley Hess; Barbara Hoover; Kay Engle; Mae Kocher; Catharine Henninger.

Confirmation Class of St. Peter's (Hoffman) Church 1919, with Pastor Wehr
Top row: Clarence Lower, Chas Hoffman, Allen Harman, Middle Row: Irene Troutman, Guy Daniels, Chas Snyder, Elwood Hoover, Russel Crabb, Harry Troutman, Webster Hoover, Leah Hoover. Front: Emma Hoover, Eva Bonawitz, Rev. Wehr, Clara Troutman, Edna Lower, Bessie Weaver.

St. Peters' Hoffman's Confirmation Class Of 1915 - with Pastor Wehr

l to r - 1st row: Lillian Wolfe; Cora Troutman; Calvin P. Wehr, Pastor; Emma Snyder; Edna Rowe. 2nd row: Lillian Hoover John H. Wolfe; Mary Hoover. 3rd row: Norman Evitts; Daniel Rowe; Harry Lower; Harry Kocher; John Boyer; Lee E. Boyer

ST. PETERS (HOFFMAN) CEMETERY

The burial ground that at this modern time is located across the street from Hoffman Church, is the final resting-place for many early settlers of Lykens Township. Among those buried there are nine Revolutionary War veterans. Numerous burials were made during the early years, whose graves are obscure today. The early burial ground at the end of Short Mountain, it the site of the very earliest graves of members of Hoffman Church. The earliest legible tombstones in existence today in Hoffman cemetery are the following:

Eve Christian Moyer, wife of Jacob b October 21, 1778, died March 27, 1812, age 33 years 5 months, 6 days

Johannes Hoffman son of Daniel, b February 10 , 1776, died June 18, 1814 age 33 years, 3 months, 28 days.

John Jacob Stauch b December 15, 1780, d July 1815, age 35 years, 7 months, born in Tulpehocken Twp, Berks Co, married 8 years to Sarah Bleystein, 2 sons and 1 daughter.

Peter Bordner, son of Jacob b March 11, 1763, died December 21, 1816, age 53 years, 9 months, 16 days. Born in Bethel Twp, Berks Co, husband of Catharina Katerman, had 6 sons and 5 daughters.

334

Hoffman Cemetery Showing Surviving Church Bell & Monument To Revolutionary Veterans

DAR PLACES REVOLUTIONARY SOLDIERS MARKER

While John S. Fisher was governor of Pennsylvania, he appropriated money to be used in providing suitable markers for the graves of veterans of the Revolutionary War. The Harrisburg Chapter of DAR began a campaign to seek burial places of these veterans. Member Mrs. J.A.W. Brubaker made an extensive search to identify the veterans of this area. She found that at least seven were buried in this cemetery, but not all graves were marked. A large boulder was approved as a monument for these veterans. It was taken from the bed of the Susquehanna River in 1930, by local ferrymen Captain Warren Hunter and his son Robert. The stone is 4 x 6 ½ feet by 15 inches and weighs 5500 pounds. Guy L. Heckert (monument dealer) of Millersburg placed the stone upon the foundation. The bronze tablet bearing the names of the known veterans was placed on the stone and a dedication service held Monday, November 24, 1930. The monument reads:

TWELVE SOLDIERS OF THE AMERICAN REVOLUTIONARY WAR LIE BURIED HERE

Captain John Hoffman	(1746 - 1831)
John Bordner	(1758 - 1812)
Nicholas Bressler	(1751 - 1825)
Andreas Daniel	(1757 - 1841)
Mathias Deibler	(1763 - 1837)
John Nicholas Hoffman	(1749 - 1814)
Jacob Huber	(1756 - 1849)
Henry Umholtz	(17__ - 1829)
John Peter Willier	(1745 - 1821)

Peter Schoffstall (1740 - 1815) is another Revolutionary Veteran who is buried at Hoffman Cemetery, his grave unmarked. His name does not appear on the marker.

Henry Hartman (Oct 14, 1752 - ____), another Revolutionary War Veteran who is buried in this cemetery, but his name is not on the marker.

The twelfth one has not been identified.

335

The Reformed Centennial Celebration Held In Isaac Daniels Grove August 12, 1893

EARLY GERMAN REFORMED MEETINGS

Hoffman's Church was affiliated with the United (Reformed) Congregation of Lykens Valley. This group held occasional business meetings relating to the individual church activities.

On Saturday September 27, 1845, a meeting of the consistory of the United (Reformed) Congregation of Lykens Valley was held at David's Reformed Church in Killinger. The group met to settle existing difficulties. The substance of this meeting gives us an interesting view of government of the early churches.

Included in the congregations were: David's, Hoffman's, Steinthal, Gratztown, Huber's Uniontown, Georgetown and Elizabethville. Officers were nominated as follows: Jacob Hoffman, elder of Hoffman's Church for President: John Seiler elder of Steinthal Conjuration, Jacob Witmer, elder of Uniontown, John Brand elder of David's Congregation for Vice-President; Henry Ditty, Trustee of Huber's Congregation, and John Buffington, Trustee of Gratztown was nominated for secretary. Several agreements were confirmed or resolved at that meeting. Some of the resolutions were:

*John Adam Leiss, received a large majority of votes in every congregation, and he should be allowed to move into the pastoral dwelling house.

*No congregation may separate from the Charge without a majority vote from the whole charge . . . no secret maneuvers, as had previously been the case.

*Only Hoffman's, Steinthal, and David's Congregations have possession of the pastoral dwelling house and the land belonging thereto, as their own property, as it is set down in the agreement adopted earlier in the year 1813.

Another meeting of the Lykens Valley Charge of the Reformed Church, was held November 13, 1848, also at David's Church. Among the resolves made:

*Appointment of a standing committee to manage the farm, rent it out on shares, and see to it that the tenant adheres strictly to the agreement. Half of the grain should be stored in the barn. Tenant to keep fences in repair.

*Cost of repair expense was estimated at eighty-four dollars.

*Always, funeral services at any house of mourning shall be started promptly at the appointed time. The brethren with the pastor shall work to the end that this is done.

THE OLD UNIONTOWN CHARGE

During the last year of Rev. Engle's pastorate the Old Uniontown Charge, of which Hoffman's Church was a member, came to a close. The following eight churches belonged to the Uniontown Charge: Uniontown; Hickory Corners (Stone Valley); Georgetown (Dalmatia); Vera Crus (Malta); Hoffman's (St. Peter's); Gratz (Simeon); Berrysburg (Peace) and Elizabethville (Salem).

At a meeting held on July 13, 1889, under the guidance of Rev. Engle, it was decided to split the Charge in two. The four churches in the valley to the north retained the name of Uniontown Charge. The four churches in Lykens Valley were called the Lykens Valley Charge. This Charge was officially formed at a meeting held September 17,1890, and was made up of St. Peter;s Church, Lykens R.D.; Peace Church, Berrysburg; Simeon Church, Gratz; Salem Church, Elizabethville. On September 28, 1969, Simeon United Church of Christ disbanded and the congregation united with Simeon Lutheran. It left three churches belonging to the Lykens Valley Charge.

MINISTERS WHO SERVED HOFFMAN'S CHURCH

The information for this section was gathered from many sources. It gives an important look at the ministers who dedicated their lives to serving humanity, by perpetuating goodness to the people who lived in the community surrounding the house of worship. Surprisingly, the list of ministers who served St. Peters (Hoffmans) Church is almost complete. Unfortunately, information about some of them is scarce. The dates given with each minister refer to the length of time they served this church.

REVEREND SAMUEL DUBENDORF. . . (Dates intersperse between, 1779 - 1799)

Rev. Samuel Dubendorff is the first known pastor of St. Peter's (Hoffmans) Church. He was born October 21, 1721 in Stettin, Mecklenburg-Schwerin (now Szczecin, Poland). His father was a weaver. In his early years, Rev. Dubendorff was an inspector of a Berlin Gymnasium, and later served as a pastor in Brandenburg-Prussia for about fifteen years. Much later in life, on November 28, 1775, at the age of fifty-four, he volunteered to travel to America to serve as a minister. He came here on a ship with mercenary Hessian troops and served as chaplain while aboard the ship arriving in New York in 1775. Due to lack of proper credentials, he was not approved and commissioned to preach until March 8, 1776.

Rev. Dubendorff first served a church in Germantown from 1777 to 1778, while the British occupied Philadelphia, and during the battle of Germantown. It was a very unhappy experience, and in 1779, he left Germantown to come to the Lykens Valley. Years later, at a Reformed Church meeting in Philadelphia, this statement was written about him: "This old gentleman had the misfortune to come over with the Hessian troops, and remained for quite a time among the British in New York. Therefore, he was suspected of siding with the British, and lost the confidence of the people in Germantown."

His task was difficult in Lykens Valley. Serving three fledgling congregations that were spread from areas of Dauphin and even Northumberland Counties, he was the only Reformed minister in the area. It was said of him at the time that like John the Baptist, he was preaching the Gospel in the wilderness. His people greatly honored and loved him but they were poor. Aside from the most necessary articles of food they could give him no salary. The church in Holland learned of his circumstances and sent him one hundred guilders. Despite financial straits, he was honored as an impressionable person. Rev. Muhlenberg described him as "the learned Reformed minister of the congregations in Lykens Valley and the Schwaben Creek." After several years he moved to Carlisle and served 1790 to 1795. He returned to Lykens Valley and served until old age and poor health compelled him to relinquish his labors.   Rev. Dubendorff purchased land in Lykens Township, where he had relatives. There is no indication that he had children, or that he had ever married. He died January 1799, and shortly after, letters of administration were issued from Dauphin County Court, to his nephew Frederick Dubendorff. An inventory of his possessions include these items: "Destemend (testament), a blow coad (blue coat), a bleak welved coad (black velvet coat), three cattekissem, fifteen Chermeny (German) books, etc. His place of burial is not known.

REVERAND ANTHONY HAUTZ . . . . . (1791 - 1799)

Rev. Anthony Hautz was born August 4, 1758 in Germany. He came to America, accompanied by his wife and family. They arrived in Philadelphia on October 10, 1768, soon moved to Lebanon County, where he was a tailor by trade. He met Reverend William Hendel, and with encouragement, he studied under him for the ministry.

Rev. Hautz was ordained in 1787, although there was some doubt about his doctrinal soundness. He made a written statement in which he pledged to "live according to the doctrine, customs and regulations of the Reformed Church according to the word of God." During most of his ministry in Pennsylvania he served in areas where revival fervor was strong, because at least to a degree, he related to it.

Rev. Hautz served in Heller's Church before coming here. While he served at Hoffman's, he also served churches in Harrisburg, Middletown, Paxton, Wenrichs and Friedens as well as other congregations in Lykens Valley.Rev. Hautz married twice, his first wife died in Carlisle November 10, 1802. He married secondly to Catharine Keller on February 1, 1803. The date of his death or place of burial has not been found.

REVEREND BRAFFEL. . . . .(1800 - 1805)

Nothing is known about this pastor, except that he came from Canada.
REVEREND CHARLES EDWARD MUENCH (1804 - 1833)

Rev. Charles Edward Muench, although not an officially ordained pastor to Hoffman's Church, had a great influence on the work of that congregation. It is difficult to separate his expertise as a schoolmaster from his religious influence on the church. More will be found written about him as the first school master at Hoffman's school.

Rev. Muench was born January 7, 1769 in Mettenheim, Wartenburg, in the Palatinate of Chur Pfaltz on the Rhine, Germany. He was of Huguenot-French descent, his grandfather, Charles Frederick Beauvoir, fleeing France during the religious persecutions. He purchased the "Muench Hoff" and took his surname from there.

Charles (Carl) Muench was sent to Heidelberg, where he studied fourteen years preparing for the ministry, learning five different languages.. It was at the time that a general war developed in Europe, and his home was invaded by the French army. He became commissioned as a captain of the company of huzzars in the allied armies. While serving, he was severely wounded by a pistol ball in the leg, and a sabre cut on the left hand. He commanded the guard that conducted Lafayette to the prison at Olmutz.

Charles and Anna Margareth Bieser (Jun 24, 1770 - Feb 19, 1834),were married in Westphalia on the Rhine, on July 8, 1794. In 1798 they came to America, and settled near Shaefferstown, Lebanon County. He immediately became a school master in Shaefferstown, by 1800 in Rehrersburg, and by 1804 he was teaching at Trinity Tulpehocken. All of these dates are confirmed by church baptismal records of his children at these church sites. In the spring of 1805, Charles Edward moved to Lykens Valley to teach school, but discouraged by the wildness of the country, he moved on to Union County. In 1806, the congregation at Hoffman's Church called him back to start the first school in Lykens Valley.

The following excerpts are from an article written by Charles F. Muench, son of Charles Edward Muench, and printed in the DAILY TELEGRAPH, Harrisburg, Monday Evening, May 5, 1879. The personal details and memories of Charles F. Muench help us to become aware of the adventures and hardships of early immigrants. It also gives us more details about the church, school, and life in general in Lykens Township early in the 1800s.

"In 1798 he (father, wife and one child Julia) embarked for the United States. While on their voyage they were overtaken by French pirates, and robbed of everything of value. The boots were taken from father's feet. One of the pirates seeing mother in her distress, told her if she had any valuables about her she should secrete it about the baby; that it would not be disturbed. She done so and saved sufficient to prevent them from being sold as *Redemptioners*. When landing at Philadelphia they had fifty cents of a fund left, a baby six months old, no clothing, having been robbed of all that was worth taking. Father learning of a German school master wanted at Sheafferstown, now Lebanon county, secured the situation, taught school there some time, moved to Rehrersburg, Berks County, then to Lykens Valley in 1804 to the Hoffman church school house property, which contained nearly 18 acres, all woods with the exception of about or nearly one and one-half acres cleared for garden purposes and potato patch, this place being a perfect *wilderness*. He became discouraged under the unfavorable circumstances, remained but a short time, then moved to Union County. During the year and one-half of his stay there the Hoffman church congregation desiring his return, proposed the clearing of certain portions of the *wilderness*, which proposition he accepted and again returned to the Hoffman church property about the year 1806.

The people of the congregation done as proposed, enabling him by strict economy and the assistance of the neighboring farmers assisting in cultivating the land for several years which had been cleared, that enabled him in a few years to be more comfortably situated, when he became reconciled to his fate, teaching school during the winter months and occupying the balance of the year in preparing that portion of the land which still remained in somewhat wild condition. In a year or two with the assistance of an occasional neighbor, Mother and three of the older children (two sisters and a brother), the *wilderness* (at one time) became a paradise, as he frequently expressed himself to visitors. The congregation erected suitable buildings for housing the products and the comfort of the small stock he was enable to support on the land. His family increasing, they built an addition to the house, which still more increased his happiness. They elected him their regular clerk, in which service he remained until his decease.

Father was a strict observer of the Sabbath, requiring his family to make all the necessary provisions for the day, so that the sanctity of it was not interfered with. The same rule was observed on all holy days. Christmas, Easter and Whitsuntide each required two days; no work of any secular character was permitted during each of those holy days. Good Friday and Ascension day was hallowed the same as the Sabbath.

During the period when the congregation was without a regular stated preacher, father was required to conduct religious services on the Sabbath by reading sermons to them and conducting regular Sabbath services. He was also required to officiate on funeral occasions. His house was the home for clergymen of all denominations. The Rev. J. P. Shindel, of the Lutheran denomination, from Sunbury, filling appointments in the valley every four weeks, invariably was his guest, Rev. Smith, Hempering, and others. The first Reformed clergyman that I have any recollection of was Rev. James R. Reily, brother of Dr. Luther Reily, late of Harrisburg. He was stationed preacher for many years. His parsonage was twelve miles from father's residence. The reverend being single, preferred father's association, would remain the entire week and on Sunday early would leave for his next appointment.

The church was built of logs without inside or outside plastering with a gallery on three sides. Some years after it was weather-boarded and plastered inside. The school house stood about one hundred and fifty yards from the church and graveyard; its size was about thirty feet square, one and a half stories high, also of logs. The school room was about twenty feet wide. The convenience for the scholars was a flat-top table about three feet wide, about sixteen feet long, with one bench on each side; another table of about twelve feet long stood across the room at the end of the long table with benches of the same length. The other portion of the house (about ten feet) was occupied as the kitchen, dining room and parlor, until after the addition was made, the family having increased to seven children, six born in America and one in Germany. (C. F. Muench in another article mentions that the school house had a large room attached, where the older portion of the congregation generally met before service and had their friendly greetings, this occurring every four weeks.)

When I was a lad of seven or eight summers, some of the neighbors presented him with fruit trees to plant on the new home. One was said to be a choice cherry; he remarked as he examined it, "this I will plant close to the graveyard fence." While planting, remarked in German, "this will shade my grave." The tree became a large growth; the congregation having learned his desire, reserved that portion of the ground where now rests his and my mother's remains, having died one year apart; father in 1833 and mother in 1834, each arriving at the age of 64 years." (About 1880, Charles F. Muench came back to visit the area, and found that the tree had grown so large that its overhanging boughs almost shut out the sun from the tombstones of his parents in that portion of the ground, and for this reason the propriety of cutting down the tree had been recently discussed. Mr. Muench stated "It is safe to say this will not be done, at least by the present generation"). The tree has of course since disappeared.

On a little farm two miles northwest of Gratz, Charles and Anna Margareth settled with their seven children in the gently mountainous "Upper End" of Dauphin County. The Muench family apparently moved back across the Susquehanna River, briefly, sometime between the winter of 1806 and 1808 because their daughter Margareth was born at Freyburg, Penn Township, Northumberland County, December 8, 1808. This is documented by a Fraktur (baptismal Certificate) drawn by her father. This Fraktur is now in the collection of the National Gallery of Art in Washington, D.C. It is of special interest because it depicts four different scenes, with the schoolmaster sitting behind his desk. It was drawn around the time of Margareth's confirmation at Hoffman's Church, May 13, 1826.

For twenty eight years, Charles served as schoolmaster and lay leader of Hoffman's Church. He frequently conducted religious services as well as funerals. He was a musician and an artist, drawing and designing books and inlaying furniture. "He was exceedingly expert with the pen" and produced many Frakturs, as well as tiny bookmarks and book plates. These may be seen today in museums or libraries, as well as reprinted in books.

Proceedings of the German Reformed Church show some of the activities that Charles Muench participated in. He was listed as an Elder at the September 1816 Synod Meeting at New Holland. On April 30, 1820 he was the lay representative from the Lykens Valley Charge which consisted of four congregations and 397 communicants. It was the first meeting of the Susquehanna Classis of the Reformed Church held at Sunbury Church, Northumberland County. In September 1821, he attended meetings in Reading, Pa. Charles Muench died on January 8, 1833, and was deeply mourned by the Hoffman congregation. Margareth died the following year. Both are buried in the old graveyard.

REVEREND WILLIAM HENDEL. . . . . . .(1805 - 1807)

Rev. William Hendel was born October 14, 1768 in Lancaster, Pennsylvania. He was a son of Reverend John William and Elizabeth (LeRoy) Hendel. William was one of eight children, and the only one to follow in his father's footsteps as a minister. Professor James I. Good once called Williams's father "the most beautiful spiritual character in the early church." He was a close friend of Reverend Henry Melchior Muhlenberg, Lutheran, and Rev. William Otterbein, United Brethren, indicating mutual friendship among early ministers of other than Reformed persuasions. William Otterbein was also his brother-in-law.

A book by Rev. Harbaugh, gives this information about the senior Reverend Hendel. "During the Revolutionary War, he often visited Lykens Valley and preached at what is called David's church. The Indians being yet numerous, it was necessary for the inhabitants to go armed with weapons, to meet him at the confines of the valley, and guard him to his place of destination. Whilst he preached the guards stood under and around the door, with their rifles, so that they could keep a lookout for enemies, and also listen to the servant of God delivering unto them the glad tidings of salvation. They thus accompanied him from place to place, and when services were ended, he was guarded, in the same manner, on his way home, till he was beyond the reach of danger." Since there is a record of the senior Rev. Hendel preaching in this area, it is very likely that he also served Hoffman's during the early years.

Young William Hendel grew up in this religious environment. He studied for the ministry at Columbia College, and the theological seminary at New Brunswick. Rev. William Hendel was ordained by the synod April 30, 1793, and served the Tulpehocken charge from 1793 - 1882). For two of those years, 1805 to 1807, he ministered to the Hoffman Church congregation. He also owned land in Lykens Township and Gratz.

From 1822 to 1829, Hendel lived in Womelsdorf and there served several congregations. Rev. Willian Hendel married Margaret Hahn (1773 - 1829), but left no descendants. He died July 11, 1846 in Womelsdorf.

REVEREND'S GREESTWEIT, HELFENSTEIN, SMITH, JACOB DEIFENBECK - no further information.

REVEREND C. L. BECKER - lived in Baltimore in 1809, became Reverend James R. Reily's instructor.
Supply pastor during the period of 1807 to 1811, no other information

REVEREND PHILIP GLONINGER . . . . . (1811 - 1812)

Supply pastor, lived in Harrisburg in 1811. He was instrumental in arranging for Rev. Reily's placement here at Hoffman's in 1812. On August 30, 1812, Rev. Gloninger baptized fifteen babies in Harrisburg. All from the Hoffman congregation, according to the records.

REVEREND JAMES R. REILY . . . . (1812 - 1819)

Rev. James Ross Reilly was born October 31, 1788, at Myerstown, Lebanon County, a son of Captain John Reily (1752 - 1810), a native of the city of Leeds, England. Captain Reily emigrated before the Revolution, served in the war, and later became a lawyer. In 1773 John Reily was married to Elizabeth Myer (1755 - 1800), a daughter of Isaac Myer, founder of Myerstown. They had three sons, Rev. James Ross, Dr. Luther, a Harrisburg physician, General William, who served in the Pennsylvania Militia.

When his mother died, James lived with Rev. William Hendel of Tulpehocken. He probably came to the Lykens Valley with Rev. Hendel when he preached in this church, so was familiar with the area. Under the influence of Rev. Hendel, James Reily was sent to Baltimore, where he studied with Reverend C. L. Becker. He was called to Lykens Valley in 1812.

In August 1812, Carl Muench, a schoolmaster and lay leader at Hoffman church, wrote to James Reily, telling him that the elders and deacons had arranged for the new pastor a beautiful comfortable dwelling. The dwelling had 3 rooms; a living room kitchen & cellar and a big barn for horses and cattle. The schoolmaster hinted that with this home, he need not remain single.

When Rev. Reily began his duties here, at the age of twenty-five years, he was given charge of numerous churches from the Susquehanna River, east to the Blue Mountain, at least twelve churches in addition to Hoffman's. During his tenure, he also became a supply pastor to vacant congregations outside of Dauphin County. In August 1813, he made a three week missionary journey on horseback through Virginia into North Carolina. When he returned to Lykens Valley, he attempted to raise a company of men to fight in the War of 1812. But the war ended before his troops were organized.

From 1816 to 1818, Rev Reily served the Penna Legislature in Dauphin County. Later that year he accepted a call from Hagerstown, Maryland. Soon after he moved to Hagerstown, he married Mary Orndorf, but she died six months later.

In 1825, Rev. Reily resigned from his pastorate because of ill health. He later crossed the Atlantic to Switzerland and Germany to solicit funds for the theological library at Carlisle (It later moved to Lancaster). Rev. Reily died in York, March 18, 1844, and is buried in the graveyard on Beaver Street, York, Pennsylvania.

REVEREND ISAAC GERHART . . . . (1819 - 1843)

Rev. Isaac Gerhart was born near Sellerville, Bucks County, Pennsylvania on February 12, 1788, a son of Abraham and Barbara (Detterer) Gerhart. His great grandfather Paul Gerhart, was an exile from France, compelled to flee his native country about 1680. He went over into the Palatinate where he settled in Gerhartsbrunn. Peter Gerhart, his grandfather immigrated to Pennsylvania about 1730, and settled in Montgomery County.

Rev. Gerhart was baptized as an infant and confirmed in the German Reformed Church of Indianfield. From early childhood his parents took Isaac along to church, where he was so impressed by the preaching that he was in the habit of imitating the minister at home by preaching from a block or chair. His wish was to become a minister. At the age of eighteen he expressed this desire to his father, who was not fully in agreement with the idea. The father thought "he was too young, and ought to learn to work first." The father approved of common school education, but thought that much education for the ministry was useless. Meeting with this opposition Isaac Gerhart gave up the idea of the ministry for the time being, but hoped that eventually he could fulfill his goal. He met his goal in 1808 at the age of twenty. He had again wrestled with the idea for several months before he approached his father. This time his father was in agreement. He began his studies in Montgomery County 1809, and in 1812, made a three month missionary journey into central and western Pennsylvania. He preached in surrounding areas such as Snyder County, Buffalo Valley, Penn's Valley, Huntingdon and Bedford Counties, Pittsburgh, Westmoreland County, York County. While he served these congregations, only one other German Reformed minister served northwest of the Blue Mountain. So, he made frequent missionary visits to Northumberland and Columbia Counties. During five years, he traveled 2,500 miles each year on his preaching circuit.

In 1818, he resigned his extensive charge due to ill health, at which time it was said, "he was not able to preach more than once a day." He accepted a call from Peter's (Hoffman's) and Zion (Klinger's) in Lykens Township, Stone Valley, and

Fetterhof's. In 1822 he added the Gratztown Simeon congregation. Better health returned to him and he continued here until 1843, when he moved to Frederick, Maryland. He died in 1865 , age 77 years, and is buried in Lancaster County.

REVEREND JOHN ADAM LEIS. . . . . . .(1844 - 1856)

Rev. John Adam Leis was born in Berks County, Pennsylvania. In his early years he worked as a carpenter. While helping to erect First Reformed Church in Lebanon, he met with a serious accident, which made such a deep impression on his mind that he felt a call to devote himself to the work of preaching the gospel. He began his public ministry in Ohio, then returned to Pennsylvania and became pastor of the Belleman and Friedensburg churches, until 1838.

Rev. John Adam Leis came to Lykens Valley from Dillsburg in 1844. He served the congregations in this area for twelve years. He resigned inn January 1856, after being troubled for several years with "indisposition and spells of dropsy and asthma." According to the minutes of January 26, 1856, the Lykens Valley Charge responded. . . "We are sorry that our congregations must give up our pastor, John Adam Leis who for the duration of twelve years served us faithfully and with much patience and great diligence." Rev. Leis was living in the Reformed parsonage in Killinger while he served this area. On January 26, 1856, he resigned his pastoral duties and left Lykens Valley. He became a pastor in Illinois, and stayed for one year. From there he went to Ohio where he preached for ten years before returning to Pennsylvania.

REVEREND RICHARD A. FISHER. . . . . .(1856 - 1857)

Rev. Richard A. Fisher was born October 25, 1805, in a rural neighborhood in Heidleberg Township, Berks County, son of John and Susanna Fisher, members of Hain's Church.

Early in life he began to feel led to become a minister. In 1822 he began to study theology under Dr. Herman of Montgomery County. He was licensed in Northumberland County, where he began his ministry in 1827.

During his pastorate in Sunbury Rev. Fisher met Amelia Weiser, to whom he was married, in 1831. Amelia was the eldest daughter of Hon. George Wieser of Sunbury. The Fisher's had six sons and four daughters.

His ministry lasted about twenty-eight years in Sunbury. He served a very large number of congregations, which required him to travel an incredible amount of miles over mountainous country. His dedication to duty caused him to develop very poor health. During the autumn of 1854 he became painfully ill leaving him unable to attend to his duties. After rest and medical help, he was able to accept a call to the Charge in Upper Dauphin Area, and came here June 1, 1856. But because of his impaired health, Rev. Fisher's ministry here was a short one. He died at David's (Killinger) parsonage, on Tuesday January 27, 1857, of consumption. He is buried in Sunbury.

During his service as a pastor Rev. Fisher recorded twelve hundred baptisms, received by confirmation between five and six hundred persons into the Church, buried nearly five hundred persons, preached about four-thousand sermons, and assisted in ordaining twelve ministers. In person he was of medium height, slim, straight, and genteel in appearance with a modest and quiet disposition. Mrs. Amelia Fisher survived her husband by fifty-eight years, having lived to be one hundred and two years of age.

REVEREND EPHRAIM KIEFFER . . . . .(1857 - 1865)

Rev. Ephraim Kieffer was born January 17, 1812, near Mercersburg, Franklin County, Pennsylvania. During his childhood he lived in Virginia, where his mother died when he was but ten years old. In about 1830, when he was eight years old, Ephraim Kieffer moved to Chambersburg, Pa. where he spent the next two years of his life as clerk in a store. It was during those years that he attained religious instructions and was confirmed on May 28, 1831. Soon after this important step he "resolved to dedicate himself more fully to Christ," and in October of that year, he moved to York and prepared himself for the ministry. His first charge consisting of five congregations was in Bellefonte, Pennsylvania, starting in November 1836. In 1840 he moved to Union County, and remained there for almost seventeen years.

Rev. Kieffer came to the Lykens Valley Charge on September 1, 1857. During his pastorate of six and one-half years in the charge, he had eight congregations extending over a wide section of the county. It was too much for him, causing his health to be impaired. He was admonished to withdraw from this large field, and take a much-needed rest. He resigned April 1, 1864, and returned to his former home in Mifflinburg. In 1866, he accepted a call to Carlisle, Pa., but poor health returned, forcing him to retire in 1870. He died May 11, 1871.

In person, Rev. Kieffer was tall, slender, and erect, with slightly curled dark hair. He was of mild and pleasing aspect, courteous, genial and warm hearted. He was twice married. The first time in 1837, he was married to Eleanor Spangler of York, Pennsylvania. To this marriage, six children were born four sons and two daughters. Three of the sons became ministers. After Eleanor died, he married in 1848, Margaret M. Linn of Union County. There were nine children, six daughters and three sons to this marriage.

REVEREND JACOB KEHM. . . . . (1865 - 1872)

Very little has been found about the person of Reverend Jacob Kehm. It is recorded that he performed seventy-one baptisms while he served Hoffman Church.

REVEREND WILLIAM G. ENGLE. . . . . . .(1872 - 1889)

Rev. William G. Engle was born at New Berlinville, near Boyertown, Pa., on April 16, 1833. He was a son of Solomon K. and Catharine (Gottschall) Engle. His mother died when he was sixteen months old; he was reared by his maternal grandparents.

As a youth, Rev. Engle learned the trade of coach making. In 1852, he was enrolled at the Mt. Pleasant Academy in Boyertown. For several terms he was a student at Union Seminary in New Berlin, Pa. After graduation, he taught in a public school and in a select school for several years. He graduated from the Theological Seminary at Mercersburg in 1862, and was licensed and ordained by the Goshenhoppen Classis the same year. He married Annie C. Herlacker of New Berlin on May 24, 1859.

Beginning in 1862, Rev. Engle served churches near Boyertown, Clarion Co., and Rehersburg. On April 1, 1872, Rev. Engle became associated with this area as pastor of Uniontown Charge. It included these congregations: Simeon (Gratz), Hoffman's (Lykens Twp), Peace in Berrysburg, Salem in Elizabethville, Uniontown (Pillow), Hickory Corners (Stone Valley), Dalmatia (Georgetown), and Vera Cruz (Maltz). He resided in the Reformed parsonage in Pillow. He took responsibility for many activities in his various congregations during his tenure. He took serious his role of keeping accurate records and preserving the churches events, for the sake of history. By-weekly sermons, in each congregation began while Rev. Engle was here. Also Union Sunday Schools held what was called HARVEST HOME CELEBRATIONS in the fall of the year.

Rev. Engle continued in his ministry here until May 22, 1889. In his farewell sermon, he included these statistics: During his seventeen years of service here, two new churches had been built, one remodeled. He baptized a total of 1,153 infants, confirmed 739, and had 494 burials.

REVEREND SAMUEL KUHN. . . . . (1889 - 1890)

Rev. Samuel Kuhn, son of John and Elizabeth (Gallatin) Kuhn was born in Franklin County, Pennsylvania, August 14, 1819. His mother died when he was six years old. He spent his childhood and youth working on his father's farm. At the age of seventeen, he learned the trade of cabinet making. Through the influence of his pastor, Rev. A. H. Kremer, he was induced to prepare for the ministry. In the spring of 1841, he entered Marshall College, but after a short time ran out of funds. He then returned to his trade of cabinet making, and continued his studies privately. On July 1, 1851, he was ordained, and served as pastor at New Bloomfield, Pennsylvania, until December 1862. From there, he accepted a call to Aaronsburg and later Hummelstown. From Hummelstown, he came to the Berrysburg Charge, and served until August of 1890.

Local records give no insight into his activities in this Charge. He left no record of baptisms or communions for his year of service at Hoffman Church. Rev. Kuhn was a skilled cabinetmaker, sometimes putting his skills to work in the church buildings. From here he moved to Liverpool and stayed until 1895. Then retired to Elizabethville, where he died in 1897.

REVEREND JOHN J. STAUFFER. . . . (1891 - 1902)

Rev. J. J. Stauffer was born at Allentown, Pa. on July 11, 1860, a son of Daniel and Fannie (Long) Stauffer. His family came from Spain in the early 1800s. His father was a cabinet and coach maker, and a staunch Prohibitionist, probably having a strong influence on his sons. Rev. Stauffer graduated from Ursinus School of Theology and was ordained in 1886. After serving several other churches, he was accepted on February 27, 1891 by the just formed East Susquehanna Classis (this area). It consisted of Simeon, Salem in Elizabethville, St. Peter's (Hoffmans), and Peace in Berrysburg. During his ministry, on August 12, 1893, the Reformed Centennial Celebration was held in the grove of Isaac Daniels in Lykens Township. A great crowd of people gathered for the event. A picture was taken, a copy of which is in this book.

Rev. Stauffer continued in his ministry here until September 1901. A newspaper piece written in July 1901, mentions that Rev. Stauffer submitted his resignation for the second time, and it was reluctantly accepted. The newspaper stated: "Rev. Stauffer had been enthusiastically engaged in the Prohibition Organization. He submitted his resignation, in order to give all of his time as pastor and energy to the overthrow of the legalized liquor traffic which is doing so much to curse humanity and neutralize the work of the church." He had helped to organize the prohibition picnic, which was held each year in Jacob Boyer's Grove in the western section of Lykens Township.

Rev. Stauffer served several other until his sudden death, of cerebral apoplexy at his home in York, September 5, 1924. He is buried in Mt. Carmel Cemetery, Littlestown, Pennsylvania. He married Ella Rebert of Littlestown, and had three children.

REVEREND ADAM ZIMMERMAN. . . . . .(1902 - 1904)

Rev. Adam Zimmerman was born April 12, 1864, in Gnadenhutten, Ohio. He was a son of Nicholas and Mary Elizabeth (Sahm) Zimmerman. He graduated from Calvin College in 1878, later attended Moravian Theological Seminary in Bethlehem, Pennsylvania, was ordained on February 26, 1888. He served in two Moravian, than six Reformed churches churches before coming here

On July 7, 1888, Rev. Zimmerman was married to Sarah L. Petry, but nothing is known of their family. Pastor Zimmerman served in two Moravian Churches between 1888 and 1894. From 1894 to 1912, he served in five Reformed Churches, before coming to Hoffman's. He eventually went back to Ohio, died in Canton May 23, 1944.

REVEREND CALVIN P. WEHR, D. D. . . (1905 - 1937)

Rev. Calvin Peter Wehr, the eldest son of Wilson and Rebecca (Werly) Wehr was born January 10, 1870, in Heidelberg Twp., Lehigh Co. on the old Wehr homestead. It was owned first by his grandfather, later by his father.

As a child, Rev. Wehr had only common school advantages. But in 1888, he was granted a certificate to teach in the public schools. In 1889, he entered Keystone state Normal School, at Kutztown. In September 1889, he entered the academic department of Ursinus College, graduating in 1895. That fall he enrolled in Ursinus College, Theological Department, graduated and was licensed to preach in 1898.

In December of 1904, Rev. Wehr received a call from the Lykens Valley Charge. On May 30, 1905, at a meeting held in Killinger, Pa., Rev. Wehr transferred his affiliation with Lehigh Classis of the Reformed Church, to East Susquehanna Classis. Years later he recalled this meeting. "I was but the stripling of a youth. This was the day of horse and buggy. When you arrived it reminded one of a great county fair. One had a hard time to find a suitable place to tie his horse and lucky to find shade. One was more lucky to have a comfortable set for himself and family as they sat in the church. Often standing room was at a premium. What devout worshippers! The local choir furnished music to the very best of their ability. The Classis usually took four or five days. When we were ready to sing the doxology, the roosters were ready to climb on top of a building for safety, and rejoiced over our departure and having escaped with their lives. Those were not only horse and buggy days, but the days when the minister was looked to as a mighty force and ruling power in the community. When he entered the pulpit the people rewarded him as a man sent from God. The Bible was none else but the Word Of God. The outstanding factor of a sermon was not its brevity but often the opposite was true. A sermon was an hour in length, and was regarded as too short and hardly worth while to drive three or four miles in mud, up over the horses feet."

Rev. Wehr remained in Lykens Valley for many years serving St. Peter's (Hoffman), Simeon, Salem and Peace Congregations. His ministry was successful in many ways.

One of the personal things remembered about Pastor Wehr, is that he loved horses. For his own use, he wanted a horse that could travel four miles per hour. One day, he was late leaving Elizabethville for a funeral in Gratz. Pressured to arrive on time, his special horse Ruby doubled her effort and ran eight miles in an hour.

On November 6, 1891, Rev. Wehr married his childhood sweetheart, Agnes E. Peters. She was born July 30, 1871, a daughter of Franklin and Catherine Peters. They had one child, Florence b August 13, 1892, did not marry.

REVEREND A. LEVAN ZECHMAN. . . . . (1937 - 1949)

In January 1938, Rev. A. Levan Zechman began his pastorate in this area, serving several churches including Hoffman's. This minister is especially remembered as having a good relationship with his parishioners. Despite the many responsibilities of serving four congregations, he frequently took time to visit those who were sick or had other personal problems. Rev. Zechman resigned this pastorate in 1949, to accept a call to the Friedensburg Charge.

REVEREND WALTER E. BOYER (supply) . 1949 - 1950)

REVEREND EARL R. MARKS. . . . . . . (1950 - 1961)

Rev. Earl R. Marks was born May 8, 1927, to Robert and Eva Marks of Myerstown, Pennsylvania. Rev. Marks attended Lebanon Valley College and Lancaster Theological Seminary. On May 28, 1950, he was ordained at Richland, Pennsylvania, and immediately accepted a call to the Lykens Valley Charge.

During the pastorate of Rev. Marks many student associates assisted in the pastoral duties of the Charge. It was during his ministry that the balcony of the church was remodeled to house three Sunday School classes. The tragic fire caused by a stroke of lightening that destroyed the building occurred while he was here.

Rev. Marks and Arlene Wiest of Reinholds, Pennsylvania were married October 28, 1950. A daughter, Holly was born to them in 1956.

REVEREND JAMES G. REED. . . . . . . (1961 -   )

Rev. James G. Reed was born at Shamokin, Pennsylvania on January 30, 1915, a son of Mr. & Mrs. Joseph L. Reed. He studied at Wheaton College and graduated from Lebanon Valley College in 1940. He did his seminary work at Eastern Baptist Theological Seminary in Overbrook, Phila. He was ordained in the East Pa. Conference of the Evangelical Congregational Church in 1944, transferred into the pastorate of the Evangelical and Reformed Church in 1950.

Rev. Reed came to this Charge in August 1960, and served for about eight years. It was during his pastorate that the Evangelical and Reformed Church merged with the Congregational Christian Church to form the United Church Of Christ.

On October 10, 1941 Rev. Reed and Eleanor L. Erdman of Shamokin were married. A daughter Nancy was born to them in 1944. Rev. Reed retired from the ministry on December 31, 1978, and eventually moved to Florida.

REVEREND MICHAEL C. ROMIG. . . . . . .(1975 - c1992)

Rev. Romig was born in Mifflinburg, Pa. area on September 1, 1950. He was married to Ruth Wertz, also of Mifflinburg.

Rev. Romig was assigned as pastor of Hoffman's church in 1975, and continued to serve that congregation for seventeen years. .He eventually went back to Mifflinburg.

REVEREND JEFFREY WAGNER...... PRESENT PASTOR

THE EARLY CHURCH HOUSE AND SCHOOL

A log house located south of the cemetery was built possibly many years before the log church was built. It was built on the land transferred from John Hoffman, Esquire and wife Ann Mary (mentioned in write-up of church) to the joint trustees of the German Reformed congregation in 1805.

The existing "church house" across the street from the present church building was the "messuage" in the deed. It is likely that the house was a residence of an early Hoffman family. The early Hoffman congregation met in homes, and it is almost certain that this house eventually became the meeting house for worshippers while they waited for the church to be built. By 1804 this house became the home of the Hoffman Church School. The class room was in one section of the house, another small area was reserved for the school master's residence. It was in fact, the first known school to be established in Lykens Township. Schoolmasters affiliated with church organizations were paid by parents to educate the local children. After 1834, when public school laws became effective, this building became the first home of Hoffman public school.

Very little documented information has been found on this early school. An 1855 school account book known to exist as late as fifty years ago has not been located. It would probably contain valuable information. A study done by Superintendent La Ross in 1877, reports that the earliest Hoffman schoolhouse was erected about one hundred yards from the old Hoffman church. It was surrounded by a wilderness of heavy pine timber, which extended along the old valley road leading to Millersburg until about 1815.

The very first teacher at Hoffman school, and probably within the Lykens Valley, was Charles (Carl) Edward Muench. As already mentioned, little early detail has been found concerning his work at the school. However, later memories of his son Charles F. Muench provide personal information about some of the pupils who received their German education from his father. "Schools in those days were not as convenient as the present (c1879) day; many scholars were obliged to walk three or four miles. Henry Peffer, well known in the county, living with his step-father, Daniel Ferree, generally came on horseback. John Paul had a four mile distance, but so great was his desire to accomplish what he had undertaken that the distance was no barrier. Jeremiah Schindle, son of Rev.

John P. Shindel of Sunbury received his German education from father; he afterwards became a Lutheran preacher; was subsequently elected State Senator from the Lehigh district. Facilities for schooling were not as convenient as the Present time – which has been fully demonstrated by the following occurrence; Benjamin Riegel, living in Northumberland County (not connected with the Riegels of Lykens Valley), sent his children to my father's school on horse back, a distance of over ten miles, bringing provision for the children and feed for the horses sufficient for the week. This family lived in Mahantongo Valley. They were compelled to pass through Hepner's Gap, a short distance above now Gratztown, to make their way to the school house, which at the period was a perfect wilderness from their home to the school house, judging from what has been stated by old settlers, that scarcely half dozen clearings, existed between the two points, and they containing but few acres of cleared land."

Carl Muench lived in this building for a time, but later lived on a farm about two miles west of the school, and taught for about twenty-eight years. Since he served in many capacities in the work of Hoffman Church, more is written in the write-up of the ministers of Hoffman Church. However, in writing about his capabilities as a schoolmaster we should give him special credit for his abilities as a musician and an artist, drawing and designing books and inlaying furniture. "He was exceedingly expert with the pen" and produced many Frakturs, as well as tiny bookmarks and bookplates. These may be seen today in museums or libraries, as well as reprinted in books. An example of his artistic skills is the record of birth of Margareta Mumch born December 8, 1808 in Freyburg, Penn Township, Northumberland County and confirmed by Isaac Gerhart in Hoffman's Church May 13, 1826. The original certificate is now in the National Gallery of Art in Washington, D.C. (The Muench family had moved from here to Freyburg for about two years1806 to1808, but came back here to stay.) [Muench genealogy with farm write-up.]

The second teacher at this school was probably Jacob Schaffner, a tenant on the Hoffman Congregation property in 1840. In 1855 the tax record lists Hoffman's Congregation with six acres, a two-story log house and log barn. In 1858 the congregation is listed with eleven acres, a log house and stable. In 1883 and for many more years, the congregation is listed as having eight acres. The church was assessed only for the house and land around it.

This house was also used for Sunday school activities. Union Sabbath School of Hoffman's Church held its first meeting April 1, 1855. The officers elected were: George Wiest, superintendent; Isaac Martz, assistant Supt; John Laudenslager, secretary; Edward Reedy, librarian; George Williard, assist. librarian; John Hartman, treasurer; George Forney, Samuel Henninger, George Daniel and Anthony Betz, managers.

A meeting was held May 19, 1855 by the members of Hoffman's Church to decide whether Sabbath School should be held in Church or the schoolhouse. By a majority of seven votes, it was decided to keep the Sunday School in this house. From May 1856 to March 19,1856, all official meetings and Sabbath School sessions were held in the house south of the cemetery. A secretary's report of May 6, 1856 should be typical of the time period. On that day ninety-three scholars and sixteen teachers were present. The boys had learned seventy-seven verses of scripture. The FARMERS & MINERS JOURNAL on September 6,1856 reported "The Union Sabbath met at Hoffman's Church Saturday the 30th at nine o'clock a.m. On that day, the school was organized by Superintendent, Mr George Wiest, and the Marshals of the day formed a procession accompanied by the Umholtz Band. They marched to a beautiful grove a mile from the church. Arrangements had been made and seats prepared for all present. An address was delivered by Rev. D. Sell, after which a collection was taken up for the benefit of the School

Very Early Church Owned School/Tenant Building

During an intermission of half an hour refreshments were taken and the band was called upon to discourse some of their delightful music. The school was then convened, and Rev. H. Hoffman of Northumberland County delivered a sermon in German. After another collection being taken up, the procession was again formed and returned to the church. Rev. D. Sell addressed the school in the German language, when they were dismissed, and all went to their respective homes."

Classes continued to be held in the basement of this old building for more than twenty more years. When the new school was built on the opposite side of the cemetery, this building lost its usefulness as a school. The basement windows were eventually filled in with bricks. The building continued to be owned by the Hoffman Congregation, and through many years it became a residence for folks who served as sexton of Hoffman Church. Since then it has become a rental property.

THE NEW HOFFMAN SCHOOL
Known As School Number SIX

Lately Home Of Gregory A. Reed

The land for the new school was part of the adjacent Sebastian Henninger farm. On April 1, 1871, George and Susanna Forney sold several tracts of land to Sebastian Henninger. A tract of eleven acres (with houses, buildings, barns and stable), was included in the sale "subject to an open road or free passageway for horses and wagons over the lot from the present main road "to the property of Sebastian Henninger. On April 14, 1879, Sebastian Henninger and his wife Dina sold forty perches of this tract to the Lykens Township School District for thirty dollars. The lot became the site of the new brick Hoffman School. [Prior arrangements apparently were made to purchase the lot, since the school appears on the 1875 map.]

The new school served surrounding Lykens Township families for many years. As will be told in some of the following recollections, attending Hoffman school was a very positive experience. However, some children were not perfect pupils as this incident indicates. The MILLERSBURG SENTINEL published this account February 7, 1890: "There was an exciting time in the school house at Hoffman's Church in Lykens Township one day last week. Solomon Wolf a young pupil on his second day's attendance, attacked the teacher, Jacob E. Boyer, threw him on the floor, and might have done him serious injury had not some of the pupils gallantly come to the assistance of the teacher. The pugilistic young fellow was arrested and on Saturday placed under $300 bail by Squire Snyder of

Berrysburg for his appearance at court. The school board of Lykens Township is considering whether they should arrest the young ruffian for disturbing the school."

PERSONAL MEMORIES

Most people look back at their Hoffman school days as fun times. Mr. Harry Troutman, now deceased, related to us some of the activities at the school. He said recess and dinner periods were happy times. They played baseball, and on rainy days played jacks. In winter they looked forward to sledding down the long hill from the schoolhouse to Baltzer Matters house. In his first year as a pupil at Hoffman's, in 1907, Harry Troutman attended school every day. His teacher, Daniel Koppenhaver, gave him an award for perfect attendance. The prize was a framed picture. Plays and spelling bees were extra curricular activities, which were enjoyed during class sessions. Harry also remembered that his teacher Daniel Koppenhaver stayed at the home of his parents during severe winter weather, rather than walk the four miles to his own home.

A few years later, between 1912 and 1915, the children continued to enjoy sledding in winter. Clara Henninger recalled that in those years, Danny Romberger, a local farmer brought a large homemade sled to the school at noon. All the children and the teacher were loaded unto the sled - about twenty-two persons. They rode along the road, over frozen snow from the top of the hill near the school, all the way down the steep incline to the bottom of the hill. Sometimes, depending on conditions, the sled continued to slide part way up the next hill towards the farm of Baltzer Matter. Then the big boys pulled the sled back up the hill to the school, and off they went again!. Many times the sledding continued well past lunch break, but that was permissible because the teacher was enjoying the fun as much as the kids.

Florence Troutman remembers the games of marbles the children played on the platform floor in the school. She also remembers a game of tag called "prisoner base." Those were the days when children could entertain themselves very well with just a bit of resourcefulness.

During the 'twenties and 'thirties, and even into the 'forties the Hoffman school pupils were involved in some of the same activities as students in other area schools. One of them was to "pen" the teacher out of the classroom on Shrove Tuesday. It worked for many years, but one year the children were disappointed because they did not succeed in having a day off. They blocked the door, but Isaac Troutman came up and took the hinges from the door allowing the teacher to have access. It was a usual day of school.

On November 13, 1948, the Board of School Directors held a public auction, and two of their buildings were offered for sale. One of them, Hoffman school, was offered at two o'clock in the afternoon. The building was sold to Mary F. Burris who several months later on February 26, 1949 sold to Charles A. and Emma E. Riegel. The Riegel family transferred the property to Sadie M. Luessenhop and her daughter Gladys Luessenhop on May 20, 1949. They used this property as a summer home for several years. Sometime later, Gladys married James Watkins and moved to Garden Grove, California. Sadie died, and by her will she provided that "my little red school house in Lykens Township shall go to my daughter Gladys to do as she pleases." On March 20,1969, Gladys and James Watkins, Robert G. and Alice Luessenhop of West Chicago, Illinois, and Rodney M. and Constance Luessenhop of Darien, Wisconson sold this property to Mr. and Mrs. Albert Reed. They have transformed the building into a very cozy and attractive dwelling, surrounded by beautiful flowers. In its present state of preservation, serving as a residence, it continues to be a special memory for folks who received their early education within its walls. After Albert N. Reed died (Mar 3, 1979, Laura lived here until her death November 15, 2001. The property was sold in February 2002 to Gregory A. Reed.

THE ATTENDANCE AWARD

This following "Award" (THE LITTLE DISASTER) is a copy of the print given in 1907 to Harry A. Troutman at the end of his first grade year at Hoffman school. He received the award for perfect attendance. It was given to Harry by his teacher Daniel Koppenhaver, whose positive influence on his students has kept his name alive these many years later. When Harry brought this copy to us for preservation, he was very pleased to be sharing. Harry was a student at Hoffman school.

THE LITTLE DISASTER

THE LITTLE DISASTER

Once there lived a little man, where a little river ran,
And he had a little farm and little dairy O!
And he had a little plough, and a little dappled cow,
Which he often called his pretty little Fairy O!

And his dog, he called Fidelle, for he loved his master well;
And he had a little pony for his pleasure O!
In a sty not very big he'd a frisky little pig,
Which he often called his little piggy treasure O!

Once his little maiden, Ann, with her pretty little can,
Went a milking when the morning sun was beautiful O!
When she fell, I don't know how,
But she stumbled o'er the plough,
And the cow was quite astonished at her screaming O!

Little maid cried out in vain, while the milk ran o'er the plain,
Little pig ran grunting after it so gaily O!
While the little dog behind,
For a share was much inclined,
So he pulled back squeaking piggy by the tail O!

Such a clatter now began as alarmed the little man,
Who came capering from out his little stable O!
Pony trod on doggy's toes,
Doggy snapped at piggy's nose,
Piggy made as great a noise as he was able O!

Then to make the story short, little pony with a snort
Lifted up his little heels so very clever O!
And the man he tumbled down,
And he nearly cracked his crown,
And this only made the matter worse than ever O!

TEACHERS WHO TAUGHT IN HOFFMAN SCHOOL

1805 to 1832 - Carl Edward Muench
1840 - Jacob Schaffner
1841 – 1884 - unknown
1885 - M. H. Zerfing
1886 - I. N. Henninger
1887 - Henry Willier of Pillow
1888 - unknown
1889 - Jacob E. Boyer
1890 - F. P. Ferree
1891 - H. W. Williard
1892 - unknown
1893 - unknown
1894 – unknown
1895- Mar 1895 I. E. Runk here
1896- Edward E. Riegel
1897 - Edward E. Riegel
1898- John Harman
1899- Charles M. Dockey
1900- Charles M. Dockey
1901- Charles M. Dockey
1902- Thomas Knecht, Jr.
1903- Jacob Koppenhaver

1904 – Jacob Koppenhaver
1905 – Jacob Boyer
1906 –Jacob Boyer
1907 – Daniel Koppenhaver
1908 – Daniel Koppenhaver
1909 –Daniel Koppenhaver
1910 – Daniel Koppenhaver
1911 – Harry C. Buffington
1912- unknown
1913 - unknown
1914 – Clayton Willier
1915 – Charles Henninger
1916- Harry Klinger
1917 – Harry Klinger
1918 & 1919 - unknown
1920 – unknown
1921 – Russell Crabb
1922 –Effie Lubold
1923 – Effie Lubold
1924 – Harry C. Klinger

1925 -Harry C. Klinger ?
1926- Harry C. Klinger
1927- Effie Lubold
1928- unknown
1929 -Effie Lubold
1930 - Katherine Grell ?
1931 - Katherine Grell
1932 - unknown
1933 - Edna Hoffman
1934- Katherine Grell
1935- Katherine Grell
1936- Edna Hoffman
1937 -Edna Hoffman
1938 - Winifred Koppenhaver
1939-- Winifred Kpenhaver
1940- Winifred Koppenhaver
1941- Pearl Miller
1942- Pearl Miller
1943- Pearl Miller
1944- Winifred Koppenhaver
1945- Winifred Koppenhaver
1946- The School close, pupils
were sent to Shepley School

CLASS PICTURES TAKEN AT HOFFMAN SCHOOL

HOFFMAN SCHOOL 1938- Winifred Koppenhaver, teacher – l to r – 1st row seated: Eugene Howard; Herbert Hoover; Russell Henninger; William Steely, Ellard Reigle, Harold Howard; Don Haward; George Dockey; William Rank; Junior Witmer. 2nd row: Renee Witmer; Barbara Reed;Phyllis Henninger; Lucille Reed; Betty Hoover; Betty Reed; Fearl Howard; Pearl Howard; Betty Lebo; Arlayne Welker. 3rd row: teacher, Hannah Dockey; Grace Shade; Gladys Riegle; Clarence Welker; Albert Lebo; Albert Billow; Robert Howard.

Hoffman School 1934 – Miss Kathryn Grell, teacher. l to r – 1st row: Leon Ryan; Robert Howard; Mark Howard; ____ Koppenhaver or Buffington; Albert Lebo; Clarence Welker; Albert Billow; Lester Welker.
2nd row: Jean Billow; Phyllis Duckey; Mary Witmer; Betty Hoover; Gladys Riegel; Alberta Howard; Effie Hoover; Betty Steely; Helen Welker. 3rd row: Edna Steely; Betty Harris; Lillian Kemble; Robert Harris; Eldred Kocher; Burnett Kocher; Leo Hoover.

HOFFMAN SCHOOL 1914 – l to r -Top Row: Cora Troutman; Minnie Riegel; Elsie Troutman; Clara Troutman; Irene Troutman; Stella Troutman; Florence Matter; Grace Straub; Mildred Matter; Eva Bonawitz; Tilly Hoke; Belton Hoke; Harry Troutman; Charles Hoffman; Bottom Row: Albert Troutman; Howard Bonawitz; Charles Bonawitz; Grace Riegel; Myrtle Matter; Mable Hoffman; Lilly Romberger; Kate Riegel; Grace Daniel; Laura Matter; Florence Troutman; Laura Troutman; Harvey Romberger; Guy Daniels; George Hoke; Clayton Willier, teacher.

350

Hoffman School September 1927 - L to r: - 1st row: William Bower; Pershing Henninger; Paul Troutman, Jr.; Harold Hoover; Lester Hoover; Lee Henninger. 2nd row: Gilbert Buffington; Hannah Buffington; ___ Howard; Paul Buffington; Lee Hoover; Loretta Howard; Martha Lebo; Marlin Buffington; Ruth Klock; John Riegel. 3rd row: Earl Longabach; Daisy Wiest; Dorothy Klock; Effie Lubold, teacher; Arlene Klinger, Paul Romberger. 4th row: Ella Troutman; Grace Weaver; Margaret Henninger; Leah Romberger.

HOFFMAN SCHOOL – 1912 - Charles Henninger, Teacher. Pupils not identified

Hoffman School - c1918 – front - Florence Troutman, Grace Daniel,
Myrtle Matter, Laura Troutman, Emma Lubold, Mabel Hoffman.
back: John Riegel, John Troutman, Forrest Weaver, Lilly Romberger seated

Charles Henninger,
Hoffman Teacher

Hoffman School – 1922 – Effie Rebuck, teacher. Kneeling, Lillie & Leah Romberger, John Harris, Ed
Buffington, Ralph Riegel, Gilbert Buffinton, John Riegel, Paul Troutman, John Troutman, Melvin Riegel,
Paul Lesher, Willie Brown. 2nd row: Marie Troutman, Emma Lubold, Marlin Straub, John Shaffer, Arlene
Klinger, Forrest Weaver above her, Ethel Louden above Kattie Riegel, Leah, Riegel, Landon Hoover, ___.3rd
row: Alma Louden, Grace Riegel, Laura Troutman, Myrtle Matter, John Kissinger, Mabel Hoffman, Earl
Lesher, Grace Daniel, Stanford Shade, Harvey Romberger, Charles Kissinger, _____ Lesher, Robert
Buffington.

HOFFMAN SCHOOL – 1945 – David Stiely front row 2nd from right

MR AND MRS. ALBERT N. MORGAN FARM
(Sebastian Henninger 67 acres -1875 - House Built c1828)

This land is part of three distinct tracts that Commonwealth of Pennsylvania conveyed. The first was 202 acres known as 'Hickory Bottom" warranted January 7, 1785, surveyed March 1785, patented February 26, 1796, and conveyed to Nicholas Hoffman. The second tract containing 270 acres known as "Walnut Bottom," was conveyed to Peter Hoffman. On August 10, 1799, Peter Hoffman conveyed the second tract to Nicholas Hoffman. On June 24, 1809 Nicholas and Margaret Hoffman conveyed part of the two tracts containing 135 1/2 acres to Daniel Hoffman. Daniel and Hannah Hoffman built a house and other buildings on the land, and on March 1, 1811 they sold the land and appurtenances to Christopher Snyder. About one year later, on April 13, 1812, Christopher Snyder sold the same to Hermonius Zerbe. Through several more transactions, (from the Hoffman's and Hermonius Zerbe), Michael Salada became the owner of about 30 acres on April 14, 1823.

Another grant known as "Hempfield" conveyed to John Hoffman, esquire (patented March 2, 1801) was divided into many tracts. One tract became the property of Jacob and Maria Wiest on March 9, 1821. They sold to Michael Salada September 3, 1821 and on January 3, 1828, and Michael and Barbara Salad sold all three portions of their land containing 57 acres, 64 perches to Simon Salada.

Simon and Jane Salada on March 13,1831, sold the fifty-seven acres, sixty-four perch farm with a two-story log house to John Forney. Along with farming, John was a blacksmith for most of his life. Starting about 1847, George son of John Forney was a tenant on the farm. He continued to work with his dad, apparently until the father became elderly.

The Forney family lived on this farm for many years, and after John Forney died, his heirs, widow Mary and daughter Lucetta married to Peter Weise conveyed it on June 18, 1866, to George Forney, subject to a dower to Mary. The plantation included two tracts, one containing the fifty-seven acre farm, and another tract of eleven acres, twenty-five perches. The land included a log house and a bank barn. [Forney genealogy on page 324.]

On April 1, 1871, George and Susanna Forney sold the two tracts, containing a total of sixty-nine acres, sixty-three perches to Sebastian Henninger. The tract of eleven acres (with houses, buildings, barns and stable), was "subject to an open road or free passage way for horses and wagons over the lot from the present main road "to the property of Sebastian Henninger. On April 14, 1879, Sebastian Henninger and his wife Dina sold forty perches of the above tract to the Lykens Township School District for thirty dollars. This lot became the site of the new brick Hoffman School. Classes had previously been held in the very old frame building that is situated south of the brick school. [More information under the Hoffman school write-up.]

Sebastian Henninger

Christiana (Deibler) Henninger

On March 15, 1902, Sebastian Henninger and his wife Leah Jane of Mifflin Township sold the same tract of 69 acres 63 perches "minus the lot leased for school purposes" to Mary Jane Riegel. Mary Jane Riegel and Husband John Riegel sold to their son Charles A. Riegel, November 23, 1905.

On December 31, 1945, Charles A. Riegel and Emma E his wife of Lykens Twp sold a messuage bounded by the land of the former Reuben Riegel, former John George Weaver, John Hartman, George Williard, church property, and former George Row to William S. Hoffman, single, of Lykens Township. This tract of land contained sixty-nine acres sixty-three and 16/100 perches, and included the lot that was leased to the school.

To the Right: Mary Jane (Forney) Riegel & children: Maggie, Charles, Cora, Minnie, baby Gurney

William S. Hoffman, a single man, immediately conveyed the property back to Charles & Emma Riegel. At the time of the sale, the land included the lot "leased for school purposes." On May 13, 1959, Charles A. and Emma E. Riegel conveyed this 69 acre 63.16 perch farm to Lloyd L. and Florence Lenker. By that time the school lot had been sold to Sadie Lussenhop. On January 12, 1967, the heirs of Lloyd L. Lenker sold the farm to Albert N. and Margaret M. Morgan. They have been the owners to the present time.

THE HENNINGER FAMILY

[The earliest found Henninger ancestor for the family that settled in this area was **JOHN HENNINGER** who was born about 1750 in Alsace-Lorraine area of Germany. In addition to Sebastian (see below) John Henninger (b c1750) may be the father of two or three others and relative to Elizabeth who were living in Lykens Valley just before 1800.

Heinrich Henninger (no dates), m Anna Maria ___ had a child <u>Susanna Maria</u> b Jun 29, 1802, bapt Klingers Church.

Michael Henninger (   ), m Eve Elisabeth Troutman b Feb 15, 1776, a dau of Peter and Eva Elisabeth (Meyer), Troutman. Michael and Anna Elisabeth Henninger were sponsors for a child of Peter Disaman at Klingers Church in 1803. Michael was on the 1810 census for Up Paxton over 45 years old and had a female age 16 to 26 in his household. **Michael and Eva Elisabeth (Troutman) Henninger children bapt Klingers Church: Simon** b Apr 6, 1811; **Michael** b May 8, 1814, m Elizabeth Sassaman (   ), a dau of _____-. **Michael and Elizabeth (Sassaman) Henninger children (bapt Davids Ch Hebe):** <u>Sarah Ann</u> b Sep 21, 1835; <u>Sophia</u> b Feb 18, 1837

Samuel Henninger (no dates), m Sarah _____ **had these children (bapt Klingers Zion Ch & David's Ch):**
  Michael b Aug 15, 1834 bapt David's Ch rec, sp Michael Henninger & Christina Zeller; Evah Maria b Jul 31, 1836, sp David Troutman and Evah Maria Henninger

Elizabeth Henninger Klinger (Jun 15, 1763 - Aug 20, 1804, bur Klingers Ch Cem), m Johannes Klinger (Apr 3, 1753 - Apr 3, 1800), a son of Alexander and ____ Klinger. Klingerstown was named for this John Klinger. [more information in the Klinger genealogy.]

354

JOHN HENNINGER (c1750 - _____) m Doroda Peters. **John and Doroda (Peters) Henninger children:**
*SEBASTIAN (Jan 20, 1790 - Feb 10, 1880, bur Hoffman Cem), m Mary Barbara Carl (Apr 30, 1787 - Feb 6, 1858, bur Old Stone Cem, E'ville. Sebastian lived in Lykens Twp in 1820. In 1850, Sebastian and Barbara lived in Washington Twp, and had Eliza Shoop age 17, and John Smith age 15, in their household. In 1860, after his wife died, Sebastian lived alone, and Sarah Smeltzer age 18, was employed as a housekeeper. **Sebastian and Barbara (Carl) Henninger children (some bapt Davids Ch, Killinger, Zion Luth, Erdman):**
SAMUEL (1815 - pre1880), m Susanna Riegel (Sep 6, 1818 - Mar 15, 1856, bur Hoffman Cem), a dau John and Susanna Riegel, lived in Mifflin Twp in 1850. By 1860, Samuel lived in Jefferson Twp, Dau Co., and was apparently married again to Catharine _____ . Joseph Grim age 10, John Grim age 8, also lived in this household, possibly children of Catharine from a first marriage? **Samuel and Susanna (Riegel) Henninger children (some bapt Hoffman Ch):
***Sebastian (Jan 6, 1840 bapt Hoffman Ch, - d 1925, bur Peace Ref Cem, Bbg), m 1st Christiana (Dina) Deibler (Apr 15, 1839 - Jun 2, 1895), dau of Mathew Deibler Jr. Sebastian was mentioned as an heir of his grandfather Sebastian in December 1880, because Samuel his father had died. After his first wife Christiana died, Sebastian m 2nd Leah Jane Poffenberger (Feb 29, 1847 - Mar 29, 1909), and later m for the 3rd time to Mary Jane Nace (Feb 1, 1846 - Oct 16, 1919). He had no children with the two later wives. **Sebastian and Christiana (Deibler) Henninger children:**
****Isaac Milton (b May 16, 1862 Lyk. Twp - d Jun 28, 1943, bur Peace Cem, Bbg), m Oct 25, 1885, Etta C Romberger (Sep 26, 1863 - Jan 14, 1919, of the flu), a dau of Isaac and Lydia (Michael) Romberger. Isaac M. m 2nd, Maggie Moyer. **Isaac and Etta C. (Romberger) Henninger children:**
Charles Edward (Oct 9, 1888 - Aug 7, 1964, bur Hoffman Cem), m Mar 3, 1917, Clara E. Troutman (1897 - 1990). He was a teacher in Mifflin and Lykens Twp Schools, also did farming and carpentry. In the spring of 1936, Charles was attempting to fell the stump of a mulberry tree in his yard. His wife and children were holding a rope attached to the trunk to prevent the tree from falling on a fence. Having completed the chopping at the base, Charles turned to help his family hold the rope. Being hard of hearing, he did not hear their warning shouts as the tree began to fall. He was struck by a limb and hurled to the ground. He was disabled the remainder of his life. **Charles E. & Clara (Troutman) Henninger children:** *Margaret* m Charles Leer; *Pershing* m Barbara Sultzbaugh, 2nd Ethel Harner; *Lee* m Jean Straub; *Russell* m Nell Wolfe of Florida, a teacher in Williams Valley.
Lillie Alverta b Feb 12, 1890, m Earl Stine (1890 - Jul 22, 1957). **Earl and Lillie Henninger Stine children:** *Floyd* m Olive Yoder; lives in Berrysburg; *Peter* m Marie Umholtz of Gratz; *Woodrow* m Marian Riegle; *Miriam* m Isaac Tressler of Herndon.
Carrie Edna (May 4, 1895 – 1975), m Eston R. Klinger (1895 – 1972). **Eston and Carrie (Henninger) Klinger children:** *Violet* m Arthur Klinger; *E. Leroy* m Renee Holtzman; *Earl* m Mildred Burrell; *Lorraine* m Clyde Witmer.
Harry Allen (Apr 20, 1898 – 1978, bur Sweitzer Cem, Bbg), m Etta M. Willier (1894 – 1964). **Harry and Etta (Willier) Henninger children:** *Kermit* m Mildred Markle: *Harold* m Carolyn Ash.
Laura May b Jul 6, 1899, m Mar 25, 1921 Lee Emerson Boyer. **Lee and Laura (Henninger) Boyer children:** *Romaine* m William Macht; *Delores* m Byron Parry.
John Philip (Mar 20, 1903 - Mar 6, 1964, bur Schweitzer Cem, Bbg), m Annie Holtzman (1903 – 1988). **John P. and Annie (Holtzman) Henninger children:** *Elwood* m Myrtle Miller; *Norwood* m Hannah Umholtz.

****Catherine Rebecca (Oct 24, 1863 - 1948, bur Simeon Cem), m Daniel L. Hartman (1850 - 1949) of Gratz;
****John F.(Nov 3,1877 - Nov 7, 1948), m Alice Hartman (Nov 21, 1881 -Jan 10,. 1919), dau of George and Leah (Herman) Hartman. **John and Alice (Hartman) Henninger children:** Mildred; Marlin George m Gertrude Matter, dau of William E. and Martha (Erdman) Matter; Lauretta Alice
****Sallie E. (Jun 16, 1879 - ____), m Cloyd Miller

***John b Jun 16,1841, moved to Franklin, Venago Co, Pa. by 1880 when he was mentioned as an heir of his grandfather Sebastian Henninger.
*** Sarah b Feb 18,1842;
***Harriet (1844 -1845)
***Amanda (b & d 1848)
*** 3 dau (triplets?) b & d Apr 16, 1850

***<u>Susanna</u> (Mar 16, 1856 - 1857)
***<u>Isaac</u> b c1858 on the 1860 census was probably born to Catherine of the second marriage.

**JOSEPH (Jun 15, 1812 bapt Klingers Ch - Aug 15, 1896, bur Davids Cem Killinger), m 1ˢᵗ Louisianna Yeager (b Jan 21, 1813 - Nov 30, 1865), lived in Up Pax Twp, in 1850 & 1860, and he was a farmer. After Louisiana died, Joseph m Adaline _____(1831 - 1900), she survived him.
Joseph Henninger and his wives had these children (some bapt David's Ch, Killinger):
<u>Sarah Ann</u> b 1835;<u>William</u> b Nov 6, 1836;***<u>John</u> (Mar 14,1838 – 1840);***<u>Joseph</u> b c1842;***<u>Loisa</u> b 1850; <u>Mary</u> (no dates); <u>Joseph Yeager</u> (Mar 5, 1855 - Jun 22, 1916 bur David's Cem, Killinger), m 1st m Louisa____(Aug 25, 1856 - Mar 18, 1900), m 2nd, Mary Alice Lenker (Sep 25, 1863 - Mar 26, 1948), a dau of Jonathan and Mary (Noll) Lenker. **Joseph and Louisa (   ) Henninger had these children:**
John (no dates, bur Davids Cem Killinger); <u>Mary</u> (no dates); <u>Charles</u> (1870 – 1944); <u>Harry H.</u> (1879 – 1956)), m Lovina F.Walborn (1856 -1900). **Joseph Yeager and Mary Alice (Lenker) Henninger children:** <u>Chester</u> b1888; <u>Irene</u> b 1895; <u>George</u> 1898; <u>Lawrence</u> 1902; <u>Bertha</u> 1902 (twins)
The following grandchildren were mentioned in orphan court records when Joseph Henninger died in 1896.
grandchildren: *Jerome, Charles, Josiah, William Etzweiler, Mary Kahler*.

**CHRISTINA (Jan 15, 1817, bapt Klingers Ch - d Feb 5, 1897, bur Hoffman Cem), m Simon Daniels (Dec 30, 1819 - Mar 22, 1884), a son of Henry B. and Maria Catharine (Buffington) Daniels.
JOHANNES b Aug 2, 1818, bapt Klingers Ch,- d Sep 6, 1900, bur Evang Cem, Bbg), m Mary Umholtz (Apr 20, 1822 - Sep 1, 1881, bur Evang Cem, Berrysburg), a dau of Henry and Susan (Hoover) Umholtz. They lived on a farm in Mifflin Twp. in 1860. In 1880, Kate Bechlter age 21 lived with them. Johannes and Mary (Umholtz) Henninger children:** ***<u>Henry Wiliiam</u> (b Jul 30, 1845 - d Jun 3, 1924, bur Berrysburg), m Nov 13, 1875, Oakdale Ch rec, to Mary Jane Romberger (Apr 29, 1852 – Dec 20, 1928), a dau of Isaac and Lydia (Michael) Romberger. He was a Civil War Vet. In 1880, Jonathan Hoke age 17, and Mary E Hoke age 14 were listed as servants in their household. **Henry William and Mary Jane (Romberger) Henninger children** (some bapt Oak Dale): ****<u>Mary Elizabeth</u> b 1879; ****<u>William Moody</u> b Dec 9, 1883; ****<u>John Isaac</u> b May 29, 1896; ***<u>Nathaniel</u> (b 1848 - Oct 6, 1919, bur Evang Cem, Berrysburg), m Nov 11, 1869 at home of Rev Jacob Kehm to Amanda Miller (Dec 19, 1852 in Curtin, Mifflin Twp – Nov 1, 1937), a dau of Daniel and Betsy (Herb) Miller, originally from Hegins Valley, but moved to brick house (was hotel) in Curtin. In 1880 they had William Bohner age 20 with them in Mifflin Twp. **Nathaniel and Amanda (Miller) Henninger had five children (3 d young):****<u>William Guy</u> (no dates) ****<u>John E.</u> (c 1872 - Jun 16, 1914 of a heart attack) ****Samuel Franklin b Aug 30, 1883; ***<u>Mary Jane</u> (May 9, 1850 – Feb 3, 1872, bur Evang Cem, Bbg); ***<u>Isaac.N</u> (b Mar 13, 1852 - Aug 24, 1922, bur Evang Cem, Berrysburg), m Feb 6, 1875, Sarah L. Keiter (Jun 10, 1853 - Oct 23, 1933), **had a son** Charles Wellington b Aug 5, 1883, bapt Oak Dale; ***<u>Jacob A.</u> (b Apr 28, 1853 - Apr 1, 1925, bur Evang Cem, Berrysburg), m Jun 22, 1882, Annie I. Romberger (1865 – 1935).
ISAAC b Apr 12, 1821, m Catharine Umholtz, a dau of John Philip and Anna Maria (Willier) Umholtz, b Mar 20, 1822. In 1850, they lived in Lykens Township on a farm, but moved to Stark County, Ohio. **Isaac and Catharina (Umholtz) Henninger children: ***<u>Henry</u> b c1843; ***<u>Sarah</u> b c1844; ***<u>Lucinda</u> b c1851; ***<u>Barbara</u> b & d 1849; ***<u>Amanda</u> b Oct 18, 1851; ***<u>Catharine</u> A b c1855; ***<u>Susannah</u> b c1857.
SUSANNA (Dec 13, 1822 - Feb 4, 1879), m Daniel Lubold (Feb 25, 1819 - Jan 25, 1905, bur Fetterhoffs Cem), a son of Frederick and Elizabeth (Ney) Lubold. **Daniel and Susanna (Henninger) Lubold children: **<u>Augustus</u> (Oct 23, 1842 - Aug 4, 1855); **<u>David</u> (Dec 1, 1844 - Jan 1, 1850); **<u>Cornelius</u> (Dec 11, 1846 - Jan 8, 1854);**<u>Elias</u> b Nov 18, 1848, m Sarah Ann Miller; **<u>Elizabeth</u> (Mar 10, 1851 - Oct 23, 1853);**<u>John</u> **Frederick** (Oct 4, 1853 - ____), m Mary Ellen Romberger; **<u>Samuel</u> (Nov 22, 1855 - Feb 13, 1863); **<u>Amanda</u> b Oct 16, 1857, m John M. Rutter, **they had one son: ***<u>Daniel</u> (1858 -1931); ***<u>Sarah</u> (1860-1862); ***<u>Daniel G.</u> b Pct 27, 1862, m Irene Workman; ***<u>Thomas</u> b Oct 17, 1865 m Margaret Eisenhower; ***<u>John Ellsworth</u> b Jan 24, 1868 m 1st Margaret Sheetz, 2nd Mrs. Minnie Hare
GEORGE b 1825, m Amanda or Sarah C. _____ b 1829, **George and ____ children: *<u>Polly</u> b Aug 18, 1849. In 1850, they lived next to Sebastian Henninger in Washington Twp. and had Catharine Row age 12, with them. By 1880, when his father died, George and his family lived in Missouri.
SALOME or SARAH b Sep 4, 1826, bapt Davids Ch, Killinger, m Jacob Rutter (b ____ - d Dec 1884), a son of George and Susanna (Lubold) Rutter, of Halifax, the parents later moved to Mercer County. **Jacob and Sarah

(Henninger) Rutter children: ***Susannah** (1843 - 1844, bur Hoffman Cem); ***Isaac** (1855 - 1856, bur Bowerman Cem);

CATHARINE (no dates) m ___Fleeden?, moved to Iowa. She apparently died before her father, leaving children.

ANGELINE (Oct 17, 1830 -Sep 1, 1910, bur Hoffman Cem), m Feb 26, 1848, Charles Yohe (Apr 15, 1823 - Mar 9,1898), a son of William Yohe of Loyalton. [More info in YOHE family genealogy page 216.]

JAMES ROMBERGER LAND
(Part of farm owned by Angeline Weaver Farm - 40 acres in 1875)

This land was part of an original grant that Commonwealth of Pa. conveyed to Baltzer Romberger in 1787. In June 1798 Baltzer Romberger and wife conveyed 33 acres 3 perches to Jacob Snyder. John Reiter also received a grant and sold some of his land to Jacob Snyder. Jacob and Catherine Snyder sold 68 acres of the accumulated land from both tracts to Peter Batdorf, Sr. Apr 2, 1814. They appeared on the tax record as early as 1815.

Peter Batdorf, Sr. owned this land for some time, but after his death, an accumulation of debts made it necessary for High Sheriff Henry Christian, Esquire of Harrisburg to seize thirty acres of the land to recover the owed funds. A one-story log house, a stable or barn, and orchards had been established on the land, and in 1828 the tax record refers to the thirty acres as the estate of Peter Baddorf. His widow was living on the property. The land was adjacent to these neighboring properties: Hermonius Zerby, Peter Hoffman, Ludwig Shietz, Nicholas Hoffman.

The property, goods and chattels were offered for sale at public outcry on January 1, 1829, but a buyer was not found. The property was then rented, and over a seven-year period, sufficient profits were realized from the rental to satisfy the debts. The property was again offered for sale on July 27, 1836, and sold to Thomas L. Boddorf, the highest bidder. He assigned the property to George and Catherine Kapp of Tulpehocken Township, Berks County, and they assigned the thirty-four acres with messuage to Johan Adam Bonawitz and his wife also of Tulpehocken Township. On April 3,1848 John Adam Bonawitz sold the property to Jacob Williard.

An adjoining tract of six acres of land was owned by Adam Romberger who sold it on June 2, 1832 to George Stough. On April 3, 1846, George Stough and his wife assigned the tract to Samuel B. Lupold. Two years later on April 3, 1848, Samuel B. Lupold and his wife assigned the same tract to Jacob Williard.

On March 31, 1849, Jacob and Sarah Williard sold three tracts of land (the two mentioned above and one near Wiconisco Creek) in Lykens Township to John George Weaver, a resident of adjoining Mifflin Township. Two of the tracts comprised this farm. The larger tract containing thirty-four acres, had a two-story log house and log barn. The smaller piece of adjoining land contained six acres, making a total of about forty acres together. The third tract containing eight acres is located on the side of Short Mountain, and because of the separation of townships, it is partly in Lykens Township and partly in Wiconisco Township.

John George Weaver owned this property for many years, and then about 1873 (about the time of his death), deeded it to his daughter Angeline with certain conditions. Angeline lived on the farm alone in 1880, but married Elias Fegley shortly after that.. Angeline died July 11, 1884, and on July 15, 1884, Elias Fegley was assigned life interest in the property. Elias Fegley went back to Jordan Township, Northumberland County, and on August 5, 1884, he sold all three tracts to John B. Weaver. Several years later, in April 1892, John B. and Elizabeth Weaver sold the two adjoining tracts (34 acres & 6 acres) to Edward Hoover who sold to Daniel I. Welker in 1893. Eventually the land became dispersed, and during the period between the 1930's and 50's the Howard family owned twenty acres of this farm.

The Romberger family later owned at least part of this land. Daniel C. Romberger transferred a small tract of his land to Lloyd and Bessie Romberger, and later part of it was conveyed to James Romberger.

WILLIAM WELKER FAMILY

[WILLIAM WELKER (b 1812 – d before wife), a son of John and Elizabeth (Messerschmidt) Welker, grandson of Valentine Welker. William m Oct 26, 1852 Elizabeth Schreffler (May 10, 1835 Upper Mahantongo Twp, Sch Co– Dec 18, 1894 of typhoid pneumonia in Gratz), a dau of Peter and Elizabeth (Kratzer) Schreffler. They were married in the German Reformed church by Rev. Leisig. Marriage record in Dauphin County court gives information. Rev. Pfleuger recorded her death, burial unknown. In 1870, William and Elizabeth Welker lived in Gratz. **William and Elizabeth (Schreffler) Welker had these children:**

John P. b c1855; **Sarah R.** b c1858; **Henry M** b c1860; **Charles** b c18862; **Hannah Casiah** b Mar 1, 1864; **Isaiah Daniel** b Dec 16, 1865, bap Simeon Ref Ch, m c1889, Emma or Edith_____ b Nov 1863. They lived in Lykens Twp in 1900 and he was a coal miner. They had Charles W. Buffington 14 a stepson, and Wellington Hoover 24, a border with them at that time. **Daniel Isaac and Emma Welker had one known child** Annie Edna b Jul 4, 1889.]

[More information under WELKER family elsewhere in book.]

THE WEAVER FAMILY

[JOHAN PETER WEAVER (WEBER), was born in Germany, and came to America in the GOOD SHIP CHANCE, sailing from Rotterdam, landing in Philadelphia September 23, 1766. With him on the ship were two brothers, Johannes and Johann George Weaver. Johan Peter was already married to Maria Elizabeth _____, and had at least one child when they arrived here. More information needed, but they are probably buried in this area.

PETER WEAVER (Jan 17, 1766 - May 14, 1839, bur Hoffman Cem), is the only known child of Johan Peter and Maria Elizabeth Weaver above. According to the Dauphin County History, Peter was one year old when he came here from Germany with his parents, probably the child mentioned above. The family lived in Lykens Twp. on a one-hundred-fifteen acre farm. When the 1790 window tax was levied Peter Weaver's residence was described as a cabin with a poor stable. His land adjoined the land of Mathias Hawk. Peter married Catherine Peiffer (Nov 11, 1765 - Mar 1836), a dau of Jacob and Margaret (probably Riegel) Peiffer, also of Lykens Township. **Peter and Catherine (Peiffer) Weaver children (some bapt Hoffman Ch):**

*JACOB (Nov 15, 1794, m Catharine Romberger b Sep 2, 1798, a dau of Adam and Anna Maria (Paul) Romberger **Jacob and Catherine (Romberger) Weaver children:** **Benjamin** (Apr 19, 1830 - Apr 21, 1897, bur Hoffman Cem), m Elizabeth Bordner (Apr 8, 1836 – Feb 18, 1910, d at home of son John in Bbg, bur St. Johns Cem), lived in Mifflin Twp 1850 to 1880. **Benjamin and Elizabeth (Bordner) Weaver children (some bapt Salem, Bbg):***** Sarah Ellen b Mar 3, 1861; ***Adam (Jun 7, 1863 - 1925, bur Hoffman Cem), m Sarah _____ (1853 -1896), **had these known children:** Bertha b 1886; Jennie b 1888; Elmer b 1890. After Sarah died, Adam was married to Lydia A. Groff of Washington Twp on Jan 23, 1897 by Rev. Stauffer ; ***Mary Catherine b May 10, 1867;***Jonas b Aug 16, d Sep 1869; ***Henry John b May 22, 1879; ** Jacob b c1837.
**Catherine b ___ m John Yeager

*ELIZABETH (b ___ d pre 1840), m Henry Metz (Mar 22, 1788 - Mar 25, 1862), a son of Sebastian and Catharine Metz. **Henry and Elizabeth (Weaver) Metz had one known child:**
Peter (Apr 2, 1829 - May 16, 1887, bur St. Johns Cem), m Jan 29, 1863 Sarah Weaver (Feb 8, 1835 - Jul 5, 1882), a dau of Daniel and Susanna (Buffington) Weaver. Peter was mentioned in the will of his grandfather.In 1880 Peter and Sarah Metz had Sarah Weaver, age 11, a niece living with them. **Peter and Sarah (Weaver) Metz children: ***Henry
Daniel (Mar 6, 1864 – Dec 6, 1912, bur St. John's Cem, Bbg), m Sarah E. _____ (Apr 26, 1866 – Feb 10, 1946). Henry became blind; ***Charles P. (1867 – 1923, bur St. Johns Hill Cem) m Anna I Lark (Sep 9, 1867 – Jun

358

19, 1957). In 1870, they lived in Mifflin Twp and had William W. Derr age 16, farm labr; also Sarah Kitzmiller age 15, domestic with them. After Elizabeth died, Henry Metz married her sister Anna Maria [see below.]

*ANNA MARIA (Apr 1, 1798 - d Jun 6, 1862, bur St Johns Cem, Berrysburg) , m Henry Metz (Mar 22, 1788 - Mar 25, 1862), a son of Sebastian and Catharine (_____) Metz. Anna Maria may have been his second wife, his first wife perhaps Elizabeth Weaver. In 1850, Henry and Anna Maria lived next to her brother Daniel Weaver in Mifflin Twp. **Henry and Anna Maria (Weaver) Metz children; ** Elizabeth** (Apr 10,1840 - Sep 29, 1894, of hemorrhage of the lung, bur St. John's Hill Cem), m Dec 20, 1863 Samuel B. Clark (Dec 16, 1841 - d Apr 2, 1921). Samuel and Elizabeth Clark probably had no children. In 1870 they lived in Mifflin Twp and had Cornelius Lebo age 18, farm labr, Henry Hassinger age 12, domestic, and Frances Cooper age 12 domestic with them. In 1880, they lived in Mifflin Twp., and these had two people in their household: a cousin Charles Clark age 17 and Clara Boddorf a servant age 24.

*PETER (May 10, 1800 - May 11, 1874, bur Hoffman Cem), m Anna Mary Schwab (Feb 13, 1806 - Jan 26, 1877), a dau of John Jacob and Anna Maria (Hetzel) Schwab. In 1850, Peter and Anna Mary Weaver lived in Mifflin Twp and he was a farmer. In 1860, Emoline Witmer age 14, lived with the family. In 1870 they lived in Mifflin Twp, and he was listed as a retired farmer. **Peter and Anna Mary (Schwab) Weaver children:**
Josiah (Mar 26, 1825 – Aug 16, 1874, of "brain fever" bur Fisherville Cem) m 1st Rebecca ___ (b c1826 – d pre 1860). Josiah and Rebecca lived in Mifflin Twp in 1850, and had sons Henry and John H. with them. Also Paul Matter age 21, Jonas Buffington age 16, son of Isaac and Hannah, and William Swab age 21, all carpenters. Josiah Weaver was a master carpenter, and conducted an extensive cabinet making and undertaking business at Berrysburg and Fisherville.
Josiah and Rebecca ( ) Weaver children; ***Henry b c1846 – d age 7); ***John H. b c1849, moved to Lock Haven.
After Rebecca died, Josiah married Margaret Buffington (Feb 10, 1826 – Feb 5, 1873, bur Fisherville Cem), a dau of ____, In 1860 Josiah and Margaret lived in Mifflin Twp, and these children lived with them: John, Agnes and Alice. Also with them were these people: Catharine Faust age 15, a servant, J. H. Shammo 21 and Sam O Nace age 18, both apprentice carpenters. **Josiah and Margaret (Buffington) Weaver children: ***Agnes L.** (1854 – 1932), m May 25, 1873 Hiram Lyter (b Aug 261850 Halifax Twp – 1923, bur Presbyterian Cem in Dauphin), a son of Henry and Susan (Miller) Lyter. Hiram took up carpentry for some years in Jackson Twp, but later Hiram and Agnes lived on a farm in Middle Paxton Twp on what later became "Speece Dairy." **Hiram and Agnes L (Weaver) Lyter had these children;** Harry Edward b Sep 22, 1875; Frank Newton b Nov 30, 1877; Annie Melinda b Oct 2, 1879; Charles Monroe b Nov 29, 1881; William Alton b Apr 9, 1886; Lizzie Lucretia b Aug 17, 1889; Susan Rebecca Mar 6, 1894.
***Alice (b c1857 – d ___), m William Shell; ***George b c1860 lived with the Emanuel Lyter family in 1880 and was an apprentice miller; ***Phoebe b c1862, m William Burrell.

**David b c1828, m Sarah ____, b c1832. **David and Sarah Weaver children: ***Mary b c1853; ***Emma b c1855; ***Lydia b c1857; ***Sarah J. b c1860; ***Eddy Mclanchton b Mar 4, 1865;
**Rebecca b c1830, m John Shutt, had a dau Isabella before she m John Shutt;
** _____ (no dates) m Noah Cluck.
**Susanna b c1832;
**Mary b c1834;
**Jonathan b c1837 m Catherine _____ b c1845. In 1870 they lived on a farm in Mifflin Twp. next to his parents, and F Bowman age 14 lived with them and was a farm laborer
Anna Elizabeth (Aug 11, 1838 – Apr 11, 1921), m Jan 22, 1877 Jonathan Holtzman (Oct 1, 1802 – Jul 21, 1884, death recorded Hoffman Ch, bur Berrysburg Cem, a son of George and Elizabeth (Lebo?) Holtzman. Anna Elizabeth was a second wife. He was married first to Elizabeth Koppenhaver (Feb 21,1805 - Apr 2, 1874), bur St. John's Hill Cem, Bbg-), a dau of Frederick and Maria Eliz (Gross) Koppenhaver. **Jonathan and Anna Elizabeth (Koppenhaver) Holtzman children: ***Mary b Sep 25, 1825, m 1847 Isaac App b in Selinsgrove, a son of Francis App. Isaac App moved to Berrysburg and purchased a farm. **Isaac and Mary (Holtzman) App children:** Francis; John G.; Daniel N; Henry Jackson; ***Jonathan B b Oct 28, 1827; ***Edward (Oct 8, 1830 - Mar 25, 1832); David K (no dates) m Oct 26, 1854 1st Mary Mattis, a dau of Aaron and Catherine Mattis, m 2nd

Margaret Neagley; ***Elizabeth** (no dates) m William Straub. Jonathan and his first wife were on the census for Mifflin Twp from 1850 to 1870. In 1870 they had John M. Straub age 14 with them. By1880 Jonathan had married Anna Elizabeth Weaver and they lived in Mifflin Twp. They had Andrew Fox age 14 with them. **Jonathan and Anna Elizabeth (Weaver) Holtzman had two sons:** ***Henry Milton** b Jun 1, 1877, bapt Hoffman Ch; ***Harry Clayton** b Nov 13, 1883;

**Sara Ann b c1843;

**Catharine A. b c1846

**Anna Eliza b c1850

**Amelia b c1853

*GEORGE JOHN** (Dec 10, 1801 - Apr 13, 1873, bur Hoffman Cem), m Catherine Bishoff (Mar 4, 1802 - Jul 19, 1872), a dau of John and Maria Christiana Bishoff of Mifflin Twp. In 1870, John G. and Catherine Weaver lived in Lykens Townshp, and daughter Angeline lived with them. In 1880 Angeline lived alone. **George John and Catherine (Bishoff) Weaver children:**

John Bishoff (b Jul 26, 1824 bapt Hoffman Ch - d Apr 30, 1902, bur Hoffman Cem), m Elizabeth Tschopp (Oct 10, 1829 - Jun 15, 1901). **John B. and Elizabeth (Tschopp) Weaver children:

***Jonathan** (b & d 1848, bur Hoffman Cem);

***Henry C.** (b Jul 3,1849 Lyk Twp - d Dec 20, 1912, of acute indigestion, bur UB Cem, Berrysburg), m Jun 23, 1870 Mary Ann Hoover (Mar 19, 1852 - Jun 24, 1912), died 6 mo before husband), a dau of John Hoover. They lived in Berrysburg. Both deaths recorded in Hoffman Church. When he was seventeen years old, Henry lived with the Peter Bishoff family, and learned the trade of chair and cabinet making with BISHOFF and SONS. He also became an expert buggy, coach and wagon painter. At intervals for thirty years before his death, he assisted William F. Wise of Tyrone, Pa., the noted scenic painter. He was also a fresco painter, and painted the interior of many of the churches in Dauphin and surrounding counties (including the Lutheran and Reformed Church in Gratz in 1904). In his relaxing hours, he played in the Berrysburg band, and was a charter member when the band was formed about 1867. He was leader of the band for at least forty years. On the day of his funeral, the band was in the funeral procession, played appropriate music at his home, and again at the gravesite. **Henry C. and Mary (Hoover) Weaver had these children:** Anna Elisabeth (Nov 18, 1870 – Apr 10, 1873, bur Hoffman Cem); Henrietta Verdilla b Sep 12,1872 - May 8, 1926, bur Berrysburg Cem), m William Deiner; Maggie Alberta (Sep 20,1875 – 1933, bur Berrysburg), m Harvey Deibler, a son of John and Mary (Updegrove) Deibler of Berrysburg; Arthur Miles (Feb 24, 1876 - Dec 5, 1948), m Annie Ditty, dau of Isaac Ditty of Rife; Harry Clayton b Nov 13, 1883, m Lizzie ____

***Franklin W.** (Jan 31, 1852 – Dec 19, 1882, bur Hoffman Cem), m Sarah Tschopp (no dates), a dau of David and Catharine Tschopp. **Franklin and Sarah (Tschopp) Weaver children:** Perlena b Feb 2, 1880; Cloyd Irvin (Jan 27, 1881 – 1935, bur Hoffman Cem), m Cora G ___ 1878 – 1950).

***Daniel** b c1853, lived with Hiram Matter family in 1870. Hiram was a coach maker, and Daniel was working as a coach painter;

Catherine A.** (b May 10, 1855, bapt Salem Union Ch, Berrysburg; ***John Allen** (Jun 26, 1861 – Sep 21, 1921), m Mar 13, 1883 Mary C. Yeartz of E'ville;Adaline E.** b Nov 9, 1863, m ____ Hawk, lived in Gratz; ***Samuel** (Jan 25, 1866 - Apr 1869); ***Emanuel** (Aug 8, 1869 - Jan 7, 1934, bur Hoffman Cem), m Anna Alvetta Riegel? (1866 - 1927), moved to Sunbury. They had a son John (Aug 16, 1907 _ Nov 9, 1968; ***Mary** d age1; several other children died in infancy.

**Angeline (Dec 22, 1826 - Jul 11, 1884), m Elias Fegley;

**George (Nov 29, 1841 - Aug 29, 1861);

*DANIEL** (b Sep 21, 1803, Lyk Twp - d Sep 30, 1882, Mifflin Twp, bur Hoffman Cem), m Susannah Buffington (Mar 21, 1810 - Jan 10, 1878), a dau of David and Eva (Schoffstall) Buffington. Daniel learned the skills of carpentry and joiner, and later purchased a forty-three acre farm in Mifflin Twp. There they operated a water-powered sawmill. They cut logs up to twenty feet in length. In 1870 they were retired, but he continued to farm. In 1880, Daniel lived in Mifflin Twp. with his son David and family. **Daniel and Susannah (Buffington) Weaver children:** **Isaac (May 4, 1833 – Apr 3, 1904, bur St. John Cem, Berrysburg), m Feb 23, 1854 Mary (Polly) Lark (Jun 3,1826 – Apr 5, 1910). They lived in Mifflin Twp. in 1870 and 1880, & he was a stone mason and bridge contractor. **Isaac and Polly ( ) Weaver children:** ***Hannah b c1848 ***Albert b c1854; ***Harriet (1857–1934, bur St. John's Cem);***Mary Ellen (Oct 8,1861 –Jun 27, 1934);***Ulyses Grant b c1867

**Sarah (Feb 8, 1835 - Jul 5, 1882), m Peter Metz (1829 - 1887), a son of Henry and Anna Maria (Weaver) Metz. [See Henry Metz write-up.]

Martin Peter (Jun 29, 1837 - Apr 10, 1887, bur Hoffman Cem), m Elizabeth Derr (Nov 1841 – Aug 1921, bur Berrysburg), a dau of Peter and Catharine (Weikel) Derr of Barry Twp, Sch Co. Elizabeth died at the home of her daughter Mrs. Henry Howe in Berrysburg..It is said that Isaac and Martin who were stone masons, helped to build the stone wall for the new Hoffman Church in 1885. Martin Peter Weaver and his family lived in Bbg in 1880. Martin Peter and Elizabeth ____ Weaver children:** ***George L. b c1866; ***Anna Alice b Aug 4, 1867; ***Clara V b c1871; ***Catherine Jane b Jan 12, 1879; ***Charles G. b c1874;***James M. b c1876; ***Alvin M. b c1878.

David B.(Dec 5, 1842 - Jan 14, 1906, bur Hoffman Cem), m May 19, 1864 St. Johns Ch in Mifflin Twp, Catherine A. Matter (Oct 28, 1839 - Sep 11, 1892), a dau of _____. In 1880, they lived in Miffllin Twp. **David and Catherine (Matter) Weaver children:
Mary S. (b c1865) m Peter Bender; ***Amanda S. (1869 - 1962), m David Norman Straub; ***Henry Franklin b Dec 1, 1873, m Dec 24, 1896, Julia Elizabeth Koppenhaver b Jun 12, 1874, a dau of Benjamin and Melissa (Gilger) Koppenhaver;Daniel Simon b Nov 13, 1875. After his first wife Catherine died, David m Jul 4,1895, Salome Engle (Feb 6, 1845 - Aug 2, 1897, bur St. John's Hill Cem)), dau of John Engle and widow of Amos Matter of Upper Paxton Twp.

*JOHN (1810 –1875, bur Hoffman Cem), m Rebecca Margaret "Peggy" Batteiger (1811 -1894), a dau of Peter Batteiger. In 1839 Peggy received an inheritance from her father Peter's estate. In 1860 John and Rebecca Margaret (Peggy) Batteiger lived in Lykens Twp. In 1880, Catherine was a widow, but most of her children lived with her. Her son Peter lived in the same house, but in different quarters. In 1894 when the property of John Weaver was sold, John's heirs as follows were mentioned: William & Rebecca, Harrison & Sarah, Cornelius and wife of Ogle, Ill; Kate, John W. and Sarah, Riley & wife, Mary, Sarah, Anne and Peter of Lykens Twp. **John and Rebecca (Batteiger) Weaver children:**
**William (Jul 28, 1834 – Feb 24, 1910, bur Hoffman Cem), m Rebecca ____ (Oct 14, 1844 - Sep 2, 1898). William was a carpenter in 1880;
Peter (Feb 4,1836 – Nov 4, 1911, bur Hoffman Cem). He lived in Lykens Twp in 1880, next to Sebastian Henninger. He was alone and single.; **Polly Mary (Aug 21, 1837 -Jun 7, 1913, bur Hoffman Cem), lived with mother in 1880; **Henry Harrison (Nov 6, b1840 – Jun 26, 1815, bur Sweitzer Mem Cem, Bbg), m Sarah E. Baddorf Jan 31, 1864 at St. Johns Hill Ch. They lived in Mifflin Twp in 1910. **Henry Harrison and Sarah (Baddorf) Weaver children: Henry b c1865; Mary R. b c1867; Emma J. b 1872; **Cornelius b c1844. A child was born to Cornelius and Louisa Hassinger August 6, 1868, bapt Hoffman Ch. He later m Catherine Tschopp b Jan 8, 1852 in Northld Co, a dau of Philip and Susan (Heckert) Tschopp. She had moved to Iillinois with her parents when she was young. Cornelius moved to Ogle Co., Illinois by 1872.
Rebecca b c1844 (She is probably the Rebecca bur Hoffman Cem (1844 - 1865); **John Adam b Dec 23, 1846, m Sarah C Tschopp b Apr 27, 1852, a dau of George and Magdalena (Schoffstall) Tschopp. They moved to Millersburg, and he was listed as a farmer;John Adam and Sarah (Tschopp) Weaver children:** ***Anne M b c1875;***George Elsworth b Aug 7, 1874; ***Reiley Edgar (Oct 9, 1875 - Dec 28, 1916, bur Hoffman Cem), m Oct 9,1883 Agnes J. Jury (Oct 13, 1864 - May 17, 1933). **They had a dau Verna Edna** m Charles Welker, no children:***Jennie Mabel (1884-1949, bur Schweitzer Cem), m Allen Louden (1884 –Jan 24, 1955) **Sarah (Mar 7,1849-Aug 4,1908, bur Hoffman Cem) lived with her mother in 1880; ** Riley b c1852, lived with his mother in 1880. He later m Catherine Bowman, **had these children:** ***Cruzie S. (Oct 22, 1912 - Apr 24, 2006, bur E'ville Cem), m George F. Hoffner (1912 - 1967), **had these children;****Rose M m ____ Shomper; ****Nancy m ___ Mattis;***Rosabella b c1915 m Galen Lentz (1908 –1977, bur E'ville):***Milton; ***Erma m ___ Enders;***Verna m ___ Lenker; ***Pansy m Shertzer;***Hanna m Shertzer
**Emma C (Sep 20,1853–Aug 1,1941, bur Hoffman Cem). She lived with her mother in 1880.]

FARM OF DAVID & NAOMI PETERSHEIM
(George Row with Two Houses and 60 Acres On 1875 Map, Nothing known of 2nd one.)

This House Was Replaced By A New House On Same Site c2001

Present Appearance Of Farm (With New House).

Peter Batteiger was living on 150 acres of warranted land as early as 1805. He sold some of his acreage, but he and his family other of his land for many years. In 1831 George Feldy was a tenant on the Batteiger property. Before Peter Batteiger died he sold three acres with appurtenances on April 17,1835 to his son Joseph (blacksmith) stipulating that there should be a dower paid to his parents. After Peter Batteiger died in 1837, fifty-seven acres, 90 perches more land was sold to son Joseph Apr 1, 1838 and that became this farm.

Joseph Batteiger sold both tracts of land to John Matter Mar 1, 1839. One tract containing 57 acres 93 perches, another 3 acres. The land was bound south by John Matter and Henry Batteiger, west by Adam Wise, north by Henry Hoyer, John Weaver and John Matter and Andrew Riegel.

By 1851, John Matter had sold about 60 acres of land to George Row. He was taxed in 1855 and 1859 for 59 acres, a two-story log house and log barn. He was also taxed for a pleasure carriage, gold watch, and a $400 promissory note. Adam Row was a tenant there in 1858. The Row family continued to live here for years.

On Nov 21, 1884, Mary J. Romberger executor of George Row est., conveyed 59 acres 55 ¾ perches to Adeline Stine. The deed was not recorded until 1902. On Apr 1, 1938 Peter E. Stine conveyed the 59 acres to George E. Finkbone. After George Finkbone died, his widow Mary E. received the two tracts of land containing 59 acres 45 ¾ perches with two-story dwelling, attached summer kitchen and frame bank barn on Feb 5, 1952. She conveyed the same to Samuel H. and Mary Weaver September 23, 1955. The next year on February 17, 1956 Samuel H. and Maria S. Weaver conveyed the farm to John E. Harris, Jr., who sold to Charles F. and Pauline Miller March 1, 1979. The next year in May 1980, Charles F. and Pauline Miller conveyed the farm to Christ and Katie Petersheim. They conveyed to David B. and Naomi Petersheim, the present owners.

[WILLIAM FINKBONE (1801 – Oct 31, 1880, bur Stone Valley Cem), probably a son of Jacob Finkbone, m Salome Shaffer (Feb 14, 1806 Low Mah Twp, Northld Co – Dec 4, 1870, bur Stone Valley Cem, Northld Co), a dau of Jacob Conrad and Maria Margaret (Lenker) Shaffer After his wife died, William lived with his son James in 1880 in Low Mah Twp, Northld Co. His death was said to have come from an accident when he fell out of an upstairs window. **William and Salome (Shaffer) Finkbone children:**
JAMES (Oct 15, 1824 – Sep 3, 1902, bur Stone Valley Cem), m Maria Magdalena Shaffer (Nov 8, 1828 – Feb 4, 1898), a dau of Jacob and Magdalena (Bachman) Shaffer.). **James and Maria Magd (Shaffer) Finkbone children:** Sarah Elizabeth b Feb 17, 1851 m Dec 28, 1872 to Levi Hoffer b Apr 1853, moved to Mbg; Maria Ellen b Dec 7, 1854; William b Sep 18, 1860 – Jul 31, 1929, bur St. John's Hill Cem), m Jul 30, 1887 ST. Paul's Ch, Urban to Alice Snyder (Apr 17, 1865 – Sep 26, 1914). William and Alice lived in Low Mah Twp, Northld Co. **William and Alice (Snyder) Finkbone children; Mary Adeline** (Dec 5, 1887 – 1953, bur St. John's Cem); **Annie Ellen** b Sep 9, 1889; Maude Irene b Aug 17, 1891; **George Elmer** (May 4, 1893 – pre 1952), m Mary E. ____;**Lottie May** b Nov 25, 1894; **Ida Belle** b Aug 28, 1896; **John Adam** b Dec 29, 1898]

THE ROW FAMILY

[FRANZ ROWE, (b c1740 - d between Jan 8 and 13th, 1806 in Lanc Co) is the earliest known member of the ROW family, supposedly of English descent. His parents are not identified. Franz m January 24, 1764, Catharine Trout (Jan 24, 1748 - ____), a dau of Wendel and Maria Magdalena (Walter) Trout. By occupation, Franz was a wagonmaker. He penned a will on January 8, 1806, stating that was very sick. He mentions only four children, but more are accounted for. **Known children of Franz and Catharine (Trout) Rowe are:**
*FRANTZ ROWE (no date)
*ADAM ROWE (Sep 21, 1770 - Sep 5, 1830, bur St. John's Luth, Berrysburg), m Mar 28, 1797 to Christiana Diller (b Sep 16, 1772 - Lancaster County - d Feb 21, 1823), a dau of John and Magdalena (Sherk) Diller.They were married in her parents home by Rev. Traugott Frederick Illing of the Episcopal Church in Churchtown. The tombstone of Adam Rowe had this inscription: "Don't mourn for me now, I am dead and moldering in my grave, but look to Christ the living head who all mankind can save."
**JOHN (1798 – 1873), m Susannah Ferree (1804 – 1846), 2nd Anna Elizabeth ___ (1810 – 1900). [More information on Adam Row with his land in Loyalton.]
**BARBARA (Sep 26, 1799 - Mar 31, 1833, bur Strasburg), m Adam Brubaker.
**FRANZ b Jul 9, 1802, bapt Strasburg,, moved to Ohio.
**ADAM (b Jun 6, 1804 - Strasburg- d Apr 39, 1868, Northld Co.), m 1st Dec 25, 1827 Leah Jane Rutter who d 1830, had two children who d in infancy. Adam m 2nd Apr 17, 1831 Rachel McCurtin, dau of Mary McCurtin, 2nd wife of Adam's father Adam Sr.
**VERONICA b Dec 9, 1805, bapt Strasburg, m Christian Conrad, lived in Lykens Twp
**MAGDALENA b Aug 10, 1807, b apt Strasburg, m John Carlin, lived in Cumberland Co.
**CORREL DAVID b Jun 22, 1809, bapt Strasburg, moved to Mifflin County, Pa.
**CHRISTIANA b Apr 30, 1811, bapt St. Johns Hill Ch, Berrysburg - d Aug 1890)., m 1st John Forney (1802 - 1828), m 2nd on Dec 14, 1831Christian Schoffstall (Aug 23, 1807 - Nov 15, 1880, bur Stueben Co, Ind), son of Solomon and Catharina (Haag) Schoffstall,and moved to Crawford Co., Ohio, later to Steuben Co., Ind. (Childrens names with Schoffstall write-up).
**ISABELLA b Apr 7, 1813, bapt Hoffman Ch, Lyk Twp, apparently not married in 1848 when father's estate was settled;

MARTIN b Nov 19, 1814 (there are three different dates given for his birth and death, depending on which source used) - d Feb 8, 1858, bur Wiconisco Cem), m Susannah Fegley (Mar 28, 1816 - Feb 18, 1895), a dau of Jacob and Elizabeth Fegley. They lived in Wiconisco Twp. In 1880, Susannah lived next to her son Tobias in Williams Twp. **Martin and Susannah (Fegley) Row children (some bapt Zion Luth, Lykens);
***Martin Cyrus b 1833, m Elizabeth ____, lived in Porter Twp, Sch Co; *****Henry** (this is probably the one b Sep 1, 1835 - Mar 18, 1914, bur Greenwood Cem, Tower City), m 1st Barbara ____ (Jul 30, 1834 - Jun 24, 1888), m 2nd Sarah ____ (Dec 28, 1841 - Oct 21, 1907). He lived in Porter Twp, Sch Co.; *****Tobias** (Nov 8, 1837 - Jul 10, 1907, bur Calvary Meth Cem, Wiconisco), lived in Williams Twp, m Margaret (Nov 24, 1841 - Jan 27, 1918). In 1880 he was a coal miner; *****Elijah** (1840 - Nov 24, 1912), m Lucetta b c1840, lived in Williams Twp, **had these children:** John H. b c1863; Andrew M b c1865; Clara b c1868; William b c1869; *****Aaron** (1843 - 1905), m Mary ____ b c1849. lived in Porter Twp, Sch Co, but in 1880 they were in Williams Twp.; *****Simon F.** (Nov 13, 1845 - Jan 13, 1915, Carbon Co, bur Oak Hill Cem, Mt. Carmel, m Lydia Dinger Kessler ((Dec 21, 1840 - Dec 15, 1926), dau of Abraham and Christina (Dinger) Kessler; *****Christina** b 1848, m Walter Row; *****Anna Elizabeth** b 1850, m Emanuel Weidel, a son of George & (Nancy Radel) Weidel; *****Leah Jane** b1852, m Jonathan Baddorff lived in Williams Twp, Dau Co.; *****Adam** b Apr 12,1855; *****Jacob** b 1856; *****Francis** b Apr 24, 1857, moved to Mt. Carmel, d 1897, bur Oak Hill Cem.

*CATHARINA ROW bapt Nov 7, 1774, eight weeks old, in Trinity Luth Ch, New Holland.
*WENDEL ROW (Aug 5, 1777 - Jan 29, 1843, bur St. John's Luth Cem, Berrysburg), m Isabella ____ (Sep 12, 1781 - Feb 9, 1867), a dau of _____. In 1860, widow Isabella Row age 75, lived with   Adam and Sarah Godshall in Lykens Twp. **Wendel and Isabella ( ) Row children:**
**JOSEPH (Sep 22, 1806 - Sep 1, 1875, bur Hoffman Cem), m Mary Catherine (Oct 15, 1806 - Sep   17, 1883), a dau of _____. [This could be #951 1860 census]
GEORGE (Aug 31, 1808   - Sep 19, 1883, bur St. John's Luth, Berrysburg), m Elizabeth Kissinger (b 1833- ____), a dau of John and Elizabeth (Hawk) Kissinger. In 1850, George was the head of the house, Adam Row age 35, his mother Isabella age 60, Susanna Row age 16, and Tobias Daniel age 7 lived with him. In 1860, George and Elizabeth Row lived on a farm in Lykens Township and Benneville Matter 16, a servant, and Adam Row 34, servant with him. In 1870, Jacob Row age 21 lived with George and his family. In 1880, George and Elizabeth Row lived in Berrysburg. **George and Elizabeth (Kissinger) Row children: ***Mary A. (Jan 24, 1852 - Oct 23, 1881, d of consumption), m Nov 23, 1871, John A. Romberger (Apr 21, 1850 -), a son of Daniel and Hannah (Bergstresser) Romberger; *****Adelina** (Apr 25, 1857 - ___), m Peter E. Stine; *****Sarah Anna** Aug 1, 1863 - Apr 15, 1865)
WENDEL (Apr 30, 1810 - Jan 9, 1884, bur St. Johns Luth Cem, Berrysburg). [Wendel has same birth date as sister below - twins?] Wendel m 1st Rachel ____ (Aug 17, 1806 - Aug 27, 1866), m 2nd Anna Bitterman (Sep 3, 1819 - Oct 30, 1890), a dau of Balthaser & Barbara Bitterman (bapt St. Johns Hill Ch), both wives bur St. Johns Luth Cem. In 1880 Wendel and Anna Row lived inWashington Twp **Wendel & Rachel (   ) Row children:*Lovina** b c1832; *****Susanna** (Jul 4, 1833 - Aug 17, 1855, bur St. Johns Luth Cem), 1st wife of Charles Stine, m Feb 6, 1854; *****Mary** (1841 - 1843); *****Sophia** (b Jun 7, 1845 - Mar 25, 1898, bur Luth Cem, E'ville), m Jan 31 1869, Jonathan Smith. In 1880 Wendel and Anna Row lived in Washington Twp and had Matilda Brandt age 55 (servant0 with them.
ISABELLA (Apr 30, 1810 - Jan 27, 1852, bur St. Johns Luth Cem), m Solomon Matter (Mar 1806 - May 13, 1877), a son of Michael and Anna Maria (Romberger) Matter. **Solomon and Isabella (Row) Matter children:
Daniel b Jan 31, 1831; *****Mary Ann** b c1833; *****Jeremiah** b c1835; *****Catharina** b c1840; *****Elisabeth** b c1844; *****Isabelle** b c1846; *****Amanda** b c1849; ** Susanna** b Jun 24, 1851;
HENRY (May 22, 1812 - Feb 5, 1838, bur St. Johns Luth Cem), m Susanna Matter (Sep 25, 1815 - Aug 12, 1903, bur Simeon Cem), a dau of Michael and Anna Maria (Romberger) Matter. She was married four years, and had two sons, one daughter. **Henry and Susanna (Matter) Row children: ***Henry b May 20, 1836; *****Polly** (no dates). After Henry died, Susanna m Jacob Ritzman.
**ADAM (Mar 24, 1814 - Mar 14, 1869, bur St. Johns Luth Cem), m Rachel _____. After Adam died, Rachel m John Bordner.
**ABRAHAM (Apr 10, 1816 - Sep 4, 1892, d of dysentery, bur St, Johns Cem), m by Rev Hemping Sep 5, 1843, Sarah (Paul) Schreffler (Mar 15, 1822 - Mar 14, 1900), a dau of _____. Abraham and Sarah Row lived in Mifflin Twp in 1870 and 1880, and he was a farm laborer. He was skilled at making fence posts and building

rail fences. Sarah along with housekeeping line coffins for an undertaker at Matterstwon and helped the undertaker to prepare the bodies for burial. She was known for her talent in making beautiful quilts, and while she quilted, she smoked a clay pipe. **Abraham and Sarah (Paul, Schreffler) Row children:** ***Joseph** (Mar 9, 1844 - May 11, 1859); ***Isabella** (Dec 29, 1845 - Sep 19, 1862), said to be a helpless invalid for twenty years [Simeon parish record]; ***Sarah** ((1849 - 1851); ***Hannah** b c1861; ***Catherine N.** (Jan 12, 1865 - 1928, bur St. Johns Cem), m May 10, 1889 Cornelius N. Miller (1860 - 1943), **had three children:** Harry N. b Jun 12, 1890; Sadie A b Oct 22, 1892; Annie E. Sep 27, 1894; ***Julia A** (Apr 9, 1868 - Feb 13, 1933, bur St. Johns Luth Cem), m Harry T. Zimmerman.

SARAH (Oct 17, 1818 - pre 1842), m Daniel Lebo (Feb 10, 1812 - Feb 20, 1871, bur St. Johns Luth Cem), died of pneumonia. They lived on a farm in Mifflin Twp, but later moved to Lykens, where Daniel and his brothers William and David helped to built the first Lykens Coal breaker. **Daniel and Sarah (Row) Lebo Children; ***Joseph** (Jul 30, 1839 - Aug 23, 1920), lived in Oregon in 1906; ***Sarah Ann** (Jun 13, 1841 - Sep 12, 1926), m Henry R. Lehr. Sarah Ann at the age of eight lived with the Solomon Martz familly in 1850.
**ANNA b Jan 24, 1820
**CATHARINA After father died had George Rohrer for guardian
**DANIEL After father died had George Rohrer for guardian

*WILLIAM ROW (c1785 - c1877, died age 92), m Barbara Rudy (b c1790 - d Dec 1881, according to obituary), probably a dau of Jacob and Susanna Rudy. A tombstone in St. Johns Luth Cem, gives this information: Jacob Rudy died 1813, bur Greensburg, Pa. ___, wife of Jacob Rudy died 1833, bur Hoffman Cem. In 1850, William and Barbara Row lived in Wiconisco Twp, and had son Joseph age 22, with them. In 1860, William and Barbara lived in Lykens Twp, and had William Adams age 7 with them. William was a farmer and carpenter. When elderly Barbara Row died, an interesting obituary appeared in the Millersburg Herald (newspaper) dated Friday December 23, 1881:

MRS. BARBARA ROW DIED

Mrs. Barbara Row - Edging on four Score and fifteen, mother of Jacob Row of Matterstown - Mrs Row lived in this area about a century, lived to see her grandchildren grow up to man and woman hood. She was comparatively unknown outside of her immediate neighborhood until speculative life insurance sought her out from among the aged and decrepit as a desirable subject for seekers of fortune. Application after application was signed and policy after policy olders chucked in their sleeves upon the approval of their risks and a "full line" was easily disposed. In the parlance of insurance speculators she was expected to drop off any day, but alas for the disappointed beneficiaries, she not only out lived her day and generation, but all the companies that had requested her name among its members. Her end came last week, but too late to reimburse the scores of policyholders who had staked hundreds of dollars on her life. On Sunday last, her mortal remains were solemnly laid to rest and if any tears were shed outside of her relatives it was because she was not permitted to "wrap the drapery of her couch about her" twelve months sooner. Mrs. Row will continue to live in the memory of her numerous beneficiaries for generations to come.

William and Barbara (Rudy) Row children:
**JACOB (b Feb 3, 1812 Lyk Twp - d Apr 21, 1894, d of Apoplexy, Porter Twp, Sch Co, bur St. Johns Luth Cem, Berrysburg), m Apr 26, 1838, Susanna Matter (b May 11, 1821 in Mifflin Twp- d Mar 20, 1882), a dau of George and Anna Catherine (Romberger) Matter. Jacob and the family lived on a farm in Washington Twp in 1850, and had Daniel Shultz age 3, and Moses Betz age 18, with them. Besides farming, Jacob was a butcher, and kept a store at Matterstown. In 1880 Jacob and Susannah Row had Jacob Stillmaker 12 servant, Anna J. Bechtel age 10, grandaughter, and Barbara Row age 89, the mother with them. Also Fannie Schrawder age 34, a servant.
Jacob and Susanna (Matter) Row children:
***Jonas** (May 11, 1839 - Apr 6, 1923, bur Maple Grove Cem, Elizabethville), m 1st on Oct 23, 1859, Susannah Sevilla Martz (Sep 23, 1845 - Dec 30, 1870, bur St. Johns Luth Cem), a dau of Jonas and Carolyn Martz. Jonas m 2nd on Mar 26, 1871, by Rev. I. W. Kunkel to Catharine Rife Matter (Oct 3, 1843 - May 16, 1928, bur beside Jonas in Maple Grove Cem). They were married at the home of her father David Matter. During his young adult life, Jonas worked for his father on the homestead, then went into butchering and eventually owned his own farm in Washington Twp. Jonas Row was a veteran of the Civil War, having served in Co. D., 26th Regt. of Pa. Vol Inf, and Co L of the 16th Pa. Cavalry. Dr. Robert E. Barto was his physician, and George

F. Buffington was the undertaker for his funeral. Jonas and Susannah lived in Washington Twp in 1870 **Jonas and Susannah Sevilla (Martz) Row children:** <u>Jacob Clinton</u> b Oct 27, 1860; <u>Theodore</u> and <u>Charles</u> (twins) b Nov 9, 1862, died young; <u>Ida Elisabeth</u> b May 15, 1864, m Henry Harman of Halifax; <u>Ira W</u>. b Jan 11, 1867, d young; <u>Eva Jennie</u> b Jan 27, 1868, d young; <u>Oliver O</u> b Apr 12, 1869, d young.

Jonas Row Pension

A copy of the application for a Civil War pension for Jonas Row is in our library. He wrote a letter to the examiner explaining more fully the negative responses he may have from acquaintances witnessing to his pension needs. It is a very unique and most interesting document detailing examples of events that he thought led to the witnesses' disapproval of a pension for him.

"William Row is spiteful because he wanted hay this winter and I didn't sell him any. And he bought a cow of me and when he came to fetch it I was not home so he took the wrong cow and I made him pay ten dollars more or take it to my place. Now he is spiteful, and is against the pension." "George Hawk must be spiteful because his wife and my wife had a quarrel and I talked in it and about trading horses. And he is against pension."

"Levi Matter and Adam Schreffler did fence the road shut between their land and my father, now they are spiteful." "William Matter farmed for Jacob Swab but they could not agree so William ask Jonas to cut the grass and thrash it for the fourth bushel. But Jacob Swab told him not to go in the field. Jonas told him he got orders so we had a little chat and since then he never visited me so I know he is spiteful, and he will keep spite forever." "Jonas had Dr. J. P. Straub as his doctor but changed to Dr. N. W. Stroub, and now he is spunky."

Jonas ends by writing "Shall I now suffer. Such enemies shall perish, all workers of iniquity shall be scattered. May God have his eye on them." (Jonas did get his pension.)

***Catherine** (Mar 12, 1840 - Sep 18, 1873), bur St. Johns Luth Cem), m 1st Jul 13, 1856, Charles Stine, m 2nd Nov 21, 1858 to Daniel Carl (Jul 6, 1834 – Aug 10, 1894), a son of Jeremiah and Juliann (Radel) Carl..

***Susanna** b c1842, m Dec 23, 1860 Jeremiah Matter, a son of _____ of Harrisburg. **Jeremiah and Susanna (Row) Matter had these children:** <u>Edwin</u> b Jul 21, 1861; <u>Noah</u> b Nov 2, 1862; <u>Jonathan</u> b Apr 25, 1864; <u>Jacob Oliver</u> b Apr 6, 1868; <u>Nathan Solomon</u> b Aug 23, 1870; <u>Mary Agnes</u> b Jun 25, 1872; <u>Amanda Susan</u> b Jan 10, 1875; <u>Jerry Jonas</u> b Mar 28, 1877; <u>Clara Catherine</u> b Sep 9, 1879.

***Melinda** (Mar 20, 1845 - Oct 3, 1913, bur Orwin Cem, Porter Twp, Sch Co), m Jun 8, 1862 Emanuel Koppenhaver (Jan 16, 1835 - Oct 24, 1889, bur St. Johns Luth Cem, Berrysburg). Emanuel was a Civil War Veteran.

***Amanda** b c1847, m Henry Bechtel, a plasterer of Elizabethville. It is probably their dau Anna J. age 10, (grandaughter) living with Jacob & Susannah Row in 1880.

***Sarah Ann** (1849 - 1927, bur Orwin Cem, Porter Twp, Sch Co.), m John Lebo, of Sch Co. John and Sarah Ann (Row) Lebo had these children: Isaac Oliver b Sep 9, 1874; Jonathan Edward b Dec 27, 1876; Ann Rebecca b Dec 27, 1878;

***Lemuel** b Aug 26, 1855, m Emma Jane Hartman (Feb 12, 1848 - Nov 11, 1883, bur St. Johns Luth Cem, Berrysburg). **Lemuel and Emma Jane (Hartman) Row had these children:** <u>Kate Margaret</u> b Mar 5, 1875; <u>Charles Oliver</u> b Jan 4, 1877; <u>Minnie Bertha</u> b Jun 6, 1878; <u>Oscar</u> b Mar 14, 1879.

***Isaac** (Aug 31, 1858 - Nov 19, 1936, bur Zion Luth Cem, Rife), m Apr 24, 1880 Caroline Webner (Dec 16, 1860 - Nov 6, 1929), a dau of George and Hannah Longabach Webner, who came to this area from Haines Twp, Centre Co. In 1880, Isaac and Caroline were living with his parents in Washington Twp.

**DANIEL (Jul 10, 1813 - Jul 31, 1871), bur St. Johns Luth, d of Brights disease), m Susanna Frantz (Mar 23, 1819 - Oct 17, 1861, of hernia), a dau of Adam and Susannah (Geiseman) Frantz.

[Susannah Geiseman was born in Tulpehocken Twp, Berks Co Mar 10, 1788 - d Feb 15, 1826, age 37, in Mifflin Twp, a dau of Johannes Wilhelm Geiseman (Mar 23, 1761 - Aug 26, 1843, bur St. Johns Luth Cem), and his wife Anna Margaret or Maria (Grube) Geiseman (Apr 2, 1759 - Jun 12, 1837). Susannah Geiseman married Adam Frantz on Oct 6, 1811, and had nine children. So states a record in St. Davids Church book.]

Daniel and Susanna (Frantz) Row lived near Matterstown, in Washington Township, children:
***Sarah (Jun 21, 1841 - Sep 7, 1859);
***Angeline (Mar 26, 1843 - Apr 24, 1936, bur Maple Grove Cem, E'ville), m Jacob Zerby (Mar 4,   1837 - Nov 19, 1913), of Elizabethviile. Jacob was a Civil War Veteran of Co B., 9th Cavalry.
***Adam (1849 - 1929, d in Halifax). He was named after the first man Adam, because several other sons died at birth. Adam served in the Civil War.
***Susanna (Feb 7, 1852 - Oct 23, 1933, bur IOOF Cem, Lykens), m Mar 17, 1872 William Henry Keiper (Nov 26, 1851 - Aug 28, 1913), a son of John and Lucanna (Buffington Keiper of Lykens. [See story of her life below.] **William and Susannah (Row) Keiper children:** Lillian May b Jul 1873, m Joseph Blanning, lived in New Castle, Pa. Lillian did much research on the history of her ancestors during the 1930s and 1940s, and most of her work has survived. **Laura Leota** (Sep 6, 1874 - May 7, 1876); Jennie Irene (Feb 15, 1876 - Feb 17, 1967), bur Simeon Cem), m Edward Deitrich, lived in Lykens Township; Weston Merrit (Oct 5, 1879 - Jan 28, 1902), worked in the mines; Drucilla Belle b Feb 11, 1882; Minnie (Dec 1883 - 1913, bur Meth Cem), m Arthur Blackway (1883 - 1955), lived in Lykens; Angeline Myrl (Dec 5, 1885 - Oct 2, 1870, bur Wiconisco Cem); Harry Herbert (Nov 1887 -   ____), moved to El Paso, Texas; Sarah Ellen (Nov 1889 - 1976, bur Calvary Meth Cem, Wiconisco), m J. Allen Rowe (1886 - 1943)]

***Amelia b c1854, m _____Chubb of Halifax
***Leah Jane (May 16, 1856 - Apr 17, 1956, bur Seyberts Cem, Williamstown), almost 102 years old, m William H. Michael (May 9, 1834 - May 6, 1911), Civil War Vet. of Williamstown
***Adeline (b Jan 2, 1859 Wash Twp – Mar 6, 1921, bur St. Johns Luth Cem, Berrysburg), m Feb 16, 1878 John H. Wert, son of David   and Catherine (Shoop) Wert. **John H. and Adeline (Rowe) Wert had these children:** Carrie; Hattie m Daniel Romberger of Loyalton; Florence m John A. Kocher (1872 – 1939), of Bbg. **John A. and Florence (Wert) Kocher had these children:** *Albert* m Ruth Weaver,   moved to Arizona; *Vernon* m Elva Matter; *Ruby* m Lester Hassinger; *Thelma* m George Klinger; *Elenore*   m Mark Engle; Sara Jane m Warren Hoffman moved to Arizona; Beulah m Ed Baddorf of Loyalton

When Susanna Row Keiper was eighty-one years old, she was interviewed January 27, 1933, by a reporter from the MILLERSBURG SENTINEL. From that interview we find an interesting account of the life of Susanna. A view of her early days gives us a glimpse of the ordinary settler who lived in the Lykens Valley. Printed below are excerpts from the interview.

"Mrs. Susan Keiper is the widow of William Keiper, and resides with two daughters in Lykens. She is one of four sisters whose ages total 327 years, the oldest being ninety and the youngest seventy-seven. The sisters are daughters of the late Daniel and Susan Frantz Row, of Lykens Valley, who passed away rather early in life. Mrs. Row was only forty-two when she died of hernia, but was the mother of twelve children. Father Row died at the age of fifty-eight, of Brights disease. His father and mother, Mr. and Mrs. William Row of Lancaster County, each lived to be ninety-two   years of age.

Susanna Keiper was born on a farm west of Matterstown, in Washington Township, February 1, 1851. Her parents were poor, hard working farmers and she says she does not remember ever seeing a cook stove in her mothers' home. There was a fireplace in the Row home, where all food was prepared. The frying pans had long legs and long handles so they could be placed in position over the blazing wood in the fireplace. For cooking, pots were suspended from chains in the fireplace. Tallow candles were used for illumination in the home at night. The Rows grew flax and raised sheep on their farm. Flax and wool were made into clothing for the Row children by Mother Row.

Mrs. Row could not speak English, but carried on all of her conversations in Pennsylvania Dutch dialect. The children speak English and the Dutch dialect very fluently.

When Susanna was old enough, she became a pupil at Holtzman's School. She recalls that at one time she had a teacher by the name of Tarbox. Andrew Pontius was another teacher at Holtzmans school.

Every minute Susanna was not in school she was working at home or on the farm, when she became old enough to be useful. When Susanna was nine years old, her mother died, leaving six children and their father. Susanna was sent to the home of William Lenker, near Reigles Church, to reside and help with the work. At the same time, she attended Neagleys school where William Lenker was teacher.

When the Civil War broke out, one of Susanna's brothers, Adam row enlisted and served eleven months. After the war was over, he enlisted in the regular army and served three years. Adam Row died four years ago, at Halifax, aged 80 years. Susanna says she recalls the Civil War days and the many boys going away to serve their country.   She remembers the shooting of President Lincoln and the panic following the war. She says "hard" times then did not impress her very much because she was young and was provided for; did not need to worry about making ends meet. She says, however, that the panic then was mild compared to the present depression.

Susanna resided at the Lenker home four years, but when Mr. Lenker purchased the Buck store at Killinger and moved his family to that place, she went to the farm of Alfred Hoover, east of Berrysburg. Susanna was fourteen then, and a strong, healthy youngster, but when she found she was supposed to do the work of two men, she rebelled and her stay there was brief. Next she became attached to the home of John Holtzman family, on a farm near Reigles Church, where she remained until she was seventeen. She then became a maid at the home of Hiram Bueck family of Lykens, and later was employed in the homes of Joseph Dunlap, Daniel Woodside and Guerney Miller, all at Lykens, all now deceased.

Susanna was a member of the United Brethren Church at Lykens, and a regular attendant. So was William Keiper of Lykens, and before long the two became good friends. William was a son of John and Lucanna (Buffington) Keiper of Lykens, and was a miner at the Short Mountain Colliery.

When Susanna was twenty years of age, she and William Keiper were united in marriage at the parsonage of the Lutheran Church at Lykens, by Rev. Mr. Glosse. They moved into the Keiper home on Main Street. Susanna and William had nine children. After her husband died, Susanna lived with her two daughters in Lykens.

SUSANNA b Apr 11, 1815
JOHANNES b Mar 17, 1817
ELIZABETH b Jan 20, 1818
SARAH
(Nov 19, 1820– Apr 4,1900)
JOSEPH b c1818

*GEORGE ROW (no info)
*SARAH ROW (no info)
*SAMUEL ROW had a
 child bapt at David's Ch, Killinger
 Hannah Margaretha b Dec 13,
 1819, mothers name not given]

This photo is said to be that of William Rowe (1785 – c1877) and his wife Barbara Rudy Rowe (1790 – 1881)

THE FREDERICK STINE/ STEIN FAMILY

[FREDERICK STINE, first of the family to arrive in America was born in Germany. In 1775 he came to America as a Hessian soldier and fought for the British in the Revolutionary War. He was captured by George Washington's troops at Trenton, New Jersey in the famous Christmas night crossing of the Delaware, and with many other soldiers was sent to a prison war camp at Carlisle. It is said that when the Quakers in Philadelphia heard of this camp they formed a raiding party and set several of the prisoners free. Frederick was one of them.

Frederick Stine settled first in Berks County, but about 1788 he came to Lykens Valley. He was a stone mason. Some of the following records were found in the family German Bible of **Friedrich Stine,** purchased at an auction in June 1977. On the inside cover it states: "This book belongs to Friedrich Stine of Heidelberger Twp. of Berks Co". Frederick Stine (b Sep 28, 1749 Hochstadt, Hessen Ger – Apr 24, 1832, bur Gratz),m Feb 24, 1784 Schwarzwald Luth Ch to Apollonia Lamm (Nov 23, 1757 – Oct 16, 1825), a dau of Johann Peter Lamm and Anna Margareta Heckert Lamm of Heidelberg Twp., Berks Co. The family moved from Heidelberg, Berks Co to Lykens Twp., Dauphin County about 1788.

When the "Window Tax" was taken in 1798, Frederick Stine was assessed for a two-story wooden 32 x 24 foot house. It had eight windows with 100 lights (panes). He also had a good barn and lived next to Daniel Salady in Wiconisco Valley.

Friedrich and Appollonia (Lamm) Stine) children:

*JOHN PETER (Dec 5, 1781 –Aug 21, 1851, bur Simeon Cem, Gratz), m Regina Coleman (Aug 6,1795 Lyk Twp – Oct 11,1878, Gratz), dau of Charles & Maria Barbara (Stine) Coleman. **John P. & Regina (Coleman) Stine children**:
**Catherine (Jun 13, 1814 – Sep 19, 1881, Ogle Co.,Il), m Sep 11, 1834 Dau Co 1st Henry Moyer, She m 2nd after May 1870 Peter Moyer, of Ogle Co., Il. [More info with Moyer genealogy.]
**Frederick (Jan 24, 1816 – Dec 26, 1832) age 17
**Eleanor (1818 – Aug 11, 1887, bur Pottsville), m James Glenn, later moved to Pottsville.
John b Feb 27,1820, m Susanna Bleistein, lived in Sch Co. **John and Susanna (Blleistein) Stine children:
***Anna Maria; ***Elizabeth Sarah; ***Anna Catherine; *** Rachel; ***John Peter b Sep 31, 1852.
**Daniel P (Mar 27, 1822 – Jun 8, 1908, bur Simeon Cem), m Aug 27, 1844 Catharine Stong (Jun 13, 1820 – Dec 6, 1897, Rhumatism) , a dau of John and Catherine Stong of Lykens Twp, bur Klinger Cem. He was a saddler and farmer. They moved to Sch Co., had two daughters, ***Mary J. b July 20 , 1845, m P. J. Artz; ***Amelia R. b Nov 28, 1847, m David Dietz.
**Elizabeth (Jan 11, 1824 – Apr 24, 1904, Gratz), m Daniel Ritzman (1804 – 1873), lived in Gratz.
**Abigail (Sep 17, 1825 – Jul 10, 1905), m Feb 22, 1849 Joseph De Frehn in Orwigsburg, son of Daniel & Susanna (Nowacer) DeFrehn. They lived in Pottsville, Joseph became a well known contractor. Had 5 children.
Peter L. (Jul 26, 1827 Lyk Twp – d Nov 10, 1902, paralysis, bur E'ville), m Dec 17, 1850 Catharine Elizabeth Buffington (Jan 24, 1830- May 15, 1893, bur E'ville), a dau of Jacob & Catherine Buffington. Peter had a grist mill in Washington Twp for 17 years, but in 1885 became a merchant in Elizabethville. **Peter L. and Elizabeth (Buffington) Stine children (had 10): some bapt St. John's Hill Ch): ***Ellen ( ), m C. A. Deibler; ***Sarah Louisa b Apr 8, 1854, m Daniel J. Deibler; ***Isaac Frederick b Sep 19, 1856 – Apr 1, 1902, consumption, bur St. John's Hill Cem), m Adeline Row (Jan 2, 1860 -), a dau of Daniel & Susanna (Frantz) Row, had these children Jennie L (1875 – 1877); George David (Sep 18, 1873- Jan 22, 1910, appendicitis); Mark (Feb 5, 1896 – Sep 1, 1967, bur St. John's Hill Cem); ***Catharine Elizabeth b May 5, 1859, m Edward Martin, moved to Kansas; ***Peter Elias (Sep 23, 1861 -1948, bur E'ville), in 1885 m Mary F. Bonawitz (May 1862 – 1937), a dau of Jonathan Bonawitz. Peter and Mary moved to Mifflin Twp in 1892 and established the Stine Creamery. It was a very successful business that continued for many years; **Peter E. and Mary F. (Bonawitz) Stine children:
Amy I., m Harry Romberger; Earle Alvin (Feb 5, 1890 – 1957), m Lillie Henninger (1890 – 1972), a dau of Isaac Henninger; Clayton Elias b Mar 10, 1891, m Bessie Minnich; Hubert Nevin bAug 26, 1892, m Beulah Shoop; Marjorie Leona b Oct 27, 1899;***David Calvin (Jan 20, 1865 – 1902, of consumption bur E'ville); ***Harry W. (1870 – 1942, bur E'ville), m Eliza J. (1866 – Oct 24, 1895 of consumption); ***Cora Elva b Aug 11, 1872; ***Carrie ( ), m Charles Cooper; ***Samuel Tobias b Oct 19, 1876;

**Charles (- 1893, Perry Co)
**Jonas went to Pottsville was an engineer on the railroad. He m Lydia
Josiah P. (Sep 9, 1837 -), m Feb 16, 1857 to Catharine Louisa Good (Nov 5, 1837, a dau of Daniel and Margaret (Reedy) Good. Before that he went to Ogle Co Ill with brother in 1855, but stayed only two months. On the way home his pocket was picked of thrity-two dollars. Back home he became a tanner apprentice to Daniel Good in Gratz.. Later he went to Wash Twp where he had a tannery business for thirty-seven years. **Josiah and Catharine L (Good) Stine children:* Franklin Peter (Aug 6, 1858 – Mar 1, 1924, bur Gratz), became a teacher; ***Daniel M b Feb 24, 1860, also a teacher, m Mary C. Frank; ***Mary L b Jan 9, 1863, m Samuel W. Cooper.

*ELISABETH (Mar 13, 1786 – m Andrew Riegle (Jan 14, 1780 – Sep 13, 1838), a son of Andrew & Anna Catherine (Hoffman) Riegle. [more information with the Riegle genealogy.]

*ROSINA (Feb 8, 1791 – Sep 2, 1870), m Jul 9, 1809 John Coleman (Jan 26, 1791 – Oct 7, 1822), a son of Charles & Barbara (stine) Coleman. They are buried at Coleman Cem, Lykens twp.[More info with Coleman genealogy.]

*CATHARINE (Apr 22, 1799 - Jan 17, 1873), m John Dietz (Mar 19, 1795 bapt date Feb 14, 1793, a son of John Conrad and Margaret Magdalena (Schornman) Dietz– Aug 31, 1853, bur Klinger Cem). Dietz ch **John and Catharine Dietz children:** **Frederick (Dec 31, 1818 – Sep 3, 1825); **Catherine b Jun 6, 1823; **William (Nov 7, 1830 – Aug 31, 1859, bur Klinger Cem); **Jacob (May 8, 1833 Gratz – Dec 1, 1907, record in Farrow Funeral book in Shamokin)

HOME OF RUTH ANN DREHER (1 ¼ ACRE)
COLONEL JOHN MATTER 1875 (acreage not given for this tract - south side of road)
(Grant to Ludwig Shietz of 53 ½ acres of land)

LUDWIG SHIETZ OR SCHIETZ (SHITZ, SHEETZ, SHOTT, SCHOTTE)
(Throughout this genealogy, the various spellings will be used as found)
(Help from various sources including Dean F. Grimm, Evelyn Hartman, Ethel Myers,

This land belonged to one of the very earliest settlers in Lykens Valley. Ludwig Shietz, Sr. born about 1713, sailed into the port of Philadelphia, September 3, 1742 on aboard ship "Loyal Judith". He moved to the East End of Hanover Township, (now in Lebanon County), where by 1750, he was taxed as a landowner. He became acquainted with Andrew Lycans, also a resident in that township, and when Lycans came to "Wiconisco Valley," Ludwig Shietz in company with a few other pioneers, came with him. They had settled before 1756 in "Wiconisco Valley " but it is difficult to determine exactly where they built their first cabins.

Ludwig was one of the men attacked by the Indians in a raid on the settlers who lived in the area now known as Loyalton. There, on March 7, 1756, a fierce attack left Andrew Lycans near death, several others including Ludwig Shietz wounded. The description of the Indian raid describes Ludwig as a neighbor who "crept out of the house to get a shot at the Indians." He was either visiting Lycans at the time, or his cabin was in the immediate vicinity. Ludwig did fire two deadly shots, but in the process he was wounded by a shot to his abdomen from the assailants. [An account of the assault can be found in the write-up of Andrew Lycans.]

After the Indian raid, many of the pioneers fled back to their original settlements. The Shietz family may have left for a brief time. However, Ludwig Shot applied for a grant of 200 acres of land on September 24, 1767 in Wiconisco Valley. Ludwig Shietz received a grant of 53 ½ acres of land (the land we are focusing on now) from Commonwealth of Pa., the date of which has not been found. Tax records substantiate the presence of Ludwig and his family here in 1775. Ludwig Shotts and his son Jacob are taxed in 1779. Both Ludwig Schots, Junior and Senior were listed in the "Wiconisco District" in 1780, as were Michael and Jacob Schotts.

By 1773, Ludwig Schott was serving as an elder in Salem Lutheran Church in Killinger. He was treasurer of the church in 1776, and later served as a deacon. Ludwig son of Ludwig Schott was confirmed at Salem Lutheran in April 1774. Two or three of his daughters were confirmed at St. David's in August 1774. Both father and son were present for communion in Salem Lutheran regularly from November 1779 to 1786. The communion record for May 31, 1789, lists Ludwig Schott and wife **Anne Barbara** and son Johann Philip. Nothing more is known about pioneers Ludwig and Anne Barbara Shietz. According to a county court record, Ludwig died about 1789, his wife died later. Two sons, Ludwig and Peter, petitioned Dauphin County Orphans Court for an inquest, dated April 19, 1796. It mentions that their father Ludwig Shott of Upper Paxton Township died "about eight years ago, leaving a widow since deceased, and eight children." When Ludwig Shietz died, he had a plantation of 240 acres. A record of burial has never been found. Perhaps Ludwig and Anne Barbara Shietz are among the early pioneers buried at the end of Short Mountain, maybe in an unmarked grave near Salem Lutheran Church in Killinger, or speculating, maybe in the old cemetery near the land where the family lived at Woodside near Rife.

Ludwig Shietz, Jr. remained in Lykens Township on this property. The 1798 "window tax" assessment describes the Ludwig Shietz property as having two acres of cleared land, with a one-story, thirty by twenty-four foot wooden house. The house had four windows, with a total of thirty glass panes. Another window tax entry records 100 acres for Ludwig with a good barn, bordering on land of Jacob Snyder. He purchased this tract from Nicholas and Margaret Hoffman December 6, 1796. By 1817, he had 126 acres of land, and was engaged in farming. On August 12, 1812, a larger part of two tracts of land was sold to John Riegel who was married to Susanna Shietz, daughter of Ludwig Shietz, Sr. Ludwig Shietz owned another eighteen acres of land that was granted to him on February 27, 1796. It bordered the road "Reading to Berrysburg, John Matter, John Searer, Mathias Haag, road Lancaster to Sunbury, John Riegel and John Hoffman." Ludwig Shietz sold it to John Riegel in August 1812, and Riegel sold the land to John Matter in May 1827.

On February 6, 1796, Commonwealth of Pennsylvania conveyed another tract of 300 acres of patented land to Ludwig Shietz (apparently Ludwig, Jr.). This land was in Upper Paxton Township, located in the vicinity of the old Woodside covered bridge, near Rife. The neighbors were Christian Bock, John Shott, James Woodside and Peter Long. Several members of the family eventually settled in that area, and had a gristmill and sawmill erected near the creek. Later the land bordered Wiconisco Creek, land of Stephen Lenker, Jacob Sandoe and George Minnich. Eventually William Kottka purchased the land and continued to operate the mill for many years. Other members of the Shietz family by 1798, owned land near Armstrong Creek, Armstrong Valley, and on the "River Road" adjacent to the land of Martin Weaver.

MORTGAGE D – 1 – page 492

The following document was very helpful in identifying the children of Ludwick Shott /Shietz etc. It also records the date (11 June, 1787) when his children (heirs) released his land to Ludwick Shott, Jr.   The document was recorded September 12, 1796.

Philip Shott & Christian Shott ⟩492
to
Ludwick Shott . . . . ⟩ To all people to whom these
presents shall come Philip Shott of Middle Paxton township
in the County of Dauphin and State of Pennsylvania yeoman
and Elizabeth his wife and Christian Shott of the township of
Upper Paxton in the County and State aforesaid yeoman send
Greeting. Whereas Ludwick Shott late of Upper Paxtan township
aforesaid was during his lifetime and at the time of his death
lawfully seized in his demesne as of fee of and in a certain tract
of land situate lying and being in the township of Upper Pax
tan, containing three hundred acres should the same be more or
less together the appurtenances And Whereas the said Ludwick
Shott died intestate leaving issue to wit Jacob Shott Michael
Shott Ludwick Shott Christina Shott who intermarried with
Adam Cooper Catharina Shott who intermarried with adam
Laudermilch anna Maria Shott who intermarried with Peter
Schweigart Mary Shott (since dead) who intermarried with the
Reverend Samuel Dubendorff Peter Shott Margaret Shott Christian
Shott and Philip Shott And whereas the aforesaid Jacob Shott
Michael Shott Adam Cooper and Christina his wife Adam Lau
dermilch and Catherine his wife Peter Schweigart and anna Maria
his wife the reverend Samuel Dubendorff Peter Shott and Margaret
Shott by deed of release dated the eleventh day of June in the year of
our Lord one thousand seven hundred and eighty seven and un
der their hands and seals duly executed for the consideration there
in mentioned did remise release and forever quit claim unto Lud
wick Shott of Upper Paxton township aforesaid (one of the sons of
the said Ludwick Shott deceased) and his heirs and assigns

THE LUDWIG SHIETZ FAMILY

[**LUDWIG SHIETZ** (b c1713 - d about May 1787 or 1789. (According to the court record the heirs of Ludwig "Shott" signed a release of land to Ludwig Shott, Jr. on June 11, **1787**. The communion date of 1789 above, raises a question as to which date is correct.) He married Barbara Maria Lauer (b c1732- d between May 1787 & April 1796). Considering the age difference, perhaps Ludwig had a previous wife. Their children and spouses are listed in two court records: Mortgage Book D-1-314 & D-I-492. Some were bapt St. Johns & St. David's Church.

*JOHN JACOB (c 1751 - Oct 1, 1808), m Elizabeth Margaret _____ (no dates). Note: bapt records of their children at St. Davids, Killinger give her name as Ann Margaret, orphan court records state her name as Elizabeth. John Jacob received the tract of 220 acres, plantation and mill in Upper Paxton Twp. from his father's estate. The land adjoined lands of John Smelzer and George Minnich. Served in Capt Albright Deibler's Co. during Rev. War. **John Jacob and Elizabeth/ Margaret (_____) Shietz had these children (some bapt Hoffman's, St. Johns, St. David's, Salem Luth church):**
CHRISTIAN (Nov 24, 1775 – 1820 in Halifax, bur Fetterhoff Cem), m Anna Mary d 1826, had **no children. They were members of Fetterhoff Church as early as 1808. In later life appointed guardian of Leonard Snyder's son Samuel.
**ANNA MARIA (Nov 17, 1776 Salem –Nov 15, 1862) m Leonard Snyder (b 1772 - Jan 19, 1815 (pastor Reilly note , pastor at Hoffman Ch) .[More information in Leonard Snyder genealogy.]
**ANNA CATHARINA (b Nov 20, 1778 – Salem Luth), m John Adam Herman b c1774
JACOB (Dec 26, 1779 – Mar 9, 1840, bur Luth Ref Cem, E'ville), His tombstone states that he was married 37 years to Anna Catharine Messner, had 10 children. Jacob m Anna Catharine Messner (Feb 26, 1784 – Jul 23, 1852), a dau of John Messner (Feb 12, 1742 – Sep 20, 1821, bur St. John's Hill Cem, Berrysburg), and Catharina (Mosser) Messner (1756 – 1822), dau of George Mosser . In 1850 widow Anna Catherine lived with her son Christian. **Jacob and Anna Catharina (Messner) Shietz children some bapt St. John's Hil, Hoffmans, or David's Killinger ch):
***Johannes b Nov 27, 1802, bapt Hoffman Ch – Feb 2, 1873), m Dec 23, 1823 Margaretha Woodside (Sep 9,1803 – Jun 25, 1863), a dau of John Woodside, lived in Jackson Twp in 1836 (Davids Ch record), in 1850 Washington Twp. In 1860 they lived in Leaf River, Ogle Ill. **Johannes and Margaretha (Woodside) Shietz children:** Catherine b Dec 23, 1823; Susanna b Aug 8, 1825; George (Dec 5, 1826 – Nov 21, 1897), m Louisa Kembel b1830; Elizabeth (Feb 2, 1831 – Jun 17, 1917), m Leonard Matter (1826 – 1896), moved to Ogle Co. Il . William b 1834; Susanna b 1840, m Isaac Novinger, moved to Ogle Co. Il; Margaretha b 1843, m Henry Stover; Jonas (1844 – 1866)
***Jacob b Oct 10, 1804 not listed in o/c, m Elizabeth Messner (Jul 26, 1806 – Oct 21, 1853), a dau of Philip and Magdalena Messner
***John George b May 14, 1807 –Oct 28, 1826) - not listed in o/c
***Lydia (Nov 13, 1811 – Jan 20,1892), , m John Heller (Mar 11,1810 – Sep 1, 1880), moved to Ogle Co.,Il.
***Christian (Sep 11, 1813 Wash Twp – 1872, bur Old Stone Cem, E'ville, m Susanna Schott (Aug 8, 1825 – Mar 26, 1918, Old Stone Cem, E'ville with Christian), later moved to Tuscola, Minnesota, m 2nd George Markhart (1818 – 1895). In 1850 lived in Jackson Twp **had children:** Margaret (1846 – 1872, bur Eville), m Wm. H. Gobel. Nathaniel b c1848, George b 1850; Catherine b c1851 m Nathaniel Snyder b c1852; Sarah b 1855; Susanna b 1856; Mary b 1858; Christian b 1862; Jacob b c1864; Charles b 1866. Most of the family lived in Jackson Twp. Christian's mother Catherine age 65 lived with them.
***Philip b 1815, m 1st Anna Lenker (Jan 16, 1814 – Mar 29, 1843), 2nd Rebecca Ann Lebo b 1829
***Michael b Oct 7, 1818, bapt David's Ref Ch, m Catherine
*** Catherine (Sep 18, 1821 – 1908), m Philip Miller (Jul 23, 1807 – Nov 11, 1889, bur St. Jacob Cem, Jacksonville), divorced. 2nd Jacob Bordner (1804 – 1879)
***Elizabeth (Jan 24, 1822 -), m John L. Buffington, b Aug 20, 1803, a son of Levi and Susannah Catharine (Hoffman) Buffington. They later moved to the mid-west by wagon train, and lived in Illinois and later Iowa.
***Peter b Dec 11, 1827

**CHRISTIANA MAGDALENA (b Oct 3, 1781   Hoffmans- d_____). m Abraham Feidt (b c1777 -   ).
Abraham & Christiana Magd (Shietz) Feidt children (some Bapt Hoffman, Fetterhoff & St. John's Hill Ch)

John b Mar 29, 1804; **Catharina** b Feb 15. 1807; **Ja. George** b Oct 12, c1808; **Magdalena** b Sep 9, 1810
Elisabeth b Aug 15, 1812; **Joseph** b Mar 2, 1815.

**LUDWIG (Sep 3, 1785 – Hoffmans Apr 24, 1823), m Margaret Messner (Jun 29, 1788 – Jun 11, 1 847), a
dau of John & Catherine Messner. Ludwig served with Capt Seal in the 8ᵗʰ Company, 152 Regt. Ludwig and
brother Jacob inherited the gristmill , from their father. By 1840 it had "fallen down". **Ludwig and Margaret
(Messner) Shietz had 4 children:**
***Catherine ( ), m Daniel Heller – lived in Crawford Co Ohio as early as 1841
***Susanna (May 19, 1817 – 1877), was the 2ⁿᵈ wife of J. Christian Lenker (Jun 22, 1801 – Nov 10, 1846), a
son of Stephen and Susanna (Deck) Lenker, who lived on an adjacent farm near E'ville. Susanna's tombstone
states that she was a daughter of Ludwig and Margaret (Messner) Schott. **J. Christian and Susanna (Shietz)
Lenker children**:
Daniel b Mar 18, 1835, went to Ohio, was a Civil War Vet.
Valentine (Jul 12, 1838 – May 1901) m Nov 28, 1865 Ellen E. Uhler (1842 – 1892), lived in Berrysburg, where
he was a saddler. He was a Civil War Vet.
Christian (Mar 10, 1842 – Nov 22, 1925), m Mary Stoddard, was a doctor in Schuylkill Haven.
Hiram (Feb 2, 1845 – 1859)
***John (Jun 21, 1819
***George (Sep 30, 1822 -   ), when his father died, Philip Messner became his guardian.
After Ludwig died, Margaret m Johann Philip Shietz, (Aug 5, 1789 – Jan 1, 1854), brother to Ludwig.

**JOHN PETER (b Aug 22, 1787 -   ), m Elizabeth Jury b 1790. **John Peter and Elizabeth (Jury) Shietz
children:**
***Catharine (Apr 16, 1809 – Dec 8, 1859), m Jonas Lebo (Dec 20, 1811- Feb 15, 1852, bur Bowerman Cem
near Halifax); *****John** b Jan 3, 1811; *****Elizabeth** b Apr 17, 1813; *****Peter** (Apr 1, 1814 – Jul 3, 1893), m
Maria ___ Jan 3, 1811 – Apr 17, 1813); *****Lydia** (Jun 3, 1817 – Jan 30, 1886), m John Heim (Jun 12, 1816 –
Oct   30, 1869); *****Rebecca** (Aug 14, 1819 – Oct 13, 1862), m Michael Hetrick (Dec 27, 1821 – Jul 24, 1843)
***Sarah (Sep 22, 1821 – Sep 3,1875), m Henry Reitz (Jan 25, 1829 – Apr 20, 1883)

**JOHAN PHILIP (b Aug 5, 1789 – Jan 1, 1854, Halifax), m 1ˢᵗ Ann Lebo (no dates, she d before Philip), had
4 children over age 21, not named in O/C. *****Mary** b c1838; *****John** b c 1839; *****Catherine** b c1841;
***James b c1842. In 1850, Philip was living in Halifax Twp. and was married to Margaret (Messner) Shietz,
widow of his brother Ludwig. These individuals were living with them: Christian age 20, Jacob 18, Polly 15.

*MICHAEL (c1753 - d before 1822), presumed to have married about 1795, Elizabeth Troxell, widow of Jacob
Troxell. This is a very interesting account, with very few details. Jacob Troxell (b c1767 – d before Oct 4, 1794,
bur in Old Matter Cem, near E'ville). The stone is unique, the name ELIZ is carved in the stone upside down, as
is the name Jacob. However Troxell and unreadable dates are in upright position on the stone. It is believed that
this is a mark of Indian culture. Jacob was a son of John and Jacobina (King) Troxell of Lebanon County. Jacob
married Elizabeth ____, (no dates), whose parents were American Indians, apparently from Upper Dauphin area.
Jacob and Elizabeth Troxell had a son: **Johannes b Jan 9, 1794. He was baptized at "Wert" Salem Lutheran
Church in Killinger, but not until February 14, 1796, when Michael and Elizabeth Schott were the sponsors.
Johannes married Hanna and they had a dau ***** Salome** (Jan 8, 1818 0 1826, bur Salem Luth, Killinger). Soon
after Salome was born, Johannes Troxell her father died. The notation of Salome's death "died Oct 15, 1826" in
the David's church book, Killinger, also records the information that her father Johannes is deceased.In the
meantime, Jacob Troxell died about November 1794. His widow apparently became the wife of Michael Schott,
and they were the sponsors at the baptism of Johannes as noted above, appearing in the record as Michael Schott
and Elisabeth. Michael and Elisabeth had two known children of their own. **Michael and Elisabeth (Troxell)
Schott had these children, bapt at Davids Ref Church, Killinger: **Michael** (Mar 31, 1796 - , m Christina
(no dates), **had these children (bapt Davids ch Killinger): ***Anna Maria** b Jan 21, 1824; *****Nathaniel** b Mar
17, 1828; *****Elizabeth** b Jun 20, 1830; **MAYBE Maria** M b Oct 12, 1834; **Susan Catherina** b Jun 29, 1798,
but nothing more is known about them.

*LUDWIG JR. (b c1754 – 1824), was confirmed April 1774 at Salem Lutheran Church in Killinger. He m Jul 9, 1780, Maria Catharine Schessley (   ), the 3rd dau of Johan and Anna Maria Schessly, mentioned in her fathers will.. The marriage is recorded in St. David's Ch, Killinger. They lived in Up. Paxton Twp in 1796. He attended communion services with his father and then alone up to 1822. In 1800, he had 5 sons, 5 dau and lived next to Michael Schott, Jacob Schott, and Jacob Sandoe. **Ludwig and Maria Catharine (Scheessly) Shietz children (some bapt Salem Luth , David's Ref, & St. Johns, Berrysburg)** :

**Maria Elisabeth b May 12, 1781; sp Peter Shott & Elis Schorah

**John Ludwig b Feb 10, 1785; sp Christoph Schussly & Magd Schottin – 1841), m Susanna Klein b Oct 6, 1793 -

Philip (b Oct 11, 1788   sp Christian Shott & Elis Schieesle single – d c1825), m Catharine _____ (no dates). **Philip and Catharine Shietz children: Mary L (no dates); Ann Eliza (no dates – both minors when Philip died. His widow later m ____ Hiney of Harrisburg.

**Maria Magdalena b Aug 7, 1790 sp Peter Shott & Magd, m Anthony Helfrich b c1786

**Anna Maria Margaretha b Feb 3, 1792 sp Margaretha Shott

**Christina Margaretha b May 25, 1793 sp Adam & Christina Cooper, m George Botz

**Johannes b Apr 17, 1795 sp Philip Lenker

**John Frederich b Feb 2, 1799 sp Stephen Lenker, Lydia Bortz b 1803

**Susanna b Mar 15, 1801 sp John Messner Sr. & Cath

**Jacob b Aug 5, 1802, m Elizabeth Messner (Feb 29, 1806 – Oct 21, 1853)

*CHRISTINA MARGARETHA (twin b Jan 23, 1758, bapt 1st Ref Ch., Lancaster – d Sep 7, 1816, bur St. David's Cem, Killinger), Christina Margaretha m Jun 29, 1783, John Adam Cooper (Jul 1, 1759 – Nov 11, 1823, bur private Cem on his land, Up Pax Twp), a son of Abraham and Elizabeth. Rev. Reily had the funeral for Christina Margaretha, and made this note: "funeral wife of Ad. Kupper May 9, 1814." The old Cemetery record of Davids Church, Killinger states: Christiana Margaretha Kupper, dau of Ludwig and Barbara Schoot, b Jan 11, 1758, m John Adam Cooper Jul 29, 1783, lived with him   30 years, 11 months 2 days and had 4 sons and 4 dau's, d 1813." John Adam Cooper came to Lykens Valley during the Revolutionary war, and was a private in Capt. Martin Weaver's company of Upper Paxtang. He took part in the campaign in the spring of 1781 to help the settlers on the West Branch. Adam Cooper was a farmer, and known for his deer hunting. **Adam and Christina Margaretha (Shietz) Cooper children:**

**John died before father.

**Elizabeth (Apr 2, 1784 – Jul 5, 1870), m John Shoop (Sr.) (Oct 12, 1769 – d after 1850). In 1850 John and Elizabeth Shoop lived in Jackson Twp., and had Susannah Sweigard 34, a widow, Sarah 5, Samuel 2 with them.

**Christianne (   ) m Jacob Weaver

Johann George (b May 28, 1788 – Sep 25, 1840), record of death in Killiner ch states: "m Anna Maria "Linburn" maybe Lenker?, lived with her 32 years, had 2 sons and 1 dau, d sep 25, 1840 age 52 yrs, 3 mo 29 days"). **Johann George and Anna Maria (Linburn) Cooper children: ***John Adam b Aug 27, 1809, m Elizabeth _____ b c1810. The family lived on a farm in Jackson Twp in 1850. **John Adam and Elizabeth Cooper children:** Caroline b c1832; James b c1833; **Margaret** b c1838; **Priscilla** b c1840; Nancy b c1843; Catharine b c1845; Elizabeth b c1849; *****Elizabeth** b Nov 27, 1811; *****Wilhelm** b Oct 19, 1813;

Anna Margaretha b Mar 28, 1790 - Mar 24, 1871, bur Davids Cem, Killinger), m John Abraham Shorah (Feb 12, 1789 bapt Salem Luth, Killinger- Feb 11, 1849). [Note that the dates for Anna Margaretha and John Abraham have several discrepancies. However, the will of John Abraham was probated Feb 28, 1849, substantiating the date given for his death.] Margaret lived in Up Paxton in 1850, and had Hannah age 21 with her. **John Abraham and Anna Margaretha (Cooper) Shora children: ***Johann Jacob b Sep 4, 1818, m Emmeline b c1823; *****Jonas** bapt Jan 7, 1822, tombstone records: Apr 18, 1820 - Feb 3, 1902, bur Davids Cem), m Margaret ____ (Dec 5, 1816 - Oct 8, 1867); *****Adam** b May 9, 1822 - Jun 2, 1906, bur Oak Hill Cem, Mbg), m Catherine ____ (Apr 13,1821 - Nov 30, 1894); *****Catharina** b Jul 3, 1826; *****Hannah** b May 2, 1829

Anna Catharina (Oct 17, 1793 - Sep 7, 1816, b ur Davids Cem), m Sep 25, 1814 by Rev. James Ross Reily Michael Matter Jr.(Mar 29, 1791 - Feb 11, 1838). **Michael and Anna Catharina (Cooper) Matter children: ***Christoph b Jun 29, 1816;

**J. Jacob b ___ 9, 1795

John (Jun 30,1797 bapt Davids Ch – c1884),m Maria Miller (- d pre-1884). John was elected to the state legislature for the year1850.He was a farmer in Mifflin Twp. **John and Maria Cooper children:** ***Philip** b Mar 27, 1820; ***Amos** lived in Washington Twp; ***Nellie** m Eli Swab, lived in Washington Twp; ***Jemina** m Daniel Lebo, lived in Up Paxton Twp; **William** b Sep 1831, m Mary A. Martin, a dau of Samuel P. and Mary (Dubendorf) Martin; ***Mary**, m Josiah P. Miller of Washington Twp; ***Silas** lived in Up Paxton Twp; ***Amanda** m Henry Hartman of Washington Twp.

*ANNA CATHARINA** (twin b Jan 23, 1758 – d before 1822). She was bapt 1st Ref Ch, Lancaster Both sisters were confirmed at David's Aug 16, 1774. Anna Catharina m Adam Laudermilch b c1754. **Adam and Anna Catharina (Shietz) Laudermilch children (some bapt Fetterhoff ch):**
John Adam (Jan 6, 1787 – Jul 8, 1841, bur Fetterhoff Cem), m Mary Magdalena (Apr 9, 1796 – May 5, 1863), **had these children(bapt Fetterhoff Ch)**;***Jacob** b Mar 21,1816;***Catharine** b Oct 22,1817;***Maria** b Aug 15, 1819;***Andreas** b Oc t 6,1821, m Lucy Ann ___ b 1820;***Adam** b Mar 6, 1824; ***Margaretha** b May 12, 1832; Sara Christina b Jun 10 1832;
children: ***Catharina** b Oct 22, 1817; ***Maria** b Aug 15, 1819; ***Margaret** b May 12, 1832; ***Elspy** b Jul 18, 1834, m Henry Grimm Feb 2, 1854;
John b May 6, 1788, m Elizabeth ___, **had these children (bapt Fetterhoff Ceh)**;***Catherine** b Nov 10, 1811;***Adam** (Oct 29, 1813 – Jan 9, 1843, bur Bowermwn Cem, Enterline);***Elisabeth** b Jan 28, 1816; ***Johannes** b 1818; ***Joseph** b Aug 18, 1820; ***Maria** b Oct 22, 1823; **Antoni**a (Nov 27, 1826 – 1898, bur St. Jacob's Cem, Waynesville), m Esther ___ (1828 –1876), lived in Jefferson Twp.
John Jacob (Dec 11, 1791 – Nov 3, 1864, bur Fetterhoff Cem), m Christina _____ (Mar 20, 1801 – Dec 10, 1875), **had these children (bap Fetterhoff Ch)**; ***Jacob** b Mar 27, 1820;***Louisa** b Nov 26, 1821; *** Susanna** (May 10 , 1824 – Feb 24, 1856, bur Fetterhoff Cem), m Samuel Fetterhoff (Feb 26, 1821 –Feb 26, 1866); ***Jacob Michael** (Aug 10, 1829- Sep 17, 1890), m Nellie (Aug 21, 1821 – Jan 1, 1915); ***Sara Christina** (Jun 10, 1832 – Oct 7, 1869, but Fetterhoff Cem), m Adam Rudisill.
Andreas b Oct 6, 1821, m Lucy Ann ___ b c1820

*ANNA MARIA** (b Nov 16, 1760, bapt Trinity Luth, Lanc – d Apr 13, 1818). She was confirmed at Davids Ch in Killinger Jul 1775, m Sep 1, 1772 John Peter Schweigart (Apr 3, 1754, bapt 1st Ref ch, Lanc – Jul 13, 1833), a son of John Peter and Christina Schweigart of Upper Paxton Twp. Peters death is recorded in Davids ch, mentions that they married in 1772, had 7 ch, 4 sons, 3 dau, and that he was a widower for 15 years and 3 months. **John Peter and Anna Maria (Shietz) Schweigart children:**
Adam (Feb 22, 1784 – Nov 21, 1849, bur St. Jacobs (Millers) Cem, Jacksonville, Dau Co), he was a vet of the War of 1812, m Elizabeth Warfel (Oct 7, 1788 – Oct 7, 1852), a dau of Henry and Christian (Stonebreaker) Warfel. **Adam and Elizabeth (Warfel) Schweigart children (Bapt Fetterhoff Ch):*****Christina** b Nov 11, 1806; ***Johannes** b Jan 8, 1810; ***Jonas** (Jan 30, 1813 -   ), m Elizabeth ___ b c1815; ***Susanna** b Jan 12, 1815; ***Regina** b Sep 27, 1816; ***Barbara** b Apr 25, 1818; ***Philip** b Sep 11, 1822, m Mary ___ b 1830; ***Catharina** b Feb 22, 1827; ***Solomon** b Aug 25, 1828; ***Johannes** b Jun 21, 1830; ***George** b Feb 18, 1832
John (Feb 20, 1786 – Aug 26, 1832, bur Millers Cem), m Elizabeth Sheesley (Jun 16, 1792 – Oct 30, 1849), a dau of Christoph & Catharina Sheesley
Ludwig (Nov 19, 1782 – Aug 26, 1854), m Regina   (Oct 18, 1784 – Mar 11, 1849)
Margaret (May 25, 1789 – Apr 20, 1865), m John Warfel (Apr 15, 1785 – Nov – 9, 1874)
Anna Barbara b Dec 16, 1792 bapt Fetterhoff Ch
Elizabeth b Dec 16, 1792
Johann Peter b Jun 26, 1795 bapt Fetterhoff Ch – Dec 29, 1855), m Eve Metz (Nov 6, 1760 – Apr 13, 1818), they lived in Jefferson Twp in 1850. **Peter and Eve (Metz) Schweigart children:** ***Joseph** b c1827; ***Catherine** b c1829; ***Elizabeth** b c1831; ***Susan** b c1833; ***John** b c1836.
*MARIA MAGDALENA** (b Nov 16, 1761 –1787 – shortly before her father), m Rev. Samuel Dubendorff (b Oct 21, 1721 Stettin, Ger – d Jan 1799), a son of Samuel and Elizabeth (Wetstein) Dubendorf. The mortgage book D-492 mentions that Mary, deceased dau of Ludwig Shott was married to Rev. Samuel Dubendorff.

Rev. Dubendorf came to America and in 1781 accepted a call to St. David's Church in Lykens Valley (Killinger). Shortly after he arrived here in this area, he wrote to the Philadelphia COETUS, telling them of his environment. He complained of the poverty of his congregation, which could not give him the necessary support. (They gave him articles of food, but not a cent of money). He also spoke of the danger of entirely perishing, since his life was in great danger because of the Indians. Rev. Dubendorf was devoted to the work of his ministry, was a beloved pastor and continued to preach in this area for many years. He took up thirty acres of land which he sold in 1798. Rev. Samuel Dubendorf is mentioned in official documents as the husband of Mary Schott. He also received a share of money on behalf of Mary, his deceased wife, from the estate of Ludwig Schott. They apparently did not have children.

*PETER (1762 – 1833, Halifax), m Margaret Magdalena Fritz (Apr 2, 1769 – Aug 24, 1855, Erie, Pa.). Peter attended Salem Luth 1791 –17 93). Peter and Magdalena later attended Fetterhoff church. **Peter and Margaret Magdalena (Fritz) Sheitz children (some bapt Salem Luth, Killinger):**
**Anna Catherina b Jan 4, 1790 bapt Salem Luth
**Maria Elisabeth b Jun 30, 1792, m Wilhelm Bowerman (c1784 – 1811)
**Johann Wendel b Feb 15, 1794
Magdalena (Feb 28, 1798 – Aug 30, 1858, in Summit, Erie, Pa.), m Jacob Hassler. **Jacob and Magdalena (Sheitz) Hassler children (bapt Fetterhoff Ch): *****Anna Elis** b Nov 7, 1823; *****Susanna** b Jul 1, 1825;
Peter (Aug 10,1802 – c1834), m Margaret Kinsinger b c1804. **Peter and Margaret (Kinsinger) Schottt, Jr children (bapt Fetterhoff Ch, Rife):
***Heinrich b Apr 20, 1829
***Catharine twin b Sep 5, 1830; **Anna Elisabeth** twin b Sep 5, 1830
Philip b Oct 21, 1805, m Susanna ____ (no dates). **Philip and Susanna Schott children (bapt Fetterhoff Ch): *****Polly** b Oct 3, 1819; *****Susanna** (Oct 4, 1822 – Mar 18, 1904), m Samuel Keiter (Nov 8, 1819 – Sep 2, 1898, bur Fetterhoff Cem. He was a Civ War Vet.; *****Jonas** b Jan 21, 1823; *****Ludwig** b Dec 28, 1830;
**Anna Maria b Dec 18, 1808
**Christian b Mar 10,1812 bapt Fetterhoff Ch

*MARGARET (b c1767 -   ) conf. Davids Ch, Killinger in 1782, age 15., m Edward Freeman. When her brother Christian died in 1822, the family did not know where she was.
*JOHN CHRISTIAN (Mar 21, 1772 – Feb 18, 1822, bur Hill Church Cem, Halifax), was a minor child in 1787, communed at Salem Luth 1793. He m Anna Maria Baker (1780 – 18847).
*PHILIP (May 5, 1775 bapt Salem Luth – Feb 1823), m Catharine Elizabeth Fritz b Sep 2, 1776, lived in Middle Paxton Twp in 1796. Communed at Salem Luth 1790 – 1793. Served in war of 1812. **Philip and Elizabeth (Fritz) Shietz children (some bapt Fetterhoffs Ch):**
**Elisabeth (Jan 12, 1796 – May 15, 1880, bur Zion Cem, Rife), m Michael Deibler (   ).
**John Wilhelm b Nov 2, 1798
**Joseph b Feb 28, 1803
**Catharine b Feb 17, 1807,
**John b Aug 18, 1809
**Christian (b & d 1812, bur Fetterhoffs Cem)

The following two Sheetz, etc families have not been identified.

Ludwig Sheetz (c1749 - d Apr 24,1823) m Anna Eliz Hoffman (Sep 4, 1757 bapt Host Ch – Apr 15, 1823), dau of John Peter and Maria Sarah (Snyder) Hoffman. **Ludwig and Anna Elizabeth (Hoffman) Sheetz children (some bapt Hoffman & St. John's Ch):**
Catharina (Mar 7, 1784 – May 28, 1858), m Aug 1802, Joseph Harmon (Sep 13, 1778 – Sep 2, 1824), moved to Tuscarawas County, Ohio by 1818.
Susannah (Dec 24, 1787 – Mar 20, 1871, bur Hoffman Cem) , m Jul 27, 1806 Johannes Riegel (Sep 16, 1772 – Jun 14, 1838, bur Hoffman Cem), a son of Andreas and Anna Catharine (Hoffman) Riegel)
Johannes b Mar 13, 1791 m Elizabeth _____ , later moved to New Philadelphia, Ohio.
Elizabeth b Jul 22, 1793

Anna Maria b Aug 17, 1795 m Christian Yergas (Apr 8, 1791 – Apr 14, 1856, bur Simeon Cem). **Christian and Anna Maria (Schietz) Yergas children (bapt Hoffman Ch):** Lydia; John b May 9, 1815; Joseph b Sep 1, 18186; Anna Maria b Nov 24, 1817; Joseph b Apr 8, 1821.
Possibly Ludwig who m Mary Catheirne Sheesley, a dau of John Sheesley (m before 1782)

George Sheetz Schitz (no dates) m Maria _____ (Jan 30, 1778 - Jun 3, 1848, bur Bowerman Cem). **George and Maria had these children:**

Jacob b Mar 20 , 1810
Samuel (Feb 5, 1814 – Feb 11, 1848, bur Fetterhoff Cem), m Catherine _____ b c 1820.. In 1850, widow Catherine lived in Jackson Twp. with four children: **Samuel and Catherine Schietz children:**
John; William b Sep 2, 1839; **Elizabeth** (1841 – Apr 1921), m Henry E. Welker (1835 – 1886, bur Bowerman Cem), a son of Jacob & Elizabeth (Seal) Welker; **Angeline** b c1841; **Harriet** b Feb 28, 1843; **Peter** b Dec 14, 1844, m Mary A.Wise Aug 22, 1867 by Rev Bressler, Jackson Twp. **Peter and Mary (Wise) Schietz children:** Samuel L b Feb 4, 1868, Buela Salome b Oct 21, 1869, Jersey or Tursey Delphen b Apr 5, 1871, Curney Agnes b Feb 4, 1874 died, Bertha Jane b Jan 13, 1875, Peter Samuel b Mar 5, 1877 dead, Catharine Eliz b Feb 20, 1880, Elsie Irene b May 15, 1882, Wonneida C b May 14, 1884, Gurney b May 14, 1886, Jacob b May 27, 1887 dead, Mary Edna b Apr 16, 1892, Virgin Lulla b May 21, 1895. They lived in Fisherville. He d Mar 14, 1929 **James** b Sep 8, 1846 bapt Fetterhoff Ch; **Samuel** b c1848.]

By several transactions, some of the land that John Riegel and John Matter had purchased from Ludwig Shietz and others, became the property of Peter Battieger. One such transaction took place in March 1833. He accumulated a total of 133 acres. Peter Batteiger died in 1837, but before his death, he appointed his eldest son Joseph Batteiger and Jospeh Miller, his executors. His son Joseph petitioned orphans court to appraise the property, and divide it, so that each of the children would get a share. It was appraised, but the twelve men chosen to divide it, could not part it in a way that would be fair. Instead they divided it into two tracts. One tract contained fifty-seven acres, ninety-three perches, the other contained seventy-five acres, seventy-six perches. Joseph, eldest son, chose to take the plantation of fifty-seven acres, ninety-three perches. On April 17, 1835, before Peter Batteiger died, he had conveyed a separate parcel of three acres with appurtenances to his son Joseph, stipulating that Joseph would pay a dower to Peter and Margaret Batteiger. Now he was to pay a share to each of his brothers and sisters, in return for this tract. On March 1, 1838, Joseph and Esther Batteiger conveyed the two tracts, fifty-seven acres, ninety-eight perches, and three acres (total of sixty acres, ninety-three perches) with appurtenances to John Matter, a tailor.

[About 1825, John Matter had purchased another plantation with a house and 33 acres of land. It was located on the northwest side of the road, and was in recent years owned by John Harris. See information on that property. The 1875 map shows the farm north of the highway as belonging to John Matter, and containing 84 acres, not 57 acres. The 33 acres is not noted, suggesting that for tax purposes both plantations were combined.]

John Matter continued to own both farms for many years. In 1846 David Kissinger was a tenant on this property, John and family lived on the other one. In 1849 the real-estate on both farms was described as two-story log houses and log barns. In 1828, John Matter had thirty two acres of land with a wooden house, and he was a tailor. In 1847, John Matter had two parcels of land, one a thirty acre seated tract, the other a fifty-three acre seated tract. He lived on the smaller tract, and had David Kissinger as a tenant on the other acreage. In 1849 the tax record describes the thirty acres as having a two-story log house and log barn. The fifty-three acres also had a two-story log house and log barn (situated on the south side of the road Gratz to Berrysburg.)

By 1858, the land was treated as one parcel, and John Matter, a farmer, was the occupant. A two-story log house and log barn continued to be on the land. John Matter lived on this property until 1868, when the tax assessor listed the property as the John Matter Estate, with eighty-three seated acres. It remained his until 1883. John Matter died in 1881. His wealth and land was distributed among his descendants. The 54 acre farm was conveyed to one of the heirs, Lavina Kissinger and her husband David Kissinger on October 16, 1883. Several years later on June 29, 1889, Lavina and David Kissinger sold the same acreage to Benjamin Romberger. After Benjamin Romberger died, his heirs conveyed the farm to his son Nathan Romberger on Sepember 23, 1905.

August 15, 1916 Jacob D. Riegel and Edna D bought the land from the heirs of Nathan Romberger. The widow Mary E. later married William Bohner, but she died March 6, 1923, and a dower left in this tract was paid to the heirs. This land bordered the south side of the road from Gratz to Berrysburg.

About 1924, Jacob Riegel opened a radio shop in this house. Radios were not very common and "Jake" was the very first merchant to sell radios in this area. In those days prize fights were very popular events, and on scheduled meets, friends would be invited to the Riegel home to listen to the meet. The living room would be wall to wall people, and sometimes seating space would extend up the stairs. In those days only one person could listen by way of the ear phones. So, some of the people took turns listening, and informed the people of the score.

On December 14, 1925, Jacob D. Riegel sold fifty four acres seventy six perches of land and this house to Harvey F. and Lottie Hoover. While the Hoover's owned the property, they had a very large peach orchard planted on the west side of the house. They also raised chickens. Mrs. Hoover liked to have her surroundings scrupulously clean. She had a separate drain and spigots installed in her kitchen so that when the family members came in from the barn they would have a place to wash their hands, other than her kitchen sink.

Severe, damaging thunderstorms were prevalent in this area during the 1930's. One day while the Hoovers lived here, a very severe storm came through. Lottie Hoover was standing outside near the house, when a bolt of lightning streaked down the side of her head knocking her unconscious. Her family believed that if they would lay her down flat on the ground she would become conscious. It worked, and she recovered. The date of this incident is not known but it may have been in June 1936, when Hoffman Church steeple was damaged, and Samuel Billow lost two horses that were stuck by lightning.

The Hoovers later decided to move to Millersburg. On January 25, 1956, Harvey and Lottie Hoover sold this fifty-four acre tract of land to Richard and Lillian Leitzel of Upper Mahantongo Township, Schuylkill Co. The Hoovers' were not happy living in town, so they moved back and purchased the house on the southeast side of the road. (More information with that house).

When he purchased this fifty-four acre tract, Richard Leitzel rented the old house to tenants. Ruth and Palmer Dreher were his tenants beginning about 1970. After Richard died, the land was conveyed to Paul and Peggy Leitzel. The new owners gave the Drehers the opportunity to purchase a little more than an acre of ground and the old house. It was sold June 27, 1984 to Palmer G. Dreher. This is a very old house with logs ranging up to three feet thick. It was difficult to install plumbing and wiring because of the thick walls. It originally did not have a basement. The Dreher's have made this a very attractive home, and have kept the colonial look. Ruth is now the owner, and she is manager of the Deli at the Crossroads Auction on a Friday night. Her husband was killed in a motorcycle accident.

Shortly after purchasing the fifty-four acres Paul and Peggy Leitzel had a new ranch style house built on the eastern section of the land. The Leitzel's have since conveyed this very attractive property to Doris Shade

Home of Doris Shade

THE POTTEIGER/PFFATTEICHER/ BATTEIGHER FAMILY
(Much of the research was done by deceased member 's Sidney & Kathleen Amick Temple & shared with us years ago.)

[The **POTTEIGER FAMILY** has been traced to Breslau, Germany as early as 1350. Several later generations of the family resided in Spock and Blankenloch, Germany. While living in those areas, the family engaged in tavern keeping, and were bakers or butchers. A brother and sister, [children of Johan Zacharias (1671 – 1719) andAnna Susanna *Wolff) Pfatteicher (1667 – 1755)] were the first immigrants to America. They were: **Anna Susanna Pfatticher** b Dec 23, 1709 and her husband Johann Conrad Ernst (1706 – 1789), and **JOHN MARTIN PFATTEICHER** (Aug 21, 1701 - Apr 23, 1761, bur Daniel's Cem, Robesonia, Berks Co.), who settled in Mt. Pleasant, Tulpehocken Twp, Berks County. John Martin m Feb 13, 1725 **Anna Barbara Suess** (Dec 16, 1702 - Apr 25, 1761), in Baden, Durlach, Germany. She was a dau of Johann Jacob Suess and Anna Catharine Fetzner. John Martin and Anna Barbara came to America together from the village of Spock (located on the Rhine River, in what had been in recent years West Germany) aboard the "Billender Towshend," and landed in America on Oct 5, 1735. John Martin Potteiger and others established the church at St. Daniel's, near Robesonia, he helped to lay out the cemetery, and was the first man buried in it. **John Martin and Anna Barbara (Suess) Potteiger had eight children (only four of them survived their parents and they are listed below):**
* <u>MARTIN</u> (b Sep 24, 1725 in Germany – d Nov 20, 1791, Berks Co), m Catherine ____. **Martin And Catherine (___) Potteiger children**:
****MARIA ELISABETH** (no dates) m Jan 3, 1775 Jacob Gerhardt (no dates) a son of Fridrich Gerhardt of Heidelberg Twp.
****MARIA CATHERINA** (no dates)
****MARIA EVA ROSINA** (Mar 30, 1754 – Aug 6, 1802), m 1st Johannes Bickel, a son of Tobias Bickel. m 2nd Philip Fuchs;
****MARTIN** (b Dec 30, 1770 Heidelberg Twp, Berks Co – d May 1, 1811, bur St. Daniels Ch), m Dec 27, 1791 Catherine Fuchs (Sep 10, 1770 – Dec 30, 1836), a dau of Philip and Anna Elisabeth (Lerch) Fuchs);

*<u>ADAM</u> b Nov 27, 1727, in Germany – d Mar 24,1807, Berks Co), m Maria Sibilla Schauer (_____). **Adam & Maria Sibilla (Schauer) Patteiger probably had these children**: ADAM (no dates), m _____, had a son **John Adam** (no dates), m Dec 29, 1778 Maria Barbara Linck, a dau of John Philip Linck.
*<u>MARIA</u> CATARINA (twin) b Jan 25, 1742, bapt Tulpehocken, m May 16, 1762 John Thomas Filbert;
* <u>CASPER</u> (twin) b Jan 25, 1742 Heidelberg Twp., Berks Co, m Maria Salome Boyer b Nov 2, 1754, a dau of Johann Henrich Boyer (b Feb 15, 1708 in Palatinte, Germany - d 1757 in Tulpehocken, Berks Co), and his wife Maria Salome Suess. Casper Batteiger served in the Berks County Malitia during the Revolutionary War, with Capt John Sheafer. **Casper and Salome (Boyer) Patteiger known children (some bapt Christ Luth, Stouchsburg , some Altalaha Luth, Rehrersburg):**
****ELISABETH** b Oct 24, 1769 to Casper and Salome Badeucher, bapt Trinity Luth Ch, Reading – not sure this must be a first wife or another Casper.)
****PETER** (Feb 16, 1783 - Jun 6, 1837, bur Hoffman Cem), m in 1801 to Anna Margaretha "Rebecca" Hoppel (Mar 2, 1778 - Dec 25, 1855), a dau of Johannes and Margaretha Hoppel. **Peter & Margaretha (Hoppel) Potteiger children:**
*****Joseph** (b May 4,1805 – Jul 17, 1888) m in 1838 to Esther Kissinger. He was a blacksmith;
*****Henry** (May 4, 1809 - Jan 24, 1865, bur Killinger Cem), m Sep 13, 1829 Maria Elizabeth Bonawitz (Jan 1, 1809 - Apr 14 or 21, 1898), a dau of George and Maria Catherine (Koppenhaver) Bonawitz. They lived on a farm in Upper Paxton Twp in 1850 and 1860. Lida Hoke lived with them in 1860, listed as 23 and a domestic. **Henry and Maria Elizabeth (Bonawitz) Batteiger had 13 children, 6 died before their mother (some bapt St. Johns Hill or Hoffman Ch):**
Emanuel (Aug 21, 1828 - Jun 26, 1838, bur Hoffman Cem;
 Sophia b Oct 18, 1830, m Daniel Batteiger b c1829. **Daniel and Sophia (Potteiger) Potteiger children:**Daniel David b Nov 1, 1854, bapt st. John's "Hill" Ch;
Daniel b Sep 21, 1832
Susanna (b Nov 21,1836 – Jun 6, 1912, bur David's Cem), m Joseph Bentz who d before 1880. Susan lived with the John A. Keefer family in Up Pax Twp in 1880 and was listed as a domestic servant;

John Henry (Aug 21, 1841 – May 1, 1917, bur Maple Grove Cem, E'ville, m Nov 22, 1863 Rachel Fry (Mar 4, 1839 – Jul 28, 1921), had a son William Harrison b Mar 2, 1869 bapt Hoover Ch, Rife; Mary Etta b Dec 14, 1866 bapt Hoovers ch
James b c1846;
George b c1848;
W. Preston b Sep 25, 1850, m Caroline b c1852, **had these children**: Nora T. b c1871; Emma P b c1872; William F. b c1874; Harry N b c1875; Mary E b c1877; Carrie S. b c1880. In 1880 they lived in Up Paxton Twp and Elizabeth age 71, mentioned as mother, lived with them;
Mary Etta b Dec 14, 1866

***Margaret Rebecca "Peggy"**(Mar 6,1811 – Jan 14,1894, died of La Grippe, bur Hoffman Cem), m Mar 18, 1834 John Weaver (1810 – 1875), a son of Peter and Catherine (Peiffer) Weaver. [More information with Weaver genealogy.]
***Daniel Bottieger** (Jul 2, 1813 - Nov 8, 1889 bur Salem Luth Cem, E'ville, m c1835 Nancy Anna Riegel (Apr 17,1814 L.T.- Feb 28, 1893), a dau of John and Susannah (Sheetz) Riegel, had 5 sons 5 dau - 3son, 1 dau Elizabeth preceded in death.. She died of old age (record in Simeon Parish). They lived in Up. Paxton Twp in 1850. In 1880 they lived in Jackson Twp., and their daughter Mary Wiest and her two children Charles and Harry lived with them.**Daniel and Nancy Anna (Riegel) Bottieger children**: Emaline b Jul 22, 1836; J.Henry (Aug 22, 1841 – Jan 5, 1917, bur Maple Grove), m Rachel or Mary Fry (Mar 4, 1839 – Jul 28, 1921), moved to Pottstown area; Peter (b c1844 Lykens Valley – d Mar 31, 1916 in Polo, Ill.). He left this area at the age of seventeen, but came back to visit frequently. He was a Civil War veteran, was married and had 6 children.
John (May 15, 1845 – Nov 15, 1872, bur Maple Grove Cem, E'ville), m Christiana ____ (Feb 7, 1846 – Sep 9, 1911) ; Rebecca (May 1 5, 1847 – Jun 10, 1913, bur Fairview Cem, Enders), m Theodore B. Kitzmiller (Oct 3, 1852 – Jun 18, 1893); Clara (no dates) m ___ Harper of Elizabethville; _____ m Wesley Witmer of Lykens; _____ m John F. Helt, lived in Jacksonville; Isabelle m Daniel K. Smith of Wiconisco; Mary Amelia (b Mar 31, 1852 – d May 18, 1907, bur Maple Grove Cem), m 1st Jacob Wiest (b ___ d prc 1892), **had three children** . After Jacob Wiest died, Mary Amelia m in March 1892 to Alfred Hoke ( ). Mary lived on a farm near Berrysburg for many years, but later moved back to her childhood home in Jackson Township, just before her death;
***John** (Mar 15, 1816 – Nov 15, 1872, bur Salem Luth Cem, E'ville)
***Peter** b 1817, lived in Schuylkill County.
***Anna** b c1825
***Nancy or Elizabeth** c1829

MARIA SALOME b Dec 27, 1784, m May 25, 1809 Adam Meyer, a son of Heinrich Meyer in Salem Luth Ch, Killinger.
JOHN JACOB (Jan 7, 1787 – Oct 9, 1829, bur Wenrich Cem, Linglestown, Dau Co) m Anna Maria ___ (Oct 23, 1793 – Mar 1, 1868). **John Jacob and Anna Maria children**: ***Jacob (Jun 20 , 1811 – Nov 3, 1853, bur Wenrich Cem), m Elizabeth Feeser (Feb 16, 1811 – Jun 25, 1868); ***Margaret b Nov 5, 1813; ***Jonathan (Aug 30, 1821 – 1904, bur Wenrich Cem), m Hannah ____ (1833 – 1910); ***Maria Anna b Jul 20, 1824;

ELIZABETH BOTTEIGER (b Dec 18, 1788 Stouchberg – d Jun 15, 1865, bur Davids, Hebe Cem, Northld Co), m Peter Troutman (Jul 13, 1790 - Feb 23, 1854, Lykens Twp), a son of Henry and Regina (Tschopp) Troutman. **Peter and Elizabeth (Batteiger) Troutman children**: ***Isaiah (Dec 25, 1812 - May 7, 1861), m c1813 Regina Schneider, lived near Ashland, Sch Co; ***Lydia b Apr 16, 1815, m Jacob Williard, moved to Ogle Co, Illinois; ***Daniel (Oct 23, 1817 - Nov 14, 1880, murdered by robbers in his home, bur Hebe Cem), m Nov 14, 1839 to Elizabeth Bush (b Jul 6, 1822 – d Dec 24, 1915); ***Elias B. (Oct 30, 1819 - Dec 30, 1884, bur Hebe Cem) m Nov 17, 1839 Mary Ruppenthal (Sep 26, 1819 - Nov 17, 1893, Lykens Twp); ***James B. (Aug 8, 1821 - Sep 26, 1894, in Gratz, bur Hebe Cem), m Sarah Ann Leitzel (May 31, 1829 - Apr 20, 1878); ***Salome b Nov 1823, m Jan 1, 1842, Isaac Mattis; ***Elizabeth b Nov 22, 1825 - Jul 29, 1881, killed by lightning, bur Klinger Cem), m Jacob K. Wiest Jun 23, 1826 - Oct 23, 1878), a son of Samuel Wiest; ***Rebecca (May 20, 1829 - Dec 10, 1909, d in Mt. Carmel, bur Klingerstown), m Nov 18, 1852, George

Shadle b Oct 12, 1827 – d Mar 8, 1899, bur Hebe); ***Anna** (May 14, 1833 - Mar 14, 1877, Jordan Twp), m Samuel Strohecker (b Jul 6, 1838 – Mar 3, 1892);
**EVA ROSINA b Nov 8, 1791
**M. MAGDALENA b May 27, 1794

**DANIEL (Apr 2, 1798 or Apr 12, 1799 –c1852?), m Jun 14, 1818, Juliana Yeakley (Jun 15, 1795 -), a dau of Conrad and Catherine (Hain) Yeakley of Mahanoy Twp, Northld Co.
[Conrad Yeakley (b Jun 4, 1768 Berks Co - d Dec 1804, Northld Co.), m Catharine Hain (Apr 10, 1774 - Oct 23, 1854, bur Davids Ch, Hebe, Northld Co.) Conrad Yeakley was operating a distillery in which an explosion occurred and caught fire, burning him severely, causing his death. Catherine, his widow, later married Henry Troutman (1764 - 1833). Her minor children lived with Catherine and her new husband.] Daniel and Juliana lived on an eighty-three acre farm in Low Mahanoy Twp, Northld. County in 1828. He was listed as a stone mason. They later moved to Jackson Twp, Dauphin Co. **Daniel and Juliana (Yeakley) Potteiger had these children (as recorded in the family Bible):**
***ELISABETH (Mar 30, 1819 bapt Hoffman Ch -Nov 24, 1875, bur Stone Valley Cem, Low Mahanoy Twp, Northld Co), m Simon Hepner (b Nov 8, 1820 - d Jan 3, 1901,Marshalltown, Iowa), a son of Peter Hepner (Feb 1,1793 - Dec 11,1856, bur Stone Valley Cem) and his wife Magdalena ( ) Hepner (Aug 14, 1795 - Jan 24, 1859). **Simon and Elizabeth (Potteiger) Hepner had these children (bapt Stone Valley Ch): Emanuel** (Jun 6, 1844 - Mar 27, 1921), m Oct 18, 1870 in Brookville, Ill, Catharine R. Moyer (b Apr 10, 1849, Gratz - d Mar 13, 1927). Her parents later moved to Forreston, Ill, some of the Hepner family (including his father) moved to Marshalltown, Iowa; **Delilah** b Mar 6, 1846, m Solomon Tschupp; **Cornelius** b Feb 28, 1850 - Nov 19, 1925), m Sarah Wert (1853 - Jul 20, 1922); **Sarah** (Nov 19, 1853 bapt Stone Valley - Jul 18, 1897), m Aaron Hassinger b Dec 23, 1859;**Louisa** (May 13, 1856 -Mar 22, 1863, bur Stone Valley Cem); **Lena** (Jan 6,1858 - Feb 8, 1937), m David Swab (1854 - 1919); **Emma** m Frank Myers; **Isreal** (Nov 16, 1860 - May 13, 1872, bur Stone Valley Cem); **Katie** (no dates), single, moved to Marshalltown, Iowa where she died. After Elizabeth (Potteiger) Hepner died, Simon Hepner married Elizabeth Salada (Faust, Clark), and moved to Gratz. After his second wife Elizabeth Salada Faust Clark died, he moved to Marshalltown, Iowa to be with his son Emanuel.
***VERONICA b Jan 4, 1820, bapt St. Johns, Berrysburg;
***ADAM (b c1821 – d ___),) m Sarah Koppenheffer b Mar 17, 1817, dau of Michael & Catharaine (Garrett) Koppenhaver. They lived in Mifflin Twp in 1850, and he was a shoemaker.Later lived in Williamstown - **Adam and Sarah (Koppenheffer) Potteiger had nine children: Elisabeth** b c1839; **Peter** b c1841, m Mary Klinger b (Aug 11, 1827 – Oct 20, 1897, bur Klinger Cem alone), a dau of John George and Eva Catherine (Smeltz) Klinger; **Louisa** b c1842; **John** b May 20, 1842 – d Apr 14, 1907, bur Fairview Cem, Wmstown), was a coal miner, and served in the Civil war in many battles. He m 1st Matilda ___ , m 2nd Mary E. ___; **Leah Jane** b c1845; **Lazarus** b c1847; **Elias** b c1849.
**GEORGE b Apr 2, 1823;
***SUSANNA b Jun 16, 1826, bapt Stone Valley;
*** ISAAC b Jul 21, 1828;
*** CATHARINA b Nov 6, 1831;
*** JAMES b Mar 5, 1834, probably moved to Snyder Co. by 1880.
***JONATHAN (Nov 6, 1837

The following ancestors have not been identified.

JOHN BOTTEIGER (b c1775 -   ), m Anna Barbara Deibler (Jul 3, 1776 – ____), a dau of Mathias and Barbara Deibler. They lived in Up Paxton Twp in 1810 and had two sons and two daughters. We haven't identified this John. **They had these known children:**
Elisabeth b Nov 10, 1805, bapt Salem Luth, Killinger
Johannes b c1806, bapt Salem, but no date
Barbara b May 11, 1813 Up Pax – Feb 13, 1891 of old age) m June 12, 1836 John Washington Lebo (Jul 16, 1814 – Jun 12, 1889) 7 ch 5 son 2 dau, husband deceased. [Simeon Parish record]. They lived in Mifflin Twp in 1850. Hugh Baddicher age 30 lived with them. **John Washington and Barbara (Botteiger) Lebo children:**

Mary Ann b c1836; Sarah Ann b c1839; Daniel M. b c1842; Jeremiah (1843-1912), m Emaline Bressler (1847 – 1928); Emanuel (1846 – 1926), m Sarah E. Martz; Cornelius b c1850, m Elizabeth Snodgrass; Jonatha (Mar 26, 1851 – 1911), m Susanna Hassinger (1857 – 1928).
Hugh b c1816 not proved – he lived in Mifflin Twp in 1860 and was a broom maker.
Margaret Potteiger confirmed in Salem Church 1819 may be their daughter.
William b Sep 24, 1819, bapt Fetterhoff Ch.

Samuel Potteiger (1841 - d 1910, bur Halifax Meth Cem), 1st Lavina ___(1839 – 1872), 2nd m Mary Jane Boyer (1848 - 1925,) a dau of Joseph and Mary L. Lyter Boyer. Samuel was a carpenter.and a Civil War Vet. **Samuel and Mary Jane (Boyer) Potteicher had these known children**: Harry W. b c1872; Warren B. b c1875; William E b c1878; John Franklin b 1880, m Sep 23, 1899 Merril Mary Brubaker, lived in Millersburg..

From Fetterolfs - **Jonathan Potteiger** (Dec 2, 1839 - Dec 22, 1918 m Mary _____ (1848 - Feb 3, 1913). They lived in Halifax Twp in 1880. **Jonathan and Mary Potteiger had these children**; Susan E b c1867; Isaiah P b c1873; Jane C b c1875; Jacob M b c1877; John F. b 1880. All children d young bur with parents.

THE MATTER FAMILY

The **MATTER** family is traced to **Hans Matter** b c1614 in Alsace Lorraine, Germany /France - d Feb 20, 1681 in Alsace Lorraine. He married about 1642 Catherina ___ b 1616 in Alsace, Lorraine - d Mar 6, 1698. The people who settled in Dauphin County descend from Hans Matter by this line: **Diebold Matter** (b c1648 - Feb 18, 1728, Alsace), m Aug 12, 1679 in Eckendorf, Margaretha Kueffer (b c1656 - d Nov 10, 1726). **Johannes Matter** (Mar 11, 1692 - May 6, 1736, Alsace Lorraine), m Feb 28, 1719 to Christina Keiser (Mar 7, 1697 - Oct 13, 1741)

[**JOHN MATTER** , The earliest known **immigrant ancestor** of the Matter family of Dauphin County arrived in the port of Philadelphia on the ship **Edinburgh**, on September 16, 1751. Several other members of the Matter family came with him. The family originated in Switzerland, but as religious refugees, they moved to France, and later migrated to Germany. At least some of the family members moved inland, and settled in Earl Township, Lancaster County soon after they arrived in America. They were listed on the tax record for that area in 1756. They attended Trinity Evangelical Lutheran Church in Lancaster, where they were recorded as having come from Altendeckendorf, Germany. Several years later, members of the Matter family migrated to Upper Paxton Township (the area which later became Washington and Mifflin Township), and were listed on the tax record of 1773. Here they became very well established, were some of the earliest members of St. John's Lutheran Church near Berrysburg.

About 1776, John Matter volunteered to serve under the command of Captain Albright Deibler, and was on active duty during the fierce Battle of Long Island. After they returned home, under the command of Captain John Hoffman, John Matter and his son John, Jr. helped to patrol the frontiers against the roving Indians and Tories.

By 1798, when the "window tax" was taken, John Matter Sr. and John Matter Jr. appeared on the list. John Matter Sr had two acres of cleared land on which a one-story, twenty-four by twenty-six foot wooden house had been erected. The house had three windows, with a total of twenty-seven small panes of glass. John Matter Jr had two acres of cleared land, having a one-story twenty-six by thirty foot house. His house had three windows with twenty-four panes of glass.

*****JOHN MATTER** (b Jan 24, 1732 in Germany - d May 22,1802, bur St. John's Luth Cem, Berrysburg), married three times. First he m Oct 24, 1758, Anna Barbara Arnold. (Marriage recorded in Trinity Evangelical Lutheran Church in Lancaster). Anna Barbara Arnold (b ____ - d c1785). After Anna Barbara (Arnold) Matter died, John m Anna Catharine ____, who died 1796, bur   St. Johns Luth Cem). John Matter m a third time in 1797 to Salome Stahlschmidt, widow of John George Stahlschmidt of Heidelberg Twp, Lebanon County.**John and Anna Barbara (Arnold) Matter children; (baptism of their first four children recorded in Trinity Evang Ch, New Holland, Earl Twp, Lancaster Co.):**

JOHANNES MATTER (Aug 17, 1759 - Jun 30, 1832, bur St. Johns Luth, Berrysburg), m Elisabeth Bergner (Apr 16, 1762 - Dec 18, 1832). John Matter and his family lived in the area known as Matterstown, in Washington and Mifflin Township. He inherited part of the land which his father owned. He served during the Revolutionary War. In 1850, Elisabeth was a widow, living with her son -in-law Christian Romberger and family in Washington Twp. **Johannes and Elisabeth (Bergner) Matter children:

*****Anna Catharine** (Aug 14, 1785 - Nov 18, 1840, bur St. Johns Luth Cem); *****Elisabeth** (b May 24, 1787 - d Nov 22, 1850), was the second wife of George Bonawitz (b Mar 22, 1774, Tulpehocken Twp - d Sep 18, 1852 of dysentery in Mifflin Twp, bur Berrysburg). George Bonawitz was a son of George and Elizabeth (Wenrich) Bonawitz who lived in the Robesonia area of Berks County. After his father died, this George purchased his fathers land and lived there briefly, working as a tailor. He moved to Berrysburg area shortly after 1800 and purchased about one hundred acres of land. George married first Maria Catharina Koppenhaver (Nov 17, 1767 - c1812), a dau of Michael and Eva Koppenhaver. **George and Maria Cath (Koppenhaver) Bonawitz known children: ****Jacob** (1796 - 1886), moved to Ohio; ******Michael** (1799 - 1883), moved to Ohio; ******John** (1801 - 1885) m 1st Salome Schoffstall (1813 -1841), 2nd Catherine Harman wid of John Messner (1805 - 1870), lived in Berrysburg; ******Daniel D** (1805 - 1886), m Mariah Jane Maurer lived in Rife, near Millersburg; ******Elizabeth** (1809 - 1898), m Henry Botteiger (1809 - 1865) bur Davids Cem, Killinger, lived in Up. Paxton Twp.;******Maria Catherine** (1811- 1892, bur Zions Cem, Lykens), m 1st Michael Radel (1807 -1864), m 2nd Jacob Witmer (1807 - 1885), near Pillow, in Northld Co., bur Stone Valley Cem. **After his first wife died, George m Elisabeth Matter, and they had these children:**

******Anna Mary** (_____ - Feb 22, 1847), m John Messner (Jun 19, 1815 – Mar 4, 1865, bur Brookville, Ill), a son of Michael & Catherine Messner. He moved to Ogle Co. Ill in 1853; **** **Susanna** (Mar 13, 1816- Aug 24, 1885, bur Stone Valley Cem, Northld Co), m Isaac Lenker (1818 – 1881), a son of Simon & Catharine (Dockey) Lenker, lived in Perry Co; ******Anna** b Apr 17, 1817, m Henry Weaver (Apr 10, 1816 – Oct 11, 1881, bur County Line Cem, Northld Co), a son of George Weaver, lived near Pillow; ******George** (Apr 6, 1818 -Aug 28, 1893, bur Enders), m Susannah Miller (Sep 12, 1816- Aug 24, 1885), moved to Ogle Twp,Ill,but later returned to Dau Co. He was a Civil War Vet. of Co A 210 Inf. Regt; ******Eva** b May 24, 1819, 2nd wife of Jacob Harman b Sep 30, 1799, lived in Crawford Co, Ohio; ******Jonas** (Jun 21, 1820 - Aug 23, 1903), m Catherine Lenker (Feb 2, 1827 - Jul 18, 1887), a dau of John Adam & Maria Magdalena (Bobb) Lenker. He purchased land from father and lived near Berrysburg; ******William** (c1820 - Feb 5, 1911) m 1848 Phoebe Ann Lower (Jul 2,1828 - Jan 16,1898), moved to Ogle Co, Il. in 1853, then to Marshall Co, Iowa where they died; ******Elias** (Jan 17,1823 - Mar 13, 1873), m 1st Mary Ann Kimes (Oct 22, 1829 - Jan 11, 1855), possibly a dau of Peter Kimes who found coal on Short Mountain in 1825, 2nd Mary Jane Felburn, lived in Perry County, then to Indiana where they died; ******Hannah** b c1828, m Daniel Messner b c1828, a son of Michael Messner, lived in Ogle Co., Ill. in 1853.; ******Mary Ann** (1829 –1904, bur Wiconisco Cem), m Peter Romberger (1826 –1906); ******Peter** b Nov 5, 1831.

*****Johannes** (Sep 30, 1788 – Jan 21, 1869, Jefferson Co., Pa.), m Eva Catherine Carmine b 1794. **Johannes & Eva Cath (Carmine) Matter children:** Elizabeth; Mary; Savina; Lydia; Anna Catharine; Amos; Isaac; Cyrus – most left this area.

*****Johan Jacob** (Feb 7, 1790 - Feb 22, 1824), m Sarah Fisher (Feb 2, 1789 - Jul 1, 1838), **had these children:** ******Joseph** (May 5, 1811- Oct 21, 1857, bur Lykens), m Anna Mary Yerges (1815- 1893), a dau of Michael Yerges. He was a shoemaker. **Joseph and Anna Mary (Yerges) Matter children:** Ann Mary b c1836; John b c1839; Henry b c1843; Jacob b c1846; William b c1848.******Henry** (Feb 18, 1818 - Nov 2, 1902), m Elisabeth DeFrehn (Aug 28, 1818 - Oct 23, 1909), **had one child:** William H. b Jan 1, 1844.

*****Johan Christian** (Jul 8,1792 - Aug 25, 1836,bur St. John's Luth Cem), m Julianna Swab (Jul 1, 1790 - Feb 18, 1875), a dau of Jacob & Anna Maria (Hetzel) Swab. He was a Vet of War of 1812; **Johan Christian and Julianna (Swab) Matter children: ****Samuel** b Nov 7, 1816; ******Jacob** Feb. 4, 1818, moved to Naporville, Ill; ******Elias** (Feb 12, 1823 - Feb 19, 1904 Jefferson Co), m Barbara Smathers (1822 - 1881), **had one child:** Barbara E. (_____ - May 1831), m Charles T. McCarty (_____ - d 1922); ******Johannes** b Oct 12, 1827 (twin); ******Jonathan** b Oct 12, 1827, this is probably the one bur in IOOF Cem Lykens (Aug 6, 1827 - Nov 3, 1897);

*****Isaac Jacob** (Sep 18, 1794 -1866, Stephenson Co., Ill), m 1st Anna Maria Umholtz (Nov 11, 1801 – Apr 24, 1825, bur St. John's Hill Cem), a dau of John & Catherine (Herman) Umholtz), had a son Moses (Dec 14, 1823

Dau Co - Jul 1898), m in Illinois Apr 24,1856 Maria Duth, had 10 children. Isaac Jacob m 2nd Hannah Lenker b May 14, 1806, a dau of Philip and Anna Margaretha (Weaver) Lenker. The family moved to Freeport area of Illinois. [From a note on an obit from Roger Kramer: Isaac Matter & family moved to Stephenson Co Ill in 1845. They traveled to the west in the way common to those times, with a team of horses and a wagon, until they reached Mt. Mahonen, Pa., where they embarked on a steamer on the Alleghaney River and went by boat on the Ohio and Mississippi Rivers to Savanna, making the rest of the way by team to Freeport.]

***Johan Philip (Apr 27, 1796 -Jan 20, 1873), bur St. Johns Luth Cem), m Anna Catharine Romberger (Oct 1, 1805 - Aug 11, 1856), a dau of Balthasar and Elisabeth Romberger. They lived In Mifflin Twp in 1850, and had Samuel Lehman age 22, shoemaker and Adam Schreffler 23, carpenter with them. **Philip and Anna Catharine (Romberger) Matter children: ****Benjamin** b Jun 7,1824, m Mary Thorg, b c1826, **they had these children:** Jonas b Feb 25, 1856, bapt St. Johns Ch, Berrysburg; m Maggie _____, b Jul 1858. Benjamin lived next to Philip Matter in 1860, and had John 11,and Philip Heller 6 with them **Jonas & Maggie children:** Harry W. b Oct 1877; John B b Jun 1879; George W b Feb 1882; Sarah A. b Jan 1892; Mary E. b Jul 1897; Katie M. b Apr 1899.

****Elisabeth b Aug 23, 1826, m probably Thomas Heller
****Angaline (Feb 11, 1828 – Mar 1, 1909, bur St. John's Hill Cem), m Adam John Schreffler (Nov 6, 1826 – Jul 10, 1896), a son of Peter & Elizabeth (Kreitzer)_ Schreffler; ****Hannah (Nov 21, 1837 - Nov 22, 1915), m James Eby (Dec 22, 1842 – Jun 12, 1819, bur Peace Cem), a son of Peter & Catharine Eby.. Hannah and James Eby were living with Philip Matter in 1860, and had two children, John 4, James 1; ****Mary b c1842, may have m Benjamin Jury b c1836, Benjamin and Mary Jury also lived with Philip Matter in 1860.;
***Susanna (Jan 26, 1798 - Mar 24, 1861, bur Sweitzer Mem Cem, Bbg), m Christian Ramberger (Jul 16, 1797 - May 30, 1874), a son of Henrich & Elizabeth (Hoffman) Romberger. [More info with Romberger genealogy.]
***Peter (Apr 4, 1801 – Aug 2, 1884), m Sarah Stell (1808 – 1880), moved to Jefferson Co, Pa.
***Maria Margaretha b Sep 14, 1803 -
***Juliana b Feb 21, 1805, m George Detweiler
***Wilhelm (Dec 8, 1809 –Apr 5, 1905 in Ill.), m 1830 Leah Troutman (Mar 31, 1814 – Mar 28, 1899), a dau of Jacob and Anna Maria (Williamson) Troutman. They moved to Illinois.

ANNA MARIA MATTER (Feb 18, 1761 Lanc Co – before 1806), m Joseph Paul (Sep 3, 1760 - Sep 1, 1844, died in Marion Co., Ohio). Joseph Paul served during the Revolutionary War, fought in the battles of Brandywine, Trenton, and Germantown, wintered in Valley Forge. He later received a pension. **Joseph and Anna Maria (Matter) Paul children (some bapt St. John's Hill Ch: ***Elisabeth b Sep 1787; ***Anna Maria (Jul 1, 1789 – Mar 18, 1866, bur St. John's Hill Cem with 2nd husband Heller), m 1st John Matter (Jul 4, 1788 – Feb 16, 1816), a son of John Michael and Anna Maria (Romberger) Matter. **John, Jr & Anna Maria (Paul) Matter children (some bapt St. John's Hill Ch):** ****Anna Maria b Oct 23, 1810; ****Elisabeth (Jul 22, 1812- post 1832), m

Christian Wirth (Oct 15, 1799 – Jul 11, 1854), a son of Johann Christian & Catharine Magd (Bretz) Wirth; ****Simon (Oct 7, 1813 – Jun 3, 1895, old age, bur St. Johns Hill Cem), m Sarah Schwab (Feb 16, 1817 – Apr 15, 1885), a dau of Jacob & Catharine (Metz) Schwab. **Simon and Sarah (Schwab) Matter children some bapt St. Johns' Hill Ceh):** Susanna (d 1838 inf); Catharine Ann (Oct 28, 1839 – Sep 11, 1892) of gravel, bur Hoffman Cem) [death recorded in Simeon parish book], m May 19, 1864 by Rev Waltz, to David Weaver (no dates), **had four children, 2 boys 2 girls.** After Catharine Ann died, David m Salome ___(Feb 6, 1845 – Aug 2, 1897, bur St. Johns Hill Cem).
John (1841 – 1863); David b c1844; Amos (Aug 16, 1845 – Jun 5, 1892 of typhoid fever) [Simeon Ch record], m Sep 3, 1865 Salome Engel b 1845. In 1880 Samuel Malick age 62, retired farmer, lived with Amos & family. Amos & Salome (Engel) Matter had 8 children, all but one died before father); Sarah b Jun 10, 1852; Elizabeth b Apr 28, 1854; Leah Jane b Aug 19, 1856; Amanda b Jul 20,1860; Ellen Elizabeth b Oct 20, 1864;
****Benjamin b May 15, 1815, m Maria Tschopp , **Benjamin and Maria (Forry) Matter children some bapt St. John's Hill Ch);** William Henry b Apr 1, 1854; Jonas b Feb 25, 1856; Lewis Milton b Feb 17, 1859;
After her husband John Matter died, Anna Maria m 2nd John Heller (Oct 28, 1779 – Aug 4, 18 47, bur St. Johns Hill Cem), a son of Isaac and Anna Catharine (Wingert) Heller. [See Heller genealogy.]

David b Apr 19, 1791; ***Maria Magdalena b Nov 31, 1796; ***Salome (Oct 4, 1799 – Aug 2, 1880, bur Hoffman Cem), m Jacob Schoffstall (Jul 16, 1799 – Oct 2, 1858), a son of Jacob & Maria Magd (Hoover) Schoffstall.[More info in Schoffstall genealogy.];Joseph b Mar 17, 1802;***Anna Catharina b Aug 4, 1806. **After his wife Anna Maria died, Joseph Paul m Missi ___ , and had these children**: ***Christina b Mar 29, 1808;***Thomas b Mar 24, 1811; ***John b Mar 27, 1814;

MICHAEL MATTER (Oct 3, 1763 - Feb 11, 1852, bur St. John's Luth Cem), m Anna Maria Romberger (Jan 12, 1770 - Feb 26, 1838, Mifflin Twp), a dau of Balthasar and Anna Maria (Trout) Romberger. Michael was the first of the Matter's to come into Lykens Valley. **Michael and Anna Maria (Romberger) Matter children:** ***Johannes (Jul 4, 1788 - Feb 16, 1816), m Anna Maria Paul (Jul 1, 1789 - Mar 18, 1866), a dau of Joseph and Anna Maria (Matter) Paul. **Johannes & Anna Maria (Paul) Matter children:** ****Anna Maria b Oct 23, 1810; ****Elisabeth b Jul 22, 1812; ****Simon Oct 7, 1813 - Jun 3, 1895, bur St. Johns's Cem), m Sarah Schwab (1819 - Apr 15, 1885); **Simon and Sarah (Schwab) Matter children:** Susanna d 1838 inf; Catharine Ann (b Oct 28, 1839 in Mifflin Twp – d Sep 11, 1892 of gravel, bur Hoffman Cem), [death recorded in Simeon parish record]. She m May 19, 1864 by Rev Waltz to David Weaver, had four children, 2 boys, 2 girls. John (1841 - 1863); David b c1844; Amos (b Aug 16,1845, Wash Twp -Jun 5, 1892 of typhoid fever), m Sep 3, 1865, Salome Engel, **had eight children, all but one died before father** [death record in Simeon parish record]; Emanuel b c1848; Maria d 1850, young; Elizabeth d 1856, young;
***Anna Maria (Jan 21, 1790 - Jan 29, 1871, bur Ebenezer EUB Cem, Halifax), m Peter Minich (Sep 17, 1785 – Sep 25, 1855), death recorded in Zion Hoover Ch, Rife), a son of George and Anna Barbara Minnich. Peter served in War of 1812. They lived in Wash Twp in 1880, Mary Ann Minnich age 12, lived with them. **Peter and Anna Maria (Matter) Minnich children:** ****Peter b Feb 19, 1808; ****Johannes b May 24, 1809, d Jun 2 32, 1894,in Stephenson Co. Il.); ****Michael (Sep 24, 1811 – Mar 10, 1891, bur Miller Cem, Jackson Twp), m Ruth Ann Kern (1812 – 1890); ****Elizabeth (Dec 29, 1813- Jun 30, 1882, bur Miller Cem), m Johannes Travitz (Jul 12, 1810 – Mar 1, 1880); ****Catherine Ann Marie (Nov 12, 1815 – Oct 28, 1893, bur Zion Hoover Cem, Rife), m in 1834 Jacob Hoover (Jan 2, 1810 – May 21, 1885); ****Sara (Dec 17, 1817 – May 10, 1890, bur St. Jacob's UM Cem, Wayne Twp), m Jacob Gipple (Jan 16, 1815 – Sep 23, 1882), a son of Christian & Johanna (Stroh) Gipple. In 1880 Jacob & Sarah lived near Loyalton. **Jacob & Sarah (Minnich) Gipple children**: Lydia b c1839 m Jacob Hassinger; Louisa b c1841; Samuel b c1848.

***Michael (b Mar 29, 1791 Mifflin Twp – d Feb 11, 1838, bur St. John's Luth Cem), m Sep 25, 1814, 1st Anna Catharine Kupper (Oct 17, 1793 - Nov 7, 1824, beside husband), a dau of John Adam & Christian Margaretha (Schott) Kupper. He m 2nd Mar 29, 1825 Margaret Rebecca Kiener (Mar 17, 1805 - May 7, 1854, bur beside husband John Harman), dau of Philip & Maria Magd Kiener. John Michael Matter's tombstone states that they had been married thirteen years, had twelve children. The last one was born after his death. Margaret Rebecca was first m to John Herman.. **Michael and first wife Anna Catharine (Kupper) Matter children:** ****David (Jun 13, 1815 - Jun 10, 1871), m Catharine Romberger (Nov 11, 1816 - Jul 17, 1889), a dau of Jacob and Sophia Romberger, The family lived in Washington Twp. in 1850, where David was a tanner. Several other tanners lived with them, Henry Snyder age 17, Isaiah Matter age 25, and Emias (?) Matter age 36. Also Sarah Matter age 30, Ann S. age 17, & Michael age 8, a son of the deceased Christopher Matter. **David and Catharine (Romberger) Matter children:** Mary Ann b c1838; Hannah b c1840; Margaretha Ann b c1842; Catharine M b c1843;

****Christian or Christopher (Jun 29, 1816 - Oct 12, 1843, bur Fetterolfs Cem), m 1838 by Rev. Hemping to Catherine Lenker (Oct 4, 1820 - Jul 16,1891, bur Old Stone Cem, E'ville), dau of Ludwig and Amelia (Dietrich) Lenker. **Christian and Catherine (Lenker) Matter children:** John L. (Feb 8, 1839 - Aug 31, 1901, bur IOOF Cem, Lykens), m Oct 31, 1865 by Rev. C. A. Fetzger in Berrysburg, to Harriet Martz,(1846- Feb 3, 1915, died of cancer, cremated in Jersey City, N.J.), a resident of Lykens. A description of her casket and funeral expenses is found in the Civil War pension record of her husband. In 1880, John & Harriet lived in Lykens Twp and had John's brother Christian Matter age 1841 with them. They also had Francis Buffington 16, and Harper Hensil 20 with them. **John and Harriet (Martz) Matter children (some bapt Zion Luth, Lykens):** *Jennie* (Oct 27, 1868 - 1940, bur Calvary Meth Cem, Wiconisco), m ____ Holmes; *Mary Edith* b Jul 23, 1873, m ____ Greismer

(___ - d before 1915), became a nurse, moved to New York; John was a Civil War Veteran , having served in Co F of the 10th Regt and Co B of the 9th Cavalry. John's father died when he was very young. John was "farmed" out to other relatives in Lykens Twp. While he was working on a farm, he was gored by a bull one day, as he was stabling the cattle. His injuries were so serious that he "carried his intestines to the house in his arms." So wrote Amos Kuntzelman who at the time was living with the nearby family of William Hawk who had a tailor shop. Kuntzelman further noted that he knew this because "the accident caused some excitement in the neighborhood." Several years later, Amos Kuntzelman opened a tailor shop in Lykens. John L. Matter later lived with the Kuntzelman family four years as an apprentice tailor, before opening his own shop in Lykens. In September 1873, John Matter was hired to make dark blue uniforms for the Gratz Coronet Band.

Michael (Apr 28, 1842 - Dec 4, 1912, bur Matters Cem, d in Highland Co, Ohio brought back for burial). Michaels father died when he was very young, and in 1850 he lived with his uncle David Matter and family in Washington Twp. Michael m Oct 3, 1865 Sarah Anne Keene (Oct 17, 1849 - Dec 7, 1907, bur Matters Cem), a dau of Joseph and Salome (Lettich) Keene. **Michael and Sarah Anne (Keene) Matter children:** *Sarah* b 1870; *Margie or Mary* b 1873; *William F. b* 1876; *Carrie J* b1878; *John M.* (Feb 28, 1881 – Nov 1, 1959, bur E'ville Cem), m Alice S. Kieffer (1875 – 1920). John M. served in Pa. 19th Co of Coast Arty during the Spanish American War. *Charles C.* b 1887. After Sarah died, Michael m Feb 20, 1912 in Hillsboro, Ohio to Mary Justice , widow of George Justice who d Feb 1908. Michael Matter was a Civil War Vet, served in Co B 9th Regt Penn Cav. During a cavalry charge at Salina, Kentucky, his horse fell and threw him to the ground. Other cavalrymen rode over him, injuring him in the back, kidneys and spine. He was also a prisoner during the war. After the war was over, he received a pension. But in the fall election of 1884, Michael voted the Democratic ticket. His neighbors and acquaintances were unhappy and threatened to create a problem for him. He said his pension ended two months later, and he thought it was because of the way he voted. Michael Matter wrote a very lengthy letter to the pension office, and apparently was reinstated. [See photo of father John Michael and son Michael below.]

Christian or Christopher (May 9, 1844 - Aug 31, 1906, bur Maple Grove Cem, E'ville). Apparently his father died several months before he was born. He lived with the Ludwig Lenker (grandparents) in Washington Township in 1850.

[A note in the interesting material from historian Clayton Willier gives this account: Christian Matter born and lived in Lykens Twp., was a farmer. He had 1 son 3 girls. His son was Jonas b Lyk Twp lived on homestead below Gratz. Later went into freight hauling business at Millersburg. One trip with his three horse team at the narrows below Millersburg, the horses shied on account of the train. He went to the horses to calm them, and they pushed him upon the railroad tract and the train went over his leg and so lost his leg. This about 1882. He was a tenant farmer and about 1899 moved to Gratz. He secured the stage from Gratz to Good Spring for 4 yrs, then 8 years to drove to Elizabethville. At winter time two horse bole sleds were in use, for several months of the year. On one trip he had Abe Gross along to Eville and the snow drifts were high and they upset and it took some time till he could find Abe in the snow, lucky no one was hurt. (The only Jonas we found was born Feb 25, 1856 to Benjamin & Mary Matter. He lived in Gratz in 1900 with wife Maggie, children: Harry, John B., George W., Sarah, Mary & Katie).

After Christian Matter died, Catherine (Lenker) Matter m about 1845 to John Shoop and had a son and daughter. He may have died before Catherine, place of his burial unknown.

****Anna (no dates).

****Margareta b Aug 16, 1817; ****Levi (Nov 24, 1820 - Dec 6, 1895, bur St. John's Cem, Berrysburg), m Esther Dubendorf (Nov 11, 1819 - Aug 28, 1904); ****Christiana b Jul 30, 1823.

Michael & second wife Margaret Rebecca (Kenner) Herman Matter children (bapt St. John's Luth, Bbg) Catharina Anna b Dec 9, 1825; Carl b Dec 2, 1826; James b Dec 14, 1827; Martin b Jan 25, 1829; Sara b Feb 3, 1830; Conrad b Mar 19, 1831; Elisabeth b May 5, 1832; Reuben b Aug 1, 1833;Magdalena b Nov 22, 1834; Ludwig b Feb 6, 1837; Mary (no dates).

***George (Feb 16, 1793 - _____), m Susan _____   **George and Susan (___) Matter children (bapt Hoffman Ch):** ****Lea b May 22, 1817; ****Joseph (Aug 23, 1818 - d Oct 21,1857 in Jefferson Twp., bur Old Lykens Cem, Wiconisco Twp) This is probably the one who m Anna Mary Yerges (common law marriage) (Sep 22, 1815 - Oct 25, 1893), and **had these children:** Ann Mary b c1836; John b c1839; Henry b c1842; Jacob (b Jun 13, 1845 or 1846 - d Sep 15, 1917, m at the home of Benjamin Umberger, by Rev. Hackman on Jan 21, 1866 to Emma Elizabeth Maurer (Dec 21, 1847 - Jul 10,1935, bur IOOF Cem, Lykens), a dau of Philip and Elizabeth (Meyers) Maurer.. **Jacob and Emma (Maurer) Matter children;** *Elizabeth E.* b Mar 21, 1868; *Philip H* . b Jun

27, 1870; *Lydia M* b Apr 27, 1873; *Jacob O* b Sep 25, 1875; *William F* b Sep 8, 1877; *James E*. Dec 11, 1879; *Charles A*. Jul 12, 1887; *Blanch E* Dec 8, 1881; *Howard B* May 12, 1884; *Emma L* b Jun 29, 1893. During his youth Jacob hired out to Adam Wilvert, and lived with that family in Halifax Twp for over a year. But later came back to Lykens and lived with his widowed mother. Jacob Matter served in Co I, 13th Regt Pa Cavalry during the Civil War. He was injured when his horse was shot from under him during a charge near Raleigh, N.C. William b Apr 3, 1848; *Grace* b ___ m ___Jarrett of Tower City. The Joseph Matter family lived in Lykens in 1850, in supposedly one of only six houses, a log cabin. William in later life remembered that one day while the father was not home, a bear came to their cabin. His mother took him to the loft where they remained until his father came home and killed the bear. William told that his father Joseph became engaged in the ice business. About 1855, Joseph Matter moved his family to Jefferson Twp, Dau Co, and he died there in 1857.
 ****Delila** b Feb 9, 1825;****Jonathan** b Aug 7,1826; ****Elisabeth** b Feb 23, 1832;****Sara** b Jan 8, 1833;

Balthasar** (Jul 7, 1795 - Dec 21, 1871, bur Union Cem, Lykens), m Catharine Ritzman (Feb 12, 1797 - Oct 17, 1864, bur Simeon Cem, Gratz), a dau of Peter and Catharine Elizabeth (Kerns) Ritzman. **Balthasar & Catharine (Ritzman) Matter children: ****Michael** b Apr 26, 1818, m Anna Maria ___ ; **Susanna** b Jun 12, 1819; ****Elizabeth** (Apr 15, 1821 - Sep 26, 1852, bur Simeon Cem), 1st wife of Daniel Keiser (Nov 17, 1820 - Feb 4, 1877, bur Evang Luth Cem, Lykens);****Benneville** (Nov 25, 1823 - Feb 28, 1899), m Veronica Snyder (b Dec 5, 1822 or May 5, 1823 Halifax Twp- May 26, 1892), a dau of Jacob Snyder, **had eight children**; Harry; ___ m Henry Miller; ___ m John Smith of Kansas; ___ m William Morgan; ___ m Otto Long; Charles, Mt. Carmel, Pa. Bennevile and Veronica were m 47 yrs (record in St Johns Luth, Lykens; ****Leonard** (b Mar 8, 1826 - Jul 21, 1896), m Nov 21, 1852 to Elizabeth Shott (b Feb 2, 1831 Mifflin Twp, Dau Co - d Jun 17, 1917, Leaf River, Ill.), a dau of Johannes and Margaret (Woodside) Schott. They moved to Leaf River Twp, Ogle Co. Ill in 1859.**Leonhart and Elizabeth (Shott) Matter children:** Amelia (b Mar 2, 1853 Dau Co -d Oct 27, 1941), m Oct 8, 1871 Benjamin F. Schreiber (b Aug 30, 1850, Hegins, Pa – d 1932, Leaf River Twp, Ill), a son of Christian Schreiber and Elizabeth (Dietrich) Schreiber. [Christian Schreiber with his family moved to Ogle Co, Ill about 1867. **The Christian Schreiber children were**: Andrew E.; Benjamin F.; Malinda; Catherine; Rudolph]
 Margaret (b Aug 3, 1854 – Feb 19, 1927, Ill.), was 3rd wife of Solomon Bell Bowerman, (b Mar 3,1829 Dau Co. Pa. - d Nov 28, 1905 Leaf River, Ill), a son of John A. and Ann Maria (Woland) Bowerman of Pa. Solomon moved to Ogle Co in 1858, and taught school in Leaf River. Then returned to Pa. and studied medicine in Phila Medical College. He practiced medicine in his home town, but when the Civil War broke out, he served as first lieutenant in Co A. 172 Pa. Vol Inf., later Capt. in Co A. 210th Pa Vol Inf. After two more years as a physician in his hometown, he moved back to Ogle Co. Ill in 1859., and began a practice in Lightsville. He and Margaret were married in 1873. John A. (Nov 25, 1855 – Jan 29, 1938), moved to Leaf River, Ogle Co., Il and married Alice A.Icely Nov 1883. Aaron (May 8, 1862 Ogle Co – Feb 12, 1956), m Martha Ann Pipher.; Amanda (Apr 6, 1864 Ogle Co – Dec 27,1929), m Philip Messner (Aug 6, 1861 Dau Co- Feb 14, 1927), a son of Philip and Hannah (Lenker) Messner; Susan (Nov 5, 1866 Ogle Co – Nov 16, 1942), m Philip Henry Schreiber, a son of Christian & Elizabeth (Dietrich) Schreiber; William Franklin (Dec 5, 1869 Ogle Co– 1963 in Yankton, SD), m Nellie Mae Kretsinger of Ogle Co.

****Abraham** (b Jun 3, 1828 Lykens Twp – d May 23, 1895 Adeline, Ill), m 1848, Elizabeth Smeltzer (b May 28, 1828 Dau Co - d Feb 25, 1916, Ill), a dau of Michael and Elizabeth (Weiss) Smeltzer of Mifflin Twp. Abraham and Elizabeth moved to Maryland Twp, Ogle Co, Ill about 1859. Abraham was a blacksmith. In 1850, Abraham lived with the Thomas Batdorf family a blacksmith in Lykens Twp. He was a veteran of the Civil War, Co A of the 64th Illinois Regt, and was taken prisoner while in the service. After Abraham died, his wife lived with their children. First with Caroline, and after her death, with Mary and Emma. **Abraham and Elizabeth (Smeltzer) Matter children:** Nathaniel (Jul 11, 1849 -1871, bur beside parents); Sarah (1852 - 1870, bur beside parents); Riley b Jun 2, 1854 - d Aug 1918), m Mary A. Light, lived in Illinois; Henry (1855 - 1940, Oregon), m Frances Jane Kuntzelman in Forreston, Ogle Co, Ill; Mary Elizabeth (Aug 29, 1858 – Jul 3, 1934), m Benjamin Franklin Kuntzelman in Forreston, Ogle Co., Ill. Caroline (1861 - 1910), m 1st John H. Heiter, 2nd m James Drumheller; Emma (1862 - 1932), m Joseph Light; Jonathan (1867 - 1936, Ogle Co, Ill.

**** **Emanuel**; ****<u>Sarah</u> b c1834; ****<u>Edward</u> (1836 - 1881, bur Calvary Meth Cem, Wiconisco), m 1st Elizabeth ___, 2nd Emaline Witmer (1846 -1908), a dau of Daniel Witmer.

***<u>Heinrich</u> (Dec 26, 1796 - Oct 1, 1868, bur Matter Cem, E'ville), m Anna Mary Dietrich (Mar 16, 1803 - Nov 11, 1865), a dau of Jacob and Anna Magdalena ( ) Dietrich, her father Jacob served as a Captain in the War of 1812. This family lived in Washington Twp in 1850, and had Rebecca Sheesley age 11, and Sarah Sheesley age 9 with them. Heinrich Matters mother-in-law Magdalena Deitrich, age 75, lived next to them. **Heinrich and Anna Mary (Dietrich) Matter children:**
****<u>Elizabeth</u> b Feb 6, 1820, m 1st David Sheesley, had a dau Rebecca (1839 - 1870, bur Matters Cem, m 2nd George Gilbert, b c 1814 , lived in Wash Twp in 18503, had these children with them: John 14, Sarah 13, Mary 11, Will 9, Catharine 7; married 3 rd Philip Bowman.
****<u>Thomas</u> (Apr 20, 1821 - May 27, 1878, bur Matters Cem, E'ville), m 1st Margaretha _____ (Jul 22, 1831 - Jul 9, 1863), m 2nd Lovina _____ Aug 28, 1840 - Feb 25, 1892), both wives bur Matters Cem.
****<u>Catharine</u> (Jan 26, 1823 - Mar 13, 1915), m 1846 Philip Wilbert (Oct 29, 1821 - Nov 2, 1893), a son of Peter and Mary (Enders) Wilbert. **Philip and Catharine (Matter) Wilbert children:** <u>Sarah</u> ****<u>Jane</u> (Jan 12, 1848 - Aug 23, 1926), m Daniel Miller (___-1901); <u>Lydia</u> <u>Ann</u> b 1854; <u>Amanda</u> b c1861; <u>Clara</u> b 1863;
****<u>Margaretha</u> <u>Rebecca</u> (Mar 18, 1825 - Jun 22, 1890), m Jacob Frederick Eisenhower (Sep 19, 1826 - May 20, 1906), a son of Frederick and Barbara (Miller) Eisenhower. This is the ancestor of President Dwight David "Ike" Eisenhower. <u>Nicholas</u> (Dec 7, 1826 - Jun 23, 1865, bur Matter Cem, E'ville); <u>Enoch</u> b c1829, m Margaret <u>Sarah</u> b c1831, m George R. Williard; <u>Washington</u> b c1832; <u>Mary A</u>. b c1842, m Emanuel Bohner

***<u>Anna Catharine</u> (Feb 14, 1798, bapt St. Johns Luth Ch)
***<u>Georgiana</u> b Feb 14, 1798
***<u>Elizabeth</u> (May 16, 1799 - Nov 16, 1837), bur Simeon Cem, Gratz, alone, m Jul 12, 1818 Jacob Ritzman (Dec 15, 1794 - May 6, 1857), a son of Peter and Catharine (Kerns) Ritzman. After Elizabeth died, Jacob Ritzman m Susanna, sister of Elizabeth. Jacob and Susanna Ritzman also bur Simeon Cem, together.
***<u>A Catharine</u> (b Oct 7, 1800 - d Aug 13, 1852 Jefferson Twp, bur Bowermans Cem)
***<u>Jonas</u> b Apr 18, 1802
<u>George Daniel</u> (Nov 3, 1803 bapt St. Johns Luth Ch, Berrysbu rg - d Oct 1, 1873, Beaver Twp, Jefferson Co, Pa.), m Aug 8, 1824, Anna Catharine Buffington (Jan 17, 1805 - d Sep 25,1839, in Jefferson Co.), a dau of David Buffington (marriage record states father). They moved to Beaver Twp, Jefferson Co, Pa. before 1833. **George <u>Daniel</u> and Catharine (Buffington) Matter known children:** *<u>AnnaMaria</u> b Mar 13, 1825, m William Garhart; ****<u>Peter</u> b Dec 14, 1826, m Oct 10, 1848 in Washington Twp, by Rev. J. N. Hemping to Catherine Wert (- d Feb 21,1885). Peter was a Veteran of Civil War, served in Co D, 127th Rebt Pa Vol. He was a shoemaker. **Peter and Catherine (Wert) Matter had these children:** <u>Mary</u> <u>Elizabeth</u> b Sep 3, 1852 <u>Martha</u> <u>Jane</u> b May 27,1859; <u>Laura</u> <u>Etta</u> b Jan 31, 1872. Peter and his family lived in Elizabethville, He was a foreman for repairs on the railroad for two years, and later he was a shoemaker. He was a Civil War Vet; ****<u>Saul</u> (1829 - Feb 1898, bur West Salem Twp, Mercer Co., Pa), m Sarah Heil (b Dec 31, 1828 , prob Crawford Co, Pa. - Jan 7, 1898), a dau of George and Christianna Heil; ****<u>Elizabeth</u> b 1831, m Daniel Pliler (Blyler?); ****<u>William</u> b c1833 Beaver Twp d young; ****<u>Susan</u> b 1842, m Ira Phillip Gurhrie; ****<u>Benjamin</u> (b 1844 d young); ****<u>Sarah</u> b 1846 m Emanuel Smith; ****<u>Rebecca</u> b 1848; ****<u>Mary</u> <u>Ellen</u> b 1856; ****<u>Melinda</u> b 1860; ****<u>Daniel</u> b 1863.
<u>Solomon</u> (Mar 3, 1806 - May 13, 1877, bur St. Johns "Hill" Cem)), m 1st Isabelle Rowe (Apr 31, 1810 - Jan 27,1852), a dau of Wendel and Isabelle Row, m 2nd Feb 20, 1853 Susanna Baer (b Apr 10, 1817, Buffalo Twp, Perry Co - Nov 26, 1891 Thanksgiving Day of old age), oldest dau of John Bair. Solomon and both wives bur St. Johns Luth Cem, Berrysburg. [Death record in Simeon Parish record]. They lived in Mifflin Twp in 1850. **Solomon and Isabelle (Rowe) Matter children:** *<u>Mary</u> <u>Ann</u> b c1833;****<u>Jeremiah</u> (Apr 18,1835 - Mar 29, 1912, bur Wiconisco, died of pneumonia and heart disease), may have m Angeline ___ b c1835; ****<u>Catharine</u> b c 1840;**** <u>Elisabeth</u> b1844; ****<u>Isabelle</u> b 1846; ****<u>Amanda</u> b Apr 5, 1849. **Solomon and Susanna (Baer) Matter had three children, one son and two dau, the dau's both died before parents.** _____ b Oct 5, 1807
***<u>Eva</u> b Jan 16, 1810 - ____), m Joseph Blystone

389

***Adam (Apr 1, 1812 - c1889 in Clinton Co., Pa.), m Sarah Dubendorf (Jun 21,1815 - c1900), a dau of Samuel and Elizabeth Voegel (Fagely) Dubendorf.

***Jacob (Jul 2, 1813 - Feb 12, 1875, bur Matters Cem, E'ville), m Elisabeth Lettich (Nov 9, 1818 – Dec 12, 1886). They lived in Washington Twp in 1850, and Jacob was a shoemaker. Jacob and Elisabeth (Lettich) Matter children: ****Emanuel b c1840; ****Elisabeth b c1842; ****Catharine b c1843; ****Cornelius b c1844; ****William b c1846; ****Emaline (Sep 4, 1847 - Mar 12, 1864); ****Henry J. (Feb 26, 1849 - Feb 23, 1865); ****Sarah J. b & d 1855; ****Thomas M. b c1858.

****Regina (____ bapt Oct 23, 1815 - d pre 1852), m Joseph Rowe

***Susanna (Sep 25, 1815 - Aug 12, 1903, bur Simeon Cem, Gratz), m 1st Henry Row (May 22, 1812 - Feb 5, 1838, bur St. John's Luth Cem), a son of George and Eliaabeth (Kissinger) Row, 2nd Jacob Ritzman, who was first m to Susanna Matters sister Elizabeth. In 1850, Jacob and Susanna Ritzman lived in Gratz and had these children with them: Eva age 12, Sarah age 16, Jacob age 17, probably Jacob and Elizabeth's children, Hetty age 7, (Susanna's dau). Susanna and Jacob Ritzman had one child: Esther "Hetty" (b c1842 - d ____), m John J. Phillips of Gratz.

ANNA CATHARINE MATTER May 20, 1765 Lanc Co - ____), m c1787, George Paul (1763 - Jun 24, 1818, bur St. John's Luth Cem), a son of Johannes & Anna Catharine Paul. He was a veteran of the Rev. War. George & Anna Catherine (Matter) Paul children: ***Anna Catherina (Apr   10, 1788 - May 9, 1862, bur Pillow), m Adam Romberger (Jun 3, 1775 – Aug 7, 1868), a son of Balthaser and Anna Maria (Trout) Romberger. [More info in Romberger genealogy.]:*Johannes (Oct 3, 1789 – Sep 15, 1868, bur Old Stone Cem, E'ville), m Hannah Paul (Jul 10, 1804 - Oct 29, 1866), a dau of Johannes & Elizabeth Paul. He was a vet of War of 1812. Had no known children. *** Johannes Jacob (Mar 6, 1791 – Nov 24, 1850, bur Old Stone Cem), m Anna Catharine Shoop (Oct 19, 1789 – Apr 24, 1857, a dau of Jacob & Anna Catherine (Yeager) Schoop Johannes Jacob & Anna Catharine (Shoop) Paul children: ****Magdalena b Dec 14, 1812; ****Anna Catharina b May 26,1814; ****Elizabeth b Nov 24, 1816- d pre Dec 1856); ****Jonathan b Sep 14, 1818; ****Jacob (May 7, 1821 – Jun 25, 1886, bur St. Jacob's (Millers) Cem, Jackson Twp), m Sarah Schreffler (Apr 13, 1818- May 31, 1869), a dau of Peter & Elizabeth (Kreiter) Schreffler. After Sarah died, Jacob Paul m 2nd Catharine Romberger (Mar 26, 1835 – Jun 5, 1923), a dau of Johan Christian & Susannah (Matter) Romberger. Jacob & Catharine (Romberger) Paul children: Eli (Jan 2, 1824 – Oct 6, 1889, bur St. Jacob's (Millers) Cem), m Susan Shive (May 4, 1827 - ___, Northld Co.), a dau of Jeremiah & Catharine Shive; Josiah (Jan 18, 1826 – May 23, 1905, bur Fairview Cem, Enders), m Salome Sarah Shoop (Aug 11, 1824 – Mar 28, 1862), a dau of Joseph & Rebecca Shoop; Eva b Nov 26, 1827, m Adam Weaver b 1827; Cores (Apr 15, 1830 – Nov 23, 1903, bur St. Jacob's Cem), m Rebecca Ritzman (Nov 7, 1824 – Sep 2, 1898), a dau of Johannes & Anna Catharine (Matter) Ritzman; Johannes b c1832; ***Isaac b Jul 6, 1792 m Sarah Paul May 2, 1822 at Killinger, a dau of Johannes & Elizabeth Paul; Isaac & Sarah (Paul) Paul children: ****John (Feb 11, 1823 – Aug 13, 1902); ****Lavina b Dec 2 9, 1825, m Daniel Crawford; ***Ludwig (Jun 17, 1794 – Nov 24, 1878, bur Zion (Hoover's) Cem, Rife, m Anna Maria Wert (Feb 6, 1799 – May 6, 1859), a dau of Johan Jacob & Anna Maria Sophia (Smith) Wert; Ludwig & Anna Maria (Wert) Paul children: ****Henry (Dec 11, 1818- Mar 27, 1883, bur Zion Hoover Cem), m Lydia ___ (Mar 24, 1816 – Jan 5, 1861); ****Wilhelm L. (Jun 5 , 1820 – Jan 20, 1882), m Elizabeth Matter (Jul 23, 1817 – Dec 16, 1896), a dau of Balthaser & Magdalena (Giseman) Matter; ****Sarah W. (May 15, 1822 – Mar 14, 1900, bur St. John's Hill Cem), m Johannes Schreffler (Nov 5, 1813 – Jun 27, 1840, bur Salem Luth Cem, Killinger), a son of Peter & Elizabeth (Kreitzer) Schreffler.After her husband Johannes died, Sarah m Abraham Rowe (Apr 10, 1816 – Sep 4, 1892), a son of Wendell & Isabella Rowe: ****Juliana (Sep 1, 1829 – Sep 26, 1849, Adair Co., Mo), m Jonas Schott (Jan 21, 1824 – Aug 7, 1902, bur Topeka, Ks.), a son of Johann Philip & Susannah (Hoffman) Schott; ***Jonas (Aug 2, 1796 – May 8, 1878, bur Umberger Cem, W. Hanover Twp), m Catharina Stroh (Dec 23, 1801 – May 11, 1868), a dau of George & Elizabeth Stroh. Jonas & Catharina (Stroh) Paul had a son ****Amos (1842 – 1906) ***George b Dec 5, 1798; ***Philip (Jan 19, 1801 – pre 1866); ***Daniel (Mar 28, 1803 – Nov 9, 1856, bur Simeon Cem, Gratz), m Susannah; ***Wilhelm (Feb 16, 1805 – pre Dec 1866); *** Elisabeth n Jun 15, 1807.

**ANNA BARBARA MATTER (b c1766 - ____), m Johannes Dietrich (Nov 7, 1771 - c May 1846), a son of Michael & Maria Sarah (Bernhard) Dietrich. Johannes & Anna Barbarar (Matter) Dietrich children. [More info with Dietrich genealogy page 87 and Botts genealogy page 95 .]

JOHAN JACOB MATTER (Aug 12 or 19, 1767 - Aug 22, 1810, bur St. Johns Luth Cem), m Catharine Bitterman (1756 – 1822), a dau of Baltzer and Anna Margaretha (____) Bitterman. After Johan Jacob Matter died, Catharine m John Adam Heller. **Johan Jacob and Catharine (Bitterman) Matter children:
***Johannes Colonel (Jan 25, 1795 - Jan 4, 1881, bur Hoffman Cem), m Christiana Deibler (Oct 21, 1798 - Feb 26, 1885), a dau of Mathias and Catherine (Etzweiler) Deibler. Johannes served from Sep 1814 - Mar 1815, in Adam Ritschers Co., York County, during the War of 1812. In 1850, John and Christiana Matter lived in Lykens Twp, and dau Catherine lived with them. In 1860 John and Christiana had Amelia Matter 18, listed as servant with them. In 1870, Washington and Rebecca Matter lived with Philip Matter. Also Sarah Matter age one year. In 1880, John and Christiana were elderly, and had Rebecca age 45, probably their daughter, Sarah Myers 11, and Monroe Heim age 15 with them. On the 1875 Lykens Twp map, John Matter is listed as Col. J, Matter. **Johannes and Christiana (Deibler) Matter had these known children:** Joel (1820 – 1901, bur Hoffman Cem) m Catherine Hoffman (Dec 30, 1819 - May 7, 1897, bur Hoffman Cem), a dau of John and Elisabeth (Bordner) Hoffman. In 1860 Joel and Catherine Matter lived next to Joel's father in Lykens Twp. **Joel and Catherine Matter children(most bapt Hoffman Ch):** Amelia b Mar 5, 1842 ; Washington b 1844, m Sarah Ellen Lebo b c1854, **had these children:** *Mary Jane* b Oct 25,1874; *Oliver O.* b Oct 7, 1875; *Harry Franklin.* b Jun 21,1879; *George Washington* b Oct 14, 1882; Benjamin F. b Oct 17, 1845 - d Oct 31, 1852, bur Hoffman Cem); Rebecca b c1846; Amanda b c1848; Emelie J. b c1849;Lovina b c1851; Lydia Ann (Apr 10, 1853 - Dec 21, 1865, bur Hoffmans Cem); Sarah b c1856;Catharina (Apr 13, 1857 - Feb 18, 1865, bur Hoffman Cem); Samuel b c1859; Joel (c1860 - 1901); John (Oct 21, 1861 - Dec 31, 1865, bur Hoffman Cem); William Henry (Oct 25, 1864 - Aug 1, 1865, bur Hoffman Cem)
****Lovina (b Apr 10, 1820 Lyk Twp - d Dec 27, 1893 of dropsy, bur Simeon Cem, Gratz), m Mar 17, 1839 to David Frederick Kissinger (Jan 1, 1816 – Apr 23, 1892), a son of George & Catharina (Hoover) Kissinger;
****Catharine Amelia (Nov 9, 1833 - May 24, 1893, bur Hoffman Cem beside her parents.), m 1st on Mar 22, 1853, Abraham Schoffstall (Dec 19, 1825 - Oct 23, 1858, bur Hoffman Cem, next to his father), a son of Jacob and Salome (Paul) Schoffstall. St. John's Luth Ch, Lykens recorded her death, and states they had four children (one son three daughters), *Ellen Clara Jane* b ____; possibly *Abraham J.* b Jun 1859; After Abraham Schoffstall died, Catharine m Vitus Linseman , they had no children.
***Maria Magdalena (Nov 20, 1796 – Sep 27, 1871, bur Peace Cem, Bbg), m George Schreffler (Feb 6, 1791 Berks Co – Feb 28, 1876), a son of Godfried & Hannah Schreffler. **George & Maria Magdalena (Matter) Schreffler children:** ******Lucetta** (Jul 17, 1816 – Sep 18, 1880, bur Peace Cem, Bbg), m Daniel Moyer (Feb 16,1812 – Dec 5, 1856), a son of Peter & Eva Catharina (Hoffman) Moyer; ******Hannah** b Apr 24, 1818; ******Catharina** b Dec 3 0, 1819; ******Elias Harper** (Dec 8, 1824 - Aug 7, 1895, bur Messiah Luth Cem, Fisherville), m Lovina Knerr (Sep 27,1820 – Jan 29, 1909); ******George** (Jan 1, 1826 – Sep 5,1884, bur Old Union Cem., Lykens), m Anna Lucetta Matter b Apr 30, 1829, a dau of Michael & Sarah (Crum) Matter; ******Jonas** (Mar 2, 1836 – Aug 7, 1854, bur Sweitzer Cem, Bbg), m Susan Kebaugh (1840 – Apr 30, 1910)

Balthaser (Mar 8, 1798 - Aug 30, 1868, bur St. John's Luth Cem), m 1st Magdalena Geseman (Jan 16, 1798 - Jan 16, 1844), m 2nd on Feb 11, 1864 to Magdalena Lettich (Aug 9, 1823 – May 3, 1891, bur Hoffman Cem), a dau of William & Magdalena (Bechtel) Lettich. She later m Peter Batdorf. **Balthaser and Magdalena (Geseman) Matter children: ****Elisabeth** (Jul 23, 1817 - Dec 16, 1896), m Jun 1843, William L. Paul (Jun 5, 1820 – Jan 20, 1882, bur Zion Hoover Cem, Rife), a son of Ludwig & Anna Maria (Wert) Paul;***William C.** (Oct 11, 1818 – Mar 23, 1853, bur Bucks Cem, Perry Co), m Susanna Radel b Sep 19, 1918, a dau of Johannes & Maria Barbara (Minnich) Radel;******Margaretha Rebecca** b Dec 24,1820, m Solomon Buffington (Oct 20, 1819 – Jan 1, 1878), a son of Solomon & Elisabeth (Romberger) Buffington; ******Daniel C** (Mar 23, 1823 – Jun 22, 1898, bur Lewistown, Pa.) ******Anna Maria** (Oct 7, 1825 - Nov 29, 1871. bur St. Johns Cem, Bbg), m Daniel Knerr (Oct 6, 1822 Up Mah Twp, Northld Co- Jan 27, 1887), a son of Issac & Anna Catharine (Schaffer) Knerr; ******George W.** (Apr 10, 1828 - Aug 20, 1876, bur Rife Cem, Up Pax Twp), m Rebecca Shoop (Mar 6, 1837 - Aug 6, 1895), a dau of Jacob and Elizabeth Shoop. **George and Rebecca (Shoop) Matter had five children (bapt Hoover Ch):** *Mary Elisabeth* b Apr 26, 1862; *Frances Rebecca* b Aug 25, 1864; *Martin Luther* b Jul 20, 1869, 2 others; ******Jacob** b Oct 6, 1829; ******Peter** (May 14, 1833 - ____); ******John** b c1836, m Sarah

Gilbert b c1838, a dau of George and Elizabeth Gilbert; ******Benjamin** (Sep 26, 837 -Apr 11,1861, bur St. Johns Luth Cem,Bbg), m Mary Tschopp (1836–Jan 23, 1911);******Catherine** b Aug 2,1841;******William** (no dates). Balthaser & Magdalena (Lettich) Matter children: Balthaser L.(Apr 22, 1864 – Aug 4,1949, bur St. John' s Hill Cem), m Sarah Priscilla Lubold (Feb 10, 1869 – Jan 14, 1955), a dau of Aaron & Sarah (Rogers) Lubold; ***Daniel** (Sep 25, 1800 - Jun 3, 1881, bur St. Johns Luth Cem Berrysburg), m Anna Mary Romberger (Oct 12, 1803 - Nov 29, 1871), dau of Baltzer and Elizabeth (Sierer) Romberger. Daniel & Anna Mary (Romberger) Matter children: ****John G. b 1822, served in Civil War; ****Jeremiah (Jun 27, 1825 - after Mar 1888, Allen Co In.), m Angeline Straub (Nov 16, 1826- Jan 1, 1861, bur St. John's Hill Cem), a dau of John & Christina (Heim) Straub. Jeremiah m 2nd Catharine Tyson, d 1879 in Wyandot Co., Ohio; **Jeremiah & Angeline (Straub) Matter children**: Aaron (18276 – 1889, in Kansas), m Sarah Hoffman b Sep 24,1821, a dau of John & Elizabeth (Bordner) Hoffman; Hiram (Jun 13, 1830 – Oct 1, 1893, of stomach disease, bur St. John's Hill Cem.), m Apr 22, 1858 Mary R. Wade (1833 – 1907, bur Sweitzer Cem, Bbg), native of E. Hanover Twp; Edward (Sep 11, 1831 – Oct 9, 1865, bur St. John's Hill Cem); Elisabeth (Jun 24, 1844 – Jan 16, 1912), m Jan 29, 1863 George W. Wade (Feb 15, 1833 – Mar 19, 1921). He was a Capt serving in Civil War.
***Anna Catharine** (Nov 14, 1801 – Mar 31, 1867, bur Hoffman Cem), m Mathias Deibler (May 13, 1794 – Feb 10, 1875), a son of Mathias & Anna Catharina Elizabeth (Etzweiler) Deibler. (More info under Deibler gen.]
***Anna** (May 15, 1806 – May 5, 1882, bur Sweitzer Cem, Bbg), m William Schwab (Jul 27, 1800 – May 4, 1869), a son of John Jacob & Anna Maria (Hetzel) Schwab.
***Elizabeth** "Betsy"(Feb 27, 1809 - ___ bur Bbg cem), m Peter Yeager (Dec 17, 1804 – Sep 10, 1845), a son of Johannes & Juli (Row), Yeager, Sr. **Peter & Elisabeth (Matter) Yeager childre**n: ******Sarah Ann** (Dec 1, 1826 – Jan 12, 1876, bur Peace Cem, Bbg), m Benjamin J. Evitts (Sep 20, 1822 – Mar 30, 1909), a son of George & Salome (___) Evitts; ******Catharine** b Sep 16, 1828. [More info under Evitts genealogy.].

JOHN GEORGE MATTER (Jan 16, 1771 - Oct 11 or 26, 1855, bur St. Johns Luth Cem, Berrysburg), m Anna Catherine Romberger (Mar 29, 1777 - Jul 3, 1851), a dau of Balthaser and Anna Maria (Bricker) Romberger. George Matter served during the War of 1812. In 1850 they lived in Mifflin Twp, had Catharine Witmer age 18, and Joseph Matter age 7 with them. **George and Catherine (Romberger) Matter children:
***Michael** (Apr 12, 1794 - Jan 14, 1880), m Sarah Crum (Mar 4, 1799 - Jun 10, 1875), a dau of Frederick Crum. **Michael and Sarah (Crum) Matter had sixteen children (most bapt St. Johns Ch, Berrysburg):**
******Catharine** (Jun 11, 1817- Nov 12, 1887, bur Peace Cem), m Samuel Stites (Feb 24, 1816 N. J.- Mar 28, 1882, Perry Co, bur Peace Cem); ******Elisabeth** (Feb 24, 1819 – Mar 16, 1872, bur Hoffman Cem), m Joseph Williard (1816 – 1883). [See Williard genealogy]; **** **A Maria** Nov 22, 1820 - Mar 22, 1896), m David Coleman b Nov 25, 1817, a son of Johannes Jacob & Maria Barbara (Artz) Coleman; ******Sara** b Apr 12, 1822, m Christian Umholtz b Apr 26, 1818, a son of Philip & Anna Maria (Williard) Umholtz; ******Amos** (Nov 28, 1823 -Aug 4, 1848, bur Simeon Cem), m Lavina Kiehl;******Washington** b Dec 14, 1825- d young; **** **Joel** b (Sep 14, 1827 - Feb 27, 1892, bur Peace Cem, Bbg), m Louisa Hoover (Jul 21, 1834 - Apr 23, 1884), a dau of Henry & Amanda (Reichert) Hoover. They lived in Lykens Twp in 1860. Catherine Keener age 16, and Elias Minnich lived with them. **Joel and Louisa (Hoover) Matter children:** Amos b c1853; Mary b c1854; Sarah b Jul 2, 1855; Uriah b Feb 17, 1857; Amanda b & d 1859;Edward b c1860; Levi b c1862; Emma Jane (b Nov 12, 1865 - d Feb 28, 1871); Clara b & d Dec 1866; Henry b c1868; Ida Sybilla b & d 1870;
******Lovina** b Apr 30, 1829 (twin), m George Hoffman;
******Lucetta** b Apr 30, 1829, m George Schreffler (Jan 1, 1826 – Sep 5, 1884, bur Old Cem, Lykens); a son of George & Maria Magdalena (Matter) Schreffler; ******Emeline** (Apr 27, 1831- Nov 2, 1894,bur Seibert Cem, Williamstown), m May 12, 1849 in the Matter home to Elias Grimm (b Feb 9, 1828 Jackson Twp - Jul 4, 1915), a son of John & Catherine (Kahler) Grimm. He was a Vet.of the Civil War, Co H 210th Reg.; ******Amanda** (Mar 14, 1833- d Jan 1916, bur in Sweitzer Cem), m Daniel Walborn (Nov 21, 1820 – Jul 22, 1865, bur Coleman Cem), a son of Jacob & Susanna (Umholtz) Walborn; ******Maria Magdalena**. b Nov 14, 1834 - d Mar 12, 1912, bur Sweitzer Cem), m ___ Hawk; ******Malinda** b Sep 11, 1836 - d Apr 21,1906, bur Simeon Cem), m Jonathan (Jonas) Hawk (May 5, 1834 – Dec 20, 1904), a son of Danieil & Elizabeth (Holtzman) Hawk; ******Lydia** (Mar 17, 1838 - Nov 25, 1915, bur Calvary Meth Cem, Wiconisco), m Samuel S. Matter (Mar 3, 1837 – Nov 16, 1903), a son of Joseph M & Catherine (Shoop) Matter; ******George** Frederick (Aug 14, 1840 - Oct 22, 1897, died in Shenandoah, Scho Co, funeral afficiated there), m Louisa J. of Logan (Aug 5, 1838 - Dec 4, 1876, bur Seybert Cem, Williamstown). Dr. George Matter m 2nd, on Jun 6, 1878 by Rev. Richard Turner

to Annie J. Yeager of Wmstown, Pa. **George & Annie (Yeager) Matter children (bapt M.E. Ch, Wmstown) :** <u>George Clare</u> b Jun 28, 1880; <u>Ralph Wilber</u> b Dec 2, 1881; <u>Pearl Etheline</u> b Oct 13, 1883; <u>Ruth Virginia</u> (so called because she was born in the state of Virginia) b Sep 28, 1886. George graduated from Jefferson Medical College in 1866. He served as a hospital steward during the Civil War.

***<u>**William H**</u>. b Aug 6, 1842, m Catherine Koppenhaver (1841 – 1904, bur Middleburg, Snyder Co), a dau of Jonathan M. and Catherine (Hepner) Koppenhaver.

***<u>**Johannes**</u> (Oct 25, 1795 – d in Ashland, Ohio)

***<u>**George**</u> b Oct 11, 1796

<u>**Joseph M**</u> (May 16, 1797 – 1845), m Susanna Ritzman (Feb 27, 1799 - Oct 22, 1821, age 22, bur St. Johns Cem, Berrysburg), **had two children.** After Susanna died, Joseph m Catherina Shoop (Mar 12, 1804 – Aug 19, 1879, bur Novinger Cem, Adair Co., Mo), a dau of Johannes & Elisabeth (Cooper) Shoop. **Joseph M & Catharina (Shoop) Matter children**:*<u>**Anna Maria**</u> (Aug 15, 1824 – Feb 3, 1880, bur Maple Grove Cem, E'ville), m Jacob Schwab (1822 – 1905), a son of Jacob and Caharine (Metz) Schwab. He was a Civil War Vet; ****<u>**Noah**</u> (Dec 16, 1825 – Jul 11, 1904, bur Adair Co., Mo), m Susanna Dubendorf (1826 – 1899), a dau of Samuel Tobias & Elizabeth (Fagely) Dubendorf. He was a Civil War Vet, served in Missouri unit; ****<u>**Isaiah Samuel**</u> (Oct 9, 1827 – Sep 22, 1900, bur Fairview Cem, Enders), m Catherine Specht (Aug 27, 1827 – Mar 25, 1916), a dau of John N & Barbara (Hoffman) Specht; ****<u>**Enoch**</u> b Feb 7, 1829, went to Calif in the Gold Rush; ****<u>**Elias**</u> b Oct 6, 1833, moved to Grand Rapids, Mo c1855; ****<u>**Hannah**</u> (Dec 15, 1834 – 1876, bur Calvary Meth Cem, Wiconisco), m Charles Wolcott (c1828 – Jun 28, 1912); ****<u>**Catharine**</u> b c1835; ****<u>**Mary**</u> b c1836; ****<u>**Samuel S.**</u> (Mar 3, 1837 – Nov 16, 1903, bur Calvary Meth Cem, Wiconisco, m Lydia Ann Matter (Mar 17, 1838 – Nov 25, 1915), a dau of Michael & Sarah (Crum) Matter; ****<u>**Henry**</u> b Aug 7, 1840, m Mary Ferguson; ****<u>**Joseph S**</u> (Nov 1, 1842 – Jun 19, 1905, bur Adair Co., Mo), m Julia Studebaker; ****<u>**George;**</u> (1845 – Mar 1890), m _____ moved to Henry Co., Ohio

***<u>**Daniel**</u> b Feb 4, 1801 twin

***<u>**Anna Catharine**</u> (twin) (Feb 4, 1801 – pre 1838), m Joseph Bleistein (Aug 11, 1798 – Apr 25, 1858, bur St. John's Hill Cem). **Joseph & Anna Catharine (Matter) Bleistein children:** <u>Elizabeth</u>, m George Hincy; <u>Susanna</u> m John Stine b Feb 20, 1820, a son of Peter & Regina (Coleman) Stine; <u>Sarah</u> d young; <u>Anna Maria</u> d young.

***<u>**Anna Maria**</u> b Feb 4,1803 (Feb 4, 1803 – pre1855), 1st wife of Abraham Miller (Dec 4, 1799 – Feb 1, 1867, bur St. John's Hill Cem). **Abraham & Anna Maria (Matter) Miller children:** <u>George</u>; <u>Sarah</u>; <u>Simon</u>; <u>Anna</u>; After his wife Anna Maria died Abraham Miller m Anna Bitterman (b ___ d 1889).

***<u>**Balthasar**</u> (Feb 4,1805- Jan 3, 1880, bur Old Dutch Cem, Ashland, O), m Barbara ___ , had large family.

***<u>**Elizabeth**</u> b Aug 21, 1807, m 1st John Weiss, 2nd Henry Miller, moved to Ashland Co., Ohio.

***<u>**Salome**</u> b Jul 15, 1810, m Samuel Witmer. Children: Catharine m Moses Betz; <u>Josiah</u>; <u>Jonas</u>; <u>Sarah.</u>

***<u>**Jacob**</u> (Nov 4, 1814 - Jul 24, 1819)

***<u>**Hannah**</u> (Nov 26, 1817 - Nov 28, 1880, bur St.Johns Luth Cem, Berrysburg), m Henry Martin (Feb 12, 1812 Perry Co – Sep 6, 1891), a son of Samuel Martin. Henry & Hannah (Matter) Martin children: George W. (Sep 17, 1839- Mar 23, 1855, bur St. Johns Hll Cem); Amanda R. b Aug 7, 1860 d young.

***<u>**Susanna**</u> (May 11, 1821- Mar 20, 1882, bur St. John's Hill Cem), m Jacob Rowe (Feb 2, 1812 – Apr 21, 1894, bur St. John's Hill Cem), a son of William & Barbara (Rudy) Rowe. [More info in Rowe genealogy.]

<u>JOHN ADAM MATTER**</u> (Apr 4, 1774, bapt Salem Luth, Killinger - ____), m Margaretha _____ (no dates). **John Adam and Margaretha ( ) Matter children:** ***<u>Johann Adam</u> b Jul 4, 1796; ***<u>Margaretha</u> b Oct 14, 1796.

<u>JOHN CHRISTIAN MATTER**</u> (Jul 20, 1776 - d pre 1803), he was a crippled son.]

To the left: Civil War Veteran Michael Matter (1842 – 1912)

John Michael Matter (1881- 1959
Spanish American War

John L. Matter (1839 – 1901)
Civil War Veteran

HOME OF MR. & MRS. LEO HOOVER
(HOUSE ON SOUTH EAST CORNER OF CROSSROADS)

The history of this land is the same as that of the adjoining Riegel homestead. In July 1902, While Andrew and Sarah Riegel owned the farm they sold a one acre lot to Lizzie E. Riegel, a single lady, and sister to Andrew. Lizzie contracted to have a house built on the lot, which is located on the southeast corner of the crossroads. It was made into a two-family home, and Lizzie lived on one side.

Many years later on June 29, 1925, Lizzie Riegel conveyed the house and land to George W. and Edna J. Straub. Several years later, on March 30, 1932, Isaac and Anna Riegel conveyed another tract from the Riegel homestead to George W. Straub. This tract contained 44 acres 85 perches.

While George W. and Edna J. Straub owned this property, they operated a store in part of the house. They sold candy, ice cream, and other light refreshments and essentials. It was a place where young folks, particularly boys, enjoyed gathering to play games and talk. George and Edna's son Marlin worked in the store, and enjoyed the company of the young people.

On August 23, 1938, George W. Straub conveyed about 21 acres of his land to Samuel Riegel. They continued to own the house and store, but on June 9, 1941, another 22 acres of their land was sold to Harvey F. Hoover. Ford Leitzel and Paul A. Leitzel became the next owners in 1956, and this became the home of the Crossroads Auction. [See more details elsewhere.]

When George Straub became retirement age, he and Edna conveyed the one acre and house to their son Marlin R. Straub on April 21, 1948. Marlin was a minister and did not live in the area. He sold the premises to Leo and Anna Hoover. The Hoover's are the present owners.

THE STRAUB FAMILY

[This Straub family came from Germany to America and settled in the Mahantango Valley, Schuylkill County.

JOHN STRAUB (Jan 16, 1806 - Jun 30, 1845, bur Sacramento Cem), m Christiana Heim (Jun 24, 1806 - May 4, 1880, bur St. Johns Cem, Berrysburg), a dau of John and Susanna Sophia (Kohl) Heim. After John died, Christiana m Valentine Savidge (no dates), bur Sacramento Cem. **John and Christiana (Heim) Straub had these children: ANGELINE** (Nov 16, 1826 - Jan 1, 1861, bur St. Johns Cem, Berrysburg), m Jeremiah Matter (Jun 27, 1825 - Mar 24, 1888), a son of Daniel and Elisabeth (Bergner) Matter. **Jeremiah and Angeline (Straub) Matter had these children: Samuel** (May 29, 1854 - pre 1860); **Catharina** b Oct 11, 1855; **Imanuel** (Oct 11, 1857 - Mar 23, 1915, bur Wharton Cem, Wyandot Co., Ohio. After Angeline died, John Straub moved to Wyandot County, Ohio, and there he married Catharina Tyson, who d c1878, near Upper Sandusky.

JOHN b 1828, m Rebecca Martz;

WILLIAM (Sep 22, 1831 - Mar 11, 1900, bur Salem Union Cem, Berrysburg), m Elizabeth Holtzman (Oct 14, 1837 - Jul 25, 1890), a dau of Jonathan and Elizabeth (Koppenhaver) Holtzman of Mifflin Twp. In 1860, William and family lived in Mifflin Twp, and had Sarah Straub age19, a servant; Samuel Clouser age 22, and Simon Gibbons age 18, noted as laborers living with them.

William and Elizabeth (Holtzman) Straub had these children (Most bapt Salem Union, Berrysburg): John Newton b Jun 15, 1856, m Mrs Emma Kinsinger, **John Newton and Emma Straub children (bapt Salem Union, Bbg): Stephen Fernando** b Apr 3, 1881; **Jerome Horatio** b Apr 25, 1885; **Justie Elila** b Nov 11, 1886;

Mary Elizabeth (Mar 31, 1858 - 1917), m Dec 9, 1876 , Salem Luth Bbg to John Dockey; **John and Mary Eliz (Straub) Dockey children: Katie Loietta** b Aug 23, 1891;

Charles M. (Apr 25, 1861 - Aug 31, 1887), m May 20, 1882, Amanda Alice Forney (Nov 18, 1865 - Nov 17, 1890), a dau of George and Rebecca Forney. **Charles M. and Amanda (Forney) Straub had onely one child: George William** (Jan 11, 1883 - Jan 29, 1949, bur Berrysburg), m Edna Josephine Riegel (Feb 19, 1884 - Feb 7, 1965), a dau of Andrew and Sarah (Radel) Riegel. George was only seven years old when his father died. He was shifted to several different homes, and eventually lived with an uncle near Liverpool, Pa. before coming back to this area. **George W. and Edna J. (Riegel) Straub had these children:**

Grace Esther (Nov 13, 1904 - Mar 14, 1966, bur C.E. Cem, Berrysburg), m Clarence Ryan (1876 - 1951) of Williamstown. **They had a son:** *Leon Ryan* (Mar 12, 1924 - Sep 4, 1987, bur Lebanon), m Grace Zerbe b Sep 19, 1924;

Marlin Straub (Feb 23, 1912 - Jun 24, 1972, bur C.E. Cem, Berrysburg), m Hilda D. Henninger b Aug 13, 1912 – d 2002), a dau of _____. Marlin was a minister and they lived in Richfield. After his death, Hilda moved to Elizabethville, where she resided until her death. **Marlin and Hilda (Henninger) Straub had one son:** Marlin b Nov 12, 1944, m Ruth Page.

David Norman (Sep 10, 1864 - 1937, bur Berrysburg), m Katie Rebecca Dockey (Jul 4, 1868 - May 9, 1905, d of Nephritis). After his first wife died, David m Amanda S. Weaver (c1869 - 1952, bur Millersburg), **had a son:** Mark E. b 1907. **David Norman and his 1st wife Katie Rebecca (Dockey) Straub had these children:**

Charles Clinton (Jul 4, 1885 - 1960), m Hannah S. Sultzbach; William Clayton (Jul 9, 1887 - 1935), m Lottie M. Shade; Herbert S. (1888 - 1981), m Mamie Flory; Verna Elizabeth (Jul 25, 1890 - 1969), m Frank Shadle; Anna Louvena (Feb 3, 1892 - 1953), m John Tschopp; Homer Elmer (Mar 18, 1894 - 1900; Harry Jacob (Apr 10, 1895 - 1971), m 1st Sarah Snavely, 2nd Helen Mease Reed; Francis McKinley (Jan 11, 1897 - 1970), m Grace Lenker; Lulu Mabel b Nov 3, 1900, m Clair Dressler; Resta Irene b 1901; Velva Ellen b 1905, m Charles R. Corsnitz.

Emma Louise (Apr 7, 1867 - 1936), m Henry Howe;

Harry Straub (Jun 9, 1869 - 1939), m Cora Schlegel. **Harry and Cora (Schlegel) Straub children:** Frederick Leo b Nov 7, 1897; Martha Edna b Jun 4, 1900; Harriet Ann b Jun 27, 1902; Russell Samuel b Feb 16, 1908;

Katey Ann (Jul 10, 1871 - ____), m Jacob Hartman. **Jacob and Katey (Straub) Hartman children:** Ottie Lovenia b Jul 11, 1902;

Harvey F. and Lottie (Zimmerman) Hoover later purchased this property. A very large peach orchard had been established on the westside of the house and many folks were familiar with "Hoovers peach orchard." They also raised chickens. Lottie was a very particular person concerning cleanliness. She had a spigot and drain installed in her kitchen so that when the men came in to the house after working in the barn, they washed their hands at the drain instead of the sink near her cooking area.

Years later, the Horace Hoover family moved to Millersburg. But they could not adjust to town life after living in the country, so they came back and purchased the farm on the eastside of the crossroads.

[**HARVEY F. HOOVER** (1893 - 1957, bur Wiconsico Cem), , son of William A. (1866 -1938, bur Wiconisco Cem) and Catherine E. (___) Hoover (1873 - 1959) of Coaldale, m Lottie M. Zimmerman (1898 - 1968), a dau of _____. Harvey was a miner, and they lived in Coaldale before moving to this area. They first lived in the house on the southwest corner of the Crossroads. When they came to the crossroads area, they brought their furnishings in a hay wagon over dirt roads. **Harvey F. and Lottie M. (Zimmerman) Hoover had these children: Harold** (b - died); **Leo** (1921 – c2007), m Ann Romberger; **Lester** (b __ d ___), m Ruby Enders b Jan 19, 1921, a dau of Daniel and Eva (Koppenhaver) Enders of Gratz; **Effie** m Marlin Noll of Millersburg; **Betty** m Gordon Matter; **Herbert** m Eddie ___ of North Carolina, they lived in York, Pa. Leo Hoover was born in the house on the southwest corner of the Crossroads, but in later life lived in the house on the eastern corner. Leo joined the U.S. Navy and was a career man from 1940 to 1963. When he first went into the Navy he was in a fighter squadron and flew in a bi-plane. During the second world war, he was on a ship that was torpedoed and sunk.]

THE CROSSROADS AUCTION

This property has the same background as the Reuben Riegel homestead (Described in the next write-up) . When Andrew Riegel became the owner of the Riegel homestead, he sold off some of the land on several different occasions. On January 1, 1926, Andrew Riegel and Sarah (she d 1826?) sold 155 acres, 44 perches of land to their son Isaac Riegel of Lykens Twp. While Isaac Riegel owned this farm, he sold a portion containing 4 acres 85 perches on March 30, 1932 to George W. Straub.

On June 9, 1941, twenty-two acres of this land was conveyed to Harvey F. and Lottie M. Hoover. On March 5, 1956 Harvey F. Hoover sold the twenty-two acres to Ford Leitzel and Paul A. Leitzel. In January 1977

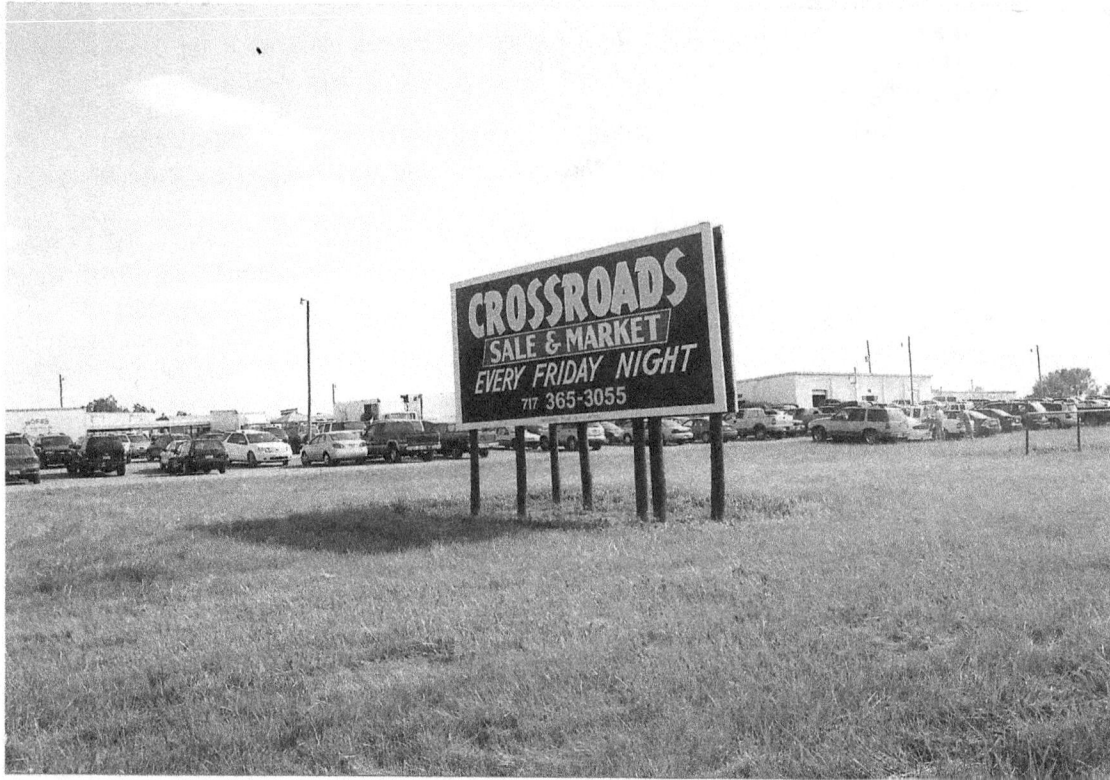

the brothers conveyed the property to Paul A. and Peggy J. Leitzel. Richard E. Leitzel became the owner in 1993.

The Leitzel brothers had previously established a market on the Gratz Fair Grounds where many people came each Friday night to purchase farm products and many other varieties of merchandise. It was also a place where people of every age could entertain themselves with bingo and other games.

The brothers later decided to create their own center, and that is when they purchased this land. The Leitzel brothers established "Crossroad Sale And Market " which over the years has become a family enterprise. Each Friday night many people from various areas enjoy a trip to the crossroads to buy fresh fruit and vegetables, as well as numerous other products. Butchers offer varieties of fresh meat. Smoked sausage is a popular product known mostly to folks acquainted with this area. Many visitors coming to this vicinity from other places plan to take some Pennsylvania Dutch sausage with them when they leave. Merchants offer candies, wearing apparel, bakery products, landscape plants, and a variety of other attractive goods. Of course, there are several food stands where sandwiches can be purchased.

Many years ago, Paul Dockey well known for his auctioneering services began to hold auctions, dispersing of antiques and other merchandise throughout the Friday evenings. After Paul Dockey died, his son Lee took over the business. He and his daughter Yvonne continue to offer their patrons the chance to come and look over the merchandise. Then hope to be the 'high bidder" and take home that special item that was offered for sale.

REUBEN RIEGEL FARM
(156 Acres in 1875)

This is part of the 202 acre tract of land known as "Hickory Bottom" that Nicholas Hoffman received from Commonwealth of Pennsylvania on January 7, 1785. Shortly after that at least part of it was conveyed to Andrew Riegel. On April 30, 1792 Andrew Riegel, a blacksmith, conveyed 194 3/4 acres of land with buildings to his son John Riegel. On June 2, 1837, John Reigel, Esquire and his wife sold 157 acres to Andrew Riegel. The father John Riegel, Sr. lived on the property for about two years, after it was sold.

Air View of the Riegel Family Homestead Taken c1955
The little house to the right of the dwelling house was near a Spring and was the "milk & butter" house

Andrew Riegel penned his will on August 9, 1835. His first concern was his wife Elizabeth's well being. He bequeathed to her a bed, bedding, a chest, a spinning wheel and reel, one cow, two hogs, and the furniture of her choosing, without charge, as long as she remains his widow. The family should divide among themselves the yarn that is woven and the linen that is woven for make clothing. They should also divide the crops stored in the barn, and the seed for planting. But the crops taken in 1839 shall belong to his estate, and Elizabeth and the children shall agree to farm the farm where he lived. If they cannot agree to do the farming, it should be rented, with Reuben the eldest son having first chance. Elizabeth should have her share of the grain, fruit and hay. She should be given sufficient house room, garden and stabling for her livestock, and firewood cut and brought to the house for her. He mentions again that if she is no longer his widow, she shall have only half of the above shares. The daughters should each receive a bed and bedding, and furniture that Elizabeth should choose for them, all in equal shares. Both sons and daughters should each receive a cow, to be raised on the farm. The sons should work on the farm as long as they are minor children. If they refuse to work, they should be given household furniture in value according to the time they remained on the farm. The sons "above age" should receive furniture according to the value of the work they did on the farm. If the family cannot agree on their value, three men should be chosen to make an award, but not "an extraordinary one, because they have been clothed in good and bad weather." Simon and Reuben should each receive a horse.

Andrew Reigel desired to have his other nearby farm rented out until his youngest son become of age, and they should build a new barn on that farm. If the family could not agree on the rental, the farm should be sold. The profits from that farm should be divided. The third farm located on the bank of the Wiconisco Creek, should also be rented. If none of the heirs wished to own these farms they were to be sold, and the money divided among the heirs.

398

**Recent Photo Of Farm House Along Route 25 Inherited By Reuben Reigel
Now Owned By Mr. and Mrs. Homer B. Campbell**

After Andrew Riegel died, the heirs sold the 155 acres 44 perches in 1838 to his son Reuben Riegel. Reuben Riegel continued to own this farm throughout his whole life. In 1850, he and his wife Amy had three small children: Anna Maria, Andrew, John, and Catherine Jane in the household. They also had Nicholas Bressler age 28, with them. In 1870, Reuben and Amy had a young daughter Elizabeth age 12 living with them on the homestead. Their sons Andrew and John and their families also resided in another section of the house or perhaps a second house on the property. By 1880, John Riegel had moved to the farm he inherited, so Reuben, Annie (Amy) and their daughter Elizabeth lived together. Andrew also had a separate home for his family.

In his last will made December 18, 1878 (recorded December 6, 1880), Reuben devised this land (this was his homestead, but he also owned the adjoining farm), to his son Andrew Riegel on the condition that he would pay a share of money to his brothers and sisters. Reuben also was supposed to give his mother possession of the house, garden, cellar, and barn during her lifetime. He was to feed her two cattle in winter, and give them pasture in summer. He had to provide coal and cut firewood that he hauled to her house, also potatoes, as many as she wants for her use, He was to allow his mother to raise chickens, and he had to provide a stable near the house where she could keep a hog, and also corn and chop to feed the hog. Other items that he should provide were cherries, apples, apple butter, fifteen bushels of wheat, which he should take to the mill and bring home the flour, fifty pounds of beef which she should receive at the time that she butchers her hog. All this should be provided each year during her lifetime, and fifteen dollars in money, six pounds of coffee, fifteen pounds of sugar, and one bushel of salt.

In November 1863, a license was issued from the office of Internal Revenue to Riegel and Frank of Lykens Township to become 2nd class peddlers. The license cost $7.50 cents and it expired on May 1, 1864. This type of license was common during those years among farmers who took their products to market in neighboring towns.

After Andrew Riegel owned this property, Reuben became the occupant from about 1840 to perhaps 1855. In 1858 Reuben Riegel was taxed for this 156 farm with a 1 ½ story log house and bank barn. Many years later, Reuben Riegel sold the 156 acres to his son Andrew. While Andrew owned the farm, his son Harry became the farm manager. On January 1, 1926, the land of Andrew Riegel and Sarah was sold to their son Isaac Riegel of Lykens Twp.

These Members Of The Riegel Family Are Believed To Be
Andrew Riegel (1841 – 1930) & Sarah (Radel) Riegel (1846 – 1923)

Wedding Photo Of Isaac Riegel (1887 – 1970)
& Annie Florence Shaffer (1894 – 1973)
They were married on August 3, 1912

Chauncey A. Riegle
(1870 - 1936)
(died at home of Wm Dietrich)

Harrison   & wife Hannah Riegle
(1840 - 1899)   also child

Charles Gerone Riegle
(1876 -1913)
Killed at Short Mt. Colliery, crushed by fall of coal
caused by car jumping tracts. Died before he could
be removed from mass of slate and coal

Minnie (Coleman) Riegle
(1880 - 1958)

While Isaac Riegel owned this farm, he and his son became involved in a dairy business during the late 1920's and 1930's. The milk was stored in the "milk house" located near a spring at the back of the main house. They also kept butter and perhaps other dairy products in this house. About the time that the Riegels ventured into the dairy business farmers began to deliver milk in bottles. The Riegels purchased bottles for their business embossed with the name "Isaac M. Riegel & Son" and "T B Tested Milk and Cream." A few of them have survived and are sought after by bottle collectors.

Another special relic from the Riegel dairy is a calendar that was handed out to their customers. This one was distributed for the year 1934.

Isaac Riegel sold a portion of his farm containing 4 acres 85 perches on March 30, 1932 to George W. Straub.

On May 29, 1957, Isaac M. and Anna F. Riegel sold the remaining about 150 acres of the155 acre, 44 perch farm to Ralph and Helen Riegel. At this time the land was adjacent to John H. Riegel and Charles Riegel, north to the public road from Pillow to Loyalton, Mrs. Isaac Stine, north to Lizzie E. Riegel and Gratz to Berrysburg road, John Harris and Charles Kocher land, John D. Riegel and Harvey Kissinger. Ralph and Helen Riegel sold 71/100 acre of land to Ray D. and Cora M.Witmer on December 16, 1860, and they built the ranch style house on the lot. Christina Riegel Walter inherited this farm from her father Ralph. Christina A. and J. Bruce Walter sold this same approximately 111 acres of land to Homer B. and Bonita Campbell on January 31, 1985. The land has been continuously owned by the Riegel family for about 175 years.

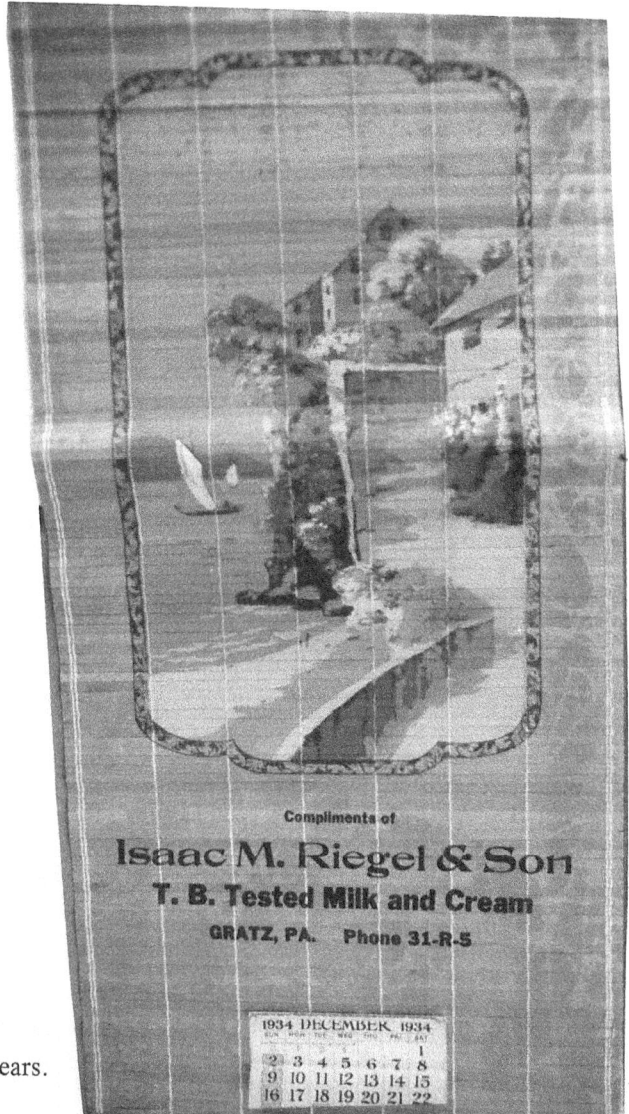

Compliments of

Isaac M. Riegel & Son
T. B. Tested Milk and Cream
GRATZ, PA.   Phone 31-R-5

1934 DECEMBER 1934

Below a scene on the Isaac Riegel farm. Elura Riegel Schadel in Buggy .   Isaac M. Riegel & Son Calendar -1934

THE RIEGEL FAMILY
Most of this information attributed to Dr. Samuel A. Riegel, whose research created the Riegel genealogy volume that is housed in the Gratz Historical Society library.

The RIEGEL family is traced to **MATTHEIS RIEGELl** b c1615 in Bad Muenster, Palatinate, Germany. He married Maria Werner, a daughter of Jost Werner. Their son **JOST RIEGELL** b 1635 in Bad Muenster, Rheinland, Germany, m Maria Hoenen, had a son: **CORNELIUS RIEGEL** (Sep 29, 1674 – c1750) b in Beckerbach, Germany, m Anna Gertrude. Cornelius and Gertrude Riegel brought their family to Philadelphia, arriving Jun 24, 1733 from Holland on the ship Brigateen. Two of their children came to America a year earlier, and landed at Philadelphia Sep 23, 1732.

Cornelius and Anna Gertrude Riegell had among other children, a son:

DANIEL RIEGELL (c1713 – May 25, 1786) in Berks Co. He m Maria Dorothea Beitler (bc1716 in Germany – d c1786 in Tulpehocken Twp, Berks Co. **Among their children was a son:**

***ANDREAS RIEGEL**, Sr. (b c1750 in Tulpehocken Twp, Berks Co – d May 14, 1815 in Lykens Twp), m c1770 Catherine Hoffman (b 1751 - d Oct 4, 1819), a dau of John Peter and Maria Sara Hoffman. Place of burial is uncertain, but it is believed they are interred in the pioneer cemetery on the Bush farm. Andreas served as a private in the Revolutionary War. He was one of the carpenters that helped to build the old Hoffman Church. He died intestate, and his children formulated a contract to disperse of his goods. An appraisal of his real estate was held at the home of his widow on Dec 23, 1815.

Andreas and Catherine (Hoffman) Riegel children:

****SUSANNA CATHARINE** b Mar17, 1771 Tulpehocken Twp, Berks Co - d _____), m George Matter. [More information in Matter genealogy.]

****JOHANNES, Esq.** (Sep 16, 1772 bapt Host Ref Ch, Tulpehocken Twp – Jun 14, 1838, bur Hoffman Cem), m Jul 26, 1806 Susanna Sheetz (Dec 24, 1787 - Mar 2, 1871), a dau of Ludwig and Elizabeth (Hoffman) Sheetz.
Johannes and Susanna (Sheetz) Riegel children (most bapt Hoffman Ch):
*****Johannes** (b Nov 2, 1806 - d Aug 14, 1855, Jordan Twp, Northld Co bur St. David's Cem, Hebe), m Susanna Rose (Jan 1, 1812 – Dec 31, 1893), died in Ohio. **Johannes and Susanna (Rose) Riegel children:** Rebecca b c1831; Susanna Catharina b May 20, 1834, bapt Hoffman Ch; Nancy b 1836, m John Schoffstall; Simon R. (May 20, 1838 – May 9, 1864, from injuries received in Civil War battle). He served in "A" Co. of the 50th Pa., Vol. of Sch Co. He m May 20, 1858 to Maria Lesher (Aug 15,1837 – 1921), a dau of John & Polly (Troutman) Lesher. After Simon died, Mary m Jun 18, 1874 Adam Bohner (Nov 4, 1838 – Mar 8, 1889), also a veteran of the Civil War. Adam had m 1st Catherine Delp. **Simon R. & Maria (Lesher) Riegel children:** Catherine b 1858; John R.Jr. b Sep 8, 1860, Sarah Ann b May 14, 1863, m James Strohecker. Susanna (Jul 23, 1839 – May 26, 1900, bur Stone Valley Cem), m May 4, 1862 Michael Dockey, Jr.a son of Michael & Margaret Rebecca Dockey. They lived in Low Mah Twp., Northld Co. **Michael & Susanna (Riegel) Dockey children:** Jonathan Francis (Nov 21, 1862 – Nov 21, 1941), m Elmira E. Buffington; Sarah A; Mary A; Catharine;John Michael b Dec 3,1871, m Mary A. ___; Emma Jane b Oct 31,1878; Cora Melinda Mar 15, 1880; Sarah (Jan 2, 1845 – Mar 15, 1930), m Reuben Lenker (Oct 11, 1843 – Aug 29, 1929), a son of Jacob & Susanna (Haupt) Lenker, lived in Shamokin.

*****Jacob** (Dec 5, 1808 – May 31, 1838, bur Hoffman Cem near the parents), m Susanna ___, had a child Karl b Jul 3, 1837; *****Elisabeth** b Aug 7, 1810, bapt St. Johns Hill Ch, m Jacob Meyer; *****Simon** (Apr 4, 1812 – Sep 28, 1902), m Jan 14, 1840 Barbara Stoner (Mar 9, 1815 – Nov 5, 1883); *****Anna** b Apr 17, 1814, m Daniel Botteiger; *****Rebecca** (Dec 11, 1816 – Feb 22, 1855, bur St. Davids Ref Cem, Hebe, Northld Co), m George Maier (Jul 3, 1815 – Aug 7, 1879; *****Susanna** b Sep 6, 1818; *****Salome** b Mar 8, 1821; *****Hannah** b Sep 12, 1824; *****Lavina** (Aug 12, 1826 – Nov 19, 1899, bur Shamokin Cem, Shamokin, Northld Co), m Jan 16, 1845 Benjamin Katterman (Nov 6, 1821 – May 17, 1892). They lived at Hickory Corners, Northld Co. He was a tailor and Civil War Vet.; *****Obed J.** (Oct 18, 1829 – Jan 11, 1891). He was a Civil War Vet. He m late 1852 to Mary Ann Farrel, by Rev. Leise of Up. Paxton Twp.

****DANIEL, Sr.** (b Sep 21, 1774 Up Tulpehocken Twp, Berks Co – d Feb 18,1839, bur Hoffman Cem), m Nov 29, 1803 Catharine Harmon b c1780, a dau of Johannes and Anna Maria Harmon
Daniel and Catharine (Harmon) Riegel children:

****Daniel, Jr. (Jun 1, 1804 - Jun 2, 1855, bur Simeon Cem, Gratz), m Dec 24, 1826 at David's Killinger Ch, Catharine Hoffman (Sep 10, 1807 – Sep 2, 1864), a dau of Peter and Magdalena (Lubold) Hoffman. Daniel owned a farm of 50 acres in Lykens Twp until 1850, when he purchased the Hoover mill property. He later moved to Gratz, and planned to open a blacksmith shop. According to the 1855 tax record the shop was already finished, but he died about that same time. On April 1, 1857, Jonas Laudenslager, administrator of his estate sold the property to Dr. Isaiah Schminky. Daniel Riegel served as County Commissioner in Dau Co from 1852 – 1855. **Daniel and Catharine (Hoffman) Riegel children:**

Elizabeth (May 12,1827 –Feb 3, 1885, bur Simeon Cem, Gratz, alone), m Elias Etzweiler, lived in Jackson Twp.
Josiah R (Nov 30,1828 - Jan 6,1886, bur Simeon Cem, Gratz), m Nov 15, 1853 by Rev. Bossler in Berrysburg, Amanda Kissinger (May 8,1831 –Jul 3, 1897), a dau of Jacob and Susannah Kissinger. Josiah served in the Civil War 1st as a Corp in 36th Pa. Regt ., 2nd as a musician in 103rd Reg. Josiah & brother Harrison mustered into service on the same day, Mar 14, 1865.**Josiah and Amanda (Kissinger) Riegel children:** Lewis b c1854; Mary b c1856; Emma b c1858; George; Annie; William Harrison b May 15, 1872; Sarah J. b May 25, 1875, m ____ Hartman; (Amanda had 8 children, but five of them plus her husband died before her);
Jonas P. (Sep 19, 1835 - d Nov 1, 1889 bur Reinerton, Sch Co), m by Justice of the Peace Jonas Laudenslager on Dec 28, 1856 to Rebecca Holtzman (Oct 19, 1836 - Apr 21, 1921), a dau of Peter John and Catharine (Kissinger) Holtzman. Jonas was a veteran of the Civil War. **Jonas and Rebecca (Holtzman) Riegel known children**: Mary B (Apr 1, 1857 - May 6, 1862), died while her father was serving in the Civil War, according to a letter written to him by the mother; Sarah (1859 - pre 1870);Charles Grant (Aug 28, 1865 - Jan 26, 1937, bur Muir, Sch Co), m Sarah Alice Sponsler (1865 - 1963), a dau of John and Malinda (Fetter) Sponsler. **Son** *Franklin Harrison* (1888 – 1969), m Flossie Ebert (1890 - 1914, **had a son** *Norman Joseph* b Oct 25, 1911. William Edward b Jan 3, 1875, m Anna Mary Straub. **Wm Edw and Anna Mary (Straub) Riegel children:** *Sarah Ann* b Mar. 1893; *Maggie Jane* b Mar 23, 1900; Emma Clara b May 10, 1878. Jonas Riegel was a veteran of the Civil War. After he came back he worked as a clerk in a store in Williamstown, also at the braker of the mines; **Harrison** (b Nov 15, 1840 - d Jul 31, 1899, bur Simeon Cem, Gratz), m 1867 Hannah Rickert (May 22, 1847 - Jul 11, 1919), a dau of Martin and Elizabeth (Yerges) Rickert. Harrison worked for Lykens Valley Coal Company, served in Civil War, later purchased a farm in Lykens Township. In 1860 Harrison lived with his widowed mother Catherine and sister Eliza. Some personal items that belonged to Harrison Riegel are housed in the Gratz Historical Society. **Harrison and Hannah (Rickert) Riegel children (four others died as infants):** Chauncey (Aug 1, 1870 twin - 1936, bur Simeon Cem, Gratz), m Emma ____ (1863 - 1934); Jancy Ellen b Aug 1, 1870 twin; Lizzie C (1872 - 1942, bur Simeon Cem); Edward A. (Apr 4,1874 –Mar 1, 1960), m Jennie Hawk, a dau of Jonathan & Melinda (Matter) Hawk. He was a teacher; Charles Gerome (Oct 10, 1876 - Mar 19, 1913, bur Simeon Cem), d in a mine accident at Lykens Valley Mines, Wiconisco, m Minnie Amanda Coleman (1880 – 1958), a dau of John and Amanda (Schneider) Coleman; Berth b 1879; Mabel; Norman b 1886.

****John (b Oct 1806 – d c1837), Susanna Louisa Muench, a dau of Charles Edw. Muench, teacher & minister at Hoffman Ch. [more info in Muench genealogy.]

***GEORGE (Aug 5, 1776 Berks Co – Aug 30, 1855 Pickaway Co., Ohio), m Maria Elizabeth ____
***JACOB (Feb 28, 1778 - Jul 19, 1846), m Nancy Anna Hartman (Sep 3, 1790 - Oct 15, 1880)
Jacob and Nancy (Hartman) Riegel children (most bapt Hoffman Ch):
****Salome b Jan 1814; ****Amos b Jul 15, 1816, m Mary Ann Hoffman who d in 1843; ****Hanna b Nov 8, 1817; ****Susanna b Apr 10, 1819; ****Juliana b Jan 1, 1822; ****Jacob b Nov 20, 1824;****Maria Ann b Oct 8, 1829;
***ANDREW, Jr. (Jan 14, 1780 - Sep 13, 1838), m Elizabeth Stine (Mar 13, 1786 - after 1850), a dau of Frederick and Apolonia (Lamm) Stine. Andrew Stine was a farmer, served in War of 1812.
Andrew and Elizabeth (Stine) Riegel children:
****Apolonia b May 27, 1812;
**** Reuben (b Feb 4, 1814 –d Nov 12, 1880, bur Simeon Cem), m Jan 21, 1836 Amy Stine (Dec 20, 1816 - Jun 20, 1898), a dau of John and Catharine (Klinger) Stine. In 1860, Reuben, Amy and family lived on their farm in Lykens Twp. Sam Wenrich, age 20 also lived with them and was listed as a servant. **Reuben and Amy (Stine) Riegel children:**

Anna Maria (Mar 14, 1840 – May 27, 1901, bur Forreston, Ogle Co, Illinois), m Jun 4, 1868 in German Ref Ch, Pillow, Pa. to Aaron F. Myers (Jan 19, 1844 – Jul 4, 1925), son of Henry Myers.

Andrew (Dec 20, 1841 – Jan 1, 1930, bur Hoffman Cem.), m Sarah Radle (Dec 6, 1846 – Nov 13, 1923), a dau of Isaac and Mary Radle. **Andrew and Sarah (Radle) Riegel had these children:** Annie Alvesetta (1866 – 1927, bur Hoffman Cem), m Emanuel Weaver (1869 – 1934), a son of Jonathan and Elizabeth (Tschubb) Weaver; William Harvey (1868 – 1900, bur Hoffman Cem), m Catherine Boyer (1869 – 1946), a dau of John and Mary Boyer; Michael Edwin (1870 – 1940, bur Maple Grove Cem, E'ville), m Mary M Lubold (1876 – 1948); Emma Sevilla (1872 – 1948, bur Hoffman Cem), m Rufus Willier (2nd wife). he d 1933, bur Simeon Cem, Gratz; John Hiram (1874 – 1941, bur Hoffman Cem), m Amanda Hoover (1873 – 1923), dau of Edmund Hoover; Jennie Caroline (1876 – 1904), m Charles M. Dockey; Katie Elizabeth (1879 – 1958, bur Hoffman Cem), m Egidius Latsha (1884 – 1968); Mary Magdalena (1880 – 1881, bur Hoffman Cem); Harry Garfield (1881 – 1960, bur Simeon Cem, Gratz), m Bertha Scheib, a dau of Monroe and Hanna (Klinger) Scheib, had a dau Avis b 1916, m Ira Gottshall b 1915; Edna Josephine (1884 – 1965, bur C.E. Cem, Berrysburg), m George Straub (1883 – 1949) [see Straub Family history]; Lura Evelena (1885 – 1973, bur Sacramento Cem, Sch Co), m Arthur Schadle (1895 – 1948); Isaac Monroe (1887 – 1973, bur Oak Hill Cem, Millersburg) , m Aug 3, 1912 to Annie Florence Shaffer (1894 – 1970), a dau of Newton Daniel and Sara E. (Phillips) Shaffer. **Isaac and Annie (Shaffer) Riegel had these children:** *Marlin Shaffer Riegel* (b & d 1912); *Ralph Melvin* (May 22, 1914 – Dec 18, 1973, bur Oak Hill Cem, Millersburg), m Aug 9, 1941, Helen Irene Updegrove (Nov 18, 1912 – Jun 12, 1968**), had a dau** *Christine Ann* b Dec 11, 1947, m Bruce Walter. Ralph m 2nd Dec 21, 1968 Ruth Goodling b Feb 1, 1929.; Helen Arabella (1890 – 1933, bur St. Andrew's Meth Cem, Valley View, Sch Co), m Harry E. Miller (1892 – 1955), a son of John and ___ (Buffington) Miller of Miller Funeral Home in Valley View; Jacob Daniel (1892 – 1948, bur Herndon Union Cem, Northld Co), m Apr 25, 1914, Edna Rieger (1895 – 1980), a dau of Samuel E. and Evey Elizabeth (Kissinger) Rieger. .

John (Apr 20, 1844 – Aug 24, 1915, bur Hoffman Cem), m Mary Jane Forney (Oct 7, 1848 – Feb 19, 1934), a dau of George and Susanna (Hoffman) Forney. **John and Mary Jane (Forney) Riegel had these children:** Miriam (1868 – 1957, bur Hoffman Cem), m Henry Wolfe Willier (1867 – 1920), principal of Frailey Twp Schools, Sch Co); Catherine Elizabeth (1870 – 1959, bur Hoffman Cem), lived with her sister Mary Jane; Annie Susan (1872 – 1955, bur St. John's Cem, Bbg), m George Lahr (1882 – 1962); Maggie Ellen (1874 - ___), m Lewis Rowe; Charles Andrew (1876 – 1962, bur Hoffman Cem), m Emma Lahr (1885 – 1969); Cora Gertrude (1879 - ___), m Cloyd Weaver. Cora and Cloyd built a house on land owned by Charles and Emma Riegel, but because of a dispute, tore down the house and moved it to Big Run, one mile east of Loyalton ; Mary Jane (1882 – 1967, bur Hoffman Cem), m Harry E. Klinger (1880 – 1969); Gurney Wellington (1886 – 1966, bur Hoffman Cem), m Mabel Estella Brosius (1890 – 1956, bur Hoffman Cem), a dau of Charles and Emma (Kiehl) Brosius; Sadie (1889 - ___), m ___ Luessenhop; Amy Caroline (1892 – 1967, bur Pillow Cem), m Samuel Isaac Snyder (1888 – 1971); Minnie Etta (1896 - ___, bur Hoffman Cem), m Gurney Jay Kissinger (1894 – 1923).

Catherine Jane b 1849, m William B. Moyer, moved to Sabetha, Kansas.

Elizabeth "Lizzie" Ellen (Jun 13, 1857 – Apr 7, 1926, bur Simeon Cem with parents). She never married and lived in the western half of the house in which her brother Andrew and his wife Sarah lived during the later days of their lives. The house is situated on the southeastern corner of the Crossroads.

****Catharina (Oct 13, 1816 – Nov 15, 1892), m Abraham Kessler (Nov 30, 1818 – Jun 12, 1881) [More information in Abraham Kessler genealogy];

**** Elisabetha b Aug 20, 1820;

****Simon b Feb 24, 1823, lived on a farm east of Gratz, once known as the Bellis farm. In 1860, Simon and Abby Riegel lived in Lykens Twp on a farm, no children listed. In 1870 Simon Riegel age 46 lived with the John Dietz family and he was listed as a laborer.

****Susanna b Nov 21, 1825;

***ANNA CATHARINE (c1782 – 1857), m George Radenbach [For more information see Radenbach family]

***MARIA ELIZABETH b Dec 23, 1785 – d _____), m Daniel Sheesley. Daniel and Maria Elizabeth (Riegel) Sheesley had one known child: ****Daniel (b Sep 16, 1815 Lyk Twp – d Jun 21, 1880 Harrisburg), m 1837, Sarah Rissing, dau of Lewis and Mary Rissing. They lived in Harrisburg where Daniel engaged in the milling business, and was an auctioneer.

***MAGDALENA (Jun 24, 1793 – Mar 24, 1868), m 1ˢᵗc1812 John Bressler (Aug 30, 1788 - c1822, bur Hoffman Cem (stone marked J + B 1822), a son of Nicholas and Magdalena (Stoner) Bressler. She m 2ⁿᵈ c1825, Mathias Haag/Hawk (b c1764 – d _____), son of John George Haag, and widower of Susanna Deibler. Magdalena m 3ʳᵈ c1837 John Bitterman (b Jul 7, 1787 Strasburg, Lanc Co – d Aug 25, 1853, bur St. John's Hill Cem), a son of Baltzer Bitterman. John Bitterman was first married to Anna Deibler (Dec 20, 1795 – Mar 16, 1826), she is bur beside him. Magdalena was widow Bitterman in 1860, and she and her son Nicholas Bressler lived in Wiconisco Twp. **John and Magdalena (Riegel) Bressler children (Some bapt Hoffman Ch):**
****Susanna b Aug 3, 1813, m Hugh Bitterman (b _____ - d 1841), **Hugh and Susanna (Bressler) Bitterman had these known children:** Catherine (no dates), m ____ Moyer; Cyrus (Apr 21, 1837 – Jan 5,1926, Harrisburg, bur Wiconisco Meth Cem), m Nov 18, 1860, by Rev. Wm Heim in Millersburg to Louisa McCoy (1841 – May 5, 1892), a dau of William and Eva (Bohner) McCoy. Cyrus was a veteran of the Civil War. Cyrus was a teamster in 1870, and they lived in Wiconisco Twp. **Cyrus and Louisa (McCoy) Bitterman had these children:** Amelia (b Nov 7, 1861 – d Jan 5, 1900); Susan Catherine b Sep 5, 1863 – d Jan 18, 1921); Howard McCoy (b Jan 7, 1865 – d Oct 11, 1932); Jacob Walter (b May 11, 1867 – d Jul 28, 1945); Joseph (b Oct 1870 – d ___); Harry Maxwell (b Oct 18, 1869 – d Dec 31, 1883, age 14, in a mining accident at Tower City); Eva Maude (b Jul 9, 1871 – d Dec 28, 1961), m William B. Pumin; John Wellington (b Oct 4, 1873 – d Sep 23, 1875, bur Hbg); William Joseph (b Feb 21, 1876 – Mar 21, 1959, in Md.); Nellie Louisa (b Mar 11, 1878 – d ____), m ____ Shepley; Louis & Paul, twins b & d 1881; Elizabeth May (May 5, 1882 – Sep 1887, Tower City); Amanda (no dates).
****George (Sep 10, 1815 – c1822). Susanna later m George Geiger (no dates), and had these children: Louisa (no dates) m _____ Dreibelbis; Joseph Henry (no dates); William Warren (no dates).
****Magdalena (Feb 2, 1818 – Jul 15, 1894, bur Calvary Meth Cem, Wiconisco), m Captain Daniel Keen (Feb 26, 1816 – Dec __, 185_), a son of Henry and Anna Keen. **Daniel and Magdalena (Bressler) Keen children:** John H. (1840 – 1919, bur Calvery Cem), m Anna Mary Mace (b 1838 in Berrysburg – d 1921), a dau of John Mace, a weaver (this from Dau Co Hist.); Samuel (Sep 18, 1844 – 1917, bur Calvary Meth Cem Wiconisco), m Miriam (1848 – 1932);Edward; Mary Emanda b Jun 6, 1849, bapt Hoffman Ch; George W. (Jul 14, 1850 – Sep 16, 1907 bur near parents);Charles; Daniel N. (Apr 20, 1853 – Sep 13, 1861, bur beside parents).
****Nicholas (Apr 7, 1819 or 1820 – Jan 26, 1880, bur Hoffman Cem), lived with the Reuben Riegel family in 1850, with his widowed mother in Wiconisco Twp. in 1860, was a teamster in adult life, not married.
****John b Feb 21, 1823
****Mary Ann
Magdalena (Riegel, Bressler) and 2ⁿᵈ husband Mathias Haag children:
Magdalena b Sep 19, 1816 – was a dau of Mathias Haag and his first wife;
****George b c1826;
****Wilhelm b 1828, m Rebecca Laudenslager
****Barbara b Nov 28, 1830
****Elmira b Aug 15, 1831, m Lemuel Rowe
Magdalena (Riegel, Bressler, Haag) and 3ʳᵈ husband John Bitterman children:
****Amanda

***MATHIAS (b c1795 -   ), m Anna Maria either Bressler or Hoffman
Mathias and Anna Maria (Bressler or Hoffman) Riegel children (some bapt Hoffman Ch):
****Rebecca b Jun 6, 1817,, m Henry Keboch , had a dau Mary (1862 –1864, bur Hoffman Cem);
****Benjamin (Dec 25, 1819 – Apr 7, 1852, bur Hoffman Cem), m Hannah Rickert (Jun 11, 1824 – Jul 24, 1849), a dau of Henry and Sarah (Romberger) Rickert.]

CHAPTER 11

SHORT MOUNTAIN LAND AND INDIAN TRAIL ROAD
(From S. Crossroads, Along Specktown Road to Gratz Borough Line)

MAP OF SHORT MT., SPECKTOWN & NORTH TO ROUTE 25

Map Drawn By Fisk
Dated 1875

Note: This 1875 map is included to help the readers find properties of interest. By following Sequence of ownership, the land can be located up to present time.

From Loyalton north on South Crossroads Road, a road known as Specktown Road cuts off to the right. This road meanders through a section that from the beginning in 1811 when it was separated from Upper Paxton was Lykens Township. It is sandwiched between Route 25 on the north, the village of Gratz to the east, and on the south, the side of Short Mountain. A vast part of this area continues to be part of Lykens Township. A very small portion at the side of Short Mountain became Wiconisco Township. Because it was originally Lykens Township, and its early history is part of Lykens Township growth, the small part of Wiconisco Twp. is included in this section of the book.

The first part of this segment will focus on the land along Specktown road to the place where Indian Trail Road veers off to the right. Specktown Road is at first surrounded by farm fields on both sides of the road, and belongs to the adjacent Clair Bush farm. But after a short distance, the land becomes part of what was known as the old Abraham Hess tavern property, later referred to as the "Lucas place." In more recent years, several lots were sold from the "Lucas place" and new homes have been built. Several homes were also built on lots on the south side of Specktown Road adjacent to the highway.

The second part of this segment will focus on the land between Route 25 and Specktown Road on the west side of Gratz. This section continued to be farms and farmland until very recent times. Now a number of new homes have been scattered throughout the territory.

HOME OF MR. & MRS. JOHN E. LUCAS 39-024-026

The land for this house was part of the farm owned by Charles E. Lucas Jr. and his wife Grace. On August 5, 1976, Charles Lucas Jr., conveyed this lot containing about one and one-half acres of land to his son John E. Lucas and his wife Linda. The house was built soon after that, and the family continues to live here.

HOME OF DENNIS J. LUCAS 39-024-029

This parcel of land also belonged to the Lucas farm. On April 3, 1978, Charles E. and Grace Lucas conveyed this lot containing over two acre of landt to Larry E. Lucas. He sold to Dennis J. Lucas on October 30, 1985.

HOME OF MR. AND MRS RAY JOHNS 39-04-024
Built 1972

This home is located a distance from the south side of Specktown Road on the side of Short Mountain. The lot was part of the farm owned by Charles E. and Grace Lucas. The deed describes the lot as being on the "western side of an ancient thirty-three foot wide road."

On May 19, 1972, Charles E. and Grace Lucas Jr. sold this lot to Charles W. George . He and his wife had the ranch style home built. Ray and Darla Johns purchased the residence on February 20, 1986, and they continue to live here. Ray is owner of Ray's Front End Shop in Gratz.

[*Ray Johns*, a son of Marlin E. Johns m Darla N. (Radel) Johns, a dau of Mark T. and Mary N (Schwalm) Radel. *Ray and Darla (Radel) Johns have one child: Penny R.* (Johns family genealogy elsewhere in this book).]

HOME OF MR. AND MRS. JOSEPH BUSH 39-024-028

This home located along the edge of Short Mountain a distance to the right of Ray Johns home was part of the Lucas property. Earl S and Pamela R. Lucas received these 4 acres of land October 15, 1973, and sold to Joseph and Monda (Ditty) Bush on May 16, 1985. This home joins the Bush farm owned by Clair Bush, who is the father of Joseph Bush.

Jay L. and Shirley J Sponsler Property
(Was Abraham Hess Hotel 1875, 2 story house built c1830's)

The Log House (Still Standing) As It Looked About 1985

This land is part of two original patents granted by Commonwealth of Pennsylvania to two different individuals. One patent was granted to Nicholas Hoffman, April 25, 1797. The other patent went to Peter Hoffman, Jr. on February 26, 1796, called Walnut Bottom. Peter Hoffman sold his land to Nicholas Hoffman.

On June 24, 1809, Nicholas and Margaretha Hoffman sold 225 acres, 114 perches of land to Jacob Hoffman. Many years later, on April 1, 1854, Jacob and Catherine Hoffman sold ninety-eight and one-half acres of their land with "two log houses, one being weather-boarded" to their son-in-law Abraham Hess. Before living on this property, Abraham Hess lived in Gratz, where he had several properties. He had been a shoemaker all of his life, and in Gratz he conducted his shoemaker business from a shop on lot fifty-three. When he decided to move to the country he sold all of his real estate in Gratz.

When Abraham Hess purchased this plantation, in addition to the two log houses, it included outhouses, other buildings, a log bank barn, stables, warps, woods, and waters. Several years later, Abraham Hess bought another small tract of original Hoffman land, and within his lifetime, accumulated about 110 acres. In 1864, Levi Leitner, a laborer, was a tenant on the Hess farm. Perhaps he was living in the second house.

When he moved to this farm, in addition to making shoes, Hess became an innkeeper. A record of his tavern license has been found for May 1873, and April 1874. He also owned a nice carriage. It is not certain how many years he was in the hotel keeping business. His tavern was known as "Short Mountain" Hotel, and is listed on the 1875 map of Lykens Township.

The1860 census for Lykens Twp. shows Benjamin and Mary Ann Rickert living in a house on one side of Abraham Hess (his daughter & her husband).Jacob and Catherine Hoffman (wife's parents) lived in the adjacent house on the other side. One of them apparently lived in the small old house on the property. By 1880, after he sold his farm, Abraham Hess lived with his son Edward and family in Loyalton, and continued to be a shoemaker.

On September 28, 1875, several years after his wife died, Abraham Hess sold his accumulated land, 110 acres and 144 perches to Benjamin Rickert, a coal miner of Williamstown, and Henry A. Grubb, a farmer in Lykens Township. These two men were Abraham Hess' son-in-laws. For two years after they purchased this property, Grubb and Rickert continued with the hotel business. In 1895, they became involved in a dairy business, and distributed their products to Lykens. The census indicates that Abraham and Catherine Kessler occupied one of the houses on this land in 1880, and Reuben Kessler, their son lived next door.

Catherine (Hoffman) Hess
(1816 – 1873)

Abraham Hess
(1817 – 1892)

Henry A. Grubb
(1850 – 1910)

Isabella Louise (Hess) Grubb
(1857 – 1944)

THE ABRAHAM HESS FAMILY

[**ABRAHAM HESS** (b Apr 7, 1817, Upper Mahanoy Twp, Northld Co - d Dec 23, 1892, bur Simeon Cem), was a son of David and Mariah (Katerman) Hess. A record of the death of Abraham Hess is recorded in St. John's Lutheran Church in Lykens. David Hess and Mariah Katerman were married after her first husband Nicholas Hetrick died. **David and Mariah (Katerman) Hess had these children: John,** moved to Clarion Co.; **David; Solomon; *Abraham; Gideon; Maria Catherine** b Jan 1, 1821, bapt Himmel's Ch, Northld Co. David Hess died about 1844, the date of death of Mariah has not been found.

*ABRAHAM HESS m Catherine Hoffman (b Mar 23, 1816, near Short Mountain - d Dec 19, 1873, in Gratz), a dau of Jacob Hoffman (Feb 4, 1782 - Feb 2, 1862) and his wife Catharine (Ferree) Hoffman (Apr 7, 1783 - Aug 1,1859). Both bur Hoffman Cem. **Abraham and Catherine (Hoffman) Hess children:**
MARY ANN (Oct 16, 1838 - Jan 16, 1916, bur Seiberts Cem, Williamstown), m Benjamin Rickert (Oct 25, 1839 -Dec 25, 1900), a son of Peter and Elizabeth (Klinger) Rickert. Benjamin apparently was a member of Oakdale Church at Loyalton. He was a member of their Quarterly Conference and attended a meeting in December 1877. In 1870 Benjamin Rickert and family lived in Williams Township, and Jacob Bellon, age 20 lived with them, and worked in the mines. **Benjamin & Mary Ann (Hess) Rickert children: ***Mary E. b c1861;*****Charles M.** b c1863, was a teacher in 1880; *****Lillie C** (b & d 1870).

JACOB A. (Jan 29, 1840 - Aug 9, 1917), had a son *****Harvey Adam Lincoln Hess with Ella Amanda Rodenbach (Feb 7, 1846 - Nov 27, 1882), a dau of John and Sarah (Holdeman) Rodenbach. Harvey A. Hess (Nov 25, 1864 - Dec 1, 1951), m Flora Clemens (Oct 18, 1866 - Oct 14, 1943). Harvey moved to Kansas about 1887. **Harvey and Flora had a son: ****Chester Clemens Hess** (Aug 26, 1909 - Jul 9, 1984), a medical doctor.
Jacob A. Hess b 1840 (from above), m in Berrysburg Aug 6, 1864, Amanda S. Klinger (Oct 7, 1845 - Sep 23, 1931), of Pillow. **Jacob and Amanda (Klinger) Hess children: ***Cora Minerva** b Apr 30, 1866; *****Anna Victoria** b Aug 4, 1867;*****Ida** (1870 - 1871); *****Mary Deborah** b Oct 26,1872; *****William Henry Harrison** b Oct 26,1874; *****John Quincy Adam** b Jun 28,1876;*****Oscar** (1882 -1883);***** Mabel Cath** b Feb 28, 1884. Jacob Hess served during the Civil War with Co H. 210th Pa. Regiment. After the war, he lived in Lykens Twp, then Minersville for 26 years, where he died.

**AMANDA (Sep 1, 1842 - Aug 31, 1876), not married
ADALINE b c1845. She lived with the Simon Hartman family in 1850, m _____ Umholtz (this is probably Jacob Umholtz, (Mar 18, 1824 - Jun 8, 1894, bur Simeon Cem), a son of John Jacob and Catharine (Harman) Umholtz. Jacob 1st. married Mary Artz b c1826, a dau of _____ . **Jacob and Mary (Artz) Umholtz children: Jonathan b c1848 - d after 1897); **Harry** (Oct 25, 1849- May 2, 1923, Phila), a stage driver, hotel keeper, m Emma Clara **Aaron A.** (Jun 9, 1855 - Jan 28, 1897, killed in mines); **Mary A.** b c1859. Jacob Umholtz m 2nd Adaline Hess. **Jacob and Adaline (Hess) Umholtz children:***Elmer Lincoln** b Aug 11, 1865, bapt Simeon Ref Ch, Gratz. In 1870, Jacob and Adaline Umholtz lived in part of the residence of Jacob and Magdalena Umholtz in Lykens Twp. In 1880, they lived in Gratz, and Elizabeth Ritzman age 56, a "lady boarder" lived with them.
EMMA (b Jan 29, 1847 in Gratz - d Oct 9, 1943 in Elizabethtown, Pa.), she was with the Simon Hartman family in 1850. Emma m 1st _____ Gratz, but later divorced. She m a 2nd time, Nov 15, 1868, to Jacob Wilt (Jun 10, 1833 - d in Linglestown), **had two known children: ***George Wellington b May 1, 1869; ***Maggie Elizabeth (Wilt) (b Aug 29, 1871, Wiconisco - 1958, Elizabathtown), m Apr 20, 1893 William Charles Gratz (b Apr 29, 1868, Lykens - d Dec 31, 1932, Delaware Co.), both bur Lykens, Pa. William was a son of David and Kate (Martz) Gratz, grandson of Edward Gratz, (founder of Lykens), great-grandson of Simon Gratz (founder of Gratz). William C. and Maggie Gratz were married in Lykens, and lived there for sometime before moving to Overbrook section of Philadelphia, where he was employed in his father's business. They later moved to Delaware Co, near Philadelphia, where William died. Maggie lived alternately with the several children until her death. **William and Maggie (Wilt) Gratz had these children: Miriam H.** b Jun 4, 1894; **Henrietta; Lester; David; Emily; Katharine**, all born in Wiconisco.
**EDWARD A . b c1852, m Mary Jane Snyder b c1856. Edward and his family lived in Washington Twp in 1880, and his father Abraham a shoemaker, by then a widower was living with the family. Edward was a

411

life insurance agent. **Edward and Mary J. (Snyder) Hess children**: ***Anna Catharine** b Sep 23, 1875; ***Beulah A** b c1878; ***John C.** b Mar 1880; Linnie Elisabeth b Dec 11, 1882; ****ISABELLA** (Dec 6, 1857 – Jul 24, 1944), was an adopted dau of Abraham and Catharine Hess. She m 1874 Henry A. Grubb.

THE GRUBB FAMILY

[**HENRY A. GRUBB** (Sep 30,1850 –May 22,1910, bur Maple Grove Cem, E'ville), son of Henry & Abbey (Moretz) Grubb, was a native of Greenwood Township, Perry County. His mother was a native of Northld. Co. His grandfather Henry A. Grubb settled in Perry County, and the family had been there many years. When Henry A. Grubb (the third) left Perry Co. he worked for George Neagley in nearby Washington Twp.

Henry A. Grubb and Isabella Hess were married in 1874. Isabella (b Dec 6, 1857 in Lykens Twp – d Jul 24, 1944, bur Maple Grove Cem), was an adopted daughter of Abraham Hess, who had been the previous hotel keeper here. **Henry and Isabella (Hess) Grubb had these children:**
*William Calvin** (Jun 25, 1876 Loyalton - 1949, bur Fairview Cem, Williamstown, alone), m Sep 16, 1899, Katie Cenora Umholtz (Aug 8, 1879 Gratz - Jul 28, 1956, bur Simeon Cem), a dau of Levi and Anna Maria (Radel) Umholtz. William was a miner in 1900, and they lived near his parents in Lykens Twp. **William and Kate (Umholtz) Grubb children: **Forrest W.** (Mar 18, 1901 - Mar 16,1941), m 1924 Marguerite Finley (b 1905 Wmstown – Jul 10, 1983), a dau of Robert & Martha (Bowen) Finley; **Floyd Henry** (Jan 31,1903 -Aug 5, 1963, bur Fairview Cem, Wmstown), m Cleo A. Wolfe (1903–1963);** **Mary Louisa** (Dec 7, 1904 - Loyalton - Oct 29, 1988, bur Fairview Cem), m 1st John E. Finley (1903 – 1936), 2nd John Weaver;**Laura Catherine** (May 28, 1908 Loyalton - Dec 9, 1993, E'ville), m Nov 23, 1935, John Albert Forney; **Orpha Arlene** (Jan 2,1910 - Dec 28, 1910, bur Simeon Cem);**Mark William** (Dec 19, 1913, Loyalton - Aug 22, 1964, bur Wiconisco Cem), m 1944 Ellen Lutz b 1914, a dau of George & Elizabeth Lutz;**Esther Naomi** (Jan 24, 1915 - Jan 22, 1928, bur Simeon Cem), she died of the result of a beating from her father which caused spinal meningitis. The father was taken away by a sheriff, and no one heard of him again for many years;**Ceylon Delbert** (Jun 11, 1918 –Aug 14, 1984, bur E'ville), m Dorothy M Thompson b 1920; Jean Eleanor b Jun 6, 1922 Coaldale, m Earl Carr Shire, Jr. b 1927, Phila, 2nd Howard Dean Hasbood b 1919, a son of John & Saraha Ellen (Wert) Hasgood; *Annie Beulah** (b Mar 3, 1878 – d Jul 8, 1948), m William Henry Boyer (Mar 26, 1877 – Jan 30, 1957, **had these children: Edna** b 1899 m George Irvin Spotts b 1898, **their children: Gladys** b 1918, m John Strohecker; Melvin b 1921, m Geraldine Straub; Richard b 1922, m Francis Lebo; Ruth b 1922 (twin), m Albert Wentzel; Mildred b 1924, m Russell Snyder; Thelma b 1929 m Robert Bellis; Grace b 1931, m Elwood Lucas, Sr, Forrest R. Otto; *Edward N.** (b May 21,1880 – 1946, bur Maple Grove Cem), m Annie A ___ (1885 – 1911). Edward m 2nd in Mar 1913 Maude Irene Harper b Oct 4, 1894; *Charles S.**(Apr 28, 1882 – Dec 22, 1928, of heart attack, bur Maple Grove Cem, E'ville), m Jul 18, 1903 Annie M. Miller (Jul 17, 1883 – Jun 11, 1971), a dau of . James and Sara A. Miller of Loyalton. **Charles and Annie (Miller) Grubb children: **Myrl Emily** (1905 – 1977, bur Maple Grove Cem., E'ville), m C. Elwood Hoover (1903 – 1975), a son of Elwood and Lillian (Wetzel) Hoover;**Arthur James Henry** 1907 –1986), m Ruth L. Bond (1907 - 1988), a dau of Thomas & Ellen (Price) Bond.. Arthur was mayor of Williamstown for 32 years: **Ruth N** m Francis A. Reichenbach; **Catharine L** d infant. *Carrie M.** (b Aug 19,1883 – Apr 11, 1951, bur Maple Grove Cem), m Oct 1901 to George A. Bonawitz (Feb 21, 1880 – Dec 8, 1928)]

In 1893 Benjamin Rickert and Mary sold one acre, 131 perches of land to Amanda Gunderman. Several years after Benjamin Rickert died, on March 20, 1911, his heirs sold the remainder of his portion of the property to James A. Kessler. On April 1, 1911, Isabella L. and Charles S. Grubb sold their share of the 109 acres, fourteen perch farm to James A. Kessler.

James Kessler was described as a very thin man. His wife Beulah was in contrast a very large woman. At first when James Kessler owned the brewery in Loyalton, he and his wife lived on this farm. One of his livelihoods was keeping bees. While the Kessler's lived here, Margaret Shadel's aunt and uncle, William C. and Kate (Umholtz) Grubb lived in the small house on or near the Kessler property. A large mulberry tree stood along side of the road, about 2000 feet from the little house. When Margaret or other relatives and friends visited her aunt, they always included a visit to the mulberry tree (in season) to enjoy the delectable berries. This aunt had four children the Kesslers had none. When the Kessler's eventually moved to Loyalton, they volunteered to take several of the youngsters to live with them.

After the family moved to Loyalton in these surrounding fields they continued to grow the corn, barley, and rye used to make their distillery products. The grain was ground at the gristmill located at the west end of Loyalton, called Fishers Mill. Shortly after son George died in 1912, at the age of forty, Reuben hired a brew-master to take his place, and the distillery continued to prosper. Jim spent most of his time on this farm. After Reuben died in 1915, at the age of sixty-nine, Jim spent all of his time on the farm with the tenant farmer.

When World War I began, grain became scarce, the tenant farmer quit, and Jim was left alone with a large farm and no one to help. He did have a pair of horses and a wagon, but needed some cattle and farm implements, which he purchased from the farmer. He planted one of the fields in corn, and had a vegetable garden. Another complication plagued Jim. A few years prior to this, he had fallen and broke a bone in his shoulder. He never went to a doctor so he was disabled and was limited in what he could do. His mother was living with him at the time, and each evening he would hitch a ride to Loyalton for supplies etc.

After Jim quit farming, the farm remained idle. Then the rumor was spread around that the tavern was haunted. The neighbors reported that they heard a baby crying. Several other people reported hearing voices and seeing ghosts. In recalling these incidents, several people have said that these things actually happened. One person suspected that rumors were began back in those days to discourage persons from searching for whiskey that could have been in the tavern.

While the Kessler's lived in Loyalton they rented this farm to tenants. One of their tenants was Morris Albert Shade. While the Shade family lived here, this farm was in very good condition. The large house was beautiful, and an older, smaller log house survived below the mansion house. Several other outbuildings were on the property, including a mill, water trough, and a very nice barn. A pond had been built below the old house, and an outdoor bake over nearby. Mr. Hoover had a dairy in Specktown, and when he died Albert purchased a small milk wagon and horses from widow Hoover. Two black horses named Ted and Mell pulled the wagon. Each day he filled a ten-gallon milk can equipped with a spigot, and placed it beside his wagon seat. He had a long handled dipper, and with it, he could fill containers that his customers brought to his wagon. The containers were of every variety, and in any state of cleanliness! In addition to milk, Albert Shade took eggs and butter on his route to Loyalton, Lykens and Wiconisco, and sometimes to Gratz. If he did not have a large supply of products, he purchased more from neighbor Johnny Snyder.

During Gratz Fair week, Albert took cattle to the exhibit. He drove them from his farm to Gratz. Walking among the cattle was a bull, which he led all the way to town. They also had geese and chickens on the farm. The Shades had many cows, and this was before fields were fenced. Ellen rode a horse and was assigned the chore of "watching" the cows in the pasture.

Ellen took piano lessons from Morris Zerfing while they lived on this farm. When her grandmother became sick, she came to live with Ellen's family. They needed the "piano room" for a bedroom for the grandmother, so that was the end of the piano lessons.

In the spring of 1920, William and Helen Deitrich purchased a small farm next to this farm. They had moved to Harrisburg in May 1918, but now they purchased Helen's grandmother Riegels' farm.

On April 13,1925, James A. and Beulah Kessler of Loyalton, sold this property to Fremont J. Mauser of Lykens Township. [Kessler genealogy included in write-up of distillery property page 155 and page 293.]

On April 6, 1939, the land of Fremont J. Mauser was sold to Samuel O. and Elva Pell. On March 13, 1943, Samuel O. Pell and his wife Elva M, of Lykens, transferred this farm with dwelling house, barn and other out buildings to Charles E. Lucas, Jr. and Grace his wife of Hegins, Schuylkill County.

During the early 1940s, the Barry family rented this farm from the Lucas family, over a period of about four years. The farm continued to be in good condition while the Barry's lived there. The buildings included the big barn, an outhouse, milk house, and the dwelling house. The interior of the house was also in good condition, except that from age, the floorboards were beginning to slope. The Barry's were farmers, and grew all types of grains and corn. Their daughter Margaret remembers that she worked in the Gratz factory, while she was here. But she also helped with the farm chores. She especially remembers helping to chop corn and make shocks, then later to husk the corn from the shocks. Earl Barry and family also raised chickens and pigs, and had a dairy herd. They sold their milk to Johns Dairy.

Pictures From The Barry Family.
(Taken when they lived in this home).

Standing: Jean Henninger; Betty Reed;
Barbara Reed.
Kneeling: Sarah Barry

This Picture Taken When Barry
Family Lived In The House

THE BARRY FAMILY

[JOHN EARL BARRY (1897 - 1962, bur Hoffman Cem), son of John I. Barry (1870 - 1943, bur Maple Grove Cem, E'ville) and Mary Ellen (Lehman) Barry (1858 - 1939) of Jackson Twp. John Earl m Jun 2, 1917, by Rev. Wehr, to Cora E. Troutman (1901 - 1993, age 92), a dau of James M. and Katie M. Troutman who had the dairy in Lykens Township. Cora came from a big family, and thought perhaps she did not want to have so many children. When she had the first child, she gave him several names, thinking he would be the only one. Then when the second son was born she gave him several names. The list of children below suggests that she needed to come up with several more names for succeeding children! **Earl and Cora (Troutman) Barry had these children:**

Floyd John James (1917 - 1941, bur Maple Grove Cem, E'ville), had polio, but it was not confirmed until fifteen years later. He m Mildred I. Lebo, b 1917, **had one dau Ann Louise**

Ralph E. (b 1919, Lyk Twp - d 1942, bur E'ville), member of Salem Ref Ch, E'ville, died age 23, of injuries sustained at Colonial Park, Harrisburg, when he fell under the wheels of a moving freight car near the Reading Railroad Company. Ralph m Pauline E. Gelnett (1919 - 1999), **had dau Mary Elizabeth**

Mildred N. m April 8, 1944, Joseph Herbert Hartman (Jun 2, 1924 - 1994), a son of Joseph H. and Elma B. (Willier) Hartman. Mildred and Joseph began dating while the Barry family lived on this farm. It all began when Mildred and her sister-in-law Mim were out driving one afternoon. They passed two young men in a convertible and Mildred whistled at them. The men turned around and came back to talk with the

414

girls. Mildred and Joe were married April 8, 1944. **Joseph and Mildred (Barry) Hartman had these children:**

Joanne, m Merlin Wirt, **has two sons:**Timothy; Andrew; **John** m Barbara Gallagher, a dau of Martin and Margaret (Hockenberry) Gallagher, originally from Carsonville. **John and Barbara (Gallagher) Hartman have these children:** Pamela Ann; John Joseph Jr.; Mathew Martin Luther; Mary Elizabeth; Benjamin Michael; Gabrielle Joanne.

Ella May b Feb 7, 1923, m Charles Bellis b Jan 25, 1918, a son of Elmer and Luma (Hartman) Bellis Ella walked from this farm to Elizabethville to attend high school, and never missed a day.

Albert Troutman m Joyce Stoneroad

Robert m Rosina Howard

Irene m Kenneth Deibler;

William L. b 1931, m Janice L. Smeal b 1934

Sarah m 1st Guy Hoffman, 2nd Henry Gunderman

Roy b c1940 on this farm, m Carolyn Starr;

Lester E. m Edith Zerby

On October 30, 1973, Charles E. Lucas Jr and his wife Grace sold about seven acres from these premises to Jay L. and Shirley J. Sponsler of Halifax. They conveyed the remaining property to Gerald F. and Linda K. Wiest on April 20, 1992.

HOME OF MR. AND MRS WALTER SHADE JR.
House built c1998

The land for this house was part of the land belonging to the Lucas farm that was sold to Gerald F. and Linda K. Wiest in 1992. It is located on the eastern side of the farm, on the north side of Specktown Road. Gerald F. and Linda K. Wiest sold about four acres of land to Walter D. and Helen L. Shade on January 6, 1995. That same year they had this ranch style home built on the lot. Walter and Helen resided in Gratz before they moved to this residence.

[**Walter Shade Jr.** is a son of Walter D. and Evelyn (Fogle) Shade of Gratz. He m Helen Witmer, b Jun 23, 1946, a dau of Kermit and Martha (Lenker) Witmer of near Pillow. **Walter and Helen have one daughter**: Linda b 1966, m Jeff Spotts, and they have adopted two children.]

HOME OF MR. AND MRS. WILLIAM R. SHADE

This is another private home that was at one time part of the property known as the Lucas farm. It does not border on Specktown Road, so access to this property is gained by a side road on the west side of Specktown Road. This parcel of 15 acres was conveyed from Charles E. Lucas, Jr. widower to Marlin L. Lucas September 29, 1979. He had the ranch style house built on the land. On July 29, 1987, Marlin L. Lucas conveyed the same to William R. Shade, Jr. and his wife Susan J. Shade. They have continued to live here with their family. William and Susan Shade own and operate SHADES GROCERY STORE, located in Gratz. A sandwich shop has been added to their store.

[William Shade, Jr, is a son of William Shade Sr and his wife Dora (Miller) Shade of Gratz. He m Susan Susan Schwalm b 1952, a dau of the late Dr. Glenn P. Schwalm and his wife the later Carolyn (Dunkelberger) Schwalm of Valley View. *William and Susan (Schwalm) Shade have three children*: *Jared*; *Laura*; *Jenny*.]

THE HARTMAN RICKERT SETTLEMENT

Hartman (Sr.) and Magdalena Rickert and their next of kin established their own permanent little village in Lykens Township. Located on the slope near end of Short Mountain, it was northeast of the early Hoffman settlement. They were natives of Germany, and along with Hartman Rickert Jr. and Christophel Rickert arrived in Philadelphia aboard the ship "Dorothea" on October 14, 1787. About two weeks later on October 31st, the names of Hartman and Magdalena Rickert appear on a "Redemptioners' Contract" as follows:

"Hartman Rickert and Magdalena his wife bound themselfs Servants to John Demlinger of Strasburg Township, Lancaster County, State of Pennsylvania farmer to Serve him four years Each, to have customary freedom, Suits or Fifteen Pounds therein Lieu of their New Suits and Cloaths for their son L38.7.6 ----. "

The Rickert family continued to reside in Strasburg, Lancaster County for several years. They were there as late as1790. But soon after that Hartman Rickert Sr. and Magdalena along with their nephew Hartman Rickert, Jr. came to what is now Lykens Township. They were affiliated with St. Peter's (Hoffman) Church during the 1790s. We have not located Christophel Rickert in this area. Perhaps he stayed in Lancaster County. A Christoph Reichart family lived in Lancaster County as early as 1757. Perhaps they were early relatives of this family.

On March 22, 1793, Hartman Rickert received a warrant of 109 acres 150 perches of land in Upper Paxton Twp. from Commonwealth of Pennsylvania. The land was surveyed on April 22, 1811. This land was located south of the land that belonged to the Lykens family, near land of Peter Hen and John Dietrich. Hartman Rickert also took up additional tracts of land. He received a15-acre grant in 1812. Another tract Commonwealth of Pennsylvania granted to Peter Hen on March 8, 1792. Peter and Elizabeth Hen conveyed 110 acres to Daniel Maurer on May 18, 1793. Several years later on December 12, 1797 Daniel and Mary Maurer conveyed 75 acres of the land to Hartman and Magdalena Rickert, and they sold this land with appurtenances on May 12,1812 (recorded 1825). All of these acres were together in the southern end of Upper Paxton Twp, beyond what is now Loyalton. Hartman and Magdalena Rickert by two separate deeds conveyed this land to Nicholas Bressler in April 1813. They apparently abandoned the idea of settling in this particular spot.

Hartman Rickert does appear on the "window tax" record of 1798 as having a twenty-one by sixteen-foot cabin in Wiconisco Valley, joining Levi Buffington. Hartman Rickert is also listed on the "1798 window tax" record as being a tenant living in the cabin owned by Daniel Ferree. This cabin measured twenty by fourteen foot and a good wood barn was also on the property that was located near Wiconisco Creek, next to Isaac Ferree. They had not yet purchased their Short Mountain land, and the exact location of this property has not been learned.

On January 3, 1785, Commonwealth of Pennsylvania warranted land known as "Chelmford" in two separate tracts to Michael Salada. The tracts were surveyed August 3, 1806, and patented January 28, 1807. The large tract contained 231 acres, 149 perches with six-percent allowance for roads. The second tract contained 50 acres, making a total of 281 acres 149 perches

Michael Salada owned the acreage briefly before his death. By his will made September 12, 1810, he gave his executors authority to sell his land (except about eleven acres which he sold before 1810 to Jacob Huber). The executors sold the remaining 271 acres, 149 perches on April 17, 1811 to (John) Hartman Rickert Sr. The Rickert family took up residency on this land, and began to form the little village on the hilly terrain on the edge of Short Mountain. The large tract of land slowly developed into small one to ten acre plots of land with dwellings that were eventually conveyed to members of the family. Over the years, some of the descendants cultivated small farms, while others worked in the mines. The neighborhood survived for many years. Over time, relatives transferred the small tracts with houses from one generation to another until well into the 1900's. Then the old log houses began to deteriorate, and one by one they fell into ruin. Today but one house has survived, and no one has lived in it for many years. Much of the cleared land has been taken over by new forest growth. The Hartman Rickert community has passed into oblivion.

The nearby coalfields may have contributed to the down hill slide of this neat little village. From early times coal was mined in most every part of Short Mountain. Speculators purchased land very close to these houses, hoping for a good source of coal. One mine tunnel was developed by Amos Hoffman and John B. Miller during the 1860's, but later abandoned. Then in 1886, Jacob Shiro received a ten-year lease to re-open the mine. He and his partners C. T. Bowman, William A. Kotka and H. B Hoffman formed a company that at various times was named NORTH SIDE COLLIERY OR KEYSTONE MINE, but better known by local residents as SHIRO'S MINE. This group was in business until about 1900. A coal washery was established during the 1920 or 1930 period, but it was not too successful. Although threatened by the coal industry, this part of Short Mountain escaped the scars of mining. Today, a person wishing to find the remains of the old houses would have to be guided to the locations by someone well acquainted with Short Mountain. As previously mentioned, until recently, it has again become mostly wood land.

Hartman and Magdalena Rickert Sr. had no children (or at least had none that grew to maturity). When Hartman Rickert, Sr. died, in April 1814 (funeral held Apr 14, 1814 by Rev. Reily, in Lykens Twp, Dauphin Co), his widow Magdalena and nephew Hartman Rickert Jr. inherited his estate jointly. It was divided after Magdalena died. A death date has not been found for Magdalena, but she was listed in 1837 under female communicants at Hoffman Church, and she appears on the 1840 Lykens Township census, over eighty years old. She probably died late spring 1840.

Hartman Rickert, Sr did not leave a will. But an inventory of the estate of (John) Hartman Rickert, yeoman was made on May 17, 1814. It is an interesting look at the household items owned by settlers at that time. The following items were listed in the inventory:

A 12 year old mare, 5 year old horse, 7 year old mare, cow, a 16 year old cow, heifer, bull, 2 calves, 5 sheep, 3 large hogs, 4 different sized hogs, 2 small hogs.

A wagon without body, hay ladder with tackling, a cutting box with apparatus, 4 scythes, 2 hay forks, 1 shovel and a wooden fork, 4 rakes, dung fork, dung hoe and shovel, meat tub, 2 flax crates, 2 pine tubs, 2 small kegs, 5 barrels, horse gear generally, 8 cow chains, a harrow, scale, double tree, chain, apple mill with apparatus, grindstone, iron kettle, rifle gun, shot gun.

Six cups and saucers & teaspoons, 6 small plates, walnut table with drawers & a lock, sundry glass and queens ware, sundry tin, pewter and other wares.

1 stove pipe, 4 chairs, a bed and bedstead, walnut chest, Bible, testament, hymn and other books, a pair of scales, looking glass, 9 pair of cotton, linen and woolen trousers, a great coat, 5 cotton, woolen and other coats, coats (long and short), an old great coat, a dressed dear skin, 2 tin buckets and 2 tin ladles, ladles and strainer, 2 pans and a pot, 2 iron pots, a copper teakettle, one dozen pewter plates, 5 pewter dishes and ½ dozen spoons, 1 dozen tin dishes, sundry tin ware, spice-box and sundries.

Shovel & tongs, bellows, etc, knives & forks, a funnel and salt box, 2 saws, an adz, a drawing knife and augurs, 3 chisels and pr of corn p____, grubbing hoe, axe & sythe, old iron, a churn, a brass kettle, hemp, 4 old sythes, 3 tubs, 3 small stands and a milch strainer, stove and pipe.

Small table, kitchen dresser, wood wheel an old saddle, plow shears, an old plough and tacklin, bed stead, chest, 12 sheets, 6 table clothes, table cloth and 2 hand towels, new coverlet, small blanket, coverlet, 3 ½ yard linen, sheet and wollet, piece of flax linen, 32 lb of soap, 31 pound of tow and 2 bags, 13 pound tallow, 5 pound beeswax, 1 ½ - pounds flax seed, 5 bushels of wheat, 7 pounds flour, 3 brooms, spinning wheel and real, flax hatchel, a dough tray, a barrel with vinegar, a small keg with vinegar, 10 bushels of potatoes, a wooden house clock, 4 acres of wheat and rye in the field, 4 acres of wheat in the ground, plough, a bond payable by Christian Hoffman $113.50, a note payable by Jacob Hoffman $40, a note payable by Jacob Huber Sr. $17, a bond payable by Nicholas Bressler $46.67, a bond payable by Nicholas Bressler $266, cash on hand in bank notes $70, cash in silver and gold $55.84.

During the early years, after Hartman Sr. died, Hartman Rickert Jr. was assessed for all of the Rickert land. At first he had at least two houses, and later as the family expanded, more land was cleared and several houses were built on the Rickert tract. At one point Martin Rickert was assessed for five houses. The Hartman family continued to live in the same neighborhood, adding new dwellings for family members as needed. Each of the sons of Hartman Rickert, Jr. developed his own skills. Henry was a weaver, Martin a shoemaker, and others were miners or farmers.

During the next years while Magdalena, widow, and Hartman Rickert, Jr. shared the estate of Hartman Rickert, Sr., several small tracts of land were sold, mostly to relatives. Those tracts will be traced later in this account. But most of the Rickert land and houses continued to be shared until about three years after Magdalena Rickert widow of Hartman Rickert Sr. died. They were then divided among the three sons. Not much is known about the life of Hartman Rickert, Jr. and his wife Catharine. We know that in 1826, Hartman Jr., expanded their little log house by building a two- story section to the front of the house. That date is carved in roman numerals into one of the attic beams. The will he penned on May 15, 1828, several weeks before his death, gives some insight into the family togetherness apparently enjoyed at least by some of the family members.

Hartman Rickert, Jr. will (May 15, 1828)

" . . . . . As for my temporal estate, consisting in a farm lying in Lykens Township and the county aforesaid, and several movables, which shall be treated as follows: All my movables, house and land that is to say all what now is found in my possession, shall all remain in the possession and in the hands of my son Martin and my beloved widow Catharina, until my youngest son Jacob has reached or should reach the age of twenty one years, furniture and all appurtenances and the said farm all in the same condition as it is found; excepting that they must take care of and support the minor children, that is to say so as we by this time leave, eat, drink and work together, and after my demise to regulate my affairs and to pay all my remaining debts; also to pay punctually to my beloved mother the allowance as required. After that my youngest son Jacob has reached or shall have reached the age of twenty one years, then do I bequeath and give the above named farm and all movables which will be found to be my property to my three sons, Martin, John and Jacob as their full and entire property, yet under the conditions that they must give to my beloved widow Catharina as long as she bears my name and remains unmarried her yearly support, and also to give her right in the whole house, kitchen and cellar, one piece in the garden, two cows and provender for two cows and to let them go in the pasture where theirs go, also to give place and room in the stable and barn, to keep the provender fresh, to make the feed, carry it home, to give her as much fine cut wood as she may need, to give her the half from one third part of summer and winter fruit from all what shall be saved, out on the said piece of ground accepting oats, one hundred and fifty pound hogs meat, one third part of the hens eggs, to give her kitchen and house furniture as much as is necessary for her use, to allow her (when there is any) as much fruit as she may want for herself. Also two sheep, food and pasture and to be kept with and in the same manner as theirs and to pay six hundred dollars good money to my six children. . . . "

In 1828, when Hartman Rickert, Jr. died, the land was listed under Hartman Rickert estate, and his two sons Henry and Martin Rickert were named as tenants on the property. Martin continued to be assessed for the land and houses. One by one as they became of age, his brothers became listed as tenants on his property. Peter and Henry were listed in 1837 as tenants, and John having reached his legal age, was listed as a single tenant. In 1840, the tax record assessed the Rickert property under Martin Rickert and company, and Peter, Jacob and John were listed as tenants. Shortly after that, when widow Magdalena Hartman died, the land was divided.

THE RICKERT /Ruckert FAMILY
Much of the genealogy research done by Norman Rickert and Lois Rickert

[This Rickert (Rueckert, Riegard, etc) family is traced to **Daniel Rueckert** born in 1670. He died in Bayern, Pfalz, Erpolzheim, Germany Jan 17, 1717, **leaving his wife Elizabeth and these children: Johann Herman** b 1707, m Anna Barbara Diehl; **Catharina** b 1709, m Johannes Diehl; **Anna Margaretha** b 1712; **Johannes Zacharias** b 1713; **Johann Simon** b 1715, m Jul 8, 1731 Anna Catharina Boeckelin , **and had these children:** Anna Margaretha b 1732; Anna Maria b Feb1735 (twin); *Johann Hartman b Feb 1735 (twin); **Johann Henrich** b May 1716, **had a son** Johann Henrich (no dates), m May 4, 1779 Anna Magdalena Koob, a dau of Peter and Margaretha Elis Koob of Erpolzheim, Germany.

Johann Henrich and Anna Magdalena (Koob) Rickert had a son **Hartman Rickert (Jr) born Dec 31, 1780. Johann Heinrich Rickert died in Germany, and Magdalena (Koob) Rickert married Hartman Rickert, Sr. ((1735 – 1814), a cousin to Heinrich Rickert. Hartman and Magdalena (Koob, Rickert) Rickert, and Hartman Rickert, Jr. came to America on board the ship "Dorothea" landing at the port of Philadelphia on October 14, 1787. If Hartman Sr. and Magdalena had children, they did not live to adulthood.

*JOHANN HARTMAN RICKERT (b Feb 1735 in Bayern, Pfalz, Friedelsheim, Germany - d 1814 of Tuberculosis (his funeral held Apr 14, 1814 by Rev. Reily, in Lykens Twp, Dau Co, Pa.), a son of Johann Simon and Anna Catharine (Boeckelin) Ruckert. He m Maria Magdalena Koob Rickert (b between 1750 & 1760 in Palatinate, Germany - d 1840/41, Lykens Twp).

HARTMAN RICKERT JR. (b Dec 31, 1780 in Germany - d Jun 8, 1828, death recorded in St. David's Church, Killinger, but states that Hartman Rickert Jr. is from Hoffman Cong). It also mentions the date they came to America (1787), and that Heinrich and A. Magdalena Rickert are his parents. Hartman m Catharine Lubold (b c1785 - d Aug 29, 1860, bur Hoffman Cem), a dau of John Martin and Catherine (Bechtel) Lubold of Lykens Township. Hartman Rickert, Jr. was naturalized on October 10, 1823 in Harrisburg.

Hartman and Catharine (Lubold) Rickert had ten children, one died before the parents (most bapt St. Johns Luth, Berrysburg):

***MAGDALENA (Aug 24, 1800- Feb 8, 1871), death recorded Hoffman Church book), m George Burd (b c1805 – d ____).A Magdalena Rickert and Daniel Heinrich had a child **Daniel** b May 21, 1821, bapt Hoffman Church. A **Daniel Henry and wife Hannah had a child Jacob** b Apr 10, 1845, bapt Hoffman Ch.George and Magdalena (Rickert) Burd had these children:

Jacob (1826 - ___), m _____ had two children bapt 1846 at St. John's Ref Ch, Orwigsburg, Sch Co: Amanda Rebecca and George Washington;

 Elizabeth A. b 1827, m William C. Messner;

 Sarah J. (Jan 26, 1829 – Feb 9, 1916, bur Hoffman Cem), m Apr 5, 1850 in Loyalton by John Womer, Justice of the Peace, to John Bellon (May 7, 1820 or May 31, 1821 (baptismal date) – May 5, 1892), a son of David and Anna Maria (Scheible) Bellon. John Bellon was born in Wurtemburg, Germany, and came to this country before 1850. The Census record for 1850 places him in Wiconisco Twp. He worked in the coal mines for eight years before being enrolled October 13, 1862 in Co I of the 177th Regt. Pa. Volunteers, and later enrolled Aug 5, 1863 with Capt. C. A. Harper in the 103rd Regt. Pa. Vol. After John died, Sarah continued to live in their home in Lykens Township, and in 1900 her daughters Ida, and Rosa lived with her. Her son Edward and granddaughter Pearly M. Rowe age 7 also was with her.

John and Sarah (Burd) Bellon had these children (bapt Hoffman Ch & Zion Luth, Lykens): Daniel (May 30, 1852 – Nov 4, 1868) Sarah A. b Nov 27, 1854; **John J.** (b Mar 27, 1855 – Oct 2, 1930, at his home, bur Hoffman Cem), m Ida Bellon. He was found dead in bed, due to a cerebral hemorrhage; Franklin (b Apr 17, 1857 – d Nov 20, 1934 in Hegins, Sch Co, bur Spring Glen Meth Cem, Hubley Twp), m 1889 to Mary Catharine Weaver b May 1867, and lived in Lykens Twp in 1900, next to Martin P. Schaffner,they had these children: Annic E b Oct 1895; Jennie M b Apr 1900.; **Louisa** b c1858; **Amanda** (Jul 15, 1859 – Mar 16, 1866, bur Hoffman Cem) Catherine b Jul 14, 865; **William** b Jul 21, 1868, m Jan 14, 1898 to Mary M. Keiter at her home in Fisherville; **Rose Ann** b c1871; **Amy E.** (Oct 13, 1871 – Nov 11, 1894, bur Hoffman Cem) Anna Elisabeth b Jul 17, 1873 – Nov 11, 1894); **Amelia** b c1874; Eddie Elsworth M. (b Sep 7, 1875 – 1957, bur IOOF Cem, Lykens), m Dec 15, 1900 in Gratz to Cora J. Keiter (1880 – 1929).

Isaac (b Dec 1832 – d Jan 1865, bur Hoffman Cem), m Mary Ann Ferree (Oct 19, 1838 – May 27, 1895), a dau of George W. and Leah (Umholtz) Ferree of Lykens Twp. **Isaac and Mary Ann (Ferree) Burd had these children: Mary Louisa** (no dates) m May 12, 1872 in Lykens to Durrell Seesholtz (1846 – 1916, bur IOOF Cem, Lykens), a son of Rebecca and _____ Seesholtz of Lykens. Durrell was a "workman in the cars in 1870." By 1911 they lived in Harrisburg. **Durrell and Mary (Burd) Seesholtz had these children:** Harry F. Jan 4, 1874 – Oct 20, 1943), Pvt in USMC, bur Simeon Cem, Gratz; Edith; Mary R.] Samuel b c1857; Elizabeth (c1858 – Apr 3, 1900, bur Union Salem Cem, Berrysburg), m Jan 3, 1875 Wiliam C. Messner, a son of John P. Messner of lykens Twp.; In 1870, after her father died, Elizabeth lived with the Cyrene Bowman family in Gratz; Susan b c 1860; George W. (Mar 1, 1861 – Apr 6, 1889, bur Simeon Cem, Gratz, bur beside his mother). He was living with the James Kolba family in 1870.The 1880 census states that he had a sore back. His obituary describes him as an unfortunate mortal who was crippled by a mine accident early in life. Henry H. b c 1863, m Ida ____ lived in Mt. Carmel; Emma Jane (1864 – Feb 26, 1927), m Oct 6, 1883 William H. Row (St. John's Luth Ch, Lykens record). She was living with her grandmother Ferree in 1880. ; Sarah b c1865, m Ambrose Reinhold of Williamstown.
Catherine b 1833.

John H. (Sep 19, 1839 – Oct 21, 1910, bur Calvary Meth Cem, Wiconisco), m 1st Feb 10, 1877, Amanda Hand . 2nd Amanda (Zerby) Keiser (Aug 15, 1832 – Dec 26, 1906, bur Calvary Meth Cem, Wiconisco), a dau of Henry and Christiana (Romberger) Zerby. Amanda was married 1st to Daniel Keiser.

Rebecca (b 1841 – d Jul 12, 1888, bur Shamokin Cem, Shamokin, Northld Co), m 1st Josiah Simmers, 2nd Amos Shomper (1839 – pre 1887).

***HENRY (Mar 30, 1802 - Dec 8, 1864, bur Hoffman Cem) m Sarah Romberger (Feb 14, 1804 - 1887), a dau of Henrich and Elisabeth Romberger.Henry was a weaver during his younger years. He and Sarah lived in Lykens Township for several years, but by 1850, they lived in Wiconisco Township, and Benjamin Riegel age 31 lived with them. They were recorded in Wiconisco Township because the land they owned was in the part of Lykens Township that was separated and became Wiconisco Township.. **Henry and Sarah (Romberger) Rickert had these children:**

Elizabeth (b Dec1822 – d after 1900), listed in 1832 under "poor children" as a child of Henry Rickert whose school tuition had to be paid by the township. She is probably the 2nd wife of Daniel Shomper (b c1807) as recorded on the 1850 census for Wiconisco Twp. **Daniel and Elizabeth (Rickert) Shomper had these children: John** b c1842; **George** (Mar 20, 1843 – Apr 19, 1904, bur Lykens Cem), m Aug 18, 1867 St. Johns "Hill" Ch Berrysbrug to Mary Ellen Woland; **Daniel** (Sep 20, 1844 – Dec 9, 1875, bur Union Cem, Lykens), m Amanda ____; **Josiah** (May 1847 – after 1910), m Hannah Machamer; **Sarah** (no dates) **William Henry** (Feb 14, 1851 – Jul 16, 1935, bur IOOF Cem, Lykens) m Emma Elizabeth Morgan; **Lawrence** (Aug 11, 1852 – Feb 15, 1884, bur Union Cem, Lykens), m Sarah A. Hain; **John Adam** (Aug 16, 1855 – Aug 7, 1933, bur Mt. Carmel Cem – Alaska, Northld Co), m 1st Oct 25, 1876 to Mary Buffington, 2nd Jan 10, 1888 to Sarah Jane Chubb

Hannah (Jun 11,1824 - Jul 24,1849, bur Hoffman Cem), listed under "poor children" as child of Henry Rickert in 1832 and 1836. Hannah m Benjamin Riegle (Dec 23, 1819 - Apr 7, 1852), a son of Mathias and Maria Polly Riegle;

William Henry b c1828 listed under "poor children" as child of Henry Rickert in 1836. He died before 1860. He m Sarah Annie Hanes (Dec 8, 1833 – Mar 5, 1912, bur Shamokin Cem), a dau of Solomon Hanes. William and Sarah Annie (Hanes) Rickert had these children: **Rebecca** (no dates), bapt Hoffman Ch Nov 6, 1853; **Valinka**; **William Henry II** (Jul 24, 1855 – Mar 15, 1915, bur IOOF Cem Shamokin), m Mary Ann Greager; **Sophia** (Feb 16, 1858 – Dec 10, 1906, bur Shamokin Cem), m Abraham Decker.

Mary (Mar 15, 1827 - Sep 30, 1847), listed under "poor children" as a child of Henry Rickert in 1832 and 1837. She m John Marckly b Mar 2, 1820, a son of John and Elisabetha Marckly.

John (Jan 4, 1829 - Nov 21, 1910, bur in Old Soldiers Home at Hampton Roads, Va.), m Jul 31, 1853 to Sarah Palmer (Feb 7, 1828 - Oct 28, 1909, bur Millersburg), a dau of Abel and Mary (Keiter) Palmer. John was also listed under "poor children" as a child of Henry Rickert in 1837. Starting at the age of nine years, John Rickert had to earn his own livelihood. He first worked on the farm of Daniel Lubold in Lykens Township, where in addition to room and board, he received one dollar per month the first year, two dollars per month the second year, three dollars per month the third year. He later worked for several years on the farm of George Rutter near Halifax. His next employer was the Summit Branch Railroad Company until 1854, when Benneville Witmer employed him at a sawmill in Millersburg.

John Rickert was a veteran of the Civil War, having served for three years, engaging in many of the very heavy battles, including Sherman's march to the sea. He also served at Gettysburg, and during that battle had a serious wound to the groin, which needed six months treatment at Teners Hospital in Philadelphia. After the war he again worked at the roundhouse at Summit Branch Railroad Company, and had various other jobs, eventually residing in Millersburg. **John and Sarah Ann (Palmer) Rickert had these children:** Benjamin Franklin (Jun 23, 1854 - Oct 4, 1943, Lock Haven,Clinton Co Pa.) m ELizabeth Keagy (Aug 24, 1852 - Dec 16, 1887, bur Oak Hill Cem, Millersburg), a dau of John and Rebecca (Luckenbach) Keagey), granddaughter of Jacob and Elizabeth (Frank) Keagey of Millersburg;

. **Benjamin and Elizabeth (Keagy) Rickert had these children:** Ellis F b Mar 1880, m Minnie C. Horner; Ralph Raymond b Sep 14,1883, m Myra Moyer; John William b 1886, Centre Co., m Alma Stoner; **Benjamin m 2nd China Ella Jordan (1870 - 1954), and had these children;** Lee Andrew b 1894; Franklin Roosevelt (b __ d 1975); Esther Queen; Sarah Mae b 1902; Hazel; Russell b 1910; **John Henry** (Jul 28, 1857 - Jun 20, 1901, bur Oak Hill Cem, Millersburg) I, m Hannah Lettich (Apr 8, 1865 - Nov 19, 1913); **Elizabeth Salome** (Oct 3, 1859 – d after 1920), m John Crawley; **George McClellan** b Mar 17, 1862, m Annie Sharon, a dau of Lawrence and Elizabeth Sharon of Perry County. Georg eand Annie lived in Steelton; **James Monroe** (Jul 7, 1866 - Jul 24, 1930), m Mary Carl (Mar 22, 1859 – May 24, 1905). Sarah (no dates), m Daniel Wiest ?

Rebecca (b Oct 1, 1837 – Sep 17, 1918, bur Hoffman Cem)

Lucetta (Jan 30, 1840 – Apr 22, 1867), m in St. John's Luth Ch, Bbg to May 3, 1857 to Jonathan (Jonas) Batdorf (b May 20, 1837 –d Aug 26, 1874, of small pox, bur Hoffman Cem), a son of Peter and Elizabeth (Welker) Batdorf. **Jonas and Lucetta (Rickert) Batdorf had these children (some bapt Hoffman Ch):** John Henry b Jul 14, 1858 – Jun 24, 1931, bur Calvary Cem, Wiconisco), m Sarah Amelia Siemons; Edward Franklin b Nov 30,1859; Sarah Elizabeth (Oct 2, 1861 – Sep 23, 1922, bur Coleman Cem,

Lykens Twp), m George Franklin Welker; **Hannah Rebecca** b Jul 16, 1863; **Amanda Ellen** d Mar 5, 1868, age one year.

Jonas H. (Jul 24, 1846 - Jun 18, 1890, bur Oak Hill Cem, Millersburg), m Sarah Romberger

***MARTIN (Sep 17, 1804 - Mar 22, 1871, bur Hoffman Cem), m Elizabeth (Betsy) Yerkes (Apr 26, 1813 bapt Klingers Ch- - Mar 5, 1877), dau of Michael and Hannah Yerkes. In 1830 Martin was a shoemaker. The Martin Rickert family was counted in the census for Wiconisco Township in 1850. In 1870 they were counted in Lykens Township. Henry Rettinger age 16, and Hannah Yerkes age 82, mother of Elizabeth was with them. **Martin and Elizabeth (Jerger) Rickert had these children:**

Elizabeth (Nov 13, 1829 – Nov 15, 1899), m May 1, 1848 to Mathias Harter (b Oct 8, 1823 – d May 13, 1903, bur Union Cem, Lykens).   Mathias was a miner.

Samuel d young 8 years old;

Susanna (Jul 1, 1833 - Dec 24, 1911), m Solomon Rettinger [see write-up where their land is described]

Henry b ____ d 1837, bur Hoffman Cem

Rebecca (Oct 1, 1837 - Sep 17, 1918, bur Hoffman Cem), not married

Catharine Rickert (1843 – 1909)

Rebecca Rickert (18837 – 1919)

Amanda (May 31, 1839 - Oct 5, 1926, bur St. Pauls Cem, Enterline, Wayne Twp), m May 3, 1854 Henry Hoover (Jan 8, 1834 - Nov 7, 1900, bur St. Pauls's Cem, Enterline), a son of John and Maria Margaret (Lebo) Hoover. Henry and Amanda lived in Wayne Twp, Dau Co in 1880. They had Hiram Corsnitz age 14 with them listed as a servant. **Henry and Amanda (Rickert) Hoover had these children: John** (b Jun 4, 1856 – Feb 29, 1936, bur Bowerman Cem, Enterline, Dau Co), m Mary J. ____ ; **Tobias** b c1859; **Priscilla** (Jul 10, 1860 – Feb 28, 1885, bur Bowerman Cem); **Catherine Elizabeth** b May 16,1862; **Isaiah** (Oct 5, 1865 – Apr 19, 1873); **Henrietta Louisa** (May 12, 1866 – May 24, 1873); **Emma J**. (May 1867 – 1946), m John J. Parmer ; **Leander** (b ___ d Feb 13, 1870); **Amanda Margaret** (Feb 28, 1872 – Mar 1873))Ida R. b c1873; Rose Ann (Sep 6, 1873 – Jun 8, 1943, bur Miller's Luth & Ref Cem, Jackson Twp), m Charles H. Parmer; Ida Rebecca b c1875 m Ira Oscar Sheesley in Enders, Dau Co; Isabella (no dates); Sadie Ellen (no dates)..

Sarah Ann (Sep 8, 1840 - Oct 11, 1912, bur Hoffman Cem), m Jan 2, 1859 by Rev. Daniel Sell of Berrysburg to Jonas W. Hoffman (Jun 15, 1838 – Feb 14, 1887, of consumption, bur Hoffman Cem), a son of John Peter and Elizabeth (Umholtz) Hoffman. **Jonas W. and Sarah A (Rickert) Hoffman had these children::); William Henry** (Apr 1, 1859 – 1880); **Dianna Elisabeth** b Oct 10, 1860; **Clinton E.** (b Aug 20, 1863 – Aug 10, 1940, bur Simeon Cem, Gratz), m Oct 9, 1886 Harriet Umholtz; **Henry Monroe** (b 1865 – 1866); **Katie Camelia** (May 12, 1867 – after 1910), m Jun 1887 Archibald A. Sergeant; **Kinda Alverta** b Apr 6, 1869, m Jan 30, 1886 Isaac Rickert b Jan 1854; **Sarah Alice** (b 1870 – d 1871); **Charles Penrose** (b & d 1872); **George Wellington** (b Nov 14, 1873 – Feb 11, 1946, bur Siemon Cem, Gratz), m Nov 18, 1894 Jennie M. Ritzman (1874 – 1956). Before his marriage to Jennie, George Wellington and Elizabeth Catherine Riegel became the parents of Helen May Hoffman (Mrs. William Dietrich). George

Wellington and Jennie (Ritzman) Hoffman had these children: Russell; Earl; Emily; **Gurney** Alvin (b Oct 6, 1875 - Nov 24, 1934, bur Hoffman Cem), m Oct 16, 1898 Amanda Elizabeth Troutman; **Harry A.** b 1876; **Edward O.** b Jul 3, 1877; **Laura May** (Oct 3, 1879 - 1953, bur Maple Grove Cem, E'ville), m Sep 17, 1904 Nathaniel B. Keiter; **Mary Ellen** (b May 1, 1881 - 1950, bur Union Cem, Fisherville), m Isaiah L. Keiter; **Jacob Arthur** (Oct 13, 1883 - 1957, bur Simeon Cem), m Maude Emma Jane Kissinger (Mar 23, 1894 - 1965), a dau of Joel and Priscilla (Engle) Kissinger. .

 Catharine M. (May 16,1843 - Jun 28, 1909, of cancer, bur IOOF Cem, Lykens), m Apr 26, 1874 Philip S. Hoffman (c1844 - Nov 21, 1878, bur IOOF Cem), 2nd m 1886 John Woland (Oct 22, 1830 - d Dec 16, 1910, killed in a mine accident, bur Lykens). John was m 1st to Lydia Heckert (b c1835 - d _____). In 1880, Catharine was a widow. She and her one year old daughter Hattie lived in Lykens Township. **Hannah Louisa** (May 22, 1847 - Jul 11, 1919, bur Simeon Cem, Gratz), m Harrison Reigle [see write-up where their land is described]

*****CATHARINA** b Oct 16, 1806, m Daniel Shomper , **Daniel and Catharina (Rickert) Shomper had these known children:** William b c1835; Heinrich (Aug 3, 1837 - 1839) bur Hoffman Cem.

*****MARGARET (GRETHLIES)** b Mar 31, 1808 m Jacob Hoover, Jr (Apr 17, 1806 - May 2, 1867), a son of Jacob and Sarah Bellis Hoover.**Jacob and Margaret "Grethlies" (Rickert) Hoover children:** Mary b c1835; **John** b c1836; **Fredrick** b c1842; **William O.** b c1845; **Samuel** (Apr 18, 1848 - Jan 1918, bur IOOF Cem, Lykens), m Oct 7, 1870 Catharine Shomper (1854 - c1941). **Samuel & Catharine (Shomper) Hoover children:** William Henry b Oct 13, 1872, m Apr 3, 1892, Emma J. Strayer; **Harvey Harper** b Aug 17, 1874; **Isaac** (Feb 28, 1851 - May 17, 1863, bur Hoffman's Cem); **Charles** b Mar 8, 1855.

*****BARBARA** (May 18, 1810 m Solomon Updegrove (b Aug 15, 1809 - d _____), a son of Conrad and Elizabeth (Angst) Updegrove of Wiconisco Twp. **Solomon and Barbara (Rickert) Updegrove had these children (some bapt St. Peters Luth Ch, Tower City:** Jacob Sylvester (b Feb 25,1829 – d Sep 5, 1913, bur Mifflinville Cem, Columbia Co, Pa.), m 1st Lavina _____ (no dates), 2nd Sarah E. _____ (no dates). He was a shoemaker in 1850; **Emma** b 1831 in Muir, Pa.; **Conrad** b c1832, m Deborah _____, **had these children:** Mary A b c1853; **Sarah J** b c1855; **Willliam A.** (1858 – 1860, bur St. Paul's Cem, Juniata Co); **James C.** b c1859; **Susan** b c1861; **George W.** (1863 – Dec 11, 1905, bur Sch Co); **Ida E** b c1867.

Catherine b Dec 3, 1833; Elizabeth b c1838; Elmirah (b Nov 2, 1839 – d Apr 21, 1908, bur Pomfret Manor Cem, Sunbury, Northld Co, Pa.), m John B. Hockenbrocht; Lusette (b Feb 5, 1842 – Feb 13, 1910, bur Riverview Cem, Northumberland, Pa., m Isaac Dressler; Solomon (b Nov 21, 1844, bapt Hoffman Ch – Mar 27, 1917, bur Grace Meth Cem, Muir, Porter Twp, Sch Co), m Melinda Brown (Jan 23, 1850 – Dec 22, 1914), a dau of William P. and Ellen (Updegrove) Brown. **Solomon and Melinda (Brown) Updegrove had these children:** Minnie b c1868; **Barbara Ellen** b Oct 1871; **Elmer Sylvester** b Feb 5, 1874; **Milton Theodore** (1875 – 1936, bur Muir); **Ira** b 1877; **Sarah** (1879 – 1910), m Henry E. Wagner; **Nora Elizabeth** 1881 – 1939) m George Unger; **Emma Katie** (1883- 1918, bur Muir Cem); **William Walter** (1885 – 1944, bur Muir Cem); **Gertie Melinda** (1887 – 1892, bur Muir Cem); **Benjamin Harrison** (1889 – 1938, bur Greenwood Cem, Tower City); **Howard Clay** (1890 – 1891); **Robert Raymond** (1893 – 1962, bur Greenwood Cem, Tower City); **Sarah** b c1847; **Mary A.** b c 1849, m William H. Long b c 1850, **and had these children:** Catherine b c1871; **Milton** b c1873; **Barbara** b c1875; **Daniel** b c1878. In 1880 they lived in Washington Twp and Solomon Updegrove her father lived with them ;Charles Henry (b Nov 19, 1852 – Jan 7, 1913, bur St. Pauls's Cem, Susquehanna Twp, Juniata Co, Pa.), m Christianna Hupp (1854 – 1925); **Theodore G.** (Apr 15, 1855 – Feb 17, 1899, bur Grace Meth Cem, Muir, Sch Co), m Kate A. Shoiller (1858 – 1906, bur Grace Meth Cem, Muir), a dau of George and Maria (Giraud) Shoiller; **Eleanor; Milton; Ira; _____** m; **William; Robert;** One of the dau m George Szeller, one m David Miller, one m George Unger.

*****PETER** (May 7, 1812 - Jun 5, 1880, bur Hoffman Cem), m Elizabeth Klinger (Nov 11, 1816 - Feb 23, 1893). **Peter and Elizabeth (Klinger) Rickert had these children:** SARAH M (b Jan 7, 1836 – after 1900), m Emmanuel Smith (1833 – pre 1880), lived in Williamstown. **Emanuel and Sarah (Rickert) Smith children:** William (May 1864 – 1933, bur Fairview Cem, Williamstwon), m Lillie Michael; **Lillie Sevilla**

(1867 – 1934, bur Seyberts Cem, Williamstown), m Charles L. Witmer; **Mary A**. (1869 – 1945, bur Fairview Cem), m John Francis Lentz; **JEREMIAH** (Sep 2, 1837- Feb 1,1839, bur Hoffman Cem); **BENJAMIN** (Oct 25, 1839 - Dec 25, 1900, bur Seibert Evang Cem, Williamstown), m Mary Ann Hess (Oct 16, 1838 - Jan 16, 1916 in Tower City), a dau of Abraham and Catherine (Hoffman) Hess. **Benjamin and Mary (Hess) Rickert children: Mary Ellen** (Sep 12, 1860 – Nov 27, 1956, bur Fairview Cem, Williamstown, Dau Co)) m Frederick Lewis Hellman; **Charles McClellan** (Mar 13, 1863 – Mar 12, 1946, bur Oak Hill Cem, Mbg), m Aug 20, 1885 to Mary Elizabeth Enterline. He m 2nd on Sep 10, 1913 to Sallie Louise Enterline. He became a doctor and practiced medicine first in Tower City, later in Harrisburg, and eventually in Millersburg. He had three children: a dau Mrs. Wm C. Hickman, Dr. W. P. of Kenton,Ohio, and Robert E. of Shepherdstown; **Lillie** (1865 – 1870, bur Seybert's Cem, Williamstown).
JUSTINA ANN (Dec 11, 1841 – Oct 21, 1892, bur Frieden's Union Cem, Hegins, Sch Co), m Elias Samuel Williard (Jul 19, 1838 – Mar 6, 1905), a son of Jacob and Lydia Williard. They lived in Hegins ; **Elias Samuel and Christina (Rickert) Williard children: Alfred Elmer** (b Dec 27, 1861 – Feb 11, 1932, bur Frieden's Union Cem, Hegins), m Susan H. Long;; **Henry Oscar** (b Mar 13,1863 – Oct 20, 1939, bur St. John's "Hill" Cem, Bbg), m Amanda Barbara Miller; **Ida Jane** (b Nov 27, 1864 – Aug 4, 1936 ,, bur Frieden's Union Cem, Hegins), m Lewis Reed; **Charles F** (Aug 30,1866 – Apr 15,1886 bur Hoffman Cem); **Edwin Elias** b Feb 12, 1874 , m Emma Williard. After Justina Ann died, Elias Samuel Williard was m Apr 12, 1893 in Hegins by Rev. Engle to Fyetta Strauser. He was a member of the Heginsville band.

SAMUEL (b 1844 – Feb 27, 1881, bur Seyberts Cem, Williamstown), m Nov 20, 1866 Mary Ann McSurdy (Nov 9, 1842 - Jul 4, 1901), a dau of Michael and Catherine (Lubold) McSurdy. They lived in Williams Twp in 1880, and he was a miner. **Samuel and Mary Ann (McSurdy) Rickert children: William** b c1862; **Henrietta** (1868 – 1916, bur Greenwood Cem, Tower City, Sch Co), m Allen Underkoffler; **George Dirvin** (Sep 16, 1869 – Jul 24, 1902, bur Williamstown) ;**Edwin** b c1872; **Kate** b c1874; **Mary May** (Oct 16, 1875 – Oct 17, 1933, bur Evang Cem, Williamstown), m David Schell; **Sarah** b c1877; **Claude Samuel** (b Sep 18, 1880. **HENRY** b 1846 m Feb 1870 Rebecca Umholtz b c1843, **no known children DANIEL** (Nov 23, 1847 bapt Hoffman Ch - Jan 7, 1911, bur Williamstown Meth Cem), m Jan 7, 1868 Angeline Snyder (Jun 8, 1846 - Mar 14, 1904), a dau of Henry and Susanna (Bellon) Snyder. They lived in Williams Township in 1880, and he was a miner; **Daniel and Angeline (Snyder) Rickert had these children: Elmer E.** b Mar 1873, m Sep 12, 1900 Amelia C. Hinke; **Annie M** (1876 – 1878, bur Seybert;s Cem, Williamstown); **CORNELIUS** (b Dec 25,1849 -Jun 23, 1905, bur UB Cem, Williamstown), m Sarah Mack (Oct 31, 1842 – after 1920), a dau of William and Anna (Funk) Mack. **Cornelius and Sarah (Mack) Rickert had these children:** Harvey b 1871; William b 1873; Allen b 1875; Bertha b 1878; Charles b 1880; Walter b 1883; Earl b 1886; **MARY JANE** (Mar 14,1852– Feb 1, 1933, bur Fairview Cem, Williamstown), m 1st Mar 13, 1870 Alfred Batdorf (1848 - 1875) of Ashland, Pa., 2nd Dec 24, 1879 Charles W. Wise (Jun 15, 1851 – Sep 25, 1927, bur Fairview Cem, Williamstown), a son of Peter and Luzetta W. (Forney) Wise. **Charles and Mary Jane (Rickert) Wise had these children:** Sarah Ann (Aug 10, 1880 – Nov 18, 1882, bur Hoffman's Cem); Samuel Milton (Jul 17, 1884 – 1943, bur Meth Episcopal Cem Williamstown), m Minnantha M Weidel; Harvey A. (Jan 8, 1888 – Jan 16, 1907, bur Hoffman's Cem); Daniel Frank b Jan 1889; Elizabeth May (May 4,1890– Jan 11,1892); Lillie B (1892 –1988, bur Fairview Cem, Williamstown), m George F. Sloan; Ruth Irene b Sep 11, 1897.

FRANKLIN K. (Aug 1854 - 1928, bur Maple Grove Cem, E'ville), m 1st Linda Messmer (divorced 1890), 2nd Jan 16, 1892 Sarah Ressler (1850 - 1922), a dau of George and Mary Ressler; **POLLY ELIZABETH** (Nov 26, 1856 - May 2, 1888, bur beside parents in Hoffman Cem), m Jan 2, 1876 Cornelius Gunderman. **Polly Elizabeth had an illegitimate dau** with Danni Schoffstall:Gertrude b Jun 19, 1874 in Mifflin Twp, who married John Good. **Elizabeth and Cornelius Gunderman had two daughters** Carrie A. b c1875; Adaline b c1877.

***JOHN** (1816 - Oct 14, 1850, bur Hoffman Cem, tombstone has no writing except states that he was 32 years old), m Elizabeth Bressler (Jan 7, 1821 - Sep 21, 1893)), dau of Michael Bressler who later m Apr 1860, George S. Deibler (Apr 10, 1825 - Jul 4, 1890, bur Hoffman Cem, next to John Rickert), a widower. He was a Civil War veteran. **John and Elizabeth (Bressler) Rickert children: Henry J.** (Nov 30, 1842 - Jan 18, 1926, bur Mt. Lebanon Cem, Lebanon, Pa.), m Sarah Witmer (Aug 26, 1842 - Dec 10, 1919, bur Hoffman Cem), a dau of Benjamin & Elizabeth (Gise) Witmer. **Henry and Sarah (Witmer) Rickert had**

these children: Salonah Amelia (1864 – 1870); Harvey Monroe (1865 – 1941, bur Ref Cem, Tremont, Sch Co); Agnes Sevilla (1867 – 1935, bur Ref Cem, Tremont), m Newton N. Badman; Wilson Elmer (1871 – 1941), m Elizabeth Light; Anna Melvina (1873 – 1957) bur Lebanon Cem, Lebanon, Pa.); John Emerson (1877 – 1941, bur U.B. Cem, Valley View), m Mary E. Wolfgang;;Elvin Oliver (1879 – 1955), m Lillian Jigen; Gurney Austin (1883 – 1964), m Marion Coleman; Nathaniel (b Dec1844 – 1864, killed while serving in the Civil War); John (Nov 23, 1846 - Oct 11, 1875, bur U.B. Andrews Cem, Valley View, Sch Co), m Dina Kroh (Apr 24, 1850 – Jan 24, 1935, bur U.B. Cem, Valley View). After John Rickert died, Dina m Amos Bixler. John and Dina (Kroh) Rickert children: Mary E. (Feb 20,1870 –Apr 4,1954, bur Maple Grove Cem, E'ville), m Michael J. Gunderman; Emma Jane (Sep 17, 1871 – Mar 25, 1947, bur Grand View Cem, Pillow), m Oct 23, 1887 to Harry W. Rickert); Tammie Catherine (Sep 17, 1873 – May 18, 1943, bur Maple Grove Cem, E'ville); Thomas H. (Mar 11, 1849 –Jul 31,1921, bur St. Andrews Cem, Valley View, Pa.), m Mary Wolfgang (1851 - 1900).Thomas H. and Mary (Wolfgang) Rickert had these children: Oscar (1870 – 1939, bur U. B. Cem, Valley View), m Nora Jane Schlegel; Ellen (1874 – 1929, bur Frieden's Union Cem, Hegins), m Joel Klouser; Salonah Amelia (1877 – 1915, bur U. B. Cem, Valley View), m Albert O. Cantner; Ludella b 1878; Ellwood Ero Jacob (1880 – 1958, bur U. B. Cem, Valley View), m Lizzie Ann Schlegel; Herbert Elwood (1883 – 1945, bur Greenwood Abbey Cem, Newton, Kansas); Verdie Dakoda (1885 – 1888, bur St. Andrew's Meth Cem, Valley View); Parker A. b 1889.

***JaCOB (Apr 16, 1817 - Feb 18, 1884, bur Hoffman Cem), m Elizabeth Hoover (Jan 18, 1826 - Jul 3, 1896),a dau of Christian and Catharine (Hinkle) Hoover. Jacob and Elizabeth (Hoover) Rickert had these children: Amanda (Feb 27, 1845 – Nov 15, 1893, bur Hoffman's Cem), m John Gunderman (b Dec 26, 1837 - Aug 7, 1913). [see information under John Gunderman].Elizabeth (1847- d c1867); Catherine (Oct 2, 1848 – Apr 1, 1941, bur Greenwood Cem, Tower City, Sch Co), m John Henry Kuntzelman (Oct 5, 1849 – Sep 22, 1918, bur Greenwood Cem, Tower City, Sch Co), a son of Elias and Elizabeth (Hoke) Kuntzelman. John Henry and Catharine (Rickert) Kuntzelman had these children: William Henry (Nov 30, 1871 – Mar 12, 1958), m May 1899 Ellen E. Wilson; Charles Franklin (Apr 1, 1873 – Mar 21, 1946, bur Greenwood Cem, Tower City), m Ella Lee Thompson; John A. (Feb 18, 1875 – Jun 4, 1930, bur Greenwood Cem, Tower City), m Mame Staple; James E. (1878 – 1885, bur Greenwood Cem). Melinda (Apr 7,1850 - d young); Isaac (Jan 1854- _____), m Jan 30, 1886 Kinda Alverta Hoffman b Apr 6, 1869, a dau of Jonas W and Sarah (Rickert) Hoffman. Isaac and Kinda (Hoffman) Rickert had these children: William Henry (Mar 5, 1886 – Sep 10, 1887);Gurney Allen (Sep 15, 1887 - Feb 17, 1957, bur Evang Cem, Wiconisco), m Dec 31, 1910 to Mae Elizabeth Miller (1892-1966); Katie Briella (Feb 11, 1889 - Dec 21, 1947, bur Wiconisco Calvary Cem), m Aug 25, 1905 George Alvin Shomper; Darwin Elvin (Feb1,1891 - Oct 30, 1957, bur Calvary Cem, Wiconisco, Pa.), m Oct 31, 1914 to Edna Mae (Shomper) Fetterhoff (May 2, 1883 - Oct 24, 1962), dau of George and Mary Ellen (Woland) Shomper, and widow of Harvey Franklin Fetterhoff b Aug 24, 1880, a son of Frank & Rachel Fetterhoff. Darvin and Edna (Shomper Fetterhoff) Rickert had a son Raymond E. (1915 - 1971); Harry Albert (Jul 18,1895 - Dec 6, 1953, bur Wiconisco Calvary Cem), m Jennie Updegrove; Charles Jacob (Apr 10, 1898 - Aug 21, 1898, bur Hoffman Cem); Sarah Elizabeth (Jun 22, 1899 – 1970, bur Wiconisco Calvary Cem), m Aug 30, 1919 to Ray Wellington George (1898 - 1953, bur Calvary Cem, Wiconisco, Pa.); Florence (Aug 30, 1903 - Jul 31,1979, bur Our Lady of Calvary Cem, Pottsville), m J. C. Foley; Minnie Irene (Oct 14, 1901 - Feb 27, 1968), m Frank J. Miller; Mary b 1907 m Harper Myers; Rose b Jul 11, 1908 - Nov 29, 1990, bur Westminster Cem, N. Middleton Twp, Cumb. Co, Pa..), m John E. Wolf. Sarah d young; Jacob Jul 25,1856 - Mar 1, 1876, bur Hoffman's Cem), killed in the mines; Harry W. b (Jun 2, 1860 – Jun 30, 1933, bur Grand View Cem, Pillow), m Oct 23, 1887 Emma Jane Rickert (Sep 17, 1871 – Mar 25, 1947), a dau of John and Dinah (Kroh) Rickert.. Harry W. and Emma Jane (Rickert) Rickert had these children: Oscar (1887 – 1954, bur Grand View Cem, Pillow);John Henry (1890 – 1918, bur Grand View Cem, Pillow); Beulah Rebecca (1892 – 1962, bur Simeon Luth Cem, Gratz), m Ralph Ezra Daniel; Mabel Elizabeth (1897 – 1952, bur Holiness Cem, Rebuck, Northld Co); Mark Emerson Evan (1900 – 1983, bur West Side Cem, Shamokin Dam, Snyder Co), m Bertha Ellen Slanker; Jennie Mae (1903 – 1981, bur Gravel Hill Cem, Lebanon Co); Harry William (1906 – 1944, bur Grand View Cem, Pillow); Mary Eva (1908 – 1994, bur Luth & Ref Cem, West Cameron Twp, Treverton), m Freeman Gottshall; Katherine Emma (1910 – 1965, bur San Fernando, Cal), m Theodore Edward Coolick; Edward Franklin (1913 – 1972, bur Stroudsburg, Monroe Co, Pa.), m Helen A. Singley.William Henry (1867 – 1871).]

The Isaac & Kinda (Hoffman) Rickert Family
(Only identified children are Gurney last on right standing, Mary (Mrs. Myers) seated 2nd from right)

SHORT MOUNTAIN & INDIAN TRAIL ROAD

RICKERT LAND IS DIVIDED

Magdalena Rickert and her nephew Hartman Rickert, Jr. continued to share the land for many years. During those years, they did sell several small tracts to other individuals, but it wasn't until the estates were settled that most of the land changed hands. On the next several pages, division of the Rickert land will be explained as accurately as possible. Most of the very old houses are gone, except for the remaining foundations, evidence of hand dug wells and a few blooming plants from the early gardens. The 1875 map again sets the course for the order of the properties. Unfortunately, some of the houses had either disappeared before 1875, or were built since then. It is difficult to describe their location.

RESIDENCE LAST OWNED BY JOHN BELLON (Buildings now gone)
(MATHIAS HARTER LAND 6 acres 81 perches 1850, RESIDENCE OF SAMUEL LEBO 6 acres in 1875)

This was part of Rickert land. On January 14, 1843, after Magdalena had died, John Rickert and wife Elizabeth, and Jacob Rickert conveyed and assigned a tract of land containing 79 acres 62 perches and a house to their brother Martin. Several years later on May 29, 1850 Martin and Elizabeth Rickert conveyed this small tract containing six acres eighty-one perches (with one-story frame house and small log stable), from their large tract of land, to Mathias Harter who was married to their daughter Elizabeth. [See Rickert genealogy page 419].This land was in both Wiconisco and Lykens Township and bordered the land of Peter Rickert, John George Weaver, south to land of Samuel Hoover and Daniel D. Boas, and other land of Martin Rickert.

In March 1864, Mathias and Elisabeth Harter purchased lot number 347 in Lykens from Henry and Catherine (Rickert) Kuntzelman. They lived in Lykens until the end of their lives. Mathias and Elisabeth Harter assigned this property to Isaac Burd on October 24, 1864. After Isaac Burd died, the land was appraised for less than $350.00, so Ann Mary Burd his widow claimed the land with buildings instead of money.

THE HARTER FAMILY

[The **HARTER /HERTER/ HERD2ER** family is traced to immigrant Andreas Harter (1698 Wuertemberg, Ger - c1757 Lanc Co) & Anna Catharina (Zahner) Harter b1702 a dau of Peter Zahner. They settled in Earl Twp, Lancaster Co. **Andreas and Catharina (Zahner) Harter had these children born in Germany:** *CATHERINE b Oct 13, 1724; *JOHN (Jan 1, 1727 - pre 1801, bur Hebe Cem, Northld Co), m Anna Maria ___ (Apr 5, 1726 –Nov 22, 1800), lived in Jordan Twp., Northld Co. **John & Anna Maria Harter children (b Bern Twp, Berks Co):** **JOHN b c1753, Bern Twp Berks Co, m Northld Co. Maria Elizabeth _____ b c 1757. John and Maria Elizabeth Harter children (Bapt Himmels & Klingers Ch):** ***PETER b Sep 14, 1783; ***ELISABETH b Jun 23, 1785; ***ANDREAS b Jan 6, 1787; ***JACOB b Sep 6,1788;***ANNA BARBARA b Jan 18, 1792;***MATHIAS b Jun 7, 1794.

ANNA MARIA b c1755; ****JACOB (Jul 9, 1757 - Jun 12, 1837 Jordan Twp, Northld Co), m Elizabeth Heim (Oct 17, 1766 - Mar 7, 1814, Northld Co), a dau of George Heim. **Jacob and Elizabeth (Heim) Harter children:** ***Jacob (Feb 3, 1786; ***John (Jul 24, 1787 – Jan 17, 1846), m Mar 29, 1818 Elizabeth ____; ***Elizabeth b May 9, 1789, bapt Klinger Ch, Lykens Twp; ***John Wilhelm b Jul 14, 1793; ***Mathias (Oct 4, 1796 – Mar 15, 1870, bur Red Cross Cem), m Hannah Eister (Feb 10, 1798 – Apr 20, 1866), a dau of Jacob & Phillippina (Kump) Eister. **Mathias and Hannah (Eister) Harter children:** Elias (1823 – Apr 15, 1886, bur Red Cross Cem); Sarah bapt Jul 17,1826; Elizabeth b Jul 4,1828; Enoch (May 12, 1830 –Oct 23, 1863), m Hannah ___ (Jul 22, 1845 - Sep 16, 1863); Henrietta (Mar 23, 1832 – Jul 25, 1905, bur Red Cross); Hannah (Oct 4, 1833 - Oct 19, 1863); Rebecca (May 8, 1838 - Jan 19, 1913, bur Red Cross Cem); Lavina b c1841; *** George b Sep 20, 1798; ***Daniel (Aug 4, 1800 - Dec 10, 1822); ***Wilhelm b Mar 6, 1803; ***Magdalena b Jun 1, 1805; ***Samuel b Apr 22, 1807

**ANNA CATHERINE b c1760
ANDREW b c1767 Berks Co - d Ohio), m Anna Magd Deibler (1774 – 1827, Ohio), **(had these children some bapt Klingers Ch): ***Catharine b Jul 1,1792; ***John b Oct 6, 1793; ***Andrew (Jan 11,1795 –May 19, 1879);***Christian b c1797; ***Joseph b 1799; ***Benjamin (Jun 1 , 1802 – 1876); ***Mary Magd b Oct 12, 1804; ***Isaac b Feb 15, 1806;***Mary Ann (1808 – 1830); ***George (1810–1830); ***Henry (1813–1851);***Jacob Aug 23, 1814 –Apr 4, 1889);***Elizabeth (1817–1821);***Daniel b c1819; ***Susanna b c1821. Moved to Delaware, Ohio after 1822.

MATHIAS (c1770– pre Apr1824, Up Mah Twp, Northld Co), m Elizabeth Bowmsn b 1774, a dau of Jacob Bowman. **Mathias & Elizabeth (Bowman) Harter children (b Northld or Dau Co):***Andrew (Sep 29, 1799– Oct 29, 1865); ***Susanne b May 1, 1803, m Apr 19, 1832, Philip Wertenberger; ***John (Apr 13, 1805 - Jul 27, 1877); ***Catharine b Jan 27, 1809; ***Sarah b Apr 7, 1811; ***Mathias b c1813; ***Henry b Apr 5, 1816, m Salome Troutman (1816–1848) a dau of Abraham & Elisabeth Troutman;***Samuel b c1817; ***Elias b Aug 7, 1819;***George b 1820; Esther c1822.
*ANNA MARIA b Dec 26, 1730;
*DOROTHEA b Feb 14, 1735;
*MATHIAS (Jun 5, 1737 - Oct 29, 1789, Mahanoy Twp, Northld Co.), m c1760 Anne Mary Shuler (c1739 Wurtemburg - Mar 1816 Centre Co). **Mathias & Anne Mary (Shuler) children (b Lanc & Dau Co):** **ANNA MARY b c1762, **GEORGE (Jun 3, 1764 Dau Co - Jun 7, 1833 Ohio), m Elizabeth Bowman (Oct 5, 1769 - Feb 13, 1864), a dau of Abraham & Christina Bowman of Leb Co. ****MARY ELIABETH** b Aug 25, 1767; ****JOHN** (1769 – May 1848);****ANDREW** b c1771; ****JACOB** b Aug 1773;****CHRISTIAN** b c1775;
*ANDREW (Feb 8, 1739 - Nov 14, 1814, Ephrata, Pa.);
*JACOB (May 16,1745 – May 2, 1812, bur Harter Cem, Northld Co), m ____ **had these known children:** **GEORGE (Aug 9, 1786 - Apr 27, 1818);**ABSALUM (1791 – May 1869);**ANDREW (1795 – after 1850);

[**Isaac Burd** (Dec 1832 – Jan1865, bur Hoffman Cem), a son of George and Magdalena (Rickert) Burd, m A. Mary Ferree (Oct 19, 1838 – May 25, 1895), a dau of George W. and Leah (Umholtz) Ferree. [More Info under Rickert genealogy.]

On March 30, 1877Ann Mary Burd conveyed the six acres 81 perches of land to Samuel Rickert. In April 1879, Benjamin Rickert assignee of the credits of Samuel Rickert of Williams Township at a public sale conveyed the same acreage with frame dwelling and other out buildings to Josiah and Elisabeth Romberger of Lykens Borough. On May 28, 1879, the Romberger's conveyed the property to Pricilla Wallace. On September 10, 1881, Priscilla and husband William conveyed the same property to Henry Kissinger. (Henry Kissinger purchased another small tract of land containing four acres seventy-seven perches with house from John and Caroline Hess on May 26, 1881. This small tract belonged to the tract of Jacob Rickert, and was conveyed to John Hess on August 29, 1878 by a sheriff sale.) John Hess sold to Henry Kissinger on May 26, 1888. [Wallace and Kissinger genealogy elsewhere.]

Both tracts of Henry Kissinger (6 acre 81 perches with dwelling and 4 acres) were conveyed to H. E. and Elisabeth Buffington on January 4, 1897. They sold both to John Bellon, Jr. on April 15, 1899, but the deeds were not recorded until June 13, 1919 when the heirs of John Bellon sold the two tracts of land to Thomas D. Berger of Pottsville, Schuylkill County. The 6 acre, 81 perch tract had a frame dwelling on it, the 4 acre, 158 perch tract was woodland.

When John Bellon died, his widow Sarah applied for a veterans pension. Henry Snyder and John Laudenslager were her witnesses and together made a statement on her behalf, to help her receive the pension. Their statement read: "In the matter of Sarah Bellon, widow of John, she has five acres of land on the slope of Short Mountain, situated about two miles south of Gratz, having a small one-story house and a small stable worth about three hundred dollars, which she occupies. The land is rocky and income of the land is not near sufficient for her support. Her personal property is a small old house, furniture worth about twenty-five dollars, and no other income. She is dependant on neighbors and other persons for her maintenance. We have known Sarah about forty years, and have seen her on the average of twenty times a year up to the present time. We were at her residence and attended the funeral of her husband John Bellon at the same place where she now resides."

On August 10, 1930, a county treasurer sale was held, and the property of Berger Coal Company was sold. C. W. Cook was the highest bidder for this land with appurtenances. Another tract of twenty-five acres was sold. Both tracts of land adjoined the land of Chauncey Riegel and Susquehanna Collieries.

Several years later on November 26, 1938, C. W. Cook and his wife sold this land to Clyde J. and Effie E. Miller of Elizabethville. Up to 1948, Clyde J. Miller was assessed for two tracts in Lykens Township, one containing six acres, and another containing four acres. In 1948, the 4 acres were described as woodland. The old house on the six acres apparently existed, but not in livable condition. The house has since been destroyed, and only part of the foundation and a whole in the ground survives. After Clyde died, his widow Effie sold the two tracts to Mabel R. Witmer on October 23, 1947. After Mabel died, her heirs conveyed the land to Ralph Tschopp May 22, 1989.

[**J. FRANKLIN COOK** (1856 – 1936, bur Maple Grove Cem), m Mary E. ____ (1856 – 1937). They lived in Washington Twp in 1880, **had these children:** Katie L b c1876; **Charles William** (Sep 29, 1879 – Jun 13, 1956, bur Maple Grove Cem), m Eva B. ____ (Feb 22, 1882 – Aug 10, 1952). **Charles W. & Eva B Cook children:** Charles Wm b m Apr 19, 1924 Barbara Elisabeth Dietrich. **Charles Wm. & Barbara E. (Dietrich) Cook children:** Charles Burton b Dec 1; 1924; Donald Edward (Apr 11, 1928 – 1996), m Ruth H. Weaver b Dec 18, 1929]

[**MABEL R. WITMER** – maiden name unknown (1910 – Jun 4, 1970,bur E'ville Cem), m Harry E. Witmer (1888-1963), **had these children:** Joyce (1933 – 1989); Robert E (1939 – 1966); Donald L. (1940 – 1987); Terrance L. b 1946.]

THE BELLON FAMILY

[The Bellon family has been known to exist as early as 1260 when they lived in Abries, France. The family that came to America is traced back to Pierre Bellon called Serre, father of David Bellon called Serre who married Susanne Martin, and were the parents of **BLASIUS BELLON** b c1673, a farmer residing in Queyras, France. Blasius married c1692 Marie Thiers b 1673, and **had these children: DAVID** (c1696 – 1775), **SUSANNA** b 1702, **JACOB, SAMUEL** (1708 - 1760), m 1836 Susanna Eckert, wid of David Armond. Susanna and David Armond had a son *DAVID b May 3, 1737, m Married Charlotte Vial in 1761 **MARIE**, The Bellon and Thiers families and 300 others eventually moved from France to Wuertemberg, Germany in the spring of 1699.

REMNANTS OF THE RICKERT VILLAGE

Chas. Schoffstall & Eugene Fetterhoff Observing the pond 0n top of Short Mountain (near parking lot) Clyde Miller owned this land & had a coal washery here in 1940's.

The house north of pond. Alvin "Red" Fetterhoff, father of Eugene Fetterhoff lived here until about 1912. He was then about 12 years old, and was employed at the washery. At that time there were cleared fields all around the house. The washery was destroyed by fire in 1918.

Old well near the above house

428 A

*David Bellon b May 3, 1737 in France, married Charlotte Vial in Germany in 1761. **David and Charlotte (Vial) Bellon had six children,** some of them came to America.

SAMUEL BELLON (Jul 25, 1764 - May 13, 1832), m Magdalena Jourdan lived in Schonenberg, where they raised seven children.

EVA SALOME BELLON (b Oct 18, 1771 in Germany - d Sep 2, 1854, bur Simeon Cem), m Aug 25, 1792 in Germany, to Jacques (Jacob) Tallman (b Oct 8, 1768 in Pinache, - d pre 1850), a son of Jean Pierre and Catharina (Brun) Tallman. In 1850 Eva Salome was living in Gratz with her daughter Charlotte. Jacob Tallman was a stocking weaver in Schoenberg, Germany. The family came to America in April1828. About five years later, Dec 23, 1833, Jacob Tallman applied for citizenship in this county. It was granted to him January 16, 1837. **Jacques (Jacob) and Eva Salome (Bellon) Tallman had these children:**

***Magdelaine** (Jul 17, 1793 in Germany - Mar 12, 1868, Ogle Co., Ill.), m Aug 25, 1819 Johan George Geyer (b Aug 15, 1793, Germany - d Sep 30, 1854, Ogle Co, Ill, bur Brookville Evang Cem). He was a son of George Conrad and Catharine (Nonneman) Geyer of Enzberg. George Geyer was a miller in Wurtemburg, Germany until 1825, when he emigrated to America. He continued that occupation here in Gratz. In 1848 George and Magdelaine Geyer decided to move their family of six sons and four daughters to Ogle County , Illinois. They were not alone in this migration. Several other families from our area moved west, many settled in that same area. It has been stated that a cemetery in that vicinity has so many burials with names common to Gratz that it looks like a transplanted cemetery. **Johan George and Magdalaine (Tallman) Geyer) had these children:** Johann Frederick (b May 25, 1820 Germany - d 1884, Kansas), m Mrs. Susann Bessler Betterman, moved to Albany, Kansas; Elizabeth Caroline b Dec 29, 1821, Schonenberg, Germany - d Feb 4, 1879, bur Dunkard Cem, Carrol, Illinois), m Christian Moyer (no dates) of Dauphin County. **Christian and Elizabeth Caroline (Tallman) Moyer had these children:** Amanda (Mar 21, 1845, Gratz - Sep 3, 1869, in Carroll Co., Illinois, bur Schreiner Cem). She was the first wife of Jacob Shiro.

Jacob Bernhard (Jul 20, 1823 - 1899), m Louisa Hall, moved to Illinois; Louisa Barbara b Nov 23, 1824-- d 1898), m John Rummel moved to Illinois; Wilhelm Conrad (Aug 16, 1826 - 1901), m in Gratz Dec 5, 1848, Mary E. Buffington (Feb 24, 183_ - Jun 10 , 1900), moved to Illinois; George Jr. b 1829, Dau Co.; Henry (b May 15, 1830, Gratz - d 1910 Ogle Co., Illinois), m Jan 11, 1855 Barbara Layman b Oct 16, 1834 in Blair Co, Pa. to John and Mary Layman. The Layman's came to America and settled in Franklin Co., Pa. Henry Geyer learned the blacksmith trade in his youth, and worked at the forge until 1869, when he retired and moved to Polo, Ogle Co. Elizabeth (1831 Dau Co- d 1876, Ill.), m Elias Snovel; John (1835-1914), died in Kansas, not married; Amanda (1837-1912), m Isaac Hamilton, moved to Illinois.

***Susanna** b Sep 20, 1794, m 1816; ***Susanna Catharina** b Jun 3, 1797, m 1818 in Enzberg. ***Jean David** (Mar 2, 1800 - Aug 13, 1881), m 1826 Regina Vollmer, remained in Germany. ***Jean Jaques** (John Jacob) (May 25, 1802 - Sep 5, 1876, bur Calvary Meth Cem, Wiconisco). Jacob was a stonecutter. m in Otisheim Jan 30, 1828 Anna Maria Bellon b Dec 14, 1802, dau of David and Anna Maria (Scheible) Bellon [see their write-up] Jacob Tallman was listed as a mason on the 1837 tax record for Lykens Twp. He was employed by Penn Railroad Company to build stone bridges. By the summer of 1856, he owned the Sheridan (Brookside) Hotel in Wiconisco earlier known as WICONISCO HOUSE. He continued to be a tavern keeper for many years. **John Jacob and Anna Maria (Bellon) Tallman had these children** born in Germany: Jakob Friedrich b Apr 9, 1826; Friedrich Matthaus b Jna 12, 1829.

Charlotte** (Sep 6,1805 in Germany - Oct 12,1861), m Mathias Bellon [see write-up for him];Margarete** b Jan 23, 1808 in Germany , m George Moyer. ***Frederic** (Dec 7, 1811- 1814). ***Anne Marie** (b & d 1814)

JOHANN DAVID BELLON (1776 - Nov 28, 1828), m Nov 26, 1797 in Schonenberg, Germany to Anna Maria Scheible b Mar 25, 1777, a dau of Johann George and Catherine (Thiers) Scheible, a butcher. They stayed in Germany, and had thirteen children, some of whom came to America. **Johann David and Anna Maria (Scheible) Bellon children (bapt record from church in Schonenberg, Ger):** ***Margaretha Catharina** b Feb 6, 1798; ***Johann George** b Sep 26, 1799; ***Johann David** b Jan 24, 1801, m Caroline Hofle (below); ***Anna Maria** (b Nov 13, 1802 or Dec 14, 1802, Schonenberg, Germany - d Feb 16, 1884, bur Calvary Meth Cem, Wiconisco), m Jan 30, 1828 Johan Jacob Tallman (Mar 25, 1802 - Sep 5, 1876), a son of Jacques and Eva Salome (Bellon) Tallman. Jacob Tallman came with his family to America in 1831. **Jacob and Anna Maria (Bellon) Tallman children (1st two bapt Otisheim, Germany):** Jakob Friedrich (Apr 9, 1826 - Nov 1, 1865, bur beside parents); Friedrich Matthaus b Jan 12, 1829; Mathias (Sep 12, 1833 Dau Co - Jan 29, 1898 in Carroll Co, Illinois). Mathias m Sarah Buffington in 1855. She was first married to _ Werntz or Wentz. Sarah Buffington (Nov

10, 1835 - Dec 15, 1910), was a dau of J. Jacob Buffington of Gratz. Mathias and Sarah Tallman were living in Wiconisco in 1860, where he was employed as a tanner. They moved to Illinois in 1866. **Mathias and Sarah (Buffington) Tallman children: James O. Werntz** b Sep 25, 1852 to Sarah and her first husband. In 1870 James was living with the Samuel Buffington family and was employed as a trainer of teams. James Werntz m Agnes H. Campbell, moved to Idaho where he died in 1926; **John J.** (b & d 1857); **George W.** b 1864, m Ida moved to Calif; **Amanda E** b 1866 m Winfree Scott Smith; **Minnie** d young; **Mary Ellen** d young;; **Bert** b 1870 m Loula Hamilton; **Edwin** b 1872 m Nettie Ekdahl; **Louella M** b 1875 m Royal B. Stone, lived in Illinois; **William W.** b 1 877 moved to North Yakima, Washington State.
<u>David</u> b c1838, Pa.; <u>George</u> b c1839, Pa. <u>Daniel</u> b c1840, Pa.; <u>John</u> (b Oct 29, 1841, Pa. - d Jun 7, 1930, Carroll Co., Illinois). John m in 1866 Sarah Sarber. He was a Civil War Veteran.

***Matthias** (b Aug 27, 1804 Ger - d Jul 16, 1865, Gratz, bur Simeon Cem),m Charlotte Tallman (Sep 5, 1805, Ger- Oct 12, 1861, Gratz), his first cousin, a dau of Jacques and Eva Salome (Bellon) Tallman [see also write-up for them]. Matthias applied for naturalization Apr 6, 1836, received Aug 20, 1838. Matthias and Charlotte had eight children, but six died young. One son moved to the west. Only one of the children lived in this area, married and had a family. **Matthias and Charlotte (Tallman) Bellon children:**
<u>George</u> (Apr 17, 1834 - Nov 29, 1855, bur Simeon Cem); <u>Christine Catherine</u> (Mar 13, 1837 - Dec 15, 1842), bur Simeon Cem)
<u>John Mathias</u> (b Nov 26, 1838, Dau Co - d Dec 12, 1899 Douglas, South Dakota), m Dec 27, 1860 in Harrisburg, Pa. to Sarah Delilah Schreffler (Dec 17, 1841 - Jun 10, 1928), a dau of Johan Heinrich and Catherine (Saltzer) Schreffler. **John Matthias and Sarah (Schreffler) Bellon children:** <u>Catherine Charlotte</u> (Oct 19, 1861, Gratz - Nov 14, 1939), m 1880   Richard Rupp in S. Dak., later moved to Utah to find work on the railroad. Eventually moved to Idaho; <u>Elizabeth</u> b 1864 Gratz d young; <u>John David</u> b Sep 4, 1868 in Pilot Mound, Boone Co, Iowa, m Lena Schroder in S. Dak; <u>Carrie Amelia</u> b Apr 26, 1871, m John Brown; <u>Ida Luella</u> b Jan 16, 1873, m John Crismore; <u>Hattie M/arie</u> b Sep 22, 1875, m Frank Strohdehm; <u>HarryEdward</u> b Nov 22, 1876 d young; <u>Minnie A</u>. b Feb 7, 1878 in Wittenburg, S. Dakota, m Lewis Hall;<u>Anna Diana</u> b Jan 2, 1882, m Simon Jemming; <u>Richard</u> b Aug 24, 1884. All children remained in South Dakota.
<u>Charlotte</u> (Sep 25, 1840 - Nov 6, 1868, bur Simeon Cem)
<u>Carolina</u> (Sep 9, 1843 - Feb 12, 1858, bur Simeon Cem)
<u>Louisa</u> (Mar 1846 - Sep 2, 1913, Coal Twp, Northld Co, bur Simeon Cem), so states her death certificate. Louisa m Henry B. Ferree (c1846 Lyke Twp - d Apr 14, 1903, bur Gratz, according to his death record.) He was a son of George W. and Leah (Umholtz) Ferree. **Henry and Louisa (Bellon) Ferree children:** *Ida Charlotte* b Jan 6,1867; *Sarah Caroline* b May 27, 1868; *George Franklin* b Apr 9, 1870; *Henry M*; *Lizzie Louisa* b Sep 6, 1875; *Mary E*; *Hattie Leah* b Sep 23, 1880; *Eva N.* b Aug 1882, was 2nd wife of Daniel S. Artz c1875, a son of Preston and Mary J. Artz.; *Charles Adam* b Dec 1885; (all bapt at Simeon Ref Ch);
<u>Mathias</u> or **Martha** (Oct 13, 1847 - Nov 24, 1860, bur Simeon Cem)
<u>Jacob</u> (Aug 19, 1854 - Nov 12, 1859, bur Simeon Cem)

***Andreas** b Aug 25, 1806, moved to Russia; ***Jakobina** b Aug 30, 1808; ***Friederich** b Feb 3, 1810; ***Catharina** b May 9, 1812 -1825; ***Susanna** (May 31,1816 – Jun 27, 1890), m 1st Jaeques Giraud (Shiro) who died about 1844 in Germany. She m 2nd Henry Snyder (b Nov 16, 1816 Baden, Ger – d Jul 3, 1899). [More family information on write-up of Henry Snyder property];
***Jakob** b Oct 4, 1818; ***Johannes** (b May 12, 1820 – d Nov 5, 1892, bur Hoffman Cem, date may not be correct), m Sarah Burd (Jan 26, 1829 – Feb 9, 1916), a dau of George and Magdalena (Rickert) Burd of Lykens Twp. In 1900 Sarah was a widow in Lykens Twp and had children Ida 38, Rosa 28, Edward 25 and grandau Pearly M Row 7, with her. **Johannes and Sarah (Burd) Bellon had these children – 6 died before parents (some bapt Hoffman Ch):** <u>Jacob</u> (Jul 26, 1850 – Jan 15, 1891, bur Seybert Cem, Wmstown), m Catherine __ (1857 – 1917); <u>Daniel</u> (May 30, 1852 – 1868) <u>Sarah A.</u> b c1854; <u>John J.</u> b Mar1855; <u>Franklin</u> b Apr 1859, m Mary ___ b c1868, had a **dau** <u>Anne E.</u> b c1896; <u>Amanda</u> (Jul 15, 1859 –1866); <u>Catherine Charloda</u> b Oct 19,1861, bapt Simeon; <u>Louisa</u> b c1862; <u>Catherine</u> b Jul 14,1865; <u>William</u> b Jul 21, 1868; <u>Rosa</u> b Jul 1871; <u>Annie Elizabeth</u> (Jul 17, 1873 – Nov 11, 1893); <u>Eddie Elsworth M.</u> b Sep 7, 1875

***JOHANN DAVID** - from above (b Jan 24, 1801, Schonenberg, Germany - d Jun 15, 1881, of palsy, death recorded in Zion Luth Ch, Lykens, bur Lykens Cem). Johann David was a farmer and innkeeper in Schonenberg. He and his entire family supposedly came to America, but not all at the same time. The pension record of son David mentions that his family left Germany in 1857. He was in fact in Wiconisco in 1861. His wife and some of the children arrived in New York on March 23, 1864. The Census record is proof that J. David Bellon and family lived in Wiconisco Township in 1870. At that time, David and his wife **had these children with them**: Joanna, Frederick, and Jacob. Also a little girl Annie age 5 was with them. It also states that he was employed as a watchman at the Williams breaker. A small but interesting detail in son David's Civil War pension record is a statement by Dr. Schminky. He wrote that he came to live in Gratz in 1855, and David Bellon was then living with his grandmother, Mrs. Loeb. Passing years play havoc with perfect memories. It accounts for the discrepancy between the dates remembered by David Bellon and Dr. Schminky. But the point that David Bellon was living with his grandmother Mrs. Loeb is interesting. A relationship between Mrs. Leopold Loeb and David Bellon has not yet been found. J. David Bellon m Aug 23, 1831 Friedrike Caroline Hofle, b Sep 20, 1812 in Zaiserweiher, a dau of Carl Friederick Hofle and wife Christina Heinrike Bauchte, who later moved to Russia. A date of death has not been found for Friederick Carline, but she is not listed on the 1880 census. David Bellon is listed on the 1880 Wiconisco Twp census with a granddaughter Annie age 15, George Keene age 27, and Magdalena Keene age 65. **John David and Friedrike Caroline (Hofle) Bellon had these children (bapt record in Schonenberg Church):**

******Caroline Johanna** (Sep 4, 1832 - d 1836); ******Carl Gottfried** (Dec 5, 1833 - 1859); ******Johanna Sophia** b Aug 13, 1836; ******Caroline Heinrike** (b Feb 27, 1839 - Oct 24, 1865, bur Old Lykens Cem, Wiconisco Twp) came to North America 1857, and in 1860 was living with the Mathias Tallman family. She m Jacob Stephen Reiff (b Aug 27, 1833 Germany - d Jun 7, 1879, bur IOOF Cem, Lykens with 2nd wife). He died of paralysis. Jacob Reiff was an undertaker and furniture maker. He came to America in 1852. The Gratz Historical Society has a set of plank bottom chairs that were made by him. **Jacob and Caroline (Bellon) Reiff children:** <u>Lucy</u> (no dates) m Abraham Snyder, lived in Harrisburg; <u>John S.</u> (Mar 23, 1861- Dec 14, 1932, bur IOOF Cem, Lykens), m Oct 30, 1894 Louise Klinger (1863 -1926); <u>Catherine Wilhelmina</u> (Feb 6, 1865- Jun 1939, bur Harrisburg Cem), m Feb 26,1884 John. Clinton Riegel, of Williamstown then moved to Harrisburg. **John Clinton and Catherine (Reiff) Riegle children:** *Nellie* m ___ Hocker; *Dr. Reiff J.*, dentist in Harrisburg. After Caroline died, Jacob Reiff m Aug 29,1868, Mary (Umholtz) Muench. **Jacob and Mary (Umholtz) Reiff had a dau** *Agnes* (May 26, 1872 bapt Zion Luth, Lykens - Jul 11, 1912, d of consumption), m Feb 15, 1894 Edward S. Grimm.

******Johann David** (b Nov 12, 1842 in Germany - d Dec 8, 1895 in Olivet, South Dakota of heart trouble and asthma). Johan David came to America in 1857 and settled in Wiconisco where he remained until 1861. He m Oct 4, 1868, in Pilot Mound, Iowa to Wilhelmina Fischer (Sep 18, 1850 in Ger- Oct 17, 1924, in Yanktop, S.D.), a dau of Henry Z. Fischer. Wilhelmina and David Bellon had no children. But at his death, in addition to his widow, he had four nieces and one nephew, offspring of two deceased sisters. David enlisted in Co A., 50th Regt Pa Vol in Sep1861, and reenlisted again in December 1863. During the battle at Spottsylvania, Court House, Va, he was captured and placed in Andersonville prison for nine months.

After David Bellon died, his widow Wilhelmina married on July 25, 1898 to M. E. Hotchkiss "believing he had title to marry me, and lived with him until his death. But after his death, his will revealed the fact that I was not his legal widow, as his divorce from his first wife was illegal. I tried to acquire the right to the property he left, but the court decided against me" Wilhelmina realizing that she was never a legal wife to M. E. Hotchkiss, later applied for a pension from her husband David Bellon.

Aaron Ossman of Tremont was a witness for Wilhelmina when she made application for a pension as the widow of David Bellon. In his statement, Aaron Ossman remarked among other things that when he was discharged in July 1865, David "took Horrace Greely's advice and went west." He did infact move to Pilot Mound, Iowa and later moved to Olivet, South Dakota where he lived out his life. He came back to Harrisburg to visit relatives in 1892, but was by then in very poor physical condition. His widow Wilhelmina came back to this area during the spring and summer of 1898 , and stayed six months, visiting her nephew John S. Reiff.

******Jakob Friedrich** (Sep 30, 1845 - Mar 3, 1881,died of a self inflicted wound, bur Old Lykens Cem.) He lived in Wiconisco with his mother Caroline in 1870 and 1880, and was employed as a cabinetmaker. In 1880, his brother David was also in the household. ******Christian Gottlob** (b Jun 15, 1848 - d 1848); ******Philipp August** (Sep 12, 1849 - Jan 17, 1868); ******Jakob Andreas** (Jun 10, 1854 - Jan 15, 1891, bur Seyfert Cem, Williamstown), m Catharine _____ (Dec 9, 1857 - Apr 29, 1917). He lived with his mother in Wiconisco in 1870. **Jakob Andreas and Catharine Bellon children:** <u>Charles H</u>. b Sep 16, 1877; <u>John H</u>. b c1878; <u>Anna L</u>. b c1880]

RESIDENCE OF PETER RICKERT
(1 acres 1875)

On April 16, 1864 the widow of John Rickert, (now wife of George S. Deibler) officially conveyed one hundred sixty square perches of land to his brother Peter Rickert. This is part of the land that John Rickert received from his parents. Sometime before he died John Rickert made a commitment to convey this land to Peter Rickert, who had already paid the purchase money. However, a deed was not executed. Peter Rickert was living here at least by 1855 when he was assessed for one acre of land, a one and one-half story wooden house, and a log stable. Several years later in 1864 his buildings were listed as "poor" on the assessment record. The land of Mathias Harter, Martin Rickert, and George Deibler bordered this land on the north, John George Weaver land on the south. The Peter Rickert family lived here for many years. Peter died in 1880, and on the 1883 tax record his land is listed as owned by his estate. It was apparently sold after 1919, but a record has not been found. The house no longer exists.

THE HOME OF JOHN FETTERHOFF
(Widow Mary Johns 1875)

Aerial Photo Showing This Property After The New Specktown Road was Constructed

This land is part of the original tract that Commonwealth of Pennsylvania granted to Nicholas Hoffman April 25, 1797. Nicholas and Margaret Hoffman sold the same tract with appurtenances to Jacob Hoffman June 24, 1809, subject to an agreement that was made between Jacob Hoffman Sr. and Abraham Hess. On April 1, 1854, Jacob and Catherine Hoffman sold the messuage and ninety-eight and one-half acres to Abraham Hess.

On May 28, 1860, Abraham Hess, a shoemaker, and his wife sold six acres from the ninety-eight acres to Jacob B. Hoffman. (He was later a tavern keeper in Loyalton). Several years later, On February 18, 1862, Jacob B. and Elizabeth Hoffman conveyed the six acres to Jacob D. Hoffman who was living in Harrisburg at the time. On March 19,1864, Jacob D. and Eva Hoffman sold the same premises to Benjamin Rickert. A few years later, Benjamin Rickert and his wife moved to Williamstown, and decided to sell this house.

On March 30, 1871, Christian R. Johns composed his will in which he requested that his executors should provide a house for his wife Mary – either the one he had or purchase one. When the Benjamin Rickert home went up for sale on April 1, 1872, Christian Johns executors were the highest bidders.

The widow Mary Johns lived here until her death in August 1897. On April 4, 1898 Christian R. Johns, surviving executor of Christian Johns sold the six acres to Henry A. and Isabella Grubb. On April 1, 1907 they sold to Hannah L. Riegel. She had been living nearby on her old family homestead. [JOHNS genealogy page 84]

Present house built c1878

On April 22, 1920, the heirs of Hannah L. Riegel sold the six acres with log house to Helen and William Dietrich. Helen was Hannah's granddaughter. Helen and William had moved to Harrisburg in May 1918, but decided to return to their native area. When they came back to Specktown, they could not move directly into their newly acquired house. They moved temporarily into the little house across the street. While they were tenants in the little house, a severe thunderstorm came through the area. Lightning struck the side of the house they were living in, causing much damage. (Later Fremont Mauser purchased the property, tore down the house and built a new one.)

When William and Helen moved into this house, Helen's mother Lizzie moved with them, and remained there until her death. William worked in the mines. Soon after the Dietrich family moved here, they opened a small store in the front room of their house. They sold ice cream, candies, sodas, bagged pretzels and potato chips. Kathryn was a young girl, and sometimes worked in the store. She remembers that one of their customers, John Bellon, spoke only Dutch. Kathryn had a difficult time understanding him, so he pointed to what he wanted. Kathryn also has the following special memories:

"My second cousin Ruth Evitts came up from Philadelphia every summer after school and stayed with her grandparents (Mr. & Mrs. William Evitts, next door), but spent most of the days with us. She brought her ukulele, and taught me to play with her. We harmonized and sang for the miners when they stopped on their way home from work. Their famous words were "sing a song for us and we'll give you a treat." "We sang songs like "Bye, Bye, Blackbird." They would pay my mother for ice cream and teaberry soda, and that was our treat. We also had a player piano, and the neighbors would come to the store on Saturday night to hear the music. We would put on rolls like "The Old Rugged Cross" and other songs, and everybody would join in the singing. This was a great pastime for the farmers to enjoy. Uncle Chauncey would come down the hill with his violin. He played "Turkey In The Straw" like no one else I've ever heard. So many people in the valley had great musical talent."

"Grandmother always enjoyed the visits of the neighbors. They always talked Dutch and eventually I picked up a few words here and there, but never to speak it well enough to hold a conversation. Grandmother crocheted and made rugs. She also spent a lot of her time acting as a mid-wife, going to homes all around the valley two weeks before time and two weeks after delivery, for which she received $25.00. Many of the maternity cases were relatives. By the time I went to high school, Daddy gave up the store and concentrated on his truck patch. He grew the big ten to twelve-pound cantaloupes and watermelons. He had a stand in the front of the house where people would come from the whole valley to buy some of his produce, and sometimes sit in the yard to eat it."

Kathryn also remembered "Often times on Sunday the Dietrich family walked through the fields to Mammy Dietrich's for dinner. It seemed an easy task for Mammy to have a roast and the trimmings ready to pull out of the oven for many guests who lined up at the table. Some sat on a long bench along the table."

Kathryn and her cousin Sarah Dietrich shared a double desk at Giese School. They took their lunch in a tin lunch box and had a folding tin cup to drink water that was carried to the school from the Sitlinger farm. (Gratz Hist. Soc. has the water cooler from Geise School.) Kathryn attended high school in Lykens. The first year she stayed with her grandmother Keiper and went home weekends. After that she rode to school with the Sitlinger's on their milk truck.

1965 - Kathryn (dau), William and Helen Dietrich, son Harold - 50th Wedding Anniversary

[WILLIAM E. DIETRICH (Nov 15, 1896 –1977, bur Simeon Cem, Gratz), a son of Edward and Jennie (Keiper) Dietrich, m Mar 2,1915 Helen May Hoffman (May 10, 1895 –1977), a dau of Elizabeth Catherine Riegle and George Hoffman. William E. and Helen May (Hoffman) Dietrich children: Kathryn Elizabeth (Feb 19, 1915 –2003), m Norman John Gasbarro, had two sons: Norman John, Jr. b Jan 27,1944; William Edward b Jul 19,1947; Harold William (b Feb 14, 1919 – Mar 12, 1988, Key West, Fla., m Irma Kapps (1929 – Jan 2003). Harold and Irma (Kapps) Dietrich children: Harold W. of N.C.; Carol Ann m __ Horan; Regina M. m _____ Soos, lives in Key West, Fla.]

After both William and Helen Dietrich died, their heirs sold this property Jun 18, 1977 to Betty J. and Eugene C. Fetterhoff. On October 6, 1977 Eugene C. and Betty J Fetterhoff sold about three acres from this property to Charles E. and Eva Kissinger of Upper Mahantongo Township, Sch. Co. Eugene C. Fetterhoff sold the remainder of the property to his son John Fetterhoff about 1995.

[FRANKLIN P. FETTERHOFF (no dates), m Rachel Graeff. Fette Franklin P. and Rachel (Graeff) Fetterhoff children: Francis Monroe (Jun 26, 1874 - 1968); Catherine Alice b Jun 30, 1876; James E.(Oct 26,1879- 1955); Harvey Franklin (Aug 24, 1880- Apr 4, 1913), m Emma Mae Shomper (May 2, 1883 - Oct 24, 1962) a dau of George and Mary Ellen (Woland) Shomper. Harvey Franklin and Emma Mae (Shomper) Fetterhoff children: Mary E. Aug 7,1903 – Dec1985); Harvey F. (Feb 27, 1905 - Jul 14, 1986), m Betty Houseknecht; Alvin F. b 1906, m Cora C. Fetterhoff, had a son Eugene C. b 1933, m Betty J. Erdman (1939 – 1989, bur Maple Grove Cem, E'ville). Eugene C. and Betty J (Erdman) Fetterhoff had a son John.; Lester b 1912; George W. b Jun 1, 1883; Samuel R. b Oct 2, 1886; Ray A. (1894 – 1941), m Lottie Williams (1897 – 1930), 2nd Maude M Hand]

DIAMOND JUBILEE MEMORIAL POST #2385
VETERANS OF FOREIGN WARS OF U.S.

Diamond Jubilee Memorial Post #2385 Grounds & Building

This land is part of the property now owned by John Fetterhoff and has the same beginning as mentioned in the write-up of his home.

On October 6, 1977, Eugene and Betty J. Fetterhoff sold 3.25 acres of land to Charles E. and Eva M. Kissinger of Up. Mahantongo Township, Schuylkill County. On October 17, 1978, Charles E. and Eva M. Kissinger sold this same acreage to Diamond Jubilee Memorial Post #2385 Vets of Foreign Wars of U.S.

Memorial To Veterans

The Diamond Jubilee Post #2385 has acquired other land during the past years, some coming from the adjoining property, and sold to the organization by Jay and Shirley Sponsler in 1994.

SAMUEL & SUSIE BLANK HOME
Was Chauncey Riegel Land – Earlier Jacob Rickert 14 acres in 1875

This land was part of the acreage received by Jacob Rickert when his father's estate was distributed. Elizabeth Rickert, wife of Jacob inherited two thousand dollars from her father Christian Hoover, and she invested most of it in this property. She and her husband made an agreement in which he would pay back her money in rent. Jacob Rickert died in 1885, and on February 17, 1892, Elizabeth his widow, executed a deed to John Kuntzelman for thirteen acres of land. It was agreed that the property would be in trust for herself for the remainder of her life. After her death, the property would be vested in her children. This land bordered on land of Jacob Hess and Martin Rickert on the north, east to Martin Rickert land, then south to other land of Jacob Rickert. Than by land of Abraham Hess and Benjamin Rickert north to land of Isaac Zitlinger.

On March 12, 1898, after Elizabeth died, the heirs sold thirteen acres forty perches of land to Chauncey Riegel. On February 21, 1906, Hannah L. Riegel sold another tract of five acres, thirty-three perches of her land to her son Chauncey.

Old House As It Appears Today

This neighborhood apparently was a close-knit group during the years that the Riegel's lived here. Chauncey was known to fully enjoy a game of cards with his fellow neighbors. The men frequently got together, many times at Chauncey's house to enjoy their leisure. Chauncey also was a talented violin player, and played at community gatherings, such as barn dances, or "down the hill" from his house at the Dietrich's little store. One of his favorite songs was "Turkey In The Straw."

This property was well supplied with mountain water that came from a big well near the house. On August 13, 1937 the administrators of the estate of Chauncey A. Riegel sold the thirteen acres to Grace Greiner, who later married John M. Foley. Grace Greiner Foley died on September 23, 1951. Title to this property was vested in her husband John M. Foley. He later married Virginia ____, and they eventually moved to Seaford, Delaware. On March 10, 1955, John M. and Virginia Foley sold the same acreage and house to Charles H. and Betty M. Maurer of Wiconisco Township, whom later moved to Lykens. On July 27, 1964 they sold these premises to Wilson H. and Mildred L. Kulp of Lykens. Wilson Kulp died November 16, 1977. His widow Mildred L Kulp sold the premises to James E. and Imogean P. Kulp on August 17, 1981. On January 29, 1996, James E. and Imogean P. Kulp sold to Ephraim K Blank and Samuel E. and Susie E. Blank. They have completely remodeled the house expanding it into a much larger home, and are the present owners.

HARRISON RIEGEL FAMILY

[*HARRISON RIEGEL (Nov 15, 1840 - Jul 31, 1899), son of Daniel Riegel Jr and Catherine (Hoffman) Riegel), m Apr 9, 1867 to Hannah Louisa Rickert (May 21, 1847 - June 11, 1919), a dau of Martin and Elizabeth (Yerkes) Rickert. In 1880, Rebecca Rickert, sister of Hannah lived with them in Lykens Twp. **Harrison and Hannah (Rickert) Riegel children (they had 14 children, but many died young:**
Nancey Ellen, twin b Aug 1, 1870, probably died young, not on 1880 census
Chauncey A., twin (Aug 1, 1870 - Dec 4, 1936, bur Simeon Cem), m Emma E. Hassinger Welker (Nov 30, 1863 - May 28, 1934), a dau of Jacob and Lydia Ann (Gipple)Hassinger. Emma was the widow of Adam Welker. Chauncey was a miner for over ten years. **Chauncey and Emma (Welker) Riegel had one child: Evelyn Christine** (1902 - 1961), m Paul Lenhart (1896–1959). ***Anna E. Welker** (1889- 1959), m Fremont J. Mauser)1890 - 1947), was a dau of Emma E. (Hassinger) Welker Riegel and Adam Welker. Anna lived with them.

**Elizabeth Catharine (Jun 30, 1872 - Oct 31,1942, bur Simeon Cem), had a dau Helen who m William Dietrich, a son of Edward and Jennie Dietrich (more information in Dietrich write-up)

Edward Austin (Apr 4,1874 - Mar 1,1960, d in Lanc Co), m Dec 28,1899 Jennie A. Hawk. He taught school at Gise School for several years & Gratz about 1900. He later moved to Lanc Co. ****Charles Gerome (Oct 10, 1876 - Mar 19, 1913, bur Simeon Cem), d in a mine accident at Lykens Valley Mines, Wiconisco, m Feb 25, 1899 Minnie Amanda Coleman (Dec 21, 1880- Aug 4, 1958), a dau of John Coleman and Amanda Schneider. **Charles & Minnie (Coleman) Riegel children** (some bapt Simeon Ch): *****Evelyn Beatrice** b Feb 27, 1900; *****Warren Coleman** (Mar19,1903- Nov 4,1982) m Dorothea O'Neill McMurray (1908-1990), lived in Memphis, Tn; *****Hannah Louisa** (Nov 24,1904 - Sep 18,1977, bus Simeon Cem), m Lawrence McMillan; *****Lucy Viola** (Jan19,1907- Jul 4,1994), m Wm. John Budd (Aug7,1905- Nov 26,1978, bur Wmstown);

**Bertha E. (Dec1879 -1952, bur Simeon Cem), m Jul 28,1900 Samuel J.Sitlinger of Speck town.

**Mabel E b Oct 1883, m Walter Evitts, a son of William Evitts. She lived with her mother in 1900, but after she and Walter were married, they moved to Philadelphia.

**Norman Lester (Oct 4,1886 – Nov 11,1942), m Apr 10, 1909 Lydia Alice Helt. He attended mortuary school, then settled in Robesonia where he had a furniture and undertaker business.

HOME OF EUGENE C. FETTEROLF
House built pre1828 (SUSAN DANIEL 1875 5 acres)

This land originally belonged to the tract of land known as "Chelmford" that Commonwealth of Penna. granted to Michael Salada on January 3, 1785. Michael Salada sold to Hartman Rickert Sr. on April 17, 1811.

On Jan 5, 1826, Magdalena Rickert, widow of Hartman Rickert Sr. and Hartman and Catharine Rickert sold four acres, sixty-one perches of land to John B. Hoffman, who was a blacksmith and had a shop on the premises. John B. and Barbara Hoffman sold the same property to Jacob Riegel on March 10, 1831, who for several years had a series of tenants living in the house. In 1831, Jacob Bordner was a tenant in the house, in 1837 George Hartman lived there, and in 1840, Jonathan Bordner was the resident. Jacob and Nancy Riegel, by signing the back of the deed, conveyed the same four acre sixty-one perches of land with a two-story log house and shop, and log stable to George Holtzman on March 28, 1842. The property also had an excellent supply of running water near the cove, and an orchard containing forty-five or forty-six trees. George Holtzman was a cooper, and apparently used the shop for his craft. He came to Lykens Township early in the 1830s, and in 1833 was listed as a single person. At least part of the time, he was a tenant on the Jacob Riegel place, perhaps after his marriage.

George Holtzman and his family lived on this farm until about 1846, when tenant William Hoover lived here. The next year, according to tax records, the Holtzman family again resided here. The property was described as having a two-story log house, shop and log bank barn. George was listed as a cooper from 1840 to 1846. He had learned the trade of cooper when he was a young man, and continued in that occupation throughout his life. In 1849, George and Hannah sponsored the baptism of Henrietta Louisa b Aug 12, 1849, daughter of Josiah and Susannah (Riegel) Folk (Apr 4, 1821 – Aug 24, 1869, bur IOOF Cem Lykens). George Holtzman died in 1850.

After George died, Hannah and her three children lived on this property (at that time under Wiconisco Twp). Sarah Hoover age sixty-six and William Hoover age thirty-four lived on the same property, but in separate quarters. Hannah continued to own this property until 1855 when she is listed on the tax record with the 6 acres, 2 story log house and small barn. William Huber is the resident. By then she had married John Andre and moved to Uniontown (Pillow).

Hannah became the administrator of her late husband George Holtzman's estate, "by consent of her husband John Andre." She supplied the information to the court that the estate of George Holtzman had insufficient funds. It was decided that the property should be sold "to pay the debts, and for the sake of the children, (Mary Ann and John, both above age fourteen years), before the real estate would go into decay." A public vendue was set for January 1, 1856, and Hannah sold "four and one-half acres of land with two-story log house, shop, stable, excellent running water near the cove, and an orchard of forty-five or forty-six trees to Isaac Sitlinger. Isaac was at the time a tenant living on the property of Eliza Riegel. The 1858 tax record shows Isaac Sitlinger as owner of this property, and George Long, a coal miner, as tenant.

George Holtzman Tombstone at Hoffman Cem. Mistake made when Hoffman stones recorded

[GEORGE HOLTZMAN (b Jul 22, 1811 - d Apr 26, 1850, Lykens Twp., bur Hoffman Cem), was a son of Peter Holtzman and Susanna Riegel. The record from Dauphin County Court is given as proof of this parentage. On May 5, 1812, Peter Holtzman pleads guilty to fathering a child born Jun 22, 1811 to Susanna Riegel. He paid $14.00 for her "lying in expense," and was ordered to pay sixty-seven cents per week until the child would reach seven years of age. Nothing more is known of Susanna Riegel. George m about 1834, Hannah _____(Oct 8, 1817 - Jul 9, 1870), probably a dau of Jacob and Anna Riegel. Only problem, the baptismal birthdate is November 8, 1817 compared to tombstone Oct 8, 1817. **George and Hannah ( ) Holtzman had these known children:** John (Feb 7, 1836 - Mar 2, 1856, bur Grandview Cem, Pillow), **Anna Maria** b Apr 20, 1838, bapt Hoffman Ch.; **Jacob** b c1840. After George died, Hannah married John Andre (Sep 11, 1807 - Aug 9, 1871, bur Grandview Cem, Pillow), a son of _____. John Andre had been married first to Catharine _____ (Dec 6, 1808 - Aug 27, 1852, bur in Pillow Cem). **John and Catharine (____) Andre had these known children:** John (c1836 – pre 1910), m Catharine Kissinger (Mar 14, 1844 – Mar 1921), a dau of Daniel and Elizabeth Kissinger. They lived on a farm between Berrysburg and Pillow, but when John died, Catharine moved to Gratz where she died. Rev. Wehr had her funeral. John and Catherine (Kissinger) Andre lived in Uniontown in 1880 and had Clara M. Eby a niece age 7 with them. John (Sr.) was a master shoemaker in 1860. In 1870, John and Catherine lived in Pillow and he is listed as a boot and shoemaker. A record at St. Johns (Hill) Ch notes the birth of John Henry Jan 19, 1860 to John Endre and Louisa Deibler (illegitimate); **Jefferson** b c1841; **Mary Ann** b c1846; **Susan** b c1842; **Jeremiah** (Sep 30, 1851 - Aug 30, 1852, bur Pillow). In 1860 , John and Hannah Andre lived in Uniontown, Mifflin Township. John was listed on the census as "making cotton tabs."

[John and Catharine ____ Andre may have had a son Jacob (Feb 16, 1830 – Aug 6, 1909, bur Maple Grove Cem, E'ville), m Angeline ___ (Jun 5, 1836 – May 12, 1913). In 1880 Jacob and Angeline lived in Halifax Twp where he was employed as a miller making flour. They had Michael Forney age 71 living with them and working at the mill. **Jacob and Angeline Andre had these children:** Hanna b c1866; Susan A b c1869; Ida M b c1873; Carrie A. b c1875; Daniel A (1877 – 1935 bur Maple Grove Cem), m Mary A. ___ (1875 – 1953).]

The 1864 and 1868 tax record shows Isaac Sitlinger with five seated acres, log house and barn. (It is not unusual for land acreage to fluctuate on the tax record, for several reasons). [See Sitlinger family information elsewhere]. Susanna Daniel was the next owner. In 1873, Susannah Daniel is taxed for four acres "that lately belonged to Zitlinger." In 1880, Susannah was a widow, had her daughter Elmira age 18 and William Daniel age 12, a hired servant living with her. Susannah appointed Harrison Riegel to be her executor, and on January 1, 1886 he sold Susannah's land to her daughter and son-in-law, Sarah Adaline and William Evitts.

The William Evitts family lived here for many years. In later years, Benjamin J. Evitts (Capt. during Civil War), his father resided with William and his family, and died here in 1909. After William and Sarah Adaline died, the property was sold on January 12, 1926, to their son Frederick Evitts and his wife Lura (Laura). Several years later, on February 13, 1930, Frederick and Lura Evitts sold the four plus acres with appurtenances to John E. and Sarah E. Rothermel. [Evitts genealogy elsewhere].

[SUSAN MOYER DANIEL (Dec 29, 1818 - Jun 18, 1885, bur Hoffman Cem), was a dau of Jacob and Elizabeth Moyer. She was the 2nd wife of John George Daniel (Aug 13, 1801 - Dec 4, 1871, bur Hoffman Cem), a son of Andreas and Susanna (Hoy) Daniel. [Children of the first wife Margaretha Buffington Daniel are listed elsewhere.] John George and Susan (Moyer) Daniel had these children: Margaret b Mar 11,1840; Elizabeth (Jan 29, 1844 - Mar 10, 1862, bur Hoffman Cem); John b c1846, m Emma J. _____ b c1851; Isaac b c1848, m Elizabeth Williard; Mary b c1852; Swingley or Finley b 1855; Louisa b 1856; Susan b c1858; Sarah Adaline (Apr 11,1859-1925, bur Hoffman Cem), m1879, William A. Evitts (Sep 5,1854 - 1928), a son of Capt Benjamin J. Evitts. William and Sarah Adline (Daniel) Evitts children: Perla May (May 19, 1879 - 1896); George Washington (1881 - 1882); Walter Albert b Dec 30, 1884, m Mabel Riegel, and moved to Philadelphia during the depression years where he became a prominent contractor. He purchased homes in the city and renovated them as tenant homes. If the bathroom fixtures were in good condition when he removed them from the city homes, he brought them to this valley and installed them in local homes. One of the houses that received a bathroom was the William Dietrich home; Benjamin b ___ lived in Llewellyn; Edwin C. b Jan 1888; Beulah A b Jan 21, 1890; Flossie b Feb 1891; Harvey B b Mar 15, 1895; Laura b May 14, 1892, m ____ Dreibelbis, moved to Phila; Henry E. b Sep 21, 1896, moved to Phila; Verna Adaline (May 18, 1899 - Dec 1937, bur Wiconisco Cem), m Carl Klinger, moved to Wiconisco; Frederick Weidel (Sep 4, 1900 - Oct 1937, bur Simeon Cem, Gratz), m Laura Hess (1900 - Feb 1975), a dau of Harvey and Kate Hess. Frederick and Kate lived here in his parents home, and took care of William in his elderly years.
Elmira b Feb 21, 1861 - 1887, bur Hoffman Cem.]

The Rothermel family lived here untilAugust 18,1942 when they conveyed the four acres with dwelling and outbuildings to Calvin L. and Catherine E. Engle. And incident has been recalled about a spring day when Kate Engle was digging her garden. As she worked, she noticed a neighbor, one of the Lucas girls walking down the road. This kindly young girl worked in the Gratz factory, and came home early because work was completed. The girl stopped, and although she put in most of the day at the factory, she busied herself digging the remainder of the garden for Mrs. Engle.

On August 26, 1966, Catherine E. Engle sold this property to Eugene C. and Betty J. (Erdman) Fetterhoff, and since Betty passed away,Eugene Fetterhoff is the present owner.

THE ENGLE FAMILY

[CALVIN L. ENGLE (1884 - Feb 1, 1950, bur Simeon Cem), was a son of Daniel and Emma (Bordner) Engle of Northld Co. He m Catherine E. Hoffman (1888 - 1973), dau of Lewis C. and Sallie Hoffman. Calvin and Catherine (Hoffman) Engle children: Mildred P. b c1908, m Charles Cooper; EARLE E. (1910 - ___, bur Simeon Cem), m Marguerite Mauser (1912 - Jul 23, 1947), a dau of Fremont and Annie (Welker) Mauser. Earl and Marguerite (Mauser) Engle children: Clair m Vivian Starr; Stanley Elersly b Jan 12, 1927, m Betty Hoffman, had a large grocery store in Millersburg; Arlene Ruth b Feb 14, 1937, m Dean Deibert, a son of Harry and Ruth (Stutzman) Deibert, lives in Gratz, had a son David who m Elizabeth Wiest; Betty (no dates), m James Grab. MARLIN D b c1916, m Mary Shade; LAWRENCE C. (1921 – Mar 8, 1945, bur Simeon Cem). He was killed in the service, during World War II. He m Estella Latsko, had a dau Eleanor Lucy b Dec 13, 1941; SARAH JANE b Nov 25, 1927, m Thomas Bressler. ROBERT LEWIS b Mar 17, 1931.]

House On Property When Engle Family
Lived Here. Art Spotts and ___Bressler on photo

Calvin & Catherine (Hoffman) Engle

RALPH TSCHOPP HOME
(EDWARD HOOVER LAND 1875 – 1 acre - Present house built c1920's)

This land was part of the Hartman Rickert land that passed down to Martin Rickert on January 14, 1843. Martin and Elizabeth Rickert on April 18, 1857 sold one acre, twenty-two perches of land to Jacob and Magdalena Huber.

The 1855 tax record describes their property as one acre of seated land with a one story log house and small barn. W. Ramberger was living on the property. In 1857 Jacob Huber conveyed the small property to John Smith who was living in Wiconisco. W. Hoover resided here. On February 22, 1864, John Smith and his wife (not named), of Wiconisco, sold this real estate to Solomon Rettinger, a coal miner who had already been living on Martin Rickerts property in Lykens Township. In 1860, Solomon's grandmother Magdalena Rettinger lived with them.

About two years after they purchased this property, on February 26, 1866, Solomon and Susanna Rettinger sold the same log house, one acre and thirty-five perches of land to Jacob Hess. The Rettinger's moved to Lykens, and Solomon worked as a brakeman on the railroad until he broke his leg. Then he sold coal oil to stores. The railroad injury caused him to walk with a cane the remainder of his life.

Jacob Hess was assessed for this property in 1868, and in 1870, he and his family lived in this house. Jacob was working in the mines.
[Jacob A. Hess (Jan 29, 1840 - Aug 9, 1917), a son of Abraham and Catherine (Hoffman) Hess was the father of a son named **Harvey Adam Lincoln Hess** (Nov 25, 1864 - Dec 1, 1951) born to Ella Amanda Rodenbach (1846 - 1882). Jacob married Aug 6, 1864 in Berrysburg, Amanda S. Klinger (Oct 7, 1845 - Sep 23, 1931), of Pillow. **Jacob and Amanda (Klinger) Hess had these children: Cora Minerva** b Apr 30, 1866; **Anna Victoria** b Aug 4, 1867; **Ida** (1870 -1871); **Mary Deborah** b Oct 26, 1872; **William Henry Harrison** b Oct 26, 1874 (he lived with the John Raudenbach family in 1880); **John Quincy Adam** b Jun 28, 1876; **Oscar** (1882 - 1883); **Mabel Catherine** b Feb 28, 1884. John Hess served in the Civil War with Co H. 210th Regt. After the war, he and the family lived in Lykens Township. In 1870, Daniel Hilbert lived with the family, and he worked in the mines. Later they moved to Minersville where he died.]

Jacob & Amanda (Klinger) Hess

RETTINGER FAMILY

[The Rettinger family is traced to **HENRY RETTINGER** who was born in Germany or Switzerland. He came to America on the ship St. Andrew, leaving from Rotterdam, arriving in Philadelphia on August 18, 1750. His wife's name is unknown, and the only known child **MICHAEL RETTINGER** (c1734 - Nov 1799), came to America with his father and settled in Ruscombmanor Twp, Berks County. He served with the Berks Co. Militia during the Revolutionary War. **Michael married Anna Margaret _____, and they had these children:**

Susanna Rickert Rettinger

***ANDREW** (b c1760 Berks Co - d Aug 26, 1822 Upper Mahantango Twp, Sch Co). He also served in the Berks Co. Militia during the Rev. War. He married Susanna Barto (Mar 20, 1768 - Jun 18, 1845, bur Klingers Ch). They came into this area at least by 1800. Andrew owned a gristmill on the Mahantango Creek near Klingerstown, and attended Klinger's Church.
Andrew and Susanna (Barto) Rettinger children:
Peter b c1780 m Sarah Bowman (c1794 Jordan Twp., Northld Co – Mar 1884)), dau of Jacob and Susannah (Leffinger) Bruch. They lived in Upper Mahanoy Twp., Northumberland Co. Peter inherited his fathers gristmill at Klingerstown on the Mahantango Creek. **Peter and Sarah (Bowman) Rettinger had one known child:**
***Benjamin** b Mar 28, 1822.
Samuel (_____ - d pre 1850), m Magdalena Paul (Mar 22, 1790 - Nov 22, 1866, bur St. Pauls Cem, Wayne Twp, Dau Co. They communicated at Hoffman Church in 1818.

Samuel and Magdalena (Paul) Rettinger children:

***Samuel** b Mar 10, 1811, bapt Klingers Ch

***Jacob** (May 30, 1813 - Dec 19, 1890, bur St.Pauls Cem, Wayne Twp, Dau Co), m Catherine Hoover (Oct 3, 1812 - Sep 29, 1884), a dau of _____ .   In 1850, Jacob and Catherine lived in Lykens Township, and he was a farmer. Jacob's mother Magdalena lived with them. **Jacob and Catherine (Hoover) Rettinger children:**
****Solomon** (Oct 28, 1834 -Jul 31, 1899, of heart failure, bur IOOF Cem, Lykens), m Aug 24,1852, Susanna Rickert (Jul 1, 1833 - Dec 24, 1911), a dau of Martin and Elizabeth (Yerges) Rickert. Susanna lived with her daughter Sarah Alice at the time of her death. **Solomon and Susanna (Rickert) Rettinger children:**
Henry (Nov 24,1852 - Sep 6, 1904, of cancer, bur IOOF Cem, Lykens), m Apr 2, 1876 Caroline Knorr (1855 - 1944). They lived in Lykens Twp in 1880. **Henry and Caroline (Knorr) Rettinger had these children**: Edgar b c1877; Rebecca b c1880; Ray (no dates); *Sarah Alice* (Aug 8, 1854 - Jul 14, 1940), m Dec 31, 1873, James H. Bailey; *Jacob Howard* (Oct 17, 1856 - Feb 24, 1939, of paralysis, bur Calvary Meth Cem, Wiconisco), m Oct 26, 1878 Mary Ellen Messner (1859 - 1935); *James F* (Jun 24, 1858 - Sep18, 1890, bur Lykens), m Kathryn Weiss (Jan 8, 1856 - Sep 20, 1943), a dau of Jacob Andrew and Charlotte (Wentz) Weiss; *Agnes* (Aug 6, 1861 - Feb 16, 1918), m Charles F. Koppenhaver; *Daniel M.* (Jan 6, 1864 - May 31, 1922), bapt Hoffman Ch , m Lydia A. Rettinger, lived in Wayne Twp, Dau Co.He later moved to Phila.; *Samuel L.* b Jul 12, 1866, m Sarah Robison (no dates), had a son Joseph Raymond Robison Rettinger b Dec 8, 1887, bapt Zion Luth, grandparents Solomon Rettingers of Halifax Twp were sponsors, Samuel later lived in Mt. Carmel; Charles (no dates); Daisy (no dates); Ethel (no dates). Samuel later moved to Mt. Carmel.; *Ida Louisa* (b Nov 21, 1868, bapt Zion Luth, Lykens, - d 1924), m Howard Bitterman; *Solomon* b Nov 14, 1871, bapt Zion Luth - Jun 28, 1946), m Minnie Haertter b Sep 1839, a dau of George and Henrietta Haertter of Lykens.; *William Howard* b Oct 28, 1874, bapt. Zion Luth.- d Jul 30, 1 938), m Mary Terressa Minnich.

****John** (Mar 13, 1839 - Sep 21, 1907, Lykens), Civil War Veteran, occupation knife sharpener.****Daniel** (Nov 10, 1841 - Nov 8, 1923, bur Fairview Cem, Jackson Twp), m Amanda Paul (Jun 7, 1848 – Feb 26, 1912). **Daniel & Amanda (Paul) Rettinger children**: Cornelius b c1870; Henry b c1874; Jennie A b c1876. In 1880 Reuben J. Wilbert lived with them;****Rebecca** (Jul 21, 1844 - Jan 12, 1913, bur St. Jacob (Millers Ch), Powells Valley), m Philip Parmer; ****Amanda** b Jul 6, 1847, bapt Hoffman Ch, m Aaron Sheesley; ****Jacob** (May 24, 1849 - Mar 29, 1862, Wayne Twp, Dau Co, St. Pauls Cem);****Elias** (Oct 3, 1853 - Jan 16, 1930, bur St. Pauls, Bowermans Cem, Enterline), m Amanda Enders (Mar 20, 1850 - Dec 18, 1829), a dau of Philip and Nancy (Sheetz) Enders. **They had these children**: *William* b c1876; *Charles* b c1878.]

HENRY (Dec 15, 1759– Sep 5,1827), served in Berks Co Militia during Revolutionary War,   remained in Ruscombmanor Twp, Berks Co. He m Anna Catherine Barto
*ANNA MARGARET (no dates), m Henry Maternus
*SOPHIA b c1764, m Jacob Laudenslager of Lykens Township. [see Laudenslager genealogy.]

On May 1, 1873 Jacob Hess and his wife Amanda sold the one acre thirty-five perches of land to Edward Hoover, who with his family lived in this log house in 1875.

Another tract of eight acres 130 perches of unseated land was conveyed to Edward Hoover on April 1, 1892. This land was also originally part of the Hartman Rickert tract. On April 8, 1843, John Rickert and his wife sold it to John Adam Bonawitz and his wife. On April 3, 1848 John Adam Bonawitz and his wife assigned the residence and land to Jacob Williard. The next year on March 31, 1849, Jacob and Sarah Williard sold the land (with several other tracts) to John George Weaver. After his death, his daughter Angeline inherited the property, but she died soon after she inherited the land. Her husband Elias Fegley of Jordan Township, Northumberland County conveyed the land on August 6, 1884 to John B. Weaver. On April 1, 1892, he sold this small tract and two other ones in another area of Lykens Township to Edward Hoover. While Edward Hoover owned this land, it bordered the land of Harrison Riegel, George Deibler, and Mrs. G. Frank Boyer.

Edward Hoover and his family lived here for many years. In1880, he was working in the mines. Before his death, Edward Hoover agreed on October 1, 1892 to sell to Daniel I. Welker for $325.00. Daniel I. Welker was subject to pay twenty-five dollars upon possession of the property, the remaining debt to be paid in a way suitable to the buyer, with six- percent interest.   Seventy-five dollars was owed when Edward Hoover died, the deed had not been delivered. Mary A.. the widow petitioned the court for another agreement and received it. On July 16, 1898, Mary A. Hoover, widow, officially transferred the one acre twenty-five perches of land to Daniel I Welker.

[DANIEL I. WELKER (Dec 1865 -   ), m c1889 Emma Hassinger Buffington (Nov 30,1863 – May 28, 1934, bur Simeon Cem, Gratz with 3rd husband Chauncey Riegle), widow of John E.   Buffington. In 1900 they lived in Lykens Twp., had dau Annie age 10, stepson Charles Warren Buffington 14, and Wellington Hoover, boarded 24 with them. Daniel was a coal miner. **Daniel I. and Emma (Hassinger Buffington)Welker had one child: Annie Edna** b Jul 4, 1889, bapt Simeon Ch. More info Hassinger gen.]

Daniel I Welker and family lived here until January 12, 1907, when they conveyed the property to Jacob Shiro. On January 9, 1909, Jacob and Mary Shiro sold the same property to Emma J. Row, and on March 24, 1921, Emma J. and William Row sold their home and small tract to Frank Gunderman with appurtenances. One month later, on April 4, 1921, Frank and Ellen Gunderman conveyed to Fremont Mauser.When Fremont Mauser purchased this property, the house was in a dilapidated condition. Several years before the purchase William and Helen Dietrich were tenants in the house. A severe thunderstorm came through, and lightening struck the side of the house causing serious damage. Soon after Fremont Mauser owned the property, he tore down the old house and built the now existing house.

When Fremont died, his wife Annie received title. Annie died on July 4, 1959, and by her will her son Clarence J. Mauser receive the land and house. On May 20, 1960, Clarence J. and Dorothea Mauser sold one acre twenty-five perches and house to John H. and Betty J. Tschopp. Their son Ralph is the present resident of this home.

[**EDWARD HOOVER** (Apr 24, 1848 - Oct 5, 1893, bur Hoffman Cem), a son of Elias and Elizabeth (Witman) Hoover, m Mary Ann Giese (Sep 12, 1854 - Nov 13,1919). **Edward and Mary Ann (Giese) Hoover children: Amanda A.** (Oct 23, 1873 - Oct 4, 1923, record in Hoffman Ch book), m c 1895 John Hiram Riegel (Nov 18, 1874 -   ), a son of Andrew and Sarah (Radel) Riegel. **John Hiram & Amanda (Hoover) Riegel children** (bapt Hoffman Ch): John b c1899; Mary Ellen b Oct 27, 1895;Elsie Seville b Aug 4, 1897; Katie Amanda b Jun 15, 1907; Leah Esther b Jun 30, 1910. Katie Celeste b Oct 29, 1880, m Jonas? Lubold. A Jonas and Katie Riegel had two children in 1910 in Lykens Twp: Fronica b c1903; Carrie b c1907. After Edward died, Mary Ann (Giese) Hoover married____Williard.]

MARTIN RICKERT LAND
(House Built 1826, 1875 Widow Betsey Rickert owned 32 acres in Lykens Twp)
Later John Gunderman 79 acres 62 perches

This Photo Taken Years Ago, Showing, Old House, Two-story Addition, Small House & Barn

On January 14, 1843 after Magdalena had died, John Rickert and wife Elizabeth, and Jacob Rickert assigned a tract of land containing 79 acres 62 perches and house to their brother Martin. This was the old homestead noted on the "window tax" of 1798 as a cabin. As previously mentioned Martin and his family had been living in this house before he officially inherited it. The property was part of a distribution made between several brothers from their father's will. In 1826 the old house expanded from the small log cabin to a two-story log addition. The new addition measured 20 by 15 feet, and was made of very large logs. The date is carved in roman numerals into one of the attic beams. The basement walls were made of round rocks. Between 1847 and 1855, Martin built the small house next to the main house. He also built a bank barn in that time period. In1855 /58 Solomon Rettinger, coal miner was a tenant.

The 1850 census records the Martin Rickert family in Wiconisco Township because the township lines had been changed, and they were no longer in Lykens Township. Martin's mother Catherine was living alone either in a separate part of his house, or in the small house on the property. Martin Rickert and family lived here for many years. After Martin died, his heirs, according to instructions in his will, kept his estate in trust for his widow for her lifetime.

When the house was being remodeled a few years ago, this picture was taken showing the log construction in the walls of the house.

Martin Rickert penned his will on March 15, 1872. He stated in part:

"I give to my beloved wife Elisabeth Rickert all my real and personal effects during her natural life. After her decease the property shall be sold and divided in equal shares to my legal heirs. I also bequeath and will to Henry Reddinger my daughter's son to have equal shares with my own legal heirs after the death of my wife Elisabeth. I give the right to my wife to sell a certain piece of mountain land being a part of my mansion tract in personal property to pay my legal debts if she wishes. My daughter Rebecca shall remain with my wife during her natural life."

Picture is of the old barn as it looked about 1966. The woman on the picture has not been identified.

444

Elisabeth Rickert widow of Martin Rickert penned her will May 9,1876. She wrote in part:
        "I give to my daughter Rebecca one bed stead and bedding, and my daughter Sarah intermarried to Jonas Hoffman shall have one of my youngest cows. My daughter Rebecca shall have out of my personal property the price of one cow and one bureau out of the money of my personal property. I give to my daughter's son William Henry Hoffman one shotgun and one bedstead and bedding. It is my desire that my son-in-law Harrison Reigle shalll be the guardian of my daughter Rebecca, responsible to manage her property." (Rebecca needed special care because of a disability.)

Harrison Riegel (1840 – 1899)

Hannah L. (Rickert) Riegel (1847 – 1919)

The next Two Photos Belonged To Lizzie Riegel, obviously family gatherings. Top: Not positive but probably Chauncey 1st man 2nd row, Lizzie & Hannah Riegel far right standing. Bottom: Hannah Riegel 3rd from l; Lizzie Riegel center front.
[We thank Norman Gasbarro, Jr. for sharing most of the photos of the Rickert and extended family with us. Norman found them in the attic of his parents home and preserved them..]

445

Martin Rickert (1804 – 1871)

Elizabeth (Yerkes) Rickert (1813 – 1877)

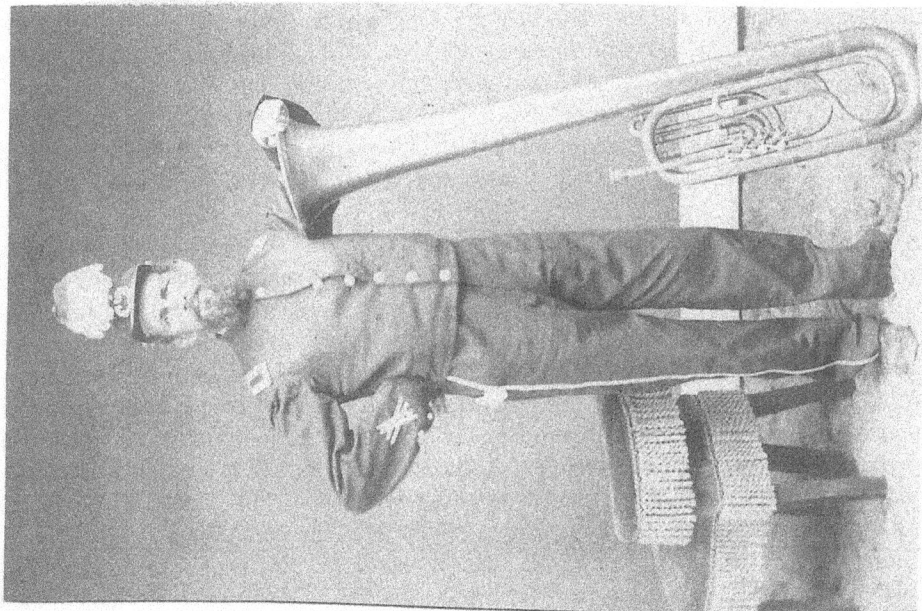

Harrison Riegle –

Perhaps while a member of the Loyalton Band

After the widow died, a public sale was held September 1, 1877, and the property containing seventy-eight acres, one hundred forty-five perches, with a log house and barn was sold to Hannah L. Riegel wife of Harrison Riegel (Elisabeth's daughter and son-in-law). The deed was recorded April 11, 1878. This land bordered the land of John Hoover to the north, Josiah Hoover, south to George Deibler, Boas and Rumford, and the public road.

Harrison Riegel grew up in Lykens Township, and worked for his father on the farm until he was about sixteen years old. Then he began working for the Lykens Valley Coal Company, and continued in that occupation until about 1855. Harrison served in the Civil War having enlisted in March 1865, and discharged in July 1865. After the war he returned to Lykens Township, and was married about two years later. Harrison went back to mining for about ten years, before purchasing this farm. He and Hannah lived here for the remainder of their lives. Harrison Riegel died Jul 31, 1899 of miners asthma. He and his brother-in-law Samuel Rettinger died on the same day, only three hours apart.

In 1900 after Harrison died, Hannah and most of her family, Chauncey, Lizzie, Bertha, Mabel and Norman lived in this house. Her granddaughter, Helen Hoffman age five, and her sister Rebecca age sixty-two also lived in her household. Her son Charles and his wife and daughter lived in the little house on their property and several children were born to them in that house. Charles was working in the mines in Wiconisco. He and his family later moved to Lykens to be closer to his employment, but he was killed in the mines in 1913. Chauncey had married Emma Welker, widow of Daniel I. Welker, and lived next door in the house on the land that he had purchased from Jacob Rickert. Anna Welker age twenty, lived with Chauncey and Emma Riegel. Anna was Emma's daughter to her husband Daniel Welker.

On February 21, 1906, five acres, thirty-three perches were sold to Chauncey Riegel. Then at an auction held on this property in the fall of 1906 (recorded April 1907), Frank Gunderman purchased the remainder of the farm with seventy-three acres 112 perches. The next spring the Gunderman family moved into the house. Several generations of the Gunderman family lived here, with several more transferals of the land.

While the Gunderman family owned this farm, the water pipe that ran from the spring on the other farm continued to serve both families. Through out those years, a trough had been placed beside the small house on the property. A continuous flow of water to the trough supplied all the water the family needed. During summer dry spells, neighbors had access to the water, and brought containers to get a supply of that good mountain water for their families. The Gunderman family used home remedies to cure some of their ills. They also rendered skunk oil for medicinal purposes. Ivy poison was treated by making a potion from the bark of a large evergreen tree located in their front yard. Frank Gunderman was known for his habit of most always wearing "gum" boots. The big hill at the Gunderman farm was a very popular place for many people to gather each winter to go sledding in the snow.

Old Rickert Homestead with Harrison & Hannah Riegel family. Photo taken c1891. l to r: _____, Edw, Norman, Mabel, Chas, Hannah standing, Lizzie seated, Becky Rickert, Chauncey age 21, Harrison

Frank and Mary E. Gunderman transferred the property to John F. Gunderman and Esther Shomper on July 16, 1949. Finally on April 23, 1966, the Gunderman family gave up their homestead. John F. and Maude R. Gunderman and Esther A. and Elmer Shomper transferred seventy-three acres, one hundred twelve perches to Edmund C. and Margaret Mae Anderson, previous residents of Bucks County. While the Andersons owned the premises, they made numerous changes to the house. The ancient barn has been gone for a number of years, leaving the stone foundation as the only reminder of the early structure. On June 11, 1982 Edmund C. Anderson died, and a year later on June 6,1983 his widow Margaret Anderson died. The land was then divided and sold to several new owners. On October 27, 1983 about 30 acres of the land was sold to Kenneth S. Bush. On November 17, 1983, 29 acres of the Anderson property was conveyed to Gerald F. Wiest. Ten acres plus the dwelling house, smaller dwelling and garage was transferred to Barbara L. and Stephen R. Evans on that same date. About 1999, the small house was demolished, leaving only the original larger dwelling with the new look.

THE GUNDERMAN FAMILY – VARIOUS SPELLINGS
(Some information from Norman Mark Rickert)

We have not succeeded in tracing the Gunderman family of this area back to those living earlier in Berks County. The following families lived in or near the Lykens Valley.

LEONHARD GUNDERMAN (Mar 11, 1778 - Jan 14, 1851), m Maria Magd _____ (Dec 2, 1784 - Feb 7, 1840).In 1850 Leonard lived in Halifax Twp. His son John age 43, Mary Wilbert 25, and William Mitchell 13 lived with him. **Leonard and Maria Magd Gunderman children (bapt Fetterhoff's Ch): Johannes** (Jan 5, 1805 - Aug 2, 1868); **Magdalena** b Feb 25, 1806; **Catherina** (Apr 25, 1816 - Jan 10, 1852) m Frederick Frank, lived next to her father in 1850; **Luisana** b Aug 26, 1820.

MICHAEL GUNDERMAN (no dates), m Magdalena _____. **Michael and Magdalena Gunderman children (some bapt St. John's (Hill) Ch, Berrysburg):**

ANNA MARY GUNDERMAN (1805– pre1870), probably a dau of Michael and Magdalena, m Jacob Buffington (1801–1877), moved to Jefferson Twp. **Children:* SUSAN** b Apr 29, 1824;*****THOMAS**;*****ISAAC** b c1825; *****JACOB Jr.** b c1832;*****JONAS** b c1835, m Catherine ___;*****EMANUEL** b c1837;*****MARY** b 1841; *****Levi** b c1848; *****LYDIA** (b___ d May 5, 1853, bur Straw's Cem), Enders.

MICHAELl GUNDERMAN (b Mar 20, 1809 - d Jul 12, 1889, bur Hoffman Cem), m Oct 17, 1833 Rebecca Riegel (b Jun 18, 1817 - d Jun 23, 1892), a dau of Mathias and Maria "Polly" Riegel. Michael and Rebecca lived in Wiconisco Township according to the census record of 1860, and he was a fence maker. All of their children were living at home with the parents. In 1880 they were living in Washington Township, and Michael was a laborer. Their children Michael, Sarah and Jacob, and granddaughter Mary age 14. lived with them. **Michael and Rebecca (Riegel)Gunderman had these children: ***HENRY (Mar 30,1836 -Oct 3,1855, bur Hoffman Cem), lived with John Riegel family in Jefferson Twp, in 1850.

***JOHN (b Dec 28, 1837 – d Aug 7, 1913, of a stroke, bur Hoffman Cem), m Amanda Rickert (Feb 27, 1845 - Nov 15, 1893), a dau of Jacob and Elizabeth (Hoover) Rickert. John was a Civil War Veteran. He served with Capt. Cornelius Harper in Co. K, 173rd Penna Regt. He took sick with typhoid fever while serving at Norfolk. When he applied for a pension, his date of birth was taken from his father's old German Bible, but the Bible later became destroyed, so offered no proof of birth date. In 1880, John and Amanda lived in Lykens Twp. and had these children with them: Emma age 13, William E age 6, Franklin age 3. In1900, John Gunderman, his son Franklin, and Caroline Mauser (a widow b May 1859) with her dau Carrie b Jun 1894, age 5, lived in the same household. Caroline was listed as a servant. In 1910, Frank Gunderman was the head of the house. His widowed father was living with him. Also in the household was John Tschopp age 22, listed as a nephew. He worked in the coal mines. **John & Amanda (Rickert) Gunderman children: ****Carrie** b c1864, died before father.

John Gunderman

448

******Emma Jane** (b Jan 9, 1867 bapt Zion Luth, Lykens - d May 26, 1899, bur Hoffman Cem), m Oct 2, 1887, George Washington Tschopp (b Oct 8, 1862 - Jul 16, 1926) , a son of George and Magdalena (Schoffstall) Tschopp. **George and Emma Jane (Gunderman) Tschopp children:**

John Henry (Feb 26, 1888 - Feb 20, 1943, bur Maple Grove Cem, E'ville), m Feb 26, 1911 Pearl Mae Rowe (Apr 14, 1893 - Mar 4, 1955), a dau of George and Annie Elizabeth (Bellon) Rowe. **John Henry and Pearl (Rowe) Tschopp children:**

George Franklin b Sep 13, 1911, bapt Oakdale Ch, - d Dec 1978) m Esther P. Tschopp; Rosa Louise (Aug 21, 1913 - ___), m John Heim, **had these children:** Roger Lee b Apr 26, 1941, bapt at home of George F. Tschopp ; Elba Mae (Feb 8, 1915 - ___) m Sep 19, 1932 Roy Austin Klinger, Klinger Ch record; Marlin Charles b Mar 2, 1917, m Sep 16, 1950 Marie Elizabeth Miller; Beulah Rebecca b Apr 19, 1919 - 1992) lived in Hubley Twp single; John Henry Jr (May 23, 1928 - Jun 25, 1997), m 1947 Betty Jean Stutzman; Betty Marie, single; Dorothy Irene m Belford Drumheller of Hubley Twp, Sch Co; Sarah (no dates)

 Beulah Rebecca p b 1890 - m Arthur Ferree; Frederick (Aug 14, 1891 - Oct 1962 in Kansas); _____ (sister) m Leroy Muldoon, Linglestown; _____ (sister) m Ray Foster of Wiconisco. bur Maple Grove Cem E;ville; Anettie Mae b Aug 11, 1893; Charles Franklin b May 29, 1896 d ___ in Texas

******John Henry** b Nov 23, 1868, died before father; ******George W.** b Apr 28, 1871, died before father; ******William Elmore** b Feb 26, 1873, died before father; ******Benjamin Franklin** (Oct 8, 1876 - Mar 8, 1954, bur Maple Grove Cem, E'ville), m Apr 21, 1901 Mary Ellen Batdorf (1881 - 1963), a dau of Jonas and Mary Batdorf. Frank lived with his father in 1900 and 1910. Frank worked in the coal mines. In 1910 Frank was listed as the head of the house. Frank's father John, his son John, and a nephew John Tschopp age 22, a coal miner lived in the household. **Benjamin Frank and Mary E Gunderman children:**

John Franklin (Dec 10, 1905 – Dec 20, 1986), m Maude Rebecca Wood; **Esther A.** (Mar 17, 1914 - Dec 23, 1998), m Aug 19, 1933 Elmer Shomper.

***JAMES** (Jan 1,1839 - Mar 10, 1905, bur Oakdale Cem, Loyalton,), m Leah A. Troutman (Dec 25, 1844 - Oct 11, 1912). **James and Leah had a son** James (1873 - 1932, bur Oakdale Cem), m Catherine _____ (1881 - 1964)

***SAMUEL** (b Mar 20, 1842 in Powells Valley - d Nov 13, 1916, bur Oak Hill Cem, Millersburg). He was found dead in bed by his wife in their home near Loyalton. Early in life, Samuel was employed by local farmers. He was a Civil War veteran, and while serving at Canasaw Mt. in June 1862, he received a gunshot wound which severed his right foot. He later received an artificial foot from the government. Samuel m 1st on January 27, 1860 to Josephine Anna Long of Halifax. According to testimony by Samuel's brother Michael in a Civil War pension application, "Samuel and Anna were married at a very young age before the war, and lived in a house in the little saloon below Loyalton. They lived together for twenty years, and then were separated and Josephine went off to Cleveland and we never saw her again." Josephine Anna died in Cleveland about 1914, and is buried in Monroe Street Cemetery.

Samuel and Josephine Anna (Long) Gunderman had two children: a son d young; Mary b c1866, m Henry Gearhart in Cleveland, Ohio, where he worked in a steel plant. Mary lived with her grandparents after her parents separated, until she was about eighteen. Then she lived with her mother in Cleveland.

Samuel Gunderman m 2nd Catherine Lettich b c1853, a dau of Jacob and Catherine Lettich of Lykens Twp. They were married by J.P George Hoffman of Gratz, on Jan 27, 1884. After Samuel died, Catharine had a little store in Millersburg, and she and her son Jacob had a broom shop. **Samuel and Catherine (Lettich) Gunderman children:** Jacob M. b Mar 23, 1882, Sarah E. b Nov 5, 1884, m Benj. Lower; Mabel Catharine b Mar 4, 1885, m Harry Wilbert, had a dau ___ whom m Samuel Burrell; Lilly Rebecca b Jun 12, 1886, m Harvey Shepley; Char Daniel (Jan 20, 1888 – Mar 1888); Henry Harrison b Mar 17, 1891.

To right: Four generations 1928: Mrs. Wilber, Mrs. Burrell, Mrs. Catherine Gunderman & grandson.

***ELIZABETH** (May 13, 1844 - Sep 26, 1908, bur Hoffman Cem, alone), m Sep 15, 1867 by Rev M. Fernsler (a Methodist minister), to Benjamin Welker (Nov 10, 1849 – Apr 1, 1926 of blood poisoning, bur Fairview Cem, Williamstown, alone), a son of Jonas and Sarah (Kocher) Welker. They were both of Wiconisco Twp. Benjamin was a Civil War veteran. On February 15, 1900, Benjamin applied for a peddler's license under veteran's law. There is a zerox copy of a Fraktur of his birth in our library files, received from the pension records in Washington D.C. Elizabeth died first, leaving a will which dispersed her goods in such a way that it displeased her husband. **Benjamin and Elizabeth (Gunderman) Welker had these children, some bapt Zion Luth, Lykens:**
****Sarah Ellen** b b Sep 18, 1864, m Jul 19, 1886, Henry Mumma of Lykens, Benjamin Welker listed as parent;
****William Francis** (May 26, 1868 - 1921, bur Greenwood Cem, Tower City), m Harriet A. ___ (1868 -1939);
****Benajmin Franklin** b Aug 12, 1874; ****Maggie Rebecca Elizabeth** (Dec 20, 1876 – 1942); ****Jennie Agnes** (b Nov 16, 1879 - Dec 7, 1913), m May 28, 1898 in Donaldson to Samuel H. Shell (1832 - 1905, bur Greenwood Cem), a Civil War veteran. Samuel was first married to Hannah __ (1838 - 1895), bur with Samuel.
****Charles Ray** (b Sep 17, 1883 – d 1973)
****Maria Francis** (no dates) m Andrew Peter Schoffstall
***CORNELIUS** (Sep 26, 1846 - Jul 17, 1919, bur Hoffman Cem), m Jan 2, 1876 Polly Eliz Rickert (Nov 26, 1856 - d May 2, 1888). They lived in Lykens Twp in 1880. **Cornelius and Elizabeth (Rickert) Gunderman known children: ****Carrie A.** b c1875 (Polly Elizabeth had a dau Gertie Ann b Jun 19, 1874 to Danni Schoffstall before Polly m Cornelius; **Adaline** b c1878.
***MICHAEL J.** b Apr 25, 1848/1849 - Apr 21, 1940, bur Maple Grove Cem, E'ville), lived in Loyalton and was a farmer, died at the age of 91. In 1880, Michael was living with his parents in Washington Twp, not married. He m Jun 9, 1894 Mary E. Rickert (Feb 20, 1870 – Apr 24, 1954), a dau of John & Christina (Kroh) Rickert. These two are buried beside him: Ida (1862 - 1946), Mary E (Feb 20, 1870 - Apr 24, 1954).
***SARAH M** (Feb 19, 1857 - Sep 26, 1934, bur E'ville), m Aug 15, 1880, Robert F. Harmon (Sep 10,1858 – Apr 15,1941), a son of John Adam and Emeline (Robinson) Harmon, lived in Elizabethville, according to details in the pension record of her brother Samuel.
***JACOB (** May 21, 1860 - Oct 19, 1886, bur Hoffman Cem), d of typhoid fever. Samuel Gunderman lists him as a brother in the pension files.
***IDA E.** (1864 – Jul 9, 1946, bur Maple Grove Cem, E'ville)
LYDIA GUNDERMAN b Mar 6, 1814
JOHANNES GUNDERMAN b Jul 31, 1819, he may have moved to Buffalo Twp, Perry Co.]

THE SPECKTOWN BRIDGE

The "Specktown" covered bridge was built over the Little Wiconisco Creek, and was a comparatively short structure. It was located in the center of the tiny village of the same name. The name "Specktown" is an unusual name although it could be said that it describes the tiny village. The origin of the name has not been learned. However, John N. Speck a fuller, lived during the 1820's & 30's west of Specktown along the Wiconisco Creek. The name may be associated with that family. More will be written about that family elsewhere.

Many folks traveled over the covered bridge on their way to Gratz from Loyalton and Lykens areas. Over the years, many folks have shared interesting memories of incidents that occurred relating to this bridge.

Some of the children who lived in the southwest section of Lykens Township walked across this bridge to get to Geise School each day. Kathryn Dietrich Gasbarro remembered that in the afternoon some of the girls walked home in a group. Sometimes the older boys ran ahead and hid in the bushes on the opposite side of the bridge. They enjoyed teasing, and when the girls arrived at the bridge, the boys jumped out and scared them.

Ellen Shade remembered that when she was a student at Geise School, she had quite a long walk to get to class. One winter day on the way home from school, instead of crossing the bridge, Ellen walked on the apparently solid ice under the bridge. Unfortunately when she was directly beneath the bridge, the ice broke, and she fell into the water. She knew that her parents would not approve of her walking on the dangerous ice, so she gave her father an excuse for being wet. When her father learned the truth, Ellen got spanked with the razor strap for lying. She never forgot that lesson.

Young folks traveling a long distance by bicycle often designated this bridge as the spot to rest. Sometimes they were on their way to visit relatives in Gratz from Loyalton or even farther away. They brought their lunch, and as they sat or loitered in the shade of the bridge, they enjoyed the meat or jelly sandwiched between two thick slices of homemade bread. Always, mom tucked in a sweet cookie, or a slice of cake or pie, which was a great finish to the special lunch.

SPECKTOWN BRIDGE
Late 1940s, Showing Chas. Schoffstall 1931 Nash

Sometime during the early 1900s there was reason to believe that a "spook" lived in or near the Specktown Bridge. Sometimes people worked late in the fields throughout the summer, and occasionally during those hours folks were said to see the spook. It would come out of the bridge, and travel toward Ellen Shades' farm and the north hills. It looked like someone who was carrying a light or lantern, but was more the color of a gas light.

Sometimes it would be seen over at the Chauncey Riegel farm. One night Clayton Sitlinger's dad was playing cards at the Riegel place, and Chauncey saw the light. People were curious about this spook, and many residents of the Specktown area believed that some extraterrestrial being existed. During the winter months after the ghost or spook was sighted, folks would go out and look for tracks in the snow, but never saw any.

Mildred Barry and a sister were traveling toward the bridge when they saw a light in the bridge. Her sister was driving and when they saw the light, not wanting to take a chance, they turned around and took Crossroads Road home. Later they found out that the Bellis brothers were the "ghosts."

One night when the auction was held at the Gratz Fairgrounds, Marlin Tshopp walked home from the auction. When he got close to the bridge, sure enough he saw a light come out of the bridge, so he turned and took a road that led to a smaller bridge on Indian Trail Road.

Another time the Dietrich boys, Marlin and Lauren waited to see the spook, guns in hand. They heard that the spook traveled near their home on it's way to the woods west from their farm. A murder was said to have been committed there in earlier days. The boys did not sight the spook. After that experience, Marlin Dietrich thinking himself brave and an unbeliever in spooks, decided to plan an adventure. He asked his brother Lauren to go with him to do a spook light. The boys planned to start over the hill to the north from their home, and travel west from the creek. Lauren was not enthused for this escapade, but Marlin was persuasive. Before they began their adventure, the boys dressed in dark clothes, and borrowed their dad's carbide lamp. They started out along the creek trail to the bridge, crossed the road that travels from Geise School to the Hoover farm. From there they started up the hill that was easily seen from Specktown. They walked arm in arm to appear as a very large "ghost" and also so that they could follow the beam of their carbide light. They walked slowly. Marlin holding the light, did some up and down and sideways maneuvers, designed to make the spook appear to be looking for something. Marlin was very calm, but Lauren was scared to death! They finally made it to the covered bridge safely. From the bridge, they stuck to the road to Geise School. From there, they didn't lose any time going home! From this episode told seventy years later, we know who some of the "spooks" were. There probably were many more.

During the late 1940s, Ethel Schoffstall married Dallas Williams. Her new husband volunteered to teach Ethel to drive. She had been practicing on several occasions, and was making progress. Then one warm sunny day Ethel was driving in the vicinity of Specktown. The windows were down, and Dallas had his arm resting on the opening. As she entered the bridge Ethel drove closer than normal to the right side of the bridge. Dallas claimed that she got so close to the wall that he had splinters in his elbow! That was the end of her practice, and she never got a drivers license.

When automobiles became the common mode of travel, young boys (and some girls) traveling in their spiffy cars, began the practice of blowing the car horn as they entered the structure. When this tradition began is unknown, but perhaps it was a throwback to giving a signal when entering a one-lane bridge. At any rate, it was a chance to use the horn!

About 1949, preparation was made to construct a new road through the Specktown area of Lykens Township. Although the bridge was in good repair, and the new road would bypass the section where the old covered bridge stood, it was decided to destroy it rather than to preserve it as a relic. It was the end of the "fun times" at the old Specktown Bridge.

LAND ALONG INDIAN TRAIL ROAD

At this point a turn to the right from Specktown Road will lead to Indian Trail Road and the next section of land that originally belonged to the Rickert family. In 1875 the road now known as Indian Trail Road did not extend from the Specktown Road to Gratz. The only access to this section was from a road closer to Gratz. [See 1875 map.]

Original JOHN RICKERT LAND 73 acres 62 perches
(1875 Elizabeth (Betsy) Rickert 32 acres - George S.Deibler ___ acres. Later divided into two farms)

On January 14, 1843, Martin Rickert and wife Elizabeth, and Jacob Rickert and wife assigned a tract of land to John Rickert. The messuage contained 73 acres 62 perches, and was situated in both Lykens and Wiconisco Township. This land was part of the distribution made between several brothers from their father Hartman Rickert's will of May 15, 1828. Each son got an equal share. The 1850 census records John Rickert and his family in Wiconisco Township, indicating that the land that was first located in Lykens Township had become part of Wiconisco Township, when the townships were separated. In 1850 Susanna McCirty age 13 lived with the Rickert family.

John Rickert died October 14, 1850, at the age of thirty-two, leaving four young sons. Through an orphan court petition, John George Daniel was appointed guardian of the four children. The court decided that this property consisting of a one story log house and a small barn, had disintegrated into a state of "dilapidation and decay, and so unproductive and expensive" that it would be in the best interest to sell. On September 26, 1863, a public vendue was held on the property. The two tracts of land and plantation were sold to George S. Deibler. The first tract contained thirty-three acres thirteen perches, and had a log house and a barn on the premises. The second contained twenty-nine acres fourteen perches, making a total of sixty-two acres twenty-seven perches of land. Beginning at the land of Martin Rickert, this land was bound by Jacob Rickert on the north, then land that was John Snyder (but at time of deed was Daniel Buffington), south and east by the public road leading from Gratz to Oak Dale, again by Daniel Buffington, Elizabeth Etzweiler, John P. Hoffman and John Bellon south to land of John G. Weaver, Peter Rickert and back to Martin Rickert land.

George S. and Susanna Deibler, his first wife came from Mifflin Township. They lived there in 1850, with their two children Henrietta and Susanna. But sometime after 1850, Susanna died, and by 1860, George had married Elizabeth widow of John Rickert, and was living on this farm. Elizabeth's children John and Thomas Rickert lived with them, and their own son George was also with them. In 1880, Emma J. Rickert age 8, their granddaughter was listed in the household.

George S. Deibler before his death appointed Harrison Riegel as the administrator of his estate. He died in 1890. On November 28, 1891 (recorded April 1893), at a public sale George A. Deibler purchased this property containing sixty-two acres twenty-seven perches, house and outbuildings, subject to two dowers. One dower was to be paid to Elizabeth Deibler, widow of George S. Deibler, heir of John Rickert. The second dower was to the heirs of George S. Deibler. Elizabeth continued to receive yearly payment of her dower amounting to about twenty-eight dollars.

George S. Deibler was a Civil War veteran of Co G, 103rd Pa. Inf. His widow Elizabeth applied for a pension after George died, and at that time Josiah Umholtz and John Laudenslager were witnesses to help her get the pension. They mentioned that her personal property consisted of "old worn house furniture valued at thirty dollars," and that she had no source of income except for the interest from her dower. The Deibler family lived here for many years. However, George A. Deibler conveyed the land in two separate conveyances to two new owners.

HOME & FARM OF CLAIR SNYDER
36 acres 57 ¼ perches

Barn On Clair Snyder Farm

On October 4, 1927, George A. Deibler, after his wife Sarah died, conveyed 36 acre 57 perches of land with buildings from the above tract to John E. and Sarah E. Rothermel. Several years later on March 8, 1930 John E. and Sarah E. Rothermel conveyed the same to Charles L. Snyder. It was bound by the southwest corner of the land of Frank Gunderman, running north to Edward Hoover land, and late Henry Buffington land to a road, then along the road south to Arthur Hoffman land. By that time Frank Gunderman owned the neighboring land. Other neighbors were Albert Shade, Charles A. Sitlinger, the public road, Arthur Hoffman, other land of Charles Sitlinger and George A. Deibler. By 1952 Gertrude M. Snyder owned the property. Clair Snyder and Helen Hoffman now own the property. A building located on this property served as a blacksmith shop for Henry Snyder many years ago. An old building foundation is said to be located on the western side of this house.

[JOHN E. ROTHERMEL (b Feb 11, 1907 – d Sep 3, 1974, bur St. Michaels Church, Klingerstown), a son of Manassas W. and Susan (Bixler) Troutman, m Sarah E. Wolfe b Apr 25, 1908 , later divorced. John E. and Sarah (Wolfe) Rothermel had these children: Edwin E. b Sep 2, 1927; Jean M b Jun 15, 1929, m Allan E. Hummel; Bryan A. b Feb 10, 1931, m Helen A. Kocher, lives in Wiconisco. Bryan has earned the reputation of being an expert at restoring antique cars; John E. b Dec 5, 1940.]

HOMER DEIBLER PROPERTY
25 ACRES 59 PERCHES

George A. Deibler continued to own the smaller portion of his land until the end of his life. After he died Darien Romberger the appointed executor of his estate sold twenty-five acres fifty-nine and four-tenth perches of the mountain land to John H. and Laura B. Deibler on June 25, 1934. They had been living here at least since 1920 as tenants. George A. and Sarah Deibler lived in a separate house nearby.

On November 5, 1942, Laura B. and John H. Deibler sold the same acreage to their son Homer A. Deibler. This land was located in both Lykens and Wiconisco Township, and was bounded by Samuel Sitlinger, south to Weaver, south to Frank Gunderman, north to John Snyder, and former George A. Deibler land.

Homer A and Alberta M. Deibler later lived in Millersburg. Paul L. and Alberta M Brown became the owners of the same farm, but sold March 1, 1978 to Kay J. and Warren Thoma, Jr.

THE GEORGE DEIBLER FAMILY

[GEORGE S. DEIBLER (b Apr 9, 1825 bapt St. Johns Luth, Berrysburg - d Jul 4, 1890/1891, bur Hoffman Cem), a son of George and Magdalena (Hepner) Deibler, m 1st probably Susanna (Speck) (Jan 23, 1824 - d before 1853), a dau of John & Elisabeth Speck of Mifflin Twp. George and Susanna (Speck) Deibler had these children bapt Hoffman Ch: Henrietta b Mar 19,1847; Susannah Elizabeth b Dec 25, 1848.

After Susannah died, George Deibler m 2nd, in April 1860 to Elizabeth (Bressler) Rickert (Jan 7, 1821 - Sep 21, 1893), widow of John Rickert who d Oct 14, 1850. In 1860 George and Elizabeth Deibler had, John 13, Thomas 11, and George age 5 with them. In 1880 George and Eliz had Emma J. Rickert age 8 with them. George and Elizabeth (Bressler, Rickert) Deibler had one child: George A. (Jun 30, 1855 - Feb 9, 1934, bur Simeon Cem), m c1878 Sarah A. Betz (Mar 24, 1858 - Aug 26, 1926), a dau of Anthony and Catherine (Row) Betz. George A. and Sarah A (Betz) Deibler children: Estelle (no dates) m _____ Heath, lived in Shamokin; John H.(Oct 1880 - Apr 30, 1952, bur Simeon Cem), m Laura Bertha Umholtz (Aug 15, 1882 - Nov 4, 1968), dau of Levi and Anna Maria (Radel) Umholtz. John and Laura Deibler lived for a time in the small house on the "Lucas" property near Specktown. John H. and Laura B. (Umholtz) Deibler children: Levi Adam (b Jun 1, 1913 - Nov 1980); Naomi Anna (Feb 20, 1915 - Nov 7, 1977); Homer Allen (b Apr 28, 1916 - Dec 8, 1951), m Alberta M. _____ ; Meda Arlene (b Jan 14, 1918 - Dec 1995); Nora E b Jul 1883, m _____ Mott, lived in Phila; Mabel S. (Feb 3, 1885 - Oct 15,1913, bur Simeon Cem); George F. (Sep 1886 -1936, bur Simeon Cem), m 1909 Thama S.Umholtz b Jan 1892, a dau of Levi and Anna (Radel) Umholtz.]

454

ORIGINAL JACOB RICKERT LAND
(75 acres 62 perches (two tracts 39 ac 142 perches & 35 ac 80 perches)

On January 14, 1843, Martin Rickert and wife Elizabeth, and John Rickert and wife conveyed and assigned two tracts of land to Jacob Rickert. One tract contained 39 acres 142 perches with dwelling and barn. Another unseated tract contained thirty-five acres 80 perches, a total of 75 acres 62 perches. The first tract of land contained a spring and pipes that had been built to carry water to Martin's house. When this deed was written, it referred to that agreement and was subject to the following: "Martin Rickert shall have free and uninterrupted use of the spring (in common with Jacob Rickert) to which pipes are now laid for the purpose of conveying water to the house of Martin Rickert with privilege at all times to enter upon, pass and re-pass to and from the spring to obtain water or for laying or repairing pipes by him to his heirs with as little damage as possible."

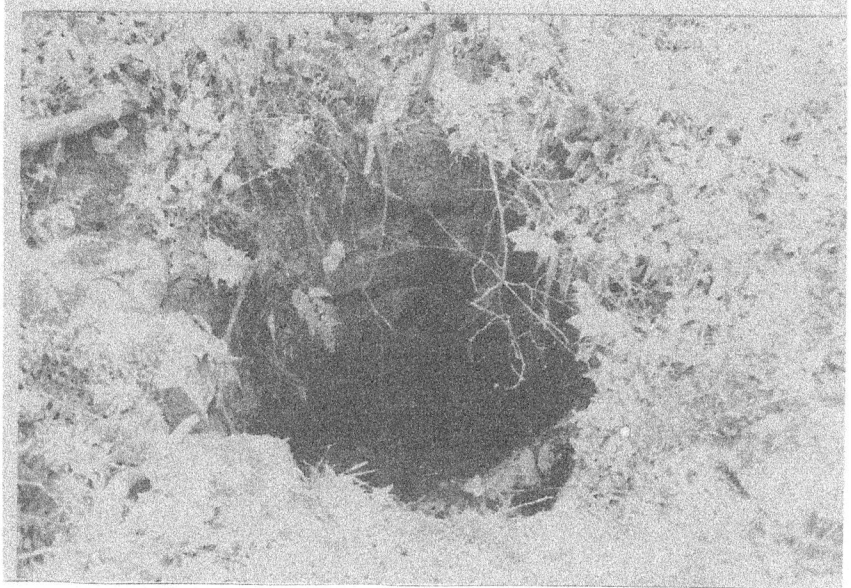

Cut stone lined well near springs. The Spring and pipes were on Jacob's property and served both Jacob & Martin Rickert's residents. This water supply served several families well into the 1900's.

Until very recently, elderly natives of that area remembered the wonderful mountain water.

By 1850, the boundaries between Lykens and Wiconisco Township were changed, so this property was partly in both townships. The tax record of 1855 describes the buildings on the land in Lykens Twp as being "poor."

The remains at the site of another old house located along the road close to the now existing power line.

455

On April 1, 1859, Jacob and Elizabeth Rickert sold six acres of their land to John Hoover, Sr. This small tract bordered land of Jacob Rickert, south to John Hoover, north to Benjamin Geise land. The Rickert's sold another 30 acres 35 perches of land from their tract to John Hoover, Sr. on April 1, 1859.

These are the remains of a foundation of a house located along the road about one-eighth mile beyond the power line near the driveway of a new brown house.

A drilled well near the foundation of a house near the now existing power line.

Another foundation and well was located on the opposite side of the road near a small coal dirt bank, remnants from the Shiro Mine. It was remembered that a Schoffstall family lived here. Perhaps it was "Danny" Schoffstall – he was remembered as having lived in this area. This site is almost obliterated and did not photograph well enough to be printed.

One more foundation on
the side of Short Mountain.

TACHOPP FAMILY PROPERTY
Was Martin P. Schaffner Place

This beautiful old structure is
the Last of the Hartman
Rickert properties to survive
on Short Mountain

Although the house is not
in a livable condition, the
owner continues to keep
the surrounding area
groomed.

For those interested in the
past it is a privilege to
view this old house, and
remember the folks who
were a part of the long
gone, unique little Rickert
family village.

457

The last described land belonging to Jacob and Elizabeth Rickert, included these four small tracts of land. They sold one tract of four acres 63 perches with a mill and sawmill to Elias Koppenhaver on June 11, 1864. Jacob Rickert is listed as a tenant of Elias Koppenhaver for that year. Years later, on May 1, 1888 Elias Koppenhaver sold this property to Anna Mariah Schaffner wife of Martin P. Schaffner. Martin was a stone mason from 1860 to just before 1880, when he became a farmer.

[ELIAS KOPPENHAVER (Jun 24, 1826 – after 1894), a son of Michael and Maria (Bordner) Koppenhaver, m Lovina ____ (b c1826, ___), a dau of _____. In 1850,1860, 1880 Elias and Lovina lived in Mifflin Twp. and he was a carpenter. **Elias and Lovina ( ) Koppenhaver children:** **Henry** b c1844; **Samuel** b c1847; **Amos** b c1850; **Ann Eliza** b c1852; **Catherine** b c1854; **Frank** b c1858; **Amanda** b c1863; **Maggie** b c1869, granddaughter, lived with Elias Koppenhaver family in 1880; **Emma** b c1870.]

Another two acre 10 perch tract of their land was sold to Mariah Schaffner in February 1876. Still another one acre 58 perch tract of land belonged to Jacob Rickert. It was part of a five acre tract with a log dwelling and out buildings, and was sold by sheriff sale to John Hess in August 29, 1878. John and Caroline Hess sold the one acre 58 perches of woodland to Mariah Schaffner on May 26, 1881. Martin was listed on the census of 1860 and 1870 as a stone mason, but in 1880, he was listed as a farmer.

After her husband Martin P. Schaffner died, Mariah sold the three tracts to Fremont J. Mauser on April 12, 1919. Fremont J. and Anna Mauser owned three these parcels of land until June 29, 1932 when they sold to John H. and Pearl Tschopp. After the death of John H.(Sr.) and Pearl Tschopp, their son George Tschopp sold **four** tracts of land to Betty M., Dorothy I. and Beulah Tschopp on March 31, 1956.

[Schaffner genealogy elsewhere in this book.]

(In April 1936, John and Pearl Tschopp had purchased a five acre 23 perch tract of land from Frank and Mary Gunderman (Deed not recorded). Fremont Mauser purchased it in 1912, sold to John J. Bellon in 1921. Bellon sold it back to the Gunderman's in April 1931.The land was located at the foot of Short Mountain, bordered the road leading to Shiro Mine, land of Martin P. Rickert and Martin P. Shaffner.) This beautiful example of an early old log house, located at the foot of Short Mountain became the home of John and Pearl until John died February 20, 1943. Pearl continued to own the property until her death in 1955, and then it was passed on to the heirs, Betty M., Dorothy and Beulah Tschopp on March 31, 1956

On February 16, 1967 Betty and Russell H. Martz, Dorothy I. and Belford Drumheller, and Beulah Tschopp conveyed the property to their brother John. H. and Betty Tschopp. In April 1979, John H. and Betty J. Tschopp conveyed some of their land to The Pennsylvania Power and Light Company for a right of way for the power line which was constructed over Short Mountain. Betty Tschopp died September 27, 1989, and her husband became sole owner.

TSCHOPP/CHUBB/SCHUPP, JOB ETC FAMILY

We have found two branches of TSCHOPP family. The first family (listed below) came originally from Mertzweller, Germany and settled first in Lancaster County. They later migrated to the Upper Dauphin area. The second branch came from Basel, Switzerland and settled in what is now known as Lebanon County. They later migrated to the lower end of Northumberland County. We have not found a connection between the two families. However, since both groups settled in our area it seems appropriate to include them in this publication.

BRANCH NUMBER ONE.

This first family has been traced back to Daniel Schupp (1600 – Dec 29, 1678) and Maria Klein b 1609, residents of Germany. The generations passed from them to **John** (1647- c1695), **John Sebastian** b 1678, m Barbara Brand, **George** b Oct 4, 1705, m Barbara ___, and then to the immigrant ancestor *Johann George b 1728.

[*JOHANN GEORGE SCHUPP (b 1728 Germany – d 1777 in Up. Pax. Twp, Dau Co.). He married Catherine Matter b in Germany May 21, 1735, a dau of John Matter (1692 – 1736) and his wife Anna Christian (Keiser) Matter. By 1773, John George and Catherine Schupp lived in the area of Up. Paxton Twp. **Johann George and Catherine (Matter) Schupp children (some bap Trinity Evang Luth, New Holland Lanc Co:**

**ANNA CATHARINA SCHUPP b Dec 13, 1752

GEORGE SCHUPP (b Aug 4,1759 Earl Twp., Lanc Co – d Aug 27, 1839 bur Salem Cem, Killinger), m Anna Maria Elisabeth Deibler (b Jan1 0, 1760 – d Mar 1, 1840), a dau of Michael and Anna Maria (Helt) Deibler of Dauphin Co. George served with Capt Deibler in the Rev. War. **George and Anna Maria Elisabeth (Deibler) Schupp children (some bapt Salem Luth, Killinger):

***GEORGE SCHUPP (Mar 10,1780–Jan 20,1854, bur Stone Valley), m Margaret ___ (Feb 12,1784 – Jul 24, 1857). **George and Margaret Schupp known child: Anna Catherine** b Jun 13, 1810

***JOHN SCHUPP (Mar 22, 1782 – Sep 11, 1862, Crawford, Ohio), m Anna Maria Yeager (Jan 22, 1787 – Sep 8, 1865), a dau of Christopher and Eva Catherine (Snug) Yeager. **John and Anna Maria (Yeager) Schupp) known children (bapt Salem Luth): Jacob** b Nov 27, 1805; **Michael** (Sep 19, 1808 – Jan 8, 1875, Holmes, Ohio), m Catharine Warner (Nov 27, 1811 – Sep 28, 1868); **Sara** b Sep 27, 1809;**Peter** b Jun 20, 1811 **Anna** b Mar 4, 1814; **John** b Apr 26, 1816; **Daniel** b Sep 10, 1817; **Anna Maria** b Dec 7, 1819; **Solomon** b Oct 22, 1821; **Christophel** b Sep 4,1823;

***DANIEL SCHUPP (Sep 11, 1783 – Apr 30, 1845), m Susanna Albright (no dates, died soon after Daniel). They lived in Jackson Twp. **Daniel and Susanna Schupp children (bapt Salem Luth):Barbara** b Oct 5, 1807 **Henry** b Sep 30, 1811;**Catharina** b Aug 26, 1813; **Frederick** b Feb 5, 1819; **Lythia** b Apr 30, 1821; **Anna Maria** b Jun 18, 1826; **Daniel** (Oct 2, 1828 – Apr 25, 1910, but Fairview Cem, Jackson Twp), m 1st Catharine Enders (Nov 1, 1829 – Jul 4, 1878), a dau of John and Sarah (Ettein) Enders. Daniel m 2nd Mary A. Enders (Sep 12, 1831 – Jun 5, 1899); **Christian** b c1835.

***JOHN MICHAEL SCHUPP (Apr 20, 1786- Dec 12, 1836), m Nov 6, 1808 Anna Marguerite Wise b Feb 14, 1789, a dau of Adam and Margaret Elisabeth (Wingert) Wise. **Michael and Marguerite (Wise) Schupp children: Michael** b Dec 19, 1809; **Elisabeth** b Nov 18, 1812; **Benjamin** b Oct 31, 1817; **Anna Maria** b Apr 3, 1820;

***CHRISTOPH SCHUPP b May 28, 1788 – 1820), m Elizabeth ___. **Christoph & Elizabeth Schupp children: Polly; David; Lydia; Sarah; Rebecca Susanna** (all under age of 14 when father died.)

***JOSEPH SCHUPP (Mar 19, 1790- Jan 14, 1852, bur Straws Cem, Enders, Dau Co), m Elisabeth Kramer (Feb 1, 1798 – Sep 11, 1858). **Joseph and Elisabeth (Kramer) Schupp children (bapt Salem Luth): Catherine** b Oct 9, 1817; **Christina** b Aug 20, 1820; **Lusette** b Jul 2, 1821

***EVA CATHERINA SCHUPP (May 1 3, 1792- Mar 2, 1866), m John Daniel Jury b Mar 5, 1790, a son of Samuel and Hanna Jury. **John Daniel and Eva Catharina (Schupp) Jury children (bapt Salem Luth): Salome** b Mar 31, 1816; **Johan** b Oct 27, 1824; **Susanna** b Mar 23, 1830.

***ELISABETH SCHUPP b Sep 27, 1794

***SUSANNA SCHUPP (Mar 21, 1797- Mar 12, 1873, bur Salem Luth Cem), m Apr 26, 1818 Daniel Wert (Dec 7, 1796 – Oct 20, 1858), twin son of Jacob and Sophia Susan (Miller) Wert. **Daniel and Susanna (Schupp) Wert children (bapt Salem Luth): Elisabeth** b Feb 11, 1819; **William** b Jan 11, 1821; **Catharina** b Mar 15, 1823; **Isaac** b Jul 21, 1825; **Emanuel** b Jan 16, 1828;

***JOHN HENRY SCHUPP b Apr 2, 1802

***ANNA MARIA ELISABETH b Apr 3, 1803

(NOT SURE if Henry is a son)

HENRY CHUBB, SR (b Mar 7, 1760 – d ____, m Mary Magdalena Kasselin (b Jan 25, 1762 – d ____), a dau of _____. They lived in the Halifax area of Dauphin County. **Henry served during the Revolutionary War. Henry and Mary Magdalena (Kassel) known children:

***JOHN CHUBB (Oct 6, 1793 – Mar 17, 1871)

***<u>HENRY CHUBB</u> (b Nov 3, 1795 – d Sep 12, 1879), m Apr 20, 1822 to Nancy Miller (1803 - 1870) of Halifax Twp. Henry learned the skill of weaving from his father, and combined that trade with farming. This family escaped a serious incident, apparently without injury about 1833. Their house caught fire while the mother was away, and all the children were at home. **Henry and Nancy (Miller) Chubb children (11):**

John (b Feb 27, 1824 – d 1870), Middletown, Pa. He was a Civil War Vet

Susan (b Aug 18, 1825 – d Jacksonville, Pa.), m John Peters who was a California gold prospector.

Henry (b Jan 13, 1827 – d ____), moved to Iowa and Kansas, later came back to this area. He was a Civil War Vet.

Jacob b Nov 23, 1828, moved to Jefferson Co. Kansas and was a farmer.

Philip b Oct 5, 1830, was a Civil War Vet – was taken prisoner at the Battle of Winchester, and held at Belle Island for six months. He later moved to Utah, where he died in 1876.

Jeremiah b Oct 14, 1832 moved to Kansas. was a carpenter & farmer. Served in Home Guards during the Civil War.

Samuel H. b Jan 22, 1835, moved to Jersey Shore, Pa. to learn carpentry, came back home later. He m Sarah J. Lyter b Jan 27, 1841. He was in the Civil War.

Catherine b Jan 7, 1838 m Eli Huff

Abigail b Jul 4, 1840 m Josiah Jury and lived in Halifax

Hiram b Mar 14, 1843, lived in Halifax

David W. (May 6, 1845 Powels Valley- Jul 8, 1921, Fisherville), m Jan 31, 1867 Susan Schaffner (Feb 17, 1845 – Apr 27, 1912), lived in Halifax Township. He was a Civil War Vet.

***NANCY ANN CHUBB** (Feb 27, 1804 – Feb 27, 1879) , moved to Kansas.

***ANNA MAGDALENA CHUBB** b Feb 27, 1805

JACOB SCHUPP (b c1765 – New Holland, Lanc Co. – d Mar 29, 1819), m Catharine Yeager b c1765. In 1808 Jacob received warrant for land in Jackson Twp. **Jacob and Catharine (Yeager) Schupp children:**

***Joseph** b c1786 –

***Anna Catherine** (Feb 19, 1789 – Apr 24, 1857, bur E'ville), m John Jacob Paul

***Jacob Jr.** (1791 – Jun 29, 1846), m Elisabeth Kemmerer b Apr 16, 1797, a dau of Dietrich & Barbara (Wieland) Kammerer. **Jacob and Elisabeth (Kemmerer) Schupp children:** Isaac (Jan 12, 1820 – Jan 3, 1876, bur Oak Hill Cem, Mbg), m Elisabeth Buffington, a dau of Solomon and Elisabeth (Romberger) Buffington; Jonas b Jun 3, 1822; Simon b Sep 23, 1824, m Catharine Sausser. **Simon & Catharine (Sausser) Schupp children:** Alice; Frank; Clinton; Annie L; Abraham b Dec 19, 1826; Lea b Jul 14, 1829; Salome b Mar 26, 1831; Elisa b Apr 27, 1833; Catharine b 1834; Lydia b Mar 17, 1834.

***Magdalena** b1793 – after Apr 5, 1830), m (twin) John Wert b Dec 7, 1796, a son of Jacob & Sophia (Miller) Wert. John and Magdalena moved to Ashland Co., Ohio. **John and Magdalena (Schupp) Wert children:** Daniel b 1817; Catherine b 1819; Lydia b 1821.

***Anna Maria** (Aug 7, 1800 – Mar 9, 18_), m Jacob Jury (Apr 15, 1799 – Feb 12, 1884, bur Sweitzer Cem, Bbg))

***George** (Feb 9, 1801-Aug 18, 1861, bur Meth Cem, Halifax), m Elisabeth Kreiner (Dec 5, 1802- Mar 31, 1856), a dau of Henry & Catharine Kreiner.

***Elizabeth** b Apr 8, 1803, m Jacob Fralich, a son of Abraham Fralich.

***John** (Sep 5, 1805 – Sep 28, 1883), m Elizabeth Fralich, a dau of Abraham Fralich.

JOHN SCHUPP (Oct 12, 1769 – Jun 11, 1855, bur Straws Cem, Jackson Twp), m Elisabeth Cooper (Apr 24, 1784 – Feb 15, 1870), a dau of John Adam and Ann Christina Margaretha (Schott) Cooper. **John and Elisabeth (Cooper) Schupp children:** ***John (Feb 8, 1803 – Jun 3, 1880), m Ann Mary __ (May 11, 1809 – Mar 22, 1865). Lived in Jackson Twp in 1850. **John & Mary Schupp children:** Jonas b c1833; Edward b c1834; Catharine b c1836; Anthony b c1838; Susanna b c1840; John b c1841; Mary b c1842; Adam b c1846; Nathaniel b c1848; Catharina b Mar 12, 1804; ***Jacob (Nov 1, 1805 – Jan 20, 1874), m Polly Snyder (Jul 16, 1805 – Jul 8 1847) ; ***George (Jul 6, 1812 – 1864), m Rachel Sweigard b c1818. Lived in Jefferson Twp. in 1850. **George & Rachel (Sweigard) Schupp children:** William (Dec 14, 1838 – Apr 28, 1916, bur Fairview Cem), m Elisabeth ___; James b c1841; Samuel (Nov 22, 1842 – Dec 5, 1872, bur Fairview Cem), m Sarah Enders (!848 – 1921), m later Henry Wilbert. Samuel a Civil War Vet; Elias (Nov 19, 1844 – May 12, 1929, bur Carsonville Cem), m Hannah Runk (1845 – 1909); Philip b c1847; Henry b c1849; John; Adam; Amanda; Nathan; Emma. ***Susannah b c1816, m ___ Sweigard who d before 1850 & Susannah was living with her parents..

DANIEL SCHUPP (1771 – 1848, Jackson Twp., Dau Co), m Margaret ____ . **Daniel and Margaret Schupp children:** Lydia b Oct 21, 1806; Lusette b Jan 8, 1809; Jonathan b Aug 22, 1816

BRANCH NUMBER TWO.

(Most of the data for the second branch of the TSCHOPP genealogy came from Steve Troutman and Beatrice Leemhuis)

[*HANS TSCHOPP (or John Job) b ____ in Waldenburg, Switzerland – d Nov 26, 1784 in Northld Co. He came to America in 1750, apparently leaving his wife and children behind. (A Jacob Tschopp came here in 1753 from Waldenberg, leaving his wife and children in Switzerland.

JOHANNES TSCHOPP (b c1740 – d 1813, Northld Co), Son of Hans Tschopp, came to America from Switzerland on the ship Sally from Rotterdam, arriving in Philadelphia on Nov 10, 1767, and settled first in Schaefferstown, Lebanon County. They later moved to Northumberland County. It is said that Johannes and his wife Magdalena (Stohler) Tschopp (Aug 31, 1740 in Bubendorf, Basellan, Switzerland – d ___ Northld Co), left secretly their native country bringing their three underage children with them.

Johannes and Magdalena (Stohler) Tschopp children (the 1st three bapt in Ziefen, Basel, Switzerland.
*****JOHANNES** bapt Jul 12, 1761 m Barbara Werner (b Nov 1, 1770 Donegal Twp, Lanc Co – d Feb 28, 1828 in Northld Co, bur Stone Valley Cem – record of death in David's Ch, Killinger), a dau of Johannes and Margaretha Werner. **Johannes and Barbara (Werner) Tschopp children** (some bapt Stone Valley, others Hoffman Ch):
******Regina** (Jul 30, 1789 – Sep 7, 1856, bur Stone Val Cem), m J. Adam Schneider (Nov 3, 1786- Aug 8, 1857), son of Nicholas & Anna Maria (Bordner) Schneider;
******Johannes** (b Mar 3, 1792 sp Felix and Maria Tschopp – d Nov 9, 1849, bur Stone Valley Cem), m Catharina Heckert (b Apr 23, 1795 – d Jul 21,1851), a dau of Casper and Anna Catharina (Steinbrecker) Heckert. **Johannes and Catharina (Heckert) Tschopp children**: <u>Anna Maria</u> (b Apr 11, 1816 – Nov 14, 1849, bur Stone Valley Cem), m Samuel Wertz (May 25, 1821 – Jan 5, 1892); <u>Michael</u> (b Jan 13, 1818 – d Feb 27, 1855, bur Stone Valley Cem); <u>Elisabeth</u> (b Sep 28, 1819 – d Nov 8, 1861, bur Davids Ch, Killinger), m Henry Jury (Mar 22, 1814 – Jul 17, 1894); <u>Magdalena</u> (b Sep 23, 1821 – Jul 22, 1852), m Elias Long (b c1828 – d ___); <u>Juliana</u> b Aug 11, 1825 (twin?), m John Lauer; <u>Lydia A.</u> b Aug 11, 1825 (twin?), m Feb 10, 1853 by Rev. John Adam Leisz in German Ref Ch, Northld Co to William Snyder Sep 1828, a son of John and Anna Magdalena Schneider (recorded in Dau Co marriage records)<u>John</u> b Oct 6, 1828 – d Mar 27, 1860, bur Stone Valley Cem), m Elizabeth Zerbe (b Dec 28, 1833 – Mar 13, 1887), a dau of Joseph and Anna Maria (Heckert) Zerbe. After John Tschopp died, Elizabeth m Michael T. Wertz (1839 –1927); Margaret Rebecca (b Dec 25, 1839 – Jun 15, 1904, bur Stone Valley), m Emanuel W. Heckert (b Jan 22, 1834 – d Aug 23, 1911), a son of Philip Heckert. He was a Civil War veteran.
******Jacob** (Apr 14, 1793 – Nov 21, 1846, bur Stone Val Cem), m Elizabeth ___ (Feb 16, 1795- Sep 12, 1857). **Jacob and Elizabeth Tschopp children**: <u>Andrew</u> b c1817, m Mary Zerbe dau of Philip & Maria (Heckert) Zerbe; <u>Caspar</u> (1821–1884), CW Vet, m Salome Dockey (Jul 17,1824 –May 2,1890), dau of John & Mary Dockey.
******Anna Catherine** b Jul 1, 1796 sp Casper Heckert & Anna Catherine; ******Margaret Magdalena** b Feb 4, 1798 sp John Warner & Margaretha; ******Barbara** b Aug 6, 1811; <u>Jesse</u> b Mar 20, 1820.

*****FELIX (PHILIP)** (bapt Dec 4, 1763 –d pre1813), not married; *****MAGDALENA** bapt Jun 30, 1765 m George Kemble; *****JOHN JACOB** b Dec 5, 1767, less than one month after they arrived in America. He was bapt Mar 28, 1768 in Heidelberg Ref. Ch.; *****CHRISTIAN** b c1769, Pa.;*****RACHEL (REGINA)** (b Feb 20, 1770 - d c1809, Northld Co), m Henry Trautman (Dec 23, 1764 Berks Co – d Dec16,1833, Northld Co). [See genealogy on write-up of Trautman family];*****HENRY** b c1772;*****CATHARINE** (b c1775 – d __), m William Fisher; *****ELISABETH** (b Oct 7, 1780 Pa. - d May 9, 1844 in Northld Co), m Abraham Trautman (b Dec 9, 1773 – Apr 1, 1852, Northld Co); *****MARIA** (b c1782 – d _____), m John Weikerly.

[**GEORGE TSCHOPP -unidentified** (Nov 28, 1827 – Jul 4, 1900, bur Simeon Cem), m Magdalena Schoffstall (Jun 2, 1833- Jan 10, 1904).**George & Magdalena (Schoffstall) Tschopp Children:** **SARAH** b Apr 27, 1852; **ELIZA** b c1859;**GEORGE WASHINGTON** (Oct 8, 1862 – Oct 2, 1887), m Emma J. Gunderman (Jan 22, 1867 – May 26, 1899, of consumption), recorded in Dau Co death records. **Children:** **John Henry** (Feb 26, 1888 twin - Feb 20, 1943, bur Maple Grove Cem, E'ville), m Feb 26, 1911 Pearl Mae Rowe (Apr 14, 1893 -Mar 15, 1955, bur E'ville). They divorced. John **Henry and Pearl (Rowe), Tschopp had these children:**
Dorothy Irene b Nov 3,1909, m Belford Drumheller lived near Fearnot; George Franklin (Sep 13, 1911 –Dec 28, 1978), m Esther Pearl Snyder (Jul 17, 1916 – Sep 30, 1989, bur Maple Grove Cem, E'ville) lived in Lykens
Rosa Louise (Aug 21, 1913 – Feb 1, 1971), m John Heim was widow in 1943;Elba (Feb 8, 1915-Jan 6, 1980), m Sep 19 , 1932 Ray A. Klinger (Aug 14, 1911-Dec 8, 1979).
Marlin Charles (Mar 2, 1917 – Apr 27, 1986), m Mayme Miller, lived in Middletown.
Beulah Rebecca (Apr 19, 1919 – May 17, 1992), lived in Calif.

l to r: back row: Frank Gunderman, (Emma's bro) Geo Tschopp & Emma. Front row: Beulah Rebecca Tschopp with gr-father John Gunderman, Amanda holding Fred. Tschopp, John H. Tschopp (twin)

461

John H. 1928 - m 1947 Betty J _____ -- (1923 - 1989, bur Maple Grove Cem, E'ville) had son Ralph who lives in house across street from Gene Fetterhoff

Bettie Marie b Dec 31,1931 -) m Russell H. Martz (1927 - 1982, bur Maple Grove Cem, E'ville))

George M. (Feb 26,1888 twin – Sep 1888); **Beulah** b 1890, m Arthur Ferree; **Frederick** (1891 – d 1962 in Kansas); **Anette** b Aug 11, 1893, m Charles Lentz; **Charles F.**b May 29, 1896, m Kate Ebberly; **Kate** m Roy Foster.

HENRY MILTON b Jun 6, 1866, m Susanna L. Ritzman (Dec 31, 1863 – May 6, 1900 of cancer, bur Simeon Cem), dau of Jacob & Lydia Ann Ritzman. Milton & Susanna children:Riley Milton d inf;Lydia Magd. b Feb 1889.

MAGDALENA b Feb 3, 1869

ANN MARY TSCHOPP b 1838 [More information in Jacob Schoffstall genealogy.]

MR. & MRS. LLOYD W. HORST FARM- WAS SAMUEL SITLINGER PROPERTY)
(JOHN HOFFMAN 1875 – 60 acres)

Present Appearance Of Farm

This farm is made up for four separate tracts. One tract containing thirty-five acres forty perches of land was part of the original Philip Umholtz grant that was sold August 21, 1840 to John Umholtz. John Umholtz and his wife sold it on March 30, 1842 to their daughter Elizabeth Hoffman, wife of John P. Hoffman. In 1855, John Hoffman was listed on the tax record with fifty-two acres of land and a one-story log house. By 1858 he also had a barn.

Barn On The Horst Farm

The second tract, containing sixteen acres ninety-seven perches, was also part of the Umholtz grant, but had been sold to Benjamin Giese. On March 31, 1867, Benjamin Giese and his wife conveyed this tract to Elizabeth Hoffman. The border of the land ran through the middle of the mill race, was bounded by former land owner David Snyder and other land of Elizabeth Hoffman.

The third tract contained eleven acres 125 perches, and was sold to Elizabeth Hoffman by Daniel Riegel on May 1, 1850. It was probably the early tract of about eleven acres that Michael Salada sold to Jacob Huber between 1806 and 1810. The tract bordered land of Benjamin Giese and other land of Elizabeth Hoffman.

John P. Hoffman, Sr and his wife Elizabeth continued to own this property for the remainder of their lives. On June 6, 1887, the heirs of John P. Hoffman, Henry B. Hoffman, John P. Hoffman, Elizabeth (Hoffman) Kimmel, Jonas Hoffman and widow Elizabeth sold the remainder of the farm to Amelia and J. Frank Boyer. The land bordered Boas and Willauver, John Hoffman, north to the former land of John G. Daniel and Sarah Bellon.

On April 11, 1908, Amelia and J. Frank Boyer sold this land to Samuel J. Sitlinger, along with a small tract of land that they purchased from James Hoffman in August 1887. This small tract was sold with a reserve, giving the new owners the right to use the north dwelling house for occupancy with yard, garden, stables for pigs and a ¼ acre plot each year for their use.

The Samuel Sitlinger Family – l to r standing: Albert & Loll (Miller) Sitlinger, Florence (Umholtz) & Harrison Sitlinger, Melva. Sitting: _____ son of Albert, Samuel (father), Melva Jane dau of Albert, Bertha (Miller) Sittlinger (mother), Lucy dau of Melva.

Samuel J. and Bertha D. Sitlinger owned this land for many years, and on February 5, 1931, conveyed sixty-one acres, thirty-one perches with house and farm buildings to their son Albert L. Sitlinger. The land bordered the race, Irvin Buffington's land, Snyder and Amelia Boyer land, north to Howard Heller, John Snyder and Charles Weiss land.

Albert L. and Laura K. Sitlinger had this property for a long time. Laura K. Sitlinger continued to own it after her husband died. On March 24, 1975 Laura added the name of her daughter Melva Jane Reinhard as a joint tenant of the property made up of sixty one acres thirty-one perches with house and farm buildings. In 1985 her son Harrison Sitlinger also became a joint tenant, and the next year Laura K and her son Harrison sold a tract from the farm containing almost three acres and a house to Melva Jane Reinhard. After Harrison Sitlnger died, Joyce M.

Sitlinger administrator of his will and Melva Jane Reinhard, a widow sold the larger tract (minus the almost three acres) containing at this time about fifty-eight acres to Leroy S. and Fannie E. Riehl of Gap, Pennsylvania. There were stipulations about access to the private road, the well water which served both houses, and a right of way for the sewage system. On March 21, 2003, Leroy S. and Fannie Riehl conveyed this farm to Lloyd Horst.

[**SAMUEL J. SITLINGER** (Jul 1871 – Sep 30, 1936), a son of Isaac and Maria (Shade) Sitlinger, m Bertha D. Riegel (1879 -1952). **Samuel J. and Bertha (Riegel) Sitlinger had these children: Melva Naomi** (Feb 23, 1901 - ___), had a dau <u>Lucy Hannah Marie Sitlinger</u> b Jul 4, 1923, m Mar 22, 1941 Paul Wesley Troutman of Loyalton; **Albert L.** (1903 - 1973, bur Simeon Cem), m Feb 25, 1925 to Laura (Loll) K. Miller (1905 - c1986?); **Albert L. and Laura K. (Miller) Sitlinger children:** <u>Melva Jane</u> b Mar 17, 1928, m John W. H. Reinhard (1930 - c1987); **Harrison Isaac** (Jul 5, 1904 – 1953), m Florence M. Umholtz (1905 – 1975). **More Sitlinger genealogy elsewhere.**]

HOME OF ROBIN & ROSE SNYDER
(HARRISON RIEGEL 1875 – 1 ACRE)

This is part of the original land from Michael Salada to Hartman and Magdalena Rickert. On April 17, 1830, Magdalena Rickert, widow of Hartman Rickert sold one acre, 138 perches of land and buildings to John Hoffman, son of Peter Hoffman. The land was bound by land of Jacob Huber, Sr., on the north and to the south, then by land of Magdalena Rickert and heirs of Hartman Rickert, Jr. north. John and Elizabeth Hoffman assigned the same property March 28, 1850 to Daniel Riegel. His heirs, Josiah R. and Amanda Riegel of Gratz conveyed this small tract to Harrison Riegel on August 28, 1866.

The 1875 map shows this land as located below the Gristmill on what is now the Sitlinger property, beside a private road. The road was at one time a public road connecting Specktown Road and Indian Trail Road.

[This is the **JOHN HOFFMAN** (1809 – 1887), son of John Peter and Susanna Magd Lubold Hoffman, m Elizabeth Umholtz (1806 – 1886), a dau of Philip and Ann Maria (Williard) Umholtz. More information in the Hoffman gen.]

DANIEL RIEGEL FAMILY

[**DANIEL RIEGEL** (Jun 1,1804 – Jun 2, 1855), m Catherine Hoffman (Sep 10, 1807 – Sep 2, 1864), a dau of John Peter and Magdalena (Lubold) Hoffman. **Daniel and Catherine (Hoffman) Riegel had these children: Elisabeth** (1827 – 1885), m Elias Etzweiler b 1828. In 1880, they lived in Jefferson Twp., Dau Co., and Lizza Laudenslager age 18 lived with them.; **Josiah** (1829 – 1886), m Amanda Kissinger (1831 – 1897); **Jonas** (no dates) m Rebecca Holtzman of Tower City; **Harrison C.** (Nov 15, 1840 – Jul 31, 1899, bur Simeon Cem, Gratz), m Hannah Louisa Rickert (May 22, 1847 – Jul 11,1919), a dau of Martin Rickert. **Harrison C. and Hannah Louisa (Rickert) Riegel had these children:** <u>Chauncey A</u> (Aug 1, 1870 twin - Dec 4, 1936, bur Simeon Cem, Gratz), m Jul 10,1909 Emma S. Hassinger d 1907); <u>Nancy Ellen</u> b Aug 1, 1870 (twin); <u>Elizabeth Catharine</u> (Jun 30, 1872 - Oct 31, 1942, bur Simeon Cem); <u>Edward Austin</u> (Apr 4, 1874 - Mar 1, 1960, bur Maple Grove Cem, E'ville), m Dec 28, 1899 to Jennie L. Hawk; <u>Charles Gerome</u> (Oct 10, 1876 - Mar 19, 1913, killed at Short Mt. Colliery, bur Simeon Luth Cem), m Minnie Amanda Coleman (Dec 21, 1880 - Aug 4, 1958); <u>Bertha Della</u> (Nov 7, 1879 - Dec 30, 1952, bur Simeon Cem, Gratz), m Jul 28, 1900 to Samuel Sitlinger; <u>Mabel E.</u> b Oct 1883, m Walter Albert Evitts; <u>Norman Lester</u> (Oct 4, 1886 – Nov 11, 1942, bur Maple Grove Cem, E'ville), m Lydia Alice Helt, a dau of D. D. Helt of Lykens.]

Sarah A. (Rickert) Hoffman

On March 30. 1878 Harrison and Hannah Riegel sold the 1 acre 138 perches of land with one-half story house and stable to Sarah A. Hoffman, wife of Jonas W. Hoffman. Jonas worked in the mines for many years. He was a Civil War Veteran, having served in Co. G of the 103rd Pa. Vol. Infantry. His obituary mentions that members of his family served in the Revolutionary War, War of 1812, and Civil War. His father died only about a week before him.

After Jonas died, his widow Sarah applied for a pension. Several people made statements in regard to Sarah's circumstances. Harrison Riegel and Jacob Shiro in 1890 wrote:

"Sarah owns one acre of land in Lykens Township, thereon erected a dilapidated frame house which she inherited from her father's estate worth about two hundred dollars. She gets some support from one of her boys who works in the coal mines. The balance of her support is from working for her neighbors such as husking corn and sifting and washing potatoes, etc."

Solomon Rettinger and Mathias Harter made another statement. They said that Jonas and Sarah were raised in Lykens Township. Both men stated that they attended the Hoffman wedding ceremony.

"It was performed January 2, 1859 by Rev. Sell, a Lutheran pastor from Berrysburg. This is a long time ago we were young then, now we are rather old men. Rev. Sell is dead as far as we know."

Sarah A. Hoffman was listed on the tax record for 1883 and 1884 with the small tract, one and one-half story house and stable. This old house of log construction dated to about 1820. It was actually a very small one and one-half story house made for two families. In 1880 The Hoffman's shared their house with the Benjamin Shadle's.

After Sarah Hoffman died, her son Jacob Arthur, nicknamed "Dickie" became the owner of the small tract and house in January 1913. Jacob Arthur and Maude Hoffman lived on this property for the remainder of their lives. The heirs sold the property on August 5, 1967 to Clair and Joyce Snyder. After Clair Snyder purchased this Property they tore down the old house and in 1968 built the existing ranch style house very close to the site of the old house. It was sold on Oct 30, 1971 to their son Robin Snyder and his wife Rose.

Modern House Built On Foundation Of Very Old House

[**Jonas W. Hoffman** (Jun 13, 1838 – Feb 14, 1887, bur Hoffman Cem), a son of Johan Peter & Elizabeth (Umholtz) Hoffman m Jan 2, 1859 Sarah A. Rickert (Sep 8, 1840 – Oct 11, 1912) a dau of Martin Rickert. Jonas was a Civil War Vet. **Jonas W. & Sarah A (Rickert) Hoffman children:** **William H.** b Apr 1, 1859; **Dianna Elisabeth** b Oct 10, 1860, m ____ Deibler; **Clinton E.** (Aug 20, 1863 – Aug 10, 1940, bur Simeon Cem), m Oct 9, 1886 Harriet Umholtz (Mar 15, 1859 – 1922), a dau of John and Magdalena Hoffman. **Clinton E and Harriet (Umholtz) Hoffman children:** John Harrison (Nov 26, 1889 – 1958); Jennie M.(Apr1887–1955, bur Simeon Cem, Gratz), m John A. Buffington (1884 – 1940), a son of J. Jacob and Clara (Kissinger) Buffington of Gratz,

Son Clinton, wife Harriet (Umholtz), gr-son Warren, dau Jennie with husband John A. Buffington

John A. and Jennie M. (Hoffman) Buffington had one child: *Warren "Mush"* (Apr 11, 1908 – Apr 1970), not married; **Henry Monroe** (Aug 14, 1865 – May 1, 1866); **Katie Camelia** b May 12, 1867, m Archibald Sergeant; **Kinda Alverta** b Apr 6, 1869, m Jan 30, 1886 Isaac Rickert; **Sarah Alice** (Nov 21, 1870-1871; **Charles Penrose** b & d 1872; **George Wellington** (Nov 8, 1873 – Feb 11, 1946), m Nov 18, 1894 Jennie M. Ritzman; **Alvin Gurney** (Oct

6, 1875 – Nov 24, 1934), m Oct 16, 1898 Amanda Elisabeth Troutman; **Harry A.** b 1876; **Edward O** b Jul 3, 1877; **Laura May** b Oct 3, 1879, m Sep 17, 1904 Nathan Keiter; **Mary Ellen** (May 1, 1881- 1950), m Isaiah L. Keiter; **Jacob Arthur** (Oct 13, 1883 -May 11, 1957, bur Simeon Cem, Gratz), m Maude Emma Jane Kissinger (Mar 23, 1894- Apr 12, 1965), a dau of Joel & Priscilla (Engle) Kissinger. More information in **HOFFMAN** and **BUFFINGTON** genealogy elsewhere in book.]

Lewis & Gertrude Shadle
(Henry Snyder land 1875)

Recent Photo Of Snyder Property (it has since been torn down)

The farm that for many years was known as the Henry Snyder farm is comprised of three separate tracts of land from the Umholtz grant. Henry Snyder was a native of Schluchtern in Baden-Wurttemberg Germany. He was married in Schoneberg on November 12, 1846 to Susanna Bellon, then a widow. Susanna had previously been married in 1837 to Jacob Giraud a native of Sengach. Jacob Giraud became a soldier in the French Army, and while on duty, he crossed into Germany during one of the religious wars. At the close of the war, he settled in Wurttemberg where he operated a public tavern until his death in 1844.It is interesting to note that when Jacob Giraud settled in Germany, his name was corrupted, and became Shiro. When he died he left Susanna with three young children.

After Henry Snyder and Susanna were married, they remained in Wurttemberg for several years, and Henry was employed as a cooper. But through news from members of Susanna Bellon's family who had earlier come to America, the Snyder's knew about this section of Pennsylvania. In the spring of 1854, Henry and Susanna Snyder and her children set sail for America. They embarked from LeHavre, France, and after a voyage of twenty-nine days they landed in the port of New York City. From there they came directly to Wiconisco, where Henry became employed in the mines. They remained in that location for a short time before they purchased this farm in Lykens Township. Susanna's brother John Bellon lived on the adjacent property, and they were neighbors for the remainder of their lives.

On July 11, 1857, Henry Snyder purchased a small tract containing seven acres seventy-two perches of land with a small log house and stable from Elizabeth Hoffman. This land adjoined the land of John Umholtz, John G. Daniel and Daniel Hawk. It had previously belonged to the Umholtz grant.

When Henry and Susanna Snyder moved from Wiconisco to this farm, Henry became a farmer, but he also worked in the mines. On April 24,1862, he purchased another tract of land containing six acres eighty-eight perches from John Umholtz. In 1864 Henry was assessed for 14 acres of land and the log house. He also built a bank barn.

On April 3, 1875 Henry Snyder purchased a third tract containing twelve acres, five perches of land from John and Magdalena Umholtz. This land was also part of the large tract that Philip Umholtz owned. This land bordered other land of John Umholtz north, other land of Henry Snyder south to land of Peter Schoffstall and John Hoffman. Several years later Henry purchased another tract of about ten acres.

Henry and Susanna Snyder continued to live here the remainder of their lives. They had a well-maintained property with white fences. They also whitewashed the tree trunks on their land giving it an attractive appearance.

Shortly after their arrival, Henry Snyder's step-son Jacob Shiro attended the public schools in Wiconisco four terms, and that was the extent of his formal education. At the age of thirteen he became employed at the mines picking slate, and was paid eight dollars per month. During the Civil War, on March 10, 1864 Jacob enlisted in Co. G of the 103rd Pennsylvania Volunteers under Capt C. A. Harper. For six months he was assigned to guard duty at Fortress Monroe and Norfolk, and while there a contagious fever broke out among the troops. It was a terrible epidemic among the soldiers causing the death of many of the men daily. Although sick, the men were ordered to march to Newberne, N.C. to guard Weldon railroad. During the march Jacob and several comrades hired an old colored man with a cart to carry their knapsacks and equipment, but the rickety vehicle proved inadequate to the strain, and their baggage was dumped on the road. Resuming their burden, the men carried their equipment, but along the way one comrade fell by the wayside and died. They completed their march, and later boarded a steamer for Baltimore in July 1865. Then they went on to Harrisburg where Jacob was discharged.

After the war, about 1867, Jacob decided to move to a section of Illinois, where many other folks from this area previously had settled. He and Amanda Moyer were married in February 1864, and now he was taking his wife and two daughters, along with his wife's parents (the Christian Moyer's), to Freeport, Illinois. Soon Jacob purchased a one hundred sixty acre farm near Brookville, Ogle County. About a year later, in August 1868, Amanda wrote a letter to her dear friend Malinda Matter Hawk who was living in Gratz. She writes:

"Been thinking of you this long time, and no time to write you till now. So I came to a conclusion to write you a little or as much as I know about this western life. I like it well so far, and we have bought a farm ourselves and we intend to move on it this fall, and I think I like it much better yet if we are on our own place.

But I will let you know a little about the harvest out here the most of us are done now with the grain, but the wheat is not so good as it could be, it was strong in the straw and then some of it fell too soon, and the people were very scarce out here, they paid from three to six dollars a day for to bind in harvest and some didn't get hand at that price.

We were up to Freeport and saw John Hawk. I spoke with him, he was on good spirit I think. D. Hopple gave up Illinois, we didn't hear from them for a long time,

We send our best respect to you and so does mother send her best respect to your parents. So write me soon and let me know all the news from my old neighbors and don't forget to write."

One year later, in September 1869, Amanda and an infant son died during childbirth, and was buried in Schreiner Cemetery. She was survived by her husband Jacob, two young daughters and her parents. Jacob was heartbroken, sold his farm, and immediately headed back to Gratz. He was living with his mother and step-father in 1870. The two very young daughters remained with their grandparents in Illinois. Jacob purchased a farm in Gratz, married again, and the Shiro family of Gratz, are his descendants. [Write-up on this family in **Comprehensive History Of Gratz**.]

Amanda Shiro Tombstone, Schreiner Cemetery, Ogle Co. Illinois

467

When Jacob Shiro came back to Pennsylvania, in addition to farming, he re-opened a mine on the Gratz side of Short Mountain. His stepfather Henry Snyder worked for him for at least a brief time.

After Susanna Snyder died of blood poisoning, Henry allowed his son John to manage the farm. Henry remained in good health and helped with the chores on the farm. The day of his death, Henry ate a hearty dinner and then went to the barn to do some work. It was there that he died suddenly, and was found a short time later.

Just before his death, Henry Snyder penned a will in July 1899, naming Jacob Shiro his executor. He requested that his land be sold and his estate be divided equally among his survivors.

On March 29, 1901, Jacob Shiro, executor of the estate of Henry Snyder officially sold the farm made up of a total of forty-four acres, forty seven perches to John Snyder, son of Henry. The land was bound by land of the late John Umholtz (then Charles Weiss), Josiah Hoover, Boas & Rupert, J. G. Daniel, John Bellon (deceased) and Peter Schoffstall. John and his family continued to live here for many years, and kept the farm in good condition. In 1910, John and Fietta had their children Daniel, John, Emma and Charles with them, and a granddaughter Mabel Weaver age four also lived with them. In 1820, Emma and Charles were again listed as living with their parents.

On January 7, 1939, the heirs of John Snyder conveyed the forty-four acres forty-seven perches of land and buildings to his son Charles L. Snyder, but the deed was not recorded. On August 20, 1945 Charles L. and Gertrude M. Snyder sold the same acreage to Lewis W. and Elva P. Shadle. The Shadle's owned the land for many years. After Elva died, a large part of her land was sold January 2004 to David H. Koppenhaver of Valley View, Sch. Co.

HENRY SNYDER FAMILY

[*HENRY SNYDER (b Nov 16, 1816, Schluchtzern, Baden, Germany - d Jul 3, 1899, in Gratz), a son of Jacob and Josephine Snyder. He m Nov 12, 1846 Susanna (Bellon , Shiro) Snyder (May 31, 1816 - Jun 27, 1890, both bur Hoffman Cem), a dau of David and Anna Maria (Scheible) Bellon. She is a sister to John Bellon, the Civil War Veteran who was her neighbor, and for whom Henry Snyder was a witness when he applied for a pension. Susanna Bellon and her first husband Jacob Shiro, Sr. (name changed from the French name Giraud), had these children (bapt. Recorded in Otisheim, Germany): ** WILHELMINA LUISE GIRAUD b Dec 2, 1839 in Germany, m James Bocker and lived in Harrisburg; **JACOB GIRAUD (Shiro) b Feb 19, 1843. Henry and Susanna (Bellon, Giraud) Snyder children (1st two recorded in Otisheim): **ANGELINE SNYDER (Jun 8, 1846 - Mar 14, 1914), m Daniel Rickert (Nov 23, 1847 - Jan 7, 1911), a son of Peter and Elisabeth Rickert of Lykens Townshp. Both bur Seybert Cem, Williamstown. _____ m Daniel Bueck and lived in Harrisburg; **PAULINA ERNESTINE SNYDER b May 8, 1847; **ROSINA MARGARETHA SNYDER b Nov 26, 1848 (nothing more known of these two children); **AMANDA L. SNYDER (Mar 1854 - 1951, bur Simeon Cem), m Oct 1875 to John C. Coleman (Oct 1852 - 1933), son of Frederick and Sophia (Klinger) Coleman. John C. Coleman was a farmer and stock raiser. He was a miner for a few years, and taught school for three terms. John C. and Amanda (Snyder) Coleman children: ***Henry L. (d 1919), m Hattie Ferree; ***Fred J. b May 1877, m Ida Haines; ***Annie B. b Dec 1878, m 1st Leander Shaffer, 2nd Harvey Kunkel; ***Minnie A. (1880 - 1958, bur Simeon Cem), m Charles G. Reigle (1866 - 1913), a son of Harrison Reigle; ***Allen E. (1882 - 1887, bur Simeon Cem); ***Maggie M. (1884 - 1967), m Willis Bingaman; ***Dora R. b Jul 1887, m ____ Wapplinger; ***Flossie S. (Jul 1888 - 1967), m Francis Laux; ***Elmer H. (Jul 1891 - 1943, bur Simeon Cem), m Jane E. Klinger (1891 - 1942); ***Foster E. b Apr 1894, served during WWII, and married a girl from France.
**HENRY SNYDER (b Mar 17, 1857 bapt Salem Union, Berrysburg - d Mar 24, 1944, bur St. Pauls Luth Cem, Tower City), m Catherine_____ d c1934. He lived in Sheridan, and worked at Brookside Colliery, later was in the poultry business. From there he moved to Douglassville and again engaged in the poultry business. He died of a stroke at the home of his dau Susan at Royerford, Pa. Henry and his wife had ten children: ***Walter H; Susan m David Watkins, lived in Royerford, Pa.; ***Edward, Wash D.C., ***Charles; ***Kate m to Landis Klinger of Reading; ***George of Birdsboro; ***Samuel of Washington D.C., ***Chester of Douglassville, ***Joseph of Tremont, ***Bessie m William Evans of Newton, N.J.
**JOHN SNYDER (Aug 18, 1860 - Sep 23, 1937, bur Hoffman Cem), m Fietta Elizabeth Klinger (Jan 16, 1863 - Mar 18, 1932), a dau of Peter Klinger. John and Fietta (Klinger) Snyder children, some bapt Hoffman Ch & Simeon Ref): ***Anna b Jul 5, 1881; ***Henry Edward b Apr 14, 1884 and ***Clara Elizabeth b Apr 14, 1884 (twins); ***Daniel b Jan 27, 1887, m Florence ____; ***Edna b Mar 26, 1889; ***John b Nov 2, 1895, m Winifred ____ lived in Shamokin; ***Emma b c1902; ***Charles L. (1904 – 1945, bur Hoffman Cem), m Gertrude M. Snyder (1914 – 1987), a dau of David and Maude (Schell) Snyder of Upper Mahantongo Twp, Sch Co .
Charles L. and Gertrude M. (Snyder) Snyder children: Robert (deceased), m Karen Scheib, had two sons; Carl

Lee b Feb 13, 1933, m Erma ____ lives in Maryland, had two sons and one dau; **Clair H**. b 1937, m Helen Enders, has a son **Robin** who m Rose Kukuk; **Lorraine**, m ____ Leitzel, divorced, has dau in Texas.]

[**DAVID O. SNYDER** (Feb 24, 1867 Up Mah Twp, Northld Co –Aug 12, 1921, E'ville, a son of David & Hetty Snyder m Dec 29, 1888 Jane Susan Bender (Jun 22, 1866-Mar 17, 1927 of dropsy, a dau of Jonathan & Christine (Bechtel) Bender of E'ville. **David O & Jane (Bender) Snyder children: ***David E**., m Maude Shell, **had these children:** Elva m Lewis Shadle; Gertrude m Charles L Snyder; Leona m Joseph Faust; Lester; Verna m __ Kress; Robert; Shirley m Carl Bauman; David; LeRoy; John; Betty m Robert E. Graff Sr., Harold; Kenneth;]

LAND OF LEROY S. AND FANNIE E. RIEHL
(WAS HOWARD H. HELLER LAND/LEWIS SHADLE -22 acres 138 Perches)

House built c1909 by Howard Heller, dismantled 2004
Barn (photo below), date of construction unknown

This piece of land originally belonged to the tract of 386 acres 51 perches of land that Commonwealth of Pennsylvania warranted to Henry Umholtz on April 16, 1787, surveyed September 15, 1818. It was patented to Philip Umholtz. When Philip died, a petition was made to Dauphin County Orphans Court to have the land appraised and divided. On August 20, 1840, his second eldest son John received a larger portion.

On February 17, 1897, John and Magdalena Umholtz sold one hundred fifty-one acres one hundred twelve perches with house and buildings to Lincoln E. Carl and his wife. Several months later, on May 18, 1897 Lincoln E and his wife conveyed the same to Andrew Weiss who was a single man. A few days later, on May 26, 1897, Andrew Weiss sold his farm to Charles Weiss.

On December 14, 1908, Charles and Henrietta Weiss sold this tract of 22 acres, 138 perches of land to Howard H. Heller their son-in law. Howard built a two-story house on this farm about 1909. He and his wife Stella lived here all of their married life. Howard had a herd of dairy cows, and sold milk to surrounding towns. But in 1921 his wife died, and about two years later he sold his milk business to Charles A. Sitlinger. He also sold the horse-drawn milk wagon that he used to transport the milk.

On November 1, 1924, Charles and Henrietta Weiss sold another tract of land containing six acres, fifteen perches of woodland on Short Mountain to Howard H. Heller. The deed was not recorded. This land belonged to Peter and Susanna Swanger, and their heirs conveyed it to William Schoffstall in 1894. On August 5, 1896, this acreage with buildings was sold for taxes, and Lincoln C. Carl and Solomon Hess became the next owners. In June 1899, Lincoln C. and Anna Carl sold their undivided share of the acreage to Solomon Hess. By "various assignments" the land was vested in Howard Heller. Howard H. Heller continued to live here until May 8,1935 when he sold the tract of land to his son Stanley E. Heller also of Lykens Township. Stanely E. Heller died n 1940, and on June 15, 1942, his wife Mazie sold the tract of land (22 acres, 138 perches) to Lewis W. and Elva P. Shadle of Lykens Twp.

The Shadle's owned this land for a long time. But in January 2003, after both Lewis and Elva passed away, a public auction was held. This property containing 22 acres, 138 perches and house was sold to adjoining neighbors Leroy S. and Fannie E. Riehl. The six acres of land known as the Schoffstall tract was conveyed April 17, 1943 to Eston Heller, but on November 27, 1946, Eston W. and Edna Heller sold to Albert and Loll Sitlinger.

THE HELLER FAMILY
(Information from ♪ Robert Howard, and various others, plus our own research)

The earliest known member of the **HELLER** family was **Conrad Heller** (1642 – 1667), a native of Canton, Zurich, Switzerland. He apparently moved to Germany where his son **Hans Jacob Heller** was born c1662, died c 1699. Hans Jacob (1662-1699), married c1688 Anna Sarah Stricker (1665 – 1728). They were the parents of **Johan Christoph Heller** (1688 – Mar 15, 1778). Johan Christoph married Feb 16, 1715 in Germany to Veronica Lawall, a dau of John and Anna (Kern) Lawall. They had a number of children born in Pfeddersheim, Hesse, Germany. Johan Christoph Heller and his family immigrated to America arriving on the ship "Winter Galley" September 5, 1738. They settled in Northampton County, Pa. The village of Hellertown was named for this family. **Johan Christoph Heller known children (bapt Low Saucon Twp. Northampton Co):**
*Joseph** (1719 – 1800);
*Simon** (Jun 18, 1721 Germany – May 20, 1783, Hamilton Twp), m Louisa Dietz b 1726 in Milford Twp. He had land in Northampton Co by 1765 and resided next to Jacob Heller. **Simon & Louisa (Dietz) Heller children:**
Veronica (Jan 24, 1747 – Oct 18, 1809), m John Peter Conrad; Elizabeth b Mar 9, 1749; Jacob (Mar 6, 1750 – Oct 8, 1822);Abraham (May 30, 1751– Oct 16, 1824);Margaret (Dec 3, 1752 – Aug 15, 1797), m Heinrich Hauser; Sarah b Feb 18, 1754; Daniel b Jul 15, 1755; John b Oct 29, 1756; Michael (Nov 19,1757 – Jul 1, 1828), m Hannah Shoener; Anthony b Feb 1,1758; Catharine b Mar 4,1759;Anna Maria b Nov 18,1760, m Jacob Hoodmacher; Louisa b Jun 10,1765;
*John Dieter** (b ___ - d pre 1818 in Shamokin, Northld Co), m Barbara Knecht; *Michael** (Feb 27, 1724 Ger – Dec 16, 1803, Hellertown), m Magdalena Catharine Keiper, a dau of Karl Ludwig and Maria (Koch) Keiper;*Daniel** (Jul 15, 1726 – Apr 20,1803), m Anna Elizabeth Keiper **had these children;** Christopher b Dec 10, 1750; Michael b Jan 9, 1758; John Dieter b Jan 1, 1760; Mathias; Jeremiah b Dec 15, 1757; *Ludwig** (Dec 31, 1728 – Feb 26, 1807 Monroe Co), m Anna Barbara ___ possibly Schlegel, after Ludwig died she m Jacob Haeffel May 25, 1767. **Ludwig and Anna Barbara children:** Anna Maria b Mar 7, 1762; Christopher Frederick b Jul 19, 1763; Christian b Feb 23, 1765. *George Christoph** (Apr 9, 1732 – Mar 23, 1805), m Mary Elizabeth Keiper, a dau of Karl Ludwig & Maria (Koch) Keiper, **had these children:** Joseph b Mar 19, 1757, Northampton Co, m Anna Margaret Butz b Nov 12, 1759, had 12 children; Jeremiah b Dec 25, 1760; Anna Helena Cath b c1765, m John Hass, moved to Ohio; Daniel b c1769; Elizabeth b c1770; Solomon b Jan 6, 1772; Catharine b Jan 8, 1774; *Maria Magdalena** b Dec 14,1734;

The early genealogy of the Heller family that migrated to Dauphin County is not positively identified at this time. We have not found a connection to the Heller family that settled in Berks County and for whom the town Hellertown was named. A variety of dates made available through many sources make it very difficult to ascertain correct information. We hope that the information given here is correct.

Isaac Heller early member of Heller family of Dauphin County had taken up his first known land consisting of 10 acres first in Tulpehocken Twp., Berks County Nov 17, 1768. But soon members of the family began to move to Upper Paxton Twp. Several of them invested in land mostly in the Upper Paxton area, that later became Mifflin Twp. On January 28, 1774 Joseph Heller received a land warrant in Upper Paxton Twp., but it was patented to Isaac and Catherine Heller May 3, 1775. Isaac appeared on the 1790 census for Upper Paxton, and the window tax of 1798 shows him established with a 30 by 25 foot one story wooden house with four windows on two acres of cleared land. In 1800 Isaac was over 45 years old. On September 17, 1803, Isaac and Catherine Heller sold the above land with appurtenances to Jacob Heller, but on August 3, 1804 Jacob and Elizabeth Heller sold the same to William Jones. On September 21, 1804 William & Elizabeth Jones sold the same to John Adam Heller. He and his wife Mary sold 48 acres 150 perches of the land June 28, 1806 to Abraham Willier. Isaac and Catherine Heller first appeared on the Hoffman Church record in Aug 1797 as a sponsor for the child of John and Anna Maria Herman.

Adam Heller (probably Isaac's brother since it would appear that he is too old to be a son) had 49 unseated acres next to Isaac "in the Wiconisco Valley" in 1790. In 1800, Adam (over 45 years old) had a large family living with him. He had seven males in addition to himself, plus a wife and three other females. Adam Heller and William Bordner took up a warrant of land in this area in 1805, but it was patented to "William Bordner et al" April 2, 1811. The sons of Isaac Heller took up warranted land beginning in 1814, and Jacob Heller had a sawmill in 1805.

Adam Heller was an early member of Hoffman Church. He participated in the construction of the old log building of Hoffman Church, and was paid three shillings for shingles for the church on January 15, 1793. He also served as a deacon in the church, but was replaced by Jacob Mayer on May 9, 1813 because Adam Heller "did move away." He and Anna Maria are listed as communicants for 1811, apparently came back to the area by 1817. In June of that year Adam is listed as a communicant at Hoffman Church. He is listed again from 1819 to November 1822. From June 1826 - 1828, he is listed as a trustee in David's Church, Killinger.

Jacob Heller received a warrant for 140 acres on June 4, 1814, but on Dec 9, 1821 he conveyed it to Mathias Deibler, Jr. Jacob and Elizabeth Heller became communicants at Hoffman Church in September 1811, and continued until 1821 when he was listed as a deacon. In 1825, Jacob Heller, Sr. is listed as an elder in place of George Bleystein, but was replaced by John Heller in 1828..

THE HELLER FAMILY OF LYKENS VALLEY
(Information from Robert M. Howard, and others as well as our own research)

ISAAC HELLER (May 26, 1752 Berks Co – 1814 in Dau Co), has not been linked to parents of the preceding generation of Hellers. He was married in Berks Co. May 26, 1772 to Anna Catharina Wingert (b 1743 – d Dec 12, 1791), a dau of Lazarus and Maria Lauck Wingert of Heidelberg Twp. Anna Catharina Wingert was also the widow of John George Walborn (Mar 15, 1740 – Nov 28, 1770), a son of Herman and Maria Margaretha (Feg) Walborn. **John George & Anna Catharina (Wingert) Walborn children:** Maria Catharine b Dec 29, 1765; Christina b Oct 11, 1767; Christian b 1771.

According to Census records Isaac had four sons and two or three daughters. In 1811 and 1815 these members of the Heller family communed at Hoffman Church: Adam, Jacob, Elisabeth and Anna Maria, and Susanna.

Isaac and Anna Catherine (Wingert) Heller had these children:

**SUSANNA b c1772

JOHN ADAM (Oct 28, 1773 in Heidelberg Twp., Berks Co d 1860, Crawford, Ohio), m 1st Feb 4, 1795 Sarah Cowen b ___ d 1803. Adam and Sarah (Cowan) Heller had a dau: *****Anna Maria (Jul 29, 1803 bap St. Johns Hill Ch (tombstone says b Apr 1, 1800 – Jan 19, 1874, bur Davids Cem, Killinger) , m 1st John Feidt (Aug 18,1798–Nov 12,1854), had a son George (Jun7,1832 bap Davids Ref Ch –1905, bur Salem Luth Cem, Killinger), m Sarah Barnhardt (1836 – 1902), a dau of Michael & Rachel Alleman. They lived in Up Paxton Twp.

Adam Heller replaced John Schoffstall as a trustee for Hoffman church council on May 27, 1821. On Jul 27, 1833 J. Adam Heller replaced John Hoffman the tailor, as Elder.

John Adam m 2nd 1804 Anna Maria Bordner (Jan 5, 1786 – 1858, Crawford, Ohio), a dau of John & Susanna (Mellinger) Bordner of Lykens Twp. Anna Maria Bordner is mentioned as one of the children of John Bordner whose estate was settled in 1812. She received money & furniture from her father. John Heller & his family lived in Wash. Twp. at the time of his death. John and Thomas were executors of his estate.
(John Adam and Anna Maria (Bordner) Heller children (some bapt David's Ch, Killinger, St. Johns Hill Bbg, Hoffman Ch. In his will prob. In Crawford, Ohio, he mentions that he has 11 children):
***John (Sep 28, 1805 – 1891) sp John Herman & Anna Maria, m Christina ___ b c1807, they were communicants at David's Church, Killinger in 1827. John received a plantation of 106 acres from his father. They lived in Logansville, Clinton Co in 1880.
John and Christina Heller children (some bapt David's Ch): ****Emanuel b1829, m Catharine ___, children: Vannie bc1860; Catharine b c1864; Ida b c1870; Harry b c1872; Calvin b c1874; ****Isaac b Oct 27, 1830; ****Susanna b Sep 1833;
***Daniel b Jun 13, 1807 sp John & Susannah Bordner (parents) m Catharine Anne ___ before 1832, had child Maria b Jan 5, 1837 bapt David's Ch, probably the one confirmed at David's Church, Killinger in May 1825. Daniel moved to Weston, Wood Co, Ohio, and there m 2nd in 1845 Margaret Campbell b c1820. In 1880 Daniel & Margaret Heller lived on a farm in that area, had a grandson George Ward age 10 with them.
Susanna (Oct 23, 1808 – Feb 23, 1891, W. Milgrove, Ohio), sp Simon & Susanna Herman, probably the one confirmed at David's Church in May 1825. She m Nov 15, 1825 (record in David's Ch), Isaac Gonder (Jan 22, 1806 – Jul 27, 1885, in Ohio), a son of Johannes & Hannah (Fralich) Gonder. **Isaac & Susanna (Heller) Gonder had these children (bapt St. David's Cem):* Salome b Feb 3, 1827;**** Elisabeth b Aug 18, 1828;****Daniel b Sep 16, 1830; ****Catherine b Sep 16, 1831; ****John Adam b Oct 13, 1837; ****David (Dec 22, 1838- 1913), Wood Co., Oh; Solomon b Aug 10, 1839; Rebecca b Mar 15, 1842; Samuel b Jun 8, 1845; Isaac Geo b Jul 13,1846; Susanna b Nov10,1849; Emanuel b Mar 25,1851; Benj. F. b Apr 25,1853. They moved to Ohio.
***Elisabeth Leah (Apr 12, 1810 – Mar 24, 1874, in Sandusky, Ohio)., m Peter Heckert (Oct 25, 1811 – Oct 23, 1881), a son of Casper & Elizabeth (Witmer) Heckert, moved to Sandusky Co., Ohio. Had many children.
***John Adam b Aug 2, 1811 sp Adam Wise & Elis, may have m 1st Anna Maria Messner (Apr 3, 1826 – Apr 19, 1855), a dau of Philip & Anna Mary Messner. **Had child Philip** b Oct 7,1834 bapt David's Ch. m 2nd Fanny McLane.
***Rebecca (Feb 7, 1813 – Feb 27,1899), m 1st in 1830 Jacob Kocher (Apr 29, 1807 – Feb 1, 1833, of typhoid fever said to be bur Hoffman Cem), a son of Levi and Magdalena Kocher. **They had two children: Daniel** (Feb 26, 1832 –1914 in Seneca, Ohio); Lydia b Nov 20, 1833, bapt Hoffman Ch. Rebecca m 2nd Jacob Ronk (1810 – 1850), moved to Crawford Co., Ohio. They had 11 children.
***Catharina b May 3, 1814 bap David's sp John Jager, m John Ronk
***Jacobus b Jun 17, 1817 sp John & Susanna Riegel, probably d young.
***Isaac b Jul 6, 1821 sp John & Maria Umholtz
***Elias (Nov 22, 1823 – Jul 4,1891 Crawford, Ohio), m 1st Elizabeth Goodale, m 2nd Margaret Beck.
***Salome b Feb 16, 1827 , m John Whitmore b Nov 1822, moved to Ohio.
***Philip b Oct 7, 1834, nothing more known. May have died young.

John Adam Heller was the founder of Hellerstettle in December 1819, the town later to become known as Berrysburg. He apparently traveled a hundred miles to Sugar Valley about 1839, and later went on to Ohio.

JACOB W. (Apr 15, 1777 Dau Co – Mar 20, 1850 Crawford Co, Ohio), m Elizabeth Wingert (Jul 31 or Aug 30, 1780– Feb 3, 1856), Jacob was a Rev. Soldier. Jacob Heller became a deacon of Hoffman Church on May 27, 1821, in place of George Bleystein, Jr. On July 10, 1825, Jacob Heller, Sr. became an elder replacing George Bleystein.
Jacob and Elizabeth (Wingert) Heller had these children (most bapt St. John Hill Ch):
*** _____ a son according to the 1810 census, a boy between 10 & 16 yrs old.
***Catharine (Jan 1, 1802 – Jul 2, 1811), sp Isaac Heller and Catharine
***Elisabeth (b Sep 27, 1803 sp Elisabeth Spat, widow – Jul 29, 1865), m Mar 24, 1822 George Steinbrecher (c1789 – d Jul 29, 1865 in Crawford Co, Ohio), **they had one known child: Johannes** b Oct 23, 1822.

***Jacob (b Oct 6, 1805 sp Philip and Magd Messner – d Mar 20, 1881, Crawford Co, Ohio), m 1847 Catherine A. Hoy (Mar 8,1809 – Mar 29,1890), dau of Peter and Susanna (Shaffner) Hoy, moved to Ohio.

*** Anna Maria (May 20, 1808 – pre 1856), m Sep 1828 Daniel Light (Jun 30, 1806 – Jul 7, 1881), a son of Adam & Ann (Ditty) Light. Both died in Crawford Co., Ohio. **Daniel & Anna Maria (Heller) Light children**: William Jacob (Jun 13, 1829- Jun 1904), m in 1859 Salome Hoy (Oct 26, 1828 Dau Co– Feb 9, 1902)- ; John b Oct 13, 1831; Emanuel b Jan 22, 1834; Adam b 1836.

***John b Aug 13, 1810 sp John and Susanna Heller – d July 1811).

***Joseph (May 12, 1812 – Mar 20, 1846), m Veronica Shaffer (1815 – 1846), **had these children:** Sara b Aug 3, 1834 bapt David's Ch, moved to Henry Co, Ohio; George b c1847; Mary b c1849.

***Daniel J. (b Aug 7, 1814 sp Simon Heller & Susanna – d Feb 28, 1894 in Crawford, Ohio), m 1833 Catharine Gingrich (Jul 15, 1816 – May 3, 1896) a dau of Jacob and Mary (Fishbaum) Gingrich of Dau Co.. Daniel and Catherine Heller moved to Holmes, Crawford Co., Ohio in 1838. In 1880 Benjamin Weber age 19, b in Pa., lived with them. They had a large family in Ohio. They had at least 13 children.

***Salome b Dec 20, 1816 sp John and Catherine Heller

***Susanna b May 23, 1821 sp Susanna Heller, m in 1838 to William Woodside (Dec 5, 1812 – 1892). They lived in Crawford Co., Ohio.

***Jonas (Jan 26, 1824 – Mar 22, 1892), moved to Crawford, Liberty Co., Ohio and married Susanna Spade (Nov 18, 1830 in Ohio.- Aug 9, 1917). They had about 7 children.

JOHANNES (Oct 28, 1779 – Aug 4, 1847, bur St. John's Hill Cem), m 1st. Susanna Bordner (Sep 12, 1786 bap Altalaha Luth, Tulpehocken Twp Berks Co – d bef 1811), a dau of William & Maria Elizabeth (Koppenhaver) Bordner. John Heller replaced Jacob Heller as Elder on Feb 25, 1828 in Hoffman Church. **Johannes and Susanna (Bordner)Heller (some bapt Hoffman & St. Johns Hill Ch):**

***Jacob D. (Nov 20, 1801 sp Jacob & Elis Heller – Dec 13, 1885, Crawford Co., Ohio), m Mar 20, 1825 (record in David's Ch Killinger) from Hoffman Ch to Margaret Daniel (Feb 11, 1805 – Dec 31, 1891), a dau of Andreas and Susanna (Hoy) Daniel. They moved to Crawford Co., Ohio in 1836. **Jacob & Margaret (Daniel) Heller children:**

Amanda b c1827, m Lair Miller in Crawford Co, Oh; Elizabeth m Daniel H. Pflieger; Isaac b 1826 Dau Co.- d 1898, Ohio, m Sevilla Rupert (Jan 17, 1832 – Apr 26,1915, Stark Co, Ohio); Sarah b 1829; John (Jul 12, 1830 – Dec 14, 1909, Ohio); Josiah (1832 – 1891), moved Crawford, Oh) in 1841, it took more than a month to get there. Later to Taylor Co., Iowa ; Edward (1834 – 1907) moved to Crawford, Oh ; William (1836 – 1912), moved to Paulding Co., Oh; Jacob Benj (1837 – 1906), to Adams Co., Ia, m in 1868 Lydia Heller b Nov 5, 1844 in Ogle Co. She was a dau of John and Lydia (Shott) Heller, ; Mary b 1840; Andrew b 1841; Catharine b 1844; Geo Lewis (1847 – 1926), Crawford, Oh..

***Elisabeth b Jun 23, 1803 bapt Hoffman Ch – may have d young – not on 1810 census.

***Susanna b Apr 2, 1805 – d before her father (1848), m John Herman (Aug 23, 1797 – Mar 22, 1874, Clinton Co or Feb 20, 1797-Mar 20 1874), a son of George and Catharine Herman She is probably the Susanna Heller a single girl that was confirmed in September 1781 at Hoffman Church. **John & Susanna (Heller) Herman known children:** ***Mary d young; ***Josiah "Jesias Isaac" (Jun 29, 1827- Mar 1, 1906, Clinton Co), m Matilda Dubendorf (Nov 28, 1831 – Jan 20, 1914) . lived in Wash Twp in 1850, moved to Clinton Co where most children born. **Josiah and Matilda (Dubendorf) Herman had these children:** Samuel M b c1850; Susanna b May 7, 1852; Rebecca (Mar 28, 1854 – Dec 6, 1922), m Samuel Eisenhower (1848- 1919), a son of Daniel & Leah (Lutz) Eisenhower, lived in Clinton Co.; William May 20, 1856 – 1928); Silas (Jan 18, 1858 -1872); Sarah b1860 in Clinton Co.; John D. (Sep 25, 1863 - 1899); ***Sarah b Nov 4, 1829, bap St. Johns Hill Ch. [See also Herman/Harman gen.]

***Anna Maria (b Sep 6, 1807 – d Apr 16, 1881, bur Jefferson Co, Pa.), m 1st Johannes Hoffman (May 13, 1809 – Aug 20, 1833, burial unknown), a son of John and Rebecca (Kuntzelman) Hoffman. She m 2nd c1837, George Weiss (1805 – 1874), a son of Johannes and Elisabeth (Bordner) Weiss, and moved to Jefferson County. In 1880 Anna Maria was living with her son John Weiss age 40, and his family.

***John E. (Mar 11, 1810 sp Wm Bordner & Elis _ – Sep 1, 1880, Maryland Twp, Ogle Co, Il), m Lydia Schott (Nov 13, 1811 – Jan 20, 1892), a dau of Johann and Anna (Messner) Schott in Dau Co. They moved to Ogle Co in 1852. **Most of their children were born in Dau Co:** Philip b c1836; Catharine Lavina b May 5, 1838; John S b Sep 15, 1840, m Emma Lantz in Ogle Co; Jacob L b 1843 m Fannie Knock in Ogle Co; Lydia (Nov 5, 1844 – Oct 20, 1925), m her cousin Jacob Benjamin Heller in Ogle Co; George b c1846;

Rebecca b 1848, m Daniel Shaffer in Ogle Co., Il; William b c1852. Two others: Henry and Charles were born in Ogle Co.

 Johannes Heller (Oct 28, 1779 –Feb 11, 1847, from above), m 2nd c1811 Catherine Bitterman Matter (1756 – 1822, bur St. John's Hill Cem), believed to be a dau of Baltzer and Ann Margaret Bitterman. Catherine was also the widow of Jacob Matter (Aug 12, 1767 – Aug 22, 1810, bur St. Johns Hill Cem).Catherine died before her mother Margaret. On April 30, 1829 the following document was entered into orphan court records: "Upon the petition of John Heller that he has been intermarried to Catharine, widow and relict of Jacob Matter of Mifflin Twp., Pa. and with her he had two daughters when she died, namely Margaret and Sarah, who have no guardian appointed to take care of a certain part of a personal estate left by their grandmother, Margaret Bitterman." **Johannes and Catherine (Bitterman, Matter) Heller had these children:**

*** **Margaret "Rebecca"** b Apr 9, 1814, bapt St. John Hill Ch, sponsors John & Catherine Bitterman.

*** **.Sarah E** b Apr 25, 1816 bapt Hoffman Ch, sp Geo Matter & Cath – d Jun 7, 1901, bur St. John's Hill Cem), m Daniel Schwab (b Jun 4, 1813 - d Jun 3, 1871), a son of John Jacob and Catherine (Metz) Schwab of Washington Twp. They lived in the spacious house on the old Swab homestead. **Daniel and Sarah (Heller) Schwab had these children;**

****Catharine (Jan 7, 1837 – Jun 20, 1926, bur St. John's Hill Cem), m Dec 9, 1855 Samuel Snyder (Jan 30, 1836 – Apr 3, 1885), a son of Daniel & Elisabeth (Hetrick) Snyder. He was a blacksmith living in Washington Twp. **Samuel and Catharine (Schwab) Snyder had these children:**

Mary Jane (Oct 20, 1855 – 1931, bur Fairview Cem, Wm.stown), m Edward A. Hess (1852 – 1929).

Jonathan Frederick (Jan 10, 1858 – 1865, bur Rife Cem); *Daniel E* (Dec 3, 1859 – Sep 15, 1924, bur St. Johns "Hill" Cem), m Lydia Ann Romberger (1861 – 1949), a dau of Isaac and Lydia (Michael) Romberger. [See Romberger history for more info.]

Sarah Elizabeth (Jan 30, 1861 in Malta, Northld Co-

Sarah (Heller) Schwab (1816 – 1901)

Sep 13, 1922, bur St. John's Hill Cem), m Joseph A. Hoke (1854 – Jul 5, 1923). **Joseph A. and Sarah (Snyder) Hoke had these children**: Josiah; Carrie A (1878 – 1950), m Peter Adam Matter (1862 – 1943). [More info in Matter info.]

Emma Louisa (May 30, 1864 – Oct 5, 1937, bur St. John's Hill Cem), m Henry Morris Spotts (1861 – 1948), a son of Samuel and Mary (Philips) Spotts.

Nathan Ellsworth (Apr 11, 1870 – May 10, 1946, bur St. John's Hill Cem), m Rosie Elnore Bonawitz (Mar 1, 1874 – 1962), a dau of David and Erlena (Rowe) Bonawitz.

****Thomas (1839 – Jan 1, 1925, bur St.John's Hill Cem), m Susanna Holtzman (May 31, 1844 – Jan 15, 1926), a dau of John and Elizabeth (Warner) Holtzman

****Mary (1840 – 1854, bur St. John's Hill Cem;

****Jonas Benj (Mar 18, 1843 – 1913, bur Maple Grove Cem, E'ville, m Ella Mattis (1848 – 1923), a dau of Isaac Mattis.   More info in Schwab family; ****Isaac (1845 – 1924, bur Maple Grove Cem), m Sarah Messner. More info in Schwab family; ****John D. (1848 – 1929, bur St. John's Hill Cem), m Lena J. Hartman (1853 – 1945), a dau of Jacob & Catherine (Deibler) Hartman, lived in Wash Twp.; ****Sarah (1851 – 1927, bur St. Johns' Hill Cem), m Frederick L. Koppenheffer. More in Schwab family. ****Aaron (1859 – 1943, bur Maple Grove Cem), m Mary Uhler (1865 – 1938), he was a buggy maker.

Johannes Heller (1779-1847 from above), m 3rd c1822 Anna Maria Paul (Jul 1, 1789 – Mar 18, 1866, bur St. Johns Hill Cem), widow of John Matter, and dau of Joseph and Anna Maria (Matter) Paul. **Johannes and Anna Maria (Paul) Heller children:**

***Thomas** (1826 – d cDec1866), m Elizabeth Matter (Aug 23, 1826 – Feb 21, 1921, bur Peace Cem, Bbg with second husband), a dau of John and Anna Elizabeth Matter. Thomas and Elizabeth Heller lived in Washington Twp in 1850, and had Joseph Harmon age 20 and his mother Mary Heller age 61 with them. After Thomas died, Elizabeth m Peter Eby (Apr 1818 or 1820 – Jun 25, 1892). The minor children of Thomas and Elizabeth (Catherine, Alfred and Philip) are mentioned after his death in an orphan court record.

Thomas and Elizabeth (Matter) Heller had these children:

****John Adam Sr.** (b Mar 23, 1849 – dJan 25, 1935, bur David's Cem, Killinger). The Rife church record mentions his death and that he was a member of that congregation. He m Catherine Weaver (1852 – Apr 1, 1925), a dau of Adam Weaver. They lived in Upper Paxton Twp. in 1880 and he was a blacksmith.
John Adam and Catharine (Weaver) Heller had these children:
<u>Charles Clinton</u> b Oct 25, 1873
<u>Samuel Peter</u> b Mar 24, 1875, m Mary Ellen Hummel.

<u>John Adam Jr</u> (b May 10, 1877 - Dec 8, 1918, bur St. Andrews Cem, Valley View, Sch Co.), m Jan 1901, Anna Mary Keiffer b Jun 29, 1880 – Jul 21, 1971, died of Cancer, bur St. Andrews Cem, Valley View), a dau of Michael E. and Catherine (Weaver) Keefer. After John Adam Heller died, Anna Mary m James Monroe Lucas (1883 – 1949).
John Adam (Jr) and Anna Mary (Keiffer) Heller had these children:
<u>Verna</u> C. b 1900 m Harry A. Snyder b 1895, a son of Andrew & Savilla (Artz) Snyder ;
<u>Eva M</u> (1905 - 1995);, m John Arthur Buffington) 1894 - 1942)
<u>Sally A</u>. (1906 - 1985), m Elvin Allen Moyer, ;
<u>Mary</u>;
<u>Bessie C</u>. (Feb 1910 - Apr 28, 2004), m Richard Null;
<u>Homer</u> b 1912 , m Mary E. Lessig b 1910, a dau of Daniel B and Mary (Dry) Lessig

<u>William H.</u> (1879 – 1918, bur Davids Cem, Killinger), m Susan Amanda Miller (1880 – 1941), dau of Daniel & Sarah (Wilbert) Miller of Jackson Twp., Dau Co.
<u>Lizzie</u> (1882 – 1959), m Arthur R. Spotts

**** *Catherine* b c 1850
**** *Philip* (1852 – 1945, bur Maple Grove Cem, E'ville), m 1st Mary Magdalena Matter (Apr 21, 1853 - Mar 18, 1887), bur Motter Cem, near Elizabethville), a dau of _____ and Elizabeth Matter.In 1880, Philip and family lived in Wash Twp. They had Elizabeth Matter age 61, his mother-in-law with them
Phillip and Mary M (Matter) Heller had two known children:
Thomas A. (May 12, 1874 - Jun 14, 1890, bur Motter Cem)
Howard Henry (May 13, 1877 - Mar 31, 1943, bur Simeon Cem), m Apr 5, 1902, Stella M. Weiss (Feb 13, 1882 - Oct 3, 1921), a dau of Charles & Henrietta (Evitts) Weiss. They lived in Lykens Twp in 1910.
Howard and Stella (Weiss) Heller had these children:
<u>Earl Leste</u>r (Sep 28, 1902 - Aug 13, 1926, bur Simeon Cem), died of a ruptured spleen;
<u>Erma Olive</u> b Jan 20, 1905, m Albert Troutman, lived first on the east side of Gratz, in Lykens Township, later moved to Halifax.
<u>Stanley Elwood</u> (Mar 20, 1908 - Nov 8, 1940,bur Simeon Cem), m Maisy E. Feger b 1916, a dau of _____ and Jane Feger of Pitman.Stnley Elwood and Maisy (Feger) Heller had a dau Betty (Feb 5, 1934 - Sep 30, 1964); After Stanley died, Maisy m Robert Adam Hopple.b Dec 18, 1914, a son of Jacob M. and Annie (Clark) Hopple.
<u>Myrtle Naomi</u> b c1910, m Donald J. Wiest, a son of Daniel & Nora (Williard) Wiest, *had a son* <u>Calvin</u> b Sep 18, 1933;.
<u>Eston W</u>. (1912 - 1977), m Edna Sitlinger b Jul 28, 1920, a dau of Norman and Elsie (Welker) Sitlinger,
Eston W. and Edma (Sitlinger) Heller had son: Dennis Clair b Jan 20, 1943, not married
Phillip Heller m 2nd, Nov 5, 1887 Clara Isabella Dietrich (Dec 19, 1865 – 1942, bur with husband), a dau of John and Mary Dietrich of Lykens.
**** *Maria Margaretha* b Oct 22, 1854;
****_Alfred Nathaniel_ b Mar 22, 1856

Erma Olive b Jan 20, 1905, m Albert Troutman, lived first on the east side of Gratz, in Lykens Township, later moved to Halifax.

Stanley Elwood (Mar 20, 1908 - Nov 8, 1940,bur Simeon Cem), m Maisy E. Feger b 1916, a dau of _____ . After Stanley died, Maisy m Robert Adam Hopple.

 Myrtle Naomi b c1910, m Donald Wiest, **had these children**: Calvin b Sep 18, 1933;.

Eston W. (1912 - 1977), m Edna Sitlinger b Jul 28, 1920, had son Dennis Clair b Jan 20, 1943]

Phillip Heller m 2nd, Nov 5, 1887 Clara Isabella Dietrich (Dec 19, 1865 – 1942, bur with husband), a dau of John and Mary Dietrich of Lykens.

**** **Maria Margaretha** b Oct 22, 1854;

******Alfred Nathaniel** b Mar 22, 1856

***Rebecca b c1818 – nothing more known

Isaac Heller (1752-1814 from above) m 2nd about 1804 to Charlotta Moor (b 1760 in Ireland – d Sep 22, 1826, a dau of Johannes Moor. (According to a record in St. David's Church in Killinger) The record is as follows:"Scharlotta Heller, daughter of Johannes Moor, born 1760 in Ireland, came to America in 1774. Confirmed in the Reformed faith. Married to Johannes Enders, had 2 daughters. Married second time to Wilhelm Power, had 2 sons. Married third time to Isaac Heller in 1804. Isaac Heller died in 1814. She died September 22, 1826. Lived with three husbands 12 years. Aged 66 years more or less." Isaac and Charlotta did not have children.

Another record from the will of William Power of Upper Paxton written August 30, 1802, probated April 16, 1804 has this statement: "To Mary Kelley daughter of reputed wife Sharlotte Kelly has lived with me some time in character of a wife and having one or two husbands alive."

[A **John Moor** died in Upper Paxton in 1805, leaving a widow Elizabeth. He is bur Old Luth Cem Killinger (1768 - 1804). His only son John petitioned the court about land etc.   The court appt Christopher Yeager guardian of his young children Charlotte, Mary and Sarah. **They had five children (Moor children bapt Salem Luth, Killinger)**: John m Philippina ___ **had these children** Jacob b Jan 30, 1800, sp John & Elix Moor; **Susanna** b 1807, date not given, Maria Mohr sp; **Littia Hanna** b Sep 4, 1807; **Catharina** b Dec 12, 1808, sp Elis Mohr; **Daniel** b Jun 11, 1811, George & Scharlotta Weise sp; **John** b Sep 26, 1813; **Wilhelm** b Apr 20, 1817; **Elizabeth** may have m John Schora or Lintner; **Charlotte** (was a minor in 1805), may have m George Weise; **Mary** b Aug 25, 1792; **Sally Ann.**]

ALBERT MORGAN FARM
(John Umholtz 70 acres in 1875)

Two brothers came to America from the German sector of Switzerland in the mid-1700s, settling first in

Swatara Township, Lebanon County. The earliest record (1764 baptism) of these brothers was found in Swatara Reformed Church near Jonestown, Lebanon County.

The brother (name unknown) was killed while fighting in Quebec during the Revolutionary War. Henry also served during the war in the units of Captain John Hoffman and Captain Michael Weaver.

Henry Umholtz married first, about 1763, Margaret Rauch, a dau of Bernard and Anna Rauch. After she died, he married Magdalena Seidensticker of Bethel Township, Lebanon County. Magdalena received an inheritance of one dollar from her brother Philip's will of 1808.

Henry and his family later came to Upper Paxton Twp. and settled near the edge of Short Mountain. He was listed in 1780 on the tax record for Wiconisco District. The "Window Tax" of 1798 shows Henry Umholtz with a 30 by 28 foot, one story wooden house with 4 windows having a total of 50 lights (small panes). He also had a good barn. and his land joined the land of Jacob Salada. John Umholtz had a 30 by 24 foot, one story wooden house with 2 windows and 24 lights, and a poor stable. His land joined the land of Jonathan Osman. Both were listed under the Wiconisco District.

The land, where the Henry Umholtz family settled was part of a tract or tracts of land that the Umholtz family received from Commonwealth of Pennsylvania. Henry received a warrant for 91 acres on April 16, 1787, but it was not patented until January 12, 1831, when Philip Umholtz received it.

Henry and his two wives are presumed buried at Hoffman's Cemetery. The death dates for the two wives is unknown. The second wife Magdalena lived as late as January 1834, when Leonard Reedy repaired a spring wheel for her, at a cost of twelve cents.

Another tract of 386 acres 51 perches of land was warranted April 16, 1787 to Henry Umholtz, patented Jan 12, 1831 to Philip Umholtz. Members of the family lived here for many years. When it was finally divided, most of it continued to be owned by later generations of the family. When Philip Umholtz died, a petition was made to Dauphin County Orphans Court to have the land appraised and divided. On August 20, 1840, his second eldest son John received the large tract. It was about this time that the land began to be divided. Those various divisions are discussed in the descriptions of the adjoining properties.

John and Magdalena Umholtz sold one hundred fifty-one acres one hundred twelve perches with house and buildings to Lincoln E. Carl and his wife on February 17, 1897. Several months later on May 18, 1897, Lincoln Carl and his wife conveyed the same acreage to Andrew Weiss who was a single man. A few days later, on May 26, 1897, Andrew Weiss sold his farm to Charles Weiss. This land was bound on the east by Andrew Schmeltz, Henry Grimm, Emanuel Umholtz. On the south by Isaac Sitlinger, George Moyer Estate, Josiah Hoover. On the west it joined with Henry Snyder and Frank Boyer. Daniel Buffington, F. P. Ferree and John W. Hoffman were on the north. Water rights were reserved for Daniel Buffington from the milldam to the mill, two rods in width.

THE UMHOLTZ FAMILY
(Much genealogy information from Evelyn Hartman)

[HENRY UMHOLTZ (b 1745 in Switzerland, d 1829, Lyk Twp, probably bur Hoffman Cem), m 1st to Anna Margaret Rauch (no dates - probably bur Hoffman Cem), a dau of Bernard and Anna Rauch. After Anna Margaret died, Henry married a second wife Magdalena Seidensticker. **Henry and his wives had these children:** *HENRY b 1764, may have died young; *JACOB b 1766, may have died young; *JOHN Sr. (b Aug 11, 1770 Leb. Co - d Jul 26, 1856 – see below; *BARNARD (Oct 22, 1772 Leb. Co- Aug 18, 1829); *MICHAEL (Aug 31, 1776 – d Jan 7, 1854); *JOHN PHILIP (Sep 14, 1779, Mifflin Twp, Dau Co - d Apr 18, 1837, Lyk Twp; *CATHARINE MAGDALENA Feb 22, 1781 d young; *HENRY, JR. (b Sep 17, 1783 Leb Co - d Dec 18, 1829; *ANNA MARIA UMHOLTZ (Jun 6, 1785 – Dec 15, 1860, bur St. John's Hill Cem),

*JOHN Sr. (b Aug 11, 1770 Leb Co - d Jul 26, 1856), m Catharine Herman (Sep 29, 1772, bapt St. Daniel's Luth Ch, in Heidelberg Twp., Berks Co - Feb 1, 1845, bur Hoffman Cem), a dau of Jacob Herman. In 1850 John lived in Mifflin Township, and had Sarah Schoffstall age 18 with him. They were living next to John Umholtz Jr.and his family. **John and Catharine (Herman) Umholtz (most bapt Hoffman Ch):**

Jacob (Feb 17, 1796 – Nov 10, 1853, bur Simeon Cem, Gratz- death record in Dau Co Court house), m Catherine Schoffstall (Apr 15, 1795 – Apr 3, 1880), a dau of Peter Schoffstall, Jr. and wife Catherine Hoffman. John Jacob was one of several gunsmith's in the vicinity, and several of his guns have survived to this day. They lived in Gratz in 1829. **John Jacob and Catherine (Schoffstall) Umholtz children;

***<u>John J.</u> (Mar 30, 1818 – Oct 17, 1888, bur in Simeon Cem), m Elizabeth Keiser (Apr 18, 1823 – Mar 10, 1882), a dau of Philip and Elizabeth (Hoffman) Keiser. Elizabeth may have died of small pox. In 1870, John J. and Elizabeth Umholtz had his mother Catherine age 75 and their grandson Milton age 9 living with them. John J. was known as "drummer John," and was probably the one who was the leader of the "Umholtz Band" during the 1850's and maybe much longer. The drum that for several years was on loan to the Gratz Historical Society museum, probably belonged to him. Unfortunately, the drum was only on loan, and eventually was sold for a price that our society could not afford. In his will probated Nov 14, 1888, John directs his heirs, Sarah Buffington, Eliza Hess, and the heirs of deceased son Edmond L. to share in three equal parts. **John J. & Elizabeth (Keiser) Umholtz children:**
****<u>Sarah</u> (Feb 13, 1842 – Dec 3, 1925, bur Simeon Cem, Gratz), m Samuel Buffington (May 26, 1837 - May 18, 1910, a son of Jacob and Rebecca (Hawk) Buffington. **They had these children:** *Catharine Elizabeth (1860 – 1929, d in Kansas),* m Edward Lloyd Umholtz, a son of Samuel and Elizabeth (Harner) Umholtz.; *Jacob John (1861-1925),* m Clara Kissinger, a dau of Daniel and Sallie (Moyer) Kissinger. He was a saddler, and barber in Gratz; *George B. (1864 – 1929),* m Mary Emma J. Laudenslager, a dau of Zacharias and Lydia (Kissinger) Laudenslager; *Henry* G. (b c1866 – 1951),m Clara Philips, a dau of John and Esther (Ritzman) Philips;*Charles E.* (1868 – 1953), m Agnes Troutman, a dau of Abraham and Elizabeth (Hartman) Troutman. *Carrie Lula (1879 – 1954),* m George Henry Kissinger, a son of Amos and Rebecca (Hoffman) Kissinger.
****<u>Edmond L.</u> (Apr 7, 1843 – Jan 10, 1882, of small pox, bur Simeon Cem), m 1st Catherine Buffington, (Oct 17, 1844 – Feb 4, 1877, bur EUB Cem, Bbg), a dau of Jacob and Catherine (Schadle) Buffington Catherine and Edmond later divorced. Edmond Umholtz was a drummer in the Civil War.
Edmond L. and Catherine (Buffington) Umholtz children:
Milton (Mar 4, 1861 – Mar 1878), traveled to Lanark, Ill to visit his uncle Matt Tallman. While visiting he was taken sick, and died of "rheumatism of the heart." The uncle arranged a funeral at the M.E. church the following Sunday morning, with internment in the nearby cemetery. Monday morning a dispatch arrived saying "He must be sent home, buried or not buried." His remains were exhumed the same day, and sent by the noon train. He is buried in Gratz Cem.
Henry O. (1863 – 1950, bur Simeon Cem), m Mary Strayer (1862 – 1929), a dau of Daniel and Sarah A. (Thomas) Strayer. **Henry O and Mary (Strayer) Umholtz had these children:** *Milton* (1881 – 1938, bur Simeon Cem), m Sallie L. Klinger (1883 – 1955); *Catherine* m Walter Wiest; *John* m Ella Kessler; *Charles* m Carrie Baum; *Carrie* m Edward Hoffman; *Claude*; *Annie* m Edman Rothermel.
Edmond L. Umholtz m 2nd Ellen L. Keiser, and had these children: *Franklin D.* (1868 – 1871, bur Simeon Cem); *Charles* (1873 – 1875); *Mary L.*; *Carrie Agnes* b Jan 18, 1875, not married, lived in Reading where she was a foot doctor; *Sallie M* (1878 – 1882, d of small pox; *Annie V* (1880 – 1882, died of small pox).
****<u>Eliza</u> (Jul 11, 1847 – Nov 11, 1917, bur Simeon Cem), m Harry Hess (Oct 22, 1845 – May 31, 1928), a son of Solomon & Eva (Saltzer) Hess. Harry was a hotel keeper at Pillow, Big Run and Lykens. **Harry & Eliza (Umholtz) Hess children:** *Elizabeth* (1865 – 1935), m Charles M. Blyler, a son of Simon and Caroline (Klinger) Blyler; *Katharine Priscilla* (1867 – 1956, bur Simeon Cem), m Cyrus M. Tobias (1864 – 1941); *Sally* (1871 – 1934, bur Simeon Cem beside M. Wiest), m 1st Morris Wiest (Dec 10, 1866 – Apr 9, 1907, bur Simeon Cem), m 2nd Joseph Laudenslager; *Harvey E.* (Dec 5,1875 – 1942, bur Simeon cem)), m Katherine Wolf (1874 – 1949), a dau of George Wolf.; *Eva* d 1898 age 20 yrs; *Lewis Edmond* (Dec 11,1881 – 1968, bur Simeon Cem), not married; *Carrie Ellen (Dec 13, 1883),* m Fred Sandt.

***<u>Joseph Adam</u> (Dec 30, 1821 – Nov 15, 1887, bur Simeon Cem), m Elizabeth Coleman (Dec 26, 1815 bapt Klinger Ch– Jun 9, 1885, bur Coleman Cem), a dau of John Jacob and Barbara (Artz) Coleman. The tombstone of Elizabeth does not agree with bapt date. In 1850 and 1860 the mother of Elizabeth lived with Joseph and the family. In 1860 Isaac Salada age 13 was also with them. In 1870 Rebecca Coleman age 69 lived with them. In his will, Joseph directs that his two sons Jonas and John Jacob shall be his sole heirs because they served him so faithfully. They should pay $100 to his granddaughter Louisa **Joseph and Elizabeth (Coleman) Umholtz had these children:**
****<u>Susannah</u> (1836 – Mar 24, 1886), m Jacob Daniel Coleman, had dau Louisa (1863 – 1918, m Milton Daniel.
****<u>Jonas</u> (Mar 17, 1842 – Feb 27, 1904, bur Simeon Cem), m Hannah Scheib (Oct 23, 1844 – Feb 23, 1906), a dau of Michael and Christiana (Alspach) Scheib of Lykens Twp. **Jonas and Hannah (Scheib) Umholtz children:** *Anna Sevilla* (c1866 – 1954, bur Oak Dale Cem, Wash Twp), m George Harper (1869 – 1945); *Charles Grant* (1866 – 1894), m Ellen Lettich; *Adam Allen* (Feb 1870 – 1947); Reiley (1873 – 1914); Elizabeth Louisa (1873 – 1956)
****<u>Susanna</u> (c1843 – pre 1886), m Daniel Coleman, **had a dau** *Louisa* who m Milton Daniel.

****John Jacob (Apr 16, 1846 – Jul 5, 1914, bur Simeon Cem), m Rebecca Scheib (Sep 13, 1847 – Jun 6, 1913), a dau of Michael and Christiana (Alspach) Scheib. **John Jacob and Rebecca Umholtz children**: *Mary Seluna* (1869 – 1942), m Harry Coltran; *Elizabeth Louisa* (Dec 11, 1873 – Nov 21, 1956, bur Simeon Cem); *Jennie Rebecca* b Jan 7, 1877, m Walter Wentzel; *Joseph Adam* (Feb 25, 1880 – Oct 5, 1942, bur Simeon Cem), m Jennie Koppenhaver (Sep 25, 1883 – Jul 21, 1930), a dau of John Koppenhaver   lived in Gratz; *Guerney Milton* (1882 – 1969), m Flora Wolfgang.

***Jacob (Mar 18, 1824 – Jun 8, 1894), m Mary Artz, **had these children**: Jonathan *A.* (1848 – 1897); Harry (1849 – 1923); Aaron A (1855 – 1897), killed in the mines, when he went to investigate a charge that did not go off. m Emma Blyler, a dau of Simon and Caroline (Klinger) Blyler..

***Johanna (no dates), m Jacob Stine, lived in Hubley Twp., Sch Co. Jacob was a major in the Pa. Militia.

***Sarah (no dates) m _____ Schoffstall

*** Daniel (Apr 10, 1833 – Aug 12, 1865, bur Simeon Cem). He lived with his widowed mother in 1860, probably did not marry.

Susanna b Mar 9, 1796, m Feb 2, 1823 Johannes Redel, record David's ch, Killinger. The only John Redel found was born Feb 20, 1799, a son of John and Susanna Redel, bapt Salem Luth Ch, Killinger. John and Susanna (Umholtz) Redel had these known children (some bapt St. John's "Hill" Ch)**: Sara (Sep 26, 1824 – Jul 14, 1842, bur St. John's Hill Cem); Susanna b Oct 23, 1825; Lydia Anna Greth b Mar 22, 1828; Catharine Menda b Jan 9, 1830; Anna Maria Elisabeth b May 30, 1831; Hannah Angeline b Oct 27, 1832; Elmira b Apr 20, 1835;

John (Feb 21, 1798 – May 13, 1859, bur Union Salem Cem, Bbg), m Anna Maria Margaretha Hoffman (Sep 7, 1796 – Sep 22, 1883), a dau of John George and Rebecca (Kunselman) Hoffman. [This Hoffman family descends from Frederick Ludwig and Catharine Hoffman who settled in Berks County near Rehrersburg. Frederick taught German at the Altallaha Luth Ch during the 1750s. In 1850 John and Anna Mary Umholtz lived in Mifflin twp and in addition to their children they had Mary Buffington age 18 and Harriet Tobias age 2 with them. In 1860, Anna Maria Margaretha was a widow living in Mifflin Twp, and   Rebecca and George William was with her. In the same house, but in separate quarters lived George Harman age 56, wife Margaret 44, Harriet 7, and William 9. They lived next to John's father on one side and John Tobias, Sr. on the other side.More info page 354 in Comprehensive History of Gratz.] **John & Anna Maria Margaretha (Hoffman) Umholt children (some bapt Hoffman Ch):

***Sarah (Mar 3, 1819 – Jan 3, 1890, bur Peace Cem, Bbg) , m Jacob Snyder (Oct 8, 1816 – Feb 19, 1901), a son of John and A. Maria Snyder. Jacob and Sarah lived in Mifflin Twp in 1860.

***Daniel (May 17, 1821 – Mar 16, 1854), m Catharine, **had son Hezekiah** d infant;

***Catharine (Jan 27, 1824 – Feb 5, 1888, bur Old Meth Cem, Bbg), m Jonathan Tobias (Dec 20, 1823 – Jan 17, 1905), a son of John and Barbara (Romberger) Tobias. He served in Co I 177th Regt during Civil War. In 1850 he was a wagon maker and wheelwright. They lived in Mifflin Twp. and in 1870 in Berrysburg. **Jonathan & Catharne (Umholtz) Tobias children**: Amanda b c1846; Harriet b c1848' Catharine b c1850; Winifred; Jacob b c1852, a coach maker in 1870. Mary Alice b c1860;

***John B. b Mar 24, 1826, m Mary Magdalena Hoffman

Jacob (Apr 20, 1832 – Nov 29, 1910, bur Peace Cem, Bbg), m 1852 Sarah Jane Tobias (Mar 9, 1836 – Jun 19, 1899, died of cancer), a dau of John and Barbara (Romberger) Tobias. **Jacob and Sarah Jane (Tobias) Umholtz children**:* Alice b c1852; ****Emma Louisa (Mar 27, 1854 – Sep 1903, bur Maple Grove Cem, E'ville), m John A. Schreiber (Mar 18, 1850 – 1924); ****Hannah b c1856; ****Sara Agnes (Dec 24, 1857 - Jun 11, 1880, bur Peace Cem, Bbg), m John A. Kambel (1856 – 1939); ****John Henry Adam (Dec 21, 1859 – Oct 28, 1945, Bbg), m Ellen Emma Whitman; ****Alice (Jul 27, 1864 – Dec 18, 1883);****Lillian (1864 – 1924), m Jacob Troxell; ****Cora E (Jan 13,1866 –1941), m George E. Troxell, lived in Lykens; ****George Robert (Apr 14,1867 – 1910), m Augusta A. Grosser, lived in Coaldale; ****Clara V. (1872 –1910), m Henry Monroe Kocher b Nov 24, 1889, a son of Cornelius and Sarah (Daniel) Kocher.

***George William (Oct 13, 1837 – Oct 22, 1898),

***Rebecca (1842 – pre Feb 1893), m May 29, 1880 to John Adam Welker (Oct 19, 1855 – Sep 13, 1891), had no children. John Adam Welker later m Hannah Snyder.

**Anna Maria (Nov 11, 1801 – Apr 24, 1825), m c1820 Jacob Matter [More info with Matter family.]

**Catharine (Jan 25, 1805 – Jan 11, 1872, bur St. John's Hill Cem)), m Aug 15, 1824 George H. Schwab (Feb 9, 1802 – Jul 29, 1888), a son of John and Anna (Hetzel) Schwab. [More info with Schwab family]

**Magdalena (Dec 23, 1813 – Feb 6, 1826), of an illness of Schuppebfieber

*BARNARD (Oct 22, 1772 Leb. Co– Aug 18, 1829), m Catharine Rissinger (no dates), said to be a dau of Michael Rissinger. They lived in the eastern part of Lykens Twp., and may be buried at Coleman Cem, but no tombstones have been found. Bernard was a member of the Pa. Militia (1790 – 1800), fought against the insurgents of Western Pa. Orphan court records were filed in Oct 1832, by Michael and Henry Umholtz. In those records only two children are named and they are minors over age 14. They are Hetty and Philip. **Bernard & Catharine (Rissinger) Umholtz children (some bapt Klingers Ch):**

**John b Jan 18, 1796 -
Michael (Feb 18, 1799 – May 27, 1855, bur Coleman Cem), m Rebecca Herman (Mar 2, 1805 – Sep 4, 1830), a dau of Philip and Magd Herman. Michael and his family lived in Lykens Twp. in a two story log house on 14 acres of land. **Michael and Rebecca (Herman) Umholtz children:* Sarah** m Isaac Rupert;*****Catharine** m Jacob Lare?;; *****Elizabeth** b Aug 22, 1825, bapt Hoffman Ch, m Daniel Heim;*****Rebecca** (Aug 28, 1830 – Mar 6, 1907), m Jonathan Hoffman, a son of George and Catharine (Troutman) Hoffman, eventually moved to Wisconsin.

Michael Umholtz m 2nd **Hannah Hollenbach** b Dec 30, 1803 bapt Hoffman Ch, a dau of George and Hannah (Hepner) Hollenbach. **Michael and Hannah (Hollenbach) Umholtz had these children (some bapt Klingers Ch):** **Maria Anna** b Jan 5, 1835; **Susannah** (Aug 15, 1836 – Mar 24, 1888), m Isaac Jacob Coleman ( ), a son of Frederick and Lydia (Shade) Coleman; **Hannah** (mentioned in o/c record) ; **Esther** (Feb 23, 1843 – Aug 7, 1908), m Daniel Artz; **William Henry** (Dec 20, 1844 –1926), m Elmira Savidge; **Daniel** (Jul 27, 1847 – 1930), m Ellen Saltzer.
**Susanna (Apr 17, 1801 – Mar 18, 1861, bur Coleman Cem), m Jacob Walborn (Apr 5, 1799 – Jan 24, 1871. [More info in Walborn genealogy.]
** Anna Margaret (Sep 15, 1803 – Sep 22, 1874), m George Hollenbach (Jun 18, 1799 – May 20, 1870), a son of George and Susanna Hollenbach, and moved to Crawford Co., Pa. [More info in Hollenbach genealogy.]
**Catharine b Nov 22, 1808, m Michael Fisher.
**Solomon (May 26, 1811 –Oct 24, 1890, bur Coleman Cem), m Elizabeth Schoffstall (Mar 31, 1815 – Nov 14, 1882), a dau of John and Magdalena Schoffstall.[More info under Schoffstall genealogy.]
**Philip (Jan 29, 1814 – Aug 29, 1883, bur Tremont) in Pottsville, Sch Co., bur in Tremont, m Susanna Carl.
**Esther (Jun 14, 1817 – May 30, 1882, Harrisburg), m Daniel Emanuel.(1808 – 1902). They lived in Gratz and he was a butcher, later moved to Harrisburg. [More info in book "Comprehensive History Of Gratz."]

*MICHAEL (Aug 31, 1776 – d Jan 7, 1854), moved to Greenwood Twp., Perry Co. He died in Millerstown. There is speculation that he married Catherine Hoover, a dau of Jacob Hoover of Lykens Twp. However, we have not found evidence. He did m Dorothea Anna Lang in Perry Co. Michael and Dorothea Anna **(Lang) had these known children: **John; **Mary** b Mar 29, 1807; ****Jacob; **Rebecca; **William** b c1815.
*JOHN PHILIP (Sep 14, 1779, Mifflin Twp, Dau Co - d Apr 18, 1837, Lyk Twp, bur possibly in Hoffman Cem), m Anna Maria Williard b Jan 10, 1782, a dau of John Peter and Magdalena (Jury) Williard. Philip and Anna Maria (Williard) Umholtz lived in Mifflin Twp. **Philip and Anna Maria (Williard) Umholtz children: **Mathias**(no dates), moved to Starke Co, Ohio, married and had about seven children;**** Susanna**(Jul 11, 1804 - Mar 3, 1874), m Jan 13, 1824 to Daniel Laudenslager (Sep 13, 1792 - Aug 29, 1867), a son of Jacob and Sophia (Rettinger) Laudenslager; [More info in Laudenslager genealogy.]****Elizabeth** (Apr 3, 1806 - Mar 4, 1886, bur Hoffman Cem), m John Peter Hoffman Jr (Oct 27, 1806 - Feb 8, 1887), a son of John Peter and Magdalena (Lubold) Hoffman; [More info in Hoffman genealogy.] ****Margaret** (Jan 10, 1807 - May 13, 1878), death record of Hoffman Ch, apparently not m.; ****Anna Margaret** b Jan 8, 1808 m Joseph Hetrick; ****John** (Dec 10, 1812 - Apr 26, 1882, death recorded in Hoffman Ch, bur Hoffman Cem), m Magdalena Schoffstall (Jun 23, 1817 - Jun 12, 1895), a dau of John and Magdalena (Hoover) Schoffstall. **John and Magdalena (Schoffstall) Umholtz children:**
Mary M. (1835 – 1906, bur with Jacob Reiff) , m 1st William Muench (Jul 28, 1835 – May 16, 1864), a son of Jacob D. and Lydia Muench. He was a Civil War soldier after being discharged started for home. But he and his brothers stopped to swim in the James River in Virginia and drowned May 16, 1864. Mary m 2nd Aug 29, 1868 Jacob Reiff (Jul 27, 1833 - Jun 7, 1879, bur IOOF Cem, in Lykens. He has lately become known for his hand painted plank bottom chairs. A set of six of those chairs were purchased for the Gratz Hist. Society. After Jacob died, Mary lived in Lykens and in 1880 she had the three children with her.**Jacob and Mary (Umholtz, Muench) Reiff children: ****Frank** b c1870;***Agnes** b May 26, 1872; ******Carrie** b c1876.
***John H. "Red" (c1836 – pre Oct 1933, bur St. Pauls Cem, Tower City). Not sure, but believed to be a son of John Jacob and Catherine Umholtz. **John H. Umholtz and Catharine Kocher had a son ****Levi** Umholtz (Aug

30, 1854 – Nov 25, 1933, bur Simeon Cem, Gratz), He was bapt at St. John's Hill Ch, sponsors were John and Catharine (Welker) Kocher. In 1880, Levi lived with the Simon Daniels family and worked in the brick yard. Levi m Anna Maria Radel (Oct 26, 1856 – Sep 14, 1940), a dau of Solomon and Catharine (Shaffer) Radel of Low Mah Twp Northld. Co. **Levi and Anna Maria (Radel) Umholtz children:**
William & *Jennie* d young;
Katie Senora (Aug 8, 1879 – Jul 31, 1956, bur Simeon Cem, Gratz), m William. Calvin Grubb (1876 – May 1949, bur Fairview Cem, Wmstown), a son of Henry and Isabella (Hess) Grubb. **Wm Calvin and Katie (Umholtz) Grubb children**: *Forrest Wm* (1901 – 1941); *Floyd Henry Levi* (1903 – 1963); *Mary Louisa* (1904 – 1988), m 1st John E. Finley, 2nd John Weaver; *Laura Catharine* (1907 – 1993), m John Albert Forney; Mark Calvin (1913 – 1964), m Ellen Lutz; *Esther Naomi* (1915 – 1928, bur Simeon Cem); *Ceylen Delbert* (1918 – 1994); *Jean Eleanor* b 1922.
Laura (Aug 1882 – 1968, bur Simeon Cem, Gratz), m John Henry. Deibler (1880 – 1952), a son of George and Sarah (Betz) Deibler. **John Henry and Laura (Grubb) Deibler children**: Levi Adam (1913 – 1980); Naomi (1915 – 1977); Homer Allen (1916 – 1951, d of heart attack on hunting trip), m Alberta Mae Howard, a dau of Isaac and Hattie (Klinger) Howard; Meda (1918 – 1995);; Chas Edwin (Nov 2, 1883 – Oct 9, 1932, bur Simeon Cem), m Cora Wiest; *Annie Amelia* b Jun 14, 1885 – m Charles P. Zimmerman; *Harry Allen* (Mar 10, 1887 – Sep 1947, bur Simeon Cem), m Minnie C. Stahl (1885 – 1964); *Eva Edna* (Sep 1889 – 1978, bur Simeon Cem), m Thomas H. Kissinger (1889 – 1932); *Thams I* b Jan 1892 – 1982), bur Simeon Cem), m George Frank Deibler (1886 – 1936), a son of George and Sarah (Betz) Deibler; *Homer Levi* (Oct 5, 1893 – 1944, bur Simeon Cem), m Hannah Pruella Shade (Jul 28, 1892 – 1963), a dau of Henry & Martha Jane (Wolfe) Shade. **Homer and Hannah Umholtz had no children**. *Meda Olive* (Nov 7, 1895 – 1993, bur Simeon Cem), m Henry J. Huntzinger (1894 – 1933, killed on Good Spring Mt. in mine accident), 2nd Jay Lahr; *Daisy Viola* (Jan 17, 1898 – 1972, bur Simeon Cem), m Frederick S. Stiely (1896 – 1968).

*** [from above]**John H. Umholtz later married Elizabeth Cline** (Jun 29, 1840 – Feb 25, 1875, bur Simeon Cem). She was living with the John Jacob Umholtz family (the gunsmith) in 1850. In 1860 John H. and Elizabeth Umholtz lived in Lykens Twp. It was a double house, and Catherine Umholtz, widow of John Jacob lived in the other half and had her son Daniel age 25 with her. **John H. and Elizabeth (Cline) Umholtz children:******Jonas or Jonathan (1859 – Dec 24, 1932), m Magdalena Snyder, a dau of Elias and Mary Schneider, moved to Phila where his family continued to live; ****Christiana E. b 1860 d young; ****Eliza b c1862;**** Edmond (Mar 27, 1864 – Jan 25, 1928, bur Wiconisco), m Mary Lily Witmer (Mar 4, 1861 – Jun 6, 1931), a dau of Henry and Amanda (Fegley) Witmer. **Edmond and Mary (Witmer) Umholtz children**: *Charles Edmond* (1884 –1946, bur Wiconisco), m Pamela L. Parson, a dau of Albert and Georgina (Stokes) Parsons, **had these children**: *Charles* b Sep 10, 1920; *Betty Lorraine* b Nov 23, 1922 ; ****Daniel Grant b May 2, 1867, bur Simeon); ****Mary Ann (c1869 – 1949, bur EUB Cem Bbg), Milton Moyer; Emma b c1872; Ellen b Feb 17, 1873.
***[from above] **John H. Umholtz married again – Rebecca Troutman** (May 11, 1849 – Oct 20, 1885, bur Simeon Cem). In 1880, John and Rebecca lived in Porter Twp., Scho Co. and he was working in the mines. They had these children with them: Jonas 22, Edmond 14, Emma 8, Ellen 7, Jane 5, Charles 1. **John H. and Rebecca (Troutman) Umholtz children (some bapt Simeon Ref.):** Charles Milton b Jun 7, 1879, m Vera Abrahamson; Sallie (Apr 29, 1882 – pre 1833); John H (Apr 14, 1884 - ____).

***Emeline (1839 – 1933), m Gabe Percival Schadle. ***Amanda (Nov 15, 1841 – Jan 1, 1922), m Rudolph Busse, an immigrant from Germany in 1878. He had a laundry plant in Lykens, but a devastating fire destroyed the plant that had not been insured. When Rudolph died, Amanda moved to Gratz to live with her sister; ***Josiah M "Jessie" (Mar 8, 1845 – Dec 14, 1894, bur Simeon Cem), m Jul 18, 1869 in Pillow Mary Anne Ritzman (Jan 23, 1852 - Sep 19, 1939), a dau of Daniel and Amanda (Buffington) Ritzman. Josiah was a veteran of the Civil War. During the battle of Gravel Run he received a gunshot wound to the side of his head. **Josiah & Mary Anne (Ritzman) Umholtz children**: Alice Celesta (Mar 13, 1871 – Oct 8, 1922, bur Simeon Cem), m John Henry "Spinny" Kissinger b Jul 30, 1874, a son of Henry and Hannah (Hoffner) Kissinger; Maggie Darella (Feb 8, 1876 – 1961, bur Simeon Cem), m Harry F. Troxell, a son of John and Ann (Rogers) Troxell; Amanda Magdalena b Jan 17, 1879; Carrie Mable b Jan 30, 1881; MaryAnn b Feb 14, 1883; Elsie Louisa (Nov 9, 1884 –Jan 12, 1918, bur Simeon Cem), m Henry Clarence Williard, a son of John and Eliza (Thomas) Williard; Minnie Elizabeth (Jan 14, 1887- c1955), m Jacob Ulsh; Thomas Adam (Dec 16, 1888 – Feb 19, 1919, bur Simeon Cem). Died while serving in the Army during WWI; Annetta Saloma (Mar 7, 1893- Apr 8, 1955, bur Sacramento Cem);, m Homer Coleman; ***Jonathan N (Mar 8, 1848 – Nov 13, 1914, in Phila, bur Simeon Cem), m Mary Magdalena "Maude" Schreiner (Feb 3,1847 – May 14, 1910 of blood poisoning. They lived in Williamstown. **Jonathan & Mary Magd (Schreiner)**

Umholtz children: ****HenryHarrison (1871 – 1954), m Myra Malinda Host, a dau of George Host and Rebecca Dockey;****Ida E. (May 25, 1877 – Sep 27, 1925), m Wilson Walhay; ****Norman Egbert (1881 – 1942); ****Charles, lived in Hbg; ****John E. (1888 – 1902, bur Simeon Cem);****MaryAnnie (1889 – 1897) ; ***Sarah b 1850, m Percival Erdman (Jan 16, 1847 – Dec 23, 1927, bur Lykens); Mary Jane b May 29, 1851; Lusetta (1855 –1856); Henry (1857 –1858); Harriet (Mar 15,1859 –1922), m Clinton Hoffman, a son of Jonas and Sarah (Rickert) Hoffman.[More info in Hoffman & Rickert genealogy.];

**SAMUEL EDWARD (b Dec 14, 1814 Lyk Twp- d Mar 18, 1883, bur Simeon Cem), m Elizabeth Harner (b Jun 1, 1820 - d Sep 6, 1855), a dau of Frederick and Mary Harner of Gratz. Samuel and Elizabeth (Harner) Umholtz had these children:

***Maria (b Feb 19, 1842 - d Dec 17, 1843)

Emanuel (b Jul 30, 1843 (the pension record say Aug 5,) – Sep 16, 1904, bur Simeon Cem), m by Rev. Shindel on Oct 23, 1866 Mary Hartman (Sep 7, 1840 - Dec 13, 1908) a dau of Henry and Magdalena (Schoffstall) Hartman. At the age of 15, Emanuel moved to Ohio, but after a year returned to his home. He had been farming most of his life, except for the period when he was in the military during the Civil War. In 1904 after Emanuel died, Mary applied for a pension. Witnesses mentioned that she had no realestate, and the only personal property she had was two horses, some farming implements and house furnishing goods, worth about $350.Her grandson was living with her and by using her team of horses provided the only income she had. Emanuel and Mary (Hartman) Umholtz children:*Isaac Monroe (May 15, 1867 – Oct 25, 1901, bur Simeon Cem)), m Nov 2, 1884 Emma Cecilia Willard (Mar 1, 1867 - ___), a dau of John L. and Eliza (Thomas) Williard. had one child Elmer;****Ida Elizabeth (Jul 29, 1869 – Apr 19, 1937), m George F. Daniel (1864 – 1943), a son of George and Elizabeth (Hoffman) Daniel, had these children: Charles b 1892; Edna (no dats, m LeRoy William.

***Isaac (1845 – Apr 2, 1865, killed in battle at Gravely Run, while serving in Civil War, bur Poplar Grove Nat'l Cem, Petersburg, Va)

***Sarah b 1847, m Henry M. Ritzman, had son Edward b 1877.

***Henry (1848 – 1851, bur Simeon Cem)

***Mary Ellen (Oct 21, 1849 – Jan 2, 1915), m Elias Klinger

***Louisa (1851 – after 1896), m Jacob Zimmerman of Williamstown;

***Edward Lloyd (Jul 15, 1853 – Jul 4, 1936, Kansas). In 1860, Edward lived with Peter and Mary Schoffstall. In 1880 he married Catherine E. Buffington (Jun 1, 1860 – Jan 23, 1929), a dau of Samuel and Sarah (Umholtz) Buffington. In Mar 1896, Edward and Catherine Umholtz moved to Iowa and later to Newton, Harvey Co., Kansas. After Elizabeth Harner Umholtz died, Samuel m 2nd Abby Maurer on Apr 5, 1857, but she deserted him a few weeks later in May 1857. Dauphin County court granted Samuel Umholtz a divorce on Aug 22, 1859. Samuel Umholtz was married the 3rd time to Elizabeth Ginter (Dec 8, 1823 – Jul 5, 1882), a dau of John and Christiana (Moyer) Ginter of Washington Twp, near Oak Dale Forge. Elizabeth had been married to Cyrus Buffington (1821 – 1856), a son of George and Catherine (Yeager) Buffington. Both Elizabeth and Cyrus buried in Peace Cem, Bbg). Samuel and Elizabeth (Ginter, Buffington) Umholtz children:

***Adaline (Aug 8, 1860 – Jan 19, 1916, bur Simeon Cem), m George Adam Welker (Sep 21, 1862 – 1933). For more info see Welker genealogy.]

***Harvey C. (Jun 2, 1862 – Jul 12, 1888, bur Simeon Cem). He was killed in a mining accident. He m Kathryn Welker, and they had a child: Harry M. (1883 – 1947)

***William P. (Aug 1865 – Jan1923), m Catharine N. Thomas (1872 – 1916), a dau of Edward and Elizabeth (Hoffman) Thomas. William and Catharine (Thomas) Umholtz children; Carrie Elizabeth (Nov 20, 1893 – 1955), Walter Franklin (1900 –1981), Clayton Jacob (1903 – 1990), m Jun 23, 1934 Hannah C. Buffington (1907 – 1971), m 2nd 1978 Thelma Ruth Parmer; Florence Margaret (1905 – 1975), m 1929 Harrison Isaac "Jack" Sitlinger, a son of Samuel and Bertha Sitlinger; Grace Ethel (1907 – 1979), m Elwood Romberger.

** CHRISTIAN (b Apr 26, 1818 Lyk Twp - ___), m 1841 Sarah Matter , a dau of Michael and Sarah (Crum) Matter. They moved to Mercer Co.

**PETER b May 17, 1820, prob. died young;

**CATHARINE b Mar 20, 1822, m Isaac Henninger b Apr 12, 1821, a son of Sebastian Henninger. They moved to Stark Co., Ohio.[More info under Henninger genealogy.]

*HENRY UMHOLTZ, JR. (b Sep 17, 1783 Leb Co - d Dec 18, 1829), m Susanna Hoover (1787 – after 1860), a dau of Jacob and Catharine (Sierer) Hoover of Lykens Twp. After her husband Henry died, Susanna m Jonas Schoffstall, but the marriage ended in divorce. **Henry and Susanna (Hoover) Umholtz children:**
**ELIZABETH b Sep or Oct 1806 -
**JOHN (b c1809 - d ___ after 1850),lived with his mother, and was recorded on the 1850 census. John was retarded, and had special mention in his grandfather Jacob Hoover's will.
**MARGARETA REBECCA (Dec 25, 1810 - May 13, 1896, bur Simeon Cem), m John Benjamin Gise (1806 – 1884), a son of Nicholas Gise. Margaret and John Gise lived on a farm that she received from her father. [More info in Benjamin Gise genealogy.]
**LEAH (Feb 7, 1815 - Jan 28, 1888), m George Washington Ferree (Nov 21, 1810 – Jan 5, 1873), a son of Isaac and Elizabeth Ferree. IMore info with Geo Wash. Ferree writeup and Ferree genealogy.]
**MARY (Apr 20, 1822 - Sep 1, 1881, bur Evang Cem, Berrysburg), m John Henninger (Aug 2, 1818 – Sep 6, 1900, bur Berrysburg). [More info in Henninger genealogy.]
**HENRY (Jul 1, 1825 - d Jun 29, 1906, near Ritzman, Sch Co), not married. He was a teacher for many years in the Lykens Twp and surrounding schools.]

*ANNA MARIA UMHOLTZ (Jun 6, 1785 – Dec 15, 1860, bur St. John's Hill Cem), m Peter Yertz (Mar 19, 1792 – Jun 10, 1866). He served in the War of 1812. **Peter and Anna Maria (Umholtz) Yertz children:**
**PETER;
ELISABETH (May 7, 1816 – Aug 9, 1874, bur Hoffman Cem), m Peter Bohner (Oct 10, 1817 – Nov 7, 1890), a son of Henry and Maria Elizabeth (Brosius) Bohner. **Peter and Elisabeth (Umholtz) Bohner children: ***Henry (1841 – 1908), m Catharine ___ (1841 – 1919);
JOHN (Nov 27, 1817 – Apr 26, 1888, bur St. Johns' Hill Cem), m Feb 18, 1855 Christiana Webner (May 29, 1829 – Mar 25, 1893), a dau of John and Christiana (Heiser) Webner. They lived in Elizabethville in 1860. **John and Christiana (Webner) Umholtz children: ***Daniel Henry (Apr 10, 1855 – Apr 7, 1924); *****Mary Christiana** (1858 – Sep 11, 1935), m Mar 13, 1883 John Weaver; **Ryanna Septima** (Nov 25, 1859 – Jan 9, 1946); **Frances Rebecca** (May 29, 1865 – May 11, 1887)
ANNA (Jul 29, 1828 – Dec 14, 1895, bur St. Johns Hill Cem), m Michael Zimmerman (Sep 19, 1826 – May 17, 1886). **Michael and Anna (Umholtz) Zimmerman children:*Emaline Jane** b Jun 15, 1854; *****Aaron Silas** (Aug 13, 1857 – Dec 30, 1890), m Aug 5, 1877 Agnes Miller; *****Edward** b Nov 28, 1873.

THE CARL FAMILY

[**CONRAD CARL** (probably b Nov 5, 1766, a son of Conrad and Magdalena Carl of Lancaster Co.), m Elisabeth _____ . **Conrad and Elisabeth Carl children (some bapt Hoffman Ch):**
*Jeremiah b 1800, m Juliana Radel b Mar 19, 1803, a dau of John Radel of Berrysburg. **Jeremiah and Juliana (Radel) Carl children (some bapt St. John's Hill Ch): **Elisabeth** b Feb 21, 1827; ****Catharina** b Mar 1, 1832; ****Daniel R.** (Jul 6, 1834 – Aug 10, 1894 bur St. Johns' Hill Cem), m Nov 21,1858 Catherine Row (Mar 12, 1840 – Sep 18, 1873), a dau of Jacob & Susanna (Matter) Row . **Daniel and Catherine (Row) Carl children:***** Daniel R. (Apr 25, 1870 – Dec 27, 1936), m Ellen Bordner (Jun 18, 1874 – Feb 6,1937), a dau of Wm and Susannah (Runk) Bordner of E'ville. **Daniel R. & Ellen (Bordner) Carl children:** Hattie; George; Elsie; Clara; Norman & Ethel (twins);*****Catherine** b Feb 27, 1873; *****Walter Clayton**; *****Ellie**; *****Herman**; *****Charles**; *****Daniel F.** Daniel Carl m 2nd Hannah Reigle b Sep 1824. Daniel Carl m 3rd Oct 9, 1879 to May E. Hoy (Jun 2, 1857 – 1933) both were from Williamstown. They had a dau *****Hannah Louisa Daisy** bap Feb 22, 1880.
**George (Feb 22, 1837 – Sep 5, 1881)
**Jeremiah R. (b Aug 4, 1841 – d ____), m May 2, 1865 Caroline Klinger b Jan 21,1844, a dau of John Adam and Lydia (Dornheim) Klinger. They lived in Williams Twp in 1880 where he was a farmer, also a potter and plasterer, engaged in the lumber business. Mary Kramer age 16, lived with them in 1880, and was listed as a servant.
Jeremiah and Caroline Carl children: **Lincoln Calvin. (1866 – 1950, bur Fairview Cem, Wmstown), m Dec 4, 1888 Anna L. Curtis (1870 – 1960), a dau of Charles F. Curtis; ****James Abram Garfield** (no dates), owned a hotel in Williamstown, and drove stage coach between Millersburg & Pottsvile; ****Hattie Cordelia.** b c1879.
**Susanna b Dec 7, 1859
*Peter b Jan 29, 1804, m Nanse _____ ;
*Daniel b Sep 1, 1806]

THE WEISS FAMILY

[**ANDREW WEISS** (Feb 12, 1828 - Jan 16, 1903) m Charlotte Wentz (b Apr 1, 1828 - d Jul 9, 1893 of pneumonia). Both Andrew and Charlotte Weiss were born in Baden, Germany. They came to America in the mid-1800s, eventually settling in Lykens Twp. Andrew worked in the mines. Charlotte was a dau of Conrad and Catherine Wents. She came to America with her parents in 1852, and they settled in Tremont, Pa. area. Charlotte and Andrew married in June 1855. **Andrew and Charlotte (Went) Weiss had six sons and five dau, only three of the children survived their parents. The known children:**
*CATHERINE b c1855;
*JACOB (May 29, 1857 - Oct 10, 1881). When the 1880 census was taken, it was noted that Jacob was "sick by fall of coal." Perhaps the incident led to his death;
*CHARLES (May 15, 1858 - Mar 13, 1936, bur Simeon Cem), m Henrietta C. Evitts (Sep 13, 1861 - Oct 30, 1936), a dau of (Capt) Benjamin J. Evitts (Sep 20, 1822 - Mar 30, 1909) and his 1st wife Ann Yeager (1820 - 1876). **Charles and Henrietta (Evitts) Weiss children:**
STELLA (1881 - 1921), m Apr 5, 1902, Howard M Heller (1877 - 1943), a son of Philip and Mary M (Matter) Heller of Loyalton, both bur Simeon Cem. **Howard and Stella (Weiss) Heller children: ***Earl L. (1902 - 1977); ***Erma Olive b Jan 20, 1905; ***Stanley E. (1908 - 1940); ***Eston W. (1912 - 1977), m Edna Sitlinger, had a son ****Dennis; ***Myrtle N m Donald Wiest.
WALTER CHARLES (Jun 1884 -1959, bur Simeon Cem), m Apr 14,1906 Sarah A. Lebo (1887 - Jan 8, 1938). **Walter & Sarah (Lebo) Weiss children:*Melvin Edw b Mar 24, 1909; ***Albert; ***Charles.
**ERMA (Jul 8, 1886 - 1933), m Mar 2, 1906 James F. Mace (1886 - 1961), both bur Simeon Cem. **James F. and Erma (Weiss) Mace children: ***Chester Emanuel b Mar 26, 1908; ***Hannah Catherine b Nov 13, 1914; ***Beatrice Erma b Jun 6, 1921; ***Herbert Henry b Feb 19, 1925; ***Betty Alverta b Mar 25, 1929.
**SALLIE OLIVE b Dec 30, 1889, m Apr 20, 1918, Charles A. Sitlinger, had one child: ***Charles Clayton b May 14, 1920, m Frances Ferree. C. Clayton and Frances (Ferree) Sitlinger children: ****Celin L. b Dec 23, 1943, m Ruth Dunmoyer, a dau of Boyd and Helen Dunmoyer of Gratz. Celin and Ruth (Dunmoyer) Sitlinger children: Leonard b Sep 21, 1971, m Jessica Lee Erdman, a dau of Donna and Greg Erdman, lives in Lykens Twp; Angeline b Jun 23, 1975, lives in Gratz.
**BENJAMIN A. (May 15, 1893- 1964), m Feb 22,1918, Mary Ellen Reigle (1895 - 1968), both bur Simeon Cem., and had a dau ***Arlene b c1819.

**HENRIETTA CATHERINE (Jul 14, 1905 -1982), m Emory I. Sitlinger (Feb 19, 1903 - 1991), a son of Alvin C and Mary Etta (Daniel) Sitlinger. **Emory & Henrietta C. (Weiss) Sitlinger children: ***Hilda Marie(b Jun 11, 1924; ***Arlene Eleanor b Sep 3, 1925; ***Robert Arland b Apr 5, 1927; ***Russell Benjamin b Jun 14, 1929; ***Carl Richard b Aug 16, 1931; ***Phyllis Marian b Mar 31, 1934; ***Evelyn Pauline b Jul 12, 1937; ***Wayne LaMar b Jan 7, 1941; ***Alvin Clayton b May 21, 1943; ***Bonita Carolyn b Jan 18, 1945; ***Margaret.

Photo below: standing l to r: M. A. Shade, Ben Weiss. Sitting: Joe Schoffstall

After Charles Weiss received this land, he sold a tract of twenty-two acres one hundred thirty eight perches December 14, 1908 to Howard H. Heller, his son-in-law. He sold other tracts of woodland to several other people.

Charles Weiss owned the remainder of the farm for many years until his death that occurred March 13, 1936. In his will, Charles Weiss requested that his son Benjamin be given the opportunity to purchase this farm for $4200.00 if he wished to have it. (Ben and his wife had already been living here in 1920.) Benjamin Weiss did

On January 12, 1949, Benjamin A. and Mary E. Weiss sold the farm and acreage (except the part that was sold to Howard H. Heller, and a few small tracts), to Albert and Martha Morgan of Pitman, Schuylkill County. The land was bordered on the east by lands of the late Andrew Schmeltz, Henry Grimm, Emanuel Umholtz, south by land of Isaac Sitlinger, George Moyer estate, Josiah Hoover, west by land of Henry Boyer, Frank Boyer, north by Daniel Buffington, F. P. Ferree and John W. Hoffman. Members of the Morgan family continue to live there.

When the Morgan's purchased this farm, a nearby spring was fed by a pipe line from the mountain, and provided their household water. Soon after they moved into the house, they installed indoor plumbing. Shutters that had been on the windows were removed and new siding was installed. The house is of old construction, but is not log. About 1986, Martha Morgan purchased a lot from Lottie Kissinger, located along the Specktown Road. She had a ranch style house built and lived there until recently.

[ALBERT L. MORGAN (Jul 23, 1912 - Mar 3, 1979), was a son of Arthur and Carrie (Stehr) Morgan of Pitman, Pa. He m Martha Rebuck b Mar 10, 1914, a dau of Joseph and Katie (Wolfgang) Rebuck. Albert LEWIS and Martha (Rebuck) Morgan had one son: ALBERT NORWOOD b Aug 22, 1934, m Margaret Weaver b Jan 12, 1938, a dau of Erma Weaver. Albert N. and Margaret (Weaver) Morgan children: David b Jan 12, 1958, m Susan ____ ; Kathy b Jul 28, 1960, m George Saltzman]

JESSE UMHOLTZ LAND – 1875

The 1875 map shows Jesse Umholtz as the owner of a tract of land situated south east of the property of John Umholtz. It was noted on an early document as being a distillery. We have not been able to locate a deed for this property. It apparently was merged with another tract of land and is no longer identified.

TWIN CEDARS GUN CLUB PROPERTY
(Andrew Schmeltz Farm - 50 acres

Home Of Twin Cedars Gun Club

This land was part of several original tracts that were warranted to several individuals by Commonwealth of Pennsylvania. One part of this land is from a tract that belonged to John Fegely. Prior to his death, John Fegely wrote his will in which he named Leonard Reedy, the executor. In his account book, Leonard Reedy made a notation on the page for John Fegely's record: "Sep 26, 1831 for going to Harrisburg on October 25th to take the will with (accompanied by) John Salada." He had to make another trip to Harrisburg on October 25th "to proof the will and deliver the appraisement." This time Benjamin Merkel accompanied him. Leonard Reedy did not list a charge in the book for this duty, but the following year April 1, 1833, he gave credit to Widow Fegely for a hog. The hog weighed

191 pounds and the going rate was five cents per pound. On April 6, 1835, part of the land of John Fegely, consisting of eighty-two acres with house and barn was conveyed to Frederick Lubolt.

Another piece of land John Salada sold to Frederick Lubolt on March 8, 1842. The third piece of land was sold by sheriff sale to Frederick Lubolt on May 1, 1845. In 1849 Jacob Rettinger was a tenant on this property, which consisted of a log house and bank barn. Frederick Lubolt conveyed all three of these tracts, containing 139 acres 77 ½ perches of land to Andrew Schmeltz, Sr. before 1855 when Andrew Schmeltz was assessed for the property that was in "middling" condition. His son Andrew Schmeltz, Jr. was living here. Several years later, on June 6, 1857, Andrew Schmeltz, Sr. conveyed this property to his son Andrew Schmeltz, Jr. In 1858, Andrew, Jr., a farmer, was assessed for sixty-nine acres of land with log house and log bank barn. The other seventy acres were unseated.

Another small tract of land was part of a warrant to Henry Umholtz in 1787, patented to Philip Umholtz in 1831. John Umholtz inherited the land in 1840, and on April 18, 1877, John and Magdalena Umholtz sold 7 acres, 35 perches of their land to Andrew Schmeltz.

The old log house (dating to the early 1800's) and log bank barn stood several hundred feet to the west of the present brick house. It was on the tax record as late as 1864, having survived at least several years past the Civil War period. But by 1883, fifty acres with brick house and a barn were noted on the assessment record. Another seventy-nine acre tract and two smaller ones were also assessed. The family remembers that the bricks for the house were made from clay found on the property. The present barn was built in 1917, but the old one stood nearby for sometime before it was torn down.

Barn Built In 1917

Members of the Schmeltz family recall several family memories that have been shared from generation to generation. One of the earliest memories is that during the Civil War period, officials of the draft board came to the house to recruit men for the service. The family gave a team of horses in place of one of the boys. Later, the recruiters returned, and accepted another team of horses in place of the son.

Andrew Schmeltz and his wife lived here for many years. In August 1899, a local newspaper printed a piece relating the names of the oldest people in the area. Andrew Schmeltz age 75, and his wife age 70 were included in the list. During their later years, Agnes Haldeman came to live with her grandfather. She was only nine years old at the time, but she was needed to take on the chores of a domestic housekeeper. She continued to live there until her marriage. During those years, she attended Geise School. But first thing each morning she prepared breakfast for the family, and whatever was left (sausage, etc.), became her lunch along with a piece of bread. A neighbor usually stopped to give her a ride to school on a horse.

When Agnes became older, she met Harry Kaufman, who came courting. He rode to her house from Sheridan on his bicycle. One Sunday, Harry and some buddies came to see her, and were told that Agnes had gone to Simeon Lutheran Church in Gratz, to attend a meeting (probably Sunday School). The boys came to Gratz, and one friend advised Harry to throw his hat through the window to get her attention. He did, but then he went in to retrieve it, and decided to stay. The friend was left alone. When Harry and Agnes married, several bolts of clothe to make dresses, and a new pair of shoes was one of their wedding gifts.

In later years, the Kaufman family drove over from Sheridan to visit their family here. They came in their Model T Ford, and the children thought their extended family was wealthy because they served two kinds of meat at their dinners. Agnes was not pleased with some of her childhood memories, and in those later years, going to Gratz was almost like a punishment.

On April 21, 1913 Andrew Schmeltz conveyed the seven plus acreage to Claudia C. Adams. Claudia C. Adams sold the same to Jonathan Schmeltz and Andrew Schmeltz in 1914.

Andrew Schmeltz penned his will in 1923, and among other things, he states that he "gives to brother Jonathan all my real and personal property." He died several weeks later on March 19th in Lykens Twp. The real estate of Andrew Schmeltz consisted of two tracts. The seven acre, thirty-five perch small tract, and the larger tract containing 139 acres, 77.5 perches. Jonathan Schmeltz was assessed for the land in 1936.

When Jonathan Schmeltz died, his executors conveyed the two tracts containing 139 acres, 71.5 perches, and seven acres, 35 perches, on November 13, 1943, to Mary E. Lentz. Many years later, the heirs of Mary E. Lentz, Leroy L. Warfel, Shirley D. Roadcap, Shirley D. Roadcap and Betty J. Fetterhoff, administrators of her estate conveyed the two tracts of land at a sale conducted June 19, 1965 to Twin Cedar Gun Club the highest bidder. The property in excellent condition, continues to be owned and preserved by the club.

[Mary E. Lentz (1900 – Apr 3, 1965, bur Maple Grove Cem, Elizabethville), **children:** Sarah Sultzbach(1917-1941, bur beside her mother, died from results of a goiter); Leroy L. Warfel m _____ Leffler; Shirley D. Erdman m _____Roadcap; Betty Erdman (b 1939 – 1989) m Eugene Fetterhoff]

THE ANDREW SCHMELTZ/SMELTZ FAMILY
(Some information from Robert G. Fisher)

[ANDREAS SCHMELTZ (b Nov 24, 1797 bapt Apr 9, 1798 1st Ref Ch, in Lancaster Co - d May 23, 1871 in Hubley Twp, Scho Co., bur Klingers Cem, Erdman), m Catharina Haag (Hawk) (b Sep 4, 1802 – d Feb 20, 1889), a dau of J. Mathias & Susanna (Deibler) Hawk. **Andreas and Catharina (Haak) Schmeltz children (most children bapt Klingers Ch):**
*SOLOMON SCHMELTZ (b Jan 31, 1823 Mahantongo Twp., Sch Co – d Aug 6, 1889, bur Hoffman Cem), m Anna Deibler (Oct 4, 1829 – Oct 19, 1891), a dau of Mathias Deibler.
*ANDREW SCHMELTZ (b Aug 14, 1824, bapt Klingers Ch - d Apr 24, 1912, bur south side Simeon Cem), a son of Andreas and Catharine (Hawk) Schmeltz. He m in 1852, Angeline Rissinger (b Sep 11, 1829, bapt Klingers Ch - d Dec 9, 1905), a dau of John and Elizabeth Rissinger. The record of her death in Dau Co Court states that she was a "farmer lady." In 1880, their three sons, Jonathan, Andrew and Daniel lived with them. Also Mary Umholtz age 11, listed as a hired girl. **Andrew and Angeline (Rissinger) Schmeltz children:**
**JONATHAN (b c1852 - d Mar 19, 1923, at 5:45 a.m., according to his will), not married in 1880 and 1900, lived with his parents and was teaching school. Richard E. Kaufman remembers that as a child he accompanied his father, two uncles Jonas and Walter, and grandmother Agnes Haldeman when they came to Jonathan's viewing. It was held in the kitchen of the brick house. He has vivid memories of the darkness of the kitchen which was illuminated only with kerosene lights. Instead of chairs in the kitchen, they had benches for people to sit on.
**ANDREW (b c1855 - 1937), lived with parents in 1880, later m Anna _____.Andrew and Anna Schmeltz had one known child: ***Anna Rebecca b Feb 7, 1900 in Hickory Corners, Northld Co.
HANNAH MARIA (Mar 8, 1856 - Aug 10, 1945), bur Hegins Evang Cem), m Jacob C. Haldeman (Dec 9, 1855 - Feb 14, 1931), a son of John Haldeman. **Jacob and Hannah (Schmeltz) Haldeman children: ***Carrie A. (b May 1877 Hegins, Sch Co - d May 1955, bur Evang Cem, Hegins), m Jeremiah E. Bohner (Sep 26, 1876 - 1949), a son of Jacob and Harietta (Bush) Bohner; ***Agnes Marie (b Jul 8, 1879 Hegins - Dec 13, 1953, bur Tower City), m Harry E. Kaufman (Feb 19, 1881 - Aug 1, 1918), of Sheridan, Sch Co. **Harry and Agnes (Haldeman) Kaufman children:** ****Jean (Jul 12, 1900 - Mar 10, 1978), m m James Wright, had no children: ****Elias Andrew, (Oct 29.1902 - May 21,1988), m Ellen Ann Evans, dau of Roland & Katie (Heckler) Evans. **Elias Andrew & Ellen Ann (Evans) Kaufman children:** Richard Evan, m Dorothy Underkoffler who was killed in an automobile accident in 1978. **Richard & Dorothy (Underkoffler) Kaufman children:** *Kim Agnes* m Robert Hassinger, lives in Berrysburg, **had two children:** *Elias; Kali; Leif Roland* , has dau *Kaitlin,*lives in Michigan. Richard E. Kaufman m 2nd Ruth E. Evans Antes, dau of Charles & Ruth Evans. *Gayle* m Joe Kobulark **had these children:** *Debra, Kathy, Linda, Joseph;* Carrie (no dates), m France Coleman.****Jonas Claude (Jul 29, 1905 - Feb 27, 1979), m Kathy Snyder of Wiconisco, **had one child:** *Clair* ****Walter Paul (Nov 27, 1907 - Jan 7, 1979),m Catherine Seeger, **no children.**

****Mark Clyde (May 22, 1912 - May 21, 1991), m Arna Lebo, has **two children**: *Mark, Valerie*

****Virginia M b Jun 6, 1915, m Albert Otto of Hegins, **has two children**: *Debra, Susie*

Clara Virgie (b Dec 7, 1881, Hegins - Apr 21, 1947, bur Evang Cem, Hegins), m Francis I. Coleman, son of John and Marie (Maurer) Coleman. **Francis and Clara Virgie (Haldeman) Coleman children: ****Bertha** (1900 - 1982); ****Maude** (1901 - 1968); ****John A**. (1908 - 1964); ****Norma** (1912 - 1990);*Helen** b 1914; ****Roy** b 1917; ****Jean** b 1921.
***Edwin (1884 - 1885);
***Nora (1886 - 1887);
***Rufus Jacob (b Feb 13, 1890, Hegins - d Sep 3, 1964), m Sadie Ellen Williard, dau of Henry and Amanda Williard. **Rufus Jacob and Sadie Ellen (Williard) Holdeman children: ****Leona Hazel** b 1914; ****June ****Marcella** b 1918.
***Annie (___ - Nov 10, 1975, Cape May Court House, N.J.), m Lennel D. Ludlam of New Jersey.
***Clayton E. (Dec 27, 1897, Hegins - Feb 22, 1966, bur Evang Cem, Hegins), m Jun 2, 1917 in Hegins to Estella Laura Sausser (1899 - 1992), dau of Harry and Carrie (Alvord) Sausser. **Clayton E. and Estella (Sausser) Holdeman children: ****Roy** Pershing "Shad" (1918 - 1982); ****Hazel** Naomi b May 28, 1919.
**SARAH b c1859
CATHERINE "KATE" (b Dec 22, 1858 – d May 12, 1946, at home of son Clayton, Hegins, Pa.), m Jorias "Jonas" Hartman, son of Simon and Hannah (Deibler) Hartman. **Jorias & Catherine (Schmeltz) Hartman had these children:
***Franklin Andrew (b Sep 30, 1880 - d Jan 14, 1954,Detroit, Mich);
***Edwin (Dec 17, 1881 - Jul 26, 1945), m Dec 17, 1904 Jennie Louisa Welker , a dau of George and Adeline (Umholtz) Welker. **Edwin and Jennie Louisa (Welker) Hartman children: Ray Edward Benjamin** (Apr 21, 1906 - Apr 30, 1996).
***Annie Lera (Jan 21, 1886 - May 18, 1899);
John Norman (Oct 25, 1888 - Jun 4, 1951), m Iva H. Minnich. **John Norman and Iva H. (Minnich) Hartman children: ****William J.** (1915 - 1941); * Clara** b Oct 2, 1920, m Victor Birunas.

***Clara Rebecca (Aug 12, 1891 - Jul 1975), m Mar 22, 1910, Thomas A. Foulk, **had one child: Margaret May** b Aug 10, 1910.
***Clayton Daniel (Jul 13, 1895 - Mar 31, 1965), m Jul 19, 1914, Bessie May Klinger, a dau of Monroe and Elizabeth (Artz) Klinger. Clayton operated the pump that supplied water up the mountain to "Good Spring" Colliery.**Clayton Daniel and Bessie May (Klinger) Hartman children: ****Alma Dorothy** b Dec 12, 1914, m 1st _____ Rickert, 2nd Ernest Hatter; ****Thomas** (Dec 26, 1919 - Feb 24, 1992), m Jul 26, 1943 in Naval Chapel, Phila, Anna Mary Brosius, a dau of Jay Brosius of Gratz, and lived in Gratz. He   served in the U.S. Marine Corp during WWII. ****Jesse** (no dates); ****Robert** b c1932, not married, lives in New   York City, and has been an accomplished actor/musician in plays and shows there.
***Joseph Benjamin (Aug 14, 1900 - Jun 1985).
***Mabel C. (c1904 - Jan 1, 1992), not married

**DANIEL b c1862, with parents in 1880.

*HANNAH SCHMELTZ (b Oct 8, 1826 Low Mahantongo Twp – d May 21, 1918, bur St. Pauls Cem), m Simon Coleman (b Nov 27, 1823 – d Oct 24,1853, in Lykens Twp, bur Simeon Cem, Gratz), a son of Johannes and Anna Marie Coleman. Simon was a blacksmith. He died of fever. In 1880, Hannah was living in Hubley Twp, and Lydia Runkel age 15, her niece lived with her. **Simon and Hannah (Schmeltz) Coleman children: **Elizabeth** b Mar 17, 1852; **Elias** (b Apr 19, 1860 – d May 14, 1916, bur Artz Cem, Sch Co), m Polly ____ b c1862. They lived in Hubley Twp in 1880, and had Lewis Miller age 16 with them.

*ELIZABETH SCHMELTZ b Nov 20, 1828 – d Aug 6, 1888, bur Klingers Cem), was 1st wife of Edward Frederick Wiest, (b Jan 18, 1828 Sacramento, Sch Co – d Jan 29, 1909, bur Klinger Cem), a son of Daniel and Justina (Fegley) Wiest. Edward and Elizabeth were married November 29, 1848, and resided on a farm near Klingers Church, where he was a farmer. After his father died, Edward became the tavern keeper at WIEST HOTEL in

Klingerstown. This hotel was established when the early pioneers began to settle in this area. It was located at the junction of the Pine and Mahantongo Creeks, and is said to be the location of an Indian village. **The History of Pottsville And Schuylkill County** by Joseph Henry Zerby mentions that an Indian carved the figure of a spead eagle on a giant sycamore tree, that stood on the banks of the Pine Creek near the hotel. The sycamore was destroyed during a severe storm in the 1870's, but the tavern took on the name "Spread Eagle Tavern" as the trademark of the Wiest family hotel.

Edward Wiest was a Civil War veteran, having served in Co. A. 50th Pa. Vol. Infantry. He was promoted to Lieutenant and served in many conflicts from November 1861 to November 1863, honored for his meritorious and gallant service.

Edward Frederick and Elizabeth (Schmeltz) Wiest children: **Daniel Andrew b Mar 1, 1849 (date from father's pension record), lived in Treverton where he was a mine foreman; **Catherine** b Jul 20, 1850, m 1st James Rhodes who died very young, m 2nd Pulaski Gensel.

After Elizabeth died, Edward Wiest married October 5, 1889 in Tremont to Caroline (Haas) Moyer, widow of Nathan Moyer. In February 1909, the second wife applied for a soldier's pension. One witness, Isreal Daniel, made a statement in behalf of the widow, noting that he was well acquainted with them. He states that he was personally acquainted with Elizabeth Wiest, first wife, and that Elizabeth and Edward attended church and Sunday school at Klinger's church. He was present and led the singing at Elizabeth's funeral.

*CATHARINE SCHMELTZ (Sep 18, 1830 – Oct 2, 1906, bur Simeon Cem), m Jacob Shade (1831 – 1891), a son of Jacob and Anna Mary (Klinger) Shade. [See write-up of Jacob Shade on Mrs. Corrine Shade property]
*JONAS (JONATHAN) SCHMELTZ (b Mar 7, 1833 – d Apr 9, 1911, bur Klinger's Cem), m Magdalena Masser (1835 – 1893)
*SUSANNA SCHMELTZ (b Mar 18, 1836 – d Oct 7, 1863, bur Klinger's Cem), m Jacob Merkel Wiest (Apr 8, 1835 – Feb 3, 1915), a son of Johannes Merkle and Catherine Wiest.
*JACOB SCHMELTZ (b Mat 16, 1838 – d Dec 5, 1916, bur Red Cross Cem, Northld Co), m Barbara Hoffa.
*LOVINA SCHMELTZ (b Sep 5, 1840 – d Dec 13, 1905, bur Klinger's Cem), m John Miller b 1843
*ELIAS SCHMELTZ (b Jan 26, 1844 - d Dec 13, 1898, bur Klinger's Cem), m Alice E. Tobias (b Jan 31, 1857 – d Feb 21, 1932). In 1900, Alice was living in Lykens Twp., and her children lived with her: Richard b 1877; Mary b 1879; Amelia b 1880; Elias b 1884; Joseph b 1891.

THE SPECKTOWN ROAD TO GRATZ

The last property described above, borders on the line that separates Lykens Township from the Borough of Gratz and is the end of Indian Trail. From here it is necessary to back tract and locate the old John Hoover estate containing 109 acres as described on the 1875 map page 406. (The present owner is Robert Rodichok). This property although visible from Specktown Road is accessed by a road which branches off to the right from South Crossroads Road. Other farms and properties located on the south side of Specktown Road as well as those scattered along the north side between Specktown Road and Route 25 will be described in this section.

ROBERT J. AND JEAN L. RODICHOK LAND
Est. OF JOHN HOOVER JR IN 1875 - 109 ACRES)
101 acres 23 perches & 8 acres 125 perches, total 109 acres 148 perches

This land is part of two separate tracts that were conveyed by Commonwealth of Pennsylvania to the Hoffman family. One tract was patented February 26, 1796 to Peter Hoffman Jr. He conveyed the same tract on August 10, 1799 to Nicholas Hoffman, whom with his wife Margaret conveyed the same with appurtenances and buildings to Jacob Hoffman on June 24, 1809. Commonwealth of Pennsylvania patented another tract of land to Nicholas Hoffman on August 10, 1799. Nicholas and Margaret Hoffman conveyed three tracts carved from his conglomeration of land to Jacob Hoffman on June 24, 1809. One tract contained fifteen acres, the second tract contained fifty acres, plus allowances for roads, with appurtenances. The third tract was a plantation with fifty-two acres one hundred twenty nine and three-fourth perches.

Over the next several years, Jacob (Sr.) and Catharine Hoffman sold several sections of their land to Amos Hoffman. In 1833 Amos Hoffman received a 15 acres parcel and 52 plus acre plantation. On January 12, 1838,

Amos Hoffman received another fifty acres with appurtenances, and in1843, he received another twenty-three acres, ninety-three perches. This land bordered Christian Moyer, Elias Huber, Henry Hartman and John Huber Jr. land.

Only Building Left On Farm

On March 30, 1850, several days after they purchased another property in Lykens Township, Amos and Amanda Hoffman sold two tracts containing over one hundred nine acres of the above land to John Huber with improvements. They sold the fifteen- acre tract mentioned above to John Huber on March 8, 1847.

The Huber family owned this land for many years. The tax record describes the land of John Huber Jr. in 1855 as having a one and one-half story log house, and log barn. They also owned a carriage. By 1868, this was the estate of John J. Hoover, having the same one hundred nine acres with log house and bank barn.

On March 31, 1917, the heirs of John Huber sold the two tracts (101 acres and 8 acres to Harry C. and Maggie Alberta Deibler of Berrysburg, a grandchild of John Huber. Harry C. and Maggie Alberta Deibler sold both tracts to Frank Hess. On February 23, 1924 Frank and Otta (Lottie) E. Hess conveyed the land known as "the Hoover Homestead" and the 8 acre tract to Morris Albert and Edna Shade. Edna died in 1965 and the farm and tract was transferred to Morris Albert and his son Thomas A. Shade as joint owners.

During the time that the Shade family owned this farm, the terrible hurricane "Hazel" came through the valley and completely wiped out this property. The wind took the barn, and a very large tree in the yard toppled and fell on the house. It was the end of this very old homestead. Since that time, temporary housing has been placed on the farm, and tenants have been living there.

When Morris Albert Shade died in 1979, Thomas A. and Marion Shade became owners and they sold December 3, 1981 to Robert J. and Jean L. Rodichok, the present owners.

[John Hoover (Sep 24, 1817 - Aug 29, 1866, bur Hoffman Cem), was a son of John Hoover, Sr. (Sep 17, 1796 – Mar 17, 1877) and Maria Margaret "Magdalena" Lebo (Dec 12, 1796 – Dec 20, 1843). He m Elizabeth Riegel (Aug 20, 1820 - Apr 19, 1906), a dau of Andreas and Elizabeth (Stine) Riegel. More information about him in the Hoover genealogy on page 494.]

FARM OF ROBERT J. RODICHOK
(LAST OWNER ELLEN SHADE, JOHN HOOVER SR. OWNED IN 1875)
117 acres 101 perches & 5 acres 107 perches

This land was originally part of the tract that Commonwealth of Pennsylvania granted to the Hoffman family. By about 1843, they conveyed this part of their land to John Hoover, Sr., and in 1847, John Hoover, Jr. was a tenant on his fathers land. From 1855 to 1864 John Hoover, Sr. was assessed for this land with a log house and barn. From 1867 to 1873 the property was listed as the estate of John Hoover Sr.

On May 14, 1880 the heirs of John Hoover Sr. sold 117 acres, 101 perches of land with appurtenances to Josiah Hoover. The land adjoined the corner of Reuben Riegel, Daniel Buffington, Isaac Zitlinger, Josiah Hoover, Lemuel Row, Reuben Riegel, and the public road. Josiah Hoover was assessed for the house and barn in 1883, and he owned this property for many years.

On December 24, 1921, Josiah Hoover, by then a widower of Washington Twp, sold five tracts of land to his son Edmund Hoover of Washington Township. Three of the tracts were in Lykens Township. The first tract was the 117 acres101 perches, that came from the heirs of John Hoover in 1880. Two others located on the north side of Short Mountain were small tracts containing ten acres and five acres one hundred seven perches. These two tracts belonged to Daniel Buffington who sold to Josiah Hoover on April 13, 1881.

On March 13, 1929, Edmund and Lillie A. Hoover of Loyalton sold the two tracts (117 acres 101 perches and 5 acres 107 perches) to Jacob D. and Edna Riegel of Gratz.

During the 'twenties and 'thirties butchering was an important event on the local farms. When the "big" day was scheduled, neighbors and relatives in this section of Lykens Township all gathered together to get the work done faster. It was really a kind of social festival. One year after Jacob Riegel purchased a radio, the usual big butchering day was scheduled at Jacob's house. After the work was finished, everyone was sitting around talking and relaxing. Then the radio was turned on, and out came the human voice of someone who was not present. Among the guests at the gathering were Chauncey Riegel who was a specialist in butchering, and Frank Gunderman. Frank was in shock as he witnessed the sound from the radio for the first time. He said "I know this is the end of the world when I hear someone talking but I can't see him."

Jacob was a carpenter, and while they lived here he cut lumber from a stand of oak timber on the land and stored it. Later when they purchased the land on the northeast corner of Crossroads and Route twenty-five, that lumber was used between 1925 and 1928 to build the bungalow style house on that lot.

These two tracts of land were conveyed to the Federal Land Bank of Baltimore on March 20, 1939. The small tract of five plus acres was subject to coal, oil, gas and mineral easements. On July 14, 1943, Federal Land Bank of

Baltimore sold the two tracts of land to Morris A. Shade. The largest tract was a farm containing 117 acres, 101 perches. The second tract contained five acres, 107 perches of mountain land located on Short Mountain.

One Sunday about noon in 1975, a severe thunderstorm came through Lykens Township, and during the storm, a twister touched down and completely destroyed Ellen Shade's barn. Shortly after that, some carpenters were hired, and in the spirit of friendship, many folks from the community volunteered to help to raise a new barn. The men and women gathered, and with all the help, a new barn was soon built. Ellen cooked a dinner for the volunteers, and set up tables in the yard where she served the food to the hungry crew. Alfreda Leffler, one of the concerned volunteers, attended her own mothers' funeral, and then went to Ellen's farm and helped with the project. During the construction, she took numerous photos as the work progressed. Alfreda had actually witnessed the twister approaching the barn from an upstairs window of her home.

New Barn Built For Ellen Shade 1975

After Edna, wife of Morris A. Shade died ownership of the two tracts was transferred on April 20, 1976, to Morris A. and Ellen E. Shade, his daughter. When the father died in 1979, Ellen became sole owner of the farm. She then lived here by herself. Ellen was involved in numerous community organizations including church, Gratz Fair Association and farm organizations.

Ellen has related the fact that her house was of log construction and very well built. She had several experiences dealing with the tough walls. Years ago, she purchased a new stove, and the merchant had a very difficult time drilling through the log wall to insert a pipe.

Knowing that eventually she would not be able to take care of her farm, Ellen made an agreement in 1982 with Robert J. Rodichok to transfer the property to him. She had an option of living in this house as long as she wished. In more recent years, Ellen suffered poor health, and eventually was deceased.

[**MORRIS ALBERT SHADE** (1893 - Jun 15, 1979, bur Simeon Cem), a son of Jacob S. and Elizabeth L. (Ritzman) Shade, m Edna M. Haag (1895 - May 15, 1965), a dau of Charles E. and Emma J. Hawk/Haag of Lykens Twp. Edna's grandparents were Daniel Hawk (Jul 26, 1853 - Nov 19, 1906, bur Simeon Cem) and Sarah (   ) Hawk (Apr 18, 1854 - d Jul 3, 1931). In 1920 the grandmother Sarah Hawk lived with Albert and Edna Shade. **Morris Albert and Edna Mae (Hawk) Shade had two children: Ellen Edna** (Mar 27, 1915 – 200_), not married; **Thomas A.** ( ), m Marion _____]

[**Daniel Hawk** (Jul 26, 1853 – Nov 19, 1906, bur Simeon Cem) m Sarah _____(Apr 18, 1854 – Jul 3, 1931), a dau of _____. They lived in Lykens Twp in 1880. **Daniel and Sarah Hawk had these children:** Charles E b c1873, m Emma J ___ b c1876. **Charles E and Emma J Hawk had these children:** Allen b c1894; Charles G b c1898; John D. b c ___; Edna M. b 1895; Grace; Stella; Daniel M b c1876. More information with the HAWK genealogy;]

THE CHARLES A. SITLINGER GRISTMILL
(Old Original Jacob Huber Gristmill)
Gristmill c1800, New barn c1862 by David Snyder – New house 1864

This tract was part of two tracts of land that Commonwealth of Pennsylvania warranted April 20, 1774, surveyed May 10, 1774 to Andreas Riegle, containing 162 acres, 80 perches. It was patented to Jacob Hoover (Huber) on February 22, 1822

The exact year that Jacob Hoover came to this area is not known. He is not listed on the Wiconisco District tax record for 1780. However, he is listed on the 1790 and 1800 census for Lykens Township (then Upper Paxton Township). The 1798 "window tax" record shows him with a wood gristmill and one pair of stones, a sawmill and small stable. He lived next to John Umholtz and the Wiconisco Creek. The "window Tax of 1798 lists Jacob Hoover again in Upper Paxton Twp on October 1, 1798 under lands "neglected by assessors." He is recorded as having a barn 61 by 30 feet, and living next to William France. However, the record is crossed out.

Jacob was taxed for the property, grist (flour) and sawmill at least as early as 1811, and at that time was listed as a miller. In 1817, he was again listed as a miller having the two mills. In 1820, Jacob and his wife lived alone in Lykens Township, and his son John and family lived as tenants on the mill property.

Jacob Hoover purchased lot number 41 in Gratz in 1818 and owned it until 1838. During the time that he owned that lot tenants George Witman and Jacob Hetrick (perhaps others) lived on the property.

Jacob Hoover was a communicant of Hoffman's church as early September 1811, and frequently attended communion services as documented in the Hoffman church records until March 1833.

This special attention is given to Jacob Hoover because for many years he was thought to be the Jacob Hoover who received a pension for his services in the militia during the Revolutionary war. In the last few years, research has questioned whether he is confused with a Jacob Hoover (same age) of Lancaster County. The Lancaster County resident was born Dec 12, 1756 - died July 31, 1848 – as established on the pension document. Jacob Hoover of Lykens Township was born 1756 - died February 6,1849 according to his tombstone in Hoffman Cemetery. Jacob was said to be physically a very large man, and he lived a very long and apparently useful life. Jacob a resident of Lykens Township wrote his will August 27, 1838, disposing of his estate including his "farm and flour and sawmill, with other buildings thereon," as well as other land in Lykens Township. He named seven children. The most substantial evidence is that the will of the Lykens Township Jacob Hoover was not recorded until February 17, 1849.

A monument in Hoffman Cemetery to Revolutionary War Soldiers, erected by Harrisburg Chapter of DAR includes the name of Jacob Hoover. It is very possible that he did serve, but he is not the one who received the pension.

THE HOOVER / HUVER FAMILY
(Help from Annabelle Hoffman and others – and Tony Hoover whose thorough research discovered the pension discrepancy for the two Jacob Hoover 's of the Revolutionary era. We thank him for sharing)

[The **HOOVER (HUBER)** name originated in Switzerland. Hube meant a measure of land. The name Huber does not appear in a Palatinate town or tax record until the 17th century. In Switzerland they had been prominent land-owners entitled to a coat of arms. They were forced out of the regions around Zurick and Bern in the 1650s by famine, bad harvests, and later for religious reasons. When they moved into France and Germany they were caught in the turmoil there.

JOHANN JACOB HUBER, first of the family to come to America was born in Ittlingen, Germany in 1684, died Aug 26, 1749 in Lancaster, Pa., bur Trinity Lutheran Cem (now removed). He was married in Germany to Anna Barbara _____ (b _____ - d Sep 21, 1749 in Lanc.) They came to America in 1747. **Johann Jacob and Anna Barbara Hoover children (all born in Germany):**

BALTHASAR (bapt Sep 27,1716 in Germany - d Sep 1747 in Montg Co., Pa., bur New Hanover Luth Cem), m Margaret _____. He came to America in 1737 on the "Charming Nancy."

ANNA DOROTHEA CHRISTINA (Sep 1718 - Jul 6, 1795), m Jan 5, 1748, Matheus Gilbert, lived in Lebanon Co., Pa. She came to America with her parents in 1747. **Matheus and Dorothea Christina (Hoover) Gilbert children: George Henrich** b Dec 1, 1748; **George Michael** b Feb 17, 1751; **Frederick** b Jul 24, 1752;

JOHANN PHILIPP DIETRICH (Aug 8, 1722 - Jan 1795, bur St. Peters Luth Cem "God's Acre," Low. Paxton Twp, Dau Co), m by Rev. Casper Stover Nov 1, 1748, Regina Franck, lived in Lanc, Perry and Dau Co. He came to America on the "Francis and Elizabeth" in 1742. Settled first near Strasburg, Lanc Co, and was a weaver. **Philipp Dietrich and Regina (Franck) Hoover had these children: Ursula** b Jul 22, 1749, bapt Trinity Luth, Lanc.; **Catharina** b Mar 13, 1754, bapt St. Michaels Luth, Strasburg, Lanc Co.; **Jacob** (b Dec 7, 1756 , Strasburg, Lanc Co - d Feb 6, 1849, bur Hoffman Cem); **Michael; Christian** b Jan 9, c1760; **John; David; Elizabeth; Anna Margaret.** Philip moved to Cumberland County (now Perry), and lived near Liverpool. He was affiliated with St. Michaels Lutheran Church in 1776.

JOHANN LUDWIG (Aug 4, 1726 - _____), m Jan 23, 1750, Margaretha Graeff, lived in Lancaster Co. He came to America on the "Francis and Elizabeth" in 1742, settled first near Strasburg, Lanc Co.

JOHANN JACOB (May 9, 1730 - _____), m Jan 1, 1750, Susanna Philippina Wetzler, lived in Lancaster Co. He came to America on the "Francis and Elizabeth" in 1742, settled first near Strasburg, Lancaster Co. **Johann Jacob and Susanna Philippina (Wetzler) Hoover had known children: Matthaeus** b Mar 23, 1765.

****

[We have not been able to link Jacob Hoover of Lykens Township to the Hoover family mentioned above. Also we were not able to identify his parents.]

*JACOB HOOVER (b 1756 in Strasburg, Lanc Co - d Feb 6, 1849, in Lyk Twp, bur Hoffman Cem), son of _____, m 1st Eva **Catharine** Elizabeth Sierer (b Mar 22, 1757 Bethel Twp, Berks Co - d c1798, probably bur Hoffman Cem, no stone.), a dau of Jacob Sierer (Jan 23, 1713 – Jan 21, 1785), and his wife Maria Catharine Bender. **Jacob and Catharine (Sierer) Hoover children:**

MARIA MAGDALENA (Dec 10 or 16, 1781 - Aug 18, 1855, bur Hoffman Cem), m John Schoffstall (Nov 15, 1771 - Jul 29, 1843), a son of Peter and Anna Elizabeth (Kornman) Schoffstall. Magdalena received one share of the estate of her father Jacob Hoover. [See write-up of Schoffstall family.]

CATHARINA (Apr 11, 1783 - Sep 21, 1861), m Jun 15, 1800, Johannes George Kissinger (Mar 20, 1775 - Dec 16, 1858). Catharina received one share of the estate of her father Jacob Hoover. [See write-up on Kissinger family.]

SUSANNA (1787 – after 1860, m 1st Henry Umholtz (Sep 17, 1783 - 1829), 2nd Jonas Schoffstall (May 15, 1782 - Feb 23, 1856), a son of Peter and Anna Elizabeth (Kornman) Schoffstall. Susanna inherited a share from her father Jacob Hoover's estate. However, she had to sign a witnessed note, that the share would be divided among her children from her first husband. Her son John received one hundred dollars, and the remaining share was divided among all her Umholtz children, including John. The legacy was made "under the provisions that Susanna should not be in want of the said part during her lifetime." [See Umholtz and Schoffstall history for more information.]

JACOB (Jul 28, 1788 - Dec 25, 1827, bur Hoffman Cem), m Sarah Bellis (no dates). Sarah was listed as a widow on the 1830 and 1840 census for Lykens Twp. When Jacob Hoover Sr. died, he bequeathed fifty dollars to Sarah, and the remainder of Jacob Jr's. share should be divided among his children. **Jacob and Sarah (Bellis) Hoover had these children:**

***Jacob Jr (Apr 17, 1806 - May 2, 1867, death recorded in Hoffman ch record), m Margaret Rickert (Mar 31, 1808 - ____), a dau of Hartman Rickert Jr and wife Catherine (Lubold), Rickert;

***Elizabeth (Feb 27, 1813 - ____);

***Samuel (May 4, 1815 - ____), m Sarah ____ (no dates). **Samuel and Sarah Hoover children:** David (1844 - 1849, bur Hoffman Cem); Ellen Jane b Feb 9, 1846; Jonathan bapt Apr 21, 1848 Hoffman Ch;

MARIA MARY (Sep 30, 1790 - Apr 11, 1869), m Jacob Bordner (Nov 2, 1787- Nov 10, 1854), a son of Wilhelm and Elisabeth Bordner, bapt Altalaha Evang. Luth Ch, Rehrersburg, Berks Co. In 1850, Jacob Bordner age 63 and Mary age 60 lived on a farm with their son William in Jefferson Twp. Maria (mentioned in her fathers will as the wife of Jacob Bordner), received one share of his estate. However, her husband had "book debts" to her father that were to be deducted from her share. If her husband objected, her share was to be put on interest, and the interest to be paid to Maria. After her death, her share should be divided among her children. **Jacob and Maria Mary (Hoover) Bordner children (bap St. John's & Hoffman Ch):

***Catharine (Jun 6, 1811 - 1868, bur Simeon Cem), m Solomon Schoffstall (Nov 25, 1803 - 1866, burial unknown), a son of Ludwig and Rebecca Schoffstall. Solomon and Catharine lived as tenants of Solomon Laudenslager from the 1840s to 1860s in Gratz on the farm now owned by Elam Stoltzfus. **Solomon and Catharine (Hoover) Schoffstall children:** William b c1826, m Susanna ___, child: Franklin Louis b Jul 14, 1853;; Henry b c1835; Elizabeth b c1837; Susanna b c1838; Rebecca b c1841; Mary b c1844; Catharine b c1845; Emma b c1845; Caroline (Jan 15, 1850 - Oct 8, 1892), m 1st Benj Kuntzelman, 2nd Benneville Hoyer.

***Anna Maria b Sep 1, 1812

***Jonathan b Dec 8, 1815

*** Veronica "Franny" (May 18, 1817 - Nov 21, 1889, bur Calvary Meth Cem, Wiconisco), m Michael Shell (Dec 21, 1810 - Apr 1, 1888), a son of _____. Michael and Veronica lived in a small log house in Gratz as tenants of either Theodore or David Gratz until about 1847, then moved to Wiconisco Twp. **Michael and Veronica (Bordner) Shell children:** John b c1835; Samuel H. (1832 - 1905, bur Greenwood Cem, Tower City), m 1st Hannah ____ (1838 - 1895), 2nd Jennie Agnes Welker. In 1870, they lived next to his parents.; Jonathan b c1838, m Louisa ____; Jacob b c1840; Mary Ann b c1843; Aaron b c1844; Elias b c1845, m Mary b c1846, **and had these children:** Sarah b c1867; David b c1868; Sarah Ann b c1846; Michael (1848 - 1916, bur Calvary Meth Cem, Wiconisco); Susan b c1850; Malinda b Oct 1, 1856 bapt Zion Luth Ch, Lykens, her sponsor was Sarah Salada; Julian b c1860.

CHRISTIAN (Aug 24, 1793 - before father), m Catherine Fegely (1794 - ____), a dau of John and Catharine Fegely. Jacob Hoover, Sr. devised one-hundred dollars to Catharine, and the remainder of Christian's share was to be divided among his children. **Christian and Catherine (Fegely) Hoover children:

*** Samuel no dates, was the first superintendent of Short Mountain Colliery. He later lived in Minnesota.

***Catharine b Sep 1812

JOHN (b Sep 17, 1796 in Lyk Twp, d Mar 17, 1877, bur Hoffman Cem), m on May 21, 1819 Maria Margaret "Magdalena " Lebo (Dec 12, 1796 - Dec 20, 1843), a dau of John Adam and Catharine (Gebhart) Lebo. She is usually called Magdalena in the records. John was a farmer, and a miller, and lived on his father's mill property. John received one share of his father's estate. In 1850, John and these children were listed on the census for Lykens Twp: "Joseph," Henry, Rebecca, Thomas. In 1860 John Hoover lived alone, but was in the same neighborhood as his children. In 1870 John lived with his son Josiah Hoover and family. **John & Maria Margaret Magdalena (Lebo) Hoover children:

***John (Sep 24, 1817 - Aug 29, 1866, bur Hoffman Cem), m Elizabeth Riegel (Aug 20, 1820 - Apr 19, 1906), a dau of Andreas and Elizabeth Riegel. In 1860, John Miller age 16 lived with this family. In 1870, Elizabeth was a widow living in her home in Lykens Township, and her three children, Elizabeth, Charles and Mary lived with her. **John and Elizabeth (Riegel) Hoover children (bapt Hoffman Ch):** ****Elizabeth Ann b Nov 11,1846 - 1929, bur Hoffman Cem), m Reily A. Haag (1853 - 1912); ****Charles Alfred (Jun 22, 1850- Mar 28, 1916, bur Hoffman Cem), m Margaret Evitts (Nov 12, 1848 - Sep 16, 1907). **Charles and Margaret (Evitts) Hoover children:** *****Sarah E. b c1871 prob. d young; *****Mary Jane b Oct 11, 1872 m Clayton Haag b c1877, lived in Gratz in 1910 and was a coal miner, but later moved to Phoenix, Arizona. **Clayton and Mary Jane (Hoover) Haag children:** *Blanche E* b c1899; Etta S. b c1906; *****Christiana Alverta b Dec 25, 1873, m Thadeous (?) Witman, and moved to Sunbury; *****William Henry (Feb 3,1876 - Sep 28, 1937, bur Hoffman Cem), m Mar 16,1907, Rebecca Kissinger, moved to Hegins, Sch Co.; *****Walter Elwood b Apr 2, 1878, m Lottie Hoover (1883-1973), a dau of Edmund & Lillian (Wentzel) Hoover; *****Margaret Ellen (Sep 14, 1880 -

Sep 19, 1927,bur Hoffman Cem), m Simon L. Daniel (Oct 1, 1882 - Oct 25, 1926); *****Henrietta Lovera Feb 7, 1884, m Leo Troutman , lived in Fear Not; *****Allen Luther b Feb 23, 1886, m Hannah,, lived Lower Northld Co; *****Florence b 1888, moved to Annville; *****Paul C. (c1895 - 1951, bur Hoffman Cem), m Lizzie Klinger (1898 - 1968); *****Clarence b c1890, lived in Dornsife; One of the dau's (Christiana?),m Wm Moyer of Annville.

****Mary Ann b Mar 19, 1852, m Henry C. Weaver . **Henry and Mary Ann (Hoover) Weaver children:** *****Ann Elizabeth b Nov 18, 1870; *****Arthur ( ), m Anne; *****Maggie Alberta (Sep 20, 1974 - 1961, bur Elizabethville), m J. Harry Deibler (1865 - 1952) of Berrysburg; *****Andy Miles b Feb 24, 1876; *****Henrietta Veerdillia (no dates), m _____Diener of Elizabethville; *****Harry Clayton (Nov 13, 1883 – 1944, bur E'ville), m Elizabeth _____of Berrysburg.

***Anna Maria b Sep 6, 1822

Elias (Aug 3, 1823 - Mar 20, 1900, bur Hoffman's Cem), m 1st Elizabeth Daniel (Sep 4, 1826 - May 13, 1856), a dau of Andrew Daniel Jr and his wife Susanna. **Elias and Elizabeth (Daniel) Hoover children some (bapt Hoffman Ch):** ****Jonas b c1837; ****Elizabeth b c1841; ****Mary b c1843; * Fredrick who died the same day as his mother, and was four months old; ****Susanna b c1842; ****John b c1843;****Sarah (Oct 20, 1845 - _____); ****Edward (Apr 24, 1848 - Oct 5, 1893, bur Hoffman Cem), m Mary N. Gise (Sep 12, 1854 - Nov 13, 1919), a dau of _____. **Edward and Mary N. (Gise) Hoover children;** *****Amanda b c1874; *****Katie Celeste b Oct 29, 1880;*****Zula Edna b Jul 31, 1887; ****Peter b c1847 ****Charles (Mar 1, 1850 - Feb 8, 1929, bur Maple Grove Cem, E'ville), m Leah A. _____ (Jun 5, 1839 - Apr 7, 1909), a dau of _____; ****Lovina b c1851;****Amanda b c1852.

After his first wife died, Elias Hoover m 2nd Nov 11, 1856, Elizabeth Riegel (Aug 20, 1820 bap Hoffman Ch - Apr 19, 1906), a dau of Andreas Riegel. [Note that the marriage records of St. John's (Hill) Ch state that Elias Hoover m Nov 11, 1856, Elisabeth Witman. Perhaps she was a widow?] **Elias and Elizabeth (Riegel) Hoover children: Daniel Franklin** (Feb 17, 1860 - 1931, bur Hoffman Cem), m Amanda Kolva (1863 - 1946), a dau of _____.

Josiah (Dec 28, 1828, bapt Hoffman Ch - Dec 28, 1923, bur Hoffman Cem), m Catharine Schmeltz (b Nov 28, 1835, Hubley Twp, Sch Co - d Dec 6, 1920), a dau of Adam and Catharine (Holdeman) Schmeltz. Josiah was a farmer and huckster, and marketed his produce in Pottsville. It was an overnight trip by horse and open wagon or sleigh. Josiah at one time owned the farm where the original Lykens cabin stood. In 1860, Mary Romberger age 10, and his brother Thomas age 19 lived with the Josiah Hoover family. In 1870, John Hoover age 74, retired farmer (his father) lived with them. Also Edward age 22, and Louisa Burd age 13. In 1880, Josiah was listed on the tax record as a farmer. He and Catharine had in their household, son Edmund age 18, and Christiane Smeltz age 18, listed as a servant.: **Josiah and Catharine (Schmeltz) Hoover had one child ****Edmund** (Jan 28, 1861 - Jul 31, 1947, bur Hoffman Cem), m Lillian Wetzel (Nov 28, 1862 - Aug 1, 1936). **Edmund and Lillian (Wetzel) Hoover children:**** Lottie May (Apr 11, 1883 – 1973, bur Hoffman Cem), m Jul 9, 1900, Walter E. Hoover (Apr 2, 1878 – Nov 23, 1918), a son of Charles & Margaret (Evitts) Hoover. **Walter and Lottie May (Hoover) Hoover children:** *Lilly Margaret* b Jan 10, 1901 m ___ Shappel; *Leah E* b c1904, m ___ Bender; *Emma E* b c1905; adopted *Webster* or Wellington Hoover ;*****Wellington Monroe b Sep 20, 1884, m Alma Bingaman; *****Carrie Alverta b May 12, 1886, m Nov 9, 1901 Harvey Crabb; *****Sula b Jul 31, 1887, m Sep 30, 1905 Edwin Dockey; *****Amelia Catharine b Dec 15, 1889, m Aug 14, 1908, Samuel Spotts; *****Alice Sevilla (Jun 22, 1893 - 1985, bur Hoffman Cem), m John E. Harris (1889 - 1959); *****John Edmund (Oct 31, 1898 - 1930, bur Hoffman Cem) m Anna Strayer G. b 1899; *****Clement Elwood b Oct 16, 1905, m Myrl Grubb; *****Landon Josiah (Jul 2, 1909 - 1958, bur Hoffman Cem), m Faye M. Hoffman b 1911.

***Daniel no dates

***Henry (Jan 1,1834 - Nov 7, 1900, bur St. Paul's Cem, Wayne Twp., Dau Co), m 1859 Amanda Richert(Apr 16, 1838 - Oct 5, 1926), a dau of Martin and Elizabeth (Yerges) Rickert. He grew up in Lykens Twp, and worked with his father on the homestead. After his marriage he continued to live on the homestead for seven years, then purchased a farm in Jefferson Twp, where he and his family lived permanently. **Henry and Amanda (Reichard) Hoover children (some bapt Hoffman Ch, others Zion Luth, Lykens. Henrietta and Isaiah were both bapt same time at Hoffman, those are the dates given):** ****John H bc1857, m Mary J. _____ moved to Halifax Twp; ****Tobias (Jun 1,1858 - Mar 13, 1896, bur St. Pauls EUB, Jackson Twp, Dau Co), m Susan E. ____ (Sep 20, 1859 - Oct 17, 1910); ****Priscilla (b Jul 10, 1860 - d pre-1896); ****Catharina Elisabeth b May 16, 1862, m Aaron Reigle; ****Henrietta Louise b May 12, 1866 - d pre-1896); ****Isaiah b Oct 5, 1865, d young; ****Emma J d young; ****Leander d young

496

****<u>Alfred</u> d young; ****<u>Amanda</u> <u>Margaret</u> b Dec 29, 1871, d Mar 25, 1873, bur St. Pauls Cem); ****<u>Rose</u> <u>Ann</u>, m Charles Palmer; ****<u>Ida</u> <u>Rebecca</u>; ****<u>Isabella</u> d young ****<u>Sadie</u> <u>Ellen</u>.

***<u>Susanna</u> - Dau Co History mentions her - no information

***<u>Rebecca</u> b c1838, m Harry Reiner, who was killed in the mines.

<u>Thomas</u> (Jan 8, 1841 - _____), m Dec 29, 1861 Mary Schreffler (_____), a dau of _____. Thomas and Mary (Schreffler) Hoover children (some bapt Hoffman Ch, some Zion Luth, Lykens): *<u>Charles</u> b c1860; ****<u>Daniel</u> b c1863; ****<u>Martha</u> <u>Jane</u> b Nov 4, 1864; ****<u>William</u> <u>Elmer</u> b Feb 22, 1866;**** <u>Mary</u> <u>Ellen</u> b Aug 31, 1869.

After Eva Catharine Elizabeth Sierer Hoover died, Jacob Hoover Sr. m Catharine Elizabeth Basshart (Nov 26,1776 - Feb 8, 1827), a dau of Johannes and Catharina Basshart, an early settler in this area. Record of the marriage is found in St. Davids Church book, Killinger. There were no children.]

[This **Jacob Hoover** (Jan 2, 1810- May 21, 1885, bur Rife Cem), m Catharine Minnich (Nov 24, 1815 – Oct 28, 1873), a dau of Peter and Anna Maria (Matter) Minnich. They lived in Wash. Twp., has not been connected to the above genealogy. **Jacob and Catharine (Minnich) Hoover children:** <u>Alfred</u> (1836 – Feb 1, 1902, bur Riegel's Cem), m Mary Deibler (Sep 27, 1839- Dec 30, 1907), a dau of Jonas Deibler; <u>Lovina</u> b 1837; <u>Susanna</u> (Oct 25, 1838 – Feb 17, 1855, bur St. John's Hill Cem), m Jacob Hassinger; <u>Anna</u> <u>Mary</u> b 1841; <u>Solomon</u> (Jan 23, 1842 – Apr 4, 1900, bur Rife Cem), m Rebecca Koppenheffer (d Feb 20, 1908, age 65 yrs., 4 mo, 9 da), a dau of Daniel and Veronica (Bordner) Koppenheffer. **Solomon and Rebecca (Koppenheffer) Hoover children:** ____ m John Cooper; ___ m Wm Eisenhower moved to Hope, Kansas; ____ m David Lenker of Curtin; <u>Peter</u> (Jan 23, 1845 – Jan 6, 1869); <u>Nicholas</u> of Rife; <u>Jacob</u> of E'ville; ____ m Charles Klinger, of Annville; <u>Elizabeth</u> <u>Jane</u> b 1847; <u>Ella</u>; <u>William</u> (1864 – 1922, bur St. John's Hill Cem), m Anna Romberger(1870 – 1943); <u>Henry</u> m . 5 sons served in the Civil War, 3 never came home.]

On April 1, 1850, the heirs of Jacob Hoover, Sr. sold a plantation with 205 acres, eight perches of land to Daniel Riegel. The tax record of 1849 describes the property as having a two-story dwelling, log bank barn, a gristmill and saw mill. John Hoover, son of Jacob was a tenant on the land.

Daniel Riegle owned this land only a short time before his death in 1855. During his lifetime, Daniel Riegle served one term as county commissioner of Dauphin County, and one term as director of the poor. After Daniel Riegel died, this land was divided into two tracts.

On April 12, 1852, Daniel Riegel and his wife Catharine sold seventy-two acres, sixty-seven perches of land, including the mills, pond and race to Josiah R. Riegel. The land transferred again on March 30, 1855, when Josiah R. and Amanda Riegle sold sixty-one acres, twenty-six perches, including the mill property to David Snyder. A few years later, complications resulted in a sheriff sale of David Snyder's property containing a two-story house, new bank barn, gristmill and sawmill, and apple orchard to Michael Wirt on August 21, 1862. The following spring, on April 1, 1863, Michael Wirt sold the sixty-one acres, twenty-six perches to John Snyder. On April 1, 1864, John and Catharine Snyder sold the same acreage with mills, dwelling house and barn to Daniel Buffington. Another small tract of land containing one acre, twenty-eight perches became the property of Daniel Buffington. This gave him the milldam, race and water rights to the adjoining spring, which had been passed from Josiah Riegle to John and Elizabeth Hoffman. The two tracts became a total of sixty-two acres, forty-six perches.

[**DAVID SNYDER** (b Apr 5, 1806 – May 28, 1883, bur IOOF Cem, Lykens), m Mary ____ b c1813 - ___), a dau of _____ . David and Mary Snyder lived in Lykens Twp in 1860 and he was listed as a farmer. **David and Mary (___) Snyder had these children:** Abram b c1842; Susan b c1843; Sarah b1844; Isreal (Oct 27, 1845 – Nov 15, 1890, bur IOOF Cem, Lykens), m Melinda ___ (Aug 7, 1846 – Jan 1, 1922); John (May 12, 1846 – Mar 8, 1893, bur IOOF Cem, Lykens), Vet of Civil War Co B, 9th Reg Pa Vol Cav; Wesley b c1848; Charles T. (1853 – 1918, bur IOOF Cem, Lykens), m Dec 7, 1873 Alice Connelly (1852 – 1920); Mary b c1856.]

The "New" House Built c1864

Daniel Buffington was about twenty-six years old, when he purchased this sixty-two plus acres. The existing log house was becoming old and in need of repair. The Dauphin County history mentions that Daniel Buffington erected a dwelling after he purchased the property. The tax record of 1864 tends to agree with the historic account, describing the property as having a log house, bank barn, gristmill and sawmill. Older members of the community remember that an old house stood south of the gristmill. A one-story ranch style house has in recent years been built on the site of the first old house. The dwelling erected by Daniel Buffington is the one built close to the private road that now leads to the mill. (The private road was the early main road leading from Gratz to Loyalton. It was reconstructed during a road project about 19__.) [Daniel Buffington also owned a lot in Gratz, see COMPREHENSIVE HISTORY OF GRATZ page 350.]

Recent Photo Of The House At The Mill

The existing mill is apparently the original one. The Dauphin County History notes that Daniel Buffington owned the mill built by Jacob Hoover. The year 1864 is carved in the plaster above the main entrance, but that may have something to do with the time that Daniel Buffington bought the property. It could also be the time that the roof was raised on the mill making it a two-story property. This gristmill is one of the mill properties that served the area from a very early period. Situated on the banks of Little Wiconisco Creek, it was powered by the flowing water, which fed the millrace, and turned the turbine wheel. In later years during summer dry spells, a steam engine was used for power. Milling was one of the most important industries when the settlers came into the area. It provided the means to turn the farmers grain into flour and meal. In later years, custom grinding was done for farmers who brought corn, oats, wheat or barley to the mill and left with feed for their livestock. The up-and-down water powered sawmill was a landmark dating to as early as the gristmill. Use of the sawmill continued to offer a thriving business until just before the era of 1900.

Daniel Buffington purchased fourteen acres of unseated land soon after he moved here. By 1883, he owned an additional sixty acres of mountain land. But in April 1898, Daniel Buffington moved to Gratz, and his son Irwin Buffington succeeded him in operating the mill. However, Daniel also continued to work at his mill. A local newspaper notes that in August 1899, "while Daniel was engaged at work in the gristmill on his farm, he was overcome by a sudden sickness which rendered him partially unconscious and helpless for sometime." His son Irwin took him home, where he recovered and was able to be about again.

On April 1, 1902, Daniel and Catharine Buffington transferred ownership of the two tracts of land (sixty-one plus acres, with gristmill, dwelling, barn and out buildings, and one plus acre with mill dam, race and water rights), to their son Irwin M. Buffington. The up-and-down water powered sawmill was not listed in the description of the property when it was sold in 1902. It had probably passed into oblivion by then, after about a hundred years of continuous operation. Other buildings known to exist on the early property were a blacksmith shop and icehouse. A small house near the mill may have been the original house on the property. In later years, it served as a residence for tenants who were employed at the mill. Chauncey Riegle lived there for a few years. A large bell stood near the mill, with a rope attached. It was a convenient way for the lady of the house to communicate with her husband and employees who were working in the area.

Another building that once stood within the boundaries of this plantation has also lost its identity. It was a very early frame one-room schoolhouse that served the immediate community for many years. The children received their "common school" education during the week, and attended "Sabbath Day" classes on Sunday at this building. A newspaper piece dated October 31, 1873 notes: "The old frame school house near Buffington mill in Lykens township has been replaced by a substantial brick structure."

[DANIEL BUFFINGTON (Nov 17, 1837 - Aug 11, 1903), bur Simeon Cem), was a son of John E. and Susan (Artz) Buffington. On Oct 28, 1860, Daniel m Catharine Hartman (Aug 1838 - Feb 28, 1923), a dau of Henry and Magdalena (Schoffstall) Hartman. **Daniel and Catherine (Hartman) Buffington had these children: Franklin Henry** (Mar 1, 1861 - _____), m Lydia Ann Ritzman, b Jan 1866, a dau of Jacob and Lydia Ritzman, **had two children:** Raymond Milton b May 1, 1885; May Lydia Catharine (Oct 9, 1891 - Nov 18, 1898, bur Simeon Cem). **Milton Ely** b Jul 4, 1864, m Mary, lived first in Denver, Colorado where he was employed as a real-estate broker. According to an newspaper piece of November 1, 1889, Milton "returned home last week from Wichita, Kansas. He will return to that flourishing town in a few weeks, where he has a position in the bank. Mr. Buffington has been in different parts of the great west during the last four years." Milton later moved to New York City, where he lived at the time of his fathers death; **Irvin Monroe** b spring 1872 - d Feb 23, 1948, bur Simeon Cem), m Lydia A. Miller (1875 - 1944), a dau of Emanuel and Caroline (Klinger) Miller.]

Irvin M. Buffington continued to operate the mill for many years, until about 1915, when he moved to Gratz. He was active in community activities, and served as assistant cashier of the Gratz Bank from 1917 to 1933, He also served as the vice-president of the bank.

After Irvin Buffington moved to Gratz, he rented the farm to tenant farmers. Morris Albert Shade became a tenant on the property for two years. During those two years, Albert used the mill to grind feed for his own livestock. One day while he was turning the flywheel, it backfired and thrust him across the building. This was the occasion that ended the use of the mill.

On December 17, 1935, William Zerby, trustee of the estate of Irvin M. Buffington sold the two tracts containing the mill property, house and barn (sixty-one acres, twenty-six perches, and one acre, twenty perches, a total of sixty-two acres, forty-six perches) to Charles C. Sitlinger.

The Sitlinger family never used the mill. But after they owned it, boys from the neighborhood frequently became curious about the interior of the building. It was also considered a challenge to find access to the second floor of the mill. One time several boys climbed up over the wheel, and were able to get inside. When they reached the interior, the thing that they found most attractive was the number of old calendars hanging on the walls. Getting back down over the wheel proved much more difficult then getting up! During earlier years, the creek usually had an abundance of flowing water, and it was not uncommon to find plenty of fish and sometimes eels in the water. Often schools of

499

fish were seen in the water near the race. The millrace was a great place to skate. One of the changes to the mill property is that the private road past the mill at one time continued to the road on Indian Trail.

Instead of milling, the Sitlinger family purchased a dairy business from Howard Heller in 1923. A fine horse-drawn milk wagon came with the business. In the beginning, they used cans furnished with spigots to deliver the milk to area towns. Their customers were in Loyalton, Lykens, and a few in Wiconisco. The usual procedure was to fill the customers' container with the amount of milk she desired. By 1928, they delivered the milk in bottles.

The Sitlingers were proud of their milk wagon. It was sometimes used for other occasions. During those years, they were farming the land that now belongs to the Crissinger farm. Soon after they received the milk wagon, Clayton used it for the first time to ride over to cultivate corn at the other farm. On the way home, he encountered a thunderstorm, and was glad for the closed-in protection from the bad weather.

The milk business continued to prosper, until one Saturday evening in 1945, lightning struck the barn, causing a heavy loss. The barn, shed, livestock, farm and dairy equipment was destroyed. The horse-drawn milk wagon, and another carriage were also destroyed. It was quite a loss, but the family purchased more equipment, and remained in the dairy business for three more years. The dairy was then sold to Big Run about 1950.

During the earlier years, the Sitlinger family also operated an ice business. Every winter they harvested chunks of ice that they cut on the Little Wiconisco Creek, and stored them in sawdust n their icehouse. They needed ice for their dairy, and the excess was sold commercially. The icehouse disappeared long ago, but patches of sawdust remained on the site for a number of years.

On November 29, 1945, Charles (Clayton). Sitlinger and his wife Francis F. sold this property with sixty-two acres, forty-six perches of land to their son Charles A. and his wife Sallie O. Sitlinger. On May 31, 1975, Charles A. and Sallie O. Sitlinger conveyed the same premises back to Charles (Clayton) and Frances F. Sitlinger. However, because on August 18, 1949, Charles A. and Sallie Sitlinger sold a small tract of more than an acre of ground to Park and Verna Ferree, there remained only 61 acres and 26 perches of land.

Photo below taken on the occasion of the 50th wedding anniversary Apr 20, 1968 of Charles A. and Sarah (Weiss) Sitlinger (seated). Standing l to r: Romaine Sitlinger, Clayton and Frances (Ferree) Sitlinger, Celin Sitlinger. Boy in middle _____.

SITLINGER/ZITLINGER FAMILY

[GEORGE SITLINGER immigrant ancestor of the Sitlinger (Zittlinger) family was born in Germany, came to Pennsylvania and settled in Schuylkill County, not far from the Dauphin County border. Harness making was his trade, but George Sitlinger was educated enough to teach in the subscription schools, both in the English and German language. He married Sarah Klinger (no dates). Family tradition carried down through several generations relates that George, or perhaps his father, left here and went back to Germany. Isaac is said to have had a stepmother, perhaps Sarah was not his mother.

George Sitlinger (dates unknown), m Sarah Klinger (no dates) a dau of _____. **George and Sarah (Klinger) Sitlinger had only two known children: *Ellemina** (Apr 6, 1853 - Sep 25, 1854, bur Simeon Cem). Since nothing more is known of George and Sarah , this is kind of a mystery; ***ISAAC** (Sep 15, 1833 - Sep 26, 1908, bur Simeon Cem), m Oct 3, 1852 in the Reformed Church to Maria Shade (Jun 23, 1834 - Oct 23, 1889), a dau o f Jacob and Catherine (Klinger) Shade. The county marriage record states that Isaac was born in "Machadimas" – Probably Mahantongo, Sch co. Maria and two of her children became ill with typhoid fever. Maria succumbed to the disease after many weeks of suffering. Isaac was a veteran of Co. G. 103rd Pa. Vol, having served with Capt C. Harper and Col Lehman. During the war, Isaac's right eye was seriously impaired due to extreme weather conditions. **Isaac and Maria (Shade) Sitlinger children:**

**Sarah (Sep 1, 1853 - Dec 3, 1912, bur Maple Grove Cem, E'ville), m Jan 10, 1875, Benjamin Shadle (1848 - 1919), of Washington Twp., Dau Co.

Jacob (Jun 13,1855 - Nov 7, 1917, bur IOOF Cem, Lykens), m Jun 29, 1878, Mary F. Stuppy (Feb 1856 - Jan 5, 1909), a dau of Ludwig and Marie (Matter) Stuppy. Jacob and Mary were both residents of Lykens when they married. Jacob worked as a miner since the age of 15, having gone to work at that early age, with his father. In later life, he became a teamster. On the day of his death, he was delivering a ton of coal to Mrs. David Sence in Lykens. The coal house was locked so he went to her house for a key. He waited in the kitchen to get warm while she unlocked the coal house. When she returned he was unconscious, the result of a heart attack. **Jacob and Mary (Stuppy) Sitlinger children: ***<u>Dorothy</u> b Sep 11, 1880, m Samuel Bateman; ***<u>Claud</u> Albert b Mar 25, 1882; ***<u>Ray</u> Edwin b Jul 3, 1884.

**Fietta (1857 - 1862, bur Simeon Cem)

Clara b 1859, m Joseph Raspatch, had dau *<u>Jamie</u> b Jul 1880, lived in Wiconisco.

**Harriet b1860

George Edward (Sep 19, 1862 - Oct 17, 1925, bur Simeon Cem), m 1st Feb 1885 in E'ville, by Rev. Hillpot, Sarah L. Good (Dec 26, 1866 - Dec15, 1889), dau of Jeremiah and Lovina Good of Gratz. George and Sarah lived in Gratz. During the fall of 1889, Sarah went to the farm of her husbands parents in Lykens Township, to care for her mother-in-law Maria. Mrs. Sitlinger was sick with typhoid fever, and died after a long struggle with the disease. Sarah while caring for her mother-in-law also became sick. She died of typhoid fever shortly before Christmas, leaving two young children. **George and Sarah (Good) Sitlinger children: ***<u>Darwin</u> E. (Jul 20, 1887 - Jun 1967, bur Simeon Cem), m Feb 12, 1916 Katie Klinger (Nov 1888 - 1965); ***<u>Katie</u> Irene (Nov 20, 1888 - 1961), m Moses A. Williard (1889 - 1953), bur Klingers Cem). **Moses and Katie (Sitlinger) Williard children:** ****<u>Alvin</u> Ray b Feb 1, 1912; ****<u>Martha</u> Irene b Jul 27, 1914.

After Sarah died, George m Jul 11, 1891, Catherine E. Hartman (May 24, 1861 - Mar 31, 1937), a dau of Simon and Hannah (Deibler) Hartman. **George and Catherine (Hartman) Sitlinger children:**

***Estella Elizabeth (May 30, 1893 - 1976, bur Simeon Cem), m Darwin Buffington (1886 - 1950)

George Isaac (Nov 22, 1894 - 1977, bur Simeon Cem), m Mar 20, 1920 Laura Florence Steely (1903 - Feb 1988), a dau of Donald and Alice (Smith) Steely. They married while George was in the service, after World War 1. **George and Florence (Steely) Sitlinger children:** *<u>Robert</u> b Aug 1, 1920, m Anna Scheib; ****<u>Blair</u> Donald b Oct 3, 1921; ****<u>Jacob</u> Isaac b May 29, 1925, m Carolyn Spotts; ****<u>Herold</u> b Jul 19, 1927; ****<u>George</u> b Oct 12, 1928; ****<u>Elwood</u> L. (1932 - 1954, bur Simeon Cem), killed during Korean Conflict); ****<u>Martha</u> m LeRoy Wiest; ****<u>Irene</u> m Jack Hepler.

John Ambrose. b Oct 6, 1896, m May 22, 1919, Florence M. Goukar, while he was serving in the U.S. Army. **John A. and Florence (Goukar) Sitlinger children:** *<u>LeRoy</u> John b Aug 1, 1920;

Norman Daniel (Oct 15 1901-1956, bur Simeon Cem), m May 1, 1920 Elsie V. Welker (Nov 23, 1899 - Jul 1978), dau of George and Adaline (Miller) Welker. **Norman and Elsie (Welker) Sitlinger had one dau:** *<u>Edna</u> Mae b Jul 28, 1920, m Eston W. Heller (Oct 12, 1912 - Dec 1977), a son of Howard H. Heller (May 13, 1877 - Mar 31, 1943), and Stella M (Weiss) Heller (Feb 13, 1882 - Oct 3, 1921). **Eston and Edna (Sitlinger) Heller had one son:** *****Dennis b Jan 20, 1943, not married, lives in Harrisburg.

Ida L (1865 - 1920, bur Simeon Cem), m Uriah H. Daniels (Feb 1, 1859 - 1923), son of George and Elizabeth Daniels. **Uriah and Ida (Sitlinger) Daniels children: ***<u>Clarence</u> Eugene (Nov 13, 1885 - 1969); ***<u>Norman</u> Alfred (Jul 7,1889 -1978, bur Simeon Cem);***<u>Elsie</u> May (Jan 29,1892 - Sep 1974, bur Simeon Cem).

Alvin C. (Nov 29, 1867 - Nov 5, 1948, bur Simeon Cem), m Jul 19, 1890, Mary Etta Daniel (Aug 2, 1873 - Sep 11, 1940). In 1900, Meta Mausser b Apr 1886, lived with the family and was listed as a niece. **Alvin and Mary Etta (Daniel) Sitlinger children:

***Florence May (Aug 24, 1895 - Apr 1897);

Charles Albert (Apr 8, 1900 - 1984), m Apr 20, 1918 Sarah Weiss. **Charles and Sarah (Weiss) Sitlinger children:** *<u>Charles</u> Clayton b May 14, 1920, m Frances Ferree, **Charles Clayton and Frances (Ferree) Sitlinger children:** *****Romaine Arlene b Jul 6, 1942, m Jay Troutman, **have these children:** *Debbie; James;* *****Celin Leonard b Dec 23, 1943, m Ruth Dunmoyer, a dau of Boyd and Helen Dunmoyer of Gratz. **Celin and Ruth (Dunmoyer) Sitlinger have two children:** *Leonard* b Sep 21, 1971, m Jessica Lee Erdman, a dau of Donna and Greg Erdman; *Angeline* b Jun 23, 1975.

Emory Isaac** Feb 19, 1903 - 1991), m May 5, 1923 Henrietta Weiss (1905 - 1982). **Emory and Henrietta (Weiss) Sitlinger children:** ****Hilda Marie b Jun 11, 1924, m Nov 30, 1946 William Robert Hay; ****Arlene Eleanore b Sep 3, 1925; ****Robert Arland b Apr 5, 1927, m May 4, 1946 Lillian Elizabeth Bellis b Dec 4, 1929, a dau of Elmer & Luma (Hartman) Bellis, **had these children:** *****Ronald Elmer b Jan 21, 1945; *****Robert Alvin b Aug 12, 1947; *****Richard Lee b Aug 12, 1848; *****Suzanna Kaye b Feb 9, 1950; *****Joanne*Russell Benjamin b Jun 14, 1929, m Apr 27, 1946 Mary A. Shadle, a dau of Lewis and Elva Pauline (Snyder) Shadle of Lykens Twp. **Russell and Mary (Shadle) Sitlinger children:** *Marilyn Elaine* b Jul 20, 1946; ****Carl Richard b Aug 16, 1931; ****Margaret Kathryn b Apr 6, 1933; ****Phyllis Marian b Mar 31, 1934; ****Evelyn Pauline b Jul 12, 1937; ****Wayne Lamar b Jan 7, 1941; ****Alvin Clayton b May 21, 1943; ****Bonita Carolyn b Jan 18, 1945, m ___ Bowman.
***Verna Kathryn** b Nov 27, 1907 , m Dec 24, 1927, Park L. Ferree (1906 - 1977, bur Simeon Cem), a son of _____;
Margaret (Mar 1870 - Sep 1870, bur Simeon Cem)
Samuel J (Jul 1871 - Sep 30, 1936), m Jul 28, 1900 Bertha D. Riegle (1879 - 1952). **Samuel and Bertha (Riegle) Sitlinger children:** ***Albert (1903 – 1973, bur Simeon Cem), m Feb 25, 1925, Laura Miller b1905, **had one known child:** ****Melva Jane b Mar 17, 1928; ***Melva Naomi b Feb 23, 1901, **had dau** ****Lucy b Jul 4, 1923; ***Harrison Isaac (Jul 5, 1904 - 1953, bur Simeon Cem), m Florence M. Umholtz (1905 - 1975), worked in the mines.
***Elsie C.** (Sep 1874 - 1966, bur Simeon Cem). In 1910 Elise lived at Rogers Hotel in Gratz, and was employed as a cook preparing meals for the dining room guests. Elsie, m May 18, 1912, Harvey S. Bellis (Jan 1885 - Nov 12, 1918), a son of David and Lillian Bellis of Lykens Twp.]

HOME OF MR AND MRS. JAY TRAUTMAN
Adjacent to Gristmill Property

The land for this residence has the same history as the adjacent gristmill property. Charles and Frances Sitlinger conveyed the lot as a residential property to Jay and Romaine Trautman. They are the present owners.

HOME OF G. B. Seibert & Gladys B. Firestone
(House Built c1949)

This lot containing one acre 126 perches of land was part of two tracts of land that belonged to the mill property as owned by the Sitlinger family. This being the small tract was conveyed to Daniel Buffington on July 29, 1876 by John and Magdalena Umholtz, and was part of the land grant to the Umholtz family.
On August 18, 1949, Charles A. and Sallie Sitlinger sold this small tract to Park and Verna Ferree. Park and Verna had the bungalow house built on the land and lived there for many years. But in July 1993, a public sale was held and the house and land was sold to G. B. Seibert and Gladys B. Firestone of Jonestown. They are the present owners.

HOME OF MR. & MRS. ROBERT SITLINGER
(Was Geise School built late c1870's)

The land for this building has the same background as the adjoining Sitlinger farm. After Isaac Sitlinger purchased his farm in 1873, he sold forty perches to Dauphin County School District for one dollar, but the date of the deed is not known. The transfer was not recorded. Daniel Blyler, school director had all the original deeds for Lykens Township schools in his possession, and in May 1886, a devastating fire at his home in Gratz destroyed them. The first Geise school was a wooden structure located across the road from the present building. It has always been known as Geise School, leading to believe that it became a school soon after 1830 when Benjamin Geise received the farm. There is evidence to show that it was there before 1856, and it appeared on the tax exemption list of schools as early as 1864. Since we do not know the wording of the deed transfer to the Dauphin County School District, it is possible that Isaac Sitlinger was trading the new school lot for the old original school lot that is now part of the Sitlinger farm. Traces of the old wooden building were seen by older folks years ago. The school building on this lot was probably built during the 1870s to replace the original nearby building. (Most of the brick township schools were constructed at that time.) The building was used continuously until 1954 when Upper Dauphin Jointure was organized. This building was sold to Robert and Lillian Sitlinger.

The following story from FARMERS & MINERS JOURNAL, dated August 16, 1856 gives an interesting account of an event that took place at this school.

SABBATH SCHOOL CELEBRATION

A Sabbath school celebration took place at number seven Gise School house, Lykens Township on Saturday the 23rd last at nine o'clock. The procession was formed by J. D. Gise, Chief Marshall and assisted by J. P. Riegel, D. Romberger & others. They marched about a mile to a beautiful grove, where seats were provided to accommodate all. Rev's Mr. Sell and Romberger addressed the assemblage in an able manner after which refreshments were served to the full gratification of all present. In the afternoon, Rev. Mr. Hambright & Mr. H. B. Hoffman made appropriate remarks, the procession was reformed and marched back to the schoolhouse. "Gratz Rifle Company" in full uniform was in attendance with its officers Messrs: O"Neill, Feagley, Shower and Moyer. The celebration passed off quietly and those connected with the arrangements deserve great credit.

TEACHERS OF GISE/GEISE SCHOOL

1854 – 1856 "possibly Joseph D. Gise
1857 – 1883 unknown
1884 – Milton E. Buffington
1885 - Charles Lubold
1886 – Frank P. Ferree
1887 – 1888 unknown
1889 - Frank P.Ferree
1890 – M. L. Williard
1891 – E. L. Dockey
1892 – 1894 – unknown
1895 – Edward Riegel (he taught several years)
1896 – Henry Williard
1897 – Charles Dockey
1898 – Edward Riegel
1899 – Jonas or Joseph A. Kissinger
1900 – Perry F. Broslus
1901 – John Keener, Jr.
1902 – 1905 – Joseph A. Ferree
1906 - Rebecca H. Thompson
1907 – Anna A. Schoffstall
1908 – Milton Schoffstall
1909 – unknown
1910 – Anna A. Schoffstall
1911 – Warren Matter
1912 – Daniel Koppenhaver
1913 – Anna A. Schoffstall
1914 – Anna A. Schoffstall
1915 – Anna A. Schoffstall
1916/17 – Warren Matter
1918 – 1929 – Henry E. Wenrich
1930/- Clayton Willier
1932/33 unknown
1934 - Clayton Willier
1935 - Harry Unger
1936 - Arlene Klinger
1937/38 – Henry E. Wenrich
1939-1947 – unknown
1948/49 – John H. Lenker
1950 - Anna A. Schoffstall
1951 - unknown
1952 - John H. Lenker
1953 - unknown
1954 - Mrs. Heisler

*Joseph D. Gise taught 14 more years in Lykens Township. Charles Henninger & Ruth Evitts taught here. Anna L. Sheesley was a substitute.

The Gratz Historical Society has an album of memorabilia from the Geise School in our library. Marlin Dietrich a deceased member of the Historical Society attended Geise School as a youth. He took on the project of gathering Geise school history. His project was the foundation of a very popular event for the historical society one year on Simon Gratz Day. The outcome is a super collection of area school data housed in the museum library.

A delightful little "Santa Claus Album" has survived these many years from1884. The album was given as a "reward of merit for good spelling" by teacher M. E. Buffington to Charles G. Riegel that year.The album preserved for several generations is owned by his grandson Charles G. Riegel, now in retirement and a resident of Florida. The verses written to "Charlie" by special friends are most interesting. Some of the pages are included below.

To Charlie
May your life be crowned
with Happiness in this world
and in the world to come
is the sincere wish of
your friend
Lydia [illegible] Hoffman

To Charlie—
When you are sitting
all alone, Reflecting on
the past, Remember that
you have a friend that
will forever last.
C. M. Boyer.

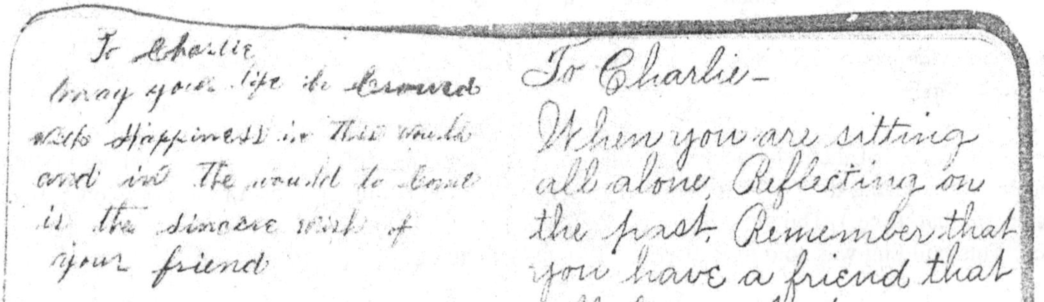

Complements of
Your Teacher,

Dise's School, Winter 1884-85.

To Charlie,
In after years, when you have outgrown boyhood's domain, and when the world asks something of you as a man, stand up nobly at a place where, as in your spelling class, you shall secure for yourself greatest honor and approbation, your Teacher
M. E. Buffington,

To Charlie.
Round went the album hither it came for me to write in, so here is my name. Your Cousin
Geo. Hoffman,

'Twas Christmas Eve! the house was still;
The good-nights had been said;
The stockings hung before the fire,
The Children were in bed.

To Charlie
Remember when far far off where the woodchucks died of whooping-cough. Your Friend
Samuel Jay Bittinger

To Charlie
In your golden chain of friendship consider me a link.
Your Friend
Laura M. Slinger

Feb-28

PHOTOGRAPHS FROM GEISE SCHOOL

Top Photo unidentified. Middle row taken March 1, 1898 – C. M.Dockey, teacher. Students with slates giving names believed to be: Norman D. Riegle, M. B ___ , J. M. K, J. C. Hoke of Gratz, Daniel Snyder. Bottom photo taken c1919 unidentified except Susan Dietrich (Schoffstall) first on left top row, & possibly Kathryn Dietrich 2nd from right front row.

Geise School March 21, 1906 – Rebecca Thompson, Teacher
L to r row 1: Helen Hoffman Dietrich; Laura Evitts; Roy Kissinger; Fred Evitts; Henry Evitts; Mark Kissinger; Jacob Kissinger; Vern Evitts; Stanley Buffington (with slate); row 2: Carrie Mauser Phillips; Ernest Kissinger; John Hoover; Allen Schoffstall; Chas Ralph Phillips; Gurney Kissinger; Florence Phillips Minnich (with hair ribbon); Henry Salada. Row 3; Laura Phillips Kissinger; Alice Hoover Harris; John Phillips; Bertha Strohecker; Annie Bellon; Flossie Evitts; Howard Phillips; Chauncey Salada; Minnie Hoke.

Geise School March 1910 – Teacher Anna Schoffstall
Std: Jacob Kissinger; Earl Dietrich; ___; Harrison Sitlinger; Albert Sitlinger; Ford Shade; Geo Shade; Ernest Kissinger; Elmer Shade; Emory Sitlinger; Charles Sitlinger; 2nd row: ___; ___; Florence Philips Minnich ____; ___;___;___; Ralph Hoffman; ___;))); Laura Dietrich; Harvey Evitts; 3rd row: Sarah Wise Sitlinger; Helen Hoffman Dietrich; Chas Shade; Benj. Wise; Albert Shade; Ralph Philips; Allen Schoffstall; Wm Dietrich; Roy Shade.

Geise School Photo - November 1924 – Henry E. Wenrich, Teacher

L to r: front row: Eston Heller, Marlin Twchopp. Row 2: Harold Spotts, Roy Evitts, Lauren Dietrich, John Hoffman. Harvey Shomper, Lester Fetterhoff. Row 3: (note – this row is not named in accurate order): Levi Kissinger, Margaret Shadle Kissinger, Kathryn Dietrich Gasbarro; Jonas Hoffman; John Mauser; Ellen Shade; Myrtle Heller Wiest; Lillian Crabb Kramer; Grant Phillips; Raymond Richert; Margaret Mauser Angle; John Dietrich; Harold Dietrich. Row 4: Marlin Dietrich; Lottie Hoffman Kissinger; Rosie Tschopp; Elba Tschopp Klinger; Esther Gunderman Shomper; Sarah

Geise School Photo 1936 – Arlene Klinger, teacher – identified next page

L to r back row: Clarence Mauser; Blair Hoffman, Warren Hoffman; Marie Kissinger; Arlene Sitlinger; Hilda Sitlinger; Lucy Sillinger; Jenny Sndyer. 3rd row: Dolores Hoffman; Betty Kissinger; Alice Minnich; Mildred Kissinger; Pauline Snyder; Melva Sitlinger; Betty Minnich; Verna Snyder; 2nd row: Miles Minnich; Orville Hoffman; Dave Snyder; Leroy Snyder; Robert Sitlinger. 1st row: Billy Gunderman; ___ Donald Koppenhaver; Stanley Engle; Blair Keefer; Carl Sitlinger; John Chubb.

Geise School Photo Taken October 5, 1949 – John H. Lenker, Teacher

L to r: front row std; Alvin Sitlinger; Cellin Sitlinger; John Mauser; JohnHoffman; Paul Leffler; Wayne Sitlinger. 2nd row: Marion Mauser; Mildred Lucas; Edna Kissinger; Gloria Lucas; Janet Leffler; Romaine Sitlinger; Shirley Mauser; Carol Lenker. 3rd row: Tommy Shade; Donald Lucas; Clair Snyder; Evelyn Sitlinger; Arlene Mauser; Betty Erdman; Guy Leffler; John Mauser; Jean & June Leffler.

EMORY SITLINGER FARM
(Original Umholtz, later Isaac Sitlinger Farm)
house built pre-1830, barn built c1875
52 acres 112 perches

This farm is made up of land from two different tracts granted by Commonwealth of Pennsylvania to the Umholtz family. It has the same history as the Albert Morgan farm.

After Henry Umholtz died, his heirs petitioned Dauphin County Orphans Court to appraise the land. It was divided into tracts, and on April 10, 1830, a part of the tract containing 55 acres, 112 perches with house was conveyed to Benjamin Geise in right of his wife Margaret, who was a daughter of Henry Umholtz. The deed was not recorded until later. Benjamin Geise was listed as a tenant on the property of Henry Umholtz estate for several years after that, and he was listed as a farmer and carpenter. By 1837 he was listed as owner of this land and wooden house. In 1855 and 1858 Benjamin Geise was assessed for a two-story log house and bank barn, and had a carriage.

The family lived on the farm for many years. In 1870, their daughter Mary, a young child Charles age 1, Ida Garber, and John Umholtz age 62 lived with them. In 1880, Benjamin and Margaret had Ida Garber age 16, and Charles Daniel age 11, a grandson living with them.

Recent Photo Of House

Recent Photo Of Sitlinger Barn Built c1875

THE GEISE/GEISS/GISE FAMILY

[*NICHOLAS GEISE (no dates) the earliest known ancestor of the Geise family was a native of Lehigh County, where he worked as a carpenter. One of his sons, **BENJAMIN GEISE (Mar 11, 1806 – Jun 4, 1884) came to Lykens Township as a young man and bought this farm in 1830. In addition to farming, Benjamin raised livestock. He married Margaret (sometimes called Rebecca) Umholtz (Dec 25, 1810 – May 13, 1896), a dau of Henry and Susanna (Hoover) Umholtz. Both bur Simeon Cem. In 1880, they had Charles Daniel age 11, their grandson with them. **Benjamin and Margaret (Umholtz) Geise children:**
Joseph D. (Apr 28, 1834 – Oct 25, 1908), m in 1840 in Berrysburg Elizabeth D. Witmer (Apr 14, 1840 – Sep 10, 1915), a dau of Benjamin Witmer, tailor of Pillow. They lived in Lykens Township beside his parents in 1870. **Joseph D. and Elizabeth D (Witmer) Geise children:** ****Henry b c1858, a professor in the public schools in Schuylkill Haven, Pa.;*Mary Amelia (1861 – 1862); ****George W. (1863 – 1938, bur Simeon Cem, Gratz), became an attorney in Sch Haven, Pa.

510

Joseph D. Geise attended New Berlin Academy in Union County. He was a teacher in Lykens Township for two years. While he continued his education, he worked on area farms in the summer, and taught in the township schools during the winter. He was eventually appointed and commissioned in the Internal Revenue service, as a storekeeper for the Fourteenth Congressional District of Pennsylvania. He continued in that job for seventeen years. After retirement, he purchased a farm in Lykens Township, and engaged in farming and raising livestock. [Write-up on his farm elsewhere in this book]. He was also a veteran of the Civil War, having served in Captain B. J. Evitts Company.

Jonathan B (John) (May 9, 1840 – Dec 10, 1915, bur Simeon Cem, Gratz), m Lila E. Boyer (Jun 30, 1847 – Nov 20, 1896), a dau of William S. Boyer. Jonathan was a Civil War veteran, having served in the 230th Regt Pa. volunteers. Jonathan and family lived in Gratz in 1880 and Aaron Miller 23, lived with them. **Jonathan B. and Lila E. (Boyer) Geise children:** ****Wellington b c1865 m Edith ____. He worked in Wash D.C. in the field of agriculture. He was a gifted muysician and composed waltz music which qualified for publication; ****Daniel W. b c1866 lived with his parents in 1880. Annie E. b c1867 m Daniel Leitzel of Leck Hill; ****Henry L. (1870 – 1928, bur Simeon Cem), m Mattie A. Deibert of Pottsville. He was a professor and taught briefly in Gratz and Millersburg before becoming a salesman for the Weaver Organ & Piano Co. in York; ****Irvin (1869 – 1872); ****Mamie (1871 – 1880); ****Sally (1872 – 1884); ****Jennie E (1873 – 1885); ****Mary E. b c1875; ****Carrie Gertrude b Jan 1877, not married, a talented musician, played the organ in Evang. Ch;*J. Darwin (1882 – 1884);****J. Arthur (1888-1896 of diphtheria). Note that most of the children died young.
***Mary A. (May 1, 1845 twin – 1934), m Jacob Shiro [write-up with Shiro family]
***Sarah Ann (May 1, 1845 twin– May 17, 1934, bur Simeon Cem, Gratz), m 1st George Garber (Dec 15, 1843 – Sep 10, 1873), whom served during the Civil War in Co. D, 25th Regt Pa Vol. Sarah and George m about 1865, while she was living near Gratz. It was a rough stormy day, and the ceremony took place in Berrysburg at the home of Rev. Yost, the Evangelical minister. Sarah's bridesmaid was her twin sister Mary, who later m Jacob Shiro. In the evening after the wedding, the newly weds were serenaded by a group of friends. Edward A. Hoffman was among the friends, and he recalled the event many years later. During their marriage, Sarah and George lived in both Pottsville and Gratz. **George and Sarah Ann (Geise) Garber children:**
****Ida Celeste (Garber) b in Gratz Aug 15, 1866, m May 13, 1884 to Dr. G. M. Schminky, son of Dr. Isaiah S. Schminky of Gratz;**** George (Garber) (1870- 1941, bur Simeon Cem), lived in Hollidaysburg, Pa. His wife's name is unknown;****Harvey (Garber) b c1873, m Mary ___, lived in Progress, Pa.
  After George Garber died, his widow Sarah married again. In a ceremony performed by Rev. J. S. Newhart at her home, Sarah Ann Geise Garber became the second wife, on Jan 20, 1877 of Captain Benjamin J. Evitts (Sep 20, 1822 – Mar 30,1909, bur Peace Cem, Berrysburg). Benjamin J. Evitts was first m to Sarah Ann Yeager.
***Amanda (Dec 30, 1846 – 1929, bur Simeon Cem), m John W. Hoffman (1843 – 1926). [More information with Hoffman write-up.]
***Edward, ***Jacob, ***Henry (Geise) – three sons preceded their father in death.]

    An unidentified George Geise age 48 lived in Lykens Twp in 1880. He had a wife Mary age 45, sons John 15, Richard 8 and a granddaughter Cora Swab age 5 living in the household.

    On April 5, 1870, Benjamin and Margaret Geise sold the farm and another small tract of land to Christian Johns, a resident of Earl Township, Lancaster County . The small tract had belonged to Amos Hoffman who sold it April 21, 1849 to Benjamin Geise. Christian Johns died shortly after the ownership transfer, but by his will dated March 30, 1871, he gave these two tracts of land with house, barn and out buildings to his son C. R. Johns, with an agreement to make yearly payments to Mary R. Rettinger, beginning April 20, 1874.
    On September 11, 1873, C. R. and Susanna Johns sold the two tracts, (fifty-five acres one hundred twelve perches with the buildings, and the six acres) to Isaac Zittlinger. While Isaac was a young youth, he came to Lykens Township and found work as a farm hand until he was fifteen years old. At that age he began to work in the coal mines, and was in the employ of Lykens Coal Company for many years. When he purchased this farm, one of the first things he did was to build a new barn. He engaged in general farming, and continued in that occupation the remainder of his life.
    Isaac Sitlinger served in the army during the Civil War, having enlisted in Harrisburg in March 1865 in Co G, 103rd Pa Vol. and served with Capt C. Harper and Colonel Lehman. During the service his right eye was seriously impaired due to exposure. He served until the close of the war.

Isaac Sitlinger (left) And His Family In Front Of Their Home (No Date – Others Not Identified)

    This picture is rather unique because when the roving photographer came, the family placed an easel in the yard so that they could display their precious pictures while they had their own pictures taken. Of course their home is also part of the display. The date of the picture is June 13, 1898. It is even more unique because we have a copy on the next page of one of the pictures displayed in the photo above! We believe that the one on the following page is a picture of George and Sarah (Klinger) Sitlinger, parents of Isaac.

Probably George Sitlinger, immigrant and wife Sarah (Klinger) Sitlinger, immigrant

On August 5, 1908, Isaac Sitlinger sold two tracts of land to Alvin Sitlinger. The first was the farm of fifty-two acres, 112 perches with the buildings. The other small, unseated six-acre tract was transferred from Amos Hoffman to Benjamin Gise in 1849.

During the years that this Sitlinger family lived here, family reunions were enjoyed. The first one was probably held at the farm owned by Samuel Sitlinger. Another was held on the Alvin Sitlinger residence, and a third one at this farm. These reunions were well attended, and it was a day of fun for all. Plenty of food was brought by each family and placed on long tables where everyone could gather and partake. Some pictures that have survived bring back memories for those who attended.

On October 19, 1943, Alvin Sitlinger sold both tracts to Charles A. Sitlinger, Emory I. Sitlinger, and Verna K. Sitlinger. On April 1, 1949, Charles A. Sitlinger and wife Sallie O, Emory I. and Henrietta C. Sitlinger, Verna K. and Park L. Ferree, heirs of Charles C. Sitlinger sold the two tracts of land to Emory I and Henrietta C. Sitlinger.

Isaac Sitlinger

HOME OF MR. AND MRS. LEONARD SITLINGER

This land was part of Sitlinger acreage. On October 16, 1992 Charles C. Sitlinger conveyed a tract of about six acres to Leonard B. Sitlinger. He and his wife Jessica had a new home on the property and this has become their residence.

The next farms are located almost directly north of the Geise School
(As marked on the 1875 map)

SAMUEL I. STOLTZFUS FARM
(William Hawk 102 acres & John Hoover Sr. 1875 map)

This land originally was part of two grants. Commonwealth of Pennsylvania patented 270 acres called "Walnut Bottom" to Peter Hoffman, Jr. February 26, 1796. Another was patented on February 29, 1796, to Nicholas Hoffman. On August 10, 1799, Peter Hoffman conveyed his acreage to Nicholas Hoffman. On June 24, 1809 Nicholas and Margaret Hoffman sold the first tract back to Peter Hoffman with buildings. About ten years later, on May 15, 1819, Peter and Magdalena Hoffman sold part of the land containing 105 acres to Jacob

Laudenslager. On September 10, 1822, Jacob and Sophia Laudenslager sold this same tract to his son Daniel Laudenslager, listed as a farmer.

Daniel Laudenslager owned the land for many years. In addition to the original acreage, he also purchased about forty acres of mountain land. Over the next years, his property is listed on the tax record as a log weatherboarded house and log barn. In 1850 and 1860, their son John Laudenslager and his family lived on the farm. Sometime during those years Daniel and his wife moved to Lykens. After Daniel Laudenslager died, his heirs made two transactions. One was an agreement made April 1, 1868 by his son John and wife Juliana Laudenslager to sell 105 acres to William and Rebecca Hawk. (Rebecca was Daniel Laudenslager's daughter). Several years later John and Juliana Laudenslager sold the adjoining tract containing forty-six acres, 113 perches to William and Rebecca Hawk.

[*DANIEL LAUDENSLAGER (Sep 13, 1792 Berks Co- Aug 29, 1867, bur Hoffman Cem), a son of Jacob and Sophia (Rettinger) Laudenslager, m Jan 24, 1824, Susanna Umholtz (Jul 11, 1804 - Mar 3, 1874), a dau of Philip and Anna Maria (Wiliard) Umholtz. In her will, Susanna mentions the following **three children**:

JOSEPH (Apr 13, 1823 - Sep 8, 1855), m Sarah Willier (May 3, 1823 - Jan 5, 1856), a dau of Adam and Sarah (Reisch) Willier. Joseph and Sarah Laudenslager are both bur at Hoffman Cem. [NOTE: The birth record for Joseph and his brother John reflect a discrepancy, but we have no baptismal record to rely on for accuracy]. **Joseph and Sarah (Willier) Laudenslager children:** ***John A. (1850 - 1937, bur Pillow Cem.), m Melinda Strohecker. In 1860 at the age of eleven, John lived with his grandmother Willier. ***Margaretha (no dates); ***Aaron d Jan 7, 1856, age eleven months.

JOHN (Feb 6, 1823 - May 18, 1895, bur Simeon Cem), m Juliana Hoffman (Feb 8, 1830 - Oct 10, 1893), a dau of John and Elizabeth (Bordner) Hoffman. **John and Juliana (Hoffman) Laudenslager children:**
***Charles Henry (Nov 5, 1847 - Mar 26, 1921, bur Wiconisco Calvery Cem), m Sarah Yeager (1850 - 1918). He was a Civil War Veteran. **Charles and Sarah (Yeager) Laudenslager children:** ****William Wilson (1868 - 1870, bur Hoffman Cem); ****Henrietta b c1870, m William Romberger of Lykens; ****Elizabeth b c1871, m _____ Kissinger; ****Henry b c1873;, lived in Wiconisco; ****Charles b c1874, m Fannie Baddorf; ****John b c1876, m Lillie Witmer, lived in Halifax; ****James d in infancy, 1878; ****Edward b Sep 17, 1880; ****George Irvin (May 14, 1882 - 1882); [Last two recorded in Oak Dale Church record] ****Sula C. (1885 - 1966), m Oscar E. Lawley (1883 - 1954, bur Wiconisco); ****Clara (no dates), m _____ Rettinger; ****Newton (1890 - 1918). The family later moved to Wiconisco, where Charles was employed as a miner.
*** Sarah (Jan 26, 1849 - 1941), m Mar 6, 1869, in Uniontown by Rev. Simon Noll, to Jacob Kratzer (Feb 1849 - Oct 7, 1941), **Jacob and Sarah (Laudenslager) Kratzer children:** ****Clarence U. (1874 - Nov 13, 1957), m 1st Oct 13, 1898 to Carrie M. Kembel (1877 - 1903), a dau of Nathaniel and Elizabeth Kembel.
Jacob m 2nd to Carrie E. Schwalm, **had these children:** ****Corbe Eugene b Apr 1, 1877; ****Henrietta Josephine b Sep 4, 1879; ****Beulah Charlotte b Aug 15, 1884; ****Guerney Harvey b Aug 15, 1886.
****Gertrude m Joshua Etzweiler, and lived in Millersburg.
***Emma b c1851 m John Daniels and moved to Humboldt, Iowa
***Mary A, (1852 - 1924) , m _____ James, had no issue.
***Henrietta (Jun 14, 1858 - 1862);
REBECCA (Aug 9, 1831 - Nov 29, 1912, bur Wiconisco Cem), m in 1849 to William Hawk (Mar 9,1828 Lyk Twp – Jan 21,1905), a son of Mathias and Magdalena (Riegel) Hawk **William and Rebecca (Laudenslager) Hawk children:** ***John Alfred (Jun 11, 1850 - 1895), d in Plymouth, Pa.; ***Ida d young; ***Lizzie A. m Alexander F. Thompson of Lykens; ***Ersula b c1858, m R. A. O'Neill, moved to St. Louis;***William B. b 1865, moved to Lorain, Ohio; ***Annie b c1869, m Byron Brand, moved to Lancaster, Pa.]

William and Rebecca Hawk lived on a twenty-acre tract in Lykens Township, and William had a tailoring business. John Bitterman also a tailor lived with them. In 1850, Amos Kuntzelman, age 17, a tailor, and Adam Byerly age 12, lived with them. The Hawk's resided here until 1854, and then moved to Wiconisco. William furnished timber for Short Mountain and Lykens Valley coalmines. He helped to construct the railroad from Millersburg to Lykens. He was also one of the contractors who helped to build the railroad from Wiconisco to Summit Branch Colliery at Williamstown.

On January 2, 1874, William and Rebecca Hawk sold this property of forty-six plus acres to Lemuel Row. Years later on April 8, 1893, Lemuel Row hired J. A. Henninger to make a new survey of the property.

Before Lemuel Row owned this farm, he was employed to haul logs for the mines. He later worked inside the mines. He eventually decided to take up farming, and purchased this farm. Lemuel and his family lived here until about 1890, then moved to Lykens where he helped his son George, who was in the ice business.

Lemuel Row penned his will on April 29, 1898, and among other things ordered that "my property be appraised and either of my two sons, George or William H. Row shall have the privilege to take the farm at the appraisement." William H. elected to take the farm with dwelling house, barn and other buildings at the appraisement. He lived here by 1900, or perhaps earlier. In August 1900, William Row took a trip to Wiconisco with his wagon and team of horses. While coming down a hill past the dye works in Wiconisco, he passed the trolley car that was going up the hill. Mr. Row did not get his team stopped in time, and a collision occurred. Fortunately, he was not seriously injured.

On March 13, 1902, George O. Row and Adam C. Long, executors of Lemuel Row's estate, sold the forty-seven acres, thirty-two perches to William H. Row.

[*LEMUEL ROW (Nov 30, 1828 Wash Twp - Dec 18, 1900, bur IOOF Cem, Lykens), a son of John and Susanna Row, m Elmira Hawk (Aug 19, 1831 - Aug 17, 1892), a dau of Mathias and Magdalena (Riegel) Hawk, of Lykens Twp. **Lemuel and Elmira (Hawk) Row children:** **Mary Ellen (Jan 5, 1854 - Jul 11, 1908, bur Lykens), m Jun 8, 1873, William Mumma, **had these children:** ***Charles Henry b Jun 10, 1873; ***William Franklin b Aug 21, 1874; ***John Wellington b Oct 9, 1880; George Oliver (1858 - Apr 17, 1936, bur Simeon Cem, Gratz), m Elmira Unger (1858 - Dec 30, 1925), a dau of _____; **William H. (Feb 10, 1864 - Jul 8, 1925, bur Simeon Cem), m Oct 6, 1883 Emma Jane Burd (May 4, 1863 - Feb 26, 1927), a dau of Isaac and A. Mary (Ferree) Burd. Emma lived with her grandmother Ferree in 1880 in Lykens Township. **William H. and Emma Jane (Burd) Row children, some bapt Simeon Ref Ch:** ***Sevilla (b & d 1881, bur Simeon Cem); ***Jennie M. (1882 - 1887, bur Simeon Cem); ***Mary Elmira b Mar 24, 1884; ***Beulah M. b Dec 1889; ***Elizabeth Louisa b Oct 7, 1892; ***Nora O. b May 1895; ***Florence b 1900.]

On October 5, 1908, William H. and Emma Jane Row sold forty-seven acres, thirty-two perches of land with dwelling house, barn and other buildings to Edward Deitrich, a resident of Lykens.

This Farm As It Looked When The Edward Dietrich Family Lived Here
Photo Taken During The 1930's

LAND FROM OTHER TRACT
(John Hoover Sr. land on 1875 map)

On April 1, 1920, Edward Deitrich purchased another thirty acres of land from Benjamin Shadle, who had come here in 1902 from Washington Township. Benjamin Shadle received this land from the estate of Elias Hoover at a public auction held at Gise School on March 31, 1902. Elias Hoover received it from the estate of John Hoover, Sr. It was probably this tract of land that William Hawk cleared when he sold timber to the Short Mountain and Lykens Valley Coal mines.

This land was probably an old homestead that disappeared long before any present resident of Lykens Township was living. The 1875 Lykens Township map shows John Hoover Sr as owner of a farm, but no acreage is given. It is said that there is or was evidence of a building on part of the land. It would be difficult to establish that fact now. The history of this early homestead has been lost.

THE LEONARD DIETRICH FAMILY
(Some information from "Our Dietrich Lines" by William Dietrich)

This **DIETRICH** family is descended from **LEONARD DIETRICH** (Sep 4,1732 – Sep1803, Lower Mahanoy Twp., Northld Co.). He married 1st Catharine _____ (__ - 1847). Leonard Dietrich came to America on the ship "BROTHERS" arriving Sep 26, 1753 in Philadelphia. He settled first in Berks Co, later coming to Hubley Twp., Sch Co by1786. He eventually moved to Lower Mahanoy Twp.

Leonard and Catharine ___ - Dietrich children all bapt Klingers Ch):

*JOHN (-1842), m M. Barbara Geiss (Mar 7, 1765 – pre 1840), a dau of George Adam and Anna Barbara (Haag) Geiss. Children:

EVA ELISABETH (Sep 21, 1787 – Aug 19, 1860, Barry Twp., Sch Co), m George Kessler (Feb 19, 1786 – Mar 29, 1866)

**JOHN (Dec 6, 1789 – Feb 18, 1868, bur St. Andrews Cem, Valley View), m Magdalena Dach (Aug 29, 1791 – after 1870, a dau of Bernard Dach. John and Magdalena Dietrich moved to Leaf River, Ogle Twp., Ill)

**GEORGE (Jan 2, 1792 – Apr 20, 1865, bur Friedens Cem, Hegins), m Susanna Catharine Stahlman (1792 – 1861)

**PHILIP (Mar 5, 1794 – Jan 28, 1871, bur St. Pauls Cem, Sacramento, Sch Co), m Eva Maria Artz (Feb 15, 1794 – Jul 11, 1885) - see below.

**LEONARD (Jun 1, 1799 – Aug 18, 1865, Wayne Co, Crawford Co. Pa.), m 1sr Barbara Kessler, m 2nd Mar 4, 1829, Lydia Brobst (Jul 14, 1810 Sch Co – Apr 12,1900, Crawford Co).

**ANDREAS (Jan 4, 1797 – Jun 15, 1888, bur Lykens), m Elizabeth Phillips b 1806. Lived in Powells Valley.

PHILIP DIETRICH - from above (Mar 5, 1794 – Jan 28, 1871, bur Sacramento, Sch Co), m Eva Artz (Feb 15,1794 – Jul 11, 1885, after a fall that broke her arm, and eventually caused her death), a dau of Philip and Barbara (Kuntzelman) Artz. **Philip and Barbara (Kuntzelman) Artz children:** ***LYDIA JUSTINA (Nov 9,1816 – Nov 12, 1875, bur Sacramento), m Daniel Zerbe (1810 – 1851), a son of John and Margareta (Schneider) Zerbe. **Daniel and Lydia (Dietrich) Zerbe children:** Caroline (1838 – 1902, bur Himmel Cem, Northld Co), m Micahel Runkle (1837 – 1913); **Sarah** (1841 – 1910, bur Sacramento), m David Herner (1836 – 1913), ; **Elizabeth** b 1843, m 1st Benjamin Myers, 2nd Cornelius Hoffman;; John D. (1845 – 1922, bur Sacramento), m 1st Elizabeth Coleman (1852 – 1873), a dau of Simon Coleman, 2nd Elizabeth Saltzer (1859 – 1932, a dau of John and Mary (Clark) Saltzer of Gratz; **Amanda** (1849 -1925), m Joel Stutzman (1844 – 1916, bur Fountain, Sch Co), a son of David and Sarah (Gehres) Stutzman ; **Lydia** (1851 – 1914, bur Sacramento);, m Wm Osman Saltzer (1850 – 1927), a son of Gabriel and Mary Marianna Saltzer; ***SOLOMON (Jun 19, 1817 – Nov 24, 1865, Barry Twp, Sch Co), m Anna Holdeman (1819 – 1900). Anna Holdeman Dietrich m 2nd Peter Klinger; Solomon and Anna (Holdeman) Dietrich **children: Elizabeth** (Dieter) b1838; **Lydia** (Dieter)(1839 – 1926 Hegins), m Paul Ney (1837 – 1908), a son of Daniel & Elizabeth (Burger) Ney; **John H.** (Dieter) 1842 – 1913, bur Ch of God Cem, Hegins), m Maria Catherine Klinger (1847 – 1922), a dau of Isreal & Caroline (Schwalm) Klinger; **Katherine** (Dieter) 1861 – 1916, bur Hegins), m Frank Boyer (1858 – 1922); ***DAVID (Feb 3, 1818 – Mar 4, 1890), m Caroline Gilbert (1824 – 1891), a dau of Johannes & Hannah (Stong) Gilbert; **David and Caroline (Gilbert) Dietrich children:** Amos (1847 – 1863, bur Sacramento); **Josiah** (1850 – 1927), m Sarah Musselman (1858 – 1928);Maria (1851 – 1925, bur Sacramento), m Henry Hoffa, Jr. (1849- 1912, bur Sacramento), a son of Henry and Elizabeth (Wiest) Hoffa; Jacob (Dieter) (1859 – 1924, Sacramento), m Sallie Carl (1872 – 1922); **Reilly** (Feb 18, 1863 – Mar 5, 1929), m 1st Mary Alice Ossman (1864 – 1907), 2nd Ellen ___ (1864 – 1941); ***NELLE HELENA (Aug 24, 1822 – 1898, bur IOOF Cem Coal Twp., Northld Co)), m James Bixler (1824 – 1901); ***ELIAS (Apr 9, 1824 – Apr 17, 1909, bur Sacramento), m Angelina Coleman (Nov 6,1830 – Jan 21, 1912). **Elias and Angelina (Coleman) Dietrich children: Franklin** 1851 – 1944), m Sarah Otto (1851 – 1929), a dau of Solomon & Lydia (Artz) Otto; **Maria** (1853 – 1936), m Charles Eby (1883 – 1941), a son of Peter & Catherine (Snyder) Eby; **Daniel** (1855 – 1920), m Catherine Maurer, a dau of Samuel & Catherine (Coleman) Maurer (1855 – 1929); ***MOSES (1827 – 1898, bur Sacramento), m Magdalena Artz (1839 – 1901), m 2nd Agatha Wiest; Moses & Magdalena (Artz) Dietrich child: Gussie Esther (1886

– 1917), m Harry D. Welker (1886 – 1966), a son of George and Sarah (Batdorf) Welker; ***EMANUEL** (1829 – 1895), see below; ***SARAH** (1831 – 1908, bur Sacramento, Sch Co), m Martin Koppenhaver (1829 – 1900), a son of Frederick & Susanna (Harner) Koppenhaver; ***JOHN** b c1832; ***SAMUEL** (1834 – 1901); ***PAUL** (Jul 26, 1837 – Jan 24,1896), m Mary Shuman (Dec 25, 1840 – Apr 29, 1915, bur Sacramento Sch Co.)

EMANUEL DIETRICH (from above) (Apr 9,1829 Low Mah, Sch Co– May 11,1895, Lyk Twp, bur IOOF Cem, Lykens), m 1st Hannah Adams (Oct 31, 1829 – Dec 6, 1851, bur Sacramento), a dau of Nicholas and Sarah (Hoffa) Adams. After Hannah died, Emanuel m 2nd Ellen Jane Adams, Hannah's sister (Mar 17, 1835 – Jan 24, 1929, bur with Emanuel). **Emanuel and Hannah (Adams) Dietrich children:**
GABRIEL - twin (Dec 21, 1850 – Dec 17, 1915); SENARY- twin (Dec 21, 1850 –Dec 12, 1895 in accident at Brookside Colliery). **Emanuel and Ellen Jane (Adams) Dietrich children:** PHILIP (Aug 15, 1853 – Nov 23, 1824); MOSES (Sep 5, 1855 – Jul 9, 1912), m Mary ___ b 1853; ISABEL (Nov 22, 1857 – Mar 30, 1899), m Charles Shadel; FRANK (1860 – Oct 2, 1936); ELIZABETH JANE (Apr 1864 – Dec 16, 1936); ALBERT (May 14, 1865 – Feb 24, 1924); DANIEL HARRISON (Aug 16, 1866 – Apr 7, 1934); AMANDA REBECCA (1868 – 1939); ELIJAH (Dec 1871 – 1965); *EDWARD (Jan 23, 1874 – Feb 7, 1948), see below.

*EDWARD DIETRICH (Jan 23, 1874 - Feb 7, 1948, bur Simeon Cem), a son of Emanuel and Ellen Jane (Adams) Dietrich), m Jennie Keiper (Feb 15, 1876 - Feb 17, 1967), a dau of William H. and Susannah (Row) Keiper.They were married May 15, 1896 at the home of her parents. **Edward and Jennie (Keiper) Dietrich children:**
WILLIAM E. (Nov 15, 1896, Lykens - Nov 9, 1977), bur Simeon Cem, m Mar 2, 1915, Helen M. Hoffman (May 10, 1895 – Jul 26,1977), a dau of Elizabeth Catherine Reigle and George Hoffman. **William and Helen (Hoffman) Dietrich children:** Kathryn Elizabeth b Feb 19, 1915 m Norman John Gasbarro, **had three children: Norman John Jr.** b Jan 27, 1944, **William Edward** b Jul 19, 1947; **James,**lives in New Jersey; **Harold William** b Feb 14, 1919 –deceased), m Erma ____, **had three children: Carol, Harold, Regina.**
EARL E. (Jul 24, 1898 – Feb 23, 1986, bur Norfolk, Va.), m 1st Elaine Anacker, had dau **Erlaine.** Earl m 2nd Viola Schnider d Jan 11, 1986), and lived in Norfolk, Va.
LAURA Ellen (Apr 23, 1900 – Sep 22, 1985, bur Simeon Cem), not married. Laura lived with her parents and worked in the Gratz factory.
ARTHUR (Aug 12, 1902 – Mar 20, 1903, bur Simeon Cem)
HARRY FRANKLIN (Feb 6, 1904 – Oct 26, 1978, bur Meth Cem, Valley View), m Laura Troutman (____), a dau of _____ **Harry and Laura (Troutman) Dietrich had two children: David** dec'd, m Hilda Schieb, **had two children: Donald, Holly** ; **Lorraine** b 1946, m Thomas Oldham. Lorraine is the librarian in the public library in Hegins.
SUSAN NAOMI (Mar 24, 1906 – Oct 12, 1991, bur Simeon Cem), m Charles A. Schoffstall (Oct 17, 1906 - Mar 9, 1957), a son of Elias and Emma (Duttry) Schoffstall. **Charles A. and Susan (Dietrich) Schoffstall children:**
Ethel Virginia b Jan 12, 1927 m Jun 27, 1948 Dallas L. Williams (Dec 13, 1926 – Dec 6, 1979, bur Halifax Cem). **Dallas and Ethel (Schoffstall) Williams had two children: Suzann Carol** b Feb 15, 1950, not m; **Judy Helen** (May 29, 1953 – d Feb 4, 2002, bur Halifax), m Dennis Gutshall (Sep 12, 1950 – Oct 7, 1999). **Dennis and Judy (William) Gutshall had one son** Jason Dennis b Jan 10, 1978.
Blair ALLEN (Mar 22, 1928 - Jun 27, 1951, bur Simeon Cem), killed while serving during the Korean War.
Charles Adam b Sep 25, 1930, m Nov 15, 1952, Lois E. Green, b Aug 21, 1931, a dau of Harvey I.and Lula P. (Yarnall) Green of Barry Twp., Sch Co., Pa.). **Charles and Lois (Green) Schoffstall children:** Debra Ann b Sep 23, 1956 Danville, Pa., m Nov 25, 1977 Thomas Henshaw b May 17, 1953, son of Jonathan and Martha Henshaw of Levittown, Pa., **have four children:** Christina Marie b Mar 21, 1981, Kelly Allison b Jun 12, 1982, Louise Michelle b Feb 3, 1984, Ryan Scott b Jul 24, 1985; **Lynne Louise** b Oct 29, 1958 Clearfield, Pa., m Apr 28, 1984 Jonathan James Baer b Oct 10, 1960,a son of Raymond and Dorothy (Potter) Baer of Millersburg , **they have two children:** Rebekah Lynne b May 20, 1985, Elliott Jonathan b Feb 13, 1989; **Lori Kay** b Jan 23, 1967, Johnson City, N.Y., m May 23, 1992 David Norris b Dec 6, 1966, a son of Blair and Louise (Altland) Norris of Thomasville, Pa. , **they have two children:** Andrew Phillip b Jan 7, 1998, Joshua Elias b Sep 7, 1999.
Joanne Marie b Aug 10, 1932, m Sep 18, 1954 Delbert Deppen b Dec 26, 1930, **they have two children:** Debra Joanne b Sep1,1958, m Jun 13, 1992 Dennis Williams, no children; **Douglas Delbert** (Jun 9, 1964 - 2002), m Jun 27, 1998 Tammy Hamlett b May 7, 1963, **had these children:** Abigail Virginia and Michaela Marie (twins) b Apr 26, 1999; Noel Alexandra b Dec 20, 2000.
Benny James b Mar 2, 1935, m 1st Eiko Sugimoto (Nov 8, 1 926 – Jan 15, 1990), 2nd Chungja Lee b Sep 30, 1943. **Two children: Ruby** b Jul 30, 1951, m 1st Michael Schlitt, had dau Kimi Catherine b Oct 17, 1977. m 2nd John

Green, had son <u>Joseph Scott</u> b May 26, 1985; <u>**Charles**</u> b Jul 27, 1964 m Emily Hansen, **have these children:**
<u>Benjamin Vaughn</u> b Mar 19, 1998<u>; Logan Charles</u> b Aug 28, 2000.

MARLIN RUSSEL (Dec 7, 1908 -   , bur St. Johns "Hill" Cem), m Marie Lark, dau of_____Lark **Marlin**
and Marie (Lark) had two children: Kenneth d in infancy; **Marlene** b Jun 1943, m _____

LAUREN ROBERT b Apr 26, 1911 - d Jul 24, 1999), m 1st Beulah Tankersley (1913 - 1974, bur Simeon Cem),
had dau **Bonnie** who lives in Utah, 2nd Anna ____, both deceased before Lauren. Lauren was the first Dietrich child
to be born on this farm. He attended Gise School, and the year that he graduated, was valedictorian of his class.
Henry Wenrich had been Lauren's teacher for several years, and was concerned that Lauren would further his
education. He came to the Dietrich farm, and told the parents that they should make arrangements for Lauren to
attend Berrysburg Vocational Tech School. Since tuition was an added cost for the family, they were reluctant, but
consented. Lauren had to walk three and one-half miles each way to attend school. Before he left home in the
morning, he walked along the line fence, checking his muskrat traps, and helped with the chores on the farm. More
chores awaited when he returned to his home in the afternoon.

LEE KEIPER (Jun 9, 1913 - Feb 8, 1939, bur Simeon Cem), killed in a mining accident, not m.

SARAH ELLEN (Jun 17, 1915 - Dec 24, 1921, bur Simeon Cem), died from smallpox vaccination.

JOHN HENRY (Apr 8, 1917 - Feb 8, 1939, bur Simeon Cem), killed in a mining accident, not m.]

Edward Dietrich was a miner when they lived in Lykens. He and his wife Jennie decided that a change to
rural life would be better for their family. The whole family enjoyed living in the country, working on the farm.

Considering that the family was made up of eleven children, the house was small. There were three
bedrooms; a small one for the girls, a larger one with several rope beds to accommodate the boys, and a room for the
parents. Access to the boys' room was made through a door in the parents room. This small detail proved to be a bit
frustrating for the teenage boys who were coming home a bit late at night!

Downstairs, the kitchen was the center of activities, day and evening. A long bench placed on one side of the
table near the wall helped to accommodate all family members and many guests who visited the farm. Grandchildren
as they arrived, headed toward the bench in hopes of getting something to eat (even though they may have just had
dinner at home). During the 'thirties and 'forties when one walked into the kitchen, the cupboard with the sink pump
was the first thing to come into view on the left. Water from the nearby springhouse was pumped to the kitchen and
provided an ample supply of water for the daily household needs. The flow of cool water through the springhouse
served as a refrigerator year round. The stove was also nearby, where coal or wood could be burned, but usually
corncobs were piled near by for a quick fire. The kitchen stove was a cozy place where folks could gather to keep
warm in cold weather. Mammy spent many hours cooking meals on her stove. Not only for her family, but for
company that dropped in. Even though she did not have modern facilities, she always had fresh or canned food so she
could prepare something to eat. The cellar walls were lined with jars of vegetables, meat, and fruit. Apples, potatoes
and walnuts were also stored there. The smokehouse near the kitchen was full of hams and sausage. In the winter,
hooks attached to the ceiling in the granary in the barn held excess smoked meats. Family members recall that one
large family had a habit of arriving at the farm for a visit just about the time that dinner was being prepared.
Although very hospitable, Mammy finally had it, and decided they would just sit and talk until these people left for
home. Time passed, hour after hour, until they finally left. But it did the trick. The visiting family was cured.

Since there was no inside plumbing, everyone used the outhouse. But at least for quite sometime, a big
nasty rooster hung out in that vicinity, and anyone leaving the outhouse was subject to being "flopped" by the rooster.
Of course chickens roamed all over the yard and barnyard. Pigs, cows and horses were housed in outbuildings and in
the barn.

If the men and boys were not working in the fields, Pappy could usually be seen outside near the
springhouse and kettle area, chopping wood for the kitchen stove or for a fire at the kettle place.

Jennie "Mammy" was busy raising and providing for the large family, so did much baking. On a morning
when she planned to bake bread, she gave Lauren a cup and three pennies, and instructed him to walk to Sitlingers'
for yeast. That was a typical chore for the young children in the family.

The boys had other chores that sometimes created problems. While Marlin and Lauren were youngsters (old
enough to travel to Gratz with horse and buggy for transportation), they were in charge of "hunting the eggs." Their
mother accumulated the eggs, and when she needed something from the store, the boys brought the eggs to
"Baugher" Rothermels store and used them for trade (the barter system). Quick thinking Marlin devised a scheme to
share his mothers' profit. He decided to keep some of the eggs each day in a separate place. That way, when he
brought the eggs to town, he would have extra money to buy candy. On one occasion when they rode up to the store,

they exchanged the eggs for the items on their mothers grocery list. Then they went to the candy counter and chose chocolate candy equal to the amount of eggs they had accumulated. It turned out to be quite a substantial amount of candy. On the way home, they realized that they would have to account for any left over candy. So, they ate and ate until it was all gone. Although they did not get sick, their stomachs did not feel too good for the remainder of the day. They lost their appetite for dinner.

In the summer of 1924, neighbor Alex Klinger came to help put lightning rods on the Dietrich barn. Edward Dietrich assigned two of his boys, Harry and Marlin to help with the installation. The barn had a tin roof, and on a hot summer day it was difficult to work without an occasional break. During the rest periods, they sat in the shade behind the barn. Alex told them stories, one that they never forgot.

"Learn to handle a gun," he said. It is a dangerous weapon. He told the story of when he was a boy and lived near Pitman on a farm. There were two houses, one for the landowner, and one for the farmer. Alex would go into the farmer's house (it was empty), where he found military rifles, and other soldier equipment stacked up in a corner. He and other boys would go out in the woods and play soldier. They hid behind trees and hollered out "boy you are dead." The pretend ramrod on the rifle had a powder charge. One fellow lifted the gun and pulled the trigger. The gun shot and hit a boy in the intestines, as he came around the tree. He was not taken to the doctor, but did recover. The moral to the story is, never trust a gun. Shortly after the lightning rods were installed, a storm came up and lightning struck the barn. Fortunately, the barn did not burn.

During the summer months, Edward and his family kept busy working on the farm, but throughout the winter months, he and some of the boys were employed in the mines. When ice and snow made it difficult to trudge over the steep Short Mountain to the colliery, the men wore cleats on the bottom of their boots. Sometimes they worked in independent mines, and one year that proved to be a disaster.

On Wednesday morning, February 8, 1939, John and Lee were working inside an independent mine slope about two miles east of Good Spring. Edward Dietrich and an eighteen-year old neighbor, Norman Howard worked outside. After hearing a signal of possible distress, Norman entered the mine. When Norman did not return, Edward went in to investigate, and found the pile of coal and rock where the boys had been working. As he started for the surface to secure help, he barely escaped another rush of rock.

A crew of men, family members, neighbors, friends, and concerned people from the area, worked diligently around the clock for the next several days to rescue the boys. After sometime, they realized no one survived. John was found Friday night, Norman was found Sunday night, and Lee's body was found the following Tuesday.

While John and Lee were entombed, their brother and sister-in-law Marlin and Marie were in the Shamokin Hospital awaiting the birth of their first child. When he received the word, Marlin came to Gratz. "Globby" Buffington told him he knew about where the mine was located, and after finishing a haircut, he would take Marlin to the mine site. Soon after they arrived at the mine, Globby found a ride home and Marlin stayed at the mine. Later, Marlin got back to the hospital, and he learned that he was the father of a baby boy, but he was born with a leakinig heart, and the baby would not survive. Another member of the family Kathryn Deitrich Gasbarro, was working in Lansdowne, Pennsylvania in a beauty shop, when she heard the news of the accident on the radio.

Viewings were held for the boys in the basement of the Hoover funeral Parlor in Berrysburg. Before this time, funerals were usually held in homes. Now the Hoover family was preparing their building for funeral services, but the first floor room was not quite finished. A funeral for Norman Howard was held one week after the entombment, on Wednesday morning, at St. Johns Church in Berrysburg. John and Lee were engaged to Mary Ellen and Lauretta Howard, sisters of Norman. Instead of the double wedding planned for later in spring, a double funeral was held for Lee and John the next morning.

Soon after the Dietrichs moved to Lykens Township, they became well acquainted with most of their neighbors. Many neighborhood gatherings took place throughout the year. One of the anticipated events was the New Years Eve party held at the Dietrich farm. People from all over the valley gathered there. Those who played string instruments formed a group to play music and many people participated in square dancing. The couples brought their children, because this was a family affair. As the evening progressed, the younger children grew tired. They were put to bed upstairs on straw beds, until the parents were ready to go home.

The young folks whom played musical instruments included Lauren Dietrich on guitar, the three Hoffman brothers, John, Charles and Clarence, and _____ Williard. Some of them played for the square dances held at Rube's hall in Loyalton on Saturday nights. One night the "caller" was sick, and someone was needed to take his place. Lauren was asked to substitute, and he continued steadily to do the "calling" until he moved to Baltimore in 1929.

During the summer months many neighborhood picnics were held in the _____ woods, west of the Dietrich farm. Each family brought food, and a huge spread was enjoyed by all.

In later years, after John and Lee were tragically killed in the mines, grandchildren Ethel and Blair frequently stayed on the farm over weekends or during the week in summer. They were extra "hands" around the farm, running errands, fetching water, churning butter. They could even mow the lawn with the hand mower. Most kids that visited enjoyed pushing the lawn mower around the yard. During those stays, if Mammy or Aunt Laura was making their special hot potato salad with the bacon, they would allow Ethel to have one little taste of her favorite dish before it was put away for the special dinner or picnic.

On December 5, 1942, Edward and Jennie Dietrich sold the two tracts of land, forty-seven acres, thirty-two perches with dwelling, barn, etc, and the thirty acres of farmland to Lincoln O. and Ellen N. Leffler of Lykens Township. Edward and Jennie retired from the farm, and moved to the house on lot seventeen in Gratz. Their daughter Laura went with them. Edward Dietrich suffered from asthma, and died in this home. About 1955, Jennie Dietrich and Laura moved to the brick house across the street on lot sixteen, now home of David and Lori Norris, and remained at that address until Jennies' death.]

Edward Dietrich Family (Photo taken on their farm c1938)
Stg l to r: sons Lee, Mary Ellen Howard, John, Loretta Howard, Earl, Lauren, Marie &Marlin Dietrich, Harold Dietrich, William, Harry. Std l to r: Chas & Susan Schoffstall, Mrs. Lark, Edward & Jennie (Keiper) Dietrich, parents, Laura, Helen (Riegel) Dietrich, Laura (Troutman) Dietrich. Bottom: Ben, Blair, Ethel & Joanne Schoffstall, Louise Lark, Chas Schoffstall.

[**LINCOLN O.LEFFLER** (1900 - 1978, bur Salem Luth, Killinger), m Ellen M. Bahner, b1908.
Lincoln O. and Ellen M. (Bahner) Leffler had these children (most bapt St. Peters Ref "Red Cross" Ch, Jackson Twp, Northld Co.): Etheleen Beatrice b Aug 29, 1923, m Clarence B_____; **Margaret Corrine** (Sep 27, 1925 –Jan 27, 1985, bur Salem Luth, Killinger), m John Holtzman (no dates); **Raymond Lincoln** (Dec 14, 1930 – Nov 28, 1981, bur Salem Luth, Killinger), m Alfreda Lenker; **Betty** m Donald Keiter; **Guy Melvin** b May 8, 1936, m Nov 27, 1958, Dotty Klinger, b Jun 16, 1941, a dau of Leon and Elva (Harner) Klinger; **Paul N.** m Mar 29, 1958, Millie Wolf b Sep 15, 1940, dau of Allen and Ada (Klinger) Wolf. **Paul and Millie (Wolf) Leffler had these children: Lori** **Ann** b Aug 29, 1958; **Brian** **Paul** b Mar 25, 1969, m Becky Morgan; **June** b _____, m Marlin Maurer; **Jean M.** m Jun 1960, Gene D. Klinger; **Janet** m _____Smith; **Carol**; **Bonnie**.

Mr. and Mrs. Lincoln O. Leffler continued to own this farm and cleared acreage for many years.
On June 25, 1979, Lincoln and Ellen M. Leffler sold both parcels to Samuel I. Stoltzfus.

The Stoltzfus family came to Lykens Township from Lancaster County. They are members of the Amish Community, and have become established in the area. After they moved to this location, they provided an area of the farm where a new Amish schoolhouse has been built. It provides a central location for private Amish schooling for the families that settled in the western section of Lykens Township. Reminiscent of the "old days" the one-story structure is conducive to elementary education.

AMISH SCHOOL

JACOB SHADE
(WAS WILLIAM SWEITZER FARM 1875- 105 acres)
Brick house built c1855, now covered with siding

Barn on Shade Farm

This land is part of a tract that Commonwealth of Pennsylvania warranted March 1, 1785, surveyed May 23, 1785 and patented July 28, 1786 to John Reiter. The grant was called "Reitersburgh" and contained 206 acres. The land became vested in many different owners during the next several years.

John and Mary Reiter sold land October 27, 1787 to Samuel McCrury, and he and his wife Ann sold to Christian Hoffman on March 28, 1794. Christian and Susannah Hoffman sold to Balthaser Romberger Sr. on June 13, 1798. On the "window tax" taken October 1798 Balthaser Romberger is assessed for a cabin and poor barn, located and joining Henry Romberger.

Several years later, on March 10, 1804, Balthaser Romberger, Sr and his wife Susanna sold a tract of eighty-two acres, 102 perches, to his son Adam Romberger. Adam owned this land for many years, but eventually he broke it up into smaller tracts. By sundry conveyances, he transferred one tract of twenty-nine acres, ninety-eight perches to Daniel Tobias. But on May 26, 1821, Daniel and Catherine Tobias transferred it back to Adam Romberger. Another small tract of four acres, four perches by sundry conveyances went to Joseph and John Tobias. But on May 9, 1824, Joseph and Mary Tobias and John and Barbara Tobias sold it back to Adam Romberger. Daniel Tobias was an early tavern keeper in Gratz, but left the area about the time they sold this property. At least some of his family members went with him.

On March 26, 1839, Adam and Catherine Romberger conveyed all three of the above tracts (forty nine acres, twenty nine plus acres and four plus acres), a total of eighty -two acres one hundred two perches to Daniel Romberger. The land was described as being a plantation, with a log house and barn. Daniel Romberger was a farmer. About 1855, while he lived here, Daniel Romberger had a two-story brick house constructed on the land. That year he was assessed for the new brick house, and a bank barn.

On August 24, 1857, Daniel and Hannah Romberger sold a messuage plantation with eighty-seven acres, four and one-half perches of land to William Sweitzer, who had lived in Mifflin Township. About five acres of this land had been transferred from Christian and Sarah Umholtz to Daniel Romberger on April 1, 1848.

THE REITER/RIDER/ REUTER/ Ryter Etc. FAMILY
[Help from Joe Rider Siphron]

John Reiter, William Reiter, and George Reiter, several members of a Reiter family settled early in the 1700s in Lancaster County. Because of border changes in the early counties, and the individual members of the family's tendency to relocate, this Reiter family can be found on tax records of Lancaster, Lebanon, Dauphin and

Northumberland Counties. Research on this family has been difficult, since church and public records for them are not easily found. Other Reiter families lived in close proximity to this branch, but have not been linked. Much time has been spent in research without total success. For one thing, the family in general did not remain in this area. Shortly after 1800, most of them had migrated to another area. A portion of the early settlers moved to Centre County, Pa. The incomplete information that we found in our research about the family is recorded below.

WILLIAM REITER (b pre 1725 - possibly in Prussia – this information handed down by his descendents), was a resident of Upper Paxton Twp as early as April 24,1776 when he signed a petition to keep stray cattle out of the settlers meadows. He paid a Continental Tax in 1778, and is also on the list of those "above 53 yrs, not eligible for military duty." He is again listed on the 1780 tax list for Wiconisco District, and in 1785, 1786, 1787 in Upper Paxton Twp. (A John Reiter is also on the tax record of 1785, 1786, & 1787). In 1783 William was a communicant at Salem Lutheran Church in Killinger. He purchased a tract of land that was patented to Martin Nissly in 1786. The land was in what is now the Lykens Township area, adjacent to John Reiter, but apparently did not stay here..

Very little has been found on the personal life of this William Reiter. From the tax records, we know that he was born before 1725, but the place of his birth is still unknown. *William Reiter had the following children:*

WILLIAM REITER (*b* May 25, 1749 Germany - d _____), m Catherine _____. He came to America and settled in Frederick County, Md. on _____. In 1778 William enlisted in the "The German Regiment of Maryland and Pennsylvania, in the Continental Army" as a substitute for Jacob Juda. He served under the command of Lt. Col. Ludwick Weltner of Frederick, Maryland, and was sent to an area near White Plains, N.Y. From there he was sent in October 1779 (with the German Regiment) to what is now Sunbury, Northumberland County "to protect the settlers around the forks of the Susquehanna River from Indian attacks." He remained on duty in that area as late as September 1780. After the war William Reiter became a resident of Mahantongo Township, Northumberland County and was taxed there in 1786, as was William Jr. He apparently did not stay there. *William and Catharine Reiter had these children baptized at either David's Reformed or Salem Lutheran Church in Killinger:*
***JOHN GEORGE b___. (There is no baptismal record, giving name of parents, but he was confirmed at David's Church at Killinger August 10, 1782.
***No name given_b May 14, 1772, sponsor the father (at Salem Luth)
***CHRISTIANA CATHARINE b Oct 8, 1778 sponsor Michael Salada and wife at Salem Luth Ch, Sp Wilhelm Reiter & Margaret Witmer.

MARGARET REITER b c1751 m Brand Fisher, had a son ***WILLIAM b Nov 4, 1779, bapt David's Ch

JOHN REITER (b c1755 In Prussia - d Jan or Feb 1805, Manada Creek, West Hanover Twp.). The inventory of his estate is dated Feb 14, 1805. John married Anna Maria _____.(b - d 1805).
This John may have come to America on the ship "Sallie" arriving in Philadelphia Oct 5, 1767 with his father William. He was taxed in Leacock Township in 1777 as the "miller at Peter Eakers (Eckerts)." That same year he was a private in Captain John Rowland's Company of the Lancaster County Militia.
John and William Reiter apparently moved to Lykens Valley about 1776. In 1779 & 1780 John Rieter and William Rieter were both living in Wiconisco District (Dauphin Co). It was five years later that John Received the Reitersburg warrant (in 1785).
In 1781 John & Anna Maria Reiter were sponsors for Catharina, a child of Jonas and Magdalena McLien.
On March 1, 1785 John Reiter received the warrant for "Reitersburg". He and William Reiter were both taxed in Upper Paxton Twp. He sold the property in October 1787 to Samuel McCrary. Earlier that year (May) he and his wife, and their son George communed at Salem Lutheran Church, Killinger
On Feb 20, 1796 an agreement was made to build a new church building for Zions Stone Valley Church. One of the people who pledged to give money in support of the new building was a John Reiter.
During the late 1780s, John Reiter moved back to West Hanover Township, and on May 15, 1790 he purchased a tract of 114 acres of land on the east bank of the Manada Creek from John and Elizabeth Weaver. The deed was not recorded until 1796. He purchased another tract of land from Jones Wilson on April 26, 1802.

After John died, Letters of administration were given to his executors William Reiter and Thomas Wenrich on Feb 14, 1805. According to orphan court records Anna Mary his widow died between February and September of that year. On September 12th, 1805, 150 acres of his land was sold to Emanuel Cassel. (probably a son of Michael Cassel (   ), who had a son Emanuel Cassel b Oct 24, 1775 in Hummelstown. Emanuel had a son Emanuel (Jr) b c1815 who married Anna Nissley (Aug 22, 1819 - Apr 11, 1845), a daughter of Martin Nissley and wife Anna Romberger.

John and Anna Mary Reiter had seven children:

***ELIZABETH b Oct 17, 1778, bapt New Holland Church, Lanc Co, May 23, 1779 sponsor Adam & Esther (Cray) Ramberger. Elizabeth must have died before her father.
***CATHERINE (Mar 17, 1780 - Sep 17, 1850), m Jan 7, 1802 in Salem Luth Ch, Lebanon to George Bartholomew Ramberger (Nov 7, 1776 - May 21, 1845), a son of Adam and Esther (Cray) Ramberger of Leacock Twp., Lanc Co.
George Bartholomew and Catharine (Reiter) Ramberger had these children:
****JOHN (Jan 7, 1805 - Oct 22, 1877), m Sep 3, 1828 Elisabeth Row (Jun 10, 1807 - Jan 29, 1854).
****ELIZABETH (Aug 21, 1808 - Mar 15,1870), m Jan 15, 1829 John Kreider (Jun 20, 1801 - Aug 9, 1886 Leb Co.)
****MARY (c1812 - 1898)
****GEORGE (1813 - Jul 27, 1850), m Margaret Leathers (1824 - 1850)
****MARGARET (no dates), m Henry Bratton

***JOHN (b c1781/2 - d between Feb and Sep 1805, had no children.
***WILLIAM (Aug 14, 1783 - Dec 7, 1863 Ferguson Twp, Centre Co), m Aug 27, 1805 (at Tabor 1st Ref Ch, Lebanon) to Elisabeth Ramberger (Oct 6, 1781 - Feb 25, 1841), bapt Bergstresser Luth Ch, Lanc Co, a dau of Adam and Esther (Cray) Ramberger of Leacock Twp., Lanc Co.
William and Elisabeth (Ramberger) Reiter had these children:
****ANNA MARY (c1806 - 1865)
****CATHERINE (Jan 12, 1813 - May 17, 1871), m Jun 19, 1833
****EVE (Nov 25, 1814 - May 16, 1899)
****JOHN (no dates)

***ANNA MARIA (b Sep 13, 1785 bapt Hoffman Ch, sp Baltzer Ramberger date of bapt not given - died before her father. - no issue

***GEORGE (___ - he was a minor child when his father died.)

***MICHAEL G. (b Feb 18, 1797 Dau Co bapt First Luth & Ref Church, Hbg- sp Philip & A. Maria Witmer - d Jan 30, 1881 in Center Co), m Barbara Kreider (b Nov 15, 1799 Leb Twp., Lanc Co - d Mar 9, 1874 Centre Co.). Michael & Barbara moved to Gatesburg, Centre Co. In 1880 he was included in the Fergueson, Centre Co. census, as a retired farmer. His niece Amy Reiter age 39 was with him.
Michael G. & Barbara (Kreider) Reiter children:

****MARY (Aug 2, 1817 - Aug 22, 1869); ****CATHERINE b Jan 29, 1821; ****ELIZABETH (Dec 21, 1822 - May 8, 1883);****LYDIA (Dec 25, 1824 - Sep 11, 1890), m Daniel Grazille; ****SARAH A. (Dec 13, 1826 - Nov 23, 1890), m Amos Clemson; ****JACOB K.. (Feb 25, 1829 - Jul 9, 1902, struck by lightening), m Barbara Rumberger (Oct 30, 1830 - Sep 27, 1925), a dau of Jacob and Elisabeth (Funk) Rumberger, lived in Gatesburg, Centre Co.; ****MICHAEL C. b Mar 14, 1832, moved to Nebraska; ****NANCY (Aug 13, 1834 - Dec 10,1914), m Samuel Musser b c1830 and lived in Fairbrook, and Fergueson, Centre Co. *Three of their children*: Anna, Edward, and William were teachers in 1880. ****JOHN G.. b May 15, 1836, m Esther Masterson (1839 - 19160. He was a farmer and huckster and lived in Gatesburg, later Fergueson. ****BARBARA b Apr 22, 1838, m Oct 21, 1859 to Isaac Beck b Oct 8, 1835, a son of Daniel and Elisabeth (Cryder) Beck of Half Moon Township, Centre County, (former residents of Warriors Mark, Huntingdon Co., Pa.); ****MATHIAS (Apr 28, 1840 - 1926), m Mary A. Ellenberger, and lived in Gatesburg and Fergueson, Centre Co.; ****ELLEN (Apr 25, 1843 - 1928), m May 18, 1891 William Hastings, a blacksmith. They lived in Gatesburg, and Fergueson, Centre Co.
***SAMUEL(no dates - he was a minor child when his father died.)

GEORGE REITER (   ), cordwainer, m 1st ___, 2nd on Jan 24, 1774, Magdalena Still, the widow of Stephen Lasch, Sr., who died in 1763, a son of George & Eva Lasch. George received two warrants of land with buildings on April 30, 1788. The land "straddled the Mahantango Creek, east of Pillow, extending into Mahanoy Township, Northumberland County and Upper Paxton Township, Dauphin County. Also east of Pillow Gap, located just over the border in Northumberland County. These tracts contained 355 acres & 114 ¼ acres. On November 16, 1789, George Reiter sold these two tracts separately to William Reiter. One tract contained 330 acres with house, the other was 100 acres (both with lesser amounts of land than original grant). That same day, George sold in open market to William Reiter the following enumerated articles: "nine head of horned cows, two mares, one horse and one lot of six sheep. Also the horses' gears and wagon, and my bed and bedding. " George Reiter does not appear on the 1790 census for Northumberland County. He apparently left the area about that time. The name of his first wife is unknown, she apparently died before 1774.

George Reiter may have been the father of the following children:

***JOHN GEORGE b c1764 ?, confirmed Davids church 1782 age 18yrs old taxed Mahanoy Twp for 150 acres 1786 – 1787 along Mahantongo Creek.
***SUSANNA b Feb 5, 1767, bapt Apr 18, 1779 Stone Valley, with Dietrich Steinbrecher & wife as sponsors.

MARGARET REITER (c1751 -) m Brand Fisher, had a son William b Nov 4, 1779, bapt David's Ch sp Wilhelm Reiter & Margaret Witmer

WILLIAM REITER, JR. (   ), m Elisabeth Lasch (   ), a dau of Stephen & Magdalena (Still) Lasch, and granddaughter of John George and Magdalena (Still) Reiter..
William and Elisabeth (Lasch) Reiter, Jr. children:

***JOHN GEORGE b Aug 10, 1786, bapt Stone Valley Ch, sp John George and Magdalena (Still or Hill) Reiter the grandparents.– mother of Elizabeth (in the old record it says grandmother – then crossed out in hand writing and . says grandparents?)
***JOHN b ____ . He is listed as a son of G. Reiter & wife in the communion list of Salem Luth Ch, Killinger on May 27, 1787.

CATHERINE REITER (____ - d pre 1800), m John Dietrich Steinbrecher, Jr. John Dietrich and Catherine (Reiter) Steinbrecher, Jr.
John Dietrich & Catherine (Reiter) Steinbrecher, Jr. children children:
***JOHN ADAM b Jan 3, 1783, bapt St. Johns Hill Church
***ANNA CATHERINE b Dec 9,1786, bapt Stone Valley, Northumberland Co.
***JOHN GEORGE b Feb 15, 1789, sp George & Magdalena Reiter
***ELIZABETH b Aug 12, 1790, sp William & Elizabeth Reiter

THE McCRURY/McCURDY FAMILY

The McCleery (McCrury, McCrary, etc) family of Scotch-Irish descent left Scotland because of religious persecutions, and settled in Northern Ireland. Two young brothers Michael and John, natives of Coleraine, Ireland, came to America. John served as a captain in the Revolutionary War, and was killed at the battle of Bunker Hill. Michael settled first in Virginia, than settled on the Conestoga, in Lancaster County, Pa. He may have come to Derry Twp, Dauphin County.

*MICHAEL McCLEERY (possibly b c1718 – d Sep 20, 1801, bur Presbyterian Cem near Hershey), m Jeanette _____, **and it is thought that these are their children:**

**SAMUEL (b May 24, 1765 - d Jun 8, 1807, bur Derry Presbyterian Cem, near Hershey), m Ann_____, and in 1800 they also lived in Up. Paxton Twp. They had two young sons, and four young daughters. They had left this area at least by 1810.

JOHN (b Oct 13, 1767, at the forks of the Conestoga in Earl Twp., Lanc Co., d Jun 21, 1851, bur Harmony Cem, Milton, Northld Co.). John m Sep 23, 1802 Mary Lytle b Mar 16, 1774, a dau of Joseph and Sarah (Morrison) Lytle, also of English and Scotch-Irish descent. John McCleery grew up in Lancaster County, then moved to Harrisburg where he became involved in a mercantile business. He lived in Halifax, Dauphin County briefly, and appeared on the 1800 Census for Up Paxton Twp, with a wife, and four young men. They moved on to Milton, Northld County in the very early 1800s. **John and Mary (Lytle) McCleery had these known children: ***William b Jul 31, 1803 at Halifax, moved early in life to Milton with his parents, m Margaret Pollock, dau of Wm Pollock, sister of James Pollock, early governor of Pa. William became a doctor; ***Sarah b Feb 18, 1805, m John L. Watson; ***Joseph b Jan 10, 1807; ***Jane b Feb 4,1809, m Rev. David Junkin; ***Elizabeth b Sep 10, 1811; ***Mary b Mar 16, 1814, m Rev. Nathan Shotwell.

**WILLIAM (Nov 15, 1770 - Nov 20, 1795, bur Derry Presbyterian Cem, Hershey), also thought to be a son of Michael McCleery, the immigrant.

**ROBERT- lived here did the valuation of land of Michael Rissinger Up Pax 1804

JONATHAN ( ), m Maria _____, had these children (bapt Hoffman Ch); ***Catarina b Aug 18, 1781 to Jona and Magd sp Johannes Reuter & Anna Maria;*Maria Catharina b Oct 17, 1789; ***Maria Elisabeth b Mar 24, 1791; ***Anna Magdalena b Mar 17, 1793; ***Samuel b May 8, 1795; ***Johannes b Apr 12, 1799

THE ROMBERGER//RAMBURGER/RUMBERGER FAMILY
(Genealogy information from many sources including Heber T. Hertzog, John A. Romberger, M. DiNinni, Ralph T. Romberger, & others and are own research.)

[The immigrant ancestor of this Romberger family to America was a miller, Bartholomaus Romberger (1716- 1800) and his wife Anna Maria Bricker. Bartholomaus was a son of J. Casper Romberger born c1684 and his wife Catharina ___ (c1684–1730) of Bavaria. He and the family arrived in Philadelphia September 24, 1753 on ship "Neptune". By 1759, Bartholomaus was settled in Leacock Twp., Lancaster Co. In 1769 he is listed as a miller, in 1770 he was listed as a weaver in Earl Twp. In 1776 he was in Leacock Twp., where he remained until the 1780's when he and his family moved to Dauphin County. He was living in Lebanon County with his son Adam at the time of his death. Shortly before his death he wrote his will (dated Aug 3, 1799), leaving his estate to his son Adam excluding all of his other relatives. Adam inherited his estate because he "kept him for 21 years."

*BARTHOLOMAUS ROMBERGER (May 4, 1716 Upper Bavaria, Ger – Sep 25, 1800, bur Hill Ch Cem, Anneville, Leb Co.), m 1st Anna Maria Bricker, **had 3 known children:**

ADAM ROMBERGER (Apr 23,1743 – Nov 1800 Annville Twp), m Jul 4, 1765 Trinity Luth, New Holland Esther Cray (____ – Sep 9, 1794), a dau of Peter Cray of Lanc Co. **Adam & Esther (Cray) Romberger children (bapt Trinity Ch, New Holland, Lanc). Many moved to western counties of Pa., possibly with members of the Reiter family:

***Anna Maria b May 15, 1768;

***Adam (Jun 24,1770 – Mar 19,1832, Huntington Co), m Mary Ann Kafroth, dau of Heinrich Kafroth of Lanc Co.

***Margaretha b Jun 4, 1772 , m John Rau of Lebanon Co b c1765, **had two known children that died young.**

***Johannes (Dec 27, 1774 – Feb 20, 1847), m Elisabeth Ellenberger, dau of Jacob Ellenberger, lived in Lanc Co.

George Bartholomew** (Nov 7, 1776, - May 21, 1845) m Catharine Reiter (1783 – 1850). **George Bartholomew & Catharine (Reiter) Romberger children:**John** (Jan 7, 1805 - Oct 22, 1877), m Oct 22, 1877 Elisabeth Row; *****Elisabeth** (Aug 21, 1808 - Mar 19, 1890), m Jan 15, 1829 John Kreider; *****George** (1813 – 1850), m Margaret Leathers (1824 – 1850, bur Rumberger Cem);*****Mary** (b ___ - d 1898); *****Margaret** (no dates) m Henry Bratton.

***Eva** b Feb 17, 1779 – d 1870), m Joseph Kreider (1773 – 1821).

Elisabeth** (Oct 6, 1781 – Feb 25, 1841), m William Reiter (Aug 14, 1783 – Dec 7, 1863, Gatesburg). [see Reiter genealogy], **William & Elisabeth (Romberger) Reiter children:**Catharine** (Jan 12, 1813 – May 17, 1871), m Isaac Way;*****Eva** (b Nov 25, 1814 – May 16, 1899), m Benjamin Way; *****John E.** (no dates) m Sarah A. Way.

***Jacob** (Jan 28, 1784 – May 4, 1852), m Elisabeth Funk (Apr 18, 1789 –Nov 20, 1884), a dau of Martin and Barbara Funk.

MARIA EVA (c1745), m Sep 29, 1765 Peter Cray. **Peter and Maria Eva (Romberger) Cray children:**
***Catherine** b Aug 13, 1765; ***John Peter** b Feb 26, 1771, bapt Trinity Luth, New Holland

BALTHASER ROMBERGER (Jul 5, 1747 Bavaria- c1825 Mifflin Co, Dau Co), m Anna Maria Traut (c1749 - ___), a dau of Johan Wendel George & Maria Magdalena (Walter) Traut. **Balthaser & Anna Maria (Traut) Romberger had 7 children (most b in Lanc Co, bapt Trinity Luth Ch, New Holland);**
***Anna Maria** (Jun 12, 1771 - Feb 26, 1838), , m Michael Matter (1763 – 1852), a son of John & Anna Barbara (Arnold) Matter. [see Matter genealogy elsewhere in book.]
***Heinrich** (Jul 12, 1773 Lanc Co – Jan 31, 1822, Lykens Twp.), m Elizabeth Hoffman (Nov 12, 1795 - Dec 19, 1873), . Henry was one of the persons who purchased a gun from Leonard Reedy the gunsmith in 1820. **Heinrich and Elisabeth (Hoffman) Romberger had these children:**
****Peter** (Nov 12, 1795 - Dec 19, 1873, Turkey Valley, Perry Co), m Catharine Bellis (Jun 6, 1796 – Nov 7, 1884), a dau of John & Catharina Bellis. Served in War of 1812. **Peter and Catharine (Bellis) Romberger had these children (some bapt St. Johns "Hill" Luth:** Sara b 1821; Jonathan b 1825, m Elisabeth ___, lived in Williamstown Twp. **Jonathan & Elisabeth Romberger children:** *William Henry* b Nov 26, 1854; *James Monroe* b Oct 17, 1856; Peter (Aug 13, 1826 – Jan 26, 1906), m Mary Ann Bonawitz. **Peter and Mary Ann (Bonawitz) Romberger had these children:** *Henry A* b c1855, lived in Phila; *James* (1856 – 1864); *Charles* (1857 – 1918), m Edith Bitterman, lived in Dalmatia; *Peter Francis* (1858 – 1923), m Susan Adaline Kissinger (1860 – 1941), a dau of Peter and Caroline (Buffington) Kissinger of Gratz. P.F. as he was better known, had several occupations throughout his life. In the 1880's he was a hotel keeper in Sacramento. In 1889 he purchased the Bear Mountain Hotel, but later gave up the hotel business and ran the stage between Gratz and Tremont. He moved to several other places but later came back to Gratz where he died. **Peter Francis & Susan Adaline (Kissinger) Romberger had these children:** *George Monroe* b Nov 30, 1879, moved to Phila; *John; Sallie Gertrude* (Jan 18, 1886 – Aug 4, 1895, bur Simeon Cem, Gratz); *Mollie; Martha* b 1891, was a teacher; *Daniel Morris* (1866 – Jan 1910, Middletown, Pa.) , m Ida Louisa Bowman (b Aug 8, 1868, a dau of Cyrene and Elizabeth (Maurer) Bowman of Gratz. D. Morris had a factory in Williamstown. **D. Morris and Ida (Bowman) Romberger had these children:** *Bertha May* b Sep 16, 1894; *Kathryn* (no dates) m ___Ince, lived in New Mexicao, taught school in Puerto Rico; *Mary* b 1867 m William Evans, lived in Middletown, later Colorado; Elias b Nov 10, 1827, m Catharine McCoy ; Joseph; b 1828; Catharine b 1830, m ____ Schroeder; Elisabeth (Jan 21, 1833 – Mar 9, 1906), m Elias Romberger; Thomas (Aug 23, 1835 – Mar 14, 1892), m Elisabeth Bitterman; Daniel b 1838; Maria b Jan 9, 1842.

****Christian** (Jul 16, 1797 – May 30, 1874, bur Sweitzer Cem, Bbg), m Susanna Matter (Jan 26, 1798 – Mar 24, 1861), a dau of Johannes and Elisabeth (Bergner) Matter. In 1850, Susanna's mother Elizabeth Matter was living with this family in Washington Twp. **Christian and Susanna (Matter) Romberger had these children:** Simon (Jan 14, 1824 – Sep 28, 1904, bur Maple Grove Cem, E'ville), m Susanna Martz (Sep 2, 1826 – Aug 31, 1898). **Simon and Susanna (Martz) Romberger had these children:** *Isaiah H* (Jul 26, 1853 – Sep 25, 1915, bur Maple Grove Cem, E'ville), m Sarah L ___ (Aug 31, 1872 – Oct 27, 1937); *Sarah Louise* b c1855, m John Sheesley b 1853; *Mary Jane* b 1857, m Fred Kemmerer (1861 – 1920); *Catherine* (Apr 23, 1858 – 1919), m George Walters (1854 – 1897)); *Henry C* (1864 – 1939), m Carrie Lebo (1865 – 1908); *Julia A* (Dec 13, 1868 – Dec 6, 1938)

Elisabeth (b 1826 - d 1877), m Solomon Dunkelberger
Jonathan (b Feb 5, 1828 – d Apr 16, 1915), m Anna Mary Zimmerman (Nov 20, 1829 – 1899) - move to Kansas.

Sarah (b Jul 3, 1830 - ___), m Adam Messersmith (1821 – 1888). Sarah apparently died or was the 2nd wife. Adam and wife Mary ___ b c1828, were listed on the 1850 census. **They had these children:** *William* b c1846; *James* b c1849. In 1850 Barbara Messersmith age 88 lived with them in Wash. Twp.

John Henry (Oct 22,1831 – Jun 22, 1864, bur Bbg), m Margaret Rebecca Deibler (Nov 26,1836 – May 4, 1916), a dau of Jonas & Christiana (Bischop) Deibler. **John Henry and Margaret (Deibler) Romberger had these children:** *Mary Ellen* (1859 – 1944), m Frederick Lubold (1853 – 1946); *Lily* m William Lesher moved to Lebanon; *Wilson Henry* (1862 – 1942), m Lillie E. Romberger (Aug 6, 1865 – Nov 7, 1955).

Susanna (1833 – 1900, bur Sweitzer Cem, Bbg), m William Mace (1832 – 1888). They lived in Mifflin Twp in 1860 and he was a blacksmith. **Their children:** *George F* b c1857; *William* b c1860.

Catharine Maria (b 1836 – 1923, bur St. Jacobs Cem, Armstrong Valley), 2nd wife of Jacob Paul.(May 7, 1821 – Jun 25, 1886).

William (b Apr 29, 1837 – Oct 28, 1876, bur Simeon Cem, Gratz), m Oct 17, 1861 Susanna Klinger (Oct 12, 1840 – Jul 8, 1877, bur Zion Klingers Cem), a dau of Daniel & Anna Klinger.. They lived in Lykens Twp in 1870 and he was a cabinet Maker and undertaker's helper. **William & Susanna (Klinger) Romberger had these children:** *Isaiah* (May 23, 1864 –Apr 21, 1919), m Elmira Clark (Mar 16, 1868 – May 14, 1926); *Chas Daniel* (Jul 14, 1866 _ Jan 20, 1895), m Ellen Jane Wolf (Aug 23, 1867 – Sep 20, 1896); *Mary Ann* (Sep 17, 1868 – May 15, 1944), m Chas Monroe Wolf (1869 – 1937)b c1869; *Wm Austin* (Dec 11, 1870 – Nov 30, 1928), m Emma Catherine Wiest (1873 – 1930); *Harry Klinger* (1873 – 1939), m Emma Jane Snyder b 1869; *John Klinger* (1876 – 1954), m Alice Troutman, 2nd Blanche (Hoffman) Klinger b 1890.

Mary (May 8, 1839 – Aug 31, 1923), bur Maple Grove Cem, m Henry Aaron Paul (Apr 10, 1852 – Nov 19, 1913 bur St. Jacobs Cem, Armstrong Valley).

****Elisabeth Romberger** b Dec 14, 1798, m Philip Matter (Apr 27, 1796 – Jan 20,1873)

****Catherine Romberger** b Oct, 3, 1800

****Jacob Romberger** (b Mar 10, 1802 – d Jul 1, 1854, bur Salem Luth Cem, Rough & Ready, Sch Co), m Catharine Klinger (Aug 10, 1802 – Sep 13, 1871). **Jacob and Catharine (Klinger) Romberger had these children:**
Sarah (Jul 23, 1823 – Jul 13, 1892), m Jan 1844 Henry Walborn (Jan 12, 1822 – Jan 13, 1893), moved to Union Co
Elisabeth (b c1824 - d Mar 17, 1916), m John Stiely Knorr. (1826 – Sep 23,1898)
Henry Klinger (Sep 11, 1825 – Apr 10 , 1901, bur Rough & Ready Cem), m Amelia Moyer (Aug 21, 1829 – Mar 20, 1908)
Elias (Mar 12, 1827 – Nov 23, 1906), m Elisabeth Romberger
William (Oct 11, 1834 – Jun 8, 1912), in Reading, Pa. m Louisa Reed. Lost his arm while serving in Civil War.
Juliana (___ - 1886), m William Walborn 1831 – 1903), moved to Centre Co.
Mary Priscilla (Jul 15, 1846 – Mar 20, 1895), m Percival Romberger, a son of Henry & Sophia Romberger.
Catharine (no dates) m ___ Foy
Daniel Klinger (Jan 30, 1830 – Mar 3, 1901), m Fromina Brown (Aug 1, 1829 – Jun 27, 1902), dau of John & Catharine (Fetter) Brown, widow of Elias Erdman (1824 – 1856).

****Sara Romberger** (Feb 14, 1804 – 1860)

****Anna Maria Romberger** (Mar 4, 1805 – Jan 4, 1877), m Jonathan Neidlinger (1807 – 1838)

****Daniel Romberger** (Dec 22, 1810 – Mar 7, 1811, bur St. Johns Hill Cem)

****Henry Romberger, Jr.** (b Dec 28, 1813- Nov 7, 1878), m Sophia Roth, lived in Up Mahantongo Twp Sch Co in 1850. **Henry and Sophia Romberger had these children:** Percival (1844 – 1878), m Mary Priscilla Romberger, dau of Jacob & Catherine Romberger ; **Hannah** b 1846; **Christina** b 1847; **Sophia** (1849 – 1913), m John S. Clark (1846 – 1934); **Sarah** b 1853; **Mary** (May 24,1855 – Nov 1885), m Samuel F. Herb (1855 – 1931); **Emilia** b 1858, m John H. Smith.

****Susanna Romberger** (Dec 18, 1815 – Mar 30, 1897), m John Klinger

ADAM (Jun 3, 1775 – Aug 7, 1867, bur Pillow, Dau Co), m Anna Maria Werner (b 1775 - 1806 in childbirth). **Adam and Anna Maria (Paul) Romberger had these children (some bapt Hoffman Ch):
***Eva Margaretha** b May 10,1795, m Peter Forney (b ___ d 1873). **Peter and Eva Margaretha (Romberger) Forney had these children:** ****Catharine** m William Metz; ****Susan** m Adam Zartman; ****Mary Ann** m George Spatz; ****Hannah** m John Q. Adams.
Anna Maria** b Aug 15, 1796, m Samuel Lehman (b Apr 15, 1797 bapt Moravian Ch, Bethel Twp, Leb Co- d Aug 12, 1859, bur St. John;s Hill Cem). **Samuel and Anna Maria (Romberger) Lehman had these children;** ****Elisabeth** b Dec 22,1819, m David Yeager; ****John** b 1821; ****Jacob** b 1823;*Daniel** b ___;

ᵀᵀᵀᵀ**Samuel** (b Sep 7, 1827 – Dec 23, 1885, bur Riegles EUB Cem);, m Catharine Deibler (Jan 15, 1831 – Aug 1, 1909), they had 15 children, several died young; ****__Moses__ b Feb 9, 1824; ****__Adam__; ****__Susanna__ b Isaac Wert.
***__Susanna__ b Sep 2, 1797, m John Jacobs (no dates). **John and Susanna (Romberger) Jacobs had these children:** ****__Daniel__; ****__John H.;__ ****__Jonathan__; ****__Cornelius__ m Elisabeth ___; ****__Matilda__ m Daniel Deibler; ****__Elisabeth__ m Peter Kehres; ****__Mary__ m George Kelly.
***__Catharine__ b Sep 2, 1798 , m Jacob Weaver (no dates), **Jacob and Catharine (Romberger) Weaver had these children:** ****__Benjamin__; ****__Jacob__; ****__Catharine__ m Yeager.
***__Elisabeth__ b May 2, 1800, m Solomon Buffington (Jan 29, 1795 – Jan 1, 1878), a son of Levi and Susannah (Hoffman) Buffington. **Solomon and Elisabeth (Romberger) Buffington had one known child:** ****__Solomon__ b Oct 20, 1819, m Rebecca Margaret ___ b 1820, lived in Jefferson Twp, Dau Co. [Information for Solomon Jr. in Buffington history.]
***__John__ (Oct 24, 1802 – May 29, 1891, bur Gratz Cem), m Jan 2, 1827 Hannah Hoffman (b Aug 16,1807 –Aug 14, 1858), a dau of Jacob (Jr) & Catherine (Ferree) Hoffman. They lived in Lykens Twp. **John and Hannah (Hoffman) Romberger had these children:**
****__William__ b Dec 30, 1827; ****__Elisabeth__ b May 15, 1829; ****__Sarah__ b Sep 15, 1830; ****__Henry__ (Jan 3, 1833 – Dec 16, 1912), m 1856 Elisabeth Hoover (Aug 28, 1832 – May 25, 1907); ****__Amos__ (Sep 12, 1834 – Jun 21, 1892, bur Church of God Cem, Valley View), m Justina ____ (May 29, 1847 – May 29, 1909); ****__Mary__ __Ann__ b 1836; ****__Jacob__ b 1839.
***__Salome__ (Jan 5, 1804 – 1887), m Henry Rickert (1802 – 1864)
__Barbara__ (May 3, 1805 – Dec 12, 1873), m John Tobias (Apr 9 , 1800 – Dec 27, 1850, bur Meth Cem), a son of John & Maria Magdalena Tobias. **John & Barbara (Romberger) Tobias children:** ****__Jonathan__ (Dec 20, 1823 – Jan 17, 1905), m Catherine Umholtz, a dau of John & Anna Maria Margaretha (Hoffman) Umholtz; ****__John__ b Jul 28, 1826; ****__Lydia__ b c1831; ****__Sarah__ (Apr 10, 1836 – Jul 1899), m Jacob Umholtz; ****__Henry__ b c1841; ****__Elias__ b c1844;*__Mary__ b c1846.
***__Jonas__ (b & d 1806)

After Anna Maria died in 1806, Adam m Catharina Paul (Apr 14,, 1788 – May 9, 1862, bur Pillow Cem), dau of George & Anna Catherine (Matter) Paul. Adam and Catharina lived in Mifflin Twp in 1860 and had Henry Romberger age 8 and Rebecca Weaver 29 with them. **Adam and Catharina (Paul) Romberger had these children:**
***__Christina__ (b Jul 6, 1809 – Feb 9, 1849) m Henry Zerbe b c1804, a son of Samuel & Barbara (Klinger) Zerbe. **Henry and Christina (Romberger) Zerbe had these children:** ****__Cyrus__; ****__Emanuel__; ****__Manda__ (Aug 15, 1832 – Dec 25, 1906, bur Wiconisco) m Daniel Keiser, 2ⁿᵈ John Burd; ****__Sarah__ b c 1831, m David Zimmerman; ****__Emeline__ b c1834, m Joseph Romberger. In 1860 Joseph & Emeline Romberger lived in Wiconisco Twp & the census records him as having a "drinking saloon". Also with them were Emanuel Gervin age 21, a miner; and John Romberger 22, also a miner. **Joseph & Ememline (Zerbe) Romberger had these children:** Mary b c1853; Alice b c1854; Samuel b c1857; Hannah b 1860; Adam (Apr 11, 1838 – Sep 27, 1856, bur Meth Cem, Wiconisco).

***__Eve__ (Jun 28, 1810 – Sep 1876), m Daniel Romberger (Mar 13, 1810 – Jun 16, 1833, bur St. Johns Hill Cem, a son of Balthasar and Elisabeth (Sierer) Romberger. Eva later m Jacob D. Hoffman. **Daniel and Eve (Romberger) Romberger had these children:**
****__Gilbert__ (Jan 19, 1829 – Mar 10, 1894, bur Peace Cem, Bbg), m 1852 to Mary Keihl (May 10, 1834 – Nov 27, 1920); ****__Luther__ (no dates), m ___ Hoffman; ****__Susan__ (no dates), m Abraham Kepler.

After Daniel Romberger died, Eve m May 19, 1836 Jacob D. Hoffman (Jul 3, 1812 – May 30, 1887), and they had these children; ****__Isaac White__ (b Mar 5, 1837- May 30, 1887), m Frances Martin; ****__Adam__ (b Oct 16, 1838 – Jan 10, 1902), m Margaret Bush; ****__Hannah__ (Oct 1, 1840 – Feb 1, 1870); ****__Sarah__ (Sep 11, 1842 – Jan 17, 1926); ****__Adeline__ b May 19, 1845; ****__Elmira__ b Mar 1, 1846; ****__Rebecca__ (b Jun 6, 1848 – Nov 30, 1908; ****__George Edward__ b Aug 29, 1849, m Sally Faust; ****__Joseph__ b 1850.

***__Nancy__ (Sep 11, 1811 – Feb 11, 1891), m Daniel Hillbish (Dec 20, 1807 – Mar 17, 1891)
***__Lydia Ann__ b May 11, 1813, m John Poffenberger
***__Julia Ann__ (Aug 24, 1814 – Mar 31, 1876), m Henry Hoy
***__Daniel__ (Feb 19, 1816–Jul 28, 1882), m Hannah Bergstresser (Sep 26, 1818 – Feb 13, 1889), dau of John & Ann (Auchmuty) Bergstresser, granddaughter of Samuel Auchmuty, Rev. Soldier. **Daniel and Hannah (Bergstresser) Romberger had these children:**

******Adam** (Aug 21, 1839 – Jan 29, 1904), m Mary A. Bohner; ******Edward** (Jul 30, 1841 – Mar 22, 1907), m Jan 10, 1867 Sarah Klinger; ******Cyrus** (Jul 14, 1843 – Apr 15, 1915), m May 25, 1875 Louisa Troutman; ******Samuel B** (Aug 9, 1845 – Mar 11, 1921), m Mar 12, 1867 Sarah Jane Brower; ******Josiah** (b Oct 9, 1847 – Apr 2, 1917), m Sarah Matter (Jul 10, 1852 – Dec 18, 1937); ******John Ambrose** (Apr 20, 1850 – Jun 9, 1916), m 1st Mary A. Row, 2nd Emma Rebecca Troutman, 3rd, Edith Koppenhaver; ******H. Howard** (Jul 12, 1853 – 1902), m Catharine Ritzman; ******Alfred D.** (Oct 9, 1854 – Sep 15, 1857.

*****Polly** b 1818 m Daniel Noll
*****Hannah** (Aug 30, 1819 – Oct 8, 1893), m Henry Samuel Wiest , a son of Jacob & Mary (Tobias) Wiest, **had these children:** ******Samuel L.** (May 10, 1844 – Feb 10, 1924), m Elisabeth Orwig. He was an ordained pastor of Evangelical Church; ******Henry Jr;** ******Oliver** m Lydia Lenker; ******Rebecca**
*****Isaac** (Jun 26, 1821 – Sep 26, 1912, bur Hoffman Cem), m Lydia Michael (Dec 14, 1827 – Jun 17, 1870). **Isaac and Lydia (Michael) Romberger had these children:** ******Rebecca** b 1846, m John Batman; ******Sarah** (Apr 24, 1850 – Sep 7, 1866; ******Mary Jane** (1852 – 1928, bur Sweitzer Cem), m Henry Henninger (1845 – 1924), ; ******Philip** (b1855 – May 29, 1847, bur Berrysburg), m Leah J. Matter (1856 – 1923). **Philip & Leah (Matter) Romberger had these children:** Sadie Ellen Mar 27, 1867 - 1956), m William Howard (Jan 8, 1865 – 1950), had Fae; William; Isaac; Edward; Charles: Lizzie Alverta (1878 – 1962), m John Lower; Lydia A. (1880 – 1959), m Wm. H. Bonawitz; Charles I b 1881 m Minerva Latsha; Harry Richard (Feb 1885 -1951), m Mary Hoover b 1890; ******Emeline** (b Aug 4, 1856 – 1857); ******Adeline E** b 1859, m Frank Beisel; ******Lydia Ann** (1861 – 1946), m ___ Snyder; ******Henrietta** (Sep 26, 1863 – Jan 14, 1919), m Isaac Henninger; ******John Elmer** (Aug 2, 1867 – Apr 8, 1926), m Sarah E. Lehman (1859 – 1931), **had these children:** Esther Mae b May b 1891, m Edward Koppenhaver (Dec 18, 1889 – Jan 4, 1965); Wm Allen (1892 – 1965), m Mabel Deibler; Mary Ellen b 1897 m George Finkbone (1893 – 1954); Roy John b 1904, m ___ Schell;.
*****Magdalena** (1801 – Feb 3,1867), m John Crawford (c1795 – after 1850). [See write-up on Crawford family. They were divorced.
_____ (no dates) m _____Jacobs
Susanna (no dates) m _____ Hollenbach

CATHARINA (Mar 29, 1777 – Jul 3, 1851, bur St. John's "Hill" Cem, Bbg)), m Johann George Matter (Jan 16, 1771 - Oct 11, 1865), a son of Johannes and Anna* Barbara (Arnold) Matter. **Johann George and Catharina (Romberger) Matter children:** ***Michael (Apr 12, 1794 – Jan 14, 1880), m Sarah Crum;***Johannes b Oct 25, 1795; ***Joseph b May 16, 1795, m Susanna Ritzman;***George b Oct 11, 1798; ***Daniel b Feb 4, 1801; ***Anna Catharina b Feb 4, 1801; ***Anna Maria b Feb 4,1803; ***Balthasar b Feb 4, 1805; ***Elisabeth b Aug 21, 1807; ***Salome b Jul 15, 1810; ***Jacob b Nov 4, 1814; ***Hanna b Nov 26, 1817; ***Susanna b May 11, 1821. [See also Matter genealogy.];

BALTHASAR (Dec 28, 1778 – Jun 16, 1839, bur Wiconisco), m Dec 25, 1802 Elisabeth Sierer (Nov 15, 1782 – Feb 2, 1858), a dau of John Conrad and Anna Maria (Stauch) Sierer. **Balthasar and Elisabeth (Sierer) Romberger had these children (bapt Salem Luth, Leb, St. Johns Luth, Mifflin Twp, Hoffman Ref, Lykens Twp:**
Anna Maria "Polly" (Oct 12, 1803 – Nov 29, 1871, bur St. Johns "Hill" Cem, Bbg), m Daniel Matter, Sr. (Sep 25, 1800 – Jun 3, 1881); **Daniel and Anna Maria (Romberger) Matter had these children:** ******Jeremiah** (Jun 27, 1825 – Mar 24, 1888, ******Allen C.**, m Angeline Straub;***Aaron** (no dates);******Hiram** (Jun 13, 1830 – Oct 1893);******Elisabeth** (Jun 24, 1844 – Jan 16, 1912); ******John G.** (no dates);******Edward** (no dates). [See Matter genealogy.]

***Anna Catharine (Oct 17, 1805 - Aug 11, 1856, bur St. John's "Hill" Cem, Bbg), m Philip Matter (Apr 24, 1796 – Jan 20, 1873); [See Matter genealogy.]
***George (Nov 12, 1807 – Jan 5, 1873, bur St. John's "Hill" Cem, Bbg), m Mary Hopple (Apr 29, 1809 – Mar 15, 1873), a dau of Henry and Nancy Hopple). In 1850 they lived in Mifflin Twp and in addition to their family had Chas A. Bressler age 3, and Calvin S. age 1 with them. **George and Mary (Hopple) Romberger had these children:** ******Jonas** (Oct 9, 1830 – Jun 13, 1906), m Amelia Pontius; ******Henry** b Dec 13, 1831; ******John George** (Sep 21, 1833 – Feb 25, 1885, bur St. Johns Hill Cem)), m Hannah Clark (Nov 10, 1842 – Feb 27, 1922), **these survived childhood:** Emma b1867, m Andrew Rutter; George Franklin (Nov 3, 1869 – May 1, 1953), m Lizzie Alverette Shaffer (1876 – 1916), dau of Wm Durrell Shaffer; Jennie b 1872 m Oliver Shroyer; Sallie b Jan 1873, m Chester Miller; John G. b Aug 1874, m Amelia Wolfgng; Hannah (1885 – 1913), m William Bucher.

****<u>Hannah</u> (Sep 5, 1834 – Aug 7, 1911), m Edward Koppenheffer (1830 – 1907), bur St. John's Hill Cem). [see Koppenhaver genealogy]; ****<u>George H.</u> (Oct 20, 1837 – Apr 6, 1907, bur St. John's Hill Cem), m Elisabeth Bressler (May 20, 1844 – Mar 20, 1920); **George and Elisabeth (Bressler) Romberger children:** Jonas Allen b May 19, 1877, went west in 1893; <u>Daniel</u> (Jan 10,1879 – Jan 5, 1959), m Hattie Wert (1881 – 1950 of burns); <u>Hannah Rebecca</u> (1885 – 1957) ****<u>Mary</u> (Jul 20, 1840 – Apr 22, 1901, bur David's Ref Cem, Killinger), m Daniel Noll (Sep 28, 1842 – Mar 9, 1922); ****<u>Leah H</u>. (Sep 20, 1841 – Nov 10, 1911, bur Davids Cem, Killinger), m Isaac Moyer (Dec 24, 1834 – Sep 20, 1860); ****<u>Baltzer</u> (Feb 23, 1843 – Nov 3, 1903, bur St. John's Hill Cem), m Hannah Deibler (1848 – 1930); ****<u>Sarah</u> (Aug 18, 1844 – Jul 4, 1904, bur Fetterhoff Cem), m John Ulrich (Aug 16, 1840 – Sep 1, 1817); ****<u>Henry</u> b 1848; ****<u>Susan</u> b 1851; ****<u>Samuel</u> b 1853.

<u>Daniel</u> (Mar 13, 1810 – Jun 16, 1833), m Eve Romberger, **had these children:** *<u>Gilbert</u> (Jan 19, 1829 – Mar 1924), m Mary Kiehl, (1834 – 1920); ****<u>Luther</u> (Apr 23,1831 – 1906), m Francesca Louise Weaver; ****<u>Susan</u> (no dates), m _____ Bowman; ***<u>Elisabeth</u> (Mar 24, 1812 – Aug 16, 1854, bur Old Meth Cem, Bbg), m Jacob Hoy (Mar 26, 1808 – Jun 19, 1889), **had several children who d in infancy;** *** <u>Susanna</u> (Jan 30, 1814- Dec 9, 1845, bur St. John's Hill Cem), m John Bordner; ***<u>Rebecca</u> (Sep 17, 1816 – Feb 8, 1887, bur St. John's Hill Cem), m Jeremiah Harner (Dec 19, 1813 – Mar 4, 1868); ***<u>Hanna</u> (Nov 11, 1818 – Apr 29, 1904, bur St John's Hill Cem), m Jacob Woodside (Jun 13, 1813); ***<u>Benjamin</u> (Jan 17, 1821 – Feb 29, 1904, bur Bbg), m Amelia Fisher (Aug 20, 1822 – Jun 20, 1868), a dau of Joseph Fisher. **Benjamin and Amelia (Fisher) Romberger had these children:******<u>Daniel Henrich</u> (Apr 4, 1844 – Sep 11, 1870); ****<u>Joseph Fisher</u> (Feb 4, 1848 – Mar 1916), m Jan 4, 1870 Mary Sophia Yeager; ****<u>Mary M.</u> (1850 – Oct 3, 1877), m Charles Mattis; ****<u>Nathan Alfred.</u> (Feb 2, 1852 – Jan 3, 1916), m Mary Ellen Shepley (Jun 26, 1855 – Mar 6, 1923); **Benjamin Romberger m 2nd Hannah (Schreffler) Troutman, widow of Elias Troutman (Jan 31, 1837 – Sep 3, 1914);**, ****<u>David J.</u> (Sep 12, 1823- May 13, 1887, burt St. John's Hill Cem)), m Anna Mary Swab (Nov 21, 1828 – Oct 6, 1903). **David J. and Anna Mary (Swab) Romberger had these children:** <u>Ann Catharine</u> (1848 – 1852); <u>Elisabeth S.</u> (Apr 12, 1851 – Mar 20, 1903); <u>George</u> d young; <u>Henry A.</u> (Aug 4, 1855 – Jan 7, 1910, bur St.John's Hill Cem), m Ann Elisabeth Koppenheffer (Jul 5, 1862 – 1941); <u>Ann Mary Ellen</u> (May 22, 1870 – 1943, bur St. John's Hill Cem), m Wm. H. Hoover (1864 – 1922); <u>Franklin Peter</u> (1874 – 1923),bur St. John's Hill Cem), m Sally Good (1868 – 1953);

****<u>Balthaser W.</u> (Dec 7, 1825 – 1905, bur Maple Grove Cem, E'ville), m 1st Sarah Orendorf (b Nov 1, 1826 – d Feb 27, 1852, bur Peace Cem, Bbg). He was a minister according to her tombstone. Balthaser and Sarah (Orendorf) Romberger had a son: <u>Henry M</u> (no dates) m Florence Smith, moved to Winona, Mississippi. After Sarah died, Balthaser m 2nd Helena Wagner (Aug 3, 1828 – Oct 2, 1914, bur Maple Grove Cem). **Balthaser and Helena (Wagner) Romberger had two children:** <u>Clara Louise</u> b 1857, m William Neil, moved to Yalobusha, Mississippi; <u>Charles E.</u> (no dates), moved to Mississippi..

*** Sarah b c1780 m Jacob Miller
<u>JOHANNES</u> (b Nov 29, 1784, bapt Hoffman Ch – c1848, bur St. Pauls Cem, Tower City), m Eva Hand (Dec 7, 1794 – Aug or Sep 1848, bur ST. Paul's Cem, Tower City). **Johannes & Eva (Hand) Romberger children:** *<u>Elizabeth</u> (1823 – 1898), m Abram Rabuck (1821 -1897); **** <u>Sarah</u> b Mar 5, 1827, m Henry Bougher; ****<u>Catherine</u> (1828 – 1913), m John Heberling;****<u>Ann</u> , m John Sharpe; ****<u>Barbara</u> (1825 – 1901), m 1st George Lenhart, m 2nd _____ Betz; ****<u>Eva,</u> m Henry Eckel;****<u>Daniel D</u> (1832 – 1920), m Selisa Weber; ****<u>Peter</u> b 1834; ****<u>Rebecca</u> (no dates).

Balthasar Romberger m 2nd Susanna Lehman (b Feb 19, 1771 Montg Co), a dau of Jacob and Martha (Pennebaker) Lehman. **Balthasar and Susanna (Lehman) Romberger children (bapt St. Johns Luth Ch, Mifflin Twp, Dau Co:** *** <u>Susanna</u> (b Apr 16, 1799 – Feb 23, 1857), m Joseph Workman b c1803, **had a dau** ****<u>Elisabeth</u> (Jul 16, 1829 – d Feb 13, 1907, Shamokin, Northld Co), m Jun 4, 1848 Isaac Smink; *** <u>Samuel</u> (May 19, 1803, bapt Jun 30, 1803 – Feb 1886), m Elizabeth Brown (1813 – 1847)), lived in Wiconisco Twp, **Samuel and Elizabeth (Brown) Romberger had these children:** ****<u>Jonathan</u> (Sep 29, 1825 – Jan 16, 1907), m Elizabeth Snodgrass (1835 – 1909, Bbg); ****<u>Elias</u> (Mar 12, 1827 –Nov 23, 1906), m Elizabeth Romberger; ****<u>Joseph</u> b Feb 22, 1829 m Emeline; ****<u>Elizabeth</u> b Nov 18, 1830, m __ Pell;****<u>John</u> (Dec 17,1836 – Sep 11, 1922), m Mary Ann Whitman (1840 – 1919). He a C. W. Vet; ****<u>Maria</u> (Oct 6, 1838 – 1936), m Augustus Walborn of Potter Co, Pa.; ****<u>Susanna</u> b Feb 4, 1844; ****<u>Simon</u> (Feb 27, 1846 – Jul 16, 1916 in N.J.), m Sep 23, 1861 Phoebe Ann Yost (1850 – Mar 5, 1890), lived in Shamokin. **Simon and Phoebe Ann (Yost)**

Romberger had these children: Mary Alice b Nov 26, 1867; William A. b 1869; Harry E. b Aug 19, 1873;John Augustus b Feb 24, 1876; Chester Logan b Jan 23, 1877; Isabella May b Jun 13, 1879; Stella E b Nov 24, 1883; ***Jacob (Jun 19, 1806 – Nov 20, 1864, Wiconisco Twp), m Margaretha Rebecca Conrad (Jan 6, 1810 p Jun 3, 1878), a dau of George and Maria (Muth) Conrad. **Jacob and Margaretha Rebecca (Conrad) Romberger had these children: ****Sarah** (Nov 28, 1829 – Feb 21, 1918, Shamokin), m Sep 6, 1846 William Franklin Hertzog (b Mar 4, 1828 Pinegrove Twp, Sch Co –d Jul 17, 1877 Shamokin, Northld Co), a son of Adam and Elisabeth (Heberling) Hertzog. **William Franklin and Sarah (Romberger) Hertzog had these children:** Franklin R. b Oct 11, 1848, m Catharine F. Betz; Theodore B. (Oct 17, 1850 – Mar 15, 1922, Shamokin), m Fietta Schminkey; Luisa (Aug 14, 1853 – pre 1860); Mary Jane b 1855 m Enos Edmonds; John b 1857; Jacob b c1860, m Lillie S.; ****Edward b 1831, m Catharine Elisabeth Weiser, moved to Lehighton, Carbon Co.Pa; ****William** (1832 – Nov 20, 1862), m Sarah Jane Kocher. **William and Sarah Jane (Kocher) Romberger had these children:** James M. (Oct 4, 1855 – Oct 25, 1938), m Josephine Siegfried; John (no dates) m Alice Klinger; Catharine Amanda (no dates) m Charles Laudenslager; Mary (no dates) m Martin Keiffer; ****Caroline Catharine** (Oct 20, 1833 – Nov 1, 1861, Richfield Twp., Juniata Co, Pa.), m Jacob Haines; ****Josiah** (Jan 20, 1836 – Jul 24, 1884), m Elisabeth Feaser. **Josiah and Elisabeth (Feaser) Romberger had these children:** Melinda b 1857; Franklin b 1859; Robert b 1864; William b c1866; ****Jacob J.** b Jan 27, 1840, m Catharine ____ . **Jacob and Catharine Romberger had these children:** Franklin H. b Dec 12, 1858; Mary Jane; George, Hannah, Carrie – all d young; ****Henry F.** b Jun 5, 1842; ****Amanda** b Mar 15, 1844, m Daniel Kerstetter;****Emanuel** b 1847 m Lavina ___ ; ****Mary** b May 7, 1849 – 1949. Steelton), m Aaron Hartman
***Salome** (Nov 22, 1808 -1890), m 1825 to Peter Bellis
***Joseph** (Nov 7, 1811 – Jan 20, 1890, of dropsy in Gratz), m Rosina Coleman (May 20, 1810 – Dec 19, 1884). **Joseph and Rosina (Coleman) Romberger children:** ****John B.** b 1832, m Elisabeth ___ b 1839. **John B. and Elisabeth Romberger had these children:** Emma C. b 1862; Maggie E. b 1869; ****Catharine** b 1835 m Josiah Schoffstall; ****Joseph D.**(Nov 1,1837 – Aug 2, 1926), not m, lived with his parents most of his life. He was a shoemaker and had a shop on lot fifty-three in Gratz.; ****Daniel** (Mar 17, 1840 – Sep 17, 1860); ****Ann M.** b 1844 m ___ Walz; ****Sarah** b 1846 m ___ Bowman; ****Hannah Lydia** (Nov 1, 1850 – Aug 7, 1832, bur Hegins, Pa.), m Martin Kiehl; ****Susanna** b 1854 m John Moser; ****Jonathan** b 1860 d young..

* BARTHOLOMAUS ROMBERGER married 2nd Anna Sabina Hess (___ Bavaria - 1776, Earl Twp., Lanc Co). They were married Mar 30, 1761 in New Holland, had 4 children (all born near New Holland, Pa.).
**MARIA CATHERINE b Feb 19, 1763
**MARIA MAGDALENA b Dec 4, 1764
**JOHANNES b Feb 27, 1767
**GEORGE BARTHOLOMAUS b Aug 2, 1768

In 1850 while residing in Mifflin Twp, the Sweitzer's had Daniel Meyer age 38, Lucetta 35, Lydia 12, Hannah 10, Jonathan 8, William 6, and Mary 3 with them. When they moved to this farm, William Sweitzer, over the next several years, purchased several more acres of unseated land from Amos and Amanda Hoffman. He also purchased a carriage. In 1860, The Sweitzer family included Catherine Forney age 50, and Daniel Behm age 14, both listed as servants.

William Sweitzer was affiliated with the United Brethren Church in Berrysburg. When he penned his will, he noted that he wished to be buried in the plot of William Sweitzer Memorial in Berrysburg. He had donated two acres of ground to the church officers "for burial of anyone." He had been liberal in his donations to the church that he belonged to for more than sixty years. He assisted financially in numerous church programs, as well as the church building. After his wife died, he gave all property to the church. His obituary states that "On the first day of his married life, he began family worship morning and evening, and never failed in that Christian duty afterwards."

[WILLIAM SWEITZER (c1816 - Jan 20, 1909, bur U.B. Cem, Berrysburg), may have married twice. A child Annie H. Sweitzer (1842 - 1855) is bur. Simeon Cem. She was a dau of William and Elizabeth (Wetcel) Sweitzer. William later m Susanna Deibler (c1825 - Aug 1913), a dau of Mathias Deibler. **William and Susanna (Deibler) Sweitzer had these children:** Rebecca (Jun 13, 1852 – Jan 23, 1889, bur Sweitzer Cem, Bbg), m J. H. Herring; **Maria** (Dec 6, 1853 - Feb 2, 1858, bur Hoffman Cem); **Catherine** (Nov 6, 1855 - Mar 13, 1858, bur Hoffman Cem); **John** (May 19, 1862 - Apr 17, 1865, bur Hoffman Cem); **Dina** or **Drucila** b c1856, bur Hoffman Cem, blank cem stone)]

On April 1, 1882, William Sweitzer and his wife Susanna sold four tracts of land containing 104 acres, sixty-eight perches, the brick house and bank barn to Daniel Buffington. Many years later, on March 30, 1907, the heirs of Daniel Buffington sold the four tracts, with same acreage, brick house and bank barn to Jacob S. Shade.

Jacob & Elisabeth (Ritzman) Shade Family – 1912, taken at brick house. L to r –Chas b 1895, Elmer b 1900, George b 1902, Morris Albert b 1893, Roy b 1897, Fred b 1905, Lillian b 1907, Susan b 1910

Jacob Shade, Sr.

Jacob Shade, Jr.

THE JACOB S. SHADE FAMILY

[**JACOB S. SHADE** (b May 19, 1866 - d Jun 11, 1928, bur Simeon Cem, Gratz), a son of Jacob and Catherine Shade, m Jul 31, 1892 Elisabeth Louisa Ritzman (Jul 23, 1873 – Jul 13, 1946), a dau of Franklin M and Susan J. (Wolfe) Ritzman of Gratz. **Jacob S. and ELisabeth ((Ritzman) Shade children (bapt Simeon Luth, Gratz):** **Morris Albert** (Jul 31, 1893 – Jun 15, 1979, bur Simeon Cem) m Oct 14, 1914 Edna M. Haag (1895 – May 15, 1965). **Morris Albert & Edna (Haag) Shade children:** Ellen Shade; Thomas Shade; **Charles Edwin** (Jun 8, 1895 - Jun 8, 1918, bur Simeon Cem, Gratz). Charles was the first area soldier killed during World War I, and Shade Post is named in his honor; **Roy Franklin** (Jul 4, 1897 – 1966, bur Simeon Cem), m Jun 10, 1922 Alice Regina Klinger (1903 – 1968), a dau of Alexander Klinger. **Roy and Alice (Klinger) Shade children:** Allen Alexander b Dec 11, 1922,_ m 1st Dora Shomper;, 2nd Doris Mauser Lillian Alice b Aug 7, 1929, m Clarence Welker; **Henry** b c1899; **Elmer Jacob** (Oct 4,1900 – 1964, bur Simeon Cem) m Mar 18, 1922 Carrie B. Steely (1905 - __), a dau of Donald and Alice Steely **Elmer& Carrie (Steely) Shade children:** Edna Irene b Sep 8, 1922, m Ernest Lenker (__ -1988), son of Marlin & Clara M. (Hollenbach) Lenker; **Ernest E. & Edna Irene (Shade) Lenker children:** Ernest E. Jr.; Ronald; Larry K; Carol M. m __ Cooper; Gloria m ___ Keffer; Nancy m ___ Deiter; Sally m ___ Troutman; Viola m ___ Witmer; Patsy m ___ Dietrich; Evelyn; **Mary Elizabeth** b Nov 13, 1924, m Marlin Engle; **Jacob Elmer** b Sep 1, 1932, m Corrine E. Snyder; **George H.** (1902 - ___, bur Simeon Cem) m Elsie A. Klinger (1907 – 1979), a dau of Monroe Klinger. **George and Elsie (Klinger) Shade children:** Grace Marie b Sep 30, 1926;; **Frederick Lawrence.** (Mar 31, 1905 – 1967, bur Simeon Cem), m Sep 18, 1926 Jennie I Hartman (1909 – 1975), dau of Charles Hartman. **Frederick & Jennie (Hartman) Shade children:** Charles Edward b Jan 29, 1927; Anna Elisabeth b Dec 17, 1932; Darlene Marie b Jun 2, 1944;; **Lillian Irene** b Apr 11, 1907, m Feb 3, 1929 Charles E. Keefer of Tower City. **Charles & Lillian (Shade) Keefer children:** Blair Edward b Aug 5, 1929; **Susan Catharine** b Jan 30, 1910 , m 1st Nevin Romberger, had a dau Fern; m 2nd ___ Uhler.[More Shade genealogy elsewhere in the book.]

After Jacob S. Shade died, his widow Elisabeth "Lizzie" conveyed this one hundred four acres sixty-eight perch farm to their son Elmer J. and his wife Carrie Shade on October 26, 1939. The property was bound at this time by Lemuel Row, George D. Moyer, the public road from Gratz to Berrysburg, Benjamin Gise, Edward Miller, George Williard. The Shade family has continued to own this property to the present time.

CHARLES CLAYTON SITLINGER FARM)
(George Williard - 85 acres 1875)

This land is comprised of various tracts of land that very early were owned by the Romberger, Walborn and Hoffman families. By sundry conveyances, two tracts, 66 acres, 148 perches, and 19 acres, 28 perches eventually became the property of Christian Moyer during the 1840's. By 1858, Christian Moyer had sold the total acreage to William Schweitzer. On May 9, 1868, William Schweitzer and wife sold the two tracts, a total of a little more than 86 acres of land to George Williard. After George Williard died, his heirs sold the two tracts to Jacob and Lavina Kissinger on Jan 15, 1886.

Jacob Kissinger was a native of Lykens Township. While growing up, he attended Kissinger school during the winter months, and worked on his fathers' farm during the summer months. In July 1863, Jacob Kissinger enlisted in Company C of the 36th Regiment Militia and served for several months. In February 1864 he enlisted in Company K of the Ninth Pennsylvania Cavalry, with Colonel Thomas J. Jordan and Captain J. Frank Miller. He served in the Atlanta Campaign with Sherman's Army. He participated in forty-two battles and skirmishes, and received a gunshot wound in his left foot, at Griswold Station, Georgia.

When Jacob Kissinger came back from the Civil War, he worked on his fathers' farm for two years. About the time he married, Jacob rented this eighty-five acre farm, which he cultivated until 1886 when he bought it. Soon after he purchased the farm he built a new dwelling.

On the day of their wedding, August 25, 1867, Jacob and Amanda traveled to Pillow, and were married at the parsonage of Rev. Kehm. It was a double wedding. The other couple was John C. and Hannah Saltzer. These couples and John W. Hoffman were neighbors, and had been friends since childhood, spending much of their time together. They continued to have gatherings at one another's homes in the township, as that was their way of socializing.

A newspaper piece recorded July 27, 1899 tells about one of the parties. "Last Thursday evening a party of sixteen ladies of Woman's Relief Corp secured a large team and made a trip to the farm of Jacob Kissinger near Gratz, where they enjoyed the evening and a splendid set out. Some one said they never had a pleasanter time. They didn't say who was along, but there is an inference that some of the widows were repeating the scenes of their younger days."

Jacob Kissinger lived to an old age, and when he decided to retire, he rented the farm to Harvey Kissinger, and moved to Gratz. When he died, his viewing was held in the Evangelical Cemetery, south of Simeon Church. It was held in the graveyard because there were so many people present. He was buried in his Civil War uniform, his cap lay on his chest.

On October 1, 1921, Thomas Kissinger became the new owner of this farm, and lived there about eight or nine years, before moving to Elizabethville. When the Thomas Kissinger family moved to this farm, their daughter Margaret started first grade at Giese School. Sometimes they had Sunday school in Giese School, and the children looked forward to those events. Before they went home, they had ice cream, and milk to drink.

While Margaret was growing up, her mother often times invited the ministers to dinner. Reverend Artz brought his wife to dinner, but Reverend Wehr came alone. This was because his mother-in-law lived with him and his wife and was not well. Reverend Wehr was always concerned about germs. One time when he was coming to dinner, Margaret had whooping cough. Her mother told her in advance that every time she had to cough, she should leave the room. She left several times, so finally Reverend Wehr told her she shouldn't leave to cough. Mrs. Kissinger always packed a lunch for Reverend Wehr to take home to his wife and mother-in-law.

During the summer months, Mrs. Kissinger always did her cooking in the summer kitchen. Most farm women utilized the summer kitchen to do their canning and other chores because it saved their house kitchen from dirt and extra wear. When the threshers came, she had to carry all that food from the summer kitchen to the main house.

When the warmer weather arrived in spring and summer, one of Margaret's chores was to "mind" the cows. She also picked stones, washed dishes, etc. and at the end of the week she was paid a nickel. She headed for Gratz to shop at Millers Store. It took her a good half- hour to look over all the different kinds of candy and then pick out what she could get for her money. When she became older, she did what everybody else did – "come to town and walk the streets up and down" - for something to do.

When Margaret was old enough to attend catechism class, she walked to Gratz to attend Reverend Artz' class. She prepared her lessons while she tended the cows. She sat near the lane at the edge of their farm. On the other side of the lane, Susan Shade Uhler was also "minding" cows, and she too studied her lessons in the same manner. The girls discussed their lessons as they studied. Reverend Artz observed that "what one of the girls knew, the other also knew, but what one did not know, the other did not know."

On March 23, 1929, Thomas H. Kissinger sold this farm to Monroe C. Snyder and moved to Elizabethville. Two years later, in 1932, Thomas Kissinger was killed in the mines. The day that the accident happened, his body was brought home from the mines and laid on the couch in the living room. The coroner came to check the body, then later he was taken upstairs until specific arrangements could be made for the funeral. Thomas Kissingers' wife never remarried, but as her daughter Margaret stated "she worked like a mule, but lived to the age of eighty-nine." She died August 19, 1978.

THE JACOB KISSINGER FAMILY

[*JACOB KISSINGER (Nov 14, 1843 - Nov 16, 1921, bur Simeon Luth & Ref Cem), a son of George   and Sarah (Knerr) Kissinger. His obituary appeared in the Elizabethville Echo, and reports:

"Mrs. Kissinger arose at 6 o'clock in the morning while the husband slept and at seven o'clock she went to call him for breakfast but found that his spirit had passed away."

Jacob m August 25, 1867, Amanda Williard (Oct 1, 1848 - Nov 20, 1936), a dau of George and Lavina (Deibler) Williard. **Jacob and Amanda (Williard) Kissinger children: ** HARVEY FREEMAN** (Nov 11, 1868 - Jun 24, 1940, bur Simeon Luth & Ref Cem), m 1st Jan 5, 1890 Abby Miller (Jul 30, 1871 - Nov 20, 1929), dau of Jonas & Mary (Dietz) Miller. Harvey m 2nd after 1929, Bertha V. Clouser. **Harvey F. and Abby (Miller) Kissinger had these children:**
***Guerney Jay (Nov 20, 1894 - Jan 8, 1923, Wash. D.C.)
***Jonas Roy (Nov 13, 1896 Wash Twp - Mar 24, 1918, bur Simeon Luth & Ref Cem). J. Roy was to be married to Crusie Daniel the day he was killed. He was working third shift at Short Mountain Colliery, and before he left for work on Saturday night, he told his mother he may be late for breakfast Sunday Morning. He and other workman at the mines were making a safety hole at the bottom of number nine slope and fired the wedge hole. When they went back to the area a piece of rock bumped out of the top striking him. He was killed instantly. He had asked Rev. Wehr the Sunday before to perform the ceremony this day. Instead, he was buried in his wedding suit. **He and Crusie Daniel had a son: ****Roy M.** (Oct 21, 1918 - 1927).
***Jacob Emanuel (Mar 12, 1898 - Aug 19, 1935, Gratz), m Sep 14, 1918, Agnes Irene Koppenhaver, dau of Charles and Agnes (Kratzer) Koppenhaver.
***Ernest Harvey (Feb 15, 1900 - Oct 27, 1938), m Feb 16, 1924, Mabel Sevilla Wagner, dau of George and Matilda (Mattern) Wagner.
***Mary Amanda (Mar 2, 1903 - Nov 1974, Halifax, Pa.), m Homer William Lebo, son of Jonathan and Susanna (Hassinger) Lebo.
***John Freeman (Aug 27, 1907 - Apr 13, 1978), m Dec 24, 1938 Helen Irene Umholtz, dau of Milton and Sallie (Klinger) Umholtz of Gratz.
***Charles Edward "Lefty" (Oct 23, 1909 - Sep 2, 1988), m Mar 22, 1940, Eva Grace Davis, dau of Walter and Elura (Erdman) Davis, **had a son ****Roy Charles** b Aug 9, 1940.
MARY ANN (Feb 8, 1870 - Nov 23, 1943, Wash D.C.), m Dec 13, 1891 Frank E. Hartman (____) a son of Michael and Catherine (Hess) Hartman. Frank had his leg crushed in an accident in Feb 1887. He had a mercantile business, and his wife Mary and daughter had a millinery shop in Gratz. **Frank and Mary Ann (Kissinger) Hartman children: ***Minnie Belle (Sep 8, 1892 - Jul 27, 1988, Santa Barbara, Ca), m William E. Lentz;
***Morris Miles (Nov 13, 1895 - Mar 30, 1963), m Aug 24, 1937 Laura Virginia Smith; ***Lottie Ella (Feb 13, 1898 - ____), m Grant Burnside.
SARAH CATHERINE (Jun 9, 1872 - Jun 14, 1950, Cortland, N.Y.), m Dec 19, 1896 in Ref parsonage, Elizabethville to Daniel Franklin Hoy, a son of Christian and Catharine (Freymoyer) Hoy. **Daniel & Sarah (Hartman) Hoy children: ***Verna May b 1897; ***Alfred E.** (1899 - 1975); ***Marion** (1900 - 1965); ***Martha Gertrude** b 1903.
GEORGE DANIEL (Jan 10, 1874 - Jan 11, 1955) at home of son Leon in Lemoyne, Pa.), m Jun 1, 1895 Mary Adeline Kocher, a dau of Henry and Elizabeth (Schoffstall) Kocher. **George D & Mary Adeline (Kocher) Kissinger children: ***Jennie b 1896; ***Minnie** (1899 - 1992), m Paul R. Laux of Loyalton; ***Anna Elizabeth** (1902 - 1957), m May 1924 Jacob Thomas Lesher, son of Cornelius and Mary (Landis) Lesher; ***Leon Jay** (1905 - 1965), m Helen Mabel Troutman, dau of Wesley and Catherine (Rebuck) Troutman.
**ANNA C. (Sep 9, ____ - ____), m
EDMUND OSCAR (Nov 9, 1876 - Apr 10, 1935, in Wiconisco, Pa.). Edmund Oscar and Daisy Magdalena Heller, dau of Philip and Clara (Dietrich) Heller **had a child: ***Daniel Franklin (Nov 10, 1898 - Dec 2, 1986),

who m Mary Amanda Hoffman, dau of Henry and Edna (Daniel) Hoffman. Edmund m Aug 27, 1898, Mary Ann Elizabeth Rowe (no dates), dau of Alfred and Jane Rowe. **Edmund Oscar and Mary A. E. (Rowe) Kissinger children:** ***Edna Mae** (Jan 9, 1899 - May 15, 1994 in Masonic Home, Elizabethtown, Pa.), m Apr 23, 1921 Blair Maurer Schminky, a son of John & Carrie (Maurer) Schminky of Gratz; ***Clarence Alfred** (Dec 9, 1899 - Feb 24, 1974), m Ruth Johns; ***Edward Mitchel** (Jan 25, 1904 - 1982), m Apr 1935, Ruth Beck; ***Verna Elan** (Oct 12, 1905 - 1996); ***Mildred Elizabeth** b Jan 3, 1913, m Raymond Hoffman; ***Robert Leroy** b 1915, Wiconisco, m Vivian June Snyder, dau of Clarence & Pauline (Weaver) Snyder; ***Paul Wilson** (1917 - 1984); ***Marian Elsie** (1920 - 1951); ***Mary Lorraine** (1924 - 1997), m 1950 Charles H. Harman.

****IDA AMANDA** (Jan 9, 1879 - Jan 19, 1881, bur Simeon Cem)

****DORA ELIZABETH** (Dec 13, 1880 - Apr 10, 1949), m Dec 25, 1901 Leander Shaffer (Oct 15, c1864 - Oct 15, 1933), died by hanging himself in his barn on his 69th birthday, lived in Matterstown.

****ANNE SEVILLA** (Sep 21, 1882 -Oct 13, 1891, bur Simeon Cem);

****CHARLES WELLINGTON** (Sep 4, 1884 - Jul 25, 1941), m 1st Feb 22, 1904, Margaret L. Snyder who died young, left three daughter's. His sister Dora raised one, Mary raised one, and another lived with the grandmother. He m 2nd Louise Richardson, and moved to Michigan.

****JACOB MILTON** (Aug 12, 1886, Gratz - Jul 31, 1970, Prescott, Ariz). He moved to Arizona and married there. Later he m Ada Whittenberg.

****THOMAS HARRISON** (Oct 6, 1888 - Jul 25, 1932, bur Simeon Cem, Gratz), killed in Short Mountain Colliery mines. While placing poles on a battery, a fall of coal from the face of the breast caught him and completely covered him), m Eva Edna Umholtz (Sep 2, 1889 - Aug 17, 1978), a dau of Levi and Anna Maria (Radel) Umholtz. **Thomas H. & Eva Edna (Umholtz) Kissinger children;** ***Margaret Arlene** b Apr 14, 1911, m Jul 7, 1928 Henry Veneda Shadle, son of Roman and Etta (Spotts) Shadle. **Henry V. and Margaret A. (Kissinger) Shadle had one child**

*****Evelyn Marie** b Jan 6, 1929, m Dean Hartman; ***Levi Jacob** (Sep 7, 1912 - Jan 27, 1998), m 1st Viola Page, dau of Charles and Vesta (Baker) Page, m 2nd Sallie Ellen Travitz, dau of Clarence and Bertha (Warlow) Travitz ; ***Marion Gilbert** (Mar 8, 1923 - Dec 12, 1939, bur Simeon Cem. died of a milk truck accident near Loyalton).]

George & Sarah (Knohr) Kissinger
Parents of Jacob Kissinger

Amanda (Williard) Kissinger
(Mrs. Jacob Kissinger)

538

Civil War Soldiers: Jacob Kissinger, Jacob Shiro, John Hoffman

On November 5, 1945, Monroe and Mary Snyder sold this eighty-five acres of land with house and buildings and another ten acres of timberland to Charles A. and Sallie O. Sitlinger. Years later on May 31, 1975 Charles A. and Sallie O. Sitlinger conveyed 86 acres 23 perches of land to Charles C. and Frances F. Sitlinger. At that time the land was bound by land of Clarence Welker, Bruce Kissinger, Ray Ferster, Carrie Shade, Charles Hoffman and Emery Sitlinger. The property continues to be owned by the Sitlinger family to the present time.

[**Monroe C. Snyder** (1878 - 1963, bur Union Cem, Pillow), a son of Johannes and Mary Ann Snyder, m Mary A. Wiest (Aug 1883 –1962) a dau of _____ of Klingerstown. **They had these children: Pauline** _____ m Harvey Sweigard **Jennie** b c1924, m Earl Wiest lives in Clarks Valley; **Mary** m Kenneth Grimm of Lykens; **Raymond**]

Photo to the right taken at a bridge over a creek near Specktown. Person unidentified. (Photo given by Sitlinger family)

JOHN P. & Ruth HOFFMAN Farm
(Jacob Andrew Weiss, 39 acres 1875)

This property has the same history as the gristmill tract. It is part of the two hundred and five acres of land that was accumulated by Jacob Hoover (Huber).

Jacob Hoover died in 1838, but just prior to his death, he penned a will designating that his 205 acres 8 perches should be distributed. His executors, John Huber and George Kissinger arranged to have a public vendue and on October 22, 1849, his daughter Susanna Hoover Umholtz ImSchoffstall was the highest bidder on a tract of 72 acres 152 perches of land with appurtenances (deed recorded April 13, 1850). Soon after she received the land she conveyed a larger portion of it to other owners. The tax record of 1858 describes Susanna's property as twenty-eight acres, with a log house and small frame barn.

Susanna died between 1858 & 1864, leaving a son John Umholtz who had mental disabilities. The heirs of his grandfather Henry Umholtz became his guardian and sold her property containing twenty-four acres and twenty perches of land and a log house on May 16, 1864, to Jacob Andrew Weiss. This property adjoined the public road from Gratz to Oak Dale, land of Jacob Shade, the millrace, and Daniel Buffington's mill property.

On September 17, 1873, Jacob Andrew Weiss purchased another 14 acres 48 perches of land from C. R. & Susannah Johns. This tract had been part of the land owned by Henry Umholtz and was conveyed to Benjamin and Margaret Gise on April 10, 1836. Benjamin and Margaret Gise conveyed the tract to Christian Johns April 2, 1840.

In March 1841, Christian Johns wrote his will, assigning this land to his son C. R. Johns. The 1883 tax record indicates that Jacob Andrew Weiss owned both tracts containing a total of 38 acres, a house and barn. That same year Jacob Andrew Weiss conveyed the same acreage to Charles W. Weiss. In February 1890, the barn on the property burned to the ground mysteriously. Three horses, five cows, hay and grain were destroyed.

Recent Photo of House

Photo of House When Walter Hoover Family Lived There
People unidentified, but believed to be Walter, Lottie & 3 daus

On April 1, 1903, Charles and Henrietta Weiss sold the two tracts as one tract containing 38 acres 87 perches to Josiah Hoover. The land bordered on the public road, and the land of F. P. Ferree and Jacob Kissinger.

On May 11, 1918 Josiah Hoover and Catherine his wife sold the same land with buildings to Walter E. and Lottie Hoover of Washington Township. By this time the surrounding land adjoined the road from Gratz to Loyalton, the mill race, and land owned by Irvin M. Buffington, R. B. Hoover, Amanda Kissinger and Alvin Sitlinger. Walter and Lottie Hoover lived here in 1910 with their three daughters.

During the outbreak of the flu in 1918, Walter Hoover became a victim. When he died on November 18th, arrangements were made for a funeral. Because the sickness was so contagious, the house was off limits to everyone but members of the household. A neighbor Thomas Kissinger, a very brave person, said that he would be willing to go in and place the body in a casket. Rev. Wehr told the family that they could not have a public funeral. On the day of the funeral friends gathered in front of the house, on the porch and in the yard. The family remained in the house. They congregated at the opened upstairs windows to hear Rev. Wehr as he conducted the service.

On April 1, 1926, Lottie, widow of Walter E. Hoover conveyed the land and house to Ernest H. Kissinger. After Ernest Kissinger died, the farm was transferred by his widow, Mabel S. Kissinger on May 31, 1938 to Charles A. and Estella Mae Hoffman. On February 11, 1991, Charles and E. Mae Hoffman conveyed 24 acres of their land to John P. and Ruth A. Hoffman.

THE HOOVER FAMILY IN PHOTOS

Margaret Evitts b 1848 wife of Charles Hoover

Lillian Wetzel Hoover (1862 – 1936)
Wife if Edmund & her mother
Mrs. _____ Reiner

Edmund Hoover (1861 – 1947)

Walter E. Hoover

Lottie (Hoover) Hoover

The Family of Edmund & Lillian (Wetzel) Hoover
Std: Alice Seville, Carrie Alverta, Amelia Kathryn, Lottie May, Sula. Sitting: Wellington Monroe, John Edmond, Clement Elwood, Edmond & Lillian (Wetzel) Hoover. (missing Landon Josiah)

542

The Six daughters of Charles A. and Margaret (Evitts) Hoover
They are (not in order) Sarah; Mary Jane; Christiana; Henrietta; Florence; Margaret
(Walter Hoover's Sisters)

Webster Hoover, adopted son of Walter and Lillian Hoover

[The Josiah Hoover genealogy can be found on page 494]

[*HARVEY F. KISSINGER (Nov 11, 1869 – Jun 24, 1940, Gratz), a son of Jacob & Amanda Kissinger, m 1st Abigail Miller (1871 – 1929), a dau of Jonas & Mary A. (Dietz) Miller. Harvey & Abigail (Miller) Kissinger children; **Gurney Nov 20, 1894 – Jun 8, 1923),m Minnie Riegle; Jacob Emanuel (Mar 12, 1898 – Aug 19, 1935), m Agnes (Kratzer) Koppenhaver (1898 – 1976); **Ernest Harvey (Feb 15, 1900 - Oct 27, 1938), m Feb 16, 1924, Mabel Sevilla Wagner, dau of George and Matilda (Mattern) Wagner; **Mary A. (1903 – 1974), m Homer W. Lebo (1893 – 1957); **John A. (1907 – 1978, bur Simeon Cem), m Helen Umholtz (1907 – 198_) a dau of Milton & Sallie Umholtz; **Charles (Oct 23, 1909 – Sep 2, 1980);, m Eva Davis b May 1900, a dau of Walter H & Elura (Erdman) Davis; **Jonas Roy (Nov 13, 1896 - Mar 24, 1918 age 21, killed in mines), bur Simeon Cem]
[See Kissinger genealogy page 537]

Catherine Schmeltz (1835 – 1920)
Wife of Josiah Hoover

MR. & MRS AMMON ASH FARM
(GEORGE WASHINGTON FERREE FARM 1875 – Now About 46 Acres)

The New House And Barn On The Old Farm Property

Part of this farm has the same history as the gristmill tract that was owned by Jacob Hoover. Another part came from the land grant that was conveyed to Philip Umholtz. When he died, a petition was made to Dauphin County Court to have the land appraised and divided. In 1842, the heirs of Philip Umholtz transferred a large portion of the land to John Umholtz, the second son of Philip Umholtz. The next owner was Henry Umholtz.

After Henry Umholtz died, his heirs conveyed on April 10, 1830 a house and fifty-five acres 112 perches of the land to Benjamin Geise in right of his wife Margaret, who was a daughter of Henry Umholtz. By 1837, Benjamin Geise conveyed 9 acres 88 perches of the 55 acres land to Margaret's sister Leah Ferree. George Washington Ferree grew up on his father's farm in Washington Twp., but in 1834, according to the tax record, he was a tenant on the farm of the Henry Umholtz estate. That was the year that he married Leah Umholtz a daughter of Henry Umholtz.

Leah and her husband G. Washington owned the 9 acres, a log house and stable at least until 1850. During that time he was a coal miner for many years. They purchased two other small tracts containing 18 acres 61 perches and 4 acres 119 perches. According to tax records of 1855 and 1858, G. Washington and Leah Ferree had a total of 28 acres with a one story house and small barn. During the 1860's they purchased lot #9 in Gratz, possibly for other members of the family. The 1860, 1870 & 1880 census shows them living on this farm. Their son Frank P. Ferree remained on the farm, and the Dauphin County history states that he took charge of the farm after his mother died in 1885. He was also a teacher in both the Geise and Hoffman schools.

Another tract of 26 acres 17 perches was owned by Susannah Schoffstall (wife of Jonas Schoffstall). It was part of a larger tract of 72 acres that she received from her father Jacob Hoover's estate on April 13, 1850. But the day she received it she sold the smaller portion (26 acres 17 perches) to Jacob Shade. This tract bordered the land described above. On November 29, 1890, Jacob Shade sold the 26 acres to Frank P. Ferree.

After both G. Washington and Leah Ferree died, the farm (including the several tracts 18 acres, 61 perches, 9 acres 88 perches, & 4 acres119 perches acres) was deeded on July 20, 1889, to their son Frank P. Ferree. In 1900, the widowed mother-in-law of Frank (Elizabeth Salada b Feb 1820) lived with the family.

Frank P. Ferree owned this land for many years. But on April 1, 1918, he conveyed the four tracts containing about 57 acres to Walter Hoover. On April 1928, the heirs of Walter Hoover conveyed all four tracts to Jacob E and Lizzie Shade. On November 15, 1938 after Jacob E. Shade died, his widow Lizzie Shade sold the fifty-eight plus acre farm to Elmer J. and Carrie Shade. Elmer died on November 19, 1964, and Carrie his widow conveyed the farm several years later to Jacob E. and Corrine E. Shade on November 13, 1975.

HOME OF CORRINE E. SHADE
(With small parcel broken from large farm)

Jacob E. and Corrine Shade sold several small tracts of this land. Two tracts, one containing about an acre, another containing about 3 acres was sold to Jacob E. Shade, Jr. (Another nine acres will be discussed elsewhere.) On Jul 16, 2001, Corrine E. Shade, by then a widow conveyed the remaining 46 acres to Ammon and Rachel Esh, the present owners. [JACOB S. SHADE Family genealogy on page 535]

[*GEORGE WASHINGTON FERREE (b Nov 21, 1810 in Wash Twp - d Jan 5, 1873, bur Hoffman Cem), a son of Isaac and Elizabeth (Seiler) Ferree, and a great grandson of Isaac Ferree, a native of France. George Washington m in 1834 to Leah Umholtz (Feb 7, 1815 - Jan 28, 1888), a dau of Henry and Susanna (Hoover) Umholtz. His grandparent Isaac and Mary Ferree lived near Wiconisco Creek, where they had a gun powder mill during the early 1800's. In 1880, Emaline Bird lived with the Ferree family. **George W. and Leah (Umholtz) Ferree children (most bur Hoffman Cem): **Cyrus** b & d 1834; **Uriah** b 1836 -d 1839; **Anna Mary** (Oct 19, 1838 - May 25, 1895, bur Simeon Cem, m Isaac Burd (1832 - 1865, bur Hoffman Cem), a son of _____. **Isaac and Ann**

Mary (Ferree) Burd children: ***Elizabeth** b c1858, lived with the Cyrene Bowman family in Gratz in 1870, after her father died. On January 3, 1875, she m William Messner, a son of John P. Messner of Lykens Twp;***Susan** b c1860; ***George W** . (Mar 1, 1861 - Apr 6, 1889), who lived with the James Kolba family in 1870. He is buried beside his mother in Simeon Cem. His obituary describes him as an unfortunate mortal who was crippled by a mine accident early in life. The 1880 census notes that he had a sore back;***Henry H**. b c1863 m Ida _____, lived in Mt. Carmel;***Emma J** . b c1864, in 1880 lived with her grandmother Ferree. She m William Row of Lykens Twp; Sarah b c1865, m Ambrose Reinhold of Williamstown; ***Mary** Louisa (no dates),m May 12, 1872, Durrell Seesholtz in Lykens. Durrell (1846 - 1916, bur IOOF Cem, Lykens), was a son of Rebecca and ____ Seesholtz of Lykens. He was a "workman in the cars in 1870." In 1911, they lived in Harrisburg. Mary and Durrell Seesholtz had these children: Harry F (Jan 4, 1874 - Oct 20, 1943), Pvt in USMC, bur Simeon Cem; Edith; Mary R.
Elizabeth (b Jun 4, 1841 - Feb 18, 1913, bur Hoffman Cem), d at the home of her brother Frank.;
Henry B. (b 1844 – Apr 13, 1903, bur Simeon Cem), m Louisa Bellon, dau of Mathias Bellon, lived in Jackson Twp in 1888.Henry and Louisa (Bellon) Ferree children (some bapt HoffmanCh): *** Ida Charlotte b Jan 6, 1867; ***Sarah Caroline** b May 27, 1868; ***George Franklin** b Apr 9, 1870, lived with Washington Ferree family in 1880;***Lizzie Louisa** b Sep 6,1875;***Hattie Leah** b Sep 21,1880, m Apr 6, 1895 to Henry L. Coleman; ***Eva N**. (no dates); ***Charles Adam** b Dec 1884; **Sarah Grace** (Apr 23, 1847 bapt Hoffman Ch - d Apr 10, 1871, bur Friedens Union Cem, Hegins), m Nathan S.Bressler. Sarah was a teacher in 1870;
George Washington Jr. (b c1849 – d pre 1896), m Emma Ritzman, **had these children**:***Hattie Louisa** b Aug 12, 1876, bapt Hoffman Ch; ***Henry Franklin** b Jul 21,1878, bapt Zion Luth, Lykens;
Franklin P. (b May 25, 1853 Lyk Twp – d _____) m 1878 Catherine A. Salada (Mar 12, 1860 - Apr 24, 1917, bur Hoffman Cem), a dau of Henry and Elizabeth (Seiler) Salada. Frank was working in the mines in 1870. **Frank P.and Catherine Salada Ferree children:**
*** Sarah E b Nov 20, 1879; ***Joseph Allen** b Dec 17, 1885;***Elizabeth Leah** (Apr 1,1889 bapt Hoffman Ch - 1897, bur Hoffman Cem); ***Henry Washington** (Apr 20, 1892 - 1897); ***Blanche Miriam** b Sep 13, 1894.
Edith Ellen b Feb 16, 1855 - d Jul 22, 1895 of cancer, bur Hoffman Cem), m John Rush (1851 - 1942), **had these children**: ***Harry Edgar** b Dec 27, 1879; ***Elizabeth Beulah** b Sep 28, 1883; ***Mary Salome** b Feb 19, 1886; ***George W**. (Jul 20, 1888 - Jul 10, 1916, bur Hoffman Cem)
**Ida Edith b c1856]

LARRY K. LENKER RESIDENCE

The land for this house had been part of a nine acre 88 perch tract of land that was owned by Jacob and Carrie Shade. After Jacob died, Carrie sold this and several other tracts of land to Jacob E. and Corrine Shade on November 13, 1975. From the nine acre tract, two smaller tracts were sold. On June 24, 1978, Jacob E. and Corrine Shade sold three acres of this land to Larry K. Lenker, a single man. It bordered on land of Charles C. and Francis Sitlinger and the highway from Gratz to Loyalton. Larry had the new house built in 1979, and is the present owner.

RONALD K. LENKER RESIDENCE

The land for this house was also part of a nine acre 88 perch tract of land owned by Jacob and Carrie Shade. After Jacob died, Carrie sold several tracts of land to Jacob E. and Corrine Shade on June 24, 1978, including this nine acre, eighty-eight perches of land. In 1986, Jacob E. and Corrine Shade sold five plus acres from the nine acres tract to Ronald Lenker. He had this house built on the land shortly after he purchased it, and continues to live here.

[These Lenker's descend from Cornelius and Rebecca (Witmer) Lenker, through Marlin Lenker (1901 – 1962), m to Clara M. Hollenbach. Marlin had a son **Ernest E. Lenker** who died in 1988, and was married to Edna Shade. **Ernest E. and Edna (Shade) Lenker children**: <u>Ronald</u> and <u>Larry</u> Lenker, owners of these two adjoining houses, as well as <u>Ernest E. Jr</u>.: <u>Carol</u>; <u>Gloria</u>; <u>Nancy</u>; <u>Sally</u>; <u>Violet</u>; <u>Patsy</u> & Evelyn.]

MR. & MRS. ALBERT N. MORGAN FARM
(Was Jacob Shade 75 acres in 1875 - later John W. Hoffman)
(Now 52 acres 70 preches)

This farm is made up of land from two different tracts. Both tracts were part of the land grant that was warranted to Henry Umholtz April 16,1787, surveyed September 15, 1818, patented to Philip Umholtz January 12, 1831. On August 20, 1840, the heirs of Philip Umholtz transferred the land to his son John Umholtz. Two years later on August 20, 1842, John & Magdalena Umholtz conveyed two tracts of land to Samuel Umholtz. One of the tracts contained 52 acres 70 perches. The other contained 38 acres 2 perches. Samuel Umholtz and his wife Elizabeth conveyed their land with houses to Jacob Shade Sr., a resident of Lower Mahantongo Twp., Schuylkill County on April 1, 1846, deed recorded April 1850. The land bordered the road from Halifax to Gratz, land of Michael Matter north, to Jonas Schoffstall, south to John Umholtz and Jacob Shade other land.

In 1850, Jacob Shade Sr., his wife Mary, and daughter Mary age 15 lived on either this farm or the adjacent farm. Their son Jacob Shade, Jr. his wife Catherine and baby Samuel lived next door. In 1860, Jacob Shade Sr., and his second wife Elizabeth lived in another section of Lykens Twp. Jacob Shade Jr and wife Catherine and their family lived on one of these farms. The adjacent farm was vacant. On February 26, 1870, Jacob Shade Sr. assigned the same acreage with houses to Jacob Shade Jr. This land was bound on the north by Elias Klinger land, south by John Umholtz estate, land of Andrew Schmeltz to the east, John W. Hoffman on the west, and Frank P. Ferree. In 1870 the census for Lykens Twp. shows Jacob and Catherine Shade living here with their family, and Jacob's father Jacob, Sr. living with them. By 1880 the Shade family had moved to their brick house (see page 522).

In March 1890, a sale was held and John W. Hoffman purchased the 52 acre, 70 perch property. This farm was adjacent to another property that Hoffman owned. Both farms gave him more than 100 acres of land to farm. He devoted much of his efforts to raising cattle.

On February 8, 1897, John W. and Amanda Hoffman conveyed this 52 acre 70 perch farm to Edwin E. Hoffman. Several years later on December 27, 1902, Edwin E. and Vietta Hoffman sold the farm to Sarah R. and John Reinohl. The Reinohl's moved to Williamstown and on June 11, 1906, they sold the farm to Frank P. Ferree. The farm was sold again on April 1, 1918, and Henry W. Hoffman became the new owner. H. W. Hoffman sold the farm to Fred E. Hoffman on March 13, 1926. Fred E. and Flora Hoffman owned this farm until December 30, 1938, when they sold it to Lottie and Harry A. Kissinger.

This farm had a lot of happy memories for Max Hoke, Esther Adams and Marie Umholtz who visited their friend Lottie Hoffman when they were youngsters. One warm Sunday afternoon, they walked down to visit Lottie. It was the perfect weather for swimming, so Lottie suggested that they could wear her brother's bathing suits, and swim in the dam. The water looked so cool and inviting, but when they stepped into the dam, they sank into mud up over their knees. They splashed around in the muddy water for a while, and then paddled around the dam in the homemade canoe. Later, when Lottie's brothers John, Charley, and Clarney came home, they got the big farm horses out of the barn and they took them down to the water trough in the meadow.

Later that year the girls were invited to the family Thanksgiving dinner because Charley won the turkey that Max and Esther's Senior Class at Lykens Valley Vocational School in Berrysburg chanced off. A large table filled the summerhouse where they ate dinner. It was filled with turkey and filling, vegetables in cream and butter, canned fruits, chocolate cake with caramel icing, and loaves of freshly baked home made bread. This meal was topped off with Mrs. Hoffman's famous cheese pie. Marie says, "Memories are made of this!"

After Henry W. Hoffman became a widower, his daughter Lottie Kissinger and family came to live with him. It was a very beautiful place to raise a family. Marie Lahr, daughter of Lottie lived in this house from her youth until 1952. She recently described the surroundings of this picturesque place. The house was an old log house with center stairway. On the first floor a kitchen stretched the length of the house, on one side, two rooms comprised the other side. The upstairs had four rooms, and a third floor was the attic. The summerhouse stood near the main house, and close by was a big stone bake oven, which served to make many loaves of bread. A well in the same vicinity provided the water. A small wooden structure was built around the well, and it was covered with a tin roof. In dry summer weather the well often went dry.

After Harry Kissinger died, Lottie sold 49 acres 133 perches with frame dwelling, barn and out buildings to Albert L. and Martha Morgan on October 31, 1970. Lottie kept a small lot near the road, and had a house built for herself. Albert L Morgan died March 3, 1979, and Martha Morgan sold to Margaret M and Albert N. Morgan on October 18, 2002. For the past several years, Randy and Brenda (Ferster) Bellon have lived as tenants on this farm.

HOME OF MRS. RAY FERSTER

The land for this house has the same background as the adjoining farm. Harry A. and Lottie Kissinger sold a small tract of land (about an acre) on December 23, 1963, to Ray E. and Edna E. Ferster. The first residence on the lot was a house trailer. They had the present house built later and it became their permanent residence. Ray Ferster died several years ago, and Edna continues to live here.

[JAMES W. FERSTER (May 20, 1857 – Feb 2, 1926, bur Krebs Luth Cem, Jackson Twp., Northld Co), son of David Ferster (Mar 2, 1828 –Aug 11, 1903, bur Urban, Jordan Twp Northld Co) & Judith (Brosius) Ferster (Mar 27, 1828 – Mar 3, 1904). James W. Ferster grandparents Peter & Christina (Rebuck) Ferster. James W. m 1st Sevilla Phillips (May 28, 1860 – Jun 25, 1901). James m 2nd Cora Brown (no dates). James W. Ferster children: Amanda m ___Lenker; Mary m ___ Lahr; Cora A. b 1913, m Adam E. Lahr (1898 – 1967 bur Krebs Cem, Northld Co); John E. (May 6, 1904 - Nov 1979), m Verna E. Brown in 1927; John & Verna (Brown) Ferster children: ___ m Earl Bordner; Mark & Guy of Dornsife; Ray (__ - c2006), m Edna Kissinger, Lykens Twp]

James & Cora Ferster, Mary, John, & Anne

HOME OF MARTHA MORGAN

About 1986, Lottie Kissinger sold a small lot of land to Martha Morgan who moved from her farm located on Indian Trail Road. Mrs. Morgan had a ranch style house built on this lot. Her son and family now live on the farm that Martha owned. [See Morgan family information on write-up of that property.]

HOME OF LOTTIE KISSINGTER

This land was part of the farm that Harry A. and Lottie Kissinger owned. Harry died in 1967, and after that Lottie sold the farm, reserving this small tract for herself. She had the house built and lived here until her death.

HOME OF MR. & MRS. RAYMOND W. LAHR

The land for this house has the same background as the adjoining farm. Harry A. and Lottie Kissinger became the owners on February 7, 1944. While they owned the land, they sold this lot with brick house on December 23, 1963 to Ray and Marie Martha Lahr. The Lahr family has lived on these premises to the present time. ([Family history on write-up of adjoining Hoffman farm.]

MR. AND MRS LEON R. CRISSINGER FARM
(WAS EDWARD ROMBERGER FARM 1875)

This land is from the original tract of patented land containing three hundred twenty four acres, seventy-three perches that Commonwealth of Pennsylvania granted to George Peiffer of Harrisburg. After George Peiffer died, his eldest son Henry petitioned orphan court of Dauphin Court to divide and appraise the estate of this father. The petition was made on September 4, 1810. On April 1, 1811, seventy acres, seven perches of the above land of George Peiffer were sold to Henry Romberger. On March 14, 1812, Henry and Elizabeth Romberger sold this same acreage with appurtenances and buildings to George Matter. Over the next several years George had a barn built on his property. He apparently later moved to Mifflin Township. After their move, On June 7, 1828, George and Catherine Matter conveyed this farm to their eldest son Michael Matter. The farm bordered on land of Sarah Schoffstall, Andrew Schmeltz, Jacob Buffington, south to Jacob Ritzman, Jacob Tallman, Jacob Shade and Christian Moyer. Many years later, on April 1, 1865, Michael and Sarah Matter of Lykens Township conveyed a plantation of seventy-six acres, forty-one perches to Daniel Romberger of Washington Township. The latest purchase included a small area of about three-quarter acre of land on the northwest corner of the property. It has not been learned what purpose that small piece of land served.

[GEORGE MATTER (Jan 16,1771 – Oct 11,1855, bur St. Johns Cem, Bbg), m Catharina Romberger (Mar 19, 1777 – Jul 3, 1851), a dau of Balthasar and Anna Maria (Traut) Romberger of Lykens Twp. George & Catharina (Romberger) Matter children; Michael (Apr 12, 1794 – Jan 14, 1880), m Sarah Crum; Johannes b Oct 25, 1795; Joseph b May 16, 1797, m Susanna Ritzman; George b Oct 11, 1798; Daniel b Feb 4,1801 (twin); Anna Catharina b Feb 4,1801 (twin);Anna Maria b Feb 4,1805; Elisabeth b Aug 21, 1807; Salome b Jul 15, 1810; Jacob (Nov 4, 1814 – Jul 24, 1816; Hanna b Nov 26, 1817; Susanna b May 11, 1821. [Find more information under Matter and Romberger genealogies.]

Daniel Romberger was born in Lykens Township, and as a youth became involved in farming with his father. In 1865, he purchased this farm and later acquired another farm in Washington Township. After settling in Wash. Twp. Daniel & Hannah Romberger sold this tract of land containing seventy-six acres strict measure, with houses & barns to their son Edward Romberger of Lykens Township March 23, 1873. Edward Romberger was born in Lykens Township, and after attending the local township schools he was enrolled in the seminary at New Berlin, Union County. He then became a teacher in a school in Williamstown for one year. He was not fond of teaching, so he purchased this farm from his father and took up farming. After his father died, Edward and his wife Sarah sold this farm on March 31,1883 to Elias Klinger. Edward purchased his fathers' farm in Washington Township, and lived on that property the remainder of his life.

[*DANIEL ROMBERGER (Feb19, 1816 -1882), a son of Adam and Catharina (Paul) Romberger, m Hannah Bergstresser (Sep 26, 1818 - Feb 13, 1889), a dau of John and Ann (Auchmuty) Bergstresser, grandaughter of Samuel Auchmuty, who served in the Revolutionary War. Daniel & Hannah (Bergstresser) Romberger children, all boys :
**ADAM (Aug 21, 1839 - Jan 24, 1904), m Mary A. Bohner, lived in Northld Co
**EDWARD (Jul 30, 1841 - Mar 22, 1907, bur Maple Grove, E'ville), m Jan 10, 1866, Sarah Klinger (Mar 29, 1842 - Jan 26, 1897), a dau of Alexander and Magdalena (Hoffman) Klinger of Washington Twp., Edward & Sarah (Klinger) Romberger children: ***Alice Celesta b Mar 19, 1870, m P.W.G. Raker , a school teacher from Williamstown. They had these children: ****Helen Evangeline b Jan 30, 1898; ***Elmer Wesley (Sep 6, 1872 - Oct 31, 1942, bur Maple Grove, E'ville), m Frances ____ (Nov 15, 1878 - Apr 8, 1911);
**CYRUS (Jul 14, 1843 - Apr 15, 1915), m May 25, 1875 to Louisa Troutman (1851 - 1943), a dau of Samuel and Catherine (Hillibush) Troutman). They lived in Elizabethville where he was a merchant. Cyrus and Louisa (Troutman) Romberger children: ***Oscar Lot (Apr 18, 1878 - 1956, bur Maple Grove Cem, E'ville); ***Daniel Homer b Nov 27, 1880; ***Steward T. b Feb 14, 1883; ***Hannah Edith b Jan 1,1888; ***Robert Raymond (1889 - 1922, bur Maple Grove Cem, E;ville), served in 1108 Aer Squadren, in WWI;

SAMUEL (Aug 9,1845 - Mar 11, 1921), learned the tanning trade with Isaac Matter at Uniontown. He later formed a partnership with Reuben Weiser and established a tanyard at Green Briar, Northld Co.which he sold several years later, and purchased the tannery east of Gratz He eventually sold that tannery and moved to Elizabethville, where he and his sons Penrose and Daniel established a business of hides and tallow. While in Green Briar, Samuel m Mar 12,1867 to Sarah Jane Brower b Oct 29, 1847, dau of Nathan and Caroline (Troutman) Brower. Samuel and Sarah Jane (Brower) children:*Daniel W. (Feb 23, 1870 - 1937, bur Maple Grove, E'ville), m Dec 5,1891, Sadie Gotshall (1874 - 1917) had these children: ****Melvin Carroll b Jan 8,1893; ****Harold LeeRoy (Apr 15, 1894 - 1971); ****Laurence Urene b Feb 2, 1896; ****Fay Olivia b Feb 21, 1898; ****Daniel Wallace (May 18, 1905 - 1960 bur Maple Grove Cem, E'ville); ***Penrose C. b 1872, attended West Chester State Normal School, and became involved in sales. He m Estella M. ____ , had ****Helen Maude b Nov 21, 1900;****Ethel Estella b Oct 18, 1902; ****Clove Winifred b Feb 15, 1905;***Elba b Jul 18, 1874, m Feb 11, 1896 to Ammon W. Krebs, of Herndon.

Samuel Romberger (1845 – 1921)

551

Ammon was a druggist at the time of the marriage. **Ammon and Elba children:********Samuel** b Oct 3, 1903; *****Ira Penrose** b 1875, m Feb 16, 1897, Kathryn Irene Lehman moved to Wilkes Barre, and worked in a branch of his father's business. **They had these children:** ******Sarah Margaret** b Oct 28, 1901; ******Mildred Susan** b Jul 19, 1904; ******Ira Penrose** b Mar 29, 1907; *****Ella J.** b 1878;

****JOSIAH** (Oct 9, 1847 - Apr 2, 1917), m Nov 3, 1870 Sarah Matter

****JOHN** A. (Apr 21, 1850 - 1916), m Nov 23, 1870, Mary A. Row

****H. HOWARD** (Jul 12, 1852 - May 11, 1902, bur Simeon Cem, Gratz), m Sep 30, 1873 to Kathryn Ritzman (Jun 11, 1855 - May 27, 1936), a dau of Michael and Elizabeth (Hartman) Ritzman..

Howard Romberger early in life engaged in farming. He enrolled in Berrysburg Seminary, with thoughts of becoming an Evangelical Preacher. In 1879 he became a licensed preacher & also continued to farm. He later was assigned to numerous Evangelical Congregations throughout eastern Penna. In 1890, he and his family came back to Gratz, and purchased a mercantile business on lot number forty in Gratz. By November he installed a steam device in the dwelling, the first central heating system in Gratz. Howard also filled positions of area ministers when needed. In 1889, the family moved to Wyomissing , Pa. to open another general store. Darwin, their son became a teacher, then the principal of Gratz Academy. He and Bessie Sebold met and married in Gratz, then moved to Wyomissing with his parents. Almost immediately, Darwin was diagnosed with well-advanced tuberculosis. He died in 1900 at the age of twenty-five. Howard and his wife in the fall of 1901, the fall of 1901, closed their store in Wyomissing , and moved to Glassport, near Pittsburgh, as senior pastor, to help build a congregation among the working people there. But by spring 1902, he was diagnosed with typhoid fever, and died in May, not quite fifty years old. **H. Howard & Kathryn (Ritzman) Romberger children:** *****Darwin Ambrose** (Aug 10, 1874 - 1900, bur Simeon Cem), m Apr 30, 1896 Bessie Sebold (1875 - 1951), a dau of George W. and Charlotte (Moyer) Sebold of Gratz, **had one son** ******Ralph**, who m Lucille Greeves, **and had two children:** *Charlotte* d young; *John Darwin*; ******Amy Agnes** b Sep 5, 1882, m Harry Albright of Reading.

****ALFRED** D. (Oct 9, 1854 - Sep 15, 1857).]

[**ELIAS KLINGER** (Nov 26, 1843 - Jan 11,1908, d of cancer, bur south side Simeon Cem), a son of Alexander and Magdalena (Hoffman) Klinger, m by Rev. William H. Weidner at Oakdale on August 2, 1868 to Mary Ellen Umholtz (Aug 20, 1848 - Jan 2, 1915, d when overcome with paralysis while butchering), a dau of Samuel and Elizabeth (Harner) Umholtz of Lykens Twp. **Elias and Mary Ellen (Umholtz) Klinger had one child: LAURA M "LOTTIE"** (Jun 1869 - Jan 17, 1949 bur south side Simeon Cem), m c 1895, John A. "Gristel" Kissinger (Jan 1865 - Mar 6, 1948), a son of Daniel and Sallie (Moyer) Kissinger. **John A. and Laura (Klinger) Kissinger had these children: Mark Klinger** (Sep 1, 1897 - Oct 26, 1973, bur south side Simeon Cem), m Anna M. Shroyer (1905 - 1968), a dau of Arthur and Christianna (Carl) Shroyer. Mark and Anna (Shroyer) Kissinger had one son: **Bruce** (Feb 21, 1936 - Dec 28, 1991) **Ella Bernice** (Feb 11, 1903 - Dec 25, 1962, bur south side Simeon Cem), not m.]

When Elias Klinger purchased this farm, it became a homestead, and remained in the family for several generations. The farm remained under the Elias Klinger estate until after 1937. Then it became the property of their daughter Laura M. and her husband John A. Kissinger. Later in life, John A. and Laura Kissinger moved to Gratz. On March 30, 1946, they sold the seventy-six acre, forty-one perch farm (less several parcels that had previously been sold containing about three acres) to their son Mark K. Kissinger.

Years later Mark K. Kissinger and his wife decided to sell the farm. On December 7, 1988, the farm was sold to Mark D. Kissinger. They decided to burn the old barn that had become in disrepair. As the structure became engulfed in flames, a strong wind developed and carried the flames to the house. The old house caught fire, and it too was destroyed.

MARK D. KISSINGER RESIDENCE

Mark D. Kissinger held a public auction in 1992, at which time Leon R. and Sharon L. Crissinger and & Kenneth W. and Karen A. Crissinger purchased the farm. Mark and his wife saved a small parcel of land for themselves along the Airport Road. They had a a ranch style house constructed and made that their retirement home. Mark has since died, and his wife is the owner and resident.

HOME OF MR. & MRS. DANIEL BLYLER
(Part of the Edward Romberger 76 acre Farm located on map of 1875)

On February 11, 1993, the Crissinger family sold more than an acre of land from the farm to Daniel E. and Carol L. Blyler. A new two-story house was built for them near the location of the Old house. The Blyler's are the presnt owners.

MR. & MRS. JOHN P. HOFFMAN
(Was Elias Snyder 49 Acres 1875, Then John W. Hoffman , He Built House c1879)

This farm was part of the tract of land that was warranted 1789, and patented 1801 to John Salada, and was called "Wilmington." On April 18, 1826, Sheriff Thomas Welker of Dauphin County sold forty-one acres, ten perches of the land of John Salada to Michael Salada. This tract contained two small houses, barns and a gristmill and sawmill. Michael Salada, son of John Salada, was a miller by trade, just as his father had been. But on April 1, 1829, he and his wife Rachel sold this same property to Jacob Hetrick, a shoemaker who was living in Gratz. Jacob Hetrick and his wife were living in Lykens Township in 1830, and had no other persons in the household. On March 31, 1830, Jacob and Rebecca Hetrick sold this forty-one acres, ten perches of land with the two small dwellings, barn, grist and saw mills to John Grimm. In 1840, the Hetrick's had a young male child with them, and lived in Gratz. In 1850, Jacob Hetrick and his wife Rebecca lived on lot sixty-one in Gratz, and had Jacob Eby age four living with them.

[**Michael Salada Jr**. (b Dec 26, 1802 in Gratz - d Oct 8, 1854 in Lycoming Co.), was a son of John Salada Jr and Anna Maria Kissinger. He received a legacy from his grandfather Abraham Kissinger, owing to the fact that his mother Anna Maria preceded her father in death. Michael Jr. married Rachel Harner (1802 - 1872). After Michael died Rachel m Frederick Stover. **Michael and Rachel (Harner) Salada Jr children**: William (Jul 18, 1826 - Apr 6, 1892); **John** b 1832; **Jeremiah** b 1834; _____ b 1836; **Frederick** b 1838; **Daniel** b 1842.]

[**Jacob Hetrick** (c1810 - pre 1852), a son of _____, m Rebecca Umholtz (c1813 - Mar 1, 1879, place of burial unknown), a dau of Philip & Anna Maria (Williard) Umholtz. Jacob was a shoemaker and tailor. He and Rebecca (Umholtz) Hetrick had one known son, **Jacob** b c1844. After Jacob Hetrick died, Rebecca m Jacob Erdman (Apr 1, 1803 - May 30, 1862, bur Simeon Cem), and continued to live in Gratz on lot sixty-one. In 1860, Rebecca's son Jacob lived with them.]

THE GRIMM ANCESTRY

[The early **GRIMM** family lived in Northampton County, Pa. in the early 1700s. **CHRISTIAN GRIMM** was born there about 1755 and later came to Lower Mahantango Twp., Schuylkill County, where he died in 1832. His wife was Magdalena _____, b in Pennsylvania about 1770, died about 1822 in Mah Twp. **Christian and Magdalena Grimm had these known children: Dau;**
*CHRISTIAN Jr. GRIMM (b Oct 9, 1790 bapt Klingers Ch - d 1825, Low Mah Twp), m Elizabeth ___ (b Mar 11, 1793 Berks Co - d Jan 29, 1855, bur Friedens Cem, Hegins, Pa) **Christian and Elizabeth Grimm had these children**: **MICHAEL** (1817 - Mar 27, 1855, Hegins Twp, Sch Co), m c1844, Catharine Fidler (b c1824 Sch Co - d probably Delaware Twp, Mercer Co, Pa.).**ELIZABETH** b 1819;
*JOHN GRIMM (b Apr 13, 1795 in Deep Creek Valley (Mahantango Twp) - d Sep 4, 1886, age 92, at the home of his son George in Halifax, bur Fairview Cem, Enders), m Catharine Kohler (b Apr18, 1800 Wash Twp, Northld Co - Jan14, 1880, a dau of George and Catherine Kehler. He was a veteran of the War of 1812. **John and Catherine (Kohler) Grimm children**: **CATHARINE** (b Jul 15, 1819 Jackson Twp, Dau Co - Feb 24, 1886, bur St. Jacobs "Millers" Cem, Jackson Twp, Dau Co), m John Samuel Barry III (b Jul 5, 1818 Dau Co - Sep 20, 1863), a son of John and Susannah (?) Barry.**LUCY ANN** b Jul 27, 1821 Sch Co - d Jul 29, 1909, bur Ebenezer EUB Cem, Jackson Twp), m Christian Zimmerman (Mar 8, 1819 - Nov 12, 1890); **GEORGE** (Oct 18, 1822 Sch Co- Nov 6, 1886, bur St. Peter's (Fetterholf's Cem, Halifax Twp, Dau Co), m Mary Laudermilch (Aug 15, 1819 - Aug 7, 1887), a dau of Adam and Maria Laudermilch; **LOVINA** (May 29, 1824 Sch Co - May 25, 1910, bur Fairview Cem, Enders), m Samuel Shoop (Jun 14, 1821 - Mar 17, 1895), a son of John and Elizabeth Shoop; **JOHN** (1825 Jackson twp - 1902, bur St. Pauls E.U.B cem, Jackson Twp, m Susanna H. Eby (1830 - 1910), **had these children**: ***Mary E. (1852 - 1862 bur Simeon Cem); ***Amos (Mar 1, 1856 - Feb 24, 1861, bur Zion Meth Cem, Jefferson Twp); **SOLOMON** (Dec 20, 1826 Sch Co - Feb 15, 1880, bur Fairview Cem, Enders), m Sarah Ann Frank (Feb 13, 1833 - May 23, 1894), a dau of David and Nancy (Kemerer) Frank, lived in Fisherville, worked as a carpenter; **ELIAS** (Feb 9, 1828, Jackson Twp - Jul 4, 1915, Seiberts Cem, Williamstown), m May 12, 1849 in her parents home, Emaline Matter (Apr 27, 1831 - Nov 2, 1894), a dau of Michael and Sarah (Crum) Matter. Elias was a Civil War Veteran, and served at first battle of Hatchers Run. Later engaged in battle at Weldon Road near Yellow House, North Carolina, where he became ill from exposure caused by lying in several inches of water for several hours. He was in the hospital at Washington D.C. for three months. Elias was a shoemaker. **Elias and Emaline (Matter) Grimm children**: ***Louisa Jane (Oct 23, 1849 - Feb 15, 1916), m 1st John Miller (d pre1876), in shock from being scalded in mine accident. Louisa Jane m 2nd in 1876 William Wingert (Nov 22, 1839 - Apr 11, 1912, bur Williamstown Cem), a son of Benjamin and Rebecca (Hoke) Wingert, lived in Williamstown; ***MaryAnn b Jun 25, 1851, m ____ Wennell, lived in Harrisburg; ***Sarah Katherine b Feb 8, 1853, m Harry Poticher, lived in Pottsville; ***Selna Rudella (Jan 16, 1855 - 1930, bur Williamstown), m Emanuel Deitrich (1849 - 1936), lived in Williamstown; ***Emmaline b 1856; ***Percival

David b 1859; ***Malinda Agnes** b Jan 27, 1861, m George Bates, lived in Reading; _____ b & d 1862; ***Milton Elias** b Sep 28, 1863, moved to Kansas City; _____ b & d 1866; ***Anna Pricilla** b Sep 13, 1867; ***Charles** b Apr 16, 1867, moved to Colorada Springs; ***Annie** b Jan 18, 1870; ***Harry Harrison** b May 3, 1873, lived in Clarks Valley.

JACOB (Jan 29,1830, Sch Co- Nov 20, 1844, bur St. Jacobs (Millers) Cem, Jackson Twp.;** **HENRY** (Jul 24, 1831, Dau Co - Feb 22, 1899, Dekalb Co, Ill), m Feb 2, 1854 (St. Johns "Hill" Ch record) Elizabeth "Abbie"Laudermilch (Aug 21, 1834-Nov 1, 1903, Hinkley, Ill), a dau of John Adam and Magdalena Laudermilch; **SARAH E.** (Feb 24,1833 Jackson Twp - Dec 27, 1864, bur Fairview Cem, Enders, Dau Co) , m Josiah McColly (b1841 - d after Jan 1917 in Iowa), a son of Robert and Anna Catherine (Lubold) McColly). Records of their children not found. After Sarah died, Josiah McColly m Mary Hoke b c1849, and moved to Iowa, where both are buried. **Josiah and Mary (Hoke) McColly children:***Annie** b c1868;***Sarah E** b c1869; ***William G.** b c1871; ***Liccie S.** b c1873;***Robert H.** b c1875; ***Thomas E.** b c1878; ***James F.** b c1880.

AMOS (Aug 7, 1836 - May 11, 1906, bur Fairview Cem, Enders), m Elizabeth "Betsy" Gilbert (Apr 15, 1843 - Mar 10, 1874); **DANIEL** (b Jan 23, 1838, near Mt. House, Jackson Twp - d Feb 3, 1910, Oklahoma City, Okla,bur Caldwell Cem, Caldwell, Kansas), m Mary Ann Shoop (Jun 26, 1842, E'ville - Nov 18, 1901, Caldwell, Kan), a dau of John (Jr) and Anna Maria (Sweigard) Shoop. After their marriage moved to DeKalb Co., Ill, 25 years later moved to Kansas. **They had 9 children;** **NATHANIEL** (Mar 31, 1839 - Oct 17, 1924, bur DeKalb Co, Kan), m 1st Lovina McColly (Apr 15, 1843 - Mar 10, 1874, bur Fairview Cem). Nathaniel m 2nd Feb 16, 1882, Mary Ann Buerer (b 1852, Ill -April 1919, DeKalb Co, Ill); **MARY AMANDA** (Jan 28, 1841, Jackson Twp, - Jun 20, 1924, bur Fairview Cem, Enders), m Oct 9, 1859, John Enders (Aug 26, 1837 - Apr 19, 1913); a son of Philip A. and Nancy (Sheets) Enders; **AARON** (1850 - 1851, bur St. Jacob's Cem);

*MARY MAGDALENA GRIMM** (b Apr 9, 1796, Sch Co - d Aug 6, 1863 in Halifax, bur Fetterhoffs Cem), m John Adam Laudermilch (Jan 6, 1787 - Jul 8, 1841, bur Fetterhoffs Cem). **John Adam and Mary Magdalena (Grimm) Laudermilch had one known child: **GEORGE WASHINGTON** (b 1836 -d 1837, bur Fetterhoffs Cem); *HENRY GRIMM** b c1800]

John and Catherine Grimm lived here for several years, then sold the forty-one acres, ten perches of land on April 23, 1835, to Charles Smith. The Grimm family moved to Jackson Township, Dauphin County, where they were living in 1850. Most of their children lived in the same household with their parents in 1850: Solomon, Henry, Sarah, Amos, Daniel, Nathaniel and Amanda. George was married, and lived nearby. He was employed as a mason.

Charles Smith was listed on the 1834 & 1837 tax record with the 40 plus acres, a sawmill & flourmill. In 1844 he bought a tavern in Gratz, and sold one year later to Solomon Laudenslager. [We have not been able to learn anything more about this family.]

About five years later, Charles & Catherine Smith sold the Lykens Twp acreage with grist & sawmills to Christian Albert, an inn keeper of Lower Mahanoy Twp., Northld Co. Christian

Elias Grimm (1828 – 1915) and wife
Emaline (Matter) Grimm (1831 – 1894)

Albert was listed on the 1840 LykensTwp., Census with three sons and a daughter. On March 30, 1842, Christian & Elizabeth Albert sold the forty-one acres with the mills buildings and improvements, plus another tract of seven acres to Jonas ImSchoffstall. Christian Albert purchased the seven acres from William & Susan Zerby in 1841. It originally belonged to the Gratz family, and was also a mill property. From here, the Christian Albert family moved to Jackson Twp. Northumberland County where they owned a farm. They continued to live there for the remainder of their lives. Christian Albert was among the men who were authorized to organize the Susquehanna & Union Bridge Company. They had two hundred dollars at their disposal "to erect a bridge across the Susquehanna River at any point within 5 miles below the mouth of Mahantongo Creek." Eventually two companies, The Treverton, Mahanoy and Susquehanna Railroad Company and the Susquehanna and Union Bridge Company were consolidated and took the name of the Trevorton and Susquehanna Railroad Company on April 25, 1854. A fourteen and one-half mile long railroad was constructed from Trevorton to the Susquehanna River, and a fourteen hundred-foot wood bridge connected the terminus of the railroad and the Pennsylvania canal on the opposite side of the river.

Louisa Jane Grimm (1849 – 1916), & husband John Miller, who died c1875 in shock from scalding in mining accident. Also children Annie & Henry

After first wife Elizabeth died, Christian married secondly Mary Stepp. But before their marriage, Mary and Christian drew up a pre-nuptial agreement on March 25, 1859. It was a rather unusual document for that early time period. The agreement gave one third of all personal property to Mary during her lifetime, should she survive Christian, the remainder to go to Christian's heirs. Mary gave up her right to any interest in Christian's real estate. However, all of Mary's property at the time of their marriage, both real and personal was to remain her sole property. The agreement was recorded on November 18, 1859.

When Christian died, by his will he stated that Mary the widow was to take her things as under the pre-nuptial agreement. Also "her cow and two hundred weight of pork and all the property she brought to me in lieu of her dower." The two sons, John and Isaac received real estate from their father's will, but daughter Polly received only two hundred dollars as her full share. The remainder of daughter Polly's share was to be divided among her sons, Franklin and George Lahr.

[*CHRISTIAN ALBERT (Nov 20, 1792 - Jan 31, 1866, bur Zion "Stone Valley" Cem,), a son of __(possibly Peter Albert who d 1799, will in Northld Co), m 1st Elizabeth Boyer (Jun 25, 1796 - Nov 24, 1857). After Elizabeth died, Christian Albert living in Jackson Township, married Mary Stepp of Lower Mahanoy Township, a widow of _____ Stepp. **Christian and Elizabeth (Boyer) Albert children:**
**Isaac (Dec 31, 1828 - Sep 29,1906, bur Herndon Cem), m Hannah ____ (Mar 1, 1827 - Jan 5, 1918), lived in Jackson Twp, Northld Co. In 1880 they had George Lahr age 24, an engineer, John Call a laborer, Laura Hollenbach 12, and Sarah Forster 19 with them.
**John (Feb 22, 1832 - Sep 2, 1902, bur Herndon Cem), m Amelia C. Stroh (Oct 22, 1835 - Feb 2, 1914), lived in Jackson Twp, later in Herndon where he had a property adjoining the river, which was used as a ferry landing. In 1880 they lived in Herndon, and he was listed as a hotel keeper. They had two children with them: Jane age 20, Martin age 22. John Kline age 32 was also with them and he was a dealer in tin and coal.
Mary (Polly), (Oct 20, 1834 - Oct 13, 1871, bur Trinity Evang Ref Cem, Dalmatia), m Daniel W. Lahr (Mar 31, 1826 - Sep 13, 1858), a son of Daniel Lahr (c1790- Dec 15, 1844, bur Dalmatia) and Sophia (Brosius) Lahr (1785 - 1859). Daniel W. Lahr was a boatman on the Penna State Canal, that ran from Sunbury to Havre de Grace, Md. He moved to Snyder Co later, and met Mary Albert there at Freeburg. **Daniel W. and Mary (Albert) Lahr had three children: Franklin b May 18, 1853, lived in Herndon and was bookkeeper for Herndon Manufacturing Co., was a talented musician, organized an orchestra in Herndon ; Geo. W., moved to Tacoma, Washington, was an electric light engr.; Sophia J. d age 8 yrs. After Daniel W. Lahr died, his widow Mary m _____ Gillespie.]

Jonas Schoffstall lived on this property, and was assessed for a house, barn, saw and flourmill from1843 until he sold a total of forty-eight acres, 112 perches of land, March 31, 1850 to Jonathan Klinger, who lived in the same area of Lykens Township. With the property, he sold the rights to access water for mill. After he sold the property, he went to live with his daughter Hannah.

Jonas Schoffstall lived in various areas of Lykens Township during his lifetime. In 1817, his occupation was listed as weller. He married first Mary Magdalena Margaretha Newbaker, and had a large family. She died in 1826. After his first wife died, Jonas had tenants on his property. In 1831 Emanuel Schoffstall was an occupant. In 1834, Moses Schoffstall at different times occupied both Jonas Sr. and Jonas Jr. properties. Jonas married a second time to Barbara

_____ in June 1831, but that marriage was short-lived. Jonas filed a petition for divorce on January 21, 1835. In testimony taken in April 1835, he stated that "he married his present wife Barbara in June of 1831 and she deserted him a considerable time past." He apparently received his divorce decree in April 1835.

Gravestone of Jonas ImSchoffstall, Ogle Co., Ill.

Jonas married a third time to Susanna Huber (Hoover) Umholtz, widow of Henry Umholtz, and daughter of Jacob and Catharine Eva Elisabeth (Sierer) Hoover. The date of the marriage is not known, but when Susanna's father penned his will in 1838, he mentioned her as the wife of Jonas Schoffstall. In 1840, Jonas and Susanna lived in this area of Lykens Township and had two young males between the ages of fifteen and thirty with them. When he purchased this mill property, Jonas was listed as a farmer, and hired Frederick Hoffner as his miller. His marriage to Susanna did not last long. In 1850, after selling this property, Jonas Schoffstall lived in a section of the house in Lykens Township that was owned by his daughter Hannah and her husband Peter Moyer. That same year, Susanna and her son John Umholtz, described as insane (and who received a legacy from his grandfather Jacob Hoover), lived on the farm adjacent to this property that she purchased from her father's estate in 1849. On Apr 6, 1852, Jonas was the plaintiff in the divorce against his wife Susnnna. He paid her twenty-five dollars" to release him from all obligations and rights to his estate."

The 1855 tax list for Lykens Township records a twenty-eight acre farm as belonging to "Susan Umholtz, Jonas Schoffstall's wife." About 1852 or1853 Jonas moved to Ogle Co., Illinois. His daughter Hannah moved there, as did his son Jonas Jr. He probably wanted to spend his last days with his children. He is buried beside his son Jonas, Jr. in West Grove Cem in Ogle County.

[*JONAS SCHOFFSTALL (May 15, 1782 - Feb 23, 1856, bur West Grove Cem, Lincoln Twp. Ogle Co. Il.,), a son of Peter and Anna Elizabeth (Kornmann) Schoffstall. He m 1st Dec 23, 1804, Mary Magdalena Margaretha Newbaker (Sep 1, 1779 Up Pax Twp - Jul 15, 1826, bur Hoffman Cem), a dau of Martin and Anna Margaretha (Hoffman) Newbaker. **Jonas and Mary Magd Marg (Newbaker) Schoffstall children:**
**AMANDA (no dates)
**ANN MARY b c1803 – d Mar 26,1879, probably m Solomon Laudenslager (Feb 8, 1802 – Jan 3, 1885, New Ulm, Brown Co, Mn), moved to Minn c1859;
HANNAH (b Mar 28, 1806 Lyk Twp - May 18, 1870, bur White Oak Cem, Forreston, Ogle Co., Il), m Jun 26, 1825 Peter Moyer (b Sep 11, 1805 in Berks Co, - d Jul 24, 1891 in Forreston Twp, Ogle Co Ill.), a son of John Jacob and Eva Christina (Koppenhaver) Moyer. They lived in Lykens Twp in 1850, but moved 1852 to Ogle Co. Ill. Peter and Hannah lived alone in Forreston in 1880. **Hannah and Peter Meyer children: ***Eliza (b Oct 17, 1825 Dau Co - d Jul 29, 1892, bur White Oak Cem Forreston, Ogle Co, Il), m Joseph A. Fisher (Aug 24, 1823 Dau Co – Mar 23, 1901), a son of Joseph and Magdalena (Dietrich) Fisher of Pennsylvania. In 1880, most of their children were living with them, namely: Hannah age 23, a dressmaker, Amelia e age 19, Benjamin H. 18, Jacob E 15. Another son Frank b c1858 was married to Abbie and lived near them; ***Jacob Peter (b Aug 5, 1827 Lyk Twp – d Jan 27, 1899 Cedar Co., Mo..), m Susan Saltzer (b Dec 13, 1832 Dau Co – Feb 20, 1903 Ft. Dodge, Webster Co., Ia). He was deaf and worked as a saddler; ***John (b Apr 14, 1829 Dau Co – d Jan 22, 1900, Wayside, Spokane Co, Wa), m Mary Ann Adams b Jan 7, 1834 Northld Co, Pa.; ***Peter S. (b Jan 7, 1835 Dau Co – d Feb 6, 1900, bur White Oak Cem, Forreston, Ogle Co.,Il), m Oct 1857 in Ogle Co., Il, Sarah Adams b 1828 Northld Co, Pa. – d Apr 25, 1871, Ogle Co, Il). Peter S. Meyer m 2nd Feb 8, 1872 Forreston Twp, Ogle Co, Il to Malinda Hoffa (b Aug 20, 1848, Pa. - d Mar 11, 1913, bur White Oak Cem), a dau of Jacob S. and Sarah (Snyder) Hoffa. **Peter had these children:** ****Alfred A. b 1860 in Illinois; ****Sarah A b c1873; ****William H. b c1874; ****Hannah M b c1876; ****Melinda b c1877; ****Daniel P b1880.
JONAS b Nov 19, 1809 Dau Co. - d Sep 15, 1866, bur St. James Luth (West Grove) Cem , m May 7, 1835 in Lykens Valley, Catherine Mayer (b Oct 31, 1815 - d Jan 15, 1901 in Ill.), a dau of John Jacob and Elizabeth (Koppenhaver) Mayer of Lykens Twp. They moved to Ogle Co, Illinois in 1836. After Jonas died, Catharine lived with their dau Melinda and William Finney. Her obit mentions that she was one of the oldest settlers of Mt. Morris Township. **Jonas and Catherine (Mayer) Schoffstall known children: ***Elizabeth Amanda b Apr 22, 1836,

bapt Hoffman Ch – d Nov 21, 1911, bur Adeline Cem, Adeline, Ogle Co., Ill.), m Joseph Fossler (b Apr 5, 1833, Pa. – d Jan 30, 1905), a son of John D. and Elizabeth (Weary) Fossler of Pa. moved to Mt. Morris, Ill. Elizabeth Fossler (b c1802), mother of Joseph moved to Illinois, and lived with her son and family in 1880. **Joseph and Elizabeth (Schoffstall) Fossler** children born in Ill: ****Lewis b c1856; Harvey C b c1865; ****Irviin F. b c1871; ****Viola b c1874; ****Charles b c1878; ***Jonathan b Oct 31, 1839 Mt. Morris Twp. Ogle Co, Il – d Jul 3, 1914, Iowa), m Jun 25, 1861 Sarah Finney b Jan 27, 1839 a dau of Wm and Elizabeth (Noll) Finney; They moved to Morrison, Iowa, **had four children:** *Jonas*; ___ m Frank Appel; *Dora* m ___ Wallace of Iowa; _____ m William Quackenbush of Iowa.***Joseph (1842 – 1848), bur St. James Luth (West Grove) Cem; ***Jared (1844–1847), bur St. James Luth (West Grove) Cem; ***Eliza b c1846, m Amos Rothermel b Northld Co, Pa.; Malinda (1848–921), m William Finney (1849–1914, bur Polo, Ill), lived in Mt Morris, Ogle Co in 1880;

SALOME (Jun 11, 1813 - Oct 19, 1841, bur St. John's near Berrysburg), m John Bonawitz (Dec 30, 1801 - Sep 10, 1885), a son of George Michael and Maria Catherine (Koppenhaver) Bonawitz. After Salome died, John Bonawitz m Catherine Harman (1805 - 1870), widow of John Messner. **John and Salome (Schoffstall) Bonawitz children:** ***Catherine; ***Henry; ***Mary; ***Jonas (b Sep 27, 1833 Mifflin Twp, Dau Co – d Ec 13, 1913, bur St. Johns (Hill) Cem. Berrysburg), m Aug 8, 1861 in Halifax Twp, Margaret Rutter (Sep 1840 Mbg - May 27, 1911), a dau of Henry Rutter. **Jonas & Margaret (Rutter) Bonawitz children:******Mary Louisa (May 28, 1862 – 1937, bur Maple Grove Cem, E'ville, m Peter Elias Stine (Sep 23, 1861 – Jul 21, 1948); ****Charles Elmer (Jan 25, 1864 – May 1, 1914); ****William Edwin (Jan 30, 1866 – Oct 2, 1911), m Anna M. Beshler; ****Kathryn b 1874, m Harry B. Ernest; ****Sarah Frances (Apr 12, 1875 – May 7, 1955 , bur Maple Grove Cem, E'ville), m Charles Edwin Deibler; ***Sarah (b Aug 16, 1835 – d Oct 17, 1869, bur Stone Valley Cem Low Mah Twp, Northld Co , m Mar 29, 1855, Jacob Lenker (b Mar 31, 1833 Low Mah Twp. Northld Co – d Oct 11, 1869), a son of Johannes Adam and Maria Magd (Bobb) Lenker.

MARGARETHA b Apr 28, 1816;

JOHANNES M. b Sep 24, 1819 Lyk Twp – d 1901, bur St. James Luth (West Grove) Cem, Lincoln Twp, Ogle Co) , m Jun 1843 Catharine Fossler (May 10,1826 – Feb 10, 1917), a native of Green Briar, Northld Co., Pa. She moved with her parents to White Eagle, Ogle Co, Illinois about 1839 along with a Byerly and Erdman family. John was a mill wright in Maryland, Ogle Co in 1880. **Johannes and Catharine (Fossler) Schoffstall children:** ***Sarah Emma b1853, m Josiah Mumma, lived in Adeline, Ill; ***Mary Catherine (1859 – 1931,in Ogle,Ill); ***Charles b c1865 in Ill.; ***John; ***Lizzie b c1869.

ELIZABETH b Jul 22, 1823 Lyk Twp – d Nov 19, 1887, bur Adeline Cem, Maryland Twp, Ogle Co, Ill), m 1846 Friedland Fossler (b c1824 Pa.- d Dec 10, 1870).

Jonas Schoffstall m 2nd Barbara ___ in June 1831. He m 3rd Susanna Hoover Umholtz (1787 – c1864), a dau of Jacob & Catharine Eva Elizabeth (Sierer) Hoover.]

Jonathan Klinger lived on this land for only about one year before transferring it to Elias Snyder on Mar 28, 1851.

[**JONATHAN KLINGER** (Aug 24, 1823 - ____), a son of Philip and Catharine Klinger, m Elizabeth _____ b c1822. In 1850 Jonathan and Elizabeth Klinger had a daughter Catharine age 3 years. [More information under the Klinger genealogy.]

Elias Snyder owned this mill property for many years, and earned his livelihood in milling. In 1855 the mill was described as being in middling condition. Elias was listed as a carpenter in 1850. Perhaps he made improvements on the building, After that it was no longer described in poor condition. A log house and bank barn plus the gristmill were the predominant buildings on the land in 1864. Unfortunately, according to an account in the LYKENS STANDARD of November 1910, under history of 1870, the Snyder gristmill "had been recently destroyed by fire."

[*ELIAS SNYDER** (Mar 29, 1819 - Apr 17, 1877, bur Simeon Cem), son of _____, m Mary M. Kissinger (Aug 18, 1819 - Jul 5, 1890), a dau of George and Catharine (Hoover) Kissinger of Lykens Twp. **Elias and Mary M. (Kissinger) Snyder children:** **CYRUS K.** b c1844, m Louisa ____ b 1844. He was a teacher in Gratz 1863 –1869, then lived in Duck Creek, Kent, Delaware in 1880. They had Frank Rumberger age 21 with them. **Cyrus K. and Louisa Snyder children:*****Isabella b c1865;***Lena H.b c1867;***Mary J b c1870;***Louisa C. b c1873;**CATHERINE** (Jun 6, 1846 – Mar 4, 1917, bur Hoffman Cem), m Isaac Lubold (Jan 10, 1845 – Apr 29, 1898)), son of Samuel & Catherine (Williard) Lubold. **Isaac & Catherine (Snyder) Lubold children:** ***Charles E. b c1867; ***Martha Amelia b Dec 11, 1872; ***Mary M b c1876; ***Annie E b c1879. **LUCY ANN** (Aug 18, 1847- Oct 13, 1923, bur Simeon Cem); **HENRY K.**(Feb 1, 1856 - Apr 26, 1893, bur Hoffman Cem), m Malinda Daniel (Mar 30, 1855 - May 12, 1895), a dau of _____, lived in Valley View. Henry was in a play in Gratz in 1874. **Henry K and Malinda (Daniel) Snyder children:** ***Mary J. (Dec 20, 1876 - Apr 7, 1895, bur Hoffman Cem); ***Laura May (Jan 28, 1877 - Aug 20, 1897, bur Hoffman Cem); ***Norman

Calvin b Jan 10, 1879, bapt Hoffman Ch; ***Alice Dina** b Jan 3, 1884; ***Charles Emery** b Mar 13, 1886; ***SARAH** b c1859, m Jonathan C Umholtz (1859 - Dec 24, 1832, Phila), a son of John and Elizabeth (Cline) Umholtz. Jonathan was a carpenter, they lived in Tower City and Phila. **ISAAC** (no dates) m Catherine ___ and lived in Washington Twp.]

On March 27, 1865, Elias and Mary M Snyder conveyed two tracts of land to Jacob Tallman. One tract contained forty-nine acres with the house and mill, another tract of mountain land contained eighteen acres, 191 perches. Jacob Tallman transferred both tracts to Cyrus K. Snyder on March 30, 1868. Several years later, on March 28, 1872, Cyrus K. Snyder and his wife sold the two tracts with buildings to John T. Hoffman of Washington Township. But John T. and Hannah Hoffman sold it all on April 14, 1875 to Elias Snyder. After Elias Snyder died his executors, Cyrus K. and Henry K. Snyder, and heirs sold the forty-nine acres and eighteen plus acres to John W. Hoffman on March 20, 1879.

John W. Hoffman was a native of this area, but his father Henry C. was born Sep 6, 1804 in Columbiana County, Ohio. He came to Harrisburg when he was a young man, and worked as a carpenter. He later came to Lykens Township, and became employed as a carpenter in Gratz. He remained in this area until his death in 1878, and was buried in Simeon Cemetery. John W. Hoffman attended the area schools, and during the summer was employed on the farm of Daniel P. Stine for about seven years during his youth. He attended Freeburg Academy in Snyder County, then taught in the local schools for twelve years. He learned the carpentry trade with his father, and worked as a journeyman until the Civil War broke out. He enlisted in the army in August 1862 for one year, participating in numerous battles before returning home. In April 1865 he re-enlisted and served until the end of the war, again suffering many hardships.

After the war, John W. Hoffman returned to teaching for several years. He also was married to Sarah Welker. On the wedding day, John and Sarah, accompanied by John L. Good and his sweetheart traveled to Pillow. A double ceremony was performed by Rev. Jacob Kehm, the Reformed minister. All of this information is recorded on John's Civil War pension record. On the application, a question was asked concerning any previous marriages. John wrote "my first wife is still living, and we are living happily together."

When John W. Hoffman bought this property The only building left was an old house. Soon after he received it, John built a new house and barn and made other improvements. Later he purchased an

John W. and Amanda (Geise) Hoffman

adjacent farm, cultivated it, and extensively engaged in raising stock. [See write-up of farm page 547.]

[*HENRY C. HOFFMAN (b Sep 6, 1804 Mercerburg, Franklin Co. Pa. - Jul 29, 1875, bur Simeon Cem), was a son of Michael and Mary Hoffman, of Columbia Co, Ohio. Early in life he came to Harrisburg, and then to Gratz. He married 1st Henrietta ____ (Jan 15, 1815 - Mar 4, 1837, bur Simeon Cem but not with husband). They had a dau Elmira who d Mar 1, 1837. He m 2nd Sarah Welker (Sep 16, 1818 - Jul 17, 1884), a dau of John and Elizabeth (Messerschmidt) Welker. **Henry C. and Sarah (Welker) Hoffman children:**Sarah (Jan 4, 1841 - Apr 22, 1915), m John B. Hoke; **John W.** (1843 - 1926) see below; **Elizabeth** (Nov 1842 -Oct 1, 1901), m Fidel K. Heitzman (1834 - 1902) of Shamokin; **Hannah** (no dates) m John Eisenhart; **Ellen** (1850 – 1914), m George Reed (1851 - 1932), of Valley View, both bur Simeon Cem. **George and Ellen Reed had two sons: ***Frances** m Bertha Agnes Dietrich; ***Harry** d age 14; **Rebecca** (Aug 7, 1852 - Oct 13, 1910), m Amos Kissinger (Nov 4, 1848 - Jan 17, 1932); **James Franklin** (Aug 1, 1855 - Jan 8, 1913), m Jun 17, 1877, **Elizabeth Kissinger** (1859 - Aug 24, 1925), both bur Trinity Luth Cem, Valley View; **Catherine**; **Amelia** (no dates) m John Getler; **Susanna** (b____ d 1849); **Ann Mary** d 1849; **Samuel; Mary.**]

[*JOHN WELKER HOFFMAN [from above],(Mar 8, 1843 - 1926,bur Simeon Cem), son of Henry C. and Sarah (Welker) Hoffman, m Jan 17, 1867 Amanda Gise (Dec 30, 1846 - 1929), a dau of Benjamin and Margaret (Umholtz) Gise. **John W. and Amanda (Gise) Hoffman children:**EDWIN ERASTUS** (Oct 5,1867 - ___), m Vietta Morgan b Oct 1872. He was a tinsmith on lot twenty-five in Gratz, later moved to Valley View. **Edwin & Vietta (Morgan) Hoffman children (some bap Simeon Evang Ch):**

Blanche b Oct 1894;Marion Bernice b Dec 26,1896;***Marlin Erastus b May 16,1899; ***Selan Albert b Sep17,1901;***Walter Sidney b May 27,1903;***Herbert Stanford b Oct 21,1905;***Kermit b1910.

EMMA CLARA (Mar 17, 1870 - pre 1915)

HENRY WILSON (Oct 8, 1872 - Sep 21, 1951), m Edna Daniel (Nov. 1873 - Oct 31, 1936, bur Simeon Cem), a dau of Isaac & Mary Ann (Coleman) Daniel. In 1900, Rebecca Kissinger lived with the family and was listed as a servant. **Henry Wilson and Emma (Daniel) Hoffman children (bapt Simeon Evang Ch):** ***Florence (Jun 24, 1894 – Nov 24, 1964), m ___ Troutman; ***Annie N. (b 1895 – d Nov 1900 from burns, bur Simeon Cem); ***Ralph H. (1897 – 1977); ***Frederick Edwin (Aug 13, 1899 – 1964, bur Simeon Cem, Gratz), m Pearl Hoffman; ***Margaret Olive (Mar 31, 1901 – Aug 30, 1 990, bur Simeon Cem, Gratz), m Marlin W. Williard; ***Charles A. (Nov 6, 1902 - 1973), m E. Mae Hoffman. **Charles A. and Mae (Hoffman) Hoffman children:** ****Kathryn L b Sep 4, 1936, m Herman Ulsh;****Joann M (no dates) m 1959 Larry D. Cooper; ****John P (no dates), m Ruth A. ___;****Nancy (no dates), m Harold Nightwine;***Mary Amanda (May 2, 1904 – Aug 20, 1988), m Daniel Franklin Kissinger, son of Edmund and Daisy (Heller) Kissinger, **had these children**:****Kermit; ****Harold; ****Leonard; ****Carolyn; ***Emma Edna (Jun 28, 1905 – 2000), m 1923 Archie H. Bohner, a son of Jeremiah and Carrie (Holdeman) Bohner. **Archie & Emma Edna (Hoffman) Bohner children:**** Kenneth;****Robert Donald;****Shirley;****Joan; ****LaMar; ****Lorraine; ****Virginia; ****William; ***Clarence Wilson b Jul 29, 1906; ***Ruby Ella (Apr 8, 1908 – 1983), m ___ Wynn; ***John Daniel (Oct 18, 1909 – 1936); ***Lottie Leona (b Sep 25, 1913 – Nov 22, 1994, bur Simeon Cem, Gratz), m Jan 23, 1932 by Rev. Hiram Weaver to Harry Allen Kissinger (Apr 13, 1908 - Mar 2, 1967), a son of Joel and Priscilla (Engle) Kissinger. **Harry and Lottie (Hoffman) Kissinger children:** ****Marie Martha b Feb 12, 1932 m Oct 12, 1963 to Raymond W. Lahr. **Ray and Marie Martha (Kissinger) Lahr children:** Carol b Apr 10, 1967, m Nov 21, 1992 Daniel E. Blyler; William b Oct 6, 1968; ****Edna Elizabeth b Jul 29, 1943, m Nov 14, 1961 Ray Elvin Ferster, son of John and Verna (Brown) Ferster. **Ray and Edna Eliz. (Kissinger) Ferster children:** Karen M b Aug 30, 1962, m Sep 20, 1980, Ronald E. Romberger Jr.; Brenda K b Feb 26, 1966, m Nov 8, 1986 Randy L. Bellon; Sandra E b Jan 2, 1968, m Kerry Matter; Daniel J. b May 16, 1969, m Susan Bowser; Barbara A b Oct 5, 1970; David R. b Mar 31, 1974; Mathew John b Jan 11, 1976; Timothy A b Dec 1, 1977; ****Charles Robert b Oct 12, 1946, m Dianne M. Lahr, **have two children**; Jennifer Lynne b Apr 7, 1973; Michael Alan b Nov 10, 1976.

MARY MARGARET (Oct 11, 1874 – Aug 8,1953, bur Hoffman Cem), m Isaac Troutman (Oct 17,1875 1960) son of Daniel B. and Sarah (Williard) Troutman. **Isaac and Mary (Hoffman) Troutman children:** ***Clara Elva (May 1, 1897 – Sep 12, 1990), m Charles Edward Henninger, son of Isaac and Etta (Romberger) Henninger; ***Harry A (Aug 15,1901 – Oct 17, 1988), m Edna Wise, lived in Lewisburg; ***Ella P m Philip Crotty of Millersburg;**MARTHA ELIZABETH** b Jul 21,1877, m Philip Boyer, a minister, lived in Allentown;

STEPHEN ARTHUR (Aug 17, 1879 - 1957, bur Simeon Cem), not married. When he was a very young man, Stephen took on an adventurous journey. About 1898, he went west and lived in Washington. Later he took a trip to Alaska where he worked in the gold mines. By 1908, he had moved to Oregon and was building houses. His leisure time was spent in hunting and fishing. About 1925, Stephen received word that his father was very sick, so he came back to Gratz to take care of him. As soon as he arrived, he purchased a Star Coupe that was his pride and joy. His father died in 1926, and Stephen continued to live with his mother until her death in 1929. After his parents died, he constructed a small one-room cabin on two acres of land near the Little Wiconisco Creek. The land had been part of the old Hoffman homestead. The cabin was sparsely furnished with one bed, one table, a stove and a chair or two. Each day Stephen walked up the Brinhouse Hallow (near Twin Cedars), to get his drinking water. At first he drove his Star Coupe to Gratz to buy his essentials, but later he parked the car because he thought it was too expensive to drive. From then on, he could be seen carrying his groceries in a sack that he threw over his back for the long walk home. He was short and stocky, ruddy faced, and looked like a gold miner.

Stephen inherited some of his father's talents, and became a skilled carpenter and mason. He also developed the ability, and occupied his time in making violins. He also learned to play the violin quite well. Unfortunately, none of his violins are known to exist. Stephen lived in his little home in the beautiful setting near the meandering creek for many years. But in 1957 when he was about seventy-eight years old he met with tragedy. The coal stove that he used for heat apparently created sulfur during the night, and he died from inhaling the fumes. It was the end of an adventurous life.

CHARLES GARFIELD (Jun 13, 1881 – Jun 16, 1955, bur Simeon Cem), m Minnie Z. Fidler (1886 – Oct 26, 1948), dau of Harvey and Catherine Fidler, lived near Millersburg; **Charles & Minnie (Fidler) Hoffman children (bapt Simeon Evang Ch):** ***Myrtle Catharine b Feb 1,1907; ***May Lillian b Aug 9, 1908; ***Charles Albert b Jul 4, 1911, m Mary Caroline Lesher, Jan 31, 1939; ***Blair Maurice b Jul 8, 1913; ***Philip Darrel b Apr 27, 1916; ***llen Myrle b Apr 22, 1918.

CLARENCE SIDNEY b Jun 11, 1883, went to Korea as a missionary in 1910 and stayed there for 30 years. He was affiliated with the Presbyterian Church, and after he retired as a missionary he became a pastor of a

Presbyterian church in Wilmington, Delaware. **Clarence and his wife Emma children;*** **John;** ***Betty;**
***Catharine; ***Stanley Bolton; ***Bobby;
CLAIRE ELLA VIRGINA b May 10, 1887, m Ira Peterson, a minister, lived in Seguin, Texas;

Henry Wilson Hoffman & Extended Family 1907
Back row: H. Wilson Hoffman, Edna (Daniel) Hoffman holding Clarence, Florence (Hoffman) Troutman; Mary Ann
(Coleman) Daniel (1851 – 1929), holding Emma Edna Hoffman, Isaac Daniel (1843 – 1914). Front: Margaret, Charles,
Mary, Fred, Ralph.

H. Wilson & Emma (Daniel) Hoffman Family 1909
L to r Standing: H. Wilson, Margaret, Mrs. Hoffman holding Clarence; middle: Charles & Emma – std: Ralph, Mary, Fred

About 1898, John and Amanda Hoffman purchased a lot in Gratz, and John and his son opened a tinsmith shop. They sold various house wares, including stoves, and hardware items. They also installed many of the standing seam roofs that continue to exit to this day.

On February 16, 1921, John W. and Amanda Hoffman conveyed two tracts of land to Henry Wilson Hoffman. The first tract was the original mill, (since gone), and farm property containing forty-nine acres. The second was a small tract containing one acre, seventy-four perches, a total of fifty acres and seventy-four perches. The small tract had previously been transferred to John W. Hoffman April 2, 1923, by Elias and Mary E. Klinger, but was not recorded.

Clarence S. and Emma Hoffman with their children:
l to r: top John, Betty, Catharine, Stanley Bolton. Front: Bobby, Clarence, Claire, Emma

Eventually, on August 21,1947, Henry Wilson Hoffman, still a widower, conveyed the farm of two tracts containing fifty acres, seventy-four perches to his daughter Lottie L. Kissinger. He also sold a tract of mountain land located on Short Mountain, and containing nine acres, sixty-five perches to Lottie. On November 30, 1951, Lottie L. and Harry A. Kissinger sold three parcels of land to Charles A. and Mae E. Hoffman. In addition to the fifty acres, they sold a tract of fourteen acres forty-eight perches that they had received from Ernest H. and Mabel Kissinger on May 31, 1938. After Charles Hoffman died, his widow Estella Mae E. Hoffman conveyed to John P. Hoffman, who died about five years later. It has since been transferred to John Hoffman, Jr.

MR. & MRS. AMMON ESH FARM
(WIDOW SCHOFFSTALL FARM in 1875)

This land is from the original tract of patented land containing three hundred twenty four acres, seventy three perches, that Commonwealth of Pennsylvania granted to George Peiffer of Harrisburg. After George Peiffer died, his eldest son Henry, executor, petitioned orphan court of Dauphin to divide and appraise the estate. The petition was made on September 4, 1810. Henry Peiffer sold the premises to Adam Romberger Jul 30, 1811.

On January 17, 1837, Adam Romberger and his wife sold a tract of land to John Tobias containing 31 acres 146 perches. On March 24, 1838, John Tobias sold the same land to Michael Matter. After many years, Michael and Sarah Matter sold the same property to George W. Moyer Apr 1, 1852.

A short time later, on January 5, 1857 George W. and Caroline Moyer of Lower Mahantongo Twp, Sch Co. sold two separate tracts of land to Jacob Schoffstall. By signing the back of the first deed, they conveyed part of their tract containing eleven acres fifty-two perches to Jacob ImSchoffstall. (This small tract was part of the

562

land Elizabeth Fry sold May 25, 1848 to Samuel and Elizabeth Umholtz. Samuel and Elizabeth Umholtz in turn sold the eleven acres fifty-two perches to George W. Moyer.) By assignment George W. and Caroline Moyer also conveyed the second tract containing twenty-three acres fifty-two perches to Jacob Schoffstall. The two tracts contained together thirty-four acres, one hundred four perches of farmland, with a log house and log barn.

New Home built By Present Owners

After Jacob Schoffstall died, his widow Sarah continued to live on this farm for many years until her death. In 1860, she was living alone. But the 1870 and 1880 census notes that her farm became a two-family residence. Sarah lived alone, and her daughter Magdalena Tschopp and family lived in another area of the house.

Magdalena was married November 15, 1848 to George Tschopp. She was only fifteen and one-half years old when they married. Rev. John A. Leis came to the house to perform the ceremony. Magdalena and George lived here with her parents for several years, and George found work as a carpenter. When the Civil War broke out, he was drafted into Co I of the 177th Infantry Regiment, and served part of the time with a neighbor, Capt B. J. Evitts. He was in the service for almost two years.

When the war ended, George & Magdalena moved to Schuylkill County, where he worked in the mines near Tremont. One day in 1869, while he was at work in the mines, a drift wagon jumped the track. By lifting it back in place, George developed a severe rupture. After the accident the Tschopps moved back to this farm, and George took up carpentry again. George seemed to be prone to ill luck.

One day in October 1890, while chopping wood in a field on this farm, he had another accident. He laid his axe on a log, the handle extending over the edge. A piece of wood that he was throwing away, hit the handle of the axe. The axe flew up and struck him in the face, breaking his jaw. It than glanced to his left arm, severing muscles and arteries. He was left partially disabled, and was not able to perform much manual work after that.

When Sarah Schoffstall died, Magdalena and George Tschopp purchased her farm containing the two tracts of thirty-four acres on February 5, 1892. But several months later, they sold the farm, on June 15, 1892, to Charles T. Phillips, who at that time was a resident of Girardville, Pa.

An Aerial View Of Original Farm Taken In 1950s

After selling the farm, George and Magdalena moved to Gratz. They continued to suffer some hardships. Their son Milton's wife Susanna gave birth to a son Riley on March 1900, but she died in Shamokin on May 6th of cancer, at the age of thirty-six, leaving three young children. George Tschopp died suddenly of heart disease several weeks later on July fourth. Little Riley became ill with "summer complaint" and died July 5th. A double funeral was held for George and his little grandson.

JACOB SCHOFFSTALL FAMILY

[*JACOB SCHOFFSTALL (Mar 16,1799– Oct 2,1858, bur Hoffman Cem), son of John Jacob and Maria Magdalena (Hoover) Schoffstall, m Salome Sarah Paul (Nov 4, 1799 – Aug 2, 1880), dau of Joseph and Anna Maria Paul. **Jacob & Salome (Paul) Schoffstall children;**

ELISABETH (Dec 4, 1823 – Nov 10, 1896, bur Ill.), m 1st John Umholtz (c1820 - ___), **had these children (all b in Pa.): *****Sarah** b 1842; *****Edward** b 1843; *****Eliza** b 1847.; m 2nd Jonas Beck (Jul 14, 1813 – Feb 2, 1895, Brookville, Ogle Co., Illinois), a son of Johan Henry and Susanna (Grunzweig) Beck, **had these children:** *****Aaron S.** b c1842, m Mary Miller; *****Julia;** *****Sarah J.** They moved to Carroll Co. Illinois in after 1847.

 **ABRAHAM (Dec 19, 1825 – Oct 23, 1858, bur Hoffman Cem), m Catharine Matter, a dau of John and Christiana Matter. [See Matter genealogy.].

**SARAH (Jan 21, 1830 – Dec 10, 1851, bur Hoffman Cem)

**JOHN b c1831

MAGDALENA (Jun 2, 1833 – Jan 10, 1904), m Nov 15, 1848 George Tschopp (b Nov 28, 1827 – Jul 4, 1900, bur Simeon Cem). **George & Magdalena (Schoffstall) Tschopp children; *****Anna Mary** b 1849; *****Salome** b Apr 27, 1852, m John Adam Weaver (   ), a son of John and ____ Weaver. **John Adam & Salome (Tschopp) Weaver children (bapt Hoffman Ch):** ******George Elsworth** b Aug 7, 1874; ******Reily Edgar** b Oct 9, 1875; ******Edwin Isaiah** b Jun 29, 1877; ******John Adam** b Aug 15, 1878; ******Bertha** b Jan 12, 1886; ******Jennie** b Aug 10, 1888; ******Elmer** b Oct 9, 1890. *****Eliza** b c1860;

*****George Washington** b Oct 8, 1862, m Emma J. Gunderman (Jan 22, 1867 – May 29, 1899 of consumption, Wmstown), a dau of John Gunderman. **George W. and Emma J (Gunderman) Tschopp children:** ******John Henry** (twin) (Feb 26, 1888 – 1943), m Pearl May Rowe (Apr 14, 1893 – Mar 15, 1955, bur Maple Grove Cem, Eville), they divorced;**** **George** (twin) b Feb 26, 1888; ******Beulah** b 1890, m Arthur Ferree; ******Frederick** b 1891; ******Annette Mae** b Aug 11, 1893, m Charles Lentz; ******Charles** b 1895 m Kate Eberly; ******Kate** m Roy Foster;

*****Henry Milton** b Jun 6, 1866, m Susanna L. Ritzman (Dec 31, 1863 – May 6, 1900, of cancer bur

Simeon Cem, Gratz), a dau of Jacob & Lydia Ann Ritzman. **Milton & Susanna had a child ****Riley Milton** (Mar 1900 – Jul 5, 1900,bur Simeon Cem)

***Magdalena** b Feb 3, 1869

SUSANNAH b c1835 m William Boyer (1830 - ____), lived in Valley View in 1880, and in addition to the family, they had Clayton Renn age 2, a nephew. **William and Susannah (Schoffstall) Boyer had these children**: ***James** b c1861; ***McLada** b 1870; ***Wilson** b 1872; ***Frances** b1877; ***Persival** b 1879.

REBECCA b 1837

CHRISTIAN b Oct 10, 1838, m Juliana ___ b c1838

ANN MARY b 1840 [More information on this family in Schoffstall genealogy.]

After Charles T. Phillips died, his heirs sold three tracts of land to his son-in-law William W. Minnich of Hegins, on April 28, 1930. The first tract contained thirty-four acres, 101 perches, and was the farm that they lived on. Another tract of land contained six acres, and was the tract that C. Elmer and Mary E. Wolf sold to Charles T. Phillips on April 1, 1907.The third tract contained eight acres, ninety-seven perches. Jonathan Smeltz sold it on April 12, 1919 to Charles T. Phillips. On April 28, 1930, the farm and acreage was sold to William W. Minnich, a son-in-law.

Charles Tobias & Susan Philips Family – Children: – William Elmer; Gertrude May; John Henry; Esther Lauretta; Oscar Howard; Charles Ralph; Grace; Florence Marie

JOHN J. PHILLIPS FAMILY

[**JOHN J. PHILLIPS** (b Aug 1, 1837 in France – d Jan 10, 1917, bur Simeon Cem, Gratz). John came to America about 1853, and in early life was a wagon-maker. He m 1st Esther "Hettie" Ritzman (b c1842 - ____), a dau of Jacob & Susanna (Matter) Ritzman. **John and Esther (Ritzman) Phillips had these children:** Jacob b c1858; Samuel b c1860; Frank (no dates) moved to Calif; *Charles b 1860 – see below; J.Cornelius b & d 1862; Susan b c1863; Joseph William (Oct 1865 – 1939), the postmaster of Gratz for many years, not married; Clara C. b 1871 Ashland Sch Co – d 1951), m Jun 15, 1890 Henry G. Buffington, lived in Gratz.]

Note – a William Phillips b c1842 was a farmer in 1870 in L.T. next to Joseph D. Gise. He had a wife Eliza b c1844, Maggie 6, Amanda 4, Eva B 2, Annie b Jan 1870 & John Romberger 67 a labr with him. In 1880, William and Eliza Phillips lived in Jordan Twp., Northld Co and had Manda 13, Cora B 10, Clara E. 9, and Sarah A. 6. Not sure if this is a branch of the Phillips that lived in Lykens Twp. John and Esther moved from here to another area after 1870. Esther apparently died in the other location. After Esther died, John J. Philips married Feb 14, 1875 to Lydia Ann Hepler (Mar 20, 1843 –

Oct 13, 1894, of typhoid pneumonia), a dau of Jacob & Hannah Hepler. In 1880 John J. and Lydia lived in Butler Twp., Sch Co., and he was listed as a breaker boss. It is not known how long they lived in Sch Co., but in 1900 John Phillips, son Joseph W., dau Agnes, and Susan Ritzman his mother-in-law were living in Gratz, all in the same household. **John J. and Lydia A (Hepler) Phillips had these children; Agnes** b Dec 1881, m Chas Zerfing; two sons died young. John J. Phillips married again before 1910. His 3rd wife was Lena Elizabeth Hartman (1853 –1939, bur Simeon Cem), a dau of John and Ann Mary (Ritzman) Hartman of Williamstown. After John died, Lena Elizabeth went back to Williamstown where she died in 1938. John Phillips is listed on the 1910 census age 71, Laura E age 58 (his wife), Joseph W. age 44, his son.

A Phillips Family Gathering About 1912 to 1914 – not identified

[*CHARLES T. PHILLIPS (Jun 13,1860 – Dec 18, 1928, bur Simeon Cem), m Susan A. Troy (b Aug 1858 – 1955). **Charles T. and Susan A. (Troy), Phillips had these children: William E.** (Mar 1884 – 1963, bur Simeon Cem), m Mary L. Knohr (May 1888 – May 26, 1940), a dau of John & Louisa Knohr of Lyk. Twp, and **had these children:** Vannie Marguerite b Jun 2, 1912, m Bill Swartz; **Effie May** (May 4, 1914 – 1985) ;**Gertrude M** (Feb 1886 -1959, bur Maple Grove Cem, E'ville), m Samuel G. Martin (1875 - 1946), of Elizabethville; **John H.**(Feb 19, 1888 – Feb 24, 1937, bur Simeon Cem), m Carrie S. Mauser (1894 – 1961), a dau of John and Caroline (Daniel) Mauser. **John H. and Carrie S. (Mauser) Phillips children:** Paul Franklin b Apr 13, 1915; **Wayne W.** b Jun 6, 1916; **Reda Caroline** (Aug 2, 1918 – Sep 1994, bur Simeon Cem), m Fred Maiden, **had two sons Larue & John; Eleanor G**. b Jan 3, 1929, m Daniel Nace of Dayton, near Wmstown; **Laura E.** (Aug 1890 - 1941, bur Simeon Cem), m John M. Kissinger (1884 –1972), **had these children:** Blair A. b Oct 24, 1913; **Ray A**. b Mar 8, 1916; **May Leona** b Feb 10, 1918; **Roy Elmer** b May 22, 1921;
Howard Oscar (Feb 3, 1893 – 1966, bur Simeon Cem), m Margaret E.Strayer (1896 – 1968), **had these children:** Delphine Lauren b Nov 20, 1923; **Herman**; **Vivian**; **Alda** . Charles Ralph (Jul 17, 1895 – 1976, bur Simeon Cem), m Lula A.Boyer b 1899, **their children:** Zerne; Iretta; Franklin Mervin b Sep 7, 1916 d of appendecites; Grant Christian b 1917, m May 1944 to Hilda M. Guy of Eastonville, Colo. He was WWII vet; Warren Ira b Oct 25, 1920; Dorothy b Sep 24, 1922; **Grace Susannah** (1898 –1900); **Florence M.**b Sep 23, 1900, m William W. Minnich of Hegins;]

William W. Minnich owned this farm and small tracts until 1938. On April 1, 1939, it was sold to Sadie E. Koons. The Koons family lived on this farm for many years, and then on April 9, 1951, sold three tracts of land comprising about twenty-five acres, to Allen A. Shade. On July 29, 1963, Allen A. and Dora T. Shade sold the same acreage to Clarence and Lillian Welker. While the Welker's owned this property, the Daniel Ferree family lived here. Clarence and Lillian Welker sold this farm to Ammon Esh during the 1990s. Soon after they purchased the farm the old house was removed and a new one constructed.

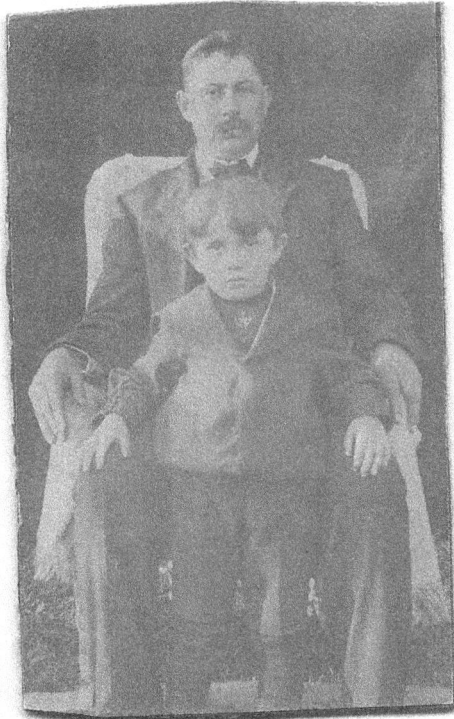

Charles Phillips and his son "Charlie."

This Phillips family photo found in an antique shop years ago. Thought to be Oscar & Chas., sons of Charles T. Philips

[JOEL ALBERT KOONS (b Sep 29,1882 bap St. John's (Kimmels) Ch, Barry Twp, Sch Co- d 1963, bur Simeon Cem), a son of Joseph & Catherine (Klauser) Koons. He m Nov 12, 1904, Catherine M. Schwartz (1886 - 1967).Joel & Catherine (Schwartz) Koons child. (bap Kimmels Ch): Dorothy May b May 13, 1905; John Elmer b Oct 12, 1906; Ray Allen b Jul 30, 1911; Sadie Ellen b Jul 26, 1914, not married; Katie Alverda b Jul 21, 1915; Helen Elmira b Jul 25, 1919; Betty J. b 1929.]

The Koons Family At Their Homestead

GIDEON AND KATIE MAE FISHER FARM
Recently CLARENCE WELKER FARM -Benjamin Gise with 32 acres 1875)

Aerial View Of Farm Taken c1950s

This land is part of two original tracts that Commonwealth of Pennsylvania conveyed to the Hoffman family. One part of the land containing 218 acres was conveyed to John Hoffman, Esquire on March 2, 1801. He and his wife Anna Mary conveyed 16 acres of it to Jacob Hoffman in September 1813. Jacob Hoffman and his wife sold the 16 acres to George Stough on May 6, 1818.

Jacob Hoffman, Jr. became the owner of another 105 acres of land but on August 19, 1833, at a sheriff sale, the land and buildings were sold to John Rehrer. Later in 1833, John Rehrer sold part of his land containing 32 acres to George Stough. This land bordered on the 16 acres that Jacob already owned. George Stough sold 32 acres 36 perches of land and 2 two-story houses (1 log, 1 frame) to Benjamin Snyder before 1855. B. Matter was a tenant in 1855. Benjamin Snyder sold March 1860 to Daniel Hopple, a plasterer, who sold to Peter Herring after 1864 with the log house.

Old Farm House With Some modern Changes

On April 1, 1869, Peter and Elizabeth Herring sold the same land to Benjamin Gise. Benjamin Gise had the land until April 4, 1882, when he and his wife Margaret Gise sold it to Mary A. Weist, wife of Daniel Wiest of Urban. The 1883 assessment record shows Mary Weist with the 32 seated acres, a house and barn, and notes that it had belonged to B. Gise.

Another tract of 55 acres 55 perches of land belonged to Henry W. Good. On April 9, 1877, his land was sold to Jeremiah C. and Lovina Good. This land was under fences and in a high state of cultivation. George D. and Sarah Mayer were the next owners, but on June 26, 1886, they assigned the 15 plus acres to Mary A.

Wiest. On March 16, 1889 Mary A. and Daniel Wiest sold the two tracts of land (described above) and a farm building to Jonathan Hawk. They contained together 47 ac 91.44 perches (32 ac 36.44 perches and 15 acres, 55 perches). Jonathan Hawk and his family lived here for many years.

On Oct 1, 1904, Jonathan and Malinda Hawk sold both tracts of land containing 47 ac 91 perches with farm buildings to their daughter and son-in-law Charles Elmer Wolfe of Loyalton. On April 1, 1907, C. Elmer and Mary Wolf sold 6 acres of the above two tracts to Charles T. Philips. They continued to own the remaining acreage until Charles Elmer Wolfe died. On December 6, 1924, the 40 acres 154 perches of land were sold to Homer W. and Mary A. Lebo.

[DANIEL WIEST (b Mar 19, 1841 Pillow – c1926, bur Pillow), a son of Jacob Wiest (Jun 11, 1797 – Mar 5, 1857) and Mary (Tobias) Wiest (Jan 28, 1796 – Jun 23, 1868), a dau of Joh Tobias, Sr. of Uniontown, m Mary A. Kurtz (b Nov 21, 1845 Bethel, Berks Co – d Mar 3, 1911 bur Simeon Cem, Gratz).Daniel and Mary (Kurtz) Wiest children: Morris Jay (Dec 10, 1867 – Apr 9, 1907, bur Gratz), m Sallie D. Hess a dau of Harry & Eliza (Umholtz) Hess. She later m Joseph Laudenslager; Jay M. (Jul 8, 1872 – 1877, bur Pillow).

[PETER HERRING (Aug 22, 1807 Berks Co – Sep 19, 1880, bur St. Andrews Meth Cem, Valley View), a son of Peter & Rosina Herring, m Elizabeth _____ (no dates). This may be the Peter Herring age 73, living in 1880 in Hegins Twp., Sch Co in the household of Susan Huber age 72, a widow and Elizabeth 14, Wiest listed as a servant. Buried next to Peter Herring in Meth Cem is John Huber (Dec 29, 1808 – Oct 11, 1876) and his wife Susan (Schoffstall) Huber (Sep 21, 1807 – Aug 3, 1882).]

[JONATHAN "JONAS" HAWK (May 5, 1834 – Dec 20, 1904, bur Simeon Cem), a son of Daniel and Elizabeth (Holtzman) Hawk, m Mar 2, 1864 Malinda Matter (Sep 11, 1836 – Apr 21, 1906), a dau of Michael and Sarah (Crum) Matter. In 1870, Jonathan and Malinda Hawk lived next to her parents in Lykens Twp. They had Phoebe Troutman age 17, listed as a domestic, with them.Jonathan & Malinda (Matter) Hawk children: Stephen, possibly m Adaline ___ had these children: Jennie Edna b Nov 8, 1890; Mary Ellen b Mar 11, 1892; Irvin (Dec 1864 – 1931, bur Simeon Cem), mentally disabled, lived with his sister Mary in 1910 & 1920; Mary E. (May 11, 1866 – Apr 30, 1932), m Elmer C.Wolf (Nov 20, 1863 – Nov 3, 1923, bur Hoffman Cem), a son of Samuel and Catherine Ann (Buffington) Wolfe, had 3 children, only two survived: Lillian b c1902; Marlin Elmer Hawk (Oct 20, 1910 – Mar 24, 1998) –[More info under Samuel Wolfe family]; Charles b Mar 1870, m Emma J. ___ b c1875. Charles and Emma Hawk children: Allen b c1894; Edna M b 1895; Grace; Stella; Clara S. b c1872, m ___ Hawthorne: Grady b c1877; Jennie b c1879, m Dec 23, 1899 Edward A. Riegle (1874 – 1960), a son of Harrison and Hannah (Rickert) Riegel.]

[HOMER WILLIAM LEBO (1893 – 1957, bur Simeon Cem), a son of Jonathan and Susanna (Hassinger) Lebo, m Mary Amanda Kissinger (Mar 2, 1903 - Nov 1974, Halifax, Pa.), a dau of Harvey F. and Abby (Miller) Kissinger. More info with Harvey Kissinger and Lebo genealogy.]

Several years later on January 2, 1930, Homer W. and Mary Lebo sold the same land to Harry E. and Elvirdia Welker Harry E. Welker died, and on March 15, 1944, and Elvirdia I. Welker his widow sold the 40 plus acres to Roy F. and Alice R. Shade of Lykens Twp. On March 25, 1944, Roy F. and Alice R. Shade sold 4.561 of the 40 plus acres to Clarence H. and Lilian S. Welker. On February 29, 1968, after Alice R. Shade died another part of the 40 acres, containing 19.187 acres were sold to Clarence and Lillian Welker. Clarence and Lillian Welker have lived on this farm for many years. Lillian died in 2004. Clarence Welker conveyed the 19 acres to his sons Harry and Ricky before his death.

The remaining parts of the above 40 acres were sold off in building lots over many years. Some were sold to family members, including the new home that Harry and Amy Welker built about 1989, and that Clarence and Lillian Welker had built for themselves. Situated behind Harry Welker's home is the home of Daniel Ferree, whose lot dates to 1979. On their property they established the business of creating cement objects, focusing on lawn ornaments. Other lots that were part of this larger tract of land include the home of William and Martha Koppenhaver whose home was built about 1974. Next to them is the home of Mr. and Mrs. Leon O. Klinger, Jr. Both of these homes are located across the street from the Weslyan Church. This area has grown into a small village of newer homes.

After Lillian died, Clarence sold 4.561 acres to Gideon A. and Katie Mae Fisher including the old homestead. The Fisher's are the present owners.

Clarence and Lillian Welker were faithful, dedicated members of the Gratz Historical Society, and were instrumental in establishing the Antique Machinery organization in this area. They were also both active in community services for the good of the community.

PURCHASED LOTS FROM WELKER FARM

HOME OF HARRY & AMY WELKER

HOME BUILT FOR CLARENCE WELKER

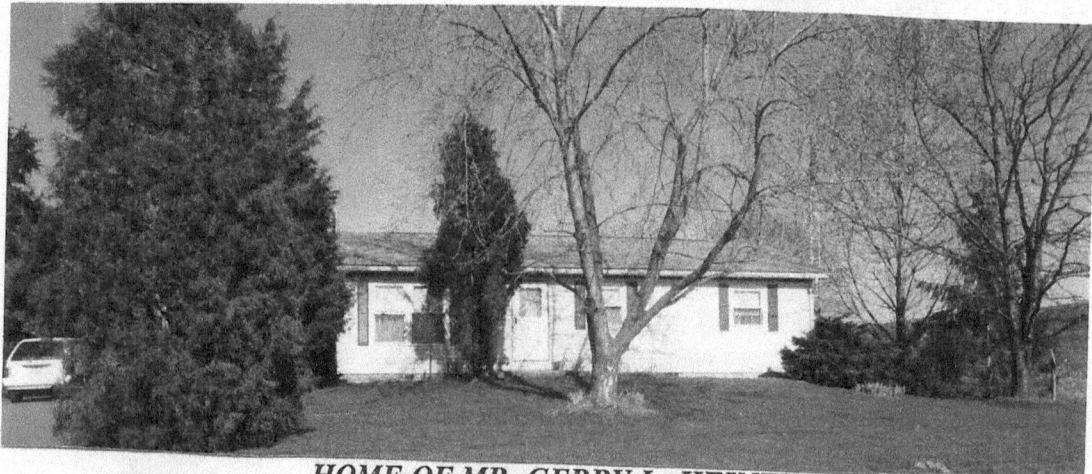

HOME OF MR. GERRY L. HEINEY.

HOME OF MR. & MRS. DANIEL FERREE

HOME OF MR. & MRS. WILLIAM KOPPENHAVER – NEAR CHURCH

HOME OF MR. & MRS. LEON O. KLINGER, JR. - NEAR CHURCH

RICK WELKER FARM
(JOHN ROMBERGER 59 ACRES IN 1875)

This land belonged to the original tract called Reiterburgh that Commonwealth of Pennsylvania conveyed to John Reiter. He and his wife Mary sold to Samuel McCrary on Oct 22, 1787. Samuel and Ann McCreary conveyed to Christian Hoffman on March 28, 1794, and he and his wife Susanna conveyed to Baltzer Romberger on June 13, 1798. The deed was not recorded. Baltzer sold to Henry Romberger, and on April 18, 1827 it was conveyed to Adam and Catherine Romberger with buildings. On April 21, 1832, Adam and Catherine Romberger transferred their land to John Romberger. He is listed on tax records with 59 acres and house in 1840, and about that same acreage for many years. In 1855 John had a 2-story weather-boarded house and bank barn. The Romberger family lived here for a long time. They sold the farm to Henry Schoffstall about 1892.

Farm House After Modernization That Took Place In Recent Years

Recent Photo Of Barn On Property

[**JOHN ROMBERGER** (Oct 14 or 24, 1802 – May 28, 1891, bur Simeon Cem), a son of Adam and Anna Maria (Werner) Romberger), m Jan 2, 1827 Hannah Hoffman (Aug 10, 1807 – Aug 14, 1858 , bur Hoffman Cem), a dau of Jacob and Catharine (Ferree) Hoffman. After Hannah died, John Romberger lived with Baltzer and Catherine Matter in 1860. In 1870 John Romberger age 67 lived with William & Eliza Phillips, probably in this house, since his neighbor was Joseph D. Gise. By 1880 John Romberger moved to Gratz and was living with Henry & Phoebe Kauderman. **John and Hannah (Hoffman) Romberger children:**
William b Dec 30, 1827
Elisabeth b May 15, 1829, m William Phillips b c1827. In 1870, they lived in Lykens Twp., on this property. **William and Elisabeth (Romberger) Phillips children:** ***Maggie** b c1864; ***Amanda** b c1866; ***Eva B** b c1868; ***Annie** b Jan 1870. They may be the William and Elizabeth Phillips living in Jordan Twp., Northld Co in 1880 **with these children:** Manda 13, Cora B 10, Clara E 9, Sarah A 6.
Sarah b Sep 15, 1830 – she is not on the 1840 or 1850 census
Henry (Jan 3, 1833 – Dec 16, 1912), m in 1856 Elisabeth Hoover (Aug 28, 1832 – May 25, 1907). **Henry and Elisabeth (Hoover) Romberger children:** ***Amos** b c1857; ***Annie C** b c1859;

572

*****Lovina** b c1860; *****Ellen E** b c1861; *****Sarah F** b c1862; *****William** b c1863; *****Adaline** b c1866; *****Harry** b c1867; *****Ambrose** b Dec 1869.
****Amos** (Sep 12, 1834 – Jun 21, 1892, bur Ch of God Cem, Valley View), m Justina ____ (May 29, 1847 –May 29, 1909). In 1880 Amos and Justina Romberger lived in Porter Twp., Sch Co., and Amos was working on the railroad. **Amos and Justina Romberger children**: *****George** b c1867; *****Lizzie** b c1869; *****Charles** b c1875; *****William** b c1878.
****Mary Ann** b 1836;
****Jacob** b 1839. (See also Romberger genealogy on page 527).]

The Henry Schoffstall family lived here for many years, and after both Henry and Emma died, the heirs conveyed the farm to John L. and Elizabeth A. Schoffstall on June 23, 19, 1944. During the years that Henry Schoffstall and his family resided here, William H. Koppenhaver married their daughter Katie. One day while William visited the Schoffstall's, a severe windstorm passed through the area. William was working at the barn when a huge gust of wind blew the barn door shut hitting him with terrific force. He died shortly after the accident leaving a wife and young daughter Mary, whom in 1920 lived with her Schoffstall grandparents.

On June 25, 1968, John L. and Elizabeth A. Schoffstall conveyed the 59 acres 54 perches to Clarence H. and Lillian A. Welker except for a lot at the intersection of Township Road and an adjoining public road.

Eventually Clarence H. and Lillian A. Welker conveyed this farm to their son Rick Welker and he is the present owner.

[**HENRY A. SCHOFFSTALL** (Nov 25, 1861 – Dec 30, 1926, bur Simeon Cem), m c1884 to Emma B. Fehler (Aug 25,1864 Feb 28, 1941), a dau of Levi and Catherine Fehler of Porter Twp., Sch Co. Catherine Fehler (b Nov 1820),lived with Henry Schoffstall and his family in 1900). **Henry A. and Emma B (Fehler) Schoffstall had 11 children:**
Katie R (Oct 12, 1884 – Apr 16, 1964, bur Simeon Cem), m William H. Koppenhaver (1881 – 1918, bur Simeon Cem). **William H. and Katie R. (Schoffstall) Koppenhaver had a Dau:** Mary E. b 1915, m Roy A. Wiest (1908 – 1963, bur Simeon Cem);
Annie A (Sep 1886 – 1970, bur Simeon Cem), not m, was a teacher in the Gratz & Lykens Twp. Schools.;
Milton H b Mar 1888 -
William H (Mar 10, 1890 – Jan 25, 1913, of acute diabetes, bur Simeon Cem);
Allen Levi (Mar 18, 1895 – Apr1, 1946, bur Simeon Cem), m Jun 12, 1920 in Valley View to Verna Kratzer (1904–1924), had dau **Jean** (no dates), m Geo McBride; **Allen Jr**. Allen L. Schoffstall m 2nd on May 22, 1933 in Valley View, to Gladys Paul. Allen was a teacher in the local schools and had military service in WWI.
Emma.Pauline b Aug 17, 1901, m Raymond Wiest.]
Jacob M (1904 – Jul 3, 1937,bur St. Andrews Cem, Valley View), m Helen ____ (Sep 7, 1909 – Jun 13, 1937)
John L. (Apr1905 – 1976, bur Simeon Cem), killed by a farm accident when his tractor ran over him, m Elizabeth ____ (1903 – 1970); More information with Schoffstall genealogy elsewhere in book.]

576

Botts, Agnes, 096	Botts, Mildred, 276	Bowman, Catharine, 078	Bowman, Josiah, 143	Boyer, Catherine, 055
Botts, Ann, 095	Botts, Mollie Snyder, 149	Bowman, Catharine, 242	Bowman, Josiah, 146	Boyer, Catherine, 123
Botts, Anna Maria, 096	Botts, Morgan, 148	Bowman, Chatarina, 025	Bowman, Katy E, 096	Boyer, Catherine, 128
Botts, Anna Sarah, 096	Botts, Morgan, 149	Bowman, Christina, 427	Bowman, Katy E, 148	Boyer, Catherine, 129
Botts, Anthony, 096	Botts, Morgan, 233	Bowman, Citi, 417	Bowman, Katy E, 149	Boyer, Catherine, 130
Botts, Anthony, 097	Botts, Morgan, 276	Bowman, Cyrene, 040	Bowman, Lana, 045	Boyer, Catherine, 294
Botts, Barbara, 096	Botts, Morgan S, 096	Bowman, Cyrene, 420	Bowman, Levi, 044	Boyer, Catherine, 404
Botts, Benjamin, 096	Botts, Moses, 095	Bowman, Cyrene, 528	Bowman, Levi B, 045	Boyer, Catherine A, 130
Botts, Caroline, 096	Botts, Moses, 096	Bowman, Cyrene, 546	Bowman, Linn, 044	Boyer, Catherine D, 130
Botts, Catharine, 095	Botts, Moses, 097	Bowman, Daniel, 325	Bowman, Louisa, 044	Boyer, Catherine H, 129
Botts, Catharine, 096	Botts, Nathaniel, 097	Bowman, Daniel A, 096	Bowman, Louisa, 096	Boyer, Catherine St, 130
Botts, Catherine, 084	Botts, Perry, 096	Bowman, Dr John F, 045	Bowman, Lucinda, 045	Boyer, Catherine T, 130
Botts, Catherine, 096	Botts, Rebecca, 097	Bowman, Edmund B, 045	Bowman, Lydia, 244	Boyer, Charles E, 185
Botts, Catherine, 097	Botts, Russeit, 148	Bowman, Eliz Maurer, 528	Bowman, Margaret, 045	Boyer, Charles I, 130
Botts, Catherine, 148	Botts, Russel, 276	Bowman, Eliza, 038	Bowman, Margret A, 045	Boyer, Christiana, 124
Botts, Charles, 095	Botts, Russell, 149	Bowman, Eliza, 044	Bowman, Maria, 038	Boyer, Christiana, 125
Botts, Charles Russel, 095	Botts, Russell, 233	Bowman, Elizabeth, 044	Bowman, Maria, 044	Boyer, Christina W, 129
Botts, Charles W, 149	Botts, Sarah Amanda, 097	Bowman, Elizabeth, 045	Bowman, Maria F, 039	Boyer, Christopher, 016
Botts, Charles W, 276	Botts, Susan, 096	Bowman, Elizabeth, 068	Bowman, Mary, 031	Boyer, Cornelius, 130
Botts, Daniel, 096	Botts, Susanna, 095	Bowman, Elizabeth, 249	Bowman, Mary, 044	Boyer, Crystal, 165
Botts, Edward, 096	Botts, William, 095	Bowman, Elizabeth, 427	Bowman, Mary, 045	Boyer, Daniel, 129
Botts, Elllen, 095	Botts, William, 096	Bowman, Emeline, 045	Bowman, Mary Ann, 242	Boyer, Daniel J, 107
Botts, Emma L, 095	Botts, William Henr, 097	Bowman, Emma, 045	Bowman, Mary F, 045	Boyer, David, 130
Botts, Fred, 276	Botz, Anna Catharin, 079	Bowman, Emma, 242	Bowman, May Wert, 044	Boyer, David A, 129
Botts, Frederick, 148	Botz, C, 099	Bowman, Emma J, 129	Bowman, Mervin, 163	Boyer, Delores, 355
Botts, Frederick, 149	Botz, Catharine, 149	Bowman, Esther, 249	Bowman, Nellie M, 044	Boyer, Edna, 412
Botts, Frederick, 233	Botz, George, 079	Bowman, Etta, 262	Bowman, Nellie M, 045	Boyer, Elias, 130
Botts, G Fred, 095	Botz, George, 375	Bowman, F, 359	Bowman, Philip, 088	Boyer, Elias D, 130
Botts, Geo William, 148	Bougher, Henry, 532	Bowman, Francis C, 039	Bowman, Philip, 242	Boyer, Eliz Coleman, 130
Botts, Geo William, 233	Bower, Chester, 069	Bowman, Francis S, 044	Bowman, Philip, 389	Boyer, Elizabeth S, 129
Botts, George, 090	Bower, Elizabeth, 315	Bowman, Frank, 044	Bowman, Rebecca Z, 174	Boyer, Elizabeth Sw, 130
Botts, George, 095	Bower, John, 017	Bowman, Frank S, 045	Bowman, Robert H, 045	Boyer, Ellen, 177
Botts, George, 095	Bower, Pauline, 132	Bowman, George, 038	Bowman, Ruth, 163	Boyer, Emaline, 130
Botts, George W, 095	Bower, Samuel, 017	Bowman, George, 044	Bowman, Ruth, 164	Boyer, Emanuel, 163
Botts, George W, 096	Bower, William, 351	Bowman, George, 249	Bowman, Samuel, 025	Boyer, Emanuel, 164
Botts, George W, 276	Bowerman, Aaron, 388	Bowman, George J, 038	Bowman, Sarah, 078	Boyer, Emeline, 055
Botts, George Wm, 149	Bowerman, Amanda, 388	Bowman, Hannah, 045	Bowman, Sarah, 441	Boyer, Frances, 192
Botts, Hannah, 095	Bowerman, Ann M, 388	Bowman, Hans R, 044	Bowman, Simon, 045	Boyer, Frances, 565
Botts, Hannah, 148	Bowerman, Anna Mary, 245	Bowman, Hay W, 045	Bowman, Simon O, 026	Boyer, Frances D, 129
Botts, Henry, 097	Bowerman, Bell, 388	Bowman, Ida Louisa, 528	Bowman, Simon Sal, 045	Boyer, Francis, 130
Botts, Hiram, 096	Bowerman, Franklin, 388	Bowman, Irene A, 045	Bowman, Sumner S, 045	Boyer, Francis E, 188
Botts, Isaac, 096	Bowerman, Geo W, 245	Bowman, Isaac, 044	Bowman, Susan, 031	Boyer, Francis Ellen, 130
Botts, Isabelle, 097	Bowerman, John A, 245	Bowman, Isaac, 045	Bowman, Susan, 045	Boyer, Frank, 477
Botts, Jacob, 096	Bowerman, John A, 388	Bowman, Jacob, 045	Bowman, Susan Bar, 038	Boyer, Frank, 485
Botts, Jeremiah, 096	Bowerman, John Jr, 388	Bowman, Jacob, 252	Bowman, Susanna L, 044	Boyer, Frank, 517
Botts, John, 096	Bowerman, Kate, 194	Bowman, Jacob, 427	Bowman, Susannah, 044	Boyer, Frank W, 065
Botts, John, 148	Bowerman, Solomon, 388	Bowman, James D, 045	Bowman, Uriah, 241	Boyer, G M, 506
Botts, John, 149	Bowerman, Susan, 388	Bowman, Jennie E, 045	Bowman, Wendell, 044	Boyer, Gabriel, 128
Botts, John, 233	Bowerman, Wilhelm, 377	Bowman, John, 044	Bowne, Leah, 272	Boyer, Gabriel, 129
Botts, John, 276	Bowerman, William, 388	Bowman, John, 078	Bowser, Susan, 560	Boyer, Gabriel, 130
Botts, John Adam, 097	Bowers, Esther Row, 144	Bowman, John, 146	Boye, J W, 146	Boyer, George, 130
Botts, John H, 095	Bowers, William, 144	Bowman, John, 244	Boye, John, 084	Boyer, George, 285
Botts, John J, 096	Bowing, Thomas, 138	Bowman, John F, 038	Boyer, ?, 239	Boyer, George Jr, 285
Botts, John Jr, 095	Bowma, Elizabeth, 427	Bowman, John F, 039	Boyer, ? , 272	Boyer, Hannah, 130
Botts, John Sr Betz, 095	Bowman, ?, 020	Bowman, John F, 044	Boyer, Abraham, 130	Boyer, Henry, 079
Botts, Jonas, 148	Bowman, ?, 502	Bowman, John F, 045	Boyer, Abraham, 244	Boyer, Henry, 130
Botts, Joseph, 096	Bowman, ?, 532	Bowman, John F, 050	Boyer, Adam, 130	Boyer, Henry, 185
Botts, Joseph, 097	Bowman, ?, 533	Bowman, John Geo, 078	Boyer, Albert D, 130	Boyer, Henry, 485
Botts, Josiah, 097	Bowman, Abraham, 241	Bowman, John Jeffer, 045	Boyer, Alfred, 130	Boyer, Irvin, 076
Botts, Leah, 097	Bowman, Abraham, 252	Bowman, John R, 044	Boyer, Amelia, 130	Boyer, Irvin D, 130
Botts, Luisiana, 096	Bowman, Abraham, 427	Bowman, John Son, 044	Boyer, Amelia, 463	Boyer, Isaac, 130
Botts, Maggie, 096	Bowman, Adam, 174	Bowman, Joshua, 045	Boyer, Amelia Mrs, 026	Boyer, J Frank, 463
Botts, Margaret, 096	Bowman, Agnes, 044	Bowman, Josiah, 031	Boyer, Ann, 099	Boyer, Jacob, 129
Botts, Mary, 095	Bowman, Agnes M, 045	Bowman, Josiah, 038	Boyer, Anna Jane G, 129	Boyer, Jacob 190,
Botts, Mary Ann, 148	Bowman, Anna, 044	Bowman, Josiah, 039	Boyer, Anna Jane G, 130	Boyer, Jacob E, 346
Botts, Mary E Schoff, 149	Bowman, Anna Eliz, 241	Bowman, Josiah, 044	Boyer, Annie, 332	Boyer, Jacob E 188,
Botts, Mary Ellen, 097	Bowman, Anna Eliz, 252	Bowman, Josiah, 050	Boyer, Annie B, 130	Boyer, James, 565
Botts, Mary Ellen, 148	Bowman, Anne J, 044	Bowman, Josiah, 053	Boyer, Benjamin, 055	Boyer, Johann Henrch, 380
Botts, Mary Ellen, 149	Bowman, Anne P, 045	Bowman, Josiah, 054	Boyer, Benjamin, 130	Boyer, John, 129
Botts, Mary Ellen, 276	Bowman, Barbara, 044	Bowman, Josiah, 066	Boyer, Benjamin A, 130	Boyer, John, 130
Botts, Mary S, 097	Bowman, Barbara, 246	Bowman, Josiah, 068	Boyer, Benneville, 079	Boyer, John, 130
Botts, Mildred, 096	Bowman, Barbara Mar, 244	Bowman, Josiah, 113	Boyer, Benneville, 129	Boyer, John, 334
Botts, Mildred, 148	Bowman, Benjamin, 044	Bowman, Josiah, 123	Boyer, Benneville, 130	Boyer, John, 404
Botts, Mildred, 149	Bowman, Benjamin, 045	Bowman, Josiah, 125	Boyer, Caroline, 130	Boyer, John B, 130
Botts, Mildred, 233	Bowman, Benjamin, 325	Bowman, Josiah, 142	Boyer, Carrie, 185	Boyer, John E, 130

Buffington, Eliz, 261
Buffington, Eliz Romb, 460
Buffington, Elizabet, 090
Buffington, Elizabeth, 234
Buffington, Elizabeth, 241
Buffington, Elizabeth, 369
Buffington, Elizabeth, 391
Buffington, Elizabeth, 428
Buffington, Elizabeth, 460
Buffington, Elmira E, 402
Buffington, Emanuel, 448
Buffington, Ethel H, 177
Buffington, Eva, 059
Buffington, Eva, 360
Buffington, Eva Schoff, 182
Buffington, Francis, 386
Buffington, Frank, 260
Buffington, Franklin H, 499
Buffington, Geo, 074
Buffington, George, 088
Buffington, George, 234
Buffington, George, 246
Buffington, George, 289
Buffington, George, 330
Buffington, George, 482
Buffington, George B, 478
Buffington, George F, 261
Buffington, George F, 365
Buffington, George F, 366
Buffington, Gilbert, 351
Buffington, Globby, 520
Buffington, H E, 428
Buffington, Hanna, 234
Buffington, Hannah, 059
Buffington, Hannah, 177
Buffington, Hannah, 182
Buffington, Hannah, 298
Buffington, Hannah, 351
Buffington, Hannah, 359
Buffington, Hannah C, 482
Buffington, Hannah S, 298
Buffington, Harry, 349
Buffington, Harry Z, 074
Buffington, Henrietta, 079
Buffington, Henry, 454
Buffington, Henry G, 478
Buffington, Henry G, 565
Buffington, Irvin, 463
Buffington, Irvin M, 541
Buffington, Irwin M, 499
Buffington, Isaac, 298
Buffington, Isaac, 359
Buffington, Isaac, 448
Buffington, J, 168
Buffington, Jacob, 369
Buffington, Jacob, 430
Buffington, Jacob, 448
Buffington, Jacob, 478
Buffington, Jacob, 550
Buffington, Jacob John, 478
Buffington, Jacob Jr, 448
Buffington, James H, 074
Buffington, Jeremiah, 128
Buffington, Joel, 036
Buffington, Johannes, 234
Buffington, John, 031
Buffington, John, 116
Buffington, John, 132
Buffington, John, 234
Buffington, John, 241
Buffington, John, 336
Buffington, John E, 083
Buffington, John E, 093
Buffington, John E, 283
Buffington, John E, 443

Buffington, John E, 499
Buffington, John Isaac, 298
Buffington, John L, 373
Buffington, Jonas, 359
Buffington, Jonas, 448
Buffington, Jonathan, 036
Buffington, Joseph, 298
Buffington, Laura, 132
Buffington, Leah J, 128
Buffington, Levi, 123
Buffington, Levi, 235
Buffington, Levi, 330
Buffington, Levi, 373
Buffington, Levi, 417
Buffington, Levi, 448
Buffington, Levi, 530
Buffington, Lucanna, 367
Buffington, Lucanna, 368
Buffington, Lydia, 234
Buffington, Lydia, 448
Buffington, M E, 505
Buffington, Mararet, 439
Buffington, Margaret, 359
Buffington, Maria, 234
Buffington, Maria Cath, 356
Buffington, Marian, 074
Buffington, Marietta, 298
Buffington, Marlin, 285
Buffington, Marlin, 351
Buffington, Mary, 074
Buffington, Mary, 234
Buffington, Mary, 287
Buffington, Mary, 421
Buffington, Mary, 448
Buffington, Mary, 479
Buffington, Mary Cat, 234
Buffington, Mary E, 429
Buffington, Mary Frise, 235
Buffington, May Lydia, 499
Buffington, Milton E, 504
Buffington, Milton O, 083
Buffington, Nancy J, 258
Buffington, Nathani, 026
Buffington, Paul, 351
Buffington, Paul W, 134
Buffington, Phoebe, 116
Buffington, Rachel, 057
Buffington, Rachel, 271
Buffington, Rachel B, 130
Buffington, Ralph F, 074
Buffington, Raymon M, 499
Buffington, Rebecca H, 478
Buffington, Reuben, 167
Buffington, Richard, 116
Buffington, Robert, 128
Buffington, Robert J, 258
Buffington, Ruth, 035
Buffington, Ruth, 036
Buffington, Ruth C, 036
Buffington, Salome, 234
Buffington, Samuel, 236
Buffington, Samuel, 430
Buffington, Samuel, 478
Buffington, Samuel, 482
Buffington, Sarah, 117
Buffington, Sarah, 236
Buffington, Sarah, 298
Buffington, Sarah, 299
Buffington, Sarah, 429
Buffington, Sarah, 478
Buffington, Sarah, 482
Buffington, Solomon, 017
Buffington, Solomon, 096
Buffington, Solomon, 391
Buffington, Solomon, 460

Buffington, Solomon, 530
Buffington, Susan, 234
Buffington, Susan, 448
Buffington, Susan Artz, 499
Buffington, Susanna, 123
Buffington, Susanna, 283
Buffington, Susanna, 358
Buffington, Susanna, 360
Buffington, Susannah, 373
Buffington, Susannah, 530
Buffington, Susannah, 036
Buffington, Thomas, 026
Buffington, Thomas, 036
Buffington, Thomas, 128
Buffington, Thomas, 157
Buffington, Thomas, 177
Buffington, Thomas, 448
Buffington, Tom, 117
Buffington, Tom, 118
Buffington, Uncle Joe, 230
Buffington, William, 035
Buffington, Wm, 036
Buffington, Wm Son, 036
Buffinton, Adam, 283
Buffinton, Charles W, 283
Buffinton, Christian, 283
Buffinton, Daniel, 283
Buffinton, Daniel, 285
Buffinton, Darwin, 501
Buffinton, Elias, 283
Buffinton, Elmira, 283
Buffinton, Emma J, 283
Buffinton, George L, 283
Buffinton, John E, 283
Buffinton, Maryetta, 283
Buffinton, Sarah A, 283
Buffinton, Susan Malin, 283
Bull, Tyrus, 055
Buman, Julius, 044
Buman, Ulie, 044
Bundy, Betsey, 092
Burckhart, John, 307
Burd, ?, 104
Burd, A Mary, 040
Burd, A Mary Ferree, 516
Burd, Amanda Rebec, 420
Burd, Ann Mary, 426
Burd, Ann Mary, 428
Burd, Ann Mary Ferre, 545
Burd, Ann Mary Ferre, 546
Burd, Elizabeth, 040
Burd, Elizabeth, 546
Burd, Elizabeth A, 420
Burd, Emma J, 040
Burd, Emma J, 041
Burd, Emma J, 546
Burd, Emma Jane, 143
Burd, Emma Jane, 516
Burd, George, 420
Burd, George, 428
Burd, George, 430
Burd, George W, 040
Burd, George W, 546
Burd, George Washing, 420
Burd, Henry H, 040
Burd, Henry H, 546
Burd, Ida, 040
Burd, Isaac, 040
Burd, Isaac, 420
Burd, Isaac, 426
Burd, Isaac, 428
Burd, Isaac, 516
Burd, Isaac, 545
Burd, Isaac, 546
Burd, Isaac Jr, 545

Burd, Jacob, 420
Burd, John, 530
Burd, Louisa, 040
Burd, Louisa, 496
Burd, Magdalelna, 428
Burd, Magdalena Cric, 430
Burd, Magdalena Rick, 420
Burd, Mary, 420
Burd, Mary Ann, 420
Burd, Mary Louisa, 040
Burd, Mary Louisa, 420
Burd, Mary Louisa, 546
Burd, Rickert, 428
Burd, Samuel, 040
Burd, Sarah, 040
Burd, Sarah, 430
Burd, Sarah, 546
Burd, Sarah J, 420
Burd, Susan, 040
Burd, Susan, 546
Burger, Elizabeth, 517
Burgert, Annette K, 092
Burkart, John H, 017
Burke, Peter Joseph Jr, 318
Burnside, Grant, 537
Burr, Henry, 018
Burr, Henry H, 017
Burr, Henry H, 050
Burr, Henry H, 051
Burr, Theodore, 020
Burr, Theodore, 021
Burrell, Carl H, 134
Burrell, Caroline, 243
Burrell, Daniel Walt, 252
Burrell, Gail E, 174
Burrell, Gary L, 174
Burrell, Gilbert, 131
Burrell, Gilbert, 189
Burrell, Gilbert E, 134
Burrell, Hattie, 253
Burrell, Hattie Eva, 252
Burrell, John David, 252
Burrell, Lillie May, 252
Burrell, Margaret, 131
Burrell, Mildred, 355
Burrell, Peg, 189
Burrell, Prudence, 177
Burrell, Ralph, 177
Burrell, Rev George, 252
Burrell, Samuel, 449
Burrell, Thomas, 270
Burrell, William, 359
Burrell, Wm Ray, 252
Burris, Mary F, 347
Bus, Xaker, 315
Bush, Albert, 249
Bush, Alice, 249
Bush, Alvin, 249
Bush, Benjamin, 249
Bush, Brad, 249
Bush, Carlos Wilson, 249
Bush, Carol, 249
Bush, Carrie, 249
Bush, Catharina, 248
Bush, Catharine, 249
Bush, Catharine Barb, 249
Bush, Catherine, 249
Bush, Cecilia E, 249
Bush, Christian, 248
Bush, Clair, 133
Bush, Clair, 247
Bush, Clair, 248
Bush, Clair, 407
Bush, Clair, 409
Bush, Clair H, 249

Bush, Clair H, 250
Bush, Clayton John, 249
Bush, Daniel, 249
Bush, David P, 249
Bush, Dorothy, 249
Bush, Earl, 249
Bush, Elias, 249
Bush, Elias K, 249
Bush, Elizabeth, 249
Bush, Elizabeth, 317
Bush, Elizabeth, 381
Bush, Emma Jane, 249
Bush, Esther, 249
Bush, Florence E, 282
Bush, Franklin, 249
Bush, George, 249
Bush, Gideon, 249
Bush, Grace, 249
Bush, Harietta, 487
Bush, Henry, 249
Bush, Hester, 249
Bush, Ida, 249
Bush, Ira C, 249
Bush, Irene, 249
Bush, Jacob, 248
Bush, Jacob, 249
Bush, James Monroe, 249
Bush, James Morris, 249
Bush, Johannes, 249
Bush, John B, 249
Bush, John Joseph, 249
Bush, Jonannes, 249
Bush, Joseph, 249
Bush, Joseph, 409
Bush, Joshia, 249
Bush, Joshua, 249
Bush, Katie Elmira, 249
Bush, Kay M, 249
Bush, Kenneth, 249
Bush, Kenneth S, 448
Bush, Lee, 249
Bush, Linda, 070
Bush, Linda, 248
Bush, Lois, 249
Bush, Lydia, 249
Bush, Margaret, 530
Bush, Margaret C, 240
Bush, Maria, 248
Bush, Maria Alien, 249
Bush, Marlin, 249
Bush, Mary, 249
Bush, Mary Matilda, 249
Bush, Millie, 249
Bush, Monda Ditty, 249
Bush, Monda Witty, 409
Bush, Moses, 249
Bush, Moses M, 249
Bush, Paul, 230
Bush, Paul, 248
Bush, Paul H, 249
Bush, Paul H, 258
Bush, Paul H, 282
Bush, Raymond, 249
Bush, Ronald, 249
Bush, Roy, 249
Bush, Samuel, 249
Bush, Sarah, 249
Bush, Shirley E, 249
Bush, Shirley Evelyn, 069
Bush, Terry, 249
Bush, William, 249
Bush, William N, 249
Buss, Dawn L, 209
Buss, Jeremy, 209
Busse, Rudolph, 481

Fagely, Sarah, 149
Fagely, Sarah A, 301
Fagley, Danial, 260
Fagley, Daniel, 261
Fagley, Maria, 261
Fagley, Sarah, 148
Fahnestock, Charles, 045
Farnsworth, Rev J S, 140
Farree, Leah, 036
Farree, Philip &Leah, 036
Farrel, Mary Ann, 402
Fasely, Amanda, 271
Fauber, Frederick, 168
Fauber, Mary Etzw, 168
Faugitt, Col William, 251
Faulkner, Eve, 035
Faulkner, Jesse, 035
Faulkner, Mary, 035
Faulkner, Mary C, 035
Faulkner, Susanna, 035
Faulkner, Thomas, 035
Faupelin, Catharina E, 251
Faust, Catharine, 359
Faust, Catherine, 238
Faust, Catherine S, 264
Faust, Chadarina, 024
Faust, Elizabeth, 382
Faust, J Amy, 024
Faust, Jonas, 025
Faust, Jonas, 238
Faust, Jonas, 264
Faust, Lewis, 025
Faust, Lewis, 238
Faust, Maryann, 024
Faust, Sally, 530
Faust, Sarah Delcamp, 264
Faust, Wever, 024
Faust, William, 197
Fawver, Adam, 276
Fawver, Emma, 276
Fawver, Johannes, 276
Fawver, John F, 276
Fawver, Leah, 276
Fawver, Magdalena, 276
Fawver, Margaret, 276
Fawver, Mary, 276
Fawver, Rebecca, 276
Fawver, Sarah Eliz, 276
Fawver, Tillie, 276
Feagley, Daniel Jr, 018
Feagley, H A, 303
Feagley, Jacob, 018
Feagley, John, 033
Feagley, Mary, 024
Feagley, Mr, 504
Feaser, Elizabeth, 533
Feather, John H, 274
Feerree, Isaac, 019
Feeser, Elizabeth, 381
Fegal, Melchoir, 015
Fegely, Catherine, 495
Fegely, John, 485
Fegely, John, 486
Fegely, John, 495
Feger, Maisy E, 476
Fegley, Amanda, 481
Fegley, Angeline, 357
Fegley, Daniel, 024
Fegley, Elias, 357
Fegley, Elias, 358
Fegley, Elias, 360
Fegley, Elias, 442
Fegley, Elizabeth, 364
Fegley, Esther, 024
Fegley, Henry Arthu, 024

Fegley, Jacob, 364
Fegley, Justina, 488
Fegley, Sarah, 024
Fegley, Susannah, 364
Fehler, Catherine, 573
Fehler, Emma B, 573
Feidt, Abraham, 373
Feidt, Catharina, 374
Feidt, Daniel, 046
Feidt, Daniel, 058
Feidt, David E, 047
Feidt, Elizabeth, 374
Feidt, George, 047
Feidt, George, 058
Feidt, George, 471
Feidt, J George, 374
Feidt, John, 374
Feidt, John, 471
Feidt, Joseph, 374
Feidt, Lidia, 046
Feidt, Magdalena, 374
Feidt, Rachel, 058
Feidt, Salome, 047
Feidt, Susanna H, 046
Feidt, Susanna H, 047
Feit, George, 147
Felburn, Mary Jane, 384
Feldy, George, 362
Felix, Jerri, 158
Fennel, Fletcher, 104
Fennel, Myrtle, 295
Fenstermacher, Rodney, 309
Fenstermacher, Sarh, 125
Ferester, Barbara A, 560
Ferester, Sandra, 560
Ferrester, Timothy A, 560
Ferguson, Mary, 393
Fernon, John, 138
Fernsler, Rev M, 450
Ferree, ?, 019
Ferree, ?, 049
Ferree, ?, 188
Ferree, A Mary, 428
Ferree, Abraham, 036
Ferree, Abraham, 037
Ferree, Agnes Ann, 040
Ferree, Allice Barba, 041
Ferree, Alvin H, 042
Ferree, Amanda, 042
Ferree, Andreas, 430
Ferree, Andrew, 032
Ferree, Andrew, 033
Ferree, Andrew Isac, 034
Ferree, Ann Eliz, 041
Ferree, Ann Mary, 040
Ferree, Ann Mary, 545
Ferree, Ann Mary, 546
Ferree, Ann McCur, 040
Ferree, Anna Maria, 032
Ferree, Anna Marie, 036
Ferree, Anna Mary, 041
Ferree, Anna Mary, 051
Ferree, Anna Mary, 545
Ferree, Anne, 176
Ferree, Arthur, 449
Ferree, Arthur, 462
Ferree, Arthur, 564
Ferree, Barbara, 034
Ferree, Barbara, 044
Ferree, Benjamin F, 042
Ferree, Beulah Rebec, 449
Ferree, Beulah Tscho, 462
Ferree, Blanche Miri, 041
Ferree, Blanche Miria, 546
Ferree, Catharina, 430

Ferree, Catharine, 239
Ferree, Catharine, 572
Ferree, Catherine, 033
Ferree, Catherine, 035
Ferree, Catherine, 036
Ferree, Catherine, 530
Ferree, Catherine, 572
Ferree, Catherine E, 039
Ferree, Catherine E, 150
Ferree, Catherine E, 165
Ferree, Catherine E, 169
Ferree, Catherine Eli, 040
Ferree, Charles, 042
Ferree, Charles A, 040
Ferree, Charles Adam, 430
Ferree, Charles Adam, 546
Ferree, Charles Ray, 041
Ferree, Clinton Augu, 040
Ferree, Conrad, 034
Ferree, Cornelius, 036
Ferree, Cyrus, 040
Ferree, Cyrus, 041
Ferree, Cyrus, 545
Ferree, Daniel, 017
Ferree, Daniel, 019
Ferree, Daniel, 030
Ferree, Daniel, 031
Ferree, Daniel, 032
Ferree, Daniel, 033
Ferree, Daniel, 034
Ferree, Daniel, 035
Ferree, Daniel, 036
Ferree, Daniel, 122
Ferree, Daniel, 123
Ferree, Daniel, 239
Ferree, Daniel, 240
Ferree, Daniel, 344
Ferree, Daniel, 417
Ferree, Daniel, 567
Ferree, Daniel, 569
Ferree, Daniel & Son, 033
Ferree, Daniel & Son, 035
Ferree, Daniel Jr, 032
Ferree, David, 033
Ferree, Dora, 039
Ferree, Dora May, 040
Ferree, Dora May, 150
Ferree, Edith Ann, 040
Ferree, Edith Ellen, 041
Ferree, Edith Ellen, 546
Ferree, Edward, 430
Ferree, Elijah, 038
Ferree, Elijah, 042
Ferree, Elisabeth, 034
Ferree, Elisah, 122
Ferree, Elisha, 035
Ferree, Elisha, 036
Ferree, Eliz Forbes, 038
Ferree, Elizabeth, 035
Ferree, Elizabeth, 036
Ferree, Elizabeth, 037
Ferree, Elizabeth, 038
Ferree, Elizabeth, 039
Ferree, Elizabeth, 040
Ferree, Elizabeth, 041
Ferree, Elizabeth, 042
Ferree, Elizabeth, 044
Ferree, Elizabeth, 051
Ferree, Elizabeth, 483
Ferree, Elizabeth, 545
Ferree, Elizabeth, 546
Ferree, Elizabeth Lea, 041
Ferree, Elizabeth Lea, 546
Ferree, Ellen C, 041
Ferree, Emeline, 042

Ferree, Emma J, 040
Ferree, Ephraim, 035
Ferree, Ephraim, 036
Ferree, Esquire, 117
Ferree, Esther, 036
Ferree, Eva N, 040
Ferree, Eva N, 430
Ferree, Eva N, 546
Ferree, F P, 477
Ferree, F P, 485
Ferree, F P, 540
Ferree, F P 189, 349
Ferree, Flora Jane, 041
Ferree, Forrest C, 041
Ferree, Frances, 501
Ferree, Francis, 484
Ferree, Frank, 546
Ferree, Frank P, 040
Ferree, Frank P, 504
Ferree, Frank P, 545
Ferree, Frank P, 548
Ferree, Franklin P, 546
Ferree, Franklin Pier, 041
Ferree, Friederich, 430
Ferree, Geo Washing, 040
Ferree, George, 016
Ferree, George, 035
Ferree, George F, 041
Ferree, George Franc, 040
Ferree, George Frank, 430
Ferree, George Frankli, 546
Ferree, George W, 420
Ferree, George W, 430
Ferree, George W Jr, 041
Ferree, George W L, 428
Ferree, George Wash, 544
Ferree, George Wash, 545
Ferree, George Wash, 546
Ferree, George Washin, 483
Ferree, Hanna, 240
Ferree, Hannah, 033
Ferree, Hannah, 034
Ferree, Hannah, 272
Ferree, Harry M, 040
Ferree, Hattie Leah, 040
Ferree, Hattie Leah, 430
Ferree, Hattie Leah, 546
Ferree, Hattie Louisa, 041
Ferree, Hattie Louisa, 546
Ferree, Henry, 040
Ferree, Henry B, 430
Ferree, Henry B, 546
Ferree, Henry Frankl, 041
Ferree, Henry Frankl, 546
Ferree, Henry M, 040
Ferree, Henry M, 430
Ferree, Henry Wash, 546
Ferree, Henry Washi, 041
Ferree, Howard Wm, 041
Ferree, Ida, 041
Ferree, Ida, 042
Ferree, Ida, 430
Ferree, Ida Charlotte, 040
Ferree, Ida Charlotte, 430
Ferree, Ida Charlotte, 546
Ferree, Ida Edith, 546
Ferree, Isaac, 017
Ferree, Isaac, 018
Ferree, Isaac, 030
Ferree, Isaac, 031
Ferree, Isaac, 035
Ferree, Isaac, 036
Ferree, Isaac, 037
Ferree, Isaac, 038
Ferree, Isaac, 041

Ferree, Isaac, 044
Ferree, Isaac, 051
Ferree, Isaac, 066
Ferree, Isaac, 113
Ferree, Isaac, 122
Ferree, Isaac, 123
Ferree, Isaac, 281
Ferree, Isaac, 292
Ferree, Isaac, 417
Ferree, Isaac, 483
Ferree, Isaac, 545
Ferree, Isaac H, 042
Ferree, Isaac Jr, 031
Ferree, Isaac Jr, 035
Ferree, Isaac Jr, 039
Ferree, Isaac Jr, 545
Ferree, Isaac Newton, 041
Ferree, Isaac Son, 036
Ferree, Isaac Sr, 545
Ferree, Isreal, 036
Ferree, Jacob, 034
Ferree, Jacob, 036
Ferree, Jacob, 037
Ferree, Jacob, 039
Ferree, Jacob, 041
Ferree, Jacob, 430
Ferree, Jacob B, 033
Ferree, Jacob Forbes, 036
Ferree, Jacob Forbes, 042
Ferree, Jacob Sr, 037
Ferree, Jakobina, 430
Ferree, James, 024
Ferree, James, 037
Ferree, James, 039
Ferree, James, 040
Ferree, James, 042
Ferree, James, 106
Ferree, James B, 150
Ferree, James Esq, 039
Ferree, James J P, 041
Ferree, James W, 039
Ferree, Jane, 037
Ferree, Jane, 038
Ferree, Jane, 039
Ferree, Jane, 042
Ferree, Jane, 111
Ferree, Jane, 116
Ferree, Jean, 031
Ferree, Joel, 015
Ferree, Joel, 018
Ferree, Joel, 030
Ferree, Joel, 034
Ferree, Joel, 036
Ferree, Joel, 037
Ferree, Joel, 038
Ferree, Joel, 044
Ferree, Joel, 111
Ferree, Joel, 113
Ferree, Joel B, 116
Ferree, Joel Barlow, 040
Ferree, Joel D, 286
Ferree, Joel Forbes, 040
Ferree, Joel Jr, 114
Ferree, Joel Sr, 037
Ferree, Joel W, 035
Ferree, Joel W, 036
Ferree, Johannes, 430
Ferree, John, 034
Ferree, John, 035
Ferree, John, 036
Ferree, John, 040
Ferree, John, 150
Ferree, John G, 040
Ferree, John G, 150
Ferree, John Milton, 040

Harper, Amanda, 239
Harper, Amanda Bar, 053
Harper, Amelia, 053
Harper, Ann, 052
Harper, Annie B, 052
Harper, Annie B, 053
Harper, Annie E, 188
Harper, Annie S, 053
Harper, Anton Frank, 052
Harper, Barbara, 051
Harper, Barbara, 052
Harper, Barbara, 251
Harper, Barbara, 258
Harper, Beatrice, 132
Harper, Beatrice, 144
Harper, Benjamin, 053
Harper, Benjamin F, 053
Harper, Benjamin F, 072
Harper, Benjamin F, 135
Harper, Capt C, 501
Harper, Capt C, 511
Harper, Capt Corneliu, 448
Harper, Carry, 053
Harper, Catharine, 052
Harper, Catharine, 053
Harper, Charles O, 053
Harper, Charlotte, 053
Harper, Clara, 052
Harper, Clara Rebec, 053
Harper, Cornelius A, 052
Harper, Cornelius A, 143
Harper, Cornelius M, 052
Harper, Dollie, 053
Harper, Elizabeth, 052
Harper, Ellen Rebe, 052
Harper, Francis, 052
Harper, Gen Thomas, 239
Harper, George, 061
Harper, George, 076
Harper, George, 478
Harper, George D, 053
Harper, George D, 072
Harper, George D, 188
Harper, Guilford, 051
Harper, Harry J, 188
Harper, Harry T, 053
Harper, Harvey O, 053
Harper, Henrietta, 052
Harper, Henry Clay, 053
Harper, Ida, 053
Harper, Ida Jones, 052
Harper, Jacob A, 053
Harper, Johannes, 089
Harper, John, 051
Harper, John, 052
Harper, John David, 052
Harper, Joseph R, 053
Harper, Lillie A, 053
Harper, Margaret, 052
Harper, Mary A, 053
Harper, Mattie, 131
Harper, Maude Irene, 412
Harper, Millie, 131
Harper, Netta Malin, 053
Harper, Nora J, 053
Harper, Nora Madda, 053
Harper, Oscar E, 053
Harper, Rebecca, 052
Harper, Rebecca, 053
Harper, Rebecca, 272
Harper, Samuel S, 052
Harper, Sarah, 052
Harper, Sarah, 143
Harper, Sarah Anna, 053
Harper, Sarah Ulrich, 052

Harper, Simeon, 051
Harper, Susan Isab, 052
Harper, Thomas, 033
Harper, Thomas, 050
Harper, Thomas, 051
Harper, Thomas, 052
Harper, Thomas, 053
Harper, Thomas, 251
Harper, Thomas, 258
Harper, Thomas Ed, 052
Harper, Thomas Wm, 052
Harper, Valentine, 052
Harper, Willard G, 053
Harper, William H, 052
Harris, Betty, 350
Harris, Bob, 137
Harris, George, 015
Harris, John, 137
Harris, John, 378
Harris, John, 401
Harris, John E, 496
Harris, John E Jr, 363
Harris, Lynn, 137
Harris, Old John, 332
Harris, Robert, 350
Harter, Absalum, 427
Harter, Andrew, 427
Harter, Anna Barbara, 427
Harter, Anna Cath Z, 427
Harter, Anna Catherin, 427
Harter, Anna Maria, 427
Harter, Anna Mary, 427
Harter, Benjamin, 427
Harter, Catharine, 427
Harter, Catherine Z, 427
Harter, Christian, 427
Harter, Daniel, 427
Harter, Dorothea, 427
Harter, Elias, 427
Harter, Elizabeth, 426
Harter, Elizabeth, 427
Harter, Enoch, 427
Harter, Esther, 427
Harter, George, 427
Harter, Hannah, 427
Harter, Henrietta, 427
Harter, Henry, 115
Harter, Henry, 427
Harter, Isaac, 427
Harter, J W, 104
Harter, Jacob, 427
Harter, John, 427
Harter, John, 427
Harter, Joseph, 427
Harter, Lavina, 427
Harter, Magdalena, 427
Harter, Maria Eliz, 427
Harter, Mary Ann, 427
Harter, Mary Eliz, 427
Harter, Mary Magd, 427
Harter, Mathias, 422
Harter, Mathias, 426
Harter, Mathias, 427
Harter, Mathias, 432
Harter, Peter, 427
Harter, Rebecca, 427
Harter, Samuel, 427
Harter, Samuel, 427
Harter, Sarah, 427
Harter, Susann, 427
Harter, Susanna, 427
Harter, Wilhelm, 427
Hartlaub, Kirk, 301
Hartlieb, Ashley M, 207
Hartman, Aaron, 533

Hartman, Alice, 355
Hartman, Alma Doroth, 488
Hartman, Ann Mary, 566
Hartman, Anna Mary, 149
Hartman, Annie Lera, 488
Hartman, Arron, 328
Hartman, Barbara Gal, 415
Hartman, Benjamin M, 415
Hartman, Catharine, 499
Hartman, Catharine D, 474
Hartman, Catherine E, 501
Hartman, Catherine H, 537
Hartman, Charles, 328
Hartman, Charles, 535
Hartman, Christian Rev, 243
Hartman, Clara, 488
Hartman, Clara Rebecc, 488
Hartman, Clayton Dan, 488
Hartman, Cornelius, 263
Hartman, Daniel, 035
Hartman, Daniel L, 355
Hartman, Dean, 538
Hartman, Dean Sch, 164
Hartman, Edwin, 488
Hartman, Eliz A Lebo, 263
Hartman, Elizabeth, 328
Hartman, Elizabeth, 478
Hartman, Elizabeth, 552
Hartman, Ella May, 415
Hartman, Elma B Will, 414
Hartman, Emma Jane, 366
Hartman, Evelyn, 157
Hartman, Evelyn, 248
Hartman, Frank E, 537
Hartman, Franklin A, 488
Hartman, Gabrielle, 415
Hartman, George, 437
Hartman, George Lear, 355
Hartman, Hani, 035
Hartman, Hannah, 501
Hartman, Hannah D, 488
Hartman, Henry, 093
Hartman, Henry, 320
Hartman, Henry, 323
Hartman, Henry, 328
Hartman, Henry, 376
Hartman, Henry, 482
Hartman, Henry, 490
Hartman, Henry, 499
Hartman, Henry J, 328
Hartman, Henry Jr, 328
Hartman, Henry Vet, 335
Hartman, Jacob, 234
Hartman, Jacob, 235
Hartman, Jacob, 236
Hartman, Jacob, 328
Hartman, Jacob, 396
Hartman, Jacob, 474
Hartman, Jennie I, 535
Hartman, Jesse, 488
Hartman, Joanne, 415
Hartman, Joanne, 415
Hartman, John, 328
Hartman, John, 345
Hartman, John, 354
Hartman, John, 415
Hartman, John, 566
Hartman, John D, 263
Hartman, John Harper, 242
Hartman, John Joseph, 415
Hartman, John Jr, 323
Hartman, John Norman, 488
Hartman, Jonathan, 328
Hartman, Jorias Jonas, 488
Hartman, Joseph, 415

Hartman, Joseph Ben, 488
Hartman, Joseph H, 414
Hartman, Joseph Herb, 318
Hartman, Joseph Herb, 414
Hartman, Judith, 289
Hartman, Lena Eliz, 566
Hartman, Lena J, 474
Hartman, Lottie Ella, 537
Hartman, Luma, 502
Hartman, Mabel C, 488
Hartman, Magdalena, 323
Hartman, Magdalena, 419
Hartman, Magdalena, 482
Hartman, Magdalena, 499
Hartman, Marie, 285
Hartman, Martha Lubo, 260
Hartman, Mary, 177
Hartman, Mary, 482
Hartman, Mary D Lebo, 263
Hartman, Mary Eliz, 415
Hartman, Mathew M L, 415
Hartman, Michael, 537
Hartman, Mildred Bar, 415
Hartman, Milton, 328
Hartman, Minnie Belle, 537
Hartman, Morris Miles, 537
Hartman, Nancy Ann, 403
Hartman, Ottie Loven, 396
Hartman, Pamela Ann, 415
Hartman, Raachael, 093
Hartman, Robert, 488
Hartman, Sarah, 093
Hartman, Sarah Hern, 328
Hartman, Sarah J, 403
Hartman, Shirley, 333
Hartman, Simon, 411
Hartman, Simon, 488
Hartman, Simon, 501
Hartman, Solomon, 328
Hartman, Theophilus, 035
Hartman, Thomas, 488
Hartman, William J, 488
Hartranft, Gen, 239
Hasgood, Howard D, 412
Hasgood, John, 412
Hasgood, Saraha El W, 412
Hass, Eva Matter, 254
Hass, John, 470
Hassinger, Aaron, 068
Hassinger, Aaron, 076
Hassinger, Aaron, 080
Hassinger, Aaron, 083
Hassinger, Aaron, 382
Hassinger, Aaron A, 079
Hassinger, Aaron E, 082
Hassinger, Abraham, 083
Hassinger, Alice L, 083
Hassinger, Allen E, 083
Hassinger, Alvena, 083
Hassinger, Alvena, 285
Hassinger, Amanda, 083
Hassinger, Anne M, 081
Hassinger, Arron E, 081
Hassinger, Carrie, 082
Hassinger, Carrie, 083
Hassinger, Catharine, 083
Hassinger, Catherine, 081
Hassinger, Catherine, 083
Hassinger, Catherine, 133
Hassinger, Christoph, 081
Hassinger, Claude R, 082
Hassinger, Clayton, 083
Hassinger, Cora, 082
Hassinger, Damon F, 082
Hassinger, Donald, 083

Hassinger, Dorothy, 080
Hassinger, Dorthy E, 083
Hassinger, Elias, 487
Hassinger, Elizabeth, 082
Hassinger, Elizabeth, 083
Hassinger, Elva H, 083
Hassinger, Elvin, 083
Hassinger, Emanuel, 082
Hassinger, Emma, 443
Hassinger, Emma E, 436
Hassinger, Emma S, 083
Hassinger, Emma S, 464
Hassinger, Esther, 080
Hassinger, Esther, 082
Hassinger, Esther, 245
Hassinger, Eugene L, 083
Hassinger, Eugene L, 134
Hassinger, Evan P, 049
Hassinger, George, 083
Hassinger, George E, 083
Hassinger, Henry, 170
Hassinger, Henry, 359
Hassinger, Henry T, 080
Hassinger, Henry T, 082
Hassinger, Herman, 081
Hassinger, Homer, 080
Hassinger, Homer E, 083
Hassinger, Homer F, 082
Hassinger, Irene, 082
Hassinger, Isaac W, 082
Hassinger, Jacob, 082
Hassinger, Jacob, 285
Hassinger, Jacob, 386
Hassinger, Jacob, 436
Hassinger, Jacob, 497
Hassinger, Jacob E, 080
Hassinger, Jacob E, 082
Hassinger, Jacob E, 099
Hassinger, Jacob J, 083
Hassinger, Jacob M, 083
Hassinger, Jacob S, 081
Hassinger, Jean, 083
Hassinger, Jennie, 082
Hassinger, Jennie, 144
Hassinger, Jennie, 145
Hassinger, Jennie, 188
Hassinger, Jeremiah, 080
Hassinger, Jeremiah, 082
Hassinger, Jeremiah, 245
Hassinger, Joel Adm, 083
Hassinger, Johannes, 082
Hassinger, John Dan, 081
Hassinger, John Hen, 083
Hassinger, John Jaco, 081
Hassinger, John Jaco, 082
Hassinger, John W, 083
Hassinger, Johnathan, 082
Hassinger, Kali, 487
Hassinger, Lester, 080
Hassinger, Lester, 367
Hassinger, Lester M, 083
Hassinger, Lillian J, 083
Hassinger, Louisa, 083
Hassinger, Louisa, 361
Hassinger, Lydia, 082
Hassinger, Lydia, 285
Hassinger, Lydia E, 083
Hassinger, M A, 278
Hassinger, Magdalen, 082
Hassinger, Maggie, 083
Hassinger, Margaret, 081
Hassinger, Maria, 081
Hassinger, Maria C, 082
Hassinger, Mary, 083
Hassinger, Mary A, 082

Hoffman, Eva Cathar, 391
Hoffman, Eva Eliz, 276
Hoffman, Eva Marie, 234
Hoffman, Family, 561
Hoffman, Fannie, 236
Hoffman, Faye, 178
Hoffman, Faye M, 496
Hoffman, Flora, 548
Hoffman, Florence, 560
Hoffman, Frances Ele, 240
Hoffman, Francis, 237
Hoffman, Francis, 238
Hoffman, Francis Cars, 243
Hoffman, Frank, 241
Hoffman, Frank C, 240
Hoffman, Frank H, 240
Hoffman, Frank J, 242
Hoffman, Fred E, 548
Hoffman, Frederich L, 479
Hoffman, Frederick E, 560
Hoffman, Frederick L, 234
Hoffman, G, 111
Hoffman, Geo Washin, 238
Hoffman, Geo Washin, 240
Hoffman, George, 018
Hoffman, George, 117
Hoffman, George, 182
Hoffman, George, 233
Hoffman, George, 237
Hoffman, George, 239
Hoffman, George, 240
Hoffman, George, 241
Hoffman, George, 242
Hoffman, George, 243
Hoffman, George, 244
Hoffman, George, 303
Hoffman, George, 392
Hoffman, George, 434
Hoffman, George, 449
Hoffman, George, 480
Hoffman, George, 505
Hoffman, George, 518
Hoffman, George Edw, 530
Hoffman, George Jr, 243
Hoffman, George L, 243
Hoffman, George M, 236
Hoffman, George M, 239
Hoffman, George W, 234
Hoffman, George W, 245
Hoffman, George Wel, 422
Hoffman, Gladys, 241
Hoffman, Grace Rebec, 301
Hoffman, Gurney Alv, 423
Hoffman, Guy, 318
Hoffman, Guy, 415
Hoffman, H B, 504
Hoffman, Hanicle, 015
Hoffman, Hanna, 033
Hoffman, Hanna, 034
Hoffman, Hanna Loui, 423
Hoffman, Hannah, 033
Hoffman, Hannah, 238
Hoffman, Hannah, 239
Hoffman, Hannah, 240
Hoffman, Hannah, 241
Hoffman, Hannah, 242
Hoffman, Hannah, 272
Hoffman, Hannah, 323
Hoffman, Hannah, 353
Hoffman, Hannah, 530
Hoffman, Hannah, 559
Hoffman, Hannah, 572
Hoffman, Hannah E, 241
Hoffman, Hannah Uhl, 241
Hoffman, Hannis John, 230

Hoffman, Harriet, 243
Hoffman, Harriet G, 129
Hoffman, Harry, 234
Hoffman, Harry A, 423
Hoffman, Harry H, 085
Hoffman, Harry H, 169
Hoffman, Harvey, 244
Hoffman, Hattie, 423
Hoffman, Helen, 446
Hoffman, Helen, 454
Hoffman, Helen M, 518
Hoffman, Helen May, 422
Hoffman, Helen May, 434
Hoffman, Henrietta, 239
Hoffman, Henrietta, 559
Hoffman, Henry, 017
Hoffman, Henry, 233
Hoffman, Henry, 237
Hoffman, Henry, 238
Hoffman, Henry, 243
Hoffman, Henry, 245
Hoffman, Henry, 538
Hoffman, Henry B, 237
Hoffman, Henry B, 463
Hoffman, Henry C, 559
Hoffman, Henry H, 239
Hoffman, Henry H, 245
Hoffman, Henry Monr, 422
Hoffman, Henry W, 244
Hoffman, Henry Wils, 562
Hoffman, Henry Wilso, 548
Hoffman, Henry Wilso, 560
Hoffman, Herbert T S, 560
Hoffman, Hester, 233
Hoffman, Hethe B, 130
Hoffman, Hir, 417
Hoffman, Hiram B, 242
Hoffman, Hohn P, 463
Hoffman, Ilen Myrle, 560
Hoffman, Irene, 234
Hoffman, Isaac, 027
Hoffman, Isaac, 233
Hoffman, Isaac, 242
Hoffman, Isaac, 243
Hoffman, Isaac, 272
Hoffman, Isaac Aaron, 242
Hoffman, Isaac B, 241
Hoffman, Isaac Petrus, 245
Hoffman, Isaac Sylve, 242
Hoffman, Isaac W, 026
Hoffman, Isaac White, 240
Hoffman, Isaac White, 530
Hoffman, Isabella, 242
Hoffman, Isaiah, 244
Hoffman, Jacob, 015
Hoffman, Jacob, 017
Hoffman, Jacob, 019
Hoffman, Jacob, 033
Hoffman, Jacob, 034
Hoffman, Jacob, 052
Hoffman, Jacob, 153
Hoffman, Jacob, 234
Hoffman, Jacob, 237
Hoffman, Jacob, 239
Hoffman, Jacob, 241
Hoffman, Jacob, 242
Hoffman, Jacob, 244
Hoffman, Jacob, 247
Hoffman, Jacob, 248
Hoffman, Jacob, 276
Hoffman, Jacob, 295
Hoffman, Jacob, 296
Hoffman, Jacob, 301
Hoffman, Jacob, 302
Hoffman, Jacob, 319

Hoffman, Jacob, 325
Hoffman, Jacob, 336
Hoffman, Jacob, 409
Hoffman, Jacob, 411
Hoffman, Jacob, 418
Hoffman, Jacob, 432
Hoffman, Jacob, 489
Hoffman, Jacob, 530
Hoffman, Jacob, 568
Hoffman, Jacob, 572
Hoffman, Jacob A, 238
Hoffman, Jacob Arth, 423
Hoffman, Jacob B, 051
Hoffman, Jacob B, 240
Hoffman, Jacob B, 432
Hoffman, Jacob D, 090
Hoffman, Jacob D, 432
Hoffman, Jacob D, 530
Hoffman, Jacob David, 240
Hoffman, Jacob Frank, 239
Hoffman, Jacob G, 240
Hoffman, Jacob H, 129
Hoffman, Jacob Jr, 024
Hoffman, Jacob Jr, 274
Hoffman, Jacob Jr, 292
Hoffman, Jacob Jr, 296
Hoffman, Jacob Jr, 303
Hoffman, Jacob Jr, 320
Hoffman, Jacob Jr, 568
Hoffman, Jacob P, 238
Hoffman, Jacob Peter, 237
Hoffman, Jacob T, 082
Hoffman, Jacob Tobias, 245
Hoffman, Jacobus, 241
Hoffman, Jame G, 234
Hoffman, James, 237
Hoffman, James, 241
Hoffman, James, 244
Hoffman, James, 463
Hoffman, James Bent, 241
Hoffman, James Frank, 559
Hoffman, Jane A, 161
Hoffman, Jane Crimby, 243
Hoffman, Jennie, 238
Hoffman, Jennie Ritz, 423
Hoffman, Joann M, 560
Hoffman, Joannah, 241
Hoffman, Johannes, 046
Hoffman, Johannes, 329
Hoffman, Johannes, 330
Hoffman, Johannes, 334
Hoffman, Johannes, 473
Hoffman, John, 015
Hoffman, John, 017
Hoffman, John, 024
Hoffman, John, 233
Hoffman, John, 234
Hoffman, John, 241
Hoffman, John, 242
Hoffman, John, 244
Hoffman, John, 247
Hoffman, John, 265
Hoffman, John, 266
Hoffman, John, 270
Hoffman, John, 272
Hoffman, John, 278
Hoffman, John, 291
Hoffman, John, 301
Hoffman, John, 303
Hoffman, John, 309
Hoffman, John, 319
Hoffman, John, 320
Hoffman, John, 327
Hoffman, John, 353
Hoffman, John, 391

Hoffman, John, 392
Hoffman, John, 462
Hoffman, John, 463
Hoffman, John, 464
Hoffman, John, 471
Hoffman, John, 473
Hoffman, John, 497
Hoffman, John, 515
Hoffman, John, 520
Hoffman, John, 548
Hoffman, John, 560
Hoffman, John, 561
Hoffman, John B, 245
Hoffman, John B, 437
Hoffman, John Benjam, 244
Hoffman, John C, 082
Hoffman, John C, 245
Hoffman, John C W V, 539
Hoffman, John Daniel, 560
Hoffman, John E, 568
Hoffman, John Esq, 017
Hoffman, John Esq, 019
Hoffman, John Esq, 286
Hoffman, John Esq, 309
Hoffman, John Esq, 329
Hoffman, John Esq, 344
Hoffman, John Gaman, 562
Hoffman, John George, 242
Hoffman, John George, 243
Hoffman, John George, 479
Hoffman, John H, 092
Hoffman, John H, 240
Hoffman, John Harper, 239
Hoffman, John Henry, 242
Hoffman, John Henry, 243
Hoffman, John III, 233
Hoffman, John Jacob, 236
Hoffman, John Jr, 232
Hoffman, John Jr, 562
Hoffman, John Lt, 232
Hoffman, John N III, 241
Hoffman, John N Jr, 241
Hoffman, John Nicho, 330
Hoffman, John Nicho, 335
Hoffman, John Nichol, 261
Hoffman, John Nickol, 235
Hoffman, John Nico, 033
Hoffman, John P, 452
Hoffman, John P, 462
Hoffman, John P, 539
Hoffman, John P, 541
Hoffman, John P, 562
Hoffman, John P Sr, 463
Hoffman, John Peter, 230
Hoffman, John Peter, 231
Hoffman, John Peter, 232
Hoffman, John Peter, 235
Hoffman, John Peter, 237
Hoffman, John Peter, 244
Hoffman, John Peter, 246
Hoffman, John Peter, 248
Hoffman, John Peter, 261
Hoffman, John Peter, 377
Hoffman, John Peter, 402
Hoffman, John Peter, 422
Hoffman, John Peter, 464
Hoffman, John Peter, 480
Hoffman, John Peter III, 237
Hoffman, John Philip, 245
Hoffman, John R, 272
Hoffman, John Robert, 239
Hoffman, John Sr, 280
Hoffman, John T, 129
Hoffman, John T, 559
Hoffman, John Tobias, 245

Hoffman, John W, 026
Hoffman, John W, 234
Hoffman, John W, 241
Hoffman, John W, 477
Hoffman, John W, 485
Hoffman, John W, 511
Hoffman, John W, 536
Hoffman, John W, 547
Hoffman, John W, 548
Hoffman, John W, 553
Hoffman, John W, 559
Hoffman, John Welker, 559
Hoffman, Jonas, 122
Hoffman, Jonas, 234
Hoffman, Jonas, 236
Hoffman, Jonas, 238
Hoffman, Jonas, 245
Hoffman, Jonas, 247
Hoffman, Jonas, 258
Hoffman, Jonas, 264
Hoffman, Jonas, 301
Hoffman, Jonas, 302
Hoffman, Jonas, 445
Hoffman, Jonas, 463
Hoffman, Jonas, 482
Hoffman, Jonas David, 245
Hoffman, Jonas J, 134
Hoffman, Jonas W, 130
Hoffman, Jonas W, 422
Hoffman, Jonas W, 425
Hoffman, Jonas W, 464
Hoffman, Jonathan, 237
Hoffman, Jonathan, 241
Hoffman, Jonathan, 243
Hoffman, Jonathan, 244
Hoffman, Jonathan, 480
Hoffman, Jonathan W, 241
Hoffman, Joseph, 034
Hoffman, Joseph, 234
Hoffman, Joseph, 237
Hoffman, Joseph, 239
Hoffman, Joseph, 241
Hoffman, Joseph, 245
Hoffman, Joseph, 530
Hoffman, Joseph F, 241
Hoffman, Joseph Hen, 240
Hoffman, Joseph R, 245
Hoffman, Joseph W, 239
Hoffman, Josiah Peter, 244
Hoffman, Jossiah, 236
Hoffman, Juliana, 242
Hoffman, Juliana, 515
Hoffman, Karen, 189
Hoffman, Karen Yvone, 301
Hoffman, Kate, 237
Hoffman, Kate C, 241
Hoffman, Kathryn L, 560
Hoffman, Katie Camel, 422
Hoffman, Katie L, 252
Hoffman, Kermit, 560
Hoffman, Kinda, 238
Hoffman, Kinda Alv, 422
Hoffman, Kinda Alver, 425
Hoffman, Larry, 241
Hoffman, Laura May, 423
Hoffman, Lewis C, 439
Hoffman, Lillian Aman, 237
Hoffman, Lizzie, 232
Hoffman, Lizzie, 241
Hoffman, Loretta, 034
Hoffman, Lottie, 241
Hoffman, Lottie, 548
Hoffman, Lottie Leon, 560
Hoffman, Louisianna, 237
Hoffman, Lucetta, 241

Hoover, Chadarina, 024
Hoover, Charles, 064
Hoover, Charles, 066
Hoover, Charles, 067
Hoover, Charles, 071
Hoover, Charles, 113
Hoover, Charles, 114
Hoover, Charles, 130
Hoover, Charles, 297
Hoover, Charles, 298
Hoover, Charles, 311
Hoover, Charles, 332
Hoover, Charles, 423
Hoover, Charles, 496
Hoover, Charles, 497
Hoover, Charles A, 311
Hoover, Charles A, 543
Hoover, Charles Alfred, 495
Hoover, Charles Elw, 162
Hoover, Christian, 425
Hoover, Christian, 435
Hoover, Christian, 494
Hoover, Christian, 495
Hoover, Christiana, 543
Hoover, Christiana A, 311
Hoover, Christiana Alv, 495
Hoover, Clarence, 311
Hoover, Clarence, 496
Hoover, Clement Elwo, 496
Hoover, Clement Elwo, 542
Hoover, D Frank, 295
Hoover, Daniel, 297
Hoover, Daniel, 496
Hoover, Daniel, 497
Hoover, Daniel Frank, 296
Hoover, Daniel Frank, 298
Hoover, Daniel Frank, 496
Hoover, David, 494
Hoover, David, 495
Hoover, Eddie, 396
Hoover, Edmond, 064
Hoover, Edmond, 065
Hoover, Edmond, 161
Hoover, Edmond, 176
Hoover, Edmund, 404
Hoover, Edmund, 491
Hoover, Edmund, 495
Hoover, Edmund, 496
Hoover, Edmund, 541
Hoover, Edmund, 542
Hoover, Edward, 297
Hoover, Edward, 298
Hoover, Edward, 357
Hoover, Edward, 358
Hoover, Edward, 440
Hoover, Edward, 442
Hoover, Edward, 443
Hoover, Edward, 454
Hoover, Edward, 496
Hoover, Effie, 350
Hoover, Effie, 396
Hoover, Elias, 067
Hoover, Elias, 296
Hoover, Elias, 297
Hoover, Elias, 298
Hoover, Elias, 320
Hoover, Elias, 322
Hoover, Elias, 443
Hoover, Elias, 496
Hoover, Elias, 516
Hoover, Elisabeth, 572
Hoover, Eliz Jane, 497
Hoover, Elizabeth, 024
Hoover, Elizabeth, 033
Hoover, Elizabeth, 067

Hoover, Elizabeth, 088
Hoover, Elizabeth, 239
Hoover, Elizabeth, 240
Hoover, Elizabeth, 296
Hoover, Elizabeth, 311
Hoover, Elizabeth, 425
Hoover, Elizabeth, 435
Hoover, Elizabeth, 448
Hoover, Elizabeth, 494
Hoover, Elizabeth, 495
Hoover, Elizabeth, 496
Hoover, Elizabeth, 530
Hoover, Elizabeth Ann, 495
Hoover, Ella, 497
Hoover, Ellen, 235
Hoover, Ellen Jane, 495
Hoover, Elwood, 136
Hoover, Elwood, 311
Hoover, Elwood, 333
Hoover, Elwood, 412
Hoover, Emma, 333
Hoover, Emma E, 496
Hoover, Emma J, 422
Hoover, Emma J, 496
Hoover, Family, 542
Hoover, Fay M, 176
Hoover, Faye Hoffm, 178
Hoover, Florence, 311
Hoover, Florence, 496
Hoover, Florence, 543
Hoover, Frank, 331
Hoover, Frank, 332
Hoover, Frederick, 297
Hoover, Frederick, 298
Hoover, Fredrick, 496
Hoover, George, 059
Hoover, Gilbert W, 134
Hoover, Grant, 238
Hoover, Hannah, 311
Hoover, Hannah, 496
Hoover, Harold, 154
Hoover, Harold, 163
Hoover, Harold, 351
Hoover, Harold, 396
Hoover, Harold C, 134
Hoover, Harold C, 162
Hoover, Harvey F, 379
Hoover, Harvey F, 395
Hoover, Harvey F, 396
Hoover, Harvey Harp, 423
Hoover, Helen, 153
Hoover, Helen, 154
Hoover, Helen Male, 178
Hoover, Henrich, 016
Hoover, Henrietta, 496
Hoover, Henrietta, 543
Hoover, Henrietta L, 311
Hoover, Henrietta Lou, 422
Hoover, Henrietta Lou, 496
Hoover, Henrietta Love, 496
Hoover, Henry, 392
Hoover, Henry, 422
Hoover, Henry, 495
Hoover, Henry, 496
Hoover, Henry, 497
Hoover, Herbert, 349
Hoover, Herbert, 396
Hoover, Ida R, 422
Hoover, Ida Rebecca, 497
Hoover, Isaac, 131
Hoover, Isaac, 423
Hoover, Isaac F, 067
Hoover, Isaac F, 130
Hoover, Isaac Frank, 164
Hoover, Isabella, 422

Hoover, Isabella, 497
Hoover, Isaiah, 422
Hoover, Isaiah, 496
Hoover, Isiah, 496
Hoover, Jacob, 019
Hoover, Jacob, 302
Hoover, Jacob, 386
Hoover, Jacob, 423
Hoover, Jacob, 480
Hoover, Jacob, 483
Hoover, Jacob, 493
Hoover, Jacob, 494
Hoover, Jacob, 497
Hoover, Jacob, 498
Hoover, Jacob, 539
Hoover, Jacob, 544
Hoover, Jacob, 545
Hoover, Jacob, 557
Hoover, Jacob, 558
Hoover, Jacob Jr, 494
Hoover, Jacob Jr, 495
Hoover, Jacob Jr, 497
Hoover, Jacob Sr, 497
Hoover, Johann Jacob, 494
Hoover, Johann Phil D, 494
Hoover, John, 024
Hoover, John, 067
Hoover, John, 131
Hoover, John, 285
Hoover, John, 297
Hoover, John, 298
Hoover, John, 311
Hoover, John, 360
Hoover, John, 422
Hoover, John, 423
Hoover, John, 446
Hoover, John, 456
Hoover, John, 491
Hoover, John, 493
Hoover, John, 494
Hoover, John, 495
Hoover, John, 496
Hoover, John, 497
Hoover, John E, 130
Hoover, John Edmond, 542
Hoover, John Edmund, 496
Hoover, John Est Jr, 489
Hoover, John H, 496
Hoover, John Jr, 490
Hoover, John Jr, 491
Hoover, John Jr, 495
Hoover, John Ludwig, 494
Hoover, John R, 139
Hoover, John Sr, 456
Hoover, John Sr, 490
Hoover, John Sr, 491
Hoover, John Sr, 514
Hoover, John Sr, 516
Hoover, John Sr, 517
Hoover, Jonas, 496
Hoover, Jonathan, 495
Hoover, Joseph, 495
Hoover, Joshiah, 065
Hoover, Josiah, 064
Hoover, Josiah, 303
Hoover, Josiah, 446
Hoover, Josiah, 477
Hoover, Josiah, 485
Hoover, Josiah, 491
Hoover, Josiah, 495
Hoover, Josiah, 496
Hoover, Josiah, 540
Hoover, Josiah, 543
Hoover, Katie A, 067
Hoover, Katie Celes, 443

Hoover, Katie Celeste, 496
Hoover, Landon, 175
Hoover, Landon J, 176
Hoover, Landon Jos, 178
Hoover, Landon Josia, 542
Hoover, Landon Josiah, 496
Hoover, Leah, 065
Hoover, Leah, 067
Hoover, Leah, 297
Hoover, Leah, 298
Hoover, Leah, 333
Hoover, Leah A, 496
Hoover, Leah Ann B, 130
Hoover, Leah E Bender, 496
Hoover, Leander, 422
Hoover, Leander, 496
Hoover, Lee, 351
Hoover, Lent, 136
Hoover, Leo, 350
Hoover, Leo, 394
Hoover, Leo, 396
Hoover, Lester, 351
Hoover, Lester, 396
Hoover, Lillian, 065
Hoover, Lillian, 065
Hoover, Lillian, 334
Hoover, Lillian, 495
Hoover, Lillian, 496
Hoover, Lillian, 543
Hoover, Lillian Wetzel, 412
Hoover, Lillian Wetzel, 541
Hoover, Lillie, 064
Hoover, Lillie, 176
Hoover, Lillie A, 491
Hoover, Lilly Margaret, 496
Hoover, Lizzie, 285
Hoover, Lottie, 379
Hoover, Lottie, 495
Hoover, Lottie, 540
Hoover, Lottie, 541
Hoover, Lottie E, 176
Hoover, Lottie H, 065
Hoover, Lottie M, 396
Hoover, Lottie May, 496
Hoover, Lottie May, 542
Hoover, Lou Gehrig, 178
Hoover, Louisa, 392
Hoover, Lovina, 496
Hoover, Lovina, 497
Hoover, Ludwig Paul, 059
Hoover, Magdalena, 480
Hoover, Margaret, 298
Hoover, Margaret, 494
Hoover, Margaret, 543
Hoover, Margaret, 543
Hoover, Margaret E, 496
Hoover, Margaret Elen, 311
Hoover, Margaret Ellen, 495
Hoover, Margaret Evit, 541
Hoover, Margaret L, 297
Hoover, Maria Magda, 386
Hoover, Maria Magdal, 494
Hoover, Maria Magdal, 564
Hoover, Maria Margar, 422
Hoover, Maria Mary, 495
Hoover, Martha Jane, 497
Hoover, Mary, 131
Hoover, Mary, 297
Hoover, Mary, 298
Hoover, Mary, 311
Hoover, Mary, 334
Hoover, Mary, 423
Hoover, Mary, 496
Hoover, Mary, 497
Hoover, Mary, 531

Hoover, Mary A, 442
Hoover, Mary Ann, 360
Hoover, Mary Ann, 443
Hoover, Mary Ann, 496
Hoover, Mary E, 067
Hoover, Mary E, 130
Hoover, Mary Ellen, 497
Hoover, Mary I, 295
Hoover, Mary J, 422
Hoover, Mary J, 496
Hoover, Mary Jane, 495
Hoover, Mary Jane, 543
Hoover, Matthaeus, 494
Hoover, Merlin C, 134
Hoover, Michael, 494
Hoover, Myrl Grubb, 161
Hoover, Myrl Grubb, 162
Hoover, Nicholas, 497
Hoover, Paty, 024
Hoover, Paul, 285
Hoover, Paul, 311
Hoover, Paul C, 496
Hoover, Peter, 496
Hoover, Peter, 497
Hoover, Priscilla, 422
Hoover, Priscilla, 496
Hoover, Rebecca, 495
Hoover, Rebecca, 497
Hoover, Rose Ann, 422
Hoover, Rose Ann, 497
Hoover, Sadie Ellen, 422
Hoover, Sadie Ellen, 497
Hoover, Samuel, 117
Hoover, Samuel, 423
Hoover, Samuel, 426
Hoover, Samuel, 495
Hoover, Sarah, 117
Hoover, Sarah, 282
Hoover, Sarah, 297
Hoover, Sarah, 298
Hoover, Sarah, 311
Hoover, Sarah, 437
Hoover, Sarah, 438
Hoover, Sarah, 495
Hoover, Sarah, 496
Hoover, Sarah, 543
Hoover, Sarah Ann, 422
Hoover, Sarah Bellis, 423
Hoover, Sarah E, 495
Hoover, Solomon, 497
Hoover, Sula, 496
Hoover, Sula, 542
Hoover, Susan, 295
Hoover, Susan, 356
Hoover, Susan Aman, 296
Hoover, Susan E, 496
Hoover, Susanna, 040
Hoover, Susanna, 483
Hoover, Susanna, 494
Hoover, Susanna, 496
Hoover, Susanna, 497
Hoover, Susanna, 510
Hoover, Susanna, 539
Hoover, Susanna, 545
Hoover, Susanna, 557
Hoover, Susanna, 558
Hoover, Thomas, 495
Hoover, Thomas, 496
Hoover, Thomas, 497
Hoover, Tobias, 422
Hoover, Tobias, 496
Hoover, Todd F, 162
Hoover, Tony, 494
Hoover, Ursula, 494
Hoover, W, 440

Kissinger, John A, 544
Kissinger, John A, 552
Kissinger, John F, 537
Kissinger, John Henry, 481
Kissinger, John M, 566
Kissinger, Jonas, 504
Kissinger, Jonas Roy, 537
Kissinger, Jonas Roy, 544
Kissinger, Joseph A, 504
Kissinger, Kermit, 560
Kissinger, Lavina, 378
Kissinger, Leon, 132
Kissinger, Leon Jay, 537
Kissinger, Leonard, 560
Kissinger, Levi Jacob, 538
Kissinger, Lottie, 485
Kissinger, Lottie, 548
Kissinger, Lottie, 549
Kissinger, Lottie, 550
Kissinger, Lottie L, 562
Kissinger, Louisa, 129
Kissinger, Lovina, 126
Kissinger, Lydia, 478
Kissinger, Mabel, 562
Kissinger, Mabel S, 541
Kissinger, Margaret, 037
Kissinger, Margaret, 164
Kissinger, Margaret, 536
Kissinger, Margaret A, 538
Kissinger, Maria E, 538
Kissinger, Maria M, 560
Kissinger, Marion, 538
Kissinger, Mark D, 552
Kissinger, Mark K, 552
Kissinger, Mary, 290
Kissinger, Mary A, 537
Kissinger, Mary A, 544
Kissinger, Mary Ann, 537
Kissinger, Mary L, 538
Kissinger, Mary M, 558
Kissinger, Maude E, 423
Kissinger, May Leona, 566
Kissinger, Michael A, 560
Kissinger, Mildred, 064
Kissinger, Mildred E, 538
Kissinger, Minnie, 537
Kissinger, Mrs Charles, 287
Kissinger, Paul W, 538
Kissinger, Pauline, 290
Kissinger, Peter, 017
Kissinger, Peter, 528
Kissinger, Priscilla, 423
Kissinger, Priscilla, 560
Kissinger, Ray A, 566
Kissinger, Rebecca, 311
Kissinger, Rebecca, 478
Kissinger, Rebecca, 495
Kissinger, Rebecca, 560
Kissinger, Robert L, 538
Kissinger, Roy Chas, 537
Kissinger, Roy Elmer, 566
Kissinger, Roy m, 537
Kissinger, Sallie, 478
Kissinger, Sallie, 552
Kissinger, Sarah, 249
Kissinger, Sarah, 537
Kissinger, Sarah, 538
Kissinger, Sarah Cath, 537
Kissinger, Susan A, 538
Kissinger, Susanna, 324
Kissinger, Susannah, 237
Kissinger, Susannah, 403
Kissinger, Thomas, 541
Kissinger, Thomas H, 481
Kissinger, Thomas H, 538

Kissinger, Thomas M, 536
Kissinger, Thomas M, 537
Kissinger, Verna Elan, 538
Kitzmiller, Maggie, 229
Kitzmiller, Sarah, 359
Kitzmiller, Theodo G, 381
Klar, Catharine, 228
Klar, Philip, 228
Klark, Christina, 249
Klauser, Catherine, 567
Klein, Maggie, 193
Klein, Maria, 458
Klein, Susanna, 375
Kline, Bill, 132
Kline, Godlep, 015
Kline, John, 556
Kline, Unc, 104
Klinger, ?, 234
Klinger, ?, 291
Klinger, A, 276
Klinger, Agnes, 126
Klinger, Agnes, 131
Klinger, Agnes, 252
Klinger, Agnes S, 252
Klinger, Alex, 138
Klinger, Alex, 520
Klinger, Alexander, 016
Klinger, Alexander, 139
Klinger, Alexander, 194
Klinger, Alexander, 242
Klinger, Alexander, 248
Klinger, Alexander, 252
Klinger, Alexander, 354
Klinger, Alexander, 535
Klinger, Alexander, 551
Klinger, Alexander, 552
Klinger, Alfred, 252
Klinger, Alice, 533
Klinger, Alice Regina, 535
Klinger, Amanda, 077
Klinger, Amanda S, 411
Klinger, Amanda S, 441
Klinger, Anna, 252
Klinger, Anna, 529
Klinger, Anna Barbara, 324
Klinger, Anna Mary, 489
Klinger, Annie, 164
Klinger, Annie, 170
Klinger, Annie, 252
Klinger, Annie B, 252
Klinger, Arlene, 351
Klinger, Arlene, 504
Klinger, Arlene, 508
Klinger, Arthur, 355
Klinger, Barbara, 530
Klinger, Benneville, 252
Klinger, Bernice Pauli, 252
Klinger, Bessie May, 488
Klinger, Betty, 133
Klinger, Blanche, 529
Klinger, Carl, 439
Klinger, Caroline, 479
Klinger, Caroline, 483
Klinger, Carolyn, 517
Klinger, Carrie, 177
Klinger, Cath Edith, 252
Klinger, Catharine, 529
Klinger, Catharine, 558
Klinger, Catherine, 252
Klinger, Catherine, 403
Klinger, Catherine, 500
Klinger, Charles, 138
Klinger, Charles, 497
Klinger, Charlotte, 324
Klinger, Clayton G, 113

Klinger, Cora L, 049
Klinger, Daniel, 113
Klinger, Daniel, 135
Klinger, Daniel, 143
Klinger, Daniel, 161
Klinger, Daniel, 251
Klinger, Daniel, 252
Klinger, Daniel, 349
Klinger, Daniel, 529
Klinger, Daniel A, 194
Klinger, Daniel L, 264
Klinger, Dotty, 522
Klinger, E Leroy, 355
Klinger, Earl, 355
Klinger, Edna, 169
Klinger, Edna I, 165
Klinger, Edna Irene, 252
Klinger, Edward, 153
Klinger, Edwin, 113
Klinger, Edwin, 180
Klinger, Edwin M, 252
Klinger, Effie E, 160
Klinger, Effie Emeline, 252
Klinger, Elba, 461
Klinger, Elba Mae, 449
Klinger, Elias, 177
Klinger, Elias, 249
Klinger, Elias, 252
Klinger, Elias, 253
Klinger, Elias, 482
Klinger, Elias, 548
Klinger, Elias, 551
Klinger, Elias, 552
Klinger, Elias, 562
Klinger, Elizabeth, 143
Klinger, Elizabeth, 168
Klinger, Elizabeth, 260
Klinger, Elizabeth, 354
Klinger, Elizabeth, 411
Klinger, Elizabeth, 423
Klinger, Elizabeth, 488
Klinger, Elizabeth, 558
Klinger, Elizabeth W, 143
Klinger, Ellen R, 077
Klinger, Elmer, 132
Klinger, Elsie A, 535
Klinger, Elva, 522
Klinger, Emaline, 113
Klinger, Emaline, 264
Klinger, Emanuel, 129
Klinger, Emeline, 183
Klinger, Emeline, 194
Klinger, Emma, 115
Klinger, Eston, 355
Klinger, Eva Alvesta, 113
Klinger, Eva Catherine, 382
Klinger, Eve, 315
Klinger, Fae, 177
Klinger, Ferle Machala, 252
Klinger, Frances, 252
Klinger, Frederick E, 252
Klinger, Gene D, 522
Klinger, George, 016
Klinger, George, 020
Klinger, George, 050
Klinger, George, 324
Klinger, George, 367
Klinger, Guy, 177
Klinger, Hanna, 404
Klinger, Harrie I, 285
Klinger, Harry C, 349
Klinger, Harry E, 328
Klinger, Harry E, 404
Klinger, Hattie, 481
Klinger, Henry, 165

Klinger, Hilda, 160
Klinger, Hilda, 180
Klinger, Homer Ramer, 252
Klinger, Howard, 101
Klinger, Israel, 517
Klinger, Jacob, 135
Klinger, Jacob, 176
Klinger, Jacob, 252
Klinger, James, 252
Klinger, Jennie L, 165
Klinger, Jeremiah, 252
Klinger, Joh Philip, 019
Klinger, Johannes, 354
Klinger, John, 238
Klinger, John, 529
Klinger, John Adam, 483
Klinger, John F, 165
Klinger, John George, 382
Klinger, John Henry, 252
Klinger, Jonathan, 135
Klinger, Jonathan, 139
Klinger, Jonathan, 180
Klinger, Jonathan, 252
Klinger, Jonathan, 556
Klinger, Jonathan, 558
Klinger, Jonathan D, 160
Klinger, Kate, 113
Klinger, Kate, 165
Klinger, Kathryn S, 252
Klinger, Katie, 309
Klinger, Katie, 317
Klinger, Katie, 501
Klinger, Katie Emeline, 252
Klinger, Kirby Jonath, 253
Klinger, Laura, 165
Klinger, Laura Agnes, 252
Klinger, Laura M, 552
Klinger, Leon, 522
Klinger, Leon, 571
Klinger, Lizzie, 285
Klinger, Lizzie, 311
Klinger, Lizzie, 496
Klinger, Lorraine, 355
Klinger, Lotta, 253
Klinger, Lottie, 552
Klinger, Louise, 431
Klinger, Lydia, 483
Klinger, Magdalena, 194
Klinger, Magdalena, 242
Klinger, Magdalena, 551
Klinger, Magdalena, 552
Klinger, Maggie, 161
Klinger, Maggie, 252
Klinger, Maggie McCl, 253
Klinger, Maria Cath, 517
Klinger, Mariah, 176
Klinger, Marie Eliz, 322
Klinger, Marietta, 253
Klinger, Mark F, 113
Klinger, Mark F, 317
Klinger, Mary, 078
Klinger, Mary, 242
Klinger, Mary, 253
Klinger, Mary, 275
Klinger, Mary, 290
Klinger, Mary, 328
Klinger, Mary, 382
Klinger, Mary Almeda, 252
Klinger, Mary E, 295
Klinger, Mary E, 562
Klinger, Mary Ellen, 177
Klinger, Minnie Bulah, 252
Klinger, Monroe, 488
Klinger, Monroe, 535
Klinger, Moody, 252

Klinger, Mr Leon Jr, 569
Klinger, Mrs Leon, 571
Klinger, Mrs Leon Jr, 569
Klinger, Olive Maria, 252
Klinger, Pat, 065
Klinger, Peter, 017
Klinger, Peter, 243
Klinger, Peter, 252
Klinger, Peter, 517
Klinger, Philip, 242
Klinger, Philip, 330
Klinger, Philip, 558
Klinger, Preston, 170
Klinger, Preston, 176
Klinger, Preston A, 164
Klinger, Preston A, 252
Klinger, Preston E, 049
Klinger, Preston Elias, 252
Klinger, R E, 104
Klinger, R M, 104
Klinger, Ralph W, 113
Klinger, Ralph Wilbert, 252
Klinger, Ray A, 461
Klinger, Ronie Druella, 252
Klinger, Ronie Druella, 253
Klinger, Roscoe, 077
Klinger, Roscoe, 099
Klinger, Roscoe Milt, 252
Klinger, Roy Austin, 449
Klinger, Ruth Ann, 309
Klinger, Ruth E, 113
Klinger, Sallie, 537
Klinger, Sallie L, 478
Klinger, Sarah, 129
Klinger, Sarah, 248
Klinger, Sarah, 253
Klinger, Sarah, 500
Klinger, Sarah, 512
Klinger, Sarah, 531
Klinger, Sarah, 551
Klinger, Simon, 078
Klinger, Simon, 252
Klinger, Stanley, 309
Klinger, Susanna, 529
Klinger, Violet, 355
Klinger, W S, 104
Klinger, Walter, 183
Klinger, Walter E, 113
Klinger, Walter Edwin, 252
Klinger, Wellington, 077
Klinger, Wellington, 078
Klinger, Wellington, 079
Klinger, Wellington, 252
Klinger, William, 252
Klinger, William A, 252
Klingere, Caroline, 499
Klock, David, 164
Klock, David, 170
Klock, David, 185
Klock, Louise, 164
Klock, Ruth, 351
Klouser, Arthur L, 196
Klouser, Ellen, 425
Klouser, Joel, 425
Klouser, Shirley L, 196
Knapp, Rebecca E, 185
Knecht, Barbara, 470
Knecht, Thomas Jr, 349
Knerr, Anna Catharina, 391
Knerr, Daniel, 391
Knerr, Isaac, 391
Knerr, Lovina, 391
Knerr, Sarah, 537
Kniley, Helen, 169
Knisely, Dr Samuel H, 108

611

Myers, John, 015
Myers, Mary, 425
Myers, Sallie, 069
Myers, Sarah, 391
Naagely, Hanna, 046
Nace, Daniel, 566
Nace, John, 566
Nace, Kate, 264
Nace, Larue, 566
Nace, Mary Jane, 355
Nace, Samuel O, 359
Nace, Sarah Ann, 058
Nagely, Benton Pierce, 047
Nagely, Catherine, 046
Nagely, Daniel, 046
Nagely, Elizabeth, 046
Nagely, Emily, 046
Nagely, George, 045
Nagely, George, 046
Nagely, George S, 047
Nagely, Hanna, 046
Nagely, Henry Calvin, 047
Nagely, Isaac, 047
Nagely, Jacob, 045
Nagely, Jo, 046
Nagely, John, 045
Nagely, John, 046
Nagely, Joseph, 046
Nagely, Magdalena, 045
Nagely, Magdalena, 046
Nagely, Mary, 046
Nagely, Mary, 047
Nagely, Mary Magd, 046
Nagely, Nevin Edgar, 047
Nagely, Rebecca, 046
Nagely, Sara, 045
Nagley, Annie, 046
Nagley, Catharine, 047
Nagley, Catherine, 046
Nagley, Charlotta, 047
Nagley, Daniel, 046
Nagley, Daniel, 047
Nagley, David, 047
Nagley, Ella A, 047
Nagley, Emelia, 047
Nagley, Emma E, 047
Nagley, Emma S, 047
Nagley, George, 047
Nagley, George Edwin, 047
Nagley, Hannah, 046
Nagley, Henrietta, 047
Nagley, Isaac, 046
Nagley, Isreal Penn, 047
Nagley, Jelania, 047
Nagley, John A, 047
Nagley, John Frede, 047
Nagley, Joseph, 046
Nagley, Katie, 047
Nagley, Leah Jane, 047
Nagley, Margaret, 046
Nagley, Maria, 046
Nagley, Mary Ann, 047
Nagley, Milton, 046
Nagley, Q Maggie, 046
Nagley, Salome, 047
Nagley, Sara, 046
Nagley, Sarah, 047
Nagley, Selesta, 047
Nagley, William, 046
Nartz, Adam, 015
Naubringer, Adam, 287
Neagley, Bob, 104
Neagley, Caroline, 044
Neagley, Caroline, 265
Neagley, George, 044

Neagley, George, 049
Neagley, George, 079
Neagley, George, 146
Neagley, George, 148
Neagley, George, 265
Neagley, George, 412
Neagley, Margaret, 276
Neagley, Margaret, 360
Neagley, Mary Magd, 056
Nece, Daniel, 025
Nece, Daniel F, 025
Nece, Sarah, 025
Neff, Jacob, 121
Neff, Margaret, 121
Negley, Anna Maria, 232
Negley, Catherine, 232
Negley, Daniel, 232
Negley, Elizabeth, 232
Negley, George, 232
Negley, Joseph, 232
Negley, Magdalena, 232
Negley, Sarah, 232
Neidlinger, Jonathan, 529
Neiffer, Sarah A, 311
Neiffer, W G, 311
Neil, William, 532
Neiman, Catharine, 300
Neiman, Charles, 252
Neiman, Conrad, 300
Neiman, Delton Wilb, 252
Neiman, Ellen, 143
Neiman, Israel, 252
Neiman, Israel, 309
Neiman, Samuel M, 072
Neiman, Sue, 252
Ncimants, Catharine, 300
Neimen, Melvin Arlin, 252
Neitz, Rev S, 148
Nelson, Anna, 011
Nelson, Brigitta, 011
Nelson, Gloria, 192
Nelson, Henry, 148
Nelson, Magdalena, 011
Nelson, Michael L, 012
Nelson, Peter, 011
Nessport, James A, 182
Nessport, Linda, 182
Netzelius, Otto, 011
Neufer, Dr P Dale, 140
Newbaker, Anna Marg, 557
Newbaker, Martin, 557
Newbaker, Mary M M, 556
Newbaker, Mary M M, 557
Newbecker, Elisabeth, 244
Newbecker, Jo Martin, 244
Newbecker, John, 243
Newbecker, Mar Sara, 244
Newbecker, Martin, 243
Newbecker, Mary Mag, 244
Newhart, Rev J S, 312
Newhart, Rev J S, 511
Ney, Daniel, 517
Ney, Elizabeth, 039
Ney, Elizabeth, 259
Ney, Elizabeth, 325
Ney, Elizabeth, 356
Ney, Elizabeth, 517
Ney, Justina, 259
Ney, Michael, 259
Ney, Paul, 517
Neyswender, Henry, 025
Neyswender, Henry P, 025
Neyswender, Rebecca, 025
Nicholas, J B, 026
Nielsson, Jonas, 011

Niger, Arthur, 015
Nigla, George, 015
Nigley, George, 016
Nillson, Annika, 011
Nilsson, Andrew, 012
Nilsson, Anna, 012
Nilsson, Catherine, 012
Nilsson, Christina, 012
Nilsson, Gertrude, 012
Nilsson, Helene, 012
Nilsson, Michael, 012
Nilsson, Michael L, 012
Nilsson, Mous, 012
Nilsson, Nicholas, 012
Nilsson, Olaf, 011
Nilsson, Peter, 011
Nilsson, Zacharius, 012
Nissly, Anne, 525
Nissly, Martin, 524
Nissly, Martin, 525
Noble, Patsy, 136
Noecker, Benjamin, 308
Noecker, Catharine, 308
Noecker, Christian, 308
Noecker, Christian Jr, 308
Noecker, Christopher, 308
Noecker, Elisabeth, 308
Noecker, Henrich, 308
Noecker, Jacob, 308
Noecker, Johannes, 308
Nolan, Annie, 067
Nolan, Asbury, 067
Nolan, Edith Cordella, 067
Nolan, Emanuel, 067
Nolan, Emeline, 067
Nolan, Howard H, 067
Nolan, Jacob, 067
Nolan, Lotta, 067
Nolan, Lucinda, 067
Nolan, Lyman F, 067
Nolan, Mary, 051
Nolan, Mary, 066
Nolan, Mary, 067
Nolan, Richard, 051
Nolan, Richard, 053
Nolan, Richard, 066
Nolan, Richard, 067
Nolan, Richard, 283
Nolan, Rickert, 017
Nolan, Sarah, 067
Nolan, Sidney Ann, 067
Nolan, Sydney, 283
Nolan, William, 067
Nolen, Richard, 117
Noll, Anna Mary, 059
Noll, Cath, 262
Noll, Daniel, 531
Noll, Daniel, 532
Noll, Elias, 262
Noll, John, 245
Noll, Marlin, 396
Noll, Mary, 356
Noll, Rev Simon, 515
Noll, Sarah, 088
Nonneman, Catharine, 429
Norris, Andrew P, 518
Norris, Blair, 518
Norris, David, 518
Norris, David, 521
Norris, Joshua Elias, 518
Norris, Lori, 521
Norris, Louise, 518
Novinger, ?, 282
Novinger, Adaline M, 148
Novinger, Adaline M, 299

Novinger, Alice, 245
Novinger, Anna Mary, 149
Novinger, Annie J, 266
Novinger, Ansella, 301
Novinger, Carl C, 301
Novinger, Catharine, 245
Novinger, Catherine, 246
Novinger, Charles E, 301
Novinger, Christina, 246
Novinger, Dewalt, 241
Novinger, Dora, 301
Novinger, Edna R, 301
Novinger, Edwin, 069
Novinger, Edwin L, 134
Novinger, Elizabeth, 301
Novinger, Harry W, 301
Novinger, Isaac, 245
Novinger, Isaac, 373
Novinger, Jacob, 148
Novinger, Jacob, 149
Novinger, Jacob, 299
Novinger, Jacob, 301
Novinger, Jake, 154
Novinger, James, 301
Novinger, Jonathan, 245
Novinger, Jonathan, 246
Novinger, Jonathan C, 245
Novinger, Jonathan Jr, 246
Novinger, Joseph A, 301
Novinger, Joseph N, 301
Novinger, Kathryn S, 301
Novinger, Leah, 266
Novinger, Lizzie V, 301
Novinger, Margaret, 275
Novinger, Margaretha, 241
Novlnger, Mary, 241
Novinger, Mary A, 301
Novinger, Raymond, 301
Novinger, Sarah Alice, 245
Nowacer, Susanna, 369
Null, John, 108
Null, John, 245
Nutt, Amanda, 100
Nutt, Ann, 100
Nutt, Anna J, 100
Nutt, Cora A, 100
Nutt, Emma, 100
Nutt, Emma D, 100
Nutt, Helen, 100
Nutt, Jane W, 100
Nutt, John, 100
Nutt, John Harper, 100
Nutt, John J, 099
Nutt, John Jacob, 100
Nutt, Jonathan, 100
Nutt, Levi, 100
Nutt, Lewis E, 100
Nutt, Liza, 100
Nutt, Martha, 100
Nutt, Martha E, 100
Nutt, Mary, 100
Nutt, Mary Ann, 100
Nutt, Mary G, 100
Nutt, Melinda, 100
Nutt, Moses, 066
Nutt, Moses, 084
Nutt, Moses, 095
Nutt, Moses, 099
Nutt, Moses, 114
Nutt, Moses E, 100
Nutt, Myron N, 100
Nutt, Nancy, 100
Nutt, Rebecca, 100
Nutt, Sarah, 066
Nutt, Sarah, 099

Nutt, Sarah, 100
Nutt, Sinette, 100
Nutt, Sumart, 100
Nutt, Thomas, 050
Nutt, Thomas, 051
Nutt, Thomas J, 100
Nutt, Thomas Lacy, 100
Nutt, Viola F, 100
O Neill, Willie, 252
O'Neal, John, 026
O'Neal, William, 026
O'Neil, Edmond Dr, 017
Ochenrider, Bertie, 074
Ochenrider, James, 074
Okizuma, Kim, 249
Oldham, Thomas, 518
Oneill, Mr, 504
ONeill, R A, 515
Orendorf, Sarah, 532
Orndorf, Amelia, 056
Orndorf, Christian, 067
Orndorf, Daniel C, 056
Orndorf, Dr John, 311
Orndorf, Eva Christina, 067
Orndorf, John, 056
Orndorf, John Dr, 017
Orndorf, John Sr, 067
Orndorf, Mary, 340
Orr, James, 090
Orwig, Elisabeth, 531
Orwig, Mary Magd, 108
Osborne, Joseph, 138
Osman, Chatarina, 025
Osman, J, 020
Osman, Jonathan, 477
Osman, Joseph, 025
Osman, Robert, 016
Ossman, Aaron, 431
Ossman, Barbara, 094
Ossman, Catharine, 093
Ossman, Catharine, 185
Ossman, Daniel Sr, 017
Ossman, George, 185
Ossman, Jacob S, 324
Ossman, James, 093
Ossman, Jay, 031
Ossman, John, 017
Ossman, John, 303
Ossman, Lydia, 094
Ossman, Magd Marg, 093
Ossman, Mary Alice, 517
Ossman, Philip, 094
Otta, Lottie E, 490
Otterbein, Rev Will, 339
Otto, Agatha, 093
Otto, Albert, 488
Otto, Daniel, 093
Otto, Debra, 488
Otto, Forrest R, 412
Otto, Lydia, 517
Otto, Magdalena, 093
Otto, Margaret, 093
Otto, Sarah, 517
Otto, Solomon, 517
Otto, Susie, 488
Otto, William, 093
Otto, William, 293
Overlady, Felty, 015
Owen, Mary Ann, 265
Owens, Anning, 138
Owens, Richard, 235
Page, Charles, 538
Page, Jane, 244
Page, Maggie, 053
Page, Ruth, 396

Romberger, Catherine, 532
Romberger, Catherine, 571
Romberger, Charles, 528
Romberger, Charles, 573
Romberger, Charles D, 529
Romberger, Charles E, 532
Romberger, Charlotte, 552
Romberger, Chas Isaac, 278
Romberger, Chester L, 533
Romberger, Christ, 018
Romberger, Christian, 089
Romberger, Christian, 384
Romberger, Christian, 385
Romberger, Christian, 528
Romberger, Christian, 529
Romberger, Christiana, 289
Romberger, Christiana, 420
Romberger, Christina, 324
Romberger, Christina, 530
Romberger, Christine, 529
Romberger, Clara, 532
Romberger, Clove W, 551
Romberger, Cyrus, 026
Romberger, Cyrus, 248
Romberger, Cyrus, 531
Romberger, Cyrus, 551
Romberger, D, 504
Romberger, Daniel, 011
Romberger, Daniel, 026
Romberger, Daniel, 084
Romberger, Daniel, 088
Romberger, Daniel, 138
Romberger, Daniel, 146
Romberger, Daniel, 247
Romberger, Daniel, 248
Romberger, Daniel, 253
Romberger, Daniel, 293
Romberger, Daniel, 324
Romberger, Daniel, 347
Romberger, Daniel, 364
Romberger, Daniel, 367
Romberger, Daniel, 523
Romberger, Daniel, 528
Romberger, Daniel, 529
Romberger, Daniel, 530
Romberger, Daniel, 532
Romberger, Daniel, 532
Romberger, Daniel, 533
Romberger, Daniel, 550
Romberger, Daniel, 551
Romberger, Daniel C, 095
Romberger, Daniel C, 099
Romberger, Daniel C, 278
Romberger, Daniel C, 357
Romberger, Daniel D, 532
Romberger, Daniel H, 532
Romberger, Daniel H, 551
Romberger, Daniel M, 528
Romberger, Daniel W, 194
Romberger, Daniel W, 551
Romberger, Darien, 454
Romberger, Darwin A, 552
Romberger, David J, 532
Romberger, Dorothy, 249
Romberger, E W, 079
Romberger, Edward, 139
Romberger, Edward, 248
Romberger, Edward, 253
Romberger, Edward, 531
Romberger, Edward, 533
Romberger, Edward, 550
Romberger, Edward, 551
Romberger, Elba, 551
Romberger, Elba, 552
Romberger, Elias, 528

Romberger, Elias, 529
Romberger, Elisa, 266
Romberger, Elisabeth, 096
Romberger, Elisabeth, 239
Romberger, Elisabeth, 278
Romberger, Elisabeth, 385
Romberger, Elisabeth, 391
Romberger, Elisabeth, 428
Romberger, Elisabeth, 460
Romberger, Elisabeth, 528
Romberger, Elisabeth, 529
Romberger, Elisabeth, 530
Romberger, Elisabeth, 532
Romberger, Elisabeth, 533
Romberger, Elisabeth, 572
Romberger, Elisabeth, 572
Romberger, Elizabeth, 101
Romberger, Elizabeth, 302
Romberger, Elizabeth, 306
Romberger, Elizabeth, 385
Romberger, Elizabeth, 392
Romberger, Elizabeth, 420
Romberger, Elizabeth, 532
Romberger, Elizabeth, 550
Romberger, Ella J, 552
Romberger, Ellen E, 573
Romberger, Elmer, 174
Romberger, Elmer, 192
Romberger, Elmer, 248
Romberger, Elmer, 248
Romberger, Elmer, 314
Romberger, Elmer W, 192
Romberger, Elmer W, 551
Romberger, Elwood, 177
Romberger, Elwood, 482
Romberger, Emaline, 278
Romberger, Emanuel, 533
Romberger, Emelia, 529
Romberger, Emeline, 530
Romberger, Emeline, 531
Romberger, Emeline, 532
Romberger, Emma, 531
Romberger, Emma C, 533
Romberger, Esther, 527
Romberger, Esther M, 275
Romberger, Esther M, 279
Romberger, Esther M, 531
Romberger, Ethel E, 551
Romberger, Etta, 560
Romberger, Etta C, 355
Romberger, Eva, 034
Romberger, Eva, 240
Romberger, Eva, 528
Romberger, Eva, 532
Romberger, Eva Marg, 326
Romberger, Eva Marg, 529
Romberger, Eve, 530
Romberger, Eve, 532
Romberger, Fay Olivia, 551
Romberger, Florence, 249
Romberger, Florence E, 249
Romberger, Frances, 192
Romberger, Frances, 248
Romberger, Frances, 551
Romberger, Franklin, 533
Romberger, Franklin P, 532
Romberger, Geo Frank, 531
Romberger, George, 026
Romberger, George, 302
Romberger, George, 528
Romberger, George, 531
Romberger, George, 532
Romberger, George, 533
Romberger, George, 572
Romberger, George B, 528

Romberger, George B, 533
Romberger, George D, 150
Romberger, George E, 265
Romberger, George H, 532
Romberger, George M, 528
Romberger, Gilbert, 530
Romberger, Gilbert, 532
Romberger, Gloria, 192
Romberger, Grace, 177
Romberger, Grace, 249
Romberger, H Howard, 531
Romberger, H Howard, 552
Romberger, Hanna, 364
Romberger, Hanna, 532
Romberger, Hanna, 551
Romberger, Hannah, 111
Romberger, Hannah, 248
Romberger, Hannah, 252
Romberger, Hannah, 274
Romberger, Hannah, 293
Romberger, Hannah, 302
Romberger, Hannah, 523
Romberger, Hannah, 529
Romberger, Hannah, 530
Romberger, Hannah, 531
Romberger, Hannah, 532
Romberger, Hannah, 533
Romberger, Hannah, 551
Romberger, Hannah, 572
Romberger, Hannah E, 551
Romberger, Hannah L, 533
Romberger, Hannah R, 532
Romberger, Harold L, 194
Romberger, Harold L, 551
Romberger, Harry, 297
Romberger, Harry, 331
Romberger, Harry, 332
Romberger, Harry, 369
Romberger, Harry, 529
Romberger, Harry, 573
Romberger, Harry E, 533
Romberger, Harry R, 278
Romberger, Harry R, 295
Romberger, Harvey, 249
Romberger, Harvey, 350
Romberger, Harvey A, 295
Romberger, Heinrich, 528
Romberger, Helen M, 551
Romberger, Helena, 058
Romberger, Helena, 064
Romberger, Helena, 068
Romberger, Henrich, 306
Romberger, Henrich, 385
Romberger, Henrich, 420
Romberger, Henrietta, 278
Romberger, Henrietta, 531
Romberger, Henry, 017
Romberger, Henry, 239
Romberger, Henry, 529
Romberger, Henry, 530
Romberger, Henry, 531
Romberger, Henry, 532
Romberger, Henry, 550
Romberger, Henry, 571
Romberger, Henry, 572
Romberger, Henry A, 085
Romberger, Henry A, 528
Romberger, Henry C, 528
Romberger, Henry F, 533
Romberger, Henry H, 248
Romberger, Henry Jr, 529
Romberger, Henry K, 529
Romberger, Henry M, 532
Romberger, Homer P, 278
Romberger, Ira P, 552

Romberger, Ira P Jr, 552
Romberger, Isaac, 248
Romberger, Isaac, 276
Romberger, Isaac, 278
Romberger, Isaac, 309
Romberger, Isaac, 311
Romberger, Isaac, 313
Romberger, Isaac, 315
Romberger, Isaac, 355
Romberger, Isaac, 356
Romberger, Isaac, 474
Romberger, Isaac, 531
Romberger, Isabella M, 533
Romberger, Isaiah, 529
Romberger, Isaiah H, 528
Romberger, Iva, 188
Romberger, Iva, 192
Romberger, J A, 078
Romberger, J Casper, 527
Romberger, J Christian, 390
Romberger, J G, 047
Romberger, J G, 152
Romberger, J G, 161
Romberger, J G, 188
Romberger, J G, 189
Romberger, Jacob, 018
Romberger, Jacob, 239
Romberger, Jacob, 386
Romberger, Jacob, 529
Romberger, Jacob, 530
Romberger, Jacob, 533
Romberger, Jacob, 551
Romberger, Jacob, 573
Romberger, Jacob J, 533
Romberger, James, 357
Romberger, James, 528
Romberger, James M, 176
Romberger, James M, 528
Romberger, James M, 533
Romberger, Jean, 132
Romberger, Jennie, 531
Romberger, Johannes, 527
Romberger, Johannes, 532
Romberger, Johannes, 533
Romberger, John, 033
Romberger, John, 196
Romberger, John, 239
Romberger, John, 275
Romberger, John, 317
Romberger, John, 528
Romberger, John, 529
Romberger, John, 530
Romberger, John, 532
Romberger, John, 533
Romberger, John, 565
Romberger, John, 571
Romberger, John, 572
Romberger, John A, 026
Romberger, John A, 364
Romberger, John A, 527
Romberger, John A, 531
Romberger, John A, 533
Romberger, John A, 552
Romberger, John B, 533
Romberger, John D, 552
Romberger, John E, 248
Romberger, John E, 275
Romberger, John E, 279
Romberger, John E, 531
Romberger, John G, 135
Romberger, John G, 157
Romberger, John G, 159
Romberger, John G, 531
Romberger, John Geo, 531
Romberger, John H, 529

Romberger, Jonas, 531
Romberger, Jonas Al, 532
Romberger, Jonathan, 528
Romberger, Jonathan, 532
Romberger, Jonathan, 533
Romberger, Joseph, 088
Romberger, Joseph, 324
Romberger, Joseph, 528
Romberger, Joseph, 530
Romberger, Joseph, 532
Romberger, Joseph, 533
Romberger, Joseph D, 533
Romberger, Joseph F, 026
Romberger, Joseph F, 532
Romberger, Josiah, 248
Romberger, Josiah, 428
Romberger, Josiah, 531
Romberger, Josiah, 533
Romberger, Josiah, 552
Romberger, Julia A, 528
Romberger, Julia Ann, 530
Romberger, Julian, 529
Romberger, Juntina, 239
Romberger, Justina, 530
Romberger, Justina, 573
Romberger, Katherine, 228
Romberger, Kathryn, 528
Romberger, Laurence, 551
Romberger, Lavina, 533
Romberger, Leah, 074
Romberger, Leah, 284
Romberger, Leah, 351
Romberger, Leah A, 295
Romberger, Leah H, 532
Romberger, Leah J, 278
Romberger, Lillie A, 295
Romberger, Lillie E, 529
Romberger, Lilly, 350
Romberger, Lily, 529
Romberger, Lizzie, 573
Romberger, Lloyd, 357
Romberger, Lovina, 572
Romberger, Luther, 530
Romberger, Luther, 532
Romberger, Lydia, 271
Romberger, Lydia, 280
Romberger, Lydia, 355
Romberger, Lydia, 356
Romberger, Lydia, 474
Romberger, Lydia A, 278
Romberger, Lydia A, 474
Romberger, Lydia A, 530
Romberger, Lydia Ann, 278
Romberger, Lydia Ann, 279
Romberger, Lydia Ann, 531
Romberger, Lydis, 315
Romberger, Lynne E, 295
Romberger, M Bertha, 174
Romberger, M Cath, 533
Romberger, M Magd, 533
Romberger, Magdalen, 531
Romberger, Maggie E, 174
Romberger, Marcy C, 248
Romberger, Margaret, 325
Romberger, Margaret, 528
Romberger, Margareth, 527
Romberger, Maria, 358
Romberger, Maria, 528
Romberger, Maria, 528
Romberger, Maria Eva, 528
Romberger, Martha, 528
Romberger, Mary, 088
Romberger, Mary, 239
Romberger, Mary, 328
Romberger, Mary, 496

Row, Susanna, 031
Row, Susanna, 052
Row, Susanna, 364
Row, Susanna, 365
Row, Susanna, 366
Row, Susanna, 367
Row, Susanna, 368
Row, Susanna, 369
Row, Susanna, 483
Row, Susanna, 516
Row, Susanna Sevilla, 366
Row, Susannah, 117
Row, Susannah, 366
Row, Theodore, 366
Row, Tobias, 364
Row, W H, 283
Row, Walter, 364
Row, Wendel, 364
Row, William, 024
Row, William, 040
Row, William, 278
Row, William, 280
Row, William, 286
Row, William, 364
Row, William, 365
Row, William, 366
Row, William, 368
Row, William, 443
Row, William, 546
Row, William H, 420
Row, William H, 516
Rowan, Thomas, 011
Rowe, Abraham, 390
Rowe, Adam, 123
Rowe, Adam, 363
Rowe, Adam David, 144
Rowe, Adam Diller, 149
Rowe, Adam Jr, 142
Rowe, Adam Jr, 143
Rowe, Adam Jr, 363
Rowe, Adam Sr, 142
Rowe, Alabama, 143
Rowe, Albert, 144
Rowe, Alfred, 047
Rowe, Alfred, 131
Rowe, Alfred, 144
Rowe, Alfred, 146
Rowe, Alfred, 165
Rowe, Alfred, 179
Rowe, Alfred, 538
Rowe, Alfred C, 145
Rowe, Alfred H, 151
Rowe, Alfred H, 153
Rowe, Alfred H, 157
Rowe, Alfred H, 196
Rowe, Amanda, 144
Rowe, Amanda, 146
Rowe, Amanda, 193
Rowe, Amos F, 144
Rowe, Ann, 144
Rowe, Anna, 132
Rowe, Anna Elizabeth, 144
Rowe, Annie, 144
Rowe, Annie Eliz, 449
Rowe, Arthur S, 134
Rowe, Arthur S, 161
Rowe, Arthur S, 162
Rowe, Barbara, 363
Rowe, Barbara, 393
Rowe, Beulah, 144
Rowe, Beulah, 155
Rowe, Beulah M, 155
Rowe, Bradley A, 161
Rowe, Carrie Grubb, 144
Rowe, Casey L, 161

Rowe, Catherine, 146
Rowe, Catherine E, 144
Rowe, Charles, 131
Rowe, Charles, 143
Rowe, Charles, 180
Rowe, Charles A, 145
Rowe, Charles A, 162
Rowe, Christiana, 123
Rowe, Christiana, 143
Rowe, Christiana, 144
Rowe, Christina, 143
Rowe, Christina, 363
Rowe, Clinton, 144
Rowe, Clinton, 146
Rowe, Clinton, 180
Rowe, Cornelius, 144
Rowe, Daniel, 183
Rowe, Daniel, 334
Rowe, David, 144
Rowe, Della Mae, 144
Rowe, Dennis E, 159
Rowe, Dennis E, 161
Rowe, Edna, 334
Rowe, Eertha Ida, 144
Rowe, Eleanor, 144
Rowe, Elizabeth, 143
Rowe, Elizabeth W, 143
Rowe, Ellen, 143
Rowe, Ellen L, 144
Rowe, Elmer Newton, 144
Rowe, Elmer Newton, 148
Rowe, Elmer Newton, 149
Rowe, Elmira, 143
Rowe, Emanuel, 144
Rowe, Emma, 143
Rowe, Erlena, 144
Rowe, Erlena, 145
Rowe, Erlena, 474
Rowe, Esther, 144
Rowe, Ethel E, 144
Rowe, Eve Bleistein, 144
Rowe, Florence, 132
Rowe, Florence, 179
Rowe, Frances, 144
Rowe, Francis, 145
Rowe, Francis M, 143
Rowe, Franklin E, 144
Rowe, Frantz, 363
Rowe, Franz, 363
Rowe, Franz Jr, 363
Rowe, George, 143
Rowe, George, 449
Rowe, George Alfred, 144
Rowe, Hannah, 146
Rowe, Hannah A, 144
Rowe, Ida, 131
Rowe, Ida C, 144
Rowe, Ira, 146
Rowe, Isabella, 363
Rowe, Isabella, 390
Rowe, J Allen, 367
Rowe, Jacob, 193
Rowe, Jacob, 393
Rowe, Jacob Herbert, 058
Rowe, James A D, 145
Rowe, Jane, 538
Rowe, Jean Peters, 145
Rowe, Jennie, 144
Rowe, Jennie, 145
Rowe, Joanne E, 159
Rowe, Joel, 143
Rowe, John, 142
Rowe, John, 143
Rowe, John, 144
Rowe, John, 146

Rowe, John, 180
Rowe, John, 363
Rowe, John D, 188
Rowe, John David, 082
Rowe, John David, 144
Rowe, John David, 146
Rowe, John Wesley, 143
Rowe, Joseph, 131
Rowe, Joseph, 390
Rowe, Joseph E, 144
Rowe, Kate, 179
Rowe, Kate M, 144
Rowe, Katie, 131
Rowe, Katie, 144
Rowe, Kaye E, 160
Rowe, Laura, 145
Rowe, Leah J, 144
Rowe, Lemuel, 143
Rowe, Lemuel, 405
Rowe, Lewis, 131
Rowe, Lewis, 404
Rowe, Lewis F, 145
Rowe, Lillian, 159
Rowe, Lillian, 160
Rowe, Lloyd, 132
Rowe, Louisiana, 047
Rowe, Louisiana, 155
Rowe, Louisiana C, 144
Rowe, Lydia, 144
Rowe, Mabel E, 148
Rowe, Magdalena, 363
Rowe, Maggie, 145
Rowe, Marguarite, 069
Rowe, Marguerite, 161
Rowe, Marguerite, 162
Rowe, Mary, 143
Rowe, Mary A, 144
Rowe, Mary A E, 145
Rowe, Mary Ann, 143
Rowe, Mary Ann Eliz, 538
Rowe, Mary Ellen, 143
Rowe, Mary Lovina, 143
Rowe, Meta, 132
Rowe, Mollie, 131
Rowe, Nathaniel, 143
Rowe, Newton, 146
Rowe, Oliver, 143
Rowe, Pearl Mae, 449
Rowe, Pearl Mae, 461
Rowe, Pearl May, 564
Rowe, Pearly M, 420
Rowe, Rebecca, 143
Rowe, Richard, 245
Rowe, Sabelle, 389
Rowe, Sally, 179
Rowe, Sarah, 143
Rowe, Sarah, 144
Rowe, Sarah Jane, 144
Rowe, Sarah Kate, 144
Rowe, Sherwood, 069
Rowe, Sherwood, 132
Rowe, Susan, 143
Rowe, Susan, 144
Rowe, Susan A, 144
Rowe, Susannah, 143
Rowe, Susannah, 193
Rowe, Sydney Ann, 144
Rowe, Theo Absolom, 144
Rowe, Veronica, 363
Rowe, Walter, 132
Rowe, Walter, 180
Rowe, Walter E, 145
Rowe, Walter Eman, 144
Rowe, Walter F, 144
Rowe, Wendel, 389

Rowe, Wendell, 390
Rowe, William, 393
Ruckert, Anna Cath, 419
Ruckert, Johann Simon, 419
Rudisill, Adam, 088
Rudisill, Adam, 101
Rudisill, Adam, 143
Rudisill, Adam, 376
Rudisill, Alfred, 143
Rudisill, Clara, 143
Rudisill, David, 052
Rudisill, David, 143
Rudisill, Mary Jane, 052
Rudisill, Solomon, 076
Rudisill, Susan, 143
Rudisill, Susanna, 052
Rudisilo, Solomon, 193
Rudy, Barbara, 280
Rudy, Barbara, 365
Rudy, Barbara, 368
Rudy, Barbara, 393
Rudy, John C, 298
Rudy, John C, 299
Rudy, Melissa M, 298
Rudy, Melissa M, 299
Rudy, Rev Fred, 140
Rueckert, Anna Marg, 419
Rueckert, Catharina, 419
Rueckert, Daniel, 419
Rueckert, Elizabeth, 419
Rueckert, Joh Henrich, 419
Rueckert, Joh Herman, 419
Rueckert, Joh Zacharia, 419
Rueckert, Johan Simon, 419
Ruhl, A Catherine, 124
Ruhl, Catherine, 124
Rumberger, Frank, 558
Rumlinger, N E, 094
Rummel, John, 429
Runk, Catherine, 168
Runk, Hannah, 460
Runk, I E, 349
Runk, Jacob, 019
Runk, Michael, 168
Runk, Susannah, 483
Runkel, Lydia, 488
Runkle, Michael, 517
Rupert, Isaac, 480
Rupert, Sevilla, 473
Rupp, Alice, 036
Rupp, Richard, 430
Ruppenthal, Mary, 381
Rusbatch, Jennie B, 307
Rusch, Henrich, 124
Rusch, Henrich, 124
Rush, Eliz Beulah, 041
Rush, Eliz Beulah, 546
Rush, George W, 041
Rush, George W, 546
Rush, Harry Edgar, 041
Rush, Harry Edgar, 546
Rush, John, 040
Rush, John, 041
Rush, John, 546
Rush, Mary Salome, 041
Rush, Mary Salome, 546
Rush, Nora Ellen, 041
Rush, Sarah, 041
Russel, Alvin S, 101
Russel, Belle, 101
Russel, Catherine, 089
Russel, Emma E, 101
Russel, Frederick L, 101
Russel, Henry M, 101
Russel, John Wesley, 101

Russel, Joseph, 084
Russel, Joseph, 101
Russel, Joseph Jr, 101
Russel, Joseph P, 101
Russel, Kate M, 101
Russel, Laura Eliz, 101
Russel, Margaret L, 101
Russel, Minnie, 101
Russel, Sarah Annie, 101
Russel, Stella, 101
Russel, Susanna, 143
Russell, Becky, 024
Russell, Bobby, 024
Russell, Family, 095
Russell, Herman, 098
Russell, John, 193
Russell, Joseph, 095
Russell, Joseph, 098
Russell, Joseph, 135
Russell, Joseph, 307
Russell, Margaret, 024
Rutherford, Anna, 045
Rutherford, Dr Cyrus, 045
Rutherford, Dr Hiram, 045
Rutherford, John, 045
Rutherford, Kate, 045
Rutherford, Luther, 045
Rutherford, William, 045
Rutherford, Wilson, 045
Rutter, Allen, 039
Rutter, Amanda, 261
Rutter, Andrew, 531
Rutter, Eliza, 039
Rutter, Eliza A, 038
Rutter, Elizabeth, 039
Rutter, Elizabeth, 044
Rutter, Elizabeth A, 038
Rutter, George, 039
Rutter, George, 260
Rutter, George, 356
Rutter, George, 421
Rutter, Hannah M, 039
Rutter, Heinrich, 039
Rutter, Henry, 030
Rutter, Henry, 039
Rutter, Henry, 558
Rutter, Isaac, 031
Rutter, Isaac, 039
Rutter, Isaac, 108
Rutter, Isaac, 357
Rutter, Jacob, 260
Rutter, Jacob, 356
Rutter, Jane, 039
Rutter, Joel, 039
Rutter, Joel W, 039
Rutter, John, 028
Rutter, John, 039
Rutter, John M, 356
Rutter, Josiah, 039
Rutter, Leah, 039
Rutter, Leah Jane, 039
Rutter, Leah Jane, 363
Rutter, Margaret, 039
Rutter, Margaret, 310
Rutter, Margaret, 558
Rutter, Margaret Ann, 039
Rutter, Mary, 039
Rutter, Mary Ann, 039
Rutter, Mary Jane, 039
Rutter, Rachel, 031
Rutter, Rachel, 039
Rutter, Rachel L, 039
Rutter, Rebecca, 310
Rutter, Sarah, 039
Rutter, Sarah, 260

Snyder, Jerry, 099
Snyder, Johannes, 539
Snyder, John, 017
Snyder, John, 060
Snyder, John, 087
Snyder, John, 089
Snyder, John, 135
Snyder, John, 270
Snyder, John, 271
Snyder, John, 272
Snyder, John, 278
Snyder, John, 286
Snyder, John, 452
Snyder, John, 454
Snyder, John, 463
Snyder, John, 479
Snyder, John, 497
Snyder, John, 497
Snyder, John A, 147
Snyder, John Adam, 148
Snyder, John Adam, 149
Snyder, John Alvin, 148
Snyder, John Alvin, 149
Snyder, John Calvin, 234
Snyder, John Calvin, 291
Snyder, John D, 058
Snyder, John D, 146
Snyder, John D, 162
Snyder, John D, 163
Snyder, John D, 271
Snyder, John D, 272
Snyder, John D, 273
Snyder, John Emory, 148
Snyder, John Emory, 149
Snyder, John Enterl, 272
Snyder, John Henry, 052
Snyder, John Nathan, 271
Snyder, John Nathan, 278
Snyder, John Sr, 192
Snyder, John T, 058
Snyder, Johnny, 413
Snyder, Jonas, 288
Snyder, Jonathan, 242
Snyder, Jonathan Frank, 474
Snyder, Joseph, 060
Snyder, Joseph F, 147
Snyder, Joseph H, 058
Snyder, Joseph H, 271
Snyder, Josiah, 060
Snyder, Josiah, 261
Snyder, Joy, 113
Snyder, Justina Marga, 069
Snyder, Kate, 291
Snyder, Katey Gippl, 261
Snyder, Katherine, 272
Snyder, Kathy, 487
Snyder, Katie Eliz, 148
Snyder, Katie Eliz, 149
Snyder, Katie Irene, 234
Snyder, Katie Irene, 291
Snyder, Katie J, 147
Snyder, Laura May, 558
Snyder, Leah Jane, 272
Snyder, Lena H, 558
Snyder, Lena M, 272
Snyder, Leon, 059
Snyder, Leona, 132
Snyder, Leona, 177
Snyder, Leona, 192
Snyder, Leonard, 148
Snyder, Leonard, 256
Snyder, Leonard, 258
Snyder, Leonard, 271
Snyder, Leonard, 272
Snyder, Leonard, 273

Snyder, Leonard, 278
Snyder, Leonard, 373
Snyder, Leonard Jr, 233
Snyder, Leonard Jr, 270
Snyder, Leonard Sr, 270
Snyder, Lidia Ann, 147
Snyder, Louisa, 558
Snyder, Louisa C, 558
Snyder, Lovina, 261
Snyder, Lucy Ann, 558
Snyder, Luisiana, 147
Snyder, Lydia, 131
Snyder, Lydia, 147
Snyder, Lydia, 192
Snyder, Lydia, 271
Snyder, Lydia, 278
Snyder, Lydia Ann, 153
Snyder, Lydia L, 461
Snyder, Lydia McCu, 261
Snyder, Mabel Edna, 278
Snyder, Magdalena, 481
Snyder, Maggie M, 147
Snyder, Malinda, 497
Snyder, Margaret, 192
Snyder, Margaret, 234
Snyder, Margaret A, 291
Snyder, Margaret L, 538
Snyder, Margaretha, 272
Snyder, Marguerite, 162
Snyder, Maria, 245
Snyder, Maria Anna, 271
Snyder, Maria Eliz, 234
Snyder, Maria Eliz, 291
Snyder, Maria Sara, 230
Snyder, Marianda, 185
Snyder, Marlyn, 132
Snyder, Mary, 192
Snyder, Mary, 272
Snyder, Mary, 276
Snyder, Mary, 497
Snyder, Mary, 539
Snyder, Mary, 539
Snyder, Mary A, 291
Snyder, Mary Alice, 147
Snyder, Mary Ann, 058
Snyder, Mary Ann, 271
Snyder, Mary Ann, 539
Snyder, Mary Edna, 148
Snyder, Mary Edna, 149
Snyder, Mary Ellen, 147
Snyder, Mary Hoke, 261
Snyder, Mary J, 412
Snyder, Mary J, 558
Snyder, Mary J, 558
Snyder, Mary Jane, 411
Snyder, Mary Jane, 474
Snyder, Mary L, 147
Snyder, Mary Louisa, 234
Snyder, Mary Louisa, 291
Snyder, Mary M, 559
Snyder, Maud Luellen, 149
Snyder, Maude, 132
Snyder, Maude Luell, 148
Snyder, Maude Shell, 162
Snyder, Minnie, 272
Snyder, Miriam, 096
Snyder, Mollie, 148
Snyder, Mollie, 149
Snyder, Monroe, 539
Snyder, Monroe C, 537
Snyder, Nathan, 180
Snyder, Nathan, 180
Snyder, Nathan, 277
Snyder, Nathan E, 144
Snyder, Nathan E, 271

Snyder, Nathan Ellswo, 474
Snyder, Nathaniel, 373
Snyder, Nellie, 272
Snyder, Nellie C, 192
Snyder, Nicholas, 031
Snyder, Nicholas, 192
Snyder, Nicholas, 240
Snyder, Nicholas, 261
Snyder, Nicholas, 270
Snyder, Nicholas, 272
Snyder, Nicholas, 272
Snyder, Norman Calvi, 558
Snyder, Norman Calvi, 559
Snyder, Orpha, 192
Snyder, Pauline, 538
Snyder, Pauline, 539
Snyder, Polly, 460
Snyder, Rachel, 271
Snyder, Rachel B, 058
Snyder, Ralph D, 085
Snyder, Ralph David, 162
Snyder, Raymond, 539
Snyder, Raymond E, 134
Snyder, Rebecca, 052
Snyder, Rebecca, 272
Snyder, Rebecca, 272
Snyder, Rebecca, 272
Snyder, Robin, 464
Snyder, Rose, 464
Snyder, Rosie Bonaw, 144
Snyder, Rosie E, 271
Snyder, Russell, 412
Snyder, Samuel, 069
Snyder, Samuel, 139
Snyder, Samuel, 270
Snyder, Samuel, 271
Snyder, Samuel, 272
Snyder, Samuel, 272
Snyder, Samuel, 272
Snyder, Samuel, 273
Snyder, Samuel, 278
Snyder, Samuel, 373
Snyder, Samuel, 474
Snyder, Samuel Edw, 234
Snyder, Samuel Edw, 291
Snyder, Samuel Isaa, 278
Snyder, Samuel Isaac, 404
Snyder, Samuel Jerom, 069
Snyder, Sara Jane, 058
Snyder, Sarah, 148
Snyder, Sarah, 149
Snyder, Sarah, 192
Snyder, Sarah, 192
Snyder, Sarah, 261
Snyder, Sarah, 271
Snyder, Sarah, 272
Snyder, Sarah, 272
Snyder, Sarah, 291
Snyder, Sarah, 497
Snyder, Sarah, 557
Snyder, Sarah, 559
Snyder, Sarah Cathe, 278
Snyder, Sarah Eliz, 148
Snyder, Sarah Elizabet, 474
Snyder, Sarah Grim, 261
Snyder, Sarah J, 147
Snyder, Sarah Jane, 271
Snyder, Sarah Jane, 271
Snyder, Sarah Jane, 272
Snyder, Sarah Zimmer, 192
Snyder, Scott A, 180
Snyder, Silvester, 147
Snyder, Simon, 015
Snyder, Simon, 299
Snyder, Squire, 346

Snyder, Steve, 249
Snyder, Steve, 249
Snyder, Stophel Chr, 270
Snyder, Susan, 147
Snyder, Susan, 192
Snyder, Susan, 261
Snyder, Susan, 497
Snyder, Susanna, 060
Snyder, Susanna, 060
Snyder, Susanna, 192
Snyder, Susanna Bell, 424
Snyder, Susanna Mc, 261
Snyder, Thomas, 052
Snyder, Thomas, 138
Snyder, Thomas, 272
Snyder, Thomas Sr, 052
Snyder, Thomas Willa, 052
Snyder, Tyrus, 234
Snyder, Tyrus, 291
Snyder, Tyrus, 291
Snyder, Uriah, 272
Snyder, Veronica, 388
Snyder, Vivian June, 538
Snyder, Wellington, 059
Snyder, Wellington E, 147
Snyder, Wesley, 497
Snyder, William, 060
Snyder, William, 147
Snyder, William, 192
Snyder, William, 192
Snyder, William, 234
Snyder, William, 272
Snyder, William, 461
Snyder, William F, 162
Snyder, William H, 113
Snyder, William H, 272
Snyer, Della Mae, 144
Solence, Constance, 159
Solence, Jenny A, 185
Solence, Jerry, 159
Soliday, Eliz, 262
Spade, Susanna, 473
Spahr, Margaret S, 243
Spangenberg, Bishop, 019
Spangler, Eleanor, 341
Spangler, Phoebe, 174
Spat, Elizabeth, 472
Spatz, George, 326
Spatz, George, 529
Spatz, Jacob, 326
Spatz, Magdalena H, 236
Spatz, Sarah M, 326
Spayd, John, 050
Spayd, Jonathan, 244
Specht, Alvaretta, 291
Specht, Angeline, 291
Specht, Anna Cath, 291
Specht, Anna Maria, 291
Specht, Asa, 291
Specht, Barbara, 393
Specht, Benjamin, 291
Specht, Catharine, 234
Specht, Catharine, 393
Specht, Catherie, 291
Specht, Daniel, 291
Specht, Daniel, 291
Specht, Eliza, 234
Specht, Elizabeth, 129
Specht, Elizabeth, 290
Specht, Elizabeth, 291
Specht, Elizabeth, 291
Specht, Elizabeth, 291
Specht, Franklin, 291
Specht, Frederick, 291
Specht, Henry, 291

Specht, Henry B, 291
Specht, Isaiah, 291
Specht, Jacob, 291
Specht, Jared, 265
Specht, Jared, 291
Specht, Jeremiah, 234
Specht, Jeremiah, 291
Specht, Jeremiah, 291
Specht, Johannes, 291
Specht, John N, 234
Specht, John N, 280
Specht, John N, 290
Specht, John N, 291
Specht, John N, 393
Specht, John N Jr, 291
Specht, John W, 234
Specht, John Wesley, 291
Specht, Josiah, 291
Specht, Kate A, 291
Specht, L Ellington, 291
Specht, Levi, 291
Specht, Louisa Leb, 265
Specht, Lydia, 291
Specht, Malinda, 291
Specht, Maria, 291
Specht, Mary, 291
Specht, Mary Salom, 265
Specht, Mary Salom, 291
Specht, Rebecca, 291
Specht, Rev Joseph, 138
Specht, Sarah, 234
Specht, Sarah, 291
Specht, Sarah, 291
Specht, Susanna, 291
Specht, Wm Edward, 291
Speck, Anna C Lebo, 264
Speck, Barbara, 283
Speck, Barbara, 319
Speck, Elizabeth, 454
Speck, Jeremiah, 265
Speck, John, 283
Speck, John, 454
Speck, John N, 319
Speck, John N, 450
Speck, Susanna, 454
Spicher, Anna, 041
Spielman, Richard, 317
Sponsler, Jay, 435
Sponsler, Jay L, 409
Sponsler, Jay L, 415
Sponsler, John, 403
Sponsler, Malinda, 403
Sponsler, Sarah Alice, 403
Sponsler, Shirley, 435
Sponsler, Shirley J, 409
Sponsler, Shirley J, 415
Spotts, Anna M, 288
Spotts, Art, 440
Spotts, Arthur R, 475
Spotts, Carolyn, 501
Spotts, Catharine, 288
Spotts, Catherine, 163
Spotts, Catherine Hoo, 164
Spotts, Catherine Hov, 161
Spotts, Emma Louisa, 164
Spotts, Etta, 164
Spotts, Etta, 538
Spotts, Etta Elizabeth, 163
Spotts, Etta Elizabeth, 163
Spotts, George Irvin, 412
Spotts, Gladys, 412
Spotts, Grace, 412
Spotts, Harold Hoover, 164
Spotts, Henry Morris, 163
Spotts, Henry Morris, 163

Wert, Anna May, 055
Wert, Carrie, 367
Wert, Catharina, 459
Wert, Catherine, 327
Wert, Catherine, 367
Wert, Catherine, 389
Wert, Catherine, 460
Wert, Daniel, 236
Wert, Daniel, 285
Wert, Daniel, 459
Wert, Daniel, 460
Wert, David, 367
Wert, Edward, 236
Wert, Elisabeth, 459
Wert, Elizabeth, 328
Wert, Emanuel, 459
Wert, Florence, 367
Wert, Hannah Amelia, 149
Wert, Hattie, 367
Wert, Hattie, 532
Wert, Ida, 054
Wert, Isaac, 328
Wert, Isaac, 459
Wert, Isaac, 530
Wert, Jacob, 270
Wert, Jacob, 459
Wert, Jacob, 460
Wert, Johan Jacob, 390
Wert, John, 460
Wert, John H, 367
Wert, Joseph, 328
Wert, Katie Salome, 096
Wert, Magdalena, 460
Wert, Mary C, 044
Wert, Mary Cath, 044
Wert, Samuel, 135
Wert, Sarah, 074
Wert, Sarah, 382
Wert, Simon, 044
Wert, Sophia, 270
Wert, Sophia, 460
Wert, Sophia Susan, 459
Wert, Susanna, 459
Wert, William, 459
Wertenberger, Philip, 427
Wertz, Anna Maria, 461
Wertz, Elizabeth, 461
Wertz, Jerima, 096
Wertz, Michael J, 327
Wertz, Michael T, 461
Wertz, Samuel, 461
Wessner, Robert H, 278
West, Daniel, 421
Wetcel, Elizabeth, 533
Wetstein, Elizabeth, 376
Wetzel, Andrew J, 316
Wetzel, Daniel, 316
Wetzel, David, 237
Wetzel, Hetty, 252
Wetzel, James, 290
Wetzel, John, 316
Wetzel, John K, 316
Wetzel, Lillian, 412
Wetzel, Lillian, 496
Wetzel, Lillian, 541
Wetzel, Maria Cath, 237
Wetzel, Wm Henry, 316
Wetzler, Susanna P, 494
Wever, Anna Margare, 385
Wever, Capt Michael, 477
Wever, John Allen, 360
Whitcomb, Linda L, 318
Whitcomb, Lizzie, 327
White, David, 312
White, Elijah, 079

White, William, 008
White, William, 009
Whitman, Ellen Emma, 479
Whitman, Isaac A, 083
Whitman, Jacob, 027
Whitman, Mary Ann, 532
Whitman, Susannah, 083
Whitman, William, 083
Whitmer, Lizzie, 300
Whitmore, John, 472
Whittenberg, Ada, 538
Widel, Alabam, 024
Widel, Emanuel, 024
Widel, George, 024
Wiedel, Alabama, 143
Wieland, Barbara, 460
Wieland, Joh Frederic, 302
Wierman, T T, 311
Wieser, Amelia, 341
Wieser, Hon George, 341
Wiest, Agatha, 517
Wiest, Alice, 288
Wiest, Arlene, 343
Wiest, Barbara, 196
Wiest, Brandy Marie, 207
Wiest, Calvin, 476
Wiest, Carolyn, 188
Wiest, Carolyn, 309
Wiest, Catherine, 058
Wiest, Catherine, 489
Wiest, Charles, 381
Wiest, Cora, 481
Wiest, Daisy, 351
Wiest, Daniel, 488
Wiest, Daniel, 568
Wiest, Daniel, 569
Wiest, Daniel A, 489
Wiest, Donald, 476
Wiest, Donald, 484
Wiest, Earl, 539
Wiest, Edward Lt, 489
Wiest, Elias, 058
Wiest, Elizabeth, 439
Wiest, Elizabeth, 517
Wiest, Elizabeth, 569
Wiest, Emme Catherin, 529
Wiest, Eve, 315
Wiest, Frank, 172
Wiest, Frederick, 488
Wiest, George, 309
Wiest, George, 345
Wiest, Gerald F, 292
Wiest, Gerald F, 294
Wiest, Gerald F, 295
Wiest, Gerald F, 415
Wiest, Gerold F, 448
Wiest, Harry, 020
Wiest, Harry, 381
Wiest, Henry Jr, 531
Wiest, Henry Samuel, 531
Wiest, Jacob, 020
Wiest, Jacob, 058
Wiest, Jacob, 353
Wiest, Jacob, 381
Wiest, Jacob, 531
Wiest, Jacob, 569
Wiest, Jacob Jr, 489
Wiest, Jacob K, 381
Wiest, Jacob Sr, 489
Wiest, James W, 058
Wiest, Jay M, 569
Wiest, John Elias, 058
Wiest, John J, 188
Wiest, John Klinger, 315
Wiest, Justina, 488

Wiest, Kerry, 207
Wiest, Kerry, 207
Wiest, Leroy, 501
Wiest, Linda K, 294
Wiest, Linda K, 295
Wiest, Linda K, 415
Wiest, Maria, 353
Wiest, Mary, 381
Wiest, Mary, 531
Wiest, Mary, 539
Wiest, Mary, 569
Wiest, Mary A, 568
Wiest, Mary A, 569
Wiest, Mary Jane, 058
Wiest, Morris, 478
Wiest, Morris Jay, 569
Wiest, Oliver, 531
Wiest, Raymond, 573
Wiest, Rebecca, 249
Wiest, Rebecca, 531
Wiest, Roy A, 573
Wiest, Samuel, 315
Wiest, Samuel, 381
Wiest, Samuel L, 531
Wiest, Walter, 478
Wiest, William, 058
Wiest, Woodrow W, 294
Wilbert, Amanda, 389
Wilbert, Carson, 078
Wilbert, Catherine, 194
Wilbert, Clara, 194
Wilbert, Clara, 389
Wilbert, George, 078
Wilbert, Harry, 449
Wilbert, Henry, 078
Wilbert, Henry, 460
Wilbert, Lydia Ann, 389
Wilbert, Mabel Cath, 449
Wilbert, Mary, 389
Wilbert, Mary, 448
Wilbert, Peter, 389
Wilbert, Philip, 389
Wilbert, Reuben, 442
Wilbert, Sarah, 475
Wild, Adam, 018
Wiley, Sarah M, 262
Wilgert, Abraham, 329
Wilhelm, C C, 104
Wilhelm, John, 427
Wilkins, Augusta F, 052
Wilkinson, Susan, 092
Will, Abraham, 046
Will, Amelia, 047
Will, Catharine, 046
Will, Conrad, 046
Will, Conrad, 232
Will, David, 047
Will, Isaac, 046
Will, Isaac, 232
Will, John William, 047
Will, Maria, 046
Will, Mary, 047
Will, Sarah, 047
Will, Sarah Jane, 047
Willard, Alfred Elmer, 424
Willard, Bertha Ida, 144
Willard, Charles F, 424
Willard, Elias Samuel, 424
Willard, Emma, 424
Willard, Henry Oscar, 424
Willard, Ida Jane, 424
Willard, Jacob, 424
Willard, Lydia, 424
Willett, Griffin W, 036
William, George, 479

William, Rebecca, 479
Williams, Adam, 117
Williams, Catherine, 117
Williams, Cylon, 137
Williams, Dallas, 452
Williams, Dallas L, 518
Williams, Daniel, 015
Williams, Dennis, 518
Williams, Emma, 071
Williams, Ethel, 452
Williams, George F, 064
Williams, George F, 068
Williams, George F, 071
Williams, Hettie E, 071
Williams, Jennie, 127
Williams, John, 117
Williams, John E, 071
Williams, Lottie, 434
Williams, Marnie Ruth, 317
Williams, Mary, 117
Williams, Mary Jane, 071
Williams, Maud Emili, 090
Williams, Mrs, 146
Williams, Richard, 090
Williams, Samuel M, 071
Williams, Sarah, 071
Williams, Suzann C, 518
Williams, Thomas, 037
Williams, William, 117
Williams, William P, 071
Williamson, A Maria, 242
Williamson, A Maria, 385
Williard, Adam, 309
Williard, Alvin Ray, 501
Williard, Amanda, 356
Williard, Amanda, 488
Williard, Amanda, 538
Williard, Amanda, 538
Williard, Anna, 194
Williard, Anna Maria, 237
Williard, Anna Maria, 392
Williard, Anna Maria, 464
Williard, Anna Maria, 480
Williard, Anna Maria, 554
Williard, Catharine, 259
Williard, Catherine, 259
Williard, Catherine, 558
Williard, Dale, 133
Williard, Dale, 137
Williard, Eertha Ida, 144
Williard, Elias, 276
Williard, Elias, 277
Williard, Eliza, 482
Williard, Eliza, 484
Williard, Elizabeth, 439
Williard, Emanuel, 276
Williard, Emma Cecili, 482
Williard, George, 153
Williard, George, 232
Williard, George, 276
Williard, George, 283
Williard, George, 294
Williard, George, 295
Williard, George, 308
Williard, George, 318
Williard, George, 319
Williard, George, 320
Williard, George, 345
Williard, George, 354
Williard, George, 389
Williard, George, 535
Williard, George, 536
Williard, George, 537
Williard, George K, 309
Williard, George R, 087

Williard, George W, 303
Williard, H W, 349
Williard, Henry, 327
Williard, Henry, 488
Williard, Henry, 504
Williard, Henry C, 481
Williard, Jacob, 357
Williard, Jacob, 381
Williard, Jacob, 442
Williard, John, 017
Williard, John, 024
Williard, John, 481
Williard, John, 482
Williard, John Peter, 303
Williard, John Peter, 480
Williard, Joseph, 392
Williard, Kathryn, 192
Williard, Lavina, 537
Williard, Lovina, 320
Williard, M L, 504
Williard, Magdalena, 303
Williard, Magdalena, 480
Williard, Marlin W, 560
Williard, Martha Irene, 501
Williard, Mary, 192
Williard, Mary Ann, 443
Williard, Michael, 017
Williard, Moses A, 501
Williard, P, 520
Williard, Peter, 259
Williard, Sadie Ellen, 488
Williard, Samuel, 303
Williard, Sara, 357
Williard, Sarah, 238
Williard, Sarah, 303
Williard, Sarah, 315
Williard, Sarah, 320
Williard, Sarah, 357
Williard, Sarah, 442
Williard, Sarah, 560
Williard, Sarah C, 317
Williard, Susanna, 242
Williard, W, 017
Williard, William, 239
Williard, William R, 134
Williard, William R, 192
Williard, Wm Burton, 192
Willier, Abraham, 471
Willier, Adam, 309
Willier, Adam, 515
Willier, Anna Cath, 471
Willier, Anna Maria, 356
Willier, Catherine, 130
Willier, Clayton, 349
Willier, Clayton, 350
Willier, Clayton, 387
Willier, Clayton, 504
Willier, Doreen, 176
Willier, Elma B, 414
Willier, Emma, 177
Willier, Emma, 290
Willier, Etta M, 355
Willier, George, 309
Willier, Henry, 238
Willier, Henry, 332
Willier, Henry, 349
Willier, Henry W, 303
Willier, Henry Wolfe, 404
Willier, John Peter, 335
Willier, Jonas, 130
Willier, Maria Ida, 303
Willier, Peter, 330
Willier, Peter Sr, 329
Willier, Rufus, 404
Willier, Sarah, 515

Witmer, Robert E, 428	Wolfe, Barbara E, 289	Wolfe, Mary, 282	Wommer, William, 069	Yeartz, Elizabeth, 253
Witmer, Salome, 146	Wolfe, Bill, 332	Wolfe, Mary, 289	Wood, Maude Rebecc, 449	Yeartz, Mary C, 360
Witmer, Samuel, 393	Wolfe, C Elmer, 287	Wolfe, Mary, 569	Woodside, Daniel, 368	Yeiser, Frederick, 035
Witmer, Sarah, 281	Wolfe, Catharine, 289	Wolfe, Mary Ann, 289	Woodside, Jacob, 302	Yentch, ?, 291
Witmer, Sarah, 393	Wolfe, Catherine, 287	Wolfe, Mary Jane, 290	Woodside, Jacob, 532	Yeo Yohe, Adam, 024
Witmer, Sarah, 424	Wolfe, Catherine, 290	Wolfe, Michael, 289	Woodside, James, 015	Yeo Yohe, Maria, 024
Witmer, Susanna, 275	Wolfe, Catherine A, 284	Wolfe, Nancy I, 290	Woodside, James, 371	Yeo Yohe, Rebecca, 024
Witmer, Terrance L, 428	Wolfe, Catherine A, 287	Wolfe, Nathan Edwin, 290	Woodside, Jane, 045	Yergas, Anna Maria, 378
Witmer, Wesley, 381	Wolfe, Catherine Ann, 569	Wolfe, Nell, 355	Woodside, Jane, 079	Yergas, Christian, 378
Witmore, Jacob, 016	Wolfe, Catherine E, 289	Wolfe, Paul, 290	Woodside, John, 373	Yergas, John, 378
Wohlford, Anna M, 263	Wolfe, Charles, 287	Wolfe, Peter, 289	Woodside, Jonathan, 015	Yergas, Joseph, 378
Wohlford, Conrad, 263	Wolfe, Charles, 290	Wolfe, Rev C N, 140	Woodside, Margaret, 387	Yergas, Ludwig, 378
Wohlford, Maria M, 263	Wolfe, Charles, 332	Wolfe, Sallie D, 287	Woodside, Margaretha, 373	Yergas, Lydia, 378
Woland, Andrew, 327	Wolfe, Charles E, 115	Wolfe, Sallie D, 290	Woodside, Mary, 241	Yerges, Anna Mary, 384
Woland, Ann Maria, 388	Wolfe, Charles Elmer, 369	Wolfe, Salome, 287	Woodside, Nathan, 053	Yerges, Anna Mary, 387
Woland, Anna Mary, 245	Wolfe, Charles K, 289	Wolfe, Samuel, 282	Woodside, William, 473	Yerges, Christian, 246
Woland, Elizabeth, 237	Wolfe, Charles K, 290	Wolfe, Samuel, 284	Woodward, P, 116	Yerges, Elizabeth, 237
Woland, Emma, 090	Wolfe, Charles K Jr, 290	Wolfe, Samuel, 285	Work, Patrick, 015	Yerges, Elizabeth, 403
Woland, J, 168	Wolfe, Chas Elmer, 290	Wolfe, Samuel, 288	Workman, Elisabeth, 532	Yerges, Elizabeth, 442
Woland, John, 089	Wolfe, Christiana, 290	Wolfe, Samuel, 289	Workman, Irene, 261	Yerges, Elizabeth, 496
Woland, John, 245	Wolfe, Christina, 289	Wolfe, Samuel, 569	Workman, Irene, 356	Yerges, H, 020
Woland, John, 423	Wolfe, Christina D, 289	Wolfe, Sarah, 290	Workman, Joseph, 532	Yerges, Kay, 133
Woland, John Jr, 245	Wolfe, Clarence J, 277	Wolfe, Sarah E, 454	Workman, Levi, 235	Yerges, Michael, 384
Woland, Lydia, 089	Wolfe, Cleo A, 412	Wolfe, Simon, 289	Workman, Susan, 242	Yergey, Rev L H, 140
Woland, Lydia, 245	Wolfe, Daniel, 290	Wolfe, Solomon S, 290	Worz, Adam, 015	Yerkes, Elizabeth, 422
Woland, Lydia, 327	Wolfe, David, 290	Wolfe, Susan, 289	Wright, Catherine, 174	Yerkes, Elizabeth, 436
Woland, Margaretha, 245	Wolfe, Earl W, 290	Wolfe, Susan J, 535	Wright, James, 487	Yerkes, Hannah, 422
Woland, Mary A, 089	Wolfe, Edward, 289	Wolfe, Susanna, 289	Wright, Joseph, 042	Yerkes, Michael, 422
Woland, Mary Ellen, 420	Wolfe, Elias, 290	Wolfe, Susanna, 289	Wynn, ?, 560	Yertz, Anna Maria, 483
Woland, Mary Ellen, 421	Wolfe, Elisabeth, 289	Wolfe, Wayne I, 290	Yarnall, Lula P, 518	Yertz, Peter, 483
Woland, Mary Ellen, 425	Wolfe, Elizabeth, 289	Wolfe, William H, 287	Yeager, A Catharine, 390	Yoder, Edward, 243
Woland, Sarah D, 327	Wolfe, Elizabeth, 290	Wolfe, Wm Henry, 289	Yeager, Andrew, 015	Yoder, Olive, 355
Wolborn, Barbara, 264	Wolfe, Ellen Salome, 290	Wolff, Anna Susanna, 381	Yeager, Ann, 484	Yohe, Charles, 357
Wolcott, Charles, 393	Wolfe, Elmer, 282	Wolfgang, Amelia, 531	Yeager, Anna Maria, 459	Yohe, Harry, 131
Wolf, Ada, 522	Wolfe, Elmer C, 569	Wolfgang, Elizabeth, 294	Yeager, Annie J, 393	Yohe, William, 357
Wolf, Allen, 522	Wolfe, Elmer Hawk, 569	Wolfgang, Flora, 479	Yeager, Catharine, 288	York, Hannah, 041
Wolf, C Elmer, 565	Wolfe, Emma Agnes, 290	Wolfgang, Gene B, 196	Yeager, Catharine, 289	York, Hannah, 042
Wolf, Catherine, 289	Wolfe, Eva, 289	Wolfgang, Katie, 485	Yeager, Catharine, 392	Yost, Phoebe Ann, 531
Wolf, Charles, 289	Wolfe, Eva Dorothea, 289	Wolfgang, Mary, 425	Yeager, Catharine, 460	Yost, Rev, 312
Wolf, Charles M, 289	Wolfe, George, 289	Wolfgang, Mary E, 425	Yeager, Catharine, 482	Yost, Rev, 511
Wolf, Charles Monroe, 529	Wolfe, Govr George, 028	Womer, John, 420	Yeager, Catharine, 530	Young, Clarence S, 318
Wolf, Christian, 018	Wolfe, Harvey F, 290	Wommer, Adam, 068	Yeager, Catherine, 326	Young, Florence, 309
Wolf, Christian, 289	Wolfe, Hattie, 290	Wommer, Catharine, 069	Yeager, Charlotte, 476	Young, Florence, 314
Wolf, Christiana, 289	Wolfe, Henry, 288	Wommer, D H, 051	Yeager, Christopher, 459	Young, George, 093
Wolf, Christina, 168	Wolfe, Henry, 289	Wommer, Daniel, 050	Yeager, Christopher, 476	Young, John, 007
Wolf, Daniel, 015	Wolfe, Ida C, 290	Wommer, Daniel, 113	Yeager, Daniel, 228	Young, John, 051
Wolf, David, 289	Wolfe, Ivan H, 290	Wommer, Daniel H, 068	Yeager, Daniel, 234	Young, John, 325
Wolf, Elias, 289	Wolfe, Ivan Jr, 290	Wommer, Elisabeth, 068	Yeager, David, 529	Young, Margaret, 051
Wolf, Eliisabeth, 274	Wolfe, Jacob Milton, 290	Wommer, Elizabeth, 068	Yeager, Elizabeth, 310	Young, Rev Harold M, 140
Wolf, Ellen Jane, 529	Wolfe, Jay, 277	Wommer, Elizabeth, 069	Yeager, Eva Catherine, 459	Young, Ruth, 315
Wolf, George, 478	Wolfe, Johannes, 289	Wommer, Elizabeth, 074	Yeager, Henry, 018	Young, Ruth, 318
Wolf, Jacob, 228	Wolfe, John H, 287	Wommer, Elizabeth, 176	Yeager, Johannes, 392	Young, William, 281
Wolf, Jacob, 289	Wolfe, John H, 290	Wommer, Gabriel, 068	Yeager, John, 358	Zacharias, Johan, 380
Wolf, John, 087	Wolfe, John H, 334	Wommer, George, 069	Yeager, Jonathan, 272	Zahner, Anna Cath, 427
Wolf, John, 289	Wolfe, John Harvey, 290	Wommer, George W, 068	Yeager, Juli, 392	Zahner, Peter, 427
Wolf, John E, 425	Wolfe, John Henry, 289	Wommer, Isabella, 069	Yeager, Louisianna, 356	Zartman, Abigail, 326
Wolf, Juliann, 228	Wolfe, John M, 290	Wommer, Jacob, 068	Yeager, Mary, 476	Zartman, Adam, 308
Wolf, Katherine, 478	Wolfe, Joseph F, 286	Wommer, Jacob Jr, 068	Yeager, Mary Ann, 282	Zartman, Adam, 325
Wolf, Maria, 289	Wolfe, Joseph Frank, 289	Wommer, John, 044	Yeager, Mary Sophia, 532	Zartman, Adam, 529
Wolf, Mary E, 565	Wolfe, Joyce, 277	Wommer, John, 054	Yeager, Paul R, 326	Zartman, Ann, 326
Wolf, Mary J, 289	Wolfe, Lillian, 290	Wommer, John, 068	Yeager, Peter, 311	Zartman, Elias, 326
Wolf, Michael, 018	Wolfe, Lillian, 334	Wommer, John, 069	Yeager, Peter, 392	Zartman, Eliza, 326
Wolf, Michael, 289	Wolfe, Lillian, 569	Wommer, John, 072	Yeager, Sarah, 476	Zartman, Eva Magd, 288
Wolf, Millie, 522	Wolfe, Lydia, 290	Wommer, John, 074	Yeager, Sarah, 515	Zartman, Hannah, 326
Wolf, Nell Ann, 317	Wolfe, M Catharine, 289	Wommer, John, 106	Yeager, Sarah Ann, 310	Zartman, Harriet, 308
Wolf, Samuel, 232	Wolfe, Mae, 333	Wommer, John Sr, 176	Yeager, Sarah Ann, 392	Zartman, Harriet, 326
Wolf, Samuel, 286	Wolfe, Magdalena, 289	Wommer, Justina, 068	Yeager, Sarah Ann, 511	Zartman, Henry, 326
Wolf, Samuel, 319	Wolfe, Margaretha, 289	Wommer, Lucinda, 237	Yeakley, Catherine, 382	Zartman, Lucy, 326
Wolf, Sarah, 289	Wolfe, Maria, 290	Wommer, Lucy Ann, 068	Yeakley, Conrad, 382	Zartman, Lydia, 326
Wolf, Solomon, 346	Wolfe, Maria Christin, 289	Wommer, M Salome, 069	Yeakley, Juliana, 382	Zartman, Malinda, 326
Wolfe, Adaline, 289	Wolfe, Marlin, 569	Wommer, Malinda, 069	Yearty, Anna, 251	Zartman, Martin, 288
Wolfe, Adam, 289	Wolfe, Marlin E H, 287	Wommer, Mary, 069	Yearty, Elisabeth, 251	Zartman, Michael, 326
Wolfe, Amelia, 277	Wolfe, Marlin Elmer, 290	Wommer, Michael, 068	Yearty, Maria, 251	Zartman, Mrs, 326
Wolfe, Andreas, 289	Wolfe, Martha Jane, 289	Wommer, Michael Jr, 068	Yearty, Peter, 251	Zartman, Phoebe, 326
Wolfe, Anna A, 290	Wolfe, Martha Jane, 481	Wommer, Susanna, 068	Yearty, Rebecca, 251	Zartman, Polly, 326

www.ingramcontent.com/pod-product-compliance
Lightning Source LLC
Chambersburg PA
CBHW062020090426

42811CB00005B/909